CAMBRID

PAPERBACK GU

# THEATRE

*Sarah Stanton and Martin Banham*

## From reviews of
## *The Cambridge Guide to Theatre*

—

'A gem of a reference tool:
it is hard to imagine anyone in the theatre who would
not benefit from owning a personal copy'
THEATRE STUDIES

\*

'Truly encyclopedic in scope and worldwide in breadth'
CHOICE

\*

'Authoritative and comprehensive ... attractive to scholars
and general readers'
LIBRARY JOURNAL

\*

'This encyclopedic volume ... both commands respect
and dispenses pleasure'
REFERENCE REVIEWS

\*

'Everything I've wanted to know about theatre
and have not dared to ask is covered'
SUNDAY TIMES

\*

'A compulsively readable theatre companion –
meatier, better written, and more attuned to contemporary
developments than its competition'
PERFORMING ARTS JOURNAL

\*

'One simply has to welcome it, with gratitude.
There has not previously been such an up-to-date
and otherwise fine guide to world theatre'
ENTRÉ THEATRE MAGAZINE

# CAMBRIDGE
## PAPERBACK GUIDE TO

# THEATRE

*Sarah Stanton and Martin Banham*

CAMBRIDGE
UNIVERSITY PRESS

7.98

Published by the Press Syndicate of the University of Cambridge
The Pitt Building, Trumpington Street, Cambridge CB2 1RP
40 West 20th Street, New York, NY 10011–4211, USA
10 Stamford Road, Oakleigh, Melbourne 3166, Australia

First published 1996

Printed in Great Britain at The Bath Press, Avon

*A catalogue record for this book is available from the British Library*

*Library of Congress cataloguing in publication data*

Cambridge paperback guide to theatre/
edited by Sarah Stanton and Martin Banham.
432 p.   23.4 cm
"Derived from The Cambridge guide to theatre" – Pref.
ISBN 0 521 44654 6 (pbk.)
1. Theater – Dictionaries.  I. Stanton, Sarah.  II. Banham, Martin.
III. Cambridge guide to theatre.
PN2035.C27  1995b
792'.03 – dc20  95-40656 CIP

ISBN 0 521 44654 6  paperback

# Preface

This book is derived from the *Cambridge Guide to Theatre*. It is an abridged version of that book, edited to meet the needs of students and theatregoers who may not have time (or money) for the longer version. Many readers will, I hope, use this book for quick reference, to seek out or remind themselves of some crucial piece of information, or in search of help for an essay, and will have neither the desire nor the leisure to tackle entries of more than 5000 words.

The original *Guide* was published in 1988 as the *Cambridge Guide to World Theatre*, and published in a revised paperback edition in 1992; the second edition, the *Cambridge Guide to Theatre*, was published in 1995 – all these editions were edited by Martin Banham. The concising of the parent *Guide* devolved to me. The resulting offspring takes its shape from two conflicting impulses: loyalty to the parent volume, and a desire to impose an independent identity and inner coherence on the compact edition. In concising, I retained as much factual information as possible, but rather than simply cut each entry in the *Cambridge Guide* by half, I tried to forge a volume with its own appeal to a slightly different market.

This entailed the complete omission of the long, scholarly essays in the *Cambridge Guide*, some of which run to ten pages or more, devoted to separate national traditions of theatre. However, so that readers should know something of the broad context of non-Western theatre, four essays on the traditions of African, Asian, Latin American and Middle Eastern theatre were commissioned in place of the national entries. Entries on Greek and Roman theatre, perennially important topics for students, have been retained in reduced form. This volume includes substantial entries on topics (theatre buildings, design, costume, censorship, copyright, feminist theatre, television and radio drama, for example), and on dramatic genres. Medieval Theatre is no longer an essay 20 pages in length, but is dealt with in short entries such as mystery play, morality play, liturgical drama and so forth.

This book pursues the broad definition of drama exemplified by the original volume, which has been praised not only for its its coverage of classical theatre, but of non-traditional forms too: musical theatre, popular theatre, singers, comedians, drag queens, nude artists. This lively and colourful component of the *Guide* has been retained as far as possible.

Entries on practitioners concentrate on non-biographical aspects – on their work rather than on their personal lives, education, marriages and so forth – except when details of a life may shed light on the course of a career.

Words in small capitals within an entry signify a cross-reference to a separate entry. This rule has has been applied systematically, except in the case of some generic words, especially 'comedy' and 'tragedy', since the cross-references would crop up so frequently as to be irritating.

Dates of plays refer to performance rather than publication, unless specified otherwise.

Where a person is known by more than one name, or started life with a different one, the alternative name appears in square brackets after the more familiar one: e.g. Astaire [Austerlitz], Fred; or Gwyn, Nell [Eleanor]. Those parts of a name not generally used appear in round brackets: e.g. Jonson, Ben(jamin). Some families of actors have been grouped in one entry, e.g. the Drew-Barrymore family, with individual members picked out in bold type during the course of the entry. Names beginning Mc have not been distinguished alphabetically from those beginnning Mac.

The breakup of the USSR has been dealt with as follows: individuals whose careers preceded 1917 or extend beyond 1991 are called Russian. Those whose careers coincided with the period 1917–91 are called Soviet. Those whose careers spanned the 1917 marker are referred to as Russian-Soviet. The exceptions are those whose republican nationality (Lithuanian, Ukrainian, Georgian) is a significant factor in their careers.

Sarah Stanton

# Acknowledgements

Very few of the entries in this book are my own, in the originating sense. Almost all have been created from longer entries in the *Cambridge Guide to Theatre*. Some have been derived from longer entries in other Cambridge *Guides*, to *American*, *African and Caribbean* and *Asian* Theatre. Those whose entries have been rewritten and updated for the purposes of this book are listed in these pages as Contributors. To all those who responded to my myriad queries, I am very grateful, and I hope that in the process of condensing your words I have not misrepresented your meanings.

Martin Banham, whom I first asked in 1984 (in my role as commissioning editor at Cambridge University Press) to edit the parent volume, has constantly rekindled my enthusiasm for theatre during many years of drama publishing, and kept alive the flame which prompted me to accept the editorship of this volume. He has remained a good friend throughout. As a publishing editor who has overseen many collaborative projects, I appreciate the true worth of that statement. Don Wilmeth, who edited the *Cambridge Guide to American Theatre*, has been a patient adviser and friend. Nobody else responds as promptly and as fully to my importunate faxes, and with such good grace. Several other people have been of especial help in selecting and vetting entries and in giving me their time to help untangle my queries. I think particularly of Arnold Aronson, David Bradby, James Brandon, George Brandt, Ruby Cohn, John Elsom, Spencer Golub, Tony Green, Errol Hill, Margaret Knapp, Peter Meredith, Tice Miller, Laurence Senelick, Russell Stephens, Peter Thomson and George Woodyard. Their willing help has kept this book on course.

Ian Ousby, who edited the complete and concise versions of *The Cambridge Guide to Literature in English*, was a close ally from the time when we began our separate tasks, and I am grateful to him for supplying help, humour and sympathy whenever they were required.

Sue Phillpott was an eagle-eyed copyeditor who paid scrupulous attention to detail and turned crude syntax into elegant sentences. Jake Bundy transferred a host of corrections to my disks and picked up several errors on the way. My sister Juliet Stanton, who combines the hobby of acting with the job of proofreading, read every word of the proofs, some of them more than once, and has saved us all from countless errors. I am especially grateful to her. Caroline Bundy was my patient editor and colleague from an early stage in the book's preparation. After years of doing that job myself, I am not one to underestimate its importance. I could not have wished for a kinder or wiser editor. I also know just how difficult authors can be, and I was no exception.

My husband Martin Walters gave me moral support at every stage, and took care of the children so that I could do this job. His own extensive knowledge of publishing, combined with a refreshing lack of expertise in theatre, have been vital to my wellbeing throughout.

I dedicate the book to my mother, Rosemary Stanton, whose love of theatre has fostered mine, and to the memory of my father, Geoffrey Stanton, who took me to my first show.

Sarah Stanton
*September 1995*

# Contributors

JAMES AIKENS

STEPHEN M ARCHER

ARNOLD ARONSON

MARTIN BANHAM

ALEC BARON†

WILLIAM O. BEEMAN

W B BLAND

DAVID BRADBY

JAMES R BRANDON

GEORGE W BRANDT

EUGENE BROGYÁNI

ANDREW BROWN

JARKA BURIAN

FRAN BZOWSKI†

OH-KON CHO

LARRY D CLARK

RUBY COHN

DAVID COLLISON

LEONARD CONNOLLY

JOHN CONTEH-MORGAN

JILL DAVIS

JILL DOLAN

LEONARD DOUCETTE

CHRIS DUNTON

JOHN ELSOM

MICHAEL ETHERTON

GERALD FITZGIBBON

DANIEL GEROULD

MARTIN VAN GINKEL

SPENCER GOLUB

FRANCES GRAY

A E GREEN

WILLIAM GREEN

IVOR GUEST

DOROTHY A HADFIELD

GEORGE HAUGER

MARY C HENDERSON

WIL HILDEBRAND

ERROL G HILL

FOSTER HIRSCH

PETER HOLLAND

ARNI IBSEN

CHRISTOPHER INNES

ANTHONY JACKSON

C LEE JENNER

ROBERT KAVANAGH

LAURENCE KEATES

DRAGAN KLAIC

MARGARET M KNAPP

JAMES KOTSILIBAS-DAVIS

RICHARD E KRAMER

HARRY LANE

THOMAS LEABHART

C I LEWIS

PETER LEWIS

FELICIA HARDISON LONDRÉ

JOHN MCCORMICK

LINDA MACKENNEY

COLIN MACKERRAS

MARGARET MACPHERSON

DOUGLAS MCDERMOTT

BROOKS MCNAMARA

HOWARD MCNAUGHTON

LAURENCE MASLON

JEFFREY D MASON

DESMOND MAXWELL

PETER MEREDITH

WALTER MESERVE

TOM MIKOWICZ

TICE L MILLER

BOGDAN MISCHIU

PENINA MLAMA

RICHARD MOODY

LYNETTE MUIR

KENT NEELY

ANDREA J NOURYEH

BOBBI OWEN

JORGEN PJETTURSON

ADRIANA POPESCU

RICHARD PILBROW

DANIEL PIRES

THOMAS POSTLEWAIT

LESLIE DU S READ

FRANCIS REID

MAARTEN REILINGH

KENNETH RICHARDS

LAURA RICHARDS

FARLEY RICHMOND

HUGH RORRISON

DONALD ROY

CHRISTOPHER SCARLES

ROBERT A SCHANKE

HENRI SCHOENMAKERS

CLAUDE SCHUMACHER

HANNA SCOLNICOV

A C SCOTT†

LAURENCE SENELICK

LOUIS SHEAFFER†

ALISA SOLOMON

SARAH STANTON

IAN STEADMAN

J R STEPHENS

ELSA STRIETMAN

JOHN E TAILBY

G THANIEL

PETER THOMSON

CLIVE WAKE

DANIEL J WATERMEIER

MARGARET WILLIAMS

SIMON WILLIAMS

DON B WILMETH

BARRY B WITHAM

GEORGE WOODYARD

MASAKO YUASA

PHYLLIS ZATLIN

**Abbey Theatre** Irish theatre. The Abbey is the Dublin playhouse by whose name the Irish National Theatre Society Ltd is popularly known. The Society's predecessors were the Irish Literary Theatre (1899–1901), founded by W. B. YEATS, AUGUSTA LADY GREGORY, Edward Martyn and George Moore; and the Irish National Dramatic Company of Frank and Willie Fay. The aim of the Society, formed by the Fay brothers, Yeats, Lady Gregory and J. M. SYNGE, was to encourage new writers, in Synge's words, to 'work in English that is perfectly Irish in essence'. The Abbey Street theatre, converted from a former morgue, was the gift in 1904 of an English admirer of Yeats, ANNIE HORNIMAN. The Fay brothers were amateurs, both capable actors with practical stage experience. Yeats and the Fays had compatible approaches to theatre, but by 1908 Miss Horniman had removed the Fays, whom she detested, and by 1911 her subsidy also. With the death of Synge in 1909 Yeats was effectively in control.

The indisputable dramatic genius of these years is Synge, whose disreputable peasant characters provoked riotous nationalist demonstrations, especially against *The Playboy of the Western World* (1907). More to the Abbey audience's taste were Lady Gregory's folk dramas. Synge's mantle passed to SEAN O'CASEY and his synthesis of poetic vernacular and urban REALISM. O'Casey's irreverent treatment of the patriotic myths of Easter 1916 in *The Plough and the Stars* (1926) caused more riots. 'You have disgraced yourselves again,' Yeats told the audience. Sadly, O'Casey abandoned the Abbey when in 1928 it rejected his part-expressionistic *The Silver Tassie*.

Alongside the uncommon brilliance of Synge and O'Casey, the Abbey had consolidated a line of essentially realist dramas on local themes, initiated by PADRAIC COLUM (*Broken Soil*, 1903), LENNOX ROBINSON (*The Clancy Name*, 1908) and T. C. MURRAY (*Birthright*, 1910). Robinson also inaugurated the DUBLIN DRAMA LEAGUE (1919–29), opening the Abbey stage to experimental European and American drama.

The relative security of an annual government subsidy from 1925 enabled the directors to accommodate a little theatre, the Peacock. Their better-known players, including CYRIL CUSACK, remained at risk to the rewards of London and Hollywood. Under the autocratic rule of Ernest Blythe, with Yeats now infrequently present, the Abbey languished but survived. In the 1930s and 40s the discipline of acting and direction slackened, vulgarizing perhaps its best writer of the period, GEORGE SHIELS. A few substantial new playwrights – including PAUL VINCENT CARROLL and M. J. MOLLOY – emerged. HUGH HUNT's tenure (play-director 1935–8) was too brief to establish reform.

The fire which destroyed the old Abbey in 1951 exiled the company for 15 years to the decrepit Queen's Theatre, a larger house requiring runs longer than the Abbey's practice. Its new home, on the old site, is a 628-seat modern theatre with sophisticated stage and lighting facilities.

After an indecisive start, the new Abbey found its confidence, enlivened by the considerable talents of the directors Tomas MacAnna, Alan Simpson, Joe Dowling, and a gifted company. However, recent times have seen both trouble and triumph. On the one hand there have been five artistic directors in about eight years, and the Abbey's primacy has been challenged by the resurgent GATE THEATRE. On the other, in recent years the Abbey has undertaken successful European and American tours, and it has had the stimulus of distinguished guest directors. It remains a writers' theatre and was an important instrument in the dramatic revival which began in the 1960s. Among the contemporary Irish writers mainly associated with it are BRIAN FRIEL, Bernard Farrell, TOM MURPHY, TOM KILROY, HUGH LEONARD, TOM MACINTYRE, FRANK MCGUINNESS and Sebastian Barry. So, despite its recent turbulent history, the Abbey continues to be at the centre of Irish theatre and a major force in Irish cultural life.

**Abbott, George** 1887–1995 American director, playwright and actor. In his 1963 autobiography Abbott praised his Harvard drama teacher GEORGE PIERCE BAKER in a way that defined his own theatrical creed: 'Professor Baker gave you no nonsense about inner meanings and symbolism; he turned your whole thoughts and energies into the practical matter of how to make a show.' Taking Baker's lessons to heart, Abbott became the most practical showman in BROADWAY history, and performer, co-author and director of over 130 productions. He first acted on a Broadway stage in 1913; in the autumn of 1989 he directed a workshop production of a new musical called *Frankie*. As both director and co-author his specialities were racy MELODRAMA (*Broadway*, 1926), split-second FARCE (*Three Men on a Horse*, 1935) and peppy musicals with vigorous choreography (*On Your Toes*, 1936; *Damn Yankees*, 1955).

**Abell, Kjeld** 1901–61 Danish playwright. He began his career designing Balanchine's ballets at the KONGELIGE TEATER. His first writing for the theatre, the ballet-scenario *The Widow in the Mirror* (1934), introduced a recurrent Abell theme, the anguish caused by alienation from life. Ballet undoubtedly influenced the plays that followed, beginning with *The Melody that Got Lost* (1935) produced at the Riddersalen cabaret theatre. His early expressionistic plays (see EXPRESSIONISM), *The Melody* and *Eve Serves Her Childhood*, sharply depict the suffocating effect of bourgeois values. His plays during and immediately after World War II, such as *Anna Sophie Hedvig*, *Judith*, *The Queen on Tour*, *Silkeborg* and *Days on a Cloud*, identify activism as essential to freedom and escapism as self-annihilation. His later plays became more complex and mystical, such as *Vetsera Does Not Bloom for Everyone*, *The Blue Pekingese* and *The Scream*.

**Abington, Frances** 1737–1815 English actress. By 1755 she was working with THEOPHILUS CIBBER at the HAYMARKET Theatre and in 1756 joined DRURY LANE. After a period acting in Ireland she returned to Drury Lane to join GARRICK's company. She played Lady Teazle in SHERIDAN's *The School for Scandal* (1777). Having retired, she made an unsuccessful return in 1799, by which time she was overweight and no longer a leader of fashion.

**above** Elizabethan stage direction denoting a practical upper level, in both public and private theatres of London. De Witt's drawing of the SWAN includes a gallery over the stage which is assumed to represent the kind of fixture normally used by actors entering 'above'. (See also BELOW.)

**absurd, theatre of the** see THEATRE OF THE ABSURD

**Accesi** Two Italian acting companies, of the COMMEDIA DELL'ARTE. Both begun under the patronage of Vincenzo I Gonzaga, Duke of Mantua, the first may have been founded around 1595, the other around 1600 by Tristano Martinelli and Pier Maria Cecchini. The troupe toured Italy and France and merged briefly with GIOVAN BATTISTA ANDREINI's troupe, the FEDELI, before dissolving about 1626, at which time SILVIO FIORILLO was the company's outstanding player in his role as Captain Matamoros.

**Achurch, Janet** 1864–1916 English actress. Her career is identified with IBSEN and SHAW. As a member of F.R. BENSON's company in the 1880s, she established a reputation as a tragedian. On taking over the management of London's Novelty Theatre in 1889 she played Nora in the first British production of A Doll's House, returning to play Mrs Linde as her final stage appearance in 1911. In 1900 she starred in the premieres of Candida and Captain Brassbound's Conversion.

**Ackermann family** The most important family of German actors in the 18th century. Having joined the SCHÖNEMANN troupe in 1740, **Konrad (Ernst)** (1712–71) soon left to set up his own troupe, along with SOPHIE SCHRÖDER (1714–92), whom he later married. The Ackermann troupe toured widely in Central and Eastern Europe and introduced to the German stage the genre of the BÜRGERLICHES TRAUERSPIEL, becoming widely known for the comparative realism of its acting, particularly after EKHOF joined the troupe in 1764. After his stepfather's death, FRIEDRICH SCHRÖDER took over the troupe, eventually settling it permanently in the Hamburg Town Theatre. Ackermann's two daughters, **Dorothea** (1752–1821) and **Charlotte** (1757–74), were also actresses.

**Acquart, André** 1922– French stage designer. He is known primarily for his work in the 1960s on such productions as The Blacks (1959), directed by ROGER BLIN, The Resistible Rise of Arturo Ui (1961), co-directed by JEAN VILAR and Georges Wilson, and Biedermann and the Firebugs (1960), directed by JEAN-MARIE SERREAU. His designs are abstract, utilizing skeletal structures such as tubes or movable flats and multiple playing levels.

**acrobatics** Form of physical entertainment. One of the most ancient and prevalent, it is represented in Egyptian and Etruscan murals by leapers and vaulters. The earliest work devoted to the subject is Arcangelo Tuccaro's Trois dialogues de l'exercice de sauter et voltiger en l'air (1599). The most basic move is the salto or leap into the air, in which neither hands nor feet must move. All sorts of combinations are possible – backwards, forwards, sideways (the Arab jump), the flip-flop (a backward somersault from a standing position), and from trampolines and flying trapezes. The salto mortale or death-defying leap is so called from its dangerousness. A double salto mortale was first performed by an Englishman named Tomkinson in 1840.

Other forms of acrobatics include the antipodean, in which one acrobat lies on his back and juggles the other performer with his feet; and its offshoot, the Icarian games, invented by the Englishman Cottrelly c.1850, in which performers are tossed, balanced and caught by the feet of their partners, lying on specially constructed cushions.

In popular amusements like the COMMEDIA DELL'ARTE and the harlequinade, acrobatics is at a premium, but it is neglected by the dramatic stage, except in actors' training. TOM STOPPARD in Jumpers (1972) used acrobatics as a metaphor for mental gymnastics.

**acting** The impulse to make-believe and PLAY is common to humanity. To act is both to do and to pretend to do. For both actor and spectator, the uncanny power of any performance springs from an ambiguous tension between what is actual and what is fictional. This ambiguity is present in all acting, however much a particular society or individual may wish to resolve it. In the 20th century many Western theories of acting have stressed the integrity of the doing, while in the 18th century, for example, Europeans were more concerned with the authentic nature of the pretence, its style and social aptness.

Throughout history, the unease aroused by this ambiguity has been reflected in the status of the actor. Even in classical Greece (see GREEK THEATRE, ANCIENT), where acting had religious and political importance, there is evidence from the 4th century BC onwards that the technitai of Dionysus were viewed with ambivalence. Certainly in Rome acting was felt to be the work of slaves and aliens (see ROMAN THEATRE), while in modern Europe players long existed on the margins of law and religion (MOLIÈRE could not be buried in consecrated ground). This ambivalence can be traced elsewhere.

In Asia, outside the confines of local prestige, religious purpose or court patronage, performers were, and often still are, equated with wanderers and beggars. Although in ancient India actors were believed to trace their ancestry to a member of the highest caste, the priestly Bharata, sacred myths tell how they were soon condemned to the lowest caste for their satire and mockery of the sages. Only through the intervention of kings could this ambivalence be allayed. In China, decrees from as early as 1369 banned actors from entering for state examinations.

The social assimilation of the acting profession in the West, around the beginning of the 20th century, was paralleled by sustained and serious evaluation of its art. In England, for example, IRVING's knighthood in 1895, the first to be bestowed on an actor, was followed not only by further theatrical knighthoods (six before 1914) but also by the founding of the Academy of Dramatic Art (later RADA). Similar developments are evident throughout Europe, most notably in Russia where for STANISLAVSKY training combined with a radical analysis of the art. Stanislavsky's accounts of his psycho-physical method constitute the first systematic examination of acting, in the West, written from the viewpoint of the actor. Earlier writings are either anecdotal or, as with DIDEROT, written from the perspective of the auditorium.

In the East, such approaches to practice can be found in works like the Natyasastra (c.200 BC) and ZEAMI's treatises on the NŌ (c.1402–30). The systematic encoding of traditional acting genres found in such manuals emphasizes a performer's obligation to embody the received wisdom and aesthetics of particular styles and techniques. Training in the genre rather than rehearsal for the individual play is paramount. In Asian theatre, the master–pupil relationship is ubiquitous. Imparting the traditional form through example, through long apprenticeship and disciplined physical preparation and practice, establishes the importance of performance over text, of the transmitted skill in its present-tense embodiment over individual expression.

The art of acting lies in showing and sharing an action, image, character or story. It is rooted in the present-tense encounter of actor with actor, and/or actor with audience. The material of the art is the body, voice and being of the performer. Different styles demand different skills of this material. Bodily skills may range from the acrobatic and pantomimic, as in traditional Chinese theatre, through schematic languages of dance and gesture, as found in *KUTIYATTAM* or *KATHAKALI*, to the faithful reproduction of everyday motions, as in Western NATURALISM. Vocal skills likewise may range from song, through chant or declamation, to conversational speech. This is not simply a contrast between a presentational mode of acting with its emphasis on display and a representational mode with its stress on verisimilitude. It relates to a range of percepts of which masks and trance are an ambiguous part. Acting works with living presence. This is of the utmost importance in performance and of the utmost contention in discussion. Contraries abound – inspiration versus technique, talent versus training. KEAN or KEMBLE, Irving or COQUELIN, DUSE or BERNHARDT?

**Acting Company** American company, originally known as the City Center Acting Company. JOHN HOUSEMAN and Margot Harley organized the first graduating class of the drama division of the Juilliard School into a permanent repertory troupe, which began performing at the City Center in New York in 1972. By 1984 it functioned as the touring arm of the JOHN F. KENNEDY CENTER FOR THE PERFORMING ARTS in Washington, DC. The company's members are selected nationally by auditions. Alumni of the company include KEVIN KLINE, PATTI LuPONE, WILLIAM HURT and Christopher Reeve.

**Actors Studio, The** American acting workshop. Founded in 1947 by GROUP THEATRE alumni ELIA KAZAN, CHERYL CRAWFORD and ROBERT LEWIS, the Actors Studio is a unique workshop for professional actors. It is not a school; it charges no tuition fees and once an actor is accepted (by a rigorous audition process) he or she becomes a member for life. Under LEE STRASBERG, its artistic director from 1951 to 1982, the Studio became renowned as the high temple of the Method. Studio actors have been both praised for their psychological revelation and attacked for self-indulgence and mannerism, but the influence of the Method is undeniable and has come to be identified as the quintessential American style. The enduring legacies are the films directed by Kazan and the performances of the Studio's many illustrious members – from MARLON BRANDO, James Dean and Montgomery Clift to DUSTIN HOFFMAN, Robert de Niro, AL PACINO, Shelley Winters, GERALDINE PAGE and Frank Corsaro, who is the Studio's present artistic director.

**Actors Theatre of Louisville** American theatre. One of the leading regional theatres, located in Louisville, Kentucky, it was founded by Richard Block and Ewel Cornett in 1964 and is noted for encouraging and producing original scripts. Block was replaced in 1969 by Jon Jory, whose leadership proved beneficial. In 1972 the company moved to their present location, the Old Bank of Louisville Building. In 1977 the Actors Theatre initiated the Festival of New American Plays. Scripts such as *Gin Game* and *Crimes of the Heart* premiered at the Actors Theatre, moved to BROADWAY, and won Pulitzer Prizes for Drama.

**Adamov, Arthur** 1908–70 French playwright. Armenian in origin, Adamov settled in Paris in 1924. Between 1947 and 1953 he completed seven plays. Influenced by STRINDBERG, they depict a world of terror and persecution stemming from Adamov's own dreams and neuroses, but with stage images that embody a whole state of mind. The masterpiece of this period is *Professor Taranne* (1953). In 1955 Adamov's *Ping-Pong* heralded a move towards a more politicized theatre. His *Paolo Paoli* (directed by ROGER PLANCHON, 1957) was praised as the first successful BRECHTian play in France. Adamov's later successes were *Off Limits* (directed by Garran and Grüber, 1969) and *Si l'été revenait* (*If Summer Returned*), published in 1970. *A. A. Théâtres d'Adamov*, a posthumous tribute directed by Planchon, was performed at the THÉÂTRE NATIONAL POPULAIRE in 1975.

**Adams, Edwin** 1834–77 American actor. He established himself during the Civil War as a travelling star distinguished for his playing of romantic or light COMEDY characters in such vehicles as *The Lady of Lyons* and *Narcisse*. In 1869, EDWIN BOOTH selected him to play Mercutio opposite his Romeo for the opening of BOOTH'S THEATRE, where he later featured in the title role in a dramatization of TENNYSON's *Enoch Arden*.

**Adams** [*née* Kiskadden], **Maude** 1872–1953 American actress. Her adult career began in New York at 16 and in 1890 she began an association with producer CHARLES FROHMAN which lasted until 1915. In 1897 she capitalized on her eternal youthfulness and whimsy as Lady Babbie in *The Little Minister*, a character rewritten for her by BARRIE. She also starred in American productions of his *Quality Street* (1901), *Peter Pan* (1905), *What Every Woman Knows* (1908), *The Legend of Leonora* (1914) and *A Kiss for Cinderella* (1916). Other parts included the title role in ROSTAND's *L'Aiglon*, the strutting hero in his *Chantecler*, and SHAKESPEARE's Viola, Juliet, Rosalind and Portia.

**Addison, Joseph** 1672–1719 English essayist, politician and playwright, who frequently wrote about drama in the periodicals the *Spectator* and the *Tatler*, often with a sharp mockery. His play *Cato* (1713), a controlled, dignified neoclassical tragedy, was politically controversial; his comedy *The Drummer or the Haunted House* (1716) was not a success.

**Ade, George** 1866–1944 American playwright and librettist. His most popular librettos, *The Sultan of Sulu* (1902) and *The Sho-Gun* (1904), were influenced by GILBERT and Sullivan. He is best remembered for two dramatic comedies of small-town life, *The County Chairman* (1903) and *The College Widow* (1904), which reveal his keen eye and ear for the residents of his native mid-America.

**Adejumo, Moses Olaiya** [Baba Sala] 1936– Nigerian actor-manager. The founder-owner of the Alawada Theatre ('theatre of the one who entertains'), Olaiya, whose stage name is Baba Sala, is the most popular comedian in Nigeria today; and his registered company (both acting and trading) is the most commercially successful, despite performances being almost entirely in Yoruba. A deeply religious Christian, since 1965 he has performed continually all over Nigeria and coastal West Africa. His satirical comedies are improvisations which debunk social pretensions. He and his Alawada Theatre perform extensively on television, and since the late 1970s he has become increasingly involved in film-making. In 1984 Olaiya made a feature film, *Orun Mooru* (*Heaven Is Heated*). Subsequently he has also turned to video as a medium.

**Adelphi Theatre** (London) Of four theatres on the same site in the Strand, the first was built in 1806 and called the Sans Pareil. It was renamed the Adelphi in 1819. During the long management (1844–74) of BENJAMIN WEBSTER, it was rebuilt to accommodate 1,500 (1858). It was well attended for most of this time, and the description 'Adelphi dramas' was familiarly attached to strong MELODRAMAS. BUCKSTONE and BOUCICAULT were among the featured dramatists. WILLIAM TERRISS's murder at the stage door of the Adelphi in 1897 brought the great years of the theatre to an abrupt end. It was subsequently twice rebuilt, in 1901 and in 1930.

**Adler, Stella** 1903–92 American actress. One of a family of Yiddish actors from Riga who achieved popular success in America, Stella studied at the AMERICAN LABORATORY THEATRE in the 1920s, joined the GROUP THEATRE in 1931 and married its founder, HAROLD CLURMAN. A tall, statuesque blonde, Adler ironically succeeded best in playing downtrodden Depression-era housewives in the Group's productions of CLIFFORD ODETS's *Awake and Sing!* (1935) and *Paradise Lost* (1935). From 1949, when she founded the Stella Adler Conservatory, she was an exhilarating teacher. Countering her arch-rival LEE STRASBERG's Method with its focus on self, she urged students to transcend their own experiences by investigating the play's circumstances rather than their own. (See also YIDDISH THEATRE.)

**Admiral's Men** English company. These Elizabethan players took their name from their patron, Lord Howard, who was created Lord High Admiral in 1585, the year in which the Admiral's Men first appeared at Court. It was EDWARD ALLEYN's acting in CHRISTOPHER MARLOWE's plays at PHILIP HENSLOWE's ROSE that established the company's reputation. In 1594 the formation of the LORD CHAMBERLAIN's MEN nudged the Admiral's Men into second place in the theatrical hierarchy. Henslowe's financial involvement helped the company to evade the general prohibition of plays after the *Isle of Dogs* affair in 1597. But Henslowe was not himself a member of the Admiral's Men: he was the owner of their theatre. When, in 1599, the Lord Chamberlain's Men opened the GLOBE, very close to the Rose, the Admiral's Men suffered in the competition for audiences. Unlike their rivals, they did not own their own theatre, and may not have commanded the same loyalty from their actors. Alleyn's increasing involvement in his business partnership with Henslowe deprived them of a star.

The move north of the river, to the FORTUNE, in 1600 brought a new audience and sufficient prosperity. As London's acknowledged second company, they were granted royal patronage and the title of Prince Henry's Men after the accession of James I. Regular writers included DEKKER, MUNDAY and CHETTLE, but the sinking reputation of the Fortune during the 1620s announced the company's creative impoverishment. As the Palsgrave's Men, they continued their occupation of the Fortune, but without much success. By 1631, when some of the Fortune actors joined a newly formed Prince Charles's Men at SALISBURY COURT, the long tradition of the Admiral's Men had been broken.

**Adriani, Placido** died c.1740 Italian actor. A Benedictine monk, residing in Naples, he played the role of Pulcinella in monastery recitals. His manuscript collection, *Selva, overo Zibaldone di concetti comici* (1734), is a rich repository of COMMEDIA DELL'ARTE scenarios, plots and *lazzi* (see LAZZO).

**Aeschylus** 525/4–456/5 BC Greek tragic playwright. A native of Eleusis, Aeschylus is said to have produced tragedies as early as 499, and won his first victory at the Great Dionysia (see GREEK THEATRE, ANCIENT) in 484. He fought against the Persians at the Battle of Marathon (490), and probably also at Salamis (480). He became the most popular tragedian of his day, winning a total of 13 victories at Athens and also visiting Sicily to produce plays for the tyrant Hieron I of Syracuse. It was on a later visit to Sicily that he died. Already by the time of ARISTOPHANES, who affectionately parodies his style in *Frogs*, he was regarded as the first of the great tragedians.

For at least part of his career he played the leading role in his own plays, as was normal until the time of SOPHOCLES. He is said to have been responsible for reducing the role of the Chorus and for introducing the second actor – clearly a momentous innovation. Many of his plays belonged to connected tetralogies.

He is said to have written 90 plays: we know the titles of over 70; seven survive under his name. *Persians* (472), which depicts the despair of the Persian court on hearing of the Greek victory at Salamis, is the earliest drama we possess and the only surviving Greek tragedy on a historical subject. It did not belong to a connected tetralogy. *Seven against Thebes* (467) was the third play of a tetralogy about Oedipus and his family, the others being *Laius*, *Oedipus* and the satyr play *Sphinx*. *Suppliant Women* (once thought to be the earliest play but now dated between 466 and 459) almost certainly belonged to a connected tetralogy about the daughters of Danaus. *Agamemnon*, *Choephori* (*Libation-Bearers*) and *Eumenides* together form the *Oresteia* (458), the only connected trilogy that survives (the lost satyr play *Proteus* completed the tetralogy). The seventh play, *Prometheus Bound*, was until recently accepted as authentic by most scholars, but detailed examination of its language, metre and stagecraft has made it very probable that it is post-Aeschylean, perhaps datable to the 440s. It was accompanied by the lost *Prometheus Unbound*, in which Prometheus was released from his torment by Heracles. Like the *Oresteia*, *Prometheus Bound* employs three actors.

Fragments also survive, not extensive but providing valuable evidence for Aeschylus' satyr plays, as well as for lost tragedies.

The surviving plays, though few in number, are extremely diverse. Each is fairly simple in plot, though those of the *Oresteia*, perhaps influenced by Sophocles, are more complex than the others. Each, except *Suppliant Women* and *Eumenides*, invests a single public event (such as the Persian defeat or the murder of Agamemnon by his wife Clytemnestra) with great moral and religious significance. Before it occurs, or is announced, the event is foreshadowed with foreboding or (in *Choephori*) with illusory hope, and we become more and more aware of the network of forces making it inevitable; afterwards its ethical implications are explored and its future consequences predicted. Characterization tends to be subordinate to the deeds which the characters perform rather than being pursued for its own sake; but this does not prevent those characters from being fully intelligible in human terms. The Chorus is constantly exploited and its songs carry much of the moral and emotional weight of the drama.

**Afinogenov, Aleksandr (Nikolaevich)** 1904–41
Soviet playwright. He searched for a new psychological
drama in the post-revolutionary years of transition
from primitive AGIT-PROP to doctrinaire socialist realism. He was a Communist Party member from 1922. His
early plays – *Robert Tim* (1923), *The Other Side of the Slot*
(adapted from Jack London, 1926), *At the Breaking Point*
(1927), *Keep Your Eyes Peeled* (1927) and *Raspberry Jam*
(1928) – were produced by the Proletkult Theatre, where
Afinogenov served as literary manager and director,
and reflected the group's proletarian bias. Tiring of the
schematic, Proletkult style, he formally broke with the
organization in 1928, joining the Russian Association
of Proletarian Writers (RAPP), whose approach to art he
helped to define in *The Creative Method of the Theatre: The
Dialectics of the Creative Process* (1931). However, in his 1929
drama *The Eccentric*, a character study of a romantic non-
communist dreamer, the author had the temerity to
cast communists as villains. His best play, *Fear* (1931),
which brings subtlety and humanity to a confrontation
between a good communist and an unenlightened but
salvageable elder scientist, was considered pivotal in
the Soviet dramatic canon, and was successfully staged
by STANISLAVSKY at the MOSCOW ART THEATRE. His
remaining plays include *Distant Point* (1935), a Soviet
philosophical drama; *Hail, Spain!* (1936), a popular
romantic piece; and *Mashenka* (1940), an amalgam of
personal and patriotic dramas. His insistence on psychological realism at the expense of ideological concerns cost Afinogenov his Party membership in 1937. It
was restored in 1938.

**African theatre** The roots of theatre in Africa are
ancient and complex and lie in areas of community festival, seasonal rhythm and religious ritual as well as in
the work of court jesters, travelling professional entertainers and storytellers. Since the late 1950s, in a movement that has paralleled the political emancipation of
so much of the continent, there has grown a theatre
that comments back from the colonized world to the
world of the colonialists, that discusses the shared
experience in the shared languages, and its own cultural and linguistic integrity. Contemporary African
theatre serves a purpose within communities and cultures that is much greater than simply that of entertainment or diversion. This functional quality gives the
theatre a sense of purpose, and influences not only its
material but also the nature of its performance and
reception. The present-day theatre is enriched and complemented by its coexistence with traditional forms,
skills and understanding.

Its vitality, diversification and variety of form and
content warn against too homogeneous a view of
African theatre, but centuries of European economic
and political domination have inevitably influenced
Africa's cultural life, and especially its theatre. During
the first half of the 20th century indigenous theatre
movements often reflected Western models, whether
in the Nigerian and Ghanaian 'concert party' or the
*vaudeville* presentations of southern African theatre.
The Western influences were, however, effectively subverted and eventually dominated or replaced by indigenous forms. The influence of Western-style education
continues to determine elements of theatrical form
and language in much contemporary drama, but here
again we can see playwrights and performers working
increasingly on their own terms and asserting a powerful cultural and political identity. Theatre in many

parts of Africa has been at the forefront of the anti-colo-
nial struggle, and has not relaxed its sense of purpose in
the post-independence world. (Witness the banning of
HUBERT OGUNDE's work not only by the colonial government of Nigeria in the 1940s but also by the independent government of the 1960s; or the imprisonment of
WOLE SOYINKA during the Nigerian civil war; or NGUGI
WA THIONG'O's exile from Kenya.)

**FESTAC**
The first World Festival of Negro Arts was held in Dakar
in 1966. This was followed by the second Black and
African Festival of Arts and Culture held in Lagos, for
which the acronym FESTAC was coined. The festivals
were planned as pan-African celebrations; and the
ingredients ranged from performance to debate, dominated primarily by dance and theatre.

**English-speaking Africa**
The universities in the anglophone nations of Africa
played an important part in developing theatre activities from the late 1950s onward, both through the playwrights they produced and through the establishment
of imaginative performance venues and initiatives. The
latter ranged from the travelling theatres in Nigeria
(see also YORUBA TRAVELLING THEATRES) and Uganda to
the Chikwakwa community theatre in Zambia. With
much of the new drama emerging from the universities, it is not surprising that a certain elitist tone characterized much of the work – both in its concern with
the problems of the young educated man or woman in
conflict with traditional manners and attitudes, and in
the choice and use of language.

The language debate remains a crucial one: calls have
been made, by Wole Soyinka amongst others, to replace
English with a pan-African language. The Nigerian playwright OLA ROTIMI proposes 'the domestication of the
English language – handling it within the terms of traditional linguistic identity'. Ngugi wa Thiong'o has
argued for the use of indignous languages. A positive
move is also being made by younger dramatists towards
exploring the use of pidgin as a lingua franca. It is
important to remember that in notionally 'English-
speaking' nations indigenous languages are often paramount, both in terms of day-to-day usage and in
government and culture. Swahili, for instance, is the
language of much theatre – published and unpublished
– in Tanzania and elsewhere in East Africa, including
the important plays of EBRAHIM HUSSEIN. Yoruba in
Nigeria is the appropriate language of the immensely
popular theatre of Baba Sala (see MOSES OLAIYA
ADEJUMO) as well as the 'operas' of DURO LADIPO, celebrating as they do the myths and history of the Yoruba
people. Shona and Ndebele are the languages of much
new writing for the theatre in Zimbabwe.

Growing alongside the literary theatre has been a
dynamic popular theatre, often using indigenous languages and unscripted, improvised material. The
nature of this theatre ranges from broad FARCE to serious commentary and protest. Protest theatre itself is,
not surprisingly, at its most effective and dynamic in
South Africa, where 'township theatre' has not only
produced an exceptional group of playwrights and performers, but has also determined a political agenda.
One of the intriguing questions for the future of South
African theatre is how a theatre geared to protest –
whether through the relatively sophisticated productions of the Johannesburg Market Theatre or Cape
Town's Space Theatre, or the street theatre productions

5

of transient radical groups – will accommodate itself to the changing political scene. Having found such a challenging role in effecting change, will the theatre be able to change itself, and contribute to the new dialogue in a post-apartheid, majority-rule South Africa? South African playwrights and performers are exploring the exciting potential of interculturalism within their own nation.

THEATRE FOR DEVELOPMENT, a community theatre activity designed either for propaganda (health care and hygiene, literacy, good agricultural practices and so on) or, in a more radical context, as a vehicle of conscientization, has also been experimented with and applied in many areas of the continent. The ideology and the practice of theatre for development has been tested and extended by the practitioners themselves in conferences and workshops, and in action through the work of companies and individuals. Typically, Oga Steve Abah in Zaria, Nigeria, through the Samaru Project, has used the resources of a university drama department to contribute to the conscientization of rural communities. ZAKES MDA in Lesotho and PENINA MLAMA in Tanzania have made important contributions to the critical literature of one of Africa's most buoyant theatre movements.

**French-speaking Africa south of the Sahara**
'Francophone' sub-Saharan Africa is the term used since the 1960s, in both English and French, to describe a group of 16 African countries where, as a result of French and Belgian colonial rule (roughly between 1885 and 1960), French is the language of government, business and administration. When independence came (in or around 1960), the continental federations of West and Equatorial Africa broke down into a series of separate states, but the influence of the French language and its culture remained. These countries, from Senegal in the west through Zaire in the centre to Chad in the east, each have a unique cultural identity, but they have also evolved, by virtue of their similar colonial experience (especially those under a centralizing power like France), a distinctive modern African culture.

This francophone African culture, a synthesis of local African and imported French and Belgian traditions, has found expression in many forms: the earliest practised genre was poetry in the 1930s, with Léopold Senghor; then came fiction in the early 1950s with Camara Laye, Mongo Beti and Abdoulaye Sadji, and almost a decade later, in terms of significant published works, the theatre. In spite of its relative youth, the theatre is now a vital aspect of the literature of sub-Saharan Africa in French, accounting for some three hundred published plays. Many of these, by playwrights like CHEIK NDAO, BERNARD DADIÉ, Sony Labou Tansi (1947–95), Félix Tchicaya U'Tamsi (1931–88) and GUILLAUME OYONO-MBIA, are of the highest standard and are regularly produced in francophone Africa. Some have been performed in France.

The performance of ancient oral narratives such as the Sunjata and Mwindo epics of old Mali and Zaire respectively by traditional bards or troubadours, commonly known as *griots*, as well as the enactment of rituals, takes on the quality of drama and theatre. European-style theatre began in French-speaking Africa in the early 1930s at two educational establishments almost simultaneously: the École Primaire Supérieure at Bingerville in the Ivory Coast, and the École Normale

William Ponty, then on the island of Gorée off Dakar in Senegal. The link between the two was Charles Béart, who taught at both institutions in the 1930s. Three of the people who contributed most to the development of theatre in the Ivory Coast – François Amon d'Aby, Coffi Gadeau and Bernard Dadié – were students at both schools. The second important development was the establishment after independence, in several states, of institutes of the arts whose drama sections provided training in a wide variety of theatre skills, and national theatres which performed, alongside European plays, the increasing number of African plays being written.

Francophone African drama falls, in terms of themes, into three broad categories: historical, social and political. The first accounts for most of the plays produced so far. In exalting language, Ndao's *L'Exil d'Albouti* (*Albouti's Exile*, 1967), Jean Pliya's *Kondo le requin* (*Kondo the Shark*, first published 1966) and Seydou Badian's *La Mort de Chaka* (*The Death of Chaka*, 1962), for example, depict the careers of various 19th-century warrior-kings and their heroic struggles to defend their territories, often against France. History (whether factual or legendary) is also used not for glorification but for the framework and the necessary safe distance that it offers for a critical reflection on the present.

The dislocating effects of modern culture on traditional beliefs and customs and the retrograde nature of some of the latter constitute the second, social, category of mostly comic plays: such as Oyono-Mbia's *Trois prétendants ... un mari* (*Three Suitors, One Husband*, 1964), Guy Menga's *La Marmite de Koka Mbala* (*Koka Mbala's Pot*, 1969) and Protais Asseng's *Trop c'est trop* (*Enough Is Enough*, 1981). The third group of plays by, among others, U'Tamsi (*Le Destin glorieux du Maréchal Nnikon Nniku, The Glorious Destiny of Marshal Nnikon Nniku*, 1979), Maxime Ndébéka (*Equatorium*, 1989) and Sony Labou Tansi explore the political corruption and ugly tyrannies that have sprung up in postcolonial African societies.

Over the past decade or so, francophone African theatre has moved in new directions. In the plays of dramatists like Nicole Werewere-Liking (1950– ) from Cameroon or Bernard Zadi Zaourou (1938– ) from the Ivory Coast, ritual ceremonies – especially healing, initiation and purification rites – have provided the bases, in content and structure, for a new type of drama.

**Portuguese-speaking (lusophone) Africa**
In the Portuguese colonies, European theatre was introduced early on by missionaries. The plays were inevitably religious in character, their objective being the propagation of Catholicism. The religion of the Africans was not taken into consideration. When independence was declared in 1975 in Angola, Cape Verde, Guinea-Bissau, Mozambique and São Tomé e Príncipe, illiteracy was higher than 90 per cent – a situation which had affected literary production and interest in drama. Portuguese colonialism had imposed severe CENSORSHIP on newspapers and books. The vast majority of the plays performed before independence were *vaudeville* pieces that came from the metropolis to amuse white spectators. After independence, Marxist regimes aimed to make good the damage done by colonialism and to build a classless society. Consequently drama was often used as a means of politicizing people, as a political instrument supporting the principles of socialist realism.

**French-speaking North Africa**
Algeria, Morocco and Tunisia are all Muslim countries

and have been so since the Arab conquest of North Africa in the 7th and 8th centuries. The dominant European influence is that of France which, starting with the annexation of Algeria in 1830, eventually brought Tunisia (1883) and most of Morocco (1912) under its control as protectorates. Independence for Morocco and Tunisia came in 1956 and for Algeria in 1962.

It has not been easy for theatre to flourish in these three countries. The Muslim tradition gave it little encouragement. French censorship was always ready to suppress criticism of the colonial authority. Theatre tended to come therefore largely from outside the region. In the 19th century shadow theatre from Turkey (see KARAGÖZ; SHADOW PUPPETS) was popular. Theatre companies from Egypt (see MIDDLE EAST AND NORTH AFRICA) visited from time to time. Touring French theatre companies provided entertainment chiefly for French expatriates (or citizens, in the case of Algeria) and the French-speaking Arab elite; their offerings were almost by definition drawn from the Parisian BOULEVARD theatres. Since independence, there has been more indigenous activity, especially in Algeria. National Theatres have been established in Algeria and Tunisia, not without difficulty. All three countries were well represented in the drama section of the 1969 pan-African festival (FESTAC), which was held in Algiers. The development of the theatre has also been hampered, even into the present, by the firm hold of classical Arabic on literary production and the barrier to communication with the ordinary people that this causes. Algeria did, however, have the major advantage of the work of Rachid Ksentini who, beween the wars, wrote and directed plays in spoken Arabic with considerable success. Directors and writers committed to the nationalist movement before independence realized the importance of Ksentini's work for the development of a people's theatre after independence. His ideas were adopted by Bachtarzi Mahiedine and Mustapha Kateb in particular, as directors of the Conservatoire Municipal d'Alger and the Théâtre National Algérien respectively.

The French-speaking Algerian playwright and novelist KATEB YACINE is well known in France for his realistic and frank attacks on French colonialism in North Africa. His plays have been directed by JEAN-MARIE SERREAU. Yacine's often violent language and style are as much those of the poet as of the dramatist, and his theatre, like his novels, offers a vision of human behaviour which is far more nuanced than the simple portraits of political theatre.

**African-American theatre** African-American theatre has a dual origin. First came the indigenous theatre consisting of folk tales, songs, music, dance and mimicry that blacks performed in cabins, at camp meetings and in open parks like Gongo Square in New Orleans. African in spirit, these expressions were transformed by the American environment. Then came the African theatre in imitation of white playhouses and scripted dramas that WILLIAM HENRY BROWN established in 1821.

The African theatre had no successors in antebellum America, except for two plays written by the ex-slave William Wells Brown. Black indigenous expressions, however, were by the 1840s adopted by white comedians and fashioned into blackface minstrelsy that caricatured black folk on Southern plantations. Ironically, the now disdained MINSTREL SHOW opened the professional stage to African-Americans. At the same time black performers were polishing their acting skills in short farces which were added to their shows. Since black playgoers were segregated in an upper gallery section in most theatres, these shows played primarily to white audiences. Yet their success ensured perpetuation of the genre into the first decades of the 20th century. Vying for popularity with the minstrels were the ubiquitous 'Tom shows', which, based on the dramatization of UNCLE TOM'S CABIN (1852), also began to employ blacks as slave characters. But eventually the play was denounced by black leaders.

Black companies of higher calibre emerged after the Civil War. The Astor Place Company of Coloured Tragedians under J. A. ARNEAUX came into being in 1884 with a Shakespearian repertoire, and in 1889 Theodore Drury gave the first performance of his Opera Company. In straight drama William Edgar Easton wrote two historical plays on the Haitian revolution: Dessalines (1893) and Christophe (1911), which were produced by HENRIETTA VINTON DAVIS. Scott Joplin composed his opera Treemonisha (1911), but it remained unproduced for decades. In 1897 Bob Cole organized a stock company and training school at Worth's Museum in New York. Others followed, urged on by black critics. In New York the Negro Players were formed in 1912 and the LAFAYETTE PLAYERS in 1915.

Blacks first appeared on BROADWAY in dramatic roles in Three Plays for a Negro Theatre (1917) by the white writer Ridgely Torrence. In 1920 CHARLES GILPIN gave a stunning performance for the PROVINCETOWN PLAYERS in The Emperor Jones (1920). W. E. B. DuBois, editor of the Crisis, urged formation of a nationwide movement of little theatres presenting plays 'about us, by us, for us, and near us'. His magazine and Opportunity sponsored playwriting competitions and published prizewinning entries. In the years ahead black college drama professors would begin writing and directing original plays with their students.

Three dramas by white playwrights demonstrated the reach of black histrionic talent. PAUL GREEN's In Abraham's Bosom (1926) shared Pulitzer Prize honours with an experienced cast including the gifted Rose McLendon; DUBOSE AND DOROTHY HEYWARD's 1927 hit Porgy inspired the operatic version by GEORGE GERSHWIN; and MARC CONNELLY's The Green Pastures (1930) earned a Pulitzer Prize and a five-year run. The 1930s witnessed an upsurge of socially relevant plays like Hall Johnson's Run Little Chillun (1933), LANGSTON HUGHES's Mulatto (1935), and Stevedore (1934) by white authors Paul Peters and George Sklar. The short-lived FEDERAL THEATRE PROJECT through its Negro units in 22 cities sponsored black playwrights and productions, including Theodore Browne's Natural Man (1937) in Seattle, Theodore Ward's Big White Frog (1938) in Chicago, and ORSON WELLES's production of the 'voodoo' Macbeth (1936) in Harlem.

In the 40s the American Negro Theatre made steady progress in training and production at its Harlem-based Library Theatre. PAUL ROBESON's record-breaking Othello (1943) belongs to this decade. After World War II the civil rights movement gained momentum. Plays such as ALICE CHILDRESS's Trouble in Mind (1955) and Loften Mitchell's A Land Beyond the River (1957) dealt unambiguously with the racial problem and used racially mixed casts. Companies like JOSEPH PAPP's NEW YORK SHAKESPEARE FESTIVAL began to cast black actors in traditionally white roles. The trend towards integration was reflected in LORRAINE HANSBERRY's award-winning drama A *Raisin in the Sun* (1959), and OSSIE DAVIS's satiric comedy *Purlie Victorious* (1961). The search for a black identity led to experimentation with new dramatic forms. In 1969 CHARLES GORDONE's *No Place to Be Somebody* captured the Pulitzer Prize. Other significant playwrights of the period were ED BULLINS, Phillip Hayes Dean, ADRIENNE KENNEDY, Ron Milner, Charlie Russell, Joseph Walker and Richard Wesley.

Among the few theatre groups to survive when funding was withdrawn were the NEGRO ENSEMBLE COMPANY of New York, the Free Southern Theatre in New Orleans and the Inner City Cultural Center in Los Angeles. African-American theatre had gained immeasurably from this period of upheaval. Important black productions of recent years include NTOZAKE SHANGE's *For Colored Girls...* and Vinnette Carroll's *Your Arms Too Short to Box with God*, both in 1976, Phillip Hayes Dean's monodrama *Paul Robeson* (1978), and CHARLES FULLER's Pulitzer Prize-winning A *Soldier's Play* (1981). The most important voice to emerge in the 1980s was that of AUGUST WILSON, who wrote and staged a series of plays chronicling black life in this century. Two met with particular success, *Fences* (1983) and *The Piano Lesson* (1990).

**Agate, James (Evershed)** 1877–1947 British critic. Theatre critic of *The Sunday Times* from 1923 until his death, Agate established himself as the most feared and most courted of theatrical judges. Determined always to write well, his views could be unreliable; he delighted in flamboyant actors, from SARAH BERNHARDT to DONALD WOLFIT, and tended to resist radical change in the London theatre. His natural conservatism was a discouragement to dramatic innovation. Agate's self-consciousness is disarmingly confessed in the title of his nine-volume diary, *Ego* (1932–47). Among his 20 volumes of selected criticism are *Buzz, Buzz!* (1918), *Brief Chronicles* (1943), *Red-Letter Nights* (1944) and *Immoment Toys* (1945). He also wrote a biography of the French actress RACHEL.

**Agathon** c.447–c.401 BC Greek tragic playwright. A tragedian at Athens, he departed c.407 for the court of Archelaus of Macedon. ARISTOTLE mentions a TRAGEDY of his (*Antheus*) in which plot and characters were entirely invented (not drawn from myth), and another which contained enough material for an epic. He also says that Agathon was the first to write choral odes which were mere interludes, irrelevant to the play's action. A few fragments survive.

**Ager Fikir** (Patriotic Theatre Association) The first professional Ethiopian theatre company. It was established in 1935, before the Italian invasion, in order to present short propaganda plays to prepare the people of Addis Ababa for resistance. After the restoration of the monarchy it was revived. Programmes were largely musical, though many short plays were performed. The present home was acquired in 1953. Today, full-length plays and music and dance shows are performed there to popular audiences four times a week.

**agit-prop** Term that describes theatre pieces devised to ferment political action (agitation) and propaganda.

**Aguilera Malta, Demetrio** 1909–79 Ecuadorian playwright, poet, novelist and diplomat. He was one-fifth of the famous Grupo de Guayaquil, a leftist literary group dedicated to social change but committed as well to literary excellence. In the early period he wrote realistic social dramas, but his best efforts clearly belong to his expressionistic period (see EXPRESSIONISM), with *El tigre*

*(The Tiger*, 1955), a play of magical realism in the supernatural tropics, *Dientes blancos* (*White Teeth*, 1955) and *Honorarios* (*Fees*, 1957). During his later years as a diplomat he wrote *Infierno negro* (*Black Hell*, 1967) and *Muerte, S.A.* (*Death Inc.*, 1970).

**Agustín, José** 1944– Mexican playwright and novelist. He combines novelistic and dramatic techniques into interesting compositions. *Abolición de la propiedad* (*Abolition of Property*), first staged in 1979, relies on television recordings and projections in dealing with an almost psychopathic perception of reality. *Círculo vicioso* (*Vicious Circle*, 1972), an exposé of corruption in the Mexican penal system, was originally censored by the Mexican authorities for its gross language.

**Aidoo, Ama Ata** 1942– Ghanaian playwright and novelist; Secretary for Education in the Rawlings government. Her reputation rests upon her two plays, *The Dilemma of a Ghost* (1964) and *Anowa* (1970). *The Dilemma of a Ghost* explores the problems of a marriage between a Ghanaian man who has achieved academic honours in the United States and a black American woman whom he brings home to Ghana. *Anowa* is concerned with the legacy of slavery, and the tragic outcome. Aidoo now lives in Zimbabwe.

**Aiken, George L.** 1830–76 American playwright. He is known for one play: *UNCLE TOM'S CABIN*, or Life Among the Lowly, a dramatization of Harriet Beecher Stowe's novel, presented in September 1852 with Aiken in the part of George Harris. In response to audience demand for more episodes from the novel, Aiken prepared a sequel, *The Death of Uncle Tom, or the Religion of the Lowly*, and in mid-November combined the two plays into one drama of six acts, now the standard version.

**Aikenvald, Yuly (Isaevich)** 1872–1928 Russian literary critic and theatre reviewer. He became embroiled in the pre-revolutionary debate over theatre's true nature and proper function. His article 'Rejecting the Theatre' (*Studio*, 1912) defied attempts by the symbolists (see SYMBOLISM) MEYERHOLD, EVREINOV and others to poeticize theatre by asserting that it had no value except as dramatic literature. Aikenvald's broadside encouraged directors NEMIROVICH-DANCHENKO and KOMISSARZHEVSKY, critic D. N. Ovsyaniko-Kulikovsky and dramatist-actor A. I. Yuzhin-Sumbatov to publish *Debating the Theatre* (1912), in which they defended their roles as artistic interpreters.

**Akalaitis, JoAnne** 1937– American actress and director. She is a founding and continuing member of the avant-garde group MABOU MINES. Her experimental works have been performed at major art centres and festivals throughout the USA and Europe. From 1990 to 1993 Akalaitis was artistic director of the NEW YORK SHAKESPEARE FESTIVAL.

**Akimov, Nikolai (Pavlovich)** 1901–68 Soviet stage and film designer. His graceful, whimsical and vibrantly colourful stage realizations defined the character of the Leningrad Theatre of Comedy, where he was artistic director (1935–49, 1955–68). As a designer in the 1920s Akimov worked in Leningrad and Moscow on Soviet dramas. He began directing in 1929 and in 1932 staged a controversial formalist production of *Hamlet* for Moscow's Vakhtangov Theatre. His sharp and witty style was most clearly demonstrated in his Theatre of Comedy productions, particularly EVGENY SHVARTS's *The Shadow* (1940, 1960), *The Dragon* (1944, 1962) and *An Ordinary Miracle* (1956), and in SUKHOVO-KOBYLIN's *The Case* (1964) and *Krechinsky's Wedding* (1966). From 1951 to

1955 he served as the Lensoviet Theatre's artistic director, where he staged SALTYKOV-SHCHEDRIN's *Shadows* (1953) and an earlier version of *The Case* (1955). He also designed theatre posters and wrote two books which blended memoirs with theatre aesthetics and practice. In 1960 he was named a People's Artist of the USSR.

**Akins, Zoë** 1886–1958 American playwright and screenwriter. She began her career with an experimental free-verse drama,*The Magical City* (1916). Early sophisticated comedies and wistful tragedies about jaded, worldly women were followed by a rash of popular comedies. Her first and best hit was *Déclassée* (1919). Others were *Papa* (1919), *Greatness: A Comedy* (1921, also called *The Texas Nightingale*), *Daddy's Gone A-Hunting* (1921) and *The Greeks Had a Word for It* (1929, later filmed as *The Golddiggers*). In 1935 she won the Pulitzer Prize for her adaptation of EDNA FERBER's *The Old Maid*.

**Aksyonov, Vasily (Pavlovich)** 1932– Soviet novelist and playwright. He is part of the intellectual tradition of literary PARODY and grotesque REALISM of GOGOL and others. As part of the Young Prose movement centred on VALENTIN KATAEV's journal *Youth* (1955), he became a spokesman for the post-World War II generation. His early novels, characterized by racy dialogue, Western-style fashions and colloquialisms, reflect the problems of youth and maturation in Soviet society. His later writing is more experimental and fantastic, reverting to the Russian avant-garde of the 1920s. *Always on Sale*, a realistic social SATIRE and highly theatricalist pastiche of popular culture, was a great success in OLEG EFREMOV's 1965 production at Moscow's Sovremennik Theatre. *Your Murderer* (published in English, 1977), subtitled 'An Anti-alcoholic Comedy in Eight Scenes with a Prologue and an Epilogue', is a grotesque, fanciful parable of an artist who is destroyed by his own creation. A third play, *The Heron* (unpublished), is a CHEKHOVian parody set at a health resort. In 1980 Aksyonov emigrated to the United States.

**Aktie Tomaat** (Action tomato, or the tomato campaign) Dutch theatre movement. Late in 1969, tomatoes were thrown at actors during a performance by the Nederlandse Comedie at the municipal theatre of Amsterdam: students from the Toneelschool (Amsterdam School of Drama) were launching a protest against the limited theatrical repertory, lacking in social relevance, and against the authoritarian status of the director, who subordinated the actors to his views. This protest linked up with the call for democracy by students and workers in Europe and America. As a result, new Dutch companies, such as WERKTEATER, organized on democratic principles, emerged: the director became a creative assistant or member of a collective; actors could start to explore their creative potential; productions were improvised and dramatic texts updated. The new theatre groups were subsidized by the Ministry of Culture.

**Alarcón, Juan Ruiz de** see RUIZ DE ALARCÓN (Y MENDOZA), JUAN

**Alawada Theatre** see ADEJUMO, MOSES OLAIYA

**Albee, Edward** 1928– American playwright. Albee made a spectacular debut with four one-act absurdist plays (see THEATRE OF THE ABSURD), beginning with *The Zoo Story* (1958), and capped his reputation with the BROADWAY productions of *Who's Afraid of Virginia Woolf?* (1962) and *Tiny Alice* (1964). He was greeted as the leader of a new theatrical movement and his name was linked with those of TENNESSEE WILLIAMS, ARTHUR MILLER and

WILLIAM INGE. Refusing to capitalize on the lacerating wit and character conflict that made *Virginia Woolf* so powerful, Albee has pursued an increasingly rarefied style. Despite critical and commercial defeats, he has continued to write prolifically in three forms: adaptations (such as Carson McCullers's *Ballad of the Sad Café*, 1963, and Nabokov's *Lolita*, 1980); short chamber plays (*Box* and *Quotations from Mao-Tse Tung*, 1968, *Listening*, 1975, and *Counting the Ways*, 1976); and full-length plays in which ordered lives are invaded and transformed. In *A Delicate Balance* (awarded the Pulitzer Prize in 1966), Harry and Edna carry a mysterious psychic plague into their best friends' living room. The title character in *The Lady from Dubuque* (1979) is an angel of death. Talking sea creatures emerge from the water to confront sedate picnickers in *Seascape* (which won the Pulitzer Prize in 1975). In recent years Albee's mainstream reputation has been low. His Broadway production *The Man Who Had Three Arms* (1983) was received poorly by the critics. *Marriage Play* (1987) premiered out of New York – as did *Three Tall Women* (1991) which, nevertheless, eventually won the Pulitzer Prize for Drama (1994).

**Albee, Edward F.** see VAUDEVILLE

**Albertazzi, Giorgio** 1925– Italian actor and director. He began his career as an actor in the early 1940s, and became internationally known in films like *L'année dernière à Marienbad* and *Morte di un bandito*. He is a strong lead player with an impressive stage presence. Among his major roles in classic drama have been SHAKESPEARE's *Hamlet*, *Macbeth* and *Richard III* (the last in his own version, most recently in 1988), PIRANDELLO's *Enrico IV* and IBSEN's *Peer Gynt* (1988). He has directed in theatre and film and, since 1985, with *Lucia di Lammermoor*, for the musical stage. He has supported the work of modern foreign dramatists on the Italian stage, most recently directing the Italian premiere of ARNOLD WESKER's *Letter to a Daughter* (1993).

**Albery, James** 1838–89 English playwright. His one outstanding success, *Two Roses* (1870), established HENRY IRVING as a star. CHARLES WYNDHAM got Albery to adapt the saucy marital farce *Les Dominos Roses* into *The Pink Dominos* (1877). *Where's the Cat?* (1880) was a disappointment for the critics, who ruined Albery's talent by expecting too much of it.

**Aldredge, Theoni** 1932– American COSTUME designer. Born in Greece, Aldredge studied and then worked at the GOODMAN THEATRE in Chicago before moving to New York in 1958. From 1962 onwards she was a principal designer for the NEW YORK SHAKESPEARE FESTIVAL. From the mid-1970s she has been part of the collaborative team – MICHAEL BENNETT, ROBIN WAGNER and THARON MUSSER – that produced *Chorus Line* and *Dreamgirls*, among others. Aldredge has designed landmark productions such as *Who's Afraid of Virginia Woolf?* and *Hair*. She also designs for ballet, opera, television and film, including *Network* and *The Great Gatsby*. Costumes for the elegant but short-lived musical *Nick and Nora* (1991) were designed by her. Aldredge is a collaborative artist; her designs are integrated with and supportive of the direction and overall visual statement of a production.

**Aldridge, Ira** 1807–67 African-American actor. Starting in New York, Aldridge moved to England at the age of 17 and became a touring provincial actor in Britain and Ireland for over 25 years. In 1833 he replaced the mortally ill EDMUND KEAN as Othello at COVENT GARDEN Theatre, and in 1852 began a series of highly successful appearances in Europe and Russia. Equally brilliant in TRAGEDY and COMEDY, he often performed Othello and Mungo (in BICKERSTAFFE's comic operetta *The Padlock*) on the same bill. He introduced psychological realism into acting in the 1850s, well before his European counterparts.

**Alekseev, K.S.** see STANISLAVSKY, KONSTANTIN

**Aleotti, Giovanni Battista** 1546–1636 Italian architect, engineer and stage designer. He spent most of his working life in the service of the court of the Estensi at Ferrara, where he built the Teatro degli Intrepidi in 1605. His finest surviving work is the Teatro Farnese in Parma (1618), one of the largest baroque theatres, with a seating capacity of 4,500. Aleotti is thought to have introduced sliding flat wings by 1618, replacing traditional Serlian (see SERLIO) fixed angle wings and permitting frequent and rapid shifts of scene. (See also TORELLI.)

**Alexander, George** [George Samson] 1858–1918 Anglo-Scottish actor and theatre manager. He was with IRVING at the London LYCEUM from 1881 to 1889, most notably as Valentine in *Faust* (1885). He bought the lease on the ST JAMES's, where his declared policy was to encourage and support the writing of new plays by British authors. The first English producer of OSCAR WILDE – *Lady Windermere's Fan* (1892) – and the creator of Jack Worthing in *The Importance of Being Earnest* (1895), he enjoyed his greatest (and boldest) success with PINERO's *The Second Mrs Tanqueray* (1893), which made a star of MRS PATRICK CAMPBELL. Later Pinero premieres included *The Princess and the Butterfly* (1897), *His House in Order* (1906), *The Thunderbolt* (1908) and *Mid-Channel* (1909). The 1902 production of STEPHEN PHILLIPS's *Paolo and Francesca* earned for Alexander an undeserved reputation as an upholder of literary standards. He was, in fact, a shrewd businessman and efficient theatre manager, who took risks only occasionally. He was knighted in 1911.

**Alexander** [*née* Quigley], **Jane** 1939– American actress. She came to stardom as the white mistress of the black boxing champion in *The Great White Hope* (1968). Dedicated to regional theatre, to which she returns frequently, she was critically acclaimed as Lavinia in O'NEILL's *Mourning Becomes Electra* at the AMERICAN SHAKESPEARE (Festival) THEATRE in 1971. Other New York theatre appearances include *Six Rms Riv Vu* (1972), *First Monday in October* (1978), WILLIAM GIBSON's *Monday After the Miracle* (1982), *Shadowlands* (1990) and *The Visit* (1992). In 1993 she was selected to head the controversial National Endowment for the Arts.

**Alfieri, Vittorio** 1749–1803 Italian playwright and poet. He wrote in both French and Italian, his first TRAGEDY *Cleopatra* appearing in 1775. Over the next decade he produced the bulk of his dramatic work, including 19 tragedies, non-dramatic verse and many political writings. At their best his plays reveal a distinctively personal blend of the classical and romantic, a taste for Aristotelian rules combined with a highly individual insistence on the exercise of heroic will. But although 19th-century actors like SALVINI performed some of Alfieri's great poetic dramas abroad, and several have survived on the modern Italian stage, none has entered the European repertoire. Of his 21 tragedies perhaps the best are *Oreste* (1778), *Virginia* (1778), *Saul* (1782) and *Mirra* (1786); none of his six comedies now attracts interest.

**Allen, Gracie** see BURNS, GEORGE

**Allen, Viola** 1869–1948 American actress. In 1884 the actor JOHN McCULLOUGH engaged her to play his daughter in *Virginius*, then made her his leading lady. Later she played opposite W.E. Sheridan, TOMMASO SALVINI and JOSEPH JEFFERSON III. She was leading lady in CHARLES FROHMAN's Empire Stock Company. An intelligent and appealing actress, she was highly regarded for such portrayals as Viola and the double roles of Hermione and Perdita. She retired in 1918.

**Alleyn, Edward** 1566–1626 English actor. He is known to have been with the ADMIRAL's MEN at the ROSE by 1592, where he played MARLOWE's towering heroes. His career, unlike that of his fellow leading actor RICHARD BURBAGE, was interrupted when he retired from the stage in 1597, and with his father-in-law PHILIP HENSLOWE ran the Bear Garden and built the FORTUNE as a new home for the Admiral's Men. When the Fortune opened in 1600, Alleyn returned to the stage. His highly rhetorical style may by then have seemed old-fashioned, but he did not finally retire until 1604. In 1613 he began the building of the College of God's Gift at Dulwich (then a few miles southeast of London).

**Alonso de Santos, José Luis** 1942– Spanish playwright, acting teacher and critic. He became associated with the independent collective theatre movement during his student years. The premiere of his first original play coincided with Franco's death in November 1975, and he is recognized as a major author of the new theatre of democratic Spain. Among important works are *La estanquera de Vallecas* (*Hostages in the Barrio*, 1981), *El álbum familiar* (*Family Album*, 1982) and *Bajarse al moro* (*Going down to Marrakesh*, 1985), the latter widely acclaimed, translated and filmed. Typically Alonso de Santos's plays are bitter-sweet comedies. Their surface humour, creative use of contemporary slang and intertextual references to filmic codes make them particularly appealing to a younger generation of theatregoers.

**Alpers, Boris (Vladimirovich)** 1894–1974 Soviet theatre critic and scholar. Following the 1917 Revolution he adopted a Bolshevik bias in his writing. A former member of MEYERHOLD's Dr Dapertutto Studio on Borodinsky Street (1914–15), Alpers helped to establish the Ligovsky Dramatic Theatre in Petrograd (1921–4), and later the Moscow Theatre of the Revolution, where he headed the literary section (1924–7) and where many of the 'social themes' originally proposed at the Ligovsky were realized. From 1921 he wrote reviews, theoretical articles and books, the most important being *The Theatre of the Social Mask* (1931), written in the late 1920s, which presented the first proper assessment of Meyerhold's work to that point.

*alta comedia* see COMEDIA

**Álvarez Lleras, Antonio** 1892–1956 Colombian playwright. Considered to be the father of the modern Colombian theatre, he wrote 15 plays. From his first effort in 1907 to his masterpiece, *El virrey Solis* (*The Viceroy Solis*, 1948), he sought to internationalize Colombian theatre with psychologically realistic plays that were didactic and often historical.

**Álvarez Quintero, Serafín** 1871–1938 and **Joaquín Álvarez Quintero** 1873–1944 Spanish playwrights. They collaborated on more than 200 plays and sketches over a period of 40 years. The brothers had an early success with *Esgrima y amor* (*Fencing and Love*, 1888) in Seville. After nine years in Madrid they gained success with *El ojito derecho* (*The Apple of His Eye*), followed by a stream of playlets, ZARZUELAS and sketches. Their work leans heavily on local Andalusian colour and custom, depicting a charming, optimistic world.

**Amalrik, Andrei (Alekseevich)** 1938–80 Soviet historian and playwright. An outspoken dissident, after years of intermittent exile and internment for his plays and political writings, Amalrik emigrated in 1976. His *Notes of a Revolutionary* (1982) is a personal biography and a cultural history of the USSR, 1966–76, focusing upon the individual's destruction by the governmental system. Amalrik's short plays reflect his childhood interest in the puppet theatre, as well as the influence of the Russian poet-dramatist Velimir Khlebnikov, BECKETT and, especially, IONESCO. *My Aunt Is Living in Volokolamsk* (1963, 1964, 1966), *East-West: A Dialogue in Suzdal* (1963), *The Fourteen Lovers of Ugly Mary-Ann* (1964), *The Story of the Little White Bull* (1964), *Is Uncle Jack a Conformist?* (1964) and *Nose! Nose? No-se!* (adapted from GOGOL's short story, 'The Nose', 1964), all one-acts, are characterized by Freudian-based sex and violence, illogical character behaviour and language which ranges from aphoristic to nonsensical.

**American Conservatory Theater** Non-commercial regional American repertory company. Combining performing with a training school, ACT was founded in 1965 by William Ball. It has made its home in San Francisco since 1967. As a result of earthquake damage, in 1990–1 ACT moved from the Geary to the Palace of Fine Arts Theater.

**American Laboratory Theatre** American acting school. Inspired by the first American appearance of the MOSCOW ART THEATRE in January 1923, the American Laboratory Theatre (originally called the Theatre Arts Institute) was founded six months later as a school for training young actors in the STANISLAVSKY system: a significant first step in translating Stanislavsky's ideas about truth in acting into an American idiom. The focus of the school was the classes taught by Richard Boleslavski and Maria Ouspenskaya, two impassioned émigrés from Stanislavsky's company. The Lab (disbanded in 1933) and its theatre (1925–30), were important links between the appearance of Stanislavsky's company and the establishment in 1931 of America's first true theatrical collective, the GROUP THEATRE.

**American Repertory Theatre** (USA) The first company of this name, founded in 1946 by EVA LE GALLIENNE, MARGARET WEBSTER and CHERYL CRAWFORD, was located on Columbus Circle, New York. It was defunct by 1948. The second company (ART) under ROBERT BRUSTEIN began an association in 1980 with Harvard University. Dedicated to neglected works from the past, to new American plays and to innovative classical productions, the theatre has staged controversial productions, innovative direction and experimental work, such as the 1985 presentation of portions of ROBERT WILSON's *the CIVIL WarS*, and inaugural productions, such as MARSHA NORMAN's *'night, Mother* (1982).

**American Shakespeare Theatre** (USA) Founded in Stratford, Connecticut, in 1951 as the American Festival Theatre under the guidance of LAWRENCE LANGNER, its name was changed in 1972. The octagonal theatre, reminiscent of the exterior of the original GLOBE THEATRE, with a thrust stage and an auditorium seating about 1,500, opened on 12 July 1955 with *Julius Caesar*. The repertoire included non-Shakespearian works. Since 1979 production has been sporadic, and since 1982 virtually non-existent.

**Ames, Winthrop** 1871–1937 American producer and director. Ames, a wealthy Bostonian, was the first American to make a serious study of the European art theatres and their scenic innovations. In 1912 he introduced the 'new stagecraft' to New York by bringing over REINHARDT's production of *Sumrun*. He encouraged NORMAN BEL GEDDES's experiments in stage lighting at his two New York theatres, the Little and the BOOTH. Ames prepared minutely detailed prompt scripts, 'mother copies', for his productions, most notably GALSWORTHY's *The Pigeon* (1912), SCHNITZLER's *The Affairs of Anatol* (1912), SHAW's *The Philanderer* (1913), *Snow White* (1913, his own adaptation), MAETERLINCK's *The Betrothal* (1918), and KAUFMAN and CONNELLY's *Beggar on Horseback* (1924).

**Amsterdamse Schouwburg** Dutch theatre. The first municipal theatre of Amsterdam, built by Jacob van Campen, was opened on 3 January 1638 with a performance of JOOST VAN DEN VONDEL's *Gijsbrecht van Aemstel*, which marked the beginning of a New Year's tradition that would continue for centuries. It was here that in 1655 the first Dutch actress, Ariana Roozemond, appeared on stage. Two subsequent theatres (1664–1772 and 1774–1890) were destroyed by fire. The present theatre was built in 1894 at the Leidseplein. The resident company chooses its repertory from all over the world.

**Anderson, J(ohn) H(enry)** 1814–74 Scottish conjuror, known as the Great Wizard of the North. His genius for publicity brought him years of success in the provinces and in London, and in 1845 he opened his 5,000-seat City Theatre in Glasgow, where for five months he produced MINSTREL SHOWS, operas and VARIETY as a setting for his demonstrations of MAGIC and second sight. Anderson originated the pulling of rabbits from top hats and of a live goose from 'The Magic Scrapbook' (Queen Victoria's favourite trick). When his theatre and apparatus burned down, he resumed touring in Europe, the USA and Australia.

**Anderson, Judith** [*née* Frances Margaret Anderson-Anderson] 1898–1992 Australian-born actress. Her reputation was made in the USA and the UK, where she consistently excelled in powerful, tragic roles. She made her debut in Sydney in 1915 and first appeared in New York in 1918. Later roles included Lavinia in *Mourning Becomes Electra* (1932), Gertrude to JOHN GIELGUD's Hamlet in New York (1936), Lady Macbeth opposite LAURENCE OLIVIER (OLD VIC, 1937), the title role in an adaptation of EURIPIDES's *Medea* (1947) and Irina Arkadina in *The Seagull* (Old Vic, 1960). In 1940 she began a film career, giving a memorable performance as the sinister housekeeper Mrs Danvers in *Rebecca*. In 1960 she was appointed DBE. In 1970 she made an unsuccessful tour playing the title role in *Hamlet*.

**Anderson, Lindsay (Gordon)** 1923–94 British director. Having begun his career by making documentary films, he became a forceful member of GEORGE DEVINE's team at the ROYAL COURT. There he directed WILLIS HALL's *The Long and the Short and the Tall* (1959) and JOHN ARDEN's *Serjeant Musgrave's Dance* (1959); and later the plays of DAVID STOREY, which began with *In Celebration* (1969) and continued through several lovingly detailed studies of contemporary life – *The Contractor* (1969), *Home* (1970), *The Changing Room* (1971), *The Farm* (1973) and *Life Class* (1974). He also worked at the NATIONAL THEATRE and on BROADWAY, and made a powerful screen impact with the film *If* (1968), about British public school life and aberrations. The success of the latter led to a new career in films and television, to which he brought his left-leaning, half-satirical NATURALISM. In his later years he worked less in the theatre, although his partnership with Storey continued at the National Theatre with *Early Days* (1980), *The March on Russia* (1989) and *Stages* (1992). In 1987 he directed a revival of PHILIP BARRY's 1928 American comedy *Holiday* at the OLD VIC.

**Anderson, Mary** 1859–1940 American actress. Her major assets were her classical physical beauty and a rich, expressive voice. She made her New York debut in 1877. W. S. GILBERT wrote a short play, *Comedy and Tragedy*, for her. Americans proudly called her 'Our Mary', though in 1890 she settled in England. During her 14-year career on both sides of the Atlantic she played 18 leading roles.

**Anderson, Maxwell** 1888–1959 American playwright and dramatic theorist. His greatest critical successes came in the 30s: *Both Your Houses* (1933), *Winterset* (1935) and *High Tor* (1937). Anderson gained a reputation as an anti-war dramatist in *What Price Glory?* (1924; co-authored with Lawrence Stallings), *Valley Forge* (1934), *Key Largo* (1939), *Candle in the Wind* (1941) and *The Eve of St Mark* (1942). He turned frequently to the lives of monarchs and other political leaders for subject-matter, e.g. *Elizabeth the Queen* (1930), *Mary of Scotland* (1933), *Knickerbocker Holiday* (1938; a musical written in collaboration with Kurt Weill), *Joan of Lorraine* (1947), *Anne of the Thousand Days* (1948) and *Barefoot in Athens* (1951). Anderson attempted to justify the use of blank verse in modern drama, and in *The Essence of Tragedy* (1939) published a detailed theoretical work.

**Anderson, Robert W(oodruff)** 1917– American playwright. He came to prominence by winning the National Theatre Conference Prize with *Come Marching Home* (1945). *Tea and Sympathy* (1953), a sensitive study of a young man's growth from innocence into experience, is still considered his outstanding work. Other plays produced by the Playwrights' Company were *All Summer Long* (1953) and *Silent Night, Lonely Night* (1959). *The Days Between* (1965) helped inaugurate the American Playwrights' Theatre. He also wrote one-act plays.

**Andrade, Jorge** 1922–84 Brazilian playwright. His plays divide into the 'rural' cycle – *O telescópio* (*The Telescope*, (1954), *A moratória* (*The Moratorium*, 1955), *Pedreira das almas* (*Stone Quarry of Souls*, 1956) and *Vereda da salvação* (*Path to Salvation*, 1964) – and the 'urban' plays, of which the best-known is *Os ossos do Barão* (*The Baron's Bones*, 1963). Born into a traditional rural aristocratic family, Andrade specialized in showing the decadence of São Paulo society. *Marta, a arvore e o relógio* (*Martha, the Tree and the Clock*, 1970) climaxed his varied production. *Rasto atrás* (*Step Backwards*), his last major play, is an autobiographical projection of a father–son relationship in a context of class decadence.

**Andreev, Leonid (Nikolaevich)** 1871–1919 Russian prose writer, playwright and journalist. Prolific and controversial, he rivalled CHEKHOV and GORKY in popularity and importance during the pre-revolutionary period (c.1905–17). Andreev is an extreme example of the soul sickness, spiritual confusion and sense of isolation suffered by the Russian artistic intelligentsia of this era. His macabre short stories, like his metaphysical dramas, contemplate man's folly, vanity and brutality and life's horror and falsity, and feature madness, death and all manner of sexual and spiritual perversion. His most representative 'cosmic' dramas include *The Life of Man* (1906), *Tsar Hunger* (1907), *Black Masks*

(1908), *Anathema* (1909) and his international classic, *He Who Gets Slapped* (1915). *The Life of Man*, which utilizes puppet-like characters and stylized speech and action, was produced by both MEYERHOLD and STANISLAVSKY in 1907. Andreev's sombreness was parodied in his time. His eventual repudiation of the revolutionary cause made his plays unpopular in the Soviet period.

**Andreini family** Italian actors, originally from Tuscany. The family's founder **Francesco Dal Gallo** (1548–1624) took the name Andreini when he entered a COMMEDIA DELL'ARTE troupe. He perfected the type of the braggart soldier and headed the GELOSI company on its pioneering visit to Paris in 1603–4. His wife **Isabella** (1562–1604) played Innamorata with the Gelosi and was the most famous actress of her time. Their eldest son **Giovan Battista** or **Giambattista** (1576 or 1579–1654) played Innamorato under the name Lelio. With TRISTANO MARTINELLI he founded the FEDELI troupe, which toured Italy (1613–14) and went to Paris, where he became a favourite of Louis XIII. He was a prolific writer of tragicomedies, comedies, mystery plays and PASTORALS. His wife **Virginia** (1583–1638) performed under the name Florinda.

**Andrianoú, Kyvéli** ?1887–1978 Greek actress. She distinguished herself in innocent girl roles and played in a great number of bourgeois dramas, captivating audiences with her melodious voice and sentimental gestures. Eventually she acted in mature roles: Mary Stuart in SCHILLER's classical drama, and the mother in BRECHT's *Mother Courage*. Several Greek playwrights wrote dramas especially for her to act in.

**Andronicus, Lucius Livius** died c.204 BC Early Roman dramatist. It is now generally accepted that he produced the first of all literary dramas in Latin in 240 BC. He wrote tragedies and comedies, all adapted from Greek originals, as well as non-dramatic works, and must have established the main conventions of Roman drama.

**animal impersonation** Possibly the earliest form of acting, as primitive tribesmen or their SHAMANS disguised themselves as animal divinities to ensure successful hunts, evoke fertility daimons or propitiate malign influences. The painting of the deer dancer in the Trois Frères cave in Ariège, France, probably shows such an impersonation, and the Indians of New Mexico preserved such a deer dance to the 20th century. The daimonic element can be traced in surviving folk customs, such as the hobbyhorses of the mummers' plays, and particularly in the combats against dragons, ranging from the grotesque Balinese *barong* to the dragon marched in procession in Suffolk as late as 1903.

The folk plays of Attica were strong on animal impersonation, and the satyr chorus from which TRAGEDY is traditionally claimed to have sprung was clad in goatskins, horsetails and fox ears. Vestiges of these practices recur in the fantastic choruses of ARISTOPHANES' comedies: birds, wasps and frogs.

The portrayal of animals as individual characters by human actors became immensely popular after the French Revolution. As a result of ROUSSEAU's ideas, the noble savage was held to exist even under the skin of an ape. English PANTOMIME was another important context for animal impersonation. The leading artists in this field were GEORGE CONQUEST the elder, George Ali and Charles Lauri. Conquest triumphed in such outlandish parts as an octopus, a crab and a giant porcupine whose costume consisted of 2,500 separate pieces. The

Brothers Griffiths kept MUSIC-HALL audiences in stitches with their wrestling lion and the famous Blondin donkey, which seemed lifelike but contorted its legs in a cartoon fashion as soon as it was forced on to the tightrope.

Modern drama, fixated on realism, has been chary of this type of performance. In a playful mode, MAETERLINCK made a dog and cat major characters in *The Blue Bird* (1908) and SHAW provided his Androcles with a waltzing lion (1913). Nevertheless, realism was challenged by such experiments as the dinosaur and mammoth in THORNTON WILDER's *Skin of Our Teeth* (1942) and the scaly amphibians in EDWARD ALBEE's *Seascape* (1975). For the most part, modern animal impersonation has been relegated to pantomime and MUSICAL COMEDY: the cat in *Dick Whittington*, Nana the St Bernard in *Peter Pan* (1904), the beagle Snoopy in *You're a Good Man, Charlie Brown*, Caroline the cow in *Gypsy* (1959), the feline cast of *Cats* and the wolf in *Into the Woods*. Horses have been merged with their riders in ANOUILH's *Becket* (1959) and KOPIT's *Indians* (1968) and stylized into elegant gymnasts in SHAFFER's *Equus* (1973). However, a more three-dimensional and moving equine hero appeared in Mark Rozovsky's dramatization of *Kholstomer*, TOLSTOY's story of a gelding (directed by GEORGY TOVSTONOGOV, Leningrad, 1975); it was recreated in English as *Strider*. Several recent adaptations of Kafka's *Metamorphosis* have provided the greatest stretch for an actor: when STEVEN BERKOFF's version was played in New York, the cockroach was interpreted by the great ballet dancer Mikhail Baryshnikov.

**animals as performers** The training of animals not to perform an agricultural or military function but simply to entertain, most specifically by imitating human behaviour, blatantly advertises man as Lord of Creation. The earliest recorded example is the lion Antam-Nekht under Pharaoh Rameses II (1292–1225 BC); and trained tigers who would allow a man to put his head safely in their mouths were known in early China and India (12th–9th centuries BC). Wandering performers in both the ancient and medieval worlds showed off simple tricks with bears and apes.

The most famous trained animal of SHAKESPEARE's day was the bay horse Morocco, shown by John Banks; as exhibited in the yard of the Belle Sauvage, London, it returned gloves to their owners, told the number of coins, and danced (warranting a mention in *Love's Labour's Lost*).

The heyday of the performing animal came in the 'Age of Enlightenment', when *animaux savants* rivalled the noble savage as exemplars of natural perfectibility. In England learned pigs were frequently on view solving mathematical puzzles. During the early romantic period of MELODRAMA and PANTOMIME, animals starred: Coco the stag, a headliner at the CIRQUE OLYMPIQUE, was seriously compared to ballet dancers when he leaped over 16 horses in 1813. COVENT GARDEN and DRURY LANE admitted horses, lions and elephants to their pantomimic spectacles, and dog drama retained its favour on the London stage well into the century. In the 1850s, when CHARLES KEAN revived 'legitimate' drama at the PRINCESS's Theatre, he put horses on stage (see HIPPO-DRAMA). Meanwhile the exhibition of wild animals at CIRCUSES was undergoing a change. New training methods stressed animal psychology and work therapy, based on Pavlov's experiments and those of the Swiss psychologist J. Gaule. The result could be seen in the

work of Carl and Wilhelm Hagenbeck who developed the round cage that filled the entire arena, allowing the animals more freedom (1888).

Almost every kind of animal has been recruited into show business, from wrestling Floridian alligators to boxing kangaroos (first shown by Prof. Landermann at the London Aquarium in 1892). Today live animals are still to be seen in grand opera and MUSICAL COMEDY – e.g. the dog Sandy in *Annie*.

***ankiya nat*** Indian theatre form. *Ankiya nat* is a kind of religious drama which originated and still exists in Assam, a beautiful, remote state in northeastern India. *Ankiya nat* was created by Sankaradeva (c.1449–1568), an ardent devotee of Lord Vishnu who in his earthly manifestation as Krishna is worshipped by many Assamese Hindus. *Ankiya* means 'act' and *nat* means 'drama'. Thus, *ankiya nat* is a one-act drama composed in a particular form. Sankaradeva wrote many popular plays for the repertory as a means of maintaining and spreading the tenets of Vaishnavism among his people.

Performances of *ankiya nat* usually take place inside prayer halls (*nam-ghar*), roofed structures open at the side, located in the sacred confines of a monastery. Companies consist of about 15 amateur actors, made up either of monks or village artists. Normally, men play all the parts in the monastery productions, but women may participate in performances in communities where taboos are not rigidly enforced. Perhaps the most striking characters are the giant effigies made of bamboo and covered with papier-mâché painted to represent demons and animals. Some of the figures are at least 15 feet high and must be manipulated by several actors at once. Masks of birds, snakes, monkeys and bears are worn when a particular play demands the presence of such fanciful characters. Typically, performances are organized to coincide with religious festivals, such as the birth of Krishna. A performance event usually begins around 9 pm and continues until sunrise.

The strength of *ankiya nat* is in its close links with the religious beliefs of the Assamese people, particularly the devotees (*bhaktas*) of Krishna. It does not seem to have changed drastically, even though the state has undergone many dramatic changes in its economic and social organization in recent times.

**Annenkov, Yury (Pavlovich)** 1889–1974 Russian designer. He assisted in the theatrical experiments by NIKOLAI EVREINOV, FYODOR KOMISSARZHEVSKY and others; and designed at NIKITA BALIEV's Moscow Bat (later, the Chauve-Souris) and (from 1913) at KUGEL's and Kholmskaya's St Petersburg Crooked Mirror Theatre. The Annenkov–Evreinov collaboration extended to expressionist designs for Evreinov's Soviet mass spectacle *The Storming of the Winter Palace* (1920) and *The Chief Thing* (1921) (see EXPRESSIONISM). Annenkov also contributed large-scale designs to *The Field of Mars May Day Celebration* (1918) and *The Hymn to Liberated Labour* (1920), staged in front of the old St Petersburg stock exchange. He helped introduce futurist theatre ideas into Russia, and his 1921 manifesto 'The Theatre to the End' posited a 'theatre of pure method', based upon gymnastic and circus performance, which inspired MEYERHOLD. In 1924 Annenkov emigrated to Germany and France.

**Annensky, Innokenty (Fyodorovich)** 1856–1909 Russian poet, critic and playwright. EURIPIDES, all of whose plays he translated, was the model for his four dramas, in which he attempted to contemporize the

ANOUILH, JEAN

Greek myths while maintaining their universality: *Melanippe, the Philosopher* (1901), *King Ixion* (1902), *Laodamia* (1906), and *Thamira, the Cither Player* (1906). These deal with the conflict between art and life, beauty and suffering. Only *Thamira* was staged, by TAIROV in a cubist production at Moscow's Kamerny Theatre (1916).

**Anouilh, Jean** 1910–87 French playwright and scriptwriter. A brilliant theatrical craftsman, he was commercially very successful. Anouilh's first plays were written in a naturalist vein, but he soon moved towards a more light-hearted style of bitter-sweet comedy, perfected in *Le Bal des voleurs* (*The Thieves' Carnival*), directed by BARSACQ (1938). This started a fruitful collaboration which included his best-known play *Antigone* (1944), derivative of PIRANDELLO and of revivals of Greek myth between the wars. The play contains references to contemporary life, and appealed both to Nazi sympathizers and to Resistance workers. After the war, Anouilh's plays bridged the gap between the classics and the BOULEVARD. His output in the 1950s and 1960s was voluminous and he set his plays in different historical periods, but his themes, notably the contrast between youthful purity and adult compromise, varied little – in e.g. *L'Alouette* (*The Lark*, 1953), *Pauvre Bitos* (*Poor Bitos*, 1956), *Cher Antoine* (*Dear Antoine*, 1969) and *Becket* (1959). Anouilh also directed revivals of MOLIÈRE and of VITRAC's *Victor*.

**Anski, S.** [Solomon Z. Rapoport] 1863–1920 Russian-born playwright. He is immortalized by his YIDDISH play *The Dybbuk*, written in 1914, which resulted from research into small mystical ethnic sects, in this case the Chassidim. It was first produced by the VILNA TROUPE just after Anski's death, and subsequently toured throughout the world. (See also HABIMAH.)

**Anthony** [Deuster], **Joseph** 1912–93 American actor and director. In 1948 he made his New York directing debut with *Celebration*. Working in both films and the theatre, Anthony's stage credits include: *The Rainmaker* (1954), *The Lark* (1955), *The Most Happy Fella* (1956), *Winesburg Ohio* (1958), *The Best Man* (1960), *Mary, Mary* (1961), *Romulus* (1962), *110 in the Shade* (1963), *Slow Dance on the Killing Ground* (1964) and *Finishing Touches* (1973).

**Antoine, André** 1858–1943 French actor and director. Between 1887 and 1894 his Théâtre Libre (Free Theatre), which had begun life as an amateur company, operated as a small experimental theatre club in Paris. It laid the foundations of stage NATURALISM, a form that was to dominate Western theatre for the next century. His lead was followed by OTTO BRAHM and J.T. Grein who founded the Independent Theatre in London in 1891.

Antoine aimed to free theatre from the conventions of bedroom farce or spectacular melodrama by performing new plays dealing with contemporary issues. He also introduced the work of major foreign naturalists to the Paris stage, e.g. IBSEN's *Ghosts* (1890), *The Wild Duck* (1891) and STRINDBERG's *Miss Julie* (1893). In 1888 he saw performances by the MEININGEN COMPANY and was deeply impressed by their ensemble playing. He aimed for similar effects, notably in HAUPTMANN's *The Weavers* (1893). In 1897 the Théâtre Libre reopened as the Théâtre Antoine, and in 1906 he was appointed director of the ODÉON. In this period he developed his techniques of naturalist theatre: he was the first French director to do away with footlights, to lower house lights completely during performances and to treat the set like a real environment rather than a decorative

background. Above all, Antoine revolutionized acting in France, rejecting grand postures and declamatory speech and encouraging an intimate acting style and realistic use of space (e.g. turning one's back on the audience). Antoine was also the first modern French director to take SHAKESPEARE seriously. During his time at the Odéon he produced the first unbowdlerized French *King Lear* (1904) as well as other plays little known at the time such as *Troilus and Cressida* (1912). After World War I he worked in films for a while.

**Anzengruber, Ludwig** 1839–89 Austrian playwright. He was happiest writing about the Austrian peasantry, whose dialect he was able to capture. Two of his greatest successes, *The Parson of Kirchfeld* (1870) and *The Cross-Makers* (1872), reflect the conflict between orthodox Catholicism and liberalism in contemporary Austria, while *The Perjured Peasant* (1871) is a grim study of family life among the peasantry. His major VOLKSSTÜCK achievement was *The Fourth Commandment* (1877), which advocated the maintenance of traditional family values and loyalties. His plays were first produced in the commercial theatres of Vienna, not at the BURGTHEATER.

**Appia, Adolphe** 1862–1928 Swiss theorist and designer. Appia reformed theatrical and operatic scenography. Having studied music and drawing, after a performance of WAGNER's *The Master Singers* in 1888 he resolved 'to reform the art of the theatre [*la mise en scène*]'. In 1891–2 he wrote his notes towards the production of *The Ring* and *La Mise en scène du drame wagnérien* (published in Paris in 1895), and in 1892 his most important work, *La Musique et la mise en scène*, first published (with his own drawings) in German as *Die Musik und die Inszenierung* (Munich, 1899). In 1906 he met Émile Jaques-Dalcroze, the creator of the system of eurhythmics, and in 1909 began sketches for his 'rhythmic spaces'. Appia and Dalcroze prepared plans for an ambitious school and festival in Hellerau (Germany), where singers, dancers, musicians and designers would work in creative harmony. The Institute operated from 1911 to 1914 and staged two festivals (1912 and 1913). In 1914 Appia met GORDON CRAIG, a kindred spirit. *L'Oeuvre d'art vivant* was published in 1921. Eventually, in December 1923, *Tristan and Isolde*, with a full design by Appia, was performed at La Scala, Milan, to a mixed reception. In 1924, the young director WÄLTERLIN asked Appia to design the whole of *The Ring* for his theatre in Basle. But after a few performances the plan was abandoned, as Appia's work was deemed 'too revolutionary'. Although his output as a theatre designer was pitifully small, his influence on scene and lighting designers cannot be overstressed. He abolished *trompe-l'oeil* scenery, called for non-naturalistic and symbolic, architectural sets, used light creatively and insisted on the alliance of music and action, of body and spirit.

**Arabic drama** see MIDDLE EAST AND NORTH AFRICA

**Arbuzov, Aleksei (Nikolaevich)** 1908– Soviet actor, director and playwright. He is one of the most prolific and popular dramatists at home and in the West; his sense of love and fantasy as twin salvations from the fragility and cruelty of life is reflected in his drama. His first full-length plays – *Class* (1930), *Six Favourites* and *The Distant Road* (1935) – were followed by the extremely popular *Tanya* (1939), centring on a dependent woman who transforms herself into a socially aware heroine. Arbuzov's next plays, written for the Moscow Theatrical Studio, which he co-founded with V.N. PLYUCHEK, include *Sunrise City* (co-written with the collective,

14

1940), *The Immortal One* (with A.K. Gladkov, 1942) and *The Little House in Cherkizovo* (1943). Following *A Meeting with Youth* (1947), a dramatization of TURGENEV's *On the Eve* (1948), and *European Chronicle* (1952), Arbuzov wrote the youth chronicle play, *The Years of Wandering* (1954), the strongly CHEKHOVian *The Twelfth Hour* (1959) and his most popular drama, *Irkutsk Story* (1959), a simple tale of young love and hardship set in a Siberian hydroelectric plant. *My Poor Marat* (English title – *The Promise*, 1965) was an international hit. His plays of the 1970s, published in the collection *Choice*, include *Tales of the Old Arbat (Once Upon a Time)*, *In This Pleasant Old House*, *My Eye-Catcher, An Old-Fashioned Comedy* (English title – *Do You Turn Somersaults?*), *Evening Light* and *Cruel Games* (1978). His most recent plays, *Remembrances* (1981) and *The Victorious One*, return to the safe, familiar conflicts between extracurricular romance and family, professional and personal life. Arbuzov's theatre studio has promoted new playwrights.

**Arch Street Theatre** (Philadelphia) Believing that Philadelphians would support a newer, more elegant playhouse than the CHESTNUT, a group of citizens pledged the money to build the Arch Street Theatre and leased it to WILLIAM B. WOOD. It opened in 1828. From 1861, it enjoyed its most prosperous and famous period when Mrs John Drew (see DREW-BARRYMORE family) became manageress. For nearly a decade, she maintained a peerless company of actors in excellent productions. The theatre was demolished in 1936.

**Archer, William** 1856–1924 Scottish journalist and drama critic. Archer's alliance with GEORGE BERNARD SHAW in the promotion of IBSEN was influential in the move to raise the literary standards of British drama at the end of the 19th century. The first of Archer's own translations from Ibsen was performed in London in 1880 under the title *Quicksands, or The Pillars of Society*. A collected edition in 11 volumes was published in 1906–8. Archer was a fierce defender of the best of contemporary drama: *The Old Drama and the New* (1923) is a vigorous defence of the plays of T.W. ROBERTSON.

**Arden, John** 1930– British playwright. His first plays were seen at the ROYAL COURT THEATRE during GEORGE DEVINE's pioneering seasons. *Serjeant Musgrave's Dance* (1959), about a band of deserting soldiers who try to recruit the inhabitants of a bleak Northern town into a dance of death, is now widely regarded as a modern classic. Other Arden plays from this period such as *Live Like Pigs* (1957) and *The Happy Haven* (1960) reveal a blend of social concern and technical experimentation. *Armstrong's Last Goodnight* was presented at the NATIONAL THEATRE in 1965. His Arthurian epic, *The Island of the Mighty* (1972), written with his wife Margaretta D'Arcy, was produced by the ROYAL SHAKESPEARE COMPANY only after violent disagreements; since 1970 Arden's Marxist convictions have increasingly distanced him from the mainstream of British theatre. He writes with Margaretta D'Arcy for non-professional groups and lives in Ireland, whose troubled history has provided them with the content of several plays, such as *The Ballygombeen Bequest* (1972) and *The Non-Stop Connolly Show* (1975). The literary preoccupations of his early years, which lent him the reputation of being an English BRECHT with a summary song for every moral, have changed towards a populist directness of speech, often harsh and polemical, but at best stirring and powerful. His views on the theatre have been collected into a book of essays, *To Present the Pretence*

(1978). Although he has largely kept to his promise, sworn after *The Island of the Mighty*, never to write for mainstream British theatres again, he has written with D'Arcy plays for smaller and touring groups, and programmes for BBC radio, including *Whose Is the Kingdom?* (1988), a nine-part series on early Christianity.

**Arena Stage** (Washington, DC) In 1950, six people associated with George Washington University founded a theatrical company, Arena Stage. They opened their first season in a cinema, presenting their plays 'in the round'. ZELDA FICHANDLER, one of the founding members, remained its director until 1991, succeeded by Doug Wager. A full company of actors, directors and designers now inhabits a 500-seat thrust stage playhouse, an 800-seat mainstage, and a CABARET theatre, the Old Vat Room.

**Aretino, Pietro** 1492–1556 Italian satirist and playwright. Noted for his vigorous SATIRES against papal and secular figures and his scurrilous dialogues I *ragionamenti* (1534–6), Aretino wrote one tragedy, *L'Orazia* (1545), and some of the most lively comedies of the period, including *La cortigiana* (*The Courtesan*, 1525) and *Il marescalco* (*The Stablemaster*, 1527). For the production of his comedy *La Talanta* at Venice in 1541 VASARI prepared a theatre in the Casa di Cannaregio, a significant early example of an indoor fitted stage.

**Ariosto, Ludovico** 1474–1533 Italian poet and playwright. He was one of the first major Italian dramatists to write in the vernacular rather than in Latin; his first play *La cassaria* (*The Chest*, performed 1508), perhaps the first *commedia erudita*, was presented with painted perspective settings. His prose comedy, *I suppositi* (1509), was widely influential and imitated in Europe, as in George Gascoigne's *The Supposes*. Ariosto later recast both plays into verse. His *La Lena* and *Il negromante* (*Lena* and *The Magician*, 1528 and 1529 respectively) were both put on during CARNIVAL at Ferrara. His non-dramatic verse epic *Orlando furioso* has been adapted for stage performance, notably by LUCA RONCONI (1968).

**Aristophanes** c.447–after 388 BC Greek comic playwright. Aristophanes was regarded as the greatest poet of the Athenian 'Old Comedy' (see GREEK THEATRE, ANCIENT), and is the only one whose work survives. He spent most of his adult life during the Peloponnesian War. He wrote about 40 plays in all, of which eleven survive. In *Acharnians* (*Men of Acharnae*, a village near Athens; 425) an Athenian makes a private peace treaty with Sparta. *Knights* (424) is a savage attack on the demagogue Cleon. *Clouds* (produced in 423) ridicules the philosopher Socrates. *Wasps* (422) satirizes the Athenians' alleged passion for jury service. *Peace* (421) celebrates an imminent peace treaty with Sparta. In *Birds* (414) two Athenians found an ideal city among the birds. In *Lysistrata* (411) the women of Greece hold a 'sex strike' to force the men to end the war. *Thesmophoriazusae* (*Women Celebrating the Thesmophoria*, a women's festival; 411) travesties EURIPIDES. In *Frogs* (405) the god Dionysus visits the underworld to fetch Euripides back. In *Ecclesiazusae* (*Women Holding an Assembly*; c.392) the women take control at Athens. In *Plutus* (*Wealth*, 388) the god Wealth is cured of his blindness.

The plots of these plays are exuberant fantasies set in a world in which anything is possible. Typically the play centres on a 'comic hero', elderly (unless female) but lusty, and a 'great idea' for setting the world, or at least the 'hero's' own problems, to rights. The 'great idea' encounters opposition, and the Chorus is called in either to assist the 'hero' or to oppose him. The 'hero' usually triumphs (but in *Clouds, Wasps* and *Frogs*, where he has ideas that Aristophanes disapproves of, he is made to see the error of his ways); and the play often ends with a series of short, farcical scenes in which enemies or spongers are beaten off.

All the plays except *Plutus* are totally lacking in moral uplift. Honesty, decency and courage barely exist, and subjects for cheerful humour include torture, rape, blindness and starvation. Aristophanes never allows considerations of relevance, dramatic illusion or consistency to get in the way of a good joke. The main targets of his political attacks are the demagogues – politicians who depended on the support of the poorer classes in Athens – and the sophists, among whom he includes Socrates and Euripides. More attractive, perhaps, is his constant devotion to the cause of peace, a devotion that is surely sincere. There is no doubt, however, that his *main* purpose was to entertain his audience and win their applause, not to alter their views.

**Aristotle** 384–322 BC Greek philosopher. A pupil of Plato, he is author of numerous works concerning logic, the natural world and human activities. Though he often alludes to drama in the *Rhetoric* and elsewhere, his importance for theatre lies mainly in his *Poetics*, which probably dates from the 330s or 320s. From this we have only one book, on tragedy and epic poetry, preserved in such a corrupt form that its meaning is often obscure. A second book, on comedy, is lost.

Aristotle approaches poetry not as a literary critic but as an analytical philosopher who must establish the highest form of poetry (in his opinion tragedy) and the best type of tragedy (exemplified for him by the *Oedipus Tyrannus* of SOPHOCLES). When Aristotle defends the existence of poetry or tragedy, the ulterior motive of replying to the charges brought against them by Plato may be detected. The factual information which Aristotle gives can seem contradictory, and may not reflect ordinary usage. His emphasis on the pre-eminence of plot over character (*Poetics* 6 etc.) may reflect the priorities of the Greek dramatists, and his guidance on effective plot construction (7–14) is widely applicable. The influence of the *Poetics* – or of doctrines purporting to be derived from it – has been immense, ever since it became known to Renaissance Europe through a Latin translation by Giorgio Valla, published in 1498. One famous 'Aristotelian' doctrine is that of the three unities – of time, place and action – which were considered canonical by, in particular, the 17th-century dramatists of France and England. The *Poetics* does insist on 'unity of action' (chapters 7–8 etc.), but the idea of 'unity of time' derives merely from a remark in chapter 5 that tragedy 'tries as far as possible to limit itself to a single revolution of the sun, or a little more', and 'unity of place' is not mentioned at all. In more recent times certain terms which do occur in the *Poetics* have become clichés of literary criticism, notably *katharsis* ('purgation' or 'purification'?) from chapter 6 and *hamartia* ('sin', 'error' or both?) from chapter 13. What Aristotle himself meant by these terms is still hotly disputed.

**Arlecchino** see *COMMEDIA DELL'ARTE*; HARLEQUIN; *ZANNI*

**Arliss, George** [George Augustus Arlis-Andrews] (1868–1946) British-born American actor.and playwright. Arliss's greatest successes occurred in the USA. Arliss, with his distinctive features (long, narrow face, pointed nose, habitual monocle), spent 40 years perfecting the playing of villains, great historical leaders and

wise old men. His most notable stage roles, in addition to the title role in *Disraeli* (1911), were in *The Second Mrs Tanqueray* (1901) with MRS PATRICK CAMPBELL, *The Darling of the Gods* (1902), *Hedda Gabler* (1904) and *Rosmersholm* (1907) with MINNIE MADDERN FISKE, *Paganini* (1915), *The Green Goddess* (1921) and *Old English* (1924). Shylock (1928) was his last formal stage appearance. In 1923 he returned to London after a 22-year absence to appear in ARCHER's *The Green Goddess*. His successful film career began in 1920. He also wrote or collaborated on six plays.

**Arlt, Roberto** 1900–42 Argentine playwright, journalist and novelist. Arlt is the link between the celebrated Golden Decade (1900–10) of Argentine theatre and the contemporary movement. His eight plays, written between 1932 and 1942, transform conventional reality by means of illusions, dreams, fantasies and the grotesque in order to create a new world. He found his inspiration in the European master painters – Goya, Dürer, Breughel. Most of his eight plays were premiered by Leónidas Barletta, the father of the Argentine independent theatre movement, in his Teatro del Pueblo. Major titles are *Saverio el cruel* (*Saverio the Cruel*), which shows the strong influence of the *Quijote*, Arlt's favourite book, *La isla desierta* (*The Desert Island*, 1937) and *La fiesta del hierro* (*The Iron Fiesta*, 1940).

**Armin, Robert** c.1568–1615 Elizabethan actor. He succeeded WILL KEMPE as leading 'clown' in the LORD CHAMBERLAIN'S MEN. We know from Armin's own *Quips upon Questions* (1600) that he inherited some of RICHARD TARLTON's skills as an extemporizer, but also that he considered himself a 'foolosopher'. The recognizable transition in SHAKESPEARE's plays from broad clown to wise fool must owe something to the contrasting playing styles of Kempe and Armin – clearly an actor whom Shakespeare trusted as well as a talented singer – for he is thought to have been the original Lavache, Pandarus and Fool to King Lear. His play, *The Two Maids of Moreclacke* (1609), was performed by the Children of the King's Revels.

**Arneaux, J. A.** 1855–? African-American actor. He took to the stage as a song-and-dance artist, then as a legitimate actor and manager of the Astor Place Company of Coloured Tragedians, the leading black dramatic troupe in America in the 1880s, based in New York. Arneaux's roles included Iago, Macbeth and Pythias, but his favourite part was Richard III, in which he ranked with MACREADY, EDWIN BOOTH and LAWRENCE BARRETT.

**Aronson, Boris** 1898–1980 Russian-American painter, sculptor and set designer. The most respected American designer of the mid-20th century, Aronson was born in Russia and emigrated to the USA in 1923. Having worked for the YIDDISH ART THEATRE, by the 1930s he was designing major shows on BROADWAY and working with the GROUP THEATRE. His early work reflected not only the influence of his Russian teacher ALEKSANDRA EKSTER but also that of Marc Chagall, whose cubist-fantastic style Aronson greatly admired. Despite his enormous output and critical success for plays by WILLIAM SAROYAN, TENNESSEE WILLIAMS, CLIFFORD ODETS, ARTHUR MILLER, WILLIAM INGE and others, and hit musicals, he did not achieve widespread recognition until he teamed up with director HAROLD PRINCE on the 1964 musical, *Fiddler on the Roof*, and later *Cabaret* and *A Little Night Music*. This collaboration seemed to bring out Aronson's creativity. His designs ranged from realistic detail for plays like *Awake and Sing* to technological fantasies such as *Company* that used steel and plexiglass and projections. His constructivist influences could be seen throughout his work. His sets always had a strong sense of line and form, and a generally subtle but evocative use of colour employed symbolically to support the mood of the play.

**Arrabal, Fernando** 1932– Spanish/French playwright. Arrabal's work is dominated by the traumas of his Spanish childhood when his mother, a Catholic, betrayed his father, a Republican, to Franco's police. His early plays, published in 1958, are dream works in which naive characters behave according to basic Freudian drives. In the 1960s he achieved notoriety with productions of *Le Labyrinthe*, *Automobile Graveyard* and *The Architect and Emperor of Assyria* (all 1967). Since then his voluminous work has appeared under the title 'panic theatre', designed to provoke psychological shock waves in its audience.

**Arriví, Francisco** 1915– Puerto Rican playwright, director and critic. His early plays – *Club de solteros (Bachelors' Club*, 1940) and *El diablo se humaniza (Humanizing the Devil*, 1941) – are fantastic and farcical. Major works include *María Soledad (María Solitude*, 1947), the trilogy *Máscara puertorriqueña (Puerto Rican Mask*, 1956–9), *Cóctel de Don Nadie (Mr Nobody's Cocktail*, 1964) and the musical *Solteros 72 (Bachelors 72)*. Arriví founded the theatre group Tinglado Puertorriqueño in 1945.

**Arrufat, Antón** 1935– Cuban playwright and poet. *El vivo al pollo (Chicken for the Living*, 1959) uses traditional BUFO theatre to parody a natural fear of death in the case of a woman who embalms her husband. With *La zona cero (Zero Zone*, 1959) the illogical patterns and comedy routines he developed earlier reached a climax in a BECKETT-style absurdism (see THEATRE OF THE ABSURD). After *La repetición (The Repetition*, 1963), and *Todos los domingos (Every Sunday*, 1965), he wrote *Los siete contra Tebas (Seven against Thebes)* which won the UNEAC prize for 1968, but he was censured for a work considered antithetical to revolutionary goals. Arrufat remains in Cuba and works as a journalist/writer. His later plays are unpublished and unstaged.

**Artaud, Antonin** 1896–1948 French poet, actor, director and theoretician. His extraordinary influence on theatre is based largely on his two short-lived attempts at directing and on his volume of essays, *The Theatre and Its Double* (1938). The double of theatre was life, the vital, metaphysical reality that shadows our everyday actions. Western society had lost contact with this life and so theatre had to be like a violent plague, from which people would emerge either dead or purged.

In 1926 he founded the Théâtre Alfred Jarry together with Robert Aron and ROGER VITRAC. Productions included STRINDBERG's *Dream Play* and Vitrac's *Victor* (both 1928). The manifestos for this theatre stressed the idea that theatre should no longer be mere entertainment but genuine action with real effects on the real world. The features of what he later called Theatre of Cruelty are all to be found here: violence, sexuality, social taboos, and the eruption of dramatic action outside the safe confines of the stage. In 1935 he founded his second theatre, the Théâtre de la Cruauté, which failed to outlive its first production, an adaptation of Shelley's *The Cenci*: primeval theatre did not harmonize with Parisian theatregoing. With his health gradually deteriorating, Artaud spent most of the rest of his life in asylums, emerging in 1946 to produce a torrent of work.

Artaud's writings move the emphasis from the writer to the director and stress the essentially physical, three-dimensional quality of theatre. Though he himself failed, his work has been enormously influential; many directors – e.g. BROOK, GROTOWSKI, PLANCHON, BLIN – have acknowledged their debt to him.

**Artef** New York Yiddish company. An acronym for Workers' Theatre Group, it was a proletarian YIDDISH THEATRE collective of amateurs led by experienced professionals. From the first 'studio' of 26 students in 1926 the collective grew to six studios by 1936 and produced over 80 plays, both AGIT-PROP and non-political, before folding in 1953.

**Arts Council of Great Britain** Agency through which funds from central government sources are distributed to the arts in Britain. The Arts Council was inaugurated in August 1946. Like its wartime predecessor CEMA, the ACGB's aims were philanthropic – to improve artistic standards and to encourage the appreciation of the arts around the country. It was allowed to subsidize only non-profit-distributing companies. The Council itself consisted of up to 16 members, appointed by the government, which was afterwards expected not to interfere with its decisions. The day-to-day running of the ACGB's affairs was left in the hands of a secretary-general and his staff, assisted by unpaid boards of expert advisers.

Initially the ACGB's funds were very small, but its influence was considerable. It helped ambitious new companies such as the English Stage Company, encouraged local authorities to lay the foundations for a new regional repertory movement, supported the establishment of two national companies, and opposed CENSORSHIP, which was abolished in 1968.

From 1965 to 1984 the ACGB became the main financial support for 12 Regional Arts Associations and subsidized most forms of theatre, apart from the amateur and narrowly commercial. Under its influence a new generation of theatre buildings came into existence, designed for 'an age of subsidy', with large foyers and uneconomically small seating capacities. As the ACGB became more central to theatre in Britain, the tensions within it emerged as conflicts. The regions objected to the preferential treatment given to London and the national companies, commercial managements complained of the unfair competition with the subsidized sector. It became more difficult for the ACGB to stay at arm's length from government; and from being the champion of the arts, it came to seem more like government's whipping boy.

Mrs Thatcher's administration was opposed in principle to such 'quangos' (quasi-autonomous non-governmental organizations), but the system was by now well established. In 'The Glory of the Garden' (1984), a modestly reformist document from the new chairman, Sir William Rees-Mogg, it was envisaged that many of the ACGB's grant-giving powers should devolve to the RAAs, while new money should be sought from sponsorship. ABSA (the Association for Business Sponsorship of the Arts) was founded; market principles were embraced.

The paradox of the 1980s was that state subsidies more than doubled within a government which did not believe in subsidy, but needed to compensate the arts for the weaknesses of its market system. In 1992 the new prime minister John Major introduced a National Heritage Ministry which embraced many arts previously scattered among several ministries. The ACGB's main role was now to fund the national companies, with the RAAs responsible for the regional ones. The beneficial effects of the the growth of the ACGB's resources and the establishment of the new ministry do not seem to have percolated down to many arts companies, which are as uncertain of their futures as ever. The wages of actors have not improved in real terms since the 1950s, and unemployment rates are still high.

**Arts Theatre** (Belfast) From 1982, known as the Belfast Civic Arts Theatre. It was built in 1961 to house the Arts Theatre Studio which, founded in 1950, presented mainly world drama – SARTRE, TENNESSEE WILLIAMS, T. S. ELIOT – employing local actors, a policy which survived until the 1960s when the economics of the new theatre enforced the more popular fare of musicals, WEST END successes and local farces. The Studio ceased its activities in 1977, the theatre becoming a venue for independent productions.

**Arts Theatre** (London) Opening in 1927, the theatre gave private performances of unlicensed experimental plays for members. Successful from the first, with a series of productions transferring to the commercial theatre, it continued this role until 1962, hosting tours by foreign artists and companies. Under the management of ALEC CLUNES from 1942 to 1950 it gained a national reputation, with premieres of work such as CHRISTOPHER FRY's The Lady's Not for Burning (1948). The intimacy of the small stage and 347-seat auditorium was particularly suited to the new wave of absurd drama in the 1950s (see THEATRE OF THE ABSURD), and BECKETT's Waiting for Godot, PINTER's The Caretaker and ALBEE's Zoo Story were all given their first English performances there. Since 1962 it has served as a WEST END transfer house for FRINGE THEATRE productions.

**Asch, Sholom** 1880–1957 Polish-born American playwright and novelist. He wrote in Yiddish. His plays mainly concern the conflict between orthodox and emancipated Jew – e.g. The God of Vengeance (1907), Downstream (1904), The Messiah Period (1906), Sabatai Zevi (1908), Wealthy Reb Shloime (1913) and Mottke the Thief (1917). (See also YIDDISH THEATRE.)

**Asche, Oscar** 1872–1936 British actor. He worked with F.R. BENSON and BEERBOHM TREE, from whom he took over the management of HER/HIS MAJESTY'S THEATRE. He made his reputation in Shakespearian roles, though he also played opposite ELLEN TERRY in GORDON CRAIG's 1903 production of IBSEN's The Vikings, and gained his greatest success in his own musical fantasy Chu Chin Chow (based on Ali Baba and the Forty Thieves), which ran from 1916 to 1921.

**Ashcroft, Peggy (Edith Margaret Emily)** 1907–91 British actress. She first took the WEST END by storm as the innocent Naemi in Jew Suss (1929). Her special quality of radiant freshness caused some critics, including JAMES AGATE, to state that she was too simple and lightweight for major classical roles, but the 1932/3 OLD VIC season revealed her range as an actress in such parts as Juliet, Rosalind, Lady Teazle and SHAW's Cleopatra. Her subsequent career was remarkable for its versatility, command and, not least, her instinct for major challenges. Against all expectations, she was a brilliantly sluttish Cleopatra to MICHAEL REDGRAVE's Antony at the Shakespeare Memorial Theatre in 1953, an electric Beatrice to JOHN GIELGUD's Benedict in 1950 and 1955, a savage Hedda Gabler in 1954, and Shen Teh in BRECHT's The Good Person of Setzuan. She played all the major

Shakespearian women except Lady Macbeth. Her roles in contemporary plays ranged from Hester in TERENCE RATTIGAN's The Deep Blue Sea (1952) to Beth in HAROLD PINTER's Landscape (1969) and Winnie in SAMUEL BECKETT's Happy Days (1975). Her last stage performance was as LILIAN BAYLIS in Save the Wells at the Royal Opera House in 1986, although she continued to act in film and television dramas until shortly before her death, appearing in Madame Soutsatzka, a film directed by John Schlesinger in 1988.

A committed socialist, Ashcroft energetically furthered the interests of her profession by serving on the council of Equity, on the ARTS COUNCIL and on the artistic committee of the English Stage Company. She was at the centre of the ROYAL SHAKESPEARE COMPANY for 30 years and became a director in 1968; among her many honours, she received a DBE in 1956 and a special Laurence Olivier award in 1991 for a lifetime's achievement in the theatre. In 1962 a new theatre in her place of birth, Croydon in south London, was named after her. At her death, glowing tributes to her talent and professional integrity defined her place in the pantheon of British actors.

**Asia-Oceania** In the enormous geographic area of the Asian mainland and adjoining islands of the western Pacific Ocean theatrical arts are ancient, highly developed, rich in diversity, and very much alive today for large segments of the population. From Pakistan in the west to the Hawaiian Islands in the east, and from China in the north to Indonesia in the south, there are 700–800 distinct forms, or genres. Each reflects the unique language, religious views, social structures and daily lives of the people who have created them. Even to the uninitiated observer, KYŌGEN comedies in Japan stand apart from KABUKI or BUNRAKU, also from Japan, and they are artistic and cultural worlds away from BHAVAI in India, or Beijing opera in China, forms which also feature comic elements. At the same time, shared features link genres within and between countries. We can even identify pan-Asian-Pacific traditions and patterns of performance.

Four major geographic (and cultural) regions may be identified within this vast sweep of land and ocean. South Asia, which encompasses the present nationstates of Bangladesh, India, Nepal, Pakistan and Sri Lanka, is the home of Hinduism and Buddhism, the source of dramatic themes from the epics, the Ramayana and the Mahabharata, and of a pervasive and multi-faceted classical dance tradition. A baroque love of brilliant theatrical display and the vibrant use of colour, emotion and rhythm in performance mark South Asian forms.

China, Hong Kong, Taiwan, Japan and Korea comprise East Asia. They share cultures based on Confucian civil ethics, systems of imperial rule and Buddhist philosophy. The Chinese writing system of calligraphic characters was adopted in all these areas, and in the process Chinese literature and Chinese arts of brush painting, music and dance were introduced. In East Asia a spirit of decorum and restraint, and a concern for structural simplicity and clarity, are apparent in the performing arts.

The countries of Southeast Asia – Burma, Cambodia, Indonesia, Laos, Malaysia, the Philippines, Singapore, Thailand and Vietnam – have welcomed religions, literature and dance from both South and East Asia, and fused these with rich indigenous performance traditions. Malay peoples settled in Indonesia, Malaysia, southern Thailand, Singapore and the Philippines, and today these people share many theatre traits. Oceania contains some 20 Pacific island nations in the sub-regions of Melanesia, Micronesia and Polynesia whose original settlement can often be traced back to common ancestors. These Pacific voyagers brought with them their religious songs, genealogical chants and dances, spreading them across the island groupings, through Fiji, Tahiti and Samoa and as far east as Hawaii.

Three quite different social milieux have nourished the region's theatre forms. First, elite forms of theatre have been created with the support of the ruling classes, propounding the ideology of rulers at centres of political and economic power. In the past these were theatres of the court, performed by court functionaries – actors, dancers, musicians, storytellers – for court occasions. Performance was a civic-political ritual demonstrating and confirming royal prerogatives, and it reflected the culture's highest literary and artistic values (e.g. in India, SANSKRIT DRAMA; in Japan, BUGAKU, NŌ. Eventually, and especially during the late 19th and early 20th centuries, the royal courts who had supported these arts lost power or were replaced, and performers were forced to turn to other audiences for support. Today, most former 'royal' theatre forms continue to be performed as important cultural artifacts, even as 'state' arts, preserved with modest levels of government support.

A completely different elite theatre was created in the 20th century by and for a new Western-oriented, university-educated, professional, managerial and student elite. The theatre of this elite was 'spoken drama', imported from the West and representing 'modernism'. It began as an amateur enterprise, idealistically motivated, in the manner of Europe's 'little theatres', and even today audiences are small and economic self-sufficiency is illusive. In the 1910s–1930s, it was primarily a theatre of REALISM, devoted to social reform. By the beginning of World War II, artists were divided sharply into two opposing groups: those committed to humanistic, psychological drama of the individual, and those allied to 'progressive' or 'socialist' ideologies who saw theatre as a means of promoting the struggle for socialist/communist societies. This division continues today, with profound consequences: countries with communist governments (China, North Korea and Vietnam) attempt to restrict or completely ban 'bourgeois' theatre, while many capitalist-democratic countries (South Korea, Taiwan, India, Indonesia, Malaysia and Thailand) censor or ban 'leftist' theatre.

Perhaps no political control of theatre has been as total as that exercised by Japan during World War II at home and throughout its Asian-Pacific empire. Consequently modern theatre is valued as a part of the modernizing process, but its creators are often at odds with whatever government is in power because they tend to be independent-minded. Direct government subsidy is usually predicated on social and political conformity. CENSORSHIP of new plays is stringent almost everywhere (Japan and the Philippines being notable exceptions). Current modern theatre in Asia and the Pacific region encompasses the older realism, Western classical drama (especially SHAKESPEARE's plays, which are performed everywhere), variations of 'socialist realism' in communist countries, avant-garde experiments with new forms often in international and 'intercultural' settings, as well as uniquely local movements.

Folk theatre is created by local villagers-turned-performers for festivals and religious occasions and for entertainment of their own communities. Although the artistic quality may be high and a performer may enjoy social esteem, performing is occasional and not an occupation. In thousands of village communities, and in urban enclaves as well, folk performances continue to be organized as religio-civic rites, expressing the solidarity of the local community. Among such forms are MANI-RIMDU in Nepal, SANDAE-GŬK in Korea, and KUTIYATTAM in India.

In Asia's large cities and towns commercial theatre forms have evolved, for a public audience. Commercial troupes perform regularly for the general ticket-buying public in permanent theatre buildings. Most important urban commercial theatre genres began as outcast theatres despised by the intelligentsia. Ironically, some are today considered reputable, even 'classical' forms of 'national theatre' (in Japan, kabuki, bunraku; in China, JINGXI, YUEJU; in Indonesia, wayang).

## Religion

Everywhere in Asia and Oceania, early performance has been associated with man's relations to the gods. In animistic belief, performance is service to the gods, a request for good health or a good harvest, a channel to invite the spirits of the sacred world into the temporary world of mankind. The belief in spirit possession, that the human performer is a mere vessel for a god's appearance, is widespread. Religious myths, legends and characters of saints, gods, spirits and demons provide the material of traditional drama in all countries. Buddhist jataka stories, tales about Lord Buddha in a former life, are the source of scores of plays in Thailand, Laos, Burma and Cambodia. The Confucian ethics of fidelity to ruler, husband and father inform Japanese bunraku, Chinese jingxi and Korean shinp'a dramas alike. Krishna and Rama, incarnations of Brahmanic god Vishnu, not only are heroes in India's regional theatres but they populate the plays of such genres as wayang in Indonesia and Malaysia, masked drama in Thailand and shadow plays in Cambodia as well. Persian and Arabic stories entered Pakistan and Bangladesh with the introduction of Islam, and the Arabian hero, Amir Hamza, appears in Malaysia and Indonesia. Muslim and Christian influences contend in Philippine komedya, and Christian biblical stories and later medieval romances are dramatized in Sri Lankan pasku and Indian CAVITTU NATAKAM.

However, this dramatic material did not travel intact and unaltered from one culture to another. Just as Japanese Buddhism is different from Chinese Buddhism (to say nothing of Sri Lankan Buddhism), Chinese stories dramatized in Korea and Japan are greatly altered and acquire a local flavour. The Hindu Ramayana contains one of the world's great mythic motifs: the withdrawal of the hero (Rama) from affairs of the world, initiation through asceticism, the gaining of spiritual power and return to temporal rule. In various forms, this quest theme occurs in dramas in Thailand, Indonesia, Malaysia and Cambodia. When Rama himself appears on the Javanese or Balinese stage he is localized into a Javanese or Balinese king.

## East–West interchange

Asian and Pacific performance styles and content have been carried by performers to neighbouring countries, resulting in performance similarities among cultures. Indian-style dance became known to performers far beyond that country's boundaries. It fused with local dance styles, creating numerous related dance forms. Korean and Japanese artists learned masked dances at the Chinese court in the early Tang Dynasty (618–907), returned home and transplanted the Chinese performing style to their own courts, in the process establishing *kiak* in Korea and *bugaku* and *gigaku* in Japan. Western entrepreneurs and colonial administrations brought popular forms of Western music, dance and theatre into India, the Philippines and Japan from the 16th century, and later into other countries. In the early decades of the 20th century, Chinese and Korean students studying in Japan discovered Western melodrama and serious drama through Japanese productions and translations.

By the time of World War II, Asian playwrights, directors and actors had travelled to Europe and the United States, learning Western spoken drama and realistic theatre. With IBSEN and STANISLAVSKY as their inspiration, they returned to create modern, serious, realistic drama in their own countries. English-language theatre became strongly established in Singapore and the Philippines, and, to a lesser extent, in Hong Kong, Malaysia and Burma, all areas under long-lasting British or American colonization. Concurrently, traditional Asian artists were performing on tour in the West for the first time. Artists of the European avant-garde were able to see MEI LANFANG, *kabuki*, and Cambodian and Balinese dance troupes. In the 50 years following the end of World War II, theatrical interchange between Asia-Oceania and Europe-America has become established as a continuous process. Happenings, absurdism, deconstructionism and multiculturalism echo in theatre practice East and West. Western actors, dancers, musicians, directors and playwrights are seriously studying performance forms of Asia and Oceania, often gaining considerable mastery of them.

### Performance training and transmission

In most Asian traditional theatre the process of preparing for performance is centred in the actor, for the actor is the source and repository of information. In many forms there are strong dramatic texts, written by specialist playwrights, that exemplify local literary standards and modes. But in other genres the centrality of the actor extends to script composition: the actor may be a playwright or improvise dialogue, and in some cases song lyrics, during performance. In order to function at this high technical level, the first task of the actor (dancer or musician) is to become proficient in the artistic and performance 'codes', the artistic languages, of the theatre form. One does not begin by training to 'act'; one begins by training to be a skilled 'artist'. The Indian KATHAKALI actor spends his childhood forming his body into a pliable instrument for the leaps and whirls of dance; for the eye, mouth and cheek movements expressive of emotion; and for the 600 hand gestures that he must flawlessly execute when on stage enacting a role. ZEAMI, writing in 15th-century Japan, said the actor should spend from the age of seven to seventeen mastering the 'two arts' (*nikyoku*) of chanting and dance before seriously studying role-playing – that is, 'acting'. The Indonesian or Malaysian puppeteer learns the 100-plus battle movements of the shadow puppets. Second, and only after this firm artistic base has been laid, the performer learns to enact roles in plays. He or she acts within a generic role type that has been developed by earlier generations of performers.

Young male hero, older male authority figure, young woman, older woman, villain (often 'foreign', or an ogre, demon or *jin*, a creature outside the human realm) and clown are roles found in most traditional theatre forms.

A performance then, is one momentary arrangement of pre-known elements, one in a series of performances which are rather like the changing patterns of a kaleidoscope. Performances are examples of an existing artistic form much more than they are the 'production of a play'. To put together a traditional performance does not require the special outside vision of a director. Actors, dancers and musicians are themselves the source of knowledge of how to perform, and they are capable of working as a self-directing ensemble.

Because the musical, dance and voice techniques are so highly developed and demanding in Asian and Oceanic performance, systems for transmitting performance knowledge to the next generation are vital to genres' survival. The most common method of professional training is for a pupil to apprentice him- or herself to a master over an extended period, perhaps a lifetime. The art may be passed from father to son, or within hereditary clans. These master–pupil relationships are strongly formalized in India, Thailand and especially Japan, with severe penalties exacted on a disciple who abandons a teacher. In some cases a master may take a group of students and train them together in a school, indicating the sacred nature of performance transmission. Today numerous formal academies also exist to teach young performers of Chinese opera, Indian classical dance, Indonesian, Thai and Cambodian dance-dramas and other forms. Most governments in Asia today either run or subsidize academy training.

### Song, dance, masks and puppetry

It is often said that all Asian performance is 'dance'. This is true in the sense that all acting follows well defined movement codes, and that every stage movement is carefully controlled. The dance is a major structural component in the dramatic composition and storytelling of many forms. Formal set dances, with opening, development and conclusion, and specific placement within the play structure, are easily recognizable. There is good reason to call such performances 'dance dramas'. Other forms are built around song. In these, sung lyrics are the major component of dramatic structure, and the 'actor' is required to have developed exceptional vocal skill. For convenience, we often call these forms 'operas' in English – for example, Korean *P'ANSORI* or Chinese *KUNQU*.

Actors in scores of genres wear masks, the mask's transformative power allowing the performer to wholly transcend self and portray gods, spirits of the dead, demons, mythological figures, and animals as well as ordinary humans.

A unique feature of theatre in Asia is the immense importance of puppetry, especially shadow theatre. Doll or MARIONETTE puppet theatre (see PUPPETS) is known in almost every country of Asia (India, Pakistan, Burma, Indonesia, China, Korea and Japan). Varieties of leather shadow play are seen from India in the west, through Malaysia, Thailand, Cambodia, Indonesia and the Philippines to the south, and into China in the east. Among Asian puppet forms are some of the most sophisticated literary and theatre arts in the world (in Japan, *bunraku*; in Indonesia, *wayang*, for example; see

SHADOW PUPPETS). Throughout Asia puppet theatre forms have served as progenitors and models for the later development of human theatre forms. Nowhere in Asia is this medium a 'child's' theatre.

Most theatre forms in Asia are interwoven fabrics of music, dance and acting, 'total theatre' in which all performance aspects are fused into a single form. The nature of each form is largely dependent upon the particular balance among its many constituent parts, upon what element is emphasized and what element is subordinated.

Throughout Asia and Oceania, governments and artistic organizations seek to preserve and invigorate traditional, indigenous theatre forms that reflect their cultural legacy. The challenge of radio, film and television for audiences is daunting. Since the 1960s and 70s avant-garde playwrights and directors have sought to return to traditional performing 'roots', rejecting the Western realist theatre imported over the past century. Realism in any case does not interest most Asian audiences, for it lacks the vital theatricality of familiar traditional forms. Burgeoning economies provide audiences in many countries with the means to support artistic pursuits. Traditional revival and radical experiments in form and content are two contrasting and significant features of present-day theatre.

**Astaire [Austerlitz], Fred** and **Adele Astaire** 1899–1987 and 1898–1981 American dancers, singers and actors. In 1917 they made their New York MUSICAL THEATRE debut in *Over the Top*. Their dances were fluid, stylish and often witty, e.g. in *Lady, Be Good!* (1924) and *Funny Face* (1927), for which GEORGE AND IRA GERSHWIN wrote the score. After Adele's retirement, Fred turned to Hollywood musical films. Equally popular in England, the Astaires took several of their American successes to the London stage during the 1920s.

**Astley, Philip** 1742–1814 English equestrian and CIRCUS manager. On leaving the cavalry, he opened a riding school outside London (1768), where he combined equestrianism with clowns and tumblers to constitute the first true circus. In 1788 he erected his Royal Amphitheatre and began staging plays without a licence, until forced by the authorities to close; he had already built his *cirque* in Paris, which prospered from1782 to 89. The French Revolution forced him home. In 1804 he rebuilt his London amphitheatre to seat 2,500 spectators, and then built the Olympic Pavilion at a cost of £800. It lost £10,000 in its first season. (See also HIPPODRAMA.)

**Aston, Anthony [Matt Medley]** c.1682–c.1753 English actor-manager. He was a strolling player with DOGGETT in the provinces and in Ireland in the late 1690s. His first play, *Love in a Hurry*, was performed in 1709. In 1710 he began performing the medleys for which he became famous. These were touring variety shows of short plays, scenes, songs and dances performed by Aston and members of his family, and their success earned him the nickname Matt Medley. In 1735 he campaigned successfully against the proposed Playhouse Bill, which would have strengthened the power of the patent companies against shows like his. His play *The Fool's Opera* contains an autobiographical sketch.

**Astor Place Opera House** (New York) Situated on Broadway at East 9th St and Astor Place, the theatre was notorious for the riot which broke out in 1849, triggered by the feud between the English star W.C. MACREADY and the American star EDWIN FORREST, and

by anti-English sentiment among the local Irish populace. The militia, called in to quell the riot, fired at the crowd. Thirty-one people were killed and 150 wounded. The theatre was renamed, and eventually torn down in 1891.

**Atelier, Théâtre de l'** (Paris) A 19th-century theatre in Montmartre, which was reopened by DULLIN in 1922 as L'Atelier and became one of the CARTEL houses, producing a wide repertoire of classic, Elizabethan and modern playwrights, notably PIRANDELLO and SALACROU. Alongside the producing company, Dullin ran a school in which many famous French actors and directors trained, e.g. ARTAUD, BARRAULT, BLIN, VILAR and BARSACQ, who took over the theatre with his Compagnie des Quatre Saisons in 1940.

**Atkinson, (Justin) Brooks** 1894–1984 American drama critic. In 1926 he undertook that role for the *New York Times*, succeeding STARK YOUNG. During the war he received a Pulitzer Prize (1947) for his reports on the Soviet Union. Afterwards he returned to reviewing the BROADWAY theatre. The most respected critic of his generation, Atkinson offered commonsense opinions in a graceful style, and was known for both his fairness and his candour, believing that his reviews were for the 'average guy who goes to the theatre'. His many books include *Broadway Scrapbook* (1948), *Brief Chronicles* (1966), *Broadway* (1970) and *The Lively Years: 1920–1973*.

**Auden, W(ystan) H(ugh)** 1907–73 British poet and playwright. Auden was a founder member of the GROUP THEATRE (London), which produced his first performed play, *The Dance of Death* (1934). This used music and ballet, doggerel verse and Marxist themes, pointing forward to his collaborations with CHRISTOPHER ISHERWOOD in *The Dog Beneath the Skin* (1935), *The Ascent of F6* (1936) and *On the Frontier* (1938). These political fables mixing symbolic quests, epic techniques derived from BRECHT and satiric pastiche are among the most powerful English plays of the 1930s. Auden was awarded the Pulitzer Prize for his modern morality play *The Age of Anxiety* (1947). As well as translations of ERNST TOLLER, Brecht and COCTEAU, Auden is known for his opera librettos.

**Audiberti, Jacques** 1899–1965 Southern French poet and playwright; author of 26 plays. The first to be staged, *Quoat-Quoat* (1946), was written without thought of performance. His poetic exuberance linked him with writers of the postwar avant-garde such as VAUTHIER. Many of his plays were produced again by Marcel Maréchal in Lyon in the 1960s. They deal with the eternal conflict between forces of good and evil in settings often borrowed from history or myth.

**Augier, Émile** 1820–89 French playwright. Augier is the most important chronicler of French society of his time. His plays – particularly his last, *The House of Fourchambault* (1878) – expose the hypocrisy, false moral values and obsession with money of the bourgeoisie. He also developed French NATURALISM by offering serious examinations of topical issues. Augier's first play, *Hemlock* (1844), had a classical theme. Later plays turned to contemporary subjects: *Le Mariage d'Olympe (The Marriage of Olympia*, 1855); *Le Gendre de Monsieur Poirier (Monsieur Poirier's Son-in-Law)*, a 19th-century version of MOLIÈRE's *Le Bourgeois Gentilhomme; A False Step (The Poor Lionesses*, 1858); *Les Effrontés (The Shameless Ones*, 1861), in which he exposed the link between manipulation of the stock exchange and the press; *Lions et Renards (Lions and Foxes*, 1869), which continues his virulent attack on the political manoeuvring of the Jesuits; *Maître Guérin* (1864), which returns to a comedy of manners, focusing on the character of a dubious lawyer; and *Madame Caverlet* (1876), which deals with the question of divorce.

**Auriol, Jean-Baptiste** 1806–81 French acrobatic CLOWN. He first worked with DUCROW, performing his famous bottle dance. After appearances throughout Europe he made his Parisian debut with Franconi (1847), where his leaps had a phenomenal success: he performed a *salto mortale* over 24 soldiers and a double *salto* over 12 horses (see ACROBATICS). Auriol's voice 'like a child's trumpet' and his jester's costume set the style for European clowns for two decades.

**auto sacramental** Spanish dramatic genre. One-act religious allegories illustrating the central dogmas of the Catholic Church, *autos sacramentales* were performed on the Feast of Corpus Christi in Spain from the 16th to the 18th century. In Madrid they were sponsored by the city authorities, CALDERÓN being the sole author from 1648 till his death (1681), and were performed in the open air on a stage. They were suppressed in 1765.

**Avignon Festival** French theatre festival. It was established by JEAN VILAR in 1947 to provide a new context for theatre-going. It is held in July, when commercial and state theatres in France are closed. Vilar's work at Avignon created an atmosphere of celebration and participation, and laid the foundations for his production style at the THÉÂTRE NATIONAL POPULAIRE in the 1950s; his choice of Avignon helped give impetus to the decentralization movement in French theatre. The festival grew rapidly in the 1960s and 1970s and is now one of the largest and most prestigious in the world.

**Ayckbourn, Alan** 1939– British playwright, director and actor. He has written nearly fifty full-length plays, as well as directing and running his own company in Scarborough. He began his career as a stage manager and actor with DONALD WOLFIT's touring company. In 1970 he became director of productions at STEPHEN JOSEPH's theatre-in-the-round at Scarborough. Ayckbourn has been the most successful writer of sharp comedies about middle-class manners and morals since the war. His major commercial successes are *Relatively Speaking* (London, 1967), *How the Other Half Loves* (1970),

*Time and Time Again* (1971), *Absurd Person Singular* (1973), *The Norman Conquests* (1974), a trilogy of plays set in different areas of one house over one weekend, *Bedroom Farce* (1977), *Sisterly Feelings* (1980), *Way Upstream* (1983) and *A Small Family Business* (1987). His brilliantly terse dialogue and intricate situations are matched with his clear observation of how people behave. His humour is tinged with sadness and sometimes even bitterness, but his most remarkable quality is his evenness of tone. In *Henceforward* (1988), with its elements of science fiction, *Man of the Moment* (1988), *Body Language* (1990) and *The Revenger's Comedies* (1991), the same qualities of craftsmanship prevail. His children's plays, *This Is Where We Come In* (1990) and *Callisto 5* (1990), are intricate puzzle games. He directed ARTHUR MILLER's *A View from the Bridge* (1987) for the NATIONAL THEATRE, where he became an associate director, and *Othello* (1990) for his Scarborough theatre, both with MICHAEL GAMBON. Ayckbourn has also written an effective musical play *Dreams from a Summer House* (1992), whose songs parody a range of musicals. *Time of My Life* (1993) is an intricate piece of dark comedy. *Wildest Dreams* (1993) is a dark comedy with the appearance of a sit-com but the substance of a sci-fi psychodrama.

**Azenberg, Emanuel** 1934– American producer. His single major client has been NEIL SIMON, for whom he has produced plays since 1972. Recent productions have included *Biloxi Blues*, SONDHEIM's *Sunday in the Park with George* and Simon's *Lost in Yonkers* (1991).

**Azevedo, Artur** 1855–1908 Brazilian playwright. Azevedo was responsible for the direction taken by Brazilian drama during the second half of the 19th century. A prolific writer, his adaptations and translations were regularly performed in Rio de Janeiro. His most popular work, *A Capital Federal* (*The Federal Capital*, 1897), itself an adaptation of one his earlier plays, turned on humorous contrasts between rural and urban lifestyles. The REVISTA (revue) form he cultivated gained quick popular acceptance. A SATIRE of customs and primarily political issues, the *revista* sometimes used a unified plot and at other times independent sketches without continuity. It attracted a greater public during those years than did the more serious theatre.

**Baba Sala** see ADEJUMO, MOSES OLAIYA

**Babel, Isaak (Emmanuilovich)** 1894–1941 Russian Jewish short story writer and playwright. He was noted for his polished language, careful attention to character and vivid sense of history. His two famous short story collections, *The Odessa Tales* (1921–3) and *Red Cavalry* (1926), are based upon personal experience of the Jewish underworld in Odessa and the brutality of the Russian Civil War. His play *Sunset* (1928) was successfully produced at the MOSCOW ART THEATRE in 1928. *Mariya* (published 1935), set in Petrograd in 1920, dramatizes the disintegration of a family in the wake of the Bolshevik victory. It was banned while in rehearsal. A third play, *The Chekist*, was seized and probably destroyed at Babel's arrest on undisclosed charges in 1939. He died in a prison camp.

**Bagnold, Enid** [Lady Roderick Jones] 1889–1981 British playwright and novelist. Her novels *Serena Blandish* (1925), *National Velvet* (1935) and *Lottie Dundas* (1943) were adapted for the stage. Her later stage plays, including *The Chalk Garden* (1955, New York; 1956, London) and *The Chinese Prime Minister* (1964, New York; 1965, London), retain a literary flavour. *The Chalk Garden* was highly praised as a fine 'artificial comedy' by KENNETH TYNAN. *The Last Joke* (1960) and *Call Me Jacky* (1967) failed to find a public in either New York or London.

**Bahr, Hermann** 1863–1934 Austrian playwright and critic. A leading light within the Jung Wien (Young Vienna) group of writers, he introduced NATURALISM and other avant-garde literary movements to his Viennese readers. He was also a prolific playwright, but only his comedy *The Concert* (1909) has proved to be durable. In 1918 he was briefly part of a directorial triumvirate at the BURGTHEATER.

**Baierl, Helmut** 1927– German playwright. Born in Czechoslovakia, from 1957 Baierl was dramaturge for the DEUTSCHES THEATER, transferring to the BERLINER ENSEMBLE in 1959. His first play, *The Finding* (1958), used Brechtian techniques to deal with peasant re-education. His reworking of BRECHT's *Mother Courage* in the contemporary GDR context, *Frau Flinz* (1961), was staged with HELENE WEIGEL in the title role.

**baiting** Popular entertainment. Now officially obsolete, baiting was notable for its cruelty. In the Roman games, specialized gladiators, the *venationes* and *bestiarii*, were set to kill exotic beasts. In the Middle Ages, the baiting of bulls was required by law as a hygienic measure prior to their slaughter by butchers, and survived in English towns like Tutbury and Stamford as 'bull-running'.

Bear-baiting began in England as an exclusively aristocratic pastime until the 15th century. By SHAKESPEARE's day public animal contests were licensed, and the Bear Garden in London was permitted to play on Sunday. It was later rebuilt as a three-storey amphitheatre, managed by HENSLOWE of the ROSE. Elizabeth I was a great enthusiast; her Treasury paid for the provisioning of the baiting animals. EDWARD ALLEYN was made Royal Keeper of Bulls and Mastiffs in 1604, a source of considerable profit. Three bear gardens existed in Restoration London, and one persisted in Birmingham until 1773. Parliament finally forbade the practice in 1835, but it was carried on in private for at least another 50 years.

Among other cities, baiting was also carried on in Dresden, Königsberg, Berlin, Moscow (till 1867) and Vienna, where a new establishment was designed in 1735 by ANTONIO GALLI DA BIBIENA and Antonio Caradini. As late as 1828, John Orlando Parry saw dogs in Paris gored and tossed by savage bulls, and a bull chained to a stake fighting an elkhound. More recently, deer-baiting has been observed at Midwestern American county fairs.

**Baker, Benjamin (A.)** (1818–90) American playwright. He deserted his prompter's post at William MITCHELL's OLYMPIC Theatre, and for Mitchell's benefit night wrote *A Glance at New York in 1848*, starring FRANK CHANFRAU as Mose. Encouraged by a run of 74 performances, Baker created more adventures for Mose: *New York as It Is* (1848), *Mose in California* (1849) and *Mose in China* (1850).

**Baker, George Pierce** 1866–1935 American educator. In 1908 he founded the Harvard Dramatic Club and in 1912 established Workshop 47 as a laboratory theatre for plays written in his playwriting course. He attracted to Harvard such promising talents as EUGENE O'NEILL, SIDNEY HOWARD, Thomas Wolfe, EDWARD SHELDON and PHILIP BARRY. From 1925 to 1933 he ran the new Yale Department of Drama. From 1927 he worked to establish the National Theatre Conference, and served as its first president in 1932. His ideas about the craft of playwriting are set forth in *Dramatic Technique* (1919). He is remembered as a teacher and mentor to the generation of American playwrights who came to the fore in the 1920s.

**Baker, Joséphine** [née Josephine Freda McDonald] 1906–75 African-American entertainer. Her outrageous comic antics had a *succès de scandale* in Paris in *La Revue Nègre* (Théâtre des Champs-Élysées, 1925). 'La Baker's' rubber-limbed Charlestons and black-bottoms, and her cincture of phalliform bananas, became a fixture of Parisian night life. Her repertory of American classics ('Always'), French nostalgia ('La Petite Tonkinoise'), and the signature tune 'J'ai Deux Amours' was sung in a thin soprano.

**Bakst, Léon** [Lev Rozenberg] 1866–1924 Russian painter and designer. He emigrated to Paris in 1909, having begun his stage career designing at the Hermitage, the Imperial private theatre. Bakst was a co-founder, with ALEXANDRE BENOIS, of the World of Art Group and was the most significant designer of the first period of the Ballets Russes, where he worked with DIAGHILEV until 1914. Bakst's use of colour revolutionized all of Western design. Drawing on ancient and eastern styles, he designed COSTUMES and sets that suggested free-flowing movement, and chose deep, rich shades for the decor. He believed that colour had significant emotional effects upon the spectators. This is most evident in *Scheherazade* (1910), *Cléopâtre*, *L'Oiseau de feu* (*The Firebird*, 1910), *Le Dieu bleu* (1912), *Thamar* (1912), *L'Après-midi d'un faune* (1912), *Daphnis and Chloë* (1912), and *La Belle au bois dormant* (1921) with the Ballets Russes in London.

**Baldwin, James (Arthur)** 1924–87 African-American novelist, essayist and playwright. A popular black author, Baldwin wrote two plays. In *The Amen Corner* (produced at Howard University in 1954 and on Broadway in 1965, but coolly received by critics), a fanatical woman pastor tries unsuccessfully to turn her son against the father whose love she has rejected; *Blues for Mr Charlie* (1964) involves the murder of an angry black youth by a white bigot.

**Bale, John** 1495–1563 English playwright. Trained as a Carmelite friar, he threw over the Roman Catholic religion and became an outspoken Protestant. The most notable of his plays is *Kynge Johan* (1538), which combines medieval abstract characters and historical drama based on actual people. Of his other surviving pieces, three are MYSTERY PLAYS transformed into Protestant polemic, and *The Three Laws* is an anti-Catholic MORALITY PLAY.

**Baliev, Nikita (Fyodorovich)** [Mkritich Balian] ?1877–1936 Russian actor and director. He co-founded (with Nikolai Tarasov) and directed Moscow's Bat (1908–22), Russia's first real CABARET. The Bat began as a MOSCOW ART THEATRE-related enterprise, whose main attraction was the rotund, moonfaced Baliev, expert at improvising horseplay with the customers from the stage and cavorting in specially designed entr'acte numbers. In 1920 Baliev emigrated to Paris with part of the company. As the Chauve-Souris they gave numerous performances in Paris, London and America.

**ballad opera** Although called a type of opera, ballad opera is more like a play interspersed with songs, the songs having new words set to already known tunes. The most famous example is *The Beggar's Opera*, which enjoyed phenomenal popularity in its own day and is now the only ballad opera to be regularly revived.

**Ballard, Lucinda** 1908–93 American COSTUME designer. An assistant to scenic designers NORMAN BEL GEDDES and Claude Bragdon early in her career, Ballard was an active designer (principally of costumes) for theatre, film and ballet. She received the first Tony Award for Costume Design for the plays *Happy Birthday*, *Another Part of the Forest*, *Street Scene*, *John Loves Mary* and *The Chocolate Soldier* in the 1947 BROADWAY season. She also won awards in 1961 for *The Gay Life* and in 1945 for *I Remember Mama*.

**Ballets Russes** see DIAGHILEV, SERGE

**Bances y López Candamo, Francisco Antonio de** 1662–1704 Spanish playwright; the last notable Spanish dramatist of the Golden Age. Many of his plays have strong political overtones, especially *El esclavo en grillos de oro* (*The Slave in Golden Shackles*, 1692), whose plot resembles SHAKESPEARE's *Measure for Measure*, and *La piedra filosofal* (*The Philosopher's Stone*, 1693). *Por su rey y por su dama* (*For King and Lady*, 1685) remained popular until the 19th century, and his treatise *Teatro de los teatros de los pasados y presentes siglos* (*Theatre of the Theatres of Past and Present Ages*, 1689–93) is the only work of dramatic theory in the age of CALDERÓN.

**Bancroft, Squire** 1841–1926 English actor-manager, who made his London debut in T. W. ROBERTSON's *Society* at the Prince of Wales's in 1865. In 1867, after creating the role of Captain Hawtree in Robertson's *Caste*, he married the theatre's lessee, MARIE WILTON, thereby entering matrimony and theatre management. The Bancrofts managed companies at the Prince of Wales's until 1879 and subsequently at the HAYMARKET (1880–5), offering an ensemble alternative to the star-centred regime of IRVING at the LYCEUM. Bancroft retired, already rich, at the age of 44. In 1897, he followed Irving to become the second actor to receive a knighthood.

**Bang-Hansen, Kjetil** 1940– Norwegian director. Much of his work has been done outside Oslo. With several associates (dubbed the 'Molde Group') Bang-Hansen established Teater Vårt in Molde in 1972, before moving to Rogaland Teater, Stavanger, and the NATIONALE SCENE, Bergen. He believes in theatre as an artistic end in itself, an encounter between performers and spectators, unrestricted by political ideology, and in the need to discover performance styles in free approaches to texts. Among many extraordinary productions, often with designer Helge Hoff Monsen, have been *Peer Gynt* (1978), *Raskolnikov* (1982) and *The Royal House of Thebes* (1985). After briefly heading NATIONALTHEATRET (1986–8), Bang-Hansen has freelanced, often at the NORSKE TEATRET, where key productions have included *The Pretenders* (1989) and *The Tidings Brought to Mary* (1993).

**Bankhead, Tallulah** 1902–68 American stage, film and television actress. She was noted for her vibrant energy, sultry voice, explosive speech and impetuous behaviour. She achieved fame in *The Dancers* (London, 1923) and later as Regina in *The Little Foxes* (1939) and as Sabina in *The Skin of Our Teeth*.

**Banks, John** c.1652–1706 English playwright. After three heroic plays, of which the best is *The Destruction of Troy* (1678), Banks established an entirely new genre dubbed 'she-tragedies', based on the sufferings of the heroine and emphasizing pathos. *The Unhappy Favourite* (1681), centring on Queen Elizabeth and Essex, was followed by one on Anne Boleyn. *The Innocent Usurper* (1683) and *The Island Queens* (1684), on Lady Jane Grey and Mary Queen of Scots, were politically sensitive, and banned from performance.

**Bannister, Jack** [John] 1760–1836 English actor. After moderate successes in tragedy at DRURY LANE, he began a new career as a comedian when he created the part of Don Ferolo Whiskerandos in SHERIDAN's *The Critic* (1779). A popular light comedian with a fair singing voice, he was particularly associated with the summer seasons at the HAYMARKET under GEORGE COLMAN THE YOUNGER, who wrote parts for Bannister and helped him to compile one of the first authentic one-man shows under the title of *Bannister's Budget*.

**Bannister, Nathaniel (Harrington)** 1813–47 American actor and playwright. The author of at least 40 plays, ranging through ancient history (*Gaulantus the Gaul*, 1836), local incidents (*The Maine Question*, 1839), romantic comedy (*The Gentleman of Lyons*, 1838) and moral dilemmas (*The Destruction of Jerusalem*, 1837), Bannister wrote mainly spectacles to please the public. *Putnam, the Iron Son of '76* (1844) enchanted audiences with horses on stage.

**Baraka, Amiri** [(Everett) LeRoi Jones] 1934– African-American poet, essayist and playwright. In the 1960s Baraka became leader of the black arts revolutionary movement which viewed theatre as a weapon in the struggle for black liberation. He has produced some 20 plays, many of them one-act, which powerfully dramatize social and racial problems with unnerving frankness from a blatantly anti-white posture. They include *Dutchman* (1964), *The Slave* (1964), *A Black Mass* (1966), and *Slave Ship* (1969). He founded the Black Arts Repertory Theatre/School in Harlem (1965–6) and Spirit House in Newark, New Jersey (1966), where his plays were produced. He later rejected black nationalism for revolutionary socialism, as shown in his play *The Motion of History* (1975).

**Barba, Eugenio** 1936– Italian theatre director and the-orist. Barba joined GROTOWSKI's Laboratory Theatre as an observer in 1961, and under his influence founded the ODIN TEATRET in Oslo, later moving to Holstebrö in Denmark, in order to explore the possibilities of what he has called 'the Third Theatre', a socially aware, exploratory, actor-oriented drama, distinct from both commercial BOULEVARD theatre and director-domi-nated, dramatist-oriented art theatre. In 1979 he founded the International School of Theatre Anthropology, as a focal point for collective research. He edited and contributed to Grotowski's *Towards a Poor Theatre* (English translation 1968), and has published many articles on actor research and theatre anthro-pology, some of which have been gathered and further developed in *The Floating Islands* (1984), *Beyond the Floating Islands* (1986), *A Dictionary of Theatre Anthropology* (with Nicola Savarese, 1991) and *The Paper Canoe* (1994).

**Barbeau, Jean** 1945– Quebec playwright. He followed MICHEL TREMBLAY in the use of *joual*, the popular French of Quebec, in plays such as *Manon Lastcall* (1970) and *Joualez-moi d'amour* (*Speak to Me of Love*, 1970) which deal humorously with the cultural schizophrenia of Quebec. *Le Chemin de Lacroix* (*The Way of Lacroix*), *0–71* and *Ben-Ur*, all three published in 1971, concern the social victims of his province's malaise. Recent plays have turned to more universal concerns, such as *Le Jardin de la Maison Blanche* (*The White House Garden*, 1979) and *Les Gars* (*The Guys*, 1984), which attack the materialistic val-ues of contemporary North American society.

**Barker, Harley Granville** see GRANVILLE BARKER, HARLEY

**Barker, Howard** 1946– British playwright. His first plays were produced at the ROYAL COURT THEATRE and the Open Space in the early 1970s. His early works looked at British society from the stance of the under-world as well as the underdog – of twin gangsters in *Alpha Alpha* (1972), of pimps in *Claw* (1975) and of a crim-inal in *Stripwell* (1975). Barker reverses moral expecta-tions: the prison governor in *The Hang of the Gaol* (1978) becomes an arsonist. *The Love of a Good Man* is a black comedy set in 1920. In *No End of Blame* (1980), he debates the issue of the different censorships, East and West, favouring the former. In *The Possibilities* (1988) and *The Last Supper* (1988) he turns religious parables inside out. *Scenes from an Execution* (1990) similarly attempts to upset expectations, denying the value of reason. There is a predictability about Barker's wildness, about his emotional extremes. *A Hard Heart* (1992), set in a besieged city, offers a grim plot, as does *The Europeans* (1993), set in Vienna after the siege of 1683. Barker has said that he tries to liberate his audiences 'from the nightmare of being entertained'. A theatre group, the Wrestling School, has been formed to realize his plays.

**Barker, James Nelson** 1784–1858 American play-wright and poet. Among his plays are *America* (1805); *Tears and Smiles* (1807); *The Embargo* (1808); the first pro-duced American play about Pocahontas, *The Indian Princess* (1808); and *Marmion; or, The Battle of Flodden Field* (1812), in which England's treatment of 16th-century Scotland was translated to America. Barker's greatest contributions are his 11 essays on drama in the *Democratic Press* and his remarkable tragedy of New England intolerance, *Superstition; or, The Fanatic Father* (1824).

**Barlach, Ernst** 1870–1938 German sculptor and play-wright. He bridges the symbolist movement (see SYM-BOLISM) and EXPRESSIONISM. His central theme is salva-tion. *Der tote Tag* (*The Dead Day*, 1917) treats the expressionist generation conflict in religious terms. The hero of *Der arme Vetter* (*The Poor Cousin*, 1919) sacri-fices his life to save his cousin from materialism. Barlach experimented with a modern form of the MYS-TERY PLAY in *Die Sintflut* (*The Flood*, 1924). *Der blaue Boll* (*Boozer Boll*, 1926) is a poetic return to his earlier themes. His writings were banned by the Nazis, and his final work *Der Graf von Ratzeburg* remained unproduced until 1956, when his plays were revived by Hans Lietzau in Berlin.

**Barnay, Ludwig** 1842–1924 German actor. After his years with the MEININGEN COMPANY as an actor of heroic roles, he made tours of England and America. In 1883 he was a co-founder with L'ARRONGE of the DEUTSCHES THEATER, though he soon left the company to start his own Berliner Theater in 1887. His last years were spent directing the BERLIN ROYAL THEATRE and the Court Theatre in Hannover.

**Barnes, Clive Alexander** 1927– English-born American dance and drama critic. Born in London, he went to the United States in 1965 as dance and later drama critic for the *New York Times* and the *New York Post*. Noted for his clever style, Barnes has been accused of being pro-British and of supporting the avant-garde more than the BROADWAY theatre.

**Barnes, Peter** 1931– British playwright. His plays com-bine trenchant SATIRE with a delight in shock effects. His first play, *Sclerosis* (1965), is an attack on British colo-nialism. It was followed by *The Ruling Class* (1968), a fierce PARODY of the English upper classes. In subse-quent plays he has chosen moral and historical themes as subjects for black comedy – the Spanish Succession in *The Bewitched* (1974), the Holocaust in *Laughter!* (1978) and the Black Death in *Red Noses* (1985). His taste for tackling large themes of Good and Evil within medieval settings was reflected in *Sunset and Glories* (1990), about the risks of electing a saintly pope, which was pre-miered at the West Yorkshire Playhouse; and his adap-tation of a Japanese play, *Tango at the End of Winter* (1991) by Kunio Shumizu, was seen at the WEST END in 1991.

**Barnum, P(hineas) T(aylor)** 1810–91 American entre-preneur and showman. A hard-headed businessman of personal integrity, he was not above commercial trick-ery. In 1835 he exhibited an ancient black woman he claimed was 160 years old and George Washington's nurse. In 1841 he purchased Scudder's American Museum, where, as Barnum's American Museum, he mixed freak-shows with 'moral' drama. He displayed the midget Tom Thumb (Charles Stratton), whose European appearances in 1844 made Barnum and the notion of 'humbug' notorious. In 1865 the museum and theatre burned to the ground. In 1881 Barnum helped to create 'The Greatest Show on Earth', a combination of circus, menagerie and side-show; the acquisition of the elephant Jumbo was his greatest feat there.

**Baron** [Michel Boyron] 1653–1729 French actor. After MOLIÈRE's death he moved from his company to the HÔTEL DE BOURGOGNE, creating some of RACINE's young heroes, and thence to the COMÉDIE-FRANÇAISE on its for-mation in 1680. At his peak his outstanding ability, good looks and intelligence enabled him to take lead-ing roles in both tragedy and comedy. He also wrote sev-eral comedies, the most interesting of which are *L'Homme à bonnes fortunes* (*The Philanderer*, 1686) and the one-act *Le Rendez-vous des Tuileries* (1685), in which several actors of the Comédie-Française appeared as themselves.

**Barrault, Jean-Louis** 1910–94 French actor and director. His first performances were at the ATELIER in the 1930s; in 1940 he joined the COMÉDIE-FRANÇAISE, where he began to direct as well as act: his production of CLAUDEL's *Le Soulier de Satin (The Satin Slipper)* in 1943 was a particular success. In 1946 he and Madeleine Renaud left to found their own company at the Marigny Theatre and, after 1959, at the ODÉON (with state subsidy), where their policy was to produce both new plays and classics. He produced six of Claudel's plays. Barrault had observed the MIME artist ÉTIENNE DECROUX whose performances were outstanding for the detail and inventiveness of their physical action. He produced many new authors, including IONESCO, DURAS and VAUTHIER, and made adaptations for the stage, the most famous being *Rabelais* (1968), performed in a Montmartre wrestling hall. In 1972 he converted the former Orsay station into a performance space and in 1981 moved to the Théâtre du Rond-Point on the Champs-Élysées. Originally identified with total theatre, Barrault became, in old age, an enormously respected star actor.

**Barrett, Lawrence** 1838–91 American actor and manager. Slender, with a sensitive face and an unusual vocal range, and often associated with EDWIN BOOTH, Barrett alternated Othello and Iago with him in 1871–2. At BOOTH'S THEATRE he was Adrian de Mauprat to Booth's celebrated Richelieu, and also starred as James Harebell in W. G. WILLS's *The Man o'Airlie*, one of his most acclaimed roles. Although estranged for a time, Booth and Barrett were reconciled in 1880 and made 'joint starring' tours. Barrett also managed theatres in San Francisco and New Orleans, and commissioned and staged original plays. His most successful roles after Harebell were Lanciotto in GEORGE HENRY BOKER's *Francesca da Rimini* (1883), Hernani, Cassius and, late in his career, Othello.

**Barrett, Wilson** 1846–1904 British actor-manager. His real gift was in MELODRAMA, preferably with religious overtones. He had major successes with George R. Sims's *The Lights o' London* (1881) and HENRY ARTHUR JONES's *The Silver King* (1882), and with his own adaptations of *The Manxman* (1894) and *Quo Vadis?* (1900). He wasted himself on inferior material, often his own – e.g. *The Sign of the Cross* (1895), a melodrama which requires a Roman patrician to face the lions for love of a Christian maiden (an outrageous success in London). Barrett was, at various times, manager of theatres in Leeds and Hull as well as in London.

**Barrie, J(ames) M(atthew)** 1860–1937 Scottish playwright and novelist. J. L. TOOLE staged his first successful play, *Walker, London* (1892). Later, in *Quality Street* (1902) and *The Admirable Crichton* (1902), Barrie discovered a profitable way of combining escapist romance with social problems. He was a craftsman, not simply the permanent adolescent, unwilling or unable to join the adult world, like the leading character of his most famous play, *Peter Pan* (1904). If *Alice Sit-by-the-Fire* (1905) and *Mary Rose* (1920) are fatally flawed by mawkishness, *What Every Woman Knows* (1908) and *Dear Brutus* (1917) are strengthened by the quiet SATIRE that is present in everything that Barrie wrote. Some of his one-act plays are good examples of the genre. He was knighted in 1913.

**Barry, Elizabeth** c.1658–1713 English actress. Barry's first known role was in OTWAY's *Alcibiades* (1675) for the Duke's Company. Her great success as Monimia in Otway's *The Orphan* (1680) showed her ability to move an audience to pity. By the late 1680s she was co-manager with BETTERTON of the United Company, and from 1695 of the new company formed at LINCOLN'S INN FIELDS THEATRE. She retired in 1710. Her acting was marked by an unusual control and intensity, and she was praised for her identification with her roles. At her best in tragedy, she had many major parts written for her by Otway, CONGREVE and others. She is regarded as the first great English actress.

**Barry, Philip (James Quinn)** 1896–1949 American playwright, popular in the 1920s and 1930s. Barry's first two plays were written in GEORGE PIERCE BAKER's Workshop 47 at Harvard: *A Punch for Judy* (1921) and *You and I* (1923), a BROADWAY success. Focusing on the problems of family relations, romance, sexual intrigue and profession vocation, he developed a modern comedy of manners: *In a Garden* (1925), *Paris Bound* (1927), *Holiday* (1928), *The Animal Kingdom* (1932), and *The Philadelphia Story* (1939), which starred Katharine Hepburn. These plays feature the 'Barry girl', a well heeled if somewhat spoiled young woman who rejects materialist culture and upper-class society. Barry's protagonists, male and female, struggle to serve liberal ideals. Less well received were his quasi-allegorical plays on metaphysical themes: *Hotel Universe* (1930), *The Joyous Season* (1934), *Here Come the Clowns* (1938, perhaps his best serious play) and *Liberty Jones* (1941). Productions in the 1940s were only moderately successful, even though Hepburn acted in *Without Love* (1942) and TALLULAH BANKHEAD starred in *Foolish Notion* (1945). His last play, *Second Threshold* (1951), was finished posthumously by ROBERT E. SHERWOOD.

**Barry, Spranger** ?1717–77 Irish actor-manager. In 1746 he left Dublin for DRURY LANE, where he played Othello and Macbeth and successfully established himself as an actor of sighing lovers, acting opposite GARRICK in plays by OTWAY and ROWE. In 1750 he joined COVENT GARDEN and for 12 nights played Romeo in direct competition with Garrick's performances in Drury Lane; Barry was praised for 'the amorous harmony of his features, his melting eyes and unequalled plaintiveness of voice'. In 1756 he played Lear with great majesty. In 1757 he built the Crow Street Theatre, Dublin.

**Barrymore** see DREW–BARRYMORE FAMILY

**Barsacq, André** 1909–1973 French theatre director. Russian in origin, he began as a designer. With JEAN DASTÉ and Maurice Jacquemont he founded the Compagnie des Quatre Saisons in 1937. In 1940 he took over from DULLIN as director of the ATELIER where, largely unsubsidized, he revived Russian classics and produced popular modern playwrights such as ANOUILH, Marcel Aymé, Félicien Marceau, René de Obaldia and Françoise Sagan. He made a fine adaptation of Dostoevsky's *The Idiot* (1966).

**Bartoli, Francesco** 1745–1806 Italian actor. A second-string actor in ANTONIO SACCO's company, Bartoli brought intelligence and a cultivated mind to his most important writing on the theatre, *Notizie istoriche de' comici italiani che fiorirono intorno all'anno MDL fino a'giorni presenti (Historical Particulars of Italian Players Who Flourished Around the Year 1550 to the Present Day*, 2 vols., 1782). It is an indispensable early source book for information on Italian performers and companies, particularly those of the *COMMEDIA DELL'ARTE*.

**Barton, John (Bernard Adie)** 1928– British director. He directed Marlowe Society productions at Cambridge during the 1950s. His particular strength lay in his detailed understanding of Elizabethan and Jacobean verse. In 1960 he joined the Shakespeare Memorial Company at Stratford (later, the ROYAL SHAKESPEARE COMPANY) under PETER HALL. Barton helped the company to make Shakespearian texts accessible to modern audiences, sometimes simplifying and reducing the originals, as in *The Wars of the Roses* (1963), which condensed the *Henry VI* trilogy and *Richard III* into three evenings of power struggles. He helped to bring the RSC's touring Theatre-go-Round into existence. In 1980 he devised a ten-play cycle, *The Greeks*. In recent years he has directed 19th- and 20th-century plays for the RSC by such writers as IBSEN, SCHNITZLER, GRANVILLE BARKER and JOHN WHITING.

**Bateman family** American theatre folk **Hezekiah Linthicum** Bateman (1812–75) was the American manager of London's LYCEUM THEATRE, where he brought HENRY IRVING to prominence in *The Bells* (1871) and then in *Hamlet* (1874). When Bateman died, his wife **Sidney** (1823–81) assumed the management and later managed SADLER's WELLS (1879). Their daughters **Kate** (1843–1917) and **Ellen** (1844–1936) began performing SHAKESPEARE in New York when they were six and five, then various Shakespearian roles, male and female, in both London and New York. Daughters **Virginia** (1853–1940) and **Isabel** (1854–1934) made their London debuts in 1865, then joined Irving.

**Bates, Alan (Arthur)** 1934– British actor. He played the passive Cliff to Kenneth Haigh's vitriolic Jimmy Porter in the ROYAL COURT production of JOHN OSBORNE's *Look Back in Anger* (1956). Bates here revealed his capacity for a taut stillness, an eloquent calm, which is evident in more demanding roles such as Mick in HAROLD PINTER's *The Caretaker* (1960), the title role in SIMON GRAY's *Butley* (1971), Simon in Gray's *Otherwise Engaged* (1975) and the Inquisitor in Pinter's *One for the Road* (1984). In 1985 he played the title role in PETER SHAFFER's *Yonadab* at the NATIONAL THEATRE, and in 1989 the title role in CHEKHOV's *Ivanov* and Benedick in *Much Ado About Nothing*. His most memorable performances have been in contemporary plays, such as DAVID STOREY's *Stages* at the NT in 1992, a thoughtful study of an artist in anguish.

**Baty, Gaston** 1885–1952 French theatre director. The only non-acting member of the CARTEL, he brought the stage techniques of EXPRESSIONISM to the Paris theatre, attacking the predominance of literary theatre in France between the wars. From 1930 to 1947 he ran the Théâtre Montparnasse, where he strove for complex staging methods with an emphasis on pictorial qualities.

**Bauer, Wolfgang** 1941– Austrian playwright. He has helped to revive the VOLKSSTÜCK tradition in contemporary terms. From *Pig Transport* in 1962, his dialect plays have presented violent images of a materialistic society in which sex, sadism, drugs and pop music are the only release from boredom. Designed as provocation, works like *Magic Afternoon* (1968), *Sylvester, or the Massacre at the Sacher Hotel* (1971), *Magnet Kisses* (1976) and *Memory Hotel* (1980) are deliberately inartistic in style.

**Bauernfeld, Eduard von** 1802–90 Austrian playwright, whose satirical comedies of Viennese manners were mostly produced at the BURGTHEATER. The best-known are *Bourgeois and Romantic* (1833), *Of Age* (1846), *The Categorical Imperative* (1850) and *From Society* (1867).

**Bax, Clifford** 1886–1962 British playwright, poet and critic. Bax wrote successful historical tragedies such as *The Rose Without a Thorn* (1932) and *The House of Borgia* (1935). He adapted KAREL ČAPEK's *The Insect Play* (1922–3) with Nigel Playfair, and experimented with COMMEDIA DELL'ARTE and PARODY in *Midsummer Marriage* (1924). During World War II he turned to radio plays on mystical themes, and in 1945 published a strong plea for the establishment of a NATIONAL THEATRE.

**Baxter, James K.** 1926–72 New Zealand playwright and poet. Having begun in radio drama, he went on to write stage plays, of which *The Wide Open Cage* (1959) was the most successful. Others on religious and social themes followed, notably *The Band Rotunda* (1967), *The Devil and Mr Mulcahy* (1967) and *The Day that Flanagan Died* (1969), as well as plays derived from Greek myth, such as *The Sore-footed Man* (1967) and *The Temptations of Oedipus* (1970).

**Bay, Howard** 1912–86 American stage and film designer. Bay's designs include *The Little Foxes, Show Boat, The Music Man, Finian's Rainbow* and *Man of La Mancha*. He became associated with the painterly, sentimental musicals of the 1940s and 1950s, although he had begun his career with a super-realistic tenement set for the FEDERAL THEATRE PROJECT's *One Third of a Nation*.

**Baylis, Lilian (Mary)** 1874–1937 British theatre manager. An eccentric lover of opera, utterly unafraid of big schemes, she began her association with the OLD VIC in 1898, when it was run as a temperance hall by her aunt, Emma Cons. Taking over in 1912, she mounted for the first time a complete cycle of SHAKESPEARE's First Folio plays (1914–23), establishing a reputation for herself and the theatre, which was eventually to become the temporary stage of the new NATIONAL THEATRE company. Appointed a Companion of Honour in 1929, she reopened SADLER's WELLS THEATRE in 1931, founding the companies that eventually became the Royal Ballet and the English National Opera.

**Bayreuth** Bavarian city. It has two notable theatres: the Margrave's Opera House, designed by members of the BIBIENA FAMILY, opened in 1748, and a perfect example of rococo theatre architecture; and the Festival Theatre, opened by RICHARD WAGNER in 1876 and built specifically for his music dramas, which are still performed there at annual music festivals. (See also THEATRE DESIGN.)

**bear-baiting** See BAITING.

**Beaton, Cecil** 1904–80 British theatre set and costume designer, and photographer. Beaton's neo-romantic style is illustrated in his costumes for the musical *My Fair Lady* (1956) and *Lady Windermere's Fan* (1946). He also created exuberant designs for film – *Gigi* (1958), *My Fair Lady* (1964) and *On a Clear Day You Can See Forever* (1970) – and designed for Frederick Ashton's ballets.

**Beatty, John Lee** 1948– American designer. Active since the early 1970s with the MANHATTAN THEATRE CLUB and CIRCLE REPERTORY COMPANY, among others, by the mid-1980s Beatty had become the most prolific designer in New York. A master of poetic or lyric REALISM, he designed the premieres of virtually all the plays of LANFORD WILSON, several by BETH HENLEY and many new plays at the NEW YORK SHAKESPEARE FESTIVAL. He also designed McNALLY's *Lips Together, Teeth Apart* (1991) and *Ain't Misbehavin'* (1978). He is known for playful and theatrical settings, such as the caricature environment for *Song of Singapore* (1991).

**Beaumarchais, Pierre-Augustin Caron de** 1732–99 French playwright. His work for the stage was only part of a busy life as government agent, financial speculator and commercial entrepreneur. Having earned himself a place at court, he wrote *Eugénie* (1767) – a domestic drama and his first serious work – but *Les Deux Amis (The Two Friends*, 1770) proved a failure. He turned to comedy with the first of his Figaro plays, *The Barber of Seville*, an exquisite confection of all the genre's traditional devices and a huge success at the COMÉDIE-FRANÇAISE (1775); but the underlying note of seriousness in its sequel, *The Marriage of Figaro*, prevented its public performance until 1784, when a record run ensued. Beaumarchais's next work was an opera, *Tarare* (1787), with music by Salieri; then in 1792 he returned to heavy-handed domestic sentiment with the last Figaro play, *La Mère Coupable (The Guilty Mother)*. The trilogy charts a progression from 'artificial' comedy to 'realistic' domestic drama. Meanwhile he had founded the Société des Auteurs, introducing an author's royalty on all theatrical performances, and established a printing press to publish the first complete edition of VOLTAIRE's works.

**Beaumont, Francis** 1584–1616 English playwright and poet. His first play, *The Woman Hater* (1605), is a COMEDY OF HUMOURS written for the BOYS OF ST PAUL'S. The only other extant play of which he was sole author is the splendidly good-humoured *The Knight of the Burning Pestle* (1607), performed by the CHILDREN OF THE CHAPEL ROYAL, in which the bourgeois taste for chivalric romance is kindly mocked. The rest of his plays were written in a famous collaboration with JOHN FLETCHER. The two succeeded SHAKESPEARE as leading playwrights for the King's Men in about 1609, providing the company with popular successes such as *Philaster* (c.1609), *The Maid's Tragedy* (c.1610) and *A King and No King* (1611), and becoming leaders of refined theatrical taste. Their natural home was the BLACKFRIARS. Of the many plays ascribed to them, only a handful (in addition to the three already mentioned) can be partly attributed to Beaumont, including *Cupid's Revenge* (c.1611), *The Coxcomb* (1612), *The Scornful Lady* (c.1613) and *The Captain* (1613).

**Beaumont, (Hugh) Binkie** [Hughes Griffiths Morgan] 1908–73 British theatre impresario. From the mid-1930s to the early 1960s this modest, retiring man was one of the most powerful impresarios in British theatre, helping such dramatists as CHRISTOPHER FRY and TERENCE RATTIGAN. He managed H. M. Tennent Ltd, which became associated with star-studded WEST END productions of small-cast, opulently dressed and staged plays, and, consequently, became a target for such 'angry young men' as KENNETH TYNAN. Beaumont became a governor of the Shakespeare Memorial Theatre in 1950 and was also a member of the NATIONAL THEATRE board from 1962 to 1968.

**Beck, Julian** see LIVING THEATRE

**Beckett, Samuel** 1906–89 Irish-French playwright and novelist. He grew up in Dublin, moved to London and then to Paris, where he lived almost continuously from 1937, writing in both French and English and doing the translating himself. Beckett became known as a playwright relatively late in life, after he had written his famous prose trilogy (*Molloy, Malone Dies* and *The Unnamable*). It was in 1953 that *En Attendant Godot* was successfully produced by ROGER BLIN in France; then in 1955 by PETER HALL in England. In both places the play, so different from anything audiences were accustomed to, had an explosive effect on theatre. In *Godot* and sub-

sequent plays – especially *Endgame* (first performed as *Fin de Partie*, directed by Blin in London, 1957), *Krapp's Last Tape* (1958) and *Happy Days* (1961) – Beckett succeeded in creating rituals for celebrating nothing which are both philosophically uncompromising and theatrically inventive. His characters' dialogue owes much to comic cross-talk acts. Through whittling away the traditional elements of plot, setting and character, he created a dynamic image for the static experience of waiting, remembering, and struggling with a sense of futility. His characters are often devoid of 'personality', possessing only the clown's self-conscious awareness that his sole function is to keep the game going. His creation of literal images for degenerating life conditions have become proverbial – e.g. Hamm's parents living in dustbins (*Endgame*) or Winnie, buried up to her waist, then her neck (*Happy Days*).

From the late 1960s Beckett wrote only short dramatic fragments, in which the clown figure of his earlier plays has been replaced by ghostly shapes, only half seen, struggling to retain a feeble hold of themselves and of their space. He also became more involved in directing his own works, e.g. *Waiting for Godot* in Berlin in 1975.

**Becque, Henry** 1837–99 French playwright. His early plays showed his committed socialism: *Michel Pauper* (1870), *La Navette (The Shuttle*, 1878) and *Les Honnêtes Femmes (Honest Women*, 1880). In 1882 *Les Corbeaux (The Crows)* received its premiere at the COMÉDIE-FRANÇAISE, a stormy event which signalled the arrival of NATURALISM in the national theatre. Becque had moved beyond the WELL MADE PLAY to the well observed play: the 'crows' are birds of prey who descend on the women of a family after the death of the father. *The Parisienne* (1885), first staged at the Renaissance with RÉJANE, had even less plot and was the prototype of the 'slice of life' play. These two major works heralded the bitter comedies, the *comédies rosses*, that would become a major feature of the Théâtre Libre repertoire.

**Bedford, Brian** 1935– British-born American actor. Since his US acting debut in PETER SHAFFER's *Five Finger Exercise* (1959) Bedford has devoted his career to the US and Canadian stages, winning awards in *The Knack* (1965) and *School for Wives* (1971). His numerous appearances at the STRATFORD FESTIVAL over a dozen seasons have included Malvolio, Angelo, Leontes, Richard II, Tartuffe, Bottom, Richard III and six roles opposite MAGGIE SMITH. He played the British actor W. C. MACREADY in RICHARD NELSON's *Two Shakespearian Actors* (1992). Since 1975 he has had starring roles in *Equus, Deathtrap, Whose Life Is It Anyway?, The Real Thing* and his own one-man show based on Shakespeare's life and works, *The Lunatic, the Lover and the Poet*.

**Beer-Hoffman, Richard** 1886–1945 Austrian playwright, director and novelist. He was one of the Young Vienna group with SCHNITZLER and HOFMANNSTHAL. After writing poetic historical tragedy and pantomime, in 1919 he presented the first part of his major work, an Old Testament cycle (*Jacob's Dream, Young David, The History of King David*) experimenting with symbolic tableaux and pageant elements. All his plays are variations on the theme of fate, and the later parts of the trilogy, banned in 1933, remain unperformed. Their portrayal of faith as the acceptance of suffering has seemed unacceptable after the Holocaust.

**Beeston family** English theatrical family. Christopher Beeston (c.1580–1639), actor and theatre manager, made his reputation at the RED BULL as autocratic business manager for Queen Anne's Men from 1612 to 1619. In 1616 he acquired the lease of the COCKPIT in Drury Lane, converting and renaming it the PHOENIX in 1617. There he exerted a major influence on the Jacobean and Caroline theatre, acknowledged in the popular name of the last company he established there, Beeston's Boys (1637–40). His son **William** (c.1606–82) inherited control of Beeston's Boys in 1639, and during and after the Interregnum maintained his theatrical ambitions at the SALISBURY COURT.

**Behan, Brendan** 1923–64 Irish playwright. At 14 he joined the IRA, and spent two years in an English Borstal, convicted in 1939 of carrying explosives. In 1942 he got 14 years for shooting at a policeman during an IRA ceremony. Amnestied in 1947, Behan continued the writing begun in prison. In 1954 the PIKE THEATRE presented *The Quare Fellow*, a grimly comic drama of the hours preceding a prison hanging. JOAN LITTLEWOOD's 1956 Theatre Workshop production in London made Behan famous. *The Hostage* (1958), derived from his one-act Gaelic play *An Giall*, was acclaimed in London, Paris and New York. His last serious work, *Borstal Boy* (1958), is an imaginatively controlled account of his Borstal years. Behan's vivid, belligerent personality illuminated the theatrical drabness of the 1950s.

**Behn, Aphra** 1640–89 English playwright and novelist. She lived for a year in Surinam, an experience on which her novella *Oroonoko* was based. In 1666 she was employed as a spy by the English government. The first English professional woman playwright, she wrote at least 17 plays, mostly comedies, but including one farce opera, *The Emperor of the Moon* (1687), which made use of massive stage spectacle. Her comedies, well crafted and vigorous, return frequently to the miseries of mercenary, loveless marriages. She wrote political comedies of Tory propaganda, e.g. *The Roundheads* (1681), as well as SATIRES on contemporary behaviour, e.g. *The Lucky Chance* (1686) and *Sir Patient Fancy* (1678). Her best play *The Rover* (1677), based on KILLIGREW's *Thomaso*, sets the rake's freedom against the independence and wit of Hellena. She produced a sequel in 1681.

**Behrman, S(amuel) N(athaniel)** 1893–1973 American playwright. Behrman produced a steady series of urbane and curiously impersonal high comedies such as *The Second Man* (1927), *Biography* (1932), *End of Summer* (1936), *No Time for Comedy* (1939) and *But for Whom Charlie* (1964). Two recurrent character types haunt his salons: fashionable, tolerant matrons and cynically detached artists. Behrman's discussion dramas (weak in story and structure) were presented by the THEATRE GUILD.

**Beijing opera** see JINGXI

**Béjart family** French actors. Their careers were intimately linked with that of MOLIÈRE. **Joseph**, the eldest brother (c.1616–59), was a co-founder in 1643 of Molière's first theatrical venture, the Illustre-Théâtre, and shared his fortunes as a strolling player in the provinces. **Madeleine** (1618–72) became Molière's touring companion and mistress. Her devoted support as performer/manager was hugely important to him for almost 30 years. She played tragic heroines and created several of Molière's outspoken soubrettes (e.g. Dorine in *Tartuffe*). Her sister **Geneviève** (1624–75), known as Mlle Hervé, also a constant member of Molière's company, was noted for tragic roles though she played Bélise in *Les Femmes savantes* (*The Learned Ladies*). **Louis** (1630–78),

known as L'Éguisé on stage, played old men and supporting roles such as La Flèche in *L'Avare* (*The Miser*), where Molière made use of his limp. **Armande** (-Grésinde-Claire-Élizabeth) (1641–1700), Madeleine's youngest sister or possibly her illegitimate daughter, was a member of Molière's itinerant company and became his wife in 1662 – an unhappy marriage but a successful stage partnership. She played most of Molière's young heroines (e.g. Célimène in *The Misanthrope*, Elmire in *Tartuffe*, Henriette in *The Learned Ladies* and Angélique in *Le Malade imaginaire* (*The Imaginary Invalid*)), parts which he had fashioned for her. With the help of LA GRANGE she rallied the company after Molière's death.

**Bel Geddes, Norman** 1893–1958 American set and industrial designer. He pioneered the use of lenses in STAGE LIGHTING equipment. Better known for his industrial work, he designed a few ambitious, visionary theatre sets – e.g. for an unrealized project based on *The Divine Comedy*, supposed to include 70ft towers and a performance area some 100ft wide. Most of his designs that were executed were detailed and naturalistic, such as *Dead End*, because of the demands of the theatre at the time. He is best known for transforming a theatre into a cavernous Gothic cathedral for MAX REINHARDT's production of *The Miracle*.

**Belasco, David** 1853–1931 American director and playwright. He moved to New York as stage manager and resident dramatist for the new Madison Square Theatre (1882), and later for DANIEL FROHMAN's Lyceum Theatre until he became an independent producer in 1890. His first successes were in collaboration with Henry C. DeMille, beginning with *The Wife* (1887). Until 1902 Belasco produced plays for the THEATRICAL SYNDICATE, including *Madam Butterfly* (1900), *Under Two Flags* (1901), *The Auctioneer* (1901) and *Dubarry* (1901). He then entered the richest phase of his career (1902–15), in which he presented 42 original productions and revivals in New York City and on tour. The most famous were *The Darling of the Gods* (1902), *The Girl of the Golden West* (1905), *The Rose of the Rancho* (1906), *The Easiest Way* (1909) and *The Governor's Lady* (1912). He also built the Belasco Theatre (1907), where he staged spectacular productions. As a playwright he affixed his name to 70 works, but none holds the stage today. His greatest theatrical contribution was in creating and managing stage effects. He pioneered the use of electric lights to create mood, and combined a scenic REALISM with melodramatic action and sentimental idealization of character. The Belasco Theatre is currently owned by the SHUBERT Organization.

**Belaval, Emilio (S.)** 1903–72 Puerto Rican playwright, director and producer. A major contributor to modern Puerto Rican theatre, in 1939 he created Areyto, a popular but short-lived theatre group. His plays are *La presa de los vencedores* (*The Victors' Prey*, 1939), *Hay que decir la verdad* (*The Truth Must Be Told*, 1940), *La muerte* (*Death*, 1950), *La vida* (*Life*, 1958) and *Cielo caído* (*Fallen Sky*, 1960).

**Bell, John** 1940– Australian actor and director. In Britain he acted with the ROYAL SHAKESPEARE COMPANY from 1964 to 1969, and acted and directed at Lincoln Repertory Theatre. A co-founder of Nimrod Theatre, Sydney, in 1970, he remained an artistic director there till 1985, directing several innovative Shakespearian productions. He is now director of the Bell Shakespeare Company, a touring company dedicated to productions that appeal to young audiences as well as to the general public. His major roles include Arturo Ui (1971, 1985), Hamlet (1973), Henry V (1964) and Cyrano de Bergerac (1980–1). He was awarded an OBE in 1978.

**Bellamy, George Anne** ?1731–88 Irish actress. Named George because she was born on St George's Day, she appeared as a child actress at COVENT GARDEN in 1741, playing Prue in CONGREVE's *Love for Love* and appearing with GARRICK in private performances. In 1744 she made her adult debut as Monimia in OTWAY's *The Orphan*. Her many lovers, extravagant lifestyle and furious rows with company members did nothing for her acting. In 1750 she played Juliet to Garrick's Romeo. Performing as Euridice in *Oedipus*, she was so 'overcome by the horror of the piece that she was carried off in a state of insensibility'. Illness made her look old and she retired in 1770; her ghosted autobiography was published in 1785.

**Bellamy, Ralph** 1904–91 American actor. He made his debut in New York in 1929 as Ben Davis in *Town Boy*. By 1943 he had made 84 films and for the rest of his career alternated between film, theatre and television. In 1958 he won awards for his performance as Franklin Delano Roosevelt in *Sunrise at Campobello*.

**Belleroche** [Raymond Poisson] c.1630–90 French actor and playwright. He acted at the HÔTEL DE BOURGOGNE until 1680, and then at the first COMÉDIE-FRANÇAISE. He developed the character of Crispin as a comic type, using his considerable bulk, large mouth and tendency to stutter to advantage, and became a favourite of Louis XIV. He also wrote farcical comedies and founded a minor theatrical dynasty.

**Bellerose** [Pierre le Messier] died 1670 French actor-manager. A leading tragedian in the first half of the 17th century, he joined the Comédiens du Roi at the HÔTEL DE BOURGOGNE in 1622 and was director from 1635–47, remaining a company member. He had a fine speaking voice, though some contemporaries preferred the greater aggression of his arch-rival MONTDORY at the MARAIS.

**Bellotti-Bon, Luigi** 1820–83 Italian actor and company manager. He acted with GUSTAVO MODENA's young company in 1845 (together with TOMMASO SALVINI). In the 1850s he was a member of the Reale Sarda with RISTORI and ROSSI, and went with them to Paris, Dresden and Berlin, on what was one of the first 'international' tours undertaken by an Italian company since the decline of the COMMEDIA DELL'ARTE. In 1859 he formed a company of his own, encouraging the leading and emerging playwrights of the day to write for it. The troupe enjoyed great success, and in 1873 he expanded his single company into three. This stretched his resources. He turned increasingly to French adaptations, but failed to hold his audience. When the financial collapse came, he shot himself. He was one of the most accomplished and innovative actor-managers of the century, and his tragedy prompted intense discussion of the problems confronting Italian drama and theatre.

**below** Elizabethan stage direction indicating the location of a character on the main stage in contrast to a character ABOVE; also the area underneath the trestle stage from which access was possible through a trap.

**Bely, Andrei** [Boris (Nikolaevich) Bugaev] 1880–1934 Russian poet, novelist, critic, theorist and playwright. His dramas – *He Who Has Come* (1903) and *The Jaws of Night* (1907) – are from the period when he championed the MYSTERY PLAY; they describe a portentous moment in time in which the earth is poised between apocalypse and the Second Coming, a situation recreated in his

1910 novel, *The Silver Dove*. Their dialogue and settings are infused with Bely's intense, hallucinogenic orchestration of rhythms, sound, light and colour. His critical essay on *The Cherry Orchard* (1904) pointed in a new direction, towards a symbolic realism in which the infinite is revealed in the instant. His essay 'Theatre and Modern Drama' rejected both the mystery play and symbolist drama (see SYMBOLISM). His final experiences with theatre involved adapting his two city novels for the stage. *Petersburg* (1913) was presented as *The Death of a Senator* at the MOSCOW ART THEATRE (1925), with MICHAEL CHEKHOV in the title role. Bely gave MEYERHOLD his *Moscow* adaptation, but it never reached the stage.

**Bemba, Sylvain** [Michel Belavin; Martial Malinda] 1934– Congolese novelist, playwright and journalist. During the 1970s he published plays, mainly for the radio. They range in theme from corruption in the old and new Africa to the intellectual's dilemma about involvement in a guerrilla war, and incorporate traditional elements and popular speech: *L'Enfer c'est Orféo* (Hell Is Orfeo, 1970, published under the pseudonym Martial Malinda), *L'Homme qui tua le crocodile* (The Man who Killed the Crocodile, 1972), *Une Eau dormante* (Sleepy Waters, 1975), *Tarentelle noire et diable blanc* (Black Tarantula and White Devil, 1976) and *Un Foutu de monde pour un blanchisseur trop honnête* (A Rotten World for an Over-Honest Laundryman, 1979).

**Ben-Ami, Jacob** 1890–1977 Russian-born American actor and director. He achieved critical acclaim on both Yiddish and English-speaking stages. Ben-Ami emigrated to New York in 1912. In 1919 he founded his own JEWISH ART THEATRE, where he discarded the old starring system. His BROADWAY acting career extended to 1972 and included Michael Cape in O'NEILL's *Welded* (1924), Arthur Kober in *Evening Song* (1934) and Forman in *The Tenth Man* (1959). He was a member of EVA LE GALLIENNE's Civic Repertory Theatre from 1929–31, portraying a memorable Trigorin in *The Seagull*. He acted and directed for the THEATRE GUILD, and toured his Yiddish productions to Africa and South America. (See also YIDDISH THEATRE.)

**Benavente, Jacinto** 1866–1954 Spanish playwright; a circus impresario before turning to the theatre. His first full-length play, *El nido ajeno* (Another's Nest, 1894), was considered too sharply critical of society. However, *Gente conocida* (People of Importance, 1896) established his career, which was to last for 50 years. He wrote 18 plays in the period 1901–4. *La noche del sábado* (Saturday Night, 1903) brought an international reputation which was confirmed by *Los intereses creados* (Bonds of Interest, 1907). *Señora ama* (M'lady, 1908) shows patient feminine virtue triumphing over a husband's philandering. *La malquerida* (The Passion Flower, 1913) is a tragedy brought on by a man's passion for his stepdaughter. In 1909 Benavente helped found a short-lived Children's Theatre, which opened with his interesting fairy-tale play *El príncipe que todo lo aprendió en libros* (The Prince Who Learned Everything Out of Books). His later plays were more conservative. He became director of the Teatro Español in 1920, but his Nobel Prize in 1922 provoked almost as much protest as that of ECHEGARAY. He declared for the Republic in 1936 but made his peace with Franco's regime. Benavente's 175 plays include all types of drama, though many are mediocre and repetitive, especially after 1920.

**Bene, Carmelo** 1937– Italian actor, director and playwright. His radical reorchestrations of classic drama, like his versions of SHAKESPEARE – *Amleto* (1975), *Romeo e Giulietta* (1976) and *Riccardo III* (1977) – or compositions such as *Nostra Signora dei Turchi* (*Our Lady of the Turks*, 1973) and *S. A. D. E.* (1974) have been highly original, controversial attempts to evolve contemporary performance styles centred on the physical and vocal qualities of the actor, but exploiting technical facilities, particularly light, sound and costuming. These have won him a wide following, but also charges of empty flamboyance and decadence. His performance skills were remarkably demonstrated in his oratorio version of MANZONI's *Adelchi* (1984), first presented on stage, then transferred to Italian television. His commitment to striking scenic adaptation has persisted in work like *Hammelette for Hamlet*, an 'operetta inqualificabile'(1987), adapted from Laforgue, and in revivals like his version of BENELLI's *La Cena delle beffe* (1989). Bene is a prolific commentator on his own approaches to the art of theatre.

**Benedetti, Mario** 1920– Uruguayan playwright, novelist and critic. After three plays, including *Ida y vuelta* (*Return Trip*, 1958), a bitter SATIRE on problems of moral decay in the national identity, Benedetti left the theatre because productions fell short of his expectations. He subsequently wrote *Pedro y el capitán* (*Pedro and the Captain*, 1979), a virulent play about torture written during the worst period of Uruguayan political repression. ICTUS, a major professional theatre in Chile, adapted his novel, *Primavera con una esquina rota* (*Spring with a Broken Corner*, 1984), for the stage.

**Benedix, Roderich** 1811–73 German playwright and director. He managed theatres in Frankfurt, Cologne and Leipzig, and was a prolific writer of popular light comedy in the manner of SCRIBE. Benedix's plays are no longer performed.

**Béneke, Walter** 1928– El Salvadorian playwright. Béneke has also been ambassador to Germany and Japan. He wrote two prize-winning plays. *El paraíso de los imprudentes* (*Paradise of the Imprudent*, 1956), with its disconcerting look at the 'lost' postwar generation in Paris was the first play published in the series Colección Teatro (Theatre Collection) of El Salvador. The English title of *Funeral Home* (1958) reflects its setting in the United States, where an anguished young widow faces an existential choice between happiness and adherence to a meaningless standard of values.

**Benelli, Sem** 1877–1949 Italian playwright and poet. His best work was done in the decade or so before the World War I: costume drama in the manner of D'ANNUNZIO, e.g. *La cena delle beffe* (*The Jest*, 1909), an exotic blank-verse tragedy of Renaissance court revenge. *La maschera di Bruto* (*The Mask of Brutus*, 1908) anticipates later experimental drama, and his comedy *Tignola* (1908) retains a certain charm.

**Bennett, Alan** 1934– British actor and playwright. He became known as part of the highly successful *Beyond the Fringe* REVUE team (1960). As a character actor, Bennett specialized in woolly-minded English eccentrics, whose nursery language revealed political realities. The satiric qualities of his acting are more fully developed in his writing, which started with a revue-like play, *Forty Years On* (1968), recalling the changes that had taken place over that period in a minor public school. *Getting On* (1971) described the disillusionment of a Labour MP, and in *The Old Country* (1977) ALEC GUINNESS played a British traitor in exile in the Soviet Union. His small-town comedy, *Habeas Corpus* (1973), contained amusing jokes about British middle-

class sexual inhibitions, while *Enjoy* (1980) offered the life-cycle of a working-class couple. In 1988 he adapted his short television play *An Englishman Abroad*, about the Moscow life of the British spy Guy Burgess, to form part of a double bill with *A Question of Attribution* for the NATIONAL THEATRE. These plays have led to further triumphs at the NT – his adaptation of *The Wind in the Willows* (1990) and *The Madness of George III* (1991). Bennett's sequence of monologues for television, *Talking Heads*, was later adapted for the stage.

**Bennett, (Enoch) Arnold** 1867–1931 British novelist and playwright. After early romantic comedies (*Cupid and Common Sense*, 1908; *The Honeymoon*, 1911) he made his reputation with *The Great Adventure* (1911), based on his own novel *Buried Alive*, about an artist who fakes his own death to escape the pressure of fame. His most successful play, *Milestones* (in collaboration with Edward Knoblock, 1912), describes an English industrial family over several generations. Later he turned to more metaphysical themes in *Sacred and Profane Love* (1919) and *Body and Soul* (1922), though these were less well received than his naturalistic comedies *London Life* (1924) and *Mr Prohack* (1927, with CHARLES LAUGHTON in the title role), both written in collaboration with Knoblock.

**Bennett [Di Figlia], Michael** 1943–87 American choreographer and director. *Promises, Promises* (1968) and *Coco* (1969) were followed by two 'concept musicals', *Company* (1970) and *Follies* (1971), with HAROLD PRINCE and STEPHEN SONDHEIM. Then came *Seesaw* (1973) and the critically acclaimed *A Chorus Line* (1975), about the lives of BROADWAY's chorus dancers, *Ballroom* (1978) and *Dreamgirls* (1981). As a choreographer, Bennett most often employed a precise, rhythmic and expressive style of jazz dance admirably suited to contemporary characters and situations.

**Bennett, Richard** 1873–1944 American stage and film actor. Among his successful roles were He in *He Who Gets Slapped*, Judge Gaunt in *Winterset*, Tony in *They Knew What They Wanted* and Robert Mayo in *Beyond the Horizon*. Bennett excited considerable controversy by berating audiences and critics, even stopping shows to lecture the audience.

**Benois, Alexandre** 1870–1960 Russian painter and designer. He emigrated to Paris in 1926. Benois designed both sets and COSTUMES, mostly for opera and ballet. Together with SERGE DIAGHILEV in 1898 he founded the journal *Mir Isskustva* (*The World of Art*), which became a focal point for the emerging modern artists of Russia. Benois served as artistic director for the early years of Diaghilev's Ballets Russes, where his crowning achievement was *Petrushka* (1911), and together with LÉON BAKST he exerted a profound influence on the development of European design and ballet. Benois's designs, which were often of 18th- and 19th-century scenes, exhibit deep, rich colours and evoke a romantic atmosphere. After the mid-1920s he designed throughout Europe, especially at La Scala in Milan.

**Benson, F(rank) R(obert)** 1858–1939 English actor-manager. While he was still an Oxford undergraduate he produced the *Agamemnon* in Greek. By the age of 25 he was manager of the F. R. Benson Company, touring SHAKESPEARE. Engaged by Charles Flower to initiate an annual Shakespeare Festival at Stratford, Benson retained his association with the Festival from 1886 to 1919. He toured the British Isles, providing for many provincial audiences their only experience of professional Shakespearian performance. He played an uncut *Hamlet* (1899) and all but two of Shakespeare's plays, and many actors did their apprenticeship in his busy company. Benson was knighted in 1916.

**Bentley, Eric (Russell)** 1916– British-born American drama critic, translator, editor, playwright and director. Bentley gained recognition in the late 1940s for his translations of BRECHT's plays. He has directed in both the US and the European theatre, and was drama critic of the *New Republic* from 1952 to 1956. Besides Brecht, he has translated PIRANDELLO and SCHNITZLER, and written ten original plays and numerous critical books.

**Berain, Jean** 1637–1711 French architect and designer. His style represents a transitional phase between baroque and rococo. Appointed official designer to Louis XIV in 1674, he devised the costumes and decorations for court ballets, operas and the open-air *fêtes* arranged by LULLY at Versailles and other royal palaces. At the Paris Opéra he succeeded VIGARANI as designer-machinist in 1680. His costume designs were sumptuous and idiosyncratic, an inspired conjunction of fantasy and fashion.

**Bérard, Christian(-Jacques)** 1902–49 French designer and painter. He combined a career as a painter and fashion designer with designs for ballet and drama. At 22 he designed the ballet *Les Elves* (1924) for Michel Fokine. He subsequently worked for other famous choreographers such as George Balanchine, Roland Petit and Léonide Massine. He designed highly stylized productions such as JEAN COCTEAU's *The Infernal Machine* (1934), the film *Beauty and the Beast*, and LOUIS JOUVET's production of JEAN GIRAUDOUX's *Madwoman of Chaillot* (1945).

**Bergman, Hjalmar** 1883–1931 Swedish novelist and playwright. His collection of one-act *Marionette Plays* (1917) is a blend of the realistic and symbolic reminiscent of MAETERLINCK. *An Experiment* (1919) is a social comedy echoing SHAW's *Pygmalion*, but with *The Gambling House* (1916–23) and *The Legend* (c.1920) he attempted ambitious symbolist fantasies (see SYMBOLISM) on moral issues. Popular success came with his final plays: *Swedenhielms* (1923), *The Rabble* (1928), *The Markurells of Wadköping* (1929) and *The Baron's Will* (1930), the last two being dramatizations of earlier novels.

**Bergman, Ingmar** 1918– Swedish director and playwright. Best known for his films, he has been constantly active in the theatre. His early work was done at provincial city theatres, including MALMÖ (1952–8), with productions of MOLIÈRE, IBSEN and especially STRINDBERG – e.g. *The Crown Bride*, *The Ghost Sonata* and *Erik XIV*. From 1963 to 1966 Bergman headed DRAMATEN, directing some extraordinary productions (including a stark *Who's Afraid of Virginia Woolf?* and his split-stage *Hedda Gabler*), returning there in the 1970s to direct Strindberg: an intimate *Dream Play* (1970), a grotesque *Ghost Sonata* (1973) and an adaptation of *To Damascus*, Parts 1 and 2 (1974). In 1976 he joined the Munich Residenztheater, where he staged Strindberg, Molière, Ibsen, CHEKHOV and GOMBROWICZ. The most ambitious was his 1981 triple production of *A Doll's House*, *Miss Julie* and his own *Scenes from a Marriage*, all opening on the same evening. In 1985 he rejoined Dramaten, reviving *Miss Julie* (1985) and a controversial *Hamlet*. In 1988 Bergman's 80th major stage production was O'NEILL's *Long Day's Journey into Night*, followed in 1989 by Yukio Mishima's *Madame de Sade*. In 1991 he staged EURIPIDES'

*The Bacchae* as a music drama at the Royal Opera, Stockholm.

Bergman's approach often involves a radical reformulation of the text, to modernize the playwright's vision. He avoids literal REALISM, preferring to suggest rather than reconstruct. Like his films, his stage productions are strikingly picturesque.

**Berkoff, Steve(n)** 1937– British playwright, performer and director. He established his reputation with three adaptations of work by Kafka – *The Penal Colony* (1968), *Metamorphosis* (1969) and *The Trial* (1970). Further adaptations included AESCHYLUS' *Agamemnon* (1973) and Edgar Allan Poe's *The Fall of the House of Usher* (1974). He formed the London Theatre Group in 1968 as a vehicle for his work both as writer and director/performer, and developed a style that combined verbal and non-verbal elements of theatre, PARODY and experiment. He often featured as his own star actor, and his intense face, savage MIME and grating voice are memorable. His writing is often a mannered parody of other styles. Original works include *East* (1975), about his East End (London) boyhood, in a blank verse which echoed both SHAKESPEARE and the football terraces; *Greek* (1979), where he treats the Oedipus story; *Decadence* (1981), where he writhed like Laocoön in the coils of upperclass vowel sounds; *Kvetch* (1987) and *Acapulco* (1992). Berkoff has also guest directed in New York and Dublin.

**Berlin, Irving** [Israel Baline] 1888–1989 Russian-born American composer. His most memorable contributions to the musical stage were individual songs rather than complete scores. In 1911 his 'Alexander's Ragtime Band' became an international sensation, launching a vogue for popular ragtime songs. Berlin wrote his first complete BROADWAY score for *Watch Your Step* (1914). In 1921–4 he and producer SAM H. HARRIS offered a series of *Music Box Revues* which introduced many of Berlin's standards, such as 'What'll I Do?' and 'All Alone'. His other shows of the 1920s were *The Cocoanuts* (1925) and *The ZIEGFELD Follies* (1927). In the 1930s Berlin created the score for *Face the Music* (1932), a SATIRE on police corruption. His score for the REVUE *As Thousands Cheer* (1933) included 'Supper Time', a lament about the lynching of a southern black. He returned from Hollywood to Broadway with the scores for *Louisiana Purchase* (1940), *This Is the Army* (1942), *Annie Get Your Gun* (1946), *Call Me Madam* (1950) and his final score, *Mr President* (1962). Berlin was never interested in experimentation or innovation; his strength was his ability to adapt to changing musical styles and to reflect in his music the thoughts and aspirations of average people.

**Berlin Royal Theatre** German theatre. In 1786 DÖBBELIN took over the Komödienhaus on the Gendarmenmarkt in Berlin, where he received a royal patent to perform plays. In 1796 AUGUST IFFLAND was appointed director of this court theatre. Under him it achieved the status of a national theatre. After Iffland's death in 1812, the direction was taken over by Count Karl von Brühl (1772–1837), who cultivated the WEIMAR STYLE. After Brühl's retirement and LUDWIG DEVRIENT's death, the pre-eminence of the National Theatre began to decline, and its influence over the development of the German theatre fell off rapidly.

**Berliner Ensemble** German theatre company. It was founded by HELENE WEIGEL in 1949 and dedicated to promoting the EPIC THEATRE of BRECHT. In 1954 it gained a permanent base at the Theater am Schiffbauerdamm, and since then has been the most influential force in German theatre. Apart from productions of all his major plays, which form about half of the repertoire, Brecht used the stage to explore his concepts of acting and directing, and to encourage work by other playwrights. The company's extensive touring gave its methods international exposure. Its visit to London in 1956 profoundly influenced the ROYAL SHAKESPEARE COMPANY and the ROYAL COURT. From its opening the Ensemble attracted major actors, and a number of directors were trained there, including BENNO BESSON, PETER PALITZSCH and MANFRED WEKWERTH, under whom the BE became a Brecht museum. Divorced from Brecht and his heirs after 1989 and German reunification, its future is uncertain. Since 1992 new directors have included Palitzsch, HEINER MÜLLER and PETER ZADEK.

**Berman, Sabina** 1953– Mexican postmodernist playwright. Her plays are complex and provocative. *Yankee* (originally named *Bill*, 1980) involves a Vietnam veteran with a Mexican novelist and his wife; *Rompecabezas* (*Puzzle*, 1982) interprets Trotsky's death in Mexico; *Aguila o sol* (*Eagle or Sun*, 1985) deals with the conquest; *Muerte súbita* (*Sudden Death*, 1988) examines value systems in a young relationship; and *Entre Villa y una mujer desnuda* (*Between Villa and a Naked Woman*, 1990) uses the figure of Pancho Villa to dramatize politics and *machismo* in Mexico.

**Bernhard, Thomas** 1931–89 Austrian playwright and novelist. Bernhard classified his plays, which are skilfully orchestrated cascades of words, set as verse without punctuation, as 'musical theatre'. *Ein Fest für Boris* (*A Party for Boris*, 1970), in which the legless Kind Lady dragoons 13 other cripples into a party for her husband – who dies unnoticed during the proceedings – is typical of his grotesque comic bleakness. In *Der Ignorant und der Wahnsinnige* (*The Ignoramus and the Lunatic*, 1972) an international soprano laments that she has become a coloratura-machine. Artistic perfectionism, with its destructive effects, is also the theme of *Die Macht der Gewohnheit* (*The Force of Habit*, 1974) and of *Der Theatermacher* (*The Showman*, 1985, Almeida Theatre, 1993). Bernhard reflects cynically on German history in *Vor dem Ruhestand* (*Before Retirement*, 1979), in which an ex-SS officer, now an MP, celebrates Himmler's birthday, and in *Heldenplatz* (1988), on Austria's continuing antisemitism . Sickness and stupidity, desperation and death, are his constant themes. The plays often take the form of interrupted monologues by one dominant character; they were written for Bernhard's favourite actors – *Minetti* (1976) for BERNHARD MINETTI and *Ritter, Dene, Voss* (1986) for GERT VOSS and two actresses in PEYMANN'S company, which premiered most of his plays.

**Bernhardt, Sarah** [Sarah Henriette Rosine Bernard] 1844–1923 French actress, incontestably the greatest star of the 19th-century French theatre. The 'divine' Sarah's reputation depended not only upon her great talent as an actress (notably the purity of her diction), but also upon her personal charisma and her extravagant lifestyle and productions. Her numerous tours abroad – to the United States, Russia and Australia – ensured her international reputation. After an unremarkable debut at the COMÉDIE-FRANÇAISE in 1862 as Iphigenia, she made her name in 1869 at the ODÉON in the BREECHES PART of Zanetto in François Coppée's *The Passer-by*. In 1872 she was back at the Comédie-Française making a triumphant appearance as the Queen in the revival of HUGO's *Ruy Blas*, and by 1875 had risen to

being a *sociétaire* of the company. *Phèdre* (1877) became one of her greatest parts, as did *Andromaque* and *Hernani*. She was at home in both classical and modern drama, notably in the plays of DUMAS *fils*. After her departure from the Comédie, she developed a pattern of long foreign tours. In 1882 she found one of her two major authors in VICTORIEN SARDOU, whose *Fédora* was written for her. From now on she was her own manager, and many of the plays chosen became vehicles for her talent and delight in sumptuous *mise-en-scène*. In 1884 she gave a memorable performance in *The Lady of the Camelias*, with her husband Jacques Damala as Armand; later that year Sardou's *Théodora* provided another lavish spectacle. In 1893 she took on the direction of the Renaissance, where she created the title roles in Sardou's *Gismonda* (1894) and *La Princesse Lointaine* (*The Distant Princess*) by ROSTAND (her other major author); and staged the first production of MUSSET's *Lorenzaccio*, in which she played Lorenzo. In 1899 she moved to the former THÉÂTRE DES NATIONS which now became the Théâtre Sarah-Bernhardt (a title it would retain until the Occupation). The most significant production of this period was Rostand's *L'Aiglon* (another breeches part for Bernhardt, as Napoleon's son). She continued playing to the bitter end, even after the amputation of one of her legs, which often required her to be propped up on stage.

**Bernini, Gian Lorenzo** 1598–1680 Italian architect, sculptor, stage designer, playwright, actor and stage manager. Perhaps the greatest artist of the Italian baroque, throughout his life he was fascinated by, and involved in, theatrical activity. No visual material has survived to illustrate his scenographic work in Rome. He stage-managed baroque spectacles such as *De'due teatri* (*The Two Theatres*, 1637) and *L'inondazione del Tevere* (*The Tiber in Flood*, 1638). He also wrote plays, including *La fontana di Trevi* (*The Trevi Fountain*, 1966), a scripted treatment of subject-matter in the COMMEDIA DELL'ARTE tradition.

**Bernstein, Aline** 1880–1955 American set and COSTUME designer. A founding member of the NEIGHBORHOOD PLAYHOUSE (1915), she later worked at the THEATRE GUILD and on BROADWAY. In 1926 actress EVA LE GALLIENNE asked her to design for a newly founded Civic Repertory Theatre. She worked with producer Herman Shumlin on *Grand Hotel* and, through the 1930s, on the plays of LILLIAN HELLMAN including *The Little Foxes*. Bernstein's early designs utilized adaptable unit sets, while some of her later work employed mechanical devices for a cinematic change of scenes. She founded the Costume Museum, later absorbed by the Metropolitan Museum of Art.

**Bernstein, Leonard** 1918–90 American composer. Bernstein wrote the scores for six musicals. In 1944 he composed the music for *On the Town*, and nine years later *Wonderful Town* gave him the opportunity to write a nostalgic score full of pastiches of the swing music of the 1930s. In 1956 he wrote the score for *Candide*, a musical adaptation of the VOLTAIRE novel. Bernstein's most famous score, that for *West Side Story* (1957), was praised for its success in embodying the tensions and passions of the show's teenage characters.

**Bertinazzi** [Bertinassi], **Carlo Antonio** [Carlino; Carlin] 1710–83 Italian actor. He was the last great Arlecchino in France (see HARLEQUIN). Already famous in Italy, he first appeared at the Théâtre Italien, Paris, in LUIGI RICCOBONI's *Arlecchino Constrained to Be Mute*. His elegant, precise movements, the wittiness of his MIME and his rapport with the audience won him the admiration of DAVID GARRICK and of GOLDONI, in whose *Arlecchino's Son Lost and Found* and *Paternal Love* he played. But his best vehicles were written by Jean-Pierre de Florian.

**Besson, Benno** 1922– Swiss director. Until 1982 he was best known for his collaboration with BRECHT and his work in East Germany. In 1949 Brecht invited him to East Berlin. His first *mise-en-scène* was MOLIÈRE's *Don Juan*, in Besson's own adaptation (BERLINER ENSEMBLE, Rostock, 1952). He remained in East Berlin until 1977: with the Berliner Ensemble, 1949–58; as director of the DEUTSCHES THEATER, 1960–9; and of the VOLKSBÜHNE, 1969–77. In 1982 he became artistic director of the Comédie de Genève. In 1985 he received the Reinhart-Ring, highest Swiss award for exceptional achievements in the theatre. Besson has directed over 50 plays, renowned for their visual inventiveness. He has modernized the classics and staged the work of young playwrights. His main productions are Brecht's *The Days of the Commune*, *The Good Person of Setzuan*, *Man Is Man*, *Saint Joan of the Stockyards*, *The Caucasian Chalk Circle*; and SHAKESPEARE's *The Two Gentlemen of Verona*, *As You Like It* and *Hamlet*. He premiered PETER HACKS's *Moritz Tassow* (1965), Gerhard Winterlich's *Horizons* (1969), Flaubert's *Le Sexe Faible* (*The Weaker Sex*, 1984) and Élie Bourquin's *Lapin Lapin* (*Rabbit Rabbit*, 1986). Besson left Geneva in 1989 to resume his international work as a freelance director in opera as well as theatre.

**Betsuyaku Minoru** 1937– Japanese playwright. His minimalist plays, profoundly influenced by the work of SAMUEL BECKETT and EUGENE IONESCO, have been a staple of the Japanese theatrical scene for three decades. *The Little Match Girl* (1966; translated 1992), one of the earliest of Betsuyaku's many works, treated the deprivation of the immediate postwar period. He subsequently rejected the style as too 'literary' and moved towards more abstract, absurdist works (see THEATRE OF THE ABSURD) like *The Move* (1973; translated 1979).

**Betterton, Thomas** 1635–1710 English actor, manager and playwright. Betterton was the greatest actor in England between RICHARD BURBAGE and GARRICK. By 1661 he had joined DAVENANT's company as their leading actor. He starred in virtually every play the company put on: playing, for instance, Bosola in WEBSTER's *The Duchess of Malfi*, Sir Toby Belch, Macbeth and Henry VIII. On Davenant's death he became co-manager, and continued after the formation of the United Company in 1682. He visited France, pursuing his interest in spectacular stage effects, and brought over Louis Grabu, a composer who collaborated with him on a series of operas of great expense and technical brilliance. By 1695, after leading the senior actors in revolt against the management, he had established a company in the LINCOLN's INN FIELDS THEATRE. But it soon failed and in 1704 he retired as manager, though continuing to act. Not long after a famous benefit performance of CONGREVE's *Love for Love* for him in 1709, he retired as an actor as well. He had played over 120 roles. Betterton was known for his careful preparation of parts, always consulting the playwright, always ready to respond to criticism. His acting style in tragedy was majestic and restrained, with an unusual self-discipline. He also wrote comedies, and adapted earlier ones for the Restoration stage.

**Betti, Ugo** 1892–1953 Italian playwright, poet and critic. After PIRANDELLO Betti is the major Italian playwright of the 20th century. He achieved his first big success with *Frana allo scalo nord* (*Landslide*, 1936), cast in the form of a judicial inquiry following an accident, and concerned with guilt, weakness and spiritual need. His standpoint is liberal and Christian, but he avoids simplicities and dogmatic judgements. The austere tone of his work was for long little appreciated in Italy until he achieved international success with plays like *Corruzione al Palazzo di Giustizia* (*Corruption in the Palace of Justice*, 1944), *Delitto all'Isola delle Capre* (*Crime on Goat Island*, 1946) and *La regina e gli insorti* (*The Queen and the Rebels*, 1949).

**Betty, William Henry West** 1791–1874 Anglo-Irish actor. A child prodigy, billed as the 'Young ROSCIUS' in 1804–6 he outshone JOHN PHILIP KEMBLE at COVENT GARDEN, threatening that theatre with bankruptcy when he was tempted over to DRURY LANE. During those heady years Betty played Hamlet, Romeo, Rolla in SHERIDAN's *Pizarro* and Young Norval in JOHN HOME's *Douglas* – to the utter delight of indulgent audiences, until the craze dwindled.

***bhagavata mela*** Indian theatre form. The *Bhagavata Puranas* are collections of epic stories about Lord Vishnu's incarnations. Those who perform these stories are known as *bhagavatars* or *bhagavatulus*. *Mela* refers to a troupe of dancers or singers. The origin of *bhagavata mela*, as found in the village of Melattur in the state of Tamil Nadu, is traced to the state of Andhra Pradesh, where it appears to have been born of the KUCHIPUDI dance drama around 1502. Today, the only village to retain *bhagavata mela* intact as an annual performance is Melattur, where, during the second half of April or early May, two troupes of devotees celebrate Vishnu's terrifying man-lion incarnation which destroyed a demon king. All the actors who participate in the production are men, the younger ones playing the female roles. The entrance songs introduce each character, and the scenes that follow depict the episodes of the drama in dialogue, song and dance. Actors combine naturalistic movement and stylized gesture to convey the meaning of the texts. The dramatic crisis usually occurs in the early hours of the morning.

One particular drama is noteworthy for its dramatic impact and RITUAL significance – that of *The Story of Prahlada* (*Prahlada Charitram*), which demonstrates the faith of Prahlada, a youthful prince who worships Lord Vishnu. When Prahlada has forsaken his father's love for that of his god, his faith is tested in various ways. With each successive test his wicked father becomes more and more furious. Eventually, the father is tricked – and dies when Lord Vishnu, in the form of a man-lion, rips open his guts and kills the tyrant king.

**Bhasa** Indian playwright. A major figure in ancient SANSKRIT DRAMA, Bhasa probably worked between the 4th and 5th centuries AD in the city of Ujjain in north central India. He composed plays based on dramatic incidents from the *Ramayana*, the *Mahabharata* and the *Purana*, as well as semi-historical tales. He also created original stories. Bhasa seems to have been a man of the theatre, as well as a capable poet. The texts of 13 plays attributed to him were discovered in 1912. The most important is *The Vision of Vasavadatta*, a play about love and political intrigue. Among Bhasa's short plays are *The Broken Thighs* and *Karna's Task*, dramatizations of episodes in the great battle which concludes the *Mahabharata*. Many modern Indian directors have been drawn to Bhasa's plays and have given them new, and often lively, modern interpretations.

***bhavai*** Indian theatre form. Raucous, obscene, satiric, poignant – all these terms describe *bhavai*, a form of rural theatre once popular in western India. Local legend has it that *bhavai*'s origins may be attributed to Asaita Thakar, an outcast Brahmin who lived during the mid-14th century in what is now Gujarat state.

The story goes that Asaita Thakar, excommunicated from his caste for helping a lower-caste girl, turned to singing and dancing, historically considered an appropriate profession for many of India's outcasts. With the help of his sons and other outcast Brahmins he formed the first company of strolling players in Gujarat, the *bhavaiyas* – 'those who arouse sentiment' in the spectators through their performance. It is this community which still preserves the hereditary right to perform *bhavai* in Gujarat. Although no longer a popular art form, *bhavai* may still be found today not only in North Gujarat and Saurashtra, but also in Malawa in the state of Madhya Pradesh and in Marwad and elsewhere in Rajasthan state. *Bhavai* is traditionally performed in connection with religious festivals in praise of mother goddesses, such as Ambaji and Bahucharaji, the latter being regarded as the patroness of the *bhavai* actors. Despite the highly charged religious atmosphere of both place and occasion, the satiric content of most of the performances centres on the vices and virtues of members of various village communities. The predominance of humour makes *bhavai* unique in the catalogue of traditional Indian theatre.

The *bhavai* stories are known as *vesa* – literally, 'costume' – and they bear the names of the chief characters around which they are composed. For example, *Ganapati-no-vesa* is the ritual introduction and dance of the elephant-headed god Ganapati; *Juthana-no-vesa* is the story about the trials of a Muslim crown prince. The musical accompaniment involves special instruments, including *bhungals*, four-foot long copper pipes.

Although the rural interest in *bhavai* has waned, urban theatre people have been attracted to it in order to preserve valuable and endangered folk traditions; they have imitated the bhavai forms, adapting the content to suit urban purposes.

**Biancolelli family** Italian actors. **Isabella** Franchini (died c.1650), the daughter of the famous Pantalone Francesco Franchini and a famous Colombina in her own right, married **Francesco** Biancolelli (died c.1640). Their son **Giuseppe Domenico** (c.1636–88) played with Locatelli's company in Paris from 1659, and from 1680 acted at the newly founded Hôtel de Bourgogne in the Comédie-Italienne, under the stage name Dominique. Short, svelte and supremely agile, he naturalized the Arlecchino (see Harlequin) type to the French stage with a mixture of dance, wisecracks and acrobatics. His children included three actors: Francesca Maria Apolline, called **Isabella** (1664–1747), a witty, brilliant *amorosa*, who made her debut in 1683; Caterina, called **Colombina** (1665–1716), who surpassed her grandmother in that role, and Pier Francesco, called **Dominique *fils*** (1680–1734), who had an extraordinary success as Arlecchino in Venice and Genoa. On his return to Paris, he took over the management of the foundering Opéra Comique. When Luigi Riccoboni reopened the newly organized Comédie-Italienne in 1716 he soon became one of its favourite players. Contemporaries unanimously hailed him as the best Arlequin of his time; he wrote a number of scenarios for the improvised comedy.

**Bibiena (Galli da) family** Italian theatre architects and scenic designers. **Ferdinando** (1657–1743) was chief court architect under the patronage of the Farnese at Parma and later under Emperor Charles VI in Vienna. His major contribution to scenic design, the scenes set at an acute angle (*scena per angolo*), revolutionized baroque staging. These were first used at Piacenza in 1687 and are described in his *L'architettura civile preparata nella geometria* (*Civic Architecture on Geometrical Principles*, 1711). His brother **Francesco** (1659–1739) built the splendid theatre at Nancy in France (1707–9) and the Teatro Filarmonico at Verona. Ferdinando's eldest son **Giuseppe** (1696–1757) was noted for the quality of his opera sets in Vienna, Dresden, Prague and Venice. In 1740 he published a rich collection of his stage designs. He was the first to use transparent scenery lit from behind. His younger brother **Antonio** (1700–74) designed a number of theatres including the Teatro Comunale in Bologna (from 1755) and the Teatro dei Quattro Cavalieri in Pavia (1773). Giuseppe's son **Carlo** (1728–87) worked with his father – e.g. on the Opera House of the Palgrave at Bayreuth, then at Vienna and Dresden.

**Bickerstaffe, Isaac** 1733–?1808 Irish playwright. In 1760 his 'dramatic pastoral' or 'ballad farce' *Thomas and Sally* was performed in London. *Love in a Village* (1762) is probably the first English comic opera. Its success led Bickerstaffe to write many more, including *The Maid in the Mill* (1765). His collaborations with Dibdin – e.g. *Love in the City*, later abbreviated as *The Romp* – influenced the whole development of musical comedy. He adapted Wycherley's *The Plain Dealer* for Garrick in 1765. His short farce *The Padlock* (1768) starred Dibdin as Mungo, the first black face comic role seen in London.

**Bill-Belotserkovsky, Vladimir (Naumovich)** 1884–1970 Soviet playwright. His propaganda tales of heroic communism and decadent capitalism introduced many of the theatrical themes which were consolidated under socialist realism (1934–53). His sojourn as an unskilled worker in the USA accounts for his nickname 'Bill'. As a member of the Proletkult and later of the Central Committee for the Control of Repertory, he helped to develop and to police the new Soviet drama. Naive and diagrammatic, his first four plays – *Beefsteak, Rare* (1920), *Stages* (1921), *Echo* (1922) and *Steer to the Left!* (1926) – traverse the path to World Revolution through Europe and America, underscoring the inevitability of the climactic struggle. *Storm* (1924) is the author's classic Civil War play, a tale of an heroic Party chairman battling to bring about a new order out of chaos. His second most influential work, *Life Is Calling* (1953), uses romantic subplots, pairings of ideological types and a climactic conversion speech within a realistic framework. His other plays include *Calm* (1926), *Moon on the Left* (1927) and *The Voice of the Depths* (1927), none of which was successful.

**Birch-Pfeiffer, Charlotte** 1800–68 German actress and playwright. Among the several plays she adapted from novels, *The Orphan of Lowood* (1856), based on *Jane Eyre*, was the most widely performed.

**Bird, Robert Montgomery** 1806–54 American playwright and novelist. His major plays were prizewinners in Edwin Forrest's playwriting contests and were performed by him: *The Gladiator* (1831), *Oralloosa* (1832) and *The Broker of Bogota* (1834). *Gladiator* and *Broker* made huge profits for Forrest and only $2,000 for Bird. *Pelopidas* (1830) was never produced. Discouraged by his bitter financial quarrels with Forest, Bird turned to novels. *Hawks of Hawk Hollow* (1836) and *Nick of the Woods* (1837) are the best-known.

**Birmingham Repertory Theatre** (England) The first purpose-built repertory theatre in Britain was opened in February 1913. Seating 464, it was designed to be intimate. Under BARRY JACKSON, the theatre's owner and artistic director, with JOHN DRINKWATER as its general manager, the resident company gave consistent, high-quality and often adventurous productions, including Eden Phillpotts's *The Farmer's Wife* (1916), Drinkwater's *Abraham Lincoln* (1918), modern-dress productions of SHAKESPEARE (1923 onwards) and SHAW's *Back to Methuselah* (1923). In 1971 a new and spacious theatre replaced the old. Jackson's policy of a mixed repertoire continues; but without a resident company and with serious cutbacks in the level of subsidy, the theatre's home-produced shows are fewer in number. Actors whose careers were launched at Birmingham include RALPH RICHARDSON, LAURENCE OLIVIER, Cedric Hardwicke, PAUL SCOFIELD and ALBERT FINNEY.

**Bjørnson, Bjørn** 1859–1942 Norwegian director and actor. Son of BJØRNSTJERNE BJØRNSON and a crucial figure in the modernization of Norwegian theatre, he first acted with the Saxe-MEININGEN COMPANY. Joining Christiania Theatre in 1884, he introduced naturalistic acting and staging (see NATURALISM), and in the next nine years acted in or directed some 130 productions, including several operas. He then campaigned for the new NATIONALTHEATRET, which opened in 1899 with Bjørnson at its head. He resigned in 1907.

**Bjørnson, Bjørnstjerne** 1832–1910 Norwegian playwright, novelist and journalist. He succeeded IBSEN as stage director of the Norwegian Theatre, Bergen (1857–9), and later successfully directed Christiania Theatre. His playwriting began in the 1850s with romantic history plays in the manner of OEHLENSCHLÄGER and SCHILLER; the most enduring is *Sigurd the Bad* (1862). From the mid-1860s his plays were more realistic, dealing with contemporary social problems: marital, as in *The Newlyweds* (1865), *Leonarda* (1879) and *A Gauntlet* (1883); business-related, as in the successful *A Bankruptcy* (1874); and political, as in *The King* (1877) and *Paul Lang and Tora Parsberg* (1898), but they were frequently marred by contrived plots and sentimental solutions. Beginning with *Beyond Our Power, I* (1883), his plays occasionally explore more spiritual issues. In 1903 he won the Nobel Prize for Literature.

**Black, George** 1891–1945 British impresario. He originated the Royal Variety Performances and injected the sumptuousness of REVUE into MUSIC-HALL. As managing director of the General Theatre Corporation (1928) and Moss Empires Ltd (1933) he controlled 40 halls, including the London Palladium, where, by conflating three teams of comedians, he created the CRAZY GANG (*U-Kay for sound*, 1936–7). His lavish revues at the HIPPODROME included *The Fleet's Lit Up* (1938), *Black Velvet* (1939) and *Black Varieties* (1941).

**blackface minstrelsy** see MINSTREL SHOW

**Blackfriars Theatre** (London) Of the two theatres built in rooms formerly part of the Blackfriars monastery, the earlier dates from 1576 and was the first private London theatre. Richard Farrant, Deputy Master of the CHILDREN OF THE CHAPEL ROYAL, converted the old refectory into an intimate theatre seating about 100. Farrant's boys were effective rivals to the BOYS OF ST PAUL's. After Farrant's death in 1580, the two BOYS' COM-

PANIES were briefly united under JOHN LYLY, but in 1584 the Blackfriars landlord recovered possession of his property. In 1597 JAMES BURBAGE bought several rooms in the Blackfriars, including the Parliament Chamber (66ft x 46ft), but his plan of conversion failed and he died leaving the unusable Blackfriars to his son, the actor RICHARD BURBAGE, who in 1600 leased it to Henry Evans, operating on behalf of the Children of the Chapel Royal. The artificial lighting and scenic refinements of the indoor stage, together with a faddish interest in boy performers, made the Blackfriars a formidable rival to the outdoor houses of the adult companies. The repertoire included many of the finest plays of the period, but Evans's management ended in disorder in 1608. It was then that Richard Burbage brought the King's Men into occupation of the prized indoor theatre, although their first performances there may have been delayed until 1610. The playhouse remained in the company's possession until the closure of the theatres in 1642, after which it fell into disrepair.

**Blake, Eubie** see SISSLE, NOBLE

**Blakely, Colin (George Edward)** 1930–87 British actor. He joined the NATIONAL THEATRE company under LAURENCE OLIVIER in 1963, where he achieved immediate success as the rugged adventurer, Pizarro, in PETER SHAFFER's *The Royal Hunt of the Sun* (1964). Equally successful as Titus Andronicus in a ROYAL SHAKESPEARE COMPANY production as in a play by HAROLD PINTER (*Old Times*, 1972), he starred in the WEST END, with the national companies, in films, TV and in FRINGE THEATRE. Dramatically un-theatrical, Blakely brought a special authenticity to his various roles. The audience was drawn into what seemed an intimate eavesdropping on human life.

**Blakemore, Michael (Howell)** 1928– Australian-born actor and director. He studied in London and, after a period as an actor, in 1966 he was appointed co-director of the Glasgow CITIZENS' THEATRE, where his sensitive productions of PETER NICHOLS's *A Day in the Death of Joe Egg* (1967) and BRECHT's *Arturo Ui* attracted attention. His association with the work of Peter Nichols continued with successful productions of *Forget-me-not Lane* (1971), *The National Health* (1969) at the NATIONAL THEATRE and *Privates on Parade* with the ROYAL SHAKESPEARE COMPANY. LAURENCE OLIVIER invited him to become an associate artistic director of the National Theatre in 1971, where he directed *Long Day's Journey into Night* (with Olivier as Tyrone), *The Front Page*, *The Cherry Orchard* and *Plunder*. He returned to being a freelance director in Britain and Australia, directing MICHAEL FRAYN's hit farce, *Noises Off* (1982). In 1987 he directed the WEST END premiere of PETER SHAFFER's *Lettice and Lovage* and a revival of ARTHUR MILLER's *After the Fall* at the NT (1990). After staging the premiere of Miller's *The Ride down Mount Morgan* (1991) in London, he directed his first major musical, Larry Gelbart's *City of Angels* in the USA, which triumphantly transferred to London in 1993.

**Bleasdale, Alan** 1946– British playwright. His comedies, musicals and dramas are often set in his home town, Liverpool. His early plays were produced in the North of England but failed to make an impact in London. National success came with two drama series on television – *Boys from the Blackstuff* (1983), about the unemployed on Merseyside, and *GBH* (1991), about the rise and fall of a leftwing leader of the Liverpool Labour Party. *On the Ledge* (1993), co-produced by the

Nottingham Playhouse and the NATIONAL THEATRE, was a bleak parable, set in Liverpool on Guy Fawkes night.

**Blin, Roger** 1907–84 French actor, director and designer. Blin acted with ARTAUD, DULLIN, BARRAULT and the OCTOBER GROUP in the 1930s, also studying MIME. After the war he began directing in avant-garde theatres, producing two of ADAMOV's plays as well as BECKETT's *En attendant Godot*, with which he made his name in 1953. He became the friend and trusted director of Beckett (*Fin de partie*, 1957; *La Dernière Bande*, 1960; *Oh les beaux jours*,1963) and also of GENET (*Les Nègres*, 1959; *Les Paravents*, 1966). For Blin, the functions of director and designer were inseparable.

**Blitzstein, Marc** 1905–64 American composer and librettist. He is best known for *The Cradle Will Rock* (1937), a pro-labour operetta developed within the FEDERAL THEATRE PROJECT. The controversial production was revived a few months later by ORSON WELLES and JOHN HOUSEMAN as part of the MERCURY THEATRE's first season. He later translated and adapted BRECHT's *The Threepenny Opera* (1952), an OFF-BROADWAY success (2,611 performances). Other musical works included *Regina* (1949), based on LILLIAN HELLMAN's *The Little Foxes*, and *Juno* (1959), based on SEAN O'CASEY's *Juno and the Paycock*.

**Bloch, William** 1845–1926 Danish director. He pioneered the introduction of naturalistic staging (see NATURALISM), particularly of IBSEN and the new drama at the KONGELIGE TEATER in the 1880s. He resigned for a period, returning (1899–1909) to revolutionize the theatre's approach to HOLBERG. Anticipating STANISLAVSKY, Bloch increased rehearsal time, planned and researched productions and strove for acting that depended on individuality, inner truth and ensemble, coordinating a mass of carefully planned details to create the atmosphere of a play's specific time and place, as in his productions of *An Enemy of the People* (1883) and *The Wild Duck* (1885).

**Blok, Aleksandr Aleksandrovich** 1880–1921 Russian poet and playwright; considered 'the last romantic' and 'the greatest symbolist'. The latter half of his career is an ironic commentary on his earlier naive romance with SYMBOLISM and the mystical philosophy of Vladimir Solovyov. When the latter's 'ideal humanity' failed to materialize with the defeat of the 1905 Revolution, Blok underwent a spiritual crisis. He rejected symbolist mysticism; and the *Lyrical Dramas* (1908) which resulted – *The Little Showbooth*, *The King on the Square* and *The Unknown Woman* (all 1906) – along with his later plays, offer a mixture of autobiography, SATIRE and elegy for what was lost. His tragi-farce *The Puppet Show* unites the GOGOLian tradition with modern absurdism (see THEATRE OF THE ABSURD), and created an exceptional furore when staged by MEYERHOLD (at VERA KOMISSARZHEVSKAYA's Theatre, 1906), who appeared as Pierrot. In 1908 the allegorical *The Song of Fate* was rejected by STANISLAVSKY for production. Blok's verse drama *The Rose and the Cross* (1913), which brings together joy (the rose) and suffering (the cross) and concludes that the former is transient while the latter may bring lasting happiness, was not produced.

**Bloom, Claire** 1931– British actress. She has developed a distinguished career on stage, in film and on television. She has played many Shakespearian roles, including Cordelia to JOHN GIELGUD's King Lear in the 1952–3 OLD VIC season, and taken major parts in both classic and modern plays, such as Hedda in *Hedda Gabler* (1971), Blanche du Bois in *A Streetcar Named Desire* (1974) and

Mary Queen of Scots in *Vivat! Vivat Regina!* (1972). Her films have included Chaplin's *Limelight* (1952) and *Look Back in Anger* (1959), and for television more Shakespearian roles and *Brideshead Revisited*. Her acting has been consistently remarkable for her great sensitivity and intelligence, as well as for her personal beauty.

**Blue Blouses** Soviet Russian workers' groups. The name refers to factory workers' loose blue smocks. Dating from 1923, the groups toured widely, presenting a LIVING NEWSPAPER montage of current events skewed to a proletarian ideology in a MUSIC-HALL format of songs and sketches. In their heyday there were over 5,000 of these groups. After 1927 the Blue Blouses were forcibly merged with the more orthodox TRAM movement.

**Boaden, James** 1762–1839 English dramatist and biographer. In 1794 his adaptation of Ann Radcliffe's *Romance of the Forest* was performed as *Fountainville Forest*, one of the first transformations of a Gothic novel into Gothic drama. Boaden led the attack on the SHAKESPEARE forgeries of WILLIAM HENRY IRELAND in 1796. The following year he adapted Mrs Radcliffe's *The Italian* as *The Italian Monk*. He wrote important biographies of KEMBLE, MRS SIDDONS, DOROTHY JORDAN, ELIZABETH INCHBALD and GARRICK.

**Boal, Augusto** 1931– Brazilian playwright, director and theorist. He premiered with *Mulher Magra, Marido Chato* (*Lean Wife, Mean Husband*, 1957). *Revolução na América do Sul* (*Revolution in South America*, 1961) by Arena Theatre opened a new epoch of political protest theatre. Teatro Oficina presented his third play, *José, do Parto a Sepultura* (*Joe, from the Womb to the Tomb*, 1962). During the 60s he worked closely with GIANFRANCESCO GUARNIERI on various classical plays about LOPE DE VEGA and GOGOL, and in 1965 they launched their famous *Arena conta...* series (on Zumbi, Tirandentes and Bolívar among others). An inveterate experimenter and Marxist ideologue, Boal was imprisoned for political reasons; in exile he developed new forms of radical theatre, such as the *teatro jornal*, a documentary drama based on current events, and the *teatro invisible*, which consists of staged performances in public places before unsuspecting audiences. His writings include *Teatro do Oprimido* (1975, translated as *Theatre of the Oppressed*, 1979), which gained international recognition as a theoretical model of revolutionary theatre.

**Boar's Head Tavern** (London) Situated in Whitechapel, just outside Aldgate, the Boar's Head was the first of London's inns to undergo radical transformation for the purpose of accommodating plays (1598–9). The conversion resulted in a stage, galleries and a TIRING HOUSE, and was intended to combine three companies – Worcester's, Derby's and Oxford's – to rival the dominance of the LORD CHAMBERLAIN's MEN at the GLOBE and the ADMIRAL's MEN at the ROSE. The combined company, renamed Queen Anne's Men under James I, soon moved to the RED BULL; by 1621 the Boar's Head was no longer a theatre.

**Bocage** 1797–1863 French romantic actor and director. He reached the peak of his career in 1831–2 with the title role in DUMAS *père's Antony*, as Didier in *Marion Delorme* and as Buridan in *La Tour de Nesle*. Antony allowed him to display a sombre, melancholy and wildly passionate nature, which established him as the romantic actor *par excellence*. In 1843 he enjoyed a huge success as Brute in PONSARD's *Lucrèce*. A great actor, a good director, but a mediocre theatre manager, during his brief and disastrous period as director of the ODÉON he staged George Sand's *François le Champi*. His final triumph was with Paul Meurice and George Sand's play *Les Beaux Messieurs de Bois Doré* (Ambigu Theatre, 1862).

**Bock, Jerry** 1925– and **Sheldon Harnick** 1924– American composer and lyricist. Their collaborations have included the musicals *The Body Beautiful* (1958), *Fiorello* (1959), *She Loves Me* (1963), *Fiddler on the Roof* (1964), *The Apple Tree* (1966) and *The Rothschilds* (1970).

**Bogusławski, Wojciech** 1757–1829 Polish actor, director, manager and playwright. He was the father of the Polish National Theatre in Warsaw, which he directed from 1783 to 1814. There he staged the first opera sung in Polish, Salieri's *Axur*, playing the title role in 1793. In 1798 in Lwów he presented the first Polish *Hamlet*. In 1811 he founded the first theatre school, where he taught and wrote a textbook on acting. Among over 80 original plays and adaptations, best known are his musical *Cracovians and Mountaineers* (1794) and the historical drama *Henry IV at the Hunt* (1792).

**Boileau(-Despréaux), Nicolas** 1636–1711 French poet and critic. His shrewd judgement and satirical style is displayed in his exposition of neoclassical doctrine, *L'Art poétique* (1674), which summarizes his thinking on literature, giving prominence to TRAGEDY and COMEDY. A powerful arbiter of contemporary taste, he was the friend and supporter of MOLIÈRE and RACINE and was elected to the Académie-Française in 1684.

**Boker, George Henry** 1823–90 American playwright and poet. His principal play, *Francesca da Rimini* (1855), in which E. L. DAVENPORT played Lanciotto, did not achieve major success until 1882 when LAWRENCE BARRETT appeared as Lanciotto and OTIS SKINNER as Paolo. Boker wrote ten other plays. The best-known are *The World a Mask* (1851) and *The Bankrupt* (1855). He also wrote several volumes of poetry.

**Bolt, Robert (Oxton)** 1924–95 British playwright. His first performed plays, *The Critic and the Heart* (1957), the notably successful *Flowering Cherry* (1957) and *The Tiger and the Horse* (1960), kept closely to the requirements of the serious, WELL MADE PLAYS of the 1950s. Bolt's training as a historian encouraged him to break away from the somewhat constricting formulae of his early work: in *A Man for All Seasons* (1960) about the life and death of Sir Thomas More, he linked together short scenes by employing a narrator, the Common Man, in a so-called BRECHTian style. Subsequent historical plays included *Vivat! Vivat Regina!* (1970) and *State of Revolution* (1977). Bolt also wrote the screenplays for such films as *Lawrence of Arabia* (1962), *Dr Zhivago* (1965), *Ryan's Daughter* (1970) and *The Mission* (1986).

**Bolton, Guy** 1883–1979 American librettist and playwright. In 1915 he joined composer JEROME KERN for the first of the Princess Theatre (New York) musicals, *Nobody Home*. The success of this modest MUSICAL COMEDY was repeated with *Very Good Eddie* (1915), *Have a Heart* (1917), *Oh, Boy!* (1917) and others. He wrote librettos for *Sally* (1920), *Lady, Be Good* (1924), *Oh Kay* (1926) and *Anything Goes* (1934).

**Bond, Edward** 1934– British playwright. His first play, *The Pope's Wedding* (1962), was naturalistic (see NATURALISM). His second, *Saved*, created a furore when it was first performed at the ROYAL COURT THEATRE in 1965. Bond used the stoning to death of a baby in a pram to illustrate the moral and cultural deprivation of contemporary life. In *Early Morning* (1968) he offered a surrealistic FARCE (see SURREALISM) on Victorian values and mock-

heroism, set in a cannibalistic heaven. *Narrow Road to the Deep North* (1968) is a myth about power lords, good and bad, the worst ones being British imperialists.

Despite his sombre views, Bond can sometimes be a funny writer, as in *The Sea* (1973), and a lyric poet capable of portraying convincingly other poets, such as John Clare in *The Fool* (1976) and SHAKESPEARE in *Bingo* (1974). The intensity of his vision can verge on the apocalyptic, as in *Lear* (1972) and particularly in his *War Plays* (1985), about life after the nuclear holocaust. In 1978 his version of the Greek myths, *The Woman*, was presented at the NATIONAL THEATRE. As with other left-wing playwrights, the collapse of the Soviet Union and international communism left Bond in ideological isolation. The 1980s were notable for the absence of his plays. In 1990 *Jackets II* was produced by the Leicester Haymarket and briefly transferred to London. *The Company of Men* was produced in Paris in 1992.

**book-holder** Elizabethan term: a person combining the functions of prompter and stage-hand.

**book-keeper** Elizabethan term. The company member responsible for the preparation and safe-keeping of copies of the plays owned by the company, he would commission a fair copy of the author's manuscript and supervise the preparation of the rolls on which individual parts, with short cues, were written out.

**Booth, Barton** ?1679–1733 English actor and manager. He joined BETTERTON's company in 1700 and played secondary roles until he joined AARON HILL's company at DRURY LANE in 1710, taking over some of Betterton's old roles. Often arguing with Hill, he rioted against him with the other actors. He scored a great triumph as Cato in ADDISON's play (1713) and became a partner in the management of the company. At his best in majestic roles in tragedy (e. g. the Ghost in *Hamlet*), he thought it 'depreciated the dignity of tragedy to raise a smile in any part of it' (Cibber).

**Booth, Edwin Thomas** 1833–93 American actor and theatre manager; the second surviving son of JUNIUS BRUTUS BOOTH. From his first major New York appearance at Burton's Theatre in May 1857 until his retirement in 1891, his acting career was a series of unbroken successes. From 1864 to 1874 Booth also managed several theatres, most notably the Winter Garden (1864–7) and his own BOOTH'S THEATRE (1869–74). His management was distinguished by his carefully mounted, visually splendid productions of *Hamlet*, *Julius Caesar*, *The Merchant of Venice*, *Othello* and *Richelieu*. After the loss of his theatre in 1873, due to poor financial management, he spent the remainder of his career touring. In 1881–2, at the height of his powers, he played at London's PRINCESS'S THEATRE and alternated Othello and Iago with HENRY IRVING at the LYCEUM THEATRE. In 1883 he also made a highly successful tour of several German cities. From 1886 to 1891 he completed several extensive national tours, in association with his close friend LAWRENCE BARRETT. Booth's last performance was as Hamlet at the Brooklyn Academy of Music in 1891. Slender and darkly handsome, studious and thoughtful, with a clear, musical voice and luminous, expressive eyes, Booth was the finest American tragedian of his time: as Iago, Richelieu and Bertuccio (*The Fool's Revenge*), and later as King Lear and Shylock. He willingly shared the stage with fellow stars, including Irving, Barrett, TOMMASO SALVINI, HELENA MODJESKA and CHARLOTTE CUSHMAN.

**Booth, John Wilkes** 1839–65 American actor, brother of EDWIN. By the early 1860s he was an established popular touring star, at his best playing romantic characters and melodramatic heroes and villains. His first New York appearance was as Richard III in 1862 at the old WALLACK's Theatre, while his last was as Pescara in *The Apostate* at FORD's Theatre in March 1865. A month later (14 April 1865) in the same theatre, Booth assassinated Lincoln while the president was watching a performance of TOM TAYLOR's *Our American Cousin*. His motive may have been a desire for notoriety or a misguided act of patriotism.

**Booth, Junius Brutus** 1796–1852 Anglo-American actor. The first of the famous theatrical family, he rose to stardom in his birthplace, London, but spent the bulk of his career in America. Booth tried various occupations before becoming an actor in 1813. After a continental tour in 1814–15, he starred in 1817 at COVENT GARDEN. KEAN, concerned with a possible new rival, invited him to DRURY LANE to play Iago to Kean's Othello. After one performance, Booth retreated to Covent Garden, then toured the provinces. In 1821 he deserted his wife and child and emigrated to America with Mary Ann Holmes. He was often compared to Kean, even accused of imitating him. Romantic, passionate, Booth's aberrant behaviour in America gained him the title of 'the mad tragedian'.

**Booth, Junius Brutus,** Jr 1821–83 American actor and theatre manager, son of JUNIUS BRUTUS and brother to EDWIN. He migrated to California in 1851, where he acted and managed several theatres in San Francisco until he returned east in 1864. At various times he managed for his brother Edwin the Boston Theatre, the WALNUT STREET THEATRE, the WINTER GARDEN and, for one season, BOOTH's THEATRE. He was a competent manager but generally an undistinguished actor, although he was well regarded for his King John and Cassius. Four of Junius's children pursued stage careers.

**Booth Theatre** (New York City) Built by the SHUBERT BROTHERS in partnership with producer WINTHROP AMES, the Booth opened in 1913 with its sister house, the Sam S. Shubert. A small house, seating about 800, Ames envisioned it for his productions of intimate dramas and comedies, which have been its staple ever since. The theatre reverted to the Shuberts after Ames's retirement, and remains in their possession.

**Booth's Theatre** (New York City) Built for EDWIN BOOTH at the corner of 6th Avenue and 23rd Street, it opened on 3 February 1869 with a production of *Romeo and Juliet*. Booth's Theatre was built of granite in an ornate Second Empire style, complete with shopping precinct, artists' studios and Booth's private flat. Among the mechanical innovations were a forced-air heating and cooling system, a set of hydraulic ramps for changing scenery and a sprinkling system for fire protection. Some of the finest Shakespearian productions of the era were mounted at the theatre during Booth's four-year tenure. After he lost control of it in 1873 – the result of poor financial management – Booth's Theatre was leased and managed by various actor-managers. In the 1960s the building, then a department store, burned down.

**Borchers, David** 1744–96 German actor. Borchers was a celebrated intuitive actor who began in the ACKERMANN troupe, then played with FRIEDRICH SCHRÖDER in the Hamburg Town Theatre. He was noted for the elemental power of his stage presence and for his wild good humour. He never learned his roles and often improvised. From 1782 to 1785 he was the director of the Linz Town Theatre. He was notorious for his irregular private life: he once gambled with his wife as the stake, and lost.

**Borchert, Wolfgang** 1921–47 German playwright and poet. His reputation derives as much from the circumstances of his life as from his single play, *Draussen vor der Tür* (*The Man Outside*, 1947). As a conscientious objector, he was imprisoned for public opposition to the Nazis. His semi-autobiographical PASSION PLAY carried particular conviction in its denunciation of a corrupted society. First staged the day after Borchert's death, with 32 productions in 1948 alone, it was performed over 130 times in the next 20 years.

**Borovsky, David** 1934– Soviet stage designer. He is best known for his work with director YURY LYUBIMOV at the Taganka Theatre in Moscow. Some of his more important productions include *Hamlet* (1972), *Comrade Believe*, GORKY's *Mother* (1978) and *Valentin and Valentina* (1978). His design is characterized by three-dimensional, interactive playing environments using real objects which can be transformed by the actors. A good example is the use of a wooden army truck in *The Dawns Are Quiet* (1972), which was transformed into trees, living quarters and coffins.

**Boston Ideal Opera Company** [the Bostonians] American company. Founded by Miss E. H. Ober in 1879 in order to present an 'ideal' production of *HMS Pinafore*, the company, which toured extensively, was noted for its high standards in comic opera. Reorganized as the Bostonians in 1887, it launched the careers of REGINALD DE KOVEN with *Robin Hood* (1891) and VICTOR HERBERT with *Prince Ananias* (1894). Its last season was 1904–5.

**Boston Museum** American theatre. Originally part of Moses Kimball's Boston Museum and Gallery of Fine Arts, the 'concert saloon' was transformed in 1843 into a standard theatre with a STOCK COMPANY. In 1844, after the phenomenal success of William H. Smith's *The Drunkard*, which played 100 performances, it provided a steady diet of moral plays – which earned it the name of 'deacon's theatre'. In 1846 it moved into its new building, and during the 1860s and 1870s housed the finest dramatic corps in America. In 1894 the company was disbanded, and in 1903 the theatre was razed.

**Bottomley, Gordon** 1874–1948 British poet and playwright. He wrote specifically for groups such as the Community Theatre and the Scottish National Theatre, though his early work also had some success on the London stage. His poetic dramas, influenced by SYNGE's REALISM, dealt with subjects from Norse history (*The Riding to Lithend*, 1907; first performed 1928), or from SHAKESPEARE (*King Lear's Wife*, 1915; *Gruach*, 1923). Discarding these as 'plays for the Theatre Outworn', he turned to experimental choral work – which he called pieces 'for a Theatre Unborn' – based on Celtic legend. He followed NŌ drama in reducing scenery to a portable folding screen, .

**Bouchard, Michel Marc** 1958– Quebec playwright and actor. He first attracted attention in 1983 with *Le Contrenature de Chrysippe Tanguay, écologiste* (*The Counter Nature of Chryippos Tanguay, Ecologist*), in which a male homosexual couple seeking to adopt a child discover the limits of social tolerance. *Les Feluettes, ou La Répétition d'un drame romantique* (1987), which also deals with homosexuality, is one of the major works of modern Canadian dramaturgy, both in French and in its English translation, *Lilies, or The Revival of a Romantic Drama* (1988).

**Bouchardy, Joseph** 1810–70 French playwright. Beginning to write for the theatre in the mid-1830s, Bouchardy was considered the direct descendant of PIXÉRÉCOURT, his name a byword for naive, old-fashioned MELODRAMA. He wrote a score of dramas – of which the most popular were *Gaspardo le pêcheur* (*Gaspardo the Fisherman*, 1837), *Le Sonneur de Saint-Paul* (*The Bell-ringer of Saint Paul's*, 1838) and *Lazare le pâtre* (*Lazarus the Shepherd*, 1840) – mostly for staging at the Ambigu or the Gaîté (see BOULEVARD) and featuring complicated plots and powerful villains who meet their deserts. His last play, *The Armourer of Santiago*, was performed at the Châtelet in 1868.

**Boucicault, Dion(ysius Lardner)** 1820–90 Irish-born playwright, actor and theatre manager. Boucicault became a leading figure in both the English and the American theatre. His successful comedy *London Assurance* (COVENT GARDEN, 1841) held the stage throughout the 19th century and has been effectively revived. It was followed by *Old Heads and Young Hearts* (1844) and a two-act comedy, *Used Up* (1844). On the strength of intelligent plagiarism he supplied the London theatres for a further decade, notably with *The Corsican Brothers* (1852) and *The Vampire* (1852). The scandal of his liaison with the actress Agnes Robertson ended his contract with CHARLES KEAN.

As Agnes Robertson's manager, Boucicault began his career in the American theatre in 1853. They toured the USA and managed theatres in New Orleans (1855), Washington (1858) and New York (1859). *The Poor of New York* (1857) established the vogue of the sensation scene in MELODRAMA, and the fashion continued in *Jessie Brown* (1858), *The Octoroon* (1859) and *The Colleen Bawn* (1860). In 1860 the pair returned to London, where they remained until 1872. The Irish melodrama *Arrah-na-Pogue* (1864) was followed by *The Shaughraun* (1874), which is among the best of the genre. Credited with nearly 200 plays, Boucicault also helped to establish the new US COPYRIGHT law, fire-proofed scenery, a profit-sharing system for playwrights and the foundation of actor-training in the USA. Famous as an actor, he relished playing his own creations, lovable Irish rogues and sensational villains alike.

**Bouffé** 1800–88 French actor. Bouffé was known particularly for his attention to nuance and accurately observed detail and for a tendency to underplay in the genre in which he excelled, the *vaudeville*. After playing at various Parisian theatres, from 1827 to 1831 he appeared in 52 plays at the Nouveautés, moving to the Théâtre du Gymnase, where he was said to be the best comic actor in Paris. His great triumph there was in *Le Gamin de Paris* (*The Urchin of Paris*), which he played 315 times between 1836 and 1844. His appointment to the Variétés (see BOULEVARD) in 1843 changed the deficit of that theatre into a handsome profit, and DÉJAZET was appointed to complement him. One of his greatest roles was in *La Fille de l'avare* (*The Miser's Daughter*) at the Porte-Saint-Martin.

**boulevard** There are two slightly different meanings of this French term. From the late 19th century it applied to the Parisian commercial, non-subsidized theatre, offering entertainment to the affluent bourgeoisie. Between 1750 and 1830 the term had referred more precisely to the Boulevard du Temple and was associated with the popular theatres, particularly those dealing in MELODRAMA, whose rise was accelerated by the abolition of the monopoly of the COMÉDIE-FRANÇAISE in 1791.

Following Napoleon's decree of 1807, which limited the number of theatres in Paris to eight, the 'secondary', non-subsidized, or boulevard theatres were the Gaîté (the theatre associated with PIXÉRÉCOURT), the Ambigu, the Variétés and the Vaudeville. The largest of the boulevard theatres was the Porte-Saint-Martin, important in the early 1800s for its *ballet-pantomimes*, forerunners of the romantic story-ballet. In 1862 the Boulevard du Temple made way for the present Place de la République. After the first Empire the number of theatres gradually increased until 1864, when Napoleon III granted freedom to build and run a theatre to anyone wishing to do so. As a result the latter part of the century saw a vast boom in theatre building, and the disappearance of theatres limited to a specific repertoire or genre.

In the 20th century these theatres changed their staple from melodrama to light comedy, though some managers have attempted to include more literary plays. The boulevard's most flourishing period was the *belle époque* (1890–1914), when GEORGES FEYDEAU, Tristan Bernard and Georges Courteline continued the tradition of the well made sex comedy, designed to entertain an affluent after-dinner audience. The obligatory wearing of evening dress and the traditional late start, not favourable conditions for serious drama, maintained the essential nature of boulevard theatre as an upper-middle-class club.

After World War II boulevard theatre again flourished and plays by more literary dramatists, especially SALACROU, SARTRE and ANOUILH, were also performed. But since the 1960s, with escalating costs and the inexorable rise of the subsidized sector, the number of commercial theatres has diminished. Some have imported successes from Britain and the USA; others have developed a particular brand of whimsical, semi-cynical, semi-poetic humour through authors such as François Billetdoux, Romain Weingarten and René de Obaldia. Today the distinctive snob value of these theatres has largely disappeared and some are even able to claim government subsidy.

**Bowery Theatre** (New York City) When wealthy and fashionable New York families began to settle near the Bowery, they decided to erect a playhouse more conveniently located for them than the PARK THEATRE. From 1830, during Thomas S. Hamblin's 20-year tenure, the greatest names of the American theatre (JUNIUS BRUTUS BOOTH, EDWIN FORREST, the WALLACKS, Mrs John Drew (see DREW-BARRYMORE FAMILY), FRANK CHANFRAU) appeared on its stage. The area became the haven for the immigrant groups who poured into New York at mid-century, and the theatre reflected the new populations: after 1879, German acting troupes performed in German, and renamed it the Thalia; in 1891 came Yiddish performers; next, Italian vaudevillians; and in 1929 it was playing Chinese VAUDEVILLE. The Bowery, renamed several times, had become the temple of entertainment for New York's Lower East Side. The theatre burned six times in its history, finally in 1929.

**box set** Scenic arrangement. The primary development associated with the realistic depiction of middle- or upper-class life on stage was the box set, a semblance of a room with three walls and a ceiling, the fourth wall supposedly removed so that the audience could see in. The introduction of the box set is frequently attributed to MME VESTRIS, who worked with PLANCHÉ at the OLYMPIC THEATRE in London from 1831 to 1838.

However, something like a box set may have been achieved as early as 1642 in Venice by TORELLI, with the production of *Il Bellerofonte*. By the early 18th century, the free placement of flats and the enclosure of space downstage practised by the BIBIENAS created at least the illusion, if not the actuality, of such an arrangement. By the late 18th century box sets were not unusual, at least on the Continent. By the mid-19th century the box set had become increasingly realistic, as actual furniture, rugs, book shelves, wall sconces, knick-knacks and the like were added to create the aura of the real world. (See also THEATRE DESIGN.)

**Boyd, John** 1912– Irish playwright; honorary director of the LYRIC THEATRE, Belfast, from 1972. Boyd's major theme is the North of Ireland's divided heritage, mainly in an urban setting and expressed in the local idiom paradoxically common to the antagonistic faiths. *The Assassin* (Gaiety, Dublin, 1969) explores the psychology of a clerical demagogue; *The Flats* (Lyric, 1971; also produced in New York and Germany) places domestic tragedy in the collective violence of Belfast. These naturalistic plays (see NATURALISM) – along with *The Farm* (1972), *The Street* (1977), *Summer School* (1987) and *Round the Big Clock* (1992), a Belfast chronicle play – are acutely discerning of the brutalities behind factional slogans.

**Boyle, Roger,** Earl of Orrery 1621–79 Irish playwright. A favourite of Charles II and one of the Lord Justices of Ireland, he wrote a tragedy in heroic couplets, *The General* (performed privately in Ireland in 1662 and in London in 1664), *Henry V* (1664), *Mustapha* (1665) and *The Black Prince* (1667). He created a new mode of heroic drama, placing the hero between love and honour. His work was much admired by DRYDEN, though his later comedies, written when heroic drama had ceased to be fashionable, were unsuccessful.

**Boyle, William** 1853–1923 Irish playwright. The ABBEY made uproarious comedies of Boyle's plays, which, except for *The Eloquent Dempsey* (1906), a FARCE about dishonest politics, are desolate enough. *The Building Fund* (1905) is a black study in avaricious competition for an inheritance; *The Mineral Workers* (1906) is about the conflict between industrial development and rural values, their representatives equally unsavoury. Boyle broke with the Abbey in the row over SYNGE's *Playboy*, but gave it his last two plays, *Family Failing* (1912) and *Nic* (1916).

**boys' companies** English children's companies. The BOYS OF ST PAUL'S and the CHILDREN OF THE CHAPEL ROYAL were the two main companies of boy players in the 16th and early 17th centuries. The Paul's Boys were probably the first English company, adult or child, to have their own theatre (c.1575), quickly followed by the Chapel Children at the BLACKFRIARS (1576). Their musical skills as choristers were exploited; many playwrights wrote plays for them, particularly JOHN LYLY, GEORGE CHAPMAN and JOHN MARSTON. Only SHAKESPEARE among the major dramatists of his day remained aloof. After the decline of the Paul's Boys and the Chapel Children, the Children of the King's Revels (1608–9) and of the Queen's Revels (1609–13) continued to perform at the less attractive WHITEFRIARS. The last of the major children's companies performed at the COCKPIT from 1637 to 1642, where they were familiarly known as Beeston's Boys after their manager, CHRISTOPHER BEESTON.

**Boys of St Paul's** English theatre company. The choristers of St Paul's Cathedral in London may have acted in plays as early as the 14th century. Certainly under the Mastership of Sebastian Westcott (1553–82), ten choristers were employed as actors. There are records of over 30 court appearances by the Paul's Boys under Westcott's direction, and evidence of a playhouse within the precinct of St Paul's. From 1582–5 the Paul's Boys combined with the CHILDREN OF THE CHAPEL ROYAL to present JOHN LYLY's courtly plays. Lyly enlisted the boy actors in the Marprelate Controversy, after which they lost their right to perform. After a ten-year silence they re-emerged as an acting company to perform in plays by MARSTON, DEKKER, CHAPMAN, MIDDLETON, WEBSTER and BEAUMONT. Around 1605 the fashion changed, and from 1606 to 1608 they were reduced to sporadic performance. (See also BOYS' COMPANIES.)

**Bracco, Roberto** 1862–1943 Italian playwright and critic. His prolific output spans a range of dramatic kinds: light, sophisticated comedies, naturalistic pieces, and explorations of social and domestic problems in the manner of IBSEN. It was for the last, with plays like *Tragedie dell'anima* (*Tragedies of the Soul*, 1899) and *Maternità* (*Maternity*, 1903), that he was particularly admired in his own day, although the play for which he is now best remembered, *Il piccolo santo* (*The Little Saint*, 1909), was more innovative in its Freudian-like treatment of the workings of the subconscious. In the 1920s his liberal views ran foul of Fascist opposition, which put an end to his career in the theatre.

**Bracegirdle, Anne** 1671–1748 English actress. From the beginning (1688) she chose to play the pathetic heroine in tragedy and the witty, sophisticated woman in comedy, particularly in BREECHES PARTS. She also possessed a good singing voice. She worked for the United Company until 1695, when she joined BETTERTON's group of seceding actors. CONGREVE wrote for her such roles as Angelica in *Love for Love* (1695) and Millamant in *The Way of the World* (1700). She successfully guarded her reputation for virtue and virginity and retired in 1707, making way for ANNE OLDFIELD.

**Brackenridge, Hugh H(enry)** 1748–1815 American novelist, poet and playwright. He wrote two plays to inspire his students at Maryland Academy: *The Battle of Bunker's Hill* and *The Death of General Montgomery in Storming the City of Quebec* (1777). As teacher, legislator and chaplain in Washington's army, Brackenridge exhibited a sense of mission. Both plays, amateur attempts in blank verse, emphasized themes of patriotic virtue to encourage the colonists. Brackenridge's best-known novel is a satire entitled *Modern Chivalry*.

**Brady, William A(loysius)** 1863–1950 American manager and producer. Brady made his debut as a producer in 1888. He purchased the rights to *After Dark* from DION BOUCICAULT in 1899 and presented it at the BOWERY THEATRE. In 1896 he leased the Manhattan Theatre, where he enjoyed several successes including *Way Down East* in 1898. Brady managed the careers of numerous players including those of his wife, Grace George, and his daughter, Alice Brady (most memorable for playing Lavinia in O'NEILL's *Mourning Becomes Electra*). His more than 260 productions included ELMER RICE's *Street Scene* (1929), which ran for 600 performances and won a Pulitzer. Also a sports promoter and film pioneer, Brady was recognized as a 'born gambler' with an 'uncanny instinct for drama'.

**Bragaglia, Anton Giulio** 1890–1960 Italian theatre director and critic. Founder and director of the Teatro degli Indipendenti – an experimental avant-garde company working in Rome between 1923 and 1930 and conceived to radically reform the conservative and conventional Italian stage of his day – he pioneered new staging techniques and introduced the work of innovative young playwrights, including BRECHT. Connected early on with the futurist movement, he looked to technology to revolutionize a moribund theatre by emphasizing spectacle. He was a theorist as well as a practitioner: many of his early ideas found expression in his controversial *Del teatro teatrale, ossia del teatro* (*About the Theatrical Theatre – that is, the Theatre*, 1927). His own experimentation was handicapped by the technical backwardness of the Italian stage. During the Fascist period he directed the Teatro delle Arti in Rome, seeking where possible to advance new work and encourage young directing talent. His last years were devoted to theatre criticism and to studies of popular theatre.

**Brahm, Otto** 1856–1912 German director and critic. Brahm began his career as drama critic of conservative tastes on the Berlin newspapers *Vossische Zeitung* and *Die Nation*. However, enthused by the European naturalist movement (see NATURALISM) and the plays of IBSEN, in 1889 he founded the FREIE BÜHNE (Free Theatre), an organization devoted to the production of naturalistic drama in established theatres and using well known Berlin actors. Brahm brought the plays of GERHART HAUPTMANN to public attention. In 1894 Brahm was appointed director of the DEUTSCHES THEATER. Limited by his unremittingly naturalistic approach to production, he was unable to adapt to changing trends in theatre. In 1904, the more versatile MAX REINHARDT took over the Deutsches Theater and Brahm's final years were spent as the director of the less prominent Lessingtheater.

**Branagh, Kenneth (Charles)** 1960– British actor, Belfast-born. In England from the age of nine, he trained at RADA and joined the ROYAL SHAKESPEARE COMPANY at 22. In 1984 he played Henry V and Laertes and in 1986 Romeo in his own production of *Romeo and Juliet* at the LYRIC THEATRE, HAMMERSMITH. He established his television career at the same time, significantly in the BBC serial *Fortunes of War* in which he played Guy Pringle and where he met the actress Emma Thompson, whom he married. In April 1987, together with David Parfit, he formed the Renaissance Theatre Company, which became one of Britain's leading touring companies. His work as an actor and director for Renaissance (including playing Benedick, Touchstone and Hamlet in 1988, directing and playing in *King Lear* and *A Midsummer Night's Dream* in 1990, co-directing *Uncle Vanya* in 1991) consolidated his reputation as a leading talent of his generation. In 1989 he played Jimmy Porter in JOHN OSBORNE'S *Look Back in Anger* (directed by JUDI DENCH), a production created to support various social causes in his native Northern Ireland and which transferred to London and was filmed for TV. By now he was already being described as a new OLIVIER, a comparison underlined by his starring part in the film of *Henry V*, which he also directed. This was the first of several successful movies in which he played the dual role of actor/director, including *Dead Again* (1990), *Peter's Friends* and *Much Ado About Nothing* (1993). In 1992 he returned to the RSC to play Hamlet in ADRIAN NOBLE'S Edwardian production, Branagh's third version of this part.

**Brandão, Raúl** 1867–1930 Portuguese playwright. Before the vogue for literary existentialism caught on anywhere, Brandão wrote plays about the existential position of man, with the emotional accent on the pain, deprivations, frustrations and brevity of life. Two apprentice plays of the turn of the century were followed by *O Gebo e a Sombra* (*Hunchback and Shadow*, 1927), the only play performed professionally in his lifetime; two longish one-acters; two dramatic monologues; and a TRAGICOMEDY, *Jesus Cristo em Lisboa* (1927). Brandão's burning compassion and his dramatic power have ensured the growth of his reputation and influence in latter years.

**Brandes, Georg** 1842–1927 Danish critic and theorist. He was the major instigator in 1870s Scandinavia of the 'modern breakthrough' of rational, progressive thinking and naturalistic literature (see NATURALISM). The controversy caused by his own questioning of accepted social views led to his spending the years 1877–83 in exile in Germany, where he had frequent contact with IBSEN, who was stirred to write his realistic plays by Brandes's campaign. Through his prolific writings, Brandes became a major promoter of Ibsen, Kierkegaard, STRINDBERG, BJØRNSON, J. P. Jacobsen and other Scandinavian writers, both at home and abroad. Equally importantly, he promoted within Scandinavia such diverse figures as John Stuart Mill, Taine, Dostoevsky and, above all, NIETZSCHE.

**Brandes, Johann Christian** 1735–99 German actor and playwright. An actor of little distinction, Brandes made his mark by his facile pen. His plays, thoroughly forgotten now, were successful in their day. He is best known now for his autobiography (1800), which is one of the chief sources for the theatre history of the late 18th century. Brandes was briefly, and unsuccessfully, manager of the Hamburg Town Theatre while FRIEDRICH SCHRÖDER was away in Vienna.

**Brando, Marlon** 1924– American actor. Although his major reputation comes from his work as a film actor (*A Streetcar Named Desire, On the Waterfront, The Godfather*), it was as Kowalski in ELIA KAZAN's stage production of TENNESSEE WILLIAMS's *A Streetcar Named Desire* (1947) that Brando first made his mark as an actor of moody intensity. His style is often seen as the most famous product of the Method school of acting (see LEE STRASBERG).

**Branner, Hans Christian** 1903–66 Danish novelist and playwright. He began writing radio plays in the early 1930s, followed in the 1950s by three stage plays: *The Riding Master*, adapted from his 1949 novel (1950), *The Siblings*, known in English as *The Judge* (1952), and *Thermopylae* (1958). While his radio work is technically innovative, his stage plays are conventionally realistic, with occasional symbolic resonances. Their power stems from his passionate concern with such themes as the crisis of humanism in an alienated postwar world and the redemptive power of love, an idea that permeates his radio play *A Play of Love and Death* (1961).

**Brassens, Georges** 1921–81 French poet and singer. The son of a mason, he moved to Paris in 1939, worked in a factory and after the war joined the anarchist movement. Although he already had an underground reputation for performing his unconventional compositions in clubs, he was 'discovered' in 1952 by Jacques Grello and his recordings soon became best-sellers. Accompanying himself on the guitar, Brassens would sing of friendship, atheism, self-sacrifice, losers and nostalgia in a gruff and ursine manner, that smacked a bit of the blues. The Académie-Française awarded him its poetry prize in 1967; he made his last public appearances at the Bobino in 1972 and 1976.

**Braun, Volker** 1939– German playwright and poet. He trained in the BERLINER ENSEMBLE, where his celebratory parable of communist utopia (*The Great Peace*, 1979) was staged. His most significant plays are critical analyses of contemporary political issues, and were consistently censored in the GDR. His biting picture of factory conditions in *Tippers* was banned in 1966, as was *Lenin's Death* in 1970, and in 1975 *Guevara or the Sun State*. The latter encapsulated Braun's own predicament – how to justify utopian communism while embroiled in the real thing. *Temporary Society* (1989) transposed CHEKHOV's *Three Sisters* to East Berlin and was popular because of the criticism of existing socialism clearly visible between the lines.

**Brayne, John** c.1540–86 English entrepreneur. Brother-in-law of the more famous JAMES BURBAGE, Brayne was a prosperous grocer who ventured his wealth in at least three London theatrical projects – firstly at the RED LION in Stepney in 1567, secondly at the THEATRE in 1576, and thirdly at the George Inn in Whitechapel in 1579. It has been too readily assumed that Burbage was the main instigator of Elizabethan theatre-building. The true (and unsung) pioneer may equally well have been Brayne.

**Bread and Puppet Theatre** American theatre company. Founded in 1961 by Peter Schumann, Bread and Puppet was a loose association of performers under Schumann's firm direction, supplemented by amateurs. It offered its services free, whenever possible, on the principle that 'theatre is like bread, more like a necessity' – literally enacted in each performance by the giving of bread to the audience. Reacting against the over-intellectualization of Western culture, members worked with larger-than-life puppets to create a non-narrative theatre which addressed contemporary issues – notably the Vietnam War – through disturbing visual images rather than words. Performances such as 'The Cry of the People for Meat' and 'The Domestic Resurrection Circus' (the latter mounted in 1970 and most years since 1974) combined religious iconography and political message. In 1974 the company nominally disbanded. In practice it has continued to regroup for summer festivals in Vermont and for specific commissions. Schumann and his associates have scripted plays such as BÜCHNER's *Woyzeck* (New York, 1981), and toured Europe and Russia in 1990 with *Uprising of the Beast*.

**Brecht, Bertolt** [Eugen Berthold Friedrich Brecht] 1898–1956 German playwright, director and poet. Brecht's work dominated 20th-century German theatre and is perhaps the most influential force in Western theatre since World War II. His first work to be staged (dates of first performance rather than composition are given), the iconoclastic *Drums in the Night* (1922), rejected political involvement, while *Baal* (1923) and *In the Jungle of Cities* (1923) are examples of nihilistic EXPRESSIONISM. These plays brought him notoriety, with riots at their premieres and instant recognition with the Kleist Prize in 1922. In his Munich staging of *Edward II* (adapted from MARLOWE, 1924) and his anti-militaristic *Man Is Man* (1926) he began to develop the anti-illusionistic staging methods and parable structures that later became the basis for his theory of EPIC THEATRE.

Moving to Berlin, he worked as a dramaturge under REINHARDT and collaborated with PISCATOR. His first popular success came with *The Threepenny Opera* in 1928, a modernization of *The Beggar's Opera* by GAY with music

by KURT WEILL, who also provided the scores for *Happy End* (1929, produced under Brecht's name, though the text was by Elisabeth Hauptmann) and *The Rise and Fall of the City of Mahagonny* (1930).

With musicians on stage, the use of placards to give spectators an objective perspective on the action, the separation of dialogue from song and a harshly cynical presentation of the material in order to prevent emotional empathy, these operas were designed as the antithesis to WAGNER. They were the first consciously developed examples of the 'distancing' or *Verfremdungseffekt*, forming the basis of a new style of acting in which the performers demonstrate the actions of a character instead of identifying with their roles. These ideas were developed in Brecht's *Small Organum for the Theatre* (1948).

Brecht's 'teaching plays', or *Lehrstücke*, derived in some ways from AGIT-PROP theatre, show his approach to his dramatic material at its clearest, abstracting political issues such as whether individuals should be sacrificed for the revolution (*He Who Says Yes* and *He Who Says No*, 1930, and *The Measures Taken*, 1931), and presenting them in historically or geographically distant contexts where their essential nature could be displayed.

Forced to flee Germany by Hitler's rise to power in 1933, Brecht collaborated with Weill, Lotte Lenya and the scene designer, Caspar Neher, in a 'ballet-cantata' – *The Seven Deadly Sins* (Paris, 1933). In exile in Denmark, Sweden, Finland, he began to write parable plays on historical or exotic subjects where the political message is oblique and the Communist premises buried deep in the structure. These are his epic masterpieces – *Mother Courage and her Children* (1941), *The Good Person of Setzuan* (1943), *The Life of Galileo* (1943) and *The Caucasian Chalk Circle* (written 1941–44, German premiere 1954). In Finland he wrote *Puntila and His Man Matti* (1948) and *The Resistible Rise of Arturo Ui* (1958), which parodies the rise of Hitler. He went via the Soviet Union to California, where he found employment in Hollywood. In 1947 he directed *Galileo*, which he had revised for CHARLES LAUGHTON to reflect the moral issues posed by Hiroshima. *The Visions of Simone Machard* (1957) and *Schweyk in the Second World War* (1957) were written in USA.

Although some of his major plays had been produced at the Zürich Schauspielhaus during his exile, it was only after his return to East Berlin in 1948 and with the establishment of the BERLINER ENSEMBLE under his wife and leading actress, HELENE WEIGEL, that they achieved wide recognition. His dramatic output during the last eight years of his life consisted of collaborations and adaptations. However, his directorial work with these and his definitive productions of his own plays affirmed the viability of his earlier theatrical theory. The work of the Ensemble established his influential position in the contemporary theatre, and his domination of the German stage continues. With the collapse of Communism, Brecht is ripe for reinterpretation.

**Bredero, Gerbrand Adriaansz** 1585–1618 Dutch poet and playwright, famous primarily for his comedies and FARCES. The impact of his plays lies in the apt portrayal of the middle classes, the farmers and citizens, seen in e.g. *The Farce of the Cow* (1612), and *The Miller's Farce* (1613). In his *Moortje* (1616), based on TERENCE's *Eunuchus*, and in *The Spanish Brabanter* (1617) his use of dialect and his depiction of ordinary Amsterdam life is striking. Today, his plays are still regularly performed. *The Spanish*

*Brabanter* has been translated and staged in England. Bredero's tragedies remain relatively unknown.

**breeches part** Male role played by an actress. PEG WOFFINGTON's portrayal of Sir Harry Wildair in FARQUHAR's *The Constant Couple* (1699) established a tradition that extends, in the English theatre, through to the principal boy in PANTOMIME. In the 19th century the breeches role often accommodated a roguish young man, of good if mischievous nature, as for instance in the part of Sam Willoughby in TOM TAYLOR's *The Ticket of Leave Man*. (See also MALE IMPERSONATION.)

**Brel, Jacques** 1929–78 Belgian song-writer and performer. He renounced his middle-class inheritance to sing in Paris. Originally, his songs were idealistic and tinged with Catholic pieties, but gradually grew more trenchant, misogynistic and obsessed with death. His performance technique used illustrative gesture to caricature his own lyrics, which he almost spat out at the adoring audience. Brel's fame spread to the English-speaking world with the musical *Jacques Brel Is Alive and Well and Living in Paris* by Mort Shuman and Eric Blau (1968). He retired from the stage in 1972.

**Brenton, Howard** 1942– British playwright. His first play, *Ladder of Fools*, was staged in 1965 in Cambridge where he was a student. He won the John Whiting Award (1970) for his short play, *Christie in Love*. Brenton was influenced by a group of intellectuals in France, the 'situationists', who described Western liberal democracies as the societies 'of the Spectacle' in which politicians deceived the public with confidence tricks, aided by the mass media. Brenton saw his task as being to 'disrupt the Spectacle', and his full-length plays, such as *Magnificence* (1973), *The Churchill Play* (1974) and *Brassneck* (with DAVID HARE, 1973), have all attempted to shock the British public out of their bourgeois complacency. In *The Romans in Britain* (1980) Brenton drew a parallel between the presence of British troops in Northern Ireland and the conquest of Britain by Julius Caesar, stressing the analogy with a graphic scene of homosexual rape. The ensuing controversy led to a private prosecution being brought under the Sexual Offences Act of 1956 – though it was eventually withdrawn. Brenton's vivid dialogue, his narrative flow of powerful incidents and his polemical attacks brought him quickly to the fore in the state-subsidized sector of British theatre, with productions at the NATIONAL THEATRE, the ROYAL COURT and major regional reps. As a translator/adapter, he has provided the National Theatre with English versions of BRECHT's *Galileo* and BÜCHNER's *Danton's Death*. During the 1980s he wrote plays which considered the end of the Cold War and its consequences, such as *Moscow Gold* (1990, with Tariq Ali) about Mikhail Gorbachev's *glasnost* and *Berlin Bertie* (1992); but his 'Three Plays for Utopia', *Bloody Poetry* (1984), *Sore Throats* (1979, revised 1988) and *Greenland* (1988), tried to revive the vision of a Marxist utopia. *Hesse Is Dead* (1989) demonstrates how history can be manipulated to suit political purposes.

**Breuer, Lee** 1937– American actor and director. A founding member of the avant-garde theatre company MABOU MINES, Breuer studied in the 60s with the BERLINER ENSEMBLE and the Polish Theatre Lab. For Mabou Mines he serves as director, author and performer. His staging and adaptation of BECKETT's work has earned him three major awards; his trilogy *Animations* was published in 1979, and *Sister Suzie Cinema* in 1986. In the 1980s, while teaching at the Yale School of Drama, he focused on creating a new theatre that merges Asian and African arts with American performance techniques. In 1988 he wrote and directed a gender-reversed adaptation of *King Lear* with Ruth Maleczech as Lear. Outside Mabou Mines his most notable effort has been *The Gospel at Colonus* (1983), which was conceived, adapted and directed for the Brooklyn Academy of Music's Next Wave Festival, as was *The Warrior Ant* (1988).

**Brice, Fanny** [Fannie; *née* Frances Borach] 1891–1951 American comedienne and singer. Her gawky walk, repertoire of comic faces, and ability to sing both satiric and serious songs with equal success made her a star of REVUES for over a quarter of a century. Brice appeared in the ZIEGFELD Follies of 1910. She remained with the *Follies* for six more editions until 1923, then switched to IRVING BERLIN's *Music Box Revue* (1924). An attempt to star in *Fioretta* (1929) was a failure. Brice appeared in four more revues: *Sweet and Low* (1930), *Billy Rose's Crazy Quilt* (1931) and two editions of the Ziegfeld Follies (1934 and 1936). In most of her songs and sketches she affected a Yiddish accent that heightened her satirical treatment of such subjects as the ballet and silent film 'vamps'.

**Bridges-Adams, William** 1889–1965 British director. He stage-managed for WILLIAM POEL before taking over the Bristol repertory theatre, where between 1914 and 1915 he introduced a programme of SHAW, MASEFIELD and STANLEY HOUGHTON. From 1919 to 1934 he directed the Festival at Stratford-upon-Avon, where he founded the New Shakespearian Company, then toured Canada and America with them after the old theatre burned down in 1926. His last production was *Oedipus Rex* at COVENT GARDEN in 1936.

**Bridie, James** [Osborne Henry Mavor] 1888–1951 Scottish playwright. Bridie, a doctor, did much to keep Scottish theatre healthy, not only through his playwriting (which included *Tobias and the Angel* (1930), *Jonah and the Whale* (1932), *Mr Bolfry* (1943), *Daphne Laureola* (1949) and *The Queen's Comedy* (1950)), but also through his association, as a founder, with the Glasgow CITIZENS' THEATRE and with the establishment of drama training in the Royal Scottish Academy of Music and Drama. His playwriting, though often on serious themes, was distinguished by a very personal wit and charm, and he created roles relished by such performers as Alastair Sim and EDITH EVANS.

**Brieux, Eugène** 1858–1932 French playwright. His naturalistic dramas (see NATURALISM) on social themes dealt frankly with matters ranging from syphilis to birth control. GEORGE BERNARD SHAW wrote a famous introduction to the English translation of three of the plays, *Les Avariés* (*Damaged Goods*, 1902), *The Three Daughters of M. Dupont* (1897) and *Maternity* (1903), in which he compared Brieux to IBSEN. In terms of Brieux as a campaigner, the comparison is valid.

**Brighouse, Harold** 1882–1958 British playwright. He wrote prolifically, mainly about the people and affairs of his home county of Lancashire. The GAIETY THEATRE in Manchester was the venue for much of his work, including his best-known play *Hobson's Choice* (1915). This play and *Zack* (1916) have established a firm place in the national repertory. His one-act plays, which are particularly well crafted, form an important part of his work. (See also STANLEY HOUGHTON.)

**Bristol Old Vic Company** Shortly after the end of World War II, the ARTS COUNCIL OF GREAT BRITAIN, in association with the OLD VIC in London, set up a permanent repertory company in Bristol, based at the recently reopened Theatre Royal (itself dating from 1766). Beginning in 1946, under the direction of HUGH HUNT, it soon became established as one of the country's leading theatre companies. Since 1972, when alterations to the Theatre Royal were completed, the company has also been able to present small-scale new and experimental work in a theatre studio, the New Vic. The Bristol Old Vic Theatre Trust also runs the highly regarded Bristol Old Vic Theatre School.

**British Theatre Association** Founded by Geoffrey Whitworth in 1919 as the British Drama League, its early causes included the establishment of a NATIONAL THEATRE, the introduction of drama into the school curriculum and the winning of public support for the arts. Of special importance has been its library and information/research service. The BTA was dissolved for financial reasons in 1990. Its collections of play scripts (presented by ANNIE HORNIMAN and including the WILLIAM ARCHER collection) are now held by the Theatre Museum in London.

**Briusov, Valery (Yakovlevich)** 1873–1924 Russian poet, novelist and critic. He was the chief theorist of the symbolist movement (see SYMBOLISM); his call for a conventional theatre of essence greatly influenced MEYERHOLD and other anti-realistic directors (see REALISM) of the early 20th century. His symbolist activities included the anthology *Russian Symbolists* (1894), which launched the movement; the editing of its journal, *The Scales* (1904); numerous volumes of poetry and short fiction; theoretical and critical articles; the novel *The Fiery Angel* (1907–8); over 20 produced plays, and sketches of many more. In his essays he argued his preference for a conventional (*uslovny*) theatre which would give the actor the centrality he enjoyed in the ancient Greek and Elizabethan theatres. Briusov attacked Meyerhold's mechanization of the actor but supported GORDON CRAIG's bid to stylize the acting in his *Hamlet* collaboration with STANISLAVSKY at the MOSCOW ART THEATRE (1912). His own dramas, which have been labelled 'cosmic' offer spectacular scenic and lighting effects, philosophical themes and heightened language, symbols and imagery. *Earth* (1904) is the only published one of four science fiction plays, the others being *Piroent* (*Pyroesis*), *The Dictator* (1921) and *The World of Seven Generations* (1923). *The Wayfarer* (1910) is a one-act 'psychodrama'. *Protesilaus Deceased* (1911–12) is a version of the myth dramatized by EURIPIDES. Briusov later broke with the symbolist movement, and in 1917 embraced the October Revolution.

**Broadway** New York commercial theatre. Broadway is to New York as the WEST END is to London – the district that is thought of as the traditional theatrical heart of the city. Since the 1890s, centred on and around the street of that name in New York City have been the major theatres that have represented the professional and commercial theatrical core of the nation, extending, from the 1950s, into OFF-BROADWAY locations (to accommodate generally smaller and somewhat more innovative theatres) as economic pressures restricted work in the big old theatres. OFF-OFF BROADWAY is distinguished from Broadway and Off-Broadway not only by a further diminution in scale and eclectic experimentation, but also by the radically different contractual relationship with actors based on non-profit-making companies. (See NEW YORK CITY THEATRES; RESIDENT THEATRE.)

**Broadway, Off-** and **Off-Off** see OFF-BROADWAY and OFF-OFF BROADWAY

**Broadway Theatre** A succession of individual New York City theatres have adopted this name:

356–8 Broadway. The original Broadway was modelled on London's HAYMARKET and, with 4,500 seats, was the largest theatre built before 1847. It never achieved the prominence of the PARK THEATRE, which it was intended to replace, and was torn down in 1859.

Broadway and 41st Street. Built in 1888, it was dedicated to MUSICAL COMEDY, operetta and spectacle. Both EDWIN BOOTH and SIR HENRY IRVING made final appearances in New York at the Broadway. Later it was used for motion pictures, and was destroyed in 1929.

1681 Broadway. Opened as B. S. Moss's Colony Theatre in 1924, renamed the Broadway in 1930, it is an 1,800-seat house, well suited for musicals, e.g. *Evita* (1979). Since 1943 it has been a SHUBERT theatre.

**Brockmann, Johann** 1745–1812 Austrian actor. Brockmann achieved prominence when, in 1776, he acted the title role in FRIEDRICH SCHRÖDER's famous production of *Hamlet* in Hamburg. The grace and naturalness of his expression were highly admired. After successful guest appearances in Berlin, Brockmann was called to the BURGTHEATER where he remained for the rest of his life. Here he helped form the characteristic style of the company.

**Brome, Richard** c.1590–1652 English playwright. He provided the Caroline theatre with plays until the closing of the theatres in 1642. Little is known about him, but the influence of BEN JONSON is detectable in his surviving plays, of which the best are *The Damoiselle* (1637), *The Antipodes* (1638), *The Court Beggar* (1640) and *A Jovial Crew* (1641). The earliest known playwright's contract was drawn up in Brome's name on 20 July 1635, providing a job description of his attachment to the company at the SALISBURY COURT playhouse.

**Bronnen, Arnolt** 1895–1959 Austrian playwright and novelist. He made his reputation on the German stage with violently emotional examples of EXPRESSIONISM (*Parricide*, 1922; *The Birth of Youth*, 1925), before turning to comedy. His plays, although frequently taken as supporting the Nazi movement, were banned in 1943, and in 1955 he moved to East Berlin as a theatre critic.

**Brook, Peter (Stephen Paul)** 1925– British director. Born in London of Russian descent, Brook first attracted attention as an Oxford undergraduate staging ambitious plays under the difficult conditions of London's little theatre clubs during the war. For BARRY JACKSON he directed *Man and Superman* and *King John* (1945) at the BIRMINGHAM REP. His enchanting *Love's Labour's Lost* (1946), designed after Watteau, began his long association with what became in 1961 the ROYAL SHAKESPEARE COMPANY. He directed plays by ANOUILH, Roussin and CHRISTOPHER FRY; but the true power of his imagination was felt through the Stratford Shakespearian productions, notably of *Measure for Measure* (1950) and of *Titus Andronicus* (1955), which starred LAURENCE OLIVIER as Titus and featured Brook's own set designs and *musique concrète*. Later Brook productions for the RSC included *King Lear* (1962) with PAUL SCOFIELD; PETER WEISS's *The Marat/Sade* (1964); *US* (1966), a documentary attack on the US involvement in Vietnam, and *A Midsummer Night's Dream* (1970), set in an adult adventure playground, with trapezes, stilts and spinning plates.

During the 1960s, Brook was influenced by the seemingly contradictory theories of ANTONIN ARTAUD and BERTOLT BRECHT, shock tactics and analytical calm, and his reconciliation of these extremes became a feature of the RSC style. His collection of four brief essays, *The Empty Space* (1968), influenced many directors in Britain and overseas as an acute analysis of the basic problems facing contemporary theatre. By 1970, however, Brook was moving towards a style of performance which would have been equally out of place in a major subsidized company as on the WEST END stage. With the help of JEAN-LOUIS BARRAULT and a Ford Foundation grant, he established an International Centre of Theatre Research (CIRT). Their first production was a play by Ted Hughes, *Orghast*, written in an ancient Persian ceremonial language and staged in Persepolis during the Shiraz Festival (1971). Brook and his co-founder Micheline Rozan found a deserted music-hall near the Gare du Nord in Paris, where he assembled a team of actors, dancers, musicians, acrobats and mimes from many countries. Brook wanted to encourage a group approach which could transcend the boundaries of national cultures. His company took myths to remote villages in the Sahara, as in *The Conference of the Birds* (1976), and the experience of living on the verge of starvation they took back to Paris and London in *The Ik* (1975).

Although the Centre has been acclaimed for its productions of *The Cherry Orchard* (1981) and *The Tragedy of Carmen* (1983), its most celebrated and daunting achievement has so far been to tell the entire story of the Indian religious epic, *The Mahabharata* (1985), in nine hours in a quarry outside Avignon. Productions since *The Mahabharata* have seemed more modest – *The Tempest* (1987) and *Pelléas and Mélisande* (1992) – but these have been distinguished by a luminous clarity and simplicity.

**Brougham, John** 1810–80 Irish-American playwright and actor. Born in Dublin, he performed in London until 1842 when he left for America, and after spells in management he was employed as actor-playwright at WALLACK's, the WINTER GARDEN and at AUGUSTIN DALY's FIFTH AVENUE THEATRE. His reputation rests principally on his outlandish Indian BURLESQUES: *Po-ca-hon-tas, or the Gentle Savage* (1855) and *Metamora, or the Last of the Pollywogs* (1857), in which he ridiculed the stage version of the 'noble savage', particularly that of EDWIN FORREST. Brougham wrote 126 wide-ranging pieces: adaptations, gothic MELODRAMAS, tearful and sensational melodramas, social SATIRES. As principal actor in most of his pieces, he was praised for his jovial versatility and impromptu 'before-the-curtain' speeches.

**Brown, John Mason** 1900–69 American drama critic. Associate editor and drama critic for *Theatre Arts Monthly* (1924–8), in 1929 Brown moved to the *New York Evening Post* and established his column 'Two on the Aisle', which remained popular throughout the 1930s. In 1944 he became associate editor and drama critic of *Saturday Review*, where his column 'Seeing Things' remained a standard for ten years. He also wrote books about theatre, in an easy informal style.

**Brown, William Henry** fl.1820s African-American theatre manager and playwright. An ex-West Indian seaman, Brown became the father of AFRICAN-AMERICAN THEATRE when he established the African Theatre in New York in 1821, with a repertoire that included condensed versions of plays such as *Richard III*, *Pizarro*, *Tom and Jerry*, *Obi, or Three-Fingered Jack*, and pantomimes. He also wrote and produced the first African-American play, *The Drama of King Shotaway* (1823), based on personal experience of the 1795 black Caribs' insurrection

on St Vincent. From his African Theatre emerged James Hewlett, the first black Shakespearian actor, and the renowned black actor IRA ALDRIDGE.

**Browne, E(lliot) Martin** 1900–80 British director. Browne was instrumental in reviving poetic religious drama. Appointed director of religious drama for the diocese of Chichester in 1930, he founded the Religious Drama Society and encouraged T. S. ELIOT to write for the theatre, directing all his plays from *Murder in the Cathedral*, in which he also acted the Fourth Tempter (1935), to *The Elder Statesman* (1958). After directing the Pilgrim Players, who toured with works by Eliot and BRIDIE, he took over the MERCURY THEATRE in 1945, making it a centre for new poetic plays that included CHRISTOPHER FRY's first success, *A Phoenix Too Frequent* (1946). In 1948 he succeeded Geoffrey Whitworth as director of the British Drama League (see BRITISH THEATRE ASSOCIATION), and in 1951 produced the first revival of the York cycle of MYSTERY PLAYS since 1572.

**Bruant, Aristide** 1851–1925 French cabaret performer. The first outstanding author-composer-performer of the French CABARET, he sang in CAFÉS CHANTANTS before opening his own cabaret Le Mirliton in 1885, where middle-class audiences flocked to be insulted by him (one refrain ran 'All customers are swine!') and hear his 'realistic songs'. These ballads, couched in the authentic slang of the Parisian slums, hymn the desperate plight of the outcast and outlawed with sardonic impassivity. Bruant, a striking combination of *apache* and lion-tamer in his black sombrero, boots and red scarf, recorded by Toulouse-Lautrec, made a fortune and in 1900 retired to the bourgeois private life he had earlier attacked.

**Bruce, Lenny** [Alfred Schneider] c.1924–66 American comedian. A stand-up comic, he became a martyr to his cult image. After World War II he studied acting and began as a night club comedian. Working out of small clubs in Greenwich Village, he first gained notoriety for his liberal use of four-letter words; gradually, he became noted for his savage attacks on establishment hypocrisy. As his act developed into intimate, improvisational harangues of the audience, he shocked the conventional with his freewheeling SATIRE on narcotics legislation, organized religion, sexual taboos and race relations. Frequently arrested for drug abuse and blasphemy (the Home Office refused to let him perform in England), he sank into paranoia and died of an overdose of narcotics. After his death, he became a totem – in KENNETH TYNAN's words, 'the man who went down on America's conscience', and a play, *Lenny*, was devoted to him.

**Bruckner, Ferdinand** [Theodor Tagger] 1891–1958 Austrian playwright. After his early experiments with EXPRESSIONISM, his plays ranged from brutally realistic studies of suicide (*Malady of Youth*, 1926) or the persecution of Jewish students (*Races*, 1933) to historical dramas such as his best-known work *Elizabeth of England* (1930). In 1936 he emigrated to America, where he worked with PISCATOR, returning in 1951 to become dramaturg at the Schiller Theater in Berlin. Though technically innovative, his post war attempts to revive verse tragedy in *Pyrrhus and Andromache* (1952) or *The Fight with the Angel* (1956) were unsuccessful.

**Brun, Johannes** 1832–90 Norwegian actor. He was the leading actor with the Bergen Norwegian Theatre (1850) and accompanied IBSEN on his 1852 study tour to Copenhagen. Brun joined Christiania Theatre in 1857 and stayed for 32 years, playing almost 400 roles, including several Ibsen premieres: Daniel Hejre in *The League of Youth*, the Dovre King in *Peer Gynt* and Old Ekdal in *The Wild Duck*. His strength was in COMEDY, to which he brought simplicity, naturalness and a fundamental gravity. He was the leading Norwegian interpreter of HOLBERG's Jeppe in his generation and, until illness restricted his range, a superb Falstaff. From the late 1870s he also directed, including the world premiere of *An Enemy of the People* (1883).

**Bruno, Giordano** 1548-1600 Italian philosopher and playwright. A Dominican priest and one of the greatest philosophers of the Renaissance, he ran foul of the Inquisition, and after a peripatetic life was burnt at the stake in Rome. His only known play, the comedy *Il candelaio* (*The Candlemaker*, Paris, 1582), is a subtle, complex and verbally difficult piece. It is rarely performed, although it was given an impressively theatrical production by LUCA RONCONI in 1968.

**Bruscambille** [Jean Deslauriers or Du Laurier] 17th-century French actor. He may have trained at fairgrounds and in Italy, where he claimed to have learned *la charlatannerie*. He was seen at Toulouse c.1598 and joined the company of the HÔTEL DE BOURGOGNE, Paris, in 1606; he was playing there still in 1632, but no trace of him survives after 1634. His prime function was as a master of ceremonies, delivering vivacious satirical prologues. Several collections of jokes attributed to him were published between 1610 and 1619, including the famous sally that his was '*une vie sans souci, et quelquefois sans six sous*'.

**Brustein, Robert** 1927- American critic, actor and director. Founder of the YALE and AMERICAN REPERTORY THEATRES, he has written several books on theatre (e.g. *The Theatre of Revolt*, 1964). He has been a respected and controversial critic for the *New Republic* since 1959 and sometimes for the *Observer* (UK). In 1979 Brustein unexpectedly left Yale for Harvard, where ART was established. At Yale and Harvard he has supervised over 170 professional productions.

**Bryden, Bill** [William Campbell Rough] 1942- British playwright and director. After writing for Scottish television he was appointed assistant director at the Belgrade Theatre, Coventry (1965-7), and at the ROYAL COURT THEATRE (1967-9). From 1971 to 1974, Bryden was an associate director at the Royal Lyceum Theatre in Edinburgh and helped to elevate it into Scotland's unofficial national theatre. Notable among many Lyceum productions were those of Bryden's own two plays, *Willie Rough* (1972), about the Greenock shop steward who led a shipyard strike during World War I, and *Benny Lynch* (1974). Both plays were distinguished by the naturalistic detail, the clear handling of complex historical material and the socialist fervour which never became blindly polemical. PETER HALL invited him to join the NATIONAL THEATRE in 1975, where he became director of the Cottesloe Theatre in 1978. Bryden developed the flexibility of the space by exploring the possibilities of 'promenade' productions, as in *Lark Rise* (1978) and TONY HARRISON's *Mysteries*, derived from the York mystery cycle (see MYSTERY PLAY), which were developed over four years from 1979 and presented in three parts. His play *Old Movies* (1977) was also seen at the Cottesloe, as were his productions of 20th-century American plays, by O'NEILL, ODETS and DAVID MAMET. To celebrate Glasgow's year as the European City of Culture he staged *The Ship* (1990), in the Govan shipyards.

**Buarque de Holanda, Chico** 1944- Brazilian composer and playwright. He brought his talent to the theatre in such plays as *Gota d'Aqua* (*Drop of Water*, 1977), the tragic theme of Medea set in the Brazilian *favela*, and *Opera do Malandro* (*The Rogue's Opera*, 1980), an adaptation of *The Threepenny Opera*, with its critique of commercial relationships between Third World countries and the United States.

**Buatier de Kolta** [Joseph Buatier] 1847-1903 French illusionist. He gave up studying for the priesthood to become assistant to the Hungarian prestidigitator De Kolta. Buatier claimed to have invented all the illusions in his act: scarves passing through bottles, a seated woman disappearing from her chair, the apparition of a giant black glove, and many others. His last great invention was 'the Growing Die', which expanded at the conjuror's command until it was the size of a trunk, at which point a woman stepped out of it. (See also MAGIC.)

**Büchner, Georg** 1813-37 German playwright. During his brief life, Büchner achieved notoriety as the leader of an abortive conspiracy to revolution in Hesse, and distinction as a lecturer in comparative anatomy at the University of Zürich, a post to which he was appointed in 1836. His first play, *Danton's Death* (1835), reflects his disillusionment with revolutionary politics; Danton's humanity is the sole positive element in this nihilistic view of the French Revolution as being nothing but the power struggle of ambitious individuals and interests. *Leonce and Lena* (1836) is a lively satirical comedy, while *Woyzeck* (1837), a possibly incomplete drama, expresses Büchner's sympathy for the socially downtrodden. Because of his unorthodox dramaturgy, his plays were not performed for several decades after his death. *Leonce and Lena* was first produced in 1895, *Danton's Death* in 1903, and *Woyzeck* in 1913. It is possible that Büchner left another play in manuscript when he died, *Pietro Aretino*; this may have been destroyed by his fiancée, who objected to the obscenity in the play.

**Buckingham** [George Villiers], 2nd Duke of 1628-87 English playwright. From 1668 he was Charles II's chief minister of state. His adaptation of FLETCHER's *The Chances* (1668) was very successful, with NELL GWYN in a minor role. In 1669 he collaborated with SIR ROBERT HOWARD on *The Country Gentleman*. His best play, *The Rehearsal*, a collaborative SATIRE on DAVENANT and Sir Robert Howard, was first performed in 1671, by which time it had become a satire on DRYDEN who was portrayed as Bayes, a pompous writer of heroic plays. A brilliant BURLESQUE of the fashionable heroic drama, the play parodies plays and playwrights unmercifully. The form, a writer outlining his ideas to his friends during a rehearsal of one of his plays, became the model for burlesque drama, evidenced particularly in SHERIDAN's *Critic*. Buckingham retired from politics after the accession of James II.

**Buckstone, J(ohn) B(aldwin)** 1802-79 English actor, playwright and theatre manager. Of the 160 or so dramatic pieces Buckstone wrote between 1825 and 1850, most were short FARCES, operettas or burlettas, but *Luke the Labourer* (1826) helped set the fashion for domestic MELODRAMA. *The Wreck Ashore* (1830) is a hyperactive adventure story with low-life comic characters. Here, as in the lively comedy of *The Irish Lion* (1838) and *Single Life* (1839) and in the tear-jerking of *The Green Bushes* (1845), Buckstone upholds manly fortitude, decency and self-sacrifice. Having early on established himself as a 'low comedian', he continued to play comic roles. He managed the HAYMARKET from 1853 to 1876, making it the home of comedy: TOM TAYLOR, WESTLAND MARSTON and, after 1870, W. S. GILBERT were his preferred playwrights.

**Buenaventura, Enrique** 1928– Colombian playwright, director and theorist. He studied architecture, painting and sculpture, which gave to his work a plastic vision of dramatic art. In 1955 he helped establish the TEC (Theatre School of Cali, renamed the Experimental Theatre of Cali in 1970), one of the most respected and enduring theatre groups in Latin America. His style and dedication to principles of Third World theatre (the so-called 'new theatre') have brought him international recognition. The early *A la diestra de Dios Padre (On the Right Hand of God the Father*, 1958) is modelled on folkloric versions of the devil and St Peter, as told by Colombian novelist Tomás Carrasquilla. His later plays have stronger messages of social and political protest. The vitriolic one-act segments of *Los papeles del infierno (Documents from Hell*, 1968) and *Historia de una bala de plata (Story of a Silver Bullet*, 1980) are representative of this change in his theatre.

**Buero-Vallejo, Antonio** 1916– Spanish playwright. He was one of the few important figures in the 1950s and 1960s. Having served six years in prison for his Republican sympathies, in 1949 his name was made with *Historia de una escalera (Story of a Staircase)*, portraying the lives of the inhabitants of a poor tenement over 30 years. This was followed by *En la ardiente oscuridad (In the Burning Darkness*, 1950), a tragedy set in a home for the blind, and *La tejedora de sueños (The Weaver of Dreams*, 1952), a reinterpretation of Ulysses' return home. These plays established the themes of man's frustrated search for happiness and the human frailty which prevents him achieving it. There followed a number of less successful plays, including *Hoy es fiesta (Today's a Holiday*, 1956), before the more socially oriented *Las cartas boca abajo (Cards Face Downwards*, 1957). A trio of historical plays followed: *Un soñador para el pueblo (A Dreamer for the People*, 1958) deals with Carlos III's idealist minister Esquilache, while *Las meninas (The Ladies-in-Waiting*, 1959) presents Velázquez as the conscience of his time.

Later plays include *Aventura en la gris (Adventure in the Grey*, 1963), *El concierto de San Ovidio (Concert at St Ovide Fair*, 1964), *El tragaluz (The Skylight*, 1967), a symbolic tragedy, and *La doble historia del Dr Valmy (The Double Story of Dr Valmy*, 1964), first performed in England in 1968. In *El sueño de la razón (The Sleep of Reason*, 1970), Goya's solitude is underscored by his deafness, which the audience is made to share by having other characters mouth words silently while he is present. Buero uses such 'immersion effects' to reveal his characters' inner nature and promote audience identification. *La fundación (The Foundation*, 1974) exploits this technique: the audience is immersed in the illusory world of a political prisoner, rather than his sordid prison cell. *Jueces en la noche (Judges in the Night*, 1979) deals with the right-wing manipulation of left-wing terror groups. His *Diálogo secreto (Secret Dialogue*, 1984) shows, since the relaxation of CENSORSHIP, a tendency to preach rather than suggest. Other recent plays include *Lázaro en el laberinto (Lazarus in the Labyrinth*, 1986) and *Música cercana (The Music Window*, 1989).

**bufo** Popular theatre form. This Caribbean, especially Cuban, equivalent of the *sainete* (see GÉNERO CHICO) incorporates the types, characters and language typical of the lower social classes. *Bufo* also implies a criticism of some aspect of life, and is normally presented with the intention of destroying false illusions. After a period of relative disuse, the form has been reincorporated into Cuba's new social theatre.

**Bugaev, Boris N.** see BELY, ANDREI

*bugaku* Japanese court dance. Dating from the 7th century, *bugaku* originated in China. A rarefied art, it is performed and taught primarily at the music department of the Imperial household agency and at large temples and shrines. Also, several times a year public performances are given at the National Theatre in Tokyo. *Bugaku* is performed on a square, raised dance floor. Unroofed, its space is demarked visually by a red-lacquered railing on four sides and by a green silk cloth that covers its surface. The stage is often set outdoors, in a garden or over a pond, to enhance the beauty of performance. Masks are worn for some roles. Costumes are court dress of the 7th century: elegant silk robes, black hats. No scenery is used. Musicians playing flute, mouth organ, gong and drums accompany the dance. There are no singers. The repertory of about 50 dances can be classified into old or modern, military or civil pieces, a classification well known in China.

Associated with the Imperial court from its beginnings, the decorous, four-square movements and ethereal music of *bugaku* evoke the refined elegance of the Japanese court of 1,000 years ago (the dances from which *bugaku* grew have long since died out in China). *Bugaku* performance was traditionally structured into an opening, a breaking apart and a fast conclusion. This fundamental aesthetic construct was later adopted in NŌ and other forms of Japanese theatre.

**Bulgakov, Mikhail (Afanasievich)** 1891–1940 Russian novelist and playwright. The medically trained son of a Kiev theologian, he soon embarked on careers in journalism and literature, the latter including such major narrative works as the story collection *Diaboliad*, the novelette *Heart of a Dog* and the epic Civil War novel *White Guard* (all 1925). His adaptation of this novel, *The Days of the Turbins* (1925), commissioned by the MOSCOW ART THEATRE (1926), realistically depicts the events leading to the destruction and exile of a White officer's family in the author's native Kiev. Its sympathetic portrayal of the White enemy resulted in Bulgakov's being labelled an 'internal émigré'.

His first major comedy, *Zoika's Apartment* (1926), is a 'satiric melodrama' similar to those by ERDMAN and FAIKO. It was eventually banned with Bulgakov's other plays in 1929. *The Crimson Island* (1927) is a comedy-allegory which parodies CENSORSHIP and officially sanctioned drama. *Flight* (1927), his most ambitious play and the first to be banned before it premiered (at MAT), is a hallucinatory epilogue to *The Days of the Turbins*. The play received its Soviet premiere in 1957. He also wrote *The Cabal of Hypocrites (Molière*, written 1929, banned 1930), a cinematically structured account of the difficulties experienced by *Tartuffe*'s author in getting his play produced. Bulgakov satirized his uneasy tenure at MAT as playwright and as an assistant director (1930–6) in his theatrical novel (*Black Snow*, 1936). Among the remaining 30-odd plays are *Last Days* (1935); *Adam and Eve* (1931); two fantasy-SATIRES on time-travel, *Bliss* (1934) and *Ivan Vasilievich* (1935); adaptations of *Dead Souls* (1932) and *Don Quixote* (1938); and *Batum* (1938), about the young Stalin. Bulgakov's brilliant novel *The Master and Margarita* was finally brought to the stage by YURY LYUBIMOV at Moscow's Taganka Theatre in 1977.

**Bullins, Ed** 1935– African-American playwright. He

began writing fiction but, seeing BARAKA's plays on stage, felt drama was more effective in reaching black audiences. Since 1965 Bullins has written several dozen plays and is produced internationally. In 1967 he joined the New Lafayette Theatre as resident playwright, became its associate director, and edited its periodical *Black Theatre*. In 1982 he moved to San Francisco. Among his best-known plays are *Goin' a Buffalo* (1966), *In the Wine Time* (1968), *The Duplex* (1970), *In New England Winter* (1971), *The Fabulous Miss Marie* (1971), *The Taking of Miss Janie* (1975), *Marvin X* and *In the Name of Love* (1988). His experiments in form combine rhythmic, racy dialogue, black ritual, jazz and blues music as integral elements of his dramaturgy.

**Buloff, Joseph** 1899–1985 Yiddish actor and director. He worked first with the VILNA TROUPE where he distinguished himself in the title role of OSSIP DIMOV's *Yoshke Musikant*, then in America where he acted with MAURICE SCHWARTZ's YIDDISH ART THEATRE and directed for the FOLKSBÜHNE, forming the New York Art Theatre in 1934/5. He eventually moved to English-speaking roles on BROADWAY, and was active in Israel during the 50s and 60s. (See also YIDDISH THEATRE.)

**Bulwer Lytton, Edward (George Earle)** [1st Baron Lytton] 1803–73 English novelist, playwright and politician. (Born Edward Bulwer, he changed his name to Bulwer Lytton on inheriting Knebworth House, and was created Baron Lytton of Knebworth in 1866.) As a member of parliament, he led an inquiry into the state of the theatre in 1832, aiming to establish an effective COPYRIGHT law, to investigate the patent theatres' monopoly over 'legitimate' drama (see THEATRICAL MONOPOLY) and to challenge the Lord Chamberlain's role as dramatic censor (see CENSORSHIP). (The first was a limited success, the second bore fruit 11 years later and the third faded into obscurity.) His analysis of contemporary theatre can be read in his social survey, *England and the English* (1833). The best of his plays, written when he was already famous as a novelist, were solicited and performed by MACREADY. They are *The Duchess de la Vallière* (1837), a Gothic drama in verse, *The Lady of Lyons* (1838), a drama of mixed verse and prose and a favourite of audiences throughout the 19th century, *Richelieu* (1839), a polished verse drama; and the prose comedy, *Money* (1840), which comments sharply on contemporary values.

**Bunn, Alfred** 1798–1860 English theatre manager. His scuffle with MACREADY made him notorious. Bunn, who had little respect for the patent theatres, followed ELLISTON's lead during his simultaneous management of both DRURY LANE and COVENT GARDEN (1833–5). His tactlessness aroused such opposition that he was never able to pursue a consistent policy, and by 1840 he was bankrupt. *The Stage: Both Before and Behind the Curtain* (1840) is his argumentative self-justification. 'Poet' Bunn, so called for his published verse, wrote several librettos, including one for Balfe's popular *The Bohemian Girl* (1843).

***bunraku*** Japanese puppet form. This is the ancient commercial doll-puppet theatre of Osaka, Japan, the name *bunraku* being relatively recent and deriving from the 19th-century theatre manager, Uemura Bunrakuen, whose troupe was the only group of professionals to continue into the Meiji period (1868–1912) – hence the association of the name with the genre.

In *bunraku* chanting is the dominant performance element. Numerous styles of chanting were in competi-

tion in the early 17th century. Until 1629 there were female chanters of considerable popularity; they were banned from public stages in that year by the same prohibition that banned *KABUKI* actresses. Since the mid-17th century Osaka and neighbouring Awaji Island have been the undisputed centres of puppet theatre in Japan.

CHIKAMATSU MONZAEMON (1653–1725), the most important playwright of *kabuki* and *bunraku* of his time, wrote both history and domestic plays. A history play, which was the major work on a programme, was written in five acts – e.g. Chikamatsu's *The Battles of Coxinga* (1715). The half-Japanese Coxinga invades China in order to dethrone a usurping emperor, which he does with the help of a tiger mount, miracles, and advice from Taoist immortals. In the concluding scene of Act 3 Coxinga's mother and sister sacrifice their lives to maintain his honour. The other four acts conclude in pitched battles. A domestic play, like Chikamatsu's *Love Suicides at Sonezaki* (1703), in one act and three scenes, was a short afterpiece. Chikamatsu wrote narrative passages of great beauty and created puppet characters of flesh and blood who wrestled with the conflict between feudal duty and human love.

The realistic puppets created up to around 1750 were capable of a wide range of visual expression. In performance a different chanter comes before the audience, to speak and sing each succeeding scene (a programme lasts nine to twelve hours). In certain scenes, such as the Ichiriki brothel scene in *The Treasury of Loyal Retainers* (1748), multiple chanters take the voices of specific characters, as if they were actors. Chanters memorize the text, which is written out in the form of a novel rather than a play. Using a highly developed vocal repertory, the chanters distinguish between the spoken prose dialogue of the puppet characters and poetic descriptions in which the voice moves back and forth between melodic song and chant, which occupies a middle ground between speech and song. The chanter shows the full gamut of human emotions vocally: wailing in suffering, rhythmic laughing in joy, raging in anger, emitting gentle tones in love. In *bunraku*, chanting is a tour de force. (See also PUPPETS.)

**Buontalenti, Bernardo** 1536–1608 Italian architect and scene designer. Assistant to GIORGIO VASARI from 1547, he designed palaces, villas and fortresses and organized firework displays for festivals. By 1574 he had succeeded Vasari as architect and supervisor of Florentine court entertainments. In honour of the marriage between Virginia de' Medici and Cesare d'Este (1585) he designed the Teatro degli Uffizi, with a system of revolving *periaktoi* and elaborate stage machinery. His decors were used for Giovanni Bardi's *L'amico fido* (*The Faithful Friend*) and the accompanying six intermezzi written for the occasion. He directed the month-long festivities honouring the marriage of Ferdinand I of Tuscany to Catherine de' Medici (1589), including the production of Girolami Bargagli's *La pellegrina* and its six intermezzi. Characteristic of his style, these elaborate and sumptuous productions were noted for the ingenious cloud machines, glories, traps, revolving *periaktoi* and moving side wings which facilitated the almost magical scene changes taking place in full view of the spectators.

**Burbage, James** c.1530–97 English actor, and builder of England's first purpose-built theatre. Trained as a joiner, he was a leading member of LEICESTER's MEN by

1572, then financed the erection of the THEATRE (1576) and devoted himself to theatre management. He planned the conversion of the old Blackfriars monastery in 1596, but died with the situation unresolved, leaving the Theatre to his elder son, Cuthbert, and the BLACKFRIARS to his younger son, RICHARD.

**Burbage, Richard** c.1568–1619 English actor, son of JAMES BURBAGE. He created many of SHAKESPEARE's greatest roles. Previously a member of STRANGE'S MEN, he was a founder and leading member of the new LORD CHAMBERLAIN's MEN (later the King's Men) from 1594 until his death. Over the next two decades he is known to have played Hamlet, Othello, Lear and Richard III, Ferdinand in WEBSTER's *The Duchess of Malfi*, Malevole in MARSTON's *The Malcontent* and 'Jeronimo', in a lost play possibly emulating KYD's *The Spanish Tragedy*. Contemporaries, comparing him perhaps with EDWARD ALLEYN, considered his acting true to life, though he was certainly faithful to rhetorical conventions. With his brother Cuthbert he owned half the shares in the GLOBE and, later, the BLACKFRIARS.

***bürgerliches Trauerspiel*** ('bourgeois tragedy') German genre. It arose in the German theatre during the latter half of the 18th century, partially as a result of the introduction of English plays into the repertoire, partially due to the rise in economic power of the bourgeoisie. It is a tragedy set neither in princely or noble courts nor in a heroic period of history, but in the home of the bourgeoisie, who are regarded as serious subject-matter for drama. The first significant examples of the genre are LESSING's *Miss Sara Sampson* (1755), written under the influence of the English writers GEORGE LILLO and Samuel Richardson, and *Emilia Galotti* (1772). SCHILLER described his *Love and Intrigue* (1783) as a *bürgerliches Trauerspiel*. The genre is universally recognized as foreshadowing the work of HENRIK IBSEN, GERHART HAUPTMANN and other late-19th-century naturalist dramatists (see NATURALISM).

**Burgtheater** (Vienna) Founded in 1741 as the court theatre of the Habsburgs. In 1776 the Emperor Josef II, influenced partially by the ideas of JOSEF VON SONNENFELS on the educative potential of the theatre, declared it to be a national theatre. Under the aegis of actors such as BROCKMANN and FRIEDRICH SCHRÖDER, the Burgtheater developed a style of acting noted for its moderation and evenness of expression among the whole ensemble. In the 19th century, under the directorship first of JOSEF SCHREYVOGEL, then of HEINRICH LAUBE, this style became widely admired and imitated. Among the greatest actors who perfected the Burgtheater style were Heinrich Anschütz (1785–1865), famous for his moving Lear; Bernhard Baumeister (1828–1917), a magnificently robust actor; Josef Lewinsky (1835–1907), a masterly player of villains; SOPHIE SCHRÖDER; Charlotte Wolter (1834–97), a great tragedienne; and Adolf von Sonnenthal (1834–1909). In 1888, the company moved from their intimate theatre in the Hofburg to a palatial construction on the Franzen-Ring. This threatened their traditional style of ensemble, but through careful direction and the acting of MITTERWURZER and KAINZ, the standard was maintained. The Burgtheater is still the pre-eminent theatre of the German-speaking world and continues to practise, in modified form, the ideals of acting developed during the 18th and 19th centuries.

**Burian, E(mil) F(rantíšek)** 1904–59 Czech director and designer. He began his career in the 1920s as composer, musician and actor, and in 1933 established his own theatre collective, D34 (the number changed annually to indicate the current season). There, his early work contained elements of PISCATOR-like AGIT-PROP, but his most successful productions combined his musical talents more artistically with his intense political concerns. Burian often created his own poetic scenarios, most strikingly in *War* (1935), a moving anti-military work of village life. An auteur of the stage, he tended to regard every text as a libretto, for which he would be editor, composer, orchestrator and conductor. Although he produced in very small spaces, he achieved sophisticated technical effects: e.g. *theatergraph*, in 1935, a system that blended cinema projections with live action in poetic ways and thus anticipated the Czech LATERNA MAGIKA of the 1950s.

**burlesque** Burlesque, PARODY, and SATIRE are often treated as synonyms for ridicule through distortion, but distinctions can be made between them. None of the three words refers exclusively to drama; yet all have been applied to drama. Burlesque as derisive imitation enters the English language in the 17th century, *after* such signal achievements as the Pyramus and Thisbe scene in SHAKESPEARE's *Midsummer Night's Dream* and the mockery of romance in BEAUMONT and FLETCHER's *Knight of the Burning Pestle*. In general, burlesque tends to be broader than parody, mocking a style, class or genre. Seventeenth-century France and 18th-century England showed a marked taste for burlesque, and plays of that genre were standard fare in the 19th-century theatres of most European countries. Twentieth-century burlesque survives in skits and REVUES, but TOM STOPPARD's *Travesties* is a rare example of a full-length burlesque.

**burlesque show, American** Popular theatre form. A raucous and bawdy style of VARIETY performance, it was partly inspired by LYDIA THOMPSON and her British Blondes, partly by blackface minstrelsy (see MINSTREL SHOW) and 'leg shows' like *The Black Crook*. Early personalities in the genre were Mme Rentz's Female Minstrels and May Howard, who ran her own company in the 1880s. The burlesque show, a preponderantly female production, rapidly developed a tripartite structure: in the first third, dance and song rendered by a female company was intermingled with low comedy from male comedians; part two was an olio of specialities in which the women did not appear; and part three comprised a grand finale. Sam T. Jack, who opened the first exclusively burlesque theatre in Chicago, pioneered 'dirty' burlesque or 'turkey show', which was especially popular in the Western 'honky-tonks'. The Empire and Mutual Circuits or Wheels revelled in such maculose entertainment, while the Columbia Circuit booked only clean shows, until 1925 when it too was forced by dwindling receipts to go dirty.

Leading entrepreneurs were the Minsky brothers: Abe, who brought belly dancers (known as 'cootchers') and the illuminated runway from Paris; the publicists Billy and Morton; and Herbert, who introduced opera. From the early 1900s to 1935 they moulded the image of American burlesque, at the Republic Theatre and the National Winter Garden, New York. By present-day standards the offerings were tame, for the girls never disrobed completely. But the blatant *doubles entendres* in the dialogue between straight man and 'talking woman', and runway interplay between strippers and audience, enraged moralists. The strip-tease (see NUDITY), which achieved extraordinary invention and daring, entered burlesque in 1921 with 'Curls' Mason, and Carrie Finnell performed the first tassel dance, twirling the fringe from her nipples; the most memorable personalities among the strippers were Millie De Leon, the urbane GYPSY ROSE LEE (a protégée of the gangster Waxy Gordon) and the indestructible Anne Corio. There were many comedians nurtured by the form, including WILLIE HOWARD.

Changing times brought classic burlesque to an end. New York courts banned the runway in 1934 and all burlesque in 1942, and the Burlesque Artists Association had its charter revoked in 1957.

**Burns, George** [Nathan Birnbaum] 1896– and **Gracie Allen** [Grace Ethel Cecile Rosalie Allen] 1895–1964 American double act. Burns and Allen was the paradigm of an American male–female duo, his wry underplaying setting in relief her staccato dizziness. Burns had been a trick roller-skater, dance teacher and song-and-dance man in VAUDEVILLE; Allen entered show business as a child in an Irish sisters act. They teamed up in 1923 and married in 1926, Burns playing the quizzical straight man to her Dumb Dora. 'Lamb Chops', one version of their cross-talk act, was signed to a six-year contract in the Keith theatres (1926–32). They had their own radio show (1932–49) and moved successfully to television. After Allen's retirement in 1958, Burns, wielding his omnipresent cigar, continued to perform, a high point being his Carnegie Hall recital in 1976.

*burrakatha* Indian theatre form. *Burrakatha* is a popular form of entertainment, especially in the rural areas of Andhra Pradesh. The form is thought to have been derived from bands of roving minstrels (*jangams*), who sang the praises of the god Shiva as they travelled the rural parts of this state in ancient times. As social and religious affiliations shifted among the population, the minstrels responded by absorbing secular materials into their shows.

The term *burra* refers to the *tambura*, a stringed instrument worn across the right shoulder of the performer (*kathakudu*). The term *katha* means a story. The *kathakudu* plays the *tambura* with his right hand as he dances rhythmically forward and back on the stage reciting a story. His co-performers are two drummers who play the earthen drums with two heads (*dakki*), which produce a distinctly metallic sound to accentuate the songs. One drummer is known as the *rajkiya*, who makes political and social comments on contemporary issues (even if the story concerns historical or mythological events). The other is the *hasyam*, who cracks jokes and generally provides comic relief.

The *burrakatha* stories fall into three categories: mythological, historical and sociopolitical. Although the form was originally improvised, today many of the most popular stories have been written down and committed to memory by the performers. In the 1940s the Indian People's Theatre Association (IPTA), which was closely associated with the Communist Party of India, made use of rural forms of theatre in many parts of India as a vehicle for conveying its political and social message. In the state of Andhra, the *Praja Natak Mandali* (IPTA) revised *burrakatha* in order to reach vast numbers of voters. Other political parties soon followed suit. Today, as a medium of traditional communication to attract audiences, *burrakatha* parties are used by a wide range of political organizations, as well as by the state and central government.

**Burrows, Abe** [Abram S.] 1910–85 American play-

wright, librettist and director. Following a successful career in radio, he first scored as a playwright in 1950 by co-authoring *Guys and Dolls* with Jo Swerling and FRANK LOESSER. Several assignments as lyricist or librettist for musicals followed, including *Three Wishes for Jamie* (1952), *Can-Can* (1953), *Silk Stockings* (1955), *Say, Darling* (1958), *First Impressions* (1959) and *How to Succeed in Business without Really Trying* (1961). He made his debut as a director with *Can-Can*, and soon became invaluable as an unbilled 'play doctor' when called on to infuse stage comedies with wit and gentle humour.

**Burstyn, Ellen** [*née* Edna Rae Gillooly] 1932– American actress. Burstyn, once a showgirl on television, is now a champion of women's status in American film and theatre. Former artistic director of the ACTORS STUDIO, she has striven to play roles that intrigued her irrespective of their size, and has played significant parts in plays as disparate as *Same Time, Next Year* (1975), *84 Charing Cross Road* (1982), *Driving Miss Daisy* (1988), *Shirley Valentine* (1989) and *Shimada* (1992). She won an Academy Award for her sensitive portrayal in *Alice Doesn't Live Here Anymore* (1974).

**Burton, Richard (Jenkins)** 1925–84 Welsh actor. His early work for the stage, in productions of FRY's *The Lady's Not for Burning* (1949) and *Hamlet* at the OLD VIC in 1953 amongst others, established him as one of the most brilliant actors of his generation. He abandoned the stage for a life of film stardom, which meant that his remarkable talent was never fully realized.

**Burton, William E(vans)** 1804–60 British-born American actor and manager. He ran one of the best stock companies (see STOCK COMPANY) in the United States, and was also the 'funniest man who ever lived'. In 1832 he appeared opposite EDMUND KEAN at the HAYMARKET Theatre. In 1834 he made his American debut, and from 1841 to 1858 managed theatres in New York, Philadelphia and Baltimore, employing a good company, largely without visiting stars. Audiences came primarily to see Burton perform such roles as Bob Acres, Tony Lumpkin, Bottom, Falstaff, and especially Timothy Toodles in his own *The Toodles*. But his own plays have not survived.

**Bury, John** 1925– British stage designer. For more than ten years after World War II he worked with JOAN LITTLEWOOD's Theatre Workshop. From 1963 to 1973 he was chief designer at the ROYAL SHAKESPEARE Theatre, and from 1973 to 1985 head of design at the NATIONAL THEATRE, in addition to freelancing at other theatres in England and abroad. With no formal training in art or design, Bury developed a mode of abstract REALISM, eschewing the consciously decorative and theatrical in favour of stark, large-scale images, and relying on authentic materials. *The Wars of the Roses* (1963) employed steel for most surfaces and shifted scenes by means of twin, mobile *periaktoi* towers. In later years a conscious sense of form and style has become more apparent in his designs: *Tristan and Isolde* (1971), *Amadeus* (1979), *Yonadab* (1985), *Salomé*, (1988) and *Elektra* (1991). Throughout his career Bury has designed his own lighting in order to increase the expressiveness of his sets.

**Bush Theatre** (London) A leading FRINGE theatre, the Bush has a remarkable record in the promotion of new plays and unknown dramatists. It was founded in 1970 by the actor Brian McDermott in the 'social functions' room of a public house. Originally self-financing, it quickly became the venue for many lively touring companies, including the PEOPLE SHOW and LINDSAY KEMP's company, whose hit show, *Flowers*, received its premiere at the Bush. In the mid-1970s the Bush Theatre received its first substantial ARTS COUNCIL grants and evolved into a 'new plays' theatre. Among the many dramatists whose early plays were promoted through the Bush are STEPHEN POLIAKOFF (*Hitting Town*, *City Sugar*) and TOM KEMPINSKI (*Duet for One*). With Dominic Dromgoole as its artistic director, the Bush has produced Billy Roche's *Wexford Trilogy* (*A Handful of Stars*, 1988; *Poor Beast in the Rain*, 1989; and *Belfry*, 1991).

**Buzo, Alex(ander John)** 1944– Australian playwright. His first success was *Norm and Ahmed* (1968), a dialogue between an old Australian and a Pakistani student. His subsequent plays tend to focus on misfit idealists in contemporary suburbia or historical settings; his style, sometimes misconstrued as realism, is a brittle comic-ironic surface with complex subtext and evocative images. His plays include *The Front Room Boys* (1969), *Macquarie*, written while he was resident playwright with Melbourne Theatre Company in 1972–3, *Coralie Lansdowne Says No* (1974), *Martello Towers* (1976), *Makassar Reef* (1978) and *The Marginal Farm* (1984).

**Byron (George Gordon), Lord** 1788–1824 English poet and playwright. Byron was keenly interested in the theatre. He wrote all his plays during his Italian exile, claiming they were not intended for the stage, while determined to write 'studiously Greek' tragedies to challenge the English tradition. Only *Marino Faliero* (DRURY LANE, 1821) was performed in his lifetime. MACREADY kept *Werner*, a gloomy Gothic MELODRAMA, in his repertoire. *Sardanapalus* was first staged by Macready in 1834 and famously revived by CHARLES KEAN at the PRINCESS's in 1853. *Manfred*, a dramatic poem rather than a play, was performed at COVENT GARDEN in 1834. *The Two Foscari*, a clumsy work, was first staged by Macready in 1838. *Cain* was directed by STANISLAVSKY for the MOSCOW ART THEATRE in 1920 and transformed by GROTOWSKI in 1960.

**Byron, H(enry) J(ames)** 1834–84 English playwright, actor, theatre manager and journalist. His prodigious punning and irreverent treatment of familiar stories made a distinctive contribution to the development of the British PANTOMIME. (To his BURLESQUE versions of *Cinderella* (1860) and *Aladdin* (1861) we owe the invention of Buttons and Widow Twankey.) In 1865, together with the star of many of his burlesques MARIE WILTON, Byron took on the management of the Prince of Wales's Theatre and of three Liverpool theatres. It was for Liverpool that he wrote *The Lancashire Lass* (1867), a melodrama full of the effects he delighted to burlesque. The popular *Our Boys* (1875) ran for four years at the Vaudeville Theatre. He returned to burlesque at the GAIETY and wrote *The Gaiety Gulliver*.

# C

**cabaret** Popular entertainment. The name derives from the Spanish *caba retta* or 'merry bowl', then the French *cabaret* or tavern. It denotes a small-scale performance, occasionally improvised, of songs, sketches, SATIRES and speeches, usually commenting on social, political or artistic conditions. Strictly an urban form, it originated as an avant-garde amusement for a select audience but later became commercialized for a broader public.

The Parisian Chat Noir club gave the generic term *cabaret artistique* to programmes put on in cafés and pubs. It was founded on 18 November 1881 by the painter Rudolphe Salis, who called it a cabaret because the songs and sketches were set forth like courses on a menu. His Montmartre premises housed not only Friday night poetry readings but elaborate shadow plays, scripted, designed and musically accompanied by leading artists. When the Chat Noir moved to elegant new premises in 1885, the old building was taken over by ARISTIDE BRUANT's Le Mirliton, one of the numerous Montmartre cabarets it inspired. The intimate milieu allowed performers like YVETTE GUILBERT to develop a subtle new manner of delivery and to treat 'naturalistic' subjects.

In Germany, the first true cabaret was the Bunte Bühne (Motley Stage), created by Baron Ernst von Wolzogen and Otto Julius Bierbaum in 1901 to offer a superior form of VARIETY show. The same year saw the founding of Berlin's Schall und Rauch (Noise and Smoke) by the young MAX REINHARDT and actors of the DEUTSCHES THEATER; and of Munich's Elf Scharfrichter (Eleven Executioners), where FRANK WEDEKIND sang his own macabre ditties to guitar accompaniment. These artistic cabarets mixed ballads, art songs, one-act plays, dance, puppet drama and instrumental music in a programme held together by a master of ceremonies. The primary aim was to amuse and to air new fashions in literature.

In Russia the gatherings were more theatrical. Letuchaya Mysh (the Bat) was developed by NIKITA BALIEV from the hilarious 'cabbage parties' held by the MOSCOW ART THEATRE, and rapidly turned into a miniature theatre presenting plays and tableaux based on classic Russian literature and folk art. As the Chauve-Souris it became world-famous after the Revolution. Krivoe Zerkalo (the Crooked Mirror), founded in St Petersburg in 1908, was, under the directorship of NIKOLAI EVREINOV, a house excelling in PARODY and experimental forms such as monodrama.

After World War I, German cabarets grew more political, breeding-grounds for dissent, particularly in Berlin. Kurt Tucholsky coined the term *Kabarett* to describe the newly engaged cabaret, with an ensemble company and a programme founded on a given theme (in German, *Cabaret* suggests a less structured series of solo numbers). They included the anti-Fascist Katakombe (Catacombs, 1929) of WERNER FINCK. Although these cabarets did not always pack the political punch they promised, by 1935 the Nazis had banned cabaret. Some performers, like Finck, were sent to concentration camps.

In the English-speaking world, cabaret was equated with nightclubs until the 1960s, when Chicago's Second City emphasized improvisation and devised sketches before the audience's eyes. It spawned a shoal of imitations, such as San Francisco's the Premise and Boston's the Proposition, manned by university graduates. Following the highly successful run of the REVUE *Beyond the Fringe*, the Establishment (1961), an after-hours club in London, tried to maintain the atmosphere of irreverence.

Recent developments include comedy clubs where untried performers air their material before uncritical audiences at little cost to the management. The haphazard nature of the enterprise is a far cry from the programmatic intentions of the artistic cabaret. More in line with the avant-garde tradition has been the short-lived New Wave Vaudeville, a lunatic musical assemblage deriving from punk rock.

*Cabaret*, a musical by Kander and Ebb (1966), popularized a somewhat distorted picture of the form in Weimar Germany. Jeremy Lawrence's revue *Cabaret Verboten* (1991) used actual material of the period, and played at the MARK TAPER FORUM, Los Angeles, and the CSC Rep, New York City.

**Cabrujas, José Ignacio** 1937– Venezuelan playwright and director. One-third of the Venezuelan 'Holy Trinity' (with CHALBAUD and CHOCRÓN), Cabrujas was a founding member of the Teatro Arte de Caracas (Art Theatre of Caracas) in 1961 and joined the NUEVO GRUPO (New Group) in 1967. A committed writer, he has composed for the New Group such plays as *Profundo* (Deep, 1970), *Acto cultural* (Cultural Act, 1976) and *El día que me quieras* (The Day You Love Me, 1979), the latter an enormously popular play that intermixes Argentine tangos with the Marxist movement of the 1930s. He also acts and directs, and since the early 60s has written and adapted for film as well. Other plays include *Los insurgentes* (The Insurgents, 1961), *El extraño viaje de Simón el malo* (The Strange Voyage of Simon the Evil, 1962) and *Fiésole* (1967).

**café chantant, café concert** French VARIETY entertainment. This leading 19th-century *divertissement* began with the musical taverns – known as *musicos*, from the Dutch – that sprang up along the Parisian boulevards in the 1770s; their growth was fostered during the Revolution by a licensing decree of the National Assembly, and they became highly popular. When theatrical freedom was suppressed under the First Empire, these *cafés* were supplanted by open-air summer theatres along the Champs-Élysées; they spread rapidly and by 1850 there were some 200 in Paris alone. However, by law, their actors had the status of fairground performers, were not allowed to perform in stage costume (until 1867), and had to pass the hat personally once or twice a night.

The *cafés chantants* multiplied under the Second Empire, but when the Boulevard du Temple and its cheap theatres were torn down, they were replaced by *cafés concerts*, long rooms with a high stage, where popular performances combined with smoking and drinking were accessible to small budgets. The *caf conc'*, as it was known, specialized in romantic ballads, erotic innuendo and *scies* (catchy, nonsensical choruses). Between 1870 and 1914 there were as many *caf conc's* in Paris as there are now cinemas. The most important were the Eldorado and the Alcazar, which showcased the talents of THÉRÉSA, JUDIC, PAULUS, POLIN, Dranem and MAYOL, among others. The types of performers included the 'comic trooper', the 'dude' or *gommeux*, the 'naturalistic' singer of urban low life, and the sentimental balladeer.

A decree of 1864 allowed some of these houses to become *cafés spectacles*, blending songs with farces and operettas, and by the turn of the century the largest had taken on the English name of 'MUSIC-HALLS'. The first was Joseph Oller's Olympia (1893), which launched MISTINGUETT and introduced American jazz. The music-hall, which dominated the scene by the end of World War I, banned smoking and drinking from the auditorium; it still offered a central role to song, but this became increasingly a recital by a single performer – e.g. Georgius, Fréhel and, later, PIAF.

**Caffe Cino** (New York City) American theatre. Caffe Cino is the prototype theatre of the OFF-OFF BROADWAY movement. Joseph Cino, a former dancer, opened his coffeehouse at 31 Cornelia Street in Greenwich Village in December 1958. Poetry recitals and songs were followed by plays, the first being a condensed version of OSCAR WILDE's *The Importance of Being Earnest*. A new generation of dramatists whose sensibilities were at odds with the commercial mainstream soon made the Cino's 8ft square stage their home, paying the expenses of their brief runs by passing the hat. Robert Patrick, Paul Foster, Tom Eyen, LANFORD WILSON, Robert Heide, MARIA IRENE FORNÉS, William M. Hoffman, Megan Terry, Leonard Melfi, Jeff Weiss, JOHN GUARE and JEAN-CLAUDE VAN ITALLIE were among the regulars whose plays Joe Cino introduced. While Cino imposed no artistic criteria, the quintessential Caffe Cino playwright was H. M. Koutoukas, whose plays had a tacky, high-camp glamour suited to an atmosphere described as a cross between 'Lourdes and Sodom'. The Cino burned down on Ash Wednesday, 1965, and was to reopen only briefly.

**Caigniez, L. C.** 1762–1842 French playwright. He excelled in MELODRAMA. His first play, *La Forêt enchantée* (*The Enchanted Forest*), a fairy extravaganza, was performed at the Gaîté in 1799. In 1802 his *Le Jugement de Salomon* (*The Judgement of Solomon*) ran for over 300 performances at the Ambigu (see BOULEVARD). He followed it with *Le Triomphe de David* (*The Triumph of King David*, 1805) and *La Forêt d'Hermanstadt, ou La Fausse Épouse* (*The Forest of Hermanstadt, or The False Wife*), set in a brigand-ridden Bulgaria. *L'Illustre Aveugle* (*The Illustrious Blind Man*, 1806), exploiting the dramatic device of switched identity, showed him at the height of his powers. He is best known for *La Pie voleuse, ou La Servante de Palaiseau* (*The Thieving Magpie, or The Servant of Palaiseau*, Porte-Saint-Martin, 1815), which provided the plot of Rossini's opera.

**Calderón, Fernando** 1809–45 Mexican playwright. His romantic dramas portrayed a desire to escape temporal and spatial boundaries in search of chivalrous themes of the European Middle Ages. His only play with a Mexican setting is *A ninguna de las tres* (*None of the Three*, 1839), a satiric comedy written as a reply to Bretón de los Herreros's *Marcela, o a cuál de las tres?* (*Marcela, or Which of the Three?*, 1831).

**Calderón de la Barca, Pedro** 1600–81 Spanish playwright. He ranks with LOPE DE VEGA as the greatest of Spain's Golden Age dramatists. Born in Madrid and educated in a Jesuit school, he rejected the priesthood to

become a gentleman poet and playwright. His first successful play dates from 1623, and after a period of military service in Flanders he devoted himself to the theatre. By 1629 his reputation was made with the martyr-play *El príncipe constante* (*The Constant Prince*) and two cloak-and-sword plays (where love usually triumphs over quarrels and secrecy), *La dama duende* (*The Phantom Lady*) and *Casa con dos puertas* (*The House with Two Doors*). The period 1629–40 showed him at the height of his creative powers, writing comedies, tragedies of the classical and honour-play type, historical plays and AUTOS SACRAMENTALES, first for the CORRALES and later for the court. He eventually became a priest in 1651, but continued playwriting until his death.

Calderón's output was prolific, with more than 110 COMEDIAS, 70 *autos sacramentales* and other works. The serious and religious side of his work and character have been emphasized, though half his plays are basically comic. He owed more to SENECA than to ARISTOTLE and rarely observed the classical unities. He combined a three-act form with a high-flown rhetorical style.

The essence of his drama is a mental and spiritual struggle between conflicting demands, especially those of love, honour, and religion. There are three controversial 'honour-tragedies' – *El médico de su honra* (*Physician to his Own Honour*, 1635), *A secreto agravio secreta venganza* (*Secret Vengeance for Secret Insult*, 1636) and *El pintor de su deshonra* (*Painter of his Own Dishonour*, 1648?). In each play a husband murders his wife because he suspects her of adultery (though in two of them she is patently innocent), and yet in each case the husband is vindicated by the king. Possibly Calderón was more interested in the tragic situation of the eternal triangle than in judging the characters involved.

The more realistic play *El alcalde de Zalamea* (*The Mayor of Zalamea*, 1642?) develops the themes of Lope de Vega's peasant honour-plays, while other serious and religious plays deal with the conflict between a harsh father and a rebellious son. Amongst these is Calderón's most famous drama, *La vida es sueño* (*Life Is a Dream*, 1635), a profound play on the themes of horoscopes, predestination and free will. Among the works on religious subjects, *El príncipe constante* tells of the heroic martyrdom of a Portuguese prince who refused to surrender Ceuta to the Moors in exchange for his own life, while *El mágico prodigioso* (*The Wonder-Working Magician*, 1637) tells the Faust-like legend of St Cyprian. The *autos sacramentales* became increasingly elaborate in structure and staging; the earlier *El gran teatro del mundo* (*The Great Theatre of the World*, 1645–50) and *La cena del rey Baltasar* (*Belshazzar's Feast*, 1632) are more appreciated by modern critics.

Calderón's plays were much translated and adapted during his lifetime by French and English playwrights, but were largely forgotten outside Spain in the 18th century. The plays had a great influence on German romantics, from GOETHE to WAGNER. In the 20th century performances of Calderón's works are rare outside Spain.

**Caldwell, James H.** 1793–1863 British-born American actor-manager. Caldwell pioneered the theatre in the Mississippi valley, having moved from Manchester to the United States in 1816. In 1824 he opened the Camp Street Theatre, the first English-language house in New Orleans and the first US theatre illuminated by gas. Caldwell built theatres for his companies in the Mississippi and Ohio river valleys. His success was such that in 1835 he opened the St Charles Theatre, but in 1837 a financial panic ruined him, in 1842 the St Charles Theatre burned down and in 1843 he retired from the stage.

**Caldwell, Zoë (Ada)** 1934– Australian-born actress and director. She has played in England, making her London debut at the Royal Court in 1960, and in Canada, Australia and the USA. While remaining active in regional theatre, she is best remembered for the award-winning title roles in *The Prime of Miss Jean Brodie* (1968) and *Medea* (1982). Her directing credits include *An Almost Perfect Person* (1977), *The Taming of the Shrew* and *Hamlet* (1985), *Park Your Car in Harvard Yard* (1991) and *Vita and Virginia* (1994). A superb technician with great power on stage, she has avoided being typecast, while leaning toward work in the classics.

**Callow, Simon** 1949– British actor and director. He has worked in a variety of theatrical situations, from the National Theatre (Mozart in Shaffer's *Amadeus*, 1979) to the innovative Joint Stock theatre company. His book *Being an Actor* (1984) offers a lively and important debate on the relationship between the actor and the director in the contemporary British theatre. Callow's actor's instincts merge with his directorial ones. After playing the title role in Goethe's *Faust* in 1988, he directed Willy Russell's *Shirley Valentine* (1988) in the West End and Alan Bennett's *A Question of Attribution* (1988) at the NT, both great successes. In 1991 he directed the musical *Carmen Jones* at the Old Vic and Sharman Macdonald's *Shades* in 1992. Callow has also written a biography of Charles Laughton. *Shooting the Actor* (1992) is a diary of his experiences while making the film *Manifesto*.

**Calmo, Andrea** 1509/10–71 Venetian actor and playwright. He is considered to be the leading literary influence on the *commedia dell'arte*. The son of a gondolier, he made his reputation playing fussy, amorous old men of the Pantalone type. His six comedies spice the intrigues of the *commedia erudita* with regional dialects, horseplay and comic invention. He is said to have retired in 1560 because pastoral and tragedy were dominating the stage.

***căluş*** Romanian dance. A Whitsuntide ritual dance of great semiotic complexity, it is performed by men who during the performance period abstain from sex and keep normal social contact to a minimum. It has a strong magical element, involving trance and the healing of people possessed by spirits. In one form the dances alternate with short comic plays, led by a paradoxical phallic clown, the 'mute' (he is not silent), on subjects such as money, sex and fighting.

**Camargo, Joracy** 1898–1973 Brazilian playwright; a precursor of the reformation of the Brazilian theatre. His career began with the revue, later shifting to the serious play. A major contribution was *Deus Lhe Pague* (*May God Pay You*, 1932), a play generally considered to mark the beginning of the social theatre in Brazil, with its examination of bourgeois values under the microscope of Marx and leftist ideology during the heady years of the 1930s.

**Campbell, Bartley** 1843–88 American playwright. The first of his 35 plays was *Through Fire* (1871). From 1876 until his mental breakdown in 1885 he was America's most popular melodramatist. His greatest success was the mining camp melodrama, *My Partner* (1879). Campbell's other outstanding plays were *The Galley Slave* (1879) and *The White Slave* (1881).

**Campbell, Ken** 1941– British actor, director, clown and playwright. As the leader of the anarchic fringe touring group, Ken Campbell's Roadshow, which featured such unlikely acts as the World 'Ferret down Trousers' Competition, Campbell became a popular entertainer around the fringe circuit during the 1960s. As a writer and director he has a particular fascination for strange and wonderful tales, including science fiction. *The Great Caper* (1974) speculated about time warps, while in 1976 he adapted with Chris Langham the science fiction novel, *Illuminatus*, for the stage, which ran for seven hours and transferred from Liverpool to open the Cottesloe auditorium at the National Theatre in 1977. Its sequel, Neil Oram's *The Warp*, transferred to the Institute of Contemporary Arts in London in 1979. In 1980 Campbell became the artistic director of the Everyman Theatre, Liverpool, for which he adapted and directed Karel Čapek's novel, *The War with the Newts*. His partly improvised monologues, *Recollections of a Furtive Nudist* (1988), have been performed successfully at fringe theatres.

**Campbell, Mrs Patrick** [née Beatrice Stella Tanner] 1865–1940 British actress. She created the title role in Pinero's *The Second Mrs Tanqueray* (1893) at London's St James's, as the superficially urbane but secretly passionate *demi-mondaine*, a character which others tried to re-create for her. She aspired higher: with Johnston Forbes-Robertson, who loved and encouraged her, she played Juliet (1896), Lady Teazle (1896), Ophelia (1897) and Lady Macbeth (1897). She staged the first English production of Maeterlinck's *Pelléas and Mélisande* in 1897, playing Mélisande against John Martin-Harvey's and later Sarah Bernhardt's Pelléas (1904). She acted in Ibsen (Rita in *Little Eyolf* (1896) and the title role in *Hedda Gabler* (1907)), but less successfully. Shaw recognized her comic potential: nearing 50, she created Eliza Doolittle in *Pygmalion* (1914), the last and greatest scandal of her London career.

**Camus, Albert** 1913–60 French novelist, essayist, playwright and director. Camus's plays, which were a significant part of the vigorous revival of French theatre following World War II, no longer seem as innovative as they did in the 1940s and 1950s. His reputation rested largely on *Le Malentendu* (*Cross-Purpose*, 1944) and *Caligula* (1945), in which Gérard Philipe played the title role. But *Les Justes* (*The Just*, 1949) confirmed Camus's tendency to write extended debates rather than true dramatic actions. He successfully directed his own adaptations of works by Faulkner and Dostoevsky in Paris in the 1950s. He once said that the only places he felt really happy were the football field and the theatre.

**Cañas, Alberto** 1920– Costa Rican playwright, director and Minister of Culture. Under his direction, the Costa Rican government launched a major new effort in the 1970s to promote theatre. Cañas is himself author of at least ten plays, including such titles as *El luto robado* (*Stolen Mourning*, 1962); *En agosto hizo dos años* (*Two Years Ago in August*, 1966), about an individual returned from the dead; *La segua* (1971), an untranslatable mythical creature in a play that used the Pirandellian techniques found in his earlier plays; and *Ni mi casa es ya mi casa* (*My House Is No Longer My Home*, 1982), in which he dealt with the socio-economic crises produced by world inflationary and recessionary spirals.

**Cano, Joel** 1966– Cuban playwright. His plays include *Fábula de insomnio* (*Insomniac Fable*) and *Beatlemania*, but his stunning play is *Timeball* (1992), combining music, time, poetry, history and imagery in a postmodern experiment.

**Cantor, Eddie** 1892–1964 American singer and comedian. Born in New York City, Cantor made his legitimate-theatre debut in a London REVUE. His first American appearance was in *Canary Cottage* (1917). FLORENZ ZIEGFELD hired him for his CABARET show, *The Midnight Frolic*, and then featured him in the *Ziegfeld Follies of 1917* (and subsequently *18,19* and *27.*) Like AL JOLSON, he often appeared in blackface, a vestige of the American MINSTREL SHOW. During his musical numbers he would skip across the stage and clap his hands while smirking his way through suggestive lyrics. He also appeared in *Whoopee* (1928) and *Banjo Eyes* (1941) in addition to film, radio and television shows.

**Cao Yu** [Wan Jiabao] 1910– Chinese playwright. In 1934 he published his play *Thunderstorm* (*Leiyu*), a dark commentary on the Chinese family system and the social degradation it caused, which was nationally toured and received instant acclaim. He followed this with five other plays written within the next six years. Two, *Sunrise* (*Dichu*) and *Wilderness* (*Yuanye*), are usually linked with *Thunderstorm* as a trilogy constituting his major achievement. Their common theme is the decadence of pre-war Chinese society. Cao Yu held a number of cultural and administrative posts in the early 1950s, but came under fire for his bourgeois thinking. He remained creatively inactive until 1956, when his new play *Bright Skies* (*Minglang de tian*) was staged at the Beijing People's Art Theatre. The play was undistinguished in both content and production, while being heavily propagandist. Cao Yu became a Communist Party member in 1957 when there was a drive to recruit older intellectuals. In 1966 he was seized from his home at night and sent to a reform school in the country. He was rehabilitated like his fellow intellectuals after 1976, and today, with state support, is recognized as a father figure of the modern theatre. He has reverted to historical themes, the never failing resource of Chinese dramatists. His play *The Gall and the Sword* (*Dan jian pian*, published 1961) describes the wars between the two ancient kingdoms of Wu and Yue in the 5th century BC; its eulogizing of 'the people' carries a clear ideological implication. His early plays have been revived, and in 1979 his master trilogy was staged to an enthusiastic reception.

*capa y espada, comedia de* see COMEDIA

**Čapek, Karel** 1890–1938 Czech playwright and novelist. A philosophical, ironic humanist, deeply committed to the democratic ideals of his nation, he achieved world recognition for several plays, especially *RUR* (1921), *The Insect Comedy* (written with his brother Josef in 1922), and *The Makropolus Affair* (1922), which became the libretto for Janáček's opera. These theatrically effective works display a fanciful, witty yet compassionate vision of humanity coping with its own weaknesses amid the stresses of a high-technology age. They were followed by the equally powerful *The White Disease* (1937), a disturbing parable of the seemingly inevitable devastation triggered by power-hungry dictators, and *The Mother* (1938).

**Capon, William** 1757–1827 English scene designer and architect. Working for JOHN PHILIP KEMBLE at DRURY LANE (1794–1809), he impressed the critics with his design of a Gothic-style chapel for Handel's *Oratorio*, performed for the opening of the reconstructed theatre (1794), and his six Gothic chamber wings designed for *Macbeth* that same year. During his tenure at Drury Lane

his most impressive designs were for Kemble's melodramas: the Gothic library and ancient baronial hall for *The Iron Chest* (1796), a chapel with side aisles and choir for *De Montfort* (1800), and a Gothic castle for *Adelmorn, the Outlaw* (1801). He moved with Kemble to COVENT GARDEN in 1809, where his designs included an Anglo-Norman hall for *Hamlet* (1812). An antiquarian, he insisted upon accurate representations of the external construction materials and architectural features of the existing historical buildings upon which he modelled his designs.

**Capuana, Luigi** 1839–1915 Italian novelist and playwright. A prolific writer, he began as a poet, and throughout his life produced a substantial body of journalistic writings and literary and theatrical criticism. The influence of SYMBOLISM is apparent and he is above all identified with the development of Italian VERISMO. Of his many plays the most enduring are his drama of peasant life, *Malia* (*The Spell*, 1895), and his study of the Sicilian petty bourgeoisie, *Lu Cavalieri Pidagna* (1909).

**Caragiale, Ion Luca** 1852–1912 Romanian playwright. His comedies are masterpieces of meticulous craftsmanship. Associated with the conservative literary circle Junimea, he lashed out violently at the Romanian society of his time. His sarcastic wit found its most celebrated expression in *A Lost Letter* (1884), the zenith of Romanian playwriting, dealing with a corrupt provincial electoral campaign won unexpectedly by a blackmailer, the basest and most empty-headed of all the candidates. His other comedy, *A Stormy Night* (1879), portrays the moral hypocrisy of the middle class, while the FARCE *Carnival Scenes* (1885), whose action takes place in a barber's shop, draws a ludicrous picture of the lower strata of urban society. Caragiale's scant dramatic output also includes the one-act farce *Mr Leonida Facing Reaction* (1880), in which a senile blockhead takes street revellers for revolutionaries; and the less successful psychological drama, *The Bane* (1890). His colourful and often nonsensical language loses much in translation. Romanian productions still invariably present these plays as period pieces, narrowing the universality of the playwright's vision. Caragiale also wrote humorous short stories, many later performed as dramatic sketches.

**Carballido, Emilio** 1925– Mexican playwright and director. He has fomented theatre in Mexico since 1948. Founder of the theatre journal *Tramoya* (1975), he has taught and promoted an entire generation of young playwrights in Mexico, where he is the premier playwright, both in quantity and quality. Drawing on both the realistic and the fantastic, he has written more than 75 plays, several novels and cinema scripts. *Rosalba y los Llaveros* (*Rosalba and the Llavero Family*, 1950), is a psychological play that contrasts the moral codes of metropolis and province; *La hebra de oro* (*The Golden Thread*, 1955) integrates the fantastic into a provincial setting with existential intentions. *Yo también hablo de la rosa* (*I Too Speak of the Rose*, 1965) dramatizes the complexities of human experience and the process of creativity through a metaphorical rose. Later titles include *Fotografía en la playa* (*Photo on the Beach*, 1977), *Mimí y Fifí en el Río Orinoco* (*Mimí and Fifí on the Orinoco River*, 1982), *Tiempo de ladrones: La historia de Chucho el Roto* (*Time of Thieves: The Story of Chucho el Roto*, 1984) and *Una rosa de dos aromas* (*A Rose with Two Scents*, 1986). The distinctive notes in his theatre are the authentic language and an irrepressible humour.

**Carey, Henry** [Benjamin Bounce] 1687–1743 English

playwright. He wrote songs for GAY's *The Beggar's Opera* (1727) and COLLEY CIBBER's *The Provoked Husband* (1728), librettos for operas like *Amelia* (1731) and a farcical afterpiece, *The Contrivances* (1715). In 1734 his brilliant PARODY of the bombast of contemporary tragedy, *Chrononhotonthologos*, was performed under the pseudonym Benjamin Bounce. In the wake of *The Beggar's Opera*, Carey attacked the excesses of Italian opera in England with his popular opera *The Dragonfly of Wantley* (1737) at COVENT GARDEN. Its sequel, *The Dragoness* (1738), was less successful. Carey committed suicide five years later.

**Carle, Richard** 1871–1941 American comedian, librettist and lyricist. Carle became a popular comedian and singer in such shows as *A Mad Bargain* (1893), *Excelsior, Jr* (1895) and *Yankee Doodle Dandy* (1898). His comic persona was that of a shrewd, worldly prankster rather than a butt or simpleton. He wrote the scripts and lyrics for many of his own shows. His last appearance was in *The New Yorkers* (1930).

**carnival** (See also TRINIDAD CARNIVAL.) Pre-Lenten festival. The features of this Christian, and especially Roman Catholic, festival vary according to both culture and climate, and can be found in May Games, the Feast of St Bartholomew (25 August), the Jamaican Christmas masquerade of *JONKONNU*, the Feast of Fools (28 December, Holy Innocents) and, outside Christianity, the Jewish PURIM PLAY. The word is known from the 11th century. Its Latin root signifies the 'removal' of flesh; Italian popular etymology gives us the metaphorically more graphic 'farewell' to flesh – the meat about to be forsworn for the Lenten fast.

The wild indulgence of carnival, though set immediately in opposition to the austerity of Lent, forms the mediating term in a shift from the *alegría* of Christmas to the *tristeza* of Ash Wednesday to Easter Sunday, so that a secular celebration of carnality stands between the year's two key spiritual occasions, looking back to one and forward to the other.

In its activities, its visual imagery and its verbal expressions, carnival is a bewildering set of variations on the theme of oppositions and their inversion or dissolution, which together create a COCKAIGNE-like universe. LIVING PICTURES are processed through the street, illustrating versions of the world turned upside down: the judge sentenced by the accused, the horseman riding backwards, the husband spinning while his wife ploughs. Distinctions between rich and poor, high status and low, are dissolved in the promiscuous mingling of the crowd in the public square, or disguised behind masks and costumes. Men and women cross-dress, and the normal rules of sexual deference are relaxed or abandoned. Informal abuse and obscenity are the order of the day, together with the bawdy or satirical song. Competitive games may be organized, but even then they are virtually rule-free and extremely robust (like the Shrove Tuesday football at Ashbourne, Derbyshire, England), or tend to deny their own rules, by ensuring that the fattest and slowest man wins the foot race. Informal associations of young men process, they mount shows, or simply roam the streets – the SCHEMBARTLÄUFER of Nuremberg, the Compagnie de la Mère Folle at Dijon, the Venetian Compagnia della Calza. Such loosely constituted associations at once express the egalitarian ideal of carnival, and parody the guilds, societies and orders of the everyday, hierarchically organized world. Above all, people eat and drink as if there is no tomorrow.

A carnival is not primarily a spectator sport, and has no need of the sequential patterning which audiences require. Nevertheless, its activities cover a spectrum from wholly informal socializing and milling about, through the relatively formal processions of floats and perambulations of societies, to the wholly proto-dramatic or dramatic performance. Some of these derive directly from the parodic thesis of carnival – mock marriages, trials, burials (such as the burial of the sardine in Madrid depicted by Goya), jousts between Carnival and Lent (Brueghel). Others extrapolate the ambiance of carnival into fully developed little farces, such as the *FASTNACHTSPIELE* of southern Germany. From plays such as these derive stock comic characters such as the German HANSWURST, and possibly the English Pickleherring.

In a sense carnival is a ritual of revolt, and sometimes this has specific political connotations. But to equate its dialectic between official and popular culture with class struggle in a general sense is too simple, for patricians as well as plebeians are involved as both organizers and participants, and share its symbolic vocabulary. For the most part, masters and servants alike seem willing to accept the collective hangover that follows the collective binge. Carnivals have led to riot and repression; they have never led directly to social revolution. Their indirect influence in posing questions of the relationship between the spiritual and the carnal, authority and equality, order and licence, and in offering an image of what the world might be like if it were turned upside down, remains a matter of speculation.

**Carnovsky, Morris** 1897–1992 American actor. Having begun his long career with the THEATRE GUILD in the 1920s, he left in 1931 to join the GROUP THEATRE. Among his performances with the Group were those in CLIFFORD ODETS's *Awake and Sing!* (1935), *Paradise Lost* (1935), *Golden Boy* (1937), *Rocket to the Moon* (1938) and *Night Music* (1940). With his mobile face, leonine profile and commanding voice, he played characters much older than himself. Like other Group members Carnovsky developed his own version of the Method; he disagreed with LEE STRASBERG's emphasis on the actor's own emotions and, in a series of acclaimed Shakespearian interpretations beginning in the 50s, achieved a fusion of the Method's psychological REALISM with the demands of poetic style. For the AMERICAN SHAKESPEARE THEATRE he performed Lear, Falstaff, Prospero and Shylock. Teaching and performing even in his 80s, he was a lifelong student of the art of acting.

**Carrillo, Hugo** 1928–94 Guatemalan playwright and director. He directed the National Theatre Company until 1968; after 1972 he was artistic director of the independent Theatre Club. His major works include *El corazón del espantapájaros* (*The Scarecrow's Heart*, 1962), *La herencia de la Tula* (*Tula's Inheritance*, 1964) and *Mortaja, sueño y autopsia para un teléfono* (*Shroud, Dream and Autopsy for a Telephone*), three one-act plays (1972); and *El señor Presidente* (*Mr President*, 1974), from the novel by Miguel Ángel Asturias. His plays are widely translated.

**Carroll, Paul Vincent** 1900–68 Irish playwright. The co-founder of Glasgow's CITIZENS' THEATRE, Carroll emigrated from Ireland aged 21 and taught in Glasgow until 1937, when his plays gave him financial independence. His early works satirize the clerical authoritarianism of his youthful experience. In 1932 the ABBEY presented *Things That Are Caesar's*, in which a woman escapes from an odious marriage engineered with the approval of the local priest. *Shadow and Substance* (1937), acclaimed in Dublin and New York, is a study of Canon Skerritt, whose cold erudition disables his care of souls. In *The White Steed* (1939), Father Shaughnessy is a ruthless puritan vigilante, credibly sinister in the Europe of 1939. Apart from two lightly satiric comedies, *The Devil Came from Dublin* and *The Wayward Saint* (1955), Carroll's later work is heavily didactic.

**Cartel** French theatre association. It was formed in France in 1927 by DULLIN, JOUVET, GEORGES PITOËFF and BATY, originally to give mutual support in the face of hostile or frivolous drama critics. Each director was to publicize the productions of the other three and encourage the audiences to see theatre as an art rather than as mere entertainment.

**Carter, Mrs Leslie** 1862–1937 American actress. Under DAVID BELASCO, her tutor and director, she became a star performer in lurid dramas. After a three-year run in *The Heart of Maryland* (1895) in which she swung on the clapper of a bell to keep it from ringing, she appeared in *Zaza* (1899), *DuBarry* (1901) and *Adrea* (1905). According to one critic, Mrs Carter would 'weep, vociferate, shriek, rant, become hoarse with passion, and finally flop and beat the floor'.

**Cartwright, Jim** 1958– British playwright. His first play, *Road* (ROYAL COURT, 1986), was a study of the unemployed in Lancashire in a sequence of short scenes with a lyrical commentary. The set for *Bed* (1989) consists of a giant bed in which seven elderly people are sleeping, their thoughts and dreams providing the action. *To* (1990) is a collection of sketches of working-class life. Cartwright's comedy, *The Rise and Fall of Little Voice* (1992), was staged at the NATIONAL THEATRE.

**Casarès, Maria** 1922– French actress. Of Spanish origin, she performed in *Cross-Purpose* and *The Just* by CAMUS and in COCTEAU's film *Orphée*, and was a permanent member of the THÉÂTRE NATIONAL POPULAIRE company during 1954–9. She has established a reputation as the outstanding French tragic actress, despite her violent style. Major performances include the Mother in *The Screens* (1966 and 1983), Medea in Lavelli's 1967 production and SHAKESPEARE's Cleopatra in 1975.

**Casino Theatre** (New York City) Designed in a Moorish style complete with turret, from 1882 to 1930 it presented musical shows of all varieties. In 1890 Rudolf Aronson opened New York's first roof garden theatre above the Casino, where light musical fare was served up with light after-theatre refreshments. The house is best remembered for *Florodora* (1900), one of the most popular musical comedies of its day. It was torn down in 1930.

**Casona, Alejandro** [Alejandro Rodríguez Álvarez] 1903–65 Spanish poet and playwright. He was director of the Teatro del Pueblo (People's Theatre), sponsored by the Republican government, in 1931–6, and in 1934 his comedy *La sirena varada* (*The Siren Castaway*) brought success and the Lope de Vega Prize. In 1937 he went into exile, and *Nuestra Natacha* (1936), on the need for educational reform, caused the Franco regime to ban his works. In exile he wrote *Prohibido suicidarse en primavera* (*No Suicide in Spring*, 1937), *La dama del alba* (*The Lady of the Dawn*, 1944) and *Los árboles mueren de pie* (*Trees Die Standing*, 1949). His plays, strongly poetic, contrast the escape into fantasy with the need to face up to unpleasant realities.

**Cassidy, Claudia** 1905– American drama critic. Cassidy began her career writing on drama and music for the *Chicago Journal of Commerce* in 1925, quickly gaining a reputation for being tough but fair. She was later hired by the *Tribune*, where, until her retirement in 1965, she wrote a daily column, 'On the Aisle', and toured Europe in the summers reporting on 'Europe on the Aisle'. Considered the most powerful Chicago critic, Cassidy was credited with stopping New York producers from putting weak companies on the road. Her major credo was that the 'only way to judge a play is to wait and see if the theatre brings it to life'.

**Casson, Lewis** 1875–1969 British actor and director. From 1904 to 1907 he was a regular player at the ROYAL COURT THEATRE during the historic VEDRENNE–BARKER seasons, and Granville Barker's influence – on his directing and commitment to the repertory movement – was life-long. In 1908 he joined ANNIE HORNIMAN's company in Manchester and was its director from 1911 to 1914. After the war he continued to mix acting with directing, and with his wife SYBIL THORNDIKE frequently toured abroad. During World War II he became a leading force in CEMA, directing and playing in *Macbeth* for the first tour of the Welsh coalfields in 1940. Knighted in 1945, he is remembered for his clear and subtly expressive stage speech, his catholicity of taste and his concern to extend the reach of the theatre.

**Castellanos, Rosario** 1925–74 Mexican novelist, poet and playwright. He wrote one play, *Eterno femenino* (*Eternal Feminine*, 1975), increasingly recognized for its statement of feminist values.

**Castelvetro, Lodovico** 1505–71 Italian playwright and theorist; perhaps the most influential of the many Renaissance translators and interpreters of ARISTOTLE. Castelvetro's liberal understanding of the dramatic unities, decorum and characterization as expounded in his *La poetica di Aristotele vulgarizata et sposta* (*Aristotle's Poetics Translated into the Vernacular and Explicated*, Vienna, 1950) generated intense critical debate on the degree of freedom that might reasonably be enjoyed by modern writers in adapting classical rules to contemporary needs and practice.

**Castro y Bellvís, Guillém de** 1569–1631 Spanish playwright. The most important exponent of the Valencian school, he later wrote from Madrid. His novelesque plays set in Central Europe are probably his earliest, and he later borrowed plots from CERVANTES (including *Don Quijote*) and from Spanish ballads, as well as writing comic plays of his own invention. He published two volumes of plays, in 1621 and 1625. His most famous work is the two-part *Las mocedades del Cid* (*The Young El Cid*), based on ballad versions of the hero's life. The first part was adapted by CORNEILLE as *Le Cid*. His comedies include *El Narciso en su opinión* (*Narcissus in His Own Eyes*) and the unbridled comedy of adultery *Los mal casados de Valencia* (*Unhappy Marriages in Valencia*).

***cavittu natakam*** Indian theatre form. In the mid-16th century, a type of theatre emerged in south India to satisfy the cravings of the Christian communities for an entertainment centred on Christian subject-matter. This was the *cavittu natakam* of Kerala state, inspired by the zeal of Roman Catholic priests who proselytized in the area under the Portuguese establishment, which had recently consolidated its power along the eastern seaboard of the Indian subcontinent.

Quasi-historical and mythological characters of Christian history and epic romance filled the stage – figures like Charlemagne, St George and St Sebastian, who are the equivalent of the great archetypal heroes of the

Hindu myths and legends such as Rama, Krishna and Arjuna. *The Play of Charlemagne* is the most famous and frequently performed: it is a rambling work requiring 15 nights to complete, and includes a cast of nearly 80 characters. The play is based on Ariosto's *Orlando Furioso* and deals with the heroic adventures of the 8th-century French emperor and his 12 valiant peers. Replete with battles and court scenes, it is the quintessential *cavittu natakam*. Other works present Old and New Testament figures, lives of the saints, and contemporary plays with social and historical significance. The dominant sentiments of this form of theatre are heroism (*vira*) and love (*srngara*).

*Cavittu* means 'step' or 'stomping' and *natakam* refers to a play or drama. The performances require a great deal of masculine dance movement in which the actors, who are all male, stamp their feet vigorously on the stage. The battle scenes loosely incorporate the martial art techniques of the region (*kalarippayatt*), adapted to suit the dramatic demands. The style of movement contrasts markedly with that of the Hindu forms of theatre popular in the region, such as KATHAKALI, KRISHNATTAM and KUTIYATTAM. The stage is unique. Located in open ground, it may be 30 feet wide and 100 feet long. Flanking each end are tall wooden platforms that must be scaled from the stage by ladders. The kings hold court on the high platforms, while the action scenes and battles take place centre stage.

*Cavittu natakam* is still performed in the Cochin and Quilon districts of central Kerala where the Latin Christians have made their home. The season lasts from December until the end of March, coinciding with the major church festivals.

**Cawthorn, Joseph** 1868–1949 American comedian. As a child, Cawthorn performed in MINSTREL SHOWS and in English MUSIC-HALLS. Returning to America, he appeared in comic operas as a 'Dutch comic', speaking fractured English with a German accent. After early successes in such musicals as *Excelsior, Jr* (1895) and *Miss Philadelphia* (1897), he played leading roles in *The Fortune Teller* (1898), *Mother Goose* (1903), *The Free Lance* (1906), *Little Nemo* (1908), *The Slim Princess* (1911) and many others.

**Céleste, Madame (Céline)** [Céleste Keppler] 1810/11–82 French dancer. Most of her career belongs to the English theatre, where she made her debut in 1830, though she was to make lucrative and popular American tours. She solicited pieces that would allow her to remain speechless or would accommodate her French accent. The first was PLANCHÉ's *The Child of the Wreck* (1837) at DRURY LANE. In 1838 she moved to the HAYMARKET. In 1844, with BENJAMIN WEBSTER, she became lessee of the ADELPHI: the part of the noble American Indian, Miami, in BUCKSTONE's *The Green Bushes* (1845) remained a favourite role. Later she became lessee of the LYCEUM (1860–1), opening as Madame Defarge in TOM TAYLOR's version of *A Tale of Two Cities*.

**CEMA** (Council for the Encouragement of Music and the Arts) British arts organization. Formed in 1940 to provide entertainment for wartime factory and evacuation areas, CEMA was responsible for transferring the bombed-out OLD VIC Company to Burnley (1941) and sponsoring tours by the Pilgrim Players and ASHLEY DUKES's Mercury Players. It took over the Bristol Theatre Royal in 1943, and through JAMES BRIDIE founded the Glasgow CITIZENS' THEATRE. In 1946 it was transformed into the ARTS COUNCIL OF GREAT BRITAIN.

**censorship** Endemic to most present-day hard-line regimes of both the right and the left, censorship of the theatre currently extends over much of Central and South America, large areas of Africa, the Middle East and parts of Asia, but since 1989–90 it has retreated from Eastern Europe. While pre-publication censorship of literature in Western Europe has been in most cases long abandoned (e.g. in Britain since 1695), censorship in the theatre survived even in several major Western democracies into the 20th century. Historically, it has been equally useful to Church and state. Fundamentally a political act, it seeks to sedate or suppress those elements in the drama which in the view of the authority that exercises it are contrary to its interests or values. A tame theatre is an ally of the state machine, an unruly one potentially its bitterest enemy and critic.

Where formal censorship no longer exists (e.g. Britain) or has never properly existed (e.g. North America), recourse to the law, though exceptional, is still open to individuals or groups who object to a play on grounds of profanity or offence to general morality. Although censorship does not have to be institutionalized to be effective, this discussion is principally concerned with pre-production censorship, which consciously aims to control the intellectual and artistic freedom of the playwright.

**Europe c.1400–1900**
The roots of modern European censorship lie within the medieval theatre. In England the Catholic Church exercised considerable control over the content of the mystery cycles – e.g. removing plays devoted to the life of the Virgin Mary from the York and Chester cycles. In France as early as 1402 Charles VI tried to assert the authority of the court over the presentation of religious drama by granting the CONFRÉRIE DE LA PASSION the right to stage *mystères* on condition that his own officials kept a critical eye on the performances.

Religious drama, disinherited by the Church and vexatious to the state, came under growing threat during the 16th century, especially in England and France. The French Parlement withdrew the privilege of the Confrérie de la Passion in 1548 and thereby banned the performance of all MYSTERY PLAYS. In England, government regulation of the drama, beginning on a restricted scale in 1543, was a vital instrument of Tudor statecraft. By 1581 Elizabeth had managed to achieve a complete prohibition of the mystery cycles, followed by a ban (lasting for over 300 years) on any kind of scriptural or biblical drama.

The key to effective censorship was already centralized control. In many parts of Western Europe (e.g. Germany and Italy) the fragmented political situation made that impossible, whereas by 1581 in Elizabethan England the MASTER OF THE REVELS had a royal patent 'to order and reform, authorise and put down' any play considered prejudicial to the state. By the time SHAKESPEARE came to London, an effective system of censorship was operating. The Master of the Revels was principal arbiter of the drama until well into the 17th century, interrupted only by the Puritans' closure of the theatres from 1642 to 1660. Plays were subjected to close official scrutiny before licensing. The text of *Sir Thomas More* (c.1594) – of which Shakespeare was probable part-author – bears the instruction: 'leave out ye insurrection and the cause'; and there is evidence of political censorship in a number of other plays of the period.

Some playwrights even went to prison for performing seditious matter, e.g. BEN JONSON, CHAPMAN and MARSTON, whose *Eastward Ho* (1605) aroused James I's wrath for its irreverent treatment of his Scottish courtiers.

The relative strength of the system of censorship in 17th-century England contrasts with its relative weakness elsewhere, even in France, where in 1641 Louis XIII abolished censorship altogether. Actors could still be punished for indecency, however, and, as MOLIÈRE discovered in the 1660s, the playwright was still not wholly free. *Tartuffe* (1664) aroused such a storm of abuse from both Parlement and the Archbishop of Paris that Louis XIV, though privately sympathetic to Molière, was obliged to ban it until 1669. In March 1701 formal censorship was reintroduced with an order that all new plays be officially scrutinized before performance. During the 18th century dramatic censorship became firmly established, with BEAUMARCHAIS its most illustrious victim.

Britain's system of censorship underwent comprehensive revision in the early 18th century. Sir Robert Walpole's 1737 Stage Licensing Act, hurriedly passed as a result of damaging lampoons on the government by HENRY FIELDING and others, granted the authorities sweeping new powers. The new law centred on the Lord Chamberlain, who was empowered to forbid any dramatic piece acted 'for hire, gain, or reward' anywhere in Great Britain. Modified only in details by the Theatre Regulation Act which replaced it in 1843, Walpole's Act established control of the theatre over the next 231 years (see THEATRICAL MONOPOLY).

Inimical to the spirit of the French Revolution, censorship was abolished by order of the Legislative Assembly, 13–19 January 1791; but by 1794 it was reinstated in an attempt to 'republicanize' the theatre. Theatres were ordered to delete all references to *duc*, *baron*, *marquis*, *comte* and *monsieur*: no playwright was immune, not even Molière and RACINE. The fear of contamination by France's revolutionary spirit induced other countries to exercise sterner vigilance in political censorship than ever before. In the Habsburg Empire the Vienna Order (1794) banned all dangerous political works, and by 1819 Metternich, supported by a spy system, sought to impose a rigid censorship through all the states of the Austrian Empire. In the 1830s and 40s FRANZ GRILLPARZER and JOHANN NESTROY were often at odds with the censor in Vienna. Political censorship was important as a weapon against the increasing use of the drama as a vehicle for the expression of national libertarian sentiment, particularly in France and in the Habsburg empire.

No formal system of censorship existed in Russia until 1804, but the tsars had brought drama into close alliance with the court, making it virtually a department of the state. Over the next 50 years the regulations were tightened. Notable victims of tsarist censorship were PUSHKIN (*Boris Godunov*, 1825, performed 1870), TURGENEV (*A Month in the Country*, 1850, performed 1872), SUKHOVO-KOBYLIN (*The Case*, 1861, performed 1882, and *Tarelkin's Death*, 1869, performed 1900) and LEV TOLSTOI (*The Power of Darkness*, 1886, performed 1895).

But the balance was slowly changing in Europe after about 1850 towards a more persistent concern with moral issues – especially in France, with the supposed immoralities of the plays of, among others, ALEXANDRE

DUMAS *fils*, VICTORIEN SARDOU and ÉMILE AUGIER, and in Britain, where many French imports proved too *risqué* in language and situation. Most notorious was the younger Dumas's *La Dame aux camélias*, first banned in England in 1853 and several times thereafter in a variety of adaptations. The 'advanced drama', heralded by IBSEN, accelerated the new anti-censorship campaign led by WILLIAM ARCHER and BERNARD SHAW. This movement was fuelled in the period 1880–1910 by the suppression in Britain on moral grounds of several European works: Ibsen's *Ghosts*, Tolstoi's *The Power of Darkness*, MAETERLINCK's *Monna Vanna*, and some plays by EUGÈNE BRIEUX. Shaw's *Mrs Warren's Profession*, HARLEY GRANVILLE BARKER's *Waste* and Edward Garnett's *The Breaking Point* were also censored, denying playwrights the opportunity to argue moral and sexual issues on the stage. In Germany censorship was strengthened after 1889: FRANK WEDEKIND's *Spring Awakening* (1891) and *Earth Spirit* (1893) were both banned from public performance until 1906 and 1902 respectively.

One solution was a theatre dedicated to private (i.e. club) performances only, which would escape the attentions of the censor and be freed from strictly commercial concerns. ANDRÉ ANTOINE's Théâtre Libre, founded in Paris in 1887, was the model for similar enterprises in Germany (FREIE BÜHNE, Berlin, 1889) and Britain (Independent Theatre Society, London, 1891). But only in France was the anti-censorship lobby victorious, with the abolition of pre-production censorship for all practical purposes in 1905, though formal abolition was delayed until after World War II. Municipalities nevertheless retained the power of local veto.

## 20th-century Europe

In Britain, censorship slowly fell into line with the public's willingness to accept what before had been considered outrageous, indecent or taboo. The rule on the ineligibility of scriptural drama on the stage was relaxed about 1912, but even as late as 1958 BECKETT's *Endgame* was censored for its references to the non-existence of God (whereas the original 1957 French version had emerged unscathed). Political censorship prohibited Shaw's *Press Cuttings* and *The Shewing Up of Blanco Posnet* in 1909. In the 1930s all references to Hitler and Mussolini were excised from play scripts, though the MUSIC-HALLS, immune from the Lord Chamberlain's jurisdiction, delighted in exploiting just the kind of material which the censors insisted on deleting.

Moral concerns, the main ingredient of British censorship in this century, resulted in temporary prohibitions on some foreign plays (including STRINDBERG's *Miss Julie*, PIRANDELLO's *Six Characters in Search of an Author*, O'NEILL's *Desire Under the Elms*, and Wedekind's *Spring Awakening* and *Earth Spirit*). Anti-censorship campaigners remained strong, and private club performances avoided official interference. Institutions like the STAGE SOCIETY, London's GATE THEATRE, the ARTS THEATRE Club, Cambridge Festival Theatre, JOAN LITTLEWOOD's Theatre Workshop and the English Stage Company at the ROYAL COURT THEATRE all contributed to the eventual abolition of censorship.

After 1956 the Lord Chamberlain was clearly on the defensive, but still had substantial power. Censorship touched dramatists such as JOHN ARDEN, ARNOLD WESKER and particularly JOHN OSBORNE (whose *A Patriot for Me* was restricted to private performance in 1964). In the late 1960s EDWARD BOND was often in trouble with the censor: the Royal Court was prosecuted for not ful-filling the necessary conditions for a private perfor-mance of *Saved* in 1965; *Early Morning* was banned in 1967, and *A Narrow Road to the Deep North* suffered cuts only months before the abolition of censorship. With the ending of censorship under the 1968 Theatres Act, British theatre has exploited its new-found freedom in such productions as *Hair* (1968) and *Oh, Calcutta!* (1969), which both featured full-frontal nudity; but the deluge of immorality predicted by supporters of censorship never really arrived. The only notable private prosecu-tion was in 1982, against Michael Bogdanov's NATIONAL THEATRE production of HOWARD BRENTON's *The Romans in Britain* (1980), which showed a simulated male rape. The case was unsuccessful and ended in confusion.

Outside Britain the pattern of European censorship was mainly political. In Germany during the 1930s and 40s (and in Austria post 1938) it was exceptionally severe. The Nazis prohibited the entire works of authors of whom they disapproved, and manipulated theatrical production and repertoire. The Nazi proscription lists included GEORG KAISER and ARTHUR SCHNITZLER (banned posthumously). BERTOLT BRECHT fled abroad in 1933 at the rise of Hitler, but returned to East Germany, under Marxist censorship, in 1949. Similar proscrip-tions operated in Nazi-occupied countries and in Fascist Italy. Official censorship ceased in West Germany at the end of World War II. Equally repressive and longer-last-ing was censorship in Franco's Spain, where pre-exis-tent Catholic censorship was overlaid with an extreme right-wing political element. After GARCÍA LORCA's mur-der by the Falangists at the start of the Civil War there was a mass exodus of intellectuals and artists, includ-ing FERNANDO ARRABAL (who became a French citizen and henceforward wrote in French). Those who stayed included ALFONSO SASTRE and ANTONIO BUERO VALLEJO, both of whom endured terms of imprisonment under Franco. Most other Spanish drama of any significance was produced abroad until the demise of Franco in 1975, when censorship was relaxed.

Until 1989, East European censorship was naturally dominated by the model of the Soviet Union. Although there was a period of relative freedom for the theatre immediately after the Bolshevik Revolution, from the 1920s the USSR perfected a system of complete state control of literature and the theatre. Soviet drama is a history of slow critical and intellectual emasculation in the name of socialist realism. Glavlit, the state censor-ship office, was established in 1922. By 1934 it was vir-tually a branch of the security police and was empowered to read all plays at least ten days before-hand and have representatives at performances. Glavrepertkom determined all theatre repertoires.

Stalinist censorship was uncompromising and vin-dictive (e.g. in 1936–7 over half the plays earmarked for production at the main theatres were banned). Among the prominent dramatists to suffer in the late 20s and 30s were VLADIMIR MAYAKOVSKY (e.g. *The Bedbug*, 1929, *The Bathhouse*, 1930), MIKHAIL BULGAKOV (e.g. *The Crimson Island*, 1928, *The Cabal of Hypocrites*, 1936), and LEONID LEONOV (*The Snowstorm*, 1939). Some dramatists man-aged to emigrate (e.g. EVGENY ZAMYATIN in 1932). Nearly all the suppressed plays and their authors were subse-quently rehabilitated during the periodic post-Stalin cultural thaws. Some of Bulgakov's work was restricted as late as 1965. In the 1960s several new dissident dramatists emerged – e.g. ANDREI AMALRIK and

Aleksandr Solzhenitsyn, whose play *The Love Girl and the Innocent* (based on first-hand experience in a Stalinist labour camp) was banned after the dress rehearsal in 1962. After the reformist Mikhail Gorbachev came to power, *glasnost* in the arts led to official approval in 1986 of *Sarcophagus* (a play based on personal observation of the aftermath of the Chernobyl nuclear disaster by Vladimir Gubarev, a senior journalist with *Pravda*). Censorship was officially abolished in Russia in August 1990.

All Soviet satellites operated systems of state censor-ship based on the parent model, with varying degrees of repressiveness. Until 1956 Hungary was relatively relaxed, as was Czechoslovakia until the Soviet invasion in 1968, after which plays of leading dramatists like Milan Kundera and Pavel Kohout were banned, as was the entire work of VÁCLAV HAVEL. He spent over four years in prison following his arrest for subversion in 1979. In Poland, where theatre has always had a distinc-tive political dimension, restrictions were relaxed when Solidarity's power was strong. But after the impo-sition of military rule under General Jaruselski in late 1981, constraints were rapidly reimposed. Kazimierz Braun's *Dzuma* (1984), based on CAMUS's *The Plague*, was permitted a few heavily censored performances, but the author was dismissed from his post as theatre director. However, by 1990, after the collapse of Soviet domina-tion, censorship ceased throughout Eastern Europe, including Czechoslovakia, where Václav Havel was state president from 1989 to 1992.

**Outside Europe**

Dramatic censorship has never existed on a formalized basis in the USA, where free speech is guaranteed under the Constitution; but occasional local action, usually by the police, may close down productions which allegedly endanger public morals or insult the state. The absence of institutionalized censorship allowed the world pre-miere of *Ghosts* to take place in Chicago in 1882, but in ARNOLD DALY's New York production of *Mrs Warren's Profession* in 1905 the actors were prosecuted and MAE WEST's debut as a waterfront whore in *Sex* (1926) earned her an eight-day prison sentence for indecency. Recent censorship in the USA tends to be through the purse-strings, by refusing public funding to productions or theatre groups deemed unsuitable.

Censorship began in Australia soon after coloniza-tion. In 1828, after the first permanent theatre was set up in Sydney, the Legislative Council regulated all places of public entertainment, drawing heavily on Walpole's 1737 Stage Licensing Act. As in Britain, it sur-vived into the late 1960s. By the 19th century the British authorities in India began to take an interest in native theatre, especially in Bengal, where the drama was used for anti-British propaganda. Formal censorship throughout the dominion was imposed from 1879. Censorship also operated in colonial Africa, where it continues under present-day dictatorships.

In the late 19th and early 20th centuries Turkish drama began to suffer censorship: the satirical shadow puppet theatre (KARAGÖZ) was deeply affected, as were the more westernized forms of theatre beginning to emerge. There were periods of severe restriction until after the 1960 Revolution. Muslim fundamentalism is not sympathetic to the stage, and Middle Eastern coun-tries under such regimes operate rigorous censorship – e.g. Iran, where during the early 1980s censorship was even more repressive than under the Shah. Theatre directors had to obtain approval of both text and the manner of performance before rehearsals were allowed to begin. In present-day Iran no play may be performed unless the text is published beforehand, which is a guarantee of its acceptability.

Japanese censorship dates back to the mid-17th century, when the irreverent KABUKI theatre was restricted. From 1629 women were prohibited from acting on the stage; and they have reappeared only in the present century. Japanese censorship was mainly political, occasionally disguised as moral. After World War I social criticism was severely restricted and by the late 1930s political drama was outlawed completely, with the government's disbanding of left-wing theatre groups.

China has laboured under strict censorship since the People's Republic was established in 1949. In the mid-60s, during the Cultural Revolution, some of China's most distinguished playwrights (e.g. T'ien Han) fell from grace in a hysterical purge of modern drama. After about 1977 there was a movement away from politically educative drama back to entertainment; but the theatre remains in a fluid state and is still a victim of conflicting reactionary and liberalizing forces.

In the restless and unstable political climate of Central and South America the predominance of censorship, usually military-inspired, has restricted growth, e.g. in Brazil between 1930 and 1960 (when the Conservatório Dramático Brasiliero assumed absolute control over the theatre), and also between 1968 and 1984; in Chile under Pinochet between 1973 and 1984; and in Argentina during the Peronist regime and the rule of the Generals. Recent political changes have partly lightened the atmosphere.

Until the 1980s, South Africa's censorship laws exercised a rigour unmatched outside the former Soviet bloc. The Entertainments (Censorship) Act (1931) and the Publications and Entertainments Act (1963) gave real force to earlier, more haphazard arrangements. Several leading black playwrights were forced into exile (e.g. Alfred Hutchinson, Lewis Nkosi); others (e.g. ATHOL FUGARD, a white writer hostile to the regime) continued to produce under increasingly daunting conditions. By 1975 theatre groups promoting black consciousness had been largely silenced. Political changes towards ending apartheid in the late 1980s and early 1990s brought about more liberal attitudes to the theatre, which assumed a less dangerous aspect in the eyes of the authorities. The arrival of majority rule in 1994 brought formally to an end what was once one of the most repressive of modern censorships.

**Centlivre, Susannah** 1669–1723 English playwright. She was a strolling player from c.1685. Her first poems and letters were published and her first play produced in 1700. Her sharp attack on gambling, *The Gamester* (1705), was her first dramatic success and was followed by *The Basset-Table*, on the same theme. Of her 20 plays the most popular were *The Busy Body* (1709) and *The Wonder: A Woman Keeps a Secret* (1714), both of which lasted well into the 19th century. Her best work, *A Bold Stroke for a Wife* (1718), provides a virtuoso acting part for the hero in his multiple disguises.

**Cervantes, Miguel de** 1547–1616 Spanish novelist and playwright. He found success in novels only after consistent failure in the theatre, to which his episodic style and lack of poetic talent were ill-suited. He wrote about 30 plays in the 1580s of which only two survive, each in four acts: *El trato de Argel* (*The Trade of Algiers*), drawing on his captivity there, and *El cerco de Numancia* (*The Siege of Numantia*), his best play in spite of its poor verse. Later he wrote eight more unperformed plays, eventually published with eight *entremeses* ( see GÉNERO CHICO) in 1615. These single-scene playlets, six of them in prose, are much superior to his full-length dramas. Cervantes initially supported the classical dramatic precepts, attacking LOPE DE VEGA in Chapter 48 of *Don Quixote*, though by 1615 his opposition had turned to warm praise and unsuccessful imitation.

**Césaire, Aimé** 1913– Martiniquan poet, politician, essayist and playwright. He helped to found (with Senghor) the negritude movement in the 1930s. He is better known as a poet than as a playwright, but he turned to the theatre to reach a broader audience and to deal directly with African politics. His plays shocked the French theatre world. His three works for the theatre were all written in the 1960s, partly under the influence of JEAN-MARIE SERREAU, who directed them. In *La Tragédie du Roi Christophe* (*The Tragedy of King Christopher*, 1964) he presents the conflicting views of black African liberation current in the 1950s and 1960s. Epic in structure, it draws on the language of Africa and the Caribbean as well as that of France. *Une Saison au Congo* (*A Season in the Congo*, 1967), in the style of the African hero play, criticizes the effects of white decolonization. This theme is taken up in *Une Tempête* (1969), a brilliant reworking of SHAKESPEARE'S *The Tempest*, in which Prospero represents a white settler and Caliban a black slave, locked in a power struggle which Prospero is doomed to lose.

**Chaikin, Joseph** 1935– American director, actor and producer. As an actor he appeared in several productions with the LIVING THEATRE and the Writers' Stage (1964). Chaikin founded the OPEN THEATRE in 1964 as an experimental company to build and perform new scripts. The success of *America Hurrah!* in 1966 established his reputation. His workshop approach to composition also produced *Terminal* and *The Serpent* in 1970, the latter a series of episodes on the history of murder. Chaikin has directed for the NEW YORK SHAKESPEARE FESTIVAL, MANHATTAN THEATRE CLUB, Magic Theatre of San Francisco, and the MARK TAPER FORUM of Los Angeles. An articulate spokesman for the 1960s avant-garde movement, he has won numerous awards. In 1991 he appeared at the American Place Theatre in plays he co-authored with SAM SHEPARD (*The War in Heaven*) and VAN ITALLIE (*Struck Dumb*).

**Chaillot Theatre** (Paris) Various theatres have been built on this site, opposite the Eiffel Tower. The first, built for the exhibition of 1878, was allotted to GÉMIER when he set up the first THÉÂTRE NATIONAL POPULAIRE in 1920. Situated at the heart of the most fashionable residential district, it could never be the centre for a popular community theatre. The present complex of museums and theatres was built for the 1937 exhibition, and its huge main theatre made a perfect debating chamber for the United Nations Organization (1947–51). VILAR managed to make a going concern of this theatre for the revived TNP between 1951 and 1963. ANTOINE VITEZ, who took over the redesigned theatre in 1981, gave bold new productions of both new plays and world classics. Since 1988 the company has been directed by JÉRÔME SAVARY.

**Chalbaud, Román** 1931– Venezuelan playwright and director. One-third of the Venezuelan 'Holy Trinity' (with CABRUJAS and CHOCRÓN), Chalbaud has written more than a dozen plays. He has also been a leading figure in Venezuelan film since the mid-50s. As a director of the NUEVO GRUPO (New Group) since 1967, he has mounted both national and foreign plays, ranging from the classics to the absurd (see THEATRE OF THE ABSURD), in order to promote a national theatre movement. His plays often depict marginal characters within society and deal with poverty, social maladjustment, sexuality, and political and ontological problems. *Caín adolescente* (*Adolescent Cain*, 1955) dealt with rural adaptation to an urban environment; later plays include *La quema de Judas* (*The Burning of Judas*, 1964), *Los ángeles terribles* (*The Terrible Angels*, 1967), *El pez que fuma* (*The Smoking Fish*, 1968) and *El viejo grupo* (*The Old Group*, 1984).

**Champion, Gower** 1921-80 American dancer, choreographer and director. Champion turned from dancing to choreography with *Small Wonder* (1948). After dancing with his wife Marge in several Hollywood films, he returned to BROADWAY as the director and choreographer of *Bye, Bye, Birdie* (1960), *Carnival* (1961), *Hello, Dolly!* (1964), *I Do! I Do!* (1966), *Irene* (1973), *Mack and Mabel* (1974) and others. He died just as his last show, *42nd Street*, was about to open in 1980. *Carnival*, in particular, was praised for its imaginative, stylized production. Along with BOB FOSSE and MICHAEL BENNETT, Champion made the choreographer-director the dominant figure in the MUSICAL THEATRE of the 1970s.

**Champmeslé, Mlle** [Marie Desmares] 1642-98 French actress. She appeared at the MARAIS from 1668, the HÔTEL DE BOURGOGNE from 1670, and after 1679 at the Hôtel Guénégaud (later the COMÉDIE-FRANÇAISE). Although not beautiful she was renowned for her touching voice, which made her a potent attraction even in indifferent plays. Having deeply impressed RACINE as Hermione in *Andromaque*, she became the playwright's mistress and created all his major heroines from Bérénice to Phèdre, which he wrote expressly for her.

**Chanfrau, Frank** 1824-84 American actor. Through his ability to imitate EDWIN FORREST he toured America, and in 1848 played Mose the fire b'hoy in *A Glance at New York*, written for him by BENJAMIN BAKER (1848). Dressed in the red shirt, plug hat and turned-up trousers of the New York fireman, Chanfrau featured in several Mose plays, particularly *The Mysteries and Miseries of New York* by Henry W. Plunkett. He performed 560 times as Kit the Arkansas Traveller in the play of that name, and played the lead character in Thomas de Walden's *Sam 783* times.

**Channing, Stockard** [*née* Susan Williams Antonio Stockard] 1944- American actress. She made her BROADWAY debut in 1971, but it was not until her appearance in *Joe Egg* (1985 Broadway revival) that her extraordinary stage talent began to be recognized. Other notable appearances include NEIL SIMON's *They're Playing Our Song* (1980), GUARE's *The House of Blue Leaves* (1986 revival, as Bunny), AYCKBOURN's *Woman in Mind* (1988), GURNEY's *Love Letters* (1989) and especially Guare's *Six Degrees of Separation* (1990; London, 1992), in which she was critically acclaimed as Ouisa. She appeared in PETER HALL's production of Guare's *Four Baboons Adoring the Sun* (1992) at the Vivian Beaumont and in the title role in STOPPARD's *Hapgood* (1994).

**Chapelain, Jean** 1595-1674 French scholar, critic and man of letters. A founder member of the Académie-Française in 1634, he was the principal author of the Academy's public censure of CORNEILLE's *Le Cid* for its irregularities. He upheld neoclassical notions of the drama of credibility (as distinct from truth to the facts), decorum, and the three unities (of time, place and action; see ARISTOTLE).

**Chapman, George** c.1560-1634 English playwright and poet-translator of Homer. Associated with HENSLOWE and the ADMIRAL'S MEN in the 1590s, he wrote *The Blind Beggar of Alexandria* (1596) and *An Humorous Day's Mirth* (1597). Several plays have been lost. The survivors from the following decade include *May Day* (c.1601), *The Gentleman Usher* (c.1602), *All Fools* (1604), *Monsieur D'Olive* (1604) and *The Widow's Tears* (c.1605), comedies written for the sophisticated audiences of the BOYS' COMPANIES, morally as well as linguistically complex. His tragedies concern deeply flawed Titanic heroes of recent French history – *Bussy D'Ambois* (1604), *The Conspiracy and Tragedy of Charles, Duke of Byron* (1608), *The Revenge of Bussy D'Ambois* (c.1610) and *Chabot, Admiral of France* (c.1613). His collaboration with JONSON and MARSTON in *Eastward Ho* (1605) had the longest theatrical life of all Chapman's plays.

**Chapman family** see SHOWBOATS

**Chappuzeau, Samuel** 1625-1701 French man of letters. In addition to comedies and farces he wrote *Le Théâtre Français* (1674), an apologia for the theatre, particularly actors, which contains a catalogue of dramatists and lives of prominent performers, including a long section on MOLIÈRE; a valuable source of information.

**charivari** Medieval processional revels. The *chalvaricum*, as 14th- and 15th-century church bans refer to it, was originally a 'tumult' directed against a marriage the community disapproved of; remarried widows and unequal matches would be treated to a barrage of catcalls (the German *Katzenmusik*). The term came to mean a procession of noisy maskers, dancers, drummers and singers who made the streets unsafe by night. Once the staid citizens realized the fun in singing and saying what one would under the anonymity of devil masks, the charivari became organized as a mass 'happening' for its own sake. Among the *buffones* or masks were depraved monks with bare behinds and lion's manes, demons rattling pots and pans (as in the modern FASTNACHTSPIEL of Basle), and the wild man Hellequin or Herlequin whose name becomes transformed into HARLEQUIN.

**Cheek by Jowl** British company. This small group, touring classic plays, was founded by its director Declan Donnellan and its designer Nick Ormerod in 1981. Its policy combined SHAKESPEARE plays (*The Tempest*, 1988, *As You Like It*, 1991) with unusual or little-known Continental classics such as CORNEILLE's *Le Cid* (1986), SOPHOCLES' *Philoctetes* (1988) and LESSING's *Miss Sara Sampson* (1990). When he pursues an idea, as with the all-male *As You Like It*, Donnellan does so consistently, which may be the secret of his successful partnership with Ormerod, who is an economical designer, precise with effects. They were invited to stage LOPE DE VEGA's *Fuente Ovejuna* (1989) at the NATIONAL THEATRE, where in 1992 they directed a new play by the American playwright TONY KUSHNER, *Angels in America*, in which AIDS offers a symbol for the downfall of Western civilization.

**Chekhov, Anton (Pavlovich)** 1860-1904 Russian playwright and short-story writer; the most notable and celebrated 20th-century Russian dramatist in the West. His plays helped establish psychological realism, although possessing symbolist, impressionist and even proto-absurdist traits (see SYMBOLISM; THEATRE OF THE ABSURD). By fragmenting the WELL MADE PLAY, scattering exposition throughout, compressing, internalizing and excising action, Chekhov created the so-called 'theatre of mood', of misdirection, non-eventfulness and partially stated meaning.

A physician by training, he began his career as a writer at medical school in Moscow. In such stories as 'The Steppe' (1888), 'A Dreary Story' (1889), 'The Duel' (1891), 'Ward No. 6' (1892), 'The Lady with the Dog' (1899) and 'In the Ravine' (1900), he learned to strike a balance between 'subjectively painful' and 'objectively comedic' perspectives on life, to link the catastrophic with the trivial.

His earliest plays are farces, vaudevilles and 'comedy-jokes' based upon his stories: On the Highroad (1884), The Harmfulness of Tobacco Smoking (1886), Swan Song and The Bear (1888), The Wedding and The Tragedian in Spite of Himself (1889), The Marriage Proposal (1890) and The Anniversary (1891). In these succinct pieces Chekhov began to erase the boundary between comedy and drama and to forge the tragi-farcical approach which confounded the audiences and critics (with notable exceptions) of his full-length plays. His uncertainty about his own career as a dramatist was reinforced by the failure of his early plays. Platonov (1878), Ivanov (1887) and The Wood Demon (1889) dealt with provincial Don Juans and Hamlets, 19th-century 'superfluous men' of the intelligentsia.

Chekhov's major plays – The Seagull (following a dismal 1896 production at the Aleksandrinsky Theatre), Uncle Vanya (a revised Wood Demon, 1899), The Three Sisters (1901) and The Cherry Orchard (1904) – all staged by STANISLAVSKY at the MOSCOW ART THEATRE (MAT) in sentimental and naturalistic productions (see NATURALISM), developed his characteristic contrapuntal use of dialogue, structure and theme, of offstage and inner action. Time moves relentlessly forward in his plays, while seeming, via home-comings and departures, memories and fixations, to cycle endlessly back, and characters manage to waste what little time they have in the present. This describes both universal human folly and the situation of the pre-revolutionary Russian intelligentsia. The grandson of a serf, Chekhov well understood the necessity of change and the burden of legacy. He befriended and supported GORKY, who later became the voice of Soviet Russia.

**Chekhov, Michael** [Mikhail (Aleksandrovich) Chekhov] 1891-1955 Russian actor and director. ANTON CHEKHOV's nephew, Michael (his professional name, following emigration in 1928) created and taught an acting system which has become increasingly influential in the West. A member of the MOSCOW ART THEATRE's First Studio from 1912 (later the Second Moscow Art Theatre, of which he became artistic director in 1924), he was taught by STANISLAVSKY and VAKHTANGOV. A self-styled mystical philosopher, Chekhov used the language of acting to reveal inner truth. His system evolved into an alternative to Stanislavsky's, emphasizing more universal, spiritual resources of energy, rather than the historical, emotional and psychological details of the actor's life. His major roles in Russia include Caleb Plummer in DICKENS's The Cricket on the Hearth (1914), Malvolio in Twelfth Night (1917), the title role in Vakhtangov's production of STRINDBERG's Erik XIV (1921), Khlestakov in The Inspector General (1921), Hamlet (1924) and Senator

Ableukov in The Death of a Senator (adapted from BELY's Petersburg, 1925). His émigré career included acting for MAX REINHARDT (1928-30) and in Hollywood, directing the HABIMAH Theatre (1930) and several companies and studios of his own, through which he disseminated his ideas as actor-director-teacher. He went to New York in 1935, where his lectures on the creative process influenced and divided GROUP THEATRE members. His books include The Path of the Actor (autobiography, 1928), On the Actor's Technique (in Russian, 1946), To the Actor (1953) and To the Director and Playwright (1963).

**Cheng Changgeng** c.1812-80 Chinese actor. He played old male (laosheng) roles in JINGXI. Cheng rose to become leader of the Three Celebrations, one of the four most prestigious acting companies in the capital. He was outstanding when portraying great statesmen and warriors, creating a style of acting which set precedents for the future. A man of great personal integrity and dignity, he was well regarded at court.

**Cheng Yanqiu** 1904-58 Chinese actor. He studied both JINGXI and KUNQU techniques under leading teachers. Specializing in women's roles (dan), he rose to professional recognition as one of the four great performers of his genre – the 'big four', as they were known in theatre circles. MEI LANFANG (1894-1961), Shang Xiaoyun (1900-76) and Xun Huisheng (1900-68) were the others. Cheng developed a very individual style of vocalization, and was noted for the grace and skill of his acting forms. In 1932 he was sent to Europe to study Western theatre and opera practices. In 1930 he was appointed head of the first coeducational Academy of Dramatic Art in Beijing. His last years were spent training a new generation of Beijing actors.

**Chéreau, Patrice** 1944- French director. He made his name with LENZ's The Soldiers in 1967 and joined PLANCHON as director of the THÉÂTRE NATIONAL POPULAIRE at Villeurbanne in 1972, moving to the Théâtre des Amandiers at Nanterre in 1982. His productions are distinguished by great scenic brilliance together with an ability to create modern archetypes. His Ring cycle at BAYREUTH in 1976-80 recast the Norse legends in images of the industrial revolution, and his revivals of MARIVAUX, IBSEN (Peer Gynt, 1981) and GENET (Les Paravents, 1983) have brought international recognition. Between 1983 and 1988 he directed the first performances of the plays of BERNARD-MARIE KOLTÈS.

**Chestnut Street Theatre** (Philadelphia) Intended to replace the deteriorating SOUTHWARK, it was completed in 1793 and leased to THOMAS WIGNELL and Alexander Reinagle. By 1805 it was considered the finest playhouse with the best acting company in America. In 1816 gaslighting was introduced for the first time in a theatre, but in 1820 the playhouse burned down. The rebuilt version looked very different. The theatre's most prosperous years occurred under the management of WILLIAM WARREN THE ELDER and WILLIAM B. WOOD, which ended in 1828. In 1855 the theatre was demolished.

**Chettle, Henry** c.1560-c.1607 English playwright and pamphleteer. Very few of his plays survive, though he had a hand in about 50, including several for the ADMIRAL'S MEN. The REVENGE TRAGEDY, Hoffman (c.1603), was probably his alone. With ANTHONY MUNDAY he wrote The Downfall and The Death of Robert, Earl of Huntingdon (1598), with JOHN DAY The Blind Beggar of Bethnal Green (1600), and with DEKKER and William Haughton Patient Grissel (1600). He printed ROBERT

GREENE's *Groatsworth of Wit* (1592), and dissociated himself from Greene's attack on SHAKESPEARE in the preface to his own dream-fable, *Kind Heart's Dream* (1593).

**Chevalier, Albert** [Albert Onésime Britannicus Gwathveoyd Louis Chevalier] 1862–1923 British actor and MUSIC-HALL singer. He made his professional debut under the BANCROFTS in 1877. In 1888 he reluctantly branched out into recitals of comic songs and monologues. He first appeared 'on the halls' at the London Pavilion, 5 February 1891, as a coster comedian and made an immediate hit; he was a favourite with royalty and the upper classes, often performing in drawing-rooms. In 1906 he toured the USA and Canada with YVETTE GUILBERT.

**Chevalier, Maurice** 1888–1972 French singer and actor. He began his career at the age of 11. In MUSIC-HALL he imitated popular comedians before developing the character of a peasant aspiring to be a dandy. At the FOLIES-BERGÈRE by 1908, he was later sponsored by MISTINGUETT, who became his mistress and his partner, leading to REVUE, operetta and singing tours, with such numbers as 'Valentine' and 'Ma Pomme'. In the 1920s Chevalier's straw boater, dinner-jacket and casual soft shoe stood for a sporty new generation. A stint in Hollywood (1928–35) earned him international fame, and he cultivated a somewhat artificial French accent, much imitated. Because of his collaboration with the Vichy government during the Occupation he temporarily fell out of favour, but he regained popularity with a series of one-man shows, begun in 1948. The chat gradually elbowed out the singing, and he bade his final farewell to the stage at the Théâtre des Champs-Élysées in 1968. Chevalier's rapport with his audiences was a triumph of manner over matter: his trivial material, weak voice and bland personality were compensated for by abundant charm and a knowing use of *Sprechgesang*.

**Chiarelli, Luigi** 1880–1947 Italian playwright. In his early years he was primarily a journalist. In 1916 the company of VIRGILIO TALLI produced his three-act *La maschera e il volto* (*The Mask and the Face*) in Rome. This ironic comedy, about the conflict between the individual and social conventions, helped to launch the TEATRO DEL GROTTESCO. Although he wrote many other plays in the 1920s and 30s, these never enjoyed the same success.

**Chiari, Pietro** 1712–85 Italian playwright. A prolific writer of competent but unambitious stock pieces, he worked mainly for the Venetian theatres and is remembered primarily for his literary and theatrical disputes with GOLDONI. His work was enormously popular in its day, mingling as it did comic, tragic and satiric elements. Much of it turned on PARODY or ridicule of Goldoni's plays, notably *La scuola delle vedove* (*The School for Widows*, 1749), a parody of Goldoni's 'reform' play, *La vedova scaltra* (*The Cunning Widow*, 1748). A former Jesuit, and known as the *abate*, Chiari also wrote romances and *novelle*, and his writing output as a whole is a useful index to the tastes of the Venetian middle classes at the time of that city's theatrical heyday.

**Chicano theatre** Spanish-American theatre. The theatre of the Mexican-American population in the United States has been known since 1965 as 'Chicano theatre'. The genre is normally written and performed in the peculiar linguistic mixture typical of the Chicano population. Words and phrases in English and Spanish are constantly interchanged, depending upon the context. Most groups perform in the 'Spanglish' dialect; others alternate performances in either language.

Chicano theatre dates from the arrival of the Spanish conquerors in the 16th century. Throughout the period of settlement and growth during the following centuries, the dominant Hispanic culture and language in the American Southwest were attentive to the theatre. During the 19th century, both San Francisco and Los Angeles were major centres of Hispanic dramatic activity; as the railway linked major cities throughout the Southwest, especially Laredo, San Antonio and El Paso, the ethnic communities with a strong sense of their heritage and traditions hosted travelling road companies en route to and from Mexico City.

By the 1920s Chicano theatre flourished from Los Angeles to Chicago. Productions of musical REVUES and ZARZUELAS coincided with serious plays which addressed issues particular to the Chicano communities. The problems of adapting culturally and linguistically to a predominantly Anglo culture were standard themes. Activity subsided during the Depression and World War II years, although it did not disappear entirely.

The more recent Chicano theatre movement coincided with the activist movement in US civil rights in the 1960s. In the summer of 1965, when LUIS VALDÉZ helped to organize the farm-workers' strike in California, using politically orientated improvisational theatre to underscore the migrant workers' cause, he became the acknowledged father of the new direction in Chicano theatre. His *actos*, as they came to be called, were short AGIT-PROP pieces that dramatized the essence and spirit of the Chicano reality. The new Chicano theatre was, suddenly, a revolutionary theatre committed to social change. From this initial experience Valdéz established EL TEATRO CAMPESINO (Farm Workers' Theatre). This group served as the model for a host of other Chicano theatre groups created throughout the West and Southwest, and extending across the country into Illinois, Indiana and Wisconsin. At the peak of the movement, 100 groups were functioning throughout the USA.

Valdéz's *Zoot Suit* opened in Los Angeles in 1978 and was the first Chicano show to arrive on BROADWAY. After Valdéz, another generation of Chicano writers has picked up the cue, including Rubén Sierra, Carlos Morton and Estela Portillo Trambley.

**Chichester Festival Theatre** (England) The first large thrust-stage theatre in Britain, seating nearly 1,400 people, it opened in 1962. It was also one of the first theatres to be built in a park, outside a small country city in the south of England. It was built largely by local subscriptions, inspired by the example of the STRATFORD (Ontario) FESTIVAL Theatre in Canada. These two theatres share the ideals for theatre construction first argued for by TYRONE GUTHRIE and derived from Elizabethan models, stressing close audience–actor contact, all-round visibility and the use of the whole auditorium as the stage set. LAURENCE OLIVIER was the first director (as well as director of the still embryonic NATIONAL THEATRE company at the OLD VIC). The productions, including *Uncle Vanya* (1962), *The Royal Hunt of the Sun* (1964) and *Armstrong's Last Goodnight* (1965), transferred from Chichester to the Old Vic. In 1965 Olivier was succeeded by John Clements. The tradition of actor-managers at Chichester continued until Peter Dews's appointment in 1978. The theatre was unusual among postwar civic theatres in that it received little grant income from the state but more from the box-office and supporters' club. It favours English repertoires. MICHAEL RUDMAN, born in the USA, was replaced as director in 1991 by a former artistic director, Patrick Garland. In 1995 DEREK JACOBI became director.

**Chikamatsu Monzaemon** 1653–1725 Japanese playwright. Chikamatsu was the most important writer of *KABUKI* and *BUNRAKU* plays in Kyoto-Osaka during his lifetime. His courtly background and education are apparent in the literary quality of his texts. Illustrated scripts of 31 of his *kabuki* plays are preserved, including *The Prostitute and the Whirlpool of Love* (1695), *The Prostitute of Buddha Field* (1699) and *The Prostitute and Prayers to Buddha* (1702). The juxtaposition of religion and eroticism is typical of early *kabuki*. Chikamatsu skilfully balanced bravura history with gentle lovers' scenes. During this period he also wrote puppet plays (see PUPPETS). He moved to Osaka in 1705 and over the next 20 years composed nearly 100 puppet plays for the Takemoto Theatre. The history play *The Battles of Coxinga* (1715), showing a Japanese hero restoring the Ming dynasty in China, was immensely successful and influential. In a dozen lovers' suicide plays Chikamatsu carried *kabuki*'s erotic themes to tragic conclusions. More than any other playwright he created significant dramatic literature for the puppet theatre.

**Children of the Chapel Royal** The choristers of the Chapels Royal in Windsor and London supplied the young Henry VIII's demand for dramatic entertainment. Most of the plays would have been in the MORALITY tradition. In 1576 Richard Farrant, Deputy Master of the Chapel Children, established an indoor theatre in the disused BLACKFRIARS monastery. Farrant's choristers became serious rivals to the BOYS OF ST PAUL'S, whom they joined briefly under JOHN LYLY before being disgraced and silenced after the Marprelate Controversy of 1589–90. From 1600 to 1608 there was intense activity, including the 'war of the theatres', which lined JONSON and the Children of the Chapel against MARSTON and the Boys of St Paul's. The talented Chapel Royal boys, including NATHAN FIELD, gave the first performances of major plays by Jonson, CHAPMAN, MIDDLETON, BEAUMONT and even Marston. Some of the material was scurrilous, and by 1608 the company was in crisis. A remnant of the Children of the Chapel Royal survived at the WHITEFRIARS, where they performed Jonson's *Epicoene* (1609) and other plays before being finally disbanded in 1615 (see BOYS' COMPANIES).

**Childress, Alice** 1920–94 African-American playwright. Born in Charleston, South Carolina, and raised in Harlem, Childress opened the New York stage to black women writers when her play *Gold through the Trees* (1952) was professionally produced OFF-BROADWAY. She had been for 12 years an actress with the American Negro Theatre and her most important play, *Trouble in Mind* (1955), voiced the protest of a veteran black actress against playing a stereotypical 'darkie' role in a BROADWAY-bound production. Other notable plays by Childress that feature strong black women of compassion and dignity are *Wedding Band* (1966) and *Wine in the Wilderness* (1969).

**Chirgwin, G. H.** 1854–1922 British comedian. 'The white-eyed kaffir', a blackface comedian, singer, instrumentalist and eccentric dancer, made his London stage debut as early as 1861. Tall and long-legged, he was a striking figure in black tights and leotard, floor length frock-coat and enormous stove-pipe hat, with a contrasting white lozenge over his right eye. Though his act never changed, his instrumental versatility (and his ability to dance while playing the bagpipes) gave it variety, as did his habit of alternating baritone and falsetto delivery in both speech and song. He is best remembered for his performance of the old Christy Minstrel tear-jerker 'The Blind Boy' and the punning 'My Fiddle Is my Sweetheart (and I'm her only Beau)'. (See MINSTREL SHOW.)

**Chocolat** see FOOTTIT, GEORGE

**Chocrón, Isaac** 1932– Venezuelan playwright, director, critic and novelist. One-third of the Venezuelan 'Holy Trinity' (with CABRUJAS and CHALBAUD), Chocrón has written more than a dozen plays plus several novels. A director of the NUEVO GRUPO (New Group) since 1967, in 1984 he was chosen to direct the newly formed National Theatre Company. His first play, *Mónica y el florentino* (*Monica and the Florentine*, 1959), used an international guest house to manifest problems of isolation and difficulties of communication. Chocrón has experimented with a variety of styles: his popular *Asia y el lejano oriente* (*Asia and the Far East*, 1966), about the selling of a country, was restaged with additional music and dance as the first offering of the National Theatre Company in 1985. *Okey* (1969) presented a *ménage à trois* addicted to consumerism, and *La revolución* (*The Revolution*, 1971) dealt frankly with homosexuality. Later plays include *La máxima felicidad* (*Maximum Happiness*, 1974), *El acompañante* (*The Accompanist*, 1978), *Mesopotamia* (1979), *Simón* (a view of young Bolívar and his mentor, 1983) and *Clipper* (1987).

**Christie** [*née* Miller]**, Agatha (Mary Clarissa)** 1891–1976 British detective novelist and playwright. Christie's dramatizations of her own novels have been successful both on stage and in film, notably *Ten Little Niggers* (1943; produced in New York as *Ten Little Indians*, 1944) and *Murder on the Nile* (1946). *The Mousetrap*, which opened in 1952 at the Ambassadors Theatre in the WEST END, and had already achieved the record for the longest continuous London run of any play before 1973, when it transferred to St Martin's Theatre, is still running.

***chuanju*** (Sichuan opera) Chinese music-drama form. Found in Sichuan, China's most populous province, this is one of the most important of the country's regional styles. Initially there were five different styles, including *KUNQU*. The only one truly native to Sichuan was the *dengxi* ('lantern theatre'), a small-scale folk style based on the mask dances of village SHAMANS.

Early in the 20th century a movement began to reform the Sichuan theatre. The first teahouse-theatres were introduced into the cities. For the first time the five styles were performed on the same stage and regarded as a unity, though every item still retained its own music. Probably the greatest of the reformers was Kang Zhilin (1870–1931), a fine actor, teacher and leader of the Sanqing (Three Celebrations) Company. Set up in 1912, this was the most famous of the Sichuan opera's troupes. Apart from the Cultural Revolution decade, the Sichuan opera has flourished under the communists, especially since 1978.

In its performance and stagecrafts, costuming and make-up, Sichuan opera is essentially similar to other Chinese regional styles, including Beijing opera (see *JINGXI*). But Sichuan opera does have its own distinctive stage arts tradition. For instance, Kang Zhilin devised a skill which enables an actor to kick up his foot, touching the middle of the lower forehead with it for a split second and leaving the image of a third eye there. This breathtaking art is still practised in Sichuan. The art of face-painting is traditionally restricted to four colours – black, red, white and grey – as against the rather larger number of shades in Beijing opera.

**Churchill, Caryl** 1938– British playwright. In the early 1960s she started to write radio plays about 'bourgeois middle-class life and [its] destruction'. A hatred of social injustice characterized Churchill's early stage plays, notably *Owners*, produced at the ROYAL COURT's Theatre Upstairs in 1972. She came to write for left-wing and feminist companies such as Joint Stock and Monstrous Regiment, for whom she wrote *Light Shining in Buckinghamshire* (1976) and *Vinegar Tom* (1976), about 17th-century witchcraft. The historical background to current social-political problems, including sexual role-playing, fascinated her, and is most fully expressed in *Cloud Nine* (1979), a lively and highly intelligent comedy of manners. In *Top Girls* (1982) she staged a dinner party for famous women of different ages, describing their various struggles to succeed in a male world. An imaginative and sceptical writer, Churchill does not tolerate political pedantry any more easily than conventional theatrical forms; and her plays (such as *Objections to Sex and Violence*, 1974, and *Fen*, 1982) are sustained by the rigorous energy of her writing. *Serious Money* (1987) proved an effective comment on the people and practices of the 'City', though Churchill's lack of didacticism was thought by some to be a weakness. Her play from Romania, *Mad Forest* (1990), developed on site in the weeks after the downfall of the Ceauşescus, attempts to understand the havoc left by totalitarianism in Eastern Europe. *The Skriker* (NATIONAL THEATRE, 1994) derives its title from a kind of northern goblin whose powers shape the lives of two Lancastrian women visiting London. The text uses an associative dream logic, which in production was realized by dance, music and MIME.

**Cibber, Colley** 1671–1757 English actor, manager and playwright. As a member of the United Company from 1690, he stayed with Christopher Rich after the secession of BETTERTON in 1695, and played Fondlewife in CONGREVE's *The Old Bachelor*. His first play, *Love's Last Shift* (1696), including a superb role for himself as a fop, Sir Novelty Fashion, contains a last-act repentance for the rake-hero and is often labelled the first sentimental comedy. He played Lord Foppington in VANBRUGH's *The Relapse* (1698); then in 1699 he produced his adaptation of SHAKESPEARE's *Richard III*, which was performed for the next 120 years, though his own performance as Richard was much ridiculed. His comedy *The Careless Husband* was first performed in 1704. In 1710 Wilks, DOGGETT and Cibber took over the management of DRURY LANE, where Cibber excelled at teaching actors. He adapted MOLIÈRE's *Tartuffe* as *The Nonjuror* and completed Vanbrugh's *A Journey to London* as *The Provoked Husband* (1728). Appointed Poet Laureate in 1730, Cibber was mocked by satirists for his snobbishness and conceit, especially by Pope, who made him King of the Dunces in *The New Dunciad* (1742). He retired as manager in 1733. His autobiography, *An Apology for the Life of Colley Cibber*, was published in 1740.

**Cibber, Susanna (Maria)** 1714–66 English actress, married to THEOPHILUS CIBBER. First a singer, she made her hugely successful debut as an actress in HILL's *Zara*. Her repertoire of roles included Desdemona, Cordelia and Monimia in OTWAY's *The Orphan*. She was particularly famed for her pathetic style and use of her handkerchief in tragic roles. She worked with GARRICK and RICH.

**Cibber, Theophilus** 1703–58 English actor, manager and playwright, son of COLLEY CIBBER. He joined the DRURY LANE company in 1719 and was a precocious and appealing actor, later assistant manager. He gained particular success as Pistol in *Henry IV Part 1* and *Henry V*, in spite of his over-acting. Distrusted by his father, he led a rebellion against the Drury Lane management and in 1734 was granted a licence for the HAYMARKET THEATRE. For attempting to sue his wife's (SUSANNA CIBBER) lover for adultery, though he had encouraged the affair, he was hissed off the stage.

**Ciceri, Pierre(-Luc-Charles)** 1782–1862 French stage designer and scene painter. From 1822 to 1847 he was scenic director for the Paris Opéra. Imaginative landscapes and classical ruins painted on flats and backdrops were characteristic of his early style. With the completion of the new opera house in 1822, the dimming and brightening of gas footlights were taken into account in his designs. In 1826, for the COMÉDIE-FRANÇAISE, he began designing detailed depictions of historical epochs. Some of his most important works were executed in his scenic studio established in 1822: designs for Liszt's *Don Sancho* (1825); and also *La Muette de Portici* (1828), *Guillaume Tell* (1829), *Robert le diable* (1831) and *Hernani* (1830). The romantic style developed at his studio dominated the scene designs of the next generation in France.

**Cinquevalli, Paul** [Paul Kestner] 1856–1918 Polish juggler. His debut took place in Odessa (1873) as an aerialist; but after a fall from a 75ft height and eight months in hospital, he switched to juggling. He was first seen in London in 1885 and was soon a headliner on MUSIC-HALL bills, as 'the Human Billiard Table'. He would often conclude his act by catching a cannon ball on the nape of his neck.

**Cinzio** see GIRALDI, GIOVAN BATTISTA

**Circle in the Square** American company. Founded in New York in 1951 by JOSÉ QUINTERO, Theodore Mann, Emilie Stevens and Jason Wingreen, the company specializes in revivals of classic plays, especially in the round (originally on Sheridan Square, whence its name). On 24 April 1952 its now famous revival of TENNESSEE WILLIAMS's *Summer and Smoke* opened, launching Circle's success and Quintero's and GERALDINE PAGE's careers, as well as marking the heyday of OFF-BROADWAY. In 1961, the company opened its training school. Circle produced many O'NEILL works directed by Quintero, plays by TERRENCE McNALLY, ISRAEL HOROVITZ and Murray Schisgal, and international classics. Many productions later ran on BROADWAY or on television.

**Circle Repertory Company** New York theatre. It was founded OFF-BROADWAY in 1969 by MARSHALL W. MASON, Robert Thirkield, Tanya Berezin and LANFORD WILSON, who had been together since 1965 at Café LA MAMA and CAFFÉ CINO. Devoted to new American writers, Circle Rep operates a playwrights' workshop, and in 1981 launched the Young Playwrights Festival (now at the NEW YORK SHAKESPEARE FESTIVAL) for writers under 19. The theatre maintains an informal alliance of actors, playwrights and designers, and many established artists frequently return. Circle Rep produced many of Lanford Wilson's plays, moving several to BROADWAY. Other productions include plays by MARK MEDOFF, JULES FEIFFER, Albert Innaurato and SAM SHEPARD.

**circus** Popular entertainment. The name derives from the Latin for 'ring', but specifically from the Circus Maximus in Rome. Circus is defined by Marcello Truzzi as 'a travelling and organized display of animals and skilled performance within one or more circular stages known as "rings" before an audience encircling these activities'.

The modern circus incorporates the individual acts into one serial, often simultaneous, presentation. It developed from the riding school in European cities of the late 18th century, often under the guidance of former cavalry officers. Fairs were declining and their entertainments could more easily be controlled within the rings of the equestrian shows (see HIPPODRAMA). Unemployed rope dancers, acrobats (see ACROBATICS) and JUGGLERS drifted to these arenas. Although Jacob Bates had set up such a show, the Cirque Équestre, in Paris in 1767, credit for the first true circus is usually bestowed on PHILIP ASTLEY in London (1768), for he supplemented the horsemanship with CLOWNS and trained animals and later added PANTOMIMES. (The Royal Circus, founded in England in 1782 by CHARLES DIBDIN, was the first theatre to use the term.) The first true circus after Bates's was that of Astley's in the rue des Vieilles-Tuileries, Paris (1772), later enlarged as the CIRQUE OLYMPIQUE (1782), where a medley of equestrian acts (including a horse minuet), rope dancing and pantomime was presented.

Once permanent buildings for the circus were created, its spontaneity diminished, but in recompense it provided an 'opera for the eyes' through its pantomime spectacles. The oval or race-track ring was characteristic, the round ring a later introduction by Americans. Astley's tradition of elegant riding was carried on in Paris by Antonio Franconi's *exercice de grâce*, in Vienna by de Bach, and in St Petersburg by Tournaire. This so-called romantic period of the circus enjoyed considerable cross-fertilization with the ballet and pantomimic MELODRAMA. But with an increasingly heterogeneous audience and larger buildings, elegant horsemanship gradually declined until the exclusively equestrian circus disappeared in 1897 with Berlin's Zirkus Renz.

Meanwhile, new genres began to dominate, with an emphasis on sensation rather than grace: aerialism, wild-beast taming and daredevil feats. Travelling circuses became a major concern only after the spread of railways, when it became easier to transport elaborate machinery, huge cages and a numerous troupe. With touring, which entailed an enormous staff to set up and strike the tents, came the need for standardization, particularly so that the horses would not be upset by any deviation in environment. The standard European arena was invariably 13 metres in diameter, surrounded by a low barrier broken by two apertures on opposite sides, and strewn with sawdust or sand six to eight centimetres thick. In the USA P.T. BARNUM entered the circus business in 1871. Later, with competition from WILD WEST EXHIBITIONS, huge operations such as the Ringling Brothers continued until the Depression. In the Soviet bloc countries circus was nationalized and heavily subsidized, organized and promoted as a tool of popular enlightenment.

Historically, the appeal of the circus has derived in part from its variety, the romantic aura of its bohemianism, and the fact that it can be appreciated on many levels. It has had a powerful influence on the modern theatre, in reaction against the psychological drama of the late 19th century. The avant-garde was attracted to its physical skills and timing, clown routines, the reduction of speech to merely one among many means of communication, and the arena itself. Although the circus is the setting for such plays as LEONID ANDREEV's *He Who Gets Slapped* and THOMAS BERNHARD's *The Force of Habit*, more significant has been the use of the circus aesthetic in modern staging. As early as 1919, YURY ANNENKOV in Russia staged TOLSTOI's *First Distiller* as a circus show, and GORKY provided a circus scenario in *The Hard-Worker Wordflow* (1920). The experiments of Eisenstein in his 'montage of attractions' and MEYERHOLD in biomechanics were grounded in circus gymnastics. JARRY, GORDON CRAIG, ARTAUD, the Futurists, and later PETER BROOK with his ingenious *Midsummer Night's Dream*, found inspiration in the circus ring.

**Cirque Olympique/Théâtre du Châtelet** Parisian theatre. In 1782 PHILIP ASTLEY established his equestrian amphitheatre in Paris (see HIPPODRAMA). After the Revolution he rented it to the Franconi family. Dramatic elements crept increasingly into the programmes, including historical pantomimes celebrating the Napoleonic victories. In 1826 the theatre moved to the Boulevard du Temple (see BOULEVARD). The Cirque Olympique was a people's theatre, with cheap seats. After the equestrian part of the programme, more spectators would arrive and an orchestra was pushed out from under the stage. In 1835 the name changed to Théâtre National du Cirque (Théâtre Impérial du Cirque from 1853). Fairy extravaganzas now dominated the repertoire. In 1862, with the demolition of the Boulevard du Temple, the whole establishment moved to a new theatre on the site of the old fortress of the Châtelet. This was the largest theatre of the time, with a stage 35 metres deep and excellently equipped for spectacular productions.

**citizen comedy** English genre. The term refers to a group of Elizabethan and Jacobean plays set in London, featuring as characters the day-by-day tradesmen of the city. Citizen (or 'city') comedy is mostly good-humoured, but characteristically moral, castigating whatever discredits the good name of London, e.g. social overreaching or fraud. Outstanding examples include DEKKER's *The Shoemaker's Holiday* (1599), *Eastward Ho* (1605) – on which CHAPMAN, JONSON and MARSTON collaborated and which outdoes the two joint works of Dekker and WEBSTER, *Westward Ho* (1604) and *Northward Ho* (1605) – and MIDDLETON's *A Chaste Maid in Cheapside* (1611). The familiar combination of a romantic plot and plain characters provoked the lively mockery of BEAUMONT's *The Knight of the Burning Pestle* (1607). Jonson evoked the teeming life of the city in *Epicoene* (1609), *The Alchemist* (1610) and *Bartholomew Fair* (1614). The hardening tone and eventual decline of citizen comedy are well represented by the distance between *Eastward Ho* and MASSINGER's darker version of the same plot in *The City Madam* (c.1632).

**Citizens' Theatre** (Glasgow) Founded in 1943 by JAMES BRIDIE, who aimed at the establishment of a Scottish National Theatre, the Citizens' began operation at the small Athenaeum Theatre but in 1945 transferred to the Royal Princess's Theatre in the Gorbals, where it has since remained. The policy continued to be the presentation of the best of British and European drama and the encouragement of new Scottish playwrights, until 1969 when Giles Havergal was appointed artistic director. Audience numbers had been dwindling and

Havergal, together with (from 1970) his co-directors PHILIP PROWSE and Robert David MacDonald, embarked on a radical new policy. Their aim was to find production styles that would make every performance, of whatever type of play, a fresh, eye-opening experience. Design (under Prowse) was accorded a high priority; NATURALISM was shunned; plays as far removed as *Hamlet*, *The Balcony* and MacDonald's *Chinchilla* (about DIAGHILEV) were invested with an assertively, sometimes outrageously, theatrical style; within 10 years the Citizens' became, and has remained, one of the most distinctive of the UK's theatre companies, with an international reputation.

**Ciulei, Liviu** 1923– Romanian director, scene designer, actor and film-maker. A seminal figure of the Romanian stage, he worked at the Lucia Sturza Bulandra Theatre in Bucharest from 1948 until the late 1970s, when he took assignments as a guest director in Germany, Canada, Australia and, finally, in the United States. Between 1981 and 1985 he was artistic director at the GUTHRIE THEATRE in Minnesota. Ciulei's eclectic, idiosyncratic and cerebral productions include *Leonce and Lena* (1974) and *Elizabeth I* (1974) at the Lucia Sturza Bulandra, and *The Tempest* (1981), *Peer Gynt* (1983), *A Midsummer Night's Dream* (1985) and *The Bacchae* (1987) at the Guthrie; and *Hamlet* (1986) at the Public Theater in New York. Like many other artists, Ciulei returned to work in Romania after 1989, and was appointed honorary director of the Bulandra Theatre. His recent Romanian performances are a spectacular *Midsummer Night's Dream* and WEDEKIND's *Spring Awakening* (1992).

**Cixous, Hélène** 1937– French feminist critic and playwright. Born into a Jewish family in Algeria, Cixous's polyglot sense of 'otherness' placed her in a powerful position to question white male perspectives on the world. Her main project has been to develop a specific *écriture féminine* and she now heads a Centre de Recherches et d'Études Féminines in Paris. In the early 1980s she became associated with the Théâtre du Soleil, who commissioned her to write two plays inspired by Shakespearean models, one on the history of Cambodia and the other on that of India. The first, *Norodom Sihanouk* (1985), was in two parts; the second, *L'Indiade* (1987), dealt with Indian history from the beginnings of the independence movement to partition. Her association with the company continued with *La Ville parjure, ou le retour des Erinnyes* (1994). An earlier success had been *Portrait de Dora* (1976).

**Clairon, Mlle** [Claire-Josèphe-Hippolyte Léris de la Tudé] 1723–1803 French actress. Considered the finest tragedienne of her age, she made a sensational debut at the COMÉDIE-FRANÇAISE as RACINE's Phèdre in 1743. This led to a series of major tragic roles, enhanced by her beautiful voice, graceful figure and range of feeling. Later she moderated the solemn, declamatory style of the day into simpler, more conversational diction and observed more historical propriety in her stage dress, as did her contemporary LEKAIN for male costume. She created many of VOLTAIRE's tragic heroines. After her retirement in 1766 she opened a school for young actors, published an interesting autobiography and died in penury.

**Clapp, Henry Austin** 1841–1904 American drama critic. He practised law in Boston, and was music and drama critic of the *Boston Daily Advertiser* from 1868 until 1902, and of the *Boston Herald* from 1902 until 1904. An authority on SHAKESPEARE, Clapp was viewed as an erudite, incorruptible and fair critic. His *Reminiscences of a Dramatic Critic* (1902) provides an overview of late-19th-century Boston theatrical life.

**claque** Organized band of applauders. Such bands have been known since ancient Greek times; their members would be under the orders of some powerful figure, or were motivated by a common desire to further the interests of some writer, performer or cause. By the 18th century claques organized on a business footing had become established in European theatres, especially in France and Italy. The first three-quarters of the 19th century probably saw the paid claque at its peak, and it had begun to disappear by the early 1900s.

Each claque had a leader, sometimes paid by the theatre but sometimes, as at the Paris Opéra, paying the theatre for acknowledging his office. He recruited applauders by distributing free tickets, adding from time to time a free drink and, very rarely, a small amount of cash. The leader was paid by, or extorted payment from, the artists and authors who desired guaranteed public approbation. Some leaders had a list of charges for different lengths and intensities of applause. The kind of reaction required at any given moment was signalled by the leader to his claqueurs.

Leaders occupied a prominent position in theatrical circles and the most celebrated took their jobs very seriously, attending rehearsals and discussing both the appropriate moments for applause and the levels at which it should be given. Louis Castel's *Memoirs of a Claqueur* (1829) deals with 'the theory and practice of the art'. Even different ways of using the hands were a matter of concern – e.g. striking both open palms together, bringing the fingers of one hand against the palm of the other or snapping the fingers.

**Clark-Bekederemo, J(ohn) P(epper)** [J.P. Clark] 1936– Nigerian playwright, poet and critic. Three early plays in English were widely acclaimed: *Song of a Goat*, a tragedy about two brothers, one of whom becomes impotent; *Masquerade*, which forms a diptych with it; and *The Raft*, an existentialist play about four men adrift on the Niger on a lumber raft (all published 1964). His research into the traditional antecedents of Nigerian theatre resulted in his own English-language play, *Ozidi* (1966). In 1982 he founded with Ebun Odutola Clark the Pec Repertory Theatre in Lagos, for the professional production of African plays in English. *The Bikoroa Plays* (a trilogy concerning one Ijo family in three ages) and a comedy, *The Wives' Revolt* (1985), maintain and develop Clark's own creative writing.

**Clarke, Austin (Augustine Joseph)** 1896–1974 Irish playwright. A major poet also, Clarke was much under the shadow of YEATS, whose ideals for verse drama fascinated him. In 1940 Clarke founded the Dublin Verse-Speaking Society, giving readings on Radio Eireann and three drama seasons (1941–3) at the Peacock. His Lyric Theatre Company presented biannual evenings (1944–51) at the ABBEY, putting on nine of Clarke's plays, reviving FITZMAURICE, and giving the first performances of Yeats's *The Death of Cuchulain* and *The Herne's Egg*. Clarke's verse plays, set mostly in the 6th–12th centuries, turn, sometimes comically, on the nature of faith, on medieval and modern Catholicism, to the latter's disadvantage: *The Flame* (1930), *Black Fast* (1941) and *The Moment Next to Nothing* (1953).

**Claudel, Paul** 1868–1955 French poet, diplomat and playwright. Considered by some the most important French dramatist of the last 100 years, Claudel had wanted to be a priest, but was turned down by the Church and joined the diplomatic service. His interest in Eastern and ancient Greek theatre (he made a fine translation of the *Oresteia*) helped him to develop a flexible dramatic style. At first influenced by SYMBOLISM, he wrote his plays in three creative bursts. The first, between about 1895 and 1905, includes *Tête d'or* (*Golden Head*, 1889), *La Ville* (*The Town*, 1890), *L'Échange* (*The Exchange*, 1893), *Partage de midi* (*Break of Noon*, 1905) and *La Jeune Fille Violaine* (*The Young Girl Violaine*, 1892), later to become *L'Annonce faite à Marie* (*The Tidings Brought to Mary*). This was the first of his plays to be staged (directed by LUGNÉ-POE, 1912). The second is a trilogy – *L'Otage* (*The Hostage*, 1909), *Le Pain dur* (*Hard Bread*, 1914) and *Le Père humilié* (*The Humiliated Father*, 1916). And the third is *Le Soulier de satin* (*The Satin Slipper*, 1924). Their power partly resides in Claudel's peculiar poetic style, which has the variety and subtlety of Shakespearian blank verse. Material confines restrict his ambitious characters (usually drawn from the Renaissance period), who constantly yearn for other spiritual worlds. His most ambitious and theatrically successful play, *Le Soulier de Satin*, ranges from high TRAGEDY to low FARCE, from soul-searching monologue to animated dialogue, and includes song, dance and MIME. BARRAULT persuaded Claudel to cut and rewrite his text for production at the COMÉDIE-FRANÇAISE in 1943. This was a triumph, and Barrault proceeded to stage plays by Claudel written much earlier: *Partage de midi* (1948), *L'Échange* (1951), *Christophe Colomb* (1953) and *Tête d'or* (1968). Since then directors such as VITEZ have made their own reinterpretations.

**Claus, Hugo** 1929– Flemish playwright, novelist, translator and director. His plays, written in Dutch, focus on themes such as loneliness, the purity of childhood in a corrupt world, love between brother and sister, and the Oedipus complex. The action is frequently of a ritual nature, lifting it above its Flemish setting. *Bruid in de morgen* (*Bride in the Morning*, 1953), *Suiker* (*Sugar*, 1958), depicting the tough life of seasonal labourers in France, and *Vrijdag* (*Friday*, 1969) have established Claus's reputation. *Vrijdag* tells, in sober, factual manner, the story of the home-coming of a prisoner, who hears his wife confess that she has given birth to another man's child. Claus has adapted several classical plays – e.g. SENECA's *Thyestes* (1966), SOPHOCLES' *Oedipus at Colonus* (1986) and *Phaedra* (1980); JONSON's *Volpone*, as *De vossenjacht* (*The Fox Hunting*, 1972) and DE ROJAS's *La Celestina* as *De spaanse hoer* (*The Spanish Whore*, 1970).

**Clive, Kitty** 1711–85 English actress. She enjoyed success as a wry actress and singer in COMEDY, BURLESQUE and BALLAD OPERA, performing at DRURY LANE until 1769, apart from a brief spell at COVENT GARDEN in the 1740s. As Portia in *The Merchant of Venice* she was attacked for high comedy and mimicry of contemporary lawyers, but was a popular success. She retired to her cottage near her old friend Horace Walpole in 1769.

**Close, Glenn** 1947– American actress. Though best known for films such as *The Big Chill*, *Fatal Attraction* and *Hamlet*, she is a versatile stage performer as well, noted for her 'charged stillness'. Her Broadway debut as Angelica in a revival of CONGREVE's *Love for Love* (1974) was followed by a series of major roles in regional theatres and OFF-BROADWAY. She has also appeared in various BROADWAY productions, including *The Crucifer of Blood* (1978) and the musical *Barnum* (1980), and played Annie in the American premiere of STOPPARD's *The Real*

*Thing* (1984). In 1992 she appeared in MIKE NICHOLS's production of *Death and the Maiden* by Ariel Dorfman.

**clown** Comic performer. The distinction between a clown and a comedian, said 'the Perfect Fool' ED WYNN, is that the former does funny things, the latter does things funny. According to the social psychologist William McDougall, there are six primary components to clowning: the fall (slipping and sliding); the blow (slaps, custard pies); surprise (incongruity between what is expected and what happens); harmless and childish naughtiness; mimicry, usually with an element of PARODY; and stupidity which can turn out to be cleverness. This last trait may be the most basic, a false contrast: the clown's assumed clumsiness is revealed to be true virtuosity, his naivety to be wisdom, his hilarity to be sorrow disguised. The mythic dimension of the clown may derive from this tension.

There are no clowns in the Hindu epic the *Mahabharata*, but its stage version features Vedusaka, a bald dwarf with fangs and drooping limbs who is teamed with Vita, a parasitic slyboots. This yoking of the dim-witted fallguy and the scheming conniver is constant in clowning: in China the contrast is between Wu Ch'ou and Wen Ch'ou; in Renaissance Italy between the two ZANNI Arlecchino and Brighella.

Clownish types also appear in the satyr choruses of classical Greek drama (see GREEK THEATRE, ANCIENT) and in the comedies of southern Italy in the 3rd century BC, and become discriminated in the Atellan farces into the pop-eyed boaster Bucco, the awkward Maccus and the hunchbacked Dossenus, and the Stupidus of the *ludi scenici*. In Roman comedy, the comic figure is usually the slave, for the clown is commonly in an underdog position, working within and hence against his social context (see ROMAN THEATRE). This anti-social aspect was confirmed by medieval distrust of the itinerant entertainer. Typically, the clown of the miracle and MYSTERY PLAYS was a devil; in the MORALITY PLAYS he becomes Vice. The first named German clown is Rubin, zany to the mountebank of the medieval PASSION PLAY; this function as stooge to a quack descends through TABARIN to HARPO MARX and Lou Costello. In the German *FASTNACHTSPIEL* the low comic is usually a peasant. Indeed, the English word 'clown' first meant a country clotpoll, and this booby begins to be polished by the professionals of SHAKESPEARE's day – THOMAS HEYWOOD, RICHARD TARLTON and WILL KEMPE. The Shakespearian comic is multiform: in *As You Like It* he runs the gamut from the thick ploughboy William to the professional jester Touchstone to the moody philosopher Jaques. (The jester or fool, native to courts, was distinctly not a clown in the modern sense; his comedy was more consciously verbal and ambiguous.)

The Elizabethan clown was conveyed to Europe by the English Comedians (see ENGLISCHE KOMÖDIANTEN). Robert Reynolds introduced Pickelhering (Pickleherring) c.1618; his bizarre costume, grotesque mask and movements were comic exaggerations of reality. Naturalized in Germany, he not only amused the audience and acted as a bridge between it and a play's action, but he also enlarged the scope of the pompous tragedies in which he appeared.

The Italian *COMMEDIA DELL'ARTE* was immensely influential in disseminating its types – the *zanni*, the Dottore, Pantalone, the Spanish Captain – throughout Europe; but over time these types became submerged into complex dramatic characters with broader dimensions. MOLIÈRE, for example, transforms Mascarille, Sganarelle and Scapin from masked clichés to recognizable human beings with individual psychologies. Only Arlecchino as Arlequin and HARLEQUIN managed to retain a being independent of the plot requirements; but even his diabolical vestiges began to be domesticated in the 18th century, in the *fêtes galantes* of MARIVAUX and Watteau and the more sophisticated figures of Figaro and Papageno. He was also gradually edged out by the melancholy, pale-faced PIERROT (created c.1682), who evolved into the elegant white clown of the European CIRCUS.

As romantic and, later, realistic drama insisted on integrating the clown into a recognizable social entity, he found a refuge in PANTOMIME and then circus. JOSEPH GRIMALDI established the type of the Joey, greedy, amoral, gloating over his triumphs and cringing at his defeats; henceforth the clown of the harlequinade would wear tufts and frills, brandish a red-hot poker, and butter slides for policemen. Clown teams dominated the latter half of the 19th century: the exchange of slaps between FOOTTIT AND CHOCOLAT, or the Price Brothers' 'Evening at Maxim's', with its demolition of a private room at a restaurant, injected social SATIRE into the ring. DAN RICE had dabbled in political commentary; this factor became dominant in pre-revolutionary Russia with the DUROV brothers and was carried on, in a carefully monitored form, under the Soviets (VITALY LAZARENKO, ARKADY RAIKIN).

Although there was a recrudescence of genius in MUSIC-HALL clowning with GROCK, the FRATELLINI and CHARLIE RIVEL, many of the clown's prerogatives were usurped by the silent film comics; circuses became overrun with Chaplin imitators. Barring such exceptions as JANGO EDWARDS who added a drug-culture anarchy to the tradition, and Coluche (Michel Colucci) who enlarged the clown's sphere of action by running for the French presidency in 1981, the clown today has become a hackneyed subject for Sunday painters, a huckster for hamburgers and cereal, a filler between circus acts, rather than a number in himself. In the USA, however, the so-called 'new vaudeville' has provided performance artists like BILL IRWIN with a chance to revive the clown as an eloquent mediator between age-old techniques and postmodern aesthetics.

The modern theatre has drawn deeply on the clown tradition, transmuting him into characters like BRECHT's Arturo Ui, Schweyk and Puntila, or absorbing his techniques, as DARIO FO has done. Germany, in particular, has been fascinated by the clown as a political symbol, and he is used by such playwrights as WEDEKIND, HANDKE, PETER WEISS and HEINER MÜLLER; but the clown has also informed the plays of MAYAKOVSKY, BECKETT and IONESCO, and the productions of the Brazilian AUGUSTO BOAL.

**Clun, Walter** died 1664 English actor. He became a leading member of KILLIGREW's company. Much admired by PEPYS, Clun played the lead in the opening production of the new playhouse in DRURY LANE in 1663. The following year he was robbed and killed in Kentish Town, London.

**Clunes, Alec** [Alexander S. de Moro] 1912–70 British actor, director and theatre manager. Clunes played a variety of roles at the OLD VIC and at the Malvern Festival; in the 1950s he joined the Shakespeare Memorial Theatre at Stratford, where he was Claudius to PAUL SCOFIELD's Hamlet in 1955. His last acting

appearance came in HOCHHUTH's *Soldiers* in 1968. His main achievement, however, began during the war years when he ran an ambitious and intellectually demanding repertory at the tiny ARTS THEATRE in the heart of London's WEST END for eight influential seasons from 1942 to 1950. In addition to pioneering the work of such writers as CHRISTOPHER FRY, he unearthed forgotten English classics and searched for plays from abroad.

**Clurman, Harold** 1901–80 American director and critic. After visiting Paris in the 1920s he became a playreader for the THEATRE GUILD (1929–31), leaving his mark on the American theatre as founder and principal director of the GROUP THEATRE (1931–40). He nurtured the talents of CLIFFORD ODETS and directed five of his plays: *Awake and Sing* (1935), *Paradise Lost* (1935), *Golden Boy* (1937), *Rocket to the Moon* (1938) and *Night Music* (1940). After the Group's demise Clurman continued directing: *The Member of the Wedding* (1950), *The Autumn Garden* (1951), *Bus Stop* (1955), *The Waltz of the Toreadors* (1957), *Incident at Vichy* (1965), and (in Tokyo) *Long Day's Journey into Night* (1965) and *The Iceman Cometh* (1968). He was also theatre critic for the *New Republic* (1949–52), the *Nation* (1953–80) and the London *Observer* (1955–63).

**Cobb, Lee J.** 1911–76 American stage, film and television actor. In 1934 he joined the GROUP THEATRE, but is best remembered for creating the bewildered Willy Loman in ARTHUR MILLER's *Death of a Salesman* (1949) on BROADWAY. In 1969 he starred in a Broadway production of *King Lear*.

**Cochran, C(harles) B(lake)** 1872–1951 British showman. Cochran's enterprises ranged from roller-skating competitions to ballet. He began in the USA, his first production being IBSEN's *John Gabriel Borkman* (New York, 1897), then returned to London in 1902. His taste was eclectic: he was capable of booking REINHARDT's *The Miracle* into the London Olympia in 1911, and then housing Hagenbeck's circus there. From 1914 he was distinguished as a producer of smart REVUES, including *Odds and Ends* (1914), *Pell Mell* (1916), *As You Were* (1918) and *London, Paris and New York* (1920). More highbrow efforts, including the first London showing of an O'NEILL play (*Anna Christie*, 1925), led to bankruptcy, but he recouped his fortunes by collaborating with NOËL COWARD and producing *On with the Show* (1925), *This Year of Grace* (1928), *Bitter Sweet* (1929), *Private Lives* (1930), *Cavalcade* (1931), *Words and Music* (1932) and *Conversation Piece* (1934). He did not adapt to postwar public taste.

**Cockaigne** Popular utopia. A land of idleness and luxury, it has been known in Europe under various names (Cocagne, Cuccagna, Schlarrafenland, Lubberland, the Land of Prester John) since the 14th century. The land where houses are thatched with pancakes, people are paid for sleeping, and pigs run around with forks stuck in them looking for diners, is an important theme of European FOLK DRAMA and CARNIVAL.

**Cockpit Theatre** (London) Built in Drury Lane in 1609 to house the popular 'game' of cockfighting, this small (c.50ft square), tiered house was permanently converted by CHRISTOPHER BEESTON in 1616 for the performance of plays. He renamed it the Phoenix and managed it until his death in 1639, employing and dispensing with several companies, the last of which was nicknamed Beeston's Boys. The Cockpit was used for surreptitious performances during the Interregnum, and two musical spectacles were staged there by DAVENANT in 1658 and 1659.

**Cockpit-in-Court** (London) Built in the Palace of Whitehall for the entertainment of Henry VIII, the royal cockpit was used periodically for play performances. Charles I decided to convert it along the lines of the COCKPIT THEATRE in Drury Lane. INIGO JONES completed it in 1629–30. His drawings show an octagonal auditorium with tiers of seats and an upper gallery, set within a 58ft-square frame. The semicircular stage had five entrance doors and was 36ft wide at the front. Only from the royal box was there a central view across the stage to the large central arch of the *scaenae frons*. The repertoire is unknown. Unused during the Interregnum, the Cockpit-in-Court was never again more than sporadically a playhouse.

**Cocteau, Jean** 1889–1963 French poet, novelist, filmmaker and playwright. Cocteau's sense of playfulness is well exemplified in the visual puns and gentle SATIRE of *Parade* (1917), *Le Boeuf sur le toit* (*The Ox on the Roof*, 1920) and *Les Mariés de la Tour Eiffel* (*The Eiffel Tower Wedding Party*, 1921). These were ballets or MIME dramas written in collaboration with such luminaries as PICASSO, Satie and Milhaud. *La Voix humaine* (1930) was a one-act play written for Édith Piaf. In his plays based on ancient Greek models – *Antigone*, *Orphée* (*Orpheus*), *La Machine infernale* (*The Infernal Machine*) – Cocteau tried to develop a modern form of tragedy but came perilously close to PARODY. *Les Parents terribles* (*Intimate Relations*, 1938), a realistic tragedy of modern family life, was banned under the Occupation as prejudicial to morality. His later plays were unoriginal: *Les Chevaliers de la Table Ronde* (*Knights of the Round Table*, 1937), an Arthurian fantasy; *Les Monstres sacrés* (*The Sacred Monsters*, 1940), a technical melodrama; *La Machine à écrire* (*The Typewriter*, 1941), a thriller; *Renaud et Armide* (1943), a fairy tale; *L'Aigle à deux têtes* (*The Eagle with Two Heads*, 1946), a love story; and *Bacchus* (1951), a philosophical drama. His real genius was for the cinema, where his gift for organizing visual images was realized in e.g. *La Belle et la bête* (*Beauty and the Beast*, 1945), *Orphée* (1950) and *Le Testament d'Orphée* (1960).

**Codron, Michael (Victor)** 1930– British producer. Codron's adventurous promotion of new playwrights during the 1960s transformed the WEST END. His first London venture came in 1957, when he took a college REVUE, *Share My Lettuce*, from Cambridge to London, recasting it to include the then unknown actors MAGGIE SMITH and Kenneth Williams. In 1958 he staged the first plays of JOHN MORTIMER (*The Dock Brief* and *Shall We Tell Caroline?*) and HAROLD PINTER's *The Birthday Party*, which ran for less than a week at the LYRIC THEATRE, HAMMERSMITH. Codron retained his faith in Pinter and in 1960 produced *The Caretaker* at the ARTS THEATRE Club, which transferred to the West End. Other dramatists whose careers began with Codron productions include HENRY LIVINGS, Charles Dyer, ALAN AYCKBOURN, JAMES SAUNDERS, CHARLES WOOD, FRANK MARCUS, JOE ORTON, DAVID HALLIWELL and SIMON GRAY, and he also enabled writers like DAVID MERCER and CHRISTOPHER HAMPTON to see their plays transferred from smaller subsidized theatres to the West End. Codron formed long-standing associations with HAMPSTEAD THEATRE, the English Stage Company and other managements. In 1984 he produced MICHAEL FRAYN's award-winning play, *Benefactors* (1984), at London's Vaudeville Theatre. At the Aldwych Theatre, London, he produced STOPPARD's *Hapgood* (1988), Ayckbourn's *Henceforward* (1988), *The Revenger's Comedies* (1991) and Frayn's *Look*,

*Look* (1990) – safe productions, perhaps, but he also helped to produce MARTIN CRIMP's *Dealing with Clair* (1988) and JIM CARTWRIGHT's *Rise and Fall of Little Voice* (1992).

**Cody, (William Frederick) Buffalo Bill** see WILD WEST EXHIBITION

**Coe, Richard (Livingston)** 1916– American drama critic. Coe wrote on drama and film for the *Washington Post* from 1938 to 1942 and from 1946 until retirement in 1979. He has been regarded as one of the most perceptive, impartial and supportive critics of the American stage.

**Cohan** [Keohane]**, George M(ichael)** 1878–1942 American performer, playwright, director and producer. He first appeared on stage as a child with his family's VAUDEVILLE team, the 'Four Cohans'. His New York debut came in 1901 with his first full-length play, *The Governor's Son*. From 1904 to 1920 he produced in partnership with SAM H. HARRIS. In 1911 he opened his own George M. Cohan Theatre. Outstanding among the 50-odd plays and musicals credited to him are *Little Johnny Jones* (1904), featuring the song that most identifies Cohan ('Yankee Doodle Dandy'), *Forty-Five Minutes from Broadway* (1905), *The Talk of New York* (1907), *Get-Rich-Quick Wallingford* (1911), *Seven Keys to Baldpate* (1913), *The Tavern* (1921) and *The Song and Dance Man* (1923). His most famous song, 'Over There' (1917), won him a Congressional medal.

**Cohen, Alexander H.** 1920– American producer. Cohen made his BROADWAY debut in 1941 with *Ghost for Sale* and *Angel Street*. In 1950 his casting of *King Lear* with blacklisted actors established him as a producer of meritorious if not always commercially successful works. In 1959 he began a series called 'Nine O'Clock Theatre' and presented 11 successive hits including *An Evening with Mike Nichols and Elaine May* (1960), *Beyond the Fringe* (1962), and a revival of JOHN GIELGUD in *The Ages of Man* (1963). A major importer of foreign productions, Cohen also has numerous WEST END presentations to his name.

**Cohen, Nathan** 1923–71 Canadian theatre critic. The first important critical voice to cover Canadian theatre from coast to coast – on radio and television and as drama critic of the Toronto *Star* from 1959 to 1971. His often provocative and acerbic reviews chronicled the growth of the regional theatre movement across the country and the emergence of a new and substantial Canadian drama.

**Cokayne, Aston** 1608–84 English playwright. His three plays may never have been performed – *The Obstinate Lady* (published 1657), a tragedy heavily influenced by FLETCHER; *Trappolin Suppos'd a Prince*, a farce later adapted by NAHUM TATE; and *The Tragedy of Ovid*, an account of the poet's life in exile. A poem of his reveals that MASSINGER collaborated on many of the plays published under the authorship of BEAUMONT and Fletcher.

**Cole, Bob** 1869–1912 and **J. Rosamond Johnson** 1873–1954 American lyricist and composer. Pioneers in bringing black musicals to the New York stage, Cole and Johnson were prolific song writers, librettists and performers. Cole, in conjunction with Billy Johnson, had written and starred in *A Trip to Coontown* (1898), the first musical entirely created and performed by African Americans. Cole and Johnson provided songs for such shows as *The Belle of Bridgeport* (1900), *Mother Goose* (1903) and *Humpty Dumpty* (1904). Their biggest hit, 'Under the Bamboo Tree', was interpolated into *Sally in Our Alley*

(1902). They wrote and appeared in two musicals, *The Shoo Fly Regiment* (1907) and *Mr Lode of Koal* (1909), but critics of the time were unwilling to accept black performers in musicals that had plots and sympathetic characters. After Cole's death, Johnson appeared in *Porgy and Bess* (1935) and *Cabin in the Sky* (1940).

**Cole, Jack** 1914–74 American choreographer and dancer. He danced in *Thumbs Up* (1934) and *Keep 'Em Laughing* (1942), and in 1943 was given his first choreographic assignment for *Something for the Boys*. Among the many other shows that he choreographed were *Alive and Kicking* (1950), in which he also appeared, *Kismet* (1953), *Jamaica* (1957) and *Man of La Mancha* (1965). A student of the Chinese dancer MEI LANFANG, Cole frequently used Oriental movements and gestures in his choreography. He is most noted for creating 'jazz dancing', a form characterized by small groupings and angular movements which became the dominant style of the 1950s and 1960s.

**Coliseum** London MUSIC-HALL and VARIETY theatre. Opened in 1904, it was the first English stage to be equipped with a revolve. Performances included actresses of the stature of ELLEN TERRY, EDITH EVANS, SARAH BERNHARDT and LILLIE LANGTRY, and companies such as DIAGHILEV's Ballets Russes (between 1918 and 1925). GROCK, the most accomplished clown of the period, presented his musical MIMES there from 1911 to 1924. After 1931 it alternated between MUSICAL COMEDY and spectacular ice-shows or Christmas PANTOMIME. From 1945 to 1960 it housed a series of American musicals, including *Annie Get Your Gun* (1947), *Kiss me Kate!* (1951) and *Guys and Dolls* (1953). After some years as a cinema, it reopened in 1968 under the SADLER'S WELLS company as the permanent home of the English National Opera.

**Collier, Jeremy** 1650–1726 English cleric and writer. In 1698 he published *A Short View of the Immorality and Profaneness of the English Stage*, a lengthy and violent attack on blasphemy, abuse of the clergy, marriage and other sacraments he cited as present in contemporary drama, particularly in the work of CONGREVE, DRYDEN, D'URFEY and VANBRUGH. The resulting pamphlet war was intense and acrimonious. By the end of 1698 Vanbrugh had written his defence, *A Vindication of The Relapse and The Provoked Wife*, Congreve his *Amendments of Mr Collier's False and Imperfect Citations*, and had been attacked in turn by Collier's supporters. Collier subsequently wrote further *Defences*. As a result, actors and playwrights were prosecuted for blasphemy. Collier's attack encouraged the establishment of Societies for the Reformation of Manners, which monitored plays. His diatribe promoted the development towards unrealistic, sentimental forms of drama.

**Collins, Lottie** [Charlotte Louise Collins] 1865–1910 English MUSIC-HALL performer. The daughter of a Jewish blackface MINSTREL, she began at the age of five as a skipping-rope dancer and joined her sisters Marie and Lizzie as a song-and-dance trio on the music-halls. In 1890 she leapt to fame with 'Ta-ra-ra-boom-de-ay', a laundered version of an American brothel song, which she introduced at the Tivoli Music-Hall, London. The infectious chorus and her high-kicking display of red petticoats has been interpreted as the revolutionary anthem of the Naughty Nineties. Collins toured America in 1892, and later became a sketch artist. Her eldest daughter Jose (1887–1958) was a popular MUSICAL COMEDY singer.

**Collins, Sam** [Samuel Vagg] 1824–65 'Irish' comic vocalist, step-dancer and entrepreneur. Despite his stage persona, he was born in London and had worked as a chimney-sweep before gaining fame at the tavern halls and concert rooms of the 1840s with still-celebrated songs such as 'Limerick Races', 'No Irish Need Apply' and 'The Rocky Road to Dublin'. He took over the Rose of Normandy in London's Edgware Road, turning it into the Marylebone Music Hall, and in 1861 converted the Lansdown Arms, Islington Green, into a thousand-seater hall which opened in 1863 as Sam Collins's Music Hall.

**Colman, George,** the elder 1732–94 English playwright and manager. In 1760, while a barrister, he began a long friendship with GARRICK when his first play, *Polly Honeycombe*, a SATIRE on the sentimental novel, was produced. His first full-length play, *The Jealous Wife* (from FIELDING's *Tom Jones*), appeared in 1761. In 1764 he turned to the theatre full-time, taking part in the management of DRURY LANE. His fine translation of TERENCE (1765) was followed by the major success of *The Clandestine Marriage* (1766), a partly serious consideration of social class and marriage, co-written with Garrick. From 1767 to 1774 he was principal manager of COVENT GARDEN. His later plays are hack work or adaptations, including burlettas. In 1773 he was persuaded by GOLDSMITH to accept SHERIDAN's *The School for Scandal*, which Garrick had turned down. In 1776 he bought the HAYMARKET Theatre from SAMUEL FOOTE and made it a financial and artistic success, later passing on the management to his son.

**Colman, George,** the younger 1762–1836 English playwright and theatre manager; son of GEORGE COLMAN THE ELDER. He inherited the HAYMARKET from his father in 1794 and, although naturally improvident, improved its status and remained manager until 1817. His fourth play, *Inkle and Yarico* (1787), a comedy with songs about the slave trade, was a success there. He was at his best as a popular entertainer. His comic verse enlivens the historical romances *The Battle of Hexham* (1789) and *The Surrender of Calais* (1791). *The Iron Chest* (1796) is an adaptation of Godwin's *Caleb Williams*. His more traditional five-act comedies are *The Heir at Law* (1797), *The Poor Gentleman* (1801) and *John Bull* (1803). Colman was Examiner of Plays from 1824 to 1836, an appointment which ironically earned him the reputation of a spoiler of other people's entertainment.

**Colum, Padraic** 1881–1972 Irish playwright. A founder member of the National Theatre Society, Colum was an influential figure in the movement. In 1906 he and other ABBEY notables, disputing YEATS's autocracy, left to form the rival Theatre of Ireland (1906–12) under Edward Martyn. His first major play, *Broken Soil* (1903), was followed by *The Land* (1905), *The Fiddler's House* (Theatre of Ireland, 1907, a revision of *Broken Soil*) and *Thomas Muskerry* (1910). Few came after. His plays are about individuals at moments of decision which reflect an era of social flux. The subdued lyricism of Colum's prose amplifies their essential realism. He established a ground between SYNGE's exuberant poetry and T. C. MURRAY's plainer speech. In 1914 he emigrated to America, where he spent most of his life, celebrated for his poetry, children's stories and travel books.

**combination company** See STOCK COMPANY.

**Comden, Betty** 1915– and **Adolph Green** 1915– American librettists, lyricists and performers. Comden and Green made their BROADWAY debuts in *On the Town*

(1944). Their wry wit appeared to best advantage in the librettos and/or lyrics they created for shows with a satirical tinge, such as *Wonderful Town* (1953), *Bells Are Ringing* (1956) and *Say Darling* (1958). Their fast-paced style of MUSICAL COMEDY declined in popularity in the 1960s, but in the late 1970s and 1980s they were again successful with *On the Twentieth Century* (1978), *Singin' in the Rain* (1985) and *The WILL ROGERS Follies* (1991).

**comedia** Spanish term. In Spain from the 16th to the 18th century, the *comedia* was simply a full-scale play, whether comic or tragic in tone, as opposed to a one-act *entremés* or other short play. Though often resisting categorization, the various types of *comedia* included the following:

**comedia de capa y espada**
(cloak-and-sword comedy) The cloak and sword were the distinctive feature of the *caballeros*, or lesser nobility. This type of play is the equivalent of middle-class comedy in other countries, and a descendant of the New Comedy of MENANDER. The main elements of the plot, a mixture of comedy and thrills, were disguises, duels, misunderstandings and deceptions involved in the secret wooing of a noble lady.

**comedia de fábrica**
A court comedy involving the more refined wooing of princes, nobles and heads of state, often incorporating long journeys and unusual events.

**comedia de figurón**
A type of comedy prevalent in the late 17th and early 18th centuries in which the main humour depends on a grotesque and ridiculous character (*figurón*), often personifying some vice.

**comedia de privanza**
A play on the rise and fall of a royal favourite (*privado*), common in the first half of the 17th century.

**comedia de santo**
A dramatization of scenes from the life of a saint.

**alta comedia**
A late-19th-century form of bourgeois social drama, popularized by such playwrights as TAMAYO Y BAUS.

**Comédie-Française** French theatre and theatre company. Formed in 1680 by a royal decree merging the troupes of MOLIÈRE and of the HÔTEL DE BOURGOGNE, the Comédie-Française is the oldest European theatre company. For its first 100 years it performed in a theatre constructed in 1688–9 on the site of a tennis court in the rue des Fossés-St-Germain-des-Prés. Until the Revolution the company enjoyed a virtual monopoly on all new plays performed in the capital (shared for just some of the time with the COMÉDIE-ITALIENNE), and so the history of its repertoire is also the history of playwriting in France.

The company has always retained a collective structure, with shares held by full members of the company and decisions about repertoire and so on taken in common. At first the main influence was wielded by LA GRANGE, one of Molière's main actors, together with ARMANDE BÉJART, Molière's widow. Under Louis XV the company was able to recruit powerful performers both in tragedy and in comedy, among whom were ADRIENNE LECOUVREUR, MLLE CLAIRON, LEKAIN and the Poisson family (see BELLEROCHE). They continued to rely on the plays of RACINE, PIERRE CORNEILLE and Molière along with the tragedies of VOLTAIRE and the *comédies larmoyantes* of LA CHAUSSÉE; their greatest success was *The Marriage of Figaro*, whose opening night in 1784 had

been delayed for several years by the censor (see CENSORSHIP). Between 1770 and 1782 the company performed in the SALLE DES MACHINES at the Tuileries palace, before moving into a new building, the present ODÉON.

From the opening of the new theatre in 1782 to the burning of the Salle Richelieu in 1900, the company had a chequered career. During the Revolution the title of the theatre was changed to Théâtre de la Nation (1789). The law of the liberty of theatres of 1791 abolished the company's monopoly, and in 1793 more conservative members were arrested and narrowly avoided execution. In 1799 a fire at the Odéon brought the troupe together again. Then in 1800 the building of the Théâtre-Français became state property, and in 1802 a regular subsidy was established. Napoleon attended some 270 performances and saw the company as essential to national prestige, installing as director of operations an imperial commissar, to which post in 1825 Baron Taylor was appointed. Taylor opened the doors of the Comédie to the romantic movement, and also to a much more elaborate *mise-en-scène* than that theatre had previously contemplated. He was responsible for *Hernani* (by Victor Hugo, 1830), for example. From 1833 a series of directors was appointed, and in 1850 Louis Napoléon fixed the rights and duties of the commissar-administrator by decree.

After World War I, as COPEAU and the CARTEL directors raised standards of production, the Comédie-Française lagged behind. Bourdet was appointed administrator in 1936, with four associate directors: BATY, Copeau, DULLIN and JOUVET. During the German occupation the theatre's reputation rose again, partly thanks to BARRAULT's production of CLAUDEL's *The Satin Slipper* (1943), but since Barrault left in 1946 the Comédie-Française, though strong in BOULEVARD comedy, has continued to be a conservative force in French theatre, claiming to preserve the traditions of 17th-century performance. Its styles have changed, both in acting and production, but always considerably *after* rather than *with* the times. There are now 40 full *sociétaires* and 30 *pensionnaires*, who are actors drawing a salary, not full shareholders. The current 350 technical and administrative staff account for the theatre's large subsidy, which is considerably higher than that of any other French theatre.

Despite many reconstructions, the theatre retains VICTOR LOUIS's basic lay-out, with a horseshoe-shaped auditorium and four shallow superimposed balconies. Originally designed to hold 2,000 spectators, it now seats about 900. The latest technology has been installed without altering the fundamental stage design. After 1968 various reforms were introduced, notably in the Conservatoire, the training school, and a policy of performing more contemporary plays was initiated. In 1988 ANTOINE VITEZ was appointed director and set in hand a new programme of reforms, but these were cut short by his unexpected death in 1990. JACQUES LASSALLE (director from 1990 to 1993) was equally unsuccessful in changing a company which many politicians are determined to maintain as a monument to the national heritage.

**Comédie-Italienne** Italian theatre company resident in France. *COMMEDIA DELL'ARTE* troupes regularly visited France from the mid-16th century, led by GANASSA, FRANCESCO and ISABELLA ANDREINI, TRISTANO MARTINELLI, TIBERIO FIORILLI and others. They were so popular with Paris audiences that Louis XIV established the last-named under royal protection, and they eventually settled at the HÔTEL DE BOURGOGNE (made available by the formation of the COMÉDIE-FRANÇAISE in 1680), where they took the name of the Comédie-Italienne. The company began to adopt whole scripted plays in French, e.g. by REGNARD, and their traditional reliance on improvisation diminished in favour of contemporary SATIRE and comedy of manners. Having displeased Mme de Maintenon, the Italians were banished, but another company, under LUIGI RICCOBONI, returned in 1716 and later enjoyed a period of great prosperity in partnership with MARIVAUX, whose plays they presented between 1720 and 1740, though their link with *commedia* weakened. Ultimately they amalgamated with the Opéra-Comique under FAVART in 1762.

**comedy** From classical Greek times, comedy has been viewed in contrast to TRAGEDY, but by the late 20th century much criticism has broken free of tragedy to comment independently on comedy and its several subgenres. Although ARISTOTLE presents rival claims to the etymology of comedy, modern scholars agree that 'comedy' means 'revel-song', and a correspondingly festive spirit has been associated with many forms of comic drama. Aristotle's definition of comedy as the painlessly ugly has proved less resonant than his famous definition of tragedy (which has more to do with his philosophy than with ordinary usage), and the centuries have brought scant agreement about the nature of dramatic comedy, its function, or its components. Critical consideration of comedy has often strayed into theories of laughter.

Played at the Dionysian Festival in the 5th century BC (see GREEK THEATRE, ANCIENT), Greek comedy by the next century was classified as Old, Middle or New, and all concerned with the laughable. Old Comedy, which is extant only in the plays of ARISTOPHANES, was a rich blend of satire and fantasy, physical farce and subtle word play; it featured an ingenious trickster and closed on a lavish choral song and dance. Middle Comedy dates from the early 4th century BC, and prevailed at Athens until about the 320s. Whatever it may be (scholars disagree), burlesque of heroes and divinities dilutes the comic brew. New Comedy, which prevailed from the late 4th century to the 2nd, depicted ordinary citizens beset by ordinary problems; the playwright's concern was with the individual. The plot of New Comedy was often structured on the most durable formula of all drama: young lovers separated by an obstacle are united at the grand finale. New Comedy thrived on asides, eavesdropping, quid pro quo and mistaken indentity, and it evolved such comic types as the old grouch, the pedant, the braggart soldier – often the obstacle in the path of the young lovers. Although MENANDER may not have invented New Comedy, he was admired for his deft creations. Admiration took the form of imitation by PLAUTUS and TERENCE (see ROMAN THEATRE), and, through them, by a host of neoclassical European playwrights in both Latin and the vulgar tongues. The scheming slave of New Comedy was the ancestor of Italian Arlecchino, German HANSWURST, and the Spanish GRACIOSO.

But long before those descendants were born, Cicero had offered a widely quoted definition of comedy as 'an imitation of life, a mirror of customs, and an image of truth'. In the Middle Ages comedy was associated with the vulgar tongue (as opposed to Latin) and with a happy ending; thus Dante called his great epic a comedy. On the late-medieval stage – both amateur and pro-

fessional – comedy displayed a spectrum of techniques from slapstick to puns, from topical satire to tropical fantasy. Moreover, in religious plays devils and vice figures were simultaneously funny and evil. For the medieval mind the comic was painfully ugly.

By the Renaissance neoclassical playwrights imposed decorum on comedy as on tragedy – the proverbial unities and five acts, as well as a realistic and prosaic tone. In contrast, neoclassical playwrights like SHAKESPEARE rejected such constraints when they created what was later called romantic comedy. Both neoclassical and romantic comedies often ended in marriage, but different paths to wedlock might suggest different subgenres of comedy, even while comedy in the Romance languages gradually came to mean any play (see *comedia*). Thus, Italian and Spanish drama introduced comedy of intrigue with elaborate plots. MACHIAVELLI's *Mandragola* may well be the pinnacle of this subgenre, but the anonymous *Ingannati (The Deceived)* became a fertile model. BEN JONSON in England created COMEDY OF HUMOURS (named after the particular humour or body fluid which was believed to determine character), but in Jacobean times the broader panoply of CITIZEN COMEDY replaced it. In France MOLIÈRE usually observed classical decorum, but ranged from a farce like *The Flying Doctor* to character comedy like *The Misanthrope*. French comedy of morals crossed the English Channel as comedy of manners, which ridiculed social foibles. Type characters from COMMEDIA DELL'ARTE sprang across national boundaries into the written comedies of several languages.

Despite such gifted practitioners of comedy as Shakespeare, Molière, LOPE DE VEGA and Jonson, critics and even practitioners tended to view comedy as a genre inferior to tragedy. In the 18th century, with the rise of the bourgeoisie, comedy tried to be serious in such subgenres as LA CHAUSSÉE's *comédie larmoyante* (tearful comedy) or STEELE's sentimental comedy (resurrected belatedly in today's sitcom). At approximately the same time, the stock type of the scheming servant towered above his master in BEAUMARCHAIS's Figaro trilogy. Romantic dramatists preferred tragedy to comedy, but MUSSET's bittersweet armchair comedies set the tone not only for BÜCHNER's *Leonce and Lena* but also for playwrights as different as CHEKHOV, GARCÍA LORCA, GIRAUDOUX and BARRIE. At the turn of the 20th century comedy gained stature, largely through BERNARD SHAW, with his comedy of ideas. Although stage humour abounds in many times and places, the 20th-century commercial stage has been particularly hospitable to frivolous entertainment that goes by the name of comedy. In contrast, the zany humour of the dadaists and surrealists (see SURREALISM) was only rarely seen in the theatre before the absurd (see THEATRE OF THE ABSURD) exploded in the 1950s.

Is dramatic comedy still with us as a distinct genre? The reply will depend on how the viewer defines comedy: the new comedy formula holds in plays as different as HARVEY FIERSTEIN's *Torch Song Trilogy* and NEIL SIMON's *Barefoot in the Park*; wit scintillates in plays as bleak as SAMUEL BECKETT's *Endgame* and HAROLD PINTER's *Betrayal*. Various comic subgenres linger residually as devices – BURLESQUE, FARCE, PARODY, SATIRE, even the grotesque – in such a play as STOPPARD's *Travesties*, of undesignated genre. Comedy has been the preferred genre of political radicals from BRECHT to FO. What is hard to find today is the festive spirit implied by the etymology of comedy, which has been periodically revived in times less threatening and threatened than our own.

**comedy of humours** A comic technique in which a play is peopled with characters dominated by a single attitude or 'humour'. Familiar from ARISTOPHANES, the English style was popularized in 1598 by the enormous success of JONSON's *Every Man in His Humour* (though CHAPMAN's *An Humorous Day's Mirth* (1597) may have been the precedent), which was followed by his less successful *Every Man out of His Humour* (1599). Jonson's work was countered by DEKKER's *Satiromastix* and MARSTON's *What You Will*, then he himself struck back with *Poetaster*. Contemporary and subsequent writers of comedy have also relied on the comic potential of 'humours' – e.g. SHAKESPEARE, in the creation of Jaques in *As You Like it* (1599) and in *Twelfth Night* (c.1600), and JOHN DAY in *Humour out of Breath* (c.1608). Restoration comedy combines humours with the sophisticated comedy of manners. Through the 18th and 19th centuries, professional dramatists put humours into FARCE, and the modern television situation comedy does the same.

*commedia dell'arte* Italian term. Literally 'comedy of the profession' – that is, the dramatic form associated with the new acting companies which sprang up in northern Italy towards the middle of the 16th century – it is to be distinguished from the *commedia erudita* of gentlemanly dilettantes. But there was never in reality a fixed distinction between the *dell'arte* and the *erudita*: some *dell'arte* actors were dramatists in their own right, and throughout their history the major companies played repertories of great generic diversity. It is useful, however, to distinguish between the *dell'arte* as an institution (professional touring companies) and as an artistic form.

The original setting of that form was the simple booth stage, easily portable or organized on the spot by a company on tour, and adaptable to any context from the public piazza to the courtly hall. On this uncluttered platform the actors improvised their plays (usually farcical comedies of sex, greed and status) from skeletal scenarios, ringing the changes on a set of masked caricatures and a repertory of traditional situations and GAGS.

Two centuries saw numerous changes of detail and nomenclature in the dramatis personae of the *commedia dell'arte*, sometimes in response to the success of particular performers (ISABELLA ANDREINI probably gave her own name to the first *inamorata* of the GELOSI company, and SILVIO FIORILLO popularized Policinella (see PUNCH)), but its basic character format remained the same: two contrasted male clowns or ZANNI, of low social status, the crafty and unscrupulous Brighella and the dim-witted and famished Arlecchino (HARLEQUIN); two older male characters of high social status, bourgeois heads of household, the avaricious, lustful and suspicious merchant Pantalone and the pedantic and ineffectual Dottore; and at least one pair of lovers, the *inamorato* (under a variety of names) and *inamorata* (often Isabella), the latter frequently the over-protected daughter or younger wife of one of the senior male characters. To this basic list were added the *capitano*, a braggart soldier; the witty serving-wench Colombina (who, as the genre developed, acquired a special stage relationship with Arlecchino); the obese and malicious Pulcinella; and numerous others – additional or alternative *zanni* such as Coviello, Pedrolino

and Tartaglia, and further female characters such as the widow, to complicate the sexual intrigue.

Most of the roles had their own half-mask and COSTUME, so that they were instantly recognizable and the actor was freed from the need to establish his character, to concentrate on improvising the action. Arlecchino, whose rise in theatrical status (partly attributable to DOMENICO BIANCOLELLI's innovative fusion of the two *zanni* into a single, paradoxical character) is itself a miniature history of popular stereotypes, wore an unembellished black or dark-brown mask and a patched and motley costume which subsequently became refined into the familiar overall pattern of lozenges, and carried a wooden slapstick. Brighella was identifiable by his green and white stripes and dagger, and sometimes played a guitar. Pantalone's attributes were a beard and long nose, loose gown, red stockings, Turkish slippers and brimless hat. The female characters were not invariably masked, but they were equally recognizable by clothes appropriate to their status, and could rely on a contemporary understanding of the emotions signified by particular colours: love or hope or jealousy.

An improvised masked comedy of traditional situation, social caricature, emblematic costume and high visual impact, with no basis in a written script – all point to a form in which action takes precedence over character, where physical skills are at least as important as verbal skills, and verbal skills are of a very particular kind. Italian actors were able to play in France or Bavaria as successfully as on their Cisalpine stamping-ground. In its early days, *commedia* made great play with local frames of reference and vernaculars, and its improvised texts must have been a pot-pourri of Italian dialects in an age when there was no spoken standard.

The scenario was a chronological plot summary which was pinned up backstage, designed as an *aide-mémoire* for actors. The scenarios provide a schematic account of the intrigue (typically concerned with the ploys of tricksters in getting the girl, or the money, or both) and indicate the interpolation of the stock comic device known as a LAZZO. The scenario was the framework which every improviser required to support a performance. The performer brought to bear on this a physical training in ACROBATICS and comic business, and a verbal training in mimicry.

The origin of the *commedia dell'arte* is unknown. There is no single, clear line of descent from Roman comedy. PLAUTUS and TERENCE were known to the educated, and their conventions mediated into popular consciousness through the plays of CALMO and RUZZANTE, who added elements of local vernacular language and anarchic comic business; patter, story-telling, clowning, acrobatics, the dancing and music of the minstrel and the mountebank contributed to *commedia* techniques. The Mantua-based ACCESI, the CONFIDENTI who toured in Spain, the DESIOSI whom Montaigne admired when visiting Pisa in 1581, and the FEDELI who played at the HÔTEL DE BOURGOGNE in 1613 and 1614, were probably constructing a new art form from classical and traditional sources, just as they combined the old financial model of aristocratic patronage with the new supply-and-demand model of performing to popular audiences in the growing cities of the early modern world.

As modern Europe's first fully fledged professional drama, the artistry of *commedia* rapidly created a demand outside its homeland. The first evidence of a company (its contracts) is from 1545: by 1568 GANASSA was working in Mantua and the Gelosi in Milan; and by 1577 DRUSIANO MARTINELLI was probably in London. Before 1600 the troupes had infiltrated every important European country, influencing actors and playwrights everywhere. France, particularly Paris, was their second home, and the later history of the form is as much French as Italian. The touring of earlier decades was consolidated, by the mid-17th century, in the long-term use of the PALAIS ROYAL by TIBERIO FIORILLI's company. In 1680 the COMÉDIE-ITALIENNE was founded, occupying the Hôtel de Bourgogne as a permanent theatre, and including among its members Domenico Biancolelli and ANGELO COSTANTINI, as well as the ageing Fiorilli. Expelled in 1697 after a scandal, the company re-formed in 1716 – with 11 actors under LUIGI RICCOBONI. By 1720, when MARIVAUX wrote *Arlequin poli par l'amour* for them, they were *ipso facto* no longer a *commedia dell'arte* troupe in the old sense.

Nor was the process confined to France. In a world of growing literacy and literature, the *commedia* had its back to the wall. In its heartland, GOLDONI wrote *The Servant of Two Masters* (1745) for SACCO's Venetian company, although he disliked masked acting and improvisation. GOZZI liked them, and his self-defeating response was to write another script, *The Love of Three Oranges* (1761). Fine plays both, but no longer *commedia dell'arte*.

The influence of *commedia* is sometimes overestimated: all regions of early modern Europe had traditions of improvised performance, and their own local comic stereotypes such as HANSWURST, but analogy does not imply derivation. The particular synthesis of demotic traditions of performance with the humanist learning of the Renaissance was, however, original and immensely influential. Among the greats, JONSON, LOPE DE VEGA, MOLIÈRE and SHAKESPEARE owe a debt to *commedia*. The Anglo-German dramatic jig, the *TURLUPINADE* and the English PANTOMIME derive some of their characteristics from it. Even puppets, possibly including Punch, have been modelled on it.

*Commedia dell'arte* may have been driven out by the literary theatre, but in the 20th century's reaction against NATURALISM it has been rediscovered. MEYERHOLD, and through him Eisenstein, were influenced by it, for reasons both technical and ideological. The notion of a non-naturalistic and non-individualistic mode of acting, demanding a range of performance skills and based in recognizable social types rather than unique human personalities, contributed to the formation of the biomechanical system. Others too have recognized the usefulness of *commedia* techniques in actor-training. JACQUES COPEAU's school (founded 1921) was an early centre of mask work as part of a programme for liberating the actor's physicality. Later, inside Italy, *commedia dell'arte* has been an important inspiration in the work of the Piccolo Teatro di Milano and of DARIO FO; outside, its techniques have been applied very successfully to modern situations and issues, on both sides of the Atlantic, by the San Francisco Mime Troupe (founded 1959) and the Belgian company INTERNATIONALE NIEUWE SCENE.

**commedia erudita** See COMMEDIA DELL'ARTE

**community theatre** (USA) see LITTLE THEATRE MOVEMENT

**Compagnie des Quinze** French theatre company. Drawn from former pupils of COPEAU, the group formed in 1929 and was directed by MICHEL SAINT-DENIS. They gave performances at the VIEUX-COLOMBIER THEATRE and the ATELIER between 1931 and 1934, creating a style of theatre both poetic and acrobatic. ANDRÉ OBEY wrote several plays for them.

**Condell, Henry** ?-1627 English actor, a long-serving member of SHAKESPEARE's company, the LORD CHAMBERLAIN's MEN. Condell played the Cardinal in WEBSTER's *The Duchess of Malfi*. He shared with his colleague HEMINGES the editing of the Shakespeare Folio of 1623 and in the churchwardenship of St Mary's, Aldermanbury, in London.

**Confidenti** Italian company. These COMMEDIA DELL'ARTE actors travelled throughout Italy and to France and Spain between 1574 and 1620. In the early years the company was headed by Vittoria Piisimi assisted by Giovanni Pellesini (Pedrolino), and for a brief time in 1584 merged with the UNITI. Its leading players were then DRUSIANO, and TRISTANO MARTINELLI as Arlecchino. From 1612 until its break-up, the troupe was managed by Flaminio Scala (Flavio), who was also its scenarist.

**Confrérie de la Passion** (Confraternity of the Passion) French medieval guild. This association of Parisian artisans and merchants was formed for the performance of religious drama and recognized by letters patent of Charles VI in 1402. The members had a monopoly on dramatic activity in Paris. In 1548 they built their own theatre, the HÔTEL DE BOURGOGNE, but were deprived of much of their repertoire by a Parlement decree banning the performance of 'sacred mysteries'. Turning to moralities, farces, romances and other secular pieces, they continued to perform until the late 16th century, afterwards leasing their theatre to itinerant companies. Their monopoly was finally abolished in 1675.

**Congreve, William** 1670–1729 English playwright. Born in Yorkshire, he was brought up in Ireland and educated at Trinity College, Dublin. He moved to London to study law and became known to DRYDEN and his circle. THOMAS SOUTHERNE and Dryden helped him revise *The Old Bachelor* (first written in Ireland) for successful performance in 1693. This witty examination of courtship and marriage, in which the rake is seen as an anachronism, was followed by *The Double-Dealer* (1694), which contrasted good with evil rather than wit with folly and was thus less appreciated. After leaving the United Company, BETTERTON's group triumphantly opened their new theatre with Congreve's *Love for Love* (1695), in which the rake is in retreat for much of the play. His only tragedy, *The Mourning Bride*, was performed in 1697.

When JEREMY COLLIER singled out Congreve in his attack on the immorality of the stage, Congreve replied with his *Amendments of Mr Collier's False and Imperfect Citations* (1698). His last COMEDY, *The Way of the World* (1700), though the greatest of all Restoration comedies, was not the success he had expected. It explores the battle for wealth and fortune as well as the search for security and constancy in courtship. Mirabell and Millamant are both witty and serious in facing the difficulty of proving their love. His libretto *The Judgement of Paris* was set in 1701 and he collaborated on a MOLIÈRE adaptation, *Squire Trelooby*, in 1704, but wrote nothing else for the stage. He briefly joined VANBRUGH to manage the Queen's Theatre in London's Haymarket in 1704. Congreve's *Works* were published in 1710. In its brilliant wit and taut control his comic style marks the greatest achievement of its age.

**Connelly, Marc** [Marcus Cook Connelly] 1890–1980 American playwright, actor, producer and director. Connelly first became known on the BROADWAY scene as a collaborator of GEORGE S. KAUFMAN on such plays as *Dulcy* (1921) and *Beggar on Horseback* (1924), the latter being the most successful of their work together. His greatest contribution as a playwright came with *The Green Pastures* (1930), with an all-black cast which held the stage for 640 performances. Connelly's Broadway acting credits include the Stage Manager in a 1944 production of *Our Town* and Professor Osman in *Tall Story* (1959).

**Conquest** [Oliver] **family** English theatrical family. **Benjamin** Oliver (Conquest) (1804–72), a low comedian famous for his rendition of 'Billie Barlow', managed the Garrick Theatre in London's Whitechapel from 1830 until 1846 when it burned down, and then took over the Grecian Theatre (1851–72), where he initiated a series of PANTOMIMES featuring his son **George (Augustus Oliver) Conquest** (1837–1901). George was the most spectacular acrobatic performer of his day, excelling in grotesque characters, strenuous leaps and aerial combats. He managed the Grecian (1872–8), and then the Surrey Theatre (1881–1901), specializing in collaborative pantomimes and full-blooded MELODRAMAS. His biggest melodramatic successes were *Mankind* (1881) and *For Ever* (1882), in which he played the man-monkey Zacky Pastrana. His son **George Benjamin** (1858–1926) rose from acrobatics to roles as giants and carried on at the Surrey till 1904. His brothers were outstanding animal impersonators (see ANIMAL IMPERSONATION): **Fred** (1871–1941) excelled as the Goose in *Mother Goose*, while **Arthur** (1875–1945), after a successful career at DRURY LANE and COVENT GARDEN, appeared as Daphne the Chimpanzee on the MUSIC-HALLS in a double act with his daughter Elizabeth.

**constructivism** see THEATRE DESIGN

**Contat, Louise** 1760–1813 French actress. She created the role of Suzanne in *The Marriage of Figaro* (1784). A particularly fine comic actress, she excelled in the plays of MARIVAUX. A tendency to stoutness made her gravitate towards matronly roles. An ardent royalist, she belonged to the anti-TALMA faction of the COMÉDIE-FRANÇAISE. She was one of the members of the troupe condemned to death in 1793 who reappeared with the reunited troupe in 1798.

**Cook, Michael** 1933– British-born Canadian playwright. *Colour the Flesh the Colour of Dust* (1972), his first stage play, is a BRECHTian examination of the political turmoil in Newfoundland in 1762 as it changed from a British to a French to a British colony. *Head, Bones and Soundbone Dance* (1973) is a powerful folk play which captures both the colourful Newfoundland speech and the fatalistic attitudes engendered by the island's harsh life. *The Gayden Chronicles* (1979), commissioned by Festival Lennoxville, tells the story of a British Navy rebel who was hanged in St John's in 1812.

**Cooke, George Frederick** 1756–1812 Irish actor. One of the first actors to achieve fame in both England and America, Cooke was probably born in Dublin. He remained a travelling actor for over 25 years, most admired in roles that gave scope for satanic humour, such as Richard III, which he played regularly from 1774; he was also notable as Shylock, Iago and, controversially, Macbeth. The actor-playwright CHARLES MACKLIN also created comic roles for him. Cooke was the star of COVENT GARDEN from 1800 to 1803, rivalling

JOHN PHILIP KEMBLE at DRURY LANE, but when Kemble moved to Covent Garden in 1803 Cooke's health and fortunes declined. His voice and style, coarsened by drink, were rough in contrast to the stately Kemble. Cooke sailed secretly for New York, where he acted and drank himself to death. His last-known performance as Sir Giles Overreach in MASSINGER's *A New Way to Pay Old Debts* took place in Providence in July 1812.

**Cooke, T(homas) P(otter)** 1786–1864 English actor; hero of nautical MELODRAMA. His most famous roles were Long Tom Coffin in FITZBALL's *The Pilot* (1825), William in JERROLD's *Black-Eyed Susan* (1829) and Harry Hallyard in J. T. Haines's *My Poll and My Partner Joe* (1835). He also provided the nautical interest in BUCKSTONE's *Luke the Labourer* (1826). His natural successor was WILLIAM TERRISS.

**Cooper, Giles** 1918–66 British playwright. Although best known in his lifetime as a prolific adapter for television (see TELEVISION DRAMA), notably the *Maigret* series, he produced 70 original plays for radio, television and theatre. He had some critical success with the stage play *Everything in the Garden* (1962) and in 1964 created one of the most spectacular television plays of its time, *The Other Man*, an alternative history of Anglo-Nazi relations. His best work was in radio (see RADIO DRAMA), a medium whose extreme flexibility suited his acerbic mixture of the absurd and the naturalistic (see THEATRE OF THE ABSURD; NATURALISM). Typically, the Cooper hero inhabits a world without meaning: he may be a small cog in an industrial machine of crushing pointlessness, or a displaced soldier in a world with no room for his values. Cooper charted the decline of the British Empire in the postwar years with a sardonic verve tinged with compassion. Despite their nihilism, his plays were charged with an economical wit. Pushing out radio's technical frontiers, he pioneered electronic SOUND EFFECTS to reinforce the cartoon-like nature of some of his stories, moving adroitly between dream and reality. Six of his radio plays were published by the BBC in 1966, a rare tribute to a single radio author.

**Cooper, Thomas A(bthorpe)** 1776–1849 British-born American actor and manager. He became the first star of the American stage and the first to travel from one company to another playing only prominent roles. His London debut was as Hamlet in 1795. He left England for Philadelphia and in 1801 joined DUNLAP at the PARK THEATRE in New York, which he then managed until 1815. With STEPHEN PRICE as his partner he played the eastern circuit, excelling in heroic characters in poetic drama, such as Pierre in *Venice Preserv'd*.

**Copeau, Jacques** 1879–1949 French actor, director, critic and playwright. The major influence on the development of French theatre since World War I, Copeau founded his own theatre company in the VIEUX-COLOMBIER on the then unfashionable Paris left bank (1913). He rejected both NATURALISM and spectacle in favour of a concentration on the actor and a bare stage; his repertoire consisted mainly of SHAKESPEARE and the French classics. Associated with the theatre was a school giving theatrical training. After the war, spent in New York, the company returned to Paris to perform on a stage remodelled by JOUVET according to the Elizabethan style. In 1924 a religious crisis led to Copeau's conversion and withdrawal to the Burgundian village of Pernand-Vergelesses, accompanied by a few students. From 1925 to 1929 he and the 'Copiaus' continued their spiritual and theatrical quest for artistic perfection. When Copeau again withdrew, some of his disciples formed the COMPAGNIE DES QUINZE. Later he staged isolated religious works in the open air and occasional productions at the COMÉDIE-FRANÇAISE, where he was briefly director (1940–1); and wrote plays and an influential essay, *Le Théâtre populaire* (1941) which articulated the theoretical foundation for the postwar decentralization movement. A huge number of directors and actors trained with him, and his search for a new performance style is still acknowledged as a source by contemporary groups such as the Théâtre du Soleil.

**Coppin, George (Selth)** 1819–1906 Australian actor-entrepreneur. A child performer and low comedian in England, Coppin arrived in Sydney with Maria Burroughs in 1843, and performed and managed theatres in several Australian colonies. By the mid-1850s he had four Melbourne theatres, including his famous Iron Pot, prefabricated in Manchester. Based at the Melbourne Theatre Royal, he established a lucrative touring circuit for international performers. A member of the Victorian parliament and a public figure for over 25 years, he retained his theatrical interests until the 1890s.

**copyright** Copyright is ownership of, and right of control over, all possible ways of reproducing a work. In this context a work is an object which is the product of an original creative act (by one or more people), in a form which makes it subject to one or other means of copying. Copyright protection is given to literary, dramatic, musical and artistic works.

There are two qualifications for protection. First, that the work is capable of being 'in copyright' – that is, that it was not created or published at a time outside the period of protection offered by the law of the country in question. Second, that the work is 'original' – that is, the product of some skill and labour in composition other than the skill and labour involved in mere copying. The emphasis here is on expression rather than content. The copyright in an article expressing a new philosophical theory, for example, is in its unique sequence of words rather than in the theory as such. You do not infringe copyright in paraphrasing this theory and publishing your paraphrase (although you may be guilty of plagiarism). Indeed, your paraphrase secures its own copyright protection as another sequence of words.

**Ownership**
The creator of a work is normally the copyright owner, and no special act (e.g. registration) is required in order to establish ownership. The main exceptions are where the creator has already assigned copyright to another party via a contract entered into before the work was finished, or where the act of creation was a legitimate part of the creator's role under a contract of employment (broadly speaking, what United States copyright legislation refers to as a 'work made for hire').

**Duration of copyright**
In the main, copyright is finite: there comes a time when a work goes out of copyright and falls into the public domain. The term of copyright varies widely from country to country – from 20 years after first publication at one extreme to 80 years after the death of the author at the other.

**Transfer of rights**
'Copyright' is really a bundle of rights, and the bundle grows as more means of reproduction and dissemina-

tion are invented. The copyright in an original play, for example, will contain the performing right, the right to publish in the original language, the right to translate and to perform and publish that translation, the right to quote, the right to turn into a film, and so on. The playwright is the original owner of all these rights by virtue of authorship; and in the normal run of events they are leased out on an exclusive basis, and possibly for a fixed period of time. An 'assignment of copyright', on the other hand, is the granting of the complete copyright to another: it is a transfer of ownership.

**Dramatic copyright**
It is a surprising fact that the United Kingdom did not establish a performing right in a play (as distinct from a right to copy words on paper) until 1833. The moving force was BULWER LYTTON, whose eloquence in parliament led to a committee of inquiry into the laws affecting dramatic literature and the condition of the drama. Other countries have their different histories: enlightenment came very early to some and very late to others. Roman law appears to have identified a performance right, for example, and playwrights sold this right to the organizers of games, whilst in pre-revolutionary France the monopoly of the COMÉDIE-FRANÇAISE led to the poor author having neither rights nor payment.

Nowadays, the copyright laws of all countries contain specific protection for drama, and almost invariably a distinction is drawn between the right of publication and the right of performance. The differences and complexities arise when one starts to try to find out what each country means by 'performance', whether it takes some types of performance out of the realm of copyright, and what performance protection it gives to works other than straightforward plays (dance or mime, for example).

**Dramatization**
In all countries which recognize an author's rights, the right to dramatize (a novel, short story or whatever) is held by the author as part of his copyright. The majority of countries assume that there is a point, however, where a dramatization is so remote from the original novel (for example) as to take it outside the dramatization right held by the novelist. The dramatist may be inspired by a dominant idea or theme in a novel, and produce a work which enshrines that idea but has its own set of characters and incidents. In any event, whether the work is a faithful dramatization of the novel or whether it is remote in everything but theme, the playwright will enjoy the copyright protection that is given to an 'original' play.

**Coquelin, Constant** 1841–1909 French actor. Coquelin's name is associated with Cyrano de Bergerac (1897), which role he played over 400 times at the Porte-Saint-Martin. He was essentially a comic actor; one of his greatest successes was as Figaro. In 1886 he broke his career at the COMÉDIE-FRANÇAISE to tour in Europe and America. In 1892 he joined SARAH BERNHARDT at the Renaissance for SARDOU's *Gismonda*. The rest of his career was spent on the BOULEVARD. His great parts included Tartuffe and Don César de Bazan in *Ruy Blas* (1879). Coquelin wrote an important manual of acting in 1880, in which he stresses the importance of the voice and the actor's control of his part, leaving nothing to chance.

**Corneille, Pierre** 1606–84 French playwright and poet. One of the dominant figures in the evolution of 17th-century neoclassical drama, equally successful in

TRAGEDY and COMEDY, he produced over 30 plays. His first play *Mélite* was presented in 1629 by MONTDORY in Paris, as were his four contemporary comedies, *La Veuve* (*The Widow*, 1631/2), *La Galerie du Palais* (*The Palace Gallery*, 1632), *La Suivante* (*The Maidservant*, 1633) and *La Place Royale* (1633). His first tragedy *Médée* (1635) was produced at the MARAIS, followed by his most original, 'theatrical' comedy, *L'Illusion comique* (*The Theatrical Illusion*, 1636). Corneille was one of five playwrights commissioned by RICHELIEU, but after a stylistic disagreement he returned to Rouen, where he wrote his most celebrated play, *Le Cid*, derived from his reading of Spanish literature. The triumph of this TRAGICOMEDY at the Marais early in 1637 signalled a resurgence in French drama, but provoked a polemical exchange of pamphlets, the *Querelle du Cid*. In its wake Corneille wrote nothing for several years, but his series of 'Roman' plays, *Horace* (1640), *Cinna* (1641), *Polyeucte* (1642) and *La Mort de Pompée* (*The Death of Pompey*, 1643), followed by *Rodogune*, *Théodore* (both 1645) and *Héraclius* (1646), led to his election to the Académie-Française in 1647. All were premiered at the Marais, where the leading roles were played by FLORIDOR, who also appeared alongside JODELET in Corneille's best comedy, *Le Menteur* (*The Liar*, 1643).

The remainder of his career was mixed. Back in Paris he continued writing. *Andromède* (1650), a 'machine-play' designed to exploit TORELLI's new mechanical installations at the PETIT-BOURBON, was followed by one of his finest tragedies, *Nicomède* (1651). He also prepared a complete edition of his plays, containing commentaries on each and a considered exposition of his dramatic theory, the three *Discours sur l'art dramatique* (1660). He wrote further tragedies for the HÔTEL DE BOURGOGNE and the Marais, but began to be eclipsed by the growing success of RACINE. As tragedians, the two evoke contrary responses: Corneille's characters are emblems of nobility and heroic virtue, inspiring admiration; Racine's are portraits of emotionally and psychologically divided individuals, arousing compassion, and thus have wider appeal today.

**Corneille (de l'Isle), Thomas** 1625–1709 French playwright, younger brother of PIERRE CORNEILLE. He wrote in a variety of genres, beginning with comedy and including opera, with librettos for LULLY. Derivative but skilfully contrived, his plays were consistently popular. His tragedy *Timocrate* was a triumph at the MARAIS in 1656, and he scored further successes with two other tragedies, *Ariane* (1672) and *Le Comte d'Essex* (*The Earl of Essex*, 1678); a comedy for JODELET entitled *Le Geôlier de soi-même, ou Jodelet prince* (*Jailer to Oneself, or Jodelet Prince*, 1655); and the 'machine-play' *La Devineresse* (*The Fortune-Teller*, 1679).

**Cornell, Katharine** 1893–1974 American actress. With HELEN HAYES and Lynn Fontanne (see ALFRED LUNT) she dominated BROADWAY during the second quarter of the 20th century. Possessing a resonant voice and a remarkably expressive face, she interpreted romantic and character roles, achieving prominence with *A Bill of Divorcement* (1921). She is best remembered as Elizabeth Barrett in *The Barretts of Wimpole Street* (1931) and as SHAW's Candida (1924). Other notable appearances included *Romeo and Juliet* (1934), *The Doctor's Dilemma* (1941), *Antony and Cleopatra* (1947), *The Dark Is Light Enough* (1955) and *Dear Liar* (as MRS PATRICK CAMPBELL) in 1959.

**Corpus Christi play** Medieval play, performed on the feast of Corpus Christi. The feast, instituted in 1264, became generally celebrated in the west of Christian Europe in the early 14th century. An essential part of the celebration was a procession. There is evidence for these plays in England, Germany, Spain and Italy. The term is medieval, but its meaning in relation to the content of the play is not fixed.

**corral de comedia** Spanish theatre. The public theatres of GOLDEN AGE Spain were set in courtyards between houses. In Madrid in 1565 a charitable organization was allowed to sponsor plays in its own courtyards to raise funds for the maintenance of its hospital. Later, other courtyards were used and a second charity joined the scheme. The COMMEDIA DELL'ARTE player GANASSA helped construct a covered stage in one of these in 1574. In 1579 the Corral de la Cruz was founded and in 1582 the Corral del Príncipe, these two remaining as Madrid's two theatres until well into the 18th century. *Corrales* were also set up in other cities in the same way.

The *corral* was a courtyard with a stage at one end, projecting forward into the yard. Most of the theatre apart from the stage was exposed to the weather, though a cloth could be stretched across to provide shade. There were no seats in the pit (*patio*), but rows of benches (*gradas*) lined the sides; and, above these, boxes (*aposentos*) were formed from the rooms in the houses on each side, which had windows giving on to the yard. The king had his own box, the others being rented by nobles. Entry, which was segregated by sex, was at the rear, as was the refreshment stall (*frutería* or *alojería*). Above this was a section for lower-class women (*cazuela*). Only in the expensive boxes were the sexes allowed to mix. A separate section for clergy (*tertulia*) was at the back at second-floor level.

All performances were in the afternoon, and had to be over before dusk. The entertainment followed a set pattern. First would be music and songs, then the LOA or prologue, perhaps ending with a dance. The COMEDIA would follow, with a brief *entremés* or *sainete* (see GÉNERO CHICO) between the acts. Then, a lively *fin de fiesta* would end with a dance.

The companies of actors for each *corral* were assembled in Lent, ready to start at Easter. They were led by an actor-manager, who bought new plays outright from authors, or adapted old ones. Each company had 12 to 14 players. From 1587, as a result of the *commedia dell'arte*'s visits, women were allowed to appear on stage and boys forbidden to take women's roles. The *corrales* declined from the middle of the 17th century, as proscenium-stage theatres began to supersede them.

**Corrie, Joe** 1894–1968 Scottish playwright. A miner, Corrie wrote for the Scottish Community Drama Association and his own amateur group, the Bowhill Village Players, which toured the mining towns in southern Scotland and Northern England. His first plays, *The Shillin'-a-Week Man* and *The Poacher*, were written for performance in the 1926 General Strike, but he rejected the more experimental techniques of AGIT-PROP theatre, calling for 'old technique' to be applied to working-class Marxist themes. The majority of his plays were short political pieces depicting everyday scenes of mining and rural life in Scottish dialect, some of which gained an international reputation, being translated into Russian, German and French; he also completed two full-length historical works – a drama on Robert Burns and *Master of Men* (1944).

**Corvan, Ned** 1830–65 British comedian and songwriter. With Billy Purvis's company he was a great hit in Tyneside in the 1850s, with his songs and patter on local issues such as the price of coal ('They ken hoo to swindle poor folks'). He then went freelance, playing the growing number of northeast MUSIC-HALLS. A versatile performer, he incorporated impromptu cartooning into his act alongside self-accompanied song and character monologue, sticking strictly to his northeastern base. His work has a concrete precision of reference that is unusual on the British VARIETY stage, as well as an anarchic imagination that looks forward to DAN LENO.

**Cossa, Roberto** 1934– Argentine playwright and journalist. His first play, *Nuestro fin de semana* (*Our Weekend*, 1964), revealed him to be a major force in Argentine theatre, at the head of the so-called 'new realistic generation'. After several plays in the 1960s, in collaboration with GERMÁN ROZENMACHER, CARLOS SOMIGLIANA and RICARDO TALESNIK he wrote *El avión negro* (*The Black Aeroplane*, 1970), a collage of scenes dealing with the myth regarding Perón's possible return to Argentina. *La nona* (*The Grandmother*, 1977), the story of a voracious nonagenarian who metaphorically consumes and destroys, is perhaps his best-known play outside of Argentina. *Los compadritos* (*The Bullies*), describing a particular style of urban strong-man, is based on the sinking of a German U-boat off the coast of Uruguay at the beginning of World War II. In 1987 his *Yepeto* (of Pinocchio fame) explored the complex relationships of art, literature and life through two men enamoured of the same young woman.

**Costantini** [in France, Constantini] **family** Italian actors. The first Costantino (c.1634-c.96) played first ZANNI under the name **Gradellino** and appeared in Paris from 1687. His son **Angelo** (c.1654–1729) alternated Arlecchino with DOMINIQUE BIANCOLELLI, but Dominique's death concentrated his powers on the role of Mezzetino, his red-and-white striped costume a contrast to the green and white livery of Brighella. He performed it in Paris (1683–97) and Dresden, where he was a successful rival in love to Duke August the Strong, who clapped him in prison for twenty years. Back in Paris, he was only sporadically successful. He wrote a life of TIBERIO FIORILLI. His brother **Giovan Battista** (died 1726) played second *amoroso* under the name Cintio, succeeding Marc Antonio Romagnesi in Paris in 1688.

***costumbrismo*** (adjective: *costumbrista*) Spanish term. It refers to a style of theatre (or other genre) that captures the customs, style, characters and local colour of a particular region. Particularly strong in Spain in the early 19th century, it became characteristic of theatre in Spanish America in later periods.

**costume** Actors often find costumes more important than scenery when making theatre. Many performance traditions throughout the world, and many 'golden ages' of theatrical history, have eschewed scenic display while lavishing resources on clothing, accessories, masks and disguises. Costumes have often been an actor's or a professional troupe's most valuable property. For companies constantly on the move, a greater reliance on dress than on scenery is understandable. The importance for the performer, however, is more intimate than this. The transformation of the human body, at rest and in motion, is central both to the craft of acting and to the craft of costuming.

**Ancient Greece and Rome**
In 5th-century Athenian drama both actors and Chorus wore masks which were fully three-dimensional. They concealed the entire head of the wearer and were designed to be viewed from all directions. These helmet masks incorporated full heads of hair and often headgear or hair adornments which served to identify the characters impersonated. Facial characteristics on comic masks were exaggerated or caricatured, but on tragic masks were more lifelike and finely delineated (the distortions usually associated with the tragic mask belong to later Hellenistic and Roman practice).

Mask and costume formed a unified image. In comedy (see GREEK THEATRE, ANCIENT) lots of padding was worn on the abdomen and buttocks, to complement the exaggerated lineaments of the mask. On top of this padding a leotard and tights – to which, when appropriate, was affixed a ludicrously long leather phallus which could be coiled and uncoiled – represented stage nudity. Over this basic costume a character wore everyday clothing that was deliberately shortened or ill-fitted to reveal something of the 'stage body' underneath. In tragedy, on the other hand, the flowing outlines of long tunics and elaborately draped cloaks complemented the finely delineated features of the masks, while subtle modifications to these everyday items of clothing served to create a sense of the familiarly unfamiliar.

The most distinctive of these modifications was the fitted sleeve, extending from shoulder to wrist, which was worn by the piper (who accomanied the lyrics and dances) and tragic actor alike. Another was the *kothornos*, or calf-length boot, which became a definitive element of tragic costume. It was soft, with thin soles, and often with a pointed toe. It could be undecorated or decorated, loose or laced, but it always covered most of the leg. Outside the theatre *kothornoi* were worn by women: in tragedy they were worn by men, irrespective of the gender of the character being portrayed. In tragic costume, ceremonial and emblematic detail seems to have taken precedence over any literal naturalism. Colour and ornamentation was used to emphasize or symbolize aspects of the tragic action, as were contrasting costume changes, as the importance of clothing as an image throughout AESCHYLUS' *Persians* clearly shows.

Chorus members in tragedy wore *kothornoi* like the actors, although it is clear that they could also perform barefoot, but appear never to have worn the fitted sleeves which distinguished both piper and characters. Comic Choruses were usually dressed in padded costumes similar to those worn by the actors but, where appropriate, they also dressed in colourful and elaborate animal disguises. A comedy such as ARISTOPHANES' *Birds*, for example, would have given an ambitious *choregos* (producer) plenty of scope for a spectacular display of avian costumes and masks. Early evidence, on vases which pre-date the beginnings of organized comedy in Athens, indicates that Choruses costumed as animals, as well as Choruses costumed as fat revellers, formed part of the prehistory of Old Comedy.

In satyr plays the Chorus wore loin-cloths, which sported an equine tail and a human phallus, and the distinctive mask of the satyr with snub nose and pointed ears. Actors in satyr plays wore the same costume as in the preceding tragedies, except for the performer playing the satyrs' father, Silenus, who donned a white-tufted, tightly fitting costume which covered the whole body, and a white-bearded mask.

From the 4th century BC onwards there were significant changes in Greek attitudes to dramatic costumes and staging conventions, which in turn influenced Roman theatre practice. The transition from Old to New Comedy saw more realistic comic masks and costumes, while the popularity of mythological burlesque (particularly in southern Italy) led to a blurring of some of the distinctions between comic and tragic genres. A 4th-century vase fragment from the theatrically active city of Taras (Taranto) shows a tragedian wearing a short fringed tunic, suggesting that a greater variety in theatrical costuming accompanied the rise of the professional actor. That costuming had a valued artistic status and played an important role in dramatic festivals throughout the Graeco-Roman world is testified by numerous inscriptions recording guild membership, or prizes and expenses, for costumiers (himatiomisthai).

Roman actors in the comedies of PLAUTUS and TERENCE wore masks and Greek costumes that were appropriate to the type of stock character portrayed. Some, like the Slave and Old Man, were grossly exaggerated, larger than life; others, like the Young Man and Young Woman, wore a more naturalistic disguise. A statue of a courtesan, found in Pompeii, shows her colourful costumes for the palliata (comedy in Greek dress) must have been. The mask has red hair and red lips, and a pale rose-violet mantle with fringes is draped over a light-blue short-sleeved robe. The influence of Italian FARCE can be detected in some of the grotesque stock disguises: the mask for the Old Man, for example, resembles that of the Attellan Pappus. Costumes in these native farces, as well as in the togata (comedy in Roman dress) which came to rival the palliata in popularity, reflected Roman and other local forms of dress. Three terracotta statuettes of masked actors, at present in the British Museum, show something of the variety that was possible: one is dressed in the Roman sagula, another in a Roman toga and the third in the Roman paenula (see ROMAN THEATRE).

A tendency, observable in late-Hellenistic tragic costume, towards vertical distortion was developed to an extreme degree on the Roman stage. The tragic actor wore boots with platform soles and heels or, eventually, stilts. The features of the tragic mask became distorted and stylized, and the forehead and hair were heightened in an increasingly two-dimensional dome. Lucian, writing in the 2nd century AD, gives an unsympathetic but graphic description of this artificial and conventional theatrical costume: 'How frightful and repellent a spectacle is a man tricked out to disproportionate size, mounted on high boots, wearing a mask that extends above his head with a mouth yawning wide as though to swallow the audience; not to mention the padding he wears on chest and paunch so that his own slender figure will not betray this excessive stature.'

## Asia

In ancient India, costume was carefully regulated in the SANSKRIT THEATRE to indicate such features as character-type, profession and social status, and to evoke emotional states and sentiments. Dress, ornaments and make-up were viewed as essential elements in the transformation that was central to the art of the actor. As the Natyasastra puts it: 'Just as the soul after renouncing the nature proper to one body assumes another character related to the body of another, so a person having a different colour and make-up adopts the behaviour connected with the clothes he wears.' The use of colour was particularly emphasized. Abhira maidens wore dark-blue clothes; wandering ascetics, sages and Buddhist monks wore dark red; ministers, bankers and merchants wore white. Colouring of the face and limbs was an important part of the overall design. Different gods and demi-gods had their appropriate colour, while human characters were painted 'in conformity with their habitation, birth and age'.

Many of the traditional theatre forms found throughout India today continue something of this elaborate codification of make-up, dress and adornment. In KATHAKALI, for example, an audience can tell from the details and colours of a character's disguise not only what type of character is being presented but also what kind of behaviour they should be prepared for. Types range from the refined and heroic (pacca, or green roles) to the grotesque and primitive (kari, or black roles). A great deal of time and care can be taken in such codified costuming; for instance, the voluminous and complexly folded skirt worn by heroic characters in KUTIYATTAM takes three hours of patient preparation before it can be tied to the performer's waist.

From the evidence of early murals, brick reliefs and figurines, it is clear that a similar emphasis on costume and make-up was a distinguishing feature of theatrical performances in ancient China. However, the symbolic system of painted-face roles encountered in modern Beijing opera (see JINGXI) is part of a tradition of stylization which appears only to have begun during the Ming dynasty. In Yuan drama, make-up was used sparingly and the range of colours was restricted. Character types could be delineated by the use of false beards, but more particularly by specific and detailed items of clothing. In a players' edition of ZAJU dramas 46 types of hat and an even larger number of different jackets are listed for the male roles.

It was during the Ming and Qing periods that elaboration, synthesis and standardization of make-up and costume occurred as part of the conventional codes and symbolic modes of acting developed both in the private and the professional troupes. The close relationship between costume and acting conventions can be seen in the way such items as the extremely long and loose 'water' sleeves, which as early as the Han dynasties had been a feature of dancers' costumes, were incorporated into the symbolic systems developed for character portrayal by the acting companies. Costumes for KUNQU and pihuang xi became increasingly luxurious, often made of silk and richly embroidered, with headgear and adornments that extended the performer's referential and aesthetic powers. The four flags sewn to the back of the Great General's costume in Beijing opera, for example, allowed an actor to indicate the presence of his army at his back, and the long silver-pheasant tail feathers that adorned his headdress could be manipulated to punctuate thoughts, words, emotions and actions.

This interplay between symbolic and formal codes in acting and in costuming is particularly marked in Japanese NŌ and KABUKI traditions. In kabuki the exaggerated embellishments in form, texture and colour of the actor's bodily image both intensify and are intensified by the convention of freezing the action at moments of heightened emotion. In the Edo style of aragoto (the heroic mode of the ICHIKAWA DANJŪRŌ acting dynasty), the thick red and black lines of face-paint on a white base form an expressive background against which 'acting with the eyes' can stand out vividly, framed by the ferocious formalism of the *kurumabin* wig. At the same time the padding, the recurved toes and fingers, and the gigantic sword fuse with the extended outlines and brilliant colours of the costume to transfigure every motion or pose and imbue the actor's patterns with a sense of superhuman energy.

Whatever the style in *kabuki*, however, the colouring and ornamenting of a costume also convey specific symbolic information. Today, each of the lavish and aesthetically spectacular dresses worn by the courtesan Agemaki in the play *Sukeroku*, which were designed by Iwai Hanshiro V, are rich with such emblematic references. In the scene where Agemaki turns away her lover's mother, for instance, her sash is composed of a bush-like profusion of poems, a design which alludes to the custom of hanging scrolls from bamboo branches at the Star Festival in celebration of the love of the Herdsman star and the Weaving Maiden star who meet briefly, once a year, across the divide of the Milky Way.

In contrast to the expressive exuberance of *kabuki* costume and acting styles, the SYMBOLISM and formalism in *nō* theatre is more restrained and subtle. The *waki* or Sideman is normally dressed in dark colours and mat fabrics to highlight the revelations encoded in the bright robes (*shozoku*) and elegant masks (*nohmen*) worn by the *shite*, or Doer. Both mask and costume are crafted so that the slightest movement pattern can alter a character's appearance and liberate, through suggestion and context, a sense of universal flux. Masks are attached to the front of the head and are usually rather small, thus emphasizing rather than disguising the performer's body. When portraying a female character, the way that outer robe and under-robe are worn in combination can indicate whether the character is a court lady or is mad or is half-dressed. The stress on the quality of material, colour, ornamentation and stylized beauty of the Doer's disguises is an essential element in *nō* theatre, guiding the audience's concentration towards the slow tempo and minimalism of the action.

## Europe before 1900

In medieval drama, theatrical costumes ranged from the exotic to the stylized and ceremonial and to the realistic and everyday. Church vestments were worn in the early *Quem queritis* tropes, but as the variety of enactment increased so MIMETIC and representational details were added. Costume specifications in an *ordo prophetarum* of the 13th century from Laon in France record this development: a beard for Isaiah, dressed in a dalmatic with a red stole, and a beard and a hunchback for Habbakuk; while the clergy playing Daniel and Elizabeth are respectively said to be 'dressed as a young man in a gorgeous robe' and 'dressed as a woman pregnant'. A 14th-century *visitatio sepulchri* from Dublin distinguishes John from Peter by dressing one in white and the other in red, one carrying a palm, the other keys (their emblems as saints).

Outside the Church, theatrical costuming often showed a similar emphasis on indicative or symbolic detail: a money-bag for Judas, a crown for Mary, and a scarlet gown with a blue tabard and a mitre 'after the old law' for Annas in the English N. town PASSION PLAY. Materials and colours could be sumptuous and varied – Herod's queen in the Bourges (France) *Acts of the Apostles* (1536) wore a purple satin cloak, lined with silver, over a gown of violet velvet which had sleeves of cloth of gold –

and wigs, masks and other elaborate bodily extensions were frequently employed.

Heads of yellow hair, suits of gold skins and pairs of iridescent wings for the angels contrasted with the distorted animality of the masks worn by the devils, who were covered all over with hair, feathers or serpent-like scales, or wore coats and trousers with bat-like flaps and ferocious faces painted on their bellies, knees and bottoms. Lucifer could descend to hell 'apparelled foul with fire about him' and then transform into 'a fine serpent made with a virgin face and yellow hair upon her head'. Death, in Saragossa in 1414, was dressed in tight-fitting yellow leather so that his body and head looked like those of a skeleton – 'quite cadaverous, without substance, without eyes' – beckoning now to one, now to another of the onlookers to come with him. The range and often lavish nature of theatrical costuming in the Middle Ages is apparent from the many references in the records that survive.

This visual exuberance, its conventions and symbolism, were developed in the English MORALITY PLAYS and Tudor moral INTERLUDES in ways which significantly influenced later practice on the Elizabethan public stage. Elizabethan fashion, with its extravagant stiffening, padding and distorting of all natural lines (in male as well as female dress), reflects the age's intense interest in clothes. It is an interest which also dominates the theatre of the time. Dramatic texts are studded with observations on their characters' clothes, costume being seen both as an expression of power, status and wealth and as a mirror of inner qualities or transitory moods. On the largely bare platform, a hero or heroine's changing fortunes were visibly emphasized by changes of costume rather than changes of scenery. The wardrobe master, or TIREMAN, had an important task to fulfil and, as we learn from HENSLOWE's diary, an actor could expect the fine for removing a costume from the playhouse to be some 40 times greater than the fine that might be imposed for missing a performance. No wonder, when the sum expended on taffeta to make two gowns for a single production in 1598 cost three times the average takings for a performance!

Some suggestion of historical or exotic dress, appropriate to the period or place depicted, may also have been employed for individual characters. Henry Peacham's drawing of characters in *Titus Andronicus* shows Titus, Aaron and two kneeling figures in fanciful versions of Roman attire, while Tamara and two soldiers are in English costumes. In the court masque, particularly in the work of INIGO JONES from 1605 onwards, this mixture of character-specific styles began to be transformed by a more unified and pictorial sense of design. Jones introduced to England, alongside Italian perspective scenery, the scholarship and ideals of the Renaissance theatre designer.

Designers like BUONTALENTI and his successor PARIGI embodied the ideals of nobility and magnificence in theatrical costume articulated by YEHUDA LEONE DE' SOMMI in his dialogues on scenic representation. The fusion of the imaginary, the contemporary and the classical in their designs proved an influential model for aristocratic display, festivities and entertainment outside, as well as inside, Italy (a model that was developed and transformed at the court of Louis XIV in the work of the great JEAN BERAIN). In particular, the dissemination – throughout the courts of Europe – of the image of the stage hero dressed as an imperial Roman conqueror affected theatrical practice for more than two hundred years. A Roman tunic and breastplate with overskirt, together with a helmet plumed with ostrich feathers, define the heroic or tragic actor throughout the baroque period. Changing notions on decorum and display continually modify details, but the exalted status of the Roman image remains a constant. Inigo Jones, when costuming Prince Henry in JONSON's *Oberon, The Fairy Prince*, eschewed an actual Roman skirt and created the illusion of its leather strips on more decorous trunk-hose; MOLIÈRE added a highly fashionable periwig when playing Julius Caesar in 1659; SPRANGER BARRY and DAVID GARRICK added contemporary long, cuffed sleeves to their armour and wore knee-breeches under their tonnelets (overskirts). Examples from the DROTTNINGHOLM COURT THEATRE of this baroque tragic attire are covered with sequins, crystals, spangles and copper threads that are designed to act as reflectors and enhance the illusion of heroic glory.

Plumes and classical overskirt also defined the baroque heroine, although the transformations due to changing tastes and fashions were even more pronounced. The overskirt might be reduced to tasselled lappets, or the hair piled higher and higher in place of the plumes. Whatever identified social superiority in high society, the theatre appropriated in order to emphasize the status of the tragic heroine. Baroque theatre costumes did not simply ape current trends and values; they also refashioned them and even, at times, created them. The *fontange* or towering hairstyle, for example, was conceived on the stage.

The quest for authenticity, REALISM or historical accuracy in theatrical costuming was a recurrent theme in stage theory and practice throughout the 19th century. Many of the costume 'reforms', initiated largely by actors and actresses, prefigured the systematic, 'scientific' 19th-century achievements that culminated in NATURALISM. These 'reforms', which at the time were lauded as authentic, realistic or historically accurate, now seem little more than tinkerings with the fashions of the day in defiance of outmoded stage conventions. Garrick and IFFLAND's concern for realism and truth in stage costume, for example, entailed adapting 'modern dress' and selected historical features to suit the characteristic and individualized details of a role. LEKAIN's concern for 'costumes appropriate to the period and manners of the action represented' amounted to little more than exotic and magnificently fulsome adaptations of conventional heroic attire, as depictions of his Oriental disguise for VOLTAIRE's *Orphelin de la Chine* clearly show.

Far more significant was TALMA's appearance, as a minor character in a 1789 revival of another of Voltaire's dramas, dressed in a toga faithfully copied from a Roman sculpture. Influenced by his friend, the painter David, Talma's innovations throughout his career were based on the conviction: 'Truth in the costume as well as in the scenery increases the illusion, takes the spectator right into the century and the country where the characters are living.'

A similar conviction sustained the unremitting researches of figures like Count Carl von Bruhl in Germany or J. R. PLANCHÉ and CHARLES KEAN in England – researches which informed every aspect of every costume in spectacular productions that sought to re-create, as it were, accurate pictures from the past. Under von Bruhl's direction, at the BERLIN ROYAL THEATRE

from 1814 onwards, even the cloth for a particular costume could be 'woven specially to reproduce the identical texture it would have had in the period concerned'. In Kean's production of *King John* (1852), the individual coat-of-arms for each noble in the play had been researched in the heraldic records and every detail was scrupulously reproduced.

This passion for exactitude was more consistently and influentially developed in the work of the MEININGEN COMPANY, who performed in most of the major cities in Europe from 1874 to 1890. Every detail of costume was intended not only to be historically correct, and actual rather than simulated in construction, but also to be harmonized with the scenery, the properties, the lighting, the sound, the movements on stage. Costume was considered as part of a total impression, of an authentic living picture. Such verisimilitude influenced ANTOINE in France, BRAHM in Germany, and STANISLAVSKY and NEMIROVICH-DANCHENKO in Moscow. For the first production of the MOSCOW ART THEATRE in 1898, the costumes of the Tsar, the boyars and the people were exact replicas of historical documents and were fashioned from genuine old materials gathered by the company from villages and markets. 'We wanted to depart from vulgar and theatrical gilding and cheap scenic luxury; we wanted to find another simpler, richer finish informed with some of the real spirit of the past.'

## The 20th century

Fidelity to period, place and psychology in theatrical dress, together with a desire for the authentic detail, 'the real spirit', is a legacy that has lingered throughout this century in spite of the numerous anti-naturalistic movements that have transformed so much of theatre practice. APPIA and CRAIG had far more influence on scenery and light than on costume. However, Craig's interest in masks, his symbolist designs for YEATS, and his fusion of costume and set in a single image (as, for instance, Claudius' enormous cloak, enveloping most of the stage, through which the courtiers of Elsinore appeared) adumbrated future developments. Many of BECKETT's arresting stage images, for example, show a similar fusion of environment and dress.

The extension of the image of the human body outside the dictates of fashion – or the conventions established through performance traditions – is perhaps the single most innovative strand in 20th-century costume design. EXPRESSIONISM in Germany and constructivism in Russia both used distortion and abstraction to play on the 'normal' expectations concerning human appearance (although stage settings were often more adventurous in this respect). Far more radical was the work of OSKAR SCHLEMMER, whose transformations of the human body in motion through mask and costume influenced modern dance and foreshadowed developments in both performance art and experimental theatre in the second half of the century. The work of BREAD AND PUPPET THEATRE, WELFARE STATE INTERNATIONAL and ODIN TEATRET is indicative of this strand.

The other major shift in this century is the triumph of the designer (see THEATRE DESIGN). Although costumiers and costume designers have been important figures in the past, actors have also been keenly involved in the issue of appearance. During the 20th century such involvement has diminished. With the rise of the modern director, the notion of a unified vision shaped from outside the action has become a standard assumption, and the individual style of a designer has become a central feature of any production.

**Coulter, John** 1888–1980 Irish-born Canadian playwright. Born in Belfast, he taught for five years in Dublin where he was much influenced by the ABBEY THEATRE. He moved to Toronto, where his play *The House in the Quiet Glen* (1937) won several awards. The Canadian Broadcasting Corporation commissioned librettos for two operas by Healey Willan: *Transit through Fire* (1942) and *Deirdre* (1946). In addition to radio and television drama, his best-known work is *Riel* (1950), an epic play about the leader of the 19th-century Métis rebellion in Western Canada. The same historic episode also yielded *The Crime of Louis Riel* (1966) and *The Trial of Louis Riel* (1968).

**court theatres** (England) Elaborate entertainments at the Tudor and Stuart courts might demand the temporary adaptation of indoor spaces, e.g. the Great Hall at Hampton Court, the Banqueting Houses and the Great Chamber at Whitehall, and the Great Halls at Greenwich, Richmond and Windsor. Under Charles I, more permanent structures were adapted or built. INIGO JONES converted the COCKPIT-IN-COURT (1629–30) into an intimate theatre similar to the COCKPIT THEATRE in Drury Lane. In 1637 the Masquing House was erected close to Jones's Banqueting Hall (1619–22). The custom of adaptation declined under Charles II.

**Courtenay, Tom** [Thomas] **(Daniel)** 1937– British actor. Courtenay helped to change the image of English acting in the early 1960s. Not conventionally handsome, with a northern accent, he played Konstantin in an OLD VIC production of CHEKHOV's *The Seagull*, stressing not just the doomed romanticism but also the provincialism of Arkadina's son. He took over from ALBERT FINNEY in the title role of *Billy Liar* (1961) and established himself quickly as a brilliant deadpan comic, starring in two ALAN AYCKBOURN comedies, *Time and Time Again* (1972) and *The Norman Conquests* (1974). In Manchester, where he was part of the 69 Company at the ROYAL EXCHANGE THEATRE for several seasons, he played Hamlet, Peer Gynt and the title role in RONALD HARWOOD's *The Dresser*. Courtenay's style of acting adapts well to television and films, retaining its down-to-earth credibility. Perhaps his most memorable London role was as John Clare, the Northamptonshire poet-peasant, in EDWARD BOND's *The Fool* (1975) at the ROYAL COURT THEATRE. His stage appearances became less frequent in the 1980s, though he was a memorable Argan in MOLIÈRE's *The Imaginary Invalid*. In 1988 he played James, the innocent victim of an estate agent in MARTIN CRIMP's *Dealing with Clair*.

**Cousin, Gabriel** 1908– French playwright and poet. Cousin's career has been entirely outside Paris. His plays deal with major world problems of our time – hunger, racism, exploitation, the nuclear threat – but approached through working-class or peasant communities. His first success, *Le Drame du Fukuryu Maru* (1962), concerned the fishermen affected by a hydrogen bomb test in the Pacific in 1954. *L'Aboyeuse et l'automate* (*The Barker and the Automaton*, 1961) is about loneliness and exploitation. *L'Opéra noir* (*Black Opera*, 1967) is a musical about racial violence and *Le Voyage de derrière la montagne* (*The Journey behind the Mountain*, 1966) is a Japanese tale of old age and poverty. His most accomplished play is *Le Cycle du crabe* (*The Crab Cycle*, directed by Cousin, 1975), about the inhabitants of a shanty town in South America. His plays are filled with songs and movement, however austere the subject.

**Covarrubias, Francisco** 1775–1850 Cuban impresario and actor. The acknowledged father of the Cuban national theatre, he wrote more than 20 plays. He was famous for his representation of the *negrito* (the white actor in blackface), probably before the famous roles created by THOMAS D. RICE and Daniel Decatur Emmett in the USA. Covarrubias integrated popular Cuban figures into forms of the Spanish *sainete* (see GÉNERO CHICO) without political implications or character development, but no play has survived.

**Covent Garden, Theatre Royal** (London) There have been three theatres on or near the Bow Street site, formerly part of a convent garden. The first was built by JOHN RICH, holder of one of the two royal patents. With a capacity of nearly 3,000, it opened with a revival of CONGREVE's *The Way of the World* in 1732. Rich's company featured opera, ballet and an annual PANTOMIME. Rivalry with DRURY LANE was a feature of these early years. After Rich's death in 1761, opera briefly predominated, but the partnership of GEORGE COLMAN THE ELDER and Thomas Harris (1767–74) restored the balance. GOLDSMITH's *The Good-natured Man* (1768) and *She Stoops to Conquer* (1773) and SHERIDAN's *The Rivals* (1775) were premiered there. Structural alterations and enlargement took place in 1792. GEORGE FREDERICK COOKE made his London debut at Covent Garden in 1800, and the first self-proclaimed MELODRAMA, THOMAS HOLCROFT's *A Tale of Mystery*, was staged there in 1802. Harris stole JOHN PHILIP KEMBLE from Sheridan's Drury Lane in 1803.

When the first theatre was destroyed by fire in 1808, a second opened in 1809. Kemble had agreed to raise prices, but the fierce Old Price Riots forced the management into submission. SARAH SIDDONS gave her farewell performance at Covent Garden in 1812, four years before MACREADY made his unwilling debut there. Gaslight for auditorium and stage was installed in 1817. In 1821, John Kemble handed over responsiblity to his brother CHARLES KEMBLE, who successfully staged *King John* there in historical costume (1823), but who nevertheless became impoverished by his involvement with the theatre. Subsequent managers – Laporte (1832–3), ALFRED BUNN (1833–5), Osbaldiston (1835–7), Macready (1837–9) and MADAME VESTRIS and CHARLES JAMES MATHEWS (1839–42) – were no luckier. The patent houses could no longer afford their supremacy. After Vestris, Covent Garden remained closed until 1847, when it entered on a new life as the Royal Italian Opera House, seating over 4,000. It was burnt to the ground in 1856.

The third theatre (capacity 2,141) opened in 1858 with a performance of Meyerbeer's *Les Huguenots* and has been associated with opera ever since, with the addition of ballet since 1946. It has been known as the Royal Opera House since 1939.

**Coward, Noël** 1899–1973 British playwright and actor. His most substantial work for the theatre was in the late 1920s to the early 1940s, with a series of rather precious but witty comedies (*Fallen Angels* (1925), *Hay Fever* (1925), *Private Lives* (1930), *Design for Living* (1933), *Blithe Spirit* (1941) and *Present Laughter* (1942)). World War II brought from him some patriotic pieces that were successful in their time (*This Happy Breed* (1942), *Peace in Our Time* (1947)), reworking a flag-waving enthusiasm first seen in *Cavalcade* (1931). As a composer and song-writer he produced popular tunes; in the theatrical orbit he was termed 'the Master'. He was knighted in 1970.

**Cowell, Sam(uel Houghton)** 1820–64 American-born British actor and MUSIC-HALL performer. The son of a DRURY LANE actor, Joe Cowell (1792–1863), he began his career in the legitimate theatre, touring the USA. Returning to England, he converted himself into a comic vocalist and BURLESQUE performer in the song and supper rooms of the WEST END – one of the first of his kind, burlesquing SHAKESPEARE among others. An ugly little man with a lugubrious expression, he specialized in cockney song-and-patter acts.

**Cowl, Jane** 1884–1950 American actress. She made her New York stage debut in 1903 in *Sweet Kitty Bellairs*. Her portrayal of the wronged woman, Mary Turner, in *Within the Law* (1912), established her as a star. Cowl appeared in plays that she wrote or co-wrote, including *Lilac Time* (1917), *Daybreak* and *Information Please* (1918), and *Smilin' Through* (1920). In 1923 she played Juliet in a production which ran for 174 consecutive performances. Her successful rendering of Larita in NOËL COWARD's *Easy Virtue* (1925) was followed by Amytis in *The Road to Rome* (1927) and Lucy Chase Wayne in *First Lady* (1935). She was famous in London as well as New York; BROOKS ATKINSON praised her 'personal beauty, impeccability of manners, humorous vitality, and simple command of the art of acting'.

**Cowley, Hannah** 1743–1809 English playwright. Her first play, *The Runaway*, was 'embellished' and produced by GARRICK in 1776. Her afterpiece *Who's the Dupe?* (1779) successfully used traditional figures of comedy such as the pedant. Her best play, *The Belle's Stratagem* (1780), and *A Bold Stroke for a Husband* (1783) make extensive and unfashionable use of Restoration comedy as sources.

**Crabtree, Lotta** [Charlotte] 1847–1924 American actress. As a dancer and singer in California, this tiny, red-haired, elfin figure became a featured performer in mining camp VARIETY troupes. She conquered San Francisco in 1859, then headed east. She turned to legitimate drama in the dual leading roles of *Little Nel and the Marchioness* (1867), dramatized for her from DICKENS's *The Old Curiosity Shop* by JOHN BROUGHAM. Her roles exhibited her skills at mimicry, banjo-picking and clog dancing.

**Craig, Edith** 1869–1947 British actress and director. The sister of GORDON CRAIG and daughter of ELLEN TERRY, she began her career performing with HENRY IRVING at the London LYCEUM in 1890. She constructed the costumes designed by her brother for his productions in 1900–1, and stage-managed her mother's 1907 American tour. She designed and directed for the Pioneer Players (between 1911 and 1921) and in London.

**Craig, (Edward Henry) Gordon** 1872–1966 British theorist, director and stage designer. Trained under HENRY IRVING, he was already a leading actor before leaving the London LYCEUM in 1897. He directed and designed a series of highly praised but financially unsuccessful productions, ranging from opera (*Dido and Aeneas*, 1900; *The Masque of Love*, 1901; *Acis and Galatea*, 1902) to LAURENCE HOUSMAN's nativity play *Bethlehem* (1902) and IBSEN's *The Vikings* (1903), before leaving for Germany where he designed productions for OTTO BRAHM and ELEONORA DUSE and influenced MAX REINHARDT, as well as beginning his association with Isadora Duncan.

In 1905 he published *The Art of the Theatre*, calling for a non-naturalistic theatre (see NATURALISM) equivalent to music or poetry, and establishing the dominant position of the modern director. This was followed by one of the first proposals for an English NATIONAL THEATRE and an attack on conventional acting, apparently demanding the elimination of the human performer, which was published in the first issue of the *Mask*. From 1908 until 1929 this quarterly journal, published and largely written by Craig himself, ranged over the whole history of the stage, arguing for an abstract and ritualistic theatre. Its basis was to be light and rhythmic movement, using a flexible stage. He founded a school of theatre in Florence in 1913 (closed by World War I in 1915), and invented movable screens to substitute for scenery. These were used by W. B. YEATS at the ABBEY THEATRE, Dublin, in 1911, and by Craig himself in the famous 1912 *Hamlet*, which he directed for STANISLAVSKY's MOSCOW ART THEATRE.

Although, apart from this production, he directed only one other play – Ibsen's *The Pretenders* in Copenhagen (1926) – the originality of Craig's writings and the visionary nature of his designs have had a lasting impact on 20th-century theatre.

**Cratinus** fl. c.450–c.423 BC Greek comic playwright. The most prominent poet of Old Comedy (see GREEK THEATRE, ANCIENT) in the generation before ARISTOPHANES, Cratinus was noted for his invective, uninhibited even by Aristophanes' standards. Numerous brief fragments survive.

**Crawford, Cheryl** 1902–86 American producer. Crawford was at the centre of American theatrical enterprise in the first half of the century. After working for the THEATRE GUILD in the late 1920s she co-founded with HAROLD CLURMAN and LEE STRASBERG the GROUP THEATRE in 1931, and created the AMERICAN REPERTORY THEATRE (1946) with EVA LE GALLIENNE and MARGARET WEBSTER. In 1947 she co-founded with ELIA KAZAN and ROBERT LEWIS the ACTORS STUDIO. A remarkably self-effacing impresario and efficient administrator, she withdrew from the organizations she helped to foster in order to produce independent musicals. Her biggest commercial success was *Brigadoon* (1947); other notable Crawford productions include the 1942 revival of *Porgy and Bess*, *One Touch of Venus* (1943), *Paint Your Wagon* (1950), *Mother Courage* (1963) and four plays by TENNESSEE WILLIAMS – *The Rose Tattoo* (1951), *Camino Real* (1953), *Sweet Bird of Youth* (1959) and *Period of Adjustment* (1960).

**Crazy Gang** British comedians. This group brought comedy techniques from VARIETY and CIRCUS to create a unique brand of knockabout satirical FARCE. (Bud) Flanagan (born Chaim Reuben Weinthrop) and (Chesney William) Allen, Jimmie Nervo (James Holloway) and Teddy Knox (Albert Edward Cromwell-Knox), Charlie Naughton and Jimmy Gold (James McConigal), with 'Monsewer' Eddie Gray, were brought together by GEORGE BLACK for 'crazy weeks' at the London Palladium in 1932. These improvisations developed into a popular series of REVUES, from *Life Begins at Oxford Circus* (1935) to *These Foolish Things* (1938); and their success was repeated at London's Victoria Palace from 1947 (*Together Again*) to 1960 (*Young in Heart*).

**creación colectiva** (collective creation) LATIN-AMERICAN THEATRE term. The technique of collective theatre that appeared in Latin America around 1968 reflected concepts of group performance seen earlier in the LIVING THEATRE, OPEN THEATRE and others. Particularly strong in Argentina, Chile, Peru and especially Colombia, this theatre served to express social and historical themes through Marxist ideology. Two good examples from Colombia are the Teatro Popular de Bogotá's *I Took Panamá* (1974), a documentary on Teddy Roosevelt's imperialistic move to gain canal rights, and La Candelaria's *Guadalupe, años sin cuenta (Guadalupe, the Fifties (Years without Number)*, 1975), which took advantage of a titular word play (*sin cuenta* means 'countless', *cincuenta* means 'fifty') to focus on the years of 'the Violence' that devastated life and politics in Colombia. In the 1990s the concept of *creación colectiva* is much diminished.

**Crébillon, Prosper Jolyot de** 1674–1762 French playwright. As if to eclipse the memory of RACINE, he cultivated passionate and sensational subject-matter. His most successful tragedies, *Atrée et Thyeste* (1707), *Electre* (1708) and *Rhadamiste et Zénobie* (1711), are rhetorical tissues of pathos, horror and complicated plotting.

**Crimp, Martin** 1956– British playwright. Crimp has been likened to HAROLD PINTER: behind his studies of apparently tranquil suburban life are signs of menace. *Dealing with Clair* (1988) concerns the relationships between an estate agent, a yuppie couple and an innocent cash buyer. *Play with Repeats* (1989) concerns a man who, feeling himself to be inadequate, seeks advice from a guru. *No One Sees the Videos* (1990) is an attack on market research, while *Getting Attention* (1991) develops from a sit-com (see TELEVISION DRAMA) into a frightening study of child abuse.

**Cronyn, Hume** 1911– Canadian-born American actor and director. Cronyn trained and acted in the States and directed his wife JESSICA TANDY as Miss Collins in TENNESSEE WILLIAMS's *Portrait of a Madonna* (1946) in Los Angeles. Cronyn and Tandy appeared together in 1951 in *The Fourposter*, in which they were compared to the LUNTS, and later co-starred in *The Physicists* (1964), ALBEE's *A Delicate Balance* (1966), *The Gin Game* (1977), Noel Coward in *Two Keys* (1974) and *Foxfire* (1982), of which Cronyn was co-author. In 1964 he played Polonius to RICHARD BURTON's Hamlet.

**Crothers, Rachel** c.1878–1958 American actress, playwright and director. Her commercially successful plays chronicled the tension in early-20th-century women between their new economic and sexual freedom and their traditional values. Her first success, *The Three of Us* (1906), was followed by some 30 BROADWAY plays, most of which she directed and staged herself. She wrote some sentimental plays in the 1910s, but her best works were her half-comic, half-serious women-centred plays: *Myself Bettina* (1908), *A Man's World* (1910), *Ourselves* (1913), *Young Wisdom* (1914), *He and She* (1920, first produced 1911), *Expressing Willie* (1924), *Let Us Be Gay* (1929), *As Husbands Go* (1931), *When Ladies Meet* (1932) and *Susan and God* (1937).

**Crouse, Russel** 1893–1966 American playwright, librettist and producer. Crouse teamed with HOWARD LINDSAY on *Anything Goes* (1934) and on many other plays and librettos, including *The Sound of Music* (1959). They also produced many plays in New York, including *Arsenic and Old Lace* (1941).

**Crowne, John** c.1640–1712 English playwright. In 1675 he wrote the last court MASQUE, *Calisto*. His heroic play *The Destruction of Jerusalem* was successful in 1677. His finest tragedy, *The Ambitious Statesman* (1679), is a serious study of political power. A favourite of the king, Crowne was given the subject for his popular comedy, *Sir Courtly Nice* (1685), by Charles himself. His political comedy, *City*

*Politiques* (1682), mocked leading lawyers and politicians. *The Married Beau* (1694), his last comedy, is a cynical SATIRE on the torture of marriage.

**Cruelty, Theatre of** see ARTAUD, ANTONIN

**Cuadra, Pablo Antonio** 1912– Nicaraguan poet, historian, journalist and playwright. Cuadra founded important cultural periodicals in Managua, such as *Vanguardia* (*Vanguard*) and *Trinchera* (*Trench*). His dramatic work includes *El árbol seco* (*The Dry Tree*); *Satanás entra en escena* (*Satan Enters on Stage*, 1938); *Pastorela* (1939); and his masterpiece, *Por los caminos van los campesinos* (*Along the Roads Go the Peasants*, 1937), which, set during the intervention of the USA in Nicaragua during the 1920s, protests against the injustices committed against the poor in the name of politics. During the Sandinista government, Cuadra served as editor of the opposition newspaper, *La Prensa*.

**Cueva, Juan de la** ?1550–1610 Spanish playwright. He wrote before the COMEDIA reached its established form under LOPE DE VEGA. His 14 extant tragedies and comedies, in four acts, were performed in the public theatres of Seville around 1579–81. His best-constructed plays are three on classical themes, but he was probably the first to adapt successfully plots from Spanish history and ballads for the stage, including the *Tragedia de los siete infantes de Lara* (*Tragedy of the Seven Princes of Lara*). His collected plays were published in 1588, and he wrote a poem on dramatic theory, the *Ejemplar poético*, in 1609.

**Cumberland, Richard** 1732–1811 English playwright. After 10 years in politics, he began his prolific career as a dramatist in 1761. Caricatured as Sir Fretful Plagiary by SHERIDAN in *The Critic*, he was rapidly successful, particularly after GARRICK's production of *The West Indian* (1771), a sentimental account of an essentially good rake making his way through London society. Among his conventional plays are some original works, particularly *The Mysterious Husband* (1783), a tragedy set in contemporary London, and *The Jew* (1794), a reasoned argument against contemporary antisemitism, which restored Cumberland's flagging reputation.

**Curtain Theatre** (London) Erected not far from the THEATRE, on which it was modelled, the Curtain was London's second purpose-built playhouse. For a brief period, between the dismantling of the Theatre and the opening of the GLOBE, it was probably the home of the LORD CHAMBERLAIN's MEN and may have staged SHAKESPEARE's *Henry V*. Briefly the home of Queen Anne's Men after 1603, it remained open until the Restoration.

**Cusack, Cyril** 1910–93 Irish stage and film actor, director and playwright. He performed with the ABBEY THEATRE in Dublin from 1932 to 1945, and again from 1968, when he started the revival of BOUCICAULT's plays in the Abbey production of *The Shaughraun* at the World Theatre Season in London. He directed the Gaelic Players in 1935–6, and in his own play *Tareis an Aifreann* (*After the Mass*) at the Dublin GATE THEATRE in 1942. After taking over the Gaiety Theatre, Dublin, in 1945, he formed his own company; in 1960 he won the International Critics' Award for his performance in BECKETT's monologue, *Krapp's Last Tape*. His daughters Sinead, Sorcha and Niamh are well known actresses.

**Cushman, Charlotte (Saunders)** 1816–76 The first native-born American actress to achieve star status. Her tall, strong body, unusual voice (she had trained as an opera singer) and powerful personality gave heroic outline to her performances. After her debut as Lady

Macbeth (1836), her first sensational success was as Nancy Sykes in *Oliver Twist* (1839). She played opposite W. C. MACREADY on his American tour in 1843–4, then appeared in 1845 at the PRINCESS'S THEATRE, London. By her return to the USA in 1849 she was widely considered the greatest living English-speaking actress. During her long career she played over 200 roles but excelled as Meg Merrilies in *Guy Mannering*, as Romeo opposite the Juliet of her sister Susan; as Lady Macbeth, and as Queen Katharine in *Henry VIII*.

**Cuzzani, Agustín** 1924–87 Argentine playwright, novelist and lawyer. Famous for his *farsátiras* (satirical farces) in the 1950s, he wrote several major plays: *Una libra de carne* (*A Pound of Flesh*, 1954), based on the Shylock story; *El centroforward murió al amanecer* (*The Centre Forward Died at Dawn*, 1955); and *Sempronio* (1958), which presents a man who has become radioactive from his Japanese stamp collection but is redeemed by the power of his family's love over the vindictive state bureaucracy. Cuzzani's plays depend on farcical situations to advocate positions of individual liberty for mankind within oppressive situations.

**da Silva, António José** 1705–39 Portuguese playwright. Probably the most noteworthy dramatist between Vicente and Ferreira and the 19th-century figure of Garrett, he was burned by the Inquisition for being allegedly a practising Jew, an iniquitous event dramatized in Santareno's *O Judeu* (1966). Da Silva's seven plays made great use of stage machinery and effects and incorporated quasi-operatic arias. The first, *Vida do Grande D. Quixote e do Gordo Sancho Pança*, had the knight, his squire and the supporting cast played by puppets. The best, *As Guerras do Alecrim e da Manjerona* (*The Wars of Rosemary and Marjoram*), contrasts the preciousness of the higher classes with the racy earthiness of the common people and is finely observed.

**Dadié, Bernard (Binlin)** 1916– Ivory Coast playwright, poet and novelist. *Assémien Déhylé, roi du Sanwi* (*Assémien Déhylé, King of the Sanwi*) was produced at the Théâtre des Champs-Élysées in Paris in 1937. After a period of poetry and fiction he published a number of plays which made him the most prolific and widely performed of African playwrights in French. In 1969 his most celebrated play, *Monsieur Thogo-gnini* (*thogo-gnini* means 'the opportunist' in Malinke), was acclaimed at the Pan-African Festival in Algiers; *Béatrice du Congo* (*Beatrice of the Congo*, published 1970) was directed by Jean-Marie Serreau at the Avignon festival in 1971. Other plays are *Min Adja-O* (*That's My Inheritance*), *Serment d'amour* (*Love Vow*) and *A Difficult Situation* (1965), *Les Voix dans le vent* (*Voices in the Wind* (1970), *Îles de tempête* (*Islands of the Storm*, 1973), *Papassidi maître escroc* (*Papassidi, Master Crook*, 1975; first version 1969), *Mhoi-ceul* (*Me Alone*, 1979). Dadié's plays depict historical, social and political themes, arising mostly from the contact between white and black.

**Dagerman, Stig** 1923–54 Swedish novelist and playwright. He was considered the most promising Swedish dramatist since Lagerkvist, a promise only partly fulfilled at the time of his suicide in 1954. His theory of 'dedramatized drama', emphasizing words and ideas rather than theatrical effects, led to plays that tend to be static, slow-moving and verbose, although he excels at building tension. Dagerman needs unusually vigorous direction, as in the case of his best (and first) play *The Condemned* (1947), brilliantly staged by Alf Sjöberg at Dramaten as a kind of Kafkaesque fantasy.

**Daldry, Stephen** 1947– British director. His Liverpool production of *The Ragged Trousered Philanthropists* in 1988 won comparisons with Joan Littlewood for liveliness and economy. In 1989 he staged Ödön von Horváth's *Judgement Day*. In 1990 he became director of the tiny Gate Theatre, Notting Hill, in London, and explored neglected European plays, including Tirso de Molina's *Damned for Despair* (1991). In 1992 he was invited by the National Theatre to direct J.B. Priestley's *An Inspector Calls*, with a magnificent set designed by Ian MacNeil. His *Machinal* (1993), a revival of Sophie Treadwell's play from 1928, and which starred Fiona Shaw as the spouse-murderer, was much admired. In 1994 Daldry triumphantly revived Wesker's *The Kitchen* at the Royal Court, where he is now established as sole artistic director.

**Dale, Alan** [Alfred J. Cohen] 1861–1928 British-born American drama critic. Dale went to New York in the early 1880s to write for the *Dramatic Times*. In 1887 Joseph Pulitzer employed him as drama critic for the *World*. Dale switched to Hearst's *Morning Journal* in 1897 and *Cosmopolitan* magazine in 1904. Except for the period 1914–17, he remained a Hearst regular until his death. He popularized a 'smart' and aggressive style of reviewing. *Who's Who in the Theatre* (1914) concluded that his opinions 'probably carry more weight than any others in New York'.

**Dallas Theater Center** (Texas) Founded in 1959, the Kalita Humphreys Theatre (named after a Texas actress) is a geometric concrete structure set in a hilly, wooded area outside Dallas. Professor Paul Baker's plan to assemble a permanent acting company to present classic and contemporary plays and to introduce new works in conjunction with a graduate programme at Baylor University was largely fulfilled, but has been discontinued. The original 516-seat theatre has been augmented by the tiny Down Center Stage.

**D'Alton, Louis** 1900–51 Irish playwright. He was associated with the Abbey from 1937 as playwright, actor and director. His plays, in the manner of Shaw, were *The Money Doesn't Matter* (1941), *They Got What They Wanted* (1947) and *This Other Eden* (1953), a witty treatment of romantic English ideas about Ireland and of Irish ideas about England.

**Daly, (Peter Christopher) Arnold** 1875–1927 American producer and actor. Daly should be remembered as Shaw's first truly effective champion in the USA. He directed and acted in a trial matinée of *Candida* in New York in 1903 and then went on tour with *The Man of Destiny*. For the 1904–5 season he produced *How She Lied to Her Husband* (written for Daly), *You Never Can Tell*; *John Bull's Other Island*; and *Mrs Warren's Profession*, whose first performance in New York was cause for Daly's arrest on moral charges, although he was acquitted. In 1906 he added *Arms and the Man* to his repertory and, under the management of the Shuberts, conducted a successful national tour, though the response of conservative critics was vitriolic.

**Daly, (John) Augustin** 1838–99 American playwright, manager, director and critic. Daly dominated theatre in the United States during the last half of the 19th century. His touring productions also influenced English theatre, and in 1893 he opened his own playhouse in London. He began as a newspaper critic (1859–1867) and playwright, with, most notably, *Leah the Forsaken* (1862) and the melodrama *Under the Gaslight* (1867) – and always secretly assisted by his brother Joseph. Ultimately, the Dalys had over 90 of their plays or adaptations performed. Among his more successful productions were *A Flash of Lightning* (1868), *Frou-Frou* (1870), *Horizon* (1871), *Divorce* (1871), *Article 47* (1872), *Needles and Pins* (1880), *Dollars and Sense* (1883), *Love on Crutches* (1884) and *The Lottery of Love* (1888). He also produced adaptations of English classics and Shakespeare. He trained and developed over 75 prominent actors, including Ada Rehan and John Drew (see Drew-Barrymore family). He managed and built several important theatres, opening Daly's in 1879. Constantly striving for an ensemble effect in his productions, Daly was one of the first directors in the modern sense and the first American *régisseur*.

**Daly's Theatre** (New York City) Originally built as a museum in 1867, John Banvard renamed it the Broadway Theatre in 1876. AUGUSTIN DALY, responding to the uptown drift of the theatres, took it over in 1879, renovated it extensively and transformed it into Daly's Theatre. Here he and his STOCK COMPANY made their last stand against the new system of booking single plays into a theatre to try for a long run. Later it met an inglorious end as a BURLESQUE house, and was razed in 1920.

**dame role** see PANTOMIME, ENGLISH; FEMALE IMPERSONATION

**Dancourt** [Florent Carton] 1661–1725 French actor and playwright. He joined the COMÉDIE-FRANÇAISE in 1685 and wrote over 80 plays, including many in one act. Most are comedies of manners in prose, based on the contemporary scene and depicting an unscrupulous and pleasure-seeking society, as in *Le Chevalier à la mode* (*The Fashionable Knight*, 1687) and *Les Bourgeoises à la mode* (1692).

**Dane, Clemence** [*née* Winifred Ashton; Diana Cortis] 1888–1965 British playwright and novelist. Trained as a portraitist, after a period as an actress (under the stage name of Cortis) she turned to writing MELODRAMATIC 'problem plays' focusing on sexual issues from a female perspective. *A Bill of Divorcement* (1921) was followed by *The Way Things Happen* (1924) and a morality play on adultery, *Granite* (1926). She also used biblical subjects (*Naboth's Vineyard*, 1925; *Herod and Marianne*, 1938) or historical settings (a dramatization of the lives of the Brontë sisters, *Wild Decembers*, 1932; *The Golden Age of Queen Elizabeth*, 1941) to illustrate her themes. Her last work, *Eighty in the Shade* (1959), was specially written for SYBIL THORNDIKE and LEWIS CASSON.

**Daniel, Samuel** 1562–1619 English poet and playwright. He wrote, for private patrons, two SENECAN tragedies, *Cleopatra* (1594) and *Philotas* (1604), supervising the production of the second by the CHILDREN OF THE CHAPEL ROYAL. He fell into royal disfavour when the Children presented *Eastward Ho* (1605), the joint work of JONSON, MARSTON and CHAPMAN, offensive to King James for its anti-Scottish jibes. Daniel re-established himself at court by devising court entertainments, including the PASTORAL *The Queen's Arcadia*, in 1605.

**D'Annunzio, Gabriele** 1863–1938 Italian poet, playwright and novelist. His flamboyant writing and decadent lifestyle rapidly made him a prominent figure in the 1880s, particularly after the publication of his experimental poetry in *Canto novo* and *Terra vergine*. His theatrical activity began comparatively late, in 1896, after the start of his seven-year relationship with the actress ELEONORA DUSE, with whom he planned a revitalization of theatre, away from the constraints of bourgeois NATURALISM. The ideals of this new theatre he passionately described in his novel, *Il fuoco* (*The Flame of Life*, 1900), and he wrote the one-act *Sogno di un mattino di primavera* (*Dream of a Spring Morning*) and *Sogno di un tramonto d'autunno* (*Dream of an Autumn Sunset*) for Duse in 1898. Audiences remained indifferent, and he won no substantially greater success with the full-length pieces which immediately followed: *La città morta* (*The Dead City*), first produced in Paris by SARAH BERNHARDT in 1898, and *La Gioconda* and *La gloria* (*The Glory*), both mounted by Duse and ERMETE ZACCONI in 1899.

D'Annunzio abandoned prose, and with his next play, *Francesca da Rimini* (1901), he attempted a verse tragedy in historical vein. It proved enormously successful and was widely imitated. Even more popular was his next

piece, *La figlia di Iorio* (*Iorio's Daughter*, 1904), a modern peasant drama set in his native Abruzzo and considered today to be by far his best stage work. Later plays, enjoying variable success, included *La nave* (*The Ship*, 1908) and *Le Martyr de Saint Sébastien* (*The Martyrdom of St Sebastian*), produced with music by Debussy in Paris in 1911.

During World War I D'Annunzio became increasingly involved in Italian political and military affairs. Of his last works perhaps the most effective was the libretto he wrote for Mascagni's *Parisina*. Increasingly from 1913 he wrote more for the cinema than for the theatre. Many films have been made from his novels, stories and plays. These last, like *La città morta* and *La gloria*, turned from the concerns of contemporary naturalistic drama to treat of the struggles of exceptional Nietzschean individuals, in a language verbally rich but flamboyant and replete with neologisms and antique terms.

***dashavatara*** Indian theatre form. The term refers to the ten incarnations (*avataras*) of Lord Vishnu, one of a trinity of deities, two of whom, Rama and Krishna, are widely worshipped in India. It also refers to a form of theatre popular in rural areas of the Konkan and Goa, on the western coast of the Indian subcontinent.

*Dashavatara* is thought to have been introduced by a Brahmin 400 years ago. Most of the actors come from the lower strata of society, although there are a few Brahmins who also perform. The troupes are itinerant, moving from village to village for half the year, sleeping in the open most of the time and performing on temporary platforms. All of the actors are male and their earnings are poor.

Performances usually begin around 11 pm with songs in praise of Ganapati, the elephant-headed god, sung by the stage manager (*sutradhara*). A Brahmin enters and comic dialogue ensues. Dances are performed by two men dressed as women. An elementary dance is then performed by an actor who impersonates Saraswati, goddess of learning. After the dance, two women enter symbolizing rivers. With them is Madhavi, a comic Brahmin. Next, the frightening figure of Shankhasura bursts onto the playing area, dressed from head to foot in black and sporting a red cloth representing a long tongue. Shankhasura is thought to be capable of exposing the scandals and private lives of the villagers. He carries on a lively improvised conversation with the stage manager. Then an actor playing the god Brahma, the creator, enters, and a story about the theft of the sacred *Vedas* is related in which Shankhasura and the stage manager participate. The events of this elaborate overture continue for approximately two hours. Finally, the drama (*akhyana*) begins, and continues until sunrise. It includes a selection of well known episodes from the epic literature and introduces mythological and historical characters with whom village audiences are familiar.

**Dasté, Jean** 1904–94 French actor and director. One of COPEAU's disciples, Dasté was a pioneer in the decentralization movement. After the Liberation he established a touring company in Grenoble, later moving to St Étienne (1947–1971). His repertoire, aimed at a working-class audience, followed Copeau's lead but included new dramatists (COUSIN, GATTI) and BRECHT – he gave the French premiere of *The Caucasian Chalk Circle* in 1956. He also played character roles in French films, notably Professor Pinel in Truffaut's *L'Enfant sauvage* (*The Wild Child*, 1970).

**Daubeny, Peter (Lauderdale)** 1921–75 British impresario. Best known as the artistic director of the World Theatre Seasons in London from 1964 to 1973, he began his career as an actor, then concentrated on management following injury in the war. His first major successes came in the early 1950s, when he brought over to London a dazzling array of dance companies from Europe and Soviet Russia. Following the triumphant success of the Compagnie Edwige Feuillère in *La Dame aux camélias* (1955), he looked to major drama companies as well. The BERLINER ENSEMBLE was brought to London's Palace Theatre in 1956, providing British audiences with their first opportunity to see BRECHT's company, which was then little known. Others included the COMÉDIE-FRANÇAISE, the MOSCOW ART THEATRE, the MALMÖ STADSTEATER Company in INGMAR BERGMAN's production of *Urfast*, and VITTORIO GASSMAN's Teatro Popolare Italiano. Daubeny introduced London audiences to the new wave of American theatre and to the Classical Theatre of China. He received no government grants for the World Theatre Seasons which ran annually, usually at the Aldwych Theatre, and were a major reason for the new-found cosmopolitanism in British drama. Daubeny was knighted in 1973, but after his death there was nobody to succeed him.

**d'Aubignac, François Hédelin,** abbé 1604–76 French critic and dramatist. He shared RICHELIEU's passion for drama and proposed radical reform of the theatre under state control. *La Pratique du théâtre*, published in 1657, elaborates neoclassical rules of composition into a systematic code of practice for the playwright. D'Aubignac insists on a strict division of the genres, on the decorum of character and incident to each, and above all on the importance of *vraisemblance* (credibility), which entails a severe interpretation of the unities of place, time and action. His own three tragedies, intended as models, were indifferently received. The *Pratique* was profoundly influential and was translated into English in 1684.

**Davenant, William** 1606–68 English playwright and manager. His comedies include *The Wits* (1634) and *News from Plymouth* (1635). He also worked with INIGO JONES, writing court MASQUES such as *Britannia Triumphans* (1638) and *Salmacida Spolia* (1640). In 1638 he succeeded JONSON as Laureate. From 1640 he ran the COCKPIT THEATRE in Drury Lane. A royalist, he avoided the government's prohibition on plays by performing operas at Rutland House in 1656, including his own heroic play *The Siege of Rhodes*, which was important for the development of English opera and was produced with changeable scenery by JOHN WEBB. Davenant and KILLIGREW persuaded Charles II to grant their two companies a monopoly on theatre performances in London. In 1661 Davenant's Duke's Company began acting at LINCOLN'S INN FIELDS, the first professional English company to act in a public theatre equipped with changeable scenery. THOMAS BETTERTON was the leading player. Davenant began adapting plays: *Hamlet* in 1661, *The Law against Lovers* from *Measure for Measure* and *Much Ado About Nothing* in 1662, and operatic versions of *Macbeth* (1663) and *The Tempest* (with DRYDEN, 1667). He also encouraged new work by ETHEREGE, BOYLE and others. The success of his very well organized company was continued under his widow's management.

**Davenport, E(dward) L(oomis)** 1815–77 American actor. Known for his versatility, grace, musical voice and gentlemanly manners, he began his career in

Providence (1835), became ANNA CORA MOWATT's leading man (1846), then went with her to London, where he remained for seven years, often playing in support of MACREADY. He returned to the USA to be acclaimed for his Lanciotto in BOKER's *Francesca da Rimini* (1855), and remained on the stage until 1876.

**Davenport, Fanny** 1850–98 English-born American actress. Daughter of actor E. L. DAVENPORT, 'Miss Fanny' was a popular child actress before her New York debut in 1862 at NIBLO'S GARDEN Theatre. In 1869 she joined AUGUSTIN DALY's FIFTH AVENUE THEATRE company and demonstrated remarkable versatility in light comedies, SHAKESPEARE, and finally serious dramatic works like Daly's *Pique* (1876) in which she created Mabel Renfew, one of her most popular roles along with Nancy Sykes in *Oliver Twist*. A beautiful, 'spirited' actress, she formed her own company and gave the American English-language premieres of four BERNHARDT vehicles by SARDOU: *Fedora* (1883), *La Tosca* (1888), *Cleopatra* (1890) and *Gismonda* (1894).

**Davidson, Gordon** 1933– American director. Davidson has directed at the Paper Mill Playhouse (New Jersey), the Barter Theatre and other venues, and stage-managed for Martha Graham. At the AMERICAN SHAKESPEARE FESTIVAL he assisted JOHN HOUSEMAN, who chose him to co-direct *King Lear* with the Theatre Group and to serve as managing director (1964–6). He is producing director of the Ahmanson (Los Angeles Theatre Center) and artistic director/producer of the MARK TAPER FORUM, where he directs nearly 20 per cent of the mainstage productions.

**Davies, Hubert Henry** 1876–1917 British playwright. By profession a journalist, he wrote a series of social comedies between 1899 and 1914. These included a depiction of female domination, *The Mollusc* (1907), and *Outcast*, his last and most successful play, about sexual double standards.

**Davies, Robertson** 1913– Canadian novelist, playwright and journalist. Born in Ontario, he was educated in Canada and England and worked at the OLD VIC before returning in 1940 to Canada and a career in journalism. Besides plays, his published writings consist of essays, novels and chronicles (with TYRONE GUTHRIE) of the early years of the STRATFORD FESTIVAL, of which he was a founding governor. His first three-act play, *Fortune My Foe* (1948), took an ironic look at the treatment of the artist in Canada. Among his later plays, the Welsh comedy *A Jig for the Gypsy* (1954) and *Hunting Stuart* (1955) were produced by Toronto's Crest Theatre. *Love and Libel* (1960) was an adaptation of his early novel, *Leaven of Malice*.

In 1966 as master of Massey College he helped establish the University of Toronto's Graduate Centre for the Study of Drama. In the 1970s he achieved international fame as a novelist, but continued to write for and about the theatre. Just as his novels often have deep roots in the theatrical tradition, his later plays such as *Question Time* (1975) develop many of the Jungian ideas that permeate his novels.

**Davis, Henrietta Vinton** 1860–1941 African-American actress. For 35 years pre-eminent on the stage, she was universally hailed by audiences across America for her powerful interpretations of a range of Shakespearian heroines. Excluded by racial prejudice from the established professional stage, she gave concert readings and performed dramatic scenes with other black actors. She produced and played leading roles in three plays by African-American dramatists: *Dessalines* (1893) and *Christophe* (1912), both by William Edgar Easton, and *Our Old Kentucky Home* (1898), written for her by the journalist John E. Bruce. From 1919 to 1931 Davis worked for racial equality and the establishment of a black nation state in Africa.

**Davis, Jack** 1917– Australian playwright and poet. He is the most distinguished and prolific of the Aboriginal dramatists who came to prominence during the 1980s. *Kullark* (1979) chronicles the conflict between European settlement and Aboriginal tribal life; *The Dreamers* (1982), *No Sugar* (1985), *Barugin: Smell the Wind* (1988) and *Wahngin Country* (1992) chart the history of Aboriginal dispossession earlier this century, juxtaposed with contemporary town life, drawn with warmth and humour. Like many Aboriginal dramas his plays fuse the realistic depiction of everyday life with traditional dance, music and poetry. Widely performed throughout Australia and overseas, Davis's plays are particularly associated with Black Swan Theatre in Perth.

**Davis, Ossie** 1917– African-American actor and playwright. He made his BROADWAY debut in the title role of *Jeb* (1946) and eventually succeeded Sidney Poitier in *A Raisin in the Sun* (1959). In 1961 Davis assumed the lead role opposite his wife RUBY DEE in his comedy *Purlie Victorious*, which pungently ridiculed racial stereotyping. Davis also wrote *Curtain Call, Mr Aldridge, Sir* (1963) and has appeared in numerous films and television shows, some of which he scripted and directed.

**Davis, Owen** 1874–1956 American playwright. The most successful MELODRAMAtist at the turn of the 20th century, between *Through the Breakers* (1899) and *The Family Cupboard* (1913) he wrote scores of plays such as *Convict 999* and *Nellie, the Beautiful Cloak Model*. He later wrote realistic plays (see REALISM), e.g. *Detour* (1921) and *Icebound* (1923), concerned with the lost illusions of a New England family. With his son Donald Davis he adapted Edith Wharton's *Ethan Frome* (1936).

**Dawison, Bogumil** 1818–72 Polish actor. His career was spent mainly in the German theatre. A celebrated virtuoso actor, he was a member of the Vienna BURGTHEATER from 1849 to 1852 and of the DRESDEN COURT THEATRE from 1852 to 1864. He was noted for his aggressive, often unpolished interpretations of Shakespearian and other classic roles. As he was a bitter rival of EMIL DEVRIENT, his acting was widely regarded as the antithesis of the WEIMAR STYLE. Dawison was one of the first German actors to tour America.

**Day, John** 1574–1640 English playwright and poet. One of HENSLOWE's circle of writers, he was part-author with CHETTLE of one of the ADMIRAL's MEN's major successes, *The Blind Beggar of Bethnal Green* (1600). Two satirical comedies for BOYS' COMPANIES, *Law Tricks* (1604) and *The Isle of Gulls* (1606), were followed by another collaboration, with WILLIAM ROWLEY and George Wilkins, on the rambling romance *The Travels of the Three English Brothers* (1607). His comedy, *Humour out of Breath* (c.1608), and the strange collection of semi-dramatic monologues in *The Parliament of Bees* (published 1641), boldly critical of Charles I's personal rule, complete his known dramatic work.

**De Filippo family** Italian actors, directors and playwrights. **Eduardo** (1900–85), like his sister **Titina** (1898–1963) and brother **Peppino** (1903–80), acted in the Neapolitan SCARPETTA troupe. In 1932 the three formed their own company, which lasted until 1945 when Peppino left to work independently, and Eduardo

and Titina set up Il Teatro di Eduardo.

A brilliant comic actor with an economic, realistic style of playing, from the late 1920s until his death Eduardo was also a prolific dramatist, acting in and directing much of his own work – the best of which ranks as the most vital in the modern Italian theatre and attests to the enduring invention of the Neapolitan dialect stage. He wrote some 40 plays, several of the finest of which – like *Filumena Maturano* (*Filumena*, 1946), *Sabato, domenica, e lunedì* (*Saturday, Sunday, Monday*, 1959) and, at least in its film version, *Napoli milionaria!* (*Affluent Naples!* 1945) – have enjoyed great popularity in Italy and considerable success abroad. Firmly placed in the language, life and attitudes of the Neapolitan petit bourgeois and working classes, with character and situation handled in naturalistic ways, they draw on a wide range of popular forms and on the Italian and dialect 'prose' theatre traditions. Eduardo's view of the world was essentially tragicomic: in many of his plays the action turns on the attempts of a good-natured, even naive individual to change a society that is rapacious and materialistic. A darker, more melancholy tone tends to emerge in his later work. At the centre of most of it, however, is the family, the one certainty in an otherwise unstable world. The subject of his play *L'Arte della commedia* (*The Art of Comedy*, 1964) is the condition of modern Italian theatre.

After forming his own company, Peppino came increasingly to specialize in Italian light COMEDY and FARCE, and excelled in much foreign comic drama. He too wrote plays and was a well-known film actor, often appearing with the comedian TOTÒ. His son **Luigi** has continued in the family's actor-management tradition. Titina de Filippo worked mainly with Eduardo, interpreting many of the female lead roles in his plays, notably Filumena Maturano.

**De Groen, Alma** 1941– Australian playwright. Her early play, *The Joss Adams Show* (1973), portrayed a teenage mother who kills her child; subsequent plays focused on social misfits and lone figures – e.g. in *The Secret Life of Arthur Craven* (1973) and *Chidley* (1977). Her more recent work is feminist. *Going Home* (1976) depicts a group of Australian art-world expatriates in Canada; *Vocations* (1982) wittily explores the conflicts in women who pursue independent careers and relationships with men; her most ambitious work, *The Rivers of China* (1987), juxtaposes the writer Katherine Mansfield's last weeks at Gurdjieff's Institute near Paris in 1923 with the story of a hospitalized man in a future female-governed world.

**De Koven, Reginald** 1859–1920 American composer. After an extensive musical education in Europe, in partnership with librettist HARRY B. SMITH De Koven set out to prove that Americans could write a comic opera in the European style. Their first show was *The Begum* (1887). In 1891 De Koven composed the score of *Robin Hood*, the most popular American comic opera of the era. Carefully mounted by the BOSTON IDEAL OPERA COMPANY, *Robin Hood* was an immediate hit and the song 'O Promise Me' became an enduring American standard.

**de la Parra, Marco Antonio** 1952– Chilean playwright. A diplomat and psychiatrist, he has an extraordinary talent for interweaving sociopolitical situations and abstract techniques. *Lo crudo, lo cocido y lo podrido* (*The Raw, the Cooked, the Rotten*) was suddenly banned in 1978 hours before its scheduled opening in the Catholic

University theatre in Santiago, after which de la Parra settled into a rhythm of regular productions. *Matatangos* (*Kill Tangos*, 1979) examines the process of myth-making regarding Carlos Gardel, famous Argentine *tanguista* (writer/singer of tango); *La secreta obscenidad de cada día* (*The Everyday Secret Obscenity*, 1984) features Karl Marx and Sigmund Freud as political assassins disguised as exhibitionists, waiting in front of a girls' school where politicians are meeting; *Infieles* (*Beds*, 1987) deals with the life of the yuppies of the Pinochet years in Chile; *El deseo de toda ciudadana* (*The Desire of Every Citizen*, 1989) is a thriller based on loneliness, invasion and an eventual homicide.

**De Liagre, Alfred,** Jr 1904–87 American producer and director. De Liagre began his professional career in 1930 as stage manager at the Woodstock Playhouse. In 1933 he began producing professionally and worked in both New York and London. He produced or co-produced more than 30 plays, a number of which he also directed. His more noteworthy credits include *The Voice of the Turtle* (1943), *The Madwoman of Chaillot* (1948), *Second Threshold* (1950), *The Golden Apple* (1954), *The Girls in 509* (1958), *J. B.* (1959), *Photo Finish* (1963), *Bubbling Brown Sugar* (1976), *Deathtrap* (1978) and *On Your Toes* (1983).

**De Loutherbourg, Philip (James)** 1740–1812 Alsatian scene designer. Born in Strasbourg, he studied painting in Paris, and in 1771 moved to London to work with GARRICK, proposing improvements in the lighting and scene systems at DRURY LANE. From 1773 he designed extravagant theatre spectacles, concentrating on light effects (e.g. sunlight, castles in moonlight) and a landscape and perspective style of romantic views of England for, e.g., SHERIDAN's *The Wonders of Derbyshire* (1779). In 1781 he left the theatre to set up the Eidophusikon, a display of scenes as panoramic pictures. His developments of stage lighting and of naturalistic landscapes prepared the ground for pictorial theatre. (See also STAGE LIGHTING; THEATRE DESIGN.)

**de Mille, Agnes** 1905–93 American choreographer and director. Trained in the techniques of classical ballet, de Mille is best remembered for her pioneering work in musicals of the 1940s and for demonstrating the potential of dance for furthering dramatic action. In 1943 RODGERS and HAMMERSTEIN hired her to choreograph *Oklahoma!*, for which she created the influential dream ballet. She went on to choreograph *One Touch of Venus* (1943), *Bloomer Girl* (1944), *Carousel* (1945) and *Brigadoon* (1947), which was acclaimed for its dramatic intensity and use of traditional Scottish dances. De Mille served as both choreographer and director for *Allegro* (1947) and *Out of This World* (1950). In the 1950s and 60s she created the dances for such shows as *Paint Your Wagon* (1951), *The Girl in Pink Tights* (1954), *Goldilocks* (1958), *Kwamina* (1961), *110 in the Shade* (1963) and *Come Summer* (1969).

**de' Sommi (de Portaleone), Yehuda Leone** [Leone di Somi (or Sommo)] 1572–92 Jewish Italian playwright and poet. He wrote the first Hebrew play, *A Comedy of Betrothal* (c.1550, English translation 1988), a typical Renaissance comedy with a racy Hebrew flavour. The main plot, based on the Midrash, tells the story of a young man, Shalom, whose father bequeathed all his possessions save one to his slave. Shalom may claim any one of them as his. He chooses the slave, thus obtaining the full inheritance. This tale is entwined with a conventional romantic plot. The play has been revived in this century.

De' Sommi was a prolific writer of poetry and plays in both Italian and Hebrew, but most of his work was destroyed by a fire in 1904. Apparently he produced plays for the Duke of Gonzaga at Mantua. He wrote an important theoretical treatise, *Four Dialogues on Scenic Representation* (English translation by Allardyce Nicoll, 1937).

**De Wahl, Anders** 1869–1956 Swedish actor. He was popular until the late 1920s, when his pre-eminence was challenged by the more natural style (see NATURALISM) of LARS HANSON. A personality actor whose lyricism and physical grace precisely reflected the ideals of *fin-de-siècle* romanticism, he excelled in emotionally troubled roles, including STRINDBERG's Erik XIV (1899) and King Magnus (1901), and in plays on religious themes such as *Everyman* (1916) or ELIOT's *Murder in the Cathedral* (1939). Firmly rooted in 19th-century tradition, he was outspokenly opposed to modernism in theatre, although the early popularity of PIRANDELLO in Sweden probably resulted from De Wahl's performances in *Six Characters in Search of an Author* (1925), *Henry IV* (1926) and *The Pleasure of Honesty* (1930).

**Dean, Basil (Herbert)** 1888–1978 British actor, director and producer. In 1907 he joined ANNIE HORNIMAN's company in Manchester as an actor, where he stayed until in 1910 he was invited to help start a new REPERTORY THEATRE in Liverpool. Before leaving in 1913, he had established the theatre as a major force in the repertory movement. From 1919 to 1926 he was in partnership with Alec Rea and, as the 'ReandeaN' management, they were responsible for a series of major productions on the London stage, including *The Skin Game*, *R.U.R.* and *Hassan*. Dean continued both to produce and to direct, staging, among others, the premieres of several plays by PRIESTLEY. In 1939 he started and became director of ENSA; in 1948 he organized the first British Repertory Theatre Festival in London. He directed a number of films, including *Lorna Doone* and the films of GRACIE FIELDS.

**Dear, Nick** 1955– British playwright. He first received national attention with *The Art of Success* (1986), set in the early 18th century and directed by ADRIAN NOBLE at the ROYAL SHAKESPEARE COMPANY's the Pit. There were echoes of Thatcherism in the tussles between its central character, William Hogarth, and the prime minister, Robert Walpole. Dear's robust language, vivid and scatalogical, made a powerful impact. He adapted OSTROVSKY's *A Family Affair* (1988) for CHEEK BY JOWL, and TIRSO DE MOLINA's *The Last Days of Don Juan* (1990) for the RSC.

**Dearly, Max** [Lucien-Max Rolland] 1874–1943 French actor and VARIETY artist. He trained in an English circus at Marseilles, and his ingratiating manners, lantern-jawed face and 'British' elegance made him a favourite. In his heyday, 1905–10, he launched the *valse chaloupée*, or apache dance, with MISTINGUETT and mimed an entire horse race in his 'Jockey américain'. As his vocal powers diminished, he abandoned operetta and REVUE for drama and the screen, where he was seen as Homais in Jean Renoir's *Madame Bovary* (1934).

**Deburau, Jean-Gaspard** [Jan Kaspar Dvorak] 1796–1846 French MIME artist. Born in Bohemia, in 1812 he went to Paris with his family of acrobats and fairground performers. From 1816 he appeared at the THÉÂTRE DES FUNAMBULES, rapidly becoming a favourite of the working-class audiences in numerous pantomimes. He developed the secondary character

PIERROT into a versatile protagonist, hapless, ingenious, often macabre and aggressive; praised by the literati, his pale-faced, elongated hero took on mythic proportions. Most modern mime artists, MARCEAU especially, acknowledge their debt to him. Deburau was the subject of a play by Sacha Guitry (1918), and Marcel Carné's film *Les Enfants du Paradis* (1945) incarnated Baptiste, the Deburau figure, in JEAN-LOUIS BARRAULT.

**Decroux, Étienne-Marcel** 1898–1991 French MIME artist. A student of CHARLES DULLIN (1926–34), he developed a systematic grammar of physical expression that he called *mime corporel* or *pantomime de style*, a method of corporal extension geared to make abstract statements. He had a strong influence on JEAN-LOUIS BARRAULT, playing DEBURAU *père* to the latter's Baptiste Deburau in the film *Les Enfants du Paradis* (1945). In 1941 he opened a school, performing for tiny audiences of two or three persons, and through his students, including MARCEL MARCEAU, his ideas were diffused throughout modern mime. He toured the Western world and Israel (1949–58), and ran a studio theatre in Paris. According to GORDON CRAIG, he 'rediscovered mime'.

**Dee, Ruby** [*née* Ruby Ann Wallace] 1923– African-American actress. She appeared in various New York productions, attracting attention as Ruth Younger in *A Raisin in the Sun* (1959). She was acclaimed as Lutiebelle, the innocent pawn in *Purlie Victorious* (1961), as the long-suffering Lena in *Boesman and Lena* (1970), and in ALICE CHILDRESS's *Wedding Band* (1973). In SHAKESPEARE, Dee has played Katharina in *The Taming of the Shrew* (1965), Cordelia to MORRIS CARNOVSKY's King Lear (1965), and Gertrude in *Hamlet* (1975). She has also written plays, including *Twin Bit Gardens* (1976).

**Déjazet, (Pauline) Virginie** 1798–1875 French actress. Her roles included a number of BREECHES PARTS. In 1828 she joined the Nouveautés, playing the youthful Napoleon in *Bonaparte à Brienne, ou Le Petit Caporal* (*Bonaparte at Brienne, or The Little Corporal*, 1830), and later played a series of *grisette* roles with a strong element of sexual suggestiveness. By 1844 she was earning 20,000 francs a year. In 1843, Béranger's *Lisette* provided her with a monologue she would use for the next 30 years. She became freelance and at the age of 70 was still touring and playing the 15-year-old Richelieu. Her funeral attracted some 30,000 people.

**Dekker, Thomas** c.1570–1632 English playwright and pamphleteer. Of the 50 or so plays on which he is known to have worked, some 20 have survived. The earliest, *Old Fortunatus* (1599), is a rambling moral comedy. The second, *The Shoemaker's Holiday* (1599), is his masterpiece. Its exuberant plotting and vivid portraits of London tradesmen established the distinctive form of CITIZEN COMEDY. *Satiromastix* (1601) is a disappointing rejoinder to JONSON's abuse of Dekker in *Poetaster* and *Every Man out of His Humour*. Careless construction also mars *The Whore of Babylon* (1606), *If It Be Not Good the Devil Is in It* (c.1610) and *Match Me in London* (c.1611). Frequently in debt and needing to accept all commissions, Dekker collaborated with CHETTLE and William Haughton on *Patient Grissel* (1600), with WEBSTER on *Westward Ho* (1604) and *Northward Ho* (1605), with MIDDLETON on *The Honest Whore* (1604) and *The Roaring Girl* (c.1610), with MASSINGER on *The Virgin Martyr* (1620) and with WILLIAM ROWLEY and FORD on *The Witch of Edmonton* (1621). His lively satirical pamphlet, *The Gull's Hornbook* (1609), contains observations of audience behaviour in the London theatres.

**Delaney, Shelagh** 1939– British playwright. Her first and most successful play, *A Taste of Honey*, about a girl who, abandoned by her lover, rears her child with the help of a maternally minded gay, was written when she was only 17 and staged in 1958 by JOAN LITTLEWOOD at the Theatre Workshop, Stratford, East London. The freshness of the writing and Littlewood's dynamic production took the play to the WEST END, and afterwards to BROADWAY. Delaney's second play, *The Lion in Love* (1960), was less successful, and she turned from the theatre to writing screenplays.

**Delavigne, (Jean François) Casimir** 1793–1843 French playwright. Liberal and anticlerical, Delavigne followed the romantics in his choice of medieval themes, but remained popular and avoided shocking his audiences. His *Sicilian Vespers*, turned down at the COMÉDIE-FRANÇAISE, ran to 300 performances at the ODÉON in 1819. In *Le Paria* (1821), set in India, he used Brahmin fanaticism as a way of attacking Catholic fanaticism, a theme he repeated in *Une Famille au temps de Luther* (*A Family in the Time of Luther*, 1836). At the 1830 revolution Delavigne's patriotic song, *La Parisienne*, was sung in all the theatres. *Marino Faliero* (1829) converted LORD BYRON's model heroine into an adulterous wife (played by MARIE DORVAL). *Louis XI*, seen by some as his greatest play, moved towards the romantic mixture of genres, and was successfully adapted by BOUCICAULT. *Les Enfants d'Édouard* (1833) reduced *Richard III* to three acts of pathos. His other main plays are *Don Juan d'Autriche*, *La Fille du Cid* (*The Daughter of the Cid*), and an opera, *Charles VI*, with music by Halévy.

**Della Porta, Giambattista** 1535–1615 Italian playwright, scientist and philosopher. His substantial output included three tragedies, a TRAGICOMEDY and 29 comedies (of which 14 have survived). The best-known of his plays are *Olimpia* (1589) and *Il moro* (*The Moor*, 1607) which, like most of his dramatic work, show the influence both of the classical tradition and of the later *novelle* and romances, uniting the example of the ancients in structure and characterization with elements more reflective of Renaissance life and assumptions. Particularly interesting are his *L'astrologo* (*The Astrologer*, 1606) and *La Trappolaria* (*The Comedy of Trappoia*, 1596), of which both scripted and scenario versions exist, indicating some of the ways in which the Italian *commedia erudita* and *COMMEDIA DELL'ARTE* interconnected.

**Delpini, Carlo (Antonio)** 1740–1828 Italian dancer, CLOWN and scenarist. He was first seen at COVENT GARDEN in 1776 as PIERROT in *Harlequin's Frolicks*, and for the rest of the century was involved in performing and creating pantomime there and at the HAYMARKET. Willson Disher credits him with having invented the Regency PANTOMIME by stressing character and scenic transformation, as in the dumb show of *Robinson Crusoe* (DRURY LANE, 1781). He also worked at Hughes's Royal Circus where, in the panto *What You Please*, he contrived a spectacular exhibition of 'The Four Quarters of the World' (1788).

**Dench, Judi** [Judith] **(Olivia)** 1934– British actress. She first attracted critical acclaim as Ophelia to JOHN NEVILLE's Hamlet at the OLD VIC in 1957. She was invited to join the ROYAL SHAKESPEARE COMPANY in the exciting first season (1961) after its transformation from the Shakespeare Memorial Company, and became an established leading actress in PETER HALL's team, playing Anya in *The Cherry Orchard*, Isabella in *Measure for Measure* and Dorcas in JOHN WHITING's *A Penny for a Song*. Her association with the RSC has continued for more than 30 years, during which time she has played a wide variety of great classical roles, from the Duchess in *The Duchess of Malfi*, Beatrice in *Much Ado* and Lady Macbeth, as well as Mother Courage in BRECHT's play. She has also appeared in the WEST END as Sally Bowles in *Cabaret* (1968), her first musical. She played Cleopatra in Peter Hall's production (1987) and Gertrude in RICHARD EYRE's *Hamlet*, both at the NATIONAL THEATRE, and directed *As You Like It* (1988) and *Look Back in Anger* (1989) for the Renaissance Theatre Company. Among the actresses of her generation Dench is technically the best equipped, with a naturally soft and expressive voice, an appearance versatile enough to match an imposing beauty for one play and dowdiness the next, and a keen intelligence which provides fresh insights into the most familiar texts.

**Denison, Michael** 1915– British actor. Denison's career has been overshadowed by his famous contemporaries, OLIVIER and GIELGUD; but, often accompanied by his wife Dulcie Gray, he excelled within a range of gentlemanly roles, becoming a star of stage and screen in the late 40s and 50s and joining the Shakespeare Memorial Theatre in 1955. He was in demand for revivals of plays by WILDE and SHAW, and was a notable Ekdal in IBSEN's *The Wild Duck* (1970). He is perhaps best known for his screen performances in *My Brother Jonathan* and *The Importance of Being Earnest* (from the 1939 stage production); his recent roles include the Earl of Caversham in PETER HALL's revival of Wilde's *An Ideal Husband* (1992).

**Dennery [D'Ennery], Adolphe** 1811–99 French playwright. Dennery was author or co-author of 200 plays, including some of the best-known MELODRAMAS of the 19th century. His plays had a strong populist appeal on the BOULEVARD. His first major success, *Gaspard Hauser* (1838), based on recent real life events, showed the inhumanity of social convention in respect of illegitimacy. The tear-jerker *La Grâce de Dieu* (*The Grace of God*, 1841) depended on the opposition of the social classes. *Les Deux Orphelines* (*The Two Orphans*, 1874) is his best-known play. Latterly, with his adaptations of Jules Verne's novels, Dennery moved towards extravaganzas and spectacular sensation drama.

**Dennis, John** 1657–1734 English critic and playwright. *The Impartial Critic* (1693) showed him an intelligent and tolerant neoclassicist. Along with other plays and adaptations, he wrote a comedy *A Plot and No Plot* (1696) and a spectacular opera *Rinaldo and Armida* (1698). He defended the stage in the COLLIER controversy in his pamphlet *The Usefulness of the Stage* (1698), and put his principles to the test in the classical tragedy *Iphigenia* (1699) and in the restrained version of *Appius and Virginia* (1709). His later criticism reveals nostalgic admiration for the drama of the Restoration.

**Dennis, Nigel (Forbes)** 1912–89 British playwright, novelist and critic. His first three satirical plays were produced at the ROYAL COURT THEATRE under GEORGE DEVINE's directorship. Unlike most other Royal Court writers, Dennis criticized society from a right-wing stance, deploring the debasement of standards under facile democracies and denouncing left-wing totalitarianism. In *Cards of Identity* (1956), which he adapted from his novel, the target is the manipulation of mass opinion, while in *The Making of Moo* (1957) he derides the idolatry of religions, Christianity included. *August for the People* (1961) concerns an aristocratic landowner who attacks the common man and finds himself besieged by

common men who agree with him. He was a brilliant journalist: the clarity of his writing style, with his acid wit, emerged from his reviews and columns for the *Sunday Telegraph*.

**Derain, André** 1880–1954 French theatrical designer, painter and sculptor. Derain's entry into the theatre came about in 1919 when SERGE DIAGHILEV recruited him and other Paris-based painters to design for the Ballets Russes. He successfully designed *La Boutique fantastique* (1919) for Léonide Massine, and *Jack-in-the-Box* (1926) for George Balanchine. Derain's theatrical design career, which lasted into the 1950s, was distinguished by a painterly style which simplified reality into a highly decorative stage picture. This style is evident in such productions as *Mam'zelle Angot* (1947) and *Les Femmes de bonne humeur* (1949). As an artist, his Fauvist style was said to have influenced early modern painting.

**D'Errico, Ezio** 1892–1972 Italian writer, painter, graphic artist, photographer and playwright. Remarkably versatile, he was keenly responsive to early-20th-century avante-garde movements, particularly FUTURISM, EXPRESSIONISM, and SURREALISM. He began to write for the theatre only in 1948, producing some 40 plays. The early work included light comedy, MELODRAMA and tradititonal pieces in the manner of the WELL MADE PLAY, which were more successful than his later, more serious work. This last was largely ignored in his lifetime by critics and practitioners alike, although it has come to attract increasing interest. His best plays, including *Tempo di cavallette* (*Time of Locusts*, 1956), *La foresta* (*The Forest*, 1956), *Il formicato* (*The Ants Nest*, 1957) and *L'assedio* (*The Siege*, 1959), are dark, pessimistic pieces treating of abstract existential issues, reflecting the influence of PIRANDELLO, IONESCO and BECKETT, and place him firmly in the 'absurdist' category (see THEATRE OF THE ABSURD). His plays were more successful abroad, particularly in Germany. D'Errico was for long associated with the influential Italian theatre journal, *Ridotto*.

**design** see THEATRE DESIGN

**Desiosi, Compagnia dei** Italian company. Literally 'those desirous' (i.e., of pleasing the public), this COMMEDIA DELL'ARTE troupe was first noted in 1581, when Montaigne saw them in Pisa and admired their comic Fargnoccola. The company also included the celebrated Arlecchino, TRISTANO MARTINELLI, and Flaminio Scala served in it both as comedian and manager; but its star from 1585 was Diana Ponti, who acted under the name Lavinia. When she joined the ACCESI in 1600, the Desiosi dispersed.

**Deslys, Gaby** [Gabrielle Caïre] 1881–1920 French REVUE artiste. Of scant talent but blonde good looks and elegant manner, she made her debut at the Parisiana in 1898. Her importance lies in her introducing Europe to American jazz styles in the revue *Laissez-les tomber* (*Let Them Fall*, 1910): dancing with her American partner Harry Pilcer to such exotic instruments as xylophones, saxophones and banjos, she opened up a New World to Paris. She was also the first to make a grand entrance, descending a staircase in ostrich plumes and pearls, setting the style for MISTINGUETT, who was her stand-in when her health failed.

**Dessoir, Ludwig** 1810–74 German actor. A virtuoso noted for the contrast in his acting between restraint and carefully judged outbursts of passion, from 1849 Dessoir was a member of the BERLIN ROYAL THEATRE. In 1853 he appeared with EMIL DEVRIENT at the ST JAMES'S THEATRE, London.

**Destouches** [Philippe Néricault] 1680–1754 French playwright. Following diplomatic service for the regent, Philip of Orleans, he was admitted to the Académie-Française in 1723 and thereafter wrote about 30 plays, gradually throwing off a MOLIÈRESque manner and discovering a more individual and moralizing voice. His most successful plays were *Le Philosophe marié* (*The Married Philosopher*, 1727) and *Le Glorieux* (*The Conceited Count*, 1732).

**Deutsches Theater** Berlin theatre company. It was founded by ADOLF L' ARRONGE in 1883 to provide the city with a repertory company that had standards of ensemble similar to those of the MEININGEN COMPANY. Thanks to the contribution of actors such as JOSEF KAINZ, L'Arronge succeeded. In 1894 the direction was taken over by OTTO BRAHM, who developed a naturalistic approach to the performance of the classics and established the plays of the naturalists firmly in the repertoire (see NATURALISM). In 1904 MAX REINHARDT, who had been a member of Brahm's ensemble, succeeded him, and in the following year established a theatre school and built a chamber theatre. The Deutsches Theater remained the centre of Reinhardt's Berlin operations until his withdrawal from Nazi Germany in 1933. It is still one of the most prominent theatre companies in Berlin.

**Devant, David (Wighton)** 1868–1941 British magician. 'The greatest magician of all times', as *The Times* called him, was discovered by J. N. MASKELYNE, who took him on as assistant and, in 1905, as partner. Devant discarded the hitherto indispensable MAGIC wand and other suspect apparatus, appeared in the first Royal Command Variety Performance of 1912, and gave matinées at London's Ambassador Theatre. His illusions, always eschewing the gruesome, included 'The Giant's Breakfast', in which a girl dressed as a chicken materialized from a huge egg, and 'Bif', in which a rattling motorcycle and its rider were pulled into the air and made to vanish. He retired in 1919.

**Devine, George (Alexander Cassady)** 1910–65 British actor and director. He established the English Stage Company at the ROYAL COURT as a 'writers' theatre'. As President of the Oxford University Dramatic Society, he invited JOHN GIELGUD to direct *Romeo and Juliet* in 1932, in which he played Mercutio. He joined Gielgud's company at the New Theatre in 1934, to act the Player King in what was recognized to be the most celebrated *Hamlet* of the time. He met MICHEL SAINT-DENIS, the innovative French director, who had founded the London Theatre Studio. The partnership between them, at the Studio from 1936 to 1939 and at the OLD VIC School with Glen Byam Shaw after the war, was fruitful both in the testing of new theatrical ideas and in the training of the next generation of actors.

The Old Vic Centre, with its school and YOUNG VIC theatre company, was intended to become the experimental heart of the proposed new NATIONAL THEATRE, but was axed in 1951. Devine returned to being a freelance actor and director, playing Tesman in a memorable *Hedda Gabler* with PEGGY ASHCROFT in 1954 and directing at SADLER'S WELLS and Stratford-upon-Avon with the Shakespeare Memorial Company. But he became convinced that the conditions within British theatre had to change before good new work could be achieved, and in 1954 he joined forces with the playwright Ronald Duncan and the businessman Neville Blond who, together with the director Tony Richardson, founded the English Stage Company for the purpose of staging contemporary plays.

In April 1956, the English Stage Company began its first season at the Royal Court and had an immediate impact upon the course of British theatre. The success of the first season was the premiere of JOHN OSBORNE's *Look Back in Anger*, an unknown play by a then unknown writer, which lent the tone of crusading radicalism, often bitter and angry but never lazy or complacent, to the Royal Court's programmes. The subsequent years provided new plays by SAMUEL BECKETT, N. F. SIMPSON, ARNOLD WESKER, JOHN ARDEN and ANN JELLICOE. As artistic director Devine bore the main burden (with Tony Richardson) of directing the early seasons, staging plays by BRECHT, ARTHUR MILLER and JEAN-PAUL SARTRE, and also acting with the company – notably in IONESCO's *The Chairs* (1957) and in John Osborne's *A Patriot for Me* (1965), his final role. The George Devine Award was instituted in his memory in 1966 to encourage young professional workers in the theatre, and has been awarded primarily to playwrights.

**Devrient family** German actors. The Devrients were the most famous German acting family in the 19th century. **Ludwig** (1784–1832) was the quintessential romantic, thanks to his celebrated interpretations of roles such as Franz Moor in SCHILLER's *The Robbers*, Shylock, and Lear. He brought to the fore the unconscious of the characters he played, fascinating and disturbing his audiences. Celebrated also for his comic roles, he played a matchless Falstaff. From 1815 he acted with the BERLIN ROYAL THEATRE, but soon chronic alcoholism caused his powers to wane. Nevertheless, he continued to act both in Berlin and on numerous tours. His three nephews were the most distinguished perpetuators of the family name. **Carl** (1797–1872) was a solid, heroic actor. **Eduard** (1801–77) was a distinguished director of the Karlsruhe Court Theatre, where he raised standards of ensemble and production; he was also author of the great *History of German Acting* (1848–74). **Emil** (1803–72) was an idolized virtuoso, his acting being considered the finest expression of the WEIMAR STYLE in the mid-19th century. Later family members continued the tradition into the 20th century.

**Dewhurst, Colleen** 1926–91 Canadian-born American actress. Her robustness made her ideal for certain EUGENE O'NEILL heroines, notably Josie in *A Moon for the Misbegotten* (1973 revival): 'I love the O'Neill women,' she said. 'They move from the groin rather than the brain.' Other O'Neill productions included *More Stately Mansions* (1967) and a 1972 revival of *Mourning Becomes Electra*. She appeared in three EDWARD ALBEE plays and with JOSEPH PAPP's NEW YORK SHAKESPEARE FESTIVAL. From 1985 to 1991 she was president of Actors' Equity.

**Dexter, John** 1925–90 British director. He joined the English Stage Company at the ROYAL COURT in 1957, primarily as an actor, but quickly became their most innovative director. He established his reputation with productions of new plays by ARNOLD WESKER, including the *Roots* trilogy (1958, 1959, 1960), *Chips with Everything* (1962) and, in 1959, *The Kitchen*, where he brilliantly choreographed the preparation of restaurant meals. His skill at MIME and movement drew him towards a West End musical, *Half a Sixpence* (1963), and he was one of two Royal Court directors to be invited to join LAURENCE OLIVIER in the formation of the NATIONAL THEATRE company.

From 1963 to 1966 Dexter was an associate director at

the NT, responsible for such revivals as *St Joan*, *Hobson's Choice* and *Othello* (with Olivier in the title role). But his most striking NT achievement was his production of PETER SHAFFER's *The Royal Hunt of the Sun* (1964), which had been rejected as unplayable by most London managements. This triumph led to other Dexter/Shaffer collaborations, particularly on *Equus* (1973). After leaving the NT, Dexter directed on BROADWAY and in the WEST END, returning sometimes to the NT on a freelance basis, e.g. for BRECHT's *Galileo* (1980). From 1974 to 1981 he was director of productions at the Metropolitan Opera House in New York. His last success before his premature death was the London production of David Henry Hwang's *M. Butterfly* (1989).

**Diaghilev, Serge** [Sergei (Pavlovich)] 1872–1929 Russian ballet impresario. The creator of the itinerant Ballets Russes, for over twenty years (1909–29) he awakened Europe to the potential of ballet as a serious and indeed major theatrical art – an art that based its claim on a collaboration between choreographer, musician and artist to an extent that had never been achieved before. He drew the finest musicians and artists to collaborate with choreographers, winning the interest and support of the cultured elite. The form of the single-act ballet became the norm in a varied and distinguished repertory that was to provide future companies with a traditional base no less strong than the classics surviving from earlier periods. For its first few tours of Western Europe the company was Russian-based, but later established itself in Monte Carlo. Under the influence of BENOIS and BAKST the early seasons were essentially Russian in flavour, but after World War I the company reflected more and more the new trends in art associated with the École de Paris. Stravinsky composed many of his most celebrated ballet scores for Diaghilev, while a series of innovative choreographers (Fokine, Nijinsky, Massine, Nijinska, Balanchine) created a body of masterworks many of which have survived to this day.

**Dias Gomes, Alfredo** 1922– Brazilian playwright. He began writing novels and plays in the 1940s. In 1960 he catapulted to national prominence with his play *O pagador de promessas* (*Payment as Pledged*), about a simple peasant whose efforts to repay a religious promise bring down upon him the entire religious and civic authority of his town. A series of successful plays followed. *A invasão* (*The Invasion*, 1962) depicted problems of the urban poor; *A revolução dos beatos* (*The Revolution of the Devout*, 1962) dealt with political and religious fanaticism and intrigue; *O berço do herói* (*The Hero's Cradle*, 1965) emphasized the humour, SATIRE and expressionistic vein of early plays (see EXPRESSIONISM); and *O santo inquérito* (*The Holy Inquisition*, 1966) dealt with a historical figure burned at the stake in the 18th century, serving as a metaphor of political repression. Dias Gomes continued with *Dr Getulio, sua vida e sua glória* (*Dr Getulio, His Life and His Glory*), written in collaboration with Ferreira Gullar; *O rei de ramos* (*The King of Boughs*, 1979), a musical collective; and *Campeões do Mundo* (*World Champions*, 1980); all have a political current strongly based in contemporary Brazilian military repression, CENSORSHIP, political intrigue and hypocrisy. *Amor em campo minado* (*Love in a Mine Field*, 1984), first published as *Vamos soltar os demonios*, chronicles the last hours of an intellectual accused of subversive activities. (See also TELEVISION DRAMA.)

**Díaz, Gregor** 1933– Peruvian playwright, actor and director. Affiliated with the Lima-based group, the Club de Teatro (Theatre Club), he has won national prizes for many of his plays. His major works are *La huelga* (*Strike*, 1966), *Los del 4* (*The Ones in 4*, 1969), *Sitio al sitio* (*Siege of the Site*, 1978), *El mudo de la ventana* (*The Mute at the Window*, 1984) and *Harina mundo* (*Flour World*, 1993). Committed to redressing political and socio-economic injustices, his theatre presents the evils of oppression with artistic sensitivity.

**Díaz, Jorge** 1930– Chilean playwright. Born in Argentina, he began his theatre career as a set designer with the group ICTUS in Santiago, Chile, in 1959. In 1965 he moved to Spain (he holds dual Chilean-Spanish citizenship). His early plays, written with ICTUS, showed the strong influence of European absurdism (see THEATRE OF THE ABSURD), such as *El cepillo de dientes* (*The Toothbrush*, 1961); and those from the first years in Spain still carried a strong Latin American influence, such as *Topografía de un desnudo* (*Topography of a Nude*, 1966). After 1970 Díaz wrote plays of strong political protest such as *Americaliente* (1971), a bombastic collage about US intervention in Latin America, and commentaries about contemporary life in Spain, such as *Mata a tu prójimo como a ti mismo* (*Kill Thy Neighbour as Thyself*, 1975). More recent works include *Piel contra piel* (*Skin against Skin*, 1982) and *El jáguar azul* (*The Blue Jaguar*, 1992). Author of more than 50 major plays, he has also written children's theatre and television scripts. Díaz is an inveterate experimenter with language who loves to challenge society's conventions regarding basic aspects of human existence.

**Dibdin, Charles** 1745–1814 English actor, playwright and composer. As singer and song-writer he collaborated with ISAAC BICKERSTAFFE on comic operas such as *The Padlock* (1768), for which Dibdin wrote the music and starred as Mungo, a black-faced servant. He also wrote text and music for numerous BALLAD OPERAS such as the excellent *The Waterman* (1774). He left DRURY LANE after a rift with GARRICK and moved to France to escape debt. Apart from numerous works for COVENT GARDEN he was also involved in an equestrian theatre (see HIPPODRAMA), the Royal Circus. From 1789 he performed one-man shows of songs, playlets and monologues, which helped to restore his fortunes. From 1796 he wrote plays and entertainments for the Sans Souci Theatre, which he managed. He wrote a five-volume *History of the Stage* (1795).

**Dickens, Charles (John Huffam)** 1812–70 British novelist. Dickens's dependence on the theatre can be sensed even where it cannot be documented. He fed off the world of MELODRAMA. His gift for eccentric characterization owed much to his observation of actors; in turn he provided actors with unrivalled opportunities in the countless adaptations of his novels. Outstanding examples include IRVING's Jingle, BEERBOHM TREE's Fagin and JOHN MARTIN-HARVEY's Sydney Carton. Among the playwrights to have dramatized Dickens are W. T. MONCRIEFF, TOM TAYLOR, T. W. ROBERTSON, BOUCICAULT, JAMES ALBERY, W. S. GILBERT and, most recently, DAVID EDGAR (*Nicholas Nickleby*, 1980). Dickens had two lightweight burlettas and a farce performed in his lifetime, but he was immensely serious about his amateur theatricals in the small private theatre in his London home.

**Diderot, Denis** 1713–84 French philosopher, novelist, playwright and critic. He argued that between classical tragedy and the traditional comedy of intrigue there is a neglected area – the 'conditions' of men, their professions and trades, their conjugal and family lives, their social virtues' – that is ripe for serious COMEDY or domestic TRAGEDY. Such drama will invite the audience's sympathy and make them better people. His thinking profoundly influenced European drama and proved more compelling than the plays that he wrote to illustrate it: Le Fils naturel (The Natural Son, published 1757 and performed 1771) and Le Père de famille (The Father of the Family, 1758 and 1761), which are too elevated in style and sentimental in tone. Paradoxe sur le comédien, his dialogue on the relative importance, to the actor, of feeling and intellect, was published posthumously in 1830.

**Digges, Dudley** 1879–1947 Irish-American actor and director. A member of the original ABBEY Players, he made his New York debut in 1904 with MINNIE MADDERN FISKE. From 1919 he performed regularly for the THEATRE GUILD and also staged four plays for them. Digges was a memorable Harry Hope in O'NEILL's The Iceman Cometh, and also appeared in over 50 films.

**Dimov, Ossip** 1878–1959 Russian-Jewish playwright. He wrote over 30 Jewish plays, first for the MOSCOW ART THEATRE, later in America. Dimov was devoted to improving the literary quality of YIDDISH THEATRE as both writer and producer. His best-known plays are The Eternal Wanderer, Hear O Israel, Yoshke Musikant and Bronx Express.

**Dingelstedt, Franz von** 1814–81 German director. After several years as a journalist and librarian, in 1851 he was appointed director of the Munich Court Theatre. Here he staged productions of unusual splendour and expense; in 1857 he was dismissed for running the theatre into debt. He was immediately appointed director of the Weimar Court Theatre, where his most significant achievement was the production in 1864 of all of SHAKESPEARE'S HISTORY PLAYS. In 1867 he was appointed director of the Vienna Opera and, in 1870, of the BURGTHEATER. Here he repeated his success with Shakespeare's histories and staged numerous other classical plays in a spectacular manner. Dingelstedt is regarded by many historians as a forerunner of both the Duke of Saxe-MEININGEN and MAX REINHARDT.

**directing** Directing is part of that complex of seeing and doing which makes theatre. At all levels the need to intervene to shape the theatrical event can be felt but, because of the processual nature of PLAY, the best of directing comes from within the activity. However, throughout the history of theatre a need can be discerned for unification, direction and encouragement from without – for leadership.

The authority to intervene on behalf of others has been, in the past, mainly the prerogative of playwright or actor (sometimes the same person, as with ZEAMI and MOLIÈRE). Social and economic power, though often influential, has rarely been directly responsible for the crafting of play. For example, in 472 BC at Athens, the politics and wealth of the young Pericles as choregos must have affected the ideology and spectacle of The Persians, but the teaching of the songs and dances, the vision and government of the overall event, was in the hands of AESCHYLUS, who was both playwright and leading actor (see GREEK THEATRE, ANCIENT). By Hellenistic times there is evidence to suggest that training was a separate professional business, but by then directorial authority had been abrogated by the 'star' performer.

Likewise in Rome (see ROMAN THEATRE), the dominus

gregis, as chief actor of the troupe, was responsible for production. In the Middle Ages the maître de jeu, or BOOK-KEEPER, worked both on the preparation and on the smooth running of the show, although often it is unclear how separate such figures were from poet or player. Many must have been similar to the 'property players' of early-16th-century England – actors engaged from the metropolis to supervise and furnish material for provincial productions; but some were, without doubt, separate managers and machinists like the two conducteurs des secrets of the Mons PASSION PLAY. With the growth of scenic illusion in the West, such stage-management increased, but it is not until late in the 19th century that the figure of the director can be discerned.

In Asia, given the historical importance of performance genres (see ACTING), masters often took control of the preparation for a production. The sutradhara in classical Indian theatre, for example, was often responsible for selecting, organizing and training the cast, overseeing the building of a theatre, conducting offerings to the gods and appearing on stage in the preliminaries to the play.

The modern concept of the director grew from the work of the Duke of Saxe-MEININGEN and his stage-manager Chronegk. It was nurtured by pioneers like ANTOINE, STANISLAVSKY and REINHARDT. The latter gave up acting completely in 1903 to devote all his time to directing. The new authority, fundamental to the thoughts of APPIA and CRAIG on the coherence of theatre as art, is exemplified in the careers of MEYERHOLD, VAKHTANGOV, TAIROV, COPEAU and PISCATOR. The work of such masters heads a rich and varied tradition, of which more recent exponents include BROOK, GROTOWSKI and PETER STEIN (all of whom began as directors). This tradition shares with film a parallel development and a common notion of the director as auteur. While this notion may be valid in film, where a final intervention is made in the cutting room, in theatre the live performance mocks its grandeur. In many ways the hegemony of the director – the director seen as an authority separate and separable from either actor or dramatist – is problematic. Reliance on this authority can sap the creativity, intelligence and initiative of the player; while for the playwright, production more and more usurps the power once held by the play. Interpretation is all! The idea of the director is the most dominant feature of Western theatre in the 20th century.

**discovery space** Elizabethan staging device. It is clear from numerous stage directions that Elizabethan theatres, both public and private, had the capacity to conceal and reveal actors and scenes. It was once assumed that the platform had a large alcove or 'inner stage' at the back, but De Witt's drawing of the SWAN undermines the theory. Perhaps a curtain was hung between the two inward-opening doors of the TIRING HOUSE. For some scenes a separate free-standing structure would have been appropriate.

**Dmitrevsky** [Dmitrevskoi], **Ivan (Afanasievich)** 1734–1821 Russian actor. He began his career with FYODOR VOLKOV's acting troupe and continued with the Moscow company co-founded by Volkov and playwright ALEKSEI SUMAROKOV in 1756. Known as 'the Russian GARRICK', Dmitrevsky is credited with having introduced into Russia the loud, artificial declamatory acting style which MIKHAIL SHCHEPKIN's simple, natural approach replaced in the 1830s. He was also teacher-director-administrator, at first with the Free Knipper

Theatre in Moscow, then with related enterprises over the next 38 years. Among his most distinguished pupils were such leaders of the next generation of actors as PYOTR PLAVILSHCHIKOV, A. S. YAKOVLEV, E. S. SEMYONOVA and I. I. SOSNITSKY. The first Russian actor of real artistic distinction and social prominence, Dmitrevsky also wrote more than 40 dramas, comedies and operas. His co-translations of Tacitus, play analyses, contributions to joint scholarly projects and his unpublished history of the Russian theatre (1792) earned him election to the Russian Academy in 1802.

**Döbbelin, Carl Theophil** 1727–93 German actor. After some years in SCHÖNEMANN's troupe, where he practised the LEIPZIG STYLE, in 1756 Döbbelin founded his own troupe; it gave the first performance of LESSING's *Götz von Berlichingen* in 1774. From 1775 on, the troupe formed a permanent company in Berlin; in 1786 it was established, still under Döbbelin's leadership, as the Berlin National and Court Theatre, later to become the important BERLIN ROYAL THEATRE.

**Dockstader, Lew** [George Alfred Clapp] 1856–1925 American comedian. He injected SATIRE into the MINSTREL SHOW. Beginning in blackface, he formed his own company with Charles Dockstader in 1876, retaining the name after his partner retired in 1883. His new partnership with George Primrose created the most popular turn-of-the-century minstrel troupe in the USA (1898–1913). Dockstader performed in two-foot-long shoes and a coat with a 30in tail; his best song was 'Everybody Works but Father'.

**Dodsley, Robert** 1703–64 English playwright and publisher. He had his greatest success with *The King and the Miller of Mansfield* (1737), a folk-tale comedy, and with *Cleone* (1758), an emotionally violent tragedy. More important to drama was his editing and publishing of *A Select Collection of Old Plays* (12 vols., 1744), in which he rescued from obscurity the work of many Renaissance dramatists.

**Doggett, Thomas** c.1670–1721 English actor, manager and playwright. He had joined the DRURY LANE company by 1691, scoring a great success as Solon in D'URFEY's *The Marriage-Hater Matched* (1692). From 1709 to 1714 he joined Wilks and COLLEY CIBBER in running the Queen's Theatre and later Drury Lane. Doggett was praised by DRYDEN for his intelligent acting and by ASTON as 'the best face-player and gesticulator'.

**Domínguez, Franklin** 1931– Dominican Republic playwright, director and actor. Instrumental in creating the experimental theatre movement in the Dominican Republic, he has served as director of the Fine Arts Theatre and has his own theatre group, Franklin Domínguez Presents. He is an eclectic writer. Among his works, which have been widely translated, are: *El último instante* (*The Last Moment*, 1957), the anguished monologue of a suicidal prostitute; *Se busca un hombre honesto* (*The Search for an Honest Man*, 1963); and *Lisístrata odia la política* (*Lysistrata Hates Politics*, 1965), a socially committed play based on ARISTOPHANES.

**Donleavy, J(ames) P(atrick)** 1926– Irish playwright and novelist. He adapted four of his novels for the stage: *The Ginger Man* (1959), *A Singular Man* (1967), *The Saddest Summer of Samuel S* and *The Beastly Beatitudes of Balthazar B* (1981). As these titles suggest, he enjoys a literary rumbustiousness which is not always suitable for the theatre, although *Balthazar* provided SIMON CALLOW with a lively, scandalous role for the WEST END. Donleavy's most successful excursion into playwriting came with

*Fairy Tales of New York* (1961), describing the sad homecoming of an American whose English wife has died on the voyage. These four short plays illustrate different aspects of New York.

**Donnellan, Declan** see CHEEK BY JOWL

**Döring, Theodor** 1803–78 German actor. A natural and versatile imitator, Döring was known for the REALISM and completeness of his characterizations, though at times he became so absorbed in a role that it was difficult to hear him. He joined the BERLIN ROYAL THEATRE in 1845.

**Dorr, Nicolás** 1947– Cuban playwright. His first work, at the age of 14, was a remarkably mature picture of human relationships, captured in a farcical and even absurdist style (see THEATRE OF THE ABSURD). In this vein are *Las pericas* (*The Parrots*, 1961), *El palacio de los cartones* (*The Cardboard Palace*, 1961) and *La esquina de los concejales* (*The Councillor's Corner*, 1962); later works are more realistic, such as *La chacota* (*The Racket*, 1974) and *Confesión en el barrio chino* (*Confession in the Chinese Quarter*). As director of the Teatro Popular Latinoamericano, Dorr launched an ambitious programme for Cuban theatre and continued writing ideologically oriented plays about the new society.

**Dorset Garden Theatre** (London) It was begun in 1669 by Christopher Wren, on a frontage facing the Thames with a site measuring 140ft by 57ft. It had seven boxes on each of the lower and middle galleries, with an undivided upper galley above. It opened in 1671, for use by the Duke's Company, with a production of DRYDEN's *Sir Martin Mar-All*. It was soon apparent that the theatre's acoustics were poor and it was increasingly used only for spectacular productions of operatic extravagances. It was demolished in 1709.

**Dorst, Tankred** 1925– German playwright. Early works such as *Grand Tirade at the Town Wall* (1961) united techniques derived from BRECHT and absurd themes (see THEATRE OF THE ABSURD). Although he rejects ideology, *Toller* (1968) aroused strong political passions. His first major play, this deals with the playwright ERNST TOLLER's role in the short-lived Munich Soviet. A REVUE structure transforms the documentary into grotesque FARCE, and this questioning of the relationship between art and reality is continued in *Ice Age* (1973) through the figure of Knut Hamsun. One of the most interesting contemporary dramatists, he has recently turned to film directing. His most ambitious work is the multimedia cycle subtitled 'German History', comprising the retrospective epilogue *On the Chimborazo* (1970); a novel, *Dorothea Merz*; a film, *Klara's Mother* (1978, also directed by Dorst); *Heinrich, or the Pains of Imagination* (1984) and *The Villa* (1984). Basically naturalistic, this cycle traces the fortunes of a representative group from the early years of the Weimar Republic to the present. His eight-hour *Merlin* (1985) is a kaleidoscopic dramatization of the decline of Christian chivalry, an Arthurian metaphor for the collapse of utopia today. *Fernando Krapp Wrote This Letter* (1992) is a critical comedy based on Miguel de Unamuno.

**Dorval, Marie** 1798–1849 French romantic actress. Her passionate temperament, tremulous voice and instinctive playing set her in opposition to the great classical actress MLLE MARS. She triumphed opposite LEMAÎTRE at the Porte-Saint-Martin in 1827 in VICTOR DUCANGE's *The Hut on the Red Mountain; or, Thirty Years of a Gamester's Life*. DELAVIGNE's *Marino Faliero* (1829) established her as the first actress of the BOULEVARD. In DUMAS *père's Antony*

(1831) she played a passionate woman trapped by society into a loveless marriage and adultery. VIGNY wrote *Quitte pour la peur* (*Getting Off with a Fright*) for her, and in *Chatterton* (1835) created the role of the silent and pathetic Kitty Bell. Other parts included the title role of PONSARD's *Lucrèce* (1842). In 1845 she was back on the boulevard in her final huge triumph, the melodrama *Marie-Jeanne*.

**Dotrice, Roy** 1923– British actor. He made his reputation after joining the ROYAL SHAKESPEARE COMPANY in 1958, where he demonstrated his versatility with memorable performances in the contrasting roles of Gaunt, Hotspur and Justice Shallow, all presented on a single day in the first half of PETER HALL's history cycle, *The Wars of the Roses* (1963). He made an international reputation with his solo adaptation of John Aubrey's *Brief Lives* (1967), which set a record for the longest-running solo performance, and has been followed by other one-man shows. His range remains eclectic, though concentrating on SHAKESPEARE and modern classics from IBSEN to PINTER.

**Douglas, James** 1929– Irish playwright. Douglas made an impressive debut with *North City Traffic Straight Ahead* (Gaiety, Dublin, 1961) which, apart from ironic echoes of SYNGE, is a sparely written drama of wasted urban lives. Since then he has written many television works and a play, *The Bomb* (1962), in whose brief span a faded Ascendancy lady's life embodies great social changes. His other stage plays – the successful *Carrie* (1963), *The Ice Goddess* (1964) and *The Savages* (1968) – more realistically scripted than *North City Traffic*, have never quite recaptured that play's force.

**Douglass, David** ?–1786 British-born American actor-manager. From his marriage in Jamaica in 1758 to the widow of LEWIS HALLAM SR, until the American Revolution, Douglass was the central figure in the history of the American theatre. Though a poor actor, he was a superb manager. In New York he became head of Hallam's company, which in 1763 he renamed the American Company of Comedians. For 17 years they played up and down the East Coast. In 1766 he built the first permanent theatre in the United States, the SOUTHWARK in Philadelphia, followed in 1767 by the JOHN STREET in New York. In April 1767 he staged the first professional production of a play by a native American, a tragedy by Thomas Godfrey: *The Prince of Parthia*. Douglass and his company returned to the West Indies in 1775.

**Dowling, Eddie** [Joseph Nelson Goucher] 1889–1976 American producer, playwright, songwriter, director and actor. He began as a singer and dancer and in 1945 co-produced TENNESSEE WILLIAMS's *The Glass Menagerie*, in which he also played Tom. The production made theatrical history and brought Williams out of obscurity. During his long career he worked with such playwrights as WILLIAM SAROYAN, PAUL VINCENT CARROLL, SEAN O'CASEY and PHILIP BARRY.

**Downes, John** fl.1661–1719 English prompter. He failed as an actor because of severe stage fright, became prompter for the Duke's Company, then worked for the United Company and BETTERTON's Company until 1706. In 1708 he published *Roscius Anglicanus*, a brief history of the stage from the Restoration.

**Downstage Theatre** (Wellington, New Zealand) Established in 1964 as a restaurant theatre specializing in local plays, it served as a stimulus for the foundation of other professional community theatres in many New Zealand cities. In 1974 Downstage moved into the new Hannah Playhouse, seating about 200, and its policy of promoting New Zealand scripts continues in the 1990s.

**drag show** SEE FEMALE IMPERSONATION

**Dragún, Osvaldo** 1929– Argentine playwright and director. Born in San Salvador, he has consistently censured the materialism and hypocrisy of our times. His *Historias para ser contadas* (*Stories to Be Told*, 1957) were written with a COMMEDIA DELL'ARTE flavour to be performed by his theatre group, Teatro Popular Fray Mocho. Internationally known, these vignettes with long titles condemn the sacrifices of human dignity on the altar of economic survival. Other titles, *La peste viene de Melos* (*The Plague Comes from Melos*, 1956) and *Tupac Amarú* (1957), show perverted economic and moral values in classical settings. Later plays include *Y nos dijeron que éramos inmortales* (*And They Told Us We Were Immortal*, 1963), *El milagro en el mercado viejo* (*Miracle in the Old Market*, 1964), *El amasijo* (*The Hodgepodge*, 1968) and sequels to the *Historias*. Dragún played a major role in the creation of the TEATRO ABIERTO (open theatre). More recent works include *Al violador* (*To the Rapist*, 1981), *Hoy comen al flaco* (*Today They Eat the Thin Man*, 1981), *Mi obelisco y yo* (*My Obelisk and Me*, 1981), *Al perdedor* (*To the Loser*, 1982), *Al vencedor* (*To the Seller*, 1982) and *Arriba corazón* (*Upward Heart!* 1987). Recently he has run the Institute for Latin American Theatre in Havana.

**Drake, Samuel** 1769–1854 American actor-manager. Born in England, where he became a provincial manager, Drake took his family of performers to America in 1810. He formed a theatrical circuit in Kentucky, which he controlled for many years. While not the first company in the American West, Drake's group improved the level of theatre in the area and firmly established the FRONTIER THEATRE.

**Drama League** American theatre society. Founded in 1909 by an Evanston (Illinois) ladies' literary society, the 'Riley Circle', they aimed 'to stimulate interest in the best drama', 'to awaken the public to the importance of the theatre as a social force'. The organization expanded rapidly: by the early 20s, they had 23,000 members and 114 centres throughout the country. They published *The Drama* (1911), a quarterly magazine on American drama and theatre, and 20 volumes of plays. After the national organization was disbanded (1931), local centres continued to function and the New York Drama League is still active.

**Dramaten** Swedish company. (The name also refers to the two connected theatre buildings where the company performs.) The Royal Dramatic Theatre in Stockholm was founded in 1788 by Gustav III for the performance of original Swedish plays. The company performed in various temporary playhouses before acquiring the New Theatre in 1863. However, until 1842 it also enjoyed a 50-year monopoly of spoken drama in the capital. It depended on royal and parliamentary subsidies until 1888, when it was denationalized and run by an association of actors. Dramaten moved to its present building and regained its subsidies in 1907 and has since become one of the world's most celebrated companies, especially under the leadership of PER LINDBERG, OLOF MOLANDER, ALF SJÖBERG and INGMAR BERGMAN. STRINDBERG, IBSEN, BRECHT and O'NEILL have been important in the modern repertory. The theatre opened its Little Stage in 1945, followed in the 1970s by the converted Paint Room and the tiny Fyran, high under the theatre's roof.

**Draper, Ruth** 1884–1956 American actress. She created and performed a repertoire of 54 different characters in her monologue sketches, finely wrought characterizations of women of all ages, types and cultures. In addition she evoked throngs of other 'unseen' characters. After her professional debut in 1920 she performed almost non-stop, on every continent.

**Dresden Court Theatre** German theatre. The first record of performances in Dresden dates from 1585, when the ENGLISCHE KOMÖDIANTEN visited the court. In the late 17th century, JOHANNES VELTEN was employed there regularly. The high point in the Court Theatre's history was the long intendancy of August von Lüttichau (1785–1863), which lasted from 1824 to 1862. During these years Dresden became known as the theatre where the WEIMAR STYLE was most assiduously cultivated. From 1831 until his death in 1872, EMIL DEVRIENT was an idolized member of the company, though his pre-eminence was challenged between 1853 and 1864, when BOGUMIL DAWISON was also in the company. In 1841 the Court Theatre was housed in a splendid new theatre designed by Gottfried Semper, which was in use until its destruction in World War II. The restored theatre was reopened in 1985.

**Dressler, Marie** [Leila Koerber] 1869–1934 Canadian comedienne. At 14 she joined the Nevada Stock Company playing ingénues, but her mastiff-like features and stocky build soon relegated her to farcical roles. She entered New York VAUDEVILLE with coon songs and impersonations, and had a real success as the MUSIC-HALL singer Flo Honeydew in the comic opera The Lady Slavey (1896). JOSEPH WEBER invited her to join his company in Higgledy-Piggledy (1904). Her most memorable role was the day-dreaming boarding-house drudge Tillie Blobbs, in Tillie's Nightmare (Herald Square Theatre, 1910), singing 'Heaven Will Protect the Working Girl'. Later she won a new Hollywood public with Anna Christie (1930), Dinner at Eight and Tugboat Annie (both 1933).

**Drew-Barrymore family** Anglo-American acting family. The name Barrymore, with Lionel, Ethel and John its foremost exponents, stands as a synonym for acting. The colour and glamour of their private lives, as well as their artistry and industry, earned them fame.

Mrs **John Drew** (1820–97), maternal grandmother to Lionel, Ethel and John, was born Louisa Lane in London, daughter of an actor and a ballad-singer. After her father's early death, the child toured provincial theatres before sailing for America with her mother. After playing such roles as the Duke of York to JUNIUS BRUTUS BOOTH's Richard III and Albert to EDWIN FORREST's William Tell (ten years later, she would graduate to Lady Macbeth opposite Forrest's Macbeth), she had a distinguished adolescent and adult career and married her third husband, **John Drew** (1827–62), whose father managed NIBLO'S GARDEN Theatre in New York. Famous for playing popular Irish characters and SHAKESPEARE's Andrew Aguecheek and Dromio, Drew briefly managed Philadelphia's National and ARCH STREET Theatres. Mrs Drew undertook the management of the Arch in 1861, and during 30 subsequent years at the helm she contributed to the achievement and acceptance of theatre in America, while continuing to act, by popular demand, in such roles as Mrs Malaprop and Mistress Quickly.

Two of her children by Drew began illustrious careers at the Arch. **John Drew** (1853–1927) trained under his mother's stern supervision before joining AUGUSTIN DALY's FIFTH AVENUE THEATRE company in New York (1875). Among his most popular old and new comedy parts were Orlando, Petruchio and Charles Surface. By the mid-1800s he and his fellow Fifth Avenue players, ADA REHAN, James Lewis and Mrs George H. Gilbert, were known as 'the Big Four'. In 1892 Drew agreed to star for manager CHARLES FROHMAN. His naturalistic acting (see NATURALISM), elegant bearing and sartorial correctness won him the uncontested title 'First Gentleman of the American Stage' and kept him a reigning star for 35 years.

**Georgiana Drew** (1856–93), after a strict Arch Street apprenticeship, followed her older brother to the Fifth Avenue in 1876. She became a popular comedienne in such hits as The Senator (1889) and Settled Out of Court (1892) with Frohman's Comedians. Her Fifth Avenue debut, in Daly's popular Pique, cast her opposite a young newcomer from England, **Maurice Barrymore** (1847–1905), who had made his debut at the Theatre Royal, Windsor, in 1872, and whom she married in 1876. His early years in America were spent in the companies of America's foremost managers: Augustin Daly, LESTER WALLACK and A. M. PALMER. His striking beauty, sharp wit and carefree manner made him a popular matinée idol and leading man. His most successful characterizations included Orlando (particularly opposite HELENA MODJESKA) and the title roles in A Man of the World and Captain Swift (1888). He also wrote eight plays, and left three children by Georgiana Drew.

**Ethel Barrymore** (1879–1959) became the first of the three siblings to achieve stardom. She had six years of apprenticeship with her grandmother, her uncle John Drew, and SIR HENRY IRVING in England, and under the astute management of Charles Frohman became a darling of fin-de-siècle society on two continents; the term 'glamour girl' was coined for her; sons of American millionaires and English notables, including Winston Churchill, courted her. 'Ethel Barrymore vehicles' such as Alice-Sit-by-the-Fire, Cousin Kate, Lady Frederick and Déclassé alternated with the stronger stuff of A Doll's House, The Second Mrs Tanqueray and The Constant Wife, and Lady Teazle, Camille, Portia and Juliet. In 1928 the SHUBERTS opened the Ethel Barrymore Theatre, with Ethel interpreting three ages of woman in The Kingdom of God. After the climax of her stage career in The Corn Is Green (1940), she opted for film work until her death.

Her older brother **Lionel Barrymore** (1878–1954) began acting at 15 under the tutelage of his grandmother and his uncle **Sidney Drew** (1868–1919, Mrs Drew's illegitimate son, a noted stage and VAUDEVILLE comedian). Lionel's inspired characterizations included boxer Kid Garvey in The Other Girl (1904), written for him by AUGUSTUS THOMAS. After three years in France as a painter he returned to America to act on stage and in film, e.g. in two co-starring ventures with his brother: Peter Ibbetson (1917) and The Jest (1919). But after the failure of his Macbeth in 1921 and a series of mediocre plays, Lionel turned irrevocably to Hollywood and nearly 200 film roles.

His younger brother **John Barrymore** (1882–1942) resisted acting for some time but, after a run of light comedy roles like The Fortune Hunter (1909), stunned critics and theatregoers with his expert delineations of tragic roles in the ARTHUR HOPKINS–ROBERT EDMOND JONES productions of Richard III (1920) and Hamlet (1922), illuminated by his beauty, vocal grandeur and subtle strength. But at the height of his powers, touted as America's greatest actor, he left the stage for films, returning only once to play a parody of himself in a travesty of a play (*My Dear Children*, 1939).

Among the later generations of Drew-Barrymore actors, John Barrymore's daughter **Diana** (1921–60) and his son, known as John Drew Barrymore Jr or **John Drew Barrymore** (1932– ), have acted on stage and screen. The latter's daughter, **Drew Barrymore** (1975– ), gained stardom at the age of seven in the film *E.T.* (1982) and continues to appear in films.

**Drexler, Rosalyn** 1926– American playwright. Her OFF-OFF BROADWAY avant-garde plays satirize sex, violence and domestic life. Drexler's first play, *Home Movies* (1964), blended her own 'camp' style with music by Al Carmines, a partnership which proved successful again with *The Line of Least Existence* (1968). She continued her anarchic humour in such plays as *Hot Buttered Roll* (1966) and *The Writer's Opera* (1979), but she also wrote in a naturalistic vein for *The Investigation* (1966). *She Who Was He* (1974) is a feminist history of Hatshepsut; *Delicate Feelings* (1984) is a poignant study of two lesbian wrestlers; *Transients Welcome* won critical acclaim in 1985.

**Drinkwater, John** [John Darnley] 1882–1937 British playwright, director, poet and biographer. Best known for his part in the revival of poetic drama, Drinkwater made a more lasting contribution to the theatre as a founder member of BARRY JACKSON's Pilgrim Players and as the first general manager of the BIRMINGHAM REPERTORY THEATRE. There he directed over 60 productions. He experimented with MASQUES before writing his first full-length play, *Rebellion* (1914), an allegorical attack on Victorian morality. This was followed by *The Storm* (1915), inspired by SYNGE's *Riders to the Sea*, but after his bitter lament against war, *X=0: A Night of the Trojan War* (1917), he abandoned verse. His most successful work was in historical drama, in particular *Abraham Lincoln* (1918); though he also wrote a popular comedy, *Bird in Hand* (1927), the first play in which PEGGY ASHCROFT and LAURENCE OLIVIER played major roles.

**Drottningholm Slottsteater** Swedish theatre. As one of the summer palaces of the Swedish kings, Drottningholm had temporary theatres from at least the 1740s, and from 1753 a permanent playhouse for Italian opera and French drama. After fire destroyed this in 1762, Carl Fredrik Adelcrantz designed the present building, which opened in 1766. It has a deep stage, with elaborate machinery in the Italian manner: wing-chariots, movable traps and cloud and wave machines. The auditorium, adjustable in size, is itself a painted setting, designed to mirror the illusory world on stage. The theatre's most brilliant era was the reign of Gustav III (1771–92), when the royal opera and acting companies spent the summers there. After Gustav's assassination it gradually fell into disuse, until rediscovered in 1921, miraculously preserved and with a store of about 30 complete 18th-century settings by such artists as CARLO BIBIENA and Louis Jean Desprez. It reopened in 1922, inaugurating a tradition of summer seasons of 18th-century opera and dance.

**Drury Lane, Theatre Royal** (London) For nearly two centuries, any of the four buildings erected along the network of narrow streets including Drury Lane could reasonably have claimed to be London's leading theatre. The first (capacity c.700), known as the Theatre Royal, Bridges Street, opened in 1663. It was built by THOMAS KILLIGREW to house the King's Men, one of the two companies licensed by Royal Patent to perform the legitimate drama in the city of Westminster. It was destroyed by fire early in 1672.

A second rectangular theatre, probably designed by Sir Christopher Wren, opened in 1674. Despite the compact elegance of its design, Restoration audiences preferred the rival DORSET GARDEN THEATRE, and Drury Lane struggled for three decades, especially under the unpopular Christopher Rich. Things improved in 1711, when three actors, Robert Wilks, THOMAS DOGGETT (replaced by BARTON BOOTH in 1713) and COLLEY CIBBER, assumed the active management and ANNE OLDFIELD was in her prime.

But the costs of satisfying public demand for opera, ballet, PANTOMIME and scenic spectacle as well as drama caused financial crises from 1733 to 1747. It was GARRICK, in association with JAMES LACY, who inaugurated the greatest years in the whole history of Drury Lane. His long management (1747–76) was a model of combined caution and daring. He surrounded himself with a strong company, including at various times SPRANGER BARRY, CHARLES MACKLIN, KITTY CLIVE, PEG WOFFINGTON, SUSANNA CIBBER and HANNAH PRITCHARD. Garrick was succeeded by the playwright SHERIDAN, whose production of his own *The School for Scandal* (1777) was the most successful opening in the theatre's history. Sheridan's financial problems were eased by the success of SARAH SIDDONS in 1782 and of her brother JOHN PHILIP KEMBLE in 1783. By 1791 the theatre had so deteriorated that Sheridan decided to demolish it.

The third Drury Lane opened in 1794, a massive building with a capacity of 3,611. Better suited to spectacle than to drama, it marked a low point in theatrical taste. Kemble defected to COVENT GARDEN in 1803, taking Sarah Siddons with him. The theatre declined and was destroyed by fire in 1809.

The fourth theatre (original capacity 3,060) opened in 1812. The sensational debut of EDMUND KEAN in 1814 delayed inevitable financial disaster, the joint fate of both patent companies in the last decades of their monopoly. For nearly five seasons, Kean reigned supreme. In 1819 ROBERT ELLISTON became manager. By 1826, Kean was past his best and Elliston bankrupt, following extensive remodelling of the interior. Equipped with gas lighting since 1817, the Drury Lane which ruined successive managers until the abolition of the patent monopoly in 1843 was a superb but costly toy. MACREADY tried, and failed, to rescue its reputation (1841–3). As a house of spectacle, sensation drama and pantomime, it survived under the managements of Sir Augustus Harris (1879–96) and Arthur Collins (1896–1923). Under Alfred Butt (1924–31) it became the home of the English musical, as it did of the American musical in the years following World War II, with Ivor Novello dominating the years between. London's greatest theatre currently presents popular musicals likely to enjoy long runs.

**Dryden, John** 1631–1700 English playwright, poet and critic. After studying at Cambridge, in 1657 he became a professional writer in London, where in addition to poetry he wrote, adapted and collaborated on over 30 plays, which were marked by an incisive intelligence and seriousness. His comedy *The Wild Gallant* was a failure at its first performances in 1663. He collaborated with SIR ROBERT HOWARD on *The Indian Queen* (1664), an attempt to create the new genre of heroic tragedy, depending on the hero's choice between love and honour in an exotic setting. His sequel, *The Indian Emperor* (1665), is a better example of the genre. In 1667 he mixed heroic TRAGEDY and contemporary COMEDY in *Secret Love*. *Sir Martin Mar-All*, a bright comedy, marked a shift of allegiance from KILLIGREW'S DRURY LANE to DAVENANT'S LINCOLN'S INN FIELDS; it was followed by an adaptation of SHAKESPEARE'S *The Tempest*, written with Davenant, playing up the spectacular and creating new characters.

In 1668 Dryden was appointed Poet Laureate and published his major critical study, *An Essay of Dramatic Poesy*, applying neoclassical principles to English drama. *Tyrannic Love*, on the martyrdom of St Catherine, was performed in 1669; his heroic drama *The Conquest of Granada* appeared in two parts, in 1670 and 1671. Of his later tragedies, *Aureng-Zebe* (1675) is more restrained and points towards *All for Love* (1678), a version of Shakespeare's *Antony and Cleopatra*, embodying neoclassical unities and morality. He adapted Milton's *Paradise Lost* into an unperformed opera, *The State of Innocence* (1677), and produced a blood-filled *Oedipus* with NATHANIEL LEE (1679). Of his comedies, *Marriage à-la-Mode* (1672) is as witty and perceptive as *The Kind Keeper* (1678) is coarse. After Dryden became Roman Catholic in 1685 he wrote *Amphitryon* (1690), which retells the myth with a surprising energy and lightness of wit, and *Don Sebastian* (1689), a dark tragedy. He also wrote operas, notably *King Arthur* (1691), with music by Purcell. In the range of his work over 30 years he dominated English drama of the Restoration.

**Držić, Marin** 1508–67 Croatian playwright. Born in Dubrovnik, he travelled in Italy, where he plotted the overthrow of the patrician rule in Dubrovnik. Between 1548 and 1559, Držić was the main animator of amateur theatricals in Dubrovnik, and creator of a small repertoire of PASTORALS and comedies, some lost. Most famous and probably the best is *Uncle Maroje*, rediscovered and restaged in Zagreb just before World War II. It became a regular feature in the Croat and Yugoslav repertoire and the national play most frequently produced abroad. In *Uncle Maroje*, *Tirena*, *The Farce of Stanac* and *The Miser*, Držić fuses the motifs and style of Italian Renaissance drama with local traditions, circumstances and temperament, but instances of melancholy and bitterness occasionally break through the spirit of merriment. He died in Venice as an exile.

**Du Maurier, Gerald (Hubert Edward)** 1873–1934 British actor-manager. He began his career under FORBES-ROBERTSON and made his reputation with HERBERT BEERBOHM TREE. He specialized in popular drama of the clubland heroes variety (Raffles, Arsène Lupin, Bulldog Drummond), though his most important roles were in the premieres of BARRIE'S *The Admirable Crichton* (1902), *Peter Pan* (1904) and *Dear Brutus* (1917). In 1910 he took over the management of Wyndham's Theatre in London, and was knighted in 1922.

**Dubé, Marcel** 1930– French Canadian playwright, poet and novelist. The most prolific and most popular dramatist of the 1950s and 60s, he began writing for Radio-Canada and national television. His stage play *Zone* won first prize at the Dominion Drama Festival in 1953. It portrays dispossessed urban youth in their defiance of social norms – in this case as smugglers on the USA/Quebec border. Even more popular was the television play *Un Simple Soldat* (*Private Soldier*, 1957), revised

for stage performance in 1958. *Le Temps des lilas* (*Lilac Time*, 1958) depicts love and disillusion in a decaying urban lodging-house.

In the 1960s, Dubé's attention turned to middle-class characters and concerns. His vision remained tragic, in works such as *Bilan* (*The Accounting*, 1960), *Florence* (1960), *Les Beaux Dimanches* (*Fine Sundays*, 1965) and, especially, in *Au retour des oies blanches* (*The White Geese*, 1966), generally considered his finest play. In the 1970s he turned his hand to comedy, in *L'Été s'appelle Julie* (*The Summer Named Julie*, 1975) and in *Dites-le avec des fleurs* (*Say It with Flowers*, 1976), written in collaboration with JEAN BARBEAU. Author of some 50 plays to date, plus a score of radio and television scripts, Dubé dominated his age.

**Dublin Drama League** Irish company. Founded in 1919 by LENNOX ROBINSON with YEATS'S support, and managed by subscribing members, the League was allowed to use the ABBEY stage on Sundays and Mondays, when the Abbey did not play. As a complement to the Abbey's almost wholly Irish repertoire, the League presented PIRANDELLO, TOLLER, STRINDBERG, CHEKHOV and ANDREEV. Abbey actors participated with amateurs, including DENIS JOHNSTON. The League succeeded in bringing world drama to a Dublin audience. It dissolved itself in 1929, recognizing the legitimate succession of the Edwards–MacLiammóir GATE THEATRE.

**Dublin International Theatre Festival** (Ireland) Originating in 1957, its purpose was to have plays by Irish and foreign dramatists staged annually by local and imported companies. Because of clerical objection to O'CASEY'S *Drums of Father Ned* and a dramatization of Joyce's *Ulysses*, its second year was cancelled. Despite hand-to-mouth funding it has admirably realized its intentions and seen many notable Irish premieres. The Festival occurs every October, and in recent years its range has greatly extended beyond conventional theatre to Brazilian, Indian, Japanese and European dance and MIME.

**Dubois, René-Daniel** 1955– Quebec playwright and actor. The Freudian overtones of *Panique à Longueil* (*Panic in Longueil*, 1980) fascinated Montreal audiences, and *Ne blâmez jamais les bédouins* (*Never Blame the Bedouins*, 1984) combined startling fantasy with REALISM. A fine actor, Dubois played all the roles in this work. *Being at Home with Claude* (1985), dealing with a homosexual's confession to the murder of his lover, is another powerful text.

**Ducange, Victor** 1783–1833 French novelist, playwright, and political journalist. Ducange's first success was *Calas* (1819), a MELODRAMA on the theme of religious fanaticism. He provoked emotion through horror and pathos, particularly in *Thérésa, ou L'Orpheline de Genève* (*Theresa, or The Orphan of Geneva*). His most lasting success was *Thirty Years of a Gamester's Life* (1827), on the evils of gambling. His anticlericalism resurfaced in *Le Jésuite* (*The Jesuit*, 1820), and his final play *Il y a seize ans* (*Sixteen Years Ago*, 1831) was another famous tear-jerker.

**Duchesnois, Mlle** [Cathérine Joséphine Rafuin] 1777–1835 French actress. She joined the COMÉDIE-FRANÇAISE, where she proved an ideal partner for TALMA and a rival to MLLE GEORGE, her warmth and strong, flexible voice compensating for lack of physical advantages. From 1804 to 1829 she created 36 roles, including Andromaque in *Hector* (1809), Marie Stuart (1820) and Clytemnestra (1822).

**Ducis, Jean-François** 1733–1816 French playwright and man of letters. He adapted SHAKESPEARE's plays according to neoclassical taste. His *Hamlet* (1769), at the end of which the prince decides to live and reign, remained popular into the 19th century. He also adapted *King Lear* (1792), *Macbeth* (1783), and *Othello* with two possible denouements (1792), as well as *Romeo and Juliet* and *King John*. His own most popular play was *Abufar, ou La Famille Arabe* (1795), which provided TALMA with one of his greatest roles.

**Ducrow, Andrew** 1793–1848 Belgian popular entertainer. A MIME artist, acrobat, equestrian and peerless contriver of spectacular shows, he won his fame in London at ASTLEY's in 1814 and at Franconi's CIRCUS in Paris. He managed Astley's with great success from 1830 to 1841, introducing brief dramas played entirely on horseback and such spectacles as his leading attraction, *The Battle of Waterloo* (1824), based on field research. Despite his theatrical acumen, he was scorned as a surly illiterate by many, who quoted his rehearsal directive, 'Cut the dialect and come to the 'osses.' (See also HIPPO-DRAMA.)

**Dudley, William** 1947– British stage designer. His work ranges from grand opera to small, intimate creations suggestive of street theatre. In recent years he has been affiliated with London's NATIONAL THEATRE. After early training in landscape painting, he gained stage experience in London FRINGE THEATRE before working for five years at the ROYAL COURT. Eventually tiring of the Court's stripped-down, unostentatious style, Dudley moved on to work that was more reflective of 19th-century romanticism expressed through contemporary techniques. Representative productions range from small-scale promenade stagings of *The Passion* (1977) and *Lark Rise* (1978), to the grander dimensions of the operas *Billy Budd* (1976), *Tales of Hoffmann* (1980) and WAGNER's *Ring* cycle at BAYREUTH (1983), and the complex scenography of *The Shaughran* (1988), *Bartholomew Fair* (1988) and *Pygmalion* (1992) at the NT.

**Duff, Mary Ann (Dyke)** 1794–1857 American actress. Born in London, she went to America in 1810. Until 1817 she was relatively unnoticed, then emerged as a star – 'the American SIDDONS' – winning fame as a tragic actress in Philadelphia and Boston rather than New York.

**Dukes, Ashley** 1885–1959 British theatre manager, drama critic and playwright. He founded the MERCURY THEATRE in London in 1933 as a permanent base for the ballet company run by his wife, Marie Rambert. In his critical writing he consistently championed new dramatists, becoming English editor of the American journal *Theatre Arts Monthly* in 1926. He adapted plays by Anatole France (1914), GEORG KAISER and ERNST TOLLER (1920–3, thus introducing German EXPRESSIONISM to the British stage), LION FEUCHTWANGER, FERDINAND BRUCKNER and CARL STERNHEIM, as well as NICCOLÒ MACHIAVELLI's *Mandragola* (1939). His most successful original play was *The Man with a Load of Mischief* (1924). In 1935 he organized a Poets' Theatre Season at the Mercury in cooperation with the GROUP THEATRE, at which T. S. ELIOT's *Murder in the Cathedral* was given its successful London premiere. In 1941 Dukes joined CEMA.

**Dullin, Charles** 1885–1949 French actor and director. Dullin was part of COPEAU's first company at the VIEUX-COLOMBIER. He ran GÉMIER's theatre school, in which actors and directors including ARTAUD, BARRAULT, BLIN and VILAR received a varied theatrical training (including ACROBATICS and *COMMEDIA DELL'ARTE* techniques), and from 1922 directed the ATELIER, attempting to com-

bine vigorous versions of the classics with modern plays by SALACROU, ROMAINS and PIRANDELLO. He helped found the CARTEL in 1927. He was also a star actor in plays by MOLIÈRE, JONSON and SHAKESPEARE. In 1937 he compiled a report which became the basis for the post-war decentralization movement in French theatre.

**Dumas, Alexandre,** *père* 1802–70 French playwright and novelist (known as Dumas *père* to distinguish him from his son). *Henri III et sa cour* (*Henry III and his Court*, 1829) was the first great romantic drama to be staged at the Théâtre-Français; in its attention to period costume and scenery it introduced the concept of *mise-en-scène*. After the 1830 revolution he wrote a play about Napoleon (no longer a forbidden subject) with LEMAÎTRE in the title role. His first real triumph was a modern-dress play, *Antony* (1831), with BOCAGE and MARIE DORVAL at the Porte-Saint-Martin (see BOULEVARD). An exciting MELODRAMA in which society is the villain, it is the first great 'problem play' of the 19th century. In 1831 the ODÉON staged *Charles VII chez ses grands vassaux* (*Charles VII with His Great Vassals*). In 1832, Dumas rewrote Gaillardet's *La Tour de Nesle*, a cloak-and-dagger piece in which past crime catches up on its perpetrators, affording Bocage a flamboyant role as hero-villain. Further dramas included *Angèle* (1833), *Cathérine Howard* (1834) and *Kean; or, Disorder and Genius* (1836), about the English actor EDMUND KEAN. In 1837 he and VICTOR HUGO rented the Ventadour and renamed it the Théâtre de la Renaissance, opening with Hugo's *Ruy Blas*. In 1839 Dumas wrote a successful historical comedy, *Mademoiselle de Belle-Isle*. In 1844 his two most famous novels appeared in serial form: *The Three Musketeers* and *The Count of Monte Cristo*. His second venture into theatre management came with the creation of the Théâtre Historique (1847) on the Boulevard du Temple, where he presented adaptations of his own novels.

**Dumas, Alexandre,** *fils* 1824–95 French novelist and playwright, son of ALEXANDRE DUMAS *père*. He examined the wealthy society of the Second Empire and Third Republic with moral severity, whilst dealing with risqué themes. Alphonsine Duplessis, a high-class courtesan, became his mistress and the model for his novel *La Dame aux camélias* (1848), which he adapted for the stage. This was finally allowed performance in 1852 (it became the basis for the libretto of Verdi's *La Traviata*, 1853). The title of his comedy *Le Demi-monde* (Théâtre du Gymnase, 1855) created a new term for the French language, as well as a new role – the woman with a past. The Théâtre-Français (see COMÉDIE-FRANÇAISE) staged *Le Supplice d'une femme* (*A Woman's Torture*, 1865) and *L'Étrangère* (1876), which explored the theme of marital infidelity. Under a pseudonym he rewrote *Les Danicheff* (1876), which was an unexpected success at the ODÉON (the cast included SARAH BERNHARDT's dog).

**dumb show** Elizabethan term. It describes the spectacular MIME element within a Tudor play, particularly in tragedy. Early dumb shows were allegorical, employing symbolic figures rather than actual characters from the play. Professional Elizabethan playwrights exploited them to focus the attention of the audience on significant deeds outside the play's narrative. Famous examples are in KYD's *The Spanish Tragedy* (c.1589), PEELE's *The Old Wives Tale* (published 1595) and the anonymous *A Warning for Fair Women* (1599). SHAKESPEARE's play-within-the-play in *Hamlet* features an introductory dumb show in a consciously archaic manner. WEBSTER and MIDDLETON continued to exploit dumb shows to sensational effect after they had been incorporated in the more spectacular MASQUE.

**Dunlap, William** 1766–1839 American playwright and manager. Often called 'the father of American drama', Dunlap began his artistic life as a painter and created many miniatures and religious canvases. He managed the PARK THEATRE from 1798 to 1805, (a financial disaster), was the first manager to write and present his own plays, and the first to champion native subject-matter and native dramatists. Among his books are a biography of the actor GEORGE FREDERICK COOKE (1813) and the first *History of the American Theatre* (1832). Dunlap translated/adapted from French and German drama, principally from KOTZEBUE. Notable among his original plays are *Darby's Return* (1789), *The Father* (1799), *André* (1798), *Leicester* (1806) and *A Trip to Niagara, or Travellers in America* (1828) with a diorama of 18 scenes along the Hudson.

**Dunlop, Frank** 1927– British director. He started his own company, the Piccolo Theatre, in 1954, directed at the BRISTOL OLD VIC, and became artistic director of the Nottingham Playhouse from 1961–4. In 1970 he founded the YOUNG VIC as a small stage adjunct to the OLD VIC, and acquired for it a reputation for lively, popular productions of classic plays. He also spotted the talents of TIM RICE and ANDREW LLOYD WEBBER, staging *Joseph and the Amazing Technicolour Dreamcoat* (1968). He was appointed director of the EDINBURGH FESTIVAL in 1983, contributed *Treasure Island* (1990) in energetic and buoyant style, and an international post-*glasnost* festival in 1991, but resigned thereafter.

**Dunnock, Mildred** 1901–91 American actress and director. She achieved stardom with such roles as Linda Loman in *Death of a Salesman* (1949) and Big Mama in *Cat on a Hot Tin Roof* (1955). She usually appeared in major supporting roles, relying on a slight stature and tremendous voice to project an ineffectual gentility. She was also a successful film and television actress.

**Dunsany** [Edward John Moreton Drax Plunkett], Lord 1878–1957 Anglo-Irish playwright, novelist and critic. His ironic fantasies in exotic settings were connected with the Irish literary revival. After *The Glittering Gates* (1909) and *King Argimenes* (1911) at the ABBEY THEATRE in Dublin, his work was mainly produced at the HAYMARKET and EVERYMAN Theatres in London and in the USA, the most successful being *If* (1921), in which time is reversed and telescoped.

**Durang, Christopher** 1949– American playwright and actor. Durang had his first play produced in 1971, emerging as a substantial dramatist in the late 1970s and early 1980s. His best-known scripts include *When Dinah Shore Ruled the Earth* (with WENDY WASSERSTEIN, 1975), *A History of the American Film* (1976), the highly controversial *Sister Mary Ignatius Explains It All for You* (1979) and *The Actor's Nightmare* (1981), *Beyond Therapy* (1981), *Baby with the Bath Water* (1983) and *The Marriage of Bette and Boo* (1973, revised 1985). Of satirical bent, in recent years he has devoted much time to CABARET and REVUE performance.

**Duras, Marguerite** 1914– French novelist, scriptwriter and playwright. Duras has blurred the distinctions between the genres: her disembodied voices speak hauntingly through novels and films as much as through the theatre. Her plays have been successful on radio. Some, like *Le Square* (*The Square*, 1956), present a stream of discourse through which characters seek to make contact with one another but seldom succeed.

Her plays include *Des Journées entières dans les arbres* (*Days in the Trees*, 1956) and *Éden-cinéma* (1977).

**D'Urfey, Thomas** 1653–1723 English playwright. A close friend of Charles II and his successors, he was mocked for his stutter and his ugliness but became known for his songs, collected as *Pills to Purge Melancholy* (six vols., 1719). He wrote 33 plays, including five poor sensationalist tragedies and four weak operas. His comedies, beginning with *Madam Fickle* in 1676, have an energy far beyond their frequently imitative plots. D'Urfey often adapted earlier plays, including a version of SHAKESPEARE's *Cymbeline* as *The Injured Princess* (1682), but his best work is sharp contemporary SATIRE, particularly on the connection between financial intrigue and marriage in *Love for Money* (1691) and *The Richmond Heiress* (1693). His three-part adaptation of CERVANTES as *The Comical History of Don Quixote* (1694–5) is a mixture of faithful recreation and coarse invention. The plays' bawdiness was attacked by JEREMY COLLIER.

**Durov family** Russian clowns and animal trainers. The brothers **Vladimir Leonidovich** (1863–1934) and **Anatoly Leonidovich** (1864–1916) became satiric clowns. Vladimir was also renowned as a trainer; with his pigs, rats and dogs in such sketches as 'The Pied Piper of Hamelin' and 'The Russo-Japanese War' he attacked bureaucratic corruption and administrative malpractice. Both brothers frequently got into trouble with the police and authorities. After the Revolution, Vladimir retired to experiment in animal behaviour. Of his progeny, four children and two grandchildren went into the CIRCUS, as did two children and two grandchildren of Anatoly.

**Dürrenmatt, Friedrich** 1921–90 Swiss playwright, novelist and essayist. He is arguably the best-known 'German' dramatist of the 20th century beside BRECHT. When his first satirical play *It is Written* was presented at the Zurich Schauspielhaus in 1947, it caused a scandal. Scandal and controversy attended many of Dürrenmatt's best plays, as he cynically asked uncomfortable questions about the complacency of post-World War II Switzerland. Success came with *Romulus the Great* (1949), 'an unhistorical historical comedy', containing already the quintessential mixture of sour comedy and unfulfilled tragedy which is Dürrenmatt's hallmark. *The Marriage of Mr Mississippi* (1952) plays freely with theatrical conventions and turns a string of murders into so many comic events. In *The Visit* (1955) and *The Physicists* (1962) he casts a desperate look over mankind and concludes that hope is not reasonable. *The Visit* concerns a millionaire's return to her small home town where, in her youth, she was seduced and abandoned. In *The Physicists* the confusion between the sane world and the asylum presented on stage, and between the responsible scientists and the mad atomic physicists, is unresolved. The bleakness of the parables is redeemed, as often in his plays, by a dazzling theatrical inventiveness. *Frank V* (1959) is an indictment of the modern totalitarian state. Dürrenmatt adapted STRINDBERG's *The Dance of Death* which became *Play Strindberg* (1969), an even sparer and harsher drama than the original, now Dürrenmatt's most performed play. *Woyzeck* followed in 1972. *The Partaker* (1973), a bleak descent into a putrid, post-Dachau netherworld where injustice rules supreme, had little success. Like IONESCO, he was convinced that the profound tragedy of our time can only be expressed through farce.

**Duse, Eleonora** 1858–1924 Italian actress. In 1879 she

joined the company of GIOVANNI EMANUEL: her parts opposite him included Desdemona and Ophelia. Later she achieved notable success in ZOLA's *Thérèse Raquin* (1879), which gave her status in the profession. In Turin in 1884 she achieved a major triumph, in VERGA's *Cavalleria rusticana (Rustic Chivalry)*. In 1887 she formed with the lead actor, Flavio Andò, the Compagnia Città di Roma, playing in 19th-century stock pieces, particularly adaptations from French dramatists like SARDOU and DUMAS *fils*, as well as in GOLDONI and GIACOSA.

The composer and librettist Arrigo Boito encouraged her to undertake artistically more ambitious work. He translated SHAKESPEARE's *Antony and Cleopatra* for her: first performed at the Teatro Manzoni in Milan in 1888, it transferred to London in 1893. Her first significant triumph abroad was in 1891, when she opened in St Petersburg with *La signora dalle camelie (The Lady of the Camellias)*; it was the start of a long international career that took her to most parts of Europe and to the United States.

In the late 90s she entered into one of the most influential and painful relationships of her life: that with the Italian poet and dramatist, GABRIELE D'ANNUNZIO. For several years from 1896 she tried to realize D'Annunzio's dream of a new and revolutionary poetic drama. In 1898 D'Annunzio gave his first play, *La città morta (The Dead City)*, to SARAH BERNHARDT for performance in Paris, but in the same year Duse acted in his short pieces – *Sogno di un mattino di primavera (Dream of a Spring Morning)* and *Sogno di un tramonto d'autunno (Dream of an Autumn Sunset)* – and went on to produce his *La Gioconda* (1899), *La gloria* (1899) and *Francesca da Rimini* (1901). Her later repertoire expanded to embrace other serious modern drama, notably the work of IBSEN, including *A Doll's House*, *Hedda Gabler*, *Rosmersholm* (for which GORDON CRAIG did the scenery), and *The Lady from the Sea*, the part of Ellida being one of her last major roles.

Duse's individual talent, her high seriousness of purpose, and her association with many of the leading cultural figures of the age brought intellectual prestige to the Italian theatre. ADELAIDE RISTORI characterized the stage persona of her younger colleague as that of the archetypal *fin-de-siècle* woman: 'the modern woman with all her maladies of hysteria, anaemia and neurosis, and with all their consequences'. BERNARD SHAW claimed she was 'the first actress whom we have seen applying the method of the great school to characteristically modern parts, or to characteristically modern conceptions of old parts'.

**Duym, Jacob** 1547-? Flemish playwright. Of a noble Brabant family, he was invalided out of the army of William of Orange after having been in captivity in Spain, then in Leyden became poetic leader (*keizer*) of the Flemish Chamber of Rhetoric in exile, the Orange Lily (founded 1590). In that capacity he wrote 12 plays, using classical and national historical material. Duym created a new type of play which combined the allegorical character and didactic moralizations of the *spel van sinnen* (see MORALITY PLAY) with the narrative epic character of both secular and religious 16th-century drama. He also made use of comic intermezzi, similar to the comic INTERLUDES in Elizabethan drama and employing lower-class characters. Each of Duym's plays is accompanied by elaborate stage directions. Costumes, decor and special effects are carefully described and complex.

**Dybwad, Johanne** 1876-1950 Norwegian actress. The greatest of her generation, Dybwad trained at the NATIONALE SCENE, Bergen, before moving to Christiania Theatre and NATIONALTHEATRET, where she acted for some 50 years, often opposite EGIL EIDE and August Oddvar. Her best work was under the direction of BJØRN BJØRNSON, who encouraged her simplicity and naturalness. Later in her career she was often accused of exploiting her virtuosity to create sensational effects. Among her 20 IBSEN roles were a complex, serious Nora, Hedvig, a very natural Hilde Wangel, Mrs Alving and Aase. From 1906 she frequently directed, sometimes with herself in the lead. Intense and demanding, she took great liberties with the text to reinforce her sometimes eccentric interpretations.

**Echegaray, José** 1832–1916 Spanish playwright. He combined a prolific output with high office in government finance. His first produced play *El libro talonario* (*The Chequebook*, 1874) was followed by more than 60 others – mostly popular successes with bourgeois audiences. They combine melodramatic and sentimental plots with exaggerated solutions. In *El hombre negro* (*The Man in Black*, 1898), for instance, an elderly guardian causes his beautiful ward to contract leprosy and persuades her to enter a convent to prevent her from marrying a young sculptor, who wins her after blinding himself to prove the purity of his love. Echegaray's historical verse MELODRAMAS such as *El hijo de don Juan* (*The Son of Don Juan*, 1892) have lasted better than his plays in the *alta* COMEDIA style, such as *El gran Galeot* (*The Great Galeoto*, 1881) in which malicious gossip forces two lovers together despite themselves. His Nobel Prize in 1904 aroused great protest from the new literary generation, and his domination of the Spanish stage for 30 years delayed the revitalization of the theatre evident in other countries.

**Edgar, David** 1948– British playwright. Edgar was one of several left-wing writers who were 'politicized' at university by the events of 1968. After a spell as a journalist he turned to writing AGIT-PROP plays for the General Will, a touring political theatre company whose targets included the Conservative government. Edgar's gift for lively writing and the telling image – cartoonist skills – resulted in ten plays between 1971 and 1973, and two collaborations, *England's Ireland* (1972) and *A Fart for Europe* with HOWARD BRENTON (1973). The best plays matched vivid popular forms with political views, as in the PANTOMIME *Tedderella* (1971) or the MELODRAMA *Dick Deterred* (1974), about the Watergate scandal. In 1973–4 Edgar started to move away from agit-prop towards social realism, taking as one of his subjects the growth of Fascism within Britain. *Destiny* (1976) concerned the rise of a fictitious political party, Nation Forward, based on the real National Front. The ROYAL SHAKESPEARE COMPANY produced it at Stratford (1976) and in London (1978). *Mary Barnes* (1979), about a disturbed child, stressed the social causes of mental illness. Edgar also adapted *Nicholas Nickleby* (1980), which became a major success for the RSC. In *Maydays* (1983) he charted the growing disillusion of British socialists since the war. In 1987 his *Entertaining Strangers* was staged by the NATIONAL THEATRE, and *That Summer* described the collapse of the 1984 miners' strike. *The Shape of the Table* (1990) showed how the political maps of Eastern Europe were redrawn after *perestroika*. *Pentecost* (1995) was a further examination of post-Communist Europe.

**Edinburgh Festival** Arts festival. The Edinburgh International Festival of Music and Drama (1947–) presents a programme of first-class international music and drama, as well as art exhibitions, opera and dance, in August and September each year. It is primarily an international occasion, but it has also provided a focus for Scottish theatrical achievement. Here, its most notable early success was TYRONE GUTHRIE's production of Sir David Lindsay's medieval MORALITY PLAY, *An Satyre of the Thrie Estaites* (first performed at Edinburgh's Assembly Halls on the Mound in 1948). From the beginning, the official Festival attracted a large number of smaller events. Their presence was ultimately recognized by the formation of the Edinburgh Fringe Festival Society (see FRINGE THEATRE). The Fringe offers a wide range of theatrical activities in halls and on the streets throughout the city. It has long been seen as a spawning ground for new talent and, on occasion, outshines its official counterpart.

**Edwardes, George** 1852–1915 Irish-born theatre manager. At London's newly opened Savoy from 1881, and under direction from Richard D'Oyly Carte, he supervised the staging of three GILBERT and Sullivan operas. From 1886 he was sole manager of the GAIETY, where he trained and made famous the chorus of Gaiety Girls and was the supreme impresario of the new style of MUSICAL COMEDY, which he introduced there and also at DALY'S, the ADELPHI, the Prince of Wales's and the Apollo.

**Edwards, Jango** [Stanley Ted Edwards] 1950– American CLOWN. He studied clowning in London. His first theatre group developed into the Friends' Roadshow, which toured Europe regularly. Obscene, anarchic and using rock-concert techniques, Edwards revolutionized the European concept of clown shows and in 1975 organized a mass international gathering of clowns, musicians and FRINGE THEATRES at his Amsterdam headquarters – a Feast of Fools, which became an annual event.

**Efremov, Oleg (Nikolaevich)** 1927– Soviet actor and director. Working in the STANISLAVSKY tradition of inward, emotional experience, he joined Moscow's Central Children's Theatre as an actor, making his directing debut in 1955. In 1957 he founded and directed the Studio of Young Actors, later the Sovremennik (Contemporary) Theatre. They concentrated on intimate, psychologically based plays, opening with VIKTOR ROZOV's family war drama *Alive Forever*, which became the theatre's signature piece.

Other notable Sovremennik productions included ALEKSANDR VOLODIN's *Two Flowers* (1959), *The Elder Sister* (1962) and *The Appointment* (1963); EVGENY SHVARTS's *The Naked King* (1962) and *The Dragon*; ROZOV's *On the Wedding Day* (1964), *The Reunion* (1967) and *From Night to Noon* (1969); VASILY AKSYONOV's social SATIRE *Always on Sale* (1965); contemporary Western plays such as WILLIAM GIBSON's *Two for the Seesaw* (1963), JOHN OSBORNE's *Look Back in Anger* (1966) and EDWARD ALBEE's adaptation of Carson McCullers's *Ballad of the Sad Café* (1967); an adaptation of Ivan Goncharov's classic novel *An Ordinary Story* (1967); and a trilogy on Russia's revolutionary history, consisting of LEONID ZORIN's *The Decembrists*, A. Svobodin's *The Populists* and Mikhail Shatrov's *The Bolsheviks* (1967), commemorating the 50th anniversary of the October Revolution.

The brilliant young company divided in 1971, some following Efremov to the MOSCOW ART THEATRE, where he became artistic director. In the hope of reviving MAT Efremov produced such plays as Volodin's *Dulcinea of El Toboso* (1973), about Don Quixote's legacy; BUERO VALLEJO's *The Sleep of Reason*, about Goya's last days; MIKHAIL ROSHCHIN's *Old New Year* (produced 1973) and

*Troop Train* (1975); and G. Bokrev's *Steel-Workers* (1974), an industrial ethics play. Although Efremov has relied heavily on guest directors, the innovative Little Stage which he opened in 1980-1 as an adjunct to MAT has helped develop young actors and directors and new Russian plays. Following his successful staging of CHEKHOV's *The Seagull* (1980), he mounted provocative productions in the 1980s, including BULGAKOV's *Molière*, in which he played the title role. In 1990 Efremov directed Chekhov's *Ivanov* at the YALE REPERTORY THEATRE, and in 1992 he staged GRIBOEDOV's *Woe from Wit* at Moscow's first Anton Chekhov International Theatre festival.

**Efros, Anatoly (Vasilievich)** 1925-87 Soviet director. Efros began his directing career in Ryazan and was artistic director of several Moscow theatres: the Central Children's Theatre (1954-63), the Lenin Komsomol (1963-7) and the Taganka (1985). From 1967 to 1985 he directed some of his most celebrated productions at the theatre on Malaya Bronnaya. He forged a uniquely athletic style of play in which characters seem always to be violently physical, the stage itself conceived as a boxing ring where anxieties escalate, via absurd repetition, into weird rituals of alternating and simultaneous acceptance and denial.

Efros sensitively staged contemporary Soviet plays dealing with confused and disaffected youth and spiritual crisis, including VIKTOR ROZOV's *On the Wedding Day* (1964) and *Brother Alyosha* (1972); EDVARD RADZINSKY's *104 Pages about Love* (1964) and *Making a Movie* (1965); and ALEKSEI ARBUZOV's *My Poor Marat* (1965). His staging of BULGAKOV's *A Cabal of Hypocrites* (*Molière*, 1967), a Soviet classic, was repeated for television with YURY LYUBIMOV in the title role and recreated at the GUTHRIE THEATRE in 1979. His highly controversial production of CHEKHOV's *The Three Sisters* (1967) emphasized enervation and repressed sexuality, dealt ironically with dreams of the future (i.e. the communist utopia) and transformed characters into convulsively moving puppets. His best production, GOGOL's *Marriage* (1974), is a frenzied and dream-like evocation of fear and loneliness. In 1984 Efros replaced Lyubimov as the Taganka Theatre's chief director, but his productions were not up to his previous standard.

**Eichelbaum, Samuel** 1894-1967 Argentine playwright. He dominated the Buenos Aires stage for nearly 50 years with more than 30 productions. His *La mala sed* (*The Bad Thirst*, 1920) deals with hereditary sexual impulses. *Un guapo del novecientos* (*A 1900s Dandy*, 1940) marks the beginning of a second period in his writing, when he departed from the earlier introspective, often abstract, plays in order to concentrate on more localized themes. Major titles include *Divorcio nupcial* (*Nuptial Divorce*, 1941), *Rostro perdido* (*Lost Face*, 1952), *Dos brasas* (*Two Live Coals*, 1952) and *Subsuelo* (*Underground*, 1966).

**Eide, Egil** 1868-1946 Norwegian actor. A leading member of NATIONALTHEATRET in the first decades of the century, he specialized in heroic figures such as IBSEN's Julian (in *Emperor and Galilean*), Ørnulf (in *The Vikings at Helgeland*) and Olav (in *Lady Inger from Østråt*). While he had little aptitude for intellectual roles, Eide was unmatched for the emotional power of his performances, as in his 1899 *Brand* and 1907 *Oedipus*. Even when his technique seemed heavy-handed, as in *When We Dead Awaken* (1934) and *King Lear* (1937), his emotional commitment carried great conviction.

**Ek, Anders** 1916-79 Swedish actor. Known internationally for his work in the films of INGMAR BERGMAN (especially as Frost in *Sawdust and Tinsel/The Naked Night*), from 1941 to 1979 he was primarily active in the theatre – much of this, also, in collaboration with Bergman, for whom he gave an extraordinary virtuoso performance as CAMUS's *Caligula* in 1946. With less than perfect diction, he possessed great emotional and intellectual intensity, and his very wide range encompassed roles by AESCHYLUS, SHAKESPEARE, MOLIÈRE, CHEKHOV, STRINDBERG, BRECHT and FUGARD.

**Ekerot, Bengt** 1920-71 Swedish actor and director. In Malmö and Göteborg he directed influential productions of BRECHT and GARCÍA LORCA, before he joined DRAMATEN in 1953. As an actor he is known internationally for his work in INGMAR BERGMAN's films, especially as Death in *The Seventh Seal*. In 1956 he directed at Dramaten the world premiere of O'NEILL's *Long Day's Journey into Night*, a brilliant orchestration of the elements of realistic theatre (see REALISM). His commitment to new Swedish drama was crucial to the early career of playwright LARS FORSSELL – from *The Coronation*, which flopped in 1956, to the much more successful *Sunday Promenade* (1963) and *The Madcap* (1964).

**Ekhof, Konrad** 1720-78 German actor. Ekhof acted mainly with the travelling troupes of JOHANN SCHÖNEMANN (from 1740 to 1764), KONRAD ACKERMANN (from 1764 to 1771) and Abel Seyler (from 1771 to 1774). He was the leading actor of the short-lived Hamburg National Theatre project. From 1774 to his death, he was director of the first troupe of actors to become permanently resident in a German court theatre, at Gotha. Deeply concerned about raising the social status of the acting profession and exploring the fundamental principles of performance, Ekhof attempted without much success to found an 'academy' to study these matters. In Gotha he was able to train young actors systematically. On stage he always gave performances that were realistic, in contrast to the still, rhetorical LEIPZIG STYLE then in vogue.

**Ekman, Gösta** 1890-1938 Swedish actor. His erratic career alternated between relatively superficial personality acting, which exploited his charm and charisma, and performances of great depth and complexity, especially in collaboration with PER LINDBERG, under whose direction he gave many of his most creative performances: Kurano in MASEFIELD's *The Faithful* (1931), Hamlet, Peer Gynt and the title role in LAGERKVIST's *The Hangman* (all 1934), Shylock, Hjalmar Ekdal and Fedja in LEV TOLSTOI's *The Living Corpse* (all 1935).

**Ekster, Aleksandra (Aleksandrovna)** 1884-1949 Soviet painter and theatrical designer. Ekster helped to introduce cubist and futurist ideas into Russia in her work with TAIROV. Her outlook was highly cosmopolitan, a result of training and studio work in Paris, where she met PICASSO, Braque, Apollinaire and MARINETTI. At Tairov's Kamerny Theatre she designed sets and COSTUMES for ANNENSKY's *Thamira, the Cither Player* (1916), WILDE's *Salome* (1917) and SHAKESPEARE's *Romeo and Juliet* (1921). Her designs orchestrated symbolic colours, rhythmic shapes, levels and spatial planes; she also designed constructivist costumes, e.g. for MICHAEL CHEKHOV's 1924 MOSCOW ART THEATRE Second Studio production of CALDERÓN DE LA BARCA's *The Phantom Lady*. She emigrated to France in 1924 and pursued an international career as a theatrical, ballet and fashion designer and book illustrator. Her legacy to Russian design includes the 'Kiev school' of artists that she trained: Pavel Chelishchev, Aleksandr Tyshler, Nisson Shifrin and Anatoly Petritsky.

**Elder, Lonne, III** 1932– African-American playwright. He had already had five plays produced when his *Ceremonies in Dark Old Men* (1969), about a Harlem family's struggle to survive with dignity, was presented by the NEGRO ENSEMBLE COMPANY with DOUGLAS TURNER WARD in the leading role. The play, 'poised between comedy and tragedy', received rave notices. Elder moved to Hollywood, where he became a successful scriptwriter for film and television. In 1988 his one-person play *Splendid Mummer*, based on the career of IRA ALDRIDGE, was performed in New York.

**Eldridge** [*née* McKechnie], **Florence** 1901–88 American actress. After several appearances on BROADWAY, she toured with her husband, FREDRIC MARCH, in the THEATRE GUILD's productions of such scripts as *Arms and the Man*, *The Silver Cord* and *The Guardsman* in 1927–8. She frequently appeared with March, e.g. in *The Skin of Our Teeth* (1942) and in RUTH GORDON's *Years Ago* (1946). One of her greatest successes was as Mary Tyrone in O'NEILL's *Long Day's Journey into Night* (1956).

**Eliot, T(homas) S(tearns)** 1888–1965 American-born British poet and playwright. Eliot's plays mark the high point in the 20th-century revival of English poetic drama. Born in St Louis and educated at Harvard, the Sorbonne and Oxford, he settled in London in 1915. He became a founder member of London's GROUP THEATRE, his first short stage pieces portraying the spiritual wasteland of contemporary social values and political movements: the fragmentary *Sweeney Agonistes* (1928) and the choral BURLESQUE *The Rock* were produced by Rupert Doone and E. MARTIN BROWNE in 1934. Eliot tried to restore poetry to the theatre by adapting popular forms, as he did in his first major play, *Murder in the Cathedral* (1935, Canterbury Cathedral), which incorporated jazz rhythms and direct address, connecting verse and religious experience. It transferred successfully to the commercial theatre and has been more frequently revived than his other plays. After *The Family Reunion* (1939), which retained Greek-style choral passages and supernatural machinery in the context of a modern detective play, he increasingly disguised the verse and spiritual themes of his drama. *The Cocktail Party* (1949), *The Confidential Clerk* (1953) and *The Elder Statesman* (1958) are comedies of manners or modern problem plays, closer to prose in rhythm and with the ritual elements played down, despite the use of plots from EURIPIDES and SOPHOCLES. The difficulties of Eliot's first marriage have recently formed the subject of a successful play, *Tom and Viv*, by Michael Hastings. The musical *Cats*, based on Eliot's 1939 poems *Old Possum's Book of Practical Cats*, promoted interest in Eliot in the 1980s.

**Eliot, Michael** 1931–84 British director. In 1959 he formed the 59 Theatre Company at the LYRIC THEATRE, HAMMERSMITH, for which he directed his highly acclaimed production of IBSEN's *Brand*. He directed at Stratford in 1961–2, was appointed artistic director of the OLD VIC for the season 1962–3, and directed for the NATIONAL THEATRE in 1965. In 1968, together with several members of the original 59 Company, he founded the 69 Theatre Company in Manchester, which in 1976 metamorphosed into the ROYAL EXCHANGE THEATRE Company. He aimed from the start to make the new theatre of front-rank quality, independent of current

London trends. His own productions helped to guarantee the success of the enterprise. He won a deserved reputation as England's foremost interpreter of Ibsen and STRINDBERG, and also directed many successful productions for television.

**Elliott, Maxine** [*née* Jessie Dermot] 1871–1940 American actress. After making her New York stage debut at PALMER's Theatre in 1890, Elliott rose rapidly in the theatre, then made her London debut as Sylvia in *Two Gentlemen of Verona* in 1895. After an Australian tour with NAT GOODWIN (1896), she became his leading lady (1897) and his wife (1898). They co-starred in numerous successes, including her first big hit as Alice Adams in *Nathan Hale* (1899). They separated in 1902, after which she established herself as a star with Georgiana Carley in *Her Own Way* (1903), written for her by CLYDE FITCH. Two years later, her Georgiana attracted the attentions of Edward VII in London. She built the Maxine Elliott Theatre in New York (1908) with help from the SHUBERTS, and appeared there in numerous comedies. She was praised as a 'rare comedienne of the drawing room'; although she appeared stiff and mechanical to some critics, all praised her dark beauty and statuesque stage presence. Her younger sister Gertrude was also an actress in England and America, and managed ST JAMES's THEATRE, London, from 1918.

**Elliston, Robert (William)** 1774–1831 English actor and theatre manager. In charge of such minor theatres as the Royal Circus (1809–14), which he converted and renamed the Surrey, and of the OLYMPIC (1813–19), Elliston fought the patent theatres' monopoly over the legitimate drama (see THEATRICAL MONOPOLY). Having failed, he assumed management of DRURY LANE (1819–26), then led by EDMUND KEAN. After a few successful years in competition with COVENT GARDEN came bankruptcy. His policy, which he bequeathed to the notorious ALFRED BUNN, was to run Drury Lane as a home for spectacle and PANTOMIME as well as the classical drama. The secret of his acting was the bond he established with his audience (as Charles Surface or Falstaff, in particular), and he managed his theatres in the same way. Almost alone among Regency managers, Elliston had the common touch.

**Eltinge, Julian** [William Dalton] 1883–1941 American female impersonator. He was first seen professionally in *Mr Wix of Wixham*, a MUSICAL COMEDY (1904). His biggest hit was *The Fascinating Widow* (1911 and subsequent tours), to whose success a grateful producer built the Eltinge Theatre on 42nd St, New York. With his own company, the Julian Eltinge Players, he worked in VAUDEVILLE during 1918–27, and starred in silent films. Eltinge was a favourite primarily with female audiences, not least for the chic of his wardrobe.

**Emanuel, Giovanni** 1848–1902 Italian actor-manager. He early became a lead player opposite the principal actresses of his day, formed his own company and, in the way of Italian players of the age, toured widely abroad, as far as Latin America and Russia. He was noted for his strongly naturalistic style (see NATURALISM) in interpreting the classics, including SHAKESPEARE, being particularly strong as Othello and Lear. The care with which he prepared productions, and the scrupulous attention he gave to detail in the roles he played, are well evidenced in his extant prompt books.

**Emery, John** 1777–1822 English comic actor, the son, father and grandfather of notable actors. From 1798 until his death he was a leading low comedian at

COVENT GARDEN. He is the first actor known to have been encored for his playing of a scene, that of Fixture's jealousy in THOMAS MORTON's *A Roland for an Oliver* (1819). Emery's pre-eminence in rustic roles established the Yorkshire dialect as an acceptable alternative to 'Mummerset' for comic country bumpkins. His Tyke in Morton's *The School of Reform* (1805) was famous in his time, and the play died with him.

**Emmet, Alfred** see QUESTORS THEATRE

**Emmett, Dan** see MINSTREL SHOW

**Empire Theatre** (New York City) When in 1893 CHARLES FROHMAN built the Empire 25 blocks north of the theatre district at Union Square, he initiated a new theatre district uptown. The Empire remained the headquarters of his activities until he died in 1915, becoming a favourite among actors and audiences alike. Until 1931 it was leased to GILBERT MILLER, then changed ownership several times before its demise in 1953.

**Encina, Juan del** c.1468-c.1530 Spanish poet, musician and playwright. Sometimes called the father of Spanish drama, he lived in Rome for several years. From 1496 Encina published dramatic *églogas* (eclogues) with his poetry and songs, exercising considerable influence on later dramatists. The early *églogas* are PASTORAL playlets performed on high feastdays by Encina himself and other courtiers, with comic shepherds, topical allusions, songs and dances. The later works are longer, more complex, and influenced by secular Italian Renaissance forms.

**Engel, Johann Jakob** 1741–1802 German playwright and aesthetician. Engel's most important contribution to theatre was his book *Ideas on Mimesis* (1786), which catalogued in detail gestures and poses of characteristic emotions. From 1787 to 1794 he was director of the BERLIN ROYAL THEATRE.

*Englische Komödianten* English acting troupes. These actors from the London theatres toured Germany from the 1580s, initially only when the London theatres were closed because of plague. By the start of the 17th century their presence was more permanent and they enjoyed some aristocratic patronage. They performed plays of the Elizabethan and Jacobean dramatists in English, but soon German came to be substituted and the troupes took on German actors. By the end of the 17th century all identification of the troupes with England had vanished, though the persistence of the *HAUPT- UND STAATSAKTIONEN* in the repertoire until the mid-18th century represents a continuation of English influence in the German theatre.

**English Stage Company** see GEORGE DEVINE; ROYAL COURT THEATRE

**Ennius, Quintus** 239-169 BC Roman playwright. One of the most important of early Latin authors, Quintus Ennius was active in various genres. His comedies seem to have been insignificant, but his tragedies, mostly adapted from EURIPIDES, were admired and influential. They are represented by 20 titles and over 400 surviving lines.

**ENSA** (Entertainments National Service Association) British arts organization. ENSA was formed in 1938 so that performing artists could contribute to the war effort by sustaining the morale of troops and support staff, wherever they were stationed, in the British Isles or abroad. The Services counterpart of CEMA, working through the NAAFI (Navy, Army and Air Force Institute), its first performance took place immediately after the outbreak of hostilities in 1939. Under the directorship

of BASIL DEAN and from its headquarters in London's DRURY LANE Theatre, it provided a touring programme that ranged from symphony orchestras, ballet companies and Shakespearian acting troupes to VARIETY shows, comedians, popular singers and mobile cinemas.

*entremés* see *GÉNERO CHICO*

**Enzensberger, Hans Magnus** 1929– German playwright and poet. He has attempted to counter conventional theatre with a radically political form of documentary drama in which dialogue is taken unaltered from legal transcripts or the news media and the performance takes place on a bare stage. His most characteristic subject has been Latin American revolution in such plays as *The Havana Inquiry* (1969), dealing with the Cuban show trial that followed the Bay of Pigs invasion, or *The Short Summer of Anarchy – Buenventura Durrah's Life and Death* (1972), but with the material presented as a media event his thematic focus is on the manipulative effects of journalism. He has also dealt with historical subjects like *The Sinking of the Titanic* (1980), in which the liner's fate symbolizes the shipwreck of Enzensberger's earlier ideals.

**epic theatre** The very juxtaposition of these two words would have horrified ARISTOTLE, and it was against Aristotle that ERWIN PISCATOR and BERTOLT BRECHT rebelled in their respective uses of the term. Aristotle declared tragedy a higher form of art than epic, partly because of the former's economy and concentration.

Reacting against EXPRESSIONISM's focus on emotion, Piscator and then Brecht separately wished theatre to embrace the larger social context of the epic. As early as 1924, in his adaptation of *Edward II*, Brecht introduced such epic elements as scene-by-scene summaries of the action and common soldiers in whiteface. In 1928 Brecht and others collaborated with Piscator in dramatizing the Hasek novel *Adventures of the Good Soldier Schweik*; Piscator translated it to the stage with the help of film, treadmills and moving cartoons by Georg Grosz. But Brecht in a 1927 newspaper article had already announced epic theatre as the contemporary theatrical style: 'The essential point of the epic theatre is perhaps that it appeals less to the feelings than to the spectator's reason.' By 1930, in connection with a production of his opera *Mahagonny*, Brecht published an essay on epic theatre, in which he tabulated the contrasts between dramatic and epic theatre. In his 1931 production of his (revised) *Man Is Man* he first introduced the devices that were thereafter associated with epic theatre – half-curtain, half-masks, summary projections, few props, visible stage machinery, songs that punctuate the action, and 'cool' or estranged acting. Brecht demanded that the spectator use reason to reflect upon the performance.

Although the term rarely refers to theatre other than Brecht's, or to adaptations of novels, the concept and devices of epic theatre have influenced playwrights as different as JOHN ARDEN, THORNTON WILDER, ROBERT BOLT, PETER WEISS, ARTHUR ADAMOV, ROGER PLANCHON and MICHEL VINAVER. It could be argued that every post-war director of stature is aware of the staging techniques of epic theatre.

**Epicharmus** 6th-5th centuries BC Sicilian comic playwright. Epicharmus was active at Syracuse in the reign of Hieron I 478–467 BC) and probably earlier. Surviving fragments of his plays, written in Doric Greek, show that they included burlesque treatments of myths as well as scenes from contemporary life; but many features are obscure.

**equestrian drama** see HIPPODRAMA

**Erdman, Nikolai (Robertovich)** 1900–70 Soviet playwright. In the tradition of GOGOL and SUKHOVO-KOBYLIN he brought grotesque SATIRE and intellectual irony to bear on the theme of the little man alienated from his technocratic society. Erdman began his theatrical career as a writer of REVUE sketches for MUSIC-HALL. His adaptation of Lensky's 1839 *vaudeville Lev Gurych Sinichkin* ran for nearly 10 years at the Vakhtangov Theatre in the 1930s. He wrote two major plays: *The Mandate* (1924), MEYERHOLD's most successful production at the Meyerhold Theatre and an influence on the work of MAYAKOVSKY; and *The Suicide* (1928), planned by the MOSCOW ART THEATRE and brought to dress rehearsal by the Meyerhold Theatre (1929) before it was closed. These two works cast ineffectual individualists and malcontents adrift in the so-called workers' utopia in search of what was promised them.

Erdman spent 1933–40 in Siberian exile, and devoted the remainder of his career to creating stage adaptations of Russian classics and to writing operetta, circus and CABARET librettos and scripts for children's films. *The Mandate* was again produced in Russia in 1956 during the Thaw period. *The Suicide*, which premiered in Sweden in 1969, played elsewhere in Europe, Canada and America in the 1970s and 1980s, and was finally produced in Russia at the Moscow Theatre of Satire in 1982. Both plays were published in the Soviet Union, and entered the official repertory in 1987.

**Ermolova, Mariya (Nikolaevna)** 1853–1928 Russian actress. She became the leading tragedienne at Moscow's Maly Theatre. With GLIKERIYA FEDOTOVA she was one of the two most prominent Russian actresses of her day, the equal of SALVINI and DUSE. She belonged to the realistic acting tradition (see REALISM) which includes SHCHEPKIN, STANISLAVSKY and KOMISSARZHEVSKAYA. She brought a mixture of romantic idealism and self-control to some 300 roles, excelling in those which emphasized heroic suffering: LESSING's Emilia Galotti (her earliest success, 1870); Judith in GUTZKOW's *Uriel Acosta* (1879); SCHILLER's Joan of Arc (*The Maid of Orleans*, her greatest success, 1884) and Maria Stuart (1886); RACINE's Phèdre (1890); and SHAKESPEARE's Ophelia (1878, 1891), Lady Anne (1878), Hermione (1887), Lady Macbeth (1896) and Volumnia (1902), among others. An interpreter of radical roles, in 1876 she portrayed Laurentia in LOPE DE VEGA's *Fuenteovejuna* in such a way that the play was banned from the Russian stage. The Maly Theatre administration sought to dismiss her in later years, but her career revived following the 1917 Revolution via a series of anti-bourgeois roles. She was the first actress to be given the honorary title of People's Artist of the Soviet Republics (1920).

**Ervine, St John** [John Greer Ervine] 1883–1971 Irish playwright, critic and manager. Emigrating to London in 1900, Ervine met SHAW, flirted briefly with Fabianism, and remained ineradicably Unionist. When appointed ABBEY manager (1915–16) he considered Ireland 'nearly a lunatic nation' and its theatre part of British theatre. Gifted and cantankerous, having sacked the entire company, he resigned.

A prolific and quarrelsome drama critic, he emerged in the 1920s as author of many successful drawing-room comedies such as *The First Mrs Frazer* (1929). His imagination found a grip in the Northern Irish plays he gave the Abbey: *Mixed Marriage* (1911), *The Magnanimous Lover* (1912), *John Ferguson* (1915), *Boyd's Shop* (1936), *William John Mawhinney* (1940) and *Friends and Relations* (1941). A craftsman of the WELL MADE PLAY, Ervine relieves his melodramatic tendency with his authentic Northern Protestant characters.

**esperpento** see VALLE-INCLÁN, RAMON DEL

**Espert, Núria** 1938– Spanish actress and director. Born in Barcelona, she began acting at 11 in Catalan theatre, achieving recognition in 1954 for her portrayal of Medea. In 1959 she and her husband, Armando Moreno, formed their own company. After establishing her reputation on the Madrid stage in classic works, she risked producing modern authors previously prohibited by CENSORSHIP; she played notable roles in BRECHT's *The Good Person of Setzuan* (1967), SARTRE's *The Respectable Prostitute* and *In Camera* (1968), and in GENET's *The Maids* (1969, directed by Víctor García). Other collaborations with García were GARCÍA LORCA's *Yerma* (1971), performed on a trampoline, and VALLE-INCLÁN's *Divine Words* (1975), which featured nudity and erotically suggestive organ pipes. The García-Espert productions toured for years, as did her ventures with another Argentine-French director, Jorge Lavelli: García Lorca's *Doña Rosita the Spinster* (1980) and SHAKESPEARE's *The Tempest* (1983). Espert began directing in 1986, with a compelling London production of García Lorca's *The House of Bernarda Alba*, starring GLENDA JACKSON. Other directing credits include several operas, staged in London and Glasgow. For the 1992 Cultural Olympics she returned to Barcelona to direct EURIPIDES' *Medea*, with Irene Papas in the role that had first brought Espert fame.

**Esslair, Ferdinand** 1772–1840 German actor. Of the romantic school, Esslair was second in popularity only to LUDWIG DEVRIENT. His grand stature, good looks and expressive, powerful voice made him an ideal interpreter of heroic roles. Reminiscent of FLECK, he was actually more reliable and methodical. He settled at the Munich Court Theatre in 1820.

**Esson, (Thomas) Louis (Buvelot)** 1879–1943 Australia's first realistic playwright (see REALISM). His early plays include *The Woman Tamer* (1910), *Dead Timber* (1911) and a Shavian political SATIRE, *The Time Is Not Yet Ripe* (1912). Between 1922 and 1926 his own company, the Pioneer Players, co-founded with Vance Palmer and Steward Macky, staged his *The Battler, Mother and Son, The Drovers* (written in London in 1919) and *The Bride of Gospel Place* – all sensitive studies of outback or underworld life, written under the strong influence of YEATS, SYNGE and the ABBEY THEATRE.

**Estorino, Abelardo** 1925– Cuban playwright and director. A practising dentist, in 1960 he joined the Studio Theatre, Cuba's first revolutionary theatre group, and in 1961 was contracted by the government as a professional writer. He directs and occasionally acts and designs sets. Estorino interprets contemporary situations and immediate problems of Cuban reality into transcendent theatrical pieces. He focuses on family units and marital issues, the need for openness, fairness and equality in human relationships. Essentially a realistic writer, he has remained loyal to the revolutionary ideals while experimenting with metatheatrical techniques in later plays. His best-known works are *El robo del cochino* (*The Theft of the Pig*, 1961), *La casa vieja* (*The Old House*, 1964), *Los mangos de Caín* (*Cain's Mangoes*, 1967), *La dolorosa historia del amor secreto de Don José Jacinto*

*Milanés (The Tragic Story of the Secret Love of Don José Jacinto Milanés*, 1974), *Ni un sí ni un no (Neither a Yes nor a No*, 1981) and *Morir del cuento (To Die from the Story*, 1983).

**Etherege, George** 1636–92 English playwright. Apprenticed to a lawyer, he went on to study at the Inns of Court in London. He became a member of a group of artistocratic courtier-wits. His first play, *The Comical Revenge, or Love in a Tub* (1663), is a brilliant mixture of four separate plots, ranging from an issue of high honour to broad farce. In 1668 *She Would If She Could* demonstrated Etherege's brilliance in a witty and thoughtful investigation of the problems of love and courtship and was highly influential on subsequent drama. After a period as a diplomat in Constantinople he wrote his last play, *The Man of Mode* (1676), which explores the conflict between sexual appetite and genuine love in the rake-hero Dorimant, and depicts one of the great stage fops, Sir Fopling Flutter. In 1685 Etherege became ambassador to Ratisbon and stayed abroad after the 1688 revolution.

**Euripides** c.485–407 BC Greek tragic playwright. Euripides came from Phyla in Attica, and was of respectable birth. Unlike his rival SOPHOCLES, he seems to have taken little part in public life. In 408 or 407 he left Athens for the court of Archelaus, King of Macedon, and it was there that he died.

He produced his first plays in 455 but did not win a victory in the Dionysian competition (see GREEK THEATRE, ANCIENT) until 441. He is said to have produced 92 plays (we know the titles of about 80), but won first prize only five times in his life (and once after his death, with plays that he had left unperformed). Nineteen plays survive under his name. Among them are *Alcestis*, 438; *Medea*, 431; *Heraclidae (Children of Heracles)*, 430–428; *Hippolytus*, 428; *Andromache*, c.425; *Hecabe*, c.424; *Suppliant Women*, c. 423 (concerning the burial of the 'Seven against Thebes'); *Electra*, c.422–416; *Heracles*, c.415; *Trojan Women*, 415; *Iphigenia in Tauris (Among the Taurians)*, c.414; *Ion*, c.413; *Helen*, c.412; *Phoenician Women*, c.409; *Orestes*, 408; *Bacchae* and *Iphigenia at Aulis*, both posthumously produced.

The tragedies open with a formal 'prologue speech', delivered by a god or a mortal character who sets the scene and sometimes foreshadows what will happen. A rhetorical *agōn*, or debate, occurs in every play. At the end a god generally appears, to remove the misapprehensions of the characters and to predict future mythical events. The Chorus tends not to be closely involved in the action, and in the later plays, especially, its songs are often evocative of a world remote from the characters' sufferings.

Euripides was not always interested in organic plot construction (as ARISTOTLE complains). While the plot of *Medea* shows 'Sophoclean' concentration and that of *Iphigenia in Tauris* is a neatly worked out adventure story, *Trojan Women* hardly has a plot at all, and some of the late plays are highly episodic. There is uniformity of structure and style, but a wide variety of tone. From the grim exploration of the mentality of child murder in *Medea*, or the bleak evocation of the sufferings of a captured city in *Trojan Women*, the plays range to such light-hearted romances as *Iphigenia in Tauris* and *Helen*, with their daring rescues and happy endings. There are also 'problem plays'; should *Alcestis* and *Ion*, for instance, be read as cheerfully romantic or as bitterly ironic? The plays leave a general impression, however, of men and women adrift in a world over which they have no control, at the mercy of passion, illusion and chance. Religion does not help, for, whatever the characters might wish, the action of the plays reveals the gods as behaving no better than mortals. In characterization Euripides is particularly fond of paradox and moral ambivalence, creating conflicts of sympathy in the audience.

The rhetoric of Euripidean speeches tends to broad generalization and theorizing, and characters can express highly unconventional views which show the influence of the sceptical 5th-century thinkers called 'sophists'. The mere expression of sophistic ideas in a tragedy could evidently be regarded as subversive. ARISTOPHANES portrays Euripides as a pretentious, atheistic intellectual, who degrades TRAGEDY by depicting trivial and vulgar subjects. After his death, however, he became by far the most popular and influential of the tragedians.

**Evans, Edith** 1888–1976 British actress. After working with WILLIAM POEL and ELLEN TERRY, she established a leading reputation in Restoration and Shakespearian comedy with Millamant (1924) and Lady Wishfort (1948) in *The Way of the World*, and Rosalind in *As You Like It* (1926, at the OLD VIC, a role she returned to in 1959 with the ROYAL SHAKESPEARE COMPANY). Her most famous performance, using her superb voice to best advantage, was as Lady Bracknell in WILDE's *The Importance of Being Earnest* (first played in 1939, filmed in 1951); but she also gave definitive interpretations of SHAW and CHEKHOV and toured widely with ENSA between 1942 and 1944. She was awarded the DBE in 1946.

**Evans, Maurice (Herbert)** 1901–89 British-born American actor, director and producer. He became an American citizen in 1941, following a 15-year acting career in England, notably as Raleigh in *Journey's End* (1929) and with the OLD VIC-SADLER's WELLS company in 1934. In the USA he became the best-known Shakespearian actor, e.g. as Romeo opposite KATHARINE CORNELL (1935) and Richard II (1937). During World War II he entertained the troops with his so-called *GI Hamlet*. After the war Evans played major roles in four Shavian comedies and presented SHAKESPEARE on television.

**Eveling, Stanley** [Harry Stanley Eveling] 1925– British playwright. He taught philosophy at Edinburgh University. Eveling's plays were first staged at the adventurous TRAVERSE THEATRE in Edinburgh during the late 1960s. *The Lunatic, the Secret Sportsman and the Woman Next Door* (1968) and *Dear Janet Rosenberg, Dear Mr Kooning* (1969) were two short plays ideally suited to the intimate, student surroundings of alternative theatre clubs. Eveling is concerned with that meaninglessness which leads to a comic despair. In the early 1970s several plays concerned suicide in some form, such as *Caravaggio, Buddy* (1972), *Shivers* (1974) and *The Dead of Night* (1975); while his *Union Jack (and Bonzo)* (1973), which successfully transferred to London, is a black FARCE about a Boy Scout camp and a serial killer.

**Everyman Theatre** (London) Founded by Norman Macdermott in 1920 as a non-commercial experimental playhouse, it became a showcase for SHAW's plays and mounted NOËL COWARD's first successful work, *The Vortex* (1924). Macdermott was also responsible for introducing many foreign dramatists to the English stage, including the first London performances of O'NEILL's early work, CHIARELLI's *The Mask and the Face* (1924) and PIRANDELLO's *Henry IV* (1925), as well as important productions of IBSEN's naturalistic dramas (see NATURALISM). This role was continued when RAYMOND MASSEY took over the management in 1926 and under Malcolm Morley, who directed the first English production of OSTROVSKY's *The Storm* in 1929. The building was subsequently used by various small companies such as the GROUP THEATRE (1932 and 1934). It was converted into a cinema in 1947.

**Evreinov, Nikolai (Nikolaevich)** 1879–1953 Russian director, playwright and theorist. The central premiss of the work of this prolific and versatile anti-realist was 'theatricality', the need to revitalize theatre by rediscovering its origin as imaginative PLAY, and the theatricalization of life in order to cure man's and society's ills, which largely derive from a fear of death. Evreinov developed these themes in his theoretical treatises *An Introduction to Monodrama* (1909), *The Theatre as Such* (1912), *The Theatre for Oneself* (three vols., 1915–17) and *Pro Scena Sua* (1915). Monodrama seeks to re-establish the audience as co-creator of the theatrical event as a first step in erasing the border between theatre and life. *The Presentation of Love* (1910) and *In the Stage-Wings of the Soul* (1911) are his earliest and best monodramas, respectively. His most significant COMMEDIA-based plays are *A Merry Death* (1908) and *The Chief Thing* (1921). He wrote over 30 plays in all.

Evreinov directed, as MEYERHOLD's successor, at VERA KOMISSARZHEVSKAYA's Theatre (1908–9); he co-founded the Ancient Theatre (1907–8, 1911–12), whose basic philosophy, 'artistic reconstruction' (as opposed to antiquarianism), was manifested in its medieval and Spanish GOLDEN AGE cycles of productions. Evreinov's love of PARODY was displayed at the Merry Theatre for Grown-up Children, co-founded with FYODOR KOMISSARZHEVSKY (1908–9), and especially at the Crooked Mirror Theatre where he served as artistic director from 1910 to 1917. Here he directed, wrote, adapted, translated and composed scores for some 100 satirical monodramas, harlequinades, pantomimes and theatrical and literary parodies, which helped transform a late-night CABARET into one of Russia's leading theatres. *The Inspector General* (1912), parodying various directors' conceptual approaches to GOGOL's play, and *The Fourth Wall* (1915), which reveals the ludicrousness of applying STANISLAVSKY's aesthetics to the staging of opera, are of particular note.

The highlight of Evreinov's Russian theatrical career was his scripting and staging of the Soviet mass spectacle *The Storming of the Winter Palace* (1920) with a cast of 10,000 on Uritsky Square in Petrograd, which realized his dream of merging theatre and life via heroic man. In 1925 he emigrated to Paris.

**expressionism** In 1901 the French painter Julien-Auguste Hervé wanted to distinguish his painting from impressionism and coined the word 'expressionism', a term that soon found its way into several European languages. Not until the *Supplement to the Oxford English Dictionary*, however, do we find a formal definition in English: 'a style of painting in which the artist seeks to express emotional experience rather than impressions of the physical world; hence, a similar style or movement in literature, drama, music, etc.'.

Despite the confusion of 'drama' with 'theatre', that definition points to one widespread use of 'expressionism' as NON-REALISM; sometimes, 'expressionism' is loosely used as a synonym of SURREALISM. The other, more rigorous, use of 'expressionism' in the context of theatre describes Central European, especially German,

productions between 1907 (date of KOKOSCHKA's *Murderer, the Hope of Women*) and the mid-1920s, with productions of plays by SORGE, HASENCLEVER, KAISER, GOERING, TOLLER, Koffka, Unruh, BRONNEN, BARLACH and KORNFELD, directed by REINHARDT, JESSNER, FALCKENBERG, Barnowsky, MARTIN, Fehling and Hartung.

Although a few expressionist dramas pre-date World War I, most of them bear the scars of that war. Aesthetically, the plays are marked by anti-mimetic predecessors, like Munch and Van Gogh in painting, and WEDEKIND, and especially STRINDBERG, in drama. Expressionists aimed at no less than the spiritual regeneration of mankind. Young men rebelling against the proprieties of the Hohenzollern Empire, they wrote of conflicts between generations, sexes and classes. They boldly treated taboo subjects, such as incest and patricide. In their plays, which verbalize emotions rather than dramatize conflicts, an autobiographical protagonist is involved not in a plot but in an apocalyptic quest, often for his essential identity. The protagonist sometimes meets avatars of himself (expressionist protagonists are unregenerately male), and other characters are schematically designed as nameless types. Short, often static, scenes are not causally linked, and the dialogue, varying from short phrases (telegraphese) to long rhapsodies, lacks interpersonal communication.

Originating in the visual arts, expressionism in the theatre was also highly visual (see also THEATRE DESIGN). The director would choose lighting to create atmosphere, stage crowd scenes, arrange movement in jagged lines, use garish colours and display distorted architecture. Staircases, revolves, treadmills, traps and bridges extended the domain of the stage. And on that stage a new generation of actors rejected verisimilitude on the one hand, and declamation on the other, in order to express passion for its own sake; a strident voice and cadaverous face became hallmarks of the expressionist actor.

It was mainly through the theatre that expressionism travelled from Germany; its most triumphant playwright was the American EUGENE O'NEILL. Expressionism is the creditor of all frankly theatrical exploitation of the modern stage.

**Eyre, Richard** 1943– British director. While at the Royal Lyceum Theatre, Edinburgh (1967–72), and later as a freelance director, Eyre gained widespread notice for his staging of contemporary drama. In 1973 he was appointed director of Nottingham Playhouse, where he remained for five years. His policy was to commission many new plays and, with premieres of such works as *Brassneck* (BRENTON and HARE) and *Comedians* (GRIFFITHS), the Playhouse quickly acquired a reputation as a major centre for adventurous and radical new drama. In 1978 he became producer of BBC TV's 'Play for Today', and in 1982 associate director at the NATIONAL THEATRE. Here he demonstrated a mastery of the stage musical, with productions of *The Beggar's Opera* and the long-running *Guys and Dolls*; other successful productions included *The Inspector General* and, for the ROYAL COURT, *Hamlet*. His several full-length feature films include *The Ploughman's Lunch* and *Laughterhouse*. In 1986 he was elected to succeed SIR PETER HALL as artistic director of the NT, from whom he took over in 1988. He developed small teams of actors and directors such as Declan Donnellan (see CHEEK BY JOWL), NICHOLAS HYTNER, STEPHEN DALDRY, the Canadian Robert Lepage and THÉÂTRE DE COMPLICITÉ. He directed CHRISTOPHER

HAMPTON's *The White Chameleon* (1991) and David Hare's trilogy (1990–3) about the three estates of Britain (of which *Racing Demon* was the first); but his regime will be especially remembered for the chances he has given to others and for a bias towards US plays and musicals (e.g. TONY KUSHNER's *Angels in America*, 1992, and the revival of *Carousel*, 1992). Eyre was due to retire from the NT at the end of 1995.

**Fabbri, Diego** 1911–80 Italian playwright. He was notable particularly for his plays of Catholic emphasis written mainly in the 1950s, like *Inquisizione* (*Inquisition*, 1950), *Processo di famiglia* (*Family Trial*, 1953) and *Processo a Gesù* (*The Trial of Jesus*, 1955). They are concerned with the serious, probing analysis of spiritual and religious issues, somewhat in the manner of the 'problem play' but strongly under the influence of PIRANDELLO. Their tone and subject-matter, however, have limited their appeal outside Italy. Although the relationship between drama and religion, and the ways in which the theatre can be used to explore religious issues, were major preoccupations – as indicated too by his collection of essays, *Ambiguità cristiana* (*Christian Ambiguity*, 1954) – not all of his work was in so serious a vein: more in the mainstream of BOULEVARD theatre are his light comedies of manners and matrimony, *Il seduttore* (*The Seducer*, 1951) and *La bugiarda* (*The Liar*, 1954). Of his later work, *Al dio ignoto* (*To the Unknown God*, 1980) and the posthumously published *Incontro al Parco Terme* (*Meeting in Terme Park*, 1982) are noteworthy. He was also an impressive stage adapter of novels, particularly those of Dostoevsky, and worked on scripts for film and television. The Italian dramatist with whom he is most frequently compared, and who shared many of his concerns, is UGO BETTI.

**Fagan, J(ames) B(ernard)** 1873–1933 British director and playwright, born in Northern Ireland. He took over the management of the ROYAL COURT THEATRE in 1918, where he mounted the British premiere of SHAW's *Heartbreak House* (1921) and a pioneering series of SHAKESPEARE productions. He also wrote over 15 plays, some specifically for GEORGE ALEXANDER and MRS PATRICK CAMPBELL. But his main contribution was in founding the Oxford Playhouse, where between 1923 and 1929 he directed a repertoire that included IBSEN, STRINDBERG, SYNGE and Shaw, and a 1925 production of *The Cherry Orchard* that was responsible for CHEKHOV's acceptance on the English stage. Here he developed a 'presentational' non-naturalistic style, and trained such young actors as JOHN GIELGUD, TYRONE GUTHRIE, RAYMOND MASSEY and FLORA ROBSON.

**Faiko, Aleksei (Mikhailovich)** 1893–1978 Soviet playwright. Among his quasi-expressionist plays (see EXPRESSIONISM) are three which are remembered chiefly for the artistic and social contexts in which they were produced. *Lake Lyul* was a detective MELODRAMA staged by MEYERHOLD at the Theatre of the Revolution (1923). The three-tiered, caged, laddered and platformed set, featuring fully operative elevators, combined with slide projections and rapidly shifting action to create the effect of cinematic montage. Meyerhold's 1924 staging of Faiko's *Bubus the Teacher* transformed that work from a naive vaudeville-operetta into a pretentious social melodrama. *The Man with a Briefcase* (1928), a melodramatic treatment of the rise and fall of a ruthless careerist doomed by a Tsarist military upbringing, was popular during the Purges of the late 1930s.

**Falckenberg, Otto** 1873–1947 German director and playwright. His work bridged SYMBOLISM and EXPRESSIONISM. After visionary plays like *Deliverance* (1899) and satirical CABARET, he became the artistic director of the Munich Kammerspiele from 1917 to 1947, establishing its reputation as one of the leading theatres for contemporary drama with productions of e.g. BRECHT's *Drums in the Night* (1922) and BARLACH's *The Dead Day* (1924).

**Falkland, Samuel** see HEIJERMANS, HERMAN

**farce** Farce as a technique is common to many forms of theatre, but since the Middle Ages it has been a popular genre which has been largely neglected in criticism. Although the word 'farce' is of medieval origin, the performance of raucous comedy is as old and as widespread as theatre. European farce has its provenance in elements of Greek and Roman theatre: for instance, the satyr plays of Greece (see GREEK THEATRE, ANCIENT) and the comedies of PLAUTUS, with their inventive manipulation of incident and character. The English word 'farce' derives from a culinary word in French, and ultimately from Latin *farsa* which means 'stuffing'. (The cook was evidently a staple character of classical farce.) The genre may therefore have its origin in the medieval theatre custom of 'stuffing' the programme with several plays of various kinds, or of stuffing the liturgy with comic scenes.

French scholars have affixed the label of *farce* to some 200 short plays, mainly dating from the second half of the 15th century, but a minority of these carried genre tags in their own time. Each consisting of a scene from daily life, these medieval farces in octosyllabic couplets (usually 300 to 500 lines) were simple in setting, sparse in properties, but inventive in acting – even though they lack scenic directions. Scholars debate whether the purpose was entertainment or edification (portraits of a fallen world), but the short plays are amazingly durable in evoking laughter. The two main subjects of medieval farce were the cuckolded husband and the deceiver deceived. The earliest extant farce – *The Boy and the Blind Man* – is a brutal but funny example of the latter. Over 50 medieval farces focus on conjugal conflict, of which *The Washbasin* is a fine example, typically reflecting medieval misogyny.

French farce influenced 15th-century German and English playwrights like JOHN HEYWOOD. After the Middle Ages, farce was perpetuated in a performing rather than a literary tradition, to which both SHAKESPEARE and MOLIÈRE in their different countries are indebted. Molière is indebted not only to Italian *COMMEDIA*, but more importantly to the great French farceurs GROS-GUILLAUME, TABARIN, GAULTIER-GARGUILLE and Turlupin (see TURLUPINADES). LABICHE must have worn out a series of collaborators to produce his 175 plays (mainly farces), some of which were preposterous, but many were grounded in the daily life of the rising French bourgeoisie in its pursuit of brides, pleasure and money. By the turn of the 20th century, FEYDEAU's farces grew increasingly sour and cynical in his variations on bedmanship. To succeed in Britain, the genre had to emerge from bedrooms and terminate in weddings, and HENRY ARTHUR JONES and PINERO were able to accomplish this feat. By the 1920s the surrealists (see SURREALISM) sang the praises of farce, e.g. ARTAUD's delight at the MARX BROS. Across the Channel the Aldwych farces (mainly by BEN TRAVERS) thrived on deception and manipulation. In the 1950s and 1960s farce was triumphant at the Whitehall Theatre, London, under the actor-manager BRIAN RIX. Silent films had given an international impetus to farce, through the brilliance of Buster Keaton, Laurel and Hardy, Harold Lloyd, and especially Charlie Chaplin.

Farce is still the favourite genre on the BOULEVARDS, on London's Shaftesbury Avenue – AYCKBOURN, FRAYN – and on BROADWAY – particularly SIMON. Since the end of World War II, however, playwrights have deftly assimilated the devices of farce to expose a serious view: e.g. BECKETT's music-hall tramps in *Waiting for Godot*, IONESCO's proliferation of chairs in *The Chairs*, GENET's clown-show in *The Blacks*, PINTER's games in *The Collection*, STOPPARD's acrobats in *Jumpers*, GRIFFITHS's comic turns in *Comedians*, or MAMET's BURLESQUE in *A Life in the Theatre*. Farce has acquired its ablest critic in ERIC BENTLEY.

**Farquhar, George** 1677–1707 Irish playwright. Born in Londonderry and educated at Trinity College, Dublin, he abandoned acting after wounding a fellow actor on stage, by forgetting to use a blunted sword. He moved from Dublin to London in 1697. His first play, a conventional comedy, *Love and a Bottle*, was produced in 1698. *The Constant Couple* (1699) was the greatest success of the Restoration. It was followed by a sequel, *Sir Harry Wildair* (1701); an adaptation of FLETCHER's *The Wild Goose Chase* as *The Inconstant* (1702); a savage comedy, *The Twin Rivals* (1702); and a farce, *The Stage Coach* (1704). Hoping for a way out of his money troubles, he became a lieutenant in the Earl of Orrery's regiment, where his experiences in recruiting soldiers in Shropshire became the source of *The Recruiting Officer* (1706). In spite of its success, Farquhar, poor and ill, was soon to write his last comedy, *The Beaux' Stratagem* – in 1707, dying soon after the first performance. Set in a country community of innkeepers and highwaymen, this play, a lasting success, explores the problems of a loveless marriage, recommending a solution of divorce by mutual consent.

**Farrah, Abdelkader** 1926– Algerian-born, British-based stage designer. Most of his work as a freelance designer has been with the ROYAL SHAKESPEARE COMPANY. Self-trained as a painter, he became a protégé and collaborator of MICHEL SAINT-DENIS in France and later in England. Farrah's scenography is marked by an architectonic and theatrically expressive shaping of stage space (especially evident in *The Balcony*, 1971, *Henry V*, 1975, and *Coriolanus*, 1977), and a painter's talent for bold design and colour in COSTUMES and props (*Doctor Faustus*, 1968, *As You Like It*, 1980, *Poppy*, 1982 and *The Balcony*, 1987). Notable instances of his interest in stylized masks occurred in *The Tempest* (1963) and *Richard III* (1970), as well as in the 1968 *Doctor Faustus*.

**Farren, Elizabeth** 1762–1829 English actress. From 1780 she acted at DRURY LANE, becoming very successful in the fine-lady roles previously played by FRANCES ABINGTON, and praised for her charm, beauty and art. Very successful and highly paid, she retired in 1797 and married the Earl of Derby.

**Farren, Nellie** [Ellen] 1848–1904 British actress. Born into a famous theatrical family, she became known as a queen of BURLESQUE and member of the famous GAIETY Quartette, with Edward Terry, Kate Vaughan and EDWARD ROYCE.

**Fassbinder, R(ainer) W(erner)** 1945–82 German playwright, film and theatre director. Although his reputation rests on a series of brilliant films (*The Marriage of Maria Braun*, 1978; *Veronika Voss*, 1982; *Querelle*, which was released posthumously; and the documentary *Berlin Alexanderplatz*, 1979, based on a novel by Alfred Döblin), Fassbinder was one of the originators of the contemporary VOLKSSTÜCK and produced film versions of plays by its leading exponents, KROETZ and SPERR. As a founding member of the Munich theatre commune Antitheater (1968), he rediscovered the work of MARIELUISE FLEISSER, which provided the catalyst for the movement, as well as staging BÜCHNER, WEISS, HANDKE and (in his own adaptation) JARRY. His own dramatic writing ranges from SURREALISM to brutally realistic images of social exploitation – e.g. *Bremen Coffee*, 1971; *Blood on the Cat's Neck*, 1972. In 1974 he became artistic director of the prestigious Theater am Turm in Frankfurt, but devoted himself entirely to the cinema after the antisemitism furore during rehearsals for his last play *Der Müll, die Stadt und der Tod* (*The Garbage, the Town and Death*, 1975; unperformed).

**Fastnachtspiel** German term. This CARNIVAL, or Shrovetide play, of German-speaking Europe has been known since the 15th century and is popular in origin and content, though incorporating some learned elements. *Fastnachtspiele* are usually farcical comedies, as the term *Schwänke* ('jests'), sometimes applied to them, indicates, or allegorical debates. They are generally supposed to have been performed by students and artisans The guild of mastersingers was also connected with them: Hans Folz, a member of the Nuremberg guild, is one of the few known 15th-century authors, and the 16th-century shoemaker and mastersinger Hans Sachs wrote a large number.

**Faucit, Helen Saville** 1817–98 British actress. She is remembered primarily for her performance as MACREADY's leading lady, creating with him the star roles in the best-known plays of EDWARD BULWER LYTTON, *The Duchess de la Vallière* (1837), *The Lady of Lyons* (1838), *Richelieu* (1839) and *Money* (1840). Her refined portrayal of romantic passion attracted fashionable theatregoers, and she was an admired Juliet, Desdemona and Cordelia. Her book *On Some of Shakespeare's Female Characters* (1892) speculates on the unwritten biographies of dramatis personae.

**Favart, Charles-Simon** 1710–92 French playwright and librettist. He wrote principally for the COMÉDIE-ITALIENNE and the Paris fair theatres, producing 150 pieces, mostly comic operas and *ballet-pantomimes* which parodied other works. Amongst his greatest successes were *La Chercheuse d'esprit* (*The Adventuress*, 1741), *Les Amours de Bastien et Bastienne* (*The Loves of Bastien and Bastienne*, 1753), a PARODY of ROUSSEAU's *Le Devin du village* (*The Village Soothsayer*), *La Fée Urgèle* (*The Fairy Urgèle*, 1753) and *Annette et Lubin* (1762). In 1757 he became director of the Opéra-Comique.

**Faversham, William** 1868–1940 British-born American actor. He migrated to America in 1887 and was in the companies of both DANIEL and CHARLES FROHMAN, playing opposite MINNIE MADDERN FISKE and MAUDE ADAMS before he became a leading man. His physical attractiveness and buoyant personality earned him the label of a 'matinée girl's idol'. Among his successful Shakespearian roles were Mark Antony in *Julius Caesar* and the title roles in *Romeo and Juliet* and *Othello*. He won his popularity, however, playing vigorous and masculine heroes in such plays as *Lord and Lady Algy*, *The Squaw May* and *The Prince and the Pauper*. His last role came in 1933 when he played Jeeter Lester in the long-running *Tobacco Road*.

**Fechter, Charles (Albert)** 1824–79 French-speaking actor. He was born in London to a German father and an English mother, and was educated in France. He became a leading MELODRAMATIC actor in Paris, but moved to London in 1860, and was a sensational success at the PRINCESS'S in a version of HUGO's *Ruy Blas*. His Hamlet had all the ease and elegance of Ruy Blas, and its ecstatic reception owed much to the innovatory blonde curls and the contrasting black suit. As manager of London's LYCEUM (1863–7) he initiated a mechanical revolution, substituting for wings and grooves the solid walls of an enclosing set and installing a system of lifts to remove complete scenes (see THEATRE DESIGN). In 1870 he sailed to the USA, where he remained for the rest of his life. His American managerial ventures failed, partly due to what his fan and friend CHARLES DICKENS called 'a perfect genius for quarrelling'.

**Fedeli** Italian company. Literally 'the faithful', they were a troupe of COMMEDIA DELL'ARTE actors founded (c.1603) and led by GIOVAN BATTISTA ANDREINI (Lelio, the male love interest), under the protection of the Duke of Mantua. Often competing with the ACCESI, the Fedeli specialized in sumptuous court spectacles and featured Florinda (VIRGINIA ANDREINI) as the languishing prima donna in her husband's plays. In 1614 they played publicly in Paris at the HÔTEL DE BOURGOGNE, when the company included TRISTANO MARTINELLI (Arlecchino), Barbieri (Beltrame) and FRANCESCO GABRIELLI (Scapino). Other French appearances occurred in 1623–4 and sometime between 1643 and 1647.

**Federal Street Theatre** (Boston, USA) The city's first theatre, it was opened in 1794 after the 1750 law prohibiting play-acting was overturned. After a succession of managers, the theatre (known as 'Old Boston') was supplanted. It closed in 1852.

**Federal Theatre Project** (USA) Established in 1935 by Congress, this was the first example in the USA of government-sponsored and -financed theatre. Under the direction of the indefatigable and intrepid HALLIE FLANAGAN (1890–1969), head of the experimental theatre at Vassar College, the FTP aimed to give employment to theatrical professionals during the Depression and to provide 'free, adult, uncensored theatre' to audiences throughout the country. At its peak 10,000 people were employed, with theatres in 40 states. The FTP lasted nearly four years and established the careers of e.g. ORSON WELLES, JOHN HOUSEMAN, ARTHUR MILLER, HOWARD BAY, PAUL GREEN, CANADA LEE and ELMER RICE. Seats were inexpensive and audiences were provided with varied fare, ranging from classics to new plays, children's theatre, foreign-language productions, puppet shows, religious plays, a Negro theatre, musical theatre, a circus and a controversial innovation called the LIVING NEWSPAPER, using documentary sources to deal with current issues. The FTP played to millions of people throughout the USA. Of the hundreds of productions, those by the black theatre were among the most innovative and included the voodoo *Macbeth* (1936), *Haiti* (1938) and *The Swing Mikado* (1939). In 1936 Sinclair Lewis's *It Can't Happen Here*, written for the FTP, was produced simultaneously in 22 cities. The FTP was boldly experimental and CENSORSHIP was a problem, leading to charges of left-wing bias, political controversy and ultimately to the disbanding of the project in June 1939.

**Fedotova, Glikeriya (Nikolaevna)** 1846–1925 Russian actress. She was the protégée of SHCHEPKIN, the father of Russian realistic acting (see REALISM), and with her husband, actor-director A. F. Fedotov, STANISLAVSKY's teacher at the Moscow Society of Art and Literature. Her range was broader than that of the tragedienne ERMOLOVA, the other great Maly Theatre actress, extending to comedy and drama, both domestic and historical. She excelled in a series of 29 character roles from the OSTROVSKY canon. She was also memorable as many of SHAKESPEARE's strong women – Beatrice (1865), Isabella (1868), Katherina (1871), Portia (1877), Lady Macbeth and Mistress Page (1890), Volumnia (1902) – and as Queen Elizabeth opposite Ermolova's Maria Stuart in SCHILLER's play.

**féerie** French spectacular show. The action derives from magical, fantastic or supernatural elements, using stage machinery. In the late 18th century the fantastic infiltrated fairground pantomimes, to produce in the 19th century the synthetic *féerie*. The first true success was *Le Pied du mouton* (Théâtre de la Gaîté, 1806), a much revived extravaganza in which a magic sheep's trotter unleashes a host of miracles. It was superseded by *Les Pilules du diable* (CIRQUE OLYMPIQUE, 1839) and successful shows based on fairy tales and romances. Since the transformations, tricks and apotheoses required a large stage, the Châtelet and then the Porte-Saint-Martin (see BOULEVARD) became favourite haunts. Romantic authors appreciated the dream-like qualities of the *féerie*; it exercised an important influence on the development of BURLESQUE, MUSICAL COMEDY and early cinema.

**female impersonation** Men impersonating women (see also MALE IMPERSONATION). The origins of theatre in religious cults meant that women were barred from performance, a prohibition sustained by social sanctions against their public exhibition in general. Therefore in Europe before the 17th century and in Asia before the 20th, female impersonation was the standard way to portray women on stage, and was considered far more normal than females playing females.

In the Oriental theatre, the female impersonator constitutes a distinct line of business – e.g. the great MEI LANFANG, voted the most popular actor in China in 1924. The *onnagata* role of Japanese KABUKI drama came about when women and boys were banished from the stage, lest they promote wantonness; mature men with shaven foreheads had to take over the female roles.

Men dressing as women was a tradition of saturnalia, Feasts of Fools and medieval New Year's celebrations, still to be seen in rag weeks and end-of-term revels. Cross-dressing is a usual accompaniment to CARNIVAL time, when norms are turned upside-down; men giving birth was enacted at some Hindu festivals, and even Arlecchino in the late COMMEDIA DELL'ARTE was shown in childbed and then breastfeeding his infant. Just as the Catholic Church attacked unruly carnivals, Protestant clerics and Puritans censured the 'sodomitical' custom of the boy-player on the Elizabethan and Jacobean stage. BOYS' COMPANIES dominated the English theatre until 1580, and NATHAN FIELD as Ophelia, Alexander Cooke as Lady Macbeth and Robert Goffe as Juliet and Cleopatra shaped the image of these characters in the minds of SHAKESPEARE's contemporaries. NED KYNASTON was the last of the line, playing well into the Restoration when PEPYS saw him in skirts. In recent decades, experimental revivals of all-male Shakespeare have been attempted, most recently the successful *As You Like It* staged by the British company CHEEK BY JOWL (1992).

Women were members of *commedia dell'arte* troupes from the 16th century but the comic characters occasionally donned petticoats – to the delight of audiences – and this travesty aspect (already present in ARISTOPHANES) grew more important as actresses gained popularity. If beauty and sex appeal were to be projected from stage by a real, nubile woman, the post-menopausal woman could as easily be played by a comic actor; parts like Mme Pernelle in MOLIÈRE's *Tartuffe* and the nanny Yeremeevna in FONVIZIN's *The Minor* were conceived as male roles, and NESTROY's mid-19th-century farces contain several of these 'dame' parts. The comic dame had become a fixture of the English PANTOMIME by the Regency period, and would be a showcase for such comedians as DAN LENO, GEORGE ROBEY and George Graves.

In the CIRCUS, boy athletes might be disguised as girls to make their stunts seem more phenomenal, e.g. the aerialist Barbette. Such transvestite performers were said to be 'in drag', a term from thieves' cant that compared the train of a gown to the drag or brake on a coach, and entered theatrical parlance from homosexual slang around 1870. 'Dragging up' provides the plot device in, e.g., BRANDON THOMAS's *Charley's Aunt* and SIMON GRAY's *Wise Child* (1968).

A new development arose in 19th-century VARIETY with the glamorous impersonator, who might be a comedian but dressed and made up to resemble a woman of taste and beauty. The baritone JULIAN ELTINGE usually selected vehicles that allowed him to vary sexes, accomplished by quick changes of costume. During and after World War II, all-male drag ensembles were popular in Britain and the USA, West Berlin (Chez Nous, 1958; Chez Romy Haag, 1972) and Paris (Alcazar, 1972; L'Ange Bleu, 1975; Chez Madame Arthur and Le Carrousel), often featuring transvestites such as Coccinelle.

The mid-1960s to 1970s saw a resurgence of female impersonation. DANNY LA RUE's club in London's Hanover Square (1964–70) was a resort of fashion, and drag MIMES were ubiquitous. This style reached an apotheosis in Paris's *La Grande Eugène*, seen in London in 1976. The drag ball in JOHN OSBORNE's *A Patriot for Me* (ROYAL COURT, 1965) hastened the demise of dramatic CENSORSHIP in England, thus enabling such impressive impersonations as Tim Curry's Dr Frank'n'furter in *The Rocky Horror Show* (1972). Androgyny had infiltrated the rock-music scene with Alice Cooper and David Bowie, and reached a logical terminus in the asexual Boy George. Comedy persisted with dames such as BARRY HUMPHRIES as Edna Everage and the piano-entertainers Hinge and Brackett (George Logan and Patrick Fyffe).

Contemporary American performance art has latched on to the conventions of drag to explore gender identity and confusion, as in the work of Los Angeles comedian John Fleck (b.1953). A mixture of avant-garde innovation and the traditions of popular culture is clear in the work of John Epperson (Lypsinka) and Ethyl (Roy) Eichelberger (1945–91). 'Alternative drag' in the UK was a shortlived phenomenon, as such FRINGE performers as the Joan Collins Fan Club (Julian Clary) became show business personalities. The success of the musical *La Cage aux folles* and David Henry Hwang's play *M. Butterfly* also testify to the co-opting of drag by the commercial theatre. The Afrikaner comedian Pieter-Dirk Uys (b.1946), who had evolved his female impersonations to attack South African society, found that his satiric creation Evita Bezuidenhout had become as beloved to Boers as to anti-apartheid activists. However, the rise of 'voguing', a transvestitic dance and beauty competition among American urban blacks and Hispanics, revealed a new strain of populism. As the politically correct gay community turned its back on drag, a radical edge was attributed to such outrageous clowns as Vaginal Creme Davis, Brenda Sexual and Glennda Orgasm of *The Brenda and Glennda Show*, and Hapi Phace, some of whom came out of the Pyramid Club in New York.

**feminist theatre (Britain)** Feminist theatre developed in the 1970s as part of the alternative/political theatre movement. The first feminist companies were set up by women involved with the women's movement (the Women's Theatre Group, 1973), and by women active in or critical of leftist theatre (Monstrous Regiment, 1975).

Feminist theatre developed rapidly in the 1970s and 1980s. Many theatre companies emerged. Some addressed feminist politics in issue-based theatre (Women's Theatre Group, Monstrous Regiment, Clean Break, Mother Hen, Siren, Spare Tyre and Theatre of Black Women). Others focused on feminist COMEDY and physical theatre (Beryl and the Perils, Bloomers, Clapperclaw, Cunning Stunts and Les Oeufs Malades), or concerned themselves primarily with the aesthetics of feminist performance (Burnt Bridges, Hesitate and Demonstrate, and the international Magdalena Project). One company, Sadista Sisters, was a band as well as a theatre group; another, Mrs Worthington's Daughters, specialized in recovering feminist plays from the early 20th century. The companies were usually worker's collectives; most were women-only and most began by group-devising their shows. All were touring companies – the aim of the Women's Playhouse Trust to establish a theatre for women has never been achieved – playing to audiences composed predominantly of women. In London two venues, Oval House and Action Space/the Drill Hall, became particularly associated with women's theatre. Funding agencies began to recognize its importance, giving grants to companies and venues.

Feminist playwrights became more numerous, nurtured by feminist theatre groups and pro-feminist policies in other theatres, notably the ROYAL COURT THEATRE in London. Feminist playwriting explored the family, gender roles and sexuality from different political (socialist feminist, radical feminist, black feminist) and national, class and ethnic perspectives. Writers whose work represents feminist writing of this period include CARYL CHURCHILL, Sarah Daniels, Andrea Dunbar, Marcella Evaristi, PAM GEMS, Bryony Lavery, Deborah Levy, Jackie Kay, Liz Lochead, Clare McIntyre, Rona Munro, Louise Page, Winsome Pinnock, Christina Reid, Sue Townsend, Michelene Wandor and TIMBERLAKE WERTENBAKER. The wider influence of feminism in the theatre was to be seen in the protests of actresses working in major theatre companies against the male 'directocracy', and in the gradual apointment of women artistic directors to major REPERTORY houses.

In the 1990s that vibrancy seems to have faded. Challenges have come from within feminism itself to the idea of an inclusive politics of 'female identity'. Protest theatre is out of favour. Public funding for the theatre has been reduced. Few feminist theatre companies have survived into the 1990s and few new ones have emerged. In women's writing for the theatre there has been a perceptible shift in tone – Wertenbaker's *Three Birds Alighting on a Field*, for example, is markedly less critical of patriarchy and masculinity than her earlier plays – and, significantly, Britain's oldest feminist theatre company changed its name from the explicitly feminist Women's Theatre Group to the feminine mystery of the Sphinx.

The emphasis of women's work in the theatre has moved away from companies and collectives to individuals, and from political issues to personal/body exploration (perhaps influenced by the feminist performance theorists' interest in HÉLÈNE CIXOUS's idea of *écriture féminine*). Performance artists Annie Griffin, Rose English and Bobby Baker, whose work explores 'the feminine', have a large following, but there are no British performance artists as radically experimental with or on the female body as, for example, the American Karen Finlay. Claire Dowle's one-woman attacks on the constraints of the sexed body are rare moments of challenge, but radical deconstruction of gender or role is now the province of gay and lesbian 'queer' theatre (see GAY THEATRE; LESBIAN THEATRE).

Women's work in the theatre continues, but there are signs that feminist theatre may be suffering the fate of popular feminism: it has become unfashionable and, fearful of the taunt of 'political correctness', it is mutating into a more fashionable 'post-feminist' humanism. Perhaps it is also significant that the Royal Court's hit of 1993 was DAVID MAMET's 'backlash' piece, *Oleanna*.

**feminist theatre (USA)** American feminist theatre is an outgrowth of the 1960s New Left, of avant-garde theatre and of the Women's Liberation Movement, which sprang from women's dissatisfaction with their roles in American life and American theatre. The first New Feminist Theatre was founded in 1969 by Anselma Dell'Olio.

The difficulty of defining the phenomenon of feminist theatre stems from its still emergent nature, the variety of its roots and the range of its ideology. All feminist theatre is radical, since it seeks to upset the status quo by scrutinizing women's position in a sexist society. However, feminist theatre groups vary between those more traditional ones designed to fight discrimination by providing a wide range of experiences for women in theatre, and the revolutionary groups that seek a total upheaval of theatrical techniques and subjects. These latter groups reject hierarchical structures, often creating their works by collective improvisation and experimental methods and drawing their political themes from their personal experiences, similar to the consciousness-raising of the Women's Liberation Movement. Many such groups exclude men and prefer female-only audiences, which join in post-performance discussions of the issues presented. Their plays generally reject standard characterizations and, instead, create women who serve as metaphorical figures to present highly didactic messages.

Feminist theatre groups since their beginning have considered a variety of women's subjects. These range from the trivial – leg-shaving, bras, ironing – to the essential – abortion, rape, domestic violence, motherhood and entrapment in the nuclear family. Many early feminist groups reflected women's anger at the start of liberation, and their perception of man as the enemy. Sometimes through the use of gender role reversal, their plays exposed the oppression of women in patriar-

chal society (*But What Have You Done for Me Lately?* by Myrna Lamb). Other feminist plays reject the destructiveness of male history and insist on a woman-oriented, visionary world of nurturing. These plays sometimes rework classical myths from a woman's point of view; create women's rituals; consider positive relationships between women as mothers and daughters, sisters and friends; rediscover women's history, or insist upon total lesbian separatism.

Many feminist theatre groups were short-lived, suffering from problems of disorganization, lack of money and media oversight. Of the numerous radical feminist theatre groups that began in the 1970s, only Spiderwomen Theatre, a collective of Native-American women operating in New York, and At the Foot of the Mountain, in Minneapolis, were continuing to produce and tour by the early 1990s. Split Britches is a popular feminist and lesbian troupe that began in the 1980s in the East Village lesbian community in New York (see GAY THEATRE; LESBIAN THEATRE).

While alternative feminist theatre practice declined in the 1980s, the decade witnessed the beginning of committed feminist theory and criticism in the theatre profession and in academia.

**Fenn, Ezekiel** 1620–? English actor. In 1635 he played two demanding female roles for Queen Henrietta's Men at London's COCKPIT: Sophonisba in Nabbes's *Hannibal and Scipio* and Winifred in a revival of *The Witch of Edmonton*, by DEKKER, FORD and WILLIAM ROWLEY. He was one of BEESTON's Boys, and the subject of a poem by Henry Glapthorne (1639), 'For Ezekiel Fenn at his first Acting a Man's Part', in which the magnitude of the transition from female to male role is revealed.

**Fennario, David** 1947– Canadian playwright. He became a writer-in-residence at Montreal's Centaur Theatre in 1974. His first play, *On the Job* (1975), was based on his own experiences as a low-paid worker. His fourth play, *Balconville* (1979), a bilingual work, treats life among the working poor of a Montreal slum. It has played across Canada and at London's OLD VIC. Fennario's plays have a strong autobiographical base. Although acclaimed as a leftist political writer, he regards the political contents of his work as an inevitable result of the milieux and characters he likes to write about.

**Fennell, James** 1766–1816 London-born American actor. Fennell made his debut in Edinburgh in 1787 as Othello, which became his most successful role, and soon appeared at COVENT GARDEN, though with minimal success. He was to have a substantial career in America. WIGNELL took him to Philadelphia in 1792, where he soon became a star. Well over six feet tall with an expressive, handsome face, he brought considerable dignity to such roles as Othello, Lear, and Jaffier in *Venice Preserv'd*; he was also much admired as Hamlet, Glenalvon in *Douglas*, and Iago.

**Ferber, Edna** 1885–1968 American novelist and playwright. A celebrated author of fiction, Ferber began her theatrical career in 1915 with *Our Mrs McChesney*, a collaboration with George V. Hobart that starred Ethel Barrymore (see DREW-BARRYMORE FAMILY). *The Eldest* (1920) was her only solo venture in playwriting, composed for the PROVINCETOWN PLAYERS. *Minick* (1924) began a lucrative partnership with GEORGE S. KAUFMAN, which also yielded *The Royal Family* (1927), depicting chaotic life in a theatrical dynasty; *Dinner at Eight* (1932), which examined the lives of guests at a fashionable dinner party; and *Stage Door* (1936), which focused on young actresses in a theatrical boarding-house. Less successful collaborations were *The Land Is Bright* (1941) and *Bravo!* (1948). Two of Ferber's novels were adapted into the musicals *Show Boat* (1927) and *Saratoga* (1959).

**Ferrari, Paolo** 1822–89 Italian playwright. His long career and substantial output provide an index to many of the tastes, characteristics and deficiencies of the mid-19th-century Italian stage. His work included dialect pieces, comedies of manners, historical dramas and plays concerned with contemporary social and moral issues. French influence, particularly of the bourgeois *drame* of AUGIER and DUMAS *père*, is pronounced in much of his later writing, little of which has continued to hold the stage. None the less, in their time plays like *Goldoni e le sue sedici commedie nuove* (*Goldoni and His Sixteen New Comedies*, 1853), *La satira e Parini* (*Parini and Satire*, 1856), *Il duello* (*The Duel*, 1868), *Cause ed effetti* (*Cause and Effect*, 1871) and *Il suicidio* (*The Suicide*, 1875) enjoyed considerable success and esteem. At its best his drama, notwithstanding a tendency to prolixity and artificiality, is marked by wit and lively characterization.

**Ferreira, António** 1528–69 Portuguese playwright. He is known mainly for his *Tragédia de D. Inês de Castro* (*The Tragedy of Lady Inês de Castro*), usually known simply as *A Castro* (*The Castro*) to underline its affinity with the plays and heroines of classical Greek tragedy; it was performed in Ferreira's lifetime at Coimbra, but published only in 1587.

Based on a real-life episode of Portuguese history, *The Castro* portrays the illicit love of the heir to the throne, D. Pedro, for the Lady Inês – a liaison which, as in RACINE's *Bérénice*, is perceived as being completely at odds with the interests of the state. The king has to choose between kingly prudence and compassion. When Inês is killed, the prince threatens vengeance and that serious social disjunction that high tragedy characteristically entails. The fine management of tensions, the poetic atmosphere of foreboding and the Chorus's highly dramatic evocation of pity and terror make this one of the most theatrically effective and enduring of neoclassical tragedies. Ferreira also wrote two comedies, *O Cioso* (*The Jealous Man*) and *O Bristo* (the protagonist's surname).

**Ferrer, José** [José Vicente Ferrer Otero y Cintron] 1912–92 Puerto-Rican born American actor, director and producer. His first substantial role came in *Brother Rat* (1936), and he achieved stardom in *Charley's Aunt* (1940). Ferrer employed his rich and powerful voice in two subsequent revivals, as Iago to PAUL ROBESON's *Othello* (1943) and in the title role of *Cyrano de Bergerac* (1946). He directed the New York Theatre Company at the City Centre, appearing in several classical revivals.

**Ferron, Jacques** 1921–85 Quebec playwright, novelist and essayist. A physician by profession, his early satirical plays such as *Le Licou* (*The Halter*, 1947) and *L'Ogre* (*The Ogre*, 1949), point towards the nationalistic political commitment of his later works. Chief among these are *Les Grands Soleils* (*The Great Sunflowers*, 1958), which re-examines the Patriote Rebellion of 1837–8; and *La Tête du roi* (*The King's Head*, 1963), dealing on intersecting historical planes with the 19th-century Métis Revolt and contemporary revolutionary violence in Quebec, crystallized in the decapitation of the statue of Edward VII, symbol of Empire. A major novelist and essayist, Ferron played an active role in the formation and victory of the separatist Parti Québécois in 1976. He was also the

founder of the parodic Rhinoceros Party, an iconoclastic grouping which perished with him.

**Feuchtwanger, Lion** 1884–1958 German playwright and novelist. After early historical dramas such as *Jew Süss* (1917, rewritten as a novel in 1925) he turned to contemporary political themes with a 'dramatic novel', *1918*, which caused an uproar when staged in 1924. He collaborated with BRECHT on several plays, including *Life of Edward II* (1924) and the adaptation of his novel, *The Visions of Simone Machard* (1957).

**Feydeau, Georges** 1862–1921 French playwright. Considered the father of French FARCE, Feydeau took over the 19th-century *vaudeville*, as perfected by LABICHE and others. His subject and audience was the wealthy bourgeoisie of the Third Republic, whose sexual and matrimonial activities he examines. Feydeau's plots move fast, invariably bringing the wrong people together at the wrong moment, presenting man helplessly out of control, in settings with multiple doors, which may open to reveal disaster. His dramatic output was relatively limited. His first full-length staged play was *Tailleur pour dames* (*A Gown for His Mistress*) at the Théâtre de la Renaissance in 1886. In 1892 *Monsieur chasse* (*Monsieur Is Hunting*) was accepted by the PALAIS-ROYAL, and *Champignol malgré lui* (*A Close Shave*) was staged at the Nouveautés, which became his main theatre. *Cat Among the Pigeons* (*Un Fil à la patte*, 1894) shows a young man trying to dispose of his *cocotte* mistress in order to make a wealthy marriage. The collaborative *Hotel Paradiso* (*L'Hôtel du Libre Échange*, 1894), like *A Flea in Her Ear* (1907), provokes laughter via the respectability of the characters and the hypocrisy of their attitudes, brought together at a dubious hotel. *The Lady from Maxim's* (1899) exposes social snobbery and was highly popular during the 1900 Exhibition. In his later years Feydeau increasingly focused on conjugal relationships, in which he was closer to the naturalistic theatre than to the fashionable BOULEVARD.

**Fialka, Ladislav** 1931–91 Czech MIME artist. Trained as a ballet dancer, he was one of the founders of the Prague Balustrade Theatre (1958), where he directed and starred in pantomimes wearing the traditional whiteface of PIERROT. Working with a regular ensemble, he based his mimodramas mainly on traditional material: *Les Amants de la lune* (1959) from DEBURAU; *The Castaways* (1959), in the style of silent films; *The Fools* (1965), which traced the type from the Bible to Kafka. He also worked in *Hamlet* (1959) and *Ubu* (1964), and toured Europe and America.

**Fichandler, Zelda** 1924– American director. Fichandler is co-founder and during 1951–90 sole producing director of the ARENA STAGE theatre (Washington, DC), the longest artistic tenure in regional theatre annals. From the beginning she was committed to having a resident acting company to present the classics, American drama and recent plays that had failed on BROADWAY. In the 1950s she articulated the promise of the regional theatre movement, and in 1961 built a permanent home for her company; there she produced new plays, such as *The Great White Hope* (1967), *Indians* (1969) and *Moonchildren* (1971). Her interest in Soviet and Eastern European drama led to productions in the 1970s of works by FRISCH, MROŻEK, ÖRKÉNY and others. In 1990 she became artistic director of New York's ACTING COMPANY.

**Field, Nathan** 1587– c.1620 English actor and playwright. Field made a reputation as an outstanding boy actor with the CHILDREN OF THE CHAPEL ROYAL. By 1613 he was the leader of the adult Lady Elizabeth's Men, from which he transferred to the King's Men c.1615. Praised by BEN JONSON, the flamboyant Field was well suited to the role of CHAPMAN's Bussy d'Ambois. His two surviving comedies, *A Woman Is a Weather-Cock* (c.1609) and *Amends for Ladies* (c.1610), are competent exercises in the style of Jonson. He collaborated with MASSINGER in *The Fatal Dowry* (c.1618) and other plays, and with FLETCHER.

**Field Day Theatre Company** Irish company. It was inaugurated in Londonderry by actor Stephen Rea and playwright BRIAN FRIEL with the premiere of Friel's forceful *Translations* (1980). The company's productions and publications have been designed to stimulate debate on current political and cultural controversies. Plays have included *Communication Cord* (Friel, 1982), *Pentecost* (STEWART PARKER, 1987), *Double Cross* (TOM KILROY, 1986), *Saint Oscar* (Terry Eagleton, 1989) and *The Madam Macadam Travelling Theatre* (Kilroy, 1991), as well as new versions of European classics. They have also published *The Field Day Anthology of Irish Writing*. Friel has since left the company.

**Fielding, Henry** 1707-54 English novelist and playwright. His reputation as the finest satirical dramatist of his age began with the production of *The Author's Farce* in 1730, a BALLAD OPERA which in its experimentation with dramatic form and the brilliance of its SATIRE established the model for his later work. His mockery of contemporary tragedy, *Tom Thumb* (1730), was later revised under the grandiose title *The Tragedy of Tragedies* (1731). *The Welsh Opera* (performed 1731) is a political satire in ballad opera form, revised as *The Grub Street Opera*. Fielding's only attempt at a serious play on sexual intrigue and marriage, *The Modern Husband* (1732), analyses marriage as prostitution and adultery by consent. With Walpole's Excise Bill threatening, he openly attacked the prime minister in *Don Quixote in England* (1734). Plays like *Pasquin* (1736) and *The Historical Register for the Year 1736* (1737) were also clear attacks on the government, using the Little Haymarket Theatre, which he managed, as a platform. Walpole was provoked to rush through the Licensing Act, which created CENSORSHIP over plays through the Lord Chamberlain's office (see THEATRICAL MONOPOLY). Fielding, censored and with his theatre closed because unlicensed, turned to the law and to writing novels, with a few infrequent plays.

**Fields** [Stansfield], **Gracie** 1898-1979 British singer and actress. 'Our Gracie' was born over a fish-and-chip shop in Rochdale and sang in working men's clubs. Her professional debut at a local cinema, as a member of a juvenile troupe, came in 1908. In 1915 she made her London debut as Sally Perkins in *Mr Tower of London*, which enjoyed a phenomenal run (1918-25) at the Alhambra, Leicester Square. She was a headliner in VARIETY by 1928, played the New York PALACE in 1930 and in 1931 first sang her signature tune 'Sally'. Audiences adored her for her ability to move smoothly from the vocal clowning of 'The Biggest Aspidistra in the World' to the mawkishness of 'Ave Maria'.

She moved to Hollywood during the war. Her theme song 'Wish Me Luck As You Wave Me Goodbye' became famous. She played ten Royal Variety Performances before retiring to Capri in 1959. She was made DBE in 1979.

**Fields, Lew** see WEBER, JOSEPH

**Fields, W. C.** [William Claude Dukenfield] 1880-1946

American comedian. He ran away from home at the age of 14. As an eccentric tramp JUGGLER he was the first American headliner at the FOLIES-BERGÈRE (1902) and a great hit at the London HIPPODROME (1904) for his trick pool game and frustrating golf lesson. The bibulous, bottlenosed Fields developed the character of a grandiloquent but seedy curmudgeon, muttering indignant asides. He starred in *The* ZIEGFELD *Follies* (1915-18, 1920, 1921, 1925), and in 1923 in *Poppy* created the type of the moth-eaten but brazen showman he would later repeat on film. After 1925 he settled in Los Angeles, filming a series of comic masterpieces.

**Fierstein, Harvey** 1954- American playwright, actor, producer and gay activist. Fierstein made his debut as an actor at LA MAMA in Andy Warhol's *Park* (1971). He garnered sudden fame in 1981 with the success of his *Torch Song Trilogy*, a play presenting various views of male homosexuality. With the commercial success of the musical *La Cage aux folles* (1983), of which he wrote the book, Fierstein was considered the most successful 1980s BROADWAY playwright concerned with gay themes, though his efforts since then have been less acclaimed.

**Fifth Avenue Theatre** (New York City) AUGUSTIN DALY began his theatre management in this converted (1865) MINSTREL hall. From 1869 to 1873 he assembled a company, staged comedies and dramas in perfectly tuned productions, and made the theatre the most fashionable and popular playhouse in New York. When it burned down in 1873, Daly transferred his company to the New Fifth Avenue Theatre on BROADWAY. In 1879 STEELE MACKAYE rebuilt the old house, renaming it the MADISON SQUARE.

**Finck, Werner** 1902-78 German CABARET performer. Co-founder of Berlin's Die Katakombe, he was compère and actor there from 1929 to 1935. His puns and word-games constituted a veritable critique of his times, for which he was interned in a concentration camp in 1935. But he survived to make numerous postwar appearances as a solo cabaretist, particularly at Die Mausefalle, Stuttgart (1948-51).

**Finlay, Frank** 1926- British actor. A versatile member of the English Stage Company at the ROYAL COURT in the late 1950s, he was a memorable Harry Khan in ARNOLD WESKER's *Chicken Soup with Barley* (1958), Attercliffe in JOHN ARDEN's *Sergeant Musgrave's Dance* (1959) and Hill in Wesker's *Chips with Everything* (1962). LAURENCE OLIVIER invited him to join the NATIONAL THEATRE Company, where he played such major roles as Willie Mossop in *Hobson's Choice*, Iago in *Othello* and Joxer Daly in *Juno and the Paycock*. Finlay acquired a certain identity as an actor, playing mainly middle-aged characters, often quiet and passive but with a controlled power which rose to emotional climaxes. As Bernard Link in DAVID MERCER's *After Haggerty* (1970) and the paterfamilias in EDUARDO DE FILIPPO's *Saturday, Sunday, Monday* (1973), Finlay retained the audience's attention with what seemed to be minimal effort until he reached the explosion of despair and anger towards the end of the play. After taking over from COLIN BLAKELY in De Filippo's *Filumena* and from PAUL SCOFIELD as Salieri in *Amadeus* (1981), he turned to a WEST END musical, *Mutiny!*, in which he played Captain Bligh (1985). In 1987 he appeared as the barrister charged with his wife's murder in Jeffrey Archer's *Beyond Reasonable Doubt*.

**Finney, Albert** 1936- British actor. He led the postwar generation of actors towards a less upper-class, less cerebral and more physical style of playing. A protégé of BARRY JACKSON at the BIRMINGHAM REPERTORY THEATRE from 1956 to 1958, he moved to the Shakespeare Memorial Theatre to play Edgar to CHARLES LAUGHTON's King Lear and to take over as Coriolanus from LAURENCE OLIVIER. He became nationally known in 1960 when he created the title role in Billy Liar, the north-country comedy by Keith Waterhouse and WILLIS HALL, and in 1961 played Luther in JOHN OSBORNE's historical epic at the ROYAL COURT THEATRE. He starred in major British films such as Saturday Night and Sunday Morning (1960) and Tom Jones (1963), making use of his rugged physique, stocky, determined manner and rich voice. He joined the NATIONAL THEATRE Company in 1965 to play a variety of parts, ranging from the rebellious border baron, Armstrong, in JOHN ARDEN's Armstrong's Last Goodnight (1965) to the limp-wristed antiques collector in PETER SHAFFER's Black Comedy (1966). He started to direct both plays and films, notably Charlie Bubbles (1967), and was considered a possible successor to Olivier as director of the National Theatre. When PETER HALL took over at the NT he invited Finney to star in the first seasons on London's South Bank, as Hamlet, Tamburlaine and Macbeth. He has appeared in films and television dramas, and recently on stage in two RONALD HARWOOD plays, Another Time (1989) and Reflected Glory (1992).

**Fiorilli, Tiberio** [Scaramuccia; Scaramouche] (c.1600–94) Italian comedian, the putative son of SILVIO FIORILLO. He popularized the character Scaramouche, an amalgam of the ZANNI and the Capitano, in a sober black costume, with no mask and a guitar in lieu of a sword. Despite his squint, deafness and withered arm, his French and Italian contemporaries were charmed by his naturalness and comic power. In 1658 he alternated performances at the PETIT-BOURBON with MOLIÈRE, who suggested a repeat of this experiment at the PALAIS-ROYAL in 1661. Fiorilli enjoyed success in London in 1673 and 1675.

**Fiorillo** [Fiorilli] **family** Italian actors. Silvio Fiorillo (died 1633) began in the COMMEDIA DELL'ARTE playing Captain Matamoros, then (c.1609) appeared in Naples as the first Policinella, brandishing a cuckold's horn; his success led to this episodic servant becoming a lead comedian. He also published some scenarios. His son Giovan Battista (fl.1614–51) played second ZANNI under the name Trappolino; his wife Beatrice Vitelli (fl.1638–54) played first amorosa.

**fireworks** As a dramatic auxiliary, fireworks were used in 14th-century religious plays, particularly for hell mouth, and became a standard requisite of the medieval and baroque theatres. In England, the 'wild men' of the Lord Mayor's show were associated with pyrotechnics; in George Whetstone's Historie of Promos and Cassandra (1578), green men enter with their clubs spouting fire. By the 18th century, fireworks displays, now with coloured lights, had been transferred to pleasure gardens, and only the COMÉDIE-ITALIENNE in Paris still employed them indoors. That they had become old-fashioned claptrap is clear in Nicholas Nickleby when Crummles proposes that a fireworks display, 'awful from the front', could be bought for 18 pence. A brief resurgence in their use came in the late 19th century in the spectaculars of the KIRALFY brothers and their competitors.

**Firmin** 1784–1859 French actor. He was lively, intelligent and sensitive, and his talents suited him to COMEDY rather than TRAGEDY. In 1810 Napoleon noticed him at

the ODÉON and had him transferred to the COMÉDIE-FRANÇAISE, where he played MARIVAUX's lovers remarkably well. In 1829 he was Saint Mégrin in Henri III et sa cour, and the original Hernani in 1830. Between 1813 and 1843 he created at least 100 parts at the Comédie, including Torquato in Tasse (1826), Frédéric in SCRIBE's Bertrand et Raton (1833) and Richelieu in Mlle de Belle-Isle (1839).

**Fiske, Harrison Grey** 1861–1942 American drama editor, critic, producer, manager and playwright. Born of wealthy parents, Fiske became a journalist, and when his father bought him one third of the Dramatic Mirror he made it an important theatrical journal by attacking corruption in the profession and working to raise the tone of the American stage. He led a crusade in 1880 to establish the Actors' Fund. In 1890 he married the actress Marie Augusta Davey (MINNIE MADDERN FISKE), and managed her career as well as that of a number of leading actors. For her he wrote or adapted numerous plays including Hester Crewe (1893) and Marie Deloche (1895). He leased the Manhattan Theatre in 1901 for Mrs Fiske, and formed the Manhattan Company to support her. His producing successes included Kismet in 1911, starring OTIS SKINNER. The death of Mrs Fiske in 1932 effectively ended his career. Fiske fought commercialism in the theatre, and did much to establish IBSEN on the American stage.

**Fiske, Minnie Maddern** [née Marie Augusta Davey] 1864–1932 American actress and director. Her adult New York debut – she had been an established child actress – was in Charles Callahan's Fogg's Ferry (1882). From 1890 to 1893, newly married to HARRISON GREY FISKE, she wrote several one-act plays and became interested in the realistic movement (see REALISM), aiming at 'natural, true acting' in her productions, especially with her Manhattan Theatre Company (1904–8). She fought, almost alone, the THEATRICAL SYNDICATE, and became a noted humanitarian. Some of her notable stage appearances were in Hester Crewe (1893), A Doll's House (1894), Tess of the d'Urbervilles (1897), Vanity Fair (1899), Hedda Gabler (1903), Leah Kleschna (1906), The New York Idea (1906), Rosmersholm (1907), Salvation Nell (1908), The Pillars of Society (1910) and Ghosts (1927). One of the most distinguished of all American actresses, she was the chief promoter of IBSEN in the USA.

**Fitch, Clyde** 1865–1909 American playwright and director. He was a highly successful and prolific writer: in 1901 four plays were running simultaneously in New York – Lover's Lane, Captain Jinks of the Horse Marines, The Climbers and Barbara Frietchie. Best known among the others are The Moth and the Flame (1898), Nathan Hale (1898), The Cowboy and the Lady (1899), The Girl with the Green Eyes (1902), Her Great Match (1905) and The Truth (1907). Fitch was a master of sprightly dialogue and documentary-like scenes from contemporary life; as a director, he meticulously controlled every detail of the staging.

**Fitzball, Edward** 1793–1873 English playwright, novelist and poet. He was most famous for his spectacular MELODRAMAS such as Jonathan Bradford (1833), based on a recent murder and provided with special music. Fitzball's other titles include The Burning Bridge (1824), The Flying Dutchman (1827), The Earthquake (1828), The Negro of Wapping (1838) and The Wreck and the Reef (1847). He was reader of plays for COVENT GARDEN (1835–8) and DRURY LANE (1838–51). His output, typical of the journeyman dramatist's, includes adaptations of popular novels, thefts from the French stage, comic operas and BURLESQUES, at the rate of six a year.

**Fitzgerald, Geraldine** 1914– Irish-born American actress and director. Fitzgerald made her stage debut at the GATE THEATRE in Dublin (1932) and her first appearance in New York as Ellie Dunn in *Heartbreak House* (1938). Working in both films and the theatre, she has played classical and modern characters including Goneril (*King Lear*, 1956), Gertrude (*Hamlet*, 1958), Mary Tyrone (*Long Day's Journey into Night*, 1971), Juno (*Juno and the Paycock*, 1973) and Amanda Wingfield (*The Glass Menagerie*, 1975), and has performed in a one-woman show, *Songs of the Streets: O'Neill and Carlotta* (1979). One of America's most distinguished character actresses, Fitzgerald was widely acclaimed for her 1973 portrayal of Juno. She has made over 30 films, including *Wuthering Heights* (1939), *The Pawnbroker* (1965), *Arthur* (1981) and *Pope of Greenwich Village* (1984).

**Fitzmaurice, George** 1877–1963 Irish playwright. A Dubliner, he is now regarded as being surpassed in the early ABBEY repertoire only by SYNGE. His first play, *The Country Dressmaker* (1907), a realistic SATIRE of peasant chicanery, was a success. His next two plays, both one-acters, *The Pie-Dish* (1908) and *The Magic Glasses*, establish his fantastic 'folk world' of reality and legend. The latter concerns witchcraft, quack, and sinister, diabolic possession. In *The Dandy Dolls*, discourteously rejected by YEATS in 1913, Fitzmaurice assumes a remarkable duality of human and supernatural, domestic and magical. The fabulous world was realized again in the extravagant comedy of *The Enchanted Land* (published 1957), where match-making goes astray in the Land-under-Wave. Discouraged by Yeats's regime, he withdrew into silence. His later, solitary work includes *One Evening Gleam* (1949), a sombre, moving tale in a realistic, urban setting.

Fitzmaurice's imagination united the macabre and the exuberant. AUSTIN CLARKE's Lyric Theatre Co. restored *The Pie-Dish* to the stage in the mid- and late 1940s; and more recently, in belated tribute, the Abbey has put on productions.

**Flanagan (Davis)** [*née* Ferguson], **Hallie** 1890–1969 American playwright, educator and administrator. She studied with GEORGE PIERCE BAKER at Workshop 47, and in 1927 went to Europe to study theatre. On her return she ran a highly successful experimental course at Vassar College. In 1935 she was invited to administer the new theatre programme that had been established to put qualified people back in work. For the next four years she managed the huge national theatre as it struggled with its double requirements of artistic merit and relief of unemployment. Franklin D. Roosevelt called her the third most powerful woman in America – 'after my wife and Frances Perkins' – during her supervision of the FEDERAL THEATRE PROJECT. In spite of government harassment, crippling bureaucratic regulations and opposition from the professional theatre, the FTP achieved a remarkable record of accomplishments including LIVING NEWSPAPERS, African-American companies, children's theatres and distinguished alumni. With the demise of the project in 1939, Flanagan returned to Vassar; she then went to Smith College, where she continued to write and direct. She left behind several books and a vision of the theatre as a vibrant social institution that must dare to be dangerous.

**Flanders, Michael** 1922–75 English VARIETY performer. He contributed lyrics for such London REVUES as *Air on a Shoestring* and translated Stravinsky's *A Soldier's Tale* for the EDINBURGH FESTIVAL (1954), but is best remembered for *The Drop of a Hat* (1956) and other entertainments created and performed with Donald Swann (died 1994).

**Fleck, Ferdinand** 1757–1801 German actor. From 1786 to his death Fleck acted with the BERLIN ROYAL THEATRE. He was adulated for his powerful, spontaneous interpretations of roles in both the classics and contemporary romantic drama. LUDWIG TIECK's ideas on acting were profoundly influenced by his experience of Fleck's acting. Fleck's performance as SCHILLER's Wallenstein provided a standard for most 19th-century actors.

**Flecker, James Elroy** 1884–1915 British poet and playwright. The sensuous lyricism of his two plays, *Don Juan* (1911, not publicly performed until 1950) and *Hassan* (1914), owes more to the decadent movement at the end of the 19th century than to the modern revival of poetic drama. However, the colourful exoticism of the second play, together with incidental music by Delius and ballets by Fokine, gave it considerable popularity when it was first produced in 1923, and it has since been revived.

**Fleisser, Marieluise** 1901–74 German playwright and novelist. Her most influential works were *Purgatory in Ingolstadt*, completed with the help of BRECHT and FEUCHTWANGER (1926), and *Pioneers in Ingolstadt* (1928), which sketches a brief encounter between a housemaid and a passing soldier and became one of the major models for KROETZ and for FASSBINDER. *Deep Sea Fish* (1980, written 1930–72) documents Fleisser's struggle to find space of her own, first with Brecht, then back home with her husband.

**Fletcher, Allen** 1922–85 American director and teacher. Born in San Francisco, he made his directing debut in 1948 at the OREGON SHAKESPEARE FESTIVAL. From 1962–5 he served as principal director and head of the professional training programme for the American Shakespeare Festival, Stratford, Connecticut (see AMERICAN SHAKESPEARE THEATRE). In 1966 he took a similar post with the Seattle Repertory Theatre where he modernized the company. Ousted in 1970, he founded the Actors' Company and became Director of the AMERICAN CONSERVATORY THEATRE. He left ACT in 1984 for a similar post with the Denver Centre Theatre. A leading classical director, Fletcher is remembered for his 1963 *King Lear* with MORRIS CARNOVSKY.

**Fletcher, John** 1579–1625 English playwright. Son of a bishop, he became associated with the King's Men (see LORD CHAMBERLAIN'S MEN). His famous collaboration with BEAUMONT provided the company with such outstanding successes as *Philaster* (c.1609), *The Maid's Tragedy* (c.1610) and *A King and No King* (1611). A 1647 edition of their work includes 34 plays and a MASQUE, and a 1679 revision adds a further 18. Fletcher's hand is present in most of these, but Beaumont's in only about ten. Fletcher may have collaborated with SHAKESPEARE on *Henry VIII*, *The Two Noble Kinsmen* and the lost *Cardenio* (all c.1613). MASSINGER became Fletcher's most frequent collaborator for the King's Men, e.g. in *Sir John van Olden Barnavelt* (1619), *The Custom of the Country* (c.1619), *The Beggars' Bush* (1622) and *The Spanish Curate* (c.1622). A happy combination of industry and facility allowed Fletcher to write or collaborate on at least four plays per year. He was the major influence on the post-Restoration comedy of intrigue. He nurtured a taste for romantic TRAGICOMEDY among the sophisticated audiences of the Jacobean private theatres. Among the plays which he may have written alone are *The Chances* (c.1617), *The Humorous Lieutenant* (c.1619), *The Wild-Goose Chase* (c.1621) and *Rule a Wife and Have a Wife* (1624).

**Floridor** [Josias de Soulas, sieur de Primefosse] c.1608–71 French actor-manager. A minor aristocrat who opted for the life of a strolling player, he led a company to London and later prospered at the MARAIS, notably in the plays of PIERRE CORNEILLE. He purchased BELLEROSE's position as director of the rival company at the HÔTEL DE BOURGOGNE in 1647. Of noble bearing, with a sonorous voice and an unforced delivery, he was most successful in roles calling for dignity and authority; some critics found him too cold, though he created the role of Nero in RACINE's *Britannicus* (1669).

**Flotats, Josep Maria** 1939– Spanish actor and director. Educated at a French institute in his native Barcelona, he played numerous roles in Paris at the THÉÂTRE NATIONAL POPULAIRE, the Théâtre de la Ville and the COMÉDIE-FRANÇAISE. Since 1985, when he assumed direction of the government-subsidized Poliorama, he has been a major figure in Catalan theatre. Serving as a bridge between Catalonia and France, he has brought to Barcelona both French theatre people and important texts. Among notable productions, directed by and starring Flotats, are ROSTAND's *Cyrano de Bergerac* (1985), Natalie Sarraute's *Per un sí o per un no* (*For the Least Little Thing*, 1986), Brian Clark's *Whose Life Is It Anyway?* (1987), MUSSET's *Lorenzaccio* (1988) and MOLIÈRE's *The Misanthrope* (1989). In 1991 he produced his first Catalan text, a dramatic monologue based on Josep Pla's narrative and written, acted and directed by Flotats.

**flyting** Stylized exchange of insults. It is a formalized debate, often in verse or formulaic prose; at its simplest, it appears as 'kidding' among friends. It is more obviously rule-bound among young American and West Indian blacks ('playing the dozens' or 'sounding'), and calls for considerable poetic skill among the Inuit, whose impromptu obscene verses are a favourite form of entertainment, and in Italy where contests in the satirical stanzas known as *contrasto a braccio* are sometimes organized enough to have a panel of judges. The pattern of the *contrasto*, in which each contestant takes on one role in an oppositional theme (wine versus water, atheist versus priest, and so on), is common in CARNIVAL plays, and influenced the dramatic work of JOHN HEYWOOD and Hans Sachs.

**Fo, Dario** 1926– Italian actor, director and playwright. A versatile MIME artist, improviser and satirist, he began his career as a writer and performer in comic sketches and political CABARET. In 1957 he and his wife, FRANCA RAME, formed a company using the techniques of popular street, fair and club theatre. The repertoire was crafted principally for bourgeois audiences: it was mocking, irreverent and anarchic, but essentially amiable.

In the mid- and later 1960s, Fo established a national reputation as a writer and performer of satirical pieces, increasingly critical of capitalism, imperialism and the scandals and abuses of Italian government. The political disturbances of 1968 caused him to abandon mainstream theatre. He and Rame formed a new company, Nuova Scena (New Stage), and under the auspices of the Communist Party toured factories, clubs and halls in search of working-class audiences. His search for a genuinely political theatre issued in some quasi-BRECHTian didactic pieces, the spectacular *Grande Pantomima* (*The Great Pantomime*, 1968), a satirical presentation of Italian politics since the fall of Fascism, and the highly original *Mistero Buffo* (1969), a unique one-man spectacle performed with great success in Italy and abroad.

Fo broke with the orthodox left, and in 1970 he and Franca Rame formed the theatre collective La Comune and turned their skills to the service of the New Left. The work of this group was more aggressively revolutionary, dramatizing topical political issues and seeking to expose the corruption, oppression and incompetence of bourgeois capitalist governments. Products of this new direction of Fo's work came in the later 70s and 80s to attract attention throughout Europe, notably plays like *Morte accidentale di un anarchico* (*Accidental Death of an Anarchist*, 1970), *Non si paga! Non si paga!* (*Can't Pay, Won't Pay*, 1974) and *Female Parts* (1981) written jointly with Franca Rame. More recent work has included *Il Papa e la Strega* (*The Pope and the Witch*, 1989) and *Johan Padan a la descoverta de la Americhe* (*Johan Padan and the Discovery of America*, 1992). Increasingly he has worked as a guest director abroad, e.g. of two MOLIÈRE farces at the COMÉDIE-FRANÇAISE (1992).

Fo is perhaps foremost a brilliant actor and exploiter of theatrical means for politico-satiric purposes. In the view of some critics his deep political commitment at times co-exists uneasily with theatrical needs, creating a gap between ideological content and dramatic form. But no one in the contemporary theatre has more effectively wedded comedy and savage political comment than Fo in pieces like *Mistero Buffo* and *Morte accidentale*.

**Folies-Bergère** Parisian MUSIC-HALL. Opening in 1869, it offered pantoMIME and operetta. Léon Sari, who managed it until 1885, indulged the prostitutes who haunted its promenade so that it became a fashionable resort of young men-about-town. Under various managements, during 1885–1918, it alternated singers like MAURICE CHEVALIER and YVETTE GUILBERT with specialty acts like LITTLE TICH and Loïe Fuller. Paul Derval, who took it over in 1918, endowed it with the style that made it world-famous: lavish *revues à grand spectacle* with cohorts of naked women, exotic tableaux, monumental staircases, and acres of sequins and ostrich plumes. The titles, always of 13 letters, had to include the word *folie*. This became the tourist trap *par excellence*. Since 1974, it has been managed by Hélène Martini.

**folk drama, European** 'Folklore' was not identified as an autonomous area of cultural activity until 1846, under the stimulus of romanticism, nationalism and rapid social change. The ensuing burst of collecting soon found its theoretical underpinning in cultural evolution, a bastard offspring of Darwin, which held that all societies pass through savagery and barbarism on their way to civilization. In the process, much is discarded, but some relics of earlier patterns live on into the modern world, particularly among the more conservative members of society, notably the peasantry (rightly or wrongly so called).

The interest of these 'survivals in culture', to the 19th-century intellectual, lay in the light they shed on the prehistory of a people; that they might have a meaning in the present, for the 'peasants' who cherished them, rarely occurred to anybody. Meaning was consigned to the past, usually so remote that no documentary source could be used to test the scholar's analysis. Folk drama, rather than being treated as an artistic genre, with its own development and conventions, was regarded as a corrupt and misunderstood RITUAL corpus. This idea of folk drama is still with us, not least among theatre historians, even though professional folklorists have abandoned it, along with the general theory of culture from which it derived.

Not all folk drama is ancient. There is graphic evidence of ANIMAL IMPERSONATION from prehistory, but lying above this ancient cultural stratum are others more recent. An important group of plays in Europe, and in Catholic Central America, celebrates major Christian feasts by the enactment of Bible stories; self-evidently, there is nothing pre-Christian about these. Though their age is unknown, they are analogous to and in some cases possibly derived from the scriptural drama of the late Middle Ages and Renaissance. They are not, however, cyclic, but concentrate rather on a specific event such as the arrival of the Magi or the adoration of the Shepherds.

Cognate with these scripturally based plays in the secular domain are the numerous performances which are related to popular or, more rarely, elite literature. The English HERO-COMBAT PLAY (often called the mummers' play) owes something textually to Richard Johnson's The Seven Champions of Christendom, which went through at least 26 editions between 1596 and 1770; the Swiss Tellspiel (William Tell play) derives from ballad and literary sources of the 15th and 16th centuries; the Wandering Jew Ahasuerus wanders off the pages of the bibliothèque bleue into a Liège PASSION PLAY for puppets; and the so-called pastorales of the Basque country draw on a variety of hagiographical and romance sources for their content. Even CONGREVE'S Love for Love lends a few lines to the admittedly unusual text of the Ampleforth sword dance: the contribution is a useful indication of folk drama's tolerant exploitation of the most unlikely-looking material.

If the 'folk' element in folk drama is problematic, the 'drama' element is no less so. Everyone would agree, in principle, that it cannot be conceptualized according to an Aristotelian thesis of plot construction (see ARISTOTLE), or to the literary theatre's preoccupation with character and motive. Even in the elite theatre, the presence or absence of a text is not easy to use as a criterion of 'drama', and in folk theatre we are faced with the question of what a text is. Some folk actors may not use language at all, or speech may be optional: processional characters in CARNIVAL, the New Year Dziady (vagabonds) of Poland, the Slovenian Kurenti with their animal-skin coats, long-nosed masks, and feathered head-dresses. But they may vocalize: grunts, snorts, roars, gibberish. Is this a 'text', and, if not, what is it? In any case, their behaviour, though apparently idiosyncratic to the point of anarchy, is neither unplanned nor incoherent. It has its own set of performance conventions, founded on the principle of reversing everyday behaviour. Other maskers engage in an improvised dialogue with their audience. Such dialogues, though improvised, follow entirely predictable lines, and occur within a recognized pattern of symbolic behaviour.

Because folk traditions are so protean, it makes sense to think in terms of a continuum of performance behaviour, rather than of clear demarcations. Structurally, folk drama lies between two poles. One is the silent or non-verbal performance by masked actors, often constantly on the move, frightening the children, grabbing girls, making mischief. The other is the virtually Aristotelian narrative of the subliterary Tellspiel, which

covers the fundamental elements of the legend. Between them lie a multitude of forms, with more or less emphasis on text or narrative development. Traditional farces, such as the Tirolean carnival-play Altweibermühle (The Mill for Old Women) or the Russian PAKHOMUSHKA, by definition develop character relationships within a plot, though often as much through the playing of variants on the same theme as through a steady and integrated forward movement.

Folk theatre is an open-space form: the normal performance environment is a street, square, public house or domestic interior, unaltered but for the presence of costumed actors. The relationship between performer and audience follows from this. When we go into somebody's house, we do not ignore the occupants; in the street or the public house, if we merely talk amongst ourselves, politeness dictates that others ignore us. Folk actors have the same way of dealing with both constraints – namely, direct address: even those performances which rely exclusively on dialogue, as many FLYTINGS do, are so formal in their construction and language as to invite a declamatory style which expressly includes the audience. Intimacy between characters is foreign to folk drama; interestingly, in the 20th century, when some traditions have been influenced in their content by film and television, the fourth wall seems to have had no effect. Characterization is, without exception, stereotypical: culture heroes and villains (including scriptural and hagiographical ones), allegorical figures, foolish old men and ugly old women, quack doctors, soldiers, schoolmasters, vagabonds. COSTUME and hand props either immediately represent these stereotypes, or are totally abstract. Finally, language and movement rarely pretend to realism. Rhymed verse, or a mixture of verse and prose, is typical, often interspersed with or framed by song. Movement is stylized, even ideographic (a fight may take the form of a metrical clashing of swords, a character decapitated may simply bow his or her head), and may become heightened into dance. Much of this also applies to performances by PUPPETS, such as PUNCH or the Turkish KARAGÖZ, which points to a high degree of stylization.

If the style of folk drama is strikingly consistent, its content is not, and the analysis of it requires close attention to particular traditions. No more than a few introductory generalizations can be advanced here.

The first, and possibly the most fundamental, is that folk drama is frequently seasonal in its performance: that is, it is one item in a festive calendar, whether liturgical (Christmas) or secular (New Year), or by reference to the pastoral or agricultural year (Anatolian shepherds perform their plays during the pregnancy of their ewes).

The idea of continuity through change is central – obviously so in the religious plays which, through the re-enactment of, say, the Nativity, make concrete the community's commitment to a particular version of human history and its meaning. Small wonder that the shepherds have been so popular. The opportunities they offer for a certain level of realism in dialect speech and local costume, together with their representation of the poor and lowly, underscore the relationship between God and ordinary people. In plays on secular themes may be seen a similar use of the past to validate the present, or particular values in relation to the present which are not necessarily those of the ruling class. The many plays about outlaws – ROBIN HOOD, the

Catalan Joán de Serrallonga, the Mexican Agustín Lorenzo – invariably show the hero as just, magnanimous and brave, thereby implying a critique of a law that makes such men criminals.

The zoomorphic figure, where it occurs, is a central metaphor. It invariably has both human and animal attributes, an ambiguity which gives it special potency in a play of taxonomy. In the Anatolian plays the speaking characters are accompanied by non-speaking animal maskers. They represent both domestic animals such as the camel, and wild animals such as the hare and fox, echoing at an ecological level of imagery the outsider–insider dialectic which the text represents at a social and racial level.

The close relationship between folk drama and its community is there in the seasonal context, in the value-laden texts, in the informal socializing that invariably accompanies them, in their strong sense of reciprocity among friends and neighbours. Theirs is an art in which text and context merge.

**Folksbiene** (People's Stage) Yiddish-American theatre group. An amalgam of several New York amateur companies, it was formed in 1915, using professional directors of the stature of JOSEPH BULOFF, Benno Schneider, DAVID HERMAN, Jacob Rotbaum, NAHUM ZEMACH and JACOB BEN-AMI. Dedicated to the highest ideals of play selection, acting and production, the Folksbiene presented at least one Yiddish play per winter season, achieving the reputation of a genuine folk theatre and serving as an inspiration to the professional YIDDISH THEATRE. In recent years it has also presented lighter entertainments, such as Yiddish translations of popular Israeli comedies.

**Folkteatern i Göteborg** The Göteborg's People's Theatre (founded in 1954) is a corporation whose members are organizations and individuals associated with the Swedish Labour movement. This is reflected in its repertoire of new Swedish plays, many by working-class writers or about local Labour concerns and history, and its ancillary services: the provision of inexpensive editions of new scripts, outreach theatre and educational programmes.

**Fonda [Jaynes], Henry** 1905–82 American actor. Fonda made his first stage appearance in 1925 at the Omaha Community Playhouse, and his BROADWAY debut in 1929. He established himself as a leading actor in *The Farmer Takes a Wife* (1934), before turning almost exclusively to making films. After World War II he played the title role in *Mister Roberts* (1948). Working in both Hollywood and New York, he won critical acclaim on Broadway in 1954 with his portrayal of Barney Greenwald in *The Caine Mutiny Court Martial*. He starred with ANNE BANCROFT in *Two for the Seesaw* (1958), and with Barbara Bel Geddes in *Silent Night, Lonely Night* (1959). Other important stage appearances include the comedy hit, *Generation*, in 1965, and the one-man show, *Clarence Darrow*, in 1974. Fonda's screen image as the quiet, unassuming man of integrity and strength dominated his appearances on stage.

**Fontanne, Lynn** see LUNT, ALFRED

**Fonvizin, Denis (Ivanovich)** 1745–92 Russian playwright. The creator of Russian national comedy, he linked SUMAROKOV's neoclassicism and the satirical, social realism of GOGOL, OSTROVSKY, SALTYKOV-SHCHEDRIN and CHEKHOV. He was a fierce moralist: his favourite targets were the egoism and Gallomania of the provincial gentry, the institution of serfdom and especially the harmfulness and abuses of foreign education (the 'tutors' in his plays are French coachmen and manicurists). Fonvizin's verse comedy *Korion* (1764) blended Russian character and linguistic traits with themes and conventions of European sentimental comedy. In his major neoclassical comedies, *The Brigadier* (written 1769, produced 1780) and *The Minor* (1782), he created such staples of the Russian actor's repertoire as Starodum ('Old Sense'), the brigadier (whose rank has been laughable ever since) and his wife. His remaining plays include *Alzire, or The Americans* (1762, adapted from VOLTAIRE's verse tragedy), *A Friend of Honest People, or Starodum* (1788) and *The Choice of a Tutor* (1790).

**Foote, Samuel** 1721–77 English actor, playwright and manager. In 1747 he published two pamphlets on acting and dramatic theory, *A Treatise on the Passions* and *The Roman and English Comedy Considered*. *The Diversions of the Morning* was a satirical REVUE, staged as a noon matinée with a tea invitation to evade the Licensing Act. *The Auction of Pictures* was a similar brief success. Almost all his plays contained satiric portraits of living people. Foote tried fortune-telling, puppet-plays, acting and theatre management. In 1760, with his SATIRE on Methodists, *The Minor*, he was at last a success in London. In 1767 he bought and remodelled the HAYMARKET, where he was a successful manager. His satire on doctors, *The Devil upon Two Sticks* (1768), exploited his own leg amputation. *The Nabob* (1722) attacked the East India Company. He was nicknamed the English ARISTOPHANES for his recurrent concern with personal satire.

**Foottit, George** [Tudor Hall] 1864–1921 and **Chocolat** [Raphaël Padilla] 1868–1917 French CLOWN act. Foottit, an Englishman trained in PANTOMIME and travelling shows, had already made a name for himself in Paris as a combination of the GRIMALDI clown and the pattering French Jocrisse when, in 1886, he teamed up with the black Cuban Chocolat at the Cirque Médrano. For 15 years, they delighted audiences with routines displaying Chocolat as 'he who gets slapped' and Foottit as his arrogant oppressor. They played the Nouveau Cirque and the Hippodrome, and in the REVUE *En selle pour la revue* (1888). After they retired, their sons carried on the tradition.

**Forbes-Robertson, Johnston** 1853–1937 British actor. He became SAMUEL PHELPS's pupil and credited the old actor with the training of his voice, one of the most praised in the English theatre. IRVING asked him to join the LYCEUM company although his new recruit was a classical actor, not, like Irving, an idiosyncratic romantic. Irving had made a virtue of his physical awkwardness. Forbes-Robertson was graceful and elegant. He played Romeo to MRS PATRICK CAMPBELL's Juliet (1895) and became the Hamlet (1897) of his generation, the role remaining in his repertoire throughout his career: grave and decorous, he displayed a feeling intelligence. SHAW cajoled him into opening *Caesar and Cleopatra* during an American tour (1906). Forbes-Robertson's last famous creation was the Stranger in JEROME K. JEROME's *The Passing of the Third Floor Back* (1908). He was knighted in 1913.

**Ford, John** c.1586–1640 English playwright. He probably wrote the subplot of *The Witch of Edmonton* (1621) and again collaborated with DEKKER on *The Welsh Ambassador* (1623) and *The Sun's Darling* (1624). Ford's subsequent fame rests on three plays. *Perkin Warbeck* (published 1634), in which the characterization of the feckless hero is a particular achievement; *The Broken Heart* (c.1629) and *'Tis Pity She's a Whore* (c.1631), two tragedies which display an interest in morbid psychology and emotional excess. The second, dealing compassionately with incestuous love, is the most acclaimed of Caroline plays. Three comedies survive, including *The Lover's Melancholy* (1628), and a tragedy, *Love's Sacrifice* (c.1632), most famous for the villainous D'Avalos.

**Ford, John T.** 1829–94 American manager. In 1855–6 he leased theatres in Richmond, Baltimore, and Washington, DC. He built Ford's Theatre in Washington in 1861, the location of the assassination of President Abraham Lincoln by JOHN WILKES BOOTH on 14 April 1865, as a result of which the theatre was closed. In the 1880s Ford became the major producer of combination companies (see STOCK COMPANY) for the entire south.

**Foreman, Richard** 1937– American director. Foreman began the Ontological-Hysteric Theatre in New York in 1968 and until 1979 that was the main outlet for his own avant-garde works. Until roughly 1975 he was concerned with 'putting [an object] on stage and finding different ways of looking at it'. In plays like *Total Recall* (1970) he used untrained performers; dialogue was disjointed, often recorded, and spoken without inflection; furniture and props were suspended from the ceiling. Later plays like *Pandering to the Masses* (1975), *Le Livre de splendeurs* (Paris, 1976), *Penguin Touquet* (1981), *Egyptology* (1983) and *Film Is Evil: Radio Is Good* (1987) display a rapid parade of images, seeking to disrupt the audience's logical thought processes. Foreman has also directed plays by BÜCHNER, VÁCLAV HAVEL, GERTRUDE STEIN and MOLIÈRE. In 1991 he took over St Mark's Church in New York City to showcase his and others' work.

**Fornés, Maria Irene** 1930– Cuban-born American playwright and director. She exemplifies the concerns and style of OFF-BROADWAY theatre. Although her plays and musicals deal with serious individual, national and global problems – *Tango Palace* (1964), *Promenade* (1965), *The Successful Life of Three* (1965), *Dr Kheal* (1968), *The Danube* (1984), *The Conduct of Life* (1985) – they are most acclaimed for their whimsical humour and the use of innovative, cinematic techniques. Fornés's greatest critical success, *Fefu and Her Friends* (1977), is a feminist perspective on female friendship and women's roles in patriarchal society. Other recent plays include *Lovers and Keepers* (1986) and *And What of the Night* (1989). She has directed classic European works and Latin American plays as well as her own.

**Forrest, Edwin** 1806–72 American actor. The first native-born star, he came to dominate the mid-19th-century American stage as Othello, Lear, Richard III, Coriolanus, Hamlet, Macbeth, Shylock and Richelieu, and in his repertoire of American plays such as JOHN AUGUSTUS STONE's *Metamora*, a winner of one of Forrest's playwriting contests (1829–47). His power derived from his commanding physique (although only 5ft 10in in height), his penetrating voice and his strenuous realism in portraying his characters' driving passions. A super-patriot, Forrest was a colourful figure off-stage and on. He appeared in London in 1836 and again in 1845 when he challenged MACREADY, a rivalry that precipitated the disastrous ASTOR PLACE OPERA HOUSE riot (1849) in which 31 people were killed.

**Forssell, Lars** 1929– Swedish playwright and poet; a member of the Swedish Academy since 1971. His plays frequently reflect his interest in socially committed CABARET and popular song. Many explore the modern dilemma of disengagement, often suggested through historical parable, as in *The Coronation* (1956), *The Madcap* (1964) and *Pirates* (1982). While his early works, such as *Mary Lou* (1962) and *The Sunday Walk* (1963), emphasize the anti-hero's cowardice, plays such as *At the Sign of the Hare and the Hawk* (1978) and *The Power and the Honesty* (1984) concern characters who overcome both their own insecurities and manipulation by society.

**Forte, Dieter** 1935– Swiss playwright. Forte writes in German. His success was established by *Martin Luther and Thomas Münzer, or the Introduction of Accountancy* in 1970. Uniting documentary with polemic farce, this deals with the relationship between finance and revolution to challenge accepted views of history, a line continued in *Jean-Henri Dunant, or the Introduction of Civilization* (1975). His irreverently iconoclastic work has systematically covered the major factors conditioning established views of Western society: he dealt with Hitler and the psychology of mass murder in *The Labyrinth of Dreams, or the Separation of the Head from the Body* (1982).

**Fortune Theatre** (London) Built in 1600 in the Liberty of Finsbury, the Fortune was intended to replace the ROSE as the home of the ADMIRAL'S MEN and rival to the GLOBE. The surviving building contract makes it clear that HENSLOWE wished to copy the Globe. But the Fortune was designed as an 80ft square (not a higher polygonal) building. There were three tiers for spectators, and a stage 43ft wide and 22–23ft deep. It was rebuilt after destruction by fire in 1621. The second Fortune was probably polygonal and was built of brick. It was demolished in 1661, but its reputation had sunk long before. The modern Fortune (1924) is near Covent Garden.

**Fosse, Bob** 1927–87 American choreographer and director. After a career as a dancer, Fosse's first choreography, created for *The Pajama Game* (1954), was influenced by JACK COLE's style of jazz dancing; it was followed by *Damn Yankees* (1955) and *New Girl in Town* (1957). With *Redhead* (1959) Fosse began to direct as well as choreograph. In the 1960s he staged a number of successful musicals, including *Sweet Charity* (1966). During the 1970s he created three unusual shows, closer in spirit to the concept musicals of SONDHEIM and PRINCE: *Pippin* (1972), *Chicago* (1975) and *Dancin'* (1978). His use of jerky, rhythmic steps and sinuous, slow-motion movement, often coupled with bowler hats and white gloves, became his choreographic trademark.

**Fox, George W(ashington) L(afayette)** 1825–77 American comedian. He was a comic actor at New York's National Theatre (1850–8), where his uproarious caricatures made him a favourite. He played Phineas Fletcher in *UNCLE TOM'S CABIN* and temporarily managed the Old BOWERY, the New Bowery and the FIFTH AVENUE, losing as lessee what he earned as a comic star. Between 1862 and 1867 he staged pantomimes at the Old Bowery, with himself as Clown and his brother Charles Kemble Fox as Pantaloon. Fox was reputed to be the funniest performer of his time; he contrived to raise American pantomime to a level of popularity it has never regained. He was more an expressive MIME artist than an acrobat. His antic drollery culminated in the immensely successful *Humpty Dumpty* (Olympic Theatre, 1868), which ran for more than 1,200 performances. He also made a hit in BURLESQUES of *Faust*, *Macbeth*, *Richelieu* and EDWIN BOOTH's *Hamlet*. In 1875 he was committed to an asylum.

**Foy, Eddie** 1856–1928 American comedian and singer. Foy brought his comic songs and acrobatic style of comedy to musicals produced at the Chicago Opera House – e.g. *Bluebeard, Jr* (1890). He was principal comedian in *The Strollers* (1901), and starred in a number of musicals including *The Wild Rose* (1902), *Mr Bluebeard* (1903), *Piff! Paff!! Pouf!!!* (1904), *The Earl and the Girl* (1905), *The Orchid* (1907), *Mr Hamlet of Broadway* (1908) and *Up and Down Broadway* (1910). Always a popular favourite in VAUDEVILLE, he spent most of his subsequent career on the VARIETY stage.

**Fragson [Fragmann], Harry [Leon Vince Philip Pott]** 1866–1913 Anglo-French MUSIC-HALL performer, the son of a Belgian brewer. His career in England met with scant success and he moved to Paris, where he became an instant hit in 1891. His English accent, chic wardrobe, eloquent gestures and self-accompaniment on the piano (a novelty at the time) won him great popularity. Returning to London in 1905, he assumed a French accent and mannerisms. In France, his repertory had been comic and sentimental; in England it was dominated by such patter songs as 'The Other Department, If You Please'. The singer of the *entente cordiale*, as he was billed, was shot by his deranged father, who coveted one of his female admirers.

**Franconi family** see CIRCUS

**Fratellini family** Italian circus performers. The Three Fratellini were a CLOWN act composed of brothers, sons of the acrobat **Gustavo** Fratellini (1842–1905). **Paul** (Paolo, 1877–1940) was the subtle comedian, dressed as a parody of bourgeois respectability. **François** (Francesco, 1879–1951) was the elegant white clown in his spangled costume, strumming the guitar and mandolin. **Albert** (Alberto, 1886–1961) played the patsy with his huge nose, fright wigs, and musical instruments that were prone to squirt water or burst into flames. The trio first formed in 1905 and settled in Paris at the Cirque Médrano and then the Cirque d'Hiver, periodically touring Europe and America. They were so successful that in 1922 they were invited to join the COMÉDIE-FRANÇAISE as affiliates. Their descendants carry on the tradition.

**Frayn, Michael** 1933– British playwright. Journalism and writing witty novels took precedence over theatre, until in 1970 he wrote four short plays which were presented together as *The Two of Us*. His true strengths were revealed in the mid-1970s when he wrote three comedies: *Alphabetical Order* (1975), about mayhem in a newspaper cuttings library; *Donkeys' Years* (1976), about university loves; and *Clouds* (1976), based on Frayn's experiences as a journalist on a visit to Cuba. In *Balmoral*, retitled *Liberty Hall* (1979), he is concerned with socialist-versus-capitalist perceptions, here satirizing a writers' collective established by the state at Balmoral Castle. He translated and adapted CHEKHOV's *The Cherry Orchard* and LEV TOLSTOI's *The Fruits of Enlightenment* for the NATIONAL THEATRE, but his greatest commercial success came with *Noises Off* in 1982, a backstage comedy about an appalling touring company. His most recent stage play *Look, Look* (1990) attempted to balance *Noises Off* with an equally jaundiced impression of audiences, but the public failed to appreciate the joke.

**Fréchette, Louis-Honoré** 1839–1908 French Canadian poet, essayist and playwright. He was the author of the most popular 19th-century Canadian play, *Félix Poutré* (1862), performed hundreds of times by amateur troupes well into the 20th century. The work draws heavily upon published memoirs of its titular hero, a participant in the 1837–8 Patriote Rebellion who feigns madness to escape the gallows – exacting delicious vengeance on stage against stereotyped representatives of British rule.

**Fredro, Aleksander** 1793–1876 Polish playwright. Between 1815 and 1835 he wrote over 20 comedies in octosyllabic rhymed couplets that have become a central part of the national repertory. Often set in pre-partition Poland, they depict the life of the landed gentry and feature lively plots and colourful, eccentric characters. Major works are *Ladies and Hussars* (1825), *Maiden Vows* (1833) and *Vengeance* (1834).

**Fregoli, Leopoldo** 1867–1936 Italian quick-change artist. In 1896 he created the Fin-de-Siècle Company to present his one-man shows; it travelled round the world with a staff of 23, 370 trunks and 800 costumes until his retirement in 1925. In the course of a three-hour performance Fregoli would perform a one-act play, taking all the roles; then present imitations of 60 well known MUSIC-HALL performers, singing, dancing, performing magic tricks, ventriloquy and hypnotism; and end by screening 10 films he had directed and starred in – the 'Fregoligraph'. Using stand-ins and dummies to effect illusions of his presence, he became synonymous with proteanism, and NIKOLAI EVREINOV used his name to baptize the mercurial hero of his play *The Chief Thing* (1921).

**Freie Bühne** (Free Stage) German theatre society. Stimulated in part by the foundation of the Théâtre Libre in Paris (see ANDRÉ ANTOINE), this Berlin society aimed to stage new plays that were not in the repertoires of the commercial and state-subsidized theatres. Under the direction of OTTO BRAHM, and with professional actors, the Freie Bühne staged IBSEN's *Ghosts* in September 1889 and the first performance of HAUPTMANN's *Before Dawn* in October 1889. Later productions included more plays by Hauptmann and works by, among others, TOLSTOI, STRINDBERG and ZOLA. The Freie Bühne was dissolved in 1894 when Otto Brahm was appointed director of the DEUTSCHES THEATER.

**French, David** 1939– Canadian playwright. Probably Canada's most produced playwright, he was born in Newfoundland, raised in Toronto and began his career as an actor and writer for television. *Leaving Home* (1972), his very successful first stage play, and *Of the Fields Lately* (1973), both produced at Toronto's TARRAGON THEATRE, explore archetypal family conflicts in the specific context of the Mercers, an 'immigrant' Newfoundland family in Toronto. French returned to the Mercers for a third work, *Salt-Water Moon* (1985); *1949* (1989) completes the tetralogy. His most widely produced and highly praised play, *Jitters* (1979), is a backstage COMEDY which offers an affectionate view of theatrical life as it is coloured by the specific problems and insecurities of producing theatre in Canada.

**Freytag, Gustav** 1816–95 German playwright, novelist and theorist. A writer of liberal sympathies, in his day Freytag was very widely read. His play *The Journalists* (1854), a genial comedy about the interrelationship of journalism and politics, was immensely popular and is still occasionally revived today. In his influential essay *The Technique of Drama* (1865) he constructed a famous model by which each play was described as being structured like a pyramid; in essence, this was a refinement of the theory of the WELL MADE PLAY.

**Friel, Brian** 1929– Irish playwright and short-story writer. Friel began by writing stories, mainly for the *New Yorker*, and radio plays for the BBC. His play *The Enemy Within* (ABBEY, 1962), was based on the exiles of St Columba. *Philadelphia, Here I Come!* brought his first wide recognition. It played at the 1964 DUBLIN INTERNATIONAL THEATRE FESTIVAL and on BROADWAY. For all the humour and devastating SATIRE of Irish cant, the tone of his work is elegiac, absorbed with memories, commemorating the solace of illusions that do not wholly deceive.

Since 1964 Friel has written the most impressive body of work in contemporary Irish drama. Its variety can be seen in *Lovers* (1967), *Crystal and Fox* (1968), *The Freedom of the City* (1973), *Aristocrats* (1979), *Faith Healer* (1979), *Translations* (1980), *The Communication Cord* (1982), an adaptation of TURGENEV's *Fathers and Sons* (1987), *Making History* (1988), the widely toured *Dancing at Lughnasa* (1990), a tender evocation of his own boyhood in the 1930s, *Wonderful Tennessee* (1993) and *Molly Sweeney* (1994). *Translations* describes the dissolution of the old Gaelic culture, reinforced by the naming into English of the Irish place names in the 1833 ordnance survey, and mirrored in the love between an Irish girl and an English soldier. All the Irish characters speak Irish and are assumed to be doing so on stage, whereas in fact they are speaking English – a richly effective illusion. While working with the essentially realist proscenium stage, in his plays Friel questions its conventions – for example, via Gar's double presence on stage in *Philadelphia* or the play-within-the-play in *Crystal*. Though his latest plays more fully deploy effects of music and dance, and even gesture towards regions of experience beyond language, words remain Friel's necessary medium.

In 1980 he founded the FIELD DAY THEATRE COMPANY in Londonderry. It has presented his own plays and, more recently, translations of MOLIÈRE and SOPHOCLES.

**fringe theatre** (UK) This movement, which began in the 1960s in Britain, corresponds to the OFF-OFF BROADWAY theatres in New York and to the 'free theatre' groups in Europe. Although London has a long tradition of adventurous little theatres, fringe theatre developed from the many small companies which gathered around the main festival offerings at the EDINBURGH FESTIVAL. The term came into use in the late 1950s, and the REVUE *Beyond the Fringe* was first seen in 1960 in Edinburgh before transferring to London and New York. In 1963 Jim Haynes, an American bookseller, started the TRAVERSE THEATRE Club in Edinburgh which became the unlikely centre for many small groups from America and Europe, including such companies as the LA MAMA troupe, GROTOWSKI's 13 Rows from Opole and, later, SZAJNA's Studio Theatre from Warsaw. The Traverse Theatre received state support and a new theatre in 1969, but Haynes was less successful in establishing his Arts Laboratory in London. Another American, CHARLES MAROWITZ, who with PETER BROOK ran the Theatre of Cruelty season at LAMDA's little theatre in 1964, opened his Open Space Theatre in London's Tottenham Court Road in 1968. By then, the fringe theatre movement had become a major force in British theatre, developing not just in Edinburgh and London but in studios around the country, sometimes attached to REPERTORY theatres but often just in back rooms of pubs or even converted garages.

Much fringe theatre has its origins in political protest movements, notably against the war in Vietnam. In the 1960s, the 'hippy' and 'flower power' movements, led by Julian Beck's LIVING THEATRE, were primarily American in origin, although they had many imitators in Britain. After 1968, and the May events in Paris, many young British writers, including DAVID HARE, HOWARD BRENTON and DAVID EDGAR, turned to fringe theatre companies to present left-wing AGIT-PROP plays. Not all fringe theatre, however, was political. In small theatre clubs, such as the Ambiance and the Almost Free, various kinds of experimentalism could be attempted which might otherwise have fallen foul of the censor, theatrical CENSORSHIP being abolished only in 1968. Improvisatory drama, environmental theatre, plays with strong sexual impact or sometimes violent spectacles were staged in clubs to avoid the restrictions of the law. Companies like the PEOPLE SHOW, which started in 1966, developed a powerful imagistic language of their own.

At first fringe theatres were unsubsidized, although by the early 1970s many had started to receive small subsidies. The financial crisis in 1973–4 caused many companies to close, while the better-established fringe theatres survived. Of these, the BUSH THEATRE and the King's Head, Islington, London, became 'new plays' theatres, encouraging unknown writers. The touring fringe companies which survived included the left-wing 7:84 and Red Ladder Companies, while Shared Experience (founded in 1975), under its director Mike Alfreds, turned the limitations of non-theatrical halls to their advantage, establishing a remarkable rapport with their audiences. The daring adventurousness of fringe theatres, the secret of their attraction in the 1960s, became less wild in the late 1970s, although the standards of production undoubtedly rose. It ceased to be polite to describe them as 'fringe', for most companies preferred the word 'alternative'. They regarded themselves as being different from mainstream theatre, but not on its edges.

This status was a sociopolitical distinction at first, claiming for the fringe its place among the avant-garde and politically radical movements, the cutting edge of modernism; but during the 1980s, shifts of political mood and outlook affected all fringe theatres. The ARTS COUNCIL became more selective in its choice of companies to support, leading to inevitable accusations of censorship by subsidy. The fringe theatres became more specialized, some concentrating on performance art, some on new plays, some (like London's Gate Theatre, Notting Hill) on plays from Europe, some on Asian or West Indian drama and some on alternative comedy.

Alternative comedy was one area where the fringe changed the course of mainstream drama, as *Beyond the Fringe* had done for the previous generation. Another lay in the field of low-cost classical touring companies, such as CHEEK BY JOWL, THÉÂTRE DE COMPLICITÉ and Shared Experience, which were supported almost as much by the British Council for their overseas visits as by the Arts Council. Their leading directors, such as Declan Donnellan, and actors, such as Kathryn Hunter, were drawn into the national companies in the early 1990s and became the state official 'alternative'.

Among the many companies established to reflect particular cultural interests, four stand out. TARA ARTS, founded in 1977, became the first professional Asian company in Britain and managed to blend Asian and Western theatrical traditions. The Black Theatre Cooperative, founded in 1982, emerged through the several Afro-Caribbean companies of the 1970s, among them Temba and the Dark and Light Theatre Club. Its pioneers were the dramatist MUSTAPHA MATURA and the director Charlie Hanson; and it was responsible for the promotion of plays by Jacqueline Rudet, Edgar White and Farrukh Dhondy.

Among the several feminist groups (see FEMINIST THEATRE (BRITAIN)), Monstrous Regiment and the Women's Theatre Group were outstanding; but the move towards establishing a theatre devoted to women's drama and performance was lead by the Woman's Playhouse Trust. The most remarkable alternative theatre company must be Graeae, a professional group formed of disabled performers in 1980 by Nabil Shaban and Richard Tomlinson, which has staged plays (by such writers as Noel Greig) that stressed the problems of isolation rather than physical handicap.

Unlike the earlier fringe theatres such as the Bush, which have their own theatres, these companies were designed to tour the arts centres and similar venues which sprang up during the 1980s, such as London's Battersea Arts Centre and Watermans and the Almeida Theatre in Islington. Most operated on a shoe-string, although by now some fringe theatres, including the Bush and HAMPSTEAD THEATRE, were generously subsidized.

**Frisch, Max** 1911–91 Swiss playwright, novelist and essayist. He worked as an architect until 1954, but his first play dates from 1945: *Santa Cruz* (staged in 1946). His second play, *Now They Are Singing Again* (1945), was the first to be seen: it deals with the problem of individual guilt in war, the dichotomy of spirit and power. *The Great Wall of China* (1946) shows the contemporary (Swiss) intellectual coming face to face with totalitarianism in the wake of Hiroshima and Nagasaki. *When the War Was Over* (1949) and *Count Oderland* (1951) are two transitional plays. *Don Juan, or The Love of Geometry* (1953) is an ironic comment on the mythical character treated as an anti-hero. Frisch's two most important and successful plays are harsh and uncompromising indictments of the Swiss mentality and of Swiss blindness to the world outside. *The Fire Raisers* (*Biedermann und die Brandstifter*, 1958), a BRECHTian parable, brought him international recognition. *Andorra* (1961), his most contentious play, concerns the growth of antisemitism in a small, peace-loving country. *Philipp Hotz's Fury* (1958), *Biography* (1968) and *Triptych* (1979) continue, in their various styles, the charting of the clash between the individual and society. Frisch received many literary prizes and academic awards in Switzerland, Germany, Israel and the USA.

**Frohman, Charles** 1860–1915 American producer and manager. Frohman's first major production was BRONSON HOWARD's *Shenandoah* (1889). In 1893 he formed the EMPIRE THEATRE Stock Company (see STOCK COMPANY) with John Drew as his leading actor and began to develop and exploit the 'star and combination' system, sending star actors, with a supporting cast, on national tours after opening in a Frohman theatre in New York. Frohman successfully employed similar methods in London, principally at the Duke of York Theatre after 1898. Actors who benefited from his patronage include MAUDE ADAMS, WILLIAM GILLETTE, ARNOLD DALY, Ethel Barrymore and John Drew (see DREW–BARRYMORE FAMILY), Margaret Anglin, JULIA MARLOWE and OTIS SKINNER. In 1896 he joined with four others to organize a monopoly known as the THEATRICAL SYNDICATE, giving him significant influence over the commercial theatre. After 1896 he regularly produced over a dozen shows a year. Frohman died with the sinking of the *Lusitania* in 1915.

**Frohman, Daniel** 1851–1940 American manager. With his brothers, CHARLES and Gustave, Frohman first came to prominence as business manager in 1880 with STEELE MACKAYE's organization at the MADISON SQUARE THEATRE, where he developed the system of 'auxiliary road companies' which toured the country while the original production was playing in New York. He was producer-manager of the old and new LYCEUM THEATRES (1887–1909), enlisting the talents of a fine acting company from which E. H. SOTHERN's career was launched. Frohman presented a fashionable repertory from contemporary authors including CLYDE FITCH, J. M. BARRIE, PINERO, HENRY ARTHUR JONES, WILDE and SARDOU. From 1899 he was manager of DALY's THEATRE for four years.

**frontier theatre** (USA) Theatre in America began in the early settlements on the eastern seaboard, the frontier of the New World. After Philadelphia, New York and Boston became theatrical centres, troupes of actors advanced into the western regions. The first theatre opened in Williamsburg (Virginia) in 1718, the second, the Dock Street in Charleston (South Carolina), in 1736, and when the LEWIS HALLAM company arrived from London in 1752 they performed in a new Williamsburg theatre. The Hallams and other troupes found makeshift halls in such settlements as Annapolis, Norfolk, Newport and Providence, and set the pattern for the western trek that followed. These companies began their journey from Albany or Philadelphia to Pittsburgh and thence by flat boat down the Ohio River to Cincinnati and Louisville, and, as the frontier expanded, down the Mississippi to St Louis, Memphis, Nashville, Montgomery, Mobile and New Orleans.

SAMUEL DRAKE's company arrived in Kentucky in 1815. Two of its actors, NOAH LUDLOW and SOL SMITH, became the leading managers on the frontier, first as competitors and then as partners. Cramped and improvised quarters were common. JAMES H. CALDWELL was the first to provide adequate facilities with his three New Orleans theatres: one of them, the ST CHARLES, seated 4,000 in a pit and had four tiers of boxes. Theatres appeared as soon as a community was settled. In the early 1850s there were a dozen theatre and MUSIC-HALLS in San Francisco. The Mormons, always theatre enthusiasts, built the elegant Salt Lake Theatre in1861, shortly after they settled in Utah.

The provincial companies who opened the frontier were quickly followed by the star players from New York and Philadelphia: JUNIUS BRUTUS BOOTH, EDWIN FORREST, W.C. MACREADY, EDWIN BOOTH, ANNA CORA MOWATT and the rest. They ranged over a wide repertoire: SHAKESPEARE, other standard British plays, the American plays of DUNLAP, JOHN HOWARD PAYNE, Mowatt and Bird, and, most frequently, the latest sentimental and spectacular MELODRAMAS.

Frontier theatres were not all land-based. SHOWBOATS on the Ohio and Mississippi began with Ludlow's 'Noah's Ark' (1817) and continued into the 20th century.

**Fry, Christopher** 1907– British playwright. His charming and witty verse plays of the 1940s and 1950s – *A Phoenix Too Frequent* (1946), *The Lady's Not for Burning* (1948), *Venus Observed* (1950) and *The Dark Is Light Enough* (1954) – were gentle successes that touched upon real concerns via unreal situations. Fry's view of mankind is marked by a tolerant Christianity that, along with their verse form, has sometimes made his plays unfashionable. His translations of ANOUILH's *L'Invitation au château* (*Ring Round the Moon*, 1950) and *L'Alouette* (*The Lark*, 1955) and of plays by GIRAUDOUX, IBSEN and ROSTAND supplied more substantial plots for his skill with words.

**Fuchs, Georg** 1868–1949 German director. Influenced by JOCZA SAVITS's experiments with the Shakespeare stage in the Munich Court Theatre, in 1908 Fuchs founded the Munich Artists' Theatre. This had a relief stage, on which no attempt was made to create a realistic illusion. Fuchs's ambitions for the theatre are to be found in his most frequently read book, *Revolution in the Theatre*.

**Fugard, Athol** 1932– South African playwright. Fugard was born of an Afrikaans mother and an English father; his plays are written in English but incorporate many regional dialects and vernacular slang. 'The family plays', including *The Blood Knot* (1961), *Hello and Goodbye* (1965) and *Boesman and Lena* (1969), show the effects of South Africa's laws and social attitudes on working-class people of different races. Later he worked through improvisation with actors to create 'the workshop plays', like *Sizwe Bansi Is Dead* (1972). *Master Harold ... and the Boys* (1982) and *The Road to Mecca* (1984) were written alone. Castigated by some for being a white liberal out of touch with the realities of black suffering and resistance, Fugard maintains that he is simply a 'regional' writer and that his concern is with individual loneliness and pain in specific situations, politics being merely the background. But his plays successfully revealed the effects of the former political system of South Africa upon its diverse peoples. *My Children! My Africa!* (1989) forcefully dramatizes the political implications of a rapidly changing apartheid society. *Playland* (1992) depicts characters searching for communication in the light of a history that has bruised every South African.

**Fulda, Ludwig** 1862–1939 German playwright. As a young man, Fulda was closely associated with the naturalist movement (see NATURALISM). His later plays were in verse.

**Fuller, Charles** 1939– African-American playwright. When *A Soldier's Play* (1981), dealing with the murder of an unpopular black army sergeant, received the Pulitzer Prize, Fuller was only the second black playwright to be so honoured. He had several plays produced OFF-BROADWAY, notably by the NEGRO ENSEMBLE COMPANY: *In the Deepest Part of Sleep* (1974), *The Brownsville Raid* (1976), *Zooman and the Sign* (1980), *A Soldier's Play*, *Sally* and *Prince* (1988–9). More recently he has worked on a series of six plays about the post-Civil War quest for black self-determination.

**Fuller, Isaac** 1606–72 English scene-painter. Fuller contracted with the King's Company in 1669 to paint 'a new scene of Elysium' for their production of DRYDEN's *Tyrannic Love*. He took longer than predicted, and was sued for £500 for the delay; he claimed he worked non-stop on it for three weeks and was awarded £325 10s as payment. The case demonstrates the colossal expenditure on sets for the Restoration stage.

**Funambules, Théâtre des** (Paris) As the name indicates, this theatre was licensed only for rope dancing and acrobatics when it opened in the Boulevard du Temple in 1813. Two years later it was allowed to stage harlequinades, provided that no word was spoken.

Topical FARCES and pantomimes were staged later. The young and unknown FRÉDÉRICK LEMAÎTRE appeared there, as did MADAME SAQUI the rope dancer. JEAN-GASPARD DEBURAU joined around 1820, and soon his pale-faced PIERROT was attracting huge crowds. After the 1830 Revolution, the manager Nicolas Michel Bertrand was enabled to add *vaudevilles* to his bill and rapidly became a millionaire. The 500-seat theatre boasted a well trapped stage that could accomplish instantaneous scene changes; since there were no intervals (the proletarian public got too restless), an average of 15 changes took place in two hours. The theatre was demolished in 1860, by which time it had had become legendary as a temple of fantasy for the Parisian populace.

**Furttenbach, Josef** 1591–1667 German architect and scene designer. In Italy he absorbed the ideas of GIULIO PARIGI and took them back to Germany. In 1631 he became municipal architect at Ulm and ten years later he designed and completed the city's Theater am Benderhof, which was used primarily for school performances. His designs are noted for their reliance upon a central vanishing point, *periaktoi*, a rear pit for the housing of special effects, and pictorial bow-shaped framing devices. He published several works on Italian architecture: *Civil Architecture* (1628); *Recreational Architecture* (1640) which illustrates *periaktoi*, cloud borders, flying machines, and the chariot-and-pole mechanism for shifting scenery; and *The Noble Mirror of Art* (1663).

**futurism** Artistic movement, founded by F. T. MARINETTI in 1909. The ideas and strategies of the futurists were rapidly diffused through manifestos, journals, exhibitions and the so-called 'futurist evenings'. The movement falls roughly into two phases, the first and most vigorous dating from Marinetti's 'The Founding and Manifesto of Futurism', published in the Paris *Figaro* of 20 February 1909, through to the early 1920s; the second during the Fascist period when it was little more than nominally avant-garde. Asserting an aesthetic of the 'new', and calling for an art attuned to the century of science and technology, futurism exalted what it claimed to be the essential characteristics of 'modernism': speed, movement, dynamism and spontaneity. It rejoiced in the machine, particularly in the motor car, aeroplane, speed boat and motor-cycle, and demanded a machine-age art. To achieve this it ruthlessly jettisoned the past, denouncing most artistic traditions and the conformism and academicism of museums, art galleries, concert halls and the regular theatre.

A distinct advance came with the synthesis proposed in *Il teatro sintetico futurista* (*The Synthetic Theatre*, 1915). Syntheses were highly compressed dramatic pieces, intended to be demonstrations of that dynamic, autonomous, alogical, anti-psychological, abstract theatre that the futurists advocated. The movement produced about 500 such syntheses, the best of which are more than mere musical GAGS and pat CABARET sketches, and anticipate certain themes and motives developed later by surrealist and absurdist theatre (see SURREALISM; THEATRE OF THE ABSURD) and by dramatists like PIRANDELLO and BECKETT. Futurism also inspired some notable scenic design work, major figures in this field including the sculptor Giacomo Balla, the designer Fortunato Depero and the painter – and one of the leading theorists of the movement – ENRICO PRAMPOLINI. Futurist staging sought a dynamic use of chromatic effects in which the role of the human was either absent altogether or relegated to a robot-like function. An impressive example of futurist scenic design is that of Balla for Stravinsky's *Feu d' artifice* (1917), but most futurist scenic projects were never realized on the stage.

**Fuzelier, Louis** 1672–1752 French playwright and librettist. He was the author of almost 200 comedies, comic operas, *vaudevilles* and *ballet-pantomimes*, many of them parodies of existing works, for performance by the COMÉDIE-ITALIENNE or the Paris fair theatres. Since an injunction outlawed spoken dialogue, the text was either sung or delivered in monologues, or written on placards suspended from the flies, to which the actors mimed and the orchestra supplied a musical accompaniment. Fuzelier frequently collaborated with other playwrights, e.g. LESAGE, and composers.

# G

**Gabrielli family** Italian actors. **Giovanni** (died between 1603 and 1611), under the name Sivello, excelled at solo pantomimes in which he presented a whole troupe of characters. His son **Francesco** (?1588-?1636), who amplified the ZANNI Scapino, toured Italy and France from 1612, mostly with the ACCESI and CONFIDENTI, though he was with the FEDELI under GIOVAN BATTISTA ANDREINI in Paris during 1624-5. Accomplished at a dozen instruments, he was noted for virtuoso musical numbers. His daughter **Giulia** was seen in Paris under the name Diana in 1645.

**gag** Theatrical term. Originally it referred to the words interpolated by an actor into his part. The term derived from 'gag' as something forced into the mouth and was current theatrical slang in the 1840s. DICKENS uses it in *Bleak House* (1852). It came to mean a comic improvisation, and then, in silent film, a surprising or unmotivated wrinkle in the plot, often an elaborately structured piece of physical comedy. Now it is used to designate any joke or creative inspiration ('What's the gag?').

**Gaiety Theatre** (London) Opening in 1868, it established a reputation for BURLESQUE, comic opera – with the first collaboration of GILBERT and Sullivan, *Thespis* (1871) – and then MUSICAL COMEDY. Its initial popularity was partly due to a famous 'quartette' of comedians – NELLIE FARREN, EDWARD ROYCE, Edward Terry and Kate Vaughan – then during the 1890s to the 'Gaiety Girls'. These were initially introduced in a PARODY form as part of *Ruy Blas; or, The Blasé Roué* (1889), a burlesque, but the name came to refer to the musical chorus line of the 1890s, who were selected as much for their legs and looks as their singing and dancing ability. Among the later stars who made their name at the Gaiety the best-known were Gertie Millar and Leslie Henson. The theatre was closed in 1939 and demolished in 1957.

**Gaiety Theatre** (Manchester, UK) Built in 1884, the theatre achieved fame with the establishment there in 1908 of ANNIE HORNIMAN's repertory company, marking the beginning of the British REPERTORY movement. The first full season set the pattern for the next six years, offering plays by (among others) EURIPIDES, SHAW and GALSWORTHY and some one-act plays by Lancashire writers Allan Monkhouse, STANLEY HOUGHTON and HAROLD BRIGHOUSE – the core of what was later to be known as the 'Manchester school'. The Gaiety under the artistic direction of BEN IDEN PAYNE and then LEWIS CASSON soon built a reputation for its ensemble playing and its fostering of new writing. During wartime the theatre's quality of output and its audiences declined, until in 1917 the company was disbanded. The theatre was finally demolished in 1952.

**Gala, Antonio** 1936- Spanish playwright, novelist and poet. He enjoys celebrity status for his television series and newspaper columns. His reputation as a major dramatist dates from the triumphant premiere of his first play, *Los verdes campos del Edén* (*The Green Fields of Eden*, 1963). *Los buenos días perdidos* (*The Bells of Orleans*, 1972), a SATIRE of contemporary materialism, and *Anillos para una dama* (*Rings for a Lady*, 1973), a feminist debunking of the Cid myth from the perspective of his widow Jimena, introduced a series of critical and box-office successes. Gala's theatre blends sparkling surface humour with an underlying tragic reality. His protagonists champion the cause of the disempowered: women, Jews, homosexuals. With occasional exceptions like *Petra regalada* (1980), an allegory of the end of the Franco era, and *La truhana* (*The Comedienne*, 1992), their battle against repression meets with failure. Recent works include the long-running musical *Carmen Carmen* (1988) and the opera libretto *Cristóbal Colón* (*Christopher Columbus*, 1989; music by Leonardo Balada).

**Galich, Manuel** 1913-84 Guatemalan playwright. He participated as a young revolutionary against Jorge Ubico (Guatemalan president 1931-44) and subsequently became Minister of Education under Arévalo, Minister of Foreign Affairs under Arbenz, and Guatemala's ambassador to Argentina. His early plays were both historical and costumbristic (see COSTUMBRISMO), but his principal thrust was anti-imperialistic, political theatre. Major titles are *El tren amarillo* (*The Yellow Train*, 1954), *El pescado indigesto* (*The Undigested Fish*, 1960) and *Míster John Tenor y yo* (*Mr John Tenor and I*, 1975). Attracted by the Castro revolution, he played a major role in the development of revolutionary theatre in Cuba and served from 1964 to 1984 as the general editor of the theatre journal *Conjunto*.

**Gallegos, Daniel** 1930- Costa Rican playwright, director, professor and actor. Gallegos was a major influence in the development of the Costa Rican theatre as director of the Teatro Universitario and professor at the University of Costa Rica. His major plays are *Ese algo de Dávalos* (*Davalos's Certain Something*, 1964), *La colina* (*The Hill*, 1968), a metaphysical play about the death of God, and *En el séptimo círculo* (*In the Seventh Circle*, 1982), about violence in the current world situation.

**Galsworthy, John** 1867-1933 British novelist and playwright. He is best known for his novel sequence *The Forsyte Saga*. His first plays, *The Silver Box* (1906), *Strife* (1909) and *Justice* (1910), were all produced by GRANVILLE BARKER. Dealing with the inequalities of justice in a class system, the causes of industrial unrest and the psychological effects of the prison system, their objective depiction of topical moral issues made Galsworthy's plays a popular staple of the provincial repertory movement as well as WEST END successes. These themes were extended in *The Fugitive* (1913), on the social victimization of women, and in *The Mob* (1914), denouncing war hysteria, then repeated in a series of plays during the 1920s: *The Skin Game*, *Loyalties*, *Escape* and *Exiled*. His call for social reform was most effective in *Justice*, which had a significant impact on the campaign for prison reform, but in general his plays have dated badly because the issues are defined too specifically in terms of a particular social context, and the WELL MADE plots, several of which end with the protagonist's suicide, are overtly conventional.

**Gambaro, Griselda** 1928- Argentine playwright and novelist. Her hard-hitting psychological plays strike at the violence and oppression which have characterized Argentina in recent years. *Los siameses* (*The Siamese Twins*, 1967) contrasts aggression and passivity in two mutually dependent individuals, while *El campo* (*The Camp*, 1968) bears the stigma of a concentration camp whose leader is named Franco. Both earlier and later plays decry the trivialization and show the absurdity of contemporary lifestyles. During virulent periods of repression Gambaro sought refuge in Spain; some of her plays have still not been performed in Argentina. Recent titles include *Decir sí* (*To Say Yes*, 1981), *La mala sangre* (*Bad Blood*, 1982), *Antígona furiosa* (*Furious Antigone*, 1986), *Effectos personales* (*Personal Effects*, 1988), *Morgan* (1989) and *Penas sin importancia* (*Unimportant Sorrows*, 1990). She is perhaps the foremost woman playwright in Latin America.

**Gambon, Michael** 1940– Irish-born British actor. Gambon has become one of the most respected actors on the British stage, especially through his work at the NATIONAL THEATRE which he first joined in 1963 (at the OLD VIC) and to which he returned in 1978, and for the ROYAL SHAKESPEARE COMPANY. He played King Lear for the RSC in 1982–3 and – as a comparable pinnacle in television – took the title role in DENNIS POTTER's play *The Singing Detective* (BBC, 1986). His association with ALAN AYCKBOURN, which began with *The Norman Conquests* (1974) in which he played Tom the vet, has continued in productions which Ayckbourn has directed, not written, such as ARTHUR MILLER's *A View from the Bridge* (1987) and *Othello* (1990). He played the Sergeant in HAROLD PINTER's chilling *Mountain Language* (1988). His is a quiet and unassuming talent, and a major one, best nurtured by those directors who respect the stillness and economy of his acting.

**Ganassa** [Zan Ganassa; Alberto Naseli or Naselli] c.1540-c.1584 Italian actor. He was one of the first COMMEDIA DELL'ARTE actors to perform beyond the borders of Italy. A specialist in ZANNI roles, he first crops up in 1568 as head of a troupe in Mantua. After giving private performances in France at the invitation of Charles IX, he spent nearly a decade in Spain (1574–84). There he was highly successful; he is often mentioned by LOPE DE VEGA, who may have based his comic GRACIOSO on commedia figures. Fifty years after Ganassa's departure, he was still cited in Spanish folk-sayings.

**Gao Xingjian** 1940– Chinese playwright. A writer of HUAJU and a theorist, Gao was influenced by Western, and especially French, ideas to become the most innovative and challenging of the younger playwrights during the 1980s in terms of concept, performance and style. He visited France in 1979 and later took up residence there. A highly prolific writer, he is best known for three spoken dramas from the first half of the 1980s: *Warning Signal*, *Bus Stop* and *Wild Man*. *Warning Signal* is about unemployed youth. The main character, Blackie, intends to take part in a train robbery to get the money he needs to marry, but in the end turns against his accomplice and kills him. Like most other spoken dramas of the time, it is really about serious social problems in Chinese society – unemployment and juvenile delinquency. What is unusual is the play's symbolism and that it offers no solutions. Blackie's murder of his intended accomplice is shown as a redemptive, not a criminal, act. He is an anti-hero of a kind virtually unique in China in 1982. *Bus Stop* concerns characters waiting in vain at a bus stop and expressing their memories, disappointments and aspirations, inviting comparison with BECKETT's *Waiting for Godot*. In *Wild Man* Gao not only adopts contemporary notions of total theatre, but returns to the traditional style of drama in which singing, recitation, dance/movement and acting are combined. The play has many messages, among which preservation of the environment is foremost.

**García Guerra, Iván** 1938– Dominican Republic playwright and director. His first play was *Más allá de la búsqueda* (*Beyond the Search*, 1963), a Promethean existentialist exercise and a combination of classical theme and Caribbean techniques and motifs. Other major plays include *Don Quijote de todo el mundo* (*Don Quixote of the World*, 1964), whose hero is a modernized revolutionary version of the idealistic dreamer, and the symbolic *Fábula de los cinco caminantes* (*The Fable of the Five Travellers*, 1965), about the irrationality of mankind within the grotesque and absurd framework of the modern world.

**García Lorca, Federico** 1898–1936 Spanish poet and playwright. The best-known dramatist of this century outside Spain, he was born in Granada, studied in Madrid and also visited France, Britain and the United States. His first play, *El maleficio de la mariposa* (*The Butterfly's Evil Spell*, 1920), a short symbolic piece, was a failure, but his historic verse drama *Mariana Pineda* (1923), recounting the life and death of the revolutionary Liberal heroine, was a great success even though such plays were no longer fashionable. Lorca continued to experiment with various styles; during his stay in the United States he wrote a surrealistic play (see SURREALISM), *Así que pasen cinco años* (*As Five Years Pass*, 1929–30, performed 1945), whose events take place in the mind of a man with only a few minutes to live, and the brief *El Público* (*The Audience*, 1930, performed 1986).

During 1932–3 he was involved with the university theatre group La Barraca, touring rural Spain, and he went on to evolve a mature style with his three great peasant tragedies of passion and frustration: *Bodas de sangre* (*Blood Wedding*, 1933), *Yerma* (1934) and *La casa de Bernarda Alba* (*The House of Bernarda Alba*, 1936, first performed 1945). The first tells of an unwilling bride who elopes with her lover on her wedding night, which leads to a tragic climax in which the husband and lover kill each other. *Yerma* deals with the tragedy of a woman whose longing for a child becomes so unbearable that she murders her indifferent husband. In *La casa de Bernarda Alba* a mother orders her daughters to mourn their father's death for eight years before marrying; her obsession with decorum produces a TRAGEDY of jealousy and frustration. A further play exploring the oppression and frustration of Spanish women is *Doña Rosita la soltera, o el lenguaje de las flores* (*Doña Rosita the Spinster, or The Language of the Flowers*, performed 1935).

Lorca was murdered by Falangists at the outbreak of the Civil War, aged only 38. His reputation abroad has been established by *Bodas de sangre*, *Yerma* and *La casa de Bernarda Alba*.

**García, Santiago** 1928– Colombian playwright and director. Founder of various theatre groups, he was also the prime force behind the Colombian Theatre Corporation, which organized the 100 or more theatre groups in Colombia into a new union. The first Colombian director to stage BRECHT and PETER WEISS he has promoted sociopolitical theatre with Marxist themes and structures. His major productions include *La ciudad dorada* (*The Golden City*, 1974) and *Guadalupe años sin cuenta* (*Guadalupe, Years without End*, 1975), both dealing with war and violence in Colombia. *Morte y vida Severina* (*Life and Death Severina*) and *Los diez días que estremecieron el mundo* (*Ten Days That Shook the World*) are adaptations of a Brazilian play and of a documentary on Russia, respectively. *Diálogo del rebusque* (*Hermetic Dialogue*, 1983) adapts the Spanish baroque poet Francisco de Quevedo.

**Garneau, Michel** 1939– Quebec playwright, poet, director and actor. His irreverence towards conservatism in politics, religion and language can be seen in his best-known play, *Quatre à quatre (Four to Four*, 1973), which explores the effects of cultural heredity on four generations of Quebec women, and in *Strauss et Pesant (et Rosa)* (1974), which deals with the unsavoury collaboration between Church and state. *Émilie ne sera plus jamais cuellie par l'anémone* (1981), translated into English as *Emilie* (1987), is a portrait of the American poet Emily Dickinson.

**Garnier, Robert** c.1545–90 French playwright and poet. His seven tragedies, based on Greek mythology or Roman history, are SENECAn in manner, relying heavily on monologue and pathos, but contain impressive choruses and lyrical passages, particularly in *Antigone* (1580) and *Les Juives (The Jewish Women*, 1583). *Bradamante* (1582), derived from ARIOSTO's *Orlando Furioso*, anticipates the TRAGICOMEDY of the next century. Two of his Roman plays were translated into English in his own time.

**Garrett, João Baptista de Almeida** 1799–1854 Portuguese playwright and administrator. After writing a neoclassical piece, *Catão (Cato)*, in 1821 and a play about the staging of one of VICENTE's MASQUES, *Um Auto de Gil Vicente*, which pointed the way to a renewal of Portuguese theatre, Garrett wrote two historical plays. From 1836 to 1841 he was Inspector-General of Theatres, with a plan to renew the national stage, set up acting schools and build a National Theatre. He built the theatre (eventually the TEATRO NACIONAL D. MARIA II) and provided its first repertoire with the above plays, five additional comedies and the century's finest drama, *Frei Luís de Sousa*, first performed in 1850. A classical tragedy, it is nevertheless attentive to period detail and based on the true story of a nobleman, presumed killed in battle, who, to the consternation of his family, returns to the Portugal of the Spanish captivity under the Philips. Frequently revived, it was played as *The Pilgrim* by the (British) New Vic Theatre Touring Company (1990–91), to considerable acclaim.

**Garrick, David** 1717–79 English actor, manager and playwright. His first play, *Lethe*, a SATIRE, was performed at DRURY LANE in 1740. He began acting as an amateur. In 1741 at GOODMAN'S FIELDS THEATRE his performance as Richard III won him immediate success, and he followed it with Bayes in BUCKINGHAM's *The Rehearsal* and King Lear. In Dublin he played Hamlet opposite PEG WOFFINGTON. One of his greatest roles was Abel Drugger in JONSON's *The Alchemist*, a realistic study of a low-comedy role. In 1742 he transferred to Drury Lane.

Garrick carefully restored many parts of SHAKESPEARE's plays that had traditionally been cut or adapted. His *Macbeth* (1744) was advertised as 'revived as Shakespeare wrote it'. Although his later notorious version of *Hamlet* (1772) cut Ophelia's madness and the gravediggers, it also reinstated other lines. During a season at COVENT GARDEN he produced the best of his 20 plays, the afterpiece FARCE *Miss in Her Teens*. In April 1747 he began his 29 years as Drury Lane's manager, establishing a standard of excellence in production and acting. In 1748 he added to his repertory Benedick in *Much Ado About Nothing* and Romeo, allowing the lovers a brief reunion in the tomb. He also inaugurated the spectacular Drury Lane PANTOMIMES. By 1754 his social and intellectual status was far beyond any previous English actor's. Most of his Shakespeare adaptations date from

this period: *The Taming of the Shrew, The Winter's Tale, The Tempest, King Lear* and *Antony and Cleopatra*.

A reformer of theatrical abuses, Garrick abolished the right of half-price admission after the third act, but the consequent riots forced him to give way. He travelled to France, where he learned about scenic innovations which he was later to introduce at Drury Lane. He collaborated with GEORGE COLMAN THE ELDER on *The Clandestine Marriage* in 1766, and in 1769 was invited to organize the Shakespeare Jubilee. The massive series of processions, orations and entertainments he paid for were largely ruined by torrential rain. Undaunted, he mounted the pageants at Drury Lane as *The Jubilee*. Eventually he sold his shares in the theatre, and his patent, to SHERIDAN, and retired in 1776. On his death he was given a grand funeral at Westminster Abbey.

Garrick's career as manager was marked by disputes with other actors and playwrights. But this intransigence also made him refuse bad plays, even from friends. He inaugurated new forms of scenery and design. His cautious balance of commercial acquiescence and artistic responsibility resulted in a rare combination of profit and artistic integrity. As a sustained success his management of Drury Lane is unparalleled. As writer, his original work was pragmatic rather than brilliant. But his adaptations show consistent theatrical intelligence, crafting scenes to maximum effect, and giving actors the best opportunities. As actor, Garrick was versatile and daring, his range in both classic and new plays unequalled. His dominance of the English stage for over 30 years was absolute, his influence as much social as theatrical; as Dr Johnson said, 'his profession made him rich and he made his profession respectable'.

**Garro, Elena** 1922– Mexican playwright and novelist. An imaginative writer, she finds abstract means of expressing external realities. *Un hogar sólido (A Solid Home*, 1956) is the title play of a collection dealing with characters and situations beyond the grave. *La señora en su balcón (The Lady on the Balcony*, 1963) is the dramatic encounter of an older woman with haunting illusions of her past.

**Gascon, Jean** 1921–88 French Canadian actor and director. One of the founders of the THÉÂTRE DU NOUVEAU MONDE, he was its artistic director until 1966. At this time the TNM attracted international acclaim for its interpretation of French classics, particularly the works of MOLIÈRE, many of them directed by Gascon. Named first director-general (1960–3) of the National Theatre School of Canada, he was also artistic director at the STRATFORD (Ontario) FESTIVAL during 1969–74.

**Gaskill, William** 1930– British director. Gaskill joined the ROYAL COURT THEATRE in 1957 as assistant to the artistic director, GEORGE DEVINE. He directed plays by N. F. SIMPSON, Donald Howarth, JOHN OSBORNE and ARNOLD WESKER at the Royal Court, *Richard III* (1961) and *Cymbeline* (1962) for the ROYAL SHAKESPEARE COMPANY and, in London, BRECHT's *The Caucasian Chalk Circle* and *Baal* (1963). LAURENCE OLIVIER invited him to join the newly formed NATIONAL THEATRE Company in 1963 as associate director, where he provided a memorable production of FARQUHAR's *The Recruiting Officer* and encouraged group acting through improvisation and discussion. After directing such NT successes as Brecht's *Mother Courage* and JOHN ARDEN's *Armstrong's Last Goodnight*, he succeeded George Devine at the Royal Court from 1965 to 1972, producing and directing

EDWARD BOND's first plays, *Saved* (1965), *Early Morning* (1968), *Lear* (1971) and *The Sea* (1973). Afterwards he helped to found a theatre cooperative, the Joint Stock Company, which brought actors and writers together in the production of radical new plays by DAVID HARE, HOWARD BRENTON and Stephen Lowe. He returned to the National Theatre to direct GRANVILLE BARKER's *The Madras House* (1977); for RICHARD EYRE's NT he has directed PIRANDELLO's *Man, Beast and Virtue* (1989) and BULGAKOV's *Black Snow* (1991), in which Bulgakov avenges himself on STANISLAVSKY.

**Gassman, Vittorio** 1922– Italian actor and director. He rapidly emerged on the postwar scene as a major stage actor. His handsome presence and strong, expressive voice made him particularly suited to classic parts like the titles roles in ALFIERI's *Oreste* (1950, directed by VISCONTI), SHAKESPEARE's *Hamlet* (1952, jointly directed by Gassman and SQUARZINA) and *Othello* (1956). He later formed and directed the Teatro Popolare Italiano, for which he played a range of lead roles. Not only classic, but modern, Italian and European drama has been prominent in his repertory, including the DUMAS *père*–SARTRE *Kean*, and plays by Zardi, Pasolini and others. He is also a successful film actor. Among his most notable achievements in Shakespeare have been his Richard III, King Lear and Prospero. His range and power were illustrated in *Ulisse e la balena bianca* (*Ulysses and the White Whale*, 1992), partly adapted from Melville's *Moby Dick*, a production in which Gassman not only performed but which he also devised and directed.

**Gate Theatre** (Dublin) The Gate generates its own productions and is run by an artistic director/producer who uses guest directors. It was created in 1928 by Micheál MacLiammóir (1899–1978) and Hilton Edwards to diversify Irish theatre. In 1930 the Gate moved from the Peacock to its own theatre, becoming noted for its brilliant productions and catholic variety: world classics, experimental plays (decreasingly), WEST END successes, FARCES. In the 1980s, with no permanent acting company, the Gate re-emerged as a theatrical force, challenging the ABBEY. In 1991, with the DUBLIN INTERNATIONAL THEATRE FESTIVAL, it staged the first complete festival of all SAMUEL BECKETT's plays. Although never a writers' theatre, it encouraged DENIS JOHNSTON, BRIAN FRIEL, HUGH LEONARD, FRANK McGUINNESS and Dermot Bolger.

**Gate Theatre** (London) First a loft near Covent Garden, then (after 1927) occupying part of the former Charing Cross Music-Hall, the Gate was opened in 1925 as an experimental theatre for presenting the work of the expressionists (see EXPRESSIONISM). Over the next nine years Peter Godfrey, a former variety performer, staged approximately 350 plays ranging from STRINDBERG, WEDEKIND, TOLLER and KAISER to O'NEILL's banned work, *Desire Under the Elms*, and PARODY performances of plays like *UNCLE TOM'S CABIN* and *Little Lord Fauntleroy*. When NORMAN MARSHALL took over in 1934 the theatre lost its experimental significance, though it continued to produce new work, e.g. JOHN STEINBECK's *Of Mice and Men* (1938) and COCTEAU's *Les Parents Terribles* (with CYRIL CUSACK, 1940), until destroyed by bombing in 1941.

**Gatti, Armand** 1924– French playwright, poet, journalist and film-maker. Having experienced a German concentration camp, Gatti struggled with the survivor complex in his early work. His plays are intended to intervene in world events, like political journalism. His autobiographical *Vie imaginaire de l'éboueur Auguste Geai*

(*Imaginary Life of Auguste Geai*, 1962) was his first big success, after which his plays – which, revolutionary in theme and form, explode the normal conventions of time and space – were hotly disputed by the decentralized theatres. Since the 1970s, he has moved away from straight plays towards the involvement of whole communities and the use of video, and has made a series of hard-hitting documentary films for television. From 1983–88 he was head of an audio-visual Atelier de Création Populaire at Toulouse.

*gaucho* theatre South American genre. Modern Argentine theatre finds its roots in the traditions of the *gaucho*, the cowboy who inhabited the endless *pampa*. After the publication of Eduardo Gutiérrez's serialized novel *Juan Moreira* in 1884, the Carlo Brothers' Circus commissioned the author to prepare a pantomimic version which was performed with José J. Podestá in the title role. This popular figure representing the fates and fortunes of the *gaucho*, the free spirit of the pampas in conflict with civil authority, captured the Argentine spirit. The CIRCUS tradition became an integral feature of Argentine theatre, and in the centennial revival of the play in 1984 the circus tent was still the dominant scenographic reminder of this heritage.

**Gaultier-Garguille** [Hugues Guéru; Fléchelles] 1572/3–1633 French actor. A famous farce-player, in 1612 he joined the company at the HÔTEL DE BOURGOGNE led by GROS-GUILLAUME, thus cementing a life-long acting partnership. In FARCE he was always masked and played old men, with black doublet, breeches, skull-cap, cane, pouch and wooden dagger, reminiscent of the Pantalone of COMMEDIA (see TURLUPINADES). He also contributed crude and licentious songs to his performance, some of them collected and published.

**Gautier, Théophile** 1811–72 French poet, novelist and critic. His importance to the theatre is as a critic of drama and ballet. From 1837–55 he had a regular column in *La Presse* and from 1855–71 in *Le Moniteur Universel*. He published a major collection of his theatre criticism in his *Histoire dramatique en France depuis vingt-cinq ans* (1858). He supported HUGO's *Hernani*, but soon distanced himself from excessive romanticism, his writing marked by its common sense and honesty. He is best known for providing the scenarios for two major romantic ballets, *Giselle* (1841) and *La Péri* (1843).

**Gay, John** 1685–1732 English playwright and poet. His topical FARCE *The Mohocks* (1712) was unacted and his Chaucer adaptation *The Wife of Bath* (1713) was performed unsuccessfully. A member of the Scriblerus Club with Swift and Pope from 1714, he failed to secure court patronage. Helped by Pope, he wrote a successful BURLESQUE of contemporary tragedy, *The What D'Ye Call It* (1715). With Pope and Arbuthnot he wrote a SATIRE on other writers, *Three Hours after Marriage* (1717). After writing the libretto for Handel's *Acis and Galatea* (1719) and a PASTORAL tragedy *Dione* (1720), he produced the first volume of *The Fables* (1727). In 1728 JOHN RICH, manager of LINCOLN's INN FIELDS THEATRE, produced Gay's BALLAD OPERA *The Beggar's Opera* with music by Pepusch, a success that made 'Gay rich and Rich gay'. Gay had invented a new form, using ballads while setting his love story in the criminal world, through which he could attack sentimental drama and contemporary politics; the work was later adapted by BRECHT as *The Threepenny Opera*. Robert Walpole banned performances of Gay's sequel *Polly* (1729). None of his later satiric plays matches the brilliance of *The Beggar's Opera*.

**gay theatre** Term used to describe theatre work by male homosexuals (see also LESBIAN THEATRE). The term usually describes performances and plays of the 1960s onwards which feature overtly gay characters and situations and/or gay political protest, but it can be extended to cover work before and since (particularly camp and drag) which exhibits a gay sensibility or aesthetic, even in the absence of a specific homosexual narrative. The key example is the work of OSCAR WILDE. Recent gay theorists have claimed Wilde as the originating point for a theatre of gay camp, and the 'bunburying' of *The Importance of Being Earnest* (1895) can be read as an image of covert homosexual practice.

The earliest play to feature a character whom the audience is invited to identify as homosexual is the British playwright HARLEY GRANVILLE BARKER's *The Madras House* (1910). The couturier, Mr Windlesham, is the first in a long history of stage representations of homosexuality as effeminacy. Interestingly, however, most early plays with discernible gay characters and/or narratives – J.R. Ackerley's *The Prisoners of War*, produced in London in 1925; MAE WEST's *The Drag*, 1927, and *The Pleasure Man*, 1928; and Mordaunt Shairp's *The Green Bay Tree* , produced in London and New York in 1933 – were written by men or, in West's case, a bisexual woman. This contrasts with the representation of lesbians in the same period, which is more overt but produced heterosexual playwrights.

In the case of the British theatre during 1920–50, it can be argued that a gay sensibility, far from being excluded to the margins of theatre, came to dominate it. Many of the major playwrights of the period (e.g. SOMERSET MAUGHAM, NOËL COWARD, TERENCE RATTIGAN) were gay, as were powerful impresarios such as BINKIE BEAUMONT of H. M. Tennent Ltd.. While none of the plays of this theatre were overtly gay, some – e.g. Coward's *The Vortex* (1924) and *Design for Living* (1932), and Rattigan's *French without Tears* (1936) – were clearly, to gay audiences, gay plays. Much of the camp performance aesthetic of the theatre of this period also signals its gay origins.

The gradual liberalization of sexual attitudes in the postwar period – one sign of which, in Britain, was the 1967 decriminaization of sex between consenting adult males – meant that sex and sexuality began to feature as issues in drama. The abolition of the Lord Chamberlain as British censor in 1968 (see CENSORSHIP) allowed for even greater freedom. It was heterosexual writers who were first to include homosexual charcters or plots in their plays, inevitably from a heterosexual and somewhat negative perspective: in the USA, for example, ARTHUR MILLER's *A View from the Bridge* (1955); in Britain, BRENDAN BEHAN's *The Hostage* (1958), SHELAGH DELANEY's *A Taste of Honey* (1958) and JOHN OSBORNE's *A Patriot for Me* (1966). The three great playwrights of the period 1940–70 – TENNESSEE WILLIAMS, JEAN GENET and JOE ORTON – included few gay characters in their plays, although their style and narratives are unmistakably gay.

Gay theatre, in the sense of upfront plays about gay subjects for gay audiences, developed in the USA in the 1960s and in Britain in the 1970s. In both places the growth of an alternative circuit of small venues where non-commercial theatre could be cheaply staged was an important factor. In the USA this provided by the OFF-BROADWAY and OFF-OFF-BROADWAY movements. The Caffé Cino, for instance, in New York's Greenwich

Village produced the work of gay playwrights Doric Wilson, Robert Patrick, Claris Nelson and William Hoffman. Off-Broadway also produced Mart Crowley's *The Boys in the Band* (1968), a huge success on both sides of the Atlantic. The 1970s in the USA saw further development with the founding of specifically gay companies and venues across America: e.g. TOSOS Theatre Company, the Glines gay arts centre and the Meridian Gay Theatre in New York, the San Francisco Gay Men's Theatre Collective and Theatre Rhinoceros in San Francisco, and other companies in Phoenix, Houston, Minneapolis and Boston.

The growth of gay theatre testifies to the growth of gay communities in large cities. In the Stonewall Riots in Greenwich Village in 1969 the New York gay community took its first direct political action – fighting back against police harassment of gays and drag queens. This was to be a politicizing moment for gays arund the world. Much of the gay theatre created post-Stonewall in both the USA and Britain was explicitly a radical, oppositional theatre. This radicalism took a variety of forms: disruptive 'situationist' spectacles (Notting Hill Street Theatre Group's drag/gender-bending performances on gay marches in London in the early 1970s, in which Betty Bourne, founder of the drag company Bloolips (see FEMALE IMPERSONATION; REVUE), took part) or transgressive /queer performance (Hot Peaches in the USA and the LINDSAY KEMP Company in Britain), or political propagandist theatre. The latter was the ethos of Gay Sweatshop, Britain's first gay theatre company, founded in 1975.

In Britain gay theatre developed in the context of the alternative political movement of the 1960s and 1970s. Gay Sweatshop was as much influenced by the political agendas of socialism, feminism and anti-racism as by the Gay Liberation Front, and its plays reflect this. Noel Greig, whose plays were a mainstay of Gay Sweatshop in its early years, came from a socialist-theatre background: his 1979 play *The Dear Love of Comrades* is about the turn-of-the-century Utopian socialist and homosexual propagandist Edward Carpenter, and his *Poppies* (1983) deals with pacifism. Throughout its history Gay Sweatshop has been a mixed gay and lesbian company, with the agenda of feminism unavoidably part of its consciousness. Furthermore, the company has had the role of political campaigner thrust upon it – it has had to fight battles with all kinds of state agencies (particularly local authorities and education authorities) to stop its productions from being summarily banned. Although it has had difficult periods, when ARTS COUNCIL funding has been withdrawn or when fatigue has threatened creativity, it has always been reinvigorated by new company members or new political campaigns – e.g. concerning Section 28 and AIDS – or new turns in gay culture, as its recent 'Queer School' events indicate.

Although in other areas of political theatre there was by the mid-1980s a feeling of weariness with overtly political or propagandist theatre, it was then, because of AIDS, that gay theatre entered its most strenuous campaigning phase. Companies produced works to educate gay communities about AIDS and safe sex, to protest against state inertia in the face of the epidemic, and to challenge 'gay plague' hysteria. In the USA, *As Is* (William Hoffman, 1985) and *The Normal Heart* (Larry Kramer, 1985) both transferred to BROADWAY, the latter also playing to full houses in London. Gay Sweatshop produced *Compromised Immunity* (Andy Kirby, 1986/7), which toured Britain, often playing in mainstream venues that did not normally book gay shows.

In the 1990s AIDS remains an inescapable fact of gay life, and all gay art is made in its shadow – not, as was the case in the 1980s, in the form of mourning and anger, but as an explosion of positive energy and creativity. Gay theatrical response has included TONY KUSHNER's huge, multidimensional epic of gay sex and politics, *Angels in America*, produced in Britain and across the USA. Gay theatre has re-embraced the older traditions (and often marginalized by gay politics) of drag (see FEMALE IMPERSONATION) and gay celebration: in Britain the collaboration of Bloolips and American lesbian company Split Britches on *Belle Reprieve*, a queer version of Tennessee Williams's *A Streetcar Named Desire*, was one of the gay theatre events of 1991. Gay bodies and sexuality have been publicly anatomized in the public health discourses centring on AIDS. Gay performers have responded with their own celebratory discourse of the body: in his show *My Queer Body* US gay performance artist Tim Miller performs a gay history – of a life in the time of AIDS – through his body, as map, as utterance. In Britain audiences, gay and straight, flock to the work of the dancer and gay performer Michael Clark and dance/performance company DV8.

While plays about gays have enjoyed occasional popular success before – *Torch Song Trilogy* and *La Cage aux folles* were great hits on Broadway and in the WEST END in the 1980s, as were Martin Sherman's *Bent* and *The Normal Heart* – what is most interesting in the mid-1990s is that a gay theatre aesthetic seems, in Britain at least, to be at the very centre of the theatre avant-garde. *Angels in America* has been one of the NATIONAL THEATRE's great critical successes; London's premier avant-garde art venue, the Institute of Contemporary Arts, is showing a great interest in gay (and lesbian) work; and Neil Bartlett, gay writer, director and performer with the theatre company Gloria as well as novelist, has become artistic director of one of London's major repertory theatres, the LYRIC THEATRE, HAMMERSMITH.

**Gélinas, Gratien** 1909– French Canadian playwright, actor and director. In 1937 he created the comic radio character Fridolin, a satiric but sympathetic observer of contemporary Canadian foibles. From 1938 to 1946 he wrote annual stage REVUES entitled *Fridolinons!*, interpreting the major role himself. Their immense popularity led to his first stage play, *'Tit-Coq* (1948), from which critics generally date the birth of modern Quebec theatre. A foundling defeated in his quest for social identity by military service in World War II and by an intransigent Catholic Church on his return, 'Tit-Coq (Lil' Rooster) incarnated, for many Québécois, their own frustrated aspirations at the end of that conflict. The play had more than 500 performances, in French and English. *Bousille et les justes* (*Bousille and the Just*, 1959), painting the bankruptcy of middle-class morality, was also a success, as was *Hier les enfants dansaient* (*Yesterday the Children Were Dancing*, 1966), which depicts a Quebec family riven by the same political forces that threatened to sunder Canada. Less topical is *La Passion de Narcisse Mondoux* (*Narcisse Mondoux's Passion*, 1986), a comedy written for himself and his actress wife Huguette Oligny. Gélinas also founded the Comédie Canadienne in 1958 and was made chairman of the Canadian Film Development Corporation in 1969.

**Gellert, Christian Fürchtegott** 1715–69 German playwright. Gellert is best known for his *Fables*, but his effective sentimental comedies are among the more significant achievements of the early German theatre. Of these, *The Affectionate Sisters* (1747) and *The Sick Woman* (1747) are probably the best.

**Gelosi** Italian company. Literally 'the jealous' – i.e. of praise – the troupe was headed by FRANCESCO and ISABELLA ANDREINI. It collaborated with TASSO on *Aminta* in 1573 and undertook numerous tours. It was the first professional Italian company to be seen in Paris (from 1576), and had a great influence on the development of the French stage. Its repertory included both COMMEDIA DELL'ARTE and *commedia erudita*. The troupe disbanded after the death of Isabella in 1604.

**Gémier, (Tonnerre) Firmin** 1869–1933 French actor and director. At first a noted actor, Gémier was the first King Ubu in 1896. His vision of a theatre for the masses led, in 1911, to the founding of a tent-based mobile touring theatre with an audience capacity of 1,650. In 1919 at the Paris Cirque d'Hiver he directed large-cast spectaculars and in 1920 was put in charge of the first THÉÂTRE NATIONAL POPULAIRE, but he was never given the means to run a permanent producing company. From 1921 to 1930 he was director of the ODÉON, where he distinguished himself with his productions of SHAKESPEARE.

**Gems, (Iris) Pam(ela)** 1925– British playwright. Gems turned to writing plays comparatively late in life. She was involved in a women's theatre season at London's Almost Free in 1975, which included her full-length play *The Amiable Courtship of Ms Venus and Wild Bill*. Two other lunchtime plays had been staged at the same theatre, *My Warren* and *After Birthday* (both in 1973). Her first great success, however, came with the production in 1977 of *Dusa, Fish, Stas and Vi*, a study of four girls rooming together in a London flat, which transferred to the WEST END from the HAMPSTEAD THEATRE CLUB. The accuracy, good humour and specific awareness of feminist (as well as feminine) issues brought her recognition as a leading woman playwright, although her appeal was never confined to female audiences. The ROYAL SHAKESPEARE COMPANY produced *Queen Christina* at the Other Place in Stratford-upon-Avon in 1977; her musical biography, *Piaf*, provided a splendid part for Jane Lapotaire (RSC) and transferred to the West End and New York (1980/1). Further productions with the RSC included *Camille* (1984) and *The Danton Affair* (1986). In 1991 she adapted *Uncle Vanya* for the Renaissance Theatre Company.

*género chico* Spanish term. It refers to the short one-act plays, originating in the medieval Church but by the 16th century entirely secular. The essence of these works, including the *paso*, the *entremés* and the *sainete*, is that they provided comic relief and variety between the acts of a full-scale COMEDIA.

*Paso* is a term (first found in use in 1585) employed by LOPE DE RUEDA for his comic interludes depicting low life characters and urban settings. It does not differ essentially from the *entremés*, which was usually performed after the first act of the *comedia*. Of many contributors to the genre, CERVANTES published eight though the greatest exponent was QUIÑONES DE BENAVENTE.

The *sainete* (term first used in 1639) was originally similar. Music was an important element, as it was though to a lesser degree, in the other two forms. In the 18th century it was revived by Ramón de la Cruz, who used it to PARODY the neoclassical tragic style. By the 19th century the genre was dominated by COSTUMBRISMO, the optimistic and conformist depiction of colourful low-life, the heyday of the genre being 1890–1910, with authors such as Carlos Arniches.

Both the *sainete* and the ZARZUELA served to inspire the popular theatre forms that began to develop in the River Plate (Argentina and Uruguay) area at the end of the 19th century: the *sainete criollo*; the *sainete gauchesco*, attuned to the specific issues of the regional cowboy of the pampas (see GAUCHO THEATRE); and the *sainete urbano*.

**Genet, Jean** 1910–86 French poet, novelist and playwright. An orphan, Genet grew up to a life of crime and made his reputation with homoerotic novels written in prison. He published five plays: *Les Bonnes* (*The Maids*), produced by JOUVET in 1947; *Haute Surveillance* (*Deathwatch*; directed by Genet and Marchat, 1949); *Le Balcon* (*The Balcony*, 1956; directed by BROOK, 1960); *Les Nègres* (*The Blacks*; directed by BLIN, 1959) and *Les Paravents* (*The Screens*), written in 1961 but not produced until 1966 by Blin at the ODÉON. Genet's plays realize some of the ideals of ARTAUD, and in their turn have been very influential: they operate on different levels of illusion, do not rely on traditional plot or psychology and are based in ritualized movements, dances, parades and interchanges of identity. There is a contrast between the sumptuousness of poetic dialogue and the sordidness of dramatic situation. But although considered subversive by right-wing forces in France, his plays do not advocate revolutionary political solutions. The Algerians of *The Screens*, the blacks in *The Blacks*, the revolutionaries of *The Balcony* are all self-destructive, and the transformations which occur are mystic rather than material.

**Gentleman, Francis** 1728–84 Irish actor, playwright and critic. His adaptations include JONSON's *Sejanus* (1750) and *The Alchemist* (as *The Tobacconist*, 1760) and SOUTHERNE's *Oroonoko* (as *The Royal Slave*, 1760). His dramatic criticism for the journal the *Dramatic Censor*, which he edited, was collected in 1771. Often pretentious and pious, his criticism provides remarkable descriptions of contemporary actors. In 1771 his SATIRE on the theatre attacked GARRICK for plagiarism. In 1772 he prepared an edition of SHAKESPEARE incorporating much material about stage business from prompt books.

**George, Mlle** [Marguerite-Joséphine Weymer] 1787–1867 French actress. She made her debut at the COMÉDIE-FRANÇAISE in 1802 in the unusual role of Clytemnestra. Her statuesque figure and sculptural beauty were suited to the great classical roles. She had a celebrated liaison with Napoleon and in 1808 left for Russia, where she was immensely popular. Back in Paris in 1813 she suffered the jealous rivalry of MLLE DUCHESNOIS. In the late 1820s the romantic drama afforded her new roles: DUMAS *père*'s *Christine* (1829) and in VIGNY's *La Maréchale d'Ancre* (1830). Under HAREL at the Porte-Saint-Martin (see BOULEVARD) her greatest roles were Marguerite de Bourgogne in *La Tour de Nesle* (1832) and Lucrèce Borgia and Marie Tudor (1833) in HUGO's plays.

**Germain, Jean-Claude** [Claude-Jean Magnier] 1939– Quebec playwright, critic and director. Active in avantgarde and experimental theatre, he founded in 1969 the Théâtre du Même Nom (TMN), a parodic anagram of the THÉÂTRE DU NOUVEAU MONDE (TNM), the most established of French Canada's troupes. Thereafter he devoted himself mainly to composing iconoclastic scripts for TMN. Relying heavily on *joual*, Quebec's popular idiom, and laden with ingenious puns, his works are virtually untranslatable. Most remarkable are *Diguidi, Diguidi, Ha! Ha! Ha!* (1969); *Le Roi des mises à bas prix* (*King of Discount Sales*, 1971); an adaptation into *joual* of 19th-century Quebec author F.-G. Marchand's *Les Faux-Brillants* (*False Diamonds*, 1977); and *A Canadian Play/Une Plaie canadienne* (1979).

**Gershwin, George** 1898–1937 and **Ira Gershwin** 1896–1983 American composer and lyricist. In 1918 the brothers teamed up to write their first song, 'The Real American Folk Song'. George's early show music was steeped in the idioms of jazz, learned from listening to black musicians. In 1924 the brothers collaborated on *Lady, Be Good!*, a musical starring FRED AND ADELE ASTAIRE, followed by other popular musicals including *Oh, Kay!* (1926), *Funny Face* (1927) and *Rosalie* (1928). Their songs of the 1920s were characterized by George's infectious, driving music and Ira's clever, slangy lyrics. In the early 1930s they created three satirical shows: *Strike Up the Band* (1930), *Of Thee I Sing* (1931), acclaimed for its trenchant political SATIRE and its good-humoured score, and *Let 'Em Eat Cake* (1933). In 1935 the THEATRE GUILD produced the Gershwins' 'American folk opera' *Porgy and Bess*. The original production was not a success, but it has proved to be their most enduring work. After George's death Ira collaborated with other composers: *Lady in the Dark* (1941) and *The Firebrand of Florence* (1945) with Kurt Weill, and *Park Avenue* (1946) with Arthur Schwartz.

As a composer, George Gershwin helped to popularize jazz on the musical stage in the 1920s. His more serious compositions for the concert hall prepared him to write *Porgy and Bess*, one of the most ambitious scores ever created for the American musical theatre. Ira's abilities as a lyricist evolved from the facile rhyming of his 1920s songs to the deeper, more eloquent style of his later work.

**Gerstein** [*née* Gersten], **Bertha** 1894–1972 American Yiddish actress. Born in Cracow and educated in America, she became the leading MUSICAL COMEDY and straight actress of the American YIDDISH THEATRE. She performed notably with BORIS THOMASHEFSKY's National Theatre and later with MAURICE SCHWARTZ's company. Married to the actor JACOB BEN-AMI, she frequently played leads opposite him.

**Gert, Valeska** [Gertrud Valesca Samosch] 1892–1978 German CABARET dancer. An exponent of grotesque pantomime, she made her Berlin debut in 1916 and appeared at the Schall und Rauch from 1920. Her pug-dog features and whirling movements were seen to advantage in macabre numbers like 'The Girl from the Mummy's Cellar'. Kurt Tucholsky called her harlot's dance, 'La Canaille', 'the boldest thing I ever saw on a stage'. She collaborated with BRECHT on a Red Revue. Later she opened the Beggar Bar in New York, the Hexenküche (Witch's Kitchen, 1950) and the Ziegenstall (Goat Pen, 1978) in West Berlin, adding parodic recitations to her dance repertory.

**Ghelderode, Michel de** [Ad(h)émar-Adolphe-Louis Martens] 1898–1962 Belgian playwright. He wrote some 60 plays as well as stories and essays. His originals are in French but a number of his plays were first performed in Flemish or Dutch translations. The most powerful and significant Belgian dramatist of the interwar years, he was heir to a mixed Flemish and French culture, with a powerful sense of his country's long and violent history. His plays (several not performed until years after they were written, several still unperformed) can be split into three groups: those set in the past, e.g. *Escorial* (Théâtre Communal, Brussels, 1929), *Chronicles of Hell* (Théâtre de l'ATELIER, Paris, 1949) and *The School for Fools* (Théâtre de l'Oeuvre, Paris, 1953); those with biblical origins, e.g. *Barabbas* (Vlaamsche Volkstooneel, Ostend, 1929), *Miss Jairus* (Atelier, 1949) and *The Women at the Tomb* (Théâtre Universitaire, Paris, 1953); and those with their roots in BURLESQUE and the MUSIC-HALL, e.g. *The Death of Doctor Faust* (Théâtre Art et Action, Paris, 1928), *Christopher Columbus* (Art et Action, 1929) and *Pantagleize* (Vlaamsche Volkstooneel, Saint-Trond, 1930). All vividly display a theatre of the senses as well as of words, a theatre of cruelty and of uneasy laughter. His plays are still largely unknown in Britain.

**Gherardi family** Italian actors. **Giovanni** (c.1645–83), a COMMEDIA DELL'ARTE player, who won his sobriquet Flautino from his virtuosity on the flute and guitar, went to Paris in 1674 or 1675. His son **Evaristo** (1663–1700) entered the COMÉDIE-ITALIENNE there as Arlequin in REGNARD's *Le Divorce* in 1689 and soon rose to manage it, often running foul of the police for his outspokenness. He wrote numerous scenarios for the HÔTEL DE BOURGOGNE, and when the Italian actors were turned out of Paris in 1697 he published 56 of them as *Le Théâtre italien*. They comprise one of the most important sources for the history of the *commedia dell'arte* in France.

**Giacometti, Paolo** 1816–82 Italian playwright. He was most important for his social dramas of which the finest, *La morte civile* (*Civil Death*, 1861), was a main piece in the repertoire of many leading actors, including SALVINI, who after first producing it at the Teatro dei Fiorentini at Naples played it successfully in both Britain and the United States.

**Giacosa, Giuseppe** 1847–1906 Italian playwright. He began as a poet and published 'a theatrical legend', *Una partita a scacchi* (*A Game of Chess*), in the journal *Nuova Antologia* in 1872. During the 1870s he wrote a number of historical plays with mainly medieval and Renaissance settings, like *Il trionfo dell'amore* (*The Triumph of Love*, 1875), and comedies in a light GOLDONIan manner like *Il marito amante della moglie* (*The Husband Lover of His Wife*, 1877). But his best work was written under the influence of NATURALISM in the 1890s: middle-class psychological dramas, the best-known of which are *Tristi amori* (*Sad Loves*, 1887) and *Come le foglie* (*Like the Leaves*, 1900), both of which were later made into films and still hold the Italian stage today. His best work is tightly constructed and is characterized by a mood of subtle melancholy. He was a distinguished librettist, collaborating with Luigi Illica on several pieces set by Puccini, including *La Bohème* (1896), *Tosca* (1899) and *Madame Butterfly* (1904).

**Gide, André** 1869–1951 French novelist, essayist and playwright. Gide was one of a group of writers concerned to reintroduce classical myth on the modern stage, as shown by his *Oedipus* (1931). He was a friend of COPEAU and interested in the VIEUX-COLOMBIER, but his talents were essentially novelistic rather than dramatic.

**Gielgud, John** 1904– British actor and director. In his first roles under GRANVILLE BARKER in 1921 and with J.B. FAGAN's Oxford Repertory Company between 1924 and 1925 – when he had his first London success as Trofimov in *The Cherry Orchard* – he developed the elegant style and expressive clarity of voice that won him immediate acclaim as the leading interpreter of Shakespearian tragedy on his appearance with the OLD VIC in 1929. His most famous role was Hamlet, which he returned to in his own production in 1933 and performed more than 500 times during his career. Another key role was John Worthing in WILDE's *The Importance of Being Earnest*, which he first played in 1930. His brilliant performances in *The Seagull* (1936), *The Three Sisters* (1937), *The Cherry Orchard* (1961) and *Ivanov* (1965), all of which he also directed, made a major contribution to CHEKHOV's acceptance on the English-speaking stage. During the 1950s he promoted the work of such modern playwrights as TERENCE RATTIGAN, GRAHAM GREENE and ENID BAGNOLD, as both actor and director, in addition to extending his Shakespearian repertoire with the ROYAL SHAKESPEARE COMPANY (Lear, Angelo, Leontes: 1950–1) and at the Old Vic. He was knighted in 1953. Since 1974 he has appeared frequently at the NATIONAL THEATRE, his most striking performances being in *The Tempest* (Prospero, 1974) – a role magnificently extended in the film *Prospero's Books* in 1988 – and in PINTER's *No Man's Land* (1975).

**Gilbert, John (Gibbs)** 1810–89 American actor. Famous for comic roles in classic English COMEDY, especially old men, Gilbert managed the CHESTNUT STREET THEATRE. For 26 years he was with WALLACK's company. A traditional actor, he resisted almost any theatrical change.

**Gilbert, Sir W(illiam) S(chwenck)** [Bab] 1836–1911 British playwright. Chiefly famous for his collaboration with Sir Arthur Sullivan in the series of Savoy Operas that made them both rich, Gilbert first trained as a lawyer and wrote comic nonsense verse, often with a satirical edge. From 1866 to 1897 he wrote over 60 plays, BURLESQUES, operas and extravaganzas. His assumption that manners are a mask for fundamental human selfishness pervades the 'fairy' plays, from *The Palace of Truth* (1870) through *Pygmalion and Galatea* (1871) to *The Wicked World* (1873), all written in blank verse that welcomes bathos. His vein of mockery was happily exploited in the collaborations with Sullivan: *The Sorcerer* (1877), *HMS Pinafore* (1878), *The Pirates of Penzance* (1879), *Patience* (1881), *Iolanthe* (1882), *Princess Ida* (1884), *The Mikado* (1885), *Ruddigore* (1887), *The Yeomen of the Guard* (1888), *The Gondoliers* (1889), *Utopia Limited* (1893) and *The Grand Duke* (1896). The fame of the Savoy Operas has eclipsed that of his best plays, notably *Sweethearts* (1874), *Engaged* (1877) and *Rosencrantz and Guildenstern* (1891), a witty swansong of Victorian burlesque.

**Gill, Peter** 1939– British director and playwright. At the ROYAL COURT he directed three hitherto underrated plays by D. H. LAWRENCE, presented as a group in 1968. In 1969 the Royal Court produced two of his first plays, *The Sleepers' Den* and *Over Gardens Out*, which revealed that Gill could evoke with lyrical skill the circumstances of his Cardiff boyhood. His best play, *Small Change* (1976), received its premiere at the Royal Court under his own directing. In 1977 he was appointed the director of RIVERSIDE STUDIOS, which he transformed into a major arts centre. On its rudimentary stages he directed classical productions as well as encouraging new dramatists and new forms of theatre. In 1980 he joined the NATIONAL THEATRE under PETER HALL, where in addition to directing such productions as TURGENEV's *A Month in* the Country (1981) and BÜCHNER's Danton's Death (1983) he pioneered new writing at the Cottesloe Theatre, running a season of premieres there in 1985. He directed Nicholas Wright's Mrs Klein (1988) and a revival of Juno and the Paycock (1989). In 1992 he staged an elegant production of CONGREVE's The Way of the World at the LYRIC THEATRE, HAMMERSMITH.

**Gillette, William (Hooker)** 1853–1937 American actor and playwright. As an actor he is remembered for his performance in his own Sherlock Holmes (1899), which he played over 1,300 times, although his Civil War spy MELODRAMA, Secret Service (1895), with its fast-moving action and tension between the demands of love and duty, was his most significant achievement as a playwright. He was the author of adaptations, dramatizations and several original plays in which he frequently appeared himself, in the USA and England. Other plays include The Private Secretary (1884), All the Comforts of Home (1890), Clarice (1905) and Electricity (1910). In 1913 Gillette delivered his influential lecture, 'The Illusion of the First Time in Acting', which explains his cool, understated approach, in contrast to the florid and romantic style that previously dominated the theatre.

**Gilpin, Charles Sidney** 1878–1930 African-American actor. In 1907 he joined the all-black PEKIN Stock Company of Chicago and later acted at the Lincoln and Lafayette Theatres in Harlem. His impressive BROADWAY performance as the slave Custis in DRINKWATER's Abraham Lincoln (1919) led to the title role in The Emperor Jones (1920), in which he scored a resounding triumph. A victim of sudden fame and racial prejudice, Gilpin took to drink, which cut short his career.

**Gilroy, Frank D(aniel)** 1925– American playwright. Gilroy first gained attention with Who'll Save the Plowboy? (1962). The Subject Was Roses (1964), a story of parents' rivalry for the affection of their son who has just returned from the war, was a major critical success, unmatched by his recent work for the stage.

**Giraldi, Giovan Battista** [Cinzio] 1504–73 Italian playwright, short story writer and literary theorist. He was a prolific and influential writer. His nine plays in the tragic or tragicomic modes, exploiting SENECAn motifs of violence and the supernatural, were much admired in Italy and abroad, particularly L'Orbecche (1541). His short stories provided plot lines or suggestions to many dramatists, among them SHAKESPEARE, who drew on his Ecatommiti (1565) for Othello and Measure for Measure. His theoretical writings on the unities of time, place and action (SEE ARISTOTLE), and the morality proper to dramatic subject-matter and treatment, were no less influential, particularly in France.

**Giraudoux, Jean** 1882–1944 French diplomat and playwright. Giraudoux's success as a dramatist was largely due to his partnership with JOUVET, who directed and acted in almost all his plays, thus realizing COPEAU's dream of bringing poetry back to the modern stage. In fact much of Giraudoux's work is verbose and lacking in action, though it has great wit and charm. His use of classical mythology encouraged a stage fashion in the 1930s and 1940s. He seems at his best in light-hearted entertainments such as Intermezzo (1933) or L'Apollon de Bellac (The Apollo of Bellac, 1942). In La Guerre de Troie n'aura pas lieu (Tiger at the Gates, 1935) he provoked a contemporary response to Hitler's power in his story of civilized Trojans and Greeks dragged unwillingly into war.

**Glaspell, Susan** 1876–1948 American playwright. She was best known as one of the founders of the PROVINCETOWN PLAYERS (along with her husband, George Cram Cook) and the LITTLE THEATRE movement. Glaspell's reputation as a playwright has grown in recent years. She was second only to EUGENE O'NEILL in the founding of a modern American drama which combined contemporary American ideas with European expressionistic techniques (see EXPRESSIONISM). Her early one-act plays satirized contemporary attitudes and interests, such as pop psychology (Suppressed Desires, 1915) and ultra-idealism (Tickless Time, 1918; both written in collaboration with Cook). But her one-act Trifles (1916) skilfully portrayed hidden psychological motivation by using realistic settings and dialogue to reveal women's inner conflicts. Here she first used the device of keeping the central female character off-stage, repeated in Bernice (1919) and in her most controversial play, The Verge (1921), in which she experimented with SYMBOLISM and expressionistic settings to reveal the state of mind of a 'new' woman striving for both abstract idealism and individual fulfilment. In The Inheritors (1921) she contrasted narrow post-World War I Americanism with earlier ideals of individual freedom and tolerance. Alison's House (1930) is loosely based on the life of Emily Dickinson.

**Globe Theatre** (London) When the lease ran out on JAMES BURBAGE's THEATRE in 1598, members of the LORD CHAMBERLAIN's MEN took most of its timbers across the Thames to a south-bank site close to HENSLOWE's ROSE, where they built the new Globe theatre. It was a polygonal structure with a three-tiered gallery surrounding an open yard. Recent scholarship claims a stage of between 40 and 50ft wide, and a seating capacity of over 3000. A system of sharing costs and profits was devised: SHAKESPEARE was among the six responsible 'housekeepers', and from 1599 to 1608 most of his finest plays were first publicly performed there. The Globe continued in use after its resident company took possession of the indoor BLACKFRIARS THEATRE in 1608–9. It was rebuilt after destruction by fire in 1613. The second Globe remained active until the closure of the theatres in 1642 and was demolished in 1644. A limited excavation was begun in 1989.

**Godber, John** 1956– British playwright and director. After an early career in radio and as a television dramatist, in 1984 Godber became artistic director of the company Hull Truck, for whom he has staged his best-known comedies, Up 'n' Under (1984; sequel, Up 'n' Under 2, 1993), Bouncers (1985), Teechers (1987), Salt of the Earth (1988) and On the Piste (1990), which transferred to the WEST END in 1993. He is closely in touch with his Northern audiences: his plays are often set in leisure centres or rugby clubs. He delights in jibes against the Establishment, which turned his production of Twelfth Night (1989) into a bunfight. Happy Families (1991) and April in Paris (1992) contributed to Godber's 1992 reputation as the fourth most performed British dramatist, after SHAKESPEARE, AYCKBOURN and WILLY RUSSELL.

**Goering, Reinhard** 1887–1936 German playwright. An exponent of EXPRESSIONISM, Goering is best known for A Sea Battle (1918), which was the first play to deal directly with the war on the German stage and introduced the anonymous characterization and telegraphic dialogue that also mark the plays of KAISER and HASENCLEVER.

**Goethe, Johann Wolfgang von** 1749–1832 German playwright, director, novelist and essayist. Goethe's achievement in the theatre was as varied and as significant as his accomplishment in other fields. His early play *Götz von Berlichingen* (1773) reflects contemporary enthusiasm for the works of SHAKESPEARE and provided the young *STURM UND DRANG* writers with a model for their own dramas. His drama gradually came to express a more classical outlook. *Egmont* (completed in 1788) is still Shakespearian in structure, but Goethe's view of his hero, whose 'daimonic' personality and trust in the goodness of those around him leads to his death, shows a distrust of the values that had enthused him in his *Sturm und Drang* period.

Perhaps his most effective works for the theatre are the classical verse plays *Iphigenie auf Tauris* (*Iphigenia at Tauris*, 1787) and *Torquato Tasso* (1790), the former reflecting his belief in the superiority of moral strength and humanitarian impulse above barbarism, the latter showing a profound scepticism as well as an appreciation of the romantic spirit of the artist. Goethe's masterpiece, *Faust Part 1* (1808) and *Part 2* (1832), while cast in dramatic form and exhibiting command of a vast range of dramatic styles, was not written with performance in mind. *Part 1* has, however, often been produced successfully; it focuses mainly on the private experience of Faust and on his erotic misadventures with Gretchen. *Part 2*, a far more formidable theatrical undertaking, has a wider scope, leading to meditations on such lofty and weighty subjects as the future of the human race.

From 1791 to 1817, as well as executing several other official duties in Weimar Goethe was director of the Court Theatre, a position he shared for some years with SCHILLER. He evolved the so-called WEIMAR STYLE of acting embodied in his 'Rules for Actors', influencing the performance of TRAGEDY in the German theatre until the end of the 19th century. *Wilhelm Meister's Apprenticeship* (1795–6), the great *Bildungsroman*, shows his obvious suspicion of the artistic integrity of the actor, but is still one of the liveliest accounts of theatre life yet written.

Initially Goethe was in the forefront of the German Shakespeare revival. Latterly, most notably in his essay of 1815 'Shakespeare und kein Ende' ('No End to Shakespeare'), he argued that Shakespeare's plays were best read and not performed. His notorious adaptation of *Romeo and Juliet* shows a lack of sympathy with Shakespeare's dramatic strategy.

**Gogol, Nikolai (Vasilievich)** 1809–52 Russian playwright and short story writer; the greatest comic writer of 19th-century Russia. His special brand of grotesque REALISM and belief in the moral and social obligation of art influenced two centuries of artists. His early exposure to the puppet plays and folk tales of his native Ukraine with their mystery, superstition and coarse humour, together with his personal cravings and doubts, combined to produce his tormented art.

During his St Petersburg career (1828–36) as lowly civil servant, bumbling history professor and developing writer he produced three volumes of short stories and miscellany: *Evenings on a Farm Near Dikanka* (1831–2), *Arabesques* and *Mirgorod* (1835), the last two containing his so-called 'Petersburg Tales'. He also composed three short comedies which feature his inimitable linguistic verve, farceur's sense of pace and plot, and his relentless dissection of opportunism, eccentricity, self-delusion and social and moral hypocrisy. These include *Marriage* (1835), *The Gamblers* (1836) and *Decoration of Vladimir of the Third Class* (1832) – this last, concerning an upwardly

mobile bureaucrat, Gogol left unfinished for fear of CENSORSHIP.

*The Inspector General* (1836) is his dramatic masterpiece. In it he creates a satirical, allegorical phantasmagoria of Tsarist Russia in the form of a provincial town whose greed, fear, pride, incomprehension and need for confession are awakened by the arrival of a nonentity mistaken for the titular government official. Variously regarded in Russia as the best early specimen of social realism and as a precursor of symbolist and formalist experiments, the play is pure Gogolian hyperbole. It amused the Tsar but confused and alienated many of the critics, upsetting the author – who fled to Rome, where he remained for 13 years. His paranoia and political conservatism intensified in his final years, as is reflected in his *Selected Passages from Correspondence with Friends* (1847) and in the picaresque epic *Dead Souls* (1842–52). The latter, a projected trilogy in the tradition of Dante's *The Divine Comedy* calling for the spiritual regeneration of Russia, was incomplete and partially burned prior to his death. The 20th century has seen several celebrated productions of his work: MEYERHOLD's and TOVSTONOGOV's *The Inspector General* (1926 and 1972, respectively), EFROS's *The Marriage* (1974) and LYUBIMOV's *The Inspector's Recounting* (1978).

**Golden Age (Spain)** A period in Spanish literature and the arts corresponding roughly to Spain's greatness as a European power, and dated as broadly as 1492–1700 by some, though in the theatre 1580–1680 is more realistic.

**Goldfadn** [Goldfaden], **Avrom** [Avraham Goldenfudim] 1840–1908 Yiddish playwright, poet and composer. Affectionately known as the father of YIDDISH THEATRE, Goldfadn presented the first public performance of a Jewish play in Mark's Biergarten in Jassy, Romania, in 1876. This event unleashed an immediate mushrooming of Yiddish theatre companies and set the pattern of a combination of laughter, tears and music in each play. Some of his songs have become Jewish folk music. His early rather naive plays were consciously directed at the masses of poor, simple and oppressed people around him. He wrote over 40 plays and operettas, including *The Two Kuni Lemels, Shmendrik* and *The Witch* (all 1877). His two greatest works approached operatic form. These were *Shulamith* (1882) based on the Talmudic legend of the love story of Shulamith and Absalom, and *Bar Kochba* (1883), an historical drama of the warrior who led the last tragic revolt of the Jews against the Romans. Goldfadn died in poverty in America, five days after his last play, *Ben Ami*, was produced. It proved a popular success.

**Goldin, Horace** [Hyman Goldstein] 1873–1939 Polish-born American magician. He emigrated to the USA at the age of 16. Because of his heavy accent and stammer he converted his MAGIC act into a rapid-fire silent routine, '45 tricks in 17 minutes', baffling audiences with a quick succession of illusions. He appeared in a MUSICAL COMEDY, *The Merry Magician* (Theatre Royal, Brighton 1911), and was the first conjuror to play the PALACE THEATRE, New York (1913). His most famous illusion was an improvement on P. T. Selbit's 1879 trick, 'Sawing a Lady in Half': Goldin eliminated the box and used a buzz-saw.

**Goldoni, Carlo** 1707–93 Italian playwright and librettist. A Venetian, Goldoni was trained as a lawyer. He wrote tragedies, tragicomedies and librettos for *opera seria*, and in 1737 he became literary director of the

Venetian opera house, the San Giovanni Grisostomo. Financial problems caused him to flee Venice in 1743 and for several years he practised law in Pisa, only occasionally writing dramatic pieces on demand. One such was *Arlecchino, servitore di due padroni* (*Arlecchino, the Servant of Two Masters*), reworked in 1745 from an old scenario at the request of ANTONIO SACCO; in 1753 Goldoni fully scripted the play into the form in which it now survives.

In 1748 he joined the actor-manager GIROLAMO MEDEBACH's company as house dramatist at the Sant' Angelo Theatre in Venice. There he began his reform of Italian comedy by gradually banishing the crudities of the old improvised comedy (see COMMEDIA DELL'ARTE), subordinating both traditional improvisation and the ornate language of baroque drama to the needs of a scripted comedy located in a recognizable social milieu. The plays of this period include *La vedova scaltra* (*The Cunning Widow*), *La famiglia dell'antiquario* (*The Antiquarian's Family*), *I due gemelli veneziani* (*The Venetian Twins*), *La putta onorata* (*The Respectable Girl*) and *La locandiera* (*The Mistress of the Inn*).

In 1753 Goldoni moved to the larger San Luca Theatre; his comic drama became increasingly refined and ambitious, e.g. *Il campiello* (*The Little Square*), *La casa nova* (*The New House*), *Gli innamorati* (*The Lovers*), *I rusteghi* (*The Boors*), *La villeggiatura* (*The Country Holiday*) and *Le baruffe chiozzotte* (*The Chioggian Squabbles*). He also wrote several librettos for *opera buffa*. In the late 1740s and 1750s his chief rival was the dramatist PIETRO CHIARI, with whom he exchanged savage dramatic parodies and offensive manifestos, leading to the introduction of CENSORSHIP to the Venetian theatre (1749). In the late 1750s a more dangerous enemy appeared in the figure of CARLO GOZZI, champion of that masked and improvised comedy supposedly undermined by Goldoni. At the end of the 1761–2 season Goldoni left Venice to join the COMÉDIE-ITALIENNE in Paris. He remained in France to the end of his life.

**Goldsmith, Oliver** 1728–74 Irish playwright, novelist and poet. He trained as a doctor in Edinburgh, toured Europe and settled in London. He began to earn a living as a writer in 1757. His first play, *The Good Natured Man*, first performed in 1768, was a serious attack on sentimentalism; the play's hero, Honeywood, suffers from an excess of good nature, though money always resolves the play's problems. *She Stoops to Conquer* (1773) mocks the snobbery of London through the manipulations of the country, embodied in Tony Lumpkin. The play celebrates the virtues of 'laughing comedy', advocated by Goldsmith in an important essay, in preference to the prevalent sentimental forms.

*gombeyatta* Indian puppet form. In this SHADOW PUPPET theatre of Karnataka, a state in the southwest part of the subcontinent, plays are adapted from stories in the *Ramayana* and the *Mahabharata* epics. About 300 families of shadow puppeteers make their living in Karnataka, where the main seasons for religious festivals are from February to April and in September and October. The puppets are made of goatskin, the largest ones (30 to 40in tall) requiring a complete skin. When constructing puppets of Ganapati, the elephant-headed god, and the epic hero-gods Krishna and Rama, the puppeteer performs ritual sacrifices and takes care in preparing and cutting the hides.

At least 50 puppets are used in a performance, and a puppeteer may have more than a hundred figures in his puppet set. Size generally indicates social rank, and puppets fall into the following categories: divinities, demons, humans, monkey generals, clowns, animals of various kinds and natural objects, such as plants and trees. As in other forms of shadow theatre, several puppets may be needed to represent the various moods of a single character.

**Gombrowicz, Witold** 1902–69 Polish playwright, novelist and memoirist. From 1939 he lived in Argentina and France. His plays are grotesque theatricalist fables that oppose conflicting images of reality in a struggle between socially imposed, restrictive forms and creative immaturity. Since the mid-1970s, *Ivona, Princess of Burgundia* (1938), *The Marriage* (1947) and *Operetta* (1966) have been central to the national repertory.

**Gómez de Avellaneda, Gertrudis** [Tula] 1814–73 Cuban poet, novelist and playwright. Her work reflected little of Cuban reality. She spent most of her life in Spain, where she aspired to courtly grandeur and where her theatre primarily belongs, although she is considered one of the major women playwrights of the Americas. With 20 plays, she dominated both tragic and comic forms. Her principal tragic works are *Munio Alfonso* (1844) and *Baltasar* (1858), the latter relating the Spanish Crown to its biblical antecedents. On the lighter side, *La hija de las flores* (*Daughter of the Flowers*, 1852) and *El millonario y la maleta* (*The Millionaire and his Suitcase*, 1870) are entertaining comedies. For the most part, she avoided the excesses of romanticism and developed characters of sound psychology.

**Goncharova, Natalya (Sergeevna)** 1881–1962 Russian designer. A painter-designer of the pre-revolutionary period (see THEATRE DESIGN), with the artist Mikhail Larionov she helped establish neo-primitivism (1910–14) as a trend in Russian art. Neo-primitivism returned to native-painted handicrafts (such as woodcuts, icons and toys) to counteract illusionism, traditional proportion, and the symbolists' (see SYMBOLISM) refined mysticism, all of which reflected the influence of the West. Goncharova embraced old Eastern forms – the Russian *SKOMOROKHI* (mummers) and *balagany* (puppet shows) – at a time when this idea was becoming attractive to Russia's most innovative directors. She designed sets and costumes for DIAGHILEV's production of the opera-ballet *The Golden Cockerel* (Paris, 1914) and the ballet *The Firebird* (London, 1926), for TAIROV's Kamerny Theatre production of GOLDONI's *The Fan* (Moscow, 1915) and for BALIEV's *Chauve-Souris* (New York, 1931). Her work also included book and fashion design. She and Larionov emigrated to Paris in 1917.

**González Dávila, Jesús** 1942– Mexican playwright. He has succeeded with several prize-winning plays. *La fábrica de juguetes* (*The Toy Factory*, 1970) and *Muchacha del alma* (*A Girl with Soul*, 1983) are representative of his efforts to penetrate the contemporary Mexican psyche with realistic, often brutal, plays.

**Goodman Theatre** (Chicago) The Goodman is America's second-oldest regional theatre, founded in 1925. The 683-seat theatre has always housed a school of drama, though the resident company operated only intermittently. In 1969–70 a professional company again took up residence and in 1978, until he became co-director of Lincoln Center, the leadership was assumed by Gregory Mosher, who emphasized new works and classic revivals. In 1986 he was replaced by Robert Falls, under whom classical and new works have been staged. World and American premieres have included MAMET's *Glengarry Glen Ross* and SOYINKA's *Death and the King's Horseman*.

**Goodman's Fields Theatre** (London) This licensed theatre was built in 1729 in Ayliffe Street, Goodman's Fields – the opposite end of London from most theatres – but after protests concerning its location royal approval was withdrawn in 1730. A new theatre opened in 1732, with a spectacular ceiling depicting the king surrounded by SHAKESPEARE, DRYDEN, CONGREVE and BETTERTON. In 1741 it was the scene of DAVID GARRICK's spectacular London debut.

**Goodwin, Nat(haniel Carl)** 1857–1919 American actor and manager. A Bostonian, Goodwin began his career as a mimic for drawing-room theatricals and then moved to the professional theatre, making his New York debut at TONY PASTOR's Opera House. He enjoyed a major success in 1876 at the New York LYCEUM in *Off the Stage* by giving imitations of popular actors. While he excelled as a mimic and eccentric comedian, he was also effective in serious parts such as the title role in *Nathan Hale* (1899). Married five times, he gained notoriety for his off-stage antics. With his third wife MAXINE ELLIOTT he starred in numerous plays, including *Nathan Hale*, *When We Were Twenty-One* (1900) and *The Merchant of Venice* (1901). He attempted Bottom in 1903, but was not successful in Shakespearian roles. In his autobiography, *Nat Goodwin's Book* (1914), he took revenge upon his many enemies.

**Gordin, Jacob** 1853–1909 Russian-born Yiddish playwright. A radical, much influenced by IBSEN and HAUPTMANN, he was appalled by the low standard of popular YIDDISH THEATRE on his arrival in America in 1890. His plays were immediately hailed by the intellectuals and the socialists. *Siberia* (1891), *The Jewish King Lear* (1892), *Mirele Efros* (1898) and *God, Man and Devil* (1890) are the best-known of some 90 plays, including translations into Yiddish of the great European classics.

**Gordon [née Jones], Ruth** 1896–1985 American actress and playwright. A revival in 1936 of WYCHERLEY's *The Country Wife*, in which she was the first American cast in an OLD VIC (London) production, led to roles that exploited her vivacity and split-second timing. In 1937 (New York) she played Nora in *A Doll's House*; in 1942 she was Natasha in *The Three Sisters*. Her most memorable stage creation was Dolly Levi in *The Matchmaker* (1954, London; 1955, New York), a role written for her by THORNTON WILDER. She was also a successful screen actress, playwright (*Over 21*, *Years Ago*) and, especially, screenwriter.

**Gordone, Charles** 1925– African-American playwright. With his only successful stage play *No Place to Be Somebody* (1969), Gordone became the first black playwright to win a Pulitzer Prize. At a time of militancy in black theatre, he dramatized in a number of highly theatrical scenes the murder of an incorrigible black pimp by his closest friend. The NEGRO ENSEMBLE COMPANY rejected the play, which was eventually staged at JOSEPH PAPP's Public Theater in New York.

**Gorelik, Mordecai** 1899–90 American stage and film designer. Born in Russia, Gorelik studied with ROBERT EDMOND JONES, NORMAN BEL GEDDES and Serge Soudeikine, and began his career with the PROVINCETOWN PLAYERS in 1920. His 1925 design for *Processional* was a rare example of successful EXPRESSIONISM on the American stage. During the 1930s he was the primary designer for the GROUP THEATRE, including *Men and White* and *Golden Boy*. He was an orga-

nizer of a short-lived leftist group, the Theatre Collective. Gorelik also designed *All My Sons* and *A Hatful of Rain*, among others, on BROADWAY. He was a strong advocate of BRECHT's EPIC THEATRE, which he emphasizes in his book, *New Theatres for Old*. Much of his design can be classified as suggestive REALISM.

**Gorky, Maksim** [Aleksei (Maksimovich) Peshkov] 1868–1936 Russian novelist, playwright, poet and critic. Born into an ignorant, cruel and impoverished milieu, Gorky became a self-educated rebel artist and in due course the official hero of Soviet art. He devoted his career to reconciling the social classes into an enlightened society built upon education and communication. His publishing house Znanie (Knowledge, 1900), although it specialized in neo-REALISM, encouraged such writers as ANDREEV, BLOK and Bunin, whose aesthetics did not always agree with Gorky's own. He was both championed and criticized by CHEKHOV.

Gorky's involvement in the 1905 and 1917 Revolutions led to arrest and an inevitable movement towards Bolshevism, which focused the remainder of his career. He wrote 12 plays between 1901 and 1913, having already established himself as a short story writer (*Sketches and Stories*, 2 vols., 1898), novelist (*Foma Gordeev*, 1899), revolutionary poet (*Song of the Stormy Petrel*, 1901) and social force. His dramas are all sociopolitically slanted, lacking in psychological and stylistic subtlety, mixing naive idealism with cynicism. They offer stereotypically 'good', i.e., strong-willed, productive peasants and workers juxtaposed with 'bad', i.e., ineffectual, self-serving and morally dishonest intellectuals, clerics and petty bourgeois. Plots are dialectically constructed so as to maximize the theme of alienation between the classes. Language is often rhetorical, building towards and often interrupted by ideological tirades that are meant to educate the audience.

His first play *The Petty Bourgeoisie* (1902), beginning Gorky's long association with the MOSCOW ART THEATRE (which originally bore his name), presents the traditional Russian generational conflict theme, resulting in the birth of the proletarian hero. *The Lower Depths* (1902) was celebrated in its time for the novelty of its tramp characters, but it suffers from all of Gorky's ideological and dramaturgical faults. *Summer Folk* (1904), *Barbarians* (1905) and *Enemies* (1906) deal with philistinism and alienation among the classes, with culpability invariably falling upon the intelligentsia and the merchants. Later plays include *Yegor Bulychov and Others* (1932) and its sequel *Dostigayev and Others* (1933), suggestive of OSTROVSKY's portraits of merchant characters.

Gorky's most fully realized human drama may well have been his own life, recorded in his autobiographical trilogy – *My Childhood* (1914), *In the World* (1916) and *My Universities* (1924). The dramatic final chapter saw the humanitarian idealist returning from self-imposed exile (1921–8) to become first president of the newly formed Union of Soviet Writers.

**Gorostiza, Carlos** 1920– Argentine playwright, actor, director and novelist. Gorostiza made theatre history when his play, *El puente* (*The Bridge*, 1949), spanned the gap between the independent theatre and the commercial theatre in Buenos Aires, and opened a new epoch in REALISM on the Argentine stage. Other major works include *El pan de la locura* (*Bread of Madness*, 1958) and *Los prójimos* (*The Neighbours*, 1966), the latter based on an incident in New York in which unconcerned witnesses to an assault failed to intervene. *¿A qué jugamos?* (*What*

*Shall We Play?*, 1968) uses a metatheatrical structure to investigate contemporary problems, especially those of the younger generation. In the Alfonsín government Gorostiza was named Secretary of Culture with broad responsibility for governmental support of the arts. Recent titles are *Los hermanos queridos* (*Beloved Brothers*, 1978), *El acompañante* (*The Accompanist*, 1981), *Hay que apagar el fuego* (*We Have to Put Out the Fire*, 1982) and *Papi* (1984).

**Gorostiza, Celestino** 1904–67 Mexican playwright and director. A major figure in the independent movement of the 1930s, Gorostiza interpreted expressionist tendencies (see EXPRESSIONISM) in vogue in the European theatre in such plays as *Ser o no ser* (*To Be or Not to Be*, 1934). In a later wave he dealt with the taboos of racism in Mexican society (*El color de nuestra piel* (*The Colour of Our Skin*, 1952)) and took a new look at the story of Cortés and Malinche in *La Malinche*, later retitled *La leña está verde* (*The Firewood Is Green*, 1958).

**Gosson, Stephen** 1554–1624 English anti-theatrical pamphleteer. His *The School of Abuse* (1579), attacking poets and actors, was dedicated, without permission, to Sir PHILIP SIDNEY, whose *The Apology for Poetry* (written c.1580) was written partly to confute Gosson. The controversy was still at its height when Gosson wrote *Plays Confuted in Five Actions*.

**Gôt, Edmond** 1822–1901 French actor. Gôt's entire career of over 50 years was at the COMÉDIE-FRANÇAISE. In 1848 he played the Abbé in MUSSET's *Il ne faut jurer de rien* (*Nothing Is Certain*), a part suited to his vein of whimsical comedy. He was equally at home in the modern and the classical repertoires. His greatest successes were in *Le Duc Job* (1859), AUGIER's *Les Effrontés* (*The Shameless Ones*, 1861), PONSARD's *L'Honneur et l'argent* and *Le Fils de Giboyer* (1862) and the splendid 1868 revival of Balzac's *Mercadet*.

**Göteborgs Stadsteater** Swedish company. Göteborg has a long theatrical tradition. In 1916 one of Europe's best-equipped theatres, the Lorensberg, was opened there and used by the Stadsteater company (founded in 1917) until it moved to its present building in 1934. Artistic achievement has varied, depending on leadership: PER LINDBERG's modernistic productions (1918–23) made the Lorensberg the theatrical focus of Scandinavia; Torsten Hammaren (1926–50) emphasized new writing, especially anti-Fascist plays; Mats Johansson (1962–82) developed its social and political profile. Conflict in the early 1980s over artistic and political aims caused long-lasting problems, but Eva Bergman has led the Backa young people's company to extraordinary success with playful productions of SHAKESPEARE and IBSEN.

**Göthe, Staffan** 1944– Swedish playwright, actor and director. In 1972 Göthe began writing children's plays for the Växjöensemble company, in which he was an actor. Plays like *A Night in February* (1972) and *The Horrible Bang* (1978) are not only *for* young audiences, but incorporate their concerns and points of view, especially their attempts to survive, sometimes tragically, in a treacherous adult world. His plays for adults include a trilogy about the Cervieng family, exploring through a mix of REALISM and fantasy the breakdown of social-democratic Sweden as a 'people's home': *La Strada del amore* (1985), *A Stuffed Dog* (1986) and *The Perfect Kiss* (1990). His plays focus, with both comedy and despair, on the vulnerability and loneliness prevalent in modern Swedish society.

**Gottsched, Johann (Christoph)** 1700–66 German playwright, critic and essayist. One of Germany's first significant men of letters, he wished to elevate German culture by modelling its literature and drama on the French. In his theatrical endeavours he was aided by CAROLINE NEUBER, whose troupe attempted to put into practice his tenets of acting, which were essentially abstracted from the acting of French companies in the German courts and developed from Gottsched's own conception of classical, rhetorical gesture. It became known as the LEIPZIG STYLE. His play *The Dying Cato* (1732), despite its woodenness, had some success when performed by the Neuber troupe. Gottsched was a man of little humour and had a limited idea of what could be achieved in the theatre. Hence, after his rupture with the Neubers in 1741, even though he had some communication with SCHÖNEMANN, his effective connections with the theatre were severed.

**Goulue, La** [Louise Weber] 1860–1919 French cancan dancer. A former washerwoman, she was notorious in her day for her hot temper, vast appetite, lesbian attachments and huge salary. Her high kicks, performed at the MOULIN-ROUGE during 1889–95, and red topknot remain familiar through the art of Toulouse-Lautrec.

**Gow, Michael** 1955– Australian playwright. His first play *The Kid* (1983), a tragedy of dispossessed adolescents in a Wagnerian context, juxtaposes contemporary life with cultural myth in a characteristic way. His most popular play *Away* (1986) links a schoolboy's imminent death with fragments from Shakespeare. His other works include *Europe* (1987), *1841* (written for Australia's bicentennial in 1988), *Furious* (1991) and the television screenplay *Edens Lost* (1988).

**Gozzi, Carlo** 1720–1806 Italian playwright. A Venetian aristocrat, he was concerned to preserve the purity of traditional language, thought and artistic activity against the threatening incursions of the Enlightenment. In the late 1750s, hostile to the bourgeois realistic and reformist tendencies of contemporary dramatists like CARLO GOLDONI and PIETRO CHIARI, he engaged first in vigorous literary polemics, then in the deliberate creation of an opposition drama. He tried to restore to the stage the masks and improvisation of the traditional *COMMEDIA DELL'ARTE*, and to reassert the courtly values of the aristocratic past.

His success did not last long, despite a 25-year association with one of the finest Venetian acting companies of the 18th century, the troupe of ANTONIO SACCO. For them he wrote the most enduring of his work, the *fiabe*: these fantastic and scenically spectacular romances included *L'Amore delle tre melarance* (*The Love of Three Oranges*, 1761), *Il corvo* (*The Raven*), *Il re cervo* (*The King Stag*, 1762), *Turandot* (1762), *La donna serpente* (*The Snake Woman*, 1762) and *L'augellino belverde* (*The Green Bird*, 1765). They often wedded the comic strategies and masked figures of the improvised drama to the fairy-tale materials of exotic Oriental stories. Underpinning Gozzi's work was his hostility to the local realism, scenographic simplicity and idiomatic language of Goldoni's new comedy. His *fiabe* provided plot lines for opera and ballet, but only began again to attract the attention of the non-musical stage with the rediscovery of a primarily non-verbal, theatrical theatre in the stagings of MEYERHOLD and VAKHTANGOV in the early years of this century, and in the avant-garde visual theatre of the 1970s and 80s.

**Grabbe, Christian Dietrich** 1801–36 German playwright. Grabbe, an army lawyer, was also a prolific writer. The manner of his plays anticipated both the EPIC THEATRE of the 20th century and the THEATRE OF THE ABSURD, and they were not produced. His most significant works are large-scale dramas on great men of history, most notable among which are two plays from a projected cycle on the Hohenstaufen family, *The Emperor Friedrich Barbarossa* (1829) and *The Emperor Henry VI* (1830). But perhaps his most durable plays are *Napoleon, or The Hundred Days* (1831) and *Hannibal* (1835), which are still occasionally revived today. The only one of his plays to be produced in his lifetime was *Don Juan and Faust* (1829), a study of the difference between the idealistic and realistic personalities. Grabbe is probably best known today for his grotesque comedy, *Joke, Satire, Irony, and Deeper Significance* (1827), though several of his plays have been revived successfully in the modern German theatre.

***gracioso*** Spanish character. A comic servant, he is one of the chief sources of humour in the Spanish *COMEDIA*.

**Graetz, Paul** 1890–1937 German CABARET artist. He made a name for himself in SCHNITZLER roles before appearing at the Schall und Rauch and Kabarett der Komiker in Berlin. With his deep, raw voice and slow movements, he excelled at Berlin loudmouths and chatterboxes. He collaborated with ARNOLT BRONNEN on the play *Katalaunische Schlacht* and worked for PISCATOR, before emigrating to the United States in 1935.

**Gramsci, Antonio** 1891–1937 Italian politician, political theorist and critic. As well as being an active politician and co-founder of the Italian Communist Party in 1921, he was a seminal commentator on a broad range of social and cultural matters, including the theatre. Between 1915 and 1920 he was theatre critic for *Avanti!*, and his penetrating articles, treating of drama and the stage from a firm and sophisticated ideological position hostile to the bourgeois and BOULEVARD values of the day, have since exercised considerable influence on thinking about the functions of theatre, both in Italy and abroad.

**Grand Duke's Opera House (New York)** see PENNY THEATRES

**Grand-Guignol** French theatre. Founded in 1895 as a *théâtre salon* by Oscar Méténier, the Théâtre de Grand-Guignol moved to its premises in the rue Chaptal, Paris, four years later, under the leadership of Max Maurey. At first merely a naturalistic theatre (see NATURALISM), it eventually specialized in horror, drawing on the works of Edgar Allen Poe in particular. Its chief playwright was André de Lorde, nicknamed The 'Prince of Terror', who preferred psychological suspense to gore, though he was not averse to the eye-gougings and acid baths that were popular features of the genre. This skilled sensationalism pleased the Parisian public, but attempts to acclimatize it to England and America were not successful. It finally closed in 1962.

**Granville Barker, Harley** 1877–1946 British actor, playwright, director and critic. He exerted a major influence on British drama and theatre. As an actor he became increasingly discontented with the low standards of commercial touring. Contact with WILLIAM POEL, WILLIAM ARCHER and BERNARD SHAW, together with membership of the STAGE SOCIETY, opened up new possibilities. In 1900 he directed his own first major play, *The Marrying of Ann Leete*. In 1904, with J. E. VEDRENNE as his business manager, Barker took a lease on the ROYAL COURT THEATRE and initiated three historic seasons of the new 'uncommercial' drama, pre-

senting 11 plays by Shaw together with new plays by Continental and British authors and new translations of three plays by EURIPIDES, thereby giving a major boost to the repertory movement.

During this period he wrote his second main play *The Voysey Inheritance* (Royal Court, 1905), and the publication during the next few years of *Waste* (1906–7) and *The Madras House* (1909) established him as an important dramatist of the new, realistic English drama. His attention now focused upon directing and upon the promotion of the REPERTORY movement in England. In 1910 he directed the experimental repertory season at the Duke of York's Theatre, London, which proved an artistic success but a financial failure – underlining for Barker the case for subsidy of repertory. In 1912 the pinnacle of his directing career was reached with productions at the Savoy Theatre of *The Winter's Tale* and *Twelfth Night*, followed in 1914 by *A Midsummer Night's Dream*. He abandoned the elaborate, conventional methods of staging SHAKESPEARE, including the domination of 'star' actors, and produced instead ensemble performances of the highest quality, stimulating a new approach to Shakespeare in the theatre.

From 1918, Barker devoted himself almost totally to writing, lecturing and scholarship. In 1919 he joined the newly formed British Drama League (see BRITISH THEATRE ASSOCIATION) and was its chairman for 13 years. He wrote several more plays and published many works on the role of theatre in society. But his most important and pioneering work of scholarship was his *Prefaces to Shakespeare* (in six vols., 1927–46), in which he bridged the gap between the academic and theatrical approaches to the plays.

**Grass, Günter** 1927– German playwright and novelist. Grass uses deliberately naive perspectives to bring out the monstrosity of the Nazi period and its distorting effect on contemporary German society. He is a leading member of the influential Group 47. Early dramas like *Flood* (1956) and *The Wicked Cooks* (1961) present political violence and moral coercion in images derived from the THEATRE OF THE ABSURD. His novel *The Tin Drum* (1959) has become a modern classic, with its picture of Fascism through the eyes of an insane dwarf; and *The Plebeians Rehearse the Uprising* (1966), which dramatizes the problematic relationship between political art and actuality through the figure of BRECHT, won an international reputation.

**Grasso, Giovanni** 1873–1930 Italian actor-manager. Born into a Sicilian family of marionette specialists, he formed his own company with an emphasis on the performance of Sicilian plays and the work of contemporary Italian dramatists in dialect versions. He was one of the last Italian stage actors to tour extensively abroad, where the REALISM of his productions of dialect plays was particularly admired. He won notable success too, at home and abroad, as Othello, his version of the Moor outdoing SALVINI's for emotionalism and sensationalism, qualities little approved by English critics when he took the play to London in 1911.

**Grau Delgado, Jacinto** 1877–1958 Spanish playwright. His works reflect his desire to raise Spanish theatre from the comfortable shallowness of ECHEGARAY and BENAVENTE. As a result his many fine plays were rarely successful in Spain, though he had some success abroad – *El señor de Pigmalión* (*Mr Pygmalion*, 1921), for instance, being produced in Paris and Prague before Spain. His early plays, reworking historical or biblical themes – e.g. *El hijo pródigo* (*The Prodigal Son*, 1917) – are classically simple. After 1918 they follow European trends, especially German EXPRESSIONISM and the concept of the superman, as in *El señor de Pigmalión* and *El caballero Varona* (*The Knight of Varona*, 1925). In exile in South America after the Civil War, he experimented with FARCE and other forms. His complete works, 25 plays, were published in Buenos Aires during 1954–9.

**Gray, John** 1946– Canadian playwright, composer and director. One of the founders of Vancouver's Tamahnous Theatre, he began writing while musical director of Toronto's Theatre Passe Muraille. His works, *18 Wheels* (1977), *Billy Bishop Goes to War* (1981) and *Rock and Roll* (1982), are finely shaped musical plays, both literate and entertaining. *Billy Bishop*, the story of a legendary Canadian World War I flying ace, has been immensely successful across Canada, in Britain and the USA, and was seen on Canadian and British television.

**Gray, Simon (James Holliday)** 1936– British playwright. His first stage play in the WEST END, *Wise Child* (1967), featured ALEC GUINNESS as a transvestite. Gray's comedies often depict lonely, alienated men, rejected by society either because of their sexual inclinations or their shyness. He can sustain a flow of comedy while exploring the nature of suffering. His first major success came with *Butley* (1971), in which ALAN BATES played a university lecturer torn between his disintegrating marriage and love for a male student. Bates also took the central role in Gray's *Otherwise Engaged* (1975), as a publisher surrounded by people whom he dislikes or distrusts and seeking solace in music, and in *Melon* (1987), again playing a publisher. In *Close of Play* (1978) a distinguished academic stays silent during his last hours, while his family bicker around him; in *Quartermain's Terms* (1981) an ineffectual but good-hearted bachelor teacher in a Cambridge language school is left defenceless against the loss of friendships and the dislocation of school routine. In *The Rear Column* (1978) Gray presented a picture of institutionalized violence, with an episode from British colonial history. *The Common Pursuit* (1984) provides a group portrait of Cambridge arts graduates, with their failures and successes in later life. The laughter in *Hidden Laughter* (1990), which he directed himself, is buried deep within the story of a family whose terrible loneliness is concealed beneath affluence.

**Gray, Spalding** 1941– American actor and playwright. A product of the avant-garde theatre movement of the 1960s, Gray spent five years as a traditional actor before joining Richard Schechner and the PERFORMANCE GROUP in 1970. With the disbanding of that group in 1980, he and colleagues formed the WOOSTER GROUP. His reputation, however, has transcended the Group, primarily because of his trilogy *Three Places in Rhode Island* (*Sakonnet Point*, 1975; *Rumstick Road*, 1977; *Nayatt School*, 1978) and a series of 13 autobiographical monologues (1979–91).

**Gray, Terence** 1895–?1987 British director and stage designer. In 1926 he founded the Cambridge Festival Theatre, where he worked with NORMAN MARSHALL mounting productions of classical Greek drama and German EXPRESSIONISM, ELMER RICE, early O'NEILL, PIRANDELLO and W. B. YEATS. His non-naturalistic style, heavily influenced by GORDON CRAIG, disregarded dramatic texts – presenting e.g. *Twelfth Night* on rollerskates and a 'flamenco' treatment of *Romeo and Juliet* – and was accompanied by 'isometric scenic design'

using pale-grey or luminous screens and columns as neutral architectural shapes for the play of light, together with arrangements of steps and multi-level rostra reminiscent of LEOPOLD JESSNER. Gray's final production was the first English performance of AESCHYLUS' *The Suppliants* in 1933.

## Greek theatre, ancient

### Dramatic festivals

Most of the Greek plays which survive were performed at Athens in the 5th century BC. All dramatic performances at this period took place at festivals of the god Dionysus. The main festival was the Great or City Dionysia, held in March or early April and centred on the temple and theatre of Dionysus beneath the Acropolis. Every year three tragedians competed for a prize, each producing four plays on one day; and five comic poets competed for another prize, each producing one play. The four plays by a tragedian usually comprised three tragedies followed by a satyr play. The four plays might be connected in theme to form a tetralogy in the proper sense (see AESCHYLUS), or might be wholly separate. (The set of three tragedies from a tetralogy is called a trilogy.)

The Great Dionysia also incorporated religious ceremonies and performances of dithyrambs (a form of non-dramatic choral song). The plays, however, were not religious rituals; they had no RITUAL function and their content had no necessary connection with Dionysus. The plays were mass entertainment, performed before an audience of several thousand (perhaps as many as 15,000) drawn from all social classes. In the 4th century at least, and perhaps earlier, the democratic state paid a small allowance to enable poor citizens to attend. Whether women attended is uncertain. The prize-giving was taken very seriously; from 449 there was a prize for the best tragic protagonist (leading actor) as well as one for the best tragedian.

The dramatists normally produced their own plays (though ARISTOPHANES did not always do so). Indeed, the Greeks generally spoke not of a 'writer' but of a 'teacher' of tragedy or comedy, since his essential task was not simply to compose a text but to instruct the Chorus and actors in the performance through which his play was to be realized. Revivals of plays already performed did not become usual at the Great Dionysia until the 4th century BC, though Aeschylus is said to have received the unique distinction of a decree allowing his plays to be revived after his death.

All actors and Chorus members were male, and wore masks. The music to accompany songs was provided by the only unmasked figure, the player of the *aulos*, which was a double pipe with reeds. The Chorus normally sang in unison (though its leader could take part in spoken dialogue with actors), and danced in formation as it sang.

Another festival of Dionysus, the Lenaea, was held around the beginning of February. From c.442 it too was the occasion for dramatic competitions in the Theatre of Dionysus, with two tragic poets producing two plays each and five comic poets producing one play each. It was more important for comedy than for tragedy.

### Greek tragedy

Tragedy contains two principal types of verse: spoken dialogue in iambic and trochaic metres, usually delivered by actors, and songs in lyric metres, usually delivered by the Chorus. There were non-dramatic precedents for both types. Iambic and trochaic poetry was composed for delivery by the poets themselves, for such purposes as attacking their enemies and giving moral and political advice to their fellow citizens. Choral songs, sometimes long and elaborate and incorporating mythical narratives, were performed on various religious and ceremonial occasions. Tragedy as we know it was born when these two traditions were combined together, verse spoken by the poet (who was at first the sole actor) being interspersed with songs sung by the Chorus. This innovation probably occurred at Athens in the second half of the 6th century, and the man responsible was probably THESPIS. Thespis also introduced the use of masks, enabling actor and Chorus to take on roles from the mythical past.

The word 'tragedy' itself (*tragōidia*) remains most mysterious. It should mean something like 'goat-singing', but the Greeks themselves seem to have had no idea how tragedy was ever connected with goats. The sacrifice of a goat on the occasion of a tragic performance is a more likely explanation than any connection between tragedy and goat-like satyrs.

As long as the poet himself was the only actor, the dramatic possibilities must have been restricted. The important step of introducing a second actor is said to have been taken by Aeschylus, who also, according to ARISTOTLE, 'reduced the choral element and gave dialogue the leading role', and who is often regarded as the true father of tragedy. The introduction of the third actor was ascribed to SOPHOCLES by most authorities but to Aeschylus by some, and evidently occurred around 460, in the period when both poets were competing. The three actors – protagonist, deuteragonist and tritagonist – shared the parts in any play between them. In addition there were mute extras, generally functioning as attendants but sometimes portraying named characters; and EURIPIDES sometimes had short singing parts for boys.

The great majority of tragedies dramatized events from the Greek myths. These traditional tales were believed to be historically true in essence, but were also felt to provide paradigms of human fortunes, against which men could measure their own experience. The mythical material was usually taken from existing poetry, whether epic, lyric or tragic. The use of this familiar material meant that the outline of the story was always known to the audience in advance, and this knowledge could be exploited for purposes of dramatic irony. Nevertheless, the tragedian had great freedom in shaping his plot, and very different plays could be based on the same myth, as can be seen by comparing the *Choephori* of Aeschylus and the *Electras* of Sophocles and Euripides. A few plays portrayed events in recent history (Aeschylus' *Persians* is the only surviving example, but see also PHRYNICHUS). These, however, were events that had already attained 'mythic' status, and the plays were set in exotic locations; no living Greek is mentioned by name in any tragedy.

The style of tragedy can be supple, lively and, up to a point, colloquial, but always retains a certain dignity; it avoids the jokes and indecencies associated with comedy and is enriched by poetic words and expressions unknown in ordinary usage. In theme and plot not all tragedies have the concentrated seriousness of Sophocles' *Oedipus Tyrannus* or Euripides' *Medea*; for those of Euripides also include sensational melodramas and plays of romance and intrigue, even of gentle humour. And there are happy endings, not only in these romantic tragedies but in such serious ones as Aeschylus' *Eumenides* or Sophocles' *Philoctetes*. The fact that a Greek tragedy *can* end unhappily, however, and can contemplate death and acute suffering without escapism or false consolation, is a remarkable feature of the genre, distinguishing it from most independent dramatic traditions in other cultures, and doubtless owing much to the example of Homer's *Iliad*.

The scene of most tragedies is set in the open air in front of a palace or other building. Occasionally there is a change of scene, marked by the departure and re-entry of the Chorus. Events on the tragic stage never include acts of violence, and seldom include deaths. Violence and death, however, were central to most of the myths portrayed, and the tragedians dealt with this by means of messengers, who come to report what has happened inside the palace or elsewhere. Every play of Sophocles and Euripides contains at least one formal messenger speech, and the dramatists make the most of the opportunities which these provide for vivid and exciting narrative. Aeschylus uses messengers in rather different and more varied ways.

In structure a tragedy consists of several acts or 'episodes', normally separated by the major choral songs, which are preceded by exits of actors and followed by entrances. Most of the spoken dialogue takes the form either of extended speeches (often highly rhetorical) or of line-by-line exchanges (stichomythia), though more irregular patterns also occur. Besides spoken dialogue, an act may contain a sung exchange between actor and Chorus (*amoibaion* or *kommos*) or a solo song by an actor (monody). The rhetorical style of tragic speeches becomes most marked in the set-piece debate (known to scholars as an *agōn* or contest) between two characters. There is at least one such debate in almost every play of Sophocles or Euripides.

A choral song can have various functions. It can influence the audience's feelings by means of moralizing comments on what the Chorus has witnessed. It can broaden the scope of the play by exploring the connections between present and past events (especially in Aeschylus). It can work ironically, evoking a mood of hope and joy before disaster strikes, or one of despair before salvation comes (especially in Sophocles). In Aeschylus the Chorus is always closely involved in what is happening on stage, and many of the actors' speeches are addressed to it. In Euripides (especially his later work) its role becomes less integral; its presence is ignored for long stretches (and can even be an embarrassment), and some of its songs are little more than interludes.

In the 4th century the tendencies seen in late Euripides (and AGATHON) – melodramatic plot, episodic structure, a decline in the role of the Chorus - were apparently carried further. The period was evidently one of decline. In the Hellenistic period (from 323 BC) tragic performances, though widespread in the Greek world, were probably no longer attended by a wide public. While comedy remained popular and continued to develop, tragedy became fossilized.

## Greek comedy

The word *kōmōdia* means singing connected with, or suitable for, a *kōmos* or drunken revel. The comedy of 5th-century Athens – 'Old Comedy' – combines the same principal types of verse as tragedy, namely iambic or trochaic dialogue and choral song. The earliest known comic dramatists were Chionides and Magnes, who seem to have competed in the earliest recorded contest, at the Great Dionysia c.486. The most admired poets of Old Comedy were CRATINUS, Eupolis and Aristophanes; and only the work of Aristophanes survives. All his extant plays have fantasy plots set at the time of their production, but burlesque treatments of mythical themes were also common.

Comedy evidently saw itself from the first as the antitype of tragedy, which it constantly parodies. Comic poets are much less concerned than tragedians with coherence and consistency of plot, and several of Aristophanes' plays degenerate by the end into a series of slapstick routines. An actor is always allowed to come out of character for the sake of a joke or a topical reference, and the 'dramatic illusion' may be deliberately broken for the sake of insulting the audience or playing with theatrical convention. There is no attempt at unity of place, a few lines of dialogue being sufficient to transform the imagined setting completely. Actors are used less economically than in tragedy, some plays requiring at least four. The language of comedy (when it is not PAR-ODYING tragedy or other literature, or foreign dialects) is an entirely colloquial Attic Greek. A startling feature is the scurrilous and often quite unfair abuse which the comic poets heaped on contemporary individuals, from defenceless private citizens to powerful politicians (even gods are treated with scant respect). There is certainly no restriction on the explicitness of the sexual and excremental jokes. A play is usually named after the character assumed by its Chorus (24 in number), which may be human (e.g. Men of Acharnae), animal (e.g. Frogs) or even inanimate (e.g. Clouds). In the middle of most of Aristophanes' plays there is a long section (sometimes two sections) called the parabasis, in which the plot simply stops and the Chorus addresses the audience directly.

The last two extant plays of Aristophanes, Ecclesiazusae and Plutus, dating from the early 4th century, exhibit the transition to Middle Comedy, which prevailed at Athens until about the 320s. We have only fragments, however, from such prolific 4th-century poets as Antiphanes, Anaxandrides and Eubulus. The importance of the Chorus declines rapidly; obscenity and satirical abuse also decline to some extent, and the pervasive cynicism of Aristophanes' earlier work is replaced by homely moralizing. Fantasy plots and burlesque treatments of myths remain popular, but familiar figures from daily life, such as cooks, parasites and courtesans, start to appear in stereotyped roles.

New Comedy, which prevailed from the late 4th century to the 2nd, is a gentle, whimsical comedy of manners, very different indeed from the anarchic fantasy of Aristophanes, and showing the influence of the romantic tragedies of Euripides. The great name here is MENANDER; other popular poets included Alexis (whose very long career spanned the transition from Middle to New), Philemon and Diphilus.

The only sign of the Chorus is now a stage direction between acts (which always number five) and a conventional warning that revellers are approaching, which signals its first entry. The scene is always set in front of two bourgeois houses in contemporary Greece, and the romantic plot, while it may be highly improbable, contains no actual impossibilities. Love, an almost unheard-of phenomenon in Old Comedy, is normally the mainspring of the action, and this proceeds through intrigues and misunderstandings to a happy ending, in which the sympathetic characters receive their reward. Most of the humour (and pathos) derives from the mistakes which the characters make and the human plausibility of their reactions. Somewhat broader humour is provided by slaves, cooks and the like, but indecency and topical allusions are very rare. While not all the sententious moralizing is to be taken at face value, an atmosphere of conventional decency and tolerance prevails.

The plays of New Comedy remained very popular throughout antiquity, but were lost in the Middle Ages. Our knowledge of them derives from imitations by PLAUTUS and TERENCE (through which they influenced the comic traditions of the Renaissance and later periods) and from more or less fragmentary texts (almost exclusively of Menander) excavated in Egypt in recent times.

## The satyr play

Satyrs are mythical subhuman creatures of the Greek countryside, drunken and lustful and often portrayed in the retinue of Dionysus or in pursuit of nymphs. On 5th-century vases they are depicted as men with bald heads, pointed ears, snub noses and horses' tails. The 5th-century satyr play was always composed by a tragedian, and normally formed a humorous tailpiece to a set of three tragedies. It consisted of a burlesque treatment of a mythical theme, which often concerned a popular figure such as Heracles, Dionysus or Odysseus, and always had a happy ending. Into this myth the satyrs (together with their father Silenus, who was regularly a character) had to be more or less artificially introduced. In metre and construction the plays were similar to tragedies, but less strict. The plot and 'dramatic illusion' were more carefully sustained than in Old Comedy, and the humour was less broad; indecencies did occur, but contemporary allusions did not. The only example to survive complete is Euripides' Cyclops, but we also have about half of Sophocles' Ichneutae (Trackers) and some interesting scraps by Aeschylus, who was regarded as the greatest exponent of the form.

## Greek theatre buildings

The Greeks positioned their first permanent theatres on hills. By the end of the 6th century BC a permanent theatron, 'watching-place', was set up in the precinct of Dionysus on the south slope of the Athenian Acropolis. Temporary timber seating gave way to durable stone carved into the hillside. The need to get large numbers of spectators close to the actors led to the adoption of a semicircular arena format with seating focused on a circular stage. The acoustics were good, and can still be experienced in the remains of the ancient theatres. Unfortunately, the only parts to survive in an understandable form are the auditorium and circular orchēstra for the movement of the Chorus at the focus of the audience sightlines. Most of the surviving plays also make use of a building, the SKĒNĒ, or scene-building, behind the orchēstra. This was used as a changing room for actors and as a sounding board, but also served to represent the palace or house in front of which most plays are set. In front of the skēnē there may also have been a low platform that raised the actors above the floor of the orchēstra. A variety of stage machinery is mentioned by late authors, but the only devices for which there is 5th-century evidence are the ekkyklēma, a low platform on wheels which could be pushed into view to reveal, in the form of a tableau, the consequence of events (normally killings) within the palace; and the *mēchanē*, a kind of crane which could transport an actor through the air to give an effect of flying. 5th-century tragedians probably did not use it for epiphanies of gods, though the 'god from the machine' (*deus ex machina*) became proverbial at an early date.

Drama spread rapidly outside Athens. Particularly well preserved, and famous for its beauty and its acoustics, is the theatre at Epidaurus in the Peloponnese, built about 300 BC by the architect Polyclitus. This is similar in size to the Theatre of Dionysus at Athens, but a hollow in the hillside allowed a more symmetrical design than was ever possible there. In the Hellenistic period (3rd and 2nd centuries BC), every town in the Greek world came to have its theatre.

### Greek masks, costumes and properties

The Greek mask covered the whole head, with holes for the eyes and mouth. It was probably made of linen on a wooden frame. Vase paintings of the 5th century show that tragic masks of this period were realistic and undistorted. There must have been a range of types to show differences of age and sex, together with some special masks for such figures as the blinded Oedipus or the Phrygian in Euripides' *Orestes*. The mask of Old and Middle Comedy seems typically to have been ugly, with goggling eyes, wide nose and gaping mouth; there is evidence that portrait masks were used by actors playing real people.

Some 5th-century paintings of tragic actors show them wearing ordinary tunics and cloaks; but it seems that the *syrma*, a long, richly embroidered robe with sleeves, was progressively adopted by the actors, becoming the standard tragic costume by the end of the century. Aristophanes repeatedly taunts Euripides with presenting his heroes in rags, and there are plays by the other tragedians in which ragged costumes seem to be called for (e.g. Aeschylus' *Persians*, Sophocles' *Philoctetes*). The standard footwear was a calf-length boot, not normally worn by men in daily life.

Actors of Old and Middle Comedy wore the tunics and cloaks of everyday life, often with padding of the stomach and buttocks. It is disputed whether all comic actors wore a leather phallus (except when playing women or effeminates); it is likely that they did, but that this could be concealed beneath clothing on occasion. In satyr plays the human characters wore tragic costume, while the satyrs wore drawers, usually of fur, equipped with phallus and horse's tail, and Silenus had a full-length costume covered with tufts of wool.

From the late 4th century the appearance of tragic actors became more stylized. The mouth of the mask opened wider; the forehead was unnaturally raised, to make the actor appear taller; and, for the same reason, the sole of the boot was thickened until the actor was walking on stilts which raised him several inches from the ground. Most surviving representations of tragic masks and costumes date from a late period, and are very different from those worn in the first performances of the surviving plays. At the same period comic masks and costumes became more lifelike and varied, in keeping with the greater realism and decorum of New Comedy.

For stage properties we are dependent on the evidence of the plays. Those few which the tragic texts mention are always dramatically significant and often memorably used (e.g. the carpet and the robe in Aeschylus' *Agamemnon* and *Choephori*, the urn and the bow in Sophocles' *Electra* and *Philoctetes*, the letter and

the head of Pentheus in Euripides' *Iphigenia in Tauris* and *Bacchae*). The properties used by Aristophanes are more numerous, and include the scientific instruments of *Clouds* 200–17 and the arms-dealer's wares at *Peace* 1210–64.

**Green, Adolph** see COMDEN, BETTY

**Green, Paul** 1894–1981 American playwright. He wrote about the life he knew – the South, its people and its religion. In *The Last of the Lowries* (1920) he re-created the rhythmic language of the African-Americans. His best play, *In Abraham's Bosom* (1926), portrays the tragedy of a black idealist, defeated by his own limitations and the people he wants to help. In both *The Field God* (1927), showing the spiritual disintegration of a man condemned by the religiosity he rejected, and *Shroud My Body Down* (1934), he dramatized the fascination and violence of religious mania. *The House of Connelly* (1931), produced by the newly formed GROUP THEATRE, dramatized plantation life against a background of family power, class and racial injustice. A man of strong opinions, Green condemned the chain-gang system in *Hymn to the Rising Sun* (1936). In *Johnny Johnson* (1936), America's most imaginative anti-war play, he satirized warmongers through a hero who is confined by society for having 'peace monomania'. With *The Lost Colony* (1937), a symphonic drama about Sir Walter Raleigh's colony, he found a new mode of expression. After World War II he continued to celebrate American history through such pageants as *The Common Glory* (1947), about the efforts of Jefferson during the Revolution, *The Founders* (1957), the story of the Jamestown colony, and *Cross and Sword* (1965).

**Greene, Graham** 1904–91 British novelist and playwright. Greene's characteristic theme is the emptiness of modern life and the rediscovery of religious belief. After dramatizing his own novel *The Heart of the Matter* in collaboration with BASIL DEAN (1950), he wrote a series of plays on adultery and the loss of faith (*The Living Room*, 1953; *The Complaisant Lover*, 1959), on the effect of a miracle on an atheistic family (*The Potting Shed*, 1957), and on the spiritual pride of an untalented artist (*Carving a Statue*, 1964). Though conventional in form, these offered satisfying roles for a number of leading performers. *The Return of A. J. Raffles* was produced by the ROYAL SHAKESPEARE COMPANY in 1975. His plays *Yes and No* and *For Whom the Bell Chimes* were staged in 1980, and he also wrote several film scripts, notably *The Third Man* (1948).

**Greene, Robert** c.1558–92 English pamphleteer and playwright, one of the UNIVERSITY WITS. His romance *Pandosto* (1588), provided SHAKESPEARE with the plot of *The Winter's Tale*, but Greene is better known for his attack on Shakespeare as 'an upstart crow, beautified with our feathers'. The attack appeared in *Greene's Groatsworth of Wit, Bought with a Million of Repentance* (1592), a death-bed pamphlet bemoaning his dissipated life. Five extant plays are ascribed to him, including the comedy *Friar Bacon and Friar Bungay* (c.1589), a light hearted treatment of the experiments with magic conducted by two 13th-century Oxford Franciscans. *James IV* (c.1591) combines Scottish history and fairy romance. *A Looking-Glass for London and England* (c.1590), written with Thomas Lodge, is a SATIRE.

**Greet, Ben** [Philip Barling] 1857–1936 British actor manager. He founded his own touring company in 1886 and is best known for his open-air performances of SHAKESPEARE, particularly *A Midsummer Night's Dream*

He followed WILLIAM POEL, with whom he had co-produced the 1902 revival of *Everyman*, in returning to the simplified staging techniques of the Elizabethan theatre. He toured widely in America and mounted a season at the New York Garden Theatre in 1910, before returning to London to become one of the leading directors at the OLD VIC, where he directed 24 Shakespeare plays between 1915 and 1918. Knighted in 1929, in 1930 he re-opened the Oxford Repertory Company (which had closed after the departure of J. B. FAGAN).

**Gregory, Andre** 1934– American director and producer. He founded the Manhattan Project, an environmental theatre group which adapted performance spaces to suit each script, and is identified closely with 1960s avant-garde. In 1970 he became famous overnight with the success of the company's *Alice in Wonderland*. *Endgame* (1973) also attracted interest, after which JOSEPH PAPP presented the company at the Public Theater in [*The*] *Seagull* (1975) and *Jinx Bridge* (1976). Always controversial, the Manhattan Project consisted of six actors performing in a highly eccentric style. Words were articulated in a strange, often comic manner, and gestures were exaggerated as the actors played the subtext more often than the text. Gregory's staging of *Uncle Vanya* was filmed as in rehearsal by Louis Malle (1994).

**Gregory, Lady Augusta (Isabella)** 1852–1932 Irish playwright and director. A staunch nationalist despite her Ascendancy background, Lady Gregory was a prime mover in founding and sustaining the Irish Literary Theatre, later the ABBEY THEATRE. She translated voluminously from Gaelic folk tales and legends, rendering them into the Kiltartan dialect, the idiom of most of her many plays – folk comedies and tragedies, histories, translations. Her one-act plays about the Irish peasantry include *Spreading the News* (1904), *The Rising of the Mood* (1906), *The Gaol Gate* (1906) and *The Workhouse Ward* (1908). Very popular in their time, particularly the comedies, and highly praised by YEATS, Lady Gregory's plays suggested, notably to SYNGE, the theatrical potential of Hibernicized English.

**Gregory, Johann (Gottfried)** 1631–75 German-born, Moscow-based director. A Lutheran minister who practised in Moscow from 1662, at the behest of Tsar Aleksei Mikhailovich he founded and directed the first official court theatre in Russia (1672). A special wooden theatre was erected; an acting company of 64, mostly the sons of German merchants, was trained; and a selection of plays on biblical themes (Esther, Judith) and adapted from English sources (MARLOWE) was drawn from the German dramatic repertory. Scenic, costume and musical effects were elaborate for their day, including perspective painting by the Dutch designer Engels. The Tsar's death in 1676 ended this theatre's brief career.

**Grenfell, Joyce** [Joyce Irene Phipps] 1910–79 British actress. She first made her name in intimate REVUE. She had entertained her friends privately with gently satiric sketches and monologues, which revealed her gifts for sharp observation and telling mimicry. After her first professional stage appearance, in *The Little Revue* (1939), she broadcast and toured throughout the war, becoming one of Britain's best-loved comediennes. She appeared in NOËL COWARD's revue, *Sigh No More* (1945), in *Tuppence Coloured* (1947), in *Penny Plain* (1951) and in her one-woman show, *Joyce Grenfell Requests the Pleasure*, which went to New York in 1955. Her one-woman sketches were similar to those of the American actress

RUTH DRAPER, and if Draper possessed a greater dramatic range, then Grenfell undoubtedly enjoyed the sharper comic instinct and, unlike Draper, was successful within a team. She was a memorable Gossage, the gawky games mistress, in the film version of John Dighton's *The Happiest Days of Your Life*. She could sing in a wistful, appealing soprano songs of her own devising, and was the author of three books: *Nanny Says* (with Sir Hugh Casson;1972); an autobiography, *Joyce Grenfell Requests the Pleasure* (1976); and *George, Don't Do That* (1977).

**Griboedov, Aleksandr (Sergeevich)** (1794–1829) Russian playwright and diplomat. The founding father of Russian stage REALISM, he made his career in the Foreign Service. Dispatched to Teheran as Russian minister in 1829, Griboedov was literally torn apart by a mob incensed by the harsh terms of the treaty which he had negotiated in order to end recent Russo-Persian hostilities.

His best early play is *All in the Family, or The Married Fiancée* (1818), but his reputation as a dramatist is based upon the verse comedy *Woe from Wit* (1824). An ironic indictment of Tsarist society, it is both romantic comedy and sociopolitical SATIRE. The protagonist Chatsky is a variant of the Hamlet-philosopher type and the ambivalent core of the play. Chatsky fiercely rejects Russia's conservatism and gallomania; but despite the play's pointed theme and characterization Griboedov largely eschewed the didactic moralizing of his contemporaries. The play's evocation of anti-government secret societies, especially the Decembrists with whom Griboedov was associated, earned its banning and underground celebrity prior to 1831. In the years following the 1917 Revolution Lenin and LUNACHARSKY declared it to be one of the earliest 'people's creations'. MEYERHOLD staged a memorable production at his theatre in 1928.

**Grieg, Nordahl** 1902–43 Norwegian poet and playwright. He was instrumental in the introduction of modernism in Norwegian theatre. He turned from journalism (in China) to playwriting with *A Young Man's Love* (1927). His mature and controversial plays *Our Power and Our Glory* (1935), *But Tomorrow!* (1936) and *The Defeat* (1937) reveal his admiration for Soviet theatre techniques, his anti-Fascism and his belief that theatre must activate the spectator. During the German occupation Grieg was close to the free Norwegian government in London, and died as an observer on a bombing raid over Berlin.

**Grieve, John Henderson** 1770–1845 English scene-painter. The first of a notable English family, long associated with COVENT GARDEN, he contributed to the vogue for picturesque SHAKESPEARE productions, encouraged by JOHN PHILIP KEMBLE. Grieve was joined at Covent Garden by his sons Thomas (1799–1882) and William (1800–44). They were superior artisans, adding to their landscapes slight antiquarian touches. Like CLARKSON STANFIELD, they made the moving diorama a regular PANTOMIME feature. Over 700 designs by members of the Grieve family have survived.

**Griffiths, Trevor** 1935– British playwright. Griffiths's debate plays for stage and television reveal his training in Marxist dialectic. His first major play, *Occupations* (1970), was brought to London by the ROYAL SHAKESPEARE COMPANY. It concerned the 1920 Fiat motor strike in Italy and the contrasting ideologies of the Marxist theorist, ANTONIO GRAMSCI, and the Soviet agent, Kabak. *Sam, Sam* (1972) describes the careers of two brothers, one who stays happily loyal to his roots and the other who becomes a member of the new bourgeoisie. *Comedians* (1975), which concerned an ageing music-hall comic, Eddie Waters, teaching his trade to aspiring comedians in a night school, is a study of the social and class implications of popular comedy. In 1973 the NATIONAL THEATRE produced *The Party*, an analysis of Britain's under-reaction to the events of May 1968, featuring LAURENCE OLIVIER as Tagg, a Glaswegian Trotskyite. Griffiths turned to television with the *Bill Brand* series (1976) and *Fatherland* (1986), then to stage-directing (*Saint Oscar*, 1990). In 1992 *The Gulf between Us*, his most ambitious stage play since *Comedians*, was produced in Leeds, a study of the Gulf War from the Arab point of view. Like SHAW, he is a political playwright more gifted at reading the left side of the argument than the right. *Thatcher's Children* (1993) brought together seven life stories from members of sample ethnic groups, expressing a similar frustration at their futures.

**Grillparzer, Franz** 1791–1872 Austrian playwright. The eclecticism of Grillparzer's work is typical of the variety of his country's dramatic tradition. His first success was a grim SCHICKSALTRAGÖDIE, *The Ancestress* (1817). His next play, *Sappho* (1819), was a classical tragedy on the irreconcilability of art and life, a work that earned him the position of house dramatist at the BURGTHEATER. *The Golden Fleece* (1821), a mighty trilogy about Medea and Jason, contains a study of male–female relationships that foreshadows the work of IBSEN; the last play of the trilogy, *Medea*, equals in power the Euripidean original. *Waves of the Sea and Love* (1829) dramatizes the story of Hero and Leander. Grillparzer was also noted for his historical tragedy *King Ottokar's Rise and Fall* (1823), while *A True Servant to His Master* (1826) owes much to the work of LOPE DE VEGA.

Calderonian drama (see CALDERÓN DE LA BARCA) in an unlikely combination with the Viennese VOLKSSTÜCK inspired Grillparzer's most popular work, *A Dream of Life* (1832). As a result of the failure of his comedy *Woe to Him Who Lies!* (1838), he withdrew from writing for the public stage. His later works, *Family Strife among the Habsburgs*, *The Jewess of Toledo* and *Libussa*, were only performed after his death. Although his plays incorporate wide-ranging political and social themes and, in *Libussa*, deal with the whole development of human civilization, their strength derives from their author's acute knowledge of human relations, especially in the sphere of sexuality. At his death he was publicly recognized as the pre-eminent dramatist of his country, and is still regarded as such today.

**Grimaldi, Joseph** 1778–1837 English CLOWN. He made his London debut at the age of four, and played sprites and fairies throughout childhood. Awkward in drama, he gravitated to PANTOMIME and first won acclaim as Clown in DIBDIN's *Peter Wilkins, or Harlequin in the Flying World* (SADLER'S WELLS, 1800), when he wore an extravagant multi-coloured costume and changed the standard ruddy complexion for a white face with two red half-moons on the cheeks. His great success came in *Harlequin Mother Goose, or The Golden Egg* (COVENT GARDEN, 1806; much revived). Grimaldi's clown was a greedy, amoral schoolboy, out to satisfy his appetites; his exuberant optimism was that of the survivor, and the fun derived from the overthrow of everyday inhibitions. His entering cry of 'Here we are again!', his songs, tricks, thieving, gluttony and violence – stealing

sausages and attacking watchmen and police with a red-hot poker – became hallmarks of the panto clown or Joey. His *Memoirs* were edited by CHARLES DICKENS in 1838; his grave in Pentonville, London, is annually commemorated by a conventicle of clowns.

**Grock** [Charles Adrien Wettach] 1880–1959 Swiss CLOWN. He began in CABARET and ACROBATICS, taking the name Grock when part of a musical-clown tour of Europe and South America in 1903. He developed a solo act, becoming a virtuoso on 13 instruments. In his routine he demonstrated his inability to play properly on anything: concertinas, miniature fiddles, grand pianos – all turned into instruments of mental anguish in his hands. Combining the elegance of the white clown with the crude childishness of the August, he made his sketches parables of the malice of inanimate objects and human fecklessness. Personally pedantic and financially astute, on stage he tinged the hilarity with melancholy. He founded his own circus in 1951, retiring three years later.

**Gropius, Walter** 1883–1969 German artist and architect. In the 1920s he founded the Staatliches Bauhaus in Weimar, Germany, a School of Fine Arts and Arts and Crafts which focused on architecture, painting, sculpture, industrial design and theatre. Working with OSKAR SCHLEMMER, Gropius hoped to fuse art with everyday life. In 1926 he conceived a new type of theatre building which he called the *Totaltheater*, intended through its design to change the actor audience relationship and intended to be used by director ERWIN PISCATOR. Gropius believed that there were only three types of theatrical stage: the thrust, the arena and the proscenium (see THEATRE DESIGN). In his new theatre design all three existed. A domed ceiling and a translucent cyclorama could display projections. When the Nazis came to power, the controversial Bauhaus was disbanded and thus the *Totaltheater* was never built. Nevertheless, its influence can be seen in many subsequent theatres.

**Gros-Guillaume** [Robert Guérin; La Fleur] ?-1634 French actor-manager. A celebrated FARCE-player, he formed his own company in 1612 and returned to Paris from the provinces as director of the Comédiens du Roi at the HÔTEL DE BOURGOGNE. A short, fat man, his belly cinctured with two belts to suggest a barrel, he powdered his face with flour which he would sprinkle over any actor who accosted him. He was a perfect foil to the other popular farce-players with whom he regularly acted in the 1620s and 30s, GAULTIER-GARGUILLE and Turlupin (see TURLUPINADES).

**Grosbard, Ulu** 1929– Belgian-born American director. Grosbard emigrated to the United States in 1948, and began directing in 1957, making his New York debut in 1962 with *The Days and Nights of Beebee Fenstermaker* at the Sheridan Square Playhouse. His notable productions include *The Subject Was Roses* (1964), *A View from the Bridge* (1965), *The Investigation* (1966), *The Price* (1968), *American Buffalo* (1977), *The Wake of Jamie Foster* (1982) and *Weekends Like Other People* (1982). Since 1961 he has worked also in films and television.

**Grossman, Jan** 1925–1993 Czech critic, dramaturge and director. He became primarily associated with Prague's Balustrade Theatre in the 1960s as VÁCLAV HAVEL's intimate collaborator (*The Memorandum*, 1965). After 1968, political factors forced Grossman to become an itinerant director, chiefly in peripheral Czech theatres. In the late 1980s he was able to return triumphantly to the Balustrade Theatre with outstanding productions of MOLIÈRE's *Don Juan* (1989) and, after the Velvet Revolution, Havel's *Largo Desolato* (1990) and *Temptation* (1992), by which time he had become artistic head of the theatre. Never an overt social critic, Grossman nevertheless imbued his work with implicit questions of contemporary social values and practices, especially in his productions of Havel and works such as JARRY's *Ubu Roi* (1964) and Kafka's *The Trial* (1966).

**Grossmith, George** (junior) 1874–1935 British actor. He also co-authored REVUES for London's Empire and GAIETY THEATRES. The son of George Grossmith, a regular performer in the Savoy operas, he introduced the stock figure of the 'dude' to MUSICAL COMEDY, in which he starred between 1893 and 1912.

**Grotowski, Jerzy** 1933– Polish director, teacher and theorist. Since 1982 he has lived in the United States and Italy. After studying at the State Drama School in Cracow and in Moscow, and directing in Cracow, he established the Theatre of 13 Rows in Opole, where from 1959 to 1964 he staged poetic works played against the texts as arguments with past cultural monuments and designed to transform traditional actor–audience relationships: BYRON's *Cain*, GOETHE's *Faust*, MAYAKOVSKY's *Mystery-Bouffe* and KALIDASA's *Shakuntula* in 1960; MICKIEWICZ's *Forefathers' Eve* in 1961; SŁOWACKI's *Kordian* and WYSPIAŃSKI's *Acropolis* (co-created with JOZEF SZAJNA) in two versions in 1962; MARLOWE's *Faustus* in 1963; a third variant of *Acropolis* in 1964. In 1965 he moved the group to Wrocław, adopting the name Laboratory Theatre. From 1965 to 1973 he created a fourth and fifth variant of *Acropolis*, three versions of CALDERÓN DE LA BARCA's *The Constant Prince* (in Słowacki's translation), and three variants of *Apocalypsis cum figuris*, his final production. Since the early 1970s he has engaged in paratheatrical activities, seminars, and teaching in Poland, Western Europe and America. Grotowski's productions and theories, his concept of a 'poor theatre' and his work on the training of actors have had a major impact on world theatre. *Towards a Poor Theatre* (1968) is a collection of his theoretical writings.

**Group Theatre, The** American company. Founded in 1931 by HAROLD CLURMAN, LEE STRASBERG and CHERYL CRAWFORD, the Group was a pioneering attempt to create a theatre collective, a company of players trained in a unified style and dedicated to presenting new American plays of social significance. With STANISLAVSKY's MOSCOW ART THEATRE as their model, Group members under Strasberg and Clurman experimented with an inner technique which became the basis of the American Method and which Strasberg continued to develop during his 35 years at the ACTORS STUDIO. The Method resulted in acting that was more natural, private, intense and psychologically charged than previous styles. Debates over method erupted in 1934 when Group member STELLA ADLER returned from her studies with Stanislavsky in Paris to announce that the Master had abandoned his earlier emphasis on inner work in favour of a new external technique, the method of physical actions. Adler and Strasberg took opposing sides in a conflict which has never been resolved, Strasberg and his followers focusing on the actor's own emotional resources while Adler concentrated on the play as opposed to the player.

The Group helped to develop excellent realistic actors, such as MORRIS CARNOVSKY, some of whom defected to film. It also produced 22 new American

plays, notably JOHN HOWARD LAWSON's *Success Story* (1932) and CLIFFORD ODETS's *Awake and Sing!* (1935) and *Paradise Lost* (1935).

**Group Theatre** (Belfast) Northern Irish company. Three amateur companies amalgamated (1939–40) to form the Ulster Group Theatre. Although it presented SHERIDAN, IBSEN, CHEKHOV and ODETS, it concentrated on Northern playwrights: ERVINE, SHIELS, James Tomelty (*The End House*, 1944; *All Souls' Night*, 1949). The theatre attained high standards and initiated some distinguished actors: Patrick Magee, J. G. Devlin, Stephen Boyd, COLIN BLAKELY and James Ellis. The major cause of the Group's demise was internal dispute over SAM THOMPSON's controversial *Over the Bridge* (1960). Its final flourish was STEWART PARKER's *The Randy Dandy* (1960).

**Group Theatre** (London) British company. Founded by Rupert Doone (a choreographer who had danced with DIAGHILEV's Ballets Russes), together with Ormerod Greenwood and TYRONE GUTHRIE, it was an ensemble company dedicated both to the performance of poetic drama and to socialist ideals comparable with those of the Workers' Theatre Movement. Its first successful production was the revival of the recently discovered INTERLUDE *Fulgens and Lucrece* by HENRY MEDWALL. It provided a stage for *Sweeney Agonistes* (1935) by T. S. ELIOT, who also wrote a choral piece, *The Rock*, in collaboration with its members; and the verse plays of W. H. AUDEN and CHRISTOPHER ISHERWOOD – *The Dog beneath the Skin* (1936), *The Ascent of F6* (1937) and *On the Frontier* (1938) – were written specifically for the Group. Louis MacNeice provided texts, as did Stephen Spender (*The Trial of a Judge*, 1938), while Benjamin Britten contributed musical scores. It also functioned briefly between 1950 and 1954, presenting the first English production of a SARTRE play, *The Flies* (1951).

**Grumberg, Jean-Claude** 1939– French actor, director and playwright. An outstanding example of a playwright who successfully combined the styles of absurdist theatre (see THEATRE OF THE ABSURD) and the social concern of the decentralized theatre in the 1970s. His use of theatre within the theatre (*Dreyfus*, 1973) and of autobiographical material (*L'Atelier* [*The Workshop*], 1979) shows a craftsmanship similar to that of ANOUILH.

**Gründgens, Gustaf** 1899–1963 German actor and director. His work epitomized the classical tradition in opposition to the REALISM of STANISLAVSKY. After working with REINHARDT in 1928, he established his reputation as the leading German actor with his performance of Mephisto in GOETHE's *Faust* in 1932. Appointed director of the Berlin Staatstheater under the Nazis from 1934 to 1944, he was attacked as a Fascist collaborator in the novel *Mephisto* by Klaus Mann. But his wartime productions of SCHILLER and LESSING had drawn contemporary parallels as oblique forms of political protest, an approach continued when he was artistic director at Düsseldorf in 1947 and at Hamburg from 1955. At BRECHT's request he directed the premiere of *St Joan of the Stockyards* in 1959.

**Grundy, Sydney** 1848–1914 British playwright. He trained as a barrister. His first play, *A Little Change* (1872), was staged at London's HAYMARKET. Grundy adapted French plays by, e.g., ALEXANDRE DUMAS *père*: *A Marriage of Convenience* (1897), *The Silver Key* (1897), *The Musketeers* (1898) and *The Black Tulip* (1899). His best-known work is *A Pair of Spectacles* (1890), adapted from LABICHE and Delacour. A reactionary opponent of IBSEN, Grundy nevertheless provided LILLIE LANGTRY with a *succès de scan-*

*dale* in *The Degenerates* (1899), and enjoyed playing with fire in *A Fool's Paradise* (1889) and *Slaves of the Ring* (1894), in which he brushed with the adulterous passion of Tristan and Isolde.

**Gryphius, Andreas** 1616–64 German playwright. Although Gryphius's plays were not performed during his lifetime, they are now generally considered to be among the most significant achievements in German drama during the baroque period. His tragedies, classical in style and structure, deal with the sufferings of high-born nobility and royalty, though *Cardenio and Celinde* (1647) is closer to middle-class drama. *Murdered Majesty, or Charles Stuart* (1649) dramatizes, not very effectively, the execution of the English king. Of Gryphius's comedies, *Horribilicribrifax* (1663) and *The Beloved Rose with a Thorn* (1661) are the most refreshing and lively.

**Guan Hanqing** c.1230–c.1300 Chinese playwright. His dates are controversial and known biographical facts are minimal. He was from Dadu, site of present-day Beijing. He may have had experience as an actor. He is regarded as the foremost of the Yuan *zaju* playwrights. Of his plays, 18 are extant out of a presumed output of 63. Eight have been translated into English, including *Injustice to Dou E* (*Dou E yuan*), perhaps his best-known piece, written towards the end of his life. It was constantly performed on the Beijing stage before 1949. It concerns the tragic fate of a young woman wrongly executed as the victim of false witness and a corrupt prefect. Her innocence is established by cosmic intervention called down with her dying cry that Heaven and Earth have failed to ensure justice in the world. Emotional vigour of characterization and an expressive lyricism were Guan's contribution to the early Chinese stage.

**Guare, John** 1938– American playwright. Some critics have found his plays too cerebral or abstract, lacking focus, but they praise his use of language. After his one-act play *Muzeeka* (1968) he received wide acclaim for his first full-length work, *The House of Blue Leaves* (1970). Since then major plays have included *Rich and Famous* (1974), *The Landscape of the Body* (1977) and *Bosoms and Neglect* (1979). *Lydie Breeze* and *Gardenia* (1982) are two parts of a projected tetralogy set in 19th-century New England. *Moon over Miami* (1988) was followed by his most successful play to date, *Six Degrees of Separation* (1990), which delves into the vulnerability under New York's brittle surface. *Four Baboons Adoring the Sun* was premièred in 1992.

**Guarini, Battista** 1538–1612 Italian poet, critic and playwright. He obtained a Europe-wide reputation with his most important work, *Il pastor fido* (*The Faithful Shepherd*), written in the early 1580s in imitation of TASSO's PASTORAL play *Aminta*, but seeking to ring changes on that work by exploring the new vein of TRAGICOMEDY. Guarini's play caught the taste of European courts, and his Preface, in which he set out a defensive theory of the genre against his critics, became widely influential: in England JOHN FLETCHER's *The Faithful Shepherdess* was a version of the new tragicomical pastoral kind, and Fletcher's Preface, in which he defined tragicomedy as a form that 'wants deaths, but brings some near it', was indebted to Guarini's theory.

**Guarnieri, Gianfrancesco** 1934– Brazilian playwright. Of Milanese birth, he arrived in Brazil as an infant and became a major influence in the develop-

ment of realistic theatre (see REALISM) during the 1950s. Affiliated with the Arena Theatre in São Paulo as actor and director, he participated in the development of the *Arena Tells ...* series (about Zumbi, Bolívar, Tiradentes, among others), which depended on concepts of open stage, simple sets, realistic dialogue and close interaction between actor and public. His *Eles Não Usam Black-tie* (*They Don't Use Tuxedos*, 1958) became a Brazilian classic for its portrayal of the social problems of the slum areas. His other plays include *Gimba, Presidente dos Valentes* (*Gimba, President of the Brave*, 1959), *Um Grito Parado no Ar* (*A Scream Silenced in Air*, 1973), *Botequim* (*Tavern*, 1973), and *Ponto de Partida* (*Point of Departure*, 1976). Guarnieri has emphasized BRECHTian techniques in portraying the reality of Brazilian political and socio-economic situations with protest against military censorship and economic repression.

**Guignol** French MARIONETTE. Guignol derives from the Lyons puppet theatre, presumably invented by the puppeteer Laurent Mourguet (1745–1844). Distinguished by a sharply satirical tongue and an earthy use of the vernacular, Guignol, costumed as a Lyons silk-weaver, was forbidden to improvise by the police of the Second Empire, became a parodist of opera, and eventually supplanted Polichinelle. The term *guignol* is now generic for any French PUNCH and Judy show.

**Guilbert, Yvette** [Emma Laure Esther Guilbert] 1865–1944 French CABARET artist. She first appeared at the Théâtre des Variétés, Paris (1889), and became a star in 1892 at the Divan Japonais and the MOULIN-ROUGE, singing verses by ARISTIDE BRUANT and Léon Xanrof. Her gaunt figure, long nose and neck, mop of red hair and invariable black gloves contrasted with the voluptuousness of her competition and were celebrated by Toulouse-Lautrec. She could be lyrical, gruesome or coquettish. After 1901 she made frequent appearances in REVUE and theatre (Mrs Peachum in the French *Threepenny Opera*, 1937); and in 1920 founded a school in New York.

**Guimerà, Àngel** 1845–1924 Catalan poet and playwright. He is one of the chief figures in the literary renaissance of Catalan. His 39 plays, following European trends, generally portray the Catalan peasantry in romantic, occasionally melodramatic, plots. His first works were historical verse love-dramas, of which perhaps the finest is *L'ànima morta* (*The Dead Soul*, 1892). He then turned to contemporary realism in such plays as *Terra baixa* (*The Lowlanders*, 1896), contrasting the morals of the lowlanders and highlanders of Catalonia, and considered his finest play. Later he wrote psychological dramas – with less success – before returning to historical sources. His drama has also succeeded in translation.

**Guinness, Alec** 1914– British actor. In 1936 he joined the OLD VIC theatre and in 1938 played Hamlet in an innovative modern dress production, a performance which firmly established his reputation. After World War II he returned to the company and played a wide variety of modern and classic roles, ranging from Lear's Fool to Klestakov in GOGOL's *The Inspector General*. He made his mark as a chameleon artist who specialized in making something out of nothing, disdaining eye-catching make-up: transformation for Guinness was done from inside. He also began to direct, with a production of *Twelfth Night* in 1948 and *Hamlet* in 1951, in which he also played the lead. His parts ranged from Macbeth in GASKILL's experimental production for the

ROYAL COURT THEATRE (1966) to the sexually backsliding MP in *Habeas Corpus* by ALAN BENNETT (1973). Guinness's film and television career developed alongside his work for the stage, including his adaptations of novels. His quizzical features became familiar in comic films such as *Kind Hearts and Coronets* (1949) and *The Lavender Hill Mob* (1951). His international stardom was established with *The Bridge on the River Kwai* (1957). For television his role as a spy-catcher in John Le Carré's *Tinker, Tailor, Soldier, Spy* (1979) and *Smiley's People* (1982) were tailored for his enigmatic presence. He was knighted in 1959.

**Gundersen, Laura** 1832–98 Norwegian actress. Gundersen was one of the first Norwegian actresses to be engaged at the Danish-speaking Christiania Theatre, where she spent almost her entire career. With her grand, declamatory style, she excelled in TRAGEDY and romantic drama, creating leading roles in many of IBSEN's early plays: Blanka in *The Burial Mound*, Hjørdis in *The Vikings at Helgeland* and, especially, Lady Inger in *Sigurd Jorsalfer*. Later in her career, she adapted sufficiently to the new realistic style to succeed as Ibsen's Mrs Borkman and Ellida (in *The Lady from the Sea*).

**Gunn, Moses** 1929–93 African-American actor. Gunn performed several Shakespearian roles in the 1960s, including an award-winning portrayal of Aaron the Moor in *Titus Andronicus* (1967). He became a founder member of the NEGRO ENSEMBLE COMPANY and appeared in several productions. His 'sensual-melodic' Othello for the AMERICAN SHAKESPEARE THEATRE in 1970 elicited ecstatic reviews from major New York critics.

**Gunter, John** 1938– British stage designer. He worked for years on the Continent and in English regional theatre (see REPERTORY THEATRE) before establishing himself as a successful realistic designer at London's ROYAL COURT THEATRE in the late 1960s. Since then his work has been seen at both the Royal Shakespeare Theatre and, more recently, at the NATIONAL THEATRE, in addition to productions in the WEST END and abroad. From 1974 to 1982 Gunter served as head of the THEATRE DESIGN programme at London's Central School, his own *alma mater*, and in 1989–90 he was head of design at the NT. Based on painstakingly selective detail, his work has lately exhibited more conscious theatricality and metaphoric imagery. Outstanding productions have included *All's Well that Ends Well* (1981), *Guys and Dolls* (1982), *The Rivals* (1983), *The Government Inspector* (1985), *Hamlet* (1989), *School for Scandal* (1990) and *Gift of the Gorgon* (1992).

**Guo Moruo** 1892–1978 Chinese playwright, poet and historian. Guo played a prominent role in the resistance in Shanghai during World War II. Under the People's Republic he was given numerous government and cultural posts and was one of the very few artists and intellectuals to remain in favour during the decade of the Cultural Revolution. He was a strong fighter for women's rights – an issue that dominates much of his prodigious literary output. Among his early spoken dramas (written in 1923), *Wang Zhaojun* and *Zhuo Wenjun*, named after their respective heroines, present intelligent and defiant historical women of the distant past whom Guo intended as positive models for his own times. In his last play, produced in 1962, *Wu Zetian*, the title character is the only woman in Chinese history ever to have become emperor (reigned 684–705). One of Guo's most productive periods was during the war against Japan. A representative play from those years is *Qu Yuan* (1942), about the famous poet of that name of the 3rd and 4th centuries BC and his struggle against tyrannical rulers.

**Gurik, Robert** 1932– Quebec playwright and novelist. Born in France, he moved to Canada in 1950. *Le Pendu (The Hanged Man*, 1967) won critical acclaim. With *Hamlet, Prince du Québec* (*Hamlet, Prince of Quebec*, 1968), a savage PARODY of the political rivalry between Quebec and Ottawa, Gurik moved towards current social issues, a commitment continued in subsequent works such as *Le Procès de Jean-Baptiste M.* (*The Trial of Jean-Baptiste M.*, 1972) and *La Baie des Jacques* (*Jacques's Bay*, 1976) – the latter consciously emulating BRECHT's *Mahagonny* (1927) and depicting the dehumanizing effects of modern industrial development upon the individual.

**Gurney, A(lbert) R(amsdell)**, [Pete] Jr 1930– American playwright. Gurney writes comedies about what he fears is an endangered species, well bred Anglo-Saxon Protestants in a time of transition. In *The Dining Room* (1981), the genteel setting is a cultural artifact threatened with extinction. In *The Middle Ages* (1983), the library of an exclusive club serves a similar thematic purpose. Other deft Gurney works include *Children* (1976), in which a matron chooses duty over pleasure; *What I Did Last Summer* (1982), about a teenager torn between propriety and bohemianism; *The Perfect Party* (1986), *Love Letters* (1989), *The Cocktail Hour* (1990), *The Snow Ball* (1991), *The Old Boy* (1991), *The Fourth Wall* (1992), *Later Life* (1993) and *A Cheever Evening* (1994).

**Guthrie, Tyrone** 1900–71 Anglo-Irish director. From the 1930s onward Guthrie was an innovative and popular international director, working extensively in Britain, the United States and Canada. His Shakespearian work included LAURENCE OLIVIER's *Hamlet* and *Henry V* (1937) and a modern-dress version of the former play in 1938 with ALEC GUINNESS. He was to repeat this experiment at the theatre named after him, the GUTHRIE THEATRE at Minneapolis, USA, in 1963. His other productions included a notable *Peer Gynt* (1944) in which RALPH RICHARDSON starred, LINDSAY's *The Three Estates* (EDINBURGH FESTIVAL, 1948) and, with DONALD WOLFIT, *Tamburlaine the Great* (OLD VIC, 1951). He was director of the STRATFORD (Ontario) FESTIVAL theatre in Canada from 1953 to 1957, and it was here that he developed (together with TANYA MOISEIWITSCH) his thrust stage theatre form that was later permanently enshrined both there and in Minneapolis and widely copied in Britain. The architecture of his theatres indicated his devotion to the Elizabethan relation between actors and audience. He was knighted in 1961.

**Guthrie Theatre** (Minneapolis) Part of the Walker Art Center, the 1,315-seat Guthrie, built in 1963, features a thrust stage, favoured by its director TYRONE GUTHRIE after whom the theatre was named. In the early seasons he presented classics and significant modern plays. In 1981, after years of declining audiences, the direction fell to LIVIU CIULEI, the Romanian-born director, who enlarged the stage and exterior and introduced new American and European plays. From 1986 to 1996 Garland Wright was director.

**Gutzkow, Karl** 1811–78 German playwright, novelist and journalist. As a young man, Gutzkow was associated with the group of liberal writers Junges Deutschland (Young Germany), and was briefly imprisoned for his views in 1836. He turned from journalism to writing plays, many of which have a historical setting but refer to contemporary politics. Among his most widely performed works were *Richard Savage* (1839), the comedies *Pigtail and Sword* (1844) and *A Model For Tartuffe* (1845), and the powerful verse tragedy *Uriel Acosta* (1846), which has racial and religious intolerance as its theme. Gutzkow was briefly dramaturge at the DRESDEN COURT THEATRE (from 1846 to 1848). After the 1848 revolution he turned to novel writing.

**Gwyn, Nell** [Eleanor] ?1642–87 English actress. After a period of selling oranges in the theatre, she began to act in 1664. Her success as Florimel in DRYDEN's *Secret Love* (1667) led PEPYS to praise her. She often attempted but was rarely successful in tragedy. In 1669 she played in Dryden's *Tyrannic Love*. Shortly afterwards she became mistress to Charles II, though she continued to act even after the birth of her first child, finally leaving the stage in the 1670s.

**Habimah** (Hebrew for 'the Stage') Israel's national theatre. Now in Tel-Aviv, it was originally founded in 1918 in Moscow by NAHUM ZEMACH as the Habimah Studio, the first Hebrew-speaking professional theatre. It soon won international acclaim with the production of S. ANSKI's *The Dybbuk* in 1922. Zemach recruited gifted actors including Menahem Gnessin, HANNA ROVINA, Yehoshua Bertonov and AARON MESKIN. They formed a collective, and the great Russian directors STANÍSLAVSKY and VAKHTANGOV worked with them. MAKSIM GORKY wrote that 'they have the element of ecstasy; theatre for them is a rite, a worship'. The problem of repertoire haunted Habimah from the very beginning, because of the scarcity of original Hebrew plays. The company travelled extensively and became a homeless wandering troupe until they finally settled in Palestine in 1931. In 1958 it became Israel's national theatre. Habimah's visit to the USSR in 1990, one of the consequences of *perestroika*, closed a circle in its history.

**Hackett, J(ames) H(enry)** 1800–71 American actor and manager. Hackett was famous in FRONTIER and Yankee roles, especially Nimrod Wildfire in *The Lion of the West* and Rip Van Winkle. He was the first American to appear in London as a star: in 1827 he played at COVENT GARDEN, but failed to win public esteem. Returning to the USA, he repeated his triumphant Dromio of Ephesus. He secured his reputation as the finest Falstaff of his time, first playing the role in 1828. He was also manager of the ASTOR PLACE OPERA HOUSE at the time of the FORREST–MACREADY riot.

**Hacks, Peter** 1928– German playwright, librettist and poet. The leading contemporary playwright in the former GDR, he was invited to Berlin by BRECHT in 1955. His early work, e.g. *The Chapbook of Duke Ernest* (1953; premiere 1967) and *The Battle of Lobkowitz* (1956), derives from EPIC THEATRE. *Anxieties and Power* (1962) offered a picture of workers' aspirations according to the precepts of socialist realism, and *Moritz Tassow* (1965) explored the relationship between utopian and practical communism. In the 1960s he attempted a 'post-revolutionary dramaturgy', rejecting both NATURALISM and epic theatre in favour of highly poetic comedies updating traditional forms. Using a light, ironic style, he takes ostensibly classical, historical or mythological subjects (*Amphitryon*, 1967, and *Prexaspes*, 1976; *Margarete in Aix*, 1966, and *Seneca's Death*, 1980; *Adam and Eve*, 1973) to present contemporary themes. He is a master of blank verse. His popularity in the GDR waned when he turned to arcane subjects and unusual verse forms in *Prexaspes* and *Seneca's Death*.

**Hagen, Uta** 1919– American actress and teacher. Hagen made her debut in 1938 in the LUNTS' production of *The Seagull*, and has acted sporadically though memorably since then: in MAXWELL ANDERSON's *Key Largo* (1939); with PAUL ROBESON and JOSÉ FERRER in *Othello* (1945); opposite Anthony Quinn in *A Streetcar Named Desire* (1950); as the lead in ODETS's *Country Girl* (1950) and, most memorably, as tortured, caustic, vulnerable Martha in EDWARD ALBEE's *Who's Afraid of Virginia Woolf?* (1962). She has an assertive presence and a deep voice that suggests enormous power in reserve. Although her understatement is ideally suited to film, she has chosen

to appear on screen only twice and has taught her craft in New York since 1947. Like most American teachers she derives her method from STANISLAVSKY; unlike LEE STRASBERG, another Stanislavsky disciple, she is strongly opposed to the use of emotional memory, which she considers both self-indulgent and self-destructive.

**Halac, Ricardo** 1935– Argentine playwright. He was a member of the realistic generation of the 1960s. Halac's first play, *Soledad para cuatro* (*Solitude for Four*, 1961), dealt with the anxieties and frustrations of a younger generation in confronting an incomprehensible and valueless society, themes echoed in *Estela de madrugada* (*Morning Wake*, 1965) and *Fin de diciembre* (*End of December*, 1965). He moved away from the realistic tradition and towards the grotesque with *El destete* (*The Weaning*, 1978), recovering some of the BRECHTian tendencies he had observed as a student in West Germany. *Lejana tierra prometida* (*Distant Promised Land*) followed in 1981, then *Ruido de rotas cadenas* (*The Noise of Broken Chains*, 1983), *Viva la anarquía!* (*Long Live Anarchy*, 1992) and *Mil años, un día* (*A Thousand Years, a Day*, 1992).

**Halbe, Max** 1865–1944 German playwright and novelist. Halbe was a prolific writer. His sole enduring success was the tragedy *Youth* (1893), one of the major works of German NATURALISM.

**Halévy, Ludovic** see MEILHAC, HENRI

**Hall, Peter (Reginald Frederick)** 1930– British director and theatre manager. Hall was largely responsible for the creation of two British national theatres, the ROYAL SHAKESPEARE COMPANY and the NATIONAL THEATRE. At Cambridge University he was an energetic amateur director, who in 1953 received a professional production at the Theatre Royal, Windsor. He inherited the mantle of ALEC CLUNES at the ARTS THEATRE Club in 1954, where he directed British premieres of new plays from overseas, including SAMUEL BECKETT's *Waiting for Godot* (1956). He went as guest director to the Shakespeare Memorial Theatre in Stratford-upon-Avon, where he was invited to become the new artistic director, taking up this post in 1960.

His plans for the Shakespeare Memorial Theatre were radical, ambitious and pursued with a dramatic speed. He wanted to create a national company modelled on Continental lines, semi-permanent, with a substantial nucleus of actors offered two- or three-year contracts. He also negotiated to take over the Aldwych Theatre in London, to enable him to present a programme of new plays, as well as the SHAKESPEARE-based repertoire at Stratford-upon-Avon. The company's name was changed to the Royal Shakespeare Company in 1961.

Hall's artistic vision transformed the verse-speaking at Stratford, encouraged contemporary interpretations of Shakespeare's plays along the lines of JAN KOTT, and backed proposals from innovative directors such as PETER BROOK. The RSC became the second-largest recipient of subsidy to non-operatic theatre, and throughout the 1960s was the major 'directors' theatre' in Britain. Hall himself was responsible for several key RSC productions, including *The Wars of the Roses* (1963), adapted from the *Henry VI* trilogy and *Richard III*, and *Hamlet* (1965) with David Warner. He also directed HAROLD

PINTER's plays *The Homecoming* (1965), *Landscape* and *Silence* (1969) and *Old Times* (1971).

In 1968 he resigned from the RSC, becoming a freelance director in both the commercial and the subsidized sectors, and extending his range of interests to opera. In 1970 he was appointed director of productions at the Royal Opera House, COVENT GARDEN, but left after a year. He was invited to succeed OLIVIER at the National Theatre and took over under acrimonious circumstances, not helped by the delays to the opening of the new building on London's South Bank.

As director of the NT, Hall was responsible for the programmes in three contrasting theatres – the Olivier, the Lyttelton with its proscenium arch stage and the Cottesloe, the smaller studio theatre. He placed individual directors, or teams of directors, in charge of the separate theatres, instead of retaining one large company structure. He himself directed such NT successes as MARLOWE's *Tamburlaine* (1976) which opened the Olivier Theatre, AYCKBOURN's *Bedroom Farce* (1977) and PETER SHAFFER's *Amadeus* (1979), which he also directed on BROADWAY. In 1983 he became artistic director of the Glyndebourne Festival, a post held jointly with his post at the NT. In 1988 he directed Shakespeare's last elegiac tragicomedies, *The Winter's Tale*, *Cymbeline* and *The Tempest*, before handing over the NT directorship to RICHARD EYRE. With his own company he took star-studded productions of classic plays on tour and to London theatres, e.g. *The Merchant of Venice* (1989) with DUSTIN HOFFMANN and *An Ideal Husband* (1992). In 1977 he was knighted for his services to the theatre.

**Hall, Willis** 1929– British playwright. Hall also writes in partnership with Keith Waterhouse. Hall and Waterhouse both come from Leeds and their plays are often set in Northern towns. These include *Billy Liar* (1960), which was based on a Waterhouse novel; *Celebration* (1961), about two different kinds of family parties; and *All Things Bright and Beautiful* (1963). They collaborated on a comedy of adulteries, *Say Who You Are* (1965), and on an adaptation of EDUARDO DE FILIPPO's *Saturday, Sunday, Monday* (1973) for the NATIONAL THEATRE. Hall's first stage hit came with his military drama set in Malaysia, *The Long and the Short and the Tall* (1958). He has written prolifically for television. With Waterhouse, he adapted De Filippo's *Filumena* for a WEST END run in 1977.

**Hallam family** Anglo-American actors. The Hallams are the first substantially documented company of English professional players to appear in North America. **William** Hallam (died 1758), manager of GOODMAN's FIELDS, sent his brother **Lewis Sr** (1714–55), Lewis's wife, their three children and an undistinguished company of ten to America. The Hallam Company opened in Williamsburg, Virginia, on 15 September 1752 with *The Merchant of Venice* and *The Anatomist*. The repertory consisted of SHAKESPEARE, ROWE, LILLO, MOORE, FARQUHAR, ADDISON, CIBBER, VANBRUGH, STEELE and GAY. They toured New York, Philadelphia and Charleston. In Jamaica (1755) they joined forces with DAVID DOUGLASS's company. After the elder Hallam's death, Douglass married **Mrs Hallam** (?–1773) in 1758, also securing **Lewis Jr** (1740–1808) as a leading man.

Mrs Hallam starred in the American Company of Comedians, as Douglass named his group from 1763, the first actress in New York to play Juliet, Cordelia and Jane Shore. Lewis Jr played the best roles in the reper-

toire for over fifty years. He appeared in Thomas Godfrey's *The Prince of Parthia* (1767), the first script by an American to be given a professional production. After Douglass's death in 1786, the younger Hallam assumed leadership of the American Company with various partners.

**Halliwell, David (William)** 1936– British playwright and actor. His first (and most successful) play was a comic study of a student Hitler, *Little Malcolm and his Struggle against the Eunuchs* (1965), which was produced in New York as *Hail Scrawdyke!* (1966). In 1966 he started the adventurous FRINGE company, Quipu, which produced (as well as his own plays) new works by other young writers, including STEPHEN POLIAKOFF. Halliwell turned towards what he called 'multi-viewpoint' drama in which, as in *K. D. Dufford ...* (1969), different versions of the same incident, the rape and murder of a child, were played side by side. The technical problems of multi-viewpoint drama preoccupied him as a director and writer for many years, and although he wrote such plays as *Muck from Three Angles* (1970), *A Last Belch for the Great Auk* (1971) and *A Process of Elimination* (1975), he has never again reached the wider audiences of *Little Malcolm*.

**Halm, Friedrich** [Baron von Münch-Bellinghausen] 1806–71 Austrian playwright. Halm wrote several romantic verse tragedies, which were produced at the BURGTHEATER. Of these, *The Gladiator of Ravenna* (1854) was the sole undisputed success of his career. Between 1867 and 1870 he was intendant of the Burgtheater.

**Hamburg style** German acting tradition. The Hamburg style was a realistic approach to acting, initially associated with FRIEDRICH SCHRÖDER, and generally posited as the opposite to the WEIMAR STYLE. Although few German actors in the 19th century can have completely realized the unvarnished REALISM normally suggested by the term, it was a valuable conception as it provided a point of reference for the discussion of various actors' styles.

**Hammerstein, Oscar, II** 1895–1960 American lyricist and librettist. His first big success came with the lyrics for *Rose-Marie* (1924), an operetta with music by Rudolf Friml. Among other shows of the 1920s for which Hammerstein provided lyrics were *Sunny* (1925) and *The Desert Song* (1926). In 1927 he wrote both the lyrics and the libretto for the era's most ambitious musical, *Show Boat*, which had a score by JEROME KERN. After writing several other musicals with Kern, Hammerstein teamed up with the composer RICHARD RODGERS in 1943 to create one of the most influential of all American musicals, *Oklahoma!*. The collaboration continued through the 1940s and 1950s, resulting in *Carousel* (1945), *South Pacific* (1949), *The King and I* (1951), *Flower Drum Song* (1958) and *The Sound of Music* (1959). While Hammerstein's lyrics have sometimes been criticized for their sentimentality, he made major innovations in the form and subject-matter of the American musical.

**Hammond, (Hunter) Percy** 1873–1936 American drama critic. After working as drama critic for the *Chicago Evening Post* (1898–1908) and the *Chicago Tribune* (1908–21) he began a 15-year career as critic for the *New York Tribune*, establishing his reputation as a master of irony and urbane humour. He wrote of the producer Al Woods: 'The anguish which Mr Woods experiences when he does a thing like *Gertie's Garter ...* is assuaged by the knowledge that with its stupendous profits he may speculate in the precarious investments of the worthier drama' (1921).

**Hampden (Dougherty), Walter** 1879–1955 American actor. Though American-born, Hampden began his career learning the classical repertory and the grand style in the British company of F. R. BENSON (1901–04). He moved to the USA in 1907 in support of ALLA NAZIMOVA in her repertory of IBSEN and other modern plays. He was always more successful in poetic and romantic roles: his desire to act in *Hamlet* was not realized until 1918. In the 1920s and 1930s he toured SHAKESPEARE's plays, and in 1923 added ROSTAND's *Cyrano de Bergerac* to his repertory and played the dauntless hero more than 1,000 times in 15 years. Hampden played Danforth in ARTHUR MILLER's *Crucible* in 1953.

**Hampstead Theatre Club** (London) The theatre opened at Moreland Hall in 1959 but moved in 1962 to a prefabricated shed by Swiss Cottage Underground station. It provides a historical link between the little theatres of pre-war London and the FRINGE THEATRE clubs of the 1960s. Its premises offered a plain end stage in a small auditorium seating about 150, now marginally more spacious. Within this simple setting successive directors, who have included James Roose-Evans, MICHAEL RUDMAN and Michael Attenborough, have pursued an adventurous policy of new plays, often tried out before WEST END runs, and visiting small companies. The Hampstead locale provides the club with loyal supporters; and its list of achievements, which include West End transfers of plays by MICHAEL FRAYN, PAM GEMS, BRIAN FRIEL and JAMES SAUNDERS, has resulted in the club's high reputation.

**Hampton, Christopher (James)** 1946– British playwright. His first play, *When Did You Last See My Mother?* (1966), was produced in London and New York while he was still an undergraduate at Oxford. From 1968 to 1970 he was resident dramatist at the ROYAL COURT THEATRE, where his study of the relationship between Rimbaud and Verlaine, *Total Eclipse* (1968), was staged, together with his comedy of linguistic misunderstanding, *The Philanthropist* (1970). Hampton disliked and resisted left-wing polemics. His plays were cool, poised, witty and cosmopolitan in outlook. An excellent linguist, he sought to provide modern, actable versions of European classics. He adapted *Uncle Vanya* (1970), *Hedda Gabler* (1970) and *A Doll's House* (1971) and later, for the NATIONAL THEATRE, MOLIÈRE's *Don Juan* (1972), IBSEN's *The Wild Duck* (1979) and two plays by the Austrian ÖDÖN VON HORVÁTH, then little known in Britain – *Tales from the Vienna Woods* (1977) and *Don Juan Comes Back from the War* (1978). Horváth also inspired him to write *Tales from Hollywood* (1983), set in the émigré community in California during the war, in which Horváth, Thomas and Heinrich Mann and BERTOLT BRECHT appear as characters. Hampton can be a technically inventive writer, as his play *Savages* (1973) revealed. His most distinctive voice, however, comes through the cleverly crafted, amusing but thoughtful comedies of which *Treats* (1976) is an underrated example. The remembrance of his childhood in Egypt provides one of his most appealing plays, *White Chameleon* (1991).

**Handke, Peter** 1942– Austrian playwright and novelist. He won immediate recognition with his first 'speaking plays' *Offending the Audience* and *Self-Accusation* (1966). Influenced by Handke's law studies and by HORVÁTH, these questioned all the conventional elements of theatre and focused on the manipulative effect of language. *Kaspar* (1968) extends this theme in exploring the social conditioning of the individual by linguistic

education. The archetypal protagonist, Kaspar Hauser – an historical figure drawn upon by expressionist poets (see EXPRESSIONISM) and by the film-maker Werner Herzog – is a clown, the traditional KASPER puppet, and the imposition of conformity results in his schizophrenia. The use of theatre figures as characters was continued in *The Ride across Lake Constance* (1970), a surreal image of the stereotypes created by stage and screen, peopled by famous actors. Handke's psychological analysis of politics is evident in *They Are Dying Out* (1973), where the surrealist second half (see SURREALISM) reveals the breakdown of the personality that underlies the preceding naturalistic presentation (see NATURALISM) of capitalism. His *Über die Dörfer* (*The Long Way Round*, 1982) is a dramatic meditation on rural roots, modernity and self-knowledge. *The Hour When We Knew Nothing of One Another* (1992) represents all human life, recorded without dialogue in the form of an extended stage direction, as it passed by Handke's café table one sunny day.

**Hands, Terry** [Terence] **(David)** 1941– British director. In 1964 he helped to found the lively Everyman Theatre in Liverpool. Two years later he joined the ROYAL SHAKESPEARE COMPANY, initially to direct its travelling offshoot, Theatre-go-round. His first production at the Shakespeare Memorial Theatre at Stratford-upon-Avon came in 1968 with *The Merry Wives of Windsor*. In the following seasons he directed *Pericles* and *Women Beware Women* (1969), *Richard III* (1970) and *The Merchant of Venice* (1971) at Stratford, and *Bartholomew Fair* (1969) and *The Man of Mode* (1971) at London's Aldwych. Hands's Stratford Centenary productions of *Henry IV* and *Henry V* (1975) and his *Henry VI* cycle in 1977 indicated his love of major challenges. In 1978 he was appointed joint artistic director with TREVOR NUNN of the RSC. There, he was not noted for his interpretations of Shakespearian texts, but he had a fine command of spectacle and worked extensively with the designer FARRAH. From 1975 to 1977 he was consultant director at the COMÉDIE-FRANÇAISE, where he had already staged a triumphant *Richard III*. His flamboyant directing has sometimes led to excess, as in his staging of PETER NICHOLS's satirical PANTOMIME, *Poppy* (1983). In 1987 Hands became the sole director of the RSC, until 1990 when he handed over to ADRIAN NOBLE. Of his later RSC productions those at the Swan Theatre seemed the most successful – *The Seagull* (1990) and *Tamburlaine* (1992), in which ANTONY SHER played the title role.

**Hankin, (Edward Charles) St John** 1869–1909 British playwright and critic. He wrote social SATIRE and, influenced by BRIEUX and SHAW, *The Return of the Prodigal* (1905, revived by JOHN GIELGUD in 1948).

**Hanlon-Lees brothers** British popular entertainers. The six brothers, aerialists and knockabout comedians, introduced a new style of stage FARCE. The sons of Tom Hanlon, manager of the Theatre Royal, Manchester, **Thomas** (1836–68), **George** (1840–1926), **William** (1842–1923), **Alfred** (1844–86), **Edward** (1846–1931) and **Frederick** (adopted; 1848–86) took the name Lees in honour of their trainer, the carpet acrobat John Lees (died 1856). After touring Europe as children they created a sensation at NIBLO'S GARDEN, New York (1860), with their daring trapeze stunts. Thereafter the troupe split up, but when reconsolidated in 1868 they made a smash in St Petersburg and Berlin, and at the FOLIES-BERGÈRE in 1878 with their original mixture of ACROBATICS and slapstick. *Le Voyage en Suisse* (1879) was a farce comedy enlivened with mechanical stunts which played in Paris, London and New York (1880-1). The troupe split up again, William and Edward developing the comic extravaganzas *Fantasma* (1884) and *Superba* (1890), which briefly revived the American taste for spectacular PANTOMIME.

**Hansberry, Lorraine** 1930-65 African-American playwright. Born into a comfortable middle-class home but surrounded by poverty in Chicago's Southside, Hansberry early confronted the plight of black families living in ghetto conditions that formed the background for her landmark drama, *A Raisin in the Sun* (1959). This first play on BROADWAY by a black woman had a black director, Lloyd Richards, and predominant black financing. It ran for 530 performances. Her next play, *The Sign in Sidney Brustein's Window* (1964), about uncommitted white intellectuals in Greenwich Village, was not successful. After her early death from cancer her former husband completed and produced two plays from her unfinished manuscripts, *To Be Young, Gifted and Black* (1969) and *Les Blancs* (1970).

**Hanson, Lars** 1886-1965 Swedish actor. Noted for both stage and screen roles, he was a leading exponent of the complex psychological realism which made DRAMATEN famous from the 1930s to the 1960s. His technical virtuosity was prodigious, enabling him to play Lear at 35 and Romeo at 49; but his acting was chiefly distinguished by its inner subtlety, especially in his many STRINDBERG roles, from his early Gustav III (1916) to a series of Dramaten performances including Master Olof (1933), the Officer in *A Dream Play* (1935), the Unknown in *To Damascus* (1937 and 1944), Hummel in *The Ghost Sonata* (1942) and the Captain in *The Father* (1953). He excelled in SHAKESPEARE, above all as Richard III (1918 and 1947). His work in O'NEILL's plays included James Tyrone in the 1956 world premiere of *Long Day's Journey into Night*.

**Hanswurst** German CLOWN. 'Jack Sausage' was the most indigenous of German clown figures. The name first appears in literature as Hans Worst in a Dutch translation of Sebastian Brant's *Ship of Fools* (1519). The earliest use of the name for a stage clown was in a *FASTNACHTSPIEL* of 1553. He became a permanent type under the influence of the ENGLISCHE KOMÖDIANTEN's Pickelhering and the Italian Arlecchino during the 17th and 18th centuries. Hanswurst received a distinctive format from JOSEF STRANITZKY in Vienna, who turned him into a phlegmatic Salzburg peasant of coarse instincts, low cunning and mother-wit, clad in blue-trimmed yellow trousers, a bright-red jacket with wide sleeves, a blue bib with a green leather heart monogrammed HW, a white ruff and a green pointed hat; he wore a short black beard, his hair in a topknot, and wielded the wooden sword or *pistolese*. Hanswurst was interpolated into the pompous doings of the HAUPT-UND STAATSAKTIONEN, to the delight of audiences and the outrage of academics, scandalized by his sexual and scatological ad libs.

Stranitzky's chosen successor was the 26-year-old GOTTFRIED PREHAUSER, who made Hanswurst more Viennese: 'gallant, charming, agreeable'. Gradually, he was effaced by the figure of KASPER (from 1769), and eventually dwindled into a dramatically integrated character, usually a small comic tradesman.

**Hardy, Alexandre** c.1575-c.1632 French playwright. The first full-time French dramatist, he reputedly wrote or adapted over 600 plays, though only 34 tragedies and

tragicomedies survive. By 1611 he was attached to the itinerant company of VALLERAN LE CONTE and later to the Comédiens du Roi under BELLEROSE. Disdaining the neoclassical unities, he believed in propelling the action forward, promoting conflict between protagonists and exploiting spectacle and violence; he was a popular success, but his verse was facile. Through animating the static SENECAN dramaturgy of the French Renaissance, he prepared the way for the emergent playwrights who disparaged but profited from his example.

**Hare, David** 1947- British playwright and director. With Tony Bicat he co-founded the influential FRINGE company, Portable Theatre (1968-72). He began his assault on male-dominated, capitalistic society with *Slag* (1970), about three teachers in a girls' school who abstain from sex as a protest. *The Great Exhibition* (1972) concerns a middle-class Labour MP who tries to opt out of parliamentary life; while *Knuckle* (1974) is a neat Raymond Chandler pastiche. With HOWARD BRENTON he wrote *Brassneck* (1973), about corruption in local government, and also contributed to several group plays.

Hare was a leader of the younger generation of dramatists politicized by the events of 1968, and was quickly absorbed into the subsidized theatre establishment. From 1970 to 1971, he was resident dramatist at the ROYAL COURT, while in 1973 he became resident dramatist at the Nottingham Playhouse under RICHARD EYRE. He was a founder member of Joint Stock, for whom he adapted William Hinton's book about the Chinese Revolution, *Fanshen* (1975). After the success of *Teeth 'n' Smiles* (1975), in which HELEN MIRREN played a drunken lead singer performing at a Cambridge May Ball to an audience she despises, Hare started to write for the NATIONAL THEATRE, which produced *Plenty* (1978), *A Map of the World* (1983) and, with Howard Brenton, *Pravda* (1985), about the subservience of journalists towards the power-mad tycoons dominating London's Fleet Street.

Hare was appointed an associate director of the National Theatre in 1984 and has directed several productions there, including *King Lear* and Brenton's *Weapons of Happiness* (1986). *The Secret Rapture* (1988) was like an Edwardian society drama, updated to suit Mrs Thatcher's Britain. His trilogy about British life consists of *Racing Demon* (1990), about the Anglican Church; *Murmuring Judges* (1991), about the law; and *The Absence of War* (1993), about British politics and the 1992 election campaign run by the Labour Party. His more domestic *Skylight* opened at the NT in 1995.

**Hare, John** 1844-1921 British actor and theatre manager. As part of the BANCROFT company at the Prince of Wales's (1865-75) he was a character actor in T. W. ROBERTSON's comedies, and successively manager of the ROYAL COURT (1875-9), the ST JAMES's with the KENDALS (1879-88) and the Garrick (1889-95), where he created his best-known role as Benjamin Goldfinch in GRUNDY's *A Pair of Spectacles* (1890). He created the title part in PINERO's *The Gay Lord Quex* (1899). Hare was knighted in 1907.

**Harel, Jean Charles** 1790-1846 French theatre manager. He had a lifelong liaison with MLLE GEORGE. From 1829-32 he managed the ODÉON, enjoying extravagant scenic effects: DUMAS *père*'s *Napoleon Bonaparte, or Thirty Years of French History* (1831), starring LEMAÎTRE, cost 80,000 francs. Harel was heading for bankruptcy when in 1831 he became manager of the Porte-Saint-Martin (see BOULEVARD). In trying to make it an alternative COMÉDIE-FRANÇAISE he had some success in staging romantic drama, but the great romantic dramatists and actors felt the lure of the Comédie-Française, forcing him to quit in 1840. He also wrote a curious *Theatrical Dictionary, or, 1,258 Truths about Various Managers, Actors and Actresses*.

**Harlequin** Comic character. Harlequin is the English name of a comic figure who has persisted throughout the modern theatre. The names Herlekin and Hellequin occur in French folk literature as early as 1100 to denominate diabolic ragamuffins. The Italian Arlecchino may, however, derive from *al lecchino*, the glutton. The character first appears as a doltish rustic, teamed as a ZANNI with the shrewder Brighella; an early portrait shows him in a loose white blouse and trousers covered with patches, a flat cap and a black moustachioed half-mask; his dagger of lath was clearly descended from the ancient comic phalloi. By nature greedy, cowardly and slow-witted but inventive under compulsion, he retained the earthiness of his origins. GANASSA is one of the first actors reputed to have played the role, which soon became a leading feature of any *COMMEDIA DELL'ARTE* company.

In France Arlecchino was first played by TRISTANO MARTINELLI, GIOVAN BATTISTA ANDREINI and ANGELO COSTANTINI. It was DOMINIQUE BIANCOLELLI who naturalized him as Arlequin and fused the two *zanni* by making his Arlecchino witty, neat and fluent in a croaking voice, which became as traditional as the squawk of PUNCH. Biancolelli's successors carried on the polishing process: EVARISTO GHERARDI gave him a *patois* of French and Italian, and Vicentini-Thomassin added the element of pathos, the ability to evoke tears as well as laughter.

With the dissolution of the COMÉDIE-ITALIENNE in 1697, Arlequin moved to the fairground theatre where he appeared in plays by MARIVAUX, Boissy, Delisle, LESAGE and others; by this time, he was the leading character in these pieces, but with the return of the Italian players was relegated to subservient status in the high comedies of Marivaux and Lesage. In Italy, GOLDONI penned vehicles for the popular Arlecchini SACCO and BERTINAZZI, but tried to confine them to the written text; his opponent GOZZI, in his attempts to revive the improvised COMMEDIA, made Arlecchino merely one of a team of comics, no more important than Tartaglia or Truffaldino. In post-revolutionary Paris, Arlequin settled into the popular BOULEVARD theatres. The character was eventually effaced by the PIERROT of JEAN-GASPARD DEBURAU.

Harlequin in England first appears in JOHN DAY's *The Travailes of the Three English Brothers* (1607), but did not catch on until the introduction of the PANTOMIME by John Weaver and JOHN RICH. Rich presented an acrobatic mute, most remarkable for his pantomimic tricks; this version was carried on by e.g. James Byrne, who devised the close-fitting costume bespangled with glittering lozenges. Harlequin was to be elbowed aside by the popular Clown of JOSEPH GRIMALDI.

In modern times, Harlequin has become emblematic of a bygone theatre, despite attempts to revive him at the VIEUX-COLOMBIER and the Piccolo Teatro di Milano with Marcello Moretti in the part. Fokine's use of the character in his ballets *Arlequinade* (1900) and *Carnaval* (1910) is typical of the svelte dandy character conjured up by many modern artists. The SAN FRANCISCO MIME TROUPE is one of the few groups to adapt Harlequin to

the needs of contemporary SATIRE, while DARIO FO has managed to absorb the *commedia* in a comic persona all his own.

**harlequinade** see PANTOMIME, ENGLISH

**Harnick, Sheldon** see BOCK, JERRY

**Harrigan, Edward** 1844–1911 and **Tony Hart** [Anthony J. Cannon] 1855–91 American playwright-actor and actor. Harrigan and Hart became the most popular comedy team on the American stage (1871–85). They sang, danced and played the principal roles (usually Harrigan as the amiable, fun-loving Irish adventurer Dan Mulligan and Hart, in blackface (see MINSTREL SHOW), as the Negro wench Rebecca Allup) in Harrigan's high-spirited 'mêlées': *The Mulligan Guard Picnic* (1878), *MG Ball* (1979), *MG Chowder* (1879), *MG Christmas* (1879), *MG Nominee* (1880), *MG Surprise* (1880), *MG Silver Wedding* (1881), *Old Lavender* (1877), *The Major* (1881), *Squatter Sovereignty* (1882), *Cordelia's Aspirations* (1883), *Dan's Tribulations* (1884) and *Investigation* (1884). Harrigan's FARCES were also documentary explorations of New York's Lower Eastside, giving striking portraits of the immigrant population, particularly the Irish. When his second BROADWAY theatre burned down (1884), the partners separated. Hart was committed to an asylum and died at the age of 35. Harrigan continued writing and acting.

**Harris, Jed** 1900–79 American producer. At the height of the 1920s Harris presented four plays celebrated for their crisp, modern style: *Broadway* (1926), *Coquette* (1927), *The Royal Family* (1927), a SATIRE about a flamboyant theatrical dynasty modelled on the Barrymores (see DREW-BARRYMORE FAMILY), and *The Front Page* (1928). He worked only sporadically thereafter, most notably on *Uncle Vanya* (1930), *The Green Bay Tree* (1933), with LAURENCE OLIVIER as a kept homosexual, *Our Town* (1938) and *The Heiress* (1947), based on HENRY JAMES's *Washington Square*. Harris directed only a few of his plays (including *Uncle Vanya* and *Our Town*) but all his productions had taste and showmanship, achieved at great cost to his collaborators. His monstrous behaviour towards his colleagues earned him GEORGE ABBOTT's epithet: 'the Little Napoleon of Broadway'.

**Harris, Julie** 1925– American film, stage and television actress. She rose to stardom as Frankie Adams in *The Member of the Wedding* (1950), as Sally Bowles in *I Am a Camera* (1951) and as Joan in *The Lark* (1955), performances she later filmed. In 1976 she successfully staged a one-woman show, *The Belle of Amherst*, which toured to London. Critics have been won over by her air of vulnerability and fragility, coupled with her remarkable stage techniques. In 1989 she toured in Alfred Uhry's *Driving Miss Daisy*, and in *Lettice and Lovage* in 1992–3. She also played in Timothy Mason's *The Fiery Furnace* (CIRCLE REPERTORY COMPANY, 1993).

**Harris, Rosemary** 1930– British actress. She has appeared in over 140 roles in England and America. A versatile artist who once described herself as 'a chameleon on a tartan', she featured prominently in GUTHRIE's 1956 production of *Troilus and Cressida*; and in *Man and Superman*, *Much Ado about Nothing*, *The School for Scandal*, *The Seagull*, *Twelfth Night*, *The Broken Heart*, *Hamlet* (Ophelia in the NATIONAL THEATRE's inaugural season), *The Lion in Winter*, *Old Times*, *Major Barbara*, *A Streetcar Named Desire*, *The Royal Family*, *All My Sons* (1981 London revival), *Hay Fever* (1985–6), *Lost in Yonkers* (1991–3) and *An Inspector Calls* (1994).

**Harris, Sam H(enry)** 1872–1941 American producer. In 1900 he became a partner in the firm of Sullivan, Harris and Woods (1900–4), which produced eight MELODRAMAS and BURLESQUES, including the hit *The Fatal Wedding*. He began a 16-year partnership with GEORGE M. COHAN in 1904, producing more than 50 plays including Cohan's own *Little Johnny Jones*, *Forty-five Minutes from Broadway* and *Seven Keys to Baldpate*. After the partnership was dissolved Harris independently produced *Rain* (1922), *Icebound* (1923), *The Jazz Singer* (1925), *Animal Crackers* (1928), *Dinner at Eight* (1932), *Of Thee I Sing* (1932), *You Can't Take It with You* (1937), *Of Mice and Men* (1938), *The Man Who Came to Dinner* (1939) and *Lady in the Dark* (1941).

**Harrison, Rex** [Reginald Carey] 1908–90 British actor. He will always be associated with the role of Henry Higgins in the musical version of SHAW's *Pygmalion*, *My Fair Lady* (by LERNER AND LOEWE) – the urbane English gentleman, stern yet sentimental, raffish yet decent. Having started his career at Liverpool Playhouse in 1924, he arrived in London in 1930. His roles were not only in the comedies of COWARD, RATTIGAN and Van Druten, but also in less obvious parts: he was the Uninvited Guest in ELIOT's *The Cocktail Party* (1950), Henry IV in PIRANDELLO's play (1973 and 1974) and appeared in SHAW, FRY, and CHEKHOV. He appeared frequently in New York from his BROADWAY debut in 1936. He made acting look easy, and rather the profession of the officer class. He was knighted in 1989.

**Harrison, Tony** 1937– British playwright, translator and poet. His brilliant adaptation of MOLIÈRE's *The Misanthrope* (1973) was followed by a version of the *Oresteia* (1981), both at the NATIONAL THEATRE. He modernized the verse of three medieval MYSTERY PLAYS in 1985 – another NT hit. From a fragment of a satyr play by SOPHOCLES he constructed a parable, *The Trackers of Oxyrhynchus* (1990), about two dons whose love for Greek culture helps them to overlook the disasters on their travels. *Square Rounds* (1992) was described as a 'theatre piece' rather than a play: a meditation on armaments manufacturers which he directed himself and illustrated by MIME, juggling, conjuring and rhymed couplets.

**Hart brothers Heinrich** 1855–1906 and **Julius** 1859–1930, German critics and playwrights. They did much to prepare the critical ground for naturalist theatre (see NATURALISM) in Berlin in the late 1880s. Their most important essays are collected in *Critical Conflicts* (1894).

**Hart House Theatre** (Toronto) A small professional theatre. It was built by the trustees of the Massey Foundation and presented to the University in 1919. During the 1920s and 1930s, under directors such as Roy Mitchell (1919–21) and Edgar Stone (1929–34), it was a major centre of new Canadian drama, introducing important new playwrights such as Merrill Denison. After World War II it became a student theatre and, under the direction of Robert Gill (1946–66), a vital training ground for a whole generation of professional actors, directors and designers.

**Hart, Lorenz** 1895–1943 American lyricist and librettist. The first complete scores by RICHARD RODGERS and Hart were for *The Garrick Gaieties* (1925) and *Dearest Enemy* (1925). In the next 18 years they created an almost uninterrupted string of successful shows, including *The Girl Friend* (1926), *A Connecticut Yankee* (1927), *America's Sweetheart* (1931), *On Your Toes* (1936), *Babes in Arms* (1937), *The Boys from Syracuse* (1938), *I Married an Angel* (1938), *Pal*

*Joey* (1940) and *By Jupiter* (1941). Hart's clever, sometimes sardonic lyrics, often employing complicated internal rhyme schemes, are considered among the finest ever written for the musical stage.

**Hart, Moss** 1904–61 American playwright, librettist and director. Although he had written several unsuccessful plays on his own, it was his teaming up with GEORGE S. KAUFMAN during the 1930s that established his career with such comic hits as *Once in a Lifetime* (1930), *You Can't Take It with You* (1936) and *The Man Who Came to Dinner* (1939). On his own in the 1940s, Hart wrote the book for the musical about psychoanalysis, *Lady in the Dark* (1941); and *Light up the Sky* (1948), about a play in rehearsal. Latterly he was a director, notably of *My Fair Lady* (1956).

**Hart, Tony** see HARRIGAN, EDWARD

**Harte, Bret** [Francis Brett Harte] 1836–1902 American short-story writer and playwright. Raised in Brooklyn, he moved to California in 1853 and became famous for stories and poems in the *Overland Monthly* (1868–71). His popularity declined as rapidly as it rose, and after 1878 he lived abroad. His best work combines sentiment and low humour in the manner of CHARLES DICKENS. As a playwright he created *Two Men of Sandy Bar* (1875) for STUART ROBSON, and collaborated with Mark Twain on *Ah Sin* (1877), a vehicle for actor Charles Parsloe. Though both failed, they established a genre that BARTLEY CAMPBELL perfected in *My Partner*.

**Hartleben, Otto** 1864–1905 German playwright, poet and short story writer. His plays, of which by far the most successful was *Rosenmontag* (*The Monday before Lent*, 1900), focus primarily upon the incompatibility of sexual attraction and social class.

**Harwood, Ronald** (1934– ) South-African born British playwright. He joined DONALD WOLFIT's British touring company as an actor. His first stage success as a playwright came with *The Dresser* (1980), in which TOM COURTENAY played the dresser to a Wolfit-like star. Harwood's mixture of affection and despair is reflected in similar studies of a loss of religious faith (*J.J. Farr*, 1987) and of South African middle-class illusions in *Another Time* (1989). *Reflected Glory* (1992) describes the rivalry between a restaurant-owner and his younger, more successful playwright brother. Harwood excels at collapses in confidence and derives humour from the grubby underside of glamour, although his technique is within the tradition of the WELL MADE PLAY.

**Hasenclever, Walter** 1890–1940 German playwright, novelist and poet. His first play, *The Son* (1916), was one of the key works of EXPRESSIONISM. Semi-autobiographical in conception, it established conflict between the generations as a typical Hasenclever subject and contains the most directly political rendering of the parricide theme. *The Decision* (1919) put forward the thesis that political action was irrelevant to real social change. His adaptation of *Antigone* (1919) as an anti-war piece was directed by KARLHEINZ MARTIN at the 3,500-seat Grosses Schauspielhaus in 1920. Hasenclever abandoned expressionism for social comedy: *A Man of Distinction* (1927) and *Marriages Are Made in Heaven* (1928) share a tragic perception of existence under an irreverently witty surface. Forced into exile by the rise of Hitler, he turned to the biblical story of Esther for his last work, *Scandal in Assyria* (performed under the pseudonym of Axel Kjellström in London in 1939). Imprisoned by the Vichy French on the invasion of France, he committed suicide.

**Hauptmann, Gerhart** 1862–1946 German playwright and novelist. From the production of his first play *Before Dawn* (1889) at the FREIE BÜHNE, Hauptmann was celebrated as the leader of NATURALISM in the German theatre. The play shows the unmistakable influence of the theories of ZOLA and the dramaturgy of IBSEN, a legacy from which Hauptmann found it difficult to escape. *Lonely Lives* (1891) was clearly inspired by *Rosmersholm*, though with *The Weavers* (1892), a play of epic structure dramatizing the plight of Silesian workers during the riots of 1844, he found a more individual tone. He continued to write naturalistic plays into the 20th century – *The Beaver Coat* (1893), *Carter Henschel* (1899) and *Rose Bernd* (1903) are notable examples – but also experimented with other genres and modes. *The Sunken Bell* (1896) was a widely performed, neo-romantic allegory that gave actors such as KAINZ an ideal opportunity to display their vocal skills. Hauptmann, who was awarded the Nobel Prize in 1912, continued to expand his range, producing historical dramas, fantasy plays, and tragedies written in both the Greek and Shakespearian forms.

***Haupt- und Staatsaktionen*** ('Monarch and State drama') German theatrical genre. The plays, performed by travelling troupes in Germany during the 17th and early 18th centuries, were derived from the Shakespearian drama that had been performed by the ENGLISCHE KOMÖDIANTEN, from the German literary drama, and from the improvised drama of the COMMEDIA DELL'ARTE troupes that toured Germany then. By all accounts, this was a debased form of theatre that encouraged bombastic acting, sensational and gory manifestations on the stage, and frequent gross obscenity. As the German theatre became 'regularized' under the influence of GOTTSCHED and the quality of drama improved as a result of the efforts of such writers as J. E. SCHLEGEL and LESSING, both the style and the genre of representation began to decline. Although *Haupt- und Staatsaktionen* continued to be performed sporadically into the 1760s by the troupes of KOCH and DÖBBELIN, by the end of that decade they had disappeared entirely from the repertoire.

**Havel, Václav** 1936– Czech playwright and president. A native of Prague, he studied at the Prague Theatre Academy and eventually became dramaturge and resident playwright at the Balustrade Theatre, for which he wrote all his plays until 1968. In his best-known works Havel focused on deformations in patterns of thinking (ideological and bureaucratic power stratagems run amok or become sclerotic). His stage world is essentially abstract, schematic and cerebral, characterized more by wit and FARCE than by humour, as is seen in *Garden Party* (1963), *Memorandum* (1965) and *The Increased Difficulty of Concentration* (1968), which form a triptych of variations on a theme. A frequently confined dissident, he continued to live and write in his homeland, although his only outlet for productions between 1969 and 1990 was abroad: e.g. *A Private View* (New York, 1983), *Largo Desolato* (Vienna, 1985), *Temptation* (ROYAL SHAKESPEARE COMPANY at the Other Place, 1987) and *Urban Rehabilitation* (1989). Following the Velvet Revolution of 1989 and the restoration of democracy, Havel was elected interim president of Czechoslovakia (1990–2) and since 1993 has been president of the Czech Republic, following the split with Slovakia. His playwriting career has been temporarily suspended.

**Hawthorne, Nigel** 1929– British actor. He moved to London from South Africa in the early 1950s and worked with JOAN LITTLEWOOD's company. He became known for playing establishment figures in a gently ironic manner, e.g. 'Roy Jenkins' in *Mrs Wilson's Diary* (1967) and the smoothly obstructive civil servant, Sir Humphrey, in the long-running BBC television series *Yes Minister* and *Yes, Prime Minister*. His acting range, however, extends from his appearance as Prince Albert in EDWARD BOND's *Early Morning* (1969) to his tender study of the writer C.S. Lewis in *Shadowlands* (1989) and the brilliant portrait of a not-mad king in ALAN BENNETT's *The Madness of George III* (1991). A subtle actor, Hawthorne is set to become the natural successor to ALEC GUINNESS.

**Hayes** [Brown]**, Helen** 1900–93 American actress. With KATHARINE CORNELL and Lynn Fontanne (see ALFRED LUNT) Hayes was one of the great ladies of American Theatre, with a stage career of over 50 years. Diminutive and homespun, she was distinctly less glamorous than the others, projecting modesty and common sense. In her youth she worked for CHARLES FROHMAN and GEORGE TYLER, acted with the THEATRE GUILD (*Caesar and Cleopatra*, 1925; *Coquette*, 1927), and had her greatest critical success as the gallant monarchs in *Mary of Scotland* (1933) and *Victoria Regina* (1935). In the 1940s and 1950s she starred in showy vehicles like *Harriet* (1943), an episodic biography of Harriet Beecher Stowe, and *Mrs McThing* (1952), in which she was a society matron transformed into a charwoman. She retired from the stage in 1971, thereafter acting occasionally in films and on television.

**Haymarket, Theatre Royal** (London) Opening in 1720, the Haymarket was the chief rival of the patent houses (see THEATRICAL MONOPOLY) for almost a century. In the 1730s HENRY FIELDING leased it to stage a series of anti-Walpole SATIRES. Walpole's Licensing Act followed in 1737, and the Haymarket was the most prominent of the illegitimate victims of this repressive legislation. In 1747 the theatre was leased by SAMUEL FOOTE, who in 1766 was licensed to stage the legitimate drama during the summer months, when the patent theatres were closed. Under the successive managements of GEORGE COLMAN THE ELDER (1776–94) and his son (1794–1817), the Haymarket provided a summer home for almost all the greatest actors and most popular plays of the period. The present theatre, with John Nash's famous portico, was built in 1820. Among its best-known managers have been BENJAMIN WEBSTER (1837–53), BUCKSTONE (1853–79), the BANCROFTS (1880–5), BEERBOHM TREE (1887–96) and Cyril Maude (1896–1905).

**Hayward, Leland** 1902–71 American producer. He was responsible for two dozen plays and musicals on BROADWAY between 1941 and his death, two-thirds of which were unqualified successes both critically and financially. His career as a producer began with *A Bell for Adano* (1944). Significant productions included *State of the Union* (1945), *Mister Roberts* (1948), *Anne of the Thousand Days* (1948), *South Pacific* (1949), *Call Me Madam* (1950), *Gypsy* (1959), *The Sound of Music* (1959) and *The Trial of the Catonsville Nine* (1971). Hayward was also a film and television producer, a pilot and a photographer.

**Hazlitt, William** 1778–1830 English essayist and critic. Hazlitt's fondness for theatre, evident in his praise of the grandeur of MRS SIDDONS, the intensity of JOHN PHILIP KEMBLE and the gusto of EDMUND KEAN, did not stop him from disparaging its faults. From his sceptical stance he was most active as a drama critic (for the *Examiner*, the

*Champion*, the *Morning Chronicle* and *The Times*) from 1813 to 1818. In 1818 he published a selection of his reviews as *A View of the English Stage*. He completed the unfinished *Memoirs of the Late Thomas Holcroft* (1816). His famous *Characters of Shakespeare's Plays* (1817) is dotted with theatrical references; the metaphor of public life as a stage pervades his most original work, *The Spirit of the Age* (1825). He also dwelt on the disparity between the actor in performance and the actor in private in two essays, 'On Actors and Acting' (*The Round Table*, 1817) and 'Whether Actors Ought to Sit in the Boxes?' (*Table Talk*, 1824).

**heavens** The canopy over the stage of an Elizabethan public theatre, supported, as in De Witt's drawing of the SWAN, by two pillars, and probably decorated with sun, moon and stars.

**Hebbel, Friedrich** 1813–63 German playwright. After a childhood of abject poverty Hebbel settled in Vienna and, in 1846, married the BURGTHEATER actress, Christine Enghaus (1817–1910). Though most of his plays have mythical or historical settings, his characters are recognizably figures of his time. The early prose drama *Judith* (1841) is an unorthodox treatment of the biblical myth, while *Maria Magdalena* (1844), a play with a contemporary setting, has been seen by many as anticipating IBSEN. *Herodes and Mariamne* (1849) treats the themes of trust and jealousy in marriage, *Agnes Bernauer* (1852) is a powerful historical drama about the guilt inherent in perfect beauty, while *Gyges and His Ring* (1856), a striking play about sexual tensions, also involves much discussion of political and moral issues. Hebbel's final work was a trilogy, *The Nibelungs* (1862).

**Heeley, Desmond** 1931– British stage and COSTUME designer. Heeley began his career at the BIRMINGHAM REPERTORY THEATRE Company and then at the Shakespeare Memorial Theatre (see ROYAL SHAKESPEARE THEATRE), where he became designer in 1955. His first shows were *Toad of Toad Hall*, notable for its masks and headdresses and depiction of animals' hands and feet, and *Titus Andronicus* under the direction of PETER BROOK. He subsequently became an internationally known designer, working at the OLD VIC, the STRATFORD (Ontario) FESTIVAL Theatre, the GUTHRIE THEATRE in Minneapolis, and COVENT GARDEN. He was hired to design *Norma* at the New York Metropolitan Opera (1970) and has subsequently designed many operas there. Heeley's lush, textured, layered and subtle but provocative use of colour in costumes has influenced a whole generation of designers. His style has been described as impressionistic SYMBOLISM combined with the texture of collage and junk art. His designs are most successful in the theatrical, larger-than-life worlds of SHAKESPEARE and opera.

**Heiberg, Gunnar** 1857–1929 Norwegian director, critic and playwright. As a critic, he argued for a more modern repertoire and acting style at Christiania Theatre, and from 1884 attempted to realize them at the NATIONALE SCENE, Bergen, where he directed the world premieres of *The Wild Duck* and *Rosmersholm*. In 1888 he began a new career as a dramatist and essayist, only occasionally returning to directing. His 14 plays are influenced by IBSEN's in their handling of ideas, but are experimental in their tendencies towards theatricalism, SATIRE and formalized characterization. *Aunt Ulrikke* (1894) and *The Tragedy of Love* (1904) have been the most enduring.

**Heiberg, Johan Ludvig** 1791–1860 Danish poet, playwright, critic and manager. Hoping to bring his country aesthetically and intellectually into Europe, he exerted a strong influence on Danish cultural life largely by promoting French classicism and GOETHE's WEIMAR classicism. He also popularized Hegelian philosophy and admired CALDERÓN DE LA BARCA and the Jena romantics for their philosophical drama. He wrote *vaudevilles*, mostly for his wife JOHANNE LUISE HEIBERG to perform, and the more enduring comedies *Elves' Hill* (1828) and *A Soul after Death* (1841). His management of the KONGELIGE TEATER (1849–56) was bitterly controversial, as he found himself opposed over repertoire by younger, more progressive minds.

**Heiberg, Johanne Luise** 1812–90 Danish actress. Her entire career was spent at the KONGELIGE TEATER. Her husband, JOHAN LUDVIG HEIBERG, wrote *vaudevilles* specifically to suit her personality, while she shared his conviction that theatre should embody idealized beauty rather than reality. Her ironic, graceful style suited the *vaudevilles* and SCRIBEAN comedies that dominated the Kongelige's repertoire in the 1830s, increasingly supplemented by the sentimental plays of Henrik Hertz in which she frequently co-starred with MICHAEL WIEHE. Though frequently criticized for her artificiality, she demanded that stage characters be complex and consistent. After her husband's death in 1860 she began her 'second career', playing Lady Macbeth and SCHILLER's Mary Stuart with depth and humanity and directing several early plays by BJØRNSON and IBSEN.

**Heijermans, Herman** [Samuel Falkland] 1864–1924 Dutch playwright and director. He reached international fame through his socio-realistic plays; a convinced socialist, he wrote in order to protest against bad social conditions. Although a Jew himself, he disliked orthodox Judaism (*Ghetto*, 1898) as well as other religious conventions and prejudices. Very popular in the 1900s, Heijermans's plays are still regularly performed today: e.g. *Schakels* (*Links*, 1903), *Uitkomst* (*Relief*, 1907), *De opgaande zon* (*The Rising Sun*, 1908) and *De wijze kater* (*The Wise Cat*, 1917). *Ahasverus* (1893) was staged in Paris by ANTOINE. *Op Hoop van Zegen* (*The Good Hope*, 1900) and *In de Jonge Jan* (*At the Jonge Jan*, 1903, a one-act mystery drama) were performed in England, the USA and Russia. *Op Hoop van Zegen*, his best-known play, deals with the oppression of poor fishermen by powerful ship-owners. The character of Kniertje, the old mother, has become a household name.

**Heiremans, Luis Alberto** 1928–64 Chilean playwright. A member of an illustrious and wealthy Santiago family, he trained as a doctor but devoted his time to some 15 plays, novels and short stories as well as translating and adapting French and English plays for the Chilean stage. He was a professor at the Teatro de Ensayo of the Catholic University in Santiago, where he promoted Chilean theatre. The Heiremans Foundation, created after his premature death from cancer, continues to provide benefits for theatre students and the arts. Interested in vanguard theatrical techniques, Heiremans dealt with existentialist themes of anguish, frustration, solitude and alienation in his early plays. *Esta señorita Trini* (*This Miss Trini*, 1958), the first Chilean MUSICAL COMEDY, enjoyed tremendous commercial success. His most mature plays are his final trilogy, *Versos de ciego* (*The Blind Man's Verses*, 1961), *El abanderado* (*The Standard-Bearer*, 1962) and *El tony chico* (*The Little Clown*, 1964), representing a combination of religious, mythic, poetic and folkloric elements that point towards a higher Christian ideal.

**Helburn, Theresa** 1887–1959 American director and producer. After a brief career as an actress, she became drama critic of the *Nation* (1918). Two years later she became executive director of the struggling THEATRE GUILD. A woman of outstanding executive ability and willpower, she was responsible for bringing ALFRED LUNT AND LYNN FONTANNE together for *The Guardsman* in 1924, which established them as the leading dual acting team in America. With LAWRENCE LANGNER she brought *Oklahoma!* to the stage in 1943, and in the same year *Othello* with PAUL ROBESON.

**Hellman, Lillian** 1906–84 American playwright. She first shocked and fascinated BROADWAY with *The Children's Hour* (1934), about the evil machinations of a child who destroys her teachers by whispering about their 'unnatural' relationship. The play ran for 691 performances. Vigorous and unyielding confrontations became her trademark in *The Little Foxes* (1939), *Watch on the Rhine* (1941), *The Searching Wind* (1944), *Another Part of the Forest* (1946), *The Autumn Garden* (1951), *The Lark* (1955, adapted from ANOUILH's *L'Alouette*), *Candide* (1956, from VOLTAIRE with music by LEONARD BERNSTEIN) and *Toys in the Attic* (1960). Only three plays failed at the box-office: *Days to Come* (1936), *Montserrat* (1949) and *My Mother, My Father and Me* (1963).

In 1931 she met detective-story writer Dashiell Hammett, who was to become her constant companion until his death in 1961. She wrote scripts for such films as *Dark Angel* (1935), *These Three* (1936, based on *The Children's Hour*), *Dead End* (1937) and *The North Star* (1943). In 1952 she was called before the House Un-American Activities Committee and her name was added to Hollywood's blacklist.

**Helpmann, Robert (Murray)** 1908–86 Australian dancer, actor, director and choreographer. He toured Australia with Anna Pavlova in 1926, and became principal dancer in J. C. WILLIAMSON's musicals. Joining the Vic Wells/SADLER'S WELLS Ballet in 1933, he remained principal dancer until 1950, also working as dancer, choreographer and director at COVENT GARDEN from 1946. After appearing as Oberon at the OLD VIC in 1937 he played many Shakespearian roles at the Old Vic and Stratford-upon-Avon, and directed and acted in many modern plays. He was co-artistic director from 1965 to 1976 of the Australian Ballet, which staged his ballets *The Display* (1964), *Yugen* (1965) and *Sun Music* (1968). He was awarded a CBE in 1964 and KBE in 1968.

**Heminges, John** died 1630 English actor and company manager. He was a sharer in the LORD CHAMBERLAIN'S/King's MEN from the company's foundation in 1594 until his death. He was an unexceptional actor, but immortalized by his initiative in the publication of the SHAKESPEARE Folio of 1623 – a task that may have fallen to him via his role as business manager of the King's Men.

**Henley, Beth** 1952– American playwright. Her comedies depict bizarre characters who survive their disastrous experiences in outlandish ways. Her first professionally produced play, *Crimes of the Heart* (1981), portrays with wit and compassion the rallying of three eccentric Mississippi sisters because one of them has shot her husband. Henley's other plays include *The Wake of Jamey Foster* (1982), *Am I Blue?* (1982), *The Miss Firecracker Contest* (1984, another black comedy about a Mississippi woman's effort to redeem her calamitous life by winning a beauty contest), *The Debutante Ball* (1985), *The Lucky Spot* (1986) and *Abundance* (1990), the exploration of a 25-year friendship of mail-order brides in the Old West.

**Hennings, Betty** 1850–1939 Danish actress. She was noted for her performances of IBSEN at the KONGELIGE TEATER. She specialized in ingénue roles, playing Agnes in *The School for Wives* and Selma in *The League of Youth*, before creating Nora in the world premiere of *A Doll's House* in 1879. Her revelation of Nora's growing inner tension was a turning point in Hennings's career, leading to her casting as other, even more complex, Ibsen characters: Hedda Gabler, Hilde Wangel, Hedvig Ekdal and Mrs Alving. Although her strength was in naturalistic modern drama (see NATURALISM), by the turn of the century her style had begun to seem too mannered for modern taste.

**Henry, John** 1738–94 American actor. Born in Ireland, he worked in London and the West Indies before joining DOUGLASS's American Company. Tall, handsome and arrogant, Henry was most successful in comedy, especially Irish characters. He made his first American appearance in Philadelphia in 1767. The matinée idol of his time, he was the first actor in America whose lamentable morals were seized on by opponents of the theatre. After the Revolutionary War, he co-managed the American Company with LEWIS HALLAM JR, and in 1792 imported JOHN HODGKINSON, who shortly forced Henry into retirement.

**Henslowe, Philip** c.1550–1616 English theatre manager. By 1592 Henslowe held the lease of the ROSE THEATRE, and may also have been in control of the theatre in London's Newington Butts. He and his son-in-law EDWARD ALLEYN formed a highly successful partnership, building the FORTUNE on the north side of the Thames (1600). Later they combined their interests in drama and animal-baiting by erecting the adaptable HOPE THEATRE on Bankside, London. Henslowe was an energetic and not over-scrupulous businessman, also engaged in pawnbroking and money-lending. Evidence of his dealings has survived in his uniquely valuable *Diary*.

**Her/His Majesty's Theatre** (London) There have been four theatres on the Haymarket site, their names varying with the sex of the reigning monarch. The first, designed by SIR JOHN VANBRUGH and named the Queen's Theatre, was intended as a home for the dissenting DRURY LANE players under the leadership of THOMAS BETTERTON. It opened in 1705, with Vanbrugh and CONGREVE in joint management, and soon became identified with opera, especially Italian. Handel wrote 29 of his 35 operas for performance there. It was destroyed by fire in 1789.

The second (King's) Theatre opened in 1791 and was recognized as a rival to La Scala in Milan (built 1788), becoming the centre of (predominantly Italian) opera until COVENT GARDEN took over that role. Renamed Her Majesty's Theatre in 1837, the second theatre was destroyed by fire in 1867.

The third theatre had an undistinguished history and was demolished in 1891. The present theatre opened in 1897 and remained under HERBERT BEERBOHM TREE's control until 1917. It was there, in 1904, that he opened the drama school that became the Royal Academy of Dramatic Art, and there that he presented his spectacular SHAKESPEARE productions. Later successes have included OSCAR ASCHE's *Chu Chin Chow* (1916), FLECKER's *Hassan* (1923), COWARD's *Bitter Sweet* (1929) and various American musicals.

**Herbert, Jocelyn** 1917– British stage designer. She became influenced by COPEAU and SAINT-DENIS while an art student in France and London. Not until her 40th year did Herbert begin a theatre career, as stage designer at the ROYAL COURT THEATRE during its most creative years, under the leadership of GEORGE DEVINE, a former associate of Saint-Denis. Her work in the austere, poetic tradition also came to reflect the spare functionality of BRECHTian theatre. In later years her scenography in England and abroad became more complex, but has never lost its essential purity and fine sense of spatial proportion. Distinctive productions include *Saint Joan of the Stockyards* (1964), *The Abduction from the Seraglio* (1979), *Galileo* (1980), *The Oresteia* (1981), *The Mask of Orpheus* (1986) and *Square Rounds* (1992).

**Herbert, Victor** 1859–1924 Irish-born American composer. Herbert went to America as a young cellist and began to compose for the theatre. Trained in the conventions and traditions of European operetta, he was adept at composing music that appealed to American audiences, and equally at home writing for comic operas, operettas and musical comedies. In 1894 his first score, *Prince Ananias*, was heard, followed by *The Wizard of the Nile* (1895) and *The Serenade* (1897). Some of his most enduringly popular songs were written for *Babes in Toyland* (1903) and *Mlle Modiste* (1905). Herbert's biggest commercial successes were *The Red Mill* (1906), *Naughty Marietta* (1910), *Sweethearts* (1913) and *Eileen* (1917).

**Herman, David** 1876–1937 Jewish director. One of the first and most influential of JEWISH ART THEATRE directors, he started with HIRSHBEIN's Troupe in Odessa in 1908, followed by the Arts Corner in Warsaw in 1910 and then the celebrated VILNA TROUPE from 1917, where his most memorable of many productions was a stylistic production of *The Dybbuk*. After periods in Warsaw and Vienna he emigrated to America in 1934, exerting a profound influence on the Yiddish theatrical scene (see YIDDISH THEATRE) with his inspired direction of the FOLKSBIENE.

**Hernández, Luisa Josefina** 1928– Mexican playwright and novelist. A professor of theatre at the National University, Mexico City, and influenced by RODOLFO USIGLI, she achieved early success with both *Los frutos caídos* (*The Fallen Fruit*, 1957) and *Los huéspedes reales* (*The Royal Guests*, 1957), the latter a brilliant study of incest. Always concerned with problems of history, she adapted several major works to the stage, such as *Clemencia* (the Altamirano novel, 1963), *Popol-Vuh* (1967), based on the Mayan myths and legends, and *Quetzalcoatl* (1968). Hernández has integrated BRECHTian techniques into many works and has been an early and steady advocate of women's rights and social justice.

**Herne, James A.** 1839–1901 American playwright. Herne's work, frequently compared to IBSEN's, began the period of modern drama in America. In San Francisco he wrote MELODRAMAS with DAVID BELASCO, e.g. *Within an Inch of His Life* (1879) and *Hearts of Oak* (1879). Among his own plays, *The Minute Men of 1774–75* (1879) suggested the New England local colour that was developed in *Drifting Apart* (1888), a temperance play, and *Shore Acres* (1892), which made him a millionaire. Herne's best-known play, *Margaret Fleming* (1890–1), about a philandering husband whose illegitimate child is accepted by his morally strong and emotionally sensitive wife, showed his interest in REALISM and social determinism, but was not successful. *The Reverend Griffith Davenport* (1899), based on a novel by Helen Gardner, dramatized the struggle of a slaveholder who opposed slavery during the Civil War. Herne developed realistic themes and characters in his plays and emphasized the 'humanity' and 'large truth' in drama, which has a 'higher purpose' than amusement.

**hero-combat play** British and Irish mumming play. The most widespread of its type, it was a comic drama of armed conflict, death and resurrection, performed seasonally. It is frequently described as medieval, or even pre-Christian, though there is no hard evidence of it until 1737. Its text appears to be based on one of the many editions of Richard Johnson's *Seven Champions of Christendom*, and on 17th-century broadside lampoons against mountebanks. It is probably a 17th- or 18th-century synthesis of popular literature with elements of indigenous mumming traditions. The hero-combat play has been extensively revived in the present century under the aegis of the folk song and dance movements: traditional gangs still perform at Antrobus, Bampton, Chipping Campden, Marshfield, Ripon and Uttoxeter in England.

**Heron, Matilda** 1830–77 American actress. Born in Ireland, she played Juliet to CHARLOTTE CUSHMAN's Romeo (1852). She made her life's work out of her own adaptation of *Camille*, opening it in New Orleans (1855) and moving to WALLACK's Theatre (1857), where audiences were captivated by her 'elemental power' and her uninhibited exploitation of a woman's sexual life. After an initial run of 100 performances, she toured the play for the next 20 years.

**Hettner, Hermann** 1821–82 German professor of literature. Hettner's most significant contribution to the theatre was his brief book *The Modern Drama* (1852), which, in validating the advances made by the bourgeois tragedy, prepared the way for the drama of IBSEN and the naturalists (see NATURALISM).

**Hewett, Dorothy** 1923– Australian playwright; initially a poet and novelist. Her first play was the working-class drama *This Old Man Comes Rolling Home* (1967). Her plays, mainly expressionistic epics (see EXPRESSIONISM) featuring music and poetry, depict complex women characters trapped in ageing, domesticity and the stereotyped images of women, or evoke an idyllic pastoral world. They include *The Chapel Perilous* (1971), *Bon-Bons and Roses for Dolly* (1972), *The Tatty Hollow Story* (1974), *Pandora's Cross* (1978), *The Man from Muckinupin* (1979) and *The Fields of Heaven* (1982).

**Heyward, Dorothy** 1890–1961 and **(Edwin) Du Bose Heyward** 1885–1940 American husband and wife playwriting team. He supplied stories from his novels and she supplied dramatic craftsmanship. Although Du Bose wrote one other play and Dorothy had five others produced, their reputation rests on their folk dramas of African-American life, *Porgy* (1927) and *Mamba's Daughters* (1939), both praised for their realistic depiction of the lives of Southern blacks. *Porgy*, the love story of a crippled black man and an erring woman, became an American legend, particularly after its conversion into a folk opera, *Porgy and Bess* (1935), by Du Bose and the GERSHWINS. The Heywards are credited with providing dramatic opportunities for black actors (ETHEL WATERS was the first black woman to star in a BROADWAY drama in *Mamba's Daughters*).

**Heywood, John** 1497–1580 English playwright. His INTERLUDES, *The Play of the Weather* (1533) and *The play called the foure P. P.* (c.1543), both jolly and simple, are regarded as his best. He was the son-in-law of JOHN RASTELL.

**Heywood, Thomas** 1573–1641 English playwright, actor, poet and pamphleteer. He claimed to have written or co-authored 220 plays, of which some 30 have survived. *The Four Prentices of London* (?1592) is a chivalric romance which may have inspired the PARODY of BEAUMONT's *The Knight of the Burning Pestle* (1607). Heywood wrote plays of many kinds. *A Woman Killed with Kindness* (1603), a domestic tragedy, is considered his masterpiece. His two-part chronicle of Elizabeth I's early years on the throne, *If You Know Not Me, You Know Nobody* (1605), and the eventful adventure play *The Fair Maid of the West* (Part 1, c.1610; Part 2, c.1630), are enlivened by a zest for the detail of Elizabethan life. The dramatizations of Greek mythology in *The Golden Age, The Silver Age, The Brazen Age* and *The Iron Age* (1611–13), tuned to an audience that liked spectacular action with their poetry, were written for Queen Anne's Men at the RED BULL THEATRE. In *An Apology for Actors* (1612) he defended his profession.

**Hibberd, Jack** [John] **(Charles)** 1940– Australian playwright. He studied medicine at Melbourne University where his first play, *White with Wire Wheels,* was staged in 1967; he later wrote for the Melbourne alternative theatres La Mama and the Pram Factory. His plays are characterized by caricature, black humour and flamboyant language: they include *Dimboola* (1969), *The Les Darcy Show* (1974) and *A Toast to Melba* (1976) – the last two both celebrations of famous Australians – the monodramas *A Stretch of the Imagination* (1972) and *Odyssey of a Prostitute* (1984), and a satirical opera, *Sin* (1978). For the present he has abandoned theatre and returned to medicine.

**Hicks, (Edward) Seymour** 1871–1941 British actor-manager and playwright. A versatile performer starring in everything from MUSIC-HALL to BARRIE's *Quality Street* (1904), he was also a prolific author of light COMEDY such as *Sleeping Partners* (1917) and Christmas plays. In 1905 he built the Aldwych Theatre, then in 1907 the Globe, both in London, which he opened with performances in his own plays. Awarded the Legion of Honour in 1931 for his promotion of French drama on the English stage, he was knighted in 1935.

**Highway, Tomson** 1951– Canadian playwright of native Cree heritage. Highway's plays give a realistic portrait of the lives of Canadian natives, with a plea for the revalidation of their culture and mythology. His earliest performance pieces, *New Song... New Dance* (1981) and *The Sage, the Dancer and the Fool* (1982), allowed him to combine his classical music training with his poetry in both English and Cree. His first full-length play, *The Rez Sisters* (1986), about the lives of a group of women on an Indian reservation, won him international attention for its 'combination of the magical and kitchen-sink REALISM'. *Dry Lips Oughta Move to Kapuskasing* (1989) is about the lives of men on the same reservation. Both plays feature the Trickster, the central figure of Cree mythology, through whom Highway tries to convey to white audiences the joyousness of Cree spirituality.

**Hilar, Karel Hugo** 1885–1935 Czech director. After early work as poet, critic and literary editor, he began his directing career in 1910 at Prague's Municipal Theatre, where he soon established himself as an expressionistic director (see EXPRESSIONISM) of great force. By his dynamic personality and artistic vision, he eventually surpassed the achievements of Jaroslav

Kvapil, the first modern Czech director, as head of drama at the National Theatre (1921–35). After the mid-1920s his work became less extravagant and more reflective. Among his principal achievements were *Hamlet* (1926), *Oedipus* (1932) and *Mourning Becomes Electra* (1934).

**Hildesheimer, Wolfgang** 1916– German playwright, novelist and painter. After writing the comedy *The Dragon Throne* (produced by GRÜNDGENS in 1955), based on *Turandot,* he became the leading German exponent of the THEATRE OF THE ABSURD with plays such as *Behind Schedule* (1961) and *Nightpiece* (1963), before turning to historical subjects like *Mary Stuart* (1970).

**Hill, Aaron** 1685–1750 English playwright, manager and critic. In 1709, as a complete novice, he was appointed manager of DRURY LANE and wrote his first plays, *Elfrid* and *The Walking Statue* (a good farce). After disputes with the actors he moved to manage the HAYMARKET Theatre for one season. He wrote the libretto for *Rinaldo* (1711), Handel's first London opera. Of his next plays, *Fatal Vision* (1716) used FERDINANDO BIBIENA's angular perspective for the first time in England, and *Fatal Extravagance* (1721) attempted domestic bourgeois tragedy. *Athelwold* (1731), a revision of *Elfrid,* tried for historical authenticity with 'old Saxon' design; *Zara* (1735), from VOLTAIRE's *Zaire,* is the first of four translations from Voltaire. Apart from his numerous inventions, Hill also founded an important theatre periodical, the *Prompter* (1734–6), and wrote the poem *The Art of Acting* (1746), encouraging the actor to imagine the emotions of the part and then embody them physically.

**Hill, George Handel** ['Yankee'] 1809–49 American actor. In the 1830s and 1840s Hill was the leading exponent of the Yankee roles in WILLIAM DUNLAP's *Trip to Niagara,* Samuel Woodworth's *The Forest Rose* and JOSEPH S. JONES's *The Green Mountain Boy.* Audiences delighted in his plausible cunning and his pliant honesty.

**Hill, Jenny** 1851–96 British comedienne. Known as 'the Vital Spark', Hill was the first female artist to achieve recognition as a MUSIC-HALL star. She and her contemporary Bessie Bellwood broke with the gentility of the lady duettist to create racy and original solo character acts, which paved the way for MARIE LLOYD, VESTA TILLEY and NELLIE WALLACE. From 1869 she played all the big London halls, performed in New York, was a popular principal boy in PANTOMIME, did BURLESQUE, and even tried her hand at the legitimate theatre. Tiny in stature, with a generous smile, she had a powerful and flexible singing voice, danced well, and excelled in character songs both male and female, concentrating on representations of the poor and downtrodden: factory girls, domestic drudges, coster boys and street vendors.

**Hillberg, Emil** 1852–1929 Swedish actor. He was important for the breakthrough of STRINDBERG's plays in the 1880s, and recognized as a leading practitioner of the realistic style (see REALISM). His impressive voice and effortless authority enabled him to excel in larger-than-life roles: Strindberg's Gustav Vasa, Bishop Brask and Gert Bookprinter and IBSEN's Bishop Nicholas. As Brand (1883) he was reportedly sublime, but at the expense of the role's humanity. Other major roles were Shylock, Iago, and Knox in BJØRNSON's *Mary Stuart in Scotland.*

**hippodrama** Play involving horses. In hippodrama trained horses are considered as actors, with their own actions. Horses had occasionally been brought on stage before the 19th century, but the hippodrama first caught on at the turn of the 18th, possibly because of cavalrymen, riding masters and grooms being made redundant after the Continental Wars, and the gradual closing of fairs. The innovation found a home in London at ASTLEY's Amphitheatre in 1803, at the Royal Circus and the Olympic Pavilion, and in Paris at the CIRQUE OLYMPIQUE. In Vienna, Christoph de Bach (1768–1834) presented equestrian pantomimes, such as *The Triumph of Diana* and *Marlborough's Heroic Death*, which constituted a synthesis of theatre and CIRCUS and introduced a broader public to mythology and history.

Astley's *The Blood Red Knight* (1810) was a financial success, prompting COVENT GARDEN to follow suit with COLMAN THE YOUNGER's *Blue Beard* and 'Monk' Lewis's *Timour the Tartar* (1811), and DRURY LANE, reluctantly, with *The Cataract of the Ganges*. The outstanding performer was ANDREW DUCROW, but women took the title role in the frequently revived *Mazeppa, or The Wild Horse of Tartary*, in which the young prince, stripped to his fleshings, is strapped to a horse set loose on a treadmill and attacked by stuffed vultures and similar impedimenta. ADAH ISAACS MENKEN made her notorious name in the part.

The hippodrama, fallen into disuse by the mid-century, enjoyed a revival of sorts at the Châtelet, Paris, with military spectaculars like *Marengo* (1863) and the immensely popular *Michel Strogoff* (1880). The invention of a graduated treadmill that could simulate races inspired one final burst of horse-play in America with *The Country Fair* by Charles Bernard (Union Square Theatre, New York, 1889) and Lew Wallace's *Ben Hur* (Broadway Theatre, New York, 1899). Thereafter, equine stardom passed to the movies, where Trigger and Rex the Wonder Horse had fan clubs of their own.

**Hippodrome** (London) Built as a circus in 1900, with a large water-tank for aquatic spectacles, the Hippodrome was reconstructed as a MUSIC-HALL in 1909, where Tchaikovsky's *Swan Lake* was first danced in England by the Russian Ballet (1910; see DIAGHILEV). Its reputation was for REVUE and MUSICAL COMEDY, among them *Mr Cinders* (1929) and Ivor Novello's *Perchance to Dream* (1938); and from 1949 to 1951 it became the London equivalent of the FOLIES-BERGÈRE. In 1958 it was reconstructed again, becoming a dinner-CABARET – the Talk of the Town – until it closed in 1982.

**Hippodrome Theatre** (New York) Built in 1905, the Hippodrome was advertised as the world's largest theatre, seating 5,000 and equipped with every device known to create magnificent spectacles. The costs of production and maintenance overwhelmed even the SHUBERTS. In 1935 Billy Rose presented his production of *Jumbo* at the theatre, the last notable event in its history. In 1939 it was torn down.

**Hirsch, John** 1930–89 Hungarian-born Canadian director. He went to Winnipeg, Canada, in 1947 as a war refugee. He co-founded the MANITOBA THEATRE CENTRE, where from 1958 to 1966 he established a reputation with productions of *Mother Courage* (1964) with ZOË CALDWELL, *Who's Afraid of Virginia Woolf?* (1964) with KATE REID, and *Andorra* (1965) with William Hutt. In 1965 he was invited to direct *The Cherry Orchard* at the STRATFORD FESTIVAL, which was followed by many other productions, particularly JAMES REANEY's *Colours in the Dark* (1967), a remarkable *Midsummer Night's Dream* (1968), and a highly successful swashbuckling version of *The Three Musketeers* (1968). During 1968–9 he was associate artistic director (with JEAN GASCON) of the

Festival. At the same time he mastered the stage of the Beaumont Theatre in New York's Lincoln Center. Notable productions were GARCÍA LORCA's *Yerma* (1966), BRECHT's *Galileo* (1967) and SOPHOCLES' *Antigone* (1971). His production of *The Seagull* (1970) opened the new home of Israel's HABIMAH National Theatre. His stage adaptation of the Yiddish parable *The Dybbuk* (1974) was immensely successful in Winnipeg, Toronto and Los Angeles. From 1981–5 he was artistic director of the STRATFORD FESTIVAL.

Hirsch was a controversial and tempestuous director, ruthless in his demands for the highest standards possible. But he was also an irrepressible popular entertainer who wrote delightful children's plays and staged many musical comedies and even night-club acts.

**Hirsch, Judd** 1935– American actor. His BROADWAY debut came in 1966 as the Telephone Repairman in NEIL SIMON's *Barefoot in the Park*. Also successful in film and television, Hirsch returns frequently to the New York stage, e.g. in *The Hot l Baltimore* (1973) as Bill, the night manager; in FEIFFER's *Knock, Knock* (1976); in Neil Simon's *Chapter Two* (1977); and in LANFORD WILSON's *Tally's Folly* (1979) as Matt Friedman, an immigrant Jewish accountant. In *The Seagull* (1983) he played Trigorin. He appeared in Herb Gardner's *I'm Not Rappaport* (1985) and *Conversations with My Father* (1992). Hirsch has a rugged 'street face, a face of interchangeable ethnicities and professions'.

**Hirschfeld, Kurt** 1902–64 German director. His major influence was in Switzerland, where he staged the premiere of BRECHT's *Puntila* and helped to shape the drama of both DÜRRENMATT and FRISCH.

**Hirshbein, Peretz** 1880–1948 Yiddish playwright. Hirshbein was raised on a farm in Lithuania. His first plays, written in Hebrew, deal with the extreme poverty he saw around him, but his later and important works, written in Yiddish (see YIDDISH THEATRE), are idyllic bucolic plays about simple country people. *The Haunted Inn* (1912), *A Forsaken Nook* (1913), *The Blacksmith's Daughter* (1914) and *Green Fields* (1916) were amongst the greatest successes, both artistically and financially, of the two leading American companies MAURICE SCHWARTZ's YIDDISH ART THEATRE and JACOB BEN-AMI's JEWISH ART THEATRE.

**His Majesty's Theatre** see HER/HIS MAJESTY'S THEATRE

**Hispanic theatre** (USA) Before the impetus of CHICANO THEATRE, popularized in the mid-1960s by LUIS VALDÉZ, and the TEATRO CAMPESINO, the Spanish-speaking theatre had an extended history in the United States. The first recorded performance took place in a Spanish mission near Miami, Florida, in 1567, in which the Spanish settlers and soldiers presented a religious play designed to catechize the local Indian population. This Spanish-speaking theatre pre-dates the first performance of English-speaking theatre in the British-American colonies, estimated to be around 1700.

From this early beginning to present times the Hispanic theatre in the United States is grouped roughly as follows: the Chicano theatre, primarily in the West and Southwest; the Cuban-American theatre, mostly in New York and Florida; and the New York theatre, which is strongly Puerto Rican.

As the turmoil in Cuban politics, especially in the latter part of the 19th century, brought a wave of immigrants to the USA, the same travelling companies from Havana and Madrid that visited New York often stopped first in Tampa or Key West, Florida. By the 1920s the

MUSICAL COMEDY, strong in the tradition of the Spanish ZARZUELA and the Cuban BUFO, was the normal fare, although some productions included the 19th-century Spanish classics of psychological realism. The Cuban Revolution of 1959 generated another migration, as thousands of Cubans sought refuge in south Florida and other parts of the United States. By the late 1960s a new Spanish-speaking theatre, written by authors with a Cuban perspective, attempted to deal with the sense of anguish and nostalgia over separation from the homeland, language and communication problems, and the generational differences between parents with a Cuban identity and the new 'American' generation. Major authors, writing in exile, included Matías Montes Huidobro (1931– ), José Sánchez-Boudy (1928– ), Julio Matas (1931– ) and Celedonio González (1923– ). Most continued to write in Spanish, although some attempted English, especially in those cases where the subject-matter had broad appeal.

New York has played a major role in fomenting Hispanic theatre. During the early part of the 20th century, travelling companies from Spain and Cuba brought Spanish MELODRAMA, zarzuelas, bufos and musical VARIETY shows to entertain the Spanish and Cuban population. From the 1920s to World War II, the New York Hispanic stage was second only to Los Angeles. The large immigrations of Spanish-speakers from Spain (because of the Civil War) and also from Puerto Rico increased the level of theatrical demand and in the late 60s generated the descriptive term 'Nuyorican', or 'New Rican', theatre.

Several established companies offered both classical and experimental plays in Spanish and English. The Festival of Latin American Popular Theatre was held five times in New York between 1976 and 1985. In addition to the best plays Spain and Latin America had to offer, the groups presented original works by local playwrights, such as Eduardo Gallardo's *Simpson Street* and Dolores Prida's *Beautiful Señoritas*. Given the heterogeneous public, these plays tended to be written in English with sufficient Spanish to capture the flavour and mood. Themes included problems of discrimination, economics, drugs, sex, street-crime and other issues that constituted the reality of this large subculture in New York.

**history play** An invented term to distinguish SHAKESPEARE's plays on subjects drawn from English history – such as the *Henry VI* trilogy and the tetralogy comprising *Richard II*, the two parts of *Henry IV* and *Henry V* – from those he wrote on subjects drawn from Roman history. The Elizabethans would not have understood the modern distinction between history and legend, seeing both in terms of story. The term loosely includes plays as various as JOHN BALE's *Kynge Johan* (1538), MARLOWE's *Edward II* (c.1592) and JOHN ARDEN's *Left-Handed Liberty* (1965).

**Hjörtsberg, Lars** 1772–1843 Swedish actor. Having trained in France, he was brought to Sweden by Gustav III, and from 1788 to 1834 became a leading member of DRAMATEN. Admired for his powers of mimicry, improvisation and attention to detail, he specialized in playing eccentrics such as the pedantic chatterbox Captain Puff, the daydreaming tailor in *The Imagined Prince* and Orgon in MOLIÈRE's *Tartuffe*. Short and somewhat plump, Hjörtsberg was unsuited to tragedy, but succeeded in serious and sentimental drama such as the title role in RICHARD CUMBERLAND's *The Jew*.

**Hochhuth, Rolf** 1931– German playwright, resident in Switzerland. More than any other single work, his first play *The Representative* (1963; in the USA, *The Deputy*) focused international attention on postwar German drama, with 73 productions in 27 countries. Accusing Pope Pius XII of complicity in the extermination of the Jews, its factual subject and historical characters were explosively controversial. Its form, however, is that of verse tragedy in the tradition of SCHILLER. The protagonist and antagonist are presented as the sacrificial Christ figure and the devil, the true focus of the play being the assertion of individual responsibility, a theme made more explicit in *Soldiers* (1970). This had a clear political aim: it takes issue with Dresden and the tactic of bombing civilians. Again, the figures are both historical and presented as symbols. In England the controversy about production of this play contributed to the abolition of stage CENSORSHIP in 1968. Hochhuth's subsequent attempts to deal with topical issues, such as the anti-CIA play *Guerrillas* (1970) or *Lysistrata and NATO*, are marred by utopian fantasy. His later work continues to attack areas of social concern such as the pharmaceutical industry and the legal system: *Female Doctors* (1982) and *Lawyers* (1980). *Wessies in Weimar* (1992) tackled West German colonization of the former GDR. Hochhuth is more highly regarded internationally than in Germany.

**Hochwälder, Fritz** 1911–86 Austrian playwright with Israeli citizenship, who lived in Switzerland. He was the first dramatist to deal with the Nazi extermination of the Jews, in *Esther* (1940), using an Old Testament parallel. Hochwälder's characteristic plays are conventional dramas of ideas focusing on general moral themes in historical examples. As in *The Public Prosecutor* (1947), a conventional problem play set in the French Revolution, analogies to contemporary political situations are left unstated. His most successful play, *The Strong Are Lonely* (*Das heilige Experiment*, 1943), uses the destruction of the autonomous Jesuit state in 18th-century Paraguay to discuss spiritual and religious utopias and the right of pacifism to self-defence. *The Princess of Chimay* was performed in 1981.

**Hodgkinson (Meadowcroft), John** 1767–1805 British-born actor and manager. After some provincial experience he accepted JOHN HENRY's invitation to join the American Company in 1792 and spent the rest of his career in the USA. He never became a star, but excelled in high and low COMEDY. From 1794 until 1798 he was joint manager of the JOHN STREET THEATRE.

**Hoffman, Dustin** 1937– American film and stage actor. Hoffman made his New York debut in 1965 as Immanuel in *Harry, Noon, and Night*. The next year he played Zoditch in *The Journey to the Fifth House*. Also in 1966 he appeared in *Eh?*, winning several awards, as he did in 1968 in the title role of *Jimmy Shine*. After an extraordinarily successful stint in films, he starred in a BROADWAY revival of *Death of a Salesman* (1984) and was acclaimed as a performer of genius and demonic intensity. In 1989 (after a successful London engagement) he played Shylock on Broadway in PETER HALL's production of *The Merchant of Venice*.

**Hoffmann, E(rnst) T(heodor) A(madeus)** 1776–1822 German poet, novelist, composer and director. Known primarily as a writer of romantic short stories and novels, Hoffmann nevertheless had important theatre experience. From 1808 to 1813 he directed the theatre at Bamberg where, in cooperation with Franz von Holbein (1779–1855), he attempted to create a theatre in which all elements – the actors, the design and the lighting – contributed towards a vision of life beyond the appearance of everyday reality. While at Bamberg, he was among the first German directors to introduce the works of CALDERÓN DE LA BARCA to the stage. After his return to Berlin in 1814, he became a close drinking companion of LUDWIG DEVRIENT. His poetic dialogue, *Strange Sorrows of a Theatre Director* (1818), apart from being an invaluable source for the acting of Devrient, also contains some of the liveliest accounts of the theatre of the time.

**Hofmannsthal, Hugo von** 1874–1929 Austrian poet, playwright and essayist. In the 1890s he was the youngest member of the Jung Wien (Young Vienna) circle, and his writings typified *fin-de-siècle* neo-romanticism and decadence. Among several plays he wrote at this time, *Death and the Fool* (1893) is notable for its elaborate verse and poetic atmosphere. As he matured, Hofmannsthal developed a profound awareness of the importance of traditional European culture and, throughout his career, worked to preserve its values in a period of radical, often violent, change. Hence he looked to the theatre of the past. *Elektra* (1906) and his two Oedipus plays (1906 and 1907), while reflecting modern interest in psyche, clearly derive from classical sources. In plays that he wrote for the Salzburg Festival, *Everyman* (1911) and *The Salzburg Great Theatre of the World* (1922), he borrowed from medieval and Spanish baroque theatre. In *The Tower* (1925), his great festival play, the central situation is taken from CALDERÓN DE LA BARCA's *Life Is a Dream*, though thematically it relates to the destruction caused in Europe by World War I. Hofmannsthal also adapted OTWAY's *Venice Preserv'd* (1905), and in his late comedy *The Difficult Man* (1921) he showed the influence of CONGREVE. Among the librettos he wrote for operas by Richard Strauss are *Elektra*, *Der Rosenkavalier* (1911) and *Ariadne auf Naxos* (1912).

**Holberg, Ludvig** 1684–1754 Norwegian-born playwright, satirist, historian and philosopher. He spent most of his life in Copenhagen, where he held several university positions. Although his major impact on Danish letters has been in the theatre, his playwriting occupied only short periods of his life. When Copenhagen acquired its first professional Danish-speaking theatre in 1722, Holberg provided 27 comedies before it closed in 1728, and then six further plays for its successor, the new Danish Playhouse (1748). Often referred to as 'the MOLIÈRE of the North', Holberg certainly owes much to the French playwright, but also directly to PLAUTUS, BEN JONSON and COMMEDIA DELL'ARTE. His most enduring comedies are those, such as *Jeppe of the Hill*, *Erasmus Montanus*, *The Political Tinker* and *The Fussy Man*, which focus on the irrationality of human behaviour. In Denmark the many plays that are built around *commedia*-like intrigues have been almost as popular, while those that satirize contemporary literary and social excesses have had a limited theatrical life. The plays seem to embody an affirmative view of human rationality typical of the Enlightenment. But Holberg is also a complex ironist, presenting a chaotic, amoral world in which reason is threatened by irrational and antisocial forces.

**Holbrook, Hal** [Harold Rowe Holbrook] 1925– American actor and writer. He developed an immensely successful one-man show, *Mark Twain Tonight!*, first appearing in New York in 1955. Recently he has turned

to classic roles such as King Lear (1990), Uncle Vanya and Shylock (1991).

**Holcroft, Thomas** 1745–1809 English playwright. For ten years he was a strolling player. His first work, a comic opera called *The Crisis* (1778), was produced at DRURY LANE. After the success of his comedy *Duplicity* (1781), his English version of BEAUMARCHAIS's *The Marriage of Figaro, The Follies of a Day*, was staged at Covent Garden in 1784. Further adaptations followed: *Seduction* (1787) from Laclos's *Les Liaisons dangereuses*; *The German Hotel* (1790) from the German of JOHANN CHRISTIAN BRANDES, and *The School for Arrogance* (1791) from *Le Glorieux* by DESTOUCHES. The source of Holcroft's best-known play, *The Road to Ruin* (1792), is not known. A moral comedy with excellent character roles, it held the stage for a century and was revived in London in 1937. Compounding Holcroft's disastrous personal life came an indictment for high treason in 1794. Though acquitted, his theatre activities were thereafter restricted. Forced to avoid contentious topics, he mixed insipid comedies with the Gothic melodramas now in vogue in Paris. The first to be advertised as a MELODRAMA, thereby importing the word into the English theatre, was *A Tale of Mystery* (1802), adapted from PIXÉRÉCOURT's *Coelina*. Holcroft's *Memoirs* (1816) were posthumously completed by WILLIAM HAZLITT.

**Holland Festival** The first Holland Festival was held in June 1947 in Amsterdam, as a result of plans made during the German occupation in World War II to organize an annual celebration of the arts. The Festival belongs to the European Association of Music Festivals and presents, as well as music, other artistic forms such as dance, the plastic arts and drama. It features experimental and controversial performances from the Netherlands and abroad.

**Holland, George** 1791–1870 British-born actor. He went to the USA in 1827 as a comic actor, making his debut at the BOWERY THEATRE in *A Day after the Fair*. Immensely popular, he toured and for a time managed theatres in the South (with NOAH LUDLOW, SOL SMITH and JAMES H. CALDWELL). For the rest of his career he was a comedian with various New York companies.

**Hollingshead, John** 1827–1904 British theatre manager and drama critic. A radical thinker, he was committed to broadening theatre audiences and improving the life of London's workers. He opened his own theatre, the GAIETY, in 1868, and it became the home to the talents of the famous BURLESQUE Quartette, NELLIE FARREN, Edward Terry, Kate Vaughan, and EDWARD ROYCE. But it was also the first theatre in London to stage an IBSEN play, WILLIAM ARCHER's translation of *The Pillars of Society* (1880).

**Hollmann, Hans** 1933– Austrian director. His productions have tended towards sensationalism. He has made a reputation for adapting the classics to reflect contemporary political issues, particularly SHAKESPEARE, and his influential productions of HORVÁTH between 1967 and 1971 helped to inspire the contemporary *VOLKSSTÜCK*.

**Holm, Celeste** 1919– American film, stage and television actress. She created Ado Annie in *Oklahoma!* in 1943. Her first film was *Three Little Girls in Blue*, 1946. She won awards for her roles in *Gentlemen's Agreement* (1947) and *Mame* (1969). In 1979 she was knighted by King Olav of Norway. She appeared with NICOL WILLIAMSON in *I Hate Hamlet* (1991).

**Holman, Robert** 1952– British playwright, born in

Yorkshire. His subtle studies of domestic and working lives express his gift for seeing wide-ranging issues in small examples, as in *Coal* (1973), *Outside the Whale* (1976), *German Skerries* (1977) and *Mucking Out* (1978) – primarily naturalistic plays. *Today* (1984), *The Overgrown Path* (1985) and *Making Noise Quietly* (1986) are encounters between people affected by war. From 1977 to 1979 Holman was resident dramatist at the NATIONAL THEATRE. *Across Oka* (ROYAL SHAKESPEARE COMPANY, 1988) contrasted two families, English and Russian, during a visit to a Soviet conservation reserve. *Rafts and Dreams* (1990) is a poetic play about a woman's visionary obsession with cleanliness.

**Holtei, Karl von** 1798–1880 German actor and playwright. Holtei's comedies were extremely popular, especially *The Viennese in Berlin* (1824) and *The Berliners in Vienna* (1825). His autobiography, *Forty Years* (1843–50), provides a lively account of the theatre of his time.

**Holz, Arno** 1863–1929 German poet and playwright. Holz is best known for his collaboration with Johannes Schlaf (1862–1941) on the naturalistic play *The Selicke Family* (1892). Though he was initially identified with NATURALISM, his later plays were poetic.

**Home, John** 1722–1808 Scottish playwright. He was a minister in the Church of Scotland. His first play, *Agis*, was rejected by GARRICK in 1749 as was his second, *Douglas*, an exploration of the love of mother for long-lost son and the first romantic tragedy. It was an extraordinary success when mounted at the Canongate Theatre in Edinburgh in 1756, making Home the first major Scots playwright. The Church, however, was outraged at a minister writing plays, and had *Douglas* denounced from pulpits. After a prolonged pamphlet war the play was brought to COVENT GARDEN by RICH and was equally successful. Home gave up the ministry and became secretary to the prime minister, Lord Bute. *Agis* was mounted at DRURY LANE by Garrick in 1758, but neither it nor Home's four subsequent plays were successful. They all aim at a romantic pathos usually intensified by remote British settings.

**Home, William Douglas** 1912–92 British playwright. His upper-middle-class comedies and dramas made him a natural successor to FREDERICK LONSDALE in the postwar WEST END theatre. He began his career as an actor and remained an actor's playwright. His first political comedy successes, *The Chiltern Hundreds* (1947) and *The Manor of Northstead* (1954), were vehicles for the eccentric talents of A. E. Matthews. SYBIL THORNDIKE starred in *The Reluctant Peer* (1964), Alastair Sim in *The Jockey Club Stakes* (1970), RALPH RICHARDSON and PEGGY ASHCROFT in *Lloyd George Knew My Father* (1972), Celia Johnson in *The Dame of Sark* (1974) and REX HARRISON in the New York version of *The Kingfisher*. His sound technique was weakened by a facile sentimentality. *Now Barabbas...* (1947), however, showed his ability with a serious theme about prison life, while *The Secretary Bird* (1968) remains a thoughtful *ménage-à-trois* comedy. His last play *Portraits* (1987) was a sympathetic study of the painter Augustus John.

**Hong Sheng** 1645–1704 Chinese playwright. He was appointed to the Imperial Academy in Beijing, where he made a reputation as a poet and playwright. His masterpiece *The Place of Eternal Youth* (*Changsheng dian*) was completed in 1688. After it came to the notice of the Kangxi Emperor (reigned 1662–1723), it was performed frequently before court society. The plot concerns the love affair of the Tang Emperor Minghuang and his favourite concubine Yang Guifei, a theme which has been a constant inspiration to poets and dramatists in China. Hong's play is still regarded by the Chinese as one of their great lyric dramas. In 1689 a group of actors staged a special performance of the play in Hong's honour. Because it coincided with a period of mourning for an Imperial family member, this was regarded as a serious breach of public etiquette. Punishment was meted out to all concerned, and Hong was dismissed from the Academy. He spent his remaining days in poverty. He was regarded as one of the two major dramatists of his time, the other being KONG SHANGREN.

**Hooft, P(ieter) C(ornelisz)** 1581–1647 Dutch playwright. Together with VONDEL, P. C. Hooft was amongst the most distinguished men of letters of the Golden Age in the Netherlands. The themes of his tragedies refer to the classics, notably SENECA, and even more to Dutch history. *Geraert van Velsen* (1613) and *Baeto* (1616), although composed in conformity with Renaissance stylistic conventions, are decidedly individual. His *Warenar* (1617), a comedy after PLAUTUS' *The Pot of Gold*, was very popular in Amsterdam during the 17th and 18th centuries. Hooft was the central figure of the so-called *Muider-kring*, a group of talented artists who had regular meetings at his official residence, the Muiderslot.

**Hope Theatre** (London) Built in 1613–14 by PHILIP HENSLOWE, the Hope was used for animal-baiting as well as plays. The surviving contract stipulates that the stage should be removable and that its roof (or HEAVENS) should be cantilevered rather than supported by the familiar pillars. JONSON's *Bartholomew Fair* (1614) was performed there. The Hope attracted no regular acting company after 1617, and was demolished in 1656.

**Hopkins, Arthur (Melancthon)** 1878–1950 American producer and director. His first BROADWAY hit was *Poor Little Rich Girl* (1913). Other early successes include *On Trial* (1914), *Good Gracious Annabelle* (1916), *A Successful Calamity* (1917), *Redemption* (1918) with John Barrymore and *The Jest* (1919) with John and Lionel Barrymore (see DREW–BARRYMORE FAMILY). He featured ALLA NAZIMOVA in revivals of IBSEN's *Wild Duck*, *Hedda Gabler* and *A Doll's House*. In the 1920s, Hopkins directed O'NEILL's *Anna Christie* (1921) and *The Hairy Ape* (1922); Stallings and MAXWELL ANDERSON's *What Price Glory?* (1924); and PHILIP BARRY's *Paris Bound* (1927) and *Holiday* (1928). His output decreased after 1930, but he staged a successful *The Petrified Forest* in 1935 and *The Magnificent Yankee* in 1946. His notable productions of SHAKESPEARE include *Richard III* (1920), *Hamlet* (1922) and *Macbeth* (1921). Hopkins placed artistic above commercial merit; he furthered the career of ROBERT EDMOND JONES. He developed the revolving stage in America, but despite his modern directing methods his reliance upon pictorial effect made his later productions seem old-fashioned.

**Hopper, De Wolf** 1858–1935 American comedian and singer. His abnormally long legs, loose-jointed movements and strong singing voice made Hopper one of the most popular performers in comic opera. His first starring role was in *Castles in the Air* (1890). His two greatest successes, *Wang* (1891) and *Panjandrum* (1893), followed. After forming the De Wolf Hopper Opera Company, he appeared in *Dr Syntax* (1894), *El Capitan* (1896) and *The Mystical Miss* (1899). He joined the WEBER AND FIELDS company for two shows, then starred in *Mr Pickwick* (1903), *Happyland* (1905), *The Pied Piper* (1908) and *A Matinée Idol* (1910). In 1911 Hopper made the first of a number of successful forays into the GILBERT and Sullivan repertoire, with a revival of HMS Pinafore. He was especially noted for his ability to handle long comic speeches and involved patter songs, and for his amusing use of props.

His wife, Edna Wallace Hopper, starred in several comic operas and musical comedies of the period.

**Hopwood, Avery** 1882–1928 American playwright. A remarkably successful writer with 18 hits in 15 years, four of them running simultaneously in New York theatres in 1920, Hopwood understood the slight and ephemeral nature of his artistry. Some of his best works were written in collaboration with others: e.g. The Bat (1920) with Mary Roberts Rinehart and Getting Gertie's Garter (1921) with Wilson Collison. Other plays demonstrate the clever, risqué character of his work: The Gold Diggers (1919), The Demi-Virgin (1921) and The Grand Illusion (1920; from the French).

**Horace** [Quintus Horatius Flaccus] 65–8 BC Roman (Augustan) poet. Though he wrote no drama himself, his verse epistle Ars Poetica (The Art of Poetry) includes advice on the writing of tragedies, comedies and satyr plays in the Greek manner (see GREEK THEATRE, ANCIENT). There is no evidence that this advice had any effect in his own day, but it influenced neoclassical drama from the Renaissance onward.

**Hordern, Michael (Murray)** 1911–1995 British actor. Hordern became associated with absent-minded, good-hearted English eccentrics. He played Riley in TOM STOPPARD's Enter a Free Man (1968) and George Moore, the traditional moral philosopher trying hard to defend his position in a world of materialists, in Stoppard's Jumpers (1972). He was the hippy vicar in DAVID MERCER's Flint (1970) and Pinfold in an adaptation of Evelyn Waugh's book, The Ordeal of Gilbert Pinfold (1977). He has also appeared with major repertory companies such as the ROYAL SHAKESPEARE COMPANY and Nottingham Playhouse in a variety of classic roles – notably Malvolio at the OLD VIC in 1954, King Lear in JONATHAN MILLER's production (1969), seen later on British television, and Prospero in The Tempest in the 1978 Stratford-upon-Avon version. He was knighted in 1983. In 1987 he appeared as the wise waiter in SHAW's You Never Can Tell.

**Hornblow, Arthur** 1865–1942 British-born American editor and novelist. Hornblow went to the United States in 1889 to pursue a career as a journalist, working for the Kansas City Globe and the New York Dramatic Mirror. From 1910 to 1926 he edited Theatre Magazine, frequently reviewing opening nights. For two years he was Dean of the John Murray Anderson–Robert Milton School of Theatre and Dance in New York. Hornblow's greatest financial success came from novelizing popular plays, including The Lion and the Mouse, The Easiest Way and Bought and Paid For. His two-volume A History of the Theatre in America (1919) remains a standard reference work.

**Horniman, Annie (E. F.)** 1860–1937 British theatre manager and patron. Born of a prosperous tea merchant's family, she inherited a large legacy in 1893 which she invested in theatrical enterprises. The first was a season at the Avenue Theatre, London, in 1894, which included W. B. YEATS's Land of Heart's Desire. She was Yeats's private secretary for five years and in 1904 financed the opening of the ABBEY THEATRE, Dublin, for the Irish National Theatre Society. In 1907 she founded a new REPERTORY company in Manchester (the first in England), opening its first season at the Midland Hotel

Theatre. She purchased the nearby GAIETY THEATRE and made it, from 1908, her company's permanent home.

**Horovitz, Israel (Arthur)** 1939– American playwright. Educated at Harvard University, Horovitz spent two years at the London Royal Academy of Dramatic Art (1961–3) and a year as resident playwright with the ROYAL SHAKESPEARE COMPANY (1965). He attracted critical attention in 1968 with the New York production of two one-acts: It's Called the Sugar Plum and The Indian Wants the Bronx, plays about urban violence in America. Also in 1968, his one-act Morning appeared on BROADWAY. Other Horovitz plays include The Good Parts (1982); The Wakefield Plays (1974–9), which include The Alfred Trilogy and The Quannatowitt Quartet; Park Your Car in Harvard Yard (1991) and Unexpected Tenderness (1994). In 1979 he founded the Gloucester Stage Company in Massachusetts, where most of his plays have since premiered (e.g. A Rosen by Any Other Name, 1987; The Chopin Playoffs, 1988). Horovitz deals in a realistic way with the angst of American life.

**Horváth, Ödön von** 1901–38 Austro-Hungarian playwright and novelist. Starting with naturalistic depictions of contemporary issues in Revolt on Côte 3018 (1927) and Sladek the Blackshirt, subtitled 'History of the Inflation Era' – which dealt with the assassination of Weimar socialists and caused a riot at its premiere in 1929 – Horváth went on to become the first exponent of the modern VOLKSSTÜCK. Influenced by NESTROY, his highly ironic comedies contrast idealized concepts of the common people with the brutal reality of a disintegrating society. He was opposed to the National Socialists. The socially conditioned language of his dialogue provides a powerful commentary on the crippling emotional effect of social exploitation. Italian Night was awarded the Kleist Prize in 1931, and Tales from the Vienna Woods, which has become a modern classic and has been translated by CHRISTOPHER HAMPTON for London's NATIONAL THEATRE, was performed the same year. But when Kasimir and Karoline was staged in 1932 Horváth felt compelled to issue guidelines for the production of his plays, and in 1933 the production of Faith, Love, Hope was banned. Figaro Gets Divorced and Day of Judgement were performed in Czechoslovakia, but his work vanished almost completely from the German stage for almost 40 years. With the difficulty of dialect translation, his plays have had little international exposure, although his 1937 novel Youth without God has been published in 15 languages. In the 1970s his plays were rediscovered in Germany, Austria and Switzerland.

**Hôtel de Bourgogne** (Paris) Built in the rue Mauconseil by the CONFRÉRIE DE LA PASSION in 1548, it was used by them until the end of the century. As the main Parisian professional stage it was then leased to itinerant companies, e.g. that of VALLERAN LE CONTE. The original building was 108ft long by 45ft wide, with a raked stage and small upper stage. Over 1,000 spectators stood in a large pit or sat in boxes, tiered benches and galleries. After 1629 it became the home of the Comédiens du Roi under the successive leaderships of BELLEROSE, FLORIDOR and Hauteroche, and until their incorporation into the COMÉDIE-FRANÇAISE in 1680 they performed there many of PIERRE CORNEILLE's later plays and most of RACINE's work. From 1680 to 1783 it was occupied by the COMÉDIE-ITALIENNE.

**Hou Baolin** 1917– Chinese performer. China's most popular exponent of xiangsheng – a branch of the storytelling genre involving comic dialogue, wisecracks and mimicry – Hou was first apprenticed to a street singer, then joined a troupe skilled in reciting plays from the Beijing repertoire to the street crowds. He studied comic monologues and dialogues and was accepted as an apprentice by the *xiangsheng* guild. After the war he was partnered for many years by Guo Qiru as his stage foil, making an irrepressible pair. Denounced during the Cultural Revolution, he left the stage, like many others. Guo died during this period, but Hou is today a national celebrity. The seemingly improvisatory nature of his craft is deceptive. He remains unsurpassed in the art of taking the audience by surprise, the essence of comic genius on the stage.

**Houdar de la Motte, Antoine** 1672–1731 French playwright, poet and critic. His dramatic theory took a modernist stance: he promoted prose, even in tragedy, rejected adherence to the ancients, and identifed the audience's pleasure as the chief criterion. His own six comedies, four tragedies (of which the most successful was *Inès de Castro*, 1723) and numerous librettos were more conservative, and he was elected to the Académie-Française in 1710.

**Houdini, Harry** [Erik Weisz] 1874–1926 American MAGICian and escape artist, born in Budapest. His stage name was a homage to ROBERT-HOUDIN. Starting in dime museums and circuses as the self-styled 'King of Cards', he gained prominence in 1895 with his escapes from handcuffs and straitjackets. A genius at self-promotion, he was soon challenging police forces throughout the world to keep him pent up, and once escaped from a chained packing crate at the bottom of a river; these escapes were often engineered by concealed keys, one passed in a kiss from his wife. Other tricks involved making an elephant vanish and swallowing 70 needles and 20 yards of thread and bringing them up threaded. Houdini was also the first to fly an aeroplane in Australia (1910), enjoyed a career as a silent-film star and, after his mother's death in 1913, exposed fraudulent mediums.

**Houghton, (Charles) Norris** 1909– American producer, educator, designer and writer. He designed eight BROADWAY productions and directed four between 1932 and 1957. As founder and co-managing director of the OFF-BROADWAY Phoenix Theatre, he helped mount almost 75 productions (1953–64). Houghton is the author of six books, including the influential *Moscow Rehearsals* (1936), *Advance from Broadway* (1941) and *Return Engagement* (1962). His autobiography, *Entrances and Exits*, was published in 1991.

**Houghton, Stanley** 1881–1913 British playwright. He was one of the Manchester writers associated with the GAIETY THEATRE. *Hindle Wakes* (1912) is typical of the genre, a good Lancashire tale told with wit and care. *The Younger Generation* (1910) shows the radical social concern that is also evident in the clearly argued woman's point of view in *Hindle Wakes*. (See also HAROLD BRIGHOUSE.)

**Houseman, John** [Jacques Haussman] 1902–88 Romanian-born American director, producer and actor. Educated in England, Houseman began producing in New York in 1934. He was affiliated for a time with the FEDERAL THEATRE PROJECT. Some of his finest work was with ORSON WELLES and the MERCURY THEATRE, which he co-founded in 1937 – notably his production of *Julius Caesar* in modern dress. He was artistic director for the AMERICAN SHAKESPEARE [THEATRE] Festival (1956–9) and for the drama division of the Juilliard School of the Performing Arts (1968–76). In 1972 Houseman founded the ACTING COMPANY.

**Housman, Laurence** 1865–1959 British playwright and novelist. Most of Housman's work was banned from the public theatre because it presented the Holy Family or the royal family on the stage (see CENSORSHIP). His early play *Bethlehem* formed the basis of a brilliant production by GORDON CRAIG in 1902, and *Prunella*, written in collaboration with GRANVILLE BARKER, was a success at London's Duke of York's Theatre in 1910. Three series of one-act dramas with the general title of *The Little Plays of St Francis* (1922, 1931, 1935) have retained their popularity on the amateur stage, but his best-known work was *Victoria Regina: A Dramatic Biography*. A sequence of ten vignettes from before Queen Victoria's accession to her Diamond Jubilee, this was first presented privately by NORMAN MARSHALL at the London GATE THEATRE, and in a much acclaimed New York production with HELEN HAYES in 1935.

**Howard, Alan (Mackenzie)** 1937– British actor. Born into a theatrical family (his uncle was the film actor, Leslie Howard), he was at the ROYAL COURT for the WESKER trilogy (1959–60) and for *The Changeling* (1961), but his aristocratic good looks, diction and stage presence were not ideally suited to the Royal Court's programme of angry, working-class plays. He joined the ROYAL SHAKESPEARE COMPANY and in 1968 played Benedick in *Much Ado About Nothing*, then in 1970 Hamlet, before touring Europe as Theseus/Oberon in PETER BROOK's revolutionary *A Midsummer Night's Dream*, where his natural athleticism was turned into circus skills on the trapeze (1970). In 1975 he played Prince Hal and Henry V in the Stratford Centenary productions of *Henry IV* and *Henry V*, which led to a remarkable association with the director TERRY HANDS, who directed him as Richard II, Richard III and, in 1977, Henry VI in SHAKESPEARE's early trilogy; these roles Howard invested with a saintly innocence and dignity. He has also played in contemporary plays, and has recently appeared in films and on television. Though seen less often now on the stage, he played Higgins in the NATIONAL THEATRE's revival of *Pygmalion* (1992) and the husband in EDUARDO DE FILIPPO's *La Grande Magia* at the NT (1995).

**Howard, Bronson (Crocker)** 1842–1908 American playwright. Howard was the first professional American playwright – and the first to frame his principles of dramaturgy – in his essay 'The Laws of Dramatic Composition'. He wrote plays which emphasized the business class, such as *Young Mrs Winthrop* (1882), about a neglected wife; *The Henrietta* (1887), a SATIRE of life on the stock exchange; and *Aristocracy* (1892), which ridiculed new and old American wealth. His awareness of social classes is evident in *Saratoga* (1870), which was adapted to English circumstance as *Brighton* (1874), and in *One of Our Girls* (1885). *The Banker's Daughter* (1878) and his Civil War MELODRAMA *Shenandoah* (1888) epitomized his success. Aided by his association with the THEATRICAL SYNDICATE, Howard raised the status of the American playwright.

**Howard, Sir Robert** 1626–98 English playwright. A fervent Royalist, at the Restoration he began a successful political career, becoming a Privy Councillor in 1688. In the 1660s he wrote six plays and argued with his brother-in-law, JOHN DRYDEN, about the relative merits of rhyming couplets and blank verse for TRAGEDY and the value of TRAGICOMEDY. *The Committee* (1662), a bitter play about the Civil War, introduced the comic Irish servant Teague to the English stage. He collaborated with Dryden on *The Indian Queen* (1664), thus helping to create the genre of heroic play in England. Howard's brothers Edward and James were also successful dramatists.

**Howard, Sidney (Coe)** 1891–1939 American playwright. In the 1920s Howard helped to lift American drama from provincial entertainment to authentic native literature. In a group of provocative plays – *They Knew What They Wanted* (1924), *Lucky Sam McCarver* (1925), *The Silver Cord* (1926), *Ned McCobb's Daughter* (1927) and *Half Gods* (1929)– he looked at such subjects as sex, psychiatry and prohibition, popularizing (like EUGENE O'NEILL) Freudian ideas about family and sexual relationships. *They Knew What They Wanted* advocates moral and sexual compromise; *Ned McCobb's Daughter* features a New Woman with more sense than any of the men in her life. Unlike O'Neill's, however, his tone was essentially comic. Howard wrote in a number of genres: spectacle, romance, the war story and both urban and rural comedy. He frequently collaborated, translated, adapted the work of other writers and wrote screenplays, including *Gone with the Wind* (1939).

**Howard, Willie** 1886–1949 and **Eugene Howard** 1880–1965 American comedians. The Howard brothers developed their comic personae in VAUDEVILLE, and their first joint appearance on the legitimate musical stage was in *The Passing Show of 1912*. Eugene served as the straight man for the act, while the sad-faced Willie got most of the laughs. Both had fine voices, with which they parodied grand opera, the latest performers and shows. They appeared in six of the *Passing Shows* and six editions of *GEORGE WHITE's Scandals*.

**Howard family** American performers. G(eorge) C(unnabel) Howard (1820–87), a Canadian-born actor, was engaged at the BOSTON MUSEUM where he met and married (1844) the actress **Caroline** Emily Fox (1829–1908). With a STOCK COMPANY that included Caroline's mother and three brothers, they toured New England in abbreviated versions of *The Drunkard* and *The Factory Girl* intermingled with an olio of songs and dances. As a respectable family unit, they acclimatized theatre in towns that had hitherto condemned all play-acting as devilish. The Howards achieved their most durable success with an adaptation of *UNCLE TOM's CABIN* (1852), carpentered by their cousin GEORGE L. AIKEN and featuring Howard as St Clare, Caroline as Topsy and their daughter **Cordelia** as Eva. When it played in an expanded text at the National Theatre (New York, 1853), it captured the imagination of the times. Cordelia became the star of the family, also creating Katy the Hot Corn Girl and Little Gerty in *The Lamplighter*.

**Howells, William Dean** 1837–1920 American novelist, critic and playwright. Known in his lifetime as the 'dean of American letters', Howells contributed to the rise of REALISM and of social comedy. *A Counterfeit Presentment* (1877) and *Yorick's Love* (1878) were acted successfully by LAWRENCE BARRETT. Howells's best dramatic work appears in 12 one-act FARCES featuring social events in the lives of two couples (the Robertses and the Campbells) – e.g. *The Garroters* (1885), in which Roberts mistakenly garrottes a friend, and *Five o'Clock Tea* (1887). A gentle satirist of Boston manners, he became bitter in later plays such as *The Impossible* (1910) and *The Night before Christmas* (1910).

**Hoyt, Charles (Hale)** 1860–1900 American playwright.

A major writer of FARCE and SATIRE, Hoyt drew on his own experiences of small-town life (*A Rag Baby*, 1884), his father's early occupation of hotel management (*A Bunch of Keys*, 1882), superstitions (*The Brass Monkey*, 1888), corrupt politics (*A Texas Steer*, 1890), prohibition (*A Temperance Town*, 1893) and baseball (*A Runaway Colt*, 1895). *A Trip to Chinatown* (1891) ran for a record 650 performances.

**Hrotsvitha of Gandersheim** c.935–73 German playwright. A noblewoman living voluntarily within an order, but not a nun, she wrote six plays – *Abraham, Callimachus, Dulcitius, Gallicanus, Pafnutius* and *Sapientia* – concerned with martyrdom for the Christian faith and the triumph of virginity over the temptations of the flesh. She wished to provide a Christian counterbalance to the plays of TERENCE, but despite successful modern productions both in the original Latin and in translation it remains unlikely that she had any idea of theatrical performance.

*huaju* Chinese theatre form. The Chinese generic description for dialogue plays in the Western style – literally, 'spoken' or 'speech drama' – *huaju* had its tentative debut in the first decade of this century. It appealed primarily to Western-educated intellectuals. The great cities remain the established centres for this genre even today.

The period 1915–19 was one of intellectual revolt against the old Chinese sociocultural order. Sweeping language reforms were introduced. Western literature was being read and translated, including the dramatists. It was the 1930s, however, that marked the first significant advance in making *huaju* credible theatre. An epoch-making event in *huaju* history was the staging of CAO YU's play *Thunderstorm* (*Leiyu*) in 1935. Treating Chinese social problems with a new sense of Western REALISM, the play was toured nationally by a cohesive travelling repertory company, a pioneer of its kind.

The war intervened, but with the foundation of the People's Republic in 1949 came a concerted attempt to reorganize *huaju* training. In 1950 the Central Drama Institute was set up in Beijing, equipped to train actors, directors and set designers for *huaju* theatre. Russian advisers and teachers presided over the modern theatre scene. The Chinese were given in-depth exposure to STANISLAVSKY's theories according to current Russian interpretation. The after-effects of this immersion are revealed in the work of many Chinese actors and directors today. However, during the Cultural Revolution (1966–76) Mao Zedong's wife Jiang Qing denounced Stanislavsky as bourgeois, along with virtually all spoken dramas performed in China since 1949. Companies were disbanded, their members dispersed and training institutions closed.

Following Jiang's downfall in 1976 much attention has been given to Western drama. A major event was the staging of ARTHUR MILLER's *Death of a Salesman* by the Beijing People's Art Theatre in 1983. It was directed by Ying Ruocheng, one of China's most talented and forward-looking actor-directors, and Miller himself. In 1986 Ying Ruocheng co-directed PETER SHAFFER's *Amadeus* under the title *The Favoured Son of God*. In the same year there was a major SHAKESPEARE festival in Beijing and other cities.

**Huerta, Jorge** 1942– Chicano director and critic. Born in Los Angeles, in 1971 he founded the Teatro de la Esperanza (Theatre of Hope) in Santa Barbara, California, and served as its artistic director until 1975.

In 1971 he was a founding member of TENAZ (Teatro Nacional de Aztlán), the national CHICANO THEATRE network.

**Hughes, Barnard** 1915– American actor. After playing a range of major supporting roles in the 1950s and 60s, Hughes became one of America's most distinguished character actors, acclaimed for his Dogberry in *Much Ado* (1972), Alexander Serebryakov in *Uncle Vanya* (1973), Falstaff in *The Merry Wives of Windsor* (1974), the title role in *Da* (1978), Father William Doherty in *Angels Fall* (1983), Philip Stone in *End of the World* (1984), Harry Hope in *The Iceman Cometh* (1985) and the father in *Prelude to a Kiss* (1990) by Craig Lucas.

**Hughes, Dusty** 1947– British playwright, critic and director. A director at the BUSH THEATRE, he wrote *Commitments* (1980) and *Heaven and Hell* (1981) before adapting two plays, by BULGAKOV and GORKY, for the ROYAL SHAKESPEARE COMPANY. His interest in Russia at the time of the Revolution is reflected in *Futurists* (NATIONAL THEATRE, 1986), set in a St Petersburg café in 1921. A *Slip of the Tongue* (1992) showed a dissident in Eastern Europe, in hiding from all but the girls sent to wheedle out his secrets in bed.

**Hughes, (James Mercer) Langston** 1902–67 African-American poet, novelist and playwright. Hughes's first play, *The Gold Piece*, was published in 1921. He gained his first BROADWAY success with *Mulatto* (1935), a MELODRAMA on race relations in a Southern town. He achieved substantial New York runs with his folk musical *Simply Heavenly* (1957) and with *Tambourines to Glory* (1963). At the interracial Karamu Theatre in Cleveland he received several premieres, including *Little Ham* (1936), *Troubled Island* (1936), *Joy to My Soul* (1937) and *Front Porch* (1938). Hughes also wrote four opera librettos and the book and lyrics for Kurt Weill's musical version of *Street Scene* (1947). He founded three short-lived theatres: the Harlem Suitcase Theatre where his polemical *Don't You Want to Be Free?* (1938) was staged, the New Negro Theatre in Los Angeles (1939) and the Skyloft Players in Chicago (1949). His plays are most appealing when his righteous anger is tempered by gentle SATIRE, humour and lyricism.

**Hugo, Victor** 1802–85 French poet, playwright, novelist – the literary colossus of the French 19th century. In the 1830s Hugo's plays had problems with CENSORSHIP, as he used historical themes to comment on the government and society of France, expressed populist ideas, and harked back to Napoleon as an idealized ruler. Napoleon could not be represented on the stage in the 1820s, so Hugo's analysis of the legitimacy of power was first expressed in the unperformed *Cromwell* (1827), which was designed to provoke understanding of its period, not simply of its historical protagonist.

The preface to *Cromwell* is often seen as the manifesto of romantic drama. Following SHAKESPEARE, Hugo advocated verse rather than prose drama, but his practice was to free the Alexandrine rhythmically, to do away with 18th-century poetic diction and to introduce banal and unpoetic vocabulary. He defied neoclassical 'unities', advocating for the serious stage a mixture of genres, the 'sublime' and the 'grotesque' together, in the manner of the BOULEVARD theatres.

*Hernani* (Théâtre-Français, 1830), albeit in a carefully cut version, created one of the famous theatre riots of history, representing the irruption into the temple of conservatism of the 'angry young men' of the romantic school. *Le Roi s'amuse* (1832), source of the libretto of

Verdi's *Rigoletto*, was banned for its portrayal of François I. Hugo's next three dramas were in prose. *Lucrèce Borgia*, a triumph at the Porte-Saint-Martin for MLLE GEORGE and FRÉDÉRICK LEMAÎTRE in 1833, resembled *La Tour de Nesle* with a sinful mother accidentally murdering her son. His *Marie Tudor*, at the same theatre the same year, was a flop. In 1835 he returned to the Théâtre-Français with *Angelo, Tyran de Padoue*. *Ruy Blas* opened DUMAS *père* and Hugo's Théâtre de la Renaissance. Despite a melodramatic framework, with clearly defined good and bad characters, the play meditated seriously on the nature of political power. A moderate success in 1838, when revived with SARAH BERNHARDT in 1872 it ran for 300 performances. Hugo's last major romantic drama, *Les Burgraves* (Théâtre-Français, 1843), was of epic proportions, but the 100-year-old lovers were not taken seriously and the play seemed old-fashioned.

His later years, spent in exile for his opposition to Napoleon III, were devoted to more novels, poetry, a study of Shakespeare (1864) and armchair plays including the modern melodrama *Mille francs de récompense* (*1,000 Francs Reward*), which was eventually performed in 1961. Hugo received a state funeral.

**Hume, Sam(uel J.)** 1885–1962 American set designer. Founder of the Detroit Arts and Crafts Theatre, Hume was one of the pioneers of the New Stagecraft and the LITTLE THEATRE MOVEMENT. He studied with GORDON CRAIG in Florence and subsequently applied Craig's idea of movable screens into 'adaptable settings' – unit sets utilizing flats, platforms, draperies, arches and pylons that could be rearranged or altered by lighting to fit individual scenes. It was thus a move away from NATURALISM towards simplification and suggestion, as well as being economical.

**Humphries, (John) Barry** 1934– Australian actor and author. He created his archetypal Australian housewife Edna Everage while working as an actor in the 1950s; his other characters include the ageing suburbanite Sandy Stone and the gross member of parliament Sir Les Patterson (Australia's 'Minister of Culture'). His satirical one-man shows, characterized by banter with the audience and a gladioli-waving finale, include *A Nice Night's Entertainment* (1962), *Excuse I* (1965), *At Least You Can Say You've Seen It* (1974), *Isn't It Pathetic at His Age* (1977), *An Evening's Intercourse with Barry Humphries* (1981), *Tears before Bedtime* (1985), *The Life and Death of Sandy Stone* (1990) and *Look at Me When I'm Talking to You!* (1993). Early in his career he created the comic strip and film character Barry McKenzie; recently 'Dame Edna' has been the provocative hostess of satirical chat shows on British television. His autobiography *More Please* was published in 1992.

**Huneker, James G.** 1857–1921 American critic. From 1890 to the early 1900s he brought continental drama to American public attention. Huneker made his debut as a music critic and in 1895 became music and drama critic for the *Morning Advertiser*. Between 1902 and 1904 he held the drama post for the *New York Sun*. In addition to his journalism he wrote 22 books. Huneker opposed the Genteel Tradition and championed the plays of IBSEN, STRINDBERG, SHAW, MAETERLINCK and SCHNITZLER. He brought a lively and impressionistic style to American criticism, and influenced a generation of writers including GEORGE JEAN NATHAN and H. L. Mencken.

**hunger artist** Sideshow performer who fasts publicly for extended periods. The practice took on after 1880, when Dr Henry Tanner (died 1893) of New York fasted for 40 days to win a bet. Most hunger artists did drink during their ordeals, among them the leading performer of the turn of the century, Giacomo Succi of Milan. The phenomenon caught on in Germany during the Inflation period, when the populace was starving anyway; Succi's record was broken in 1926 by Ventego (47 days). As late as 1950 fasting could still be seen at European fairs, though it has now become a property of political protest in prisons. TADEUSZ RÓŻEWICZ's play *The Hunger Artist Departs* (1976), based on Franz Kafka, converts the starveling into a metaphor for the visionary artist in an uncomprehending world.

**Hunt, Hugh (Sidney)** 1911–93 British director, playwright and critic. He was a director at the ABBEY THEATRE, Dublin, from 1935 to 1938, where his first play *The Invincibles* (1937), written in collaboration with Frank O'Connor, was performed. In 1946 he was appointed the first director of the BRISTOL OLD VIC COMPANY, moving to the London OLD VIC in 1949, where he directed a series of SHAKESPEARE and SHAW productions. From 1955 to 1960 he helped to develop theatre in Australia as director of the Elizabethan Theatre Trust in Sydney, where he founded the Trust Players, the Young Elizabethan Players and the Elizabethan Opera Company. Returning to England, he was instrumental in creating the Contact Company in Manchester, now the ROYAL EXCHANGE THEATRE Company. He was professor of drama at Manchester University during 1961–73, and between 1969 and 1971 was also artistic director of the Abbey Theatre.

**Hunt, (James Henry) Leigh** 1784–1859 English drama critic, essayist, poet and playwright. The volume of *Critical Essays on the Performers of the London Theatre* (1808) is a selection of reviews first written for the *News*, the product of independent observation, seriousness and verbal facility. As editor of the *Examiner* (1808), he continued to enhance the status of English theatre criticism. In 1815 he expressed memorably his disappointment in EDMUND KEAN as Richard III, speedily recanting after watching him as Othello. Of the ten or so plays that he wrote, two were staged in his lifetime, the verse tragedy *A Legend of Florence* (1840) at COVENT GARDEN, and a verse comedy, *Lovers' Amazements* (1858), at the LYCEUM. Hunt always aspired to be more than he actually was, a superior journalist.

**Hunter, N(orman) C(harles)** 1908–71 British playwright. He began by writing amusing, if unoriginal, comedies with slick plotting and dialogue. After the war his style became more leisurely, intricate and concerned with shifts in mood. His two dramas of middle-class households in decline, *Waters of the Moon* (1951) and *A Day by the Sea* (1953), gave him the reputation of being an English CHEKHOV. The casting of *A Day by the Sea*, with JOHN GIELGUD, RALPH RICHARDSON, SYBIL THORNDIKE and IRENE WORTH, illustrates the esteem in which this autumnal play was held. *A Touch of the Sun* (1958) and *The Tulip Tree* (1962) were less successful; and the fashion for N. C. Hunter's plays was one casualty of the new ROYAL COURT-led wave of angry young writers.

**Hurt, William** 1950– American actor. The OFF-BROADWAY debut of this actor of 'distilled and concentrated intensity' was in *Henry V* (NEW YORK SHAKESPEARE FESTIVAL, 1977) and his BROADWAY debut was in

*Hurlyburly* (1984). Later work includes Pintauro's *Beside Herself* (CIRCLE REPERTORY COMPANY, 1989) and *Ivanov* (YALE REPERTORY THEATRE, 1990), as well as the films *Body Heat* (1981), *The Big Chill* (1983), *Kiss of the Spider Woman* (1984), *Children of a Lesser God* (1986), *The Accidental Tourist* (1988) and *The Doctor* (1991).

**Hurwitz, Moishe** 1844–1910 and **Jacob Lateiner** 1853–1935 Yiddish playwrights. These two main writers of SHUND theatre characterized the lowest quality of popular American YIDDISH THEATRE during the 1890s. Deliberately writing down to the tastes of the most uneducated and unsophisticated of the 'green' immigrants, 'Professor' Hurwitz (as he called himself) wrote about 90 plays and Lateiner turned out over 150.

**Hussein, Ebrahim** 1943– Tanzanian playwright. Published plays include *Kinjeketile* (1970), originally in Swahili and translated into English; *Time Is a Wall* and *The One Who Got What She Deserved* (both 1970), *Devils* (1971), *Wedding* (1980), *The Cock in the Village* and *The Traditional Shield* (both 1976). Hussein depicts the struggle for a just society in Tanzania, from the Maji Maji uprising against the Germans in *Kinjeketile* to his portrayal of the unfulfilled dream for a better society in *Wedding*.

**Huston, Walter** 1884–1950 Canadian-born American stage and film actor. For almost 18 years he toured North America. He achieved stardom as Ephraim Cabot in *Desire Under the Elms* (1924). Noted for his artistic integrity, lack of affectation and economic style, he was also acclaimed for his title role in Sinclair Lewis's *Dodsworth* and for his work in *Knickerbocker Holiday*, in which he introduced 'September Song'.

**Hyman, Earle** 1926– African-American actor. Renowned in classical and contemporary roles, Hyman began with the American Negro Theatre and at 17 appeared in *Anna Lucasta* (1944) on BROADWAY and in London's WEST END. His earliest Shakespearian role was Hamlet (1951), followed by the first of six Othellos played over a 25-year period. Hyman performed ten other roles with the AMERICAN SHAKESPEARE THEATRE (1955–60), received rave notices for his Broadway performance in *Mr Johnson* (1956) and for his portrayal of the title role in *The Emperor Jones* (1965). In 1989 he played in the stage version of *Driving Miss Daisy* in Norway and Denmark. In 1991 he was Pickering in New York's Roundabout Theatre's untraditionally cast *Pygmalion*. In 1994 he starred in the Public Theatre's *East Texas Hot Links* by Eugene Lee.

**Hytner, Nicholas** 1956– British director. His debut with the ROYAL SHAKESPEARE COMPANY, a clear and visually brilliant production of *Measure for Measure* (1987), was followed by a poetic production of *The Tempest* (1988), with JOHN WOOD as Prospero. His debut at the NATIONAL THEATRE was a staging of Joshua Sobol's *Ghetto* (1989), about the sufferings of the Lithuanian Jews, which showed his confident handling of a large cast without losing a sense of detail. Hytner has demonstrated a remarkable range. He directed the musical *Miss Saigon* (1989) at DRURY LANE, an instant hit, then a much shortened *Volpone* (1990) at London's Almeida; and *King Lear*, again with John Wood, for the RSC (1990). His productions of *The Wind in the Willows* (1991), *The Madness of George III* (1991), *The Recruiting Officer* (1992) and the revival of *Carousel* (1992) were all memorable.

**Ibargüengoitia, Jorge** 1928–85 Mexican playwright; author of a dozen plays. His early light comedies were followed by black-humoured satiric comedies. His master work was *El atentado* (*The Assault*, 1966), with its sardonic view of the assassination of Mexican president Alvaro Obregón.

**Ibsen, Henrik** 1828–1906 Norwegian playwright and poet. His playwriting benefited greatly from his early practical experience in the theatre. Having written only *Catiline* and *The Warrior's Barrow*, he was appointed resident dramatist and then stage director at the new Norwegian Theatre in Bergen; his next plays were written to meet his contract for a new play every year. In 1852 the theatre sent Ibsen on a study tour to Dresden and Copenhagen, where he learned much from the methods and principles enforced by JOHAN LUDVIG HEIBERG at the KONGELIGE TEATER and from its acting ensemble. He also discovered HERMANN HETTNER's book *The Modern Drama*, which stressed psychological conflict as the basis of drama. From Heiberg he probably learned a new respect for the dramaturgical mechanics of SCRIBE. The Bergen years were valuable but difficult, and in 1857 Ibsen took the opportunity to move to Christiania (now Oslo) to manage the recently opened Norwegian Theatre, where conditions were even worse. When it closed in 1862, he was briefly engaged at Christiania Theatre to direct his own *The Pretenders*, his final direct involvement in practical theatre. In 1864 he moved to Rome, the beginning of a 27-year voluntary exile.

Apart from the contemporary *St John's Night* (1852) and *Love's Comedy* (1862), his early plays (including *The Pretenders*) owe much to OEHLENSCHLÄGER and to the national romantic movement's fascination with Norway's past. His major transformation as a playwright occurred abroad, first in the magnificent dramas *Brand* (1865) and *Peer Gynt* (1867). Ibsen's characters are typically caught in a tension between the possible and the impossible, driven to strive for the latter and tormented by guilt when they give in to the former. The motif of vocation, seized but imperfectly understood by Brand and evaded (but perhaps partly understood) by Peer Gynt, is drawn from Kierkegaard and was to hold together the sprawling two-part *Emperor and Galilean*, completed in 1873. In it Ibsen uses Julian the Apostate (AD 331–63) to explore the ironies of a confused search for a vocation, while history progresses regardless.

Despite Ibsen's protests that he was a poet rather than a social reformer, his next plays were widely understood to be primarily blows struck in favour of social and political reform. For example, *A Doll's House* (1879) seemed to be a feminist tract (shocking to many), rather than a study of self-realization and vocation. *Ghosts* (1881) was taken to be about venereal disease, rather than the more insidious social diseases it exposes. *An Enemy of the People* (1882) provoked more discussion of its supposed political targets than of its theme of the vocation to truth. However, with *The Wild Duck* (1884), the critics were bewildered. Ibsen had entered a new phase, in which his normally ambivalent perception of life became mysterious, raising more questions than he answered. In the character Gregers

Werle, the motif of vocation was perceived in a satirical and sinister light, an effect to be echoed in *Rosmersholm* (1886) and *Hedda Gabler* (1890), in which the female protagonists pursue missions that lead to disaster.

Ibsen's plays were now concerned more with individual destinies than with general moral or social principles, and his focus narrowed (and intensified) even more in *The Lady from the Sea* (1888) and the plays that followed: *The Master Builder* (1892), with its complex interweaving of guilt, ambition and fantasy; *Little Eyolf* (1894), in which Alfred and Rita seem possessed by a confused blend of guilt and frustrated personal ambition; *John Gabriel Borkman* (1896), which exposes the frustrating failure of a family to live through others. Finally, in 1899, came *When We Dead Awaken*, which draws together many of the images and themes employed in earlier plays – a final statement of his characters' spiritual dilemma, caught as they are between the temptations of the possible and the terrible demands of the ideal.

**Ichikawa Danjūrō** Japanese acting family. Twelve generations of actors in the Ichikawa family of *KABUKI* actors have attained the illustrious name Danjūrō. Danjūrō is sometimes called the 'emperor of *kabuki*'. The head (*soke*) is responsible for preserving the family's famous acting style and passing it to the next generation. **Danjūrō XII** (1946– ) was so designated in a three-month name-taking ceremony in 1985. A modern person, he has combined a college education with a career as a classical *kabuki* actor. He is a genuine star, admired for restrained acting in modern plays as well as bravura performances of *aragoto* classics in the family line. Several Danjūrōs were adopted, in order to continue the family acting line when there was no son.

**Ichikawa Ennosuke III** 1939– Japanese actor and director. The first son of Ichikawa Danshirō III, he succeeded to this stage name in 1963. Ennosuke challenges and revitalizes *KABUKI* theatre, emphasizing acrobatic movements, spectacle and liveliness. His company, the 21st Century Kabuki Gumi, produces 'super *kabuki*' such as the plays *Oguri* (1982) and *Yamato Takeru* (1987), regularly visiting Europe and the USA.

**Iffland, August (Wilhelm)** 1759–1814 German actor, director and playwright. After being trained by EKHOF at Gotha, in 1779 Iffland joined the new MANNHEIM COURT THEATRE. He left in 1796 to become the director of the BERLIN ROYAL THEATRE, where he remained until his death. He was honoured throughout Germany for the extraordinary versatility of his acting, noted for the completeness of his characterization, his subtlety and his finely judged transitions. GOETHE was among his greatest admirers. Iffland was also a prolific playwright, specializing in *Rührstücke*, sentimental, melodramatic pieces, generally with a domestic setting. Of these, *The Huntsmen* (1785) may be seen occasionally in Germany today. As director Iffland presented the plays of SHAKESPEARE, SCHILLER and contemporary historical dramatists in extremely spectacular productions, which foreshadowed the work of later directors such as DINGELSTEDT and the Duke of Saxe-MEININGEN.

**'illegitimate' theatre** see THEATRICAL MONOPOLY

**Imbuga, Francis** fl.1970s Kenyan playwright. His plays

include *The Fourth Trial and Kisses of Faho* (1972), *The Married Bachelor* (1973), *Betrayal in the City* (1976), *Games of Silence* (1977) and *The Successor* (1979). *Betrayal in the City* was Kenya's entry to the second World Black and African Festival of Arts and Culture (FESTAC) in Lagos in 1977. The play satirizes the problems of independence and freedom in postcolonial African states. The same themes are seen in Imbuga's other plays, where the clashes between individuals or classes in society are used to comment on political and social tensions.

**Immermann, Karl** 1796–1840 German director, playwright and novelist. Immermann's most important contribution to the German theatre occurred during his directorship of the Düsseldorf Town Theatre between 1835 and 1837. Here, despite modest resources, he developed a company that achieved national renown for the standards of its ensemble playing. At this time most German theatres were subject to the pre-eminence of the virtuoso actor. In February 1840, Immermann staged *Twelfth Night* on a specially constructed stage that incorporated features of the Elizabethan and Italian Renaissance stages – a highly unusual enterprise in those days. Of his plays, only his tragedy *Andreas Hofer* (1834) has any individual distinction. Immermann is remembered today primarily for his novel *Münchhausen*.

**Incháustegui Cabral, Héctor** 1912–79 Dominican Republic poet, critic and playwright. He belonged to the so-called group of independent poets who produced important social poetry from the 1930s to the 1950s. His *Miedo en un puñado de polvo* (*Fear in a Handful of Dust*, 1968) is a collection of three plays based on Greek classics that express universal constants of the human spirit, but his theatre is one of ideas rather than action.

**Inchbald, Elizabeth** 1753–1821 English playwright and novelist. She ran away from home to become an actress and later fell in love with JOHN PHILIP KEMBLE, who served as the model for Dorriforth in her novel, *A Simple Story* (1791). After 1789 she devoted herself to writing. Her first play, *A Mogul Tale* (1784), exploited the craze for hot-air balloons. Of her comedies, the most successful include *I'll Tell You What* (1785), *Everyone Has His Fault* (1793), *Wives as They Were, and Maids as They Are* (1797) and *To Marry, or Not to Marry* (1805). *The Child of Nature* (1788) is more ambitious, derived from ROUSSEAU. She adapted KOTZEBUE's *Das Kind der Liebe* as *Lovers' Vows* (1798), the play whose rehearsal in the Bertram household features in Jane Austen's *Mansfield Park* (1814). Inchbald defied male prejudice by editing three collections of plays, *The British Theatre* (25 vols., 1808), *Farces* (7 vols., 1809) and *The Modern Theatre* (10 vols., 1809).

**Independent Theatre Society** British theatre club. A private club modelled on ANDRÉ ANTOINE's Théâtre Libre, it was founded in London in 1891 by J. T. Grein in order to provide a platform for 'special performances of plays which have a literary and artistic, rather than a commercial value', including those which had fallen victim to the Lord Chamberlain's CENSORSHIP. The Society opened on 13 March 1891, to hostile reviews, with the British premiere of IBSEN's *Ghosts*, which did not receive a licence for public performance until 1914. But the Society's controversial character was not sustained, and no further banned plays were staged because London managers proved unwilling to risk their theatres by upsetting the Lord Chamberlain, who sanctioned their annual licences. A second Ibsen premiere, *The Wild Duck*, which was considered too heavy in its SYMBOLISM for commercial exposure, took place in 1894. Between 1891 and the Society's closure in December 1898, just over half the 28 pieces produced were of British origin, including the premieres of SHAW's *Widowers' Houses* (1892) and George Moore's only play *The Strike at Arlingford* (1893). Most plays were restricted to a single performance, and Grein never had a permanent venue for his programme. A branch theatre was opened in Manchester in 1893, taking the London productions. A number of similar, though smaller, club ventures appeared over the next decade, including the Pioneer Players (under EDITH CRAIG), to which Grein gave his support; but the Independent Theatre Society's main successor was the STAGE SOCIETY (founded 1899), which performed on Sunday evenings.

**Inge, William (Motter)** 1913–73 American playwright. He was born and educated in mid-America, and his works reflect this background. On the strength of his first play, *Come Back Little Sheba* (1950), the critics touted Inge as having the promise to join ARTHUR MILLER and TENNESSEE WILLIAMS – a promise he never fulfilled, although he made considerable impact on American theatre with *Picnic* (1953), *Bus Stop* (1955) and *The Dark at the Top of the Stairs* (1957). He cherished the weaknesses of his lonely characters, recording their speech with an accurate, appreciative ear. His later works, such as *A Loss of Roses* (1959), *Natural Affection* (1963) and *Where's Daddy?* (1966), received little attention.

**inner stage** see DISCOVERY SPACE

**interlude** English theatrical form. The first recorded use of the term, at the beginning of the 14th century, is in the title of the fragmentary English play of *The Clerk and the Girl* (*Interludium de Clerico et Puella*). It seems not to have been used elsewhere in Europe. During the 14th and 15th centuries it is applied to a variety of entertainments, some solo (e.g. the 1494 account of King Alfred disguised as a minstrel performing 'enterludes and songs' to the Danes). It is often associated with singing, but there are references which clearly indicate that it was also used of plays proper. The first-known named 'interlude' is MEDWALL's *Fulgens and Lucres* (late 15th century), and during the 16th century it is used for any type of play: comedy, tragedy, biblical play, morality. It goes out of use in the later 17th century and was revived, as a critical term, by J. P. Collier to refer specifically to JOHN HEYWOOD's plays. It has since become a term for the miscellaneous, short, often comic, English plays of the first half of the 16th century.

**International Centre of Theatre Research** see BROOK, PETER

**International Theatre Institute (ITI)** UNESCO-based organization dedicated to furthering the cause of theatre world-wide. It was founded in 1948 and is based in various national centres.

**Internationale Nieuwe Scene** (New International Stage) Antwerp-based company. A bilingual political company founded in 1973, its main theoretical influence is BRECHT; its main practical influences are DARIO FO and Arturo Corso. The company's first production was a reworking of Fo's *Mistero Buffo*. For preference the INS performs in a circus tent, whose connotations of popular entertainment and informal pleasure suit it better than a purpose-built theatre. The techniques of *COMMEDIA DELL'ARTE* are central to the company's work, in that they enable the actor to fulfil Brecht's criterion of showing rather than identifying with the character. The style is one element in a thoroughly considered socialist aesthetic, seen at its most mature in *De Herkuls* (*Hercules*, 1980), a group-created piece about the life and work of dockers on the River Scheldt.

**Ionesco, Eugène** 1909–94 French playwright. Ionesco's youth was divided between France and Romania (he was the child of separated parents), but his plays were written from Paris. The performance in 1950 of his first play, *La Cantatrice chauve* (*The Bald Prima Donna*), astonished its author by its comic force: he imagined he had written 'the tragedy of language'. A stream of one-act plays followed, e.g. *La Leçon* (*The Lesson*, 1951) and *Les Chaises* (*The Chairs*, 1952), which present strong concrete images of anguished mental states and merit the author's epithet 'tragic farce'. Story-line, character and discussion are abandoned; surreal events take their place (see SURREALISM; THEATRE OF THE ABSURD). *Tueur sans gages* (*The Killer*, 1959), was his first three-act play, and his subsequent work, e.g. *Rhinoceros* (directed by BARRAULT, 1960) and *Le Roi se meurt* (*Exit the King*, 1962), was more conventional in form. Into the plays of this period Ionesco introduced an autobiographical character named Bérenger – naive, imaginative, alternately ecstatic or depressed – with whom audiences could identify. In the 1960s his plays were performed all over the world. *La Soif et la faim* (*Hunger and Thirst*) was performed at the COMÉDIE-FRANÇAISE (1966). In 1981 a new play, *Voyages chez les morts* (*Journeys to the Homes of the Dead*), recaptured the hallucinatory quality of the early work. It formed the basis of PLANCHON's massive biographical production *Ionesco* (1982).

**Ireland, William Henry** 1775–1835 English forger. In 1794, desperate to please his father, Samuel Ireland, an obsessive idolizer of SHAKESPEARE, he began to forge legal documents with Shakespeare's signature. He went on to produce manuscripts of *King Lear*, part of *Hamlet* and a new play, *Vortigern*, which was accepted for production at DRURY LANE by SHERIDAN. Two days before the first performance of *Vortigern* the noted Shakespeare scholar Edmond Malone published *An Inquiry into the Authenticity of Certain Miscellaneous Papers*, which convincingly proved the forgery. *Vortigern* was performed in April 1796 and was a disaster. Ireland's *Henry II*, another supposed Shakespeare play, was never performed. He admitted the fraud in his pamphlet *An Authentic Account*. His later play, *Mutius Scaevola* (1801), was unperformed. His full *Confessions* were published in 1805.

**Irish Literary Theatre** see ABBEY THEATRE

**Irons, Jeremy** 1948– British actor. After training at the BRISTOL OLD VIC Theatre School he gained experience in REPERTORY. His reputation was initially established through films (*The French Lieutenant's Woman*) and television (*Brideshead Revisited*). In 1986 he joined the ROYAL SHAKESPEARE COMPANY at Stratford-upon-Avon, playing the title role in SHAKESPEARE's *Richard II* and the lead in APHRA BEHN's *The Rover* (at the first season of the Swan Theatre). He has since appeared in many films.

**Irving, Henry** [John Henry Brodribb] 1838–1905 British actor. Risking disapproval from his Methodist relations, he entered the professional stage in 1856, first in the provinces and from 1866 in London, acting with ELLEN TERRY for the first time in 1867. His playing of Digby Grant in JAMES ALBERY's *Two Roses* (1870) gave the first sign of his idiosyncratic genius. The American

manager of the LYCEUM, H. L. BATEMAN, yielded to Irving's suggestion that they stage LEOPOLD LEWIS's version of *Le Juif polonais*. *The Bells*, as Lewis agreed to call it, gave Irving his first great part, that of the guilt-ridden burgomaster Mathias. In a revival of EDWARD BULWER LYTTON's *Richelieu* (1873) Irving's embodiment of will-power mesmerized audiences. His tender, sensitive Hamlet (1874) was an unexpected contrast.

In 1878, Irving became manager of the Lyceum. For over 20 years he made it an actor's theatre, himself the star. For the opening revival of *Hamlet* he invited Ellen Terry to play Ophelia. She, all grace, charm and flowing lines, complemented his angular eccentricity. All their Shakespearian triumphs were shared: Shylock and Portia (1879), Iago and Desdemona (1881), Benedick and Beatrice (1882), Malvolio and Viola (1884), Wolsey and Katherine of Aragon (1892), Lear and Cordelia (1892), Iachimo and Imogen (1896). Irving's SHAKESPEARE productions were pictorially splendid and embellished with commissioned music and scenery, using famous artists such as Alma-Tadema and Burne-Jones. He kept a regular orchestra and large technical staff. Despite his reputation as an interpreter of Shakespeare and the intellectual leader of his profession, Irving was primarily a showman, quite as likely to stage a tired melodrama as a classic revival, as long as it contained a part in which he could startle audiences. It was acting that interested Irving, not writing. He was knighted in 1895, the first actor to be so honoured.

Irving's two sons were both active in the theatre. The elder, Henry, known as H. B. Irving (1870–1919) was an actor; the younger, Laurence (1871–1914), was a minor playwright and actor. H. B. Irving's son, Laurence (1897–1983), was a regular designer for stage and films and author of his grandfather's biography (1951).

**Irving, Jules** 1924–79 American producer and director. Together with teaching colleague Herbert Blau, Irving founded the San Francisco Actors Workshop (1952–64), which became known for its experimental productions. In 1965 they became co-directors of the repertory theatre of Lincoln Center (see VIVIAN BEAUMONT AND MITZI E. NEWHOUSE THEATRES), where Irving continued until 1972, when he became a producer-director of television movies in Hollywood. During his controversial tenure at Lincoln Center, he became known for his carefully crafted productions of the classics and for innovative presentations of plays by BRECHT, BECKETT and PINTER. In 1971 he staged the United States premiere of Pinter's *Landscape* and *Silence*.

**Irwin, Bill** 1950– American actor, entertainer and playwright. Irwin is the best-known among practitioners of the so-called New Vaudeville. These performers focus on the creation of theatre works which draw upon American popular entertainment traditions, from the CIRCUS to VAUDEVILLE, and experimental theatre techniques. A 'postmodern clown', he makes innovative use of his CLOWN skills to create exciting visual metaphors for the broader actions and emotions of a play. His best work to date has been *The Regard of Flight*, a 1982 performance at New York's American Place Theatre that satirized the postmodern theatre. He created and performed in the nonverbal *Largely New York* (1989), Beckett's *Texts for Nothing* (1992) and the CLOWN show *Fool Moon* (1993).

**Isherwood, Christopher** 1904–86 British novelist and playwright. Between 1935 and 1938 he collaborated with W. H. AUDEN on the series of expressionistic verse plays (see EXPRESSIONISM) that established the reputation of the London GROUP THEATRE – *The Dog beneath the Skin*, *The Ascent of F6* and *On the Frontier*. His novel *Goodbye to Berlin* (1939) was dramatized by John Van Druten as *I Am a Camera*, and formed the basis for the film *Cabaret* (1966). Moving to Hollywood in 1940, he became an American citizen in 1946.

**Isola brothers** French impresarios. **Émile** (1860–1945) and **Vincent** Isola (1862–1947) began as conjurors in their native Algeria and made a Parisian debut at the FOLIES-BERGÈRE in 1892 in a thought-transference act. That same year they founded the Théâtre Isola and were hailed for such illusions as 'The Muscovite Trunk'. Succumbing to competition, they gave up MAGIC to become the managers of, in succession, Parisiana, the Olympia, the Folies-Bergère, the Gaieté-Lyrique, the Opéra-Comique (for 12 years), the Mogador and the Théâtre Sarah-Bernhardt, which they ran with taste and acumen. Failing to create a MUSIC-HALL monopoly after the British model and losing their money in the Depression, they returned to magic. Vincent, with his aristocratic profile and monocle, presented grand illusions, while Émile specialized in shows of dexterity with cards and scarves.

**Ivanov, Vsevolod (Vyacheslavovich)** 1895–1963 Soviet playwright. His 15 plays mostly relate to the Russian Civil War, in which he fought on the Red side, and to his native Siberia and Asiatic Russia. GORKY encouraged him in his early naturalistic short story writing (1915). Ivanov's early work included the novelistic Civil War trilogy *The Partisans* (1921), *Coloured Winds* (1922) and *Armoured Train 14–69* (1922), the last of which he adapted for the stage in 1927 and which became his most important play. Commissioned by the Moscow ART THEATRE for the 10th anniversary of the Revolution, directed by STANISLAVSKY and starring KACHALOV, it was the first Soviet play to be successfully produced by MAT. In it a group of partisans, led by a peasant only recently converted to the Bolshevik cause, seize a train of White refugees in Siberia during the Civil War. Ivanov's other plays on Civil War themes include *Blockade* (1929), *The Compromise of Naib-Khan* (1931), *The Doves See the Departing Cruisers* (1937) and *Uncle Kostya* (1944); *Twelve Youths from a Snuffbox* (1936) is about Tsar Paul I's assassination in 1801; *Inspiration* (1940) is set in the 17th century in the time of the false Dmitry; and *Lomonosov* (1953) concerns the 18th-century Russian scientist and man of letters. Ivanov's plays and narrative fiction after 1930 bear the unmistakable imprint of socialist realism.

**Ivanov, Vyacheslav (Ivanovich)** 1866–1949 Russian poet, playwright and theorist. Ivanov was the leader of the St Petersburg symbolists (see SYMBOLISM). A Hellenic scholar, he linked the Dionysian cult to later Christian mysteries in an effort to establish a philosophical foundation for a modern liturgical theatre. He wrote two plays – *Tantalus* (1905) and *Prometheus* (1919) – which imitated AESCHYLUS in structure, mythological subject-matter and obscure, archaic language. The most scholarly and profound of the symbolists, his ideas greatly influenced MEYERHOLD. Apart from contributing to the major symbolist journals of the day and publishing several volumes of poetry, he collected his major aesthetic essays in the volumes *Along the Stars* (1909) and *Furrows and Landmarks* (1916). He emigrated to Italy in 1924.

**Iwamatsu Ryō** 1952– Japanese playwright, director and actor. In the mid-1970s performances of improvised comic pieces were popular on the Tokyo fringe, and the Tokyo Kanenchi (Electric Battery) Theatre Company was formed (1976). Iwamatsu was invited to create the situations and characters for improvisations, but when the company turned to scripted drama in the mid-1980s he became playwright, director and actor. Some elements of slapstick and absurdity (see THEATRE OF THE ABSURD) remain in the plays, but his naturalistic style (see NATURALISM) is reminiscent of early SHINGEKI. He discloses the problems of Japanese society in such plays as *O-cha to Sekkyo* (*Tea and a Lecture*, 1986), *Futon to Daruma* (*Futon and Daruma*, 1988; translated 1992) and *Tonari no Otoko* (*The Man Next Door*, 1990; translated 1994).

**Izenour, George** 1912– American designer. Inventor of the electronic console for theatre lighting control, the synchronous winch system and the steel acoustical shell, Izenour has been a design and engineering consultant for over 100 theatres around the world since the 1950s and a dominant force in theatre design and technology. Because economics dictates that a single theatre must be employed for many uses (spoken drama, opera, concerts, and so on), he is an advocate of the multiple-use and multiple-form theatre in which the size and shape and auditorium can be altered for different needs and acoustical requirements.

# J

**Jackson, Barry (Vincent)** 1879–1961 British theatre director, manager and patron. Born in Birmingham, he founded the amateur Pilgrim Players in 1907 and the professional BIRMINGHAM REPERTORY THEATRE in 1913, for which he financed the building of a purpose-designed theatre. As owner and artistic director until 1935 he established the theatre as the country's leading REPERTORY venture committed to both new and classic plays. He occasionally designed and directed productions himself. He was founder-director of the Malvern Theatre Festival from 1929 to 1937 and director of the Stratford Memorial Theatre, 1945–8 (see ROYAL SHAKESPEARE COMPANY). He also wrote and adapted a number of plays for adults and children, and was knighted in 1925.

**Jackson, Glenda** 1936– British actress. Her performance as Charlotte Corday in PETER BROOK's production of PETER WEISS's *The Marat/Sade* (1965) was celebrated for its intensity and eroticism. In 1967 she was a notable Masha in CHEKHOV's *The Three Sisters* at the ROYAL COURT THEATRE, became known to wider audiences through her film appearances, such as in *Women in Love* (1970), and in 1975 played Hedda Gabler in the ROYAL SHAKESPEARE COMPANY's production of IBSEN's play. Not conventionally pretty, Jackson could radiate an emotional directness and intellectual honesty which transformed her *gamine* attractiveness into outright beauty. Her independence of mind prevented her from working consistently within a permanent company such as the RSC. She returned to Stratford-upon-Avon in 1978 to play Cleopatra in Peter Brook's production of *Antony and Cleopatra* – with less than her usual success. Of her several starring WEST END performances in recent years, she achieved her most notable triumph in EUGENE O'NEILL's *Strange Interlude* (1984). She appeared in GARCÍA LORCA's *The House of Bernarda Alba* (1987), in the title role of GLASGOW CITIZENS' THEATRE's *Mother Courage* (1990), and memorably in HOWARD BARKER's *Scenes from an Execution* (1990). A lifelong supporter of the British Labour Party, she was elected to parliament as the MP for Hampstead, London, in 1992.

**Jacobi, Derek (George)** 1938– British actor. His debut was at BIRMINGHAM REPERTORY THEATRE in 1960, and in 1963 he joined the NATIONAL THEATRE at the OLD VIC, playing Laertes in *Hamlet*, Cassio in *Othello* and Lodovico in *The White Devils*, among other major roles. He joined the Prospect Theatre Company in 1972, working with them for six years. He played a memorable Hamlet in 1978, and Peer Gynt and Prospero for the ROYAL SHAKESPEARE COMPANY in the 1982–3 season. He made a major popular impact as Claudius in the television drama serial, *I, Claudius*. He played both title roles in *Richard II* (1988) and *Richard III* (1989), and appeared as the actor himself in *Kean* (1990) at the Old Vic, as Becket in *Becket* (1991) and as Byron in *Mad, Bad and Dangerous to Know* (1992), showing his ability to take centre stage and impose his strong but thoughtful personality on productions. He was knighted in 1994, while playing Macbeth for the RSC.

**Jahnn, Hans Henny** 1894–1959 German playwright and novelist. His early work *Pastor Ephraim Magnus* (1917, first produced 1923; adapted by BRECHT and BRONNEN, 1925) is the most extreme example of the violent, anti-idealistic line in EXPRESSIONISM. Later plays, in which the tragic artist is a frequent figure, re-established his reputation, with productions of his *Thomas Chatterton* by GRÜNDGENS (1956) and of *The Dusty Rainbow* by PISCATOR (1961).

**James, Henry** 1843–1916 American-born novelist, playwright and critic. James settled in England in 1876. His occasional essays on the theatre were published in 1949 in a collection entitled *The Scenic Art*. His play *Guy Domville* failed at the ST JAMES'S THEATRE, London, in 1895. The performance of his comedy *The American* had passed virtually unnoticed in 1891. A one-volume collection of his plays was published in 1948.

**Janauschek, Fanny** [Francesca] 1830–1904 Czech actress. She made her debut in Prague and was engaged as leading actress at the State Theatre, Frankfurt, for ten years. Established as an eminent tragedienne, she performed Medea in German for her 1867 New York debut, while the rest of the cast acted in English, as did EDWIN BOOTH opposite her German Lady Macbeth in 1868. Having learned English, she launched her English-speaking career in 1870. With her statuesque figure, emotional power and vibrant but controlled voice, she excelled in heroic roles like Brunhilde, Deborah, Mary Stuart and, later, Meg Merrilies. But the public preferred her dual role as the coquettish French maid Hortense and the haughty Lady Dedlock in *Chesney Wold*, adapted from DICKENS's *Bleak House*. She was one of the last great actresses in the 'grand style', but after 1898 she was reduced to playing in cheap MELODRAMAS.

**Janin, Jules** 1804–74 French critic. Known as the 'prince of critics', Janin commanded enormous influence and respect. For 41 years he wrote the theatre column in the *Journal des débats*, particularly important for his championship of RACHEL and PONSARD. He disapproved of HUGO, and also of the COMÉDIE-FRANÇAISE. His theatre criticism appeared in two collections, *Histoire de la littérature dramatique* (1853–8) and *La Critique dramatique* (1877). He also published volumes on MLLE MARS (1843), on MLLE GEORGE (1862) and on ALEXANDRE DUMAS (1871).

**Janis** [*née* Bierbower], **Elsie** 1889–1956 American VAUDEVILLE entertainer. From her debut in 1897 to the end of her career in 1932, Elsie appeared as a headliner in vaudeville (in which she was considered unsurpassed), MUSICAL COMEDY and REVUE. She specialized in impersonations and comic songs, introducing such popular songs as 'Fo' de Lawd's Sake, Play a Waltz' and 'Florrie Was a Flapper'.

**Jaques-Dalcroze, Émile** see APPIA, ADOLPHE

**Jardiel Poncela, Enrique** 1901–52 Spanish novelist, journalist and playwright. He wrote more than 40 comic plays whose combination of word-play and absurd situations was intended to parody the trivial normality of the Spanish theatre. Among his successes were *Eloisa está debajo de un almendro* (*Eloisa Is under an Almond Tree*, 1940), *Los ladrones somos gente honrada* (*We Thieves Are Decent Folk*, 1942) and *Los habitantes de la casa deshabitada* (*The Inhabitants of the Uninhabited House*, 1944).

**Jarry, Alfred** 1873–1907 French playwright. Jarry was

the creator of King Ubu, a grotesque, puppet-like figure who embodies every mean, destructive and ignoble quality. Ubu appeared first as a puppet, then in two performances by FIRMIN GÉMIER, directed by LUGNÉ-POE (1896). The play caused a legendary stir in literary circles. Jarry wrote three other Ubu plays and associated writings, but none of them matched the brutal simplicity of *Ubu Roi*. It is a Shakespearian PARODY, in which a lazy 'little man' is goaded by his wife into terrible acts of violence. The unscrupulous Ubu thinks only of his own satisfaction, but he is also devoid of imagination. Jarry's simple stagecraft challenged both naturalists and symbolists. He drank himself to death at the age of 34 but his work was championed by the surrealists (see SURREALISM) and finally achieved 'classic' status in the 1950s, when the THEATRE OF THE ABSURD adopted similar techniques and characters.

**jatra** Indian theatre form. The most popular theatre genre in the rural areas of Bengal and among the Bengali-speaking people of eastern Bihar, Orissa, Assam and Tripura, *jatra* also holds sway over the villages of Bangladesh.

*Jatra* means procession. It may have come into existence in the 16th century as a part of the Vaishnava devotional movement. Up to the early 19th century, *jatra* focused primarily on religious themes and was instructive and moralistic in tone. In the early to mid-19th century, it adopted more secular themes. From the late 19th to the mid-20th century *jatra* remained a rural art form. But after independence in 1947 the Communist Party employed it to win sympathetic support for its cause. Since that time, artists have taken a neutral political position so that they may please the widest possible audience. In the early 1960s, *jatra* underwent something of a revival among the middle classes of Calcutta. In 1961 a *jatra* festival was held in the palace courtyard of the Shabhabazar Rajas in north Calcutta, and has been repeated annually. In recent years, the form has served as the model for various contemporary stage directors, actors and playwrights who have experimented with contemporary social issues as themes.

*Jatra* companies are professional itinerant concerns. Around 20 major troupes operate from their headquarters in Calcutta. The wages are handsome by Indian standards. The owner-managers of the companies are entrepreneurs who take a large share of the profits. Generally, the actors come from the lower strata of society.

The *jatra* season runs from September to early June. *Jatra* is highly melodramatic in character, with a liberal dose of songs and dramatic scenes. Among the more interesting of the old *jatra* characters are the Conscience (*bibek*) and Fate (*niyati*), allegorical figures who move in and out of the action, commenting on its meaning and warning of dangers.

**Jefferson family** Anglo-American actors. Thomas Jefferson (1732–1807) was an actor with GARRICK and manager of various provincial English theatres. One of his children, Joseph Jefferson I (1774–1832), went to America in 1795 and became a favourite at the JOHN STREET and PARK THEATRES in New York. In 1803 he moved to the CHESTNUT STREET THEATRE in Philadelphia, remaining there until 1830. Most of his children worked in the theatre, including Joseph Jefferson II (1804–42), who succeeded as a scene painter. The greatest of the family was Joseph Jefferson III

(1829–1905), who toured with his family, visited Europe in 1856 and joined LAURA KEENE's company. In London in 1865 he first performed the role for which he was most noted, Rip Van Winkle, dramatized for him by DION BOUCICAULT. His acting won praise from the critic WILLIAM WINTER: 'an exquisite blending of humour, pathos, grace and beauty'. Of his children, four went on the stage, the most successful being **Charles Burke** Jefferson (1851–1908).

**Jelinek, Elfriede** 1946– Austrian playwright and novelist. Her experimental sequel to IBSEN's *Doll's House, Was geschah nachdem Nora ihren Mann verlassen hatte* (*What Happened after Nora Had Left Her Husband*, 1979), shows Nora unsuccessfully trying to make a living for herself in the early 1930s. Her 'musical tragedy' *Clara S* (1982) juxtaposes pianist Clara Schumann and her composer husband with the Fascist poet GABRIELE D'ANNUNZIO to examine the historical predicament of women artists. *Burgtheater* (1985) explores the behaviour of a popular acting dynasty at the Vienna BURGTHEATER during Nazi rule. *Krankheit oder moderne Frauen* (*Sickness, or Modern Women*, 1987) is a female vampire fantasy involving Emily Brontë and Heathcliff in a drama of lust and female emancipation. *Totenauberg* (1992) reunites German racist, existentialist philosopher Heidegger in the Alps with his ex-pupil, the Jewish émigrée philosopher Hannah Arendt, for a wide-ranging discourse on post-Communist Europe.

**Jellicoe, Ann** 1927– British playwright and director. Her first full-length play, *The Sport of My Mad Mother* (1956), was staged at the ROYAL COURT THEATRE. Its speech rhythms, defiantly non-literary, were based on listening to young teenagers at play and the 'mad mother' of the title was Kali, the Hindu goddess. Jellicoe was a pioneer of community theatre in Britain and sought to release in her casts impulses towards drama which might otherwise be confined by formal texts. Her first successful plays, however, were conventionally written, notably *The Knack* (1961), contrasting two young men, one who has the knack of attracting women, the other who has not. *Shelley* (1965) was a clear, almost documentary account of the poet's life. In contrast, *The Rising Generation* (1967), originally written for but not performed by the Girl Guides' Association, was conceived in a spirit of orgiastic feminism. Jellicoe was a founder-director of the Cockpit Theatre Club in 1950 and the literary manager of the Royal Court from 1973 to 1975. She founded the Colway Theatre Trust in Dorset in 1979 to stage community plays in village areas and west-country towns, but resigned as its director in 1985.

**Jerome, Jerome K(lapka)** 1859–1927 British playwright, novelist and journalist. Remembered for the comic idyll *Three Men in a Boat* (1889), he wrote several comedies and farces, such as *The Prude's Progress* (1895) and *The MacHaggis* (1897) in collaboration with Eden Phillpotts. *The Passing of the Third Floor Back* (1908) gave JOHNSTON FORBES-ROBERTSON a famous part as the Christ-like stranger whose presence in a Bloomsbury boarding-house transforms the lives of his fellow lodgers.

**Jerrold, Douglas (William)** 1803–57 British playwright and journalist. The leading contributor to *Punch* from 1841 until his death, Jerrold also wrote some 70 plays, revealing a humane concern for the poor and oppressed. Among them are the ebullient nautical MELODRAMA, *Black-Eyed Susan* (1829), domestic dramas such as *The Rent Day* (1832) and *The Factory Girl* (1832), and comedies such as *Nell Gwynne; or, The Prologue* (1833), *The Housekeeper* (1833), *The Wedding Gown* (1834), *The Schoolfellows* (1835) and *Doves in a Cage* (1835).

**Jessner, Leopold** 1878–1945 German director. One of the early exponents of NATURALISM, he later made his name by replacing representational scenery with multiple acting levels arranged in ascending steps on a bare stage (*Jessnertreppe*). He transformed SCHILLER's *Wilhelm Tell* and SHAKESPEARE's *Richard III* into key examples of EXPRESSIONISM in 1919 and 1920, using single colours and lighting to represent different moods, and developing a rhetorical acting style in which exaggerated gesture and facial masking were designed to project inner vision.

**Jesuitendrama** Jesuit plays. Performed at Jesuit colleges throughout Europe, *Jesuitendrama* is associated generally with colleges in Bavaria and Austria. It was performed from approximately the mid-16th to the mid-18th century. The purpose of these dramas was to educate the student performers in the art of speaking and rhetoric and to instil in both audiences and actors a belief in the values of the Catholic Church, as propagated by the Society of Jesus after the Counter-Reformation. Initially the plays were in Latin, but in the course of the 17th century performance in the German vernacular became increasingly common. Jesuit drama demonstrated an increasing tendency towards spectacular and musical embellishment, anticipating the tradition of spectacular opera of Austrian and southern German cities in the late 17th century. The most notable writers of Jesuit drama were Nikolaus Avancini (1611–86), an Austrian Jesuit of noble birth, and Jakob Bidermann (1578–1639), whose *Cenodoxus* (1609), written initially in Latin, might stand revival today.

**Jewish Art Theatre** American company. Closely modelled on STANISLAVSKY's MOSCOW ART THEATRE, it was set up by JACOB BEN-AMI in 1919 at the New York Garden Theatre, with EMANUEL REICHER, associate of REINHARDT and a founder of the German FREIE BÜHNE, as play director. Rave reviews greeted PERETZ HIRSHBEIN's *The Haunted Inn* and *Green Fields*, with Ben-Ami scoring a personal triumph in both. In spite of further successes, including DAVID PINSKI's *The Dumb Messiah*, OSSIP DIMOV's *Bronx Express* and TOLSTOI's *The Power of Darkness*, internal dissension brought the venture, probably the high point of YIDDISH THEATRE, to a close after two seasons and 14 productions.

**Jewish theatre** see YIDDISH THEATRE

**jig** Elizabethan theatrical form. An inclusive term, it described a broadside ballad, a short satirical scene with music and rhyme and, most frequently, a broad and often bawdy FARCE in which doggerel and dance played a prominent part and in which a CLOWN was the central figure. RICHARD TARLTON's example provided the model for later clowns, e.g. WILL KEMPE. As an afterpiece, the jig concluded an afternoon performance, even a tragedy. In 1612 there was an Order 'for the suppressing of jigs at the end of plays', but the jig retained its popularity in fairgrounds and among strolling players until well into the 18th century.

**jingxi** Beijing drama. Literally it means drama (*xi*) of the Chinese capital (*jing*). Loosely named Beijing opera in English, by the early 19th century *jingxi* dominated the Beijing stage and eventually usurped the national popularity of KUNQU. Enthusiastically patronized by the court, it was essentially an urban form and until 1949

dominated all other traditional styles. Accepted as the national form of dramatic expression, it achieved international recognition when a Beijing troupe led by MEI LANFANG toured America in 1930.

The great success of the *jingxi* was due in part to a style which, by prevailing dramatic standards, was neither too complicated nor precious. Literary and musical content was easily memorized and touched the collective unconscious. The plays derive from the historical epics and romantic novels of China's past, familiar to everybody. The musical content is limited and repetitive in form, serving a strictly theatrical function. The leader of the orchestra manipulates a pair of wooden clappers rather like castanets and uses a hardwood drum with a skin head to beat out the measures. Singing is accompanied by a bowed two-stringed instrument, a *huqin*, which has a florid, rippling line. The bowing is characterized by vibrato and glissando effects. Brass gongs and cymbals are used to mark entries, exits and emotional climaxes in the song and action of a play. They are particularly evident in the combat scenes, ACROBATICS and dance passages which are integral to all *jingxi* performance. Singing is used to indicate human emotions and psychological reactions, melodramatically accentuated by musical rhythms. Stanzas of four lines rhyming alternately are standard practice, whether in monologue or dialogue.

After the establishment of the People's Republic in 1949 *jingxi* was reformed along the lines directed by the Chinese Communist Party. During the Cultural Revolution (1966–76), virtually all items were forbidden. *Jingxi* has been revived today and is once more being staged in its entirety.

**Jodelet** [Julien Bedeau] c.1590–1660 French comedian. He acted at the MARAIS, then the HÔTEL DE BOURGOGNE, then went back to the Marais for 16 years, playing Cliton in PIERRE CORNEILLE's *Le Menteur* (*The Liar*, 1643) and the eponymous lead in several FARCES written especially for him, notably *Jodelet, ou Le Maître-Valet* (*Jodelet, or The Master-Servant*, 1645) by SCARRON and *Jodelet Prince* (1655) by THOMAS CORNEILLE. With the floured face traditionally associated with farce, a large mouth, long snout-like nose and bushy eyebrows, his appearance and nasal speaking voice alone provoked laughter. MOLIÈRE persuaded him to join his company when they arrived in Paris and wrote for him the part of the Vicomte de Jodelet in *Les Précieuses ridicules* (*The Affected Ladies*, 1659).

**Jodelle, Étienne** 1532–73 French playwright and poet. One of the Pléiade group, he pioneered an indigenous classical literary drama. Of his three extant plays, the tragedy *Cléopâtre captive* and the comedy *Eugène* were performed before Henri II in 1552. *Didon se sacrifiant* (*Dido Sacrificing Herself*) dates from 1558. Both tragedies follow SENECA, with no development of character, little action and lengthy soliloquizing. *Eugène* is about adultery and cuckoldry and owes much to medieval FARCE, despite the classical claims of its prologue.

**Joffré, Sara** 1935– Peruvian playwright and director. She founded Homero, Teatro de Grillos (Homer, Cricket Theatre) in Lima in 1963. Author and director of one-act plays for adults, Joffré is primarily known for her work with children's theatre in Peru.

**John F. Kennedy Center for the Performing Arts** (Washington, DC) This national cultural centre opened in 1971 on the banks of the Potomac. It now encompasses four theatres: the Eisenhower with 1,140 seats for dramatic presentations, the Concert Hall with 2,670 seats, the Opera House with 2,200 seats, and the Terrace Theatre with 500 seats, for films, concerts, experimental productions and children's theatre. The complex has been guided by ROGER STEVENS (1961–88), Ralph Davidson (1989–90) and James Wolfensohn (1990–).

**John Golden Theatre** (New York City) Built as the Theatre Masque in 1927 to seat 800, it was intended to present intimate or experimental plays. It was bought by the SHUBERTS in 1934 and leased to John Golden. It is considered ideal for small-cast plays; such performers as COMDEN AND GREEN, CORNELIA OTIS SKINNER and EMLYN WILLIAMS have presented their own shows there. In 1956, SAMUEL BECKETT's *Waiting for Godot* appeared at the Golden, marking the first and only time a Beckett play has appeared on BROADWAY. It remains a Shubert house.

**John Street Theatre** (New York City) The third and most substantial theatre to be built in New York by DAVID DOUGLASS. From 1777 British troops took it over and performed there. From 1785 LEWIS HALLAM JR established a permanent resident company and was joined by actor JOHN HENRY. The theatre served until 1798, when it was replaced by the PARK.

**Johnson, J. Rosamond** see COLE, BOB

**Johnson, Dr Samuel** 1709–84 English critic, poet and man of letters. Johnson befriended GARRICK, at whose request he wrote the prologue for the opening of Garrick's management of DRURY LANE in 1747, formulating his managerial policy in the couplet 'The Drama's laws the Drama's patrons give,/ For we that live to please must please to live.' His only play, *Irene*, was produced by Garrick in 1749. A sterile tragedy, it survived for nine nights through Garrick's advocacy. Johnson's edition of SHAKESPEARE, published in 1765, contains this remarkable preface as well as notes of acute critical perception, if vulnerable scholarship. Many of his *Lives of the Poets* (1779–81) are studies of dramatists, written with great sensitivity.

**Johnston, (William) Denis** 1901–84 Irish playwright. Johnston had a remarkably varied career: barrister, actor, war correspondent, BBC producer, critic and teacher. His *Nine Rivers from Jordan* (1953) is an impressionistic account of his wartime experiences. *In Search of Swift* (1959) is a controversial examination of Swift's relationship with Stella and Vanessa. *The Brazen Horn* (1977) speculates around a personal mystical philosophy.

Johnston's first play, rejected by the ABBEY (hence its title, *The Old Lady Says 'No!'*, 1929), is a sparkling expressionist SATIRE of Ireland after independence, produced by the GATE at the Peacock. He followed it with *The Moon in the Yellow River* (1931), a wryly tragic version of the same theme, realist in manner. Of his subsequent plays, only two use expressionist techniques (see EXPRESSIONISM), *A Bride for the Unicorn* (1933) and *The Dreaming Dust* (1940), in which seven actors from a Masque of the Seven Deadly Sins explore the enigmas of Swift's life. His other plays include two intelligent *pièces à thèse*, *The Golden Cuckoo* (1939) and *Strange Occurrence on Ireland's Eye* (1956). Based on law cases, they subject the law's inadequacies to witty and searching scrutiny. Johnston's last play, *The Scythe and the Sunset* (1958), is a treatment of the Easter Rising blending farce and tragedy, and, as its title suggests, a counterpart to O'CASEY.

Johnston's plays command both traditional and experimental forms. They mix prose and verse, combine human scepticism with a visionary consciousness, and salute and deride the mythology of the new Ireland.

**Jolly, George** fl.c.1630–73 English actor-manager. From 1648 he continued the old tradition of touring Germany with a troupe of English actors performing in English and German. In 1651 the company contained actresses and used changeable scenery, long before such innovations had been adopted on the professional stage in London. In 1662, while Jolly was on tour in East Anglia, DAVENANT and KILLIGREW convinced Charles II that Jolly's theatrical licence had been sold to them and he was prevented from performing in London. As a scant recompense, they allowed him to run various NURSERIES.

**Jolson, Al** 1886–1950 American singer and comedian. Jolson played the blackfaced servant Gus in a series of musicals beginning with *The Whirl of Society* (1912) and including *Robinson Crusoe, Jr* (1916), *Bombo* (1921) and *Big Boy* (1925). The use of blackface, derived from the MINSTREL SHOWS where Jolson had received his early training, gave racist overtones to his humour. His repertoire of hit songs drew large audiences, for whom he would often stop the performance, dismiss the other actors, and spend the rest of the evening singing. After his film debut in *The Jazz Singer* (1927) Jolson moved to Hollywood, except for the BROADWAY REVUE *The Wonder Bar* (1931) and the MUSICAL COMEDY *Hold on to Your Hats* (1940).

**Jones, David (Hugh)** 1934– British director. He worked under PETER HALL in an experimental season at the Arts Theatre Club (1962) and in 1964 he joined the ROYAL SHAKESPEARE COMPANY, primarily in an administrative capacity. In 1968 he became a co-director of the RSC's operations at the Aldwych, and from 1975 to 1977 he was the director of the Aldwych Theatre, responsible for the London wing of the RSC's programmes. Although he directed a wide variety of plays for the RSC by such writers as BRECHT, GÜNTER GRASS, DAVID MERCER and SEAN O'CASEY, he was best known for introducing the plays of MAKSIM GORKY to British audiences. From 1979 to 1981, he was the artistic director of the Brooklyn Academy of Music Theatre Co. in New York. His strengths as a director lie in the clear dramatic expositions, the encouragement of sensitive performances from his casts and his awareness of European theatrical traditions. In 1982 his first full-length feature film appeared, of HAROLD PINTER's *Betrayal*. In 1993 he returned to the RSC to direct a new play by an American-Russian writing team, *Misha's Party*.

**Jones, Henry Arthur** 1851–1929 British playwright. His first success was WILSON BARRETT's staging of his sensational MELODRAMA, *The Silver King* (1882), written in collaboration with Henry Herman. *Breaking a Butterfly* (1884) was a collaborative version of IBSEN's *A Doll's House*, which solemnly distorted the original by having Flossie (Nora) decide to stay with her husband. *Saints and Sinners* (1884), *The Middleman* (1889), *Judah* (1890), *The Dancing Girl* (1891), *The Crusaders* (1891) and *Michael and His Lost Angel* (1896) dramatize the war of flesh and spirit with some vigour, but without much subtlety, exposing rather than challenging moral polarities. CHARLES WYNDHAM launched Jones into producing his finest work, *The Case of Rebellious Susan* (1894), *The Liars* (1897) and *Mrs Dane's Defence* (1900). In his last years he made several outbursts against GEORGE BERNARD SHAW.

**Jones, Inigo** 1573–1652 English architect and scene designer. England's first scene designer, Jones introduced Renaissance, particularly Italian, staging practices to the English court, supervising the design and construction of the notable Stuart MASQUES until the Civil War, many of them (until 1631) in collaboration with BEN JONSON. Among his innovations were the adoption of SERLIO's raked stage, the introduction of perspective scenery for Jonson's *The Masque of Blackness* (1605) and the decoration of the proscenium arch, which owed its dominance over the English stage to the triumphant practice of Jones. Visits to Paris and Italy encouraged experiments with swivelling and folding scenes; he achieved coloured lighting effects for *The Masque of Queens* (1609). The Banqueting House at Whitehall, which he designed (1619–22), was equipped with machinery enabling the raising and lowering of whole scenes. After his conversion of the COCKPIT-IN-COURT he designed masques for texts by WILLIAM DAVENANT. His last great architectural project was the Masquing House at Whitehall (1637). A collection of his drawings and designs survives in Chatsworth House, Derbyshire. (See also THEATRE DESIGN.)

**Jones, James Earl** 1931– African-American actor. Son of the actor Robert Earl Jones, James Earl trained with LEE STRASBERG before making his 1958 BROADWAY debut in *Sunrise at Campobello*. He was unforgettable as the despised prizefighter Jack Jefferson in *The Great White Hope* (1968). An actor of magnetic physical presence and vocal power, he appears frequently in non-black roles. He has played King Lear, Macbeth, Coriolanus, Lopahin in *The Cherry Orchard* (1973), Hickey in *The Iceman Cometh* (1973) and Lenny in *Of Mice and Men* (1974). He gave a memorable performance in the monodrama *Paul Robeson* (1978), despite the controversy surrounding the production, and he won further acclaim for his Othello to CHRISTOPHER PLUMMER's Iago on Broadway in 1982. He has appeared in several of ATHOL FUGARD's South African plays under the direction of Lloyd Richards. In 1987 he was acclaimed in AUGUST WILSON's *Fences*.

**Jones, Joseph S(tevens)** 1809–77 American actor, manager and playwright. Beginning with *The Liberty Tree* (1832), he wrote about 150 plays, infusing his heroes with the qualities of individuality, personal conviction and freedom of spirit that identified Jacksonian America. For GEORGE HANDEL HILL he wrote *The Green Mountain Boy* (1833) and *The People's Lawyer* (1839), a favourite with several Yankee actors. MELODRAMAS such as *The Surgeon of Paris* (1838) and *The Carpenter of Rouen* (1840) were popular, but his most lasting play was *The Silver Spoon* (1852) in which WILLIAM WARREN THE YOUNGER acted until 1883. A professional man of the theatre, associated largely with Boston, he supported COPYRIGHT protection and adequate recompense for playwrights.

**Jones, Margo** [Margaret] **(Virginia)** 1913–55 American director and producer. In the 1940s she directed several BROADWAY successes and from 1947 until her death managed a theatre in Dallas, Texas, dedicated to the production of new plays. During its 12 seasons 133 plays were presented, 86 of which were new, including INGE's *The Dark at the Top of the Stairs*, TENNESSEE WILLIAMS's *Summer and Smoke* and LAWRENCE AND LEE's *Inherit the Wind*. Jones's theatre became the most celebrated home of arena staging in the United States and a pioneer in the decentralization of the American theatre.

**Jones, Robert Edmond** 1887–1954 American set and COSTUME designer. Jones's 1915 design for *The Man Who Married a Dumb Wife*, directed by HARLEY GRANVILLE BARKER, is considered the beginning of the New Stagecraft in America. Rebelling against the romantic realism of DAVID BELASCO and other producers of the late 19th century, Jones evolved a style of simplified sets that were suggestive, rather than a reproduction of the real world. Influenced by the work of MAX REINHARDT at the DEUTSCHES THEATER, he advocated a style of design that elicited an underlying feeling for the play and revealed his appreciation for the power of symbolic or emblematic elements. For director ARTHUR HOPKINS he designed the sets for several SHAKESPEARE plays in the early 1920s, employing unit sets – then, virtually unknown – and a strong use of light and shadow in the style of APPIA. For *Macbeth*, the three witches were portrayed by three large masks hanging over the stage. Jones was also an early member of the PROVINCETOWN PLAYERS, and designed most of EUGENE O'NEILL's plays including *Anna Christie*, *The Great God Brown* and *Mourning Becomes Electra*. From 1923 to 1929 he served as a producer with Kenneth MacGowan and O'Neill of the Experimental Theatre, Inc. – the successor to the Provincetown. His book *The Dramatic Imagination*, in which he expressed his visionary ideas, made him an inspiration to theatre artists in the next generation.

*jongleur* see JUGGLER

**Jonkonnu** Jamaican Christmas custom. Since the 18th century records show costumed characters such as Cow Head, Horse Head, Jack-in-the-Green, Actor Boy, Devil, Policeman and Belly Woman processing through the streets accompanied by 'fife and drum music'. The actors, all male, do not remove their masks in public. The custom appears to be a synthesis of European mumming and West African masquerade.

**Jonson, Ben(jamin)** 1572–1637 British playwright, poet and actor. Born and educated in Westminster, Jonson may have worked with his stepfather, a master bricklayer, before serving as a mercenary in Flanders. HENSLOWE's *Diary* reveals that by 1597 he was employed as both actor and writer. Jonson's earliest surviving play is *The Case Is Altered* (c.1597). *Every Man in His Humour* (1598, SEE COMEDY OF HUMOURS) turned him into a celebrity and was followed, less successfully, by *Every Man out of His Humour* (1599) and *Cynthia's Revels* (1600), satirical comedies which displayed his classical scholarship and his delight in formal experiment. He contributed *The Poetaster* (1601) to the 'war of the theatres'. His next play, the classical tragedy *Sejanus, His Fall* (1603), brought charges of 'popery and treason'. Always controversial – he had been imprisoned in 1597 over the *Isle of Dogs*, co-authored with THOMAS NASHE, and in 1598 was arrested for killing the actor GABRIEL SPENCER in a duel – he was briefly imprisoned in 1604, when the anti-Scottish jokes of *Eastward Ho*, written in collaboration with CHAPMAN and MARSTON, offended James I. In 1605 he began a long association with the Stuart court by collaborating with the designer INIGO JONES on *The Masque of Blackness*. Jonson's MASQUES are far more numerous than his plays. For *The Masque of Queens* (1609) he introduced the discordant anti-masque, an exuberantly grotesque feature of his subsequent masques.

Jonson's enduring reputation is based on his comedies: *Volpone* (1605), *Epicoene: or, The Silent Woman* (1609), *The Alchemist* (1610) and *Bartholomew Fair* (1614). In these plays, peopled with deceivers and dupes, his stagecraft is at its most brilliant. The comparative failure of *The Devil Is an Ass* (1616) may have discouraged him. *The Staple of News* (1625), *The New Inn* (1629) and *A Tale of a Tub* (1633) completed his dramatic output. Jonson's belief in his talent is represented by the unprecedented publication, in folio, of his dramatic and poetic *Works* (1616) and by his provision of masques for the Stuart court, for which he was rewarded with a royal pension and appointment as Poet Laureate. *Epigrams* and *The Forrest* (both 1616) and *Underwoods* (1640) were poetic publications. His classical prose style is recalled in the published notes of William Drummond of Hawthornden (1632), based on conversations held during Jonson's visit to Scotland in 1618–19. He was buried at Westminster Abbey.

**Jordan [née Bland], Dorothy** 1761–1816 British actress. She acted with JOHN PHILIP KEMBLE at Dublin's Smock Alley Theatre in 1781–2, came to England, was hired by TATE WILKINSON, reached the London theatres by 1785 and became a huge success in BREECHES PARTS and hoyden roles like Peggy in GARRICK's *The Country Girl* and Priscilla Tomboy in *The Romp*. She became mistress of the Duke of Clarence, had ten children and continued to star successfully, even though, as HAZLITT commented, 'her person was large, soft and generous like her soul'. She was highly praised as Viola and Ophelia, particularly for her delivery of verse.

**Joris, Charles** 1935– Swiss director and actor. In 1961 he founded the Théâtre Populaire Romand, the first professional French-speaking theatre ensemble in Switzerland. The TPR tours all linguistic regions of the country and neighbouring France, producing mostly Swiss or world premieres. The scenography is highly inventive and relies on sophisticated acting skills (ACROBATICS, free improvisation). In 1975 Joris was awarded the Reinhart-Ring, the highest Swiss distinction for work in the theatre. In 1993, to mark the bicentenary of GOLDONI's death the TPR collaborated with the Piccolo Teatro of Milan (see STREHLER) to great public acclaim.

**Joseph, Stephen** 1927–67 British director. He was the pioneer of theatre-in-the-round in England. Son of actress Hermione Gingold and publisher Michael Joseph, he founded, in 1955, the Studio Theatre Company in Scarborough with which he toured the atreless towns in the North of England for several years, exploring at the same time the potential for performances 'in the round'. With minimal financial support he set up the country's first permanent such theatre in Stoke-on-Trent in 1962 as a home for his company, the VICTORIA THEATRE. He also wrote books about theatre, and was Fellow of the newly created drama department of Manchester University from 1961. The Stephen Joseph Theatre in the Round at Scarborough was opened in 1976 as a memorial to his work.

**Jouvet, Louis** 1887–1951 French actor and director. Jouvet joined COPEAU's first company at the VIEUX-COLOMBIER as technical and lighting director, only gradually revealing his qualities as a star actor. In 1922 he founded his own company and in 1923 scored a hit with *Dr Knock, or The Triumph of Medicine* by JULES ROMAINS. In 1927 he was a co-founder of the CARTEL and in 1928 he produced the first of a sequence of plays by GIRAUDOUX. When the Popular Front government offered him the directorship of the COMÉDIE-FRANÇAISE he suggested instead a group of directors. After the war years he produced Giraudoux's last play, *The Madwoman of Chaillot* (1945), and GENET's first, *The Maids* (1947). He died while working on SARTRE's *The Devil and the Good Lord* in 1951. From 1934 he often worked with the designer CHRISTIAN BÉRARD, whose picturesque style fitted Jouvet's theatrical performances.

**Juana Inés de la Cruz, Sor** 1651–95 Mexican playwright and poet. Her essays and plays rivalled the European masters in quality. Her theatre corresponds to the cycle of CALDERÓN DE LA BARCA. *El divino Narciso* (*The Divine Narcissus*, c.1680) was a prime example of the *AUTO SACRAMENTAL* destined for the festivities of CORPUS CHRISTI. *Amor es más laberinto* (*Love Is a Greater Labyrinth*, c.1668) was a typical cloak-and-dagger play, and *Los empeños de una casa* (*The Obligations of a Household*, c.1680) parodied the title of Calderón de la Barca's play, *Los empeños de un acaso* (*The Obligations of Chance*). A long-lost Sor Juana manuscript was discovered in Mexican archives in the late 1980s.

**Judic [Anne-Marie-Louise Damiens]** 1850–1911 French actress and singer. She was an immediate hit at her music-hall debut (see CAFÉ CHANTANT) at the Paris Eldorado in 1869, because of her superb diction and talent for innuendo, which won her the nickname 'the School for Mimes'. Later she made a brilliant career in comic opera, especially in Offenbach, touring the United States. Her last appearance as a singer was at the FOLIES-BERGÈRE in 1900.

**juggler** Person skilled in the art of balancing, tossing and catching objects in different rhythms. This may be the oldest performance skill, known in ancient Egypt, Assyria, China, Greece and Rome. Roman jugglers were usually denominated by their specialities, as *ventilatores* (knife throwers) and *pilarii* (ball players), whereas the medieval Latin term *joculator* referred more broadly to the lower level of strolling entertainer. Hence its derivatives, 'juggler' in English, *jongleur* in French, *giullare* in Italian and *Gaukler* in German, bore pejorative connotations, suggesting deception for criminal purposes. The Spanish *malabarista* came to mean an illusionist who also juggles. The first named juggler was Pierre Gringore (1475–?).

On the 19th- and 20th-century VARIETY stage a distinction is made between strength jugglers and salon jugglers. The former juggle heavy objects, including human beings, occasionally work on horseback or unicycle, and catch cannon balls on the backs of their necks; the most celebrated have been Karl Rappo (1800–54), Paul Conchas (Huett, died 1916) and John Holtum (1845–?). The latter juggle billiard balls, cigar boxes, diabolos and similar paraphernalia, sometimes with their mouths; among the most adroit have been PAUL CINQUEVALLI, ENRICO RASTELLI, Kara (Michael Steiner, 1867–1939) and W. C. FIELDS. The Flying Karamazov Brothers have introduced comic juggling into stagings of classic works, such as *The Comedy of Errors*.

Once a staple in the repertory of every itinerant performer, juggling is now a common item in the curriculum of drama schools, used to train in agility and coordination.

**Julia, Raul** 1940–94 American film and stage actor, born in Puerto Rico. His New York debut was as Astolfo in CALDERÓN DE LA BARCA's *Life Is a Dream* in Spanish. He was an actor of striking looks and versatility, whose principal stage appearances included classical roles at the Delacorte and the VIVIAN BEAUMONT in New York. In 1982 he starred in *Nine* as Guido Contini. His performances in *The Threepenny Opera* (1976), *Where's Charley?* (1974) and *Two Gentlemen of Verona* (1971) were also acclaimed, although his Macbeth at the NEW YORK

SHAKESPEARE FESTIVAL (1990) was largely unsuccessful. He was seen as Don Quixote in a national tour of the musical *Man of La Mancha* in 1991.

**Juvarra, Filippo** 1676–1736 Italian architect and scene designer. In 1706 he became assistant designer at the San Bartolomeo opera house in Naples. He adopted the use of angled perspective, or SCENA PER ANGOLO. From 1708 to 1714 he designed and built the theatre at the Palazzo della Cancelleria and created the scenic effects for its productions. In 1713 he also designed elaborate opera sets for the private theatres of both Prince Capricanica and the queen of Poland. By 1714 he became chief architect at the Savoy court in Turin. His style is characterized by the use of curvilinear settings which draw the observer's eye in a circle and then to the foreground. The effect is accomplished with the use of free-standing units and a permanent foreground with changing vistas, depicting tropical foliage and Eastern architecture.

**juvenile drama** SEE TOY THEATRE

**kabuki** Japanese theatre form. The most important urban Japanese genre from its beginnings c.1600 until the early 20th century, *kabuki* means unorthodox, strange, new. Because it depended on a popular audience, it was always up-to-date, adapting its plays, music, dance, acting and staging styles to the taste of the times. Throughout *kabuki* history, plays and performing techniques have been borrowed from NŌ, KYŌGEN and BUNRAKU. The ideal performer was one who carried on the acting traditions of his family, while adding his own creativity to that style. Only within the past half-century or so has *kabuki* become a 'classical' theatre, repeating a known repertory in a relatively fixed fashion.

*Kabuki* has many musical styles to match its many styles of drama and performance. Today, percussion, lute players and singers are its basic musical components. The bravura acting style of heroic figures (*aragoto*), developed by the ICHIKAWA DANJŪRŌ acting family of Tokyo, is often considered synonymous with *kabuki*. The exaggerated costumes and properties and the bold red and black lines of make-up of this style are familiar through wood-block portraits of actors. Yet other styles are equally important. Comic-erotic acting (*wagoto*) is appropriate for playing the gentle good-for-nothing heroes of the domestic plays of the Kyoto-Osaka area. Both *aragoto* and *wagoto* acting may occur in the same play, balancing each other. When puppet plays were brought into the *kabuki* repertory, actors mimicked the actions of the puppets; in dance plays actors may move stiffly, like puppets, for comic effect. The overall style of dance in *kabuki*, called *shosa* – showing-the-body – fuses rural and urban dances of the common people, characterized originally by lively leaping, and dancing. Actors of female roles (*onnagata*) developed over three centuries a highly stylized art that suggests femininity but is wholly unlike a flesh-and-blood woman. The *onnagata* is a 'third sex' in which the strength of a man and the delicacy of a woman are fused (see FEMALE IMPERSONATION).

A *kabuki* performance is structured to provide constantly evolving moods and emotional states over time. The annual season consisted of six productions, and the nature of the play matched the season: love in spring, martial vigour on Boys' Day (5th month), lament for the spirits of the dead in the summer, for example. Major changes have occurred in staging *kabuki* during the 20th century. Cavernous new theatres have been constructed, modelled in part on European opera houses. Their auditoriums and stages were as much as three times the size of the traditional theatre, an oblong box in which actors and audience were part of the same space. As a result, the actor, who used to stand out on the traditional small *kabuki* stage, is dwarfed by the theatre's dimensions; acres of painted scenery fill the stage and compete with the actor for attention. The transformation of *kabuki* from a plebeian, popular, even despised, theatre into a classic art has been accompanied by the phenomenon of gigantism in theatre architecture.

**Kachalov** [Shverubovich], **Vasily (Ivanovich)** 1875–1948 Russian-Soviet actor. In 1900 he joined the MOSCOW ART THEATRE (MAT), where between then and 1948 he played 55 roles. He excelled at impersonating idealists and humanists, including the original Tuzenbach and Trofimov in *The Three Sisters* (1902) and *The Cherry Orchard* (1904), respectively, as well as the title role in CHEKHOV's *Ivanov* (1904); the Baron in the premiere of GORKY's *The Lower Depths* (1902) and Protasov in his *Children of the Sun* (1905); Julius Caesar in SHAKESPEARE's tragedy (1903); Chatsky in GRIBOEDOV's *Woe from Wit* (1906 and 1914); Don Juan in PUSHKIN's *The Stone Guest* (1915); IBSEN's Brand (1906); and Hamlet in the famous GORDON CRAIG–STANISLAVSKY collaboration (1912). He also appeared as the definitive thinking man, Ivan Karamazov, in NEMIROVICH-DANCHENKO's famous 1910 production of Dostoevsky's *The Brothers Karamazov*. Kachalov's career continued unabated after the October Revolution. He also appeared in the new Soviet drama, e.g. as Vershinin in VSEVOLOD IVANOV's *Armoured Train 14–69* (1927). In 1936 he was named a People's Artist of the USSR.

**Kainz, Josef** 1858–1910 Austrian actor. As a young man Kainz acted with the MEININGEN COMPANY (1877–80) and with the Munich Court Theatre (1880–83). He was hired in 1883 by ADOLF L'ARRONGE to become a founding member of the company of the DEUTSCHES THEATER, Berlin. Here his emotional interpretation of the title role in *Don Carlos* brought him national fame. Kainz remained the leading actor of the Deutsches Theater until 1899, when he joined the Vienna BURGTHEATER. Here he remained until his death. He was undoubtedly the most popular actor of his day, on account of his aristocratic appearance, his flexible and accurate voice, and his unusual physical dexterity. His technique has been described as 'impressionist', and in his day his acting was compared to that of SARAH BERNHARDT, COQUELIN and ELEONORA DUSE. A common feature in his interpretation of the tragic roles of SHAKESPEARE, GOETHE, SCHILLER and GRILLPARZER was his representation of them as victories of the human spirit over adversity, rather than defeats. During the last decade of his life, these interpretations became darker and his acting revealed reserves of violent passion in the characters. Most famous among his celebrated roles were Romeo, Hamlet, Mark Antony and Torquato Tasso, not to mention his masterpieces of comic characterization in the plays of MOLIÈRE and NESTROY.

**Kaiser, Georg** 1878–1945 German playwright. Kaiser wrote over 60 plays in a wide variety of styles and genres. After early satiric treatments of mythical and biblical subjects, he gained international recognition with *The Burghers of Calais* (1914, performed 1917), which celebrates anti-militarism and self-sacrifice. His modern MORALITY PLAY *From Morn to Midnight*, produced the same year, portrays the spiritual pilgrimage of a bank clerk. The action is dreamlike and distorted, and his suicide following the discovery that even religion has become corrupted is portrayed as a crucifixion. These elements had a decisive influence on later EXPRESSIONISM, and are extended in his most ambitious work, the trilogy of *Coral* (1917), *Gas I* (1918) and *Gas II* (1920). Here the expressionist 'new man' emerges, the son of the billionaire owner of a plant producing the gas that fuels modern industrialization and makes the dehumanizing of man possible. His rejection of the capitalist ethos reforms the father who represents it, but the succeeding plays dismiss the hope of meaningful change. The melodramatic plots, simplified characters and abstraction in this key expressionist work make the flaws of this dramatic style all too obvious. But thematically the work is also a rejection of the expressionist outlook, and by 1923 Kaiser had discarded its techniques.

**Kalidasa** 5th century AD Indian playwright. The most revered writer of classical SANSKRIT theatre, Kalidasa may have been court poet for King Chandragupta II of Ujjain in north central India during the mid-5th century AD. His most important work is the play *Sakuntala and the Ring of Recognition* (*Abhijnanasakuntala*), which has served as the ideal example of the *nataka* type of classical Sanskrit drama. He adheres to the classical rules without sacrificing his own artistic integrity, and his works emerge as some of the finest examples of Sanskrit poetry.

Kalidasa took liberties with the epic sources to suit his own particular needs. The plot of *Sakuntala* centres on King Dusyanta's infatuation and love for, then marriage, separation from and reunion with, Sakuntala, daughter of a heavenly nymph and a sage. The first three acts explore the delicate relationship between the king and the modest young maiden. After agreeing to marriage, Sakuntala prepares to follow her husband to the city to take up residence in his palace as his chief queen. On account of a seemingly minor offence to a saintly guest, on her arrival at court Sakuntala is punished by the king's forgetting who she is. Suffering from anguish, she is whisked away by a heavenly nymph and, up to the final act, the story revolves around the torments of the king whose memory is restored – only too late – to learn that Sakuntala has disappeared. Ultimately, fate intervenes and the king finds her; she has given birth to a handsome son, his only child, who bears the marks of royalty. Dusyanta identifies the child as his and experiences a tearful but happy reunion.

**Kamban, Gudmundur** 1888–1945 Icelandic playwright and director. Like SIGURJÓNSSON he wanted to break the isolation of Icelandic literature, writing mostly in Danish, although his best plays, *Marble* (1918) and *We Murderers* (1920), are set in New York. His neoromantic *Hadda-Padda* (1914) made his name in Iceland and Denmark. Mainly treating modern urban society, Kamban frequently deals with moral dilemmas, e.g. the question of Western legislation regarding crime and punishment. Another important play is the historical tragedy *Skálholt* (1934). An active director in Copenhagen and Germany during the 1920s, he staged his own work as well as plays by BJÖRNSTJERNE BJÖRNSON, Knut Hamsun and others. He was the first Icelandic film director. His plays are still performed in Iceland.

**Kamińska, Esther (Rachel)** 1862–1930 and **Ida Kamińska** 1899–1980 Polish actresses. Variously known as 'the Jewish DUSE' and 'mother of the YIDDISH THEATRE', Esther Kamińska began as an actress in 1892 and achieved fame particularly in the fine series of female roles in JACOB GORDIN's plays, her most notable being that of *Mirele Efros*, with her young daughter Ida playing her stage daughter. In 1921 the Warsaw Yiddish Art Theatre (VYKT) was formed by the Kamińska family. In 1950 the Polish Jewish State Theatre was founded, housed in the specially built E. R. Kamińska Theatre in Warsaw; Ida Kamińska was its artistic director until her death.

**Kamiriithu** (Kenya) The aim of the Kamiriithu Community Educational and Cultural Centre at Limuru was 'integrated rural development'; it was set up in 1976 by disillusioned workers and peasants in collaboration with NGUGI WA THIONG'O, Ngugi wa Mirii, an educationist, and other intellectuals. The collaborative production of *I'll Marry When I Want* (1977) was a powerful attack on the betrayal of the Kenyan masses by local *comprador* classes and their alliance with exploitative 'foreign interests'. The play was banned and Ngugi wa Thiong'o detained. A year later he returned to Kamiriithu and they performed *Maitu Njugira* (*Mother Sing To Me*), about the resistance to colonial oppression of the various Kenyan nationalities. The authorities closed the centre, but the Kamiriithu experience had become an inspiration to artists and cultural workers in neo-colonial African countries.

**Kantor, Tadeusz** 1915–90 Polish scene designer and director. A graduate of the Cracow Academy of Fine Arts, during the Nazi occupation he founded the underground Independent Theatre, staging SŁOWACKI's *Balladyna* (1943) and WYSPIAŃSKI's *Return of Odysseus* (1944). After the war he created avant-garde stage designs for the Teatr Stary in Cracow, including *Saint Joan* (1956), and for the Teatr Ludowy in Nowa Huta, notably *Measure for Measure* (1956). Dissatisfied with institutionalized avant-garde, he organized his own theatre in 1956 with a group of visual artists, calling it Cricot II, to mark continuity with the painters' theatre Cricot of the 1930s. In the 1960s Kantor produced happenings, exhibited widely, and travelled with his company, creating an autonomous theatre in which actors are used as props and manikins, and the text (usually by WITKIEWICZ) exists as an object, one component of the production. In the 1970s he developed 'the Theatre of Death', where time, memory and the interpenetration of life and death hold sway, and Kantor himself appeared as a master of ceremonies at the seance. Major productions were *The Cuttlefish* (1956), *In a Small Country House* (1961), *The Madman and the Nun* (1963), *The Water Hen* (1968), *The Green Pill* (1973), *The Dead Class* (1975), *Wielopole, Wielopole* (1980, created in Florence), *Where Are the Snows of Yesteryear?* (1982), *Let the Artists Die* (1985, created in Nuremberg), *I Shall Never Return* (1988) and *Today Is my Birthday* (1990).

**Kanze Hisao** 1924–78 Japanese actor. The finest NŌ actor of the post-World War II era, he was named an Important Intangible Cultural Asset. Born into nō, he was trained by his grandfather and studied with JEAN-LOUIS BARRAULT in Paris. He brought new vitality to his performances of traditional plays, *The Fulling Block*, *The Feather Robe* and *Komachi on the Stupa*. He also acted in significant experimental productions: in SUZUKI TADASHI's *The Trojan Women* (1974), as PIERROT in Takechi Tetsuji's *Moonstruck Pierrot* (1955), leading roles in four productions of Yokomichi Mario's adaptation of YEATS's *At the Hawk's Well* (1967–71), and as Oedipus in a 1971 production of the Dark Group (Mei no Kai) of which he was co-founder, with two KYŌGEN actors.

**Kapnist, Vasily (Vasilievich)** 1757–1823 Ukrainian playwright and poet. His satirical play *Chicanery* (1793) was the only 18th-century Russian COMEDY to approach FONVIZIN's work in skill and ferocity. Its tone is suggestive of GRIBOEDOV's later *Woe from Wit* and its subject, judicial corruption in a provincial town, foreshadows

GOGOL's *The Inspector General*. Kapnist's play was refused permission for production and publication until after the death of Catherine the Great (1798), when it was performed for a brief time before being removed from the repertoire. It was subsequently revived. Kapnist also translated MOLIÈRE's *Sganarelle* (1780, revised 1806).

**Karagöz** [Karaghioz, Karagheuz, Kara-Goze] Oriental puppet. The name in Turkish literally means Dark Eyes. He is the comic character in Oriental shadow-plays of Turkish origin, *karagöz*, said to have been invented by a sheikh Kishteri. An entertainer named Karagöz may have lived in the 13th century, but from the mid-17th century the characterization was heavily influenced by Persian and Chinese puppet plays (see PUPPETS). Karagöz is the quick-witted, impudent young roisterer, endowed with a huge phallus, who is constantly misconstruing Hacivat (Hadj'Iwâz), the older, more pretentious show-off, and his wife Lachampiyya, in a series of bawdy, scatological dialogues. Secondary characters, usually racial stereotypes, were added later. The *karagöz* plays (see MIDDLE EAST AND NORTH AFRICA) were first performed only at nightfall during Ramadan in coffee-houses. They greatly influenced puppet drama throughout the Islamic world: in North Africa Karagöz pops up as Karagush or Karogheuz, a kind of priapic picaroon with a flexible leather member. The Greek version Karaghiosis emerged from the 1821 revolution as an exemplary spokesman for freedom and morality, who travelled the countryside accompanied by musicians.

**Karatygin, Vasily (Andreevich)** 1802–53 Russian tragedian. His declamatory approach to acting created a coldly technical and unsurprising, if often heroic, impression. His handsome figure and basso voice suited the neoclassical, melodramatic and historical-patriotic roles he was mostly called upon to play in the works of OZEROV, KUKOLNIK and POLEVOI. Karatygin was the original Chatsky in GRIBOEDOV's *Woe from Wit* (1831), Don Juan and the Baron in PUSHKIN's 'little tragedies', *The Stone Guest* (1847) and *The Covetous Knight* (1852), respectively, and Arbenin in LERMONTOV's *Masquerade* (1852). His wife, A. M. Kolosova, was a noted actress.

**Kartún, Mauricio** 1946– Argentine playwright, with some notable successes in recent years. After *Gente muy así* (*People Like That*, 1976), *El hambre da para todo* (*Hunger for Everything*, 1978) and *Chau Misterix* (1980) he wrote *Pericones* (*Dances*, 1987), which presents a political intertext from the 19th century. *El partener* (*The Partner*, 1980) depends upon the tragicomic Argentine tradition of the *sainete criollo* (Creole FARCE) to consider the loss of family values in contemporary society.

**Kasper** [Kasperl, Kasperle] Viennese clown. The CLOWN of the old Viennese folk comedy, Kasper became the PUNCH of the Austro-German puppet play (see PUPPETS). He was originally created by stout Johann Laroche (1745–1806), leading player at the Leopoldstadt Theatre, Vienna, from 1781; for 40 years, audiences rejoiced to hear his beery voice call 'Auwedl' ('Deary me') from the wings. When Metternich forbade the good-natured dunce to speak, he cultivated his pantoMIME, giving rise to the Viennese expression 'To laugh as if you were watching Kasperl'. The name was adopted by a hand-puppet who wielded a wooden bat. In Munich there was an attempt to refine the dialect-speaking figure into the more literary Kasper Larifari, and early-20th-century educators used Kasperl as a spokesman for programmes of enlightenment. In the late 1920s, Max Jacob (1888–1967) developed a sardonic Kasperl, a displaced person given to officious preachments. The most popular puppet in the German-speaking world, Kasper has become a standard term for any puppet.

**Kataev, Valentin (Petrovich)** 1897–1986 Soviet playwright and novelist. A survivor of Stalinism, he is best known for his upbeat romantic social comedy of the New Economic Policy period, *Squaring the Circle* (1928), a tale of mismatched newly-wed couples – one staunchly communist, the other quasi-bourgeois – thrown together in a Soviet housing shortage, who eventually swap mates. It premiered at the MOSCOW ART THEATRE under NEMIROVICH-DANCHENKO's direction and played successfully in New York and London. Most of his comedies, *vaudevilles* and adaptations are characterized by a generosity of spirit combined with acute SATIRE. *The Embezzlers* (1928), from his best-known novel, is an NEP adventure story with satirical overtones. *The Vanguard* (1930) is one of the first plays about collectivization. A *Lonely White Sail* (1937), describing the picaresque adventures of two young boys during the 1905 Revolution, was adapted from his novel (1936). Along with the wartime dramas *The Soldier at the Front* (1937), *The Blue Scarf* (1943) and *Son of the Regiment* (1945), it reflects the author's sensitivity to young adults, children and sentimental themes. The drama *Time Forward!* (1932) optimistically posits its theme of social progress through industrialization. Kataev was one of the few Soviet writers who successfully and acceptably coaxed comedy and even farce from sobering reality.

*kathakali* Indian theatre form. The word means 'story play'. *Kathakali* is a kind of dance-drama popular in the state of Kerala, south India, which has gained a considerable international reputation in recent years for its vigorous masculine style of movement, bold superhuman characterizations and dance. This blend of dance, music and acting dramatizes stories, most of which are adaptations from the Indian epics – *Ramayana*, *Mahabharata* and the *Puranas*.

*Kathakali* emerged in the 17th century. The actors were originally Nairs, a caste of individuals trained in martial art techniques. Today, the actors hail from many different castes and communities. Actor training is a long and arduous process, often taking from six to ten years to complete, and a lifetime to achieve greatness. Stress is placed on eye and facial exercises, as well as mastery of an elaborate code of about 600 hand gestures. As part of the training, dance sequences that are suited to specific plays are taught and choreographic sections are committed to memory. The texts of the *kathakali* plays are learned by heart. Since the ideas of a play are conveyed by actors almost entirely through hand gestures and facial and body expressions, precision is crucial. The text is chanted by two singers who stand behind the actors and provide the basic tempo and rhythm of the music. The singers interweave their voices throughout the show and three chief drums accompany the entire dramatic action.

Any spot is considered appropriate for a *kathakali* performance, be it a temple compound, family home, large hall or proscenium arch stage. The atmosphere of a *kathakali* is charged with excitement, though the exact play may not be decided until several hours before the show begins, just in time for the actors quickly to put on the appropriate costumes and make-up. A show may include favourite scenes from various *kathakali* plays or it may be an entire play. Village performances begin in the late evening and conclude around 6 a.m., often with a band of enthusiastic devotees awake to the very end.

**kathputli** Indian puppet form. The string puppets of Rajasthan, India, are known as *kathaputli*. *Katha* means 'story' and *putli* means 'puppet'. These doll figures, seldom more than two feet tall, usually lack legs and feet because the lower part of their bodies is covered by a long, colourful skirt. They wear bright turbans and crowns, and painted beards and moustaches, to identify their social status. Women, too, have a special iconography. The puppeteers come from the Bhatt community and are known as *nat Bhatt* – 'those who perform plays'. They lead nomadic lives, travelling from village to village to entertain the public and earn a meagre livelihood. The troupes of puppeteers include musicians. Today, although *kathputli* is among the best-known of India's puppet forms, it has deteriorated to little more than a side-show, lasting barely an hour.

The plays' themes centre on the heroic deeds of Amar Singh Rathor, a Rajput warrior king, Prithvi Raj Chauhan of Ajmer and Delhi and King Vikramaditya of Ujjain. The lives of these famous individuals provide ample material for the puppeteers to demonstrate their expert skills, such as juggling, tumbling, horseback riding, swordsmanship and dancing.

**Katona, József** 1791–1830 Hungarian playwright. He wrote *Bánk Bán* (*The Viceroy*) in 1815 for a competition held by the theatre in Kolozsvár, which never acknowledged the play. Discouraged, Katona had it published in 1821, and wrote no more for the stage. He died without realizing that *Bánk Bán* would eventually be considered the greatest Hungarian play of the century. Set in 13th-century Hungary, this tragedy details the psychological undoing of Bánk, an honourable palatine, who is placed in a situation where his loyalties to his country, his king and his wife become irreconcilable. The 1845 production at the National Theatre made clear not only its dramatic merits, but also its political implications: the play treats the issue of foreign exploitation of the nation.

**Kaufman, George S(imon)** 1889–1961 American playwright and director. A founding father of the American popular theatre, Kaufman enjoyed a long and productive BROADWAY career. On his own he wrote only one play, a SATIRE of the theatre called *The Butter and Egg Man* (1925); in collaboration he wrote 40 plays, most of them certified hits. His partners included MARC CONNELLY (*Dulcy*, 1921, and *Beggar on Horseback*, 1924); Edna Ferber, Morrie Ryskind (including *Of Thee I Sing*, 1931) and MOSS HART (*Once in a Lifetime*, 1930; *You Can't Take It with You*, 1936; and *The Man Who Came to Dinner*, 1939). His speciality was dialogue, which he enlivened with witty, sarcastic rejoinders. He was a satirist of the New York theatre world, Hollywood, big business, politics and provincialism. He began his directing career in 1928 with a frenetic production of *The Front Page*. Like a terse Kaufman script, a Kaufman-directed show had remarkable precision. Swift timing was his trademark; he had no patience for analysis or introspection.

**Kawadwa, Byron** c.1940–77 Ugandan playwright. He founded Kampala City Players and the Uganda Schools Drama Festival and was director of the Uganda National Theatre from 1973 to 1977. He was a staunch royalist. His two most important works combine music and words, in collaboration with musician Wassanyi Serukenya: *Makula ga Kulabako* (1970) tells the love story of princess Kulabako and a commoner; *Oluimba lwa Wankoko* (*The Song of Mr Cock*, 1971), which is said to have caused Kawadwa's murder, concerns the attempt to oust the rightful heir by an ambitious politician.

**Kazan, Elia** 1909– American director. A member of the GROUP THEATRE and co-founder of the ACTORS STUDIO, Kazan has long been considered America's leading director of actors for both stage and film. His stage productions of *A Streetcar Named Desire* (1947), *Death of a Salesman* (1949), *Cat on a Hot Tin Roof* (1955) and *Sweet Bird of Youth* (1959), and his films *Streetcar* (1951), *On the Waterfront* (1954) and *East of Eden* (1955), have earned him the reputation of pre-eminent Method director whose highly strung, naturalistic performances are notable for the depth and intensity of their feeling. A Kazan-directed performance is notable too for its verbal stammers and backtracking, its emotional ambivalences and its sexual vibrancy. Based on STANISLAVSKY and on LEE STRASBERG, Kazan's method depends on personal contact with his actors. In 1964 he resigned from co-directorship of the VIVIAN BEAUMONT THEATRE.

**Kazantzákis, Nikos** 1884–1957 Greek playwright and novelist. Better known for his novels and the long epic *Odyssey* (a sequel to Homer), Kazantzákis was also a prolific author of plays, some of them in verse and most of them on subjects derived from Greek myth and history. *It Is Dawning* (1906) was passionately anti-conformist. The one-act tragedy *Comedy* (1908) has been likened to SARTRE's *Huis Clos* and BECKETT's *Waiting for Godot*. The *Master Builder* (1910) and all subsequent dramas show a Nietzschean influence with the Buddhist credo as a counterpoint: *Christ* (1921), *Odysseus* (1922), *Nikiphóros Phokás* (1927), *Mélissa* (1937), *Julian the Apostate* (1939), *Prometheus* (1943), *Capodistria* (1944), *Sodom and Gomorrah* (1948), *Koúros* (1949), *Christopher Columbus* (1949), *Constantine Paleológhos* (1951) and *Buddha* (1922–56). Kazantzákis wrote his dramas with little attention to the practicalities of the stage and, stressing their poetic and philosophic elements, tackling important existential issues.

**Kean, Charles** 1811–68 English actor and theatre manager. His parentage – he was the son of EDMUND KEAN – combined with an Eton education made him a gentlemanly actor and a pedagogic manager. His name helped to sustain him in Britain and on American tours before he became manager of the PRINCESS'S THEATRE in 1850. With a judicious mixture of SHAKESPEARE, BYRON and BOUCICAULT, Kean made the Princess's a centre of fashion. Queen Victoria appointed him director of her private theatricals at Windsor in 1848. His productions of classical plays were meticulously researched: for *Macbeth* (1852) he sought advice on pre-Norman building from the architectural historian, George Godwin. Each production was accompanied by lengthy documentation of historical sources. He was the first person to deploy focused limelight effectively, and it is for the care he lavished on the look of his stage that Kean deserves to be remembered, rather than for his rather wooden acting.

**Kean, Edmund** 1789–1833 English actor. Kean embodied the spirit of the romantic movement at its most turbulent. The illegitimate son of a minor actress, small, wiry and swarthy, he was also a skilful acrobat and MIME artist, capable of playing the dumb HARLEQUIN as well as speaking roles in the stock companies (see STOCK COMPANY) of Irish and English towns and cities. After ten years as a struggling provincial actor, he was brought to London by ROBERT ELLISTON and made his debut at DRURY LANE as Shylock, playing the Jew as a monster of energetic evil (1814) – which marked a turning point in the fortunes of both theatre and actor. During the same season he added his finest role, Richard III, as well as Hamlet, Othello, Iago and Luke Frugal in MASSINGER's *The City Madam*. Evidently demonic passions were his forte.

Coleridge's famous observation that 'To see him act is like reading SHAKESPEARE by flashes of lightning' reveals Kean's reliance on the making of startling 'points' rather than on the sustained character study of a JOHN PHILIP KEMBLE. Those admired sudden shifts from high to low became mechanical only in his decline, which began all too soon. HAZLITT perceived a loss of concentration even during his second season at Drury Lane (1814–15), when he added a controversial Macbeth and an often inert Romeo to his Shakespearian roles as well as restoring the neglected *Richard II* to the stage. Timon (1816), King John (1818), Coriolanus (1819), Lear (1820), Cardinal Wolsey (1822), Posthumus in *Cymbeline* (1823) and a dismal fiasco as Henry V (1830) complete the catalogue of Kean's Drury Lane Shakespeare.

There were excesses of drink and sex behind the scenes and he was taken to court in January 1825 . He was forced to absent himself to the USA, and on returning was only intermittently fit to perform. He made his last appearance in March 1833, as Othello to the Iago of his son, CHARLES KEAN, but collapsed on stage and died a few weeks later. The supreme example of the charismatic actor, he had burned himself out by 1821.

**Keane, John B(rendan)** 1928– Irish playwright. Most of Keane's plays have been locally produced and revive the traditional Irish themes of land hunger, made marriages and emigration. The most notable are *Sive* (1959), *The Year of the Hiker* (1963), *The Field* (1966 – later filmed) and *Big Maggie* (1970; revived, New York, 1984). The enduring popularity of his plays led to critical re-evaluation, and in the 1970s the ABBEY, which originally rejected all but the uncharacteristically urban, English-set *Hut 42* (1962), belatedly staged major revivals.

**Keeley** [*née* Goward], **Mary Ann** 1806–99 British actress. Extremely popular in FARCE and low COMEDY, she achieved fame with her playing of below-stairs characters. Two of her most successful parts required MALE IMPERSONATION, the title roles in BUCKSTONE's *Jack Sheppard* (1839) and Edward Stirling's *The Fortunes of Smike* (1840). After her marriage to Robert Keeley (1793–1869), a round-faced comedian who specialized in FEMALE IMPERSONATION, they always acted together and were considered the safest 'draw' in the London theatre.

**Keene** [*née* Mary Frances Moss], **Laura** ?1826–1873 British-born American actress and manager. While facts about her origins, training and name are disputed, Laura Keene apparently made her London debut in 1851, a year before J. W. WALLACK hired her as leading lady for his company in New York. Her grace and charm as well as her comic ability endeared her to New York audiences in her favourite roles of Lady Teazle, Lady Gay Spanker and Beatrice in *Much Ado*. After touring Australia with young EDWIN BOOTH, in 1855 she returned to New York and opened her own Laura Keene Varieties Theatre. From 1856 to 1863 she managed and acted in her Laura Keene's New Theatre, which became known for its lavishly mounted comedies. She encouraged the production of new American plays and closely supervised an excellent company which included E.A.

SOTHERN, JOSEPH JEFFERSON III and Agnes Robertson. She was performing in *Our American Cousin* at Ford's Theatre in Washington, DC, when President Lincoln was assassinated. During her career, she became closely identified with the emotional drama (e.g. *Camille*).

**Keith, B. F** see VAUDEVILLE

**Kellar, Harry** [Heinrich Keller] 1849–1922 American MAGICian. Kellar tended to appropriate and refashion tricks conceived by others. A master of publicity, he won fame with BUATIER DE KOLTA's 'Vanishing Birdcage'; from MASKELYNE he derived the disappearing act 'The Witch, the Sailor and the Monkey' and his supreme illusion 'The Levitation of the Princess Karnac' (1904). After touring the world in 1880, he resettled in the USA and was a popular success in Philadelphia and New York (1886–7). HOWARD THURSTON was his successor.

**Kelly, Fanny** [Frances] **(Maria)** 1790–1882 Anglo-Irish actress and singer. A regular member of the DRURY LANE company from 1810 to 1833, she played leads in musical pieces. Fanny Kelly owes her immortality to CHARLES LAMB, who wrote a famous essay about her under the deceiving title 'Barbara S—' and whom she refused to marry. She asserted the rights of women by promoting the all-female *Belles without Beaux* (1819). In 1833 she established a Theatre and Dramatic School at the Strand Theatre, boosting her income with a one-woman show. She was proud of such famous pupils as BOUCICAULT and MARY ANN KEELEY.

**Kelly, George E.** 1887–1974 American playwright. He began his career as an actor on the VAUDEVILLE circuit and had three major BROADWAY successes in the 1920s: *The Torchbearers* (1922), a SATIRE of LITTLE THEATRE enthusiasts; *The Show-Off* (1924), a battle between a commonsensical mother and braggart son-in-law; and *Craig's Wife* (1925), an exposure of an American ice maiden whose immaculate home is more important to her than her husband. Kelly insisted on directing each of his plays to preserve their distinctive rhythms. In later work such as *The Deep Mrs Sykes* (1945) and *The Fatal Weakness* (1946), he deliberately muted comic elements. His satires were designed to scold as well as to amuse; his targets were smug suburban matrons, untalented would-be actors and playwrights.

**Kelly, Hugh** 1739–77 Irish playwright. He moved to London in 1760 where his journalism included a SATIRE on actors, *Thespis* (1766). *False Delicacy* (1768) was more immediately popular than its rival, GOLDSMITH's *The Good Natured Man*. *A Word to the Wise* (1769) closed after riots against Kelly for being a government apologist. Though he was often damned as a writer of sentimental comedy, his plays, particularly his version of Molière's *The School for Wives* (1773), mock the absurd excesses of sentimentalism.

**Kemble, Charles** 1775–1854 English actor, the youngest brother of SARAH SIDDONS and JOHN PHILIP KEMBLE. His finest Shakespearian roles were Mercutio and Faulconbridge in *King John*, though, unlike his siblings, he was effective also in comedy – as Benedick, Orlando and Charles Surface in *The School for Scandal*. An intelligent actor, he rarely excited audiences. His reign as manager of COVENT GARDEN (1822–32) was uneasy, with rare triumphs such as the historically accurate *King John* (1823). His daughter FANNY KEMBLE's appearance as Juliet (1829) revived the theatre's fortunes, and they toured America with their favourite parts. Kemble was Examiner of Plays from 1836 to 1840.

**Kemble, Fanny** [Frances] **(Anne)** 1809–93 English

actress, daughter of CHARLES KEMBLE. More ambitious to write than to act, she made her debut as Juliet in 1829 in a bid to rescue her father from financial disaster at COVENT GARDEN. She performed many of the parts from the repertoire of her aunt, SARAH SIDDONS, in addition to Portia, Beatrice and Lady Teazle, and created the part of Julia in SHERIDAN KNOWLES's *The Hunchback* (1832). When the American tour with her father was over she married an American, separated and reluctantly returned to the English stage, where her Lady Macbeth to MACREADY's Macbeth (1848) was not a success. But from 1848 to 1874 she gave public readings from SHAKESPEARE, which became famous on both sides of the Atlantic.

**Kemble, John Philip** 1757–1823 English actor-manager. Son of a theatre manager, after training for the priesthood he became an actor in 1775. He made his London debut at DRURY LANE in 1783 as Hamlet, praised for his gentleness and aristocratic grace, though there were already signs of the eventual stiff technique and idiosyncratic pronunciation. In 1786 he published *Macbeth Reconsidered*, an erudite study of Macbeth's courage which defined his later approach to the role. In 1787 his performance as Lear was praised for its tremendous grandeur, while his Othello was too studied and insufficiently passionate. In 1788 he took over the management of Drury Lane, inaugurating a series of spectacular productions like *Henry VIII* and *Coriolanus*, with an original interest in antiquarian realism and a disciplined classicism. His noble acting style reached its peak with Roman roles such as Coriolanus. His limitations were obvious as Charles Surface in SHERIDAN's *The School for Scandal*, in which he was 'as merry as a funeral and as lively as an elephant'.

Kemble opened the new, large Drury Lane in 1794. In 1796 he moved to COVENT GARDEN with a repertory of classical and Shakespearian revivals. The theatre burned down and was rebuilt in 1809, but arguments about prices led to the Old Price Riots, which lasted 67 nights and left him disillusioned. EDMUND KEAN's triumphant debut in 1814 made him look old-fashioned. He retired from the stage in 1817. His adaptations of earlier plays were published as *British Theatre* in 1815. The greatest English classical actor, he created performances that were studied and lacking in spontaneity. Kemble is often regarded as progenitor of the director: his productions had aesthetic unity as well as atmospheric scenery.

**Kemp, Lindsay** 1939– British mime artist, choreographer, actor and director. He studied with Ballet Rambert and, in Paris, with MARCEL MARCEAU. During the 1960s he formed his own company but earned an income by staging outlandish 'happenings' and Soho strip shows. His MIME ballet *Flowers* (1974) toured widely and established his stage presence as a slow-moving, vulnerable coquette, surrounded by athletic male dancers, an image exaggerated in his version of OSCAR WILDE's *Salomé* (1977). He staged two ballets for the Ballet Rambert but later moved his company to Italy and Spain, though he has returned to stage productions at SADLER's WELLS, including *Alice* (1989), *A Midsummer Night's Dream* (1989) and *Onnagata, the Song of Orpheus* (1991). Kemp's blend of campness and kitsch can outrage his critics, but an instinct for beauty lies beneath his deliberate bad taste.

**Kempe** [Kemp], **Will(iam)** died c.1603 English CLOWN. Kempe was the popular successor to RICHARD TARLTON,

whom he may have replaced in the company of LEICESTER's MEN in 1583. He acted in France, the Netherlands and Denmark. After a period with STRANGE's MEN, he was a sharer in the newly formed LORD CHAMBERLAIN's MEN from 1594 to 1599. His JIG routines were popular, and in addition he played Peter in *Romeo and Juliet* and Dogberry in *Much Ado About Nothing*. It is a reasonable guess that he also featured as Lancelot Gobbo and Bottom in *The Merchant of Venice* and *A Midsummer Night's Dream*. Kempe left the Chamberlain's Men either just before or just after they had moved from the THEATRE to the GLOBE in 1599, then began a fantastic morris dance from London to Norwich, written up in his pamphlet, *Kempe's Nine Days Wonder* (1600). He joined Worcester's Men in 1601.

**Kempinski, Tom** 1938– British playwright. Born in London of Jewish parents, he was once an actor. Kempinski's first major success was *Duet for One* (1980), premiered at the BUSH THEATRE, in which his then wife, Frances de la Tour, played a concert violinist stricken with multiple sclerosis, attempting to cope with her illness through psychotherapy. Psychoanalysis features in his other plays, notably in *When the Past is Still to Come* (1992), an account of his own ten years in analysis, where he describes his struggle against fear, including his family memories of the Holocaust. He excels in intimate conversations between stricken individuals, as in *Self-Inflicted Wounds* (1985) and *Separation* (1987). He handles Freudian theory with insight, but his plays can seem sentimental to those not sharing his beliefs. When he has tried to broaden his range, as in *No Sex Please, We're Italian* (1991) the results have been unconvincing.

**Kendal, Madge** [Margaret Sholto Robertson] 1848–1935 British actress. The younger sister of T. W. ROBERTSON, she made her London debut in 1865, as Ophelia at the HAYMARKET. She established her reputation there in society comedy. She partnered W. H. Kendal (1843–1917), then married him in 1869, and they starred together in *The Rivals* (1870), *As You Like It* (1875), *She Stoops to Conquer* (1875) and in a sequence of W. S. GILBERT premieres and at the ROYAL COURT (1875–9). The Kendals were joint managers with JOHN HARE of the ST JAMES's from 1879 to 1888, where they were adventurous and prosperous. Kendal was less notable as an actress than as a theatrical *grande dame*. She was appointed DBE in 1926.

**Kennedy, Adrienne** 1931– African-American playwright. Kennedy blends symbols, historical figures, racial images and myths to create surreal, highly personalized one-act plays. *Funnyhouse of a Negro* (1964) depicts the final moments before the suicide of Sarah, a mulatto unable to reconcile herself to her mixed racial heritage. *The Owl Answers* (1969) portrays another mulatto woman caught in a hallucinatory nightmare of confused racial identity in which biographical and historical characters emerge, dissolve and metamorphose. Her other plays include *A Rat's Mass* (1966), a fantasy of war and prejudice; *In His Own Write* (1967), an adaptation of musician John Lennon's autobiographical writings; *A Movie Star Has to Star in Black and White* (1976) and *A Lancashire Lad* (1980), a children's play based on the early life of Charlie Chaplin.

**Kennedy, Charles Rann** 1871–1950 British-born American playwright. An ardent Christian, he helped bring the Social Gospel Movement to the American stage. In *The Servant in the House* (1907), his best-known play, he presented a Christ figure who reveals the hypocrisy of organized religion. Later plays include *The Idol Breaker* (1914) and *The Terrible Meek* (1912), a daring anti-war play.

**Kente, Gibson** 1932– South African playwright and director. In 1967 Kente became South Africa's first black independent producer of theatre, remaining unrivalled as a theatrical entrepreneur for the next quarter century, the leading exponent of the 'township musical'. As writer, choreographer, composer and director of all his productions, he ranges from plays with a political message, such as *How Long?* (1971), *I Believe* (1972) and *Too Late* (1973) to melodramas like *Hard Road* (1978), *Lobola* (1980) and *Mama and the Load* (1981).

**Kern, Jerome** 1885–1945 American composer. Kern began his theatrical career as a house composer for producer CHARLES FROHMAN in London. Returning to America, he was given his first opportunity to compose a complete score for *The Red Petticoat* (1912), followed by *Nobody Home* (Princess Theatre, 1915), which enchanted critics and audiences with its contemporary setting and lively score and gave rise to *Very Good Eddie* (1915). With librettist GUY BOLTON and lyricist P. G. WODEHOUSE, Kern created *Have a Heart* (1917), *Oh, Boy* (1917), *Leave It to Jane* (1917) and *Oh, Lady! Lady!* (1918). By replacing the mythical kingdoms and stilted language of European operetta with recognizable characters and situations and with American musical idioms, these shows influenced the direction in which American MUSICAL COMEDY was to evolve in the 1920s.

Kern again pioneered a new style of MUSICAL THEATRE with his score for *Show Boat* (1927), with book and lyrics by OSCAR HAMMERSTEIN II, proving that shows with serious librettos and songs that grew naturally out of the dramatic action could be successful. His shows of the 1930s, although containing many fine songs, were more traditional operettas and musical comedies.

**Kerr, Walter** 1913– American drama critic, playwright, teacher and director. From 1938 Kerr taught drama at Catholic University, Washington, DC, where he wrote and directed new scripts, four of which reached BROADWAY. With his wife Jean he collaborated on several shows including the MUSICAL COMEDY *Goldilocks* (1958). From 1951 to 1966 he was drama critic for the *New York Herald Tribune*, and then for the Sunday edition of the *New York Times* until his retirement in 1983. Regarded as the most perceptive critic reviewing the Broadway theatre during the 1960s and 1970s, Kerr brought intelligence, knowledge and a graceful style to his work. He believed that a play should be understood by an audience intuitively rather than intellectually, producing a 'single unified response'. His views are expressed in his several books on theatre.

**Kerz, Leo** 1912–76 German-American theatre and film set designer. Born in Berlin, Kerz studied with BERTOLT BRECHT and from 1927 worked as an assistant designer to ERWIN PISCATOR. These influences remained with him throughout his career, and his sets tended towards sweeping proportions and emblematic scenic elements. Like Piscator, he also incorporated film and projections into many of his designs. He left Berlin soon after Hitler assumed power and worked in London, Amsterdam and Prague before founding the Pioneer Theatre in Johannesburg. Kerz went to the USA in 1942 and made his BROADWAY debut in 1947 with the KATHARINE CORNELL production of *Antony and Cleopatra*. He is best known for his opera designs for the Metropolitan and New York City Operas, among others, and for his work at the ARENA STAGE from 1969 to 1971.

**Kessler, David** 1860–1920 Yiddish actor. Moldavian-born star of the American YIDDISH THEATRE and a leading exponent of the plays of JACOB GORDIN in America, he achieved such fame that in 1909 the Second Avenue Theatre was built for him. Amongst many notable roles were Yekel Boyle in Leon Kobrin's play of that name and Yekl Shapshovitch in *The God of Vengeance*.

**Khmelnitsky, Nikolai (Ivanovich)** 1789–1845 Russian playwright. An early skilled practitioner of *vaudeville* and *haute comédie*, he reacted against the moralizing tendency of Russian drama. Wit took precedence over didacticism in Khmelnitsky's plays, which were above all noteworthy for the native vitality of their dialogue; they advanced Russian comedy in the manner perfected by GRIBOEDOV. His works include *The Chatterbox* (1871), adapted from the comedy *Le Babillard* by Louis de Boissy; *Castles in the Air* (1818) and translations of MOLIÈRE's *School for Wives* (1821) and *Tartuffe* (1828).

**khyal** *[khyala]* Indian theatre form. This kind of village theatre is popular in the northern state of Uttar Pradesh and in the western state of Rajasthan. Various regional styles exist. *Khyal* stages are generally more elaborate than most village acting areas in north India, featuring a main stage, a subsidiary platform and a balcony-like structure erected on poles. Plays begin with prayers to Ganapati, the elephant-headed god, and include invocations to other gods and goddesses as well. This is followed by comic antics by clowns. The plays that are performed are mythological, semi-historical or fanciful. Male actors play all the roles. The accent is, typically, on melodrama, romance, valour and pathos. Like other rural theatre forms, the performances include musical accompaniment, here played on drums, bell-metal cymbals and the harmonium.

**Kiesler, Frederick** 1890–1965 Austrian-American architect and designer. Very little of Kiesler's visionary theatre was ever fully realized, yet his plans and projects exerted a strong influence on the development of mid-20th-century theatre architecture and on the emergence of environmental theatre. Most of his projects were variations on the so-called Endless Theatre – a futuristic theatre of ramps and spirals within an ellipsoidal shell projected to hold 10,000 or more spectators. His main concept was 'integrated space', allowing performance and spectators to blend. His more practical projects included flexible theatres capable of changing size and configuration, and 'space stages': non-scenic architectural stages. He was head of design for the 1924 Vienna Music and Theatre Festival. Other significant designs include *The Emperor Jones* (Berlin, 1923) and *Francisca* (Berlin and Vienna, 1925). He went to the United States in 1926 with the International Theatre Exhibit – the first look many Americans had at new European design – and stayed, but never achieved the prominence he had known in Europe. Despite many projects, the only significant theatre fully realized in the USA was the Eighth Street Cinema in New York (1930).

**Killigrew, Thomas** 1612–83 English playwright and theatre manager. Though lacking a formal education, he had established himself as a courtier by 1633. His first tragicomic romances were produced at the Phoenix (see COCKPIT THEATRE). His best play, *The Parson's Wedding* (c.1640), is a bawdy, energetic comedy. During the Interregnum he went into exile with the king, wrote c.1654 a romanticized dramatic semi-autobiography, *Thomaso the Wanderer*, and a number of unperformable closet dramas. In 1660, with DAVENANT, he secured a monopoly patent to set up the King's Company at a converted tennis court, using the patent to close down all other companies except Davenant's. Claiming descent for his company from the earlier King's Men, Killigrew took for it the rights to much of the earlier drama but failed to encourage new writers. In 1663 they moved to the Theatre Royal in Bridges Street. He established a nursery theatre (see NURSERIES) for the training of young actors in 1667. Innovative as a manager, Killigrew was financially unsuccessful and inefficient. He handed over management to his son Charles in 1671. He was MASTER OF THE REVELS from 1673 to 1677.

**Kilroy, Tom** [Thomas] 1934– Irish playwright and novelist. His novel *The Big Chapel* (1971) won a number of Irish and English awards, but outside his academic pursuits Kilroy has been primarily a dramatist: *The Death and Resurrection of Mr Roche*, a success at the 1968 DUBLIN INTERNATIONAL THEATRE FESTIVAL, then in London; *The O'Neill* (1969); *Tea and Sex and Shakespeare* (1976); *Talbot's Box* (1977); *Double Cross* (1986); *The Madam Macadam Travelling Theatre* (1991). In *Mr Roche* strange events permeate a seedy Dublin flat and an all-male drinking party with other-worldly anticipations. In *Talbot's Box*, kaleidoscopic, stylized scenes enact the life and agonized death of Matt Talbot, Dublin's 'workers' saint', searching the mystery of his frenzied devotion and its corruption by power-seekers. *Double Cross* uses two linked plays to explore questions of nationality and identity through the lives of contemporaries Brendan Bracken and William Joyce.

**Kim U-jin** 1897–1927 Korean director and playwright. Educated at Waseda University in Japan, in 1921 he led the Tongwuhoe Group and introduced realistic drama. The subjects of the plays produced by the Group were largely to do with the freedom of man and the principle of self-determination. He wrote five plays in which he experimented with REALISM, NATURALISM and EXPRESSIONISM - the first such attempt by a Korean playwright. The plays are about the conflict between old ethics and new ideas, and the suffering of women.

**King's Men** see LORD CHAMBERLAIN'S MEN

**Kingsley, Sidney** 1906–1995 American playwright. Kingsley made his reputation with realistic social MELODRAMAS. *Dead End* (1935), concerned with a group of slum kids in New York, was his most memorable success, but *Men in White* (1933), about a young doctor's experiences in a hospital, won him a Pulitzer Prize. His anti-war play, *Ten Million Ghosts* (1936), failed; *The Patriots* (1943), contrasting the political theories of Thomas Jefferson and Alexander Hamilton, was a weak effort. Forsaking propaganda for realistic and vivid melodrama, he wrote *Detective Story* (1949), featuring a conscientious police detective whose emotional involvement drives him to sadism, and a dramatization of Arthur Koestler's novel *Darkness at Noon* (1951). Later plays include a farce entitled *Lunatics and Lovers* (1954) and *Night Life* (1962), a murder melodrama with overtones of labour relations and politics.

**Kinoshita Junji** 1914– Japanese playwright. Arguably the most influential playwright of the postwar period, Kinoshita produced an eight-volume translation of SHAKESPEARE's works. An ambivalent Christian, he is deeply influenced by Hegelian theology and theory. Like ARTHUR MILLER, he reinvented tragedy in a modern idiom. In works spanning over two decades – from *Turbulent Times* (1939, rewritten 1947) to *A Japanese Named Otto* (1963) – an individual confronts history only to be simultaneously crushed and redeemed by it. Kinoshita has also written numerous 'folktale plays', the most famous of which is *Twilight Crane* (1949; translated 1956). The tension between his Christianity and his fascination with Japanese shamanism on the one hand and his Hegelian universalism and his sense of Japanese uniqueness on the other informs virtually all of his plays. A good example is *Between God and Man* (1970; translated 1979), a two-part work that approaches the problem of Japanese war crimes through the Tokyo War Crimes Tribunal in the first part and through the eyes of a SHAMAN in the second.

**Kipphardt, Heinar** 1922–82 German playwright. He pioneered documentary theatre with *In the Matter of J. Robert Oppenheimer* (1964), concerned with the creation of the nuclear bomb. It was developed for the stage by PISCATOR and set new standards for the objective treatment of factual material. It was followed by *Joel Brand, the Story of a Deal* (1965). The transaction in question was the Nazi proposal to exchange a million Jews for 10,000 trucks, turned down by the Allies. *Brother Eichmann* (1983) is a retrospective biography of a mass murderer, showing his attitudes to be commonplace.

**Kiralfy family** Hungarian dancers and impresarios. The three brothers **Imre** (1845–1919), **Arnold** (died 1908) and **Bolossy** (1848–1932) moved to New York with their sister **Haniola** (died 1889) as dancers in GEORGE W. L. FOX's *Hiccory Diccory Dock* (1869). They soon branched out on their own, staging lavish spectacles. Arnold and Bolossy built the Alhambra Palace in Philadelphia (1876). Imre produced *Around the World in 80 Days*, *The Fall of Babylon*, an open-air spectacular with 1,000 performers, and, with BARNUM, *Columbus* (1890) in the USA. He then settled in London, where his projects included *Venice in London* (1892), a refurbishment of the Earl's Court exhibition hall (1893), *India* (1896), the Victorian Era Exhibition (1897), the Military Exhibition (1901), *Paris in London* (1902) and the Coronation Exhibition (1912). The Kiralfy spectacles were distinguished by their magnificent deployment of extras and their innovative use of electricity.

**Kirshon, Vladimir (Mikhailovich)** 1902–38 Russian-Soviet playwright. Kirshon's staunch advocacy (along with AFINOGENOV) of social and psychological realism (as opposed to romantic monumentalism) as the basis for the new drama encountered strong opposition from playwrights VISHNEVSKY and POGODIN, and in official circles. His first major play, *Konstantin Terekhin* (co-written with Andrei Uspensky, 1926), which deals with the problems of post-revolutionary Soviet youth, was produced under the title *Red Rust* by New York's THEATRE GUILD (1929), with LEE STRASBERG, Luther Adler and Franchot Tone in the cast. His most important play, *Bread* (1930), deals with the suppression of the kulaks – the prosperous peasant class – during the years of the First Five Year Plan and warns against oversimplification and idealization in confronting social problems. His other plays include *The Rails Are Humming* (1927), one of the first Soviet dramas to portray heroic labour; *City of the Winds* (1929), a revolutionary drama from which he created the libretto for Lev Knipper's opera *Northern Wind* (1930); *The Court* (1932), concerning the Social

195

Democrats in Germany; *The Miraculous Alloy* (1934), a popular social comedy about youth; and *A Great Day* (1936), about life in the Soviet army. Kirshon was arrested and executed on a charge of Trotskyism during the Stalinist purge trials.

**Kishon, Ephraim** 1924– Israeli satirist and playwright. Born in Budapest, he survived the Holocaust, emigrated to Israel in 1949 without a word of Hebrew, and three years later produced his first Hebrew play, *His Name Goes before Him* (1952). He brought to the Hebrew stage a background of Central European culture and humour. For many years he wrote a daily satirical column. Kishon's plays and books have been widely translated and some have become international best-sellers, although he is less appreciated at home. Among his plays are *Black on White* (1955), on racism amongst mice; *The Marriage Contract* (1961); *Plug It Out, the Water's Boiling* (1966), an attack on modern art and its upholders; and *Oh, Julia* (1973), about Romeo and Julia in their forties. His play *Sallah Shabbati*, a spoof on the cultural misunderstandings between European oldtimers and new North African immigrants in the 1950s, was made into a successful film (1964) with TOPOL in the title role.

***kkoktu kaksi*** Korean PUPPET theatre. This traditional theatre depicts humans and animals. It is largely humorous, dealing with the corruption of Buddhist monks and with domestic problems, and satirizing immoral officials. The puppeteer manipulates a single puppet (*kkoktu*) at a time as he delivers lines and songs.

**Kleist, Heinrich von** 1777–1811 German playwright. In a brief life terminated by suicide, Kleist found neither acceptance in the military or civil service nor recognition as a writer. Today, however, his plays are regarded as being among the greatest achievements of a time when German culture was being enriched by both classicism and romanticism in art and literature. In fact they do not fit easily into either category. Although it failed when first staged by GOETHE at Weimar in 1808, *The Broken Jug* has since been accepted as one of the greatest comedies in the language, especially because of the Falstaffian central figure, the corrupt judge Adam. *Amphitryon* (1807) offers a striking example of romantic irony. Among the later plays, *Penthesilea* (1808) is a remarkable portrayal of sexual frenzy, while *Das Käthchen von Heilbronn* (1810) is a moving tale of love and devotion in a medieval environment. Kleist's final play, *The Prince of Homburg* (1811), is his masterpiece, in which he reveals his ambiguous response to Prussian militarism. Virtually unknown during his lifetime, his plays were later produced through the agency of, among others, LUDWIG TIECK.

**Kline, Kevin** 1947– American actor. As a founding member of the ACTING COMPANY, he played numerous roles including Charles Surface in *The School for Scandal*, Vaska Pepel in *The Lower Depths* (1972), Vershinin in *The Three Sisters*, MacHeath in *The Beggar's Opera* (1973) and Jamie Lockhart in *The Robber Bridegroom* (1975). Kline won recognition as Bruce Granit in *On the Twentieth Century* (1978) and as Paul in *Loose Ends* (1979), followed by critical acclaim as the Pirate King in *The Pirates of Penzance* (1980), which established him as a star, and as Bluntschli in a 1985 revival of *Arms and the Man*. Frank Rich (1981) thought that he had all the ingredients for conventional stardom – 'big voice, dashing good looks, infinite charm – and ... the grace and timing of a silent-movie clown'. In 1986 Kline played Hamlet at the NEW YORK SHAKESPEARE FESTIVAL. His recent film appearances include *The Big Chill* (1983), *A Fish Called Wanda* (1988) and *Grand Canyon* (1991).

**Klingemann, Ernst** 1777–1831 German director and playwright. Klingemann directed two theatres in Brunswick, including the Court Theatre. Here he staged the first performance of GOETHE's *Faust, Part 1* in January 1829. He was moderately successful as a playwright, writing his own stageworthy version of the Faust legend. His travel volumes *Art and Nature* (1819–29) are an invaluable source for the theatre historian.

**Klotz, Florence** c.1920– American COSTUME designer. Klotz, by her own admission, became involved in design almost by accident. Through the 1960s she designed several light contemporary comedies. In 1971 she teamed up with director HAROLD PRINCE to design *Follies*, which had 140 costumes ranging from rags to lavish show costumes spanning half a century. She subsequently designed several Prince–STEPHEN SONDHEIM musicals, each of a distinctly different style and period. Her costumes manage to combine contemporary sensibilities with period style.

**Knipper(-Chekhova), Olga (Leonardovna)** 1868–1959 Russian-Soviet actress. She joined the original company at the newly formed MOSCOW ART THEATRE (MAT) in 1898. In the premiere season she played Tsaritsa Irina in A. K. TOLSTOI's historical tragedy *Tsar Fyodor Ioannovich*, and the actress Arkadina in CHEKHOV's *The Seagull*. The latter led to a personal and professional association with Chekhov. She married him in 1901 and played leading roles in all his major plays staged at MAT: Elena Andreevna in *Uncle Vanya* (1899); Masha in *The Three Sisters* (1901); Anna Petrovna in *Ivanov* (1904); and Ranevskaya in *The Cherry Orchard* (1904). She was Nastya in the original MAT production of GORKY's *The Lower Depths* (1902) as well as Anna Andreevna in *The Inspector General* and Natalya Petrovna in TURGENEV's *A Month in the Country* (1909). She was named a People's Artist of the USSR in 1937.

**Knowles, (James) Sheridan** 1784–1862 Anglo-Irish playwright. Variously a doctor, actor, teacher and evangelical preacher (after 1844), he was considered in his time a rival to SHAKESPEARE. Almost forgotten today, Knowles's reputation was due to W. C. MACREADY, whose moving portrayal of suffering fatherhood in Knowles's *Virginius* (1820) brought the playwright into prominence. His blank-verse tragedies are too sentimental to survive 20th-century appraisal; the romances are more successful. They include *The Beggar's Daughter of Bethnal Green* (1828), revised as *The Beggar of Bethnal Green* (1834), and the understandably popular *The Hunchback* (1832). His comedies, *The Love-Chase* (1837) and *Old Maids* (1841), though entirely neglected because of Knowles's claims as a writer of tragedies, are much better.

**Knyazhnin, Yakov (Borisovich)** 1742–91 Russian playwright. He succeeded his father-in-law ALEKSEI SUMAROKOV as a writer of tragedy after the French neoclassical models of RACINE and VOLTAIRE. In 1783 he elected one of the 30 charter members of the Russian Academy. His seven tragedies, beginning with *Dido* (1769) and extending through to his best-known and most controversial plays, *Rosslav* (1784) and especially *Vadim of Novgorod* (1789), are characterized by intricate plotting and dramatic stage effects. *Vadim*, which contrasted the virtues of republicanism and monarchism, so threatened Catherine the Great in the wake of the French Revolution that she ordered it to be burned. The complete text was not published until 1914. Knyazhnin was far better as a writer of verse comedies (earlier Russian comedies were largely written in prose) which satirized the abuses of serfdom and the corrupt nobility's pursuit of title and rank. They include *The Unsuccessful Mediator* (1785), *The Braggart* (1786) and *The Odd Fellows* (1790). His comic operas are highly successful: *The Mead-Seller* (1784) and his best single work, *Misfortune from a Carriage* (written 1772, produced 1779), which offered SHCHEPKIN one of his earliest roles. Knyazhnin's popularity was eclipsed by the Russian romantic writers of the early 1880s.

**Koch, Heinrich Gottfried** 1703–75 German actor. He worked with CAROLINE NEUBER and JOHANN SCHÖNEMANN and took over the leadership of the Schönemann troupe when EKHOF was still a member. But the two had differences, especially over Koch's tendency to improvise, so Ekhof left to join the ACKERMANN troupe. Koch's troupe continued to travel in the Leipzig area until his death.

**Kochergin, Edvard (Stepanovich)** 1937– Soviet stage designer. Schooled under Soviet artists Bruni and AKIMOV, Kochergin became head of design of the Leningrad Theatre of Drama and Comedy in 1963. In 1966, he was appointed head designer of the Komissarzhevskaya Dramatic Theatre. He was later promoted to chief artist of the Gorky Theatre in Leningrad. Kochergin has refined a style which has been compared to GROTOWSKI's 'poor theatre' productions. His sparse, textured yet simple settings have been integral to such Gorky Theatre productions as *Hamlet* (1972), *Boris Godunov* (1973) and NIKOLAI GOGOL's *Notes of a Madman* (1978). His design for LYUBIMOV's *The Inspector's Recounting* (based upon Gogol's works) at the Taganka made use of a textured background, a huge piece of felt representing the famous overcoat of Gogol's Akaky Akakyevich, which is being stitched together on numerous machines operated by clerks. The felt contained openings through which performers could make sudden appearances. Kochergin's design for Dodin's Maly Dramatic Theatre production of *Brothers and Sisters* (1985) featured tall, thin poles resembling bare trees and an adjustable log platform which became a film screen on which were projected the Stalin era's idealized images of rural peasant life. Kochergin is generally considered to be one of Russia's greatest living scene designers.

**Kokoschka, Oskar** 1886–1980 Austrian painter and playwright. His works were the earliest examples of EXPRESSIONISM, with their direct externalization of subconscious states. *Sphinx and Strawman* (1907) became one of the influences for dadaist theatre, while *Murderer, the Hope of Women* (1907), staged in 1918 and 1919 and as an opera with music by Hindemith in 1922, was a forerunner of ARTAUD's Theatre of Cruelty.

***kolam*** Sri Lankan theatre form. *Kolam* is a kind of folk theatre that was once popular along the southern coastal region of Sri Lanka. It may have arisen as an ancient pregnancy rite, since, according to one of the dramas, a certain queen suffered from a pregnancy craving for dances and amusements. The Sinhalese word means either an appearance, an impersonation or an assumed guise – usually one that is comic and exaggerated so as to provoke laughter. Since full face masks are used to identify the various characters, *kolam* includes a wide range of at least 50 stock character types, many of whom are introduced through a ritual prologue and some of whom assume importance in the dramatic action which follows. The entrance of each character is highlighted by dances appropriate to his or her station in life. Among the characters that appear in the dramas are the king and the queen, the king's herald, his wife, a policeman, a washerman, the washerman's wife and a paramour, a village dignitary, plus various celestial beings, demons and animals. Despite the large range of possible characters which compose a drama, fewer than a dozen plays were written in the form.

**Koltai, Ralph** 1924– German-born British stage designer. He is noted for his bold imagery and conscious sense of style in the service of a production concept. Suggesting the art of sculpture and architecture, his designs usually centre on highly expressive forms and constructions that often employ untraditional scenic materials such as plexiglass, styrofoam, steel and fibreglass. Primarily a freelance designer with almost half of his work in opera, Koltai has also had extensive association with both the ROYAL SHAKESPEARE COMPANY and the NATIONAL THEATRE. From 1965 to 1973 he was head of the THEATRE DESIGN programme at London's Central School. Notable productions have included *Doctor Faustus* (1964), *Back to Methuselah* (1968), the opera *Taverner* (1972), WAGNER's *Ring* (1970–3), *Brand* (1978), *Much Ado About Nothing* (1982), *Othello* (1985) and *Metropolis* (1989). With a production of *The Flying Dutchman* in 1987, he began to direct as well as design.

**Koltès, Bernard-Marie** 1948–89 French playwright. PATRICE CHÉREAU produced all of Koltès's major plays at his Théâtre des Amandiers in the 1980s: *Combat de nègre et de chiens* (*Struggle of the Dogs and the Black*, 1983), *Quai ouest* (*Western Dock*, 1986), *Dans la solitude des champs de coton* (*In the Solitude of the Cotton Fields*, 1987) and *Le Retour au désert* (*Return to the Desert*, 1988 – this last at the Théâtre du Rond Point). His posthumous *Roberto Zucco* was first produced by PETER STEIN at the Berlin Schaubühne in 1990. Observing the classical unities and written in a sumptuous prose style, Koltès's plays are the most important body of new work to emerge in France in the 1980s.

**Komissarzhevskaya, Vera (Fyodorovna)** 1864–1910 Russian actress. A mystical, poetic performer, Komissarzhevskaya captured the restiveness and yearning of pre-revolutionary Russia's artistic elite. With her extreme nervousness, sensitivity and sincerity, she became the perfect icon for the Russian symbolists (see SYMBOLISM) and a useful conduit for MEYERHOLD's directorial ideas. The daughter of a noted opera tenor, she possessed a hypnotic, resonant voice.

By the time she joined St Petersburg's Aleksandrinsky Theatre company, she had appeared in well over 60 roles in two separate professional theatres, mostly as ingénues and in musical *vaudevilles*. At the Aleksandrinsky she originated the role of Nina in the disastrous first production of *The Seagull*. She was the only company member who appreciated the play and remained CHEKHOV's favourite interpreter of the role. She left this theatre in 1902 and after two years touring founded the Dramatic Theatre of V. F. Komissarzhevskaya in St Petersburg. It immediately became a haven for symbolist artists and progressive students. She appointed Meyerhold as the theatre's artistic director and played the title role in BRIUSOV's translation of MAETERLINCK's *Pelléas and Mélisande* (1907). Here, and as IBSEN's Hedda Gabler, she subordinated her talent to Meyerhold's master plan, which at this time called for extreme stylization, immobility and puppet-like actors intoning in strangely rhythmic cadences. In 1908 she replaced Meyerhold with EVREINOV and her half-brother, FYODOR KOMISSARZHEVSKY, in an effort to reclaim authority for the actor, but she continued to perform Meyerhold's symbolist play choices. She even approved Evreinov's frankly erotic production of WILDE's *Salomé* with Kalmakov's set design resembling huge female genitalia, which the Holy Synod banned in 1908. She closed the theatre in 1909 and died of small-pox soon after.

**Komissarzhevsky, Fyodor (Fyodorovich)** [Theodore Komisarjevsky] 1882–1954 Russian director, teacher and theorist. The half-brother of VERA KOMISSARZHEVSKAYA, he ran her theatre with EVREINOV following MEYERHOLD's dismissal (1908). From 1910 he worked in Moscow, staging productions of OSTROVSKY, MOLIÈRE and GOETHE at the Maly and at Nezlobin's Theatre. Between 1910 and 1918 he directed productions at his own studio. In his many opera productions at the Bolshoi Theatre and elsewhere – such as *The Golden Cockerel* (1917), *Lohengrin* (1918) and *Boris Godunov* (1918) – he tried to realize his concept of a cultured, synthetic theatre, philosophically romantic in tone, created around a universal actor-singer-dancer. In 1919 he emigrated and continued to design and direct 'synthetic' productions of classical dramas and operas in London, Stratford-upon-Avon, Rome, Paris, New York and Vienna; he also directed films in England and wrote books about theatre.

**Kong Shangren** 1648–1718 Chinese KUNQU playwright. An authority on ancient rites and music and a semi-recluse until his mid-thirties, between 1684 and 1699 he held a series of official posts following the Emperor's recognition of his talents and erudition. In 1699 he published his play *The Peach Blossom Fan (Taohua shan)*. A long piece in 40 scenes written in southern style, it is still considered a masterpiece of poetic composition by the Chinese today. It records the treachery and intrigue which facilitated the Manchu overthrow of the Ming dynasty in 1644. The characters are based on real personalities, and central to the theme is one of the great love stories of Chinese literature. The play won immediate popularity but resulted in the playwright's dismissal from office by the Manchu authorities. Kong was considered one of the two great masters of his day, the second being HONG SHENG.

**Kongelige Teater** (Copenhagen) Denmark's national theatre, located on Kongens Nytorv since 1748, comprises four related organizations, performing on several stages: the theatre company, the Royal Opera, the Royal Danish Ballet and the Royal Orchestra. Its present building dates from 1874; the recently restored Old Stage is used almost exclusively for opera and ballet, with spoken drama relegated to the adjacent New Stage and to studio theatres elsewhere in the city. The theatre company originated in the first Danish-speaking theatre founded in Lille Grønnegade street in 1722. Traditionally, a peak in its history was the mid-19th century, when a company of fine actors was assembled around the HEIBERGS. In the 20th century it has nurtured actors of undisputed genius such as Bodil Ipsen, POUL REUMERT, Bodil Kjer and MOGENS WIETH, and enjoyed a period of particular success under Peer Gregaard's management in 1966–75.

**Koonen, Alisa (Georgievna)** 1889–1974 Russian-Soviet actress. One of STANISLAVSKY's favourite pupils, Koonen made her acting debut at MOSCOW ART THEATRE in 1906 and performed with the company until 1913, when she left to join Mardzhanov's Free Theatre. She and her future husband TAIROV co-founded the Kamerny (Chamber) Theatre (1914), where Koonen played a series of spiritually strong women searching for love, freedom and self-realization, either at odds with social conventions and demands or in service to a new social ideal. These roles included Sakuntala (1914); Salome (1917); Adrienne Lecouvreur (1919 and 1949); Juliet (1921); Phèdre (1922); St Joan, HASENCLEVER's Antigone (1927); O'NEILL's Abbie and Ella in *Desire Under the Elms* (1926) and *All God's Chillun' Got Wings* (1929); the heroic commissar in VISHNEVSKY's *An Optimistic Tragedy*; Cleopatra in the compilation *Egyptian Nights* (1934); Madame Bovary in her own adaptation (1940); and Nina Zarechnaya in CHEKHOV's *The Seagull* (1944). Koonen was named a People's Artist of the Russian Soviet Federated Socialist Republic in 1935.

**Kopit, Arthur (Lee)** 1937– American playwright. He first received international attention with *Oh Dad, Poor Dad, Mama's Hung You in the Closet and I'm Feelin' So Sad* (1960), a PARODY of the Oedipus complex. He has since experimented with dramatic form, most notably in *The Day the Whores Came Out to Play Tennis* (1964), a comic portrayal of social-climbing country-clubbers; *Indians* (1968), a study of genocide of the Indians by white Americans; *Wings* (1978), a portrait of a stroke victim; *The End of the World* (1984), a dark comedy about nuclear proliferation; and *The Road to Nirvana* (1990), about Hollywood. A serious and inventive writer, he has rarely achieved popular acceptance.

**Korneichuk, Aleksandr (Evdokimovich)** 1905–72 Ukrainian playwright. The optimistic and heroic socialist realist melodramas of this prolific writer made him popular with both the government and the theatregoing public. With a few exceptions, his plays eschew regional for national issues. The most famous include *The Wreck of the Squadron* (1933), an account of heroic Red seamen during the Revolution; *Platon Krechet* (1934, revised 1963), which offers a dedicated young surgeon as a symbol of the intelligent and humane new Soviet man; and *Front* (1942), a popular, patriotic drama, growing out of the Soviet Union's early defeats in World War II. Korneichuk's *Why the Stars Smiled* (1957) and *Where the Dnieper Flows* (1960) are more intimate, comic and romantic treatments of the trials and entanglements of parents and their offspring, better suited to the climate of the post-1953 Thaw period in Soviet culture.

**Körner, Theodor** 1791–1813 German playwright. Körner's promising career was cut short by his death while fighting in the Napoleonic wars. His most successful play was the tragedy *Toni* (1812). He was briefly official dramatist to the BURGTHEATER.

**Kornfeld, Paul** 1889–1942 Czech playwright born in Austria. His tragedies *The Seduction* (1919) and *Heaven and Hell* (1920) marked the high point of German EXPRESSIONISM, while his essays provided a theoretical basis for the movement. In his later plays he turned to social comedy. He died in a concentration camp.

**Kortner, Fritz** 1892–1970 Austrian actor and director. He established his reputation as the leading interpreter of EXPRESSIONISM with his 1919 role in TOLLER's *Transfiguration* and, under JESSNER, in *Wilhelm Tell*, *Richard III* and WEDEKIND's *The Marquis of Keith*. After his return to Germany in 1948 he directed in Munich, Berlin and Düsseldorf where his meticulous productions of the classics were particularly influential, though he also introduced BECKETT's *Waiting for Godot* to the German stage.

**Kotopoúli, Maríka** 1887–1954 Greek actress. Born into a theatrical family, she played tragic roles as well as VAUDEVILLE parts. For more than 30 years she managed her own theatrical group, Elefthéra Skiní (Independent Stage), after a successful start at the Greek Royal Theatre (1901–8), hosting a variety of plays from classical and modern theatre. Towards the end of her career, Kotopoúli helped revive ancient Greek drama by playing Electra, Clytemnestra and other heroines of tragedy. She was likened to SARAH BERNHARDT.

**Kott, Jan** 1914– Polish theatre critic. His book *Shakespeare, Our Contemporary* (1964) argues exactly what its title suggests, and many directors – PETER BROOK among them – have taken Kott's ideas about the power of the fool in periods of change into the dimension of theatrical action.

**Kotzebue, August von** 1761–1819 German playwright. Although Kotzebue spent much of his life in the political service of the Russian Tsars, he was also an extraordinarily prolific writer. His early work, *Misanthropy and Repentance* (1798), was adapted by Benjamin Thompson as *The Stranger* (1798) to become one of the most popular plays of the 19th century in England. Equally popular in Germany were *The Two Klingsbergs* (1801) and *The Small-Town Germans* (1803). Several of Kotzebue's plays had historical settings. His work, which was deliberately written to appeal to as broad a cross-section of the populace as possible, reflects the transition from sentimentalism to MELODRAMA.

**Kraus, Karl** 1874–1936 Austrian critic and playwright. He published the radical journal *Die Fackel* (the *Torch*) from 1899 to 1936 and was the first to promote WEDEKIND. His plays *The Last Days of Mankind* (1919) and *The Unconquerable Ones* (1928) present a satiric panorama of the era.

**Krejča, Otomar** 1921– Czech director. His career has spanned six decades. He joined the National Theatre as an actor in 1951, and later began to direct CHEKHOV and SHAKESPEARE as well as the work of new playwrights (Hrubín, Topol, Kundera). He left the National Theatre in 1965 to establish his own Gate Theatre, which soon gained international acclaim. While maintaining fidelity to a text, Krejča would subject it to exhaustive analysis, define his concepts and interpretations meticulously to his cast, and encourage his designers (e.g. SVOBODA) to create bold stage embodiments. His theatre was forced to close in 1972, and by 1976 his only outlet for work was abroad. In 1990 he returned to Prague to reactivate Gate Theatre II. Especially dedicated to the works of Chekhov, he has also shaped powerful productions of SOPHOCLES, Shakespeare and BECKETT.

***krishnattam*** Indian theatre form. *Krishnattam*, meaning 'the dramas of Krishna', is a kind of dance-drama practised by one company at the famous Guruvayur Temple in Kerala state, south India. The form was conceived in the mid-17th century by Raja Manaveda, who apparently beheld Krishna, dressed as a small boy, while praying at the temple. Inspired by his miraculous vision, Manaveda wrote *Krishnagita*, incidents from the life of Krishna which are based on the *Bhagavata Purana* and which serve as the basis for the eight plays which comprise the entire dramatic repertory of the form. In recent years *krishnattam* has been played in towns and cities elsewhere in India and in several engagements in Europe and the United States.

Kerala possesses a long history of notable forms of theatre, such as the KUTIYATTAM and KATHAKALI, and *krishnattam* shares some features with them. As in the *kutiyattam* and *kathakali*, the dancer-actors employ a highly sophisticated code of gesture language to interpret the plays, but the dance movements display a lyrical, feminine quality of group movement rather than the masculine vigour of *kathakali*. The actors of the troupes, all of whom are male, are devotees of the god, their devotion echoed by the religious fervour of the pilgrims who watch the performances. The texts of all the plays are sung by two chief singers in the soprano style of singing popular in Kerala. The actor-dancers do not speak, but perhaps grunt or groan when their character demands it.

Traditionally, performances are commissioned by pilgrims from all over India who pay the temple authorities to have a *krishnattam* enacted as a part of their ritual sacrifice. The devotee may choose any of the eight stories – favourite ones are associated with requests for particular boons. The play which includes Krishna's marriage is thought particularly auspicious for a devotee celebrating a marriage in his family; the story which depicts Krishna's miraculous birth is thought to ensure the birth of a male child to barren parents; and the story which shows the destruction of the wicked King Kamsa is thought to ward off the evil eye.

**Krleža, Miroslav** 1893–1981 Croatian playwright, poet and novelist. He spent most of his life in Zagreb. An early supporter of the idea of a Yugoslav state and of socialism, Krleža belongs to the same Central European orbit as KRAUS, Musil, HORVÁTH and Canetti. His early plays, written in symbolist and expressionist manner (see SYMBOLISM; EXPRESSIONISM) – *The Legend* (1913), *Salome* (1913), *Kraljevo* (1915), *Christopher Columbus* (1917), *Michelangelo Buonarroti* (1918) and *Adam and Eve* (1922) – were successfully staged in Yugoslav theatres only after 1955. Between the two world wars, he was a productive novelist, poet, essayist and polemicist. As a playwright he became established only after a gradual transition to REALISM, as marked by *Vučjak* (1923) and his trilogy *The Noble Glembays*, *In Agony* and *Leda* (1928–31). Isolated from the left for his early critique of Stalinism and persecuted by the right for his leftist ideas, Krleža was a lonely figure from the late 1930s until Yugoslavia's break with Stalin in 1948; then he emerged as the towering figure of the domestic cultural scene, instrumental in rejecting socialist realism and inaugurating aesthetic pluralism. In the last three decades of his life he established and led the Yugoslav Lexicography Institute in Zagreb; edited the *Encyclopaedia Yugoslavica*; wrote a long novel and one new play *Aretheius* (1958), whose prophetic value became evident only with the recent demise of the Yugoslav state: in it, intellectuals are forced to emigrate and savage human rights violators clash in a dream-like time frame fusing Roman and contemporary epochs. Krleža's plays remain practically unknown in the English-speaking world, although they have been translated into all the Slavic languages, as well as German, French and Hungarian.

**Kroetz, Franz Xaver** 1946– German playwright. He is the most significant exponent of the contemporary VOLKSSTÜCK (folk play). FASSBINDER directed his first play *Wildwechsel* (*Wild Game Crossing*, 1969). Kroetz's typical themes are the brutalized existence of the proletariat, moral repression and linguistic deprivation. *Homeworker* and *Pig-headed*, dealing with emotional degradation, casual sex and abortion in harshly realistic terms, provoked riots at their premiere in 1971. But the most complete example of the genre comes in the double play *Stallerhof* (*Dairy Farm*, 1972) and its sequel *Ghost Train* (1975). The under-age, mentally retarded daughter of a farmer runs away to keep her child, joining the elderly labourer who seduced her, only to kill the baby in desperation when the social services commit it to an orphanage after he dies of cancer. The range of social analysis is extended in *Oberösterreich* (*Morecambe*, 1972) and *The Nest* (1975). Cultural values are exposed as sentimental in *Maria Magdalena* (1973), where HEBBEL's 19th-century classic is parodied in a contemporary adaptation.

The violence in these plays tends to MELODRAMA, as in the sexually motivated duel-to-the-death of *Men's Business*. Later work like *Neither Fish nor Flesh* (1981) is far more stylized. Kroetz's approach is in conscious contrast to BRECHT, and this is recognized in *Fear and Hope in the FRG* (1984, derived from *Fear and Misery in the Third Reich*, 1938).

**Krog, Helge** 1889–1962 Norwegian playwright and essayist. Author of 16 sometimes playful social problem plays, he was partly influenced by IBSEN and GUNNAR HEIBERG. A recurrent theme is the unliberated position of women in modern society, especially in his strongest plays *The Conch Shell* (1929) and *Break-Up* (1936). Krog is particularly admired for the wit and subtle dexterity of his dialogue, which may owe something to SHAW, and the ironic tone that qualifies his treatment of human nature.

**Kruchonykh, Aleksei (Eliseevich)** 1886–1969 Russian-Soviet poet and librettist. An extremist, he promoted *zaum*, or transrational, universal language based solely upon expressive sounds. Along with his fellow futurists, Kruchonykh exploded grammar and syntax, invented new words and cultivated dissonance in his art. He became attached to cubo-FUTURISM in 1912. He was librettist for the first and only pre-revolutionary futurist opera *Victory over the Sun* (1913), with music by Mikhail Matyushin. The libretto represented 'a complete break between concepts and words', and the music suggested 'a distorted Verdi'. These combined with the abstract sets, hastily assembled amateur actors and out-of-tune piano to create the desired anti-aesthetic effect and to arouse audience abuse and laughter.

**Krylov, Ivan (Andreevich)** 1769–1844 Russian fabulist and playwright. Before he wrote the majority of his nine volumes of satirical *Fables* (1809–20), Krylov was a dramatist and satirical journalist of some note. His malicious but largely accurate portrayal of rival dramatist KNYAZHNIN as an embezzler and plagiarist, and of his wife, SUMAROKOV's daughter, as an adulteress, kept his coarse comedy *The Bombastics* (written 1787, produced 1793) from the stage until after Knyazhnin's death. In his comedies Krylov also attacked the Russian literary vogue for sentimental heroines; classical tragedy's weakness for depicting enlightened monarchs; and the abuses of serfdom. His prose comedy *The Fashionable Boutique* (1805) captures the growing anti-French feeling following Louis XVI's execution. His most popular play *A Lesson to Daughters* (1806) reflects MOLIÈRE's continued influence on Russian comic dramatists. Despite his nationalist sympathies, Krylov's satirical comedies and comic operas received no public

performances in St Petersburg, the seat of government, during his lifetime.

**kuchipudi** Indian theatre form. Kuchipudi is the name of a village in the Krishna river delta of Andhra Pradesh, south India. The word has come to refer to a form of classical dance-drama performed by Brahmin citizens of the village. More recently, it has been applied to any dance in this particular style, e.g. on the concert stages of India's cities.

Siddhendra Yogi, who lived during the 17th century, is regarded as the father of modern *kuchipudi* because he composed dance-dramas for the players. The Brahmin men and boys of *kuchipudi* village families who still practise the art are believed to be the direct descendants of those who were the beneficiaries of Siddhendra Yogi's instruction. *Kuchipudi* troupes are, and have always been, touring companies who usually perform in the open, e.g. in front of a temple. On the concert stage, dances are adapted from the dance-drama repertory and performed as solo items. Owing to its popular reputation as a branch of classical Indian dance, few members of urban audiences are aware that the form is still practised as a full-scale dramatic performance in the villages of Andhra Pradesh.

*Kuchipudi* is the best-known 'classical' form of dance-drama in the Telugu language. As with BHAGAVATA MELA, the stories are drawn from sources which deal with the incarnations of the god Vishnu. The form exhibits considerable feats: in one of the items, a dancer performs on the sharp edge of a metal plate holding a round-bottomed water pot on his head and executes intricate rhythmic patterns by manipulating the plate, using difficult hand gestures correctly – and all without spilling a drop of water.

**Kugel, Aleksandr (Rafailovich)** [Homo Novus] 1864–1928 Russian playwright and critic. Under the pseudonym Homo Novus he edited the influential journal *Theatre and Art* (1897–1918). With his wife, Z. V. Kholmskaya, he founded the Crooked Mirror Theatre, where he served as director and spokesman (1908–28). Kugel argued in his articles and editorials for an actor's theatre to counter the directorial dominance of MEYERHOLD and EVREINOV and the 'anarchic individualism' of the new dramatists. Athough he hired Evreinov to become artistic director at the Crooked Mirror (1910), he was opposed to extremism in the arts. Evreinov later hired Kugel to help stage the Soviet mass spectacle *The Storming of the Winter Palace* (1920). After 1920 Kugel briefly headed the Petrograd People's Theatre, which during his tenure produced historical plays, and published some notable books on theatre.

**Kukolnik, Nestor (Vasilievich)** 1809–68 Russian playwright. He was one of the best-known reactionary writers of patriotic historical plays during the reign of Tsar Nikolai I. His characters are unchanging declamatory figures who eulogize king, country and the good old days. Nevertheless, they served as colourful starring vehicles for two of the great actors of Kukolnik's day, V. A. KARATYGIN and PAVEL MOCHALOV. His most famous blank verse historical epic was *The Hand of the Almighty Has Saved the Fatherland* (1833), set during the election of the first Romanov to the throne (1613). The title and its author have become synonymous in the annals of Russian drama with artist compliance to state demands. Kukolnik's other historical plays with Russian settings and themes include *Prince Mikhail Vasilievich Skopin-Shuisky* (1835), *Ivan Ryabov* and *Archangel*

*Fisherman* (1839) and *Prince Daniil Vasilievich Kholmsky* (1841). Kukolnik also composed a series of dramatic verse 'fantasies', most notably *Torquato Tasso* (1833) and *Giulio Mosti* (1833), which treated the theme of the suffering artist.

**kunqu** Chinese musical style. Originating in the Kunshan area in Jiangsu province, it was developed by the singer-composer WEI LIANGFU. Liang Chenyu, who had worked with Wei, used it as the structural basis for a play he composed entitled *Washing the Silk Yarn* (*Huansha ji*). It was widely acclaimed and marked the debut of a literary-musical genre. There were two schools of thought concerning dramatic composition. One, led by Shen Jing (1553–1610), a theorist first and playwright second, sought to codify a theory of prosody in relation to rhyme and tone and their correlation with the sung text. The second was dominated by the playwright TANG XIANZU, who advocated poetic licence and free rein to the imagination at the expense of rigid musical theory.

In its elemental form *kunqu* is performed as chamber music accompanied by a seven-holed horizontal bamboo flute (*dizi*), wooden clappers and a small hardwood drum slung on a tripod. On stage, string and percussion instruments are added and singing is synthesized with dance, gesture, song and speech. Dance movements have great fluency of line. Plays are predominantly romantic and tend to emphasize the situations and dilemmas of young love.

By the end of the 19th century it had been superseded in popularity by the more robust theatricality of the *JINGXI*, which drew considerable artistic nourishment from the stage practices of the older form. In the 1920s a school was set up in Shanghai, where excellent young performers were trained under YU ZHENFEI. Today *kunqu* is being sponsored and promoted for contemporary audiences. *Kunqu* troupes have performed in the USA and in Europe, including the widely acclaimed *Kunqu Macbeth* (1987).

**Kunst, Johann (Christian)** died 1703 German-born actor and director. He was approached in 1701 by an emissary of Peter the Great to found the first national public theatre in Moscow as part of the Tsar's overall cultural programme. Kunst and a company of seven German actors undertook the training of Russian performers and presented three comedies at the palace of General Lefort in Moscow's foreign quarter. Before a separate wooden theatre in Moscow's Red Square facing the Kremlin could be completed for the company, Kunst died. He was succeeded by another German, Otto Fürst, who continued to draw upon the native population for actors. On 31 May 1706 the company was disbanded and the theatre dismantled. The 450-seat theatre averaged only 25 admissions per performance. Its failure has been attributed to the absence of Russian plays in its repertoire and the lack of a literary language into which foreign plays could be translated.

**Kurbas, Aleksandr (Stepanovich)** [Les] 1887–1937 Ukrainian actor and director. He looked towards European (REINHARDT, CRAIG, FUCHS) stylization and ensemble and socialist political awareness. He organized the Kiev Young Theatre (1917–19), where he staged European classics and contemporary plays in Ukrainian. In 1922 the Young Theatre became the Berezil (the month of March in Ukrainian) Artistic Association, which Kurbas directed until 1933, organizing six studios for the technical training and humanis-

tic education of the new 'universal' actor. The Berezil produced AGIT-PROP and expressionist plays (see EXPRESSIONISM) interwoven with stage and film action and MEYERHOLDian human machines constructed from group movement. His tragi-farcical staging of *Macbeth* concluded with the crowning and stabbing of a 'line of kings'. His 1928 presentation of Ukrainian playwright Mikola Kulish's *The People's Malakhy*, about a would-be reformer who is declared insane, foreshadowed Kurbas's arrest (1934) and execution for 'formalism'.

**Kushner, Tony** 1957– American playwright. Although Kulmer is the author of only one major play – the two-part *Angels in America*, promoted as 'A Gay Fantasia on National Themes' (*Part One: The Millennium Approaches*; *Part Two: Perestroika*) – his work marked a possible new direction for BROADWAY. *Part One*, directed by George C. Wolfe, won all major awards in America (1992) and was also seen in London and Los Angeles. This daring play, focusing on three households in turmoil, deals with the politics of sexuality and sex through the central character of the historical figure Roy Cohn, a lawyer who died of AIDS while denying his homosexuality to his deathbed. *Part Two* joined the earlier play in repertory on Broadway and London in 1993. A third part is planned. Kushner is also the author of *A Bright Room Called Day* (1985), *Slavs* (1993–4) and adaptations of CORNEILLE's *L'Illusion comique*, BRECHT's *Good Person of Setzuan* and ANSKI's *The Dybbuk*.

**kutiyattam** Indian theatre form. *Kutiyattam* is perhaps India's oldest kind of continuously performed theatre, and one of the oldest surviving art forms of the ancient world. It is unique to the state of Kerala on the southwestern coast of the Indian subcontinent. Historical evidence points to its existence as early as the tenth century AD, but it may well be linked with the traditions of the ancient SANSKRIT theatre.

*Kutiyattam* preserves a tradition of performing plays in Sanskrit, the classical language. Some of the plays were composed by well known classical playwrights. The artists who are responsible for preserving this unique theatre form for so many centuries are the few, but dedicated, members of a sub-branch of temple servants. Traditionally, the actors are members of the Cakyar caste, whose duty has been to perform *kutiyattam* in selected temples, accompanied by the *nambiars*, a sub-caste of drummers who play the *mizhavu* – a large pot-shaped drum peculiar to *kutiyattam* – and the *Nanyars*, women of the Nambiar community, who act the female roles.

The unique contribution of *kutiyattam* to world theatre architecture has been the development of permanent theatres (*kuttampalam*). About nine theatres have been built in various temples in Kerala since the 16th century, the largest and most impressive of which is located in the Vatukumnathan Temple of Trichur. Although *kutiyattam* performances are rarely seen today, the Vatukumnathan Temple generally schedules at least one show a year. A typical performance extends over several days. During the first few days the characters are introduced to the audience, and historical incidents concerning them are explored in detail. On the final day of the performance the entire action of the play is performed in chronological order, from beginning to end, just as it was written.

**Kuzmin, Mikhail (Alekseevich)** 1875–1936 Russian poet, composer and playwright. A dandyish, decadent aesthete, he played a significant role in CABARET and the 'theatre of small forms' in pre-revolutionary St Petersburg. His period of major output, 1907–21, includes contributions to the symbolist journal the *Scales* (1904–9), controversial poetry and prose on homosexual themes, and his multi-faceted work in the theatre. This last category includes early attempts to realize a WAGNERian *Gesamtkunstwerk* combining music, dance, poetry and the visual arts, galvanized by World of Art aestheticism; the epic 'dramatic poem' *The History of the Knight d'Alessio* (his first published work, 1905); music for MEYERHOLD's production of BLOK's *Puppet Show* (1906); numerous pantomimes, operettas, comic operas, mimic and mythological ballets, children's plays, puppet shows, pastorales and masquerades; three lyrical 'mysteries'; and his major play, *The Venetian Madcaps* (1912; produced 1914), a dark *COMMEDIA* piece on a temptress's destruction of a male friendship. Despite the appealing theatricality of his plays, Kuzmin continues to be known primarily as a poet.

**kwangdae** Korean performer. Traditionally this term refers to a low-class entertainer who performed all forms of *divertissements*, such as P'ANSORI, tumbling and dance.

**Kyd, Thomas** 1558–94 English playwright. He is remembered for a single masterpiece, *The Spanish Tragedy* (c.1589), though his authorship is in some doubt. He associated with MARLOWE and was arrested and imprisoned for heresy in 1593. *The Spanish Tragedy* adapted SENECAN tragedy for the more visual taste of the Elizabethan stage and influenced the development of REVENGE TRAGEDY. Kyd's other known play, *Cornelia* (c.1594), is a version from the French of ROBERT GARNIER. Some scholars think Kyd wrote a lost *Hamlet*, used as a source by SHAKESPEARE.

**Kynaston, Ned (Edward)** c.1640–1706 English boy actor. He specialized in women's roles – probably the last of his profession. He was a favourite on the Restoration stage, and after he had grown beyond female portrayal played effectively in other roles.

**kyōgen** Japanese theatre genre. The kyōgen repertory consists of some 260 short plays, celebratory and usually comic, that are performed by specialist kyōgen actors on a NŌ stage, normally as part of a joint programme. *Kyōgen* humour arises in part from poking fun at human foible: greed, lust, chicanery, cowardice. Characters are not idealized as they are in nō – their social weaknesses are shown: e.g. a priest is ignorant or useless (*Mushrooms*, *The Crow*), a wife is domineering (*Fortified Bread*), a servant dishonest (*Poison Sugar*). Humour comes from punning, onomatopoeia and physical action. The language is the vernacular prose of the 15th and 16th centuries and readily understood by today's audiences. Actors perform energetically in controlled, clearly articulated vocal and movement patterns which, while stylized, are derived from daily speech and actions. *Kyōgen* is one of the few traditional theatre genres in Asia that are primarily spoken. Usually the actor performs without mask or make-up, in costume based on the real clothing people wore in medieval times.

# L

**La Chaussée, Pierre-Claude Nivelle de** 1692–1754
French playwright and man of letters. After a life of dissipation he produced edifying material for the theatre, particularly in his *comédies larmoyantes*, tearful comedies influenced by the contemporary sentimental novel, full of pathos, simplistic characterization and rhetorical artifice. *Mélanide* (1741) is regarded as his best play, but two others on the subject of unhappy marriage, *La Fausse Antipathie* (*The False Antipathy*, 1733) and *Le Préjugé à la mode* (*The Fashionable Prejudice*, 1735), are worthy of note, as is his adaptation of Richardson's novel, *Paméla* (1743). As forerunners of domestic drama they have historical value.

**La Grange** [Charles Varlet] 1635–92 French actor. Friend and assistant to MOLIÈRE, whose company he joined in 1659, he played the young lover in most of the repertoire, and also more challenging parts like Don Juan and Acaste in *The Misanthrope* (1666). As company secretary and archivist he kept a daily register of plays and takings, with comments on other company matters – an invaluable source of information. After Molière's death he helped to rebuild the company and in 1680 became the first 'orator' of the new COMÉDIE-FRANÇAISE, responsible for the formal address to the audience. In 1682 he brought out the first collected edition of Molière's plays.

**La MaMa** (New York City) OFF-OFF BROADWAY theatre. It was founded in 1962 by Ellen Stewart, who began Café La MaMa in a cramped Manhattan basement and in 1969 moved to East 4th Street where the theatre now operates. The Café became La MaMa ETC (Experimental Theatre Club) and Stewart still functions as artistic director. La MaMa introduced important American playwrights and directors like ROCHELLE OWENS, MEGAN TERRY, Jeff Weiss, SAM SHEPARD, HARVEY FIERSTEIN, H.M. Koutoukas, LANFORD WILSON, Julie Bovasso, ADRIENNE KENNEDY and Tom O'Horgan, also presenting works by avant-garde directors such as RICHARD FOREMAN and MEREDITH MONK. In addition, La MaMa has brought to America such artists as JERZY GROTOWSKI, ANDREI SERBAN, PETER BROOK, EUGENIO BARBA and TADEUSZ KANTOR. In 1980 La MaMa established the Third World Institute of Theatre Arts and Studies (TWITAS). Through the 1980s and 1990s the La MaMa CABARET has provided a venue for new experimentation in comedy and performance art.

**La Rue, Danny** [Daniel Patrick Carroll] 1928– British actor, born in Ireland. He has made his reputation in CABARET, PANTOMIME (*Queen Passionella and the Sleeping Beauty*, 1968) and VARIETY shows (*Danny La Rue at the Palace*, 1970) as the leading female impersonator (see FEMALE IMPERSONATION).

**La Taille, Jean de** c.1535–c.1608 French playwright and poet. He wrote two biblical tragedies, *Saül le furieux* (*Saul Enraged*), published in 1572, and its sequel *La Famine, ou Les Gabéonites* (*The Famine*, 1573). The first is prefaced by a treatise on the art of TRAGEDY which typifies 16th-century humanist theory. *Les Corrivaux* (*The Rivals*, 1574) is the first French comedy in prose.

**Laberge, Marie** 1950– Quebec playwright, actress, director and novelist. She first came to national attention in 1981 with *C'était avant la guerre à l'Anse à Gilles*
(*Before the War, Down at L'Anse à Gilles*), which depicts the inferior status of women in rural Quebec in the 1930s. Her eloquent feminism informs *L'Homme gris* (*The Tipsy Man*, 1984, published in English as *Night*, 1988). *Jocelyne Trudelle, trouvée morte dans ses larmes* (*Jocelyne Trudelle, Discovered Dead in Her Tears*, 1986) is a haunting study of a woman's suicide. Other plays of note are *Le Night Cap Bar* (1987), *Oublier* (1987), translated as *Take Care* (1988); *Aurélie, ma soeur* (*My Sister, Aurélie*, 1988) and *Le Faucon* (*The Falcon*, 1991).

**Labiche, Eugène** 1815–88 French playwright. The majority of his 175 plays (many were collaborations) are *vaudevilles*, one-act comedies with songs, but a few are more serious comedies of manners. Labiche followed EUGÈNE SCRIBE, but gradually transformed the genre into the 'French FARCE' that FEYDEAU would bring to perfection. He wrote for and about the bourgeoisie of the Second Empire, his accurate social analysis combining with a strong sense of the grotesque. His first real success came in 1848, *Un Jeune Homme pressé* (*A Young Man in a Hurry*). *An Italian Straw Hat* (1851) was one of his most popular plays (and survived into the 20th century with René Clair's classic film), in which the hapless hero is pursued by an entire wedding party. *Le Voyage de Monsieur Perrichon* (*Monsieur Perrichon's Holiday*, 1860) showed a more developed sense of characterization. In *Célimare le bien-aimé* (*Célimare the Beloved*, 1863) he used the theme of the *ménage à trois*, which he developed fully in one of his last plays, *The Happiest of the Three* (1870).

**Lacy, James** 1696–1774 English actor and manager. In 1744 he joined the partnership running DRURY LANE and in 1747 persuaded GARRICK to take a half-share in the company. Drury Lane had been in severe decline, but the huge success of the Lacy–Garrick partnership enabled them to recoup their investment within four years.

**Lacy, John** 1615–81 English actor and playwright. After the Restoration he joined BEESTON'S company and then the King's Men (see LORD CHAMBERLAIN'S MEN), playing Ananias in JONSON's *The Alchemist*. A major shareholder in the Theatre Royal in London's Bridges Street, he co-managed the company for KILLIGREW with Mohun and Hart. In 1667 he was arrested for mocking the court in his role as a rustic in *The Change of Crowns*. He was a brilliant clown, famous as Teague, an Irish footman, in SIR ROBERT HOWARD's *The Committee*, in the title role of his own *Sauny the Scot* and as MOLIÈRE's Sganarelle. His own plays included FARCES like *The Old Troop* and adaptations of SHAKESPEARE.

**Ladipo, Duro** 1931–78 Nigerian playwright, composer and performer. Ladipo's Yoruba folk operas are inspired by Yoruba history. He established the Mbari-Mbayo Centre (1962) in Oshogbo with a performance of his first opera *Oba Moro* (*The Ghost Catcher*, published 1964). His most famous opera, *Oba Ko So* (*The King Did Not Hang*, 1964), concerns the figure of Sango, god of lightning in the Yoruba pantheon. Others were *Oba Waja* (*The King Is Dead*), based on an incident in colonial Nigeria when a British District Officer tried to stop a sacred ritual suicide; *Moremi*, based on the legend of a Yoruba woman who allowed herself to be captured so that she might learn the secret of the success of her people's enemy; and *Eda*, his adaptation of HOFMANNSTHAL's *Jedermann* (*Everyman*).

**Lafayette Players** 1915–32 African-American company. A STOCK COMPANY organized by the actress Anita Bush, it provided dramatic entertainment for the Harlem community in place of VAUDEVILLE and MINSTREL SHOWS that often ridiculed black people. On a weekly schedule the company presented at the Lafayette Theatre abridged versions of popular BROADWAY comedies and melodramas, using black actors. In 1928 they moved to Los Angeles where they played successfully to mixed audiences, compiling a production record of 250 plays over 17 years before becoming a casualty of the Depression. Among well-recognized former players are CHARLES GILPIN, Clarence Muse, Dooley Wilson, Inez Clough, Evelyn Ellis and Abbie Mitchell.

**Lagerkvist, Pär** 1891–1974 Swedish playwright, novelist and poet. Winner of the 1951 Nobel Prize for Literature, he is best known in the English-speaking world as a novelist. In Scandinavia he was also an innovative dramatist who relentlessly explored new dramatic forms. His concern with form was proclaimed in his essay 'Modern Theatre: Points of View and Attack' (1918), in which he dismissed NATURALISM (especially IBSEN's plays) as untheatrical and applauded the theatricalism of STRINDBERG's later plays. His own are exploratory variations on a single theme, that of evil as an abstract force in life and as an irrepressible instinct in the individual mind. His early plays, especially the one-act trilogy *The Difficult Hour* (1918) and the short *The Secret of Heaven* (1919), are grotesque expressionistic fantasies (see EXPRESSIONISM), showing humanity trapped within and poisoned by a meaningless, ferocious world. In the 1920s his faith in humanity seemed to increase, as in *He Who Lived His Life Over* (1928), but with the rise of Fascism in the 1930s, his plays focused increasingly on the dangerous religion of brutality, often contrasting it with some feminine figure representing motherly protection. *The Hangman* (1933) was given productions all over Scandinavia by PER LINDBERG, Lagerkvist's most understanding director. His most popular play was his most accessible, the moral parable *The Philosopher's Stone* (1947), which uses the story of a medieval alchemist to examine the complexities of faith.

**Lahr, Bert** [Irving Lahrheim] 1895–1967 American comic actor. After VAUDEVILLE and BURLESQUE, Lahr's first feature part was a punch-drunk fighter in *Hold Everything* (1928), which won him critical acclaim and starring roles in musical comedies *Flying High* (1930), *Hot-Cha!* (1932) and *The Show Is On* (1936). His 'stock-in-trade included a grimace like that 'of a camel with acute gastric disorder' and a laryngeal bleat 'like a lovesick ram'. His style was too broad for film, although he is immortalized as the Cowardly Lion in *The Wizard of Oz* (1938). He returned to BROADWAY in *Du Barry Was a Lady* (1939). Lahr considered the turning point in his career to be Estragon in *Waiting for Godot* (1956). This association with the avant-garde brought him roles in SHAW, MOLIÈRE and SHAKESPEARE (Bottom).

**Lahr, John** 1941– American drama critic and author. Lahr studied at Yale and Oxford Universities and worked as a dramaturge for the GUTHRIE THEATRE (1968) and for the Repertory Theatre of Lincoln Center (1969–71; see VIVIAN BEAUMONT AND MITZI E. NEWHOUSE THEATRES). In his theatre criticism (*Evergreen Review*, *Grove Press* and *Village Voice*) he expects theatre to be socially responsible and to forge new images to 'revitalize the imaginative life of its audience'. Such theatre must be 'shocking, violent, and unpredictable'. Lahr is the author of at least ten books, including a biography of his father, the comedian BERT LAHR, and a biography of JOE ORTON. His stage version of *The Manchurian Candidate* premiered in London in 1991 and was first seen in the USA in 1994.

**Lamarche, Gustave** 1895–1987 French Canadian playwright, director, poet and a Catholic priest. His collected works comprise 34 plays in six volumes. In the 1930s and 40s his vast medieval pageant plays, generally staged outdoors, attracted huge crowds. Based on biblical themes, the best-known are *Jonathas* (1935), *La Défaite de l'enfer* (*Hell Defeated*, 1938), *Notre-Dame-des-Neiges* (*Our Lady of the Snows*, 1942) and *Notre-Dame-de-la-Couronne* (*Our Lady of the Crown*, 1947). In conjunction with Father ÉMILE LEGAULT, Lamarche succeeded in making theatre, long suspect to the Catholic Church in French Canada, a respectable and worthwhile occupation.

**Lamb, Charles** 1775–1834 English essayist and critic. An inveterate theatregoer, he included many theatrical subjects in his *Essays of Elia*. His theatrical criticism was robust. His influential *Specimens of English Dramatic Poets who Lived about the Time of Shakespeare* (1808) raised awareness of the great age of English drama, and the *Tales from Shakespeare* (1807), written with his sister Mary, was a children's classic. His own farce, *Mr H* – – (1806), was hissed off the DRURY LANE stage; he also wrote a tragedy, *John Woodvil* (published 1802).

**Lang, Matheson** 1879–1948 British actor-manager, born in Canada. He appeared in GRANVILLE BARKER's productions of IBSEN and SHAW at the ROYAL COURT THEATRE. From 1910 he toured with his own company, until 1913 when he returned to London in the title role of *Mr Wu*, a melodramatic part he revived repeatedly all over the world. In 1914 he directed and acted in the first SHAKESPEARE season at the OLD VIC.

**Långbacka, Ralf** 1932– Finnish director. Långbacka is active internationally, especially in Sweden. In the 1960s and 1970s he was the first in Scandinavia to articulate the need for artistic theatres of totally committed artists, rejecting outworn ideology and methods and presenting coherent, purposeful repertoires dealing with fundamental issues. He was particularly successful at Turun Kapunginteatteri, Finland, in 1971–7 (with co-director Kalle Holmberg). In Sweden his brilliant work at GÖTEBORG STADSTEATER in 1967–9 inspired directors like PETER OSKARSON and companies like FOLKTEATERN I GÖTEBORG. His productions of BRECHT, SHAKESPEARE and CHEKHOV have been especially important in revealing the contradictory forces at work in their texts.

**Langdal, Peter** 1957– Danish director. Langdal became known in the mid-1980s for his bold and playful productions of classics, including SCHILLER's *The Robbers* and HOLBERG's *Erasmus Montanus* (1984) and *Jeppe of the Hill* (1986). With the frequent collaboration of scenographer Karin Betz, his productions are often visually breathtaking and make extraordinary use of space, as in *The Robbers* in Gladsaxe Teater's huge arena and SHAKESPEARE's *A Winter's Tale* (1986) in Centralteatret, Oslo. The CLOWN has been a recurrent figure in his work, and in 1986 he and Betz inaugurated Copenhagen's former East Gasworks as a theatre with a CIRCUS-like production of *A Midsummer Night's Dream*.

Langdal has worked frequently at Betty Nansen Teatret, and became its director in 1992.

**Lange, Harmut** 1937– German playwright. After his work was banned in the GDR he escaped to the West. His best-known play *The Countess of Rathenow* (1969) attacks German traditionalism, but his characteristic style is political allegory (*Hercules*, 1968; *The Murder of Ajax*, 1971).

**Langham, Michael** 1919– British director. In the 1950s Langham became known as a classical director in England and Scotland, but his North American work has comprised most of his career. From 1955 to 1968 he was TYRONE GUTHRIE's successor as artistic director of the STRATFORD (Ontario) FESTIVAL. Langham expanded the Festival to include touring, film and television projects, a training programme and school performances. In 1971 he became artistic director at the GUTHRIE THEATRE, Minneapolis, which he rescued from financial near-disaster. During 1979–92 he was director of drama at the Juilliard School.

**Langner, Lawrence** 1890–1962 London-born American producer. Langner trained as a lawyer and in 1911 emigrated to New York where he headed an international firm. In 1914 he helped organize the WASHINGTON SQUARE PLAYERS and wrote several one-act plays for the group. After it disbanded he brought members together in 1918 to form the THEATRE GUILD. With THERESA HELBURN he managed the Guild and built a subscription audience of 25,000 by 1925. The success of *John Ferguson* (1919) established them artistically and commercially. Langner encouraged the production of foreign plays, including works by TOLLER, KAISER, MOLNÁR and PIRANDELLO. He obtained for the Guild several plays by SHAW. In the early 1950s he founded the AMERICAN SHAKESPEARE THEATRE at Stratford, Connecticut. Langner was one of the most enlightened of American producers, and an able businessman.

**Langtry, Lillie** 1853–1929 British actress. Originally from Jersey, she made her theatrical debut under the BANCROFTS at the HAYMARKET in 1881, when she played Kate Hardcastle in *She Stoops to Conquer*. A society beauty, competent actress and shrewd company manager, she numbered Rosalind in *As You Like It* and Lady Teazle in *The School for Scandal* among her most effective roles, but it was in SYDNEY GRUNDY's *The Degenerates* (1899) that she offered autobiographical glimpses of her notorious affairs in high society.

**Languirand, Jacques** 1931– French Canadian playwright, essayist and producer. Much influenced by the dramatists he met and the plays he saw during his studies in Paris, 1949–51, he became on his return Canada's most important exponent of the European THEATRE OF THE ABSURD. His first stage play, *Les Insolites* (*The Unusual Ones*, 1956), was followed by *Le Roi ivre* (*The Drunken King*, 1956) and his best-known work, *Les Grands Départs* (*Great Departures*, televised 1957, staged 1958). Languirand continued to write and produce plays for the next dozen years, principally *Les Violons de l'automne* (*Violins of Autumn*, 1961), the multi-media *Man, Inc.* (1970) and MUSICAL COMEDY *Klondyke* (1970), but despite performances in France and Great Britain his work has had little appeal for Canadian audiences. Since 1970 he has abandoned the theatre in favour of philosophic essays.

**Lansbury, Angela (Brigid)** 1925– British-born American actress and singer. She went to the USA to start her film career. In 1957 she made her BROADWAY debut in *Hotel Paradiso*, and her musical debut as the Mayor in the ill-fated *Anyone Can Whistle* (1964), before achieving fame as the madcap 'Auntie Mame' Dennis in *Mame* (1966). She also played the eccentric Countess Aurelia in *Dear World* (1968), the compulsive Mama Rose in a revival of *Gypsy* (1974) and the maniacal Mrs Lovett in *Sweeney Todd* (1979). She brought a powerful singing voice, a flair for comedy and a rare depth of characterization to her musical roles. She has also appeared with the ROYAL SHAKESPEARE COMPANY and at the NATIONAL THEATRE in Britain. Since the mid-1980s she has starred as a quirky and personable writer and crime buff in the popular television series 'Murder, She Wrote'.

**Lao She** [Shu Qingchung] 1899–1966 Chinese playwright and novelist. He was born and educated in Beijing. After various posts in education, he worked in England for five years from 1924, and began to write. He returned to China an acknowledged comic novelist with a keen sense of character. His masterpiece, *Xiangzi the Camel* (*Luotuo Xiangzi*), the story of the corruption and tragic fate of a good-natured Beijing rickshaw puller, brought him international fame through an unauthorized English edition with a changed conclusion. The original Chinese version was published in serial form during 1936–7. Lao She spent the war years in Chongqing, where he began to write plays and work with theatre groups. In 1951 he wrote *Dragon Beard Ditch* (*Longu gou*), a play concerning the successful rehabilitation of a Beijing slum area which earned him the title of People's Artist. In 1957 he published *Teahouse* (*Chaguan*), a three-act play in which he demonstrated his skilful command of the colloquial and sensitive insight into a changing society.

**Larivey, Pierre de** c.1540–1619 French playwright. Of Italian descent, he was inspired by the COMMEDIA DELL'ARTE players visiting France and wrote a number of Italianate comedies transposed to a French milieu, of which six were published in 1579 and a further three in 1611. Employing the type characters and familiar plot devices of *commedia*, they are written in a racy, colourful idiom and were widely performed. *Les Esprits* (*The Ghosts*, 1579) is echoed in plays by MOLIÈRE and REGNARD.

**Larochelle** [Boullanger], **Henri** 1827–84 French theatre manager. In the early 1850s Larochelle ran several Parisian theatres, including the Théâtre Montparnasse. In 1866 he opened the Cluny, aiming at a high-quality repertoire, often doing plays rejected by other managements, such as Erckmann-Chatrian's *Le Juif Polonais* (*The Polish Jew*; in England, *The Bells*). After 1870 he turned his attention to larger theatres, becoming director of the Porte-Saint-Martin (see BOULEVARD) in 1872, mounting HUGO's *Marie Tudor*, with the aged FRÉDÉRICK LEMAÎTRE; DENNERY and Cormon's *Les Deux Orphelines* (*The Two Orphans*); and the vastly successful *Around the World in Eighty Days*. In 1877 he took on the direction of the Ambigu. In 1878 he 'retired', taking on the management of the Gaîté, where one of his most spectacular productions was Paul Meurice's adaptation of Victor Hugo's *Quatre-vingt-treize* (*Ninety-three*).

**L'Arronge, Adolf** 1838–1908 German director, playwright and musician. A successful writer of light comedies, L'Arronge is best known as a founding member of the DEUTSCHES THEATER in Berlin and as its first director, from 1887 to 1894.

**Lassalle, Jacques** 1936– French director. Particularly associated with the work of MICHEL VINAVER, he has been successful in discovering new playwrights as well as neglected classics. From 1983 to 1990 he was director of the Théâtre National de Strasbourg, where he put on notable productions such as MOLIÈRE's *Tartuffe* with Gérard Depardieu. From 1990 to 1993 he was director of the COMÉDIE-FRANÇAISE.

**Lateiner, Jacob** see HURWITZ, MOISHE

**Laterna Magika** Czech staging system. Devised by the Czechs ALFRED RADOK and JOSEF SVOBODA, this system integrates live performance with film projections of the performers themselves on multiple screens. It premiered in the Czechoslovakian pavilion at the Brussels Expo in 1958. Subsequently it degenerated into tourist entertainment, but occasionally its mixed-media principle appeared in serious drama: e.g. *The Last Ones* (1966), a Radok–Svoboda collaboration. Svoboda explored its scenographic application in a version of *The Odyssey* (1987), in *Minotaur* (1991) and in *Magic Flute* (1993). Since the early 1960s Laterna Magika has also been the name of the Prague theatre where the technique is practised.

**Latin American theatre** To deal with the theatre of Latin America as a unit is to presuppose that a homogeneity exists with certain common denominators. As with all generalizations, this one contains both truth and fiction. The Spanish conquest began with Columbus's arrival in 1492, and the Portuguese explorers who claimed the territory of Brazil followed soon after. The geographic size and population diversity render a comprehensive term somewhat unsatisfactory, but despite its limitations 'Latin America' acknowledges common historical, linguistic and cultural developments.

Theatre, or at least theatrical forms, existed in the Americas before the arrival of the Spanish and Portuguese. For the most part, these manifestations were not well documented by the conquerors; in fact, from the perspective of a religious conquest of the New World, their 'heretical' nature generally caused them to be suppressed. Some indigenous forms are described in the early Spanish chronicles, but the only authentic non-European work to survive is the *RABINAL ACHÍ* of the *maya-quiché*. *El baile de El Güegüence* and *Ollantay* are both cited as early plays with indigenous flavour, but both are of dubious origin and have European characteristics.

## Colonial theatre

Early religious plays in the colonies, at a time when the Spanish theatre itself was still rudimentary, often drew on local traditions and customs to facilitate comprehension by the American Indians. Performed in the church atriums and plazas, these plays soon shared time with more secular manifestations dramatizing important events in the colonies, such as the arrival or departure of a viceroy, or the saint's day of an important personage. Traffic between Spain and Portugal and their colonies was constant throughout the colonial period, and the advanced state of development of peninsular theatre during the Siglo de Oro (GOLDEN AGE), dominated by LOPE DE VEGA and CALDERÓN DE LA BARCA and their respective schools, contributed to the early transfer of theatrical interest from Spain and Portugal to Latin America. Both JUAN RUIZ DE ALARCÓN (born in Mexico) and TIRSO DE MOLINA spent time in the colonies, but neither had a significant impact on the development of national dramaturgy, in spite of critics' claims to the contrary. By the end of the 17th century, Mexico had produced one great playwright, the extraordinary nun SOR JUANA INÉS DE LA CRUZ.

Throughout the colonial years the theatre tended to be either an imported phenomenon or an artistic form that paralleled closely the prevailing modes of the mother countries. During the 17th century the aesthetic trends ranged from early Renaissance to baroque in tone, language and form. The *AUTOS SACRAMENTALES* popular during the 17th century were banned by Charles III in 1765, as religious drama became increasingly corrupted.

## The 19th century

The period of independence in Latin America lasted from 1810 to 1825, but political independence did little to ensure cultural independence. Neoclassic and romantic plays characterized the first half of the 19th century with the strong influence of both French and Spanish themes and techniques. The indigenous elements lacked a coherent expression, although some writers turned their attention to local matters, which gave rise to the *costumbrista* theatre (see COSTUMBRISMO). Also, with the awakening of national consciousness coinciding with independence, the new political and literary freedom generated innumerable works, many barely worthy of mention. The principal exponent of Mexican romanticism was FERNANDO CALDERÓN (1809–45), most of whose dramas portrayed a desire to escape temporal and spatial boundaries in search of European themes, especially chivalrous themes of the Middle Ages.

Even though REALISM and the psychological theatre marked the latter half of the 19th century in Spain, a second wave of romantic influences impeded the development of a realistic, autochthonous theatre in the New World, and romanticism continued to prevail in many countries until about 1910. The single event of greatest importance in the development of the River Plate theatre (i.e. of Argentina and Uruguay) occurred in 1884, when the Carlo Brothers' North American Circus, on tour in Argentina, incorporated the little Uruguayan clown José J. Podestá (1858–1937) into their initial rendition of *Juan Moreira*, a romanticized version of a *gaucho* (see GAUCHO theatre) whose adventures had been published serially by Eduardo Gutiérrez. The instantaneous success of the original pantomime version led subsequently to a more developed version with dialogue, and eventually to a host of imitations about upstanding and virtuous *gauchos* persecuted unjustly by the civil authorities.

## The 20th century

Only in the 20th century did theatre in Latin America begin to find its own expression. The Golden Decade (1900–10) in Argentina and Uruguay sprang from these popular traditions of the CIRCUS and *gaucho*. Before the turn of the century, impoverished European emigrants had begun to deluge the area in search of opportunities and prosperity. The fusion of the new arrivals with the national atmosphere provided the raw material for the modernized *sainete* (see GÉNERO CHICO), the principal mouthpiece of this social class. For all their faults, the plays had the merit of depicting the local reality. The realistic-naturalistic influence of the European theatre and the local *sainete criollo* tradition merged to produce the most renowned dramatist of South America: FLORENCIO SÁNCHEZ (1875–1910). After his untimely death a host of successors continued the tradition.

## Mexico

In the other major theatrical capital of the hemisphere, to the north, Mexico was experiencing a very different environment. The peace, order and economic progress proclaimed by Porfirio Díaz during the early 20th century did little to foment the development of Mexican theatre, which was still closely tied to the Spanish tradition. The outbreak of the Mexican Revolution in 1910, following by exactly 100 years the wars of independence, brought some insignificant political drama. After the constitutional consolidation at the end of the Revolution, coinciding with the end of World War I, the nationalist current became stronger and the period of the 1920s was characterized by a desire for reconstruction and reforms. Popular customs of local life and colour were captured in the light forms of the *sainete* and ZARZUELA. By the mid-20s the Unión de Autores Dramáticos (Playwrights' Union) organized the reading of plays and translations, thus preparing the way for the formation of the Grupo de los Siete Autores (Group of Seven Authors), which started the process of modernization by discarding quaint procedures such as asides and by accepting Mexican Spanish instead of Madrid Spanish for stage dialogue.

The renovation that was lacking in the Latin American professional companies was fostered by a series of experimental groups, starting in Mexico in 1928 with the TEATRO DE ULISES (Ulysses Theatre) established by XAVIER VILLAURRUTIA and SALVADOR NOVO under the patronage of Antonieta Rivas Mercado. This vanguard theatre experiment lasted only two seasons but it presented six plays, all foreign, to counteract the outmoded influence of the Mexican comedy. Other groups followed in the 1930s, relying on intimate settings, new lighting and new concepts of staging promoted by European directors and artists such as CRAIG, REINHARDT, STANISLAVSKY, PISCATOR and others, to achieve the greatest plasticity. The role of the theatre director in balancing all aspects of the performance became paramount.

## Argentina

In Argentina the rise of the independent theatre movement in 1930 achieved similar objectives. The first group formed was the Teatro del Pueblo (People's Theatre) by Leónidas Barletta, whose motivation was to develop a new public, to give new importance to the role of the director and to impose vanguard techniques of production. This independent theatre movement also had a political commitment, inspired by Marxism, to address social concerns and vices. Other groups formed in the 1930s shared the problems, anxieties and successes of this original effort.

## Puerto Rico

Throughout the 1930s and early 1940s the spirit of vanguardism swept across the theatre of Latin America, taking shape as local conditions permitted. In Puerto Rico the stimulus for new theatre came in 1938 when EMILIO BELAVAL, as president of the Ateneo Puertorriqueño (Puerto Rican Atheneum), sponsored the national dramaturgy through a contest that produced three prize-winning new plays: one of these, *Tonight the Joker Plays* by Fernando Sierra Berdecía, broke new ground in dealing with the painful issue of the Puerto Rican immigrant in New York.

## Brazil

In Brazil the new orientation took solid form in 1938 with the formation of Os Comediantes (The Comedians), an amateur group, later professional, that dared to disobey the traditional rules and customs by experimenting with new techniques of lighting, staging and acting. The arrival of the Polish refugee Zbigniew Ziembinski added substance to their efforts, and their 1943 production of *Vestido de Noiva* (*Bridal Gown*) by NELSON RODRIGUES in Rio was ideally suited to expressionistic techniques (see EXPRESSIONISM) in lighting, rhythm and movement. The Brazilian theatre now began to reflect the aesthetic revolution that had occurred in other genres during the modernist movement of 1922.

## Chile

Chile's entrance into vanguard theatre came not through the independent theatre but rather via the university theatre, a unique case in Latin America. In 1941 the renovation began with the creation of the University of Chile Experimental Theatre under the leadership of Pedro de la Barra who brought new concepts of acting and staging, assisted the following year by a visit from LOUIS JOUVET and his French company. In 1943 a similar thrust at the Catholic University led to the creation of their Experimental Theatre. Both groups brought together the most important theatre practitioners in the country and provided theatre training for a new generation of directors, actors and technicians. In their formative years both staged the best foreign plays. Meanwhile, a new generation of national playwrights was in the making.

## After World War II

These events, and similar ones in other countries, set the stage for a wave of new and exciting theatre activity throughout the Americas in the 1950s and 60s as the Latin American theatre came into its own, not only seeking but establishing its own identity. The post-World War II period presented a new level of theatrical sophistication which, for the first time, placed Latin America in serious competition on the world stage. Conflicts between reality and illusion and the concepts of alienation and absurdity (see THEATRE OF THE ABSURD) found expression through young playwrights eager to show themselves as valid interpreters of the human condition. Dozens of new playwrights – including those who were to establish the canon for the remainder of the century, such as EMILIO CARBALLIDO (Mexico), RENÉ MARQUÉS (Puerto Rico), JOSÉ TRIANA (Cuba), OSVALDO DRAGÚN and GRISELDA GAMBARO (Argentina), JORGE DÍAZ and EGON WOLFF (Chile), and ALFREDO DIAS GOMES (Brazil) – came to the fore during these years with hundreds of new plays. The economics of production and publication, while never ideal, were reasonably favourable and led to a boom of activity.

In 1968 several significant events took place that marked changing times. The year was difficult on a global scale because of American involvement in Vietnam; student and political protests struck Paris and Chicago and led to the massacre at Tlatelolco in Mexico during the Olympics. On a more positive note, 1968 was the year of many Latin American theatre festivals – in Peru, Mexico, Costa Rica and other venues. One festival in particular, in Manizales, Colombia, established for the first time what was to become an enduring tradition of bringing together Latin Americans from all over the hemisphere to perform and to discuss their own theatre. Instead of looking for inspiration in Europe or the United States, these theatre people looked into their own hearts and souls and discovered their roots and their essence.

This festival coincided with the emergence of the CREACIÓN COLECTIVA (collective creation), the development of theatre through group participation. As a form of protest against bourgeois theatre, the collective creation systematically disregarded the importance of text author and director in favour of an egalitarian collaborative process – or at least it did so in theory. It became a commonplace to say that if existing texts did not speak to the needs of the people, then it was necessary to generate new ones. If the theatre created was often light in linguistic sophistication, it compensated with imagery that could support the message of the text. The sociopolitical importance of the performances created (at times no written text outlived the event) meant that images of violence, cruelty and human suffering were common. Brechtian principles were adopted to transform the theatre and BRECHT became, in fact, the foreign author most often staged throughout Latin America. The collective creation became the staging process for a new set of social and political configurations. These options were especially noteworthy in Cuba, where the theatre served as a vehicle to advance the ideology of the Revolution, but they were applied with equal enthusiasm in Colombia, Peru and many other settings.

### The 1980s

By the mid-1980s it was clear that the theatre was emerging from its period of most strident political activity and was again searching for new means of expression. Popular theatre groups were taking advantage of masks, colourful costumes and rich musical rhythms indigenous to their cultures. Street theatre was common, with actors on stilts creating exaggerated effects. Playhouses' offerings ranged from neo-realistic sets and staging interspersed with manifestations of 'poor theatre', virtually naked in design, to productions of pure fantasy with elaborate and imaginative techniques. All was possible, and all could be seen, depending upon the human, fiscal and imaginative resources of each theatre group. Authors searched for new forms of expression, and found in historical theatre a particularly effective medium for interpreting present reality in terms of some previous event or personage. Women playwrights emerged as a real force, and feminist issues expressed by both women and men were well received in countries with strong *machista* traditions. The study of this theatre and the quality of theatre criticism also improved, as a reflection of its sustained importance. While national and cultural differences still characterized theatre throughout the hemisphere, improved communications and the sense of identification with Latin American values and traditions vitalized both text and performance.

**Laube, Heinrich** 1806–84 German playwright and director. As a young journalist he was closely associated with the Junges Deutschland (Young Germany) movement and was briefly imprisoned for his writings in 1837. After his release he turned to playwriting, producing several dramas in the fashion of SCRIBE. Among Laube's most frequently performed plays were *Monaldeschi* (1841), *Rococo* (1842), *Struensee* (1845), *Gottsched and Gellert* (1845) and *The Karlschüler* (1846). Despite his liberal views, in 1849 he was appointed director of the BURGTHEATER where, over the next 18 years, he developed the ensemble style of the company.

**lauda** The sung vernacular drama of 13th-century Italy, closely linked to the liturgical year. The most famous of the early *laude* is the *Donna del Paradiso* (*Queen of Heaven*), in which the Virgin Mary speaks to Christ, John and the Cross.

**Lauder, Harry** [Henry MacLennan Lauder] 1870–1950 Scottish MUSIC-HALL performer. He worked in a flax mill and in coal mines for 10 years, before playing in concert parties as an Irish comic. His London debut in 1900 as an extra turn made him a star overnight, and he soon became the highest-paid British performer of his time. His repertory originally contained a whole gallery of Scottish types, but eventually he settled into a cosy, chuckling caricature of the canny Scot, invariably singing 'I Love a Lassie' and 'Roamin' in the Gloamin''. He made 22 tours of the USA between 1909 and 1932, organized the first front-line entertainment units during World War I and was knighted in 1919. He was also the most prolific recording artist of the music-hall.

**Laughton, Charles** 1899–1962 British-born actor. He became an American citizen in 1950. At the OLD VIC (1933–4) he played in seven productions, including leading roles in *The Cherry Orchard*, *The Tempest* and *Macbeth*. He was the first English actor to perform at the COMÉDIE-FRANÇAISE, in *Le Médecin malgré lui* (1936). After a decade of film work he returned to the stage in 1947 with *Galileo*, adapted with BRECHT and first performed in Los Angeles. For several years he toured the USA reading from the Bible, SHAKESPEARE and modern classics. He directed and played the Devil in SHAW's *Don Juan in Hell* (1951). He also played Bottom in *A Midsummer Night's Dream* and King Lear at Stratford-upon-Avon (1959).

**Laurents, Arthur** 1918– American screenwriter, director and playwright. *Home of the Brave* (1945) was concerned with a Jewish soldier's wartime problems. In *The Time of the Cuckoo* (1952), *A Clearing in the Woods* (1957) and *Invitation to a March* (1960) he wrote about women whose psychological problems drive them towards disaster. *The Bird Cage* (1950) builds upon the sexual frustrations of a vicious nightclub owner. Laurents is celebrated for writing the books for the musicals *West Side Story* (1957) and *Gypsy* (1960) and such screenplays as *Anna Lucasta* (1949) and *Anastasia* (1956). His later work – *The Enclave* (1973) and *Heartsong* (1974) – has been less appreciated. His most recent play, *Jolson Sings Again* (1995), premiered at the Seattle Repertory Theatre.

**Lawler, Ray** 1921– Australian playwright. As an actor in Melbourne he achieved fame when *Summer of the Seventeenth Doll* (1955), depicting two Queensland cane-cutters' annual holiday with their city girls, gained Australian and international success. After living in Britain and Ireland he returned to Australia in 1975, becoming literary adviser to the Melbourne Theatre Company. His plays include *The Piccadilly Bushman* (1959), *The Man Who Shot the Albatross* (1971), and *Kid Stakes* (1975) and *Other Times* (1977), depicting the characters of *The Doll* in earlier years and completing the *Doll* trilogy.

**Lawrence, D(avid) H(erbert)** 1885–1930 British novelist, poet and playwright. The sexual explicitness of his novels prevented Lawrence's plays from reaching the public stage until 1967–8 (see CENSORSHIP), though a biblical epic (*David*) was performed by the STAGE SOCIETY (1927), as was *The Widowing of Mrs Holroyd* (1926). This – like *A Collier's Friday Night* (written 1906), *The Daughter-in-Law*, based on the coal strike of 1912, and *The Fight for Barbara*, reflecting his own relationship with a married woman – superimposed the class struggle on the struggle of the sexes. Written from Lawrence's personal experience as the son of a miner and more starkly realistic than the plays of a contemporary like GALSWORTHY, these were well received when revived in repertory at the ROYAL COURT THEATRE in 1965–7, leading to performances of his other social plays, *The Merry-Go-Round* (1973) and *Touch and Go* (1979).

**Lawrence, Gertrude** 1898–1952 British singer, actress and dancer. A MUSICAL COMEDY star, 'Gertie' played opposite NOËL COWARD in his plays *Private Lives* (1930) and *To-night at 8.30* (1936). She had a brilliant American career in which *Lady in the Dark* (1941) and *The King and I* (1951) were high points. Vivacity, warmth and a sense of fun characterized her stage presence.

**Lawrence, Jerome** 1915– and **Robert E(dwin) Lee** 1918–94 American playwriting team. This pair of Ohio-born dramatists joined in formal partnership in 1942 and wrote dozens of plays, many produced in New York. *Inherit the Wind* (1955) was a faithful dramatization of the famous Scopes 'monkey trial'. Also extremely popular was their libretto for the musical *Mame* (1966). Their play *The Night Thoreau Spent in Jail* (1970) was an early offering of the American Playwrights' Theatre. They have also been responsible for many one-act operas, screenplays, television and radio shows.

**Lawson, John Howard** 1895–1977 American playwright and screenwriter. In the theatre of the 1920s Lawson was an anomaly, a dramatist of fiery left-wing convictions. Striking out against the convention-bound commercial theatre on the one hand and the ivory tower art theatre on the other, he attempted to forge a new theatrical style which he called 'political VAUDEVILLE'. His most successful experiment was *Processional* (1925), a staccato, fragmented series of sketches set in West Virginia during a coal strike. In 1926 he was a co-founder of the short-lived, politically radical New Playwrights' Theatre, for which he wrote a strident political SATIRE called *Loud Speaker*. Lawson changed his style in the 1930s, replacing extravagance with an idiomatic REALISM that had a strong influence on CLIFFORD ODETS. The embittered working-class anti-heroes of his *Success Story* (1932) and *Gentlewoman* (1934) speak a racy urban poetry.

**Laya, Jean-Louis** 1761–1833 French playwright. His political comedy, *L'Ami des lois* (*The Friend of the Laws*, 1793), staged at the Théâtre de la Nation (the COMÉDIE-FRANÇAISE), vigorously attacked political extremists, in particular Marat and Robespierre. Laya was imprisoned. The play became a rallying point for former aristocrats and continued to be regarded as subversive after the revolutionary period.

**Lazarenko, Vitaly (Efimovich)** 1890–1939 Russian CLOWN. He began in CIRCUS as a trapeze gymnast, later developing a vein of satiric comedy, and established a world record by leaping over three elephants. After the Revolution he came into his own as a proletarian star, playing in many satirical pantomimes, including two pieces written for him by VLADIMIR MAYAKOVSKY: 'The Universal Class Struggle Championship' and 'ABC'. He performed for soldiers during both world wars. MEYERHOLD cast him as the devil in his second staging of Mayakovsky's *Mystery-Bouffe*.

*lazzo* (plural, *lazzi*) Italian term. An important constituent element in improvised Italian COMMEDIA DELL'ARTE, a *lazzo* may be a play on words, a quid pro quo, a piece of comic business, a sleight-of-hand trick or a pantomimic joke, usually intended to prompt laughter independent of the plot. Often sadistic and scatological, some *lazzi* became traditional, such as HARLEQUIN's fly-catching or JOHN RICH's hatching from an egg.

**Le Fartere, Roland** [Rolland le Pettour] French or English or Anglo-Norman popular performer. He is recorded c.1250 as holding land in Hemmingstone, Suffolk (England), on condition that he appear before the king every Christmas Day to perform the jump, whistle and fart ('*unum saltum et unum siffletum et unum bumbulum*'). Farting is well attested as an amateur performing art to the present day, and artists such as LE PÉTOMANE have occasionally achieved success with it on the commercial stage.

**Le Gallienne, Eva** 1899–1991 British-born American actress, translator, director and producer. Best known as an actress, Le Gallienne participated in every aspect of American theatre. Her New York debut was in *Mrs Boltay's Daughter* (1915), but her first big success was as Julie in *Liliom* (1921). For the next 60-plus years she played most of the major female roles in Western drama, receiving critical acclaim for performances in plays by IBSEN, CHEKHOV, SHAKESPEARE and SCHILLER. She introduced audiences throughout the USA to European drama through her translations and productions. A lifelong believer in repertory theatre, she founded the Civic Repertory Theatre (1926–33). There she produced, directed and starred. In 1946 Le Gallienne, CHERYL CRAWFORD and MARGARET WEBSTER founded the AMERICAN REPERTORY THEATRE, which lasted only one season.

**Leach, Wilford** 1929–88 American director, teacher, playwright and designer. From 1970 to 1977 he was artistic director of LA MAMA ETC (Experimental Theatre Club). From 1977 he worked for the NEW YORK SHAKESPEARE FESTIVAL, designing as well as directing productions. His major credits include *Mandragola* (1977), *All's Well* and *The Taming of the Shrew* (1978), *Othello* (1979), *Mother Courage* (1980), *The Pirates of Penzance* (1980), *The Human Comedy* (1983), *La Bohème* (1984) and *The Mystery of Edwin Drood* (1985). Leach's highly original style drew on VAUDEVILLE, film, animated cartoon, opera and PUPPET theatre.

**LeCompte, Elizabeth** 1944– American director and playwright. Since 1979 she has been artistic director of the experimental WOOSTER GROUP. With SPALDING GRAY and other members she wrote and directed *Sakonnet Point* (1975), *Rumstick Road* (1977) and *Nayatt School* (1978), a trilogy called *Three Places in Rhode Island*. In 1979 LeCompte and the Group created an 'epilogue' (without dialogue) to this trilogy called *Point Judith*. She was also instrumental in the creation of *Route 1 & 9* (1981) and *L. S. D.* (1984). In 1984 she was appointed associate director at the JOHN F. KENNEDY CENTER FOR THE PERFORMING ARTS. In the 1980s and early 1990s she has fostered radical avant-garde theatre in New York.

**Lecoq, Jacques** 1921– French actor, director, MIME artist and teacher. Lecoq researched the masks of the COMMEDIA in Italy and helped to found the theatre school of the Piccolo Theatre in Milan (see GIORGIO STREHLER). In 1956 he set up his international mime school in Paris, which has attracted students from all over the world. Here he developed a teaching technique centred on the physical expressivity of the actor.

**Lecouvreur, Adrienne** 1692–1730 French tragic actress. Her success at the COMÉDIE-FRANÇAISE in 1717 in the title role of CRÉBILLON's *Électre* won her a series of leading roles in the classical repertoire of PIERRE CORNEILLE and RACINE as well as in contemporary TRAGEDY. Though not a natural beauty, she was an instinctive performer with an imposing stage presence. Her vocal range was limited but she was credited with a simpler, less declamatory style of playing than was the norm. After a fêted career she died mysteriously and was refused Christian burial.

**Lee, Canada** [Leonard Canegata] 1907–52 African-American actor. A successful boxing career was halted by an eye injury, but his fighting spirit was manifested in several memorable roles. He played Blacksnake in the 1934 revival of the anti-lynching drama *Stevedore*, Banquo in the FEDERAL THEATRE PROJECT's 'voodoo' *Macbeth* (1936), and the emperor Christophe in *Haiti* (1938). His finest performance was as Bigger Thomas in Richard Wright's *Native Son* (1941). Lee played Caliban in MARGARET WEBSTER's 1945 production of *The Tempest* and a whiteface Bosola in *The Duchess of Malfi* (1946). He was a powerful actor of animal-like grace who was committed to a theatre of social relevance.

**Lee, Eugene** 1939– American set designer. Lee is unique among American designers in both concept and execution. Approaching each production without preconceptions, he treats the whole space of the theatre, not only the stage, as a place to be designed. From the late 1960s onward he was resident designer for the Trinity Square Repertory Company in Providence, Rhode Island, and together with director Adrian Hall created iconoclastic, often environmental, settings. He took environmental design to OFF-BROADWAY and BROADWAY with *Slaveship*, *Alice in Wonderland* and *Candide*. Lee has worked with PETER BROOK in Shiraz and Paris and with HAROLD PRINCE on several shows, including *Sweeney Todd*. He also designed television's 'Saturday Night Live' from its inception to 1980.

**Lee, Gypsy Rose** [Rose Louise Hovick] ?1914–70 American BURLESQUE artist and writer. By the age of 17 she was starring in Minsky's Burlesque . Her act comprised more 'tease' than 'strip', tantalizing with suggestive silk stockings, lace panties and a rose-garter tossed into the audience as a coda. H. L. Mencken coined the term 'ecdysiast' to label her speciality, and her sophisticated songs were parodied in the musical *Pal Joey* (1940). Seen in the ZIEGFELD *Follies* of 1936, nightclubs, fairs and carnivals, she was the first celebrity stripper. Her writings include a play, *The Naked Genius* (1943), and some murder mysteries; and a memoir, *Gypsy* (1957), turned into a popular MUSICAL COMEDY (1959). (See also NUDITY.)

**Lee, Ming Cho** 1930– American set designer. Born in Shanghai, he studied Chinese watercolour before emigrating to the USA in 1949. In 1954 he became an assistant to JO MIELZINER. The spare, minimalist, emblematic style that became Lee's trademark was, in part, a response to the poetic realism of Mielziner. It is best exemplified in the 1964 production of *Electra* at the NEW YORK SHAKESPEARE FESTIVAL. Lee is usually associated with pipe-work scaffolding, textured surfaces and collage. But since the late 1970s his work has turned to detail and ultra-REALISM, as in the production of *K2* in which he created a mountain on the stage. Despite his influence on opera and THEATRE DESIGN since the mid-1960s, he has designed little on BROADWAY. He also heads the design programme at the Yale School of Drama.

**Lee, Nathaniel** c.1650–92 English playwright. Lee was briefly an actor. His play *Nero* was performed in 1674. *The Rival Queens* (1677) was a substantial success, frequently revived as a vehicle for two actresses playing Roxana and Statira. In 1678 he collaborated with DRYDEN on a bloodthirsty version of *Oedipus*. *Lucius Junius Brutus* (1680), the best political play of the Restoration, was soon banned. Intense and restrained, it avoids the extravagance of his other work. His only comedy, *The Princess of Cleves*, turns Mme de la Fayette's novel into a vicious SATIRE on the sexual excesses of Restoration society.

**Lee, Robert E.** see LAWRENCE, JEROME

**legitimate theatre** see THEATRICAL MONOPOLY

**Leicester's Men** Elizabethan acting company. The first of the great household companies of the era, formed in 1559, was highly prosperous from c.1570 to 1583 but dwindled thereafter. JAMES BURBAGE, who built the THEATRE, and WILL KEMPE, who became its star attraction, were both former members of Leicester's Men.

**Leigh, Mike** 1943– British director and playwright. He studied acting and became the associate director of the Midlands Arts Centre in Birmingham. His distinctive contribution to the British stage (and TELEVISION DRAMA) has been the plays that he has devised together with the actors involved. Leigh's technique is to offer actors a basic idea and to encourage them to develop characters and situations which he then shapes into the final product. Significant successes have included *Abigail's Party* (1977) and *Goose-Pimples* (1981). *Smelling a Rat* (1988) and *Greek Tragedy* (1989) were effective but somewhat shapeless studies of social behaviour, lacking the wit of his earlier works. For television his credits are longer. The strength of his group-created plays is in their acute observation; their weakness a tendency for the observation to become petty and malicious.

**Leigh, Vivien** [Vivian Mary Hartley] 1913–67 British actress. She was married to LAURENCE OLIVIER, with whom she played in a number of striking Shakespearian performances: *Hamlet* at Elsinore (1937), *Romeo and Juliet* in New York (1940), *Antony and Cleopatra* in London (1951) and *Titus Andronicus* at Stratford-upon-Avon (1955). Her success in *The Doctor's Dilemma* (1942) prompted SHAW to suggest she play Cleopatra in the film of *Caesar and Cleopatra* (also staged with Olivier, 1951). She is best-remembered for her film roles in *Gone with the Wind* and *A Streetcar Named Desire* (re-creating her acclaimed 1949 theatrical performance). The sensitivity and precision of her acting were widely admired. After touring with the OLD VIC and in GIRAUDOUX's *Duel of Angels* she gave her final performance with GIELGUD in CHEKHOV's *Ivanov* (New York, 1966).

**Leipzig style** German acting tradition. This formal, wooden performance style of the early 18th century was encouraged by JOHANN GOTTSCHED in an effort to elevate the way in which tragic drama was acted. It was practised initially by the NEUBER troupe. Although such acting was highly unsubtle, based as it was on misconceptions of classical gesture and French tragic acting, it was for many a suitable alternative to the rough improvisation that, until the time of the Neubers, was standard on the German stage. The Leipzig style remained the dominant acting mode until the rise of the BÜRGERLICHES TRAUERSPIEL required a quieter realism.

**Leis, Raúl** 1947– Panamanian playwright, journalist and poet. In addition to several children's plays, he is author of *Viaje a la Salvación y otros países* (*Journey to Salvation and Other Countries*, 1973) and *Viene el sol con su sombrero de combate puesto* (*The Sun Comes Up with its Combat Helmet On*) dealing with sovereignty issues over the Panama Canal. *María Picana* (1979) captures the inherent violence in Latin America through a woman torturer, raised as a child by animals. *El nido de Macúa* (*The Nest of the Macúa*, 1981) treats syncretism and magic in Panamanian social issues. Other works include *Lo peor del boxeo* (*The Worst of Boxing*), *Primero de mayo* (*First of May*) and *El señor Sol* (*Mr Sun*, 1983).

**Lekain** [Henri-Louis Kain] 1729–78 French actor. Discovered by VOLTAIRE, he became the leading tragedian at the COMÉDIE-FRANÇAISE. Despite modest stature and bow legs, he was renowned for his majestic bearing and passionate playing – well suited to Voltaire's tragedies, whose heroic roles he created. Helped by the example of MLLE CLAIRON, rejecting stage convention he espoused period accuracy in COSTUME, initially by wearing ancient Greek dress for RACINE's *Andromaque*. He also campaigned for the reform of acting conventions and the removal of audience seating on the stage, finally abolished in 1759. He planned an acting school associated with the Comédie-Française. Widely admired by contemporary critics, he was likened to GARRICK.

**Lemaître, Frédérick** 1800–76 French actor. Perhaps the greatest, certainly the most flamboyant actor of the century, Frédérick, as he was usually known, began his career in pantomimes, harlequinades and, from 1817 to 1820, in the *mimodrames* of the CIRQUE OLYMPIQUE. The turning point came in 1824 at the Ambigu (see BOULEVARD) when, with FIRMIN, he made a hilarious parody of a particularly pathetic melodrama, *L'Auberge des Adrets*, creating the character of Robert Macaire, who took on an independent existence in popular literature and later became a means of attacking the government and society of Louis Phillipe.

In 1827 Lemaître went to the Porte-Saint-Martin, the new temple of romanticism, where he created the role he would play for over 40 years, Georges de Germany in *Thirty Years of a Gamester's Life*. There he met an ideal partner in MARIE DORVAL. After a spell at the ODÉON he was back at the Porte-Saint-Martin, which HAREL had now acquired, and created DUMAS père's Richard Darlington with enormous success, following it with Gennaro in HUGO's *Lucrèce Borgia* (MLLE GEORGE played Lucrèce). In 1834 he took a new satirical piece, *Robert Macaire*, to the Folies Dramatiques, where it became very fashionable. In 1836 he triumphed at the Variétés in Dumas's *Kean* and in 1838 at the Théâtre de la Renaissance in Hugo's *Ruy Blas*. In 1840 he gave the first performance of Balzac's *Vautrin* at the Porte Saint-Martin, and the play was immediately banned (possibly because Lemaître made himself up to look like the king). He went from theatre to theatre (but never to the COMÉDIE-FRANÇAISE), playing high romantic drama and popular MELODRAMA, always touring, sometimes running into trouble with the censor for introducing political SATIRE into his performances. In 1852 the re-establishment of CENSORSHIP hit his major roles, including Robert Macaire and Ruy Blas. By the 1870s he was in a state of near destitution, playing the suburban theatres.

**Leñero, Vicente** 1933– Mexican playwright and novelist. His first serious novel, *Los albañiles* (*The Bricklayers*, 1964), was a major contribution to the revitalization of Latin American letters. His introduction to the theatre was *Pueblo rechazado* (*Rejected People*, 1968), a controversial documentary piece based on a monastery that promulgated psychoanalysis for its monks instead of slavish attention to prayer. Most of his subsequent plays are also documentaries: *Compañero* (*Companion*, 1971), based on Che Guevara; *El juicio* (*The Trial*, 1971), on the trial of the assassin of Mexican president-elect Obregón in 1928; *Los hijos de Sánchez* (*The Children of Sánchez*, 1972), about a Mexican village; plus several others including *El martirio de Morelos* (*The Martyrdom of Morelos*, 1981), about the Mexican national hero, and *La noche de Hernán Cortés*

(*The Night of Hernán Cortés*, 1990). His *Vivir del teatro* (*Life in the Theatre*) recounts the vicissitudes of staging his several plays.

**Leno, Dan** [George Galvin] 1860–1904 British VARIETY artist. Long before he reached manhood he had acquired an impressive range of skills as contortionist, clog-dancer, Irish comedian and character vocalist. His solo London debut came in the East End in 1885. He performed in an illustrious run of Christmas shows, including 15 consecutively at DRURY LANE from 1888. By 1897, when he made his first American appearance, he was billed as 'the funniest man on earth'. Trained in physical techniques since he could walk, he applied these to the creation of the multitude of vivid caricatures that throng his career. Leno's ambiguous comic vision was of a recalcitrant physical world inhabited by unreliable people.

**Lenormand, Henri-René** 1882–1951 French playwright. Lenormand's plays were performed by the PITOËFF company between the wars. They employed techniques pioneered by CHEKHOV and PIRANDELLO to convey the psychological life, drawing on the insights of Freudian psychoanalysis. His plays have not been revived recently but his *Confessions d'un auteur dramatique* (*Confessions of a Playwright*, 1952) gives insight into both his period and the profession of playwright.

**Lenz, Johann (Michael Reinhold)** 1751–92 German playwright. Among the most prominent of the STURM UND DRANG dramatists, Lenz is best known for his comedies of contemporary life, *The Soldiers* (1776) and *The Tutor* (1778), which are among the first German plays of genuine quality to exhibit the influence of SHAKESPEARE. His essay 'Observations on the Theatre' (1774) is among the most perceptive documents of German Shakespeare criticism of the 18th century. Lenz's creative career was cut short by a severe decline in his mental faculties, which led to his early death.

**Leonard, Hugh** [John Leyes Byrne] 1926– Irish playwright. The ABBEY produced Leonard's first two long plays, *The Birthday Party* (1956) and *A Leap in the Dark* (1958). Afterwards he wrote for television: plays, many adaptations, and a farcical series, *Me Mammy*. He is skilled in FARCE: he has adapted LABICHE's *Célimare*; his *The Patrick Pearse Motel* (1971) and *Time Was* (1976) use the genre to satirize Dublin's fashionable outer suburbs. *Da* (1973), successful in New York, is a serio-comic treatment of the same location. *A Life* (1976) retraces Mr Drumm's path to his desiccated marriage, accounting for, perhaps disturbing, his defensive reserve. By repeating a basic story in two time frames, his comedy *Moving* (1990) explores the ironies of social 'progress'. Technically highly proficient, Leonard has been suspected of glibness in these experiments with time.

**Leonardo da Vinci** 1452–1519 Italian artist, scientist and stage designer. Little is known of his work for the theatre, but extant designs suggest a keen interest in scenic decoration and stage machinery; from these several attempts have been made to construct models of the machinery and stages he intended, like those for Isabella of Aragon's entry into Milan (1489), and the scene and revolving stage prepared for Poliziano's *Orfeo* (c.1495).

**Leonov, Leonid (Maksimovich)** 1899–1994 Soviet novelist and playwright. He tried to make psychological and social realism the bases for the new Soviet literature. His work, which tends to be symbolic and even in places allegorical, consciously evokes Dostoevsky,

CHEKHOV, GORKY and other predecessors in its treatment of the crises experienced by individuals as a result of social change. His 13 plays include dramatizations of two of his novels, *The Badgers* (1927) and *Skutarevsky* (1934). The former, like his first original play, *Untilovsk* (1928), employs a Siberian setting. The latter, a character study of an old-guard scientist converted to Bolshevism, reflects the familiar Soviet conflict between service to the collective and to the individual. His best-known play, *The Orchards of Polovchansk* (1938), embodies a Chekhovian sense of society on the brink of change. Written during the purges of 1936–8, under official pressure it was transformed by its author from a psychological character study to a sociopolitical tale with an anti-Soviet villain. His most popular play, *Invasion* (1942), like *Lyonushka* (1943), is a patriotic picture of wartime heroism, notable for demonstrating the character-building potential of war.

**Léotard, Jules** 1838–70 French aerialist. He abandoned his law studies to become a trapeze artist, winning almost immediate success on his debut at the Cirque Napoléon, Paris, on 12 November 1859. Léotard perfected the trapeze act, inventing the *salto mortale* (see ACROBATICS) through the moving apparatus and giving his name to the tight-fitting garment he wore; and, after an engagement at the London Alhambra, inspiring the song 'The Daring Young Man on the Flying Trapeze'. His career was an unbroken series of triumphs.

**Lepage, Robert** 1957– Canadian director and theatre artist. Lepage studied with Alain Knapp in Paris, returning to Quebec in 1980 to help found Théâtre Repère, a company whose productions take shape from an initial focus on a tangible 'resource' object. Lepage's creations are collaborative: the writing, acting, set design and stage direction evolve 'globally'. In his one-man shows *Vinci* (1986) and *Needles and Opium* (1991), this resulted in a sense of playfulness and freedom of movement in an atmosphere of stylistic, multi-media effects. Productions change as the cast and venue change: *La trilogie des dragons* began as a 90-minute piece (1985), grew to a three-hour performance (1986) and reached its final form as three autonomous two-hour shows (1987). *Plaques Tectoniques/Tectonic Plates* (1983) was recreated for its Glasgow production (1990) to reflect the interaction between Canadian and Scottish cast members. A similar evolution has been planned for *Seven Streams of the River Ota*, which opened at the EDINBURGH FESTIVAL in 1994.

Lepage is internationally acclaimed. To create his 'global' theatre, he frequently explores intercultural collaboration of theme and structure. His bilingual production of *Romeo and Juliet* (1989) recast Shakespeare's story in the light of the tensions between the French and English cultures in his native Canada. His *Midsummer Night's Dream* (1992) at the NATIONAL THEATRE rivalled PETER BROOK's 1970 production in originality.

**Lermontov, Mikhail (Yurievich)** 1814–41 Russian poet, novelist and playwright. The five dramas of Russia's greatest romantic poet after PUSHKIN palely reflect his career as an artist and military man. *The Spaniards* (written 1830, published 1880, produced 1924) employs the romantic locale of Spain during the Inquisition as a metaphor for the repressive reign of Tsar Nikolai I. It is replete with poisonings, abduction, pathos, frenzy and a semi-autobiographical protagonist who murders the thing he loves. His best play,

*Masquerade* (written 1836, censored production 1852, uncensored production 1862), combines romanticism and social realism. The langour of the protagonist Arbenin masks a tormented soul, much as the court society which victimizes him and his wife masks cruelty and hypocrisy with gaiety and fashion. The play was opulently staged at the Aleksandrinsky Theatre in 1917 by MEYERHOLD. Lermontov's remaining plays include *Men and Passions* (written 1830, published 1880); *The Strange Man* (written 1831, published 1860), a rewritten version of the former; and *The Two Brothers* (written 1836, produced 1915), which he reworked as the psychological novel *Princess Ligovskaya*. His celebrated novel, *A Hero of Our Time* (1840), features the fatalistic hero Pechorin, whom CHEKHOV spoofs via Solyony in *Three Sisters*. Lermontov was killed in a duel with a former schoolmate.

**Lerner, Alan Jay** 1918–86 and **Frederick Loewe** 1904–88 American lyricist and composer. Loewe, a classically trained composer born in Vienna, and Lerner collaborated on their first musical score, *What's Up*, in 1943. Four years later the team had its first major success with *Brigadoon*, a fantasy set in a magical Scottish village. Their next show, *Paint Your Wagon*, achieved a modest run. In 1956 Lerner and Loewe wrote the score for *My Fair Lady*, a musical version of GEORGE BERNARD SHAW's *Pygmalion*. *My Fair Lady*'s score was a perfect blending of Loewe's operetta music with Lerner's pseudo-Shavian lyrics: the two combined to produce one of the most successful musical comedies ever. Their next show, *Camelot* (1960), was less successful. They collaborated on only one other BROADWAY musical, a 1973 adaptation of their film *Gigi*.

Loewe's music successfully combined the older operetta tradition with more modern Broadway musical idioms. Lerner's versatility as a lyricist was demonstrated in songs whose styles ranged from the sophisticated verbal trickery of LORENZ HART to the simple treatment of OSCAR HAMMERSTEIN II.

**Lesage, Alain-René** 1668–1747 French novelist and playwright. His novel *Le Diable boiteux* (*The Devil on Two Sticks*, 1707) gives a realistic picture of contemporary French society. His first theatrical success, in the same year, was the COMEDY *Crispin rival de son maître* (*Crispin Rival of his Master*), which portrays an opportunistic valet who impersonates his master. In *Turcaret* (1709), still part of the classic repertoire, Lesage takes a sardonic view of a society motivated entirely by greed and self-interest. Fiercely opposed in financial quarters, it was withdrawn from the COMÉDIE-FRANÇAISE after only seven performances. Thereafter Lesage wrote for the fair theatres, producing over 100 *vaudevilles*, comic operas and *pièces à écriteaux* (placard plays). His best-known work is the picaresque tale of *Gil Blas de Santillane* (published in 12 books between 1715 and 1735), which influenced the evolution of the European novel.

**lesbian theatre** A term used to describe theatre made by or for lesbians, and to differentiate this from work by gay men (see GAY THEATRE).

Examples of lesbian work in the theatre before 1968 are rare. Lesbians in a theatre context are triply invisible: as women, as homosexual, as women in a male theatre tradition. Lesbian theatre history has focused on figures and texts 'readable' as homoerotic (e.g. the 18th-century cross-dressing actress Charlotte Charke, daughter of COLLEY CIBBER) and has found past evidence of the occasional lesbian presence or voice. The dominant view, however (Michel Foucault's), is that the social, and thus representable, identity of the 'lesbian' was not created until the late 19th and early 20th-centuries, through sexology and psychoanalysis.

Key figures in the British FEMINIST THEATRE of the period were undoubtedly lesbian. EDITH CRAIG (daughter of ELLEN TERRY) founded the Pioneer Players (1911–20), a theatre company dominated by women and feminist ideas; her partner Christopher St John (Christabel Marshall) co-authored plays for the Actresses' Franchise League with Cicely Hamilton, whom a recent biographer proposes as lesbian. St John wrote novels and further plays with discernible lesbian narratives. The first British play in which female homoeroticism can clearly be read is Edith Ellis's *The Mothers* (1915), a one-act that uses the contemporary feminist image of the heroic mother to figure women's erotic bonding. Ellis's husband was the British sexologist Havelock Ellis, and one of the interesting features of the play is its opposition to his depiction of the 'mannish' lesbian.

Feminism as a movement declined after World War I, and with it women's theatre and the potential for a lesbian drama. (This contrasts with the history of gay men's theatre: the 1920s and 1930s in Britain saw the 'homosexualization' of the theatre.) The first plays containing recognizable 'lesbian' characters were produced in this period: German playwright Christa Winsloe's *Children in Uniform* (1932) and US playwright Lillian Hellman's *The Children's Hour* (1934) are two well known examples: others are documented in K. Curtin's *We Can Always Call Them Bulgarians*. But none was written by a lesbian and the lesbian characters are presented within the descriptive framework of the sexologists or psychoanalysts. It was against these 'negative images' of lesbianism as hysteria, as failed heterosexuality or as masculinity complex that the first phase of a truly lesbian theatre protested, in the USA and in Britain, in the 1970s and 1980s.

Lesbian theatre in Britain developed as part of the alternative political theatre movement. In its early phase it was allied to gay men's theatre. Gay Sweatshop, Britain's first gay theatre company (founded in 1975) presented its first lesbian piece, *Any Woman Can* by Jill Posner, in 1976. Like many first lesbian and gay plays this tells the story of 'coming out', the first lesbian RITE OF PASSAGE. Fairly soon, however, the alliance with gay men was challenged by an increasingly radical lesbian feminism. Although lesbians continued to work with Gay Sweatshop, for some time there were separate male and female companies, and other, specifically lesbian, theatre companies developed. *Care and Control* (devised by the company and scripted by Michelene Wandor, 1977) was the Gay Sweatshop women's company's first production. A documentary account of the problems faced by lesbian mothers in custody cases, it inaugurated the feminist phase of lesbian theatre. There were further plays about lesbian mothers: *Aid Thy Neighbour*, Michelene Wandor (1978); *Neaptide*, Sara Daniels (1986); plays challenging male violence (*Curfew*, Siren Theatre, 1981) and patriarchal control of women's bodies and sexuality (*Basin*, Jacqueline Rudet (1985); *Byrthrite*, Sara Daniels (1986); and plays celebrating the 'lesbian continuum' (*The Fires of Bride*, Ellen Galford/Red Rag (1990); *Twice Over*, Jackie Kay (1988)).

Lesbian theatre expanded throughout the 1970s and 1980s. Specifically lesbian companies were formed: in Britain – Hormone Imbalance, Siren, Hard Corps, Parker and Klein, Character Ladies, Red Rag, Dramatrix Productions and Shameful Practice. Lesbian playwrights were commissioned by other companies including the Women's Theatre Group, the English Stage Company at the ROYAL COURT and – astonishingly, given its poor record of producing women's plays – the NATIONAL THEATRE; and venues particularly or exclusively associated with lesbian theatre developed (Oval House and the Drill Hall in London, the WOW Café in New York). In London encouragement was given in the first half of the 1980s by the radical left administration of the Greater London Council and its generous funding for gay and lesbian work. Lesbian theatre was part of an expanding gay and lesbian cultural scene, alongside publishing houses, bookshops, bars and cafés, music and visual arts, much of which was also funded by the GLC.

That the audience for lesbian theatre is drawn from a metropolitan lesbian community raises questions about the point of address of lesbian theatre. Some at least of the issue-based lesbian feminist theatre implied a male heterosexual spectator as recipient of protest about heterosexism or of new positive images of lesbians. Although these plays were important in promoting lesbian audiences' sense of community, from the late 1980s lesbian theatre has seemed to be turning away from political protest towards a celebration of the specificity of lesbian difference and desire. From address to undress...

Not that sex was absent from earlier lesbian theatre. The British lesbian comedy duo Parker and Klein, and Hard Corps, a company with which they worked, were dedicated, in Debby Klein's phrase, to 'putting the sex back into sexual politics'. In Klein's 1986 comedy *Coming Soon* taboo figures, the nun and the butch, play havoc with the heroine's political correctness. Siren Theatre and Tasha Fairbanks's plays *Pulp* (1985) and *Hotel Destiny* (1987) use the 'noir' thriller and Country and Western images respectively to represent lesbian desire. Dramatrix productions' annual lesbian PANTOMIMES at London's Drill Hall – beginning in 1987 with Cheryl Moch's *Cinderella*, which premiered in 1985 at the WOW Café in New York, and followed by lesbian versions of *Peter Pan* by Bryony Lavery, and *The Adventures of Robyn Hood* and *The Snow Queen* by Nona Sheppard – have been popular for their cross-dressing and flagrant transgression of classical heterosexual narratives.

Generally, these have been *stories about* sex, in which the erotic exchange between performer and audience has been rather coyly acknowledged. Recent work by US performers Split Britches (*Split Britches*, 1981; *Beauty and the Beast*, 1982; *Upwardly Mobile Home*, 1984; *Little Women*, 1988; *Anniversary Waltz*, 1989; *Lesbians Who Kill*, Deborah Margolin, 1992) and Holly Hughes (*The Well of Horniness*, 1983; *The Lady Dick*, 1985: *Dress Suits to Hire*, 1987; *World without End*, 1990; *No Trace of Blonde*, 1992) is much more – to use the title of Gay Sweatshop's 1994 lesbian show – in your face. Their work is saturated with sexuality. The banished figures of lesbian culture and desire, the butch and the femme, have been reinvested with desire; erotic power and play have returned as the lesbian performance. A new aesthetic of lesbian theatre eschews 'representation' for a live/now performance of the lesbian body. Dressing, undressing, cross-dressing, PARODY, allusion, self-referentiality and camp mark this theatre. In 1991 Split Britches collaborated with the

British drag company Bloolips (see FEMALE IMPERSON-ATION; REVUE) on Belle Reprieve, a butch/femme/drag version of *A Streetcar Named Desire* which played on both sides of the Atlantic; one half of Split Britches, Lois Weaver, is now also joint artistic director of Gay Sweatshop and Peggy Shaw, the other half, plus US per-former Pamela Sneed, opened their double bill of butch performance pieces – *Two Big Girls* – at London's Institute of Contemporary Arts in February 1994.

In the mid-1990s the term 'lesbian theatre' seems to be becoming outmoded. Having moved away from femi-nism, and from presenting as real/nice girls, what is now drawing lesbian audiences is Queer Performance – Queer as something outside, disruptive, excessively sex-ual, incapable of assimilation; and the performance of the lesbian as neither real, nor nice, nor girl.

**Lescarbot, Marc** ?1570–1642 French historian, poet and playwright. He was author of the first dramatic text composed and performed in French in the New World, the verse play *Le Théâtre de Neptune en la Nouvelle-France* (*The Theatre of Neptune in New France*), enacted on the waters before Port Royal, Acadia (today's Annapolis Royal, Nova Scotia) in November 1606. It portrays Neptune and his Tritons, who along with four American Indians welcome the colony's leaders on their return from a dangerous exploration, and ends with an invitation to all present to share a celebratory banquet. Replete with neoclassical allusions, this slen-der text, first published in 1609, is a good-humoured example of the dramatic sub-genre known in France as a *réception*, a form that would long remain popular in French Canada. It was performed again on the same spot in 1956, marking the 350th anniversary of the birth of the theatre in North America.

**Leslie, Fred** [Frederick Hobson] 1855–92 British actor. The greatest star of early MUSICAL COMEDY was made famous in a musical version of BOUCICAULT's *Rip Van Winkle* at London's Comedy Theatre in 1882. At the GAIETY, he played opposite NELLIE FARREN in the BUR-LESQUE *Little Jack Sheppard* (1885) and *Monte Cristo, Jr* (1886), as well as in his own *Ruy Blas; or, the Blasé Roué* (1889).

**Lessing, G(otthold) E(phraim)** 1729–81 German playwright and critic. He was a journalist, critic and dramaturge during the short-lived Hamburg National Theatre project, and his essays emphasized the short-comings of the French drama, then still widely admired and imitated in Germany. Lessing was among the first to recognize the strengths of SHAKESPEARE and the warm humanity of the English dramatic tradition. In the *Hamburg Dramaturgy* (1768) he attempted to rid the German stage of its dependence on the French and in so doing engaged in a radical interpretation of ARISTOTLE, focusing in particular on the nature of pity and fear. The end of drama, he maintained, is compassion; by arousing compassion, the drama fulfils its important social function.

He wrote several plays, the most notable of which are *Miss Sara Sampson* (1755), a domestic tragedy, highly popu-lar in its day, that owed much to GEORGE LILLO and the novels of Samuel Richardson; *Minna von Barnhelm* (1767), widely regarded as the first major comedy in the German language; *Emilia Galotti* (1772), a tense, disturbing, and theatrically effective tragedy that contains much criti-cism of the egoism and venality of the rulers of contem-porary petty states; and *Nathan the Wise* (1779), a moving and noble plea for religious tolerance. Though Lessing claimed that he did not create with the spontaneity of the true artist, these four plays were among the first works of enduring quality written for the German stage.

**Levin, Hanoch** 1943– Israeli playwright. His plays depict petit-bourgeois life in Tel-Aviv as the antithesis of the idealism of the pioneers. His irreverent and pes-simistic debunking of society has earned him the repu-tation of a misanthropic decadent writer. But he has won recognition and popularity for his unflinching naturalism of speech and his satirical barbs. In the greatest of his plays, *The Passion of Job* (1981), he created the Jewish equivalent of the Gentile myth. Among his many plays are *You and I and the Next War* (1969), *Queen of the Bath* (1970), *Hefetz* (1972), *Yaacobi and Leidental* (1972; English version, *Domino*), *Vardaleh's Youth* (1974), *Shitz* (1975), *Krum* (1975), *The Patriot* (1982), *The Suitcase Packers* (1983), *The Lost Trojan Women* (1984), *Hops and Hopla* (1991) and *The Child Dreams* (1993). He has also directed many of his own plays. Although admired at home, they have not found favour with audiences abroad, perhaps because of the local idiom of his SATIRE.

**Lewes, G(eorge) H(enry)** 1817–78 British critic and playwright. A man of many parts, he enjoyed amateur acting (e.g. before CHARLES DICKENS at Tavistock House) and had 14 plays, mostly adaptations from the French, performed in his lifetime, the most successful of which was *The Game of Speculation* (1851). Lewes's dramatic crit-icism was written for the *Leader* (1850–4) and the *Pall Mall Gazette*. He campaigned against CHARLES KEAN and wrote eloquent, penetrating essays on EDMUND KEAN, RACHEL and CHARLES JAMES MATHEWS, collected in *On Actors and the Art of Acting* (1875). His own distinction as a writer has been engulfed by interest in his long liaison with George Eliot.

**Lewis, Leopold** 1828–90 British playwright. His single claim to fame was his adaptation as *The Bells* of *Le Juif Polonais* by Erckmann and Chatrian. The role of Mathias was memorably played by HENRY IRVING in 1871. Of three later plays staged in London, none succeeded.

**Lewis, Robert** 1909– American director, producer and actor. From 1931 to 1941 he worked with the GROUP THEATRE, for whom he directed the road company of *Golden Boy* in 1938. After the war he directed extensively on BROADWAY; among his hit productions were *Brigadoon* (1947) and *Teahouse of the August Moon* (1953). With ELIA KAZAN and CHERYL CRAWFORD he founded the ACTORS STUDIO in 1947.

**Leybourne, George** 1842–84 British MUSIC-HALL star. He made his London debut as a vocalist around 1863 working with a mechanical donkey. Imposingly tall and handsome, Leybourne perfected the image of the *lion comique*, the free-spending, hard-drinking sport. His most famous number was 'Champagne Charlie', a per-sona he carried into private life, treating all and sundry. He beat all rivals in the breadth of his repertory and the magnetism of his personality.

**Li Yu** 1610–80 Chinese playwright and theatre practi-tioner. Born in Jiangsu, he ran his own theatre troupe of actresses whom he trained and directed, travelling round the country to perform at the homes of high offi-cials. He was a talented and versatile playwright, author and critic. His work revealed a profound knowledge of stage practices and dramatic composition based on first-hand experience. He rejected the stigma laid upon theatre by his contemporaries. His book on dramatic theory *A Temporary Lodge for My Leisure Thoughts* (*Xianqing ouji*), published in 1671, is the most outstanding work of its genre written in 17th-century China.

**Lifshits, A. M.** see VOLODIN, ALEKSANDR

**lighting** see STAGE LIGHTING

**Ligier** 1796–1872 French actor. Of large voice, small stature and a considerable talent for make-up, he made his debut at the COMÉDIE-FRANÇAISE in 1820 as Néron in *Britannicus*. In 1829 he created DELAVIGNE's *Marino Faliero* at the Porte-Saint-Martin (see BOULEVARD). Re-admitted to the Comédie-Française as a *sociétaire* in 1831, he continued his line of sinister historical figures with *Louis XI* (1832) and others, including one of his greatest roles, Frédéric in HUGO's *Les Burgraves*.

**Lillie, Beatrice (Gladys)** [Lady Robert Peel] 1898–1989 Canadian comedienne. She found her niche as a comic in André Charlot's REVUES of 1917 and 1924, which took her to the USA where her New York successes included *This Year of Grace* (1929) with NOËL COWARD, *The Show Is On* (1936) with BERT LAHR, *Set to Music* (1939) and *Inside USA* (1948). Lillie was the consummate revue performer, wielding the slapstick with a raised pinky, puncturing her own poses of sophisticated grandeur with lapses into raucous vulgarity.

**Lillo, George** ?1691–1739 English playwright. His reputation is based on two works, *The London Merchant* (1731) and *Fatal Curiosity* (1736). The former, also known as *The History of George Barnwell*, is a rare example of English domestic tragedy, about an apprentice lured to steal from his master by his passion for an evil woman. Lillo's drama is much more dominated by pathos than its Elizabethan forebears and was influential in the development of European 'bourgeois' tragedy by ROUSSEAU, DIDEROT and LESSING. *Fatal Curiosity*, recounting an impoverished old couple's desperate decision to murder a wealthy stranger who turns out to be their long-lost son, is more fatalistic and affected the development of the German SCHICKSALTRAGÖDIE.

**Lincoln Center** see VIVIAN BEAUMONT AND MITZI E. NEWHOUSE THEATRES

**Lincoln's Inn Fields Theatre** (London) In March 1660 WILLIAM DAVENANT leased Lisle's Tennis Court and enlarged it for use as a theatre. It opened in June 1661 with performances of his play *The Siege of Rhodes*, the first production in England to use changeable scenery in a permanent professional theatre. In November 1671 Davenant's company moved into DORSET GARDEN. In February 1672 KILLIGREW's King's Company moved into Lincoln's Inn Fields until March 1674. It then reverted to use as a tennis court until 1695 when BETTERTON's company, seceding from the United Company, refurbished and opened it with CONGREVE's *Love for Love*. In 1714 JOHN RICH rebuilt it with a capacity of 1,400. His company used it until 1732.

**Lindau, Paul** 1839–1919 German journalist, playwright and director. Lindau's comedies enjoyed some success in his lifetime. In 1895 he directed the MEININGEN COMPANY, after it had concluded its tours. In 1904, he was briefly director of the DEUTSCHES THEATER before MAX REINHARDT took it over.

**Lindberg, August** 1846–1916 Swedish actor and manager. He was influential in the breakthrough of NATURALISM in 19th-century Scandinavian theatre. Impatient with the outmoded and commercial principles of most established theatres of his time, he toured Scandinavia with companies that were often compared to the MEININGEN for their ensemble playing. A relentless champion of IBSEN, he directed the European premiere of *Ghosts* (1883) and the Norwegian premieres of *Brand* (1895) and *John Gabriel Borkman* (1897). As an actor,

he excelled in such diverse Ibsen roles as Oswald, Peer Gynt, Solness and Borkman, giving them an emotional complexity that also distinguished his Hamlet and Richard II. Late in life, he won acclaim for his overseas tours reading *The Tempest*, *Peer Gynt*, *Faust* and *Oedipus the King*.

**Lindberg, Per** 1890–1944 Swedish director. He introduced to Scandinavia the non-illusionistic principles of such modernists as CRAIG, REINHARDT and MEYERHOLD. He made an early impact at the Lorensberg Theatre, Göteborg (1918–23), with theatrical productions of SHAKESPEARE, STRINDBERG and contemporary European dramatists; he also tried to create a people's theatre, based on a socially relevant repertoire, inexpensive subscription schemes and the physical unification of stage and auditorium. These ideas were later pursued in Stockholm at the huge Concert Hall Theatre (1926–7 and 1931–2) and the Club Theatre that he created at DRAMATEN. During the 1930s, Lindberg's work was increasingly dominated by his fight against Fascism, especially in his productions in Bergen (1934) and Oslo (1935) of *The Hangman* by PÄR LAGERKVIST, with whom he shared a long and close collaboration.

**Lindsay, Howard** 1889–1968 American playwright, director, actor and producer. Following numerous stage appearances in VAUDEVILLE and BURLESQUE, he established himself on BROADWAY in the 1920s as both director and actor. He starred with his actress-wife Dorothy Stickney in *Life with Father* (1939), a play he co-wrote with RUSSEL CROUSE. Other collaborations with Crouse included the book for *Anything Goes* (1934), *State of the Union* (1945), the book for *Call Me Madam* (1950), *The Great Sebastians*, which featured ALFRED LUNT AND LYNN FONTANNE, and the books for *The Sound of Music* (1959) and *Mr President* (1962). He was a craftsman more than an artist, able to 'pull together' stageworthy theatrical pieces with his collaborators.

**Linney, Romulus** 1930– American director and playwright. Linney's career has been nurtured primarily by the non-profit professional RESIDENT THEATRE outside New York and by OFF-BROADWAY. His plays include *The Sorrows of Frederick* (1967), *The Love Suicide at Schofield Barracks* (1972), *Holy Ghosts* (1976), *Childe Byron* (1978), *Tennessee* (1979), *Laughing Stock* (1984), *Woman without a Name* (1985), *Pops* (1986), *Three Poets* (1989) and *Unchanging Love* (1991).

**Lipman, Maureen** 1946– British actress. She became a household name in Britain by her appearances as the archetypal Jewish mother Beattie in a series of 35 television commercials for British Telecom. Her gift for comedy was immediately apparent, although her versatility was less obvious. She played a demanding, fur-coated camp follower in Richard Harris's cricket comedy, *Outside Edge* (1979), and a single woman with a thirst problem in Philip King's farce, *See How They Run* (revived in 1984), two memorable comic performances; although she also appeared in two more sombre plays, Martin Sherman's *Messiah* (1981) and ALAN PLATER's biographical drama about Old Mother Riley, *On Your Way, Riley* (1981), at the Theatre Royal, Stratford East, in London. Her first major WEST END success came in 1986 in a revival of LEONARD BERNSTEIN's *Wonderful Town*. In 1988 her one-woman show, based on the songs and sketches of JOYCE GRENFELL, *Re-Joyce*, was an immediate hit.

**Liston, John** 1776–1846 English actor. His first major success was as Caper in J. T. Allingham's *Who Wins?*

(1808). Snub-nosed, red-cheeked, broad-bottomed, Liston provoked laughter by the contrast between his extravagant appearance and his comparatively restrained performance. He was allotted buffoon roles at COVENT GARDEN (1805–22): Ophelia in John Poole's *Hamlet Travestie* (1813), Bottom (1816), Pompey Bum (1816), Cloten (1817), Dromio of Syracuse (1819), Sir Andrew Aguecheek (1820) and Launce (1821). It was at the HAYMARKET that Liston created his greatest role, that of Paul Pry in Poole's play of that name (1825). At DRURY LANE he became the most highly paid comic actor in the history of English theatre and spent his last active years at the OLYMPIC under MADAME VESTRIS (1831–7).

**Little Theatre movement** (USA) Essentially an amateur movement, Little Theatres took off in the second decade of this century in Providence, Wisconsin, Boston, North Dakota and Chicago. Dissatisfaction with the offerings of the commercial theatre was complemented by a passionate belief that theatre arts could be grasped by enthusiastic and ambitious amateurs. The sudden and simultaneous flowering of groups is attributable to various causes, among them the founding of the DRAMA LEAGUE (1909), the visit of LADY GREGORY's Irish Players (1911) and GEORGE PIERCE BAKER's Workshop 47 at Harvard (1912).

The movement spread. By 1920 there were more than 50 groups scattered across the country, who found further support from the PROVINCETOWN PLAYERS (1914) and WASHINGTON SQUARE PLAYERS (1915). They performed in improvised quarters (family mansions, livery stables, churches, community centres) on temporary platforms, specializing in one-act plays which required minimal scenery and few rehearsals and offered undemanding roles. The more ambitious attempted the plays of SHAW, IBSEN and STRINDBERG. Little Theatres (now numbering more than 5,000) have become an integral part of the cultural life of their communities, and many have built their own theatre complexes. Some have been transformed into regional professional theatres (e.g. Cleveland, Houston, Washington, Dallas), and even those that have maintained their amateur (or semi-amateur) status operate on large budgets and present full seasons of major plays, both old and new.

**Little Tich** [Harry Relph] 1867–1928 British comedian. A diminutive singer and eccentric dancer, he was initially a 'nigger MINSTREL' (billed as Little Tichborne after the notorious claimant), in which role he perfected the big boot dance which became his trademark. He went solo in 1884. Cosmopolitan and linguistically gifted, he worked in the USA and Europe, particularly in France where he played the Olympia and the FOLIES-BERGÈRE and was made an officer of the Académie-Française (1910). He was a master of surrealistic patter: his caricatures of the Territorial, the Gas Inspector, the Ballerina and others trod a delicate line between the realistic and the bizarre. He appeared in the first Royal Command Charity Performance at London's Palace Theatre in 1912, and was an important influence on Chaplin.

**Littler, Prince** 1901–73 and Sir **Emile Littler** 1903–85 British actors. The two brothers became the leading impresarios in popular theatre after World War II. Prince Littler began by staging major PANTOMIMES in the WEST END and continued for more than 20 years with light entertainment, bringing over musicals like *Brigadoon* (1950) and *Carousel* (1951) from the USA. His great talent, however, lay as a businessman, who became chairman and managing director of Stoll Theatres Corporation, chairman of Moss Empire and, through Prince Littler Consolidated Trust, came to own or control nearly half the West End theatres and 57 of the main out-of-London touring theatres. When he diverted some of his assets into commercial television in 1955, he caused a major slump in regional theatre. His younger brother Emile, who was knighted in 1974, was a more orthodox impresario who excelled in comedies, pantomimes and musicals, producing *Annie Get Your Gun*, *Son of Norway*, *Zip Goes a Million* and many other hits. From 1964 to 1967 he was president of the Society of West End Theatre Managers, and a governor of the ROYAL SHAKESPEARE COMPANY until he retired in 1973. From 1946 to 1983 he controlled the Palace Theatre in London, where many of his successes were staged.

**Littlewood, (Maudie) Joan** 1914– British director. She was the driving force behind the establishment of the Theatre Workshop company at the Theatre Royal, Stratford, East London. Although she trained at the Royal Academy of Dramatic Art, she was always contemptuous of WEST END theatrical values and left London to go to Manchester as a radio producer. In 1935 she met the folk-singer and playwright Ewan MacColl (Jimmy Miller), whom she married, and together they founded an adventurous, left-wing touring company, Theatre Union. This became a pioneering example for the FRINGE companies of the 1960s, using AGIT-PROP techniques borrowed from German theatre.

In 1953 Littlewood took her small company to a decaying music-hall in London's East End. The ambitiousness of her programmes, combining contemporary documentary drama with classic productions of little-known plays, attracted interest from the EDINBURGH FESTIVAL in 1955. The next five years were crucial for the Theatre Workshop, Stratford. New plays (BRENDAN BEHAN's *The Quare Fellow* and *The Hostage*, SHELAGH DELANEY's *A Taste of Honey*), new musicals (FRANK NORMAN and Lionel Bart's *Fings Ain't Wot They Used T'Be*) and, above all, new character actors and actresses emanated from her theatre, often to the despised West End. In 1963 she directed her greatest success, *Oh, What A Lovely War!*, a documentary SATIRE about World War I, set within a seaside concert party framework.

Subsequently, although she directed the successful *Mrs Wilson's Diary* (1967) and *The Marie Lloyd Story* (1967) at the Theatre Workshop, of which the first transferred to the West End, she lost her old energy and passion for people's theatre. Her last Stratford production was *So You Want To Be in Pictures?* (1973), but her influence on other British directors and companies has been profound. In 1994 she published her autobiography, *Joan's Book*.

**liturgical drama** Medieval Christian drama. This earliest recorded post-classical drama flourished in all the countries of Western Europe between the 10th and 16th centuries. More recently, ceremonies and texts have been extracted from medieval church service books and anthologized as 'liturgical drama'. Originally, their performance would have been distinguished only marginally from the liturgy itself. Most such drama is associated with Easter, the most important feast of the Christian year. The *Quem queritis?* (Whom do you seek?) trope was sung, not spoken, originally by monks, for a monastic congregation, with no purpose-made costumes or staging, except for the sepulchre. The dialogue is echoed in a thousand texts associated with the Easter liturgy in Western Europe. The elaborated versions of the *Quem queritis?*, usually called the *Visitatio Sepulchri* (*Visit to the Sepulchre*), include such incidents as the buying of the ointment to anoint Christ's body, the appearance of Christ to Mary Magdalene and the running of Peter and John to the sepulchre. At Christmas a trope developed around the Shepherds' visit to the stable. Other stories produced their own dramas: the visit of the Magi, the Slaughter of the Innocents and the *Ordo Prophetarum* (*The Play of the Prophets*). Developments independent of Easter and Christmas took place at various times, such as the French play of the *Presentation of Mary in the Temple* by Philippe de Mézières (late 14th-century). Many such plays contain extensive stage directions for performance. By the time of the Reformation and Counter-Reformation liturgical drama had become an archaism. The monastic communities which had nourished it had by the 16th century been radically transformed or disestablished.

**Liverpool Playhouse** Britain's oldest continuously operating REPERTORY theatre (excluding the war years) was inspired by the achievements of the GAIETY company in Manchester. In 1911 city shareholders reopened the old Star Theatre as the Liverpool Repertory Theatre (from 1916 known as the Playhouse), with BASIL DEAN as artistic director. Perhaps less adventurous than its sister theatres in Manchester and Birmingham, it has had a more stable history than either, benefiting from the consistent support of its shareholders and audiences, a more cautious choice of plays, long-lived directorship (of William Armstrong, 1922–40) and management (of Maud Carpenter, 1923–62) and the reputations of the actors it has nurtured (such as Robert Donat, MICHAEL REDGRAVE and REX HARRISON). A fresh emphasis on recent and new writing, inaugurated in 1981, was short-lived.

**living newspaper** American documentary theatre. The form is usually associated with the FEDERAL THEATRE PROJECT and involved unemployed newspaper men and theatre personnel who used documentary sources to stage representations of contemporary problems such as housing, health care, labour unions, natural resources and racial issues. The method was to define a problem and then call for specific action. The three most successful attempts of the New York unit were by Arthur Arent: *Triple-A-Plowed Under* (1936), about the need for farmers and consumers to unite for improved incomes and cheaper food; *Power* (1937), a plea for public ownership of utilities; and *One-Third of a Nation* (1938), an exposé of urban housing conditions. Units in other cities developed living newspapers on local problems, though few were produced.

**living picture** [tableau vivant] Arrangement of performers to reproduce a scene from art, literature or the imagination. Displayed by the medieval Church on the Feast of the Resurrection to reproduce episodes from the Gospels, such pictures were often borne in procession on a float; similar, allegorical *tableaux* were staged at Renaissance banquets. The *tableau*, as a device enabling the spectator to take in clearly visible signs of emotional and moral states, was promoted as an important dramatic device by DIDEROT and became a component fixture of the MELODRAMA, especially at the ends of acts.

The *pose plastique*, in which the performer purports to imitate classical statuary, introduced a sensual note and became an allegedly artistic means of exhibiting nudes. Such shows provided finales at the song-and-supper rooms of Regency London as well as the private gatherings of courtiers under Napoleon III. More respectable showings included the Court of Beauties, arranged at the OLYMPIC in 1835 by MADAME VESTRIS, based on portraits by Peter Lely, and the operatic *tableaux vivants* to be seen at the Royal Victoria Coffee Music Hall (OLD VIC).

The principle of the living picture underlay much 19th-century staging, and paintings were enacted as climactic moments in melodrama. The 'picturesque' quality was pursued in the productions of CHARLES KEAN, the Duke of Saxe-MEININGEN, HENRY IRVING and the young STANISLAVSKY, as a primary responsibility of the director. A recent artistic employment of the *tableau vivant* has been in STEPHEN SONDHEIM's musical *Sunday in the Park with George* (1983), in which Seurat's *Sunday on the Isle of La Grande Jatte* gradually comes to life on stage. (See also NUDITY.)

**Living Theatre** American company. When Julian Beck and his wife, Judith Malina, founded the Living Theatre in 1948, they inaugurated the experimental OFF-OFF BROADWAY movement in New York. This avant-garde company is one of the most influential and long-lasting in American history, and from the beginning it sought the marriage of a political and aesthetic radicalism. The Theatre began producing plays by Paul Goodman, GERTRUDE STEIN, GARCÍA LORCA, PIRANDELLO, COCTEAU and BRECHT, seeking an anti-REALISM that could match the contemporary fervour in the visual arts and music.

The company had no permanent performance space except for the four years from 1959. Early landmark productions included Jack Gelber's *The Connection* (1959), about heroin addicts awaiting a promised fix, Brecht's *Man Is Man* and Kenneth Brown's *The Brig* (1963). This detailed documentary of daily brutal routine in a US Marine Corps brig in Japan was the company's last New York production. From 1964 to 1968 the LT performed only in Europe, concentrating on collective improvisatory work which culminated in *Paradise Now* (1968), a 'spiritual and political voyage for actors and spectators'. The company went to Brazil for a year in 1970, experimenting with CREACIÓN COLECTIVA before returning to the USA to work with coal miners and steel mill workers in Pittsburgh. In 1984 they settled once again in New York.

Since Julian Beck's death in 1985 the company has continued under the direction of Judith Malina and Hanon Reznikov. They now have a base in Manhattan and have been presenting plays based on poetry, collaborations with homeless people from the neighbourhood (East 3rd Street), and annual street theatre spectacles.

**Livings, Henry** 1929– British playwright. Livings was once an actor with JOAN LITTLEWOOD's Theatre Workshop company. The anarchic cheerfulness of his plays, the sympathy with the underdog and his feeling for north-country towns were all aspects of his writing encouraged by the Littlewood style. His first play, *Stop It, Whoever You Are* (1961), was staged at the Arts Theatre Club during a new plays season and featured Wilfred Brambell as a downtrodden lavatory attendant in a factory plotting the downfall of all bosses. The heroes of his comedies are all underdogs – Stanley the television mechanic in *Big Soft Nellie* (1961), the cook in *Nil*

*Carborundum* (1962) and Valentine Brose in *Eh?* (1964) – although Kelly in *Kelly's Eye* (1963) is someone who believes in punching first, to teach others a lesson. A prolific writer, Livings has television and radio plays to his credit and more than 30 stage plays and, with ALAN PLATER and PETER TERSON, established a tradition of northern playwriting which flourished in the 1980s with JOHN GODBER, WILLY RUSSELL and ALAN BLEASDALE. His reputation has declined, partly because the improvising energy, on which his humour relied, is rarely found in British theatre now. In 1992 he wrote *Stop the Children's Laughter*, based on a Victorian true story about foster children.

**Lizárraga, Andrés** 1919–82 Argentine playwright. Lizárraga is known primarily for his historical plays that use national themes to speak to contemporary issues. In 1960 *Tres jueces para un largo silencio* (*Three Judges for a Long Silence*), *Santa Juana de América* (*Saint Joan of America*) and *Alto Perú* (*High Peru*) constituted a 'May trilogy', based on moments and figures of the Revolution and counter-revolution. The BRECHTian techniques fit well with the development of social themes throughout his dramatic production.

**Lloyd, Marie** [Matilda Alice Victoria Wood] 1870–1922 British MUSIC-HALL star. After choosing the name Marie Lloyd (from *Lloyd's Newspaper*), she rose to prominence, becoming notorious for her saucy songs, delivered with an assortment of winks, ogles and chuckles. She entertained troops and factory workers during the Boer War and World War I. Ageing rapidly, she switched her stage persona from knowing clotheshorse to cheerful harridan, in such numbers as 'Don't Dilly Dally' and 'One of the Ruins that Cromwell Knocked About a Bit'. 'Our Marie' became legendary; at least three unmemorable musical comedies have been based on her life.

**Lloyd Webber, Andrew** 1948– British theatre composer. His first major success came when he was only 20, with *Joseph and the Amazing Technicolour Dreamcoat*, with lyrics by TIM RICE. *Jesus Christ Superstar* (1970), *Evita* (1976), *Cats* (1981), *Song and Dance* (1981) and *Starlight Express* (1984) provided an unparalleled sequence of hit musicals, which not only established him as the leading theatre composer of his time, against competition from such American composers as STEPHEN SONDHEIM, but also transformed the respective roles of London and New York as centres for musicals in the 1980s. *The Phantom of the Opera* (1986) and *Aspects of Love* (1989) were hits on both sides of the Atlantic. A more recent venture is a musical based on the Hollywood film *Sunset Boulevard* (1993). Lloyd Webber's gift for lilting tunes has provided one ingredient of his success, but he is also an astute businessman and producer.

*loa* Spanish term. A *loa* is a short theatre piece of sacred origin, normally with music, common in Spain and Latin America during the years of conquest and colonization. The principal object was to praise high-level officials on special occasions. These pieces were popular with audiences and served to introduce full-length works.

**Loesser, Frank** 1910–69 American composer and lyricist. Loesser spent 12 years in Hollywood writing lyrics for numerous motion picture musicals. He returned to BROADWAY with the score for *Where's Charley?* (1948), a musical version of *Charley's Aunt*. Two years later he wrote his most memorable songs for *Guys and Dolls*, a musical based on Damon Runyan's short stories about tough but soft-hearted New York gamblers and their girlfriends, revived to acclaim in 1992. His score for *The Most Happy Fella* (1956) ranged from operatic arias to typical Broadway numbers. After a failure with *Greenwillow* (1960), Loesser wrote his last Broadway score for *How to Succeed in Business without Really Trying* (1961), a SATIRE on corporate politics and chicanery. He also operated a music publishing house to further the careers of several young composers.

**Loewe, Frederick** see LERNER, ALAN JAY

**Logan, Joshua** 1908–88 American director, producer and playwright. Logan was associated with many of BROADWAY's most successful plays and musicals as director, co-producer or co-author. They include *South Pacific* (1949, with OSCAR HAMMERSTEIN II), *The Wisteria Trees* (1950), *Wish You Were Here* (1952) and *Fanny* (1954). He was director and co-producer of *John Loves Mary* (1947) and *Picnic* (1953). He co-authored and directed *Mister Roberts* (1948). Other plays and musicals are *On Borrowed Time* (1938), *Knickerbocker Holiday* (1938), *Mornings at Seven* (1939), *Charley's Aunt* (1940), *By Jupiter* (1942), *Annie Get Your Gun* (1946) and *Happy Birthday* (1946). He also directed films: *Bus Stop* (1956), *South Pacific* (1958) and *Camelot* (1967).

**Lohenstein, (Daniel) Caspar von** 1635–83 German baroque playwright. Lohenstein's plays contain much overt violence and are written in an extremely florid style. They have rarely been performed.

**Lomonosov, Mikhail (Vasilievich)** 1711–65 Russian grammarian, literary critic, poet and playwright. The lawgiver of Russian literature, Lomonosov was a true Renaissance man of the peasant class and among the best-educated and most influential of his generation. Trained at the Imperial Academy of Sciences in St Petersburg and in Germany, he mastered the various disciplines of literature, science and philosophy. He published a major study of Russian grammar (1757) and set forth the principles of versification which have dominated Russian poetry since the 18th century. In his two verse tragedies for the stage, *Temira and Selim* (1750) and *Demophon* (1752), he transformed the classical opposition of love versus duty into a politico-moral consideration of the natural man forced to endure unnatural forms such as tyranny. Lomonosov also helped to found Moscow University (1755).

**Londemann, Gert** 1718–73 Danish actor. He was the leading comedian of the Danish Playhouse (later the KONGELIGE TEATER), which opened in Copenhagen in 1747. The supreme Danish HARLEQUIN of his era, he was an expert CLOWN, JUGGLER and acrobat (see ACROBATICS), admired for his spontaneity and quicksilver improvisations. He specialized in playing charming but cunning servants, such as HOLBERG's Henrik (especially in *The Political Tinker*) and MOLIÈRE's Sganarelle. Londemann was particularly successful when he partnered Niels Clementin, whose dry, refined style was an excellent foil for his exuberance.

**Long Wharf Theatre** (New Haven, Connecticut) Founded in 1965 by Jon Jory and Harlan Kleiman, this is a non-profit RESIDENT THEATRE. Known as an actors' theatre, with its two intimate performance spaces it emphasizes the production of new and established, homegrown and foreign works. Many important productions have transferred to New York, including *Shadow Box*, *Streamers*, *The Changing Room*, *Sizwe Banzi Is Dead*, *The Gin Game* and *Quartermaine's Terms*, and revivals of *A View from the Bridge* (1982) and *American Buffalo* (1984).

**Lonsdale, Frederick** 1881–1954 British playwright. He wrote a series of librettos for MUSICAL COMEDY including *The Maid of the Mountains* (1917). After *Madame Pompadour* in 1923, he turned to social comedies dealing ironically with polite manners and modern marriage, which at the time were compared with those of SOMERSET MAUGHAM. Epigrammatic wit and neatly constructed, near-farcical situations made his work highly successful, and the best of his eleven plays, *The Last of Mrs Cheney* (1925), in which the maid in a gang of burglar-servants gives up her criminal career to marry into the aristocracy, still retains its popularity.

**Loos, Anita** ?1893–1981 American actress, screenwriter and playwright. Noted for her satiric comedies, Loos, who wrote some 200 scripts for both silent and sound movies, created the art of writing film captions, beginning with D.W. Griffith's silent films, such as *Intolerance* (1916). In 1926 she and her husband, John Emerson, dramatized her successful novel *Gentlemen Prefer Blondes*. Famous for Lorelei Lee, the stereotypical 'dumb blonde', the play was made into a musical in 1949 by Loos and Joseph Fields. She wrote several other plays, e.g. *Happy Birthday* (1946), and screenplays and adaptations such as *Gigi*, from the French play (1951).

**Lope de Vega** see VEGA (CARPIO), LOPE (FÉLIX) DE

**López, Willebaldo** 1944– Mexican playwright, actor and director. Many of his plays have dealt with problems of Mexican youth – adolescents facing multiple problems of drugs, sex, unemployment and social pressures. His *Los arrieros con sus burros por la hermosa capital* (*The Muleteers with Their Animals in the Beautiful Capital*, 1967) is a study in provincial/urban prejudices; *Cosas de muchachos* (*Kids' Things*, 1968) dramatizes the ubiquitous tensions and frustrations of adolescence. Other major works include *Yo soy Juárez* (*I am Juárez*, 1972), *Pilo Tamirano Luca* (1973) and *Vine, vi y mejor me fui* (*I Came, I Saw, and I Should Have Gone*, 1971).

**Loquasto, Santo** 1944– American set and COSTUME designer. Loquasto deals equally well with detailed realism and conceptual or theatricalist productions. His early BROADWAY and regional theatre successes such as *That Championship Season* and *American Buffalo* were often typified by clutter and detail, while his work with the NEW YORK SHAKESPEARE FESTIVAL's outdoor productions often employed towering sets and constructivist and emblematic designs (see THEATRE DESIGN). His sculptural design and angularity create a strong sense of three-dimensional space. He designs frequently for dance, especially for choreographer Twyla Tharp. His costumes possess the same detail, sense of colour and texture as his sets. His award-winning design for Broadway's *Grand Hotel: The Musical* (1990) brought together many of his themes. Since the late 1970s Loquasto has worked frequently on films, notably with Woody Allen.

**Loranger, Françoise** 1913– Quebec playwright and novelist; radio and television writer. Her first stage play, *Une Maison ... un jour* (*One House ... One Day*, 1965), was a psychological drama. It was followed by *Encore cinq minutes* (*Five More Minutes*, 1967), one of the first Canadian plays to raise feminist concerns. The author's growing political commitment is evident in the savage SATIRE of *Le Chemin du roy* (*The King's Highway*, 1968) and *Médium saignant* (*Medium rare*, 1970), which focuses on the struggle for francophone rights. *Double jeu* (*Double Game*, 1969) reverts to her earlier psychodramas, but in an experimental vein that requires audience participation in the resolution of its romantic plot.

**Lorca** see GARCÍA LORCA, FEDERICO

**Lord Chamberlain's Men** Elizabethan theatre company. It was founded in 1594 under the patronage of the Lord Chamberlain, Lord Hunsdon. Most of its senior members had been previously together in STRANGE'S MEN, including Cuthbert and RICHARD BURBAGE, Thomas Pope, AUGUSTINE PHILLIPS, JOHN HEMINGES, WILL KEMPE and WILLIAM SHAKESPEARE. The Chamberlain's Men took up residence at the THEATRE and quickly gained access to the court. When the Theatre lease ran out in 1597, using the CURTAIN as a stop-gap home, they built the GLOBE south of the Thames in 1599, where they staged work by JONSON, WEBSTER, TOURNEUR, MIDDLETON, MARSTON, BEAUMONT and FLETCHER, and the finest of Shakespeare's plays. They continued to use the Globe even after occupation of the BLACKFRIARS – access to which had hitherto been blocked by a residents' petition – in 1608–9. Their theatrical supremacy was acknowledged in 1603, when King James I adopted them as the King's Men, and they maintained it throughout the reigns of the first two Stuart kings. Heminges was business manager from c.1611 until his death, when he was succeeded by JOSEPH TAYLOR and JOHN LOWIN. After his retirement in c.1613 Shakespeare's place as 'ordinary' playwright was taken successively by Fletcher and MASSINGER.

**Lorde, André de** see GRAND-GUIGNOL

**Lortel, Lucille** 1902– American producer. After a brief career in acting she gave up the stage until 1947, when she offered her barn in Westport, Connecticut, for dramatic readings. The White Barn Theatre served as a showcase for new talent. Lortel acquired the Théâtre de Lys in New York in 1955. Her first Théâtre de Lys production, *The Threepenny Opera*, ran for seven years. In 1956 she began offering a Matinée Series, which continued for 20 years. At both theatres she presented lesser-known plays by BRECHT, IONESCO, GENET, Mario Fratti and ATHOL FUGARD. The more successful presentations at the Théâtre de Lys include *Dames at Sea*, *A Life in the Theatre*, *Buried Child*, *Getting Out*, *Cloud Nine* and *Woza Albert*. In 1981 the theatre was rechristened the Lucille Lortel Theatre in her honour. She is the co-founder of the AMERICAN SHAKESPEARE THEATRE Festival.

**Louis, Victor** 1731–1802 French theatre architect. Louis's Bordeaux theatre, which opened in 1780, is generally considered the finest in France, with its grand staircase, 12-column façade and circular auditorium. In 1781, after a fire at the Opéra in Paris, Louis was commissioned to build a new Opéra in the Duke of Orleans's palace. This eventually (1799) became the permanent home of the COMÉDIE-FRANÇAISE. In 1791 he transformed MLLE MONTANSIER's small theatre in the PALAIS-ROYAL, increasing the seating to 1,300 and doubling the stage dimensions in the space of a fortnight. By 1793 he had built her the Théâtre National de Montansier, with a magnificent auditorium and a stage 75ft square and 100ft high. But it was the Opéra, not Mlle Montansier, who then occupied the theatre (until 1820). Louis's much admired auditorium was reconstituted for the new Opéra in the rue Lepeletier.

**Løveid, Cecilie** 1951– Norwegian playwright. Although her stage plays have been produced with lamentable infrequency in Norway, Løveid's fragmentary, imagistic writing is richly textured, and has been appropriately compared to that of BOTHO STRAUSS and HEINER MÜLLER. Among several important radio plays is her award-winning *Seagull Eaters* (1983). Stage plays such as

*The Ice Breaks Up* (1983), *Tightrope-Lady* (1984), *Rational Animals* (1986) and *Double Delight* (1990) received mixed receptions in Bergen and Oslo. Since 1989 she has found more sympathetic audiences in her collaborations with project theatres like Verdensteatret (*The Bath House*, 1989) and performance groups like Lilith (*Time between Times*, 1990, and *Baroque Frieze*, 1991).

**Lowell, Robert** [Traill Spence Jr] 1917–77 American poet and playwright. Considered by many the best English-language poet of his generation, he is also known in the theatre for the trilogy of plays adapted from Nathaniel Hawthorne and Herman Melville entitled *The Old Glory* (*Benito Cereno; My Kinsman, Major Molineux* and *Endecott of the Red Cross*), first performed at the American Place Theatre, New York, in 1964. Lowell also adapted RACINE's *Phèdre* (published 1960) and AESCHYLUS' *Prometheus Bound* (1966).

**Lowin, John** 1576–c.1659 English actor. He was with Worcester's Men at the ROSE in 1602, and from 1603 until 1642 was a member of the King's Men (see LORD CHAMBERLAIN'S MEN), possibly as business manager after the death of HEMINGES. Among his parts are Falstaff, Volpone, Morose in JONSON's *Epicoene* and Bosola in WEBSTER's *The Duchess of Malfi*. Lowin's longevity, according to *Roscius Anglicanus* (1708), enabled him to advise DAVENANT on SHAKESPEARE's ideas for the playing of Henry VIII.

**Lucie, Doug** 1953– British playwright. His hard-bitten, amusing and brittle comedies satirized and then came to symbolize Mrs Thatcher's yuppies. His early plays, *John Clare's Mad Nuncle* (1975), *Rough Trade* (1977), *We Love You* (1978), *The New Garbo* (1978) and *Heroes* (1979), were satirical; *Hard Feelings* (1983), about a group of Oxford graduates living in cynical self-indulgence in Brixton in the midst of the 1981 riots, began a sequence of plays about the seamier side to privilege. *Fashion* (1988), produced by the ROYAL SHAKESPEARE COMPANY, was about an advertising executive; *Grace* (1992) attacked the millionaire evangelists of US religious missions.

**Ludlam, Charles** 1943–87 American actor, director and playwright. He was an early member of John Vaccaro's Play-House of the Ridiculous, an OFF-OFF BROADWAY theatre which presented his *Big Hotel* (1967) and *Conquest of the Universe* (1967). Splitting with Vaccaro in 1967, Ludlam started his own theatre, The Ridiculous Theatrical Company, where his plays included *Bluebeard* (1970), *Camille* (1973), *Stageblood* (1975), *Professor Bedlam's Punch and Judy Show* (1975), *Der Ring Gott Farblonjet* (1977), *Le Bourgeois Avant-Garde* (1982) and *The Mystery of Irma Vep* (1984). These mixed scatological humour and FEMALE IMPERSONATION with plots and styles drawn from high drama and opera. But his treatments of *Hamlet*, WAGNER's *Ring* and *Camille* transcend PARODY. One of the first New York theatres to deal explicitly with homosexual themes, the Ridiculous Theatrical Company often featured Ludlam in female roles. In 1984 Pittsburgh's American Ibsen Theatre invited him to play Hedda Gabler.

**Ludlow, Noah (Miller)** 1795–1886 American actor-manager. After employment in Kentucky with SAMUEL DRAKE, Ludlow formed his own company, which played New Orleans and remote corners of the South and West. With SOL SMITH he formed the Ludlow and Smith Theatrical Company. From 1835 to 1853 he took the legitimate theatre to the Ohio and Mississippi valleys, building theatres in Mobile, New Orleans, St Louis and other cities, and engaging many of the leading stars of the day. Ludlow's autobiography, *Dramatic Life as I Found It* (1880), offers a factual account of the FRONTIER THEATRE in America.

**Ludwig, Otto** 1813–65 German playwright and theorist. Although Ludwig had a theoretical rather than a creative bent, *The Hereditary Forester* (1850) is an effectively melodramatic tragedy, while *The Maccabeuses* (1852), a romantic verse tragedy set in ancient Rome, has some power. His most durable writings are probably his *Shakespeare Studies* (published 1871).

**Lugné-Poe** [Lugné], **Aurélien** 1869–1940 French actor and director. Remembered as the leader of the symbolist reaction (see SYMBOLISM) against NATURALISM, Lugné started as an actor under ANTOINE but soon moved to Paul Fort's Théâtre d'Art, becoming its director in 1893 and renaming it the Théâtre de l'Oeuvre. The characteristic style of Oeuvre performances was a stylized or abstract decor, artificial intonation of dialogue and a pervasive dream-like atmosphere. Here he produced IBSEN (e.g. *Brand, Rosmersholm*), MAETERLINCK, HAUPTMANN, D'ANNUNZIO and CLAUDEL. He is remembered especially for *Ubu Roi* (1896), which he produced against his better judgement. His *Cocu magnifique* by Crommelynck (1920) was influential.

**Lully, Jean-Baptiste** 1632–87 Italian musician, dancer and composer. Lully lived in France and became a French citizen in 1661. Appointed composer to Louis XIV in 1653 and then superintendent of music at court, he dominated French musical life for three decades. At court he arranged and conducted instrumental concerts and all theatrical entertainments, collaborating with Benserade on ballets, with MOLIÈRE on *comédies-ballets* and with QUINAULT on operas. From 1672 he controlled and directed the French Opéra as the Académie Royale de Musique. An able administrator, Lully enjoyed royal favour and amassed a personal fortune.

**Lunacharsky, Anatoly (Vasilievich)** 1875–1933 Soviet minister, playwright and critic. This intelligent, cosmopolitan and humane Soviet First People's Commissar for Education (1917–29), with his great enthusiasm for the theatre (he was married to an actress), helped to save many artists and institutions in the years following the October Revolution. A revolutionary from 1897 and a Bolshevik from 1904, he helped to create the 1919 decree which nationalized all theatres in regions under Bolshevik control. He tried to preserve what was best in Russian and European culture while the new Soviet culture was evolving. Sometimes protective of avant-garde artists – e.g. STANISLAVSKY, MEYERHOLD, VAKHTANGOV and TAIROV – he nevertheless remained loyal to the Party. He urged the theatres to adopt the new Soviet drama, championed REALISM and proletarian art and encouraged new theatres built since the Revolution, including the First State Theatre for Children (Moscow, 1920), which he directed. He opposed Meyerhold's plan to 'revolutionize' the MOSCOW ART THEATRE. Lunacharsky was the author of 14 plays in which historical or legendary themes were contemporized so as to gain revolutionary resonance. These included *Faust and the City* (1918), *Oliver Cromwell* (1920), *Foma Campanella* (two-thirds of a trilogy, 1921) and *The Liberated Don Quixote* (1921). His historical plays were attacked by Marxist extremists, who saw his dimensionalized character portraits as emphasizing the role of the individual in history.

**Lunt, Alfred** 1892–1977 and **Lynn (Lillie Louise) Fontanne** 1887–1983 American actors. Alfred Lunt became a star in BOOTH TARKINGTON's *Clarence* in 1919.

Lynn Fontanne's first major role was in KAUFMAN and CONNELLY's 1921 SATIRE, *Dulcy*. But it wasn't until they appeared together, two years after their marriage, in the THEATRE GUILD's 1924 production of *The Guardsman*, MOLNÁR's comedy of sexual intrigue, that their reputations were assured. From then on they were known as the Lunts, and until their farewell in *The Visit* in 1958 they enjoyed the most successful American acting partnership of the 20th century. Although to later generations they came to represent an outmoded stylized tradition, in their own time they broke with old-fashioned BROADWAY acting techniques. They surprised audiences in the 1920s by the conversational tone of their comic dialogues and the charged intimacy of their love scenes. Their favourite playwrights, ROBERT E. SHERWOOD and S. N. BEHRMAN, provided them with vehicles in which the war between the sexes is a duel of wit and sly manipulation. Highlights of their career include Behrman's *The Second Man* (1927), *Amphitryon 38* (1937) and *I Know My Love* (1949); Sherwood's *Reunion in Vienna* (1931), *Idiot's Delight* (1936) and *There Shall Be No Night* (1940); Sil-Vara's *Caprice* (1928); a rollicking *Taming of the Shrew* (1935); *The Seagull* (1938); and NOËL COWARD's *Design for Living* (1933).

The Lunts played more one-night stands in remote towns than any other stars. They were also remarkable for resisting Hollywood, except for one film (*The Guardsman*, 1931). Although they could have commanded higher salaries from independent producers, they maintained their loyalty to the Theatre Guild. The Lunt-Fontanne Theatre in New York City, so named in 1958, is now owned by the NEDERLANDER Organization.

**Lupino family** English performers and designers. **George Richard Estcourt Luppino** (*sic*) (1710–87) played in PANTOMIME with JOHN RICH, designed scenery and costumes for Galuppi's opera *Enrico* (1743) and was a ballet master in Dublin and Edinburgh. His son **Thomas Frederick** (1749–1845) painted pantomime scenery at the King's Theatre and COVENT GARDEN, a trade carried on by his son **Samuel George** (died 1830). The modern branch of the family, which shortened the name to Lupino, is descended from Samuel's son **George Hook Luppino** (1820–1902), a HARLEQUIN. Of his progeny, **George** (1853–1932) was the best CLOWN, a stalwart of the Britannia Theatre pantomimes; **Henry Charles** (1865–1925), an eccentric dancer, married into the Lane family that managed the Britannia; and **Arthur** (1864–1908) created the role of Nana in *Peter Pan* (1904).

George's sons **Barry** (1882–1962) and **Stanley** (1893–1942) were stalwarts in pantomime and musical comedy for many years. Barry specialized in dame roles (see FEMALE IMPERSONATION) and wrote over 50 musical comedies, making his last appearance in *Dick Whittington* (1954). Stanley was seen in *So This Is Love* (1928), *Love Lies* (1929) and *Room for Two* (1932), as well as in numerous plays of his own composition; his daughter **Ida** (1914– ) became a Hollywood star. Their cousin **Lupino Lane** (Henry George Lupino, 1892–1959) toured widely in MUSIC-HALL, MUSICAL COMEDY and pantomime before enjoying his greatest success as Bill Snibson in *Me and My Girl* (1937), in which he introduced the Lambeth Walk; he also popularized the songs 'Chase Me, Charlie' and 'Knees Up, Mother Brown', and was an expert tumbler.

**LuPone, Patti** 1949– American actress. A founding member of the ACTING COMPANY, she has demonstrated her versatility in a variety of roles: Lady Teazle in *The*

*School for Scandal*, Kathleen in *The Hostage* (1972), Irina in *The Three Sisters*, Lucy Lockit in *The Beggar's Opera* (1973), Rosamund in *The Robber Bridegroom* and Kitty in *The Time of Your Life* (1975). LuPone's portrayal of the title character in *Evita* (1979) won praise from WALTER KERR for 'rattlesnake vitality'. She played Reno Sweeney in the 1987 revival of *Anything Goes!* and appeared in ANDREW LLOYD WEBBER's *Sunset Boulevard* in London (1993).

**Lyceum Theatre** (London) Situated near the Strand, this intended exhibition hall was converted into a theatre in 1794, and named the English Opera House in 1810. But it was not until HENRY IRVING made his first appearance in *The Bells* (1871) that the Lyceum, rebuilt and renamed, entered its period of unique greatness, when (1878–99) it became virtually a national theatre, the standard of dramatic excellence in Britain. After Irving made his last Lyceum appearance in 1902, still with ELLEN TERRY at his side, the theatre fell into disuse. In 1945 it became a dance hall.

**Lyceum Theatre** (New York City) Built for DANIEL FROHMAN, it opened in 1903 as the New Lyceum to distinguish it from Frohman's earlier playhouse, and became the home of first-class productions until the Depression. It is presently owned by the SHUBERT Organization and houses their archive. Seating approximately 900, it is the oldest BROADWAY theatre still in operation.

**Lyly, John** c.1553–1606 English playwright. Under the patronage of the Cecil family Lyly made his literary reputation with the prose romance, *Euphues* (1578), which set a fashion for ornate English and donated the word 'euphuism' to the language. His plays were all written for BOYS' COMPANIES, and had in mind a sophisticated audience. His use of prose in refined comedy was innovatory. He became involved in the management of the BOYS OF ST PAUL's, who performed his first two plays, *Campaspe* and *Sappho and Phao* (1584). *Galathea* (c.1585) and *Mother Bombie* (c. 1587) followed. Lyly's best-known play, *Endimion* (c.1588), includes a transparently flattering portrait of Elizabeth I as Cynthia. He involved the Paul's Boys in the debate about the established Church, thereby causing a ten-year halt to their activities. His last play, *The Woman in the Moon* (c.1593), may never have been performed.

**Lyric Theatre** (Belfast) The Lyric Players Theatre was inaugurated in 1951 by Mary and Pearse O'Malley at their Lisburn Road home, Belfast. Since 1968 it has occupied a new 300-seat, well-equipped theatre, now subsidized by the Northern Ireland Arts Council, and has consolidated a stock of local players. The Lyric has presented world theatre from ARISTOPHANES to STOPPARD, and all the major Irish dramatists, maintaining its commitment to poetic drama, YEATS's particularly, and more recently appointing resident dramatists to foster new writing.

**Lyric Theatre, Hammersmith** (London) Originally the Lyric Opera House, opened in 1890 and specializing in MELODRAMA and PANTOMIME, in 1918 it was taken over by Nigel Playfair. With ARNOLD BENNETT Playfair established a distinctive style of simplified REALISM, stylized gesture and formalized composition in a brilliant series of elegant productions, performing himself together with young actors of the stature of GIELGUD and EDITH EVANS. The production that established the theatre's reputation was Playfair's revival of GAY's *The Beggar's Opera*. Its unprecedented run of 1,463 performances was followed by other Restoration and 18th-century works, as well as classic productions of CHEKHOV and WILDE and contemporary light comedy. Playfair left the theatre in 1933, after which it declined; it closed in 1966 and was demolished in 1972, although the name was transferred to a new, smaller theatre built nearby.

**Lytton, Edward Bulwer,** Lord see BULWER LYTTON, EDWARD

**Lyubimov, Yury (Petrovich)** 1917– Soviet director. Lyubimov was the most controversial and socially important director of the later Soviet period before he was fired as artistic director of the Moscow Theatre of Drama and Comedy on Taganka Square ('the Taganka') in April 1984 and subsequently expelled from the USSR. Known as 'the theatrical conscience of his nation', he is a moral artist and a theatrical innovator. There has always been a strong AGIT-PROP element in his work.

He trained at the Second Moscow Art Theatre Studio and then at the Vakhtangov Theatre School. After the war he joined the Vakhtangov Theatre's acting company. In 1964 he became artistic director of the moribund Taganka Theatre (1964). With MEYERHOLD, STANISLAVSKY, VAKHTANGOV and BRECHT as his spiritual guides, Lyubimov eschewed Soviet drama for the more imaginative worlds of poetry and narrative fiction, which he dramatized, and the classics, which he reinvented from a pronounced critical perspective. His carefully orchestrated MISES-EN-SCÈNE are often co-created with his designer DAVID BOROVSKY.

Lyubimov's productions feature complex lighting, interpolated poetry, songs and direct audience address.

They include John Reed's *Ten Days That Shook the World* (1965), an exercise in cinematic montage produced through a light curtain; Chernyshevsky's *What Is to Be Done?* (1971); and Boris Vasiliev's sentimental patriotic tale of female heroism in World War II, *And Here the Dawns Are Silent* (1971). He has also produced poetry-based recitals on the lives of famous Russian poets, and socially minded contemporary plays and radical stagings of the classics, including *Tartuffe* (1969), on MOLIÈRE's play in crisis, under attack by Church and state; *Hamlet* (1974), featuring a huge mobile woven rope curtain, representing a redemptive theatrical life force; and BULGAKOV's *The Master and Margarita* (1977), composed of recycled theatrical props and scenic pieces.

Between 1983 and 1989 (when his citizenship and position as the Taganka's artistic director were restored), Lyubimov mounted productions in Europe and the USA, e.g. of Dostoevsky's *Crime and Punishment* and *The Devils*, PUSHKIN's *A Feast in Plague-Time* (from his *Little Tragedies*), various operas, and BABEL's *Sunset* at Israel's HABIMAH Theatre. His recent Taganka stagings include Pushkin's *Boris Godunov* (1988) as a folk-theatre presentation with an omnipresent chorus; *Alive* (1989); and a musical VARIETY show version of ERDMAN's *The Suicide* (1990). In 1992 Lyubimov successfully staged his own adaptation of Dostoevsky's *A Raw Youth* and the OSTROVSKY montage *Comedians* at the Finnish National Theatre. He is planning a musical version of Pasternak's novel *Doctor Zhivago*.

**Mabou Mines** American company. An experimental group, Mabou Mines was founded formally in 1970 after years of collaborative work among its founding members Jo ANNE AKALAITIS, LEE BREUER and Ruth Maleczech in San Francisco, and later in Europe with Philip Glass and David Warrilow. The company has developed a performance style that synthesizes traditional acting and narrative techniques with mixed media, revealing their regular collaboration with painters, sculptors, video artists, film-makers and composers. The group's directors leave their own particular stamps. Breuer's *The Red Horse Animation* (1970), *The B-Beaver Animation* (1974) and *The Shaggy Dog Animation* (1978) are theatrically clever and inventive, funny and self-reflexive – as opposed, for instance, to Akalaitis's hyper-real production of KROETZ's *Through the Leaves* (1984). In addition to creating original works, Mabou is one of the foremost interpreters of SAMUEL BECKETT; influential productions of *The Lost Ones*, *Play*, *Come and Go*, *Cascando* and *Company* have combined narration and elaborate visual spectacle. More recent productions include Linda Hartinian's *Flow My Tears, the Policeman Said* (1988) and a gender-reversed *King Lear* (1990).

**McCabe, Eugene** 1930– Irish playwright. The subjects of McCabe's work range from his *Swift*, another attempt to illuminate Swift's complex nature, to a television trilogy about contemporary Northern Irish violence (*Cancer*, *Heritage*, *Siege*, 1976). His first stage play remains the most impressive: *The King of the Castle* (1964) brings 1960s rural Ireland into a view of its past, and makes remarkably coherent the domestic tragedy of Scober (the King), the dispersed peasantry, and the Big House vandalized by Scober's improvements. McCabe's novel *Death and Nightingales* was published in 1992.

**McCarthy, Lillah** 1875–1960 British actress and theatre manager. After touring with BEN GREET and WILSON BARRETT's companies, she became closely associated with SHAW's work, playing in the first productions of *Man and Superman* (1905), *The Doctor's Dilemma* (1906) and *Androcles and the Lion* (1913) under her first husband GRANVILLE BARKER, for whom she also created the title role in JOHN MASEFIELD's *The Tragedy of Nan* (1908). In 1911 she took over the Little Theatre in London, playing a repertoire of IBSEN, Shaw and SCHNITZLER under her own management, and after repeating some of her most famous roles in New York she became manager of the Kingsway Theatre in 1919.

**McClintic, Guthrie** 1893–1961 American actor, director and producer. After a career as an actor, McClintic began directing and producing in 1921 by presenting A.A. MILNE's *The Dover Road*. He married the actress KATHARINE CORNELL and directed her major successes. Recognized as one of the most distinguished directors in the American theatre, McClintic staged more than 90 productions including the award-winning *The Old Maid* (1935) and *Winterset* (1935). His other major credits include *The Barretts of Wimpole Street* (1931), *Yellow Jack* (1934), *Ethan Frome* and *The Wingless Victory* (1936), *High Tor* and *Candida* (1937), *No Time for Comedy* and *Key Largo* (1939), *The Doctor's Dilemma* (1941), *You Touched Me* (1945), *The Playboy of the Western World* (1946), *Antony and Cleopatra* (1947), *Life with Mother* (1948), *Medea* (1949), *The Constant Wife* (1951) and *Bernadine* (1952).

**McCowen, Alec** [Alexander] **(Duncan)** 1925– British actor. He joined the OLD VIC company in 1959. His first major international success came with Peter Luke's *Hadrian VII*, where he played the man-who-would-be-pope with an unforgettable irony and wit. Sheer intelligence has been a feature of his acting, shining through his Hamlet in Birmingham in 1969, and it led him towards roles of intellectuals and academics, notably in CHRISTOPHER HAMPTON's *The Philanthropist* (1970), as Alceste in *The Misanthrope* and Dysart in SHAFFER's *Equus* (two outstandingly successful NATIONAL THEATRE productions), and as Higgins in the 1974 WEST END revival of SHAW's *Pygmalion*. In 1978, he devised his remarkable solo performance of St Mark's Gospel, with which he toured widely in Britain and the States. He returned to the National Theatre to play Crocker-Harris in the revival of RATTIGAN's *The Browning Version*, and in 1984 devised a new solo production, *Kipling*. His autobiographical writings include *Young Gemini* (1979) and *Double Bill* (1980). He appeared at the NT in BRIAN FRIEL's version of TURGENEV's *Fathers and Sons* (1987) and as Vladimir in *Waiting for Godot* (1987). He achieved notable West End successes in two modern Irish plays, Friel's *Dancing at Lughnasa* (1991) and FRANK McGUINNESS's *Someone Who'll Watch Over Me* (1992). In 1972 he was awarded an OBE.

**McCullough, John** 1832–85 American actor. Born in Ireland, he made his stage debut at the ARCH STREET THEATRE in Philadelphia in 1857 in *The Belle's Stratagem*. He subsequently toured with E. L. DAVENPORT and EDWIN FORREST. A tall, classically handsome man in the heroic mould, McCullough had a volatile, physically robust acting style that resembled Forrest's. After the latter's death in 1872, he assumed several of Forrest's major roles, including Spartacus in *The Gladiator*, Virginius and Jack Cade. He also excelled in Shakespearian roles. From 1866 to 1877 he managed the California Theatre in San Francisco, initially in association with LAWRENCE BARRETT.

**MacDonagh, Donagh** 1912–68 Irish playwright and poet. MacDonagh wrote three verse plays: *Happy as Larry* (1946), *God's Gentry* (1951) and *Step-in-the-Hollow* (1957). Rather in the manner of JOHN GAY's *Beggar's Opera*, MacDonagh combines song and street ballads with an easily spoken, at times doggerel, verse. In its period his work was associated with the supposed revival of verse drama represented by FRY and ELIOT.

**McGee, Greg** 1950– New Zealand playwright. He achieved immediate prominence with his first play, *Foreskin's Lament* (1980), a treatment of violence and cultural obtuseness, ostensibly within the context of rugby football. Various television plays have followed, as well as two notable stage plays: *Out in the Cold* (1983) and *Tooth and Claw* (1982).

**McGrath, John (Peter)** 1935– British playwright and director. McGrath's early plays, *Events While Guarding the Bofors Gun* (1966) and *Bakke's Night of Fame* (1968), were written in a conventional social drama idiom – showing his sympathies with the underdogs of society – and produced in mainstream 'new plays' theatres such as HAMPSTEAD THEATRE CLUB. After 1968, with the new spirit of revolution which entered British theatre then, McGrath developed a style of popular theatre which introduced songs, MUSIC-HALL GAGS and dances into a loose 'epic' play structure. For three years he worked at the Liverpool Everyman (1969–72), where he had nine plays put on. The most successful of his epic plays were written for his adventurous left-wing 7:84 Theatre Company, founded in 1971, which owed its odd name to the statistic that 7 per cent of the British population owned 84 per cent of the national wealth. *The Cheviot, The Stag and the Black* and *Black Oil* (1973), *Little Red Hen* (1975) and *The Imperial Policeman* (1984) are distinguished by their liveliness, conviction and popular fervour. For the Scotttish 7:84 he wrote some 20 plays, resigning in 1988. Through a trilogy of Scottish history plays and *John Brown's Body* (1990) he has maintained his socialist beliefs, to the point of not taking the WEST END or NATIONAL THEATRE road to fame and fortune. In *Watching for Dolphins* (1991) he portrays an elderly revolutionary dying with the remains of her old idealism. *The Wicked Old Man* (West Yorkshire Playhouse, 1992) is a black FARCE about a rich dead man.

Since 1959 McGrath has also been working in film and television, mainly as a writer and director, but increasingly as a producer since 1983.

**McGuinness, Frank** 1953– Irish playwright. Since the ABBEY produced *The Factory Girls* (1982), McGuinness has produced seven full-length plays, eight new versions of European classics, THEATRE-IN-EDUCATION pieces, one-acters and television plays. The award-winning *Observe the Sons of Ulster Marching towards the Somme* (1985) explores the blood loyalties of a group of Northern Irish Protestant men facing battle. *Innocence* (1986), centred on Caravaggio, probes creativity and exploitation in increasingly nightmarish style, and McGuinness's anti-naturalist energy explodes in *Mary and Lizzie* (1989), a dream journey through 19th-century politics. By contrast, *Someone Who'll Watch Over Me* (1992) treats the plight of three hostages in an unnamed Middle-Eastern country with surprising naturalistic understatement. McGuinness is the most daring and productive of recent Irish playwrights.

**Machiavelli, Niccolò** 1469–1527 Italian political theorist, historian and playwright. He served in the Florentine diplomatic service until the return to power of the Medici family in 1512 forced him into premature retirement. Most of his writings, including *Il principe* (*The Prince*, 1513) and *I discorsi* (*The Discourses*), were a product of that retirement, as probably were the versions he made of TERENCE's *Andria*, PLAUTUS' *Aulularia* and the play by which he is best remembered, *La mandragola* (c.1518) – generally considered the finest comedy of the Italian Renaissance. A witty, sharp, cold-eyed view of the more provincial aspects of Florentine society, it has been variously interpreted as a social comedy exposing the hypocrisy of pseudo-Christian values, a light *jeu d'esprit* expressive of the high summer of Renaissance confidence, and a deep, cunning and admonitory political allegory. It was probably first produced in Florence in 1518. In 1524 Machiavelli wrote his last play, *La Clizia*, closely based on Plautus' *Casina*. An early piece, based on ARISTOPHANES' *The Clouds* and apparently written about 1504, is now lost. *Il principe* exerted considerable influence on Elizabethan and Jacobean dramatists' conceptions of Italian court life and political intrigue, the devious Machiavellian schemer becoming a stock figure in many plays.

**MacIntyre, Tom** 1933– Irish playwright. In MacIntyre's early plays, relatively realistic in manner, groupings and lighting suggest rather than depict the detail of scene and action. *Eye-Winker, Tom-Tinker* (1972) dissects the inertia and the self-absorbed rhetoric of a vacillating Irish revolutionary. Here, words are paramount. Since then MacIntyre has turned increasingly to MIME, gesture and visual and aural effects, as in his highly acclaimed adaptation of Patrick Kavanagh's *The Great Hunger* (1983). *The Bearded Lady* (1984) similarly enlarges its text with visual effects developed from *Gulliver's Travels*, with Yahoos and Houyhnhnms as metaphors of Swift's own tormented psyche. *Chickadee* (1993) is more accessible, a surreal (see SURREALISM) satirical romp centred on the Pope.

**MacKaye, Percy** 1875–1956 American playwright and novelist. His best-known plays were *The Scarecrow* (1909) and *Jeanne d'Arc* (1906). His grand dramatic visions resembled those of his father, STEELE MACKAYE: *St Louis Masque* (1914), celebrating the 150th anniversary of the city's founding; *Caliban by the Yellow Sands* (1916, in Central Park, New York), to commemorate the tercentenary of SHAKESPEARE's death; and his tetralogy, *The Mystery of Hamlet* (1949), exploring 30 years of the Hamlet saga prior to Shakespeare's play.

**MacKaye, (James Morrison) Steele** 1842–94 American actor, playwright and inventor. He founded a school of acting in New York (1871) for propagating the Delsartian system; made his professional debut as actor, playwright and manager with *Monaldi* (New York, 1872); played Hamlet in London (Crystal Palace, 1873); and then achieved success as a playwright with *Rose Michel* (1875) and *Won at Last* (1877). Of his 30 plays the best was *Hazel Kirke* (1880), presented in his MADISON SQUARE THEATRE, with a new elevator stage. At New York's LYCEUM (1885) he incorporated an orchestra pit on an elevator, and quarters for America's first dramatic school. A brilliant, if erratic, dreamer, MacKaye coupled his innovations in stage mechanics with a crusade for REALISM in acting and for 'true-to-life' dialogue. His ultimate theatrical dream, a massive 'spectatorium' (480ft long) for the Chicago World's Fair (1893) to house his chronicle of Columbus's adventures, was scaled down to a 'scenitorium'.

**McKellen, Ian (Murray)** 1939– British actor. He first emerged as a major classical actor through the Prospect Theatre Company, and his twin performances as SHAKESPEARE's Richard II (1968) and MARLOWE's Edward II (1969) established his reputation as one of the most sensitive and intelligent actors in Britain. He was a founder member of the touring acting cooperative, the Actors' Company, playing both leading and small character parts with equal panache. He joined the ROYAL SHAKESPEARE COMPANY in 1974 where, despite several major roles in the main theatre, he will be best remembered for an outstanding studio Macbeth with JUDI DENCH as Lady Macbeth. He led the small-scale touring RSC company in 1978, playing major roles in *Three Sisters* and *Twelfth Night*. In 1979, he appeared as one of two homosexuals imprisoned in a Nazi concentration camp in Martin Sherman's *Bent* (see GAY THEATRE) which transferred to the WEST END, and in 1980 took the part of Salieri in the New York production of PETER SHAFFER's *Amadeus*. In 1984 he joined the NATIONAL THEATRE as an associate director, playing Coriolanus in a major PETER HALL production. In 1990 RICHARD EYRE directed him in *Richard III* and as Kent in *King Lear*, in EDUARDO DE

FILIPPO's *Napoli Milonaria* (1991) and as Vanya in *Uncle Vanya* (1992). One earlier memorable performance took place in an RSC studio production (subsequently televised), *Othello* (1989), directed by TREVOR NUNN, in which McKellen played Iago as a punctilious NCO.

**McKern, Leo (Reginald)** 1920– Australian actor. Having played initially in Sydney, he appeared with the London OLD VIC in 1949 and has since played many classical and modern roles at the Old Vic, at Stratford-upon-Avon and in the WEST END, including Peer Gynt, Iago and Toad of Toad Hall; he directed the London production of *The Shifting Heart* (1959). He returned to Australia with the 1952–3 Shakespeare Memorial Theatre tour, and to play in Douglas Stewart's *Ned Kelly* (1955) and RAY LAWLER's *The Man Who Shot the Albatross* (1971). His best-known television role is as the BBC's 'Rumpole of the Bailey'.

**Mackintosh, Cameron (Anthony)** 1946– British producer and impresario. Mackintosh was a prime force behind the revival of WEST END musicals in the 1980s, drawing on a new generation of singers and dancers who dispelled the old belief that British actors were 'talking heads'. After serving an apprenticeship in stage management, he produced his first London musical, *Anything Goes*, in 1969. He gained experience with small-scale touring productions before producing a sequence of ANDREW LLOYD WEBBER musicals in the 1980s – *Cats* (1981), *Song and Dance* (1982) and *Phantom of the Opera* (1986). In addition, he went into partnership with the ROYAL SHAKESPEARE COMPANY to produce *Les Misérables* (1985) and with the NATIONAL THEATRE for a revival of *Carousel* (1993); and produced two other major hits, *Miss Saigon* (1989) and *Five Guys Named Moe* (1990), which he took to the West End from the Theatre Royal, Stratford (London). He succeeded in turning the tables on BROADWAY, in that the West End became the place where the most ambitious and lavish musicals were usually staged. While his greatest successes may have been with British writers, he promoted STEPHEN SONDHEIM's musicals as well, including *Follies* (1987).

**Macklin, Charles** 1699–1797 Irish actor, manager and playwright. His first major success came in 1736 as Peachum in GAY's *The Beggar's Opera*. A remarkably versatile actor, in 1740 he played Shylock, turning him from a comic character into a fierce, harsh and powerful figure opposite KITTY CLIVE's Portia. By 1742 he was helping to train actors, including GARRICK. In 1747 Macklin's Shylock opened Garrick's first season at DRURY LANE. In 1759 his seventh play, *Love à-la-Mode*, gave him his first success as a playwright. In his eighties he starred as Sir Pertinax Macsycophant in his own play *The Man of the World*, and finally retired in 1789. His plays attempt colloquial dialogue and realistic detail. In his own acting style and his teaching he advocated a restrained NATURALISM.

**Mackney, E(dmund) W(illiam)** 1825–1909 British blackface performer. Mackney began in London VARIETY at the Royal Standard, Pimlico, offering a one-man show in the style of THOMAS D. RICE, accompanying himself on piano, banjo, bones, guitar and violin, the last providing farmyard imitations. However, he was better at ballad parodies and topical songs than as an interpreter of Negro life, and eventually achieved success when booked by CHARLES MORTON at London's Canterbury Hall. He also toured the provinces with his own concert party, playing at town halls and mechanics' institutes for a public that regarded theatres as immoral.

**MacLeish, Archibald** 1892–1982 American poet and playwright. His dramatic reputation relies on the success of one script, *J.B.* (1958), a 20th-century version of the book of Job. BROOKS ATKINSON said, 'It portrays in vibrant verse the spiritual dilemma of the twentieth century.' MacLeish's other verse dramas did not succeed.

**McMahon, Gregan** 1874–1941 Australian director. Initially an actor, in 1911 he founded the Melbourne Repertory Theatre to stage serious drama and promising Australian works. Throughout his career he moved between commercial and amateur theatre, working with the J. C. WILLIAMSON and Tait managements, and establishing the Sydney Repertory Society in the 1920s and the semi-professional Gregan McMahon Players in the 1930s, both known for high standards and a serious repertoire.

**McNally, Terrence** 1939– American playwright. His first produced script was *And Things That Go Bump in the Night* at the GUTHRIE THEATRE in 1964. *Bad Habits*, a double bill of *Ravenswood* and *Dunelawn*, moved to BROADWAY in 1974. Other Broadway productions include *The Ritz* in 1975 and *Broadway* in 1979. *Where Has Tommy Flowers Gone?* (1971) is often considered McNally's best script. He described with anger the major concerns of the late 1960s and early 1970s – assassination, the Vietnam War, rebellion and the sexual revolution. His later work is more lyrical and positive. More recent plays include *It's Only a Play* (1982), *The Lisbon Traviata* (1985), *Frankie and Johnny in the Clair de Lune* (1987), *Lips Together, Teeth Apart* (1991), *The Perfect Ganesh* (1993), *L'Age d'Or* (1994), *Love! Valour! Compassion!* (1994) and *Master Class* (1995).

**MacNamara, Gerald** [Harry C. Morrow] 1866–1938 Irish playwright and actor. For the ULSTER LITERARY THEATRE MacNamara wrote two popular comedies. *Thompson in Tir nan Og* (1918) deposits an Orangeman in the Gaelic Land of Youth; the title of *The Mist That Does Be on the Bog* (1909), a PARODY of the ABBEY peasant play, gave a phrase to the language.

**Macready, W(illiam) C(harles)** 1793–1873 English actor. Forced on to the stage through parental debt, he made his debut as Romeo in Birmingham in 1810. His lifelong bitterness over his early family difficulties remained, evident in the angry, fascinating *Diaries* he kept from 1833 to 1851. In 1816, with JOHN PHILIP KEMBLE newly retired and EDMUND KEAN reigning at DRURY LANE, Macready was hired at COVENT GARDEN. In 1819 he played Richard III, and was the first Covent Garden actor to be summoned for a curtain call. He followed this with the first of many portrayals of paternal love, in SHERIDAN KNOWLES's *Virginius* (1820), forging a strong link between playwright and actor. In 1834 he first played Lear, perhaps his finest role. Industrious and observant rather than charismatic, he aimed always to make passion intelligible. Macready hoped to raise the standards of English drama by encouraging playwrights like Knowles, Talfourd, Barry Cornwall, DICKENS, Browning and, more successfully, BULWER LYTTON. In addition to his appearances at Covent Garden, Drury Lane (he was manager of both at different times) and the HAYMARKET, he also made regular provincial tours and three to the USA, the last of which (1848) was scarred by the enmity of EDWIN FORREST and the tragic conclusion of the ASTOR PLACE riot. He took his farewell in 1851, in his favourite part of Macbeth, concluding his diary with the exclamation 'Thank God!'.

**McVicker's Theatre** (Chicago) Built in 1857 by actor-manager James H. McVicker (1822–96), the theatre was a commodious clapboard version of an Italianate palazzo, and the best playhouse in the West. Although he maintained a STOCK COMPANY, McVicker presented a succession of stars from SARAH BERNHARDT to EDDIE FOY. During its history, the theatre was rebuilt four times, and was finally demolished in 1984.

**Madách, Imre** 1823–64 Hungarian playwright. His masterpiece, the dramatic poem *The Tragedy of Man*, written in 1860, is a panoramic, epic statement about mankind's destiny, in the genre of GOETHE's *Faust*, BYRON's *Cain* and IBSEN's *Peer Gynt*. In a dream Lucifer leads Adam through episodes in human history, past and future, culminating in the demise of civilization and of life itself. The work ends with an enigmatic affirmation of faith in the need to struggle on against all odds. Adam, Eve and Lucifer play the historical figures throughout. *The Tragedy of Man* was premiered in 1883 at the National Theatre, and remains one of Hungary's most enduring theatrical successes. It has been widely translated and performed outside Hungary.

**Maddy, Yulisa Amadu** 1936– Sierra Leonean playwright, director and novelist. Maddy depicts the West African urban milieu. His characters rarely find easy solutions to their oppression as they struggle towards a fairer society. *Yon Kon* (published 1968) is about a criminal who is top dog amongst the prisoners in the gaol. In *Life Everlasting* some recognizable Sierra Leonean types arrive, dead, in Hell, and are organized by 'Big Boy'. *Obasai* is about community renewal led by unlikely ringleaders. *Gbana Bendu* experiments with the masquerade and the secret cult in order to explore contradictory paths to social justice. His two Krio plays are *Big Breeze Blow*, a SATIRE on family planning amongst other things, and *Big Berin* (for which he was imprisoned in Sierra Leone), set in a compound of multiple occupancy among the urban poor. Since the early 1980s his productivity as both director and playwright has diminished.

**Madison Square Theatre** (New York City) The FIFTH AVENUE THEATRE burned down in 1873. In 1879 STEELE MACKAYE gutted and redesigned the house, installing his famous double stage, experimenting with atmospheric lighting and relocating the orchestra above the stage. He renamed it the Madison Square. In 1884 A. M. PALMER took over and brought great prosperity to the house. In 1891, CHARLES HOYT secured the lease to show his own plays and eventually changed the name to Hoyt's Theatre. It was pulled down in 1908.

**Maeterlinck, Maurice** 1862–1949 Belgian poet, playwright and essayist. Winner of the Nobel Prize (1911), he wrote in French and reached international fame through plays like *La Princesse Maleine* (1889), *Les Aveugles* (The Blind, 1890), *L'Intruse* (The Intruder, 1890) and *Pelléas et Mélisande* (1892; performed in Paris by LUGNÉ-POE; inspired Debussy's opera of 1902). Maeterlinck represents the victory of SYMBOLISM over NATURALISM. He was fascinated by mysterious forces and by blindness. His plays are characterized by their lack of action or conflict, and by their suggestive force. His early work in particular made him, in the eyes of some, a precursor of absurdism (see THEATRE OF THE ABSURD). Mysterious forces evoke an atmosphere resembling early PINTER. Later work included three *drames pour marionnettes* (1894: *Alladine et Palomides*, *Intérieur* (The Interior), *La Mort de Tintagiles* (The Death of Tintagiles)), a 'classical'

tragedy *Monna Vanna* (1902), a theatrical fantasy *L'Oiseau bleu* (The Blue Bird, 1908; first performed in Moscow and filmed several times), *La Princesse Isabelle* (1935), *L'Ombre des ailes* (The Shadow of the Wings, 1937), *L'Autre Monde, ou Le Cadran Stellaire* (The Other World, or The Star System, 1941) and *Jeanne d'Arc* (1943).

**Maffei, Francesco Scipione** 1675–1755 Italian playwright and antiquarian. He spent most of his life in his home town of Verona dedicated to the study of its antiquities. His verse tragedy *Merope* (1713) ranks as one of the major Italian plays of the century and was admired and imitated by VOLTAIRE and ALFIERI, but was indifferently received when staged by LUIGI RICCOBONI as part of his attempt to reform, and raise the standards of, the Italian literary theatre.

**Magaña, Sergio** 1924–91 Mexican playwright. He achieved early success with his popular *Los signos del zodíaco* (Signs of the Zodiac, 1951), a play with sometimes simultaneous action in various settings of a lower-class neighbourhood. Later plays include *Moctezuma II* (1953) with its view of pre-Hispanic Mexico and an emperor destined to fall, and *Los argonautas* (The Argonauts, 1967), which presents a jaundiced view of Cortés and the conquest of Mexico. *Los enemigos* (The Enemies, 1990) was a moving interpretation of the RABINAL ACHÍ.

**Maggi, Carlos** 1922– Uruguayan playwright and novelist. One of Uruguay's best writers, he has utilized absurdist techniques (see THEATRE OF THE ABSURD) to uncover the social and political problems of the nation. His black humour, sharp dialogue and inventive techniques were evident in his earliest plays: *La trastienda* (The Backstore, 1958), *La biblioteca* (The Library, 1959) and *Esperando a Rodó* (Waiting for Rodó, 1961), the latter an obvious play on BECKETT's title but with Maggi's particular vision of national corruption that foiled the great Uruguayan essayist's dream of an American utopia. *Las llamadas* (The Calls, 1965) decried the loss of national identity through the dehumanizing effects of television, with a resulting imbecilic language. *El patio de la Torcaza* (The Patio of the Torcaza, 1967) is a complex analysis of the disintegration of the national welfare state. After the dictatorship, Maggi returned with *Frutos* (1985) and *Un cuervo en la madrugada* (A Crow in the Morning, 1988).

**magic** (Europe; USA) Magic had long been a fairground and street amusement before it entered the theatre in the mid-18th century. Many magic acts posed as scientific demonstrations, or centred on ingenious automata that played chess and performed lightning calculations. Much spectacular theatre was predicated on technical magic, the instantaneous transformations of scenery and the tricks of the harlequinade.

With the peace that followed Napoleon's defeat, solo conjurors criss-crossed Europe, among them the great cup-and-ball artist Bartolomeo Bosco (1793–1863), Ludwig Leopold Döbler (1801–64) who caught a chosen card from a flung pack on the tip of a sword, and J. H. ANDERSON, 'the Great Wizard of the North'. But it was ROBERT-HOUDIN and Wiljalba Frikell (1816–1903) who first worked on a stage denuded of apparatus and supernatural frills, lending their acts the respectable charm of a drawing-room entertainment.

A fresh impetus was given by the spiritualist movement that gained popularity in the 1860s. Mediums like the Davenport brothers (Ira Erastus, 1838–1911, and William Henry Harrison, 1841–77) claimed to effect miraculous escapes from knots and locked cabinets with the aid of ectoplasmic assistants; in turn, debunkers like J. N. MASKELYNE made an evening of demonstrating how such tricks could be accomplished naturally. The rise of VARIETY required conjurors to dazzle an audience in 20 minutes. Innovations such as mentalism or mind-reading (invented by the Chicago newspaperman John Randall Brown and later performed over the radio by Joseph Dunniger) arose, and there were vogues for Chinese or Hindu conjurors – commonly Europeans in masquerade, such as the Great Lafayette (Sigmund Neuberger, 1871–1911) and William Ellsworth Robinson known as Chung Ling Soo (1861–1918), who was killed in his own catch-the-bullet act. The palatial *fin de siècle* music-halls and variety theatres encouraged flashy and gigantic illusions, vanishing acts and mid-air transformations, as devised by e.g. BUATIER DE KOLTA, DAVID DEVANT, KELLAR, THURSTON and HORACE GOLDIN. Typically, HARRY HOUDINI began as a card and coin manipulator before gaining fame as an 'escapologist', capable of keeping an audience in suspense for several minutes as it watched a static tank in which he was encased.

Cinematic trickery was introduced by the stage conjuror GEORGES MÉLIÈS, and, with the decline of live variety entertainments, the more lavish acts folded. Magicians continued to play wherever variety shows were offered, but in America conjurors often drifted into chautauquas (lecture meetings of an educational or religious nature), CIRCUSES and fairgrounds. Television provided a new arena for old techniques, and there was a stage resurgence of sorts in the 1970s. BROADWAY, which had proved cool to Houdini in 1926, warmed to the musical *The Magic Show* (by Bob Randall and Stephen Schwartz, 1974) in which the Canadian Doug Henning (1947– ) performed Houdini's water torture cell in blue jeans and T-shirt and made a tiger vanish. He and colleagues like David Copperfield have invigorated the magic act with 'show biz' glamour and cunning lighting techniques. CABARET and casinos are now common venues for conjurors: the Las Vegas-style REVUE makes a congenial setting for the wild-beast illusions of Siegfried (Fischbacker) and Roy (Horn).

The fantastic aspects of the magical tradition have influenced much avant-garde theatre, particularly the surrealist obsession (see SURREALISM) with the *insolite*: COCTEAU's *Orphée* (1926) is a knowing adaptation of illusionism to a poetical conceit. John Vaccaro's transvestite production *The Magic Show of Dr Ma-Gico* (by Kenneth Bernard, LA MAMA, 1973) exploited the structure of the magic act for anarchic audience-bashing, a technique more subtly and amiably wielded by JÉRÔME SAVARY's Grand Magic Circus shows.

**Magnani, Anna** 1908–73 Italian actress. In the 1930s and 1940s she worked in both the 'straight' and REVUE theatres, notably in the early 1940s with the comedian TOTÒ, developing also a career in cinema that increasingly kept her from the stage but brought her international status in Italian films and later in Hollywood. She made occasional postwar stage appearances, notably in O'NEILL's *Anna Christie* (1945) and VERGA's *La Lupa* (1965).

**Mahelot, Laurent** fl.1620s-30s French scene designer. Mahelot was resident designer and machinist of the Comédiens du Roi at the HÔTEL DE BOURGOGNE and compiled a *Mémoire* which represents a unique record of 17th-century stage practice. The manuscript lists all 71 plays in the company's repertoire in the early 1630s and gives an illustrated description of the scenery, machin-

ery and other effects required for their performance. Mahelot's designs mark a transition between medieval multiple staging and Italian Renaissance scenography.

**Maillet, Antonine** 1929– French Canadian playwright and novelist; the leading voice of francophone Acadia. Her greatest success was *La Sagouine* (*The Slattern*, 1971), performed in French and English. In 16 monologues an unlettered Acadian washerwoman reflects, in the archaic dialect of New Brunswick, on the injustices she and her people have suffered. *La Sagouine*'s themes and language return in most of Maillet's subsequent works, such as *Gapi et Sullivan* (1973), *La Veuve enragée* (*The Mad Widow*, 1977) and *La Contrabandière* (*Smuggler Woman*, 1981), but most notably in her other critical and popular success, *Évangéline Deusse* (*Evangeline the Second*, 1976), in which she sets out to replace Longfellow's tragic heroine, too long the symbol of a passive Acadia. Maillet is also a major novelist.

**Mairet, Jean** 1604–86 French playwright. In *Silvanire* (1629) he created a pastoral tragicomedy which observed the three unities ( SEE ARISTOTLE). His tragedy *Sophonisbe* (1634) was a model of classical decorum. Predictably, he took part in the critical attack on PIERRE CORNEILLE's *Le Cid* in 1637. He was commissioned by RICHELIEU to write plays, and was attached to MONTDORY's company at the MARAIS before 1640.

**male impersonation** Women impersonating men. Unlike FEMALE IMPERSONATION in the theatre, women dressing as men has had little sanction from ancient religion or folk tradition; it has usually been condemned as a wanton assumption of masculine prerogative. When women first came on to the Western stage, costuming them in men's garb was simply a means to show off their limbs and provide freedom of movement. This was certainly the case during the Restoration, when PEPYS remarked of an actress in knee-breeches, 'She had the best legs that I ever saw, and I was well pleased by it.' NELL GWYN, Moll Davis and others took advantage of these BREECHES PARTS, but few could, like ANNE BRACEGIRDLE, give a convincing portrayal of a man. Often, the part travestied was that of a young rake – Sir Harry Wildair in *The Constant Couple* and Macheath in *The Beggar's Opera* – providing a thrill from the pseudo-lesbian overtones of the plot's situations.

The leading 'breeches' actresses of the early 19th century, MADAME VESTRIS and MARY ANN KEELEY, noted for their delicacy, made an impression less mannish than boyish. The same holds true for the first 'principal boys' in English PANTOMIME, and as Aladdins and Dick Whittingtons became more ample in flesh throughout the Victorian period no real effort was made to pretend they were men. JENNY HILL on the MUSIC-HALLS and Jennie Lee as Jo in various adaptations of *Bleak House*, Vernet in Paris and Josefine Dora and Hansi Niese in Vienna, represented the proletarian waif, a pathetic or cocky adolescent, not a mature male.

True male impersonation was first introduced on the American VARIETY stage by the Englishwoman Annie Hindle (c.1847-?) and her imitator Ella Wesner (1841–1917) in the guise of 'fast' young men, swaggering, cigar-smoking and coarse. They performed in the English music-hall as well. Bessie Bonehill, with her mezzo-soprano voice, blended the coarse-grained fast man with the principal boy into a type that could be admired for its lack of vulgarity. Her example was followed by the celebrated VESTA TILLEY, whose soprano voice never really fooled any listener; her young men-about-town were ideal types for the 1890s, sexually ambiguous without being threatening. Even so, at the Royal Command Performance of 1912 Queen Mary turned her back on Tilley's act.

After World War I, with radical changes in dress and manners, the male impersonator became a relic, although the tradition persisted in e.g. ELLA SHIELDS. Ironically, contemporary FEMINIST THEATRE groups have revived the type for political reasons, as in Eve Merriam's revue The Club (1976) and TIMBERLAKE WERTENBAKER's New Anatomies (1981). In a work like CARYL CHURCHILL's Cloud Nine (1979), sexual cross-casting is an important aspect of the play's enquiry into gender identity.

Another aspect of male impersonation is the assumption of Shakespearian men's roles by actresses. It was long a practice to cast women as such children as Mamillius, as well as supernatural beings like Puck and Ariel. More ambitious was the usurpation of leading parts. The powerful American actress CHARLOTTE CUSHMAN played Romeo to her sister's Juliet and later aspired to Cardinal Wolsey. Women have undertaken Shylock and Falstaff on occasion, but Hamlet has proven to be irresistible. The most distinguished in our time, JUDITH ANDERSON and Frances de la Tour have tried the experiment, though this has proved less successful than the all-male As You Like It attempted by CHEEK BY JOWL (1991).

During the last decades, male impersonation has been used to explore sexual politics and wider gender issues, as at the WOW Café in New York's Greenwich Village, where both heterosexual and homosexual roles have been shuffled continually. The lesbian Split Breeches company, founded there in 1981 by Lois Weaver and Peggy Shaw, specialized in gender-bending, and in 1991 linked up with the gay male Bloolips to stage Belle Reprieve, a PARODY of A Streetcar Named Desire. San Francisco nurtured Elvis Herselvis, Leigh Crow's exposé of impersonators; the hard-edged macho caricatures of Shelly Mars; and the lesbian transsexual Kate Bornstein whose shows (Hidden: a Gender and The Three-Dollar-Bill Opera) thoroughly deconstruct assumptions about gender identity.

**Malina, Judith** see LIVING THEATRE

**Malleson, Miles** 1888–1969 British actor and playwright. One of Nigel Playfair's company at the LYRIC THEATRE, HAMMERSMITH (London), he made his name in Shakespearian and Restoration comedy, and after 1950 helped to win popularity for MOLIÈRE on the English stage in his own adaptations.

**Malmö Stadsteater** (Sweden) Opening in 1944, this large theatre was an attempt to realize the ideal of a people's theatre. It was inspired by REINHARDT's Grosses Schauspielhaus; its fan-shaped auditorium seats up to 1,695 people around a shallow thrust stage, backed by an enormously wide proscenium. Movable walls allow changes in its capacity – e.g. to a more intimate format – but in practice spoken drama is increasingly relegated to the Intimate and New Theatres, leaving the main stage to opera, musicals and ballet. One of the few to use the Stadsteater successfully for spoken drama was INGMAR BERGMAN, who made it one of the most important Scandinavian theatres during the 1950s. Particularly acclaimed were his productions of STRINDBERG's The Crown Bride (1952) and The Ghost Sonata (1954), IBSEN's Peer Gynt and MOLIÈRE's The Misanthrope (both 1957), and GOETHE's Ur-Faust (1958). The company

declined in quality from the late 1970s, but was resuscitated in 1992–3.

**Mamet, David** 1947– American playwright. One of the most important dramatists to emerge from the 1970s, Mamet first attracted attention with such one-acts as Sexual Perversity in Chicago and Duck Variations. The 1977 production of American Buffalo marked his BROADWAY debut. It involves three thugs plotting to steal an especially valuable American buffalo nickel, which they never accomplish. Traditional plot is minimal; subtle character development emerges in its place. A similarly minimal script, A Life in the Theatre (1977), presents an elderly and a youthful actor, both on and back stage, contrasting their different attitudes towards their work. While many traditionalists have been hostile towards or bewildered by Mamet's work or offended by his liberal use of profanity and sexual language, the 1983–4 London and New York productions of Glengarry Glen Ross led to the Pulitzer Prize for Drama. Another success was the Lincoln Center (see VIVIAN BEAUMONT AND MITZI E. NEWHOUSE THEATRES) production of Speed-the-Plow (1988). Much of Mamet's attention since the late 1980s has been devoted to film-writing, directing and adaptation. In 1992 a new play, Oleanna, a two-hander tackling issues of political correctness within a university setting, was produced in Boston and caused controversy both in the USA and the following year at the ROYAL COURT THEATRE, London. The protagonist of Mamet's The Cryptogram (1994), a short three-hander, is an 11-year old boy who confuses his haunted dream world with his actual life. The Old Neighbourhood (1995) was inspired by Mamet's Jewish background.

**Mamoulian, Rouben** 1897–1987 Russian-born American director. While preparing for a law career in Moscow, Mamoulian attended VAKHTANGOV's Studio Theatre. After graduation he went to London, and in 1922 successfully staged The Beating on the Door at the ST JAMES'S THEATRE. From 1923 to 1926 he headed the Eastman Theatre in Rochester, New York. In 1926 he became a teacher at the THEATRE GUILD, and a year later made his BROADWAY directing debut with Porgy, gaining a reputation for integrating music, drama and dance into a rhythmic whole. He staged six plays in 1928 including O'NEILL's Marco Millions, two plays in 1929 and four in 1930. His other outstanding stage credits include Porgy and Bess (1935), Oklahoma! (1943), Carousel (1945) and Lost in the Stars (1949). He also directed 16 films.

**Manaka, Matsemela** 1955– South African poet, playwright, musician and artist. A well known figure on the Witwatersrand, he first achieved prominence in 1980 when his play Egoli (The Golden One, 1979) was performed at a German festival. His earlier musical, The Horn (1977), inspired by GIBSON KENTE's How Long?, was based on the theme of the dispossession of the migrant worker. In 1979 Manaka created, out of improvisation, the play Imbumba (Unity), the first production of his newly formed Soyikwa Africa Theatre. Later plays were Pula (1982), Vuka (1982) and Children of Asazi (1984).

**Manhattan Theatre Club** (New York City) American company. This OFF-BROADWAY organization was founded in 1970. Under its artistic director (since 1972) LYNNE MEADOW, MTC is 'committed to presenting the provocative work of the world's best writers' of drama, opera, poetry and music. Recent premieres or significant productions include HENLEY's Crimes of the Heart (1981) and The Miss Firecracker Contest (1984), new translations of CHEKHOV's plays by VAN ITALLIE, BRIAN FRIEL's *Aristocrats* (1989), AUGUST WILSON's *The Piano Lesson* (1990) and AYCKBOURN's *A Small Family Business* (1991–2).

**mani-rimdu** Nepalese theatre form. *Mani-rimdu* is a kind of dance-drama popular among the Sherpa people of Nepal. Performances are presented as seasonal three-day rituals held in May or November in the confines of Buddhist monasteries. Monks serve as the actors, and the spectators assemble from nearby villages. The main purpose is to reinforce traditionally held beliefs in Buddhism and to depict its superiority over the ancient Bon religion, the tenets of which are denigrated during the performance. It is a colourful outdoor spectacle against the grand backdrop of Mount Everest and surrounding peaks.

The courtyard in front of the monastery temple is used for the acting area. The first day's performance, known as the 'life-consecration' rite, is intended to bless the entire ceremony. On the second day the laymen dress in their finest apparel for the performance, which is divided into 13 short separate units consisting of simple group dances and two short improvised comic dramas. The events are punctuated by distribution of ritual foods and rice beer. The monks wear a variety of masks representing deities, mythological characters and human beings. Musicians accompany the performers and play a very important role in the progress of the action. Ten-foot-long brass horns and a trumpet fashioned from a human thigh bone are among the more unusual musical instruments.

On the third day, rituals are performed to symbolize the final destruction of evil forces in the Khumbu valley and the supremacy of Buddhism as a means of protecting the laity from harm during the coming months.

**Manitoba Theatre Centre** (Canada) Founded in 1958, the company built upon firm roots in the community and developed audiences through its theatre school and touring children's programmes. Under JOHN HIRSCH the MTC became a model for similar regional theatres across Canada and the United States. For several years in the 1960s it served as an unofficial winter home for much of the STRATFORD FESTIVAL company. A new home opened in 1970.

**Mannheim Court Theatre** German theatre. Under the direction of Baron Heribert von Dalberg (1750–1806) the Mannheim Court Theatre exercised much influence on the development of German theatre. Dalberg hired many of the actors from the Gotha Court Theatre after EKHOF's death in 1778. Among them was IFFLAND. For the next 12 years Dalberg encouraged them to develop a moderate, idealized REALISM in acting that became known as the Mannheim style. He insisted on his actors being educated and capable of playing together in a unified whole.

**Mansfield, Richard** 1854–1907 American actor-producer. Hailed by many as America's answer to HENRY IRVING after the death of EDWIN BOOTH, this strong personality generated critical controversy whenever he performed. He played his first important role, Baron Chevrial in *A Parisian Romance*, in 1883. In 1886 he starred in his own production of *Prince Karl*, beginning an annual tour of New York and the regions, presenting a regularly updated repertory. A compelling, intense actor and a skilful, if autocratic, producer, his notable roles and productions included the dual role *Dr Jekyll and Mr Hyde* (1887), *Richard III*, *Henry V*, CLYDE FITCH's *Beau Brummell* (1890), Bluntschli in *Arms and the Man*

(1894), *Cyrano de Bergerac* (1889) and *Peer Gynt* (1907). His productions were characterized by lavish spectacle and a meticulous attention to realistic detail.

**mansion** and **platea** Medieval theatre structure. The *mansion* was an emblematic structure suggesting a location, person or idea (e.g. Bethlehem, Herod, Paradise); the *platea* was the neutral space in front of or surrounding the *mansion*. Emblematic design involves the suggestion of a place or idea by use of an image or device. For example, in certain medieval productions Jerusalem was depicted simply by a gate, and hell by an open-mouthed monster head spewing fire and smoke. In some medieval theatre the spectators moved from one scene to the next; but the scenes could also exist side by side on a raised stage (scaffold).

Most medieval theatres used some variant of the *mansion* and *platea* design. The pageant wagons of English and Spanish MYSTERY PLAY cycles were essentially rolling *mansions* with the street or square as *platea*.

**Mantell, Robert Bruce** 1854–1928 Scottish-born American actor. Mantell received a classical English training and went to America in 1878 as a member of HELENA MODJESKA's touring company. In 1886 he made his first star appearance in *Tangled Lives*, a modern domestic MELODRAMA. He added the tragedies of SHAKESPEARE and the romances of BULWER LYTTON to his touring repertory in the 1890s, and in 1904 he made a triumphant return to New York as the last representative of a robust, passionate 'old school' of tragic acting in America. Amongst his more celebrated roles were Othello, Shylock, King John, King Lear, Macbeth, Richard III, Richelieu and Louis XI.

**Manzoni, Alessandro** 1785–1873 Italian novelist and playwright. His best-known novel, *I promessi sposi* (*The Betrothed*, 1840–2), has several times been adapted for stage and screen. He wrote two plays, *Il Conte di Carmagnola* (*The Count of Carmagnola*, 1815–19) and *Adelchi* (1820–2), both essentially literary works in the tradition of romantic poets like Shelley and BYRON; they are rarely performed today, although versions of the second have been given interesting stagings by VITTORIO GASSMAN (1960) and CARMELO BENE (1984), the last in the style of an oratorio. Manzoni was much influenced by SHAKESPEARE and helped to establish the English dramatist's reputation in Italy in the early decades of the 19th century.

**Marais, Théâtre du** Parisian theatre. As an indoor tennis court in the rue Vieille-du-Temple, it was rented by itinerant actors until MONTDORY's company settled there in 1634, acquiring a reputation with their performances of PIERRE CORNEILLE's plays which nearly eclipsed the Comédiens du Roi at the HÔTEL DE BOURGOGNE. The Marais's fortunes declined after 1647, except for the comic popularity of JODELET, and in 1673 the king amalgamated its leading actors with MOLIÈRE's former company and they moved to a theatre in the rue Guénégaud, before a further fusion with the Hôtel de Bourgogne in 1680 gave birth to the COMÉDIE-FRANÇAISE.

**Marble, Danforth** 1810–49 American actor. He began telling YANKEE stories in 1832. In competition with GEORGE HANDEL HILL and J. H. HACKETT, Marble developed a distinctive Yankee character with broad American idiosyncrasies. His vehicles included *The Forest Rose*, *The Vermont Wool Dealer*, *Yankee Land* and *The Backwoodsman; or The Gamecock of the Wilderness*, but his particular success was in the title role of *Sam Patch; or,*

*The Daring Yankee* (1836). The real Sam Patch made a career of jumping from high places; his last jump was from the top of the Genesee Falls in 1829, a distance of 125 feet. Marble made his jumps in theatres as spectacular as possible. He enjoyed a successful visit to England in 1844, playing before the king and queen. He died of cholera on the night of his benefit, the play being *A Cure for the Cholera*.

**Marceau, Marcel** 1923– French MIME artist. This most influential and best-loved of modern mimes made his debut in 1947 at the Théâtre de Poche, Paris. Inspired by both silent film comics and the *COMMEDIA DELL'ARTE*, his character Bip, recognizable by his striped jersey, whiteface and the red rose in his top hat, was adaptable to all kinds of pantomime. Starting with simple stylistic exercises ('The Tug of War', 'Chasing Butterflies'), he moved on to such philosophical and elliptical *mimodrames* as 'The Cage' and 'The Mask Maker', and with his company (1948–60) could even expand into an adaptation of GOGOL's 'The Overcoat'. Marceau's international standing was confirmed at the Berlin Festival of 1951, where he won the friendship of BRECHT, and tours of 66 countries disseminated his abstract style throughout the world. In 1974 he presented a retrospective of his work and in 1978 founded the École de Mimodrame de Paris.

**March, Fredric** [Frederick McIntyre Bickel] 1897–1975 American actor. His first major role was in WILLIAM A. BRADY's production of *The Law Breaker* (1922). He performed in MOLNÁR's *The Swan* with the actress FLORENCE ELDRIDGE (1926). They married and worked together for the rest of their careers, co-starring in *Ye Obedient Husband* (1938). He created the roles of Mr Antrobus in *The Skin of Our Teeth* (1942), Major Victor Joppolo in *A Bell for Adano* (1944), Nicholas Denery in *The Autumn Garden* (1951) and, perhaps his finest performance, James Tyrone in O'NEILL's *Long Day's Journey into Night* (1956). He also had an extensive career on screen. March considered the role of James Tyrone his finest work.

**Marcos, Plínio** 1935– Brazilian playwright. Lacking formal education, Marcos was a manual labourer and soccer player, became an actor and administrator and eventually a playwright. *Dois Perdidos numa Noite Suja* (*Two Lost Men in a Dirty Night*, 1966) scandalized the São Paulo public for its brutally realistic treatment of the marginal society of two 'bums' who eventually destroy each other. *Navalha na Carne* (*Knife in the Flesh*, 1967) elevates in lyrical terms the brutal world of a prostitute, a pimp and a homosexual. Other plays include *Homens de Papel* (*Paper Men*), *Quando as Máquinas Param* (*When the Machines Stop*, 1967), *Jornada de un Imbécil até o Entendimento* (*Journey of an Imbecile to Understanding*, 1968), and *Balbina de Iansã* (1970), the latter dealing with *umbanda* (São Paulo-style voodoo). Marcos experienced serious problems with CENSORSHIP during the 1970s. As political restrictions were lifted in the 1980s, he returned to the stage with *Madame Blavatsky* (1985).

**Marcus, Frank** 1928– British actor, director, playwright and critic. Born in Germany, he emigrated to Britain in 1939. His German background helped him to produce a thoughtful translation/adaptation of ARTHUR SCHNITZLER's *Reigen*, presented in London as *Merry-Go-Round* (1952), and some traces of Schnitzler's cool analysis of sexual behaviour appeared in his first WEST END success, *The Formation Dancers* (1964), and in *Cleo* (1965), which is like a female version of Schnitzler's *Anatol*. *The Killing of Sister George* (1965) established his reputation as

one of Britain's leading writers of serious comedies, describing how the BBC got rid of a leading radio star because of her lesbian proclivities. His subsequent plays, which include *Mrs Mouse, Are You Within?* (1968) and *Notes on a Love Affair* (1972), were less successful, and from 1968 until 1980 Marcus was best known as the perceptive theatre critic of the *Sunday Telegraph*.

**Mardzhanov, Konstantin** [Kote Mardzhanishvili] 1872–1933 Soviet Georgian director. After acting and directing in his native republic (1893–1909), he Russified his name and established himself in Moscow. He co-founded the Georgian Drama Studio with A. I. Yuzhin, directed at the MOSCOW ART THEATRE (1910–13), and organized the Sukhodolskys' Free Theatre (1913–14) where, along with the actress KOONEN and directors TAIROV and A. A. Sanin, he staged opera, drama and pantomime and sought to develop a singing, dancing actor. In Kiev (1919) he staged a notable production of *Salome* and a May Day presentation of LOPE DE VEGA's *Fuenteovejuna* in which rebellious villagers overthrow oppressive royals. Mardzhanov's experiments with festive staging in Rostov-on-Don (1914–15) and Petrograd (1916–17) prepared him to coordinate the mass spectacle *Toward a Worldwide Commune* (1920). He returned to Georgia to head Tblisi's Rustaveli Theatre. Criticized for attempting to 'Europeanize' the troupe, he founded the Second State Georgian Theatre (after 1933 the Mardzhanishvili Theatre). He also worked in films (1916–28) and directed at Moscow's Korsh, Maly and Operetta Theatres (1931–3).

**Margalit, Meir** 1906–73 Israeli actor. Born in Poland, he went to Palestine as a pioneer in 1922, where he joined the Ohel Theatre. His performance as the brave soldier Schweik in Hašek's play (1936) established him as the greatest comic actor in the country. The play was performed over 800 times. Margalit is especially remembered for the lead roles in MOLIÈRE's *L'Avare*, *Le Bourgeois Gentilhomme* and *Le Malade Imaginaire*, and as Falstaff in *The Merry Wives of Windsor*.

**Marinetti, F(ilippo) T(ommaso)** 1876–1944 Italian poet, playwright and polemicist. Founder and most active publicist of the futurist movement, he moved for some time in the French literary world, announcing the principles of the new art he championed with 'The Futurist Manifesto' in *Le Figaro*, 20 February 1909. He pioneered a new literary form, the manifesto, and in the next few years many of these poured from his pen, concerned with all the arts that FUTURISM embraced including theatre: the most important were *Il teatro di varietà* (*The Variety Theatre*, 1913) and *Il teatro sintetico futurista* (*The Synthetic Theatre*, 1915).

Marinetti's dramatic output was basically of two kinds: syntheses and full-length plays, including *Poupées électriques* (*Electric Puppets*, 1909), later adapted under various titles; *Il tamburo di fuoco* (*Fire Drum*, 1922); *Luci veloci* (*Rapid Light*, 1929); and *Simultanina* (1931). The last three combine spectacular effects with an empty verbosity. The futurist exaltation of machines and technology, of man dominating the natural world through science, had latent Fascist elements which came to the fore with the rise to power of Mussolini. In 1924 Marinetti lauded the new political nationalism in *Futurismo e fascismo* (*Futurism and Fascism*) and became a propagandist for Fascist values.

**marionette** Puppet type. A marionette hangs from a cross-piece or stick; its articulated limbs are worked from above by strings or wires. The name may derive from the medieval French word used for little statues of the Virgin Mary. Marionettes were known as well to the ancient Greeks as *neurospasta*, wooden figures on strings.

During the Middle Ages, the Church employed marionettes to illustrate Bible stories, especially the nativity, and in Spain they played an important part in religious processions. The Council of Trent (1563) banned their use in church, but to little effect. Between the 17th and 19th centuries marionettes enjoyed their most widespread popularity in Europe, often replacing live actors. Each major Italian city had its own theatre devoted to the favourite local character: Cassandrino in Rome, Girolamo in Milan, Gianduja in Turin. Ambulant showmen used lightweight and easily portable booths. The Teatro Fiando in Milan specialized in fairy plays and even operas. In Spain the *títeres* dramatized saints' legends and chivalric romances.

Marionettes appeared in Germany as early as the 10th and 12th centuries as *Tokkespill*, animated statuettes employed by itinerant minstrels. German and Dutch marionettes were greatly influenced by the ENGLISCHE KOMÖDIANTEN (English Comedians) who toured in the 16th and 17th centuries, mingling them with live actors. *Dr Faustus* (c.1589) by CHRISTOPHER MARLOWE was adapted as a marionette show which was seen by the young GOETHE in Frankfurt-am-Main. Marionettes travelled through Saxony, Bohemia, South Germany and Austria (where KASPER would become the leading comic figure). Haydn wrote music for five puppet operas (1773–8) on classic themes, sung at the court of Prince Esterházy.

A well established marionette theatre existed in Paris c.1590, when the classic characters Polichinelle and La Mère Gigogne were created. During the early reign of Louis XIV, the leading impresario was Jean Brioché (Giovanni Briocci) on the Pont-Neuf, who was paid 1,365 livres for a performance before the Dauphin. The legitimate theatre found the competition too great and in 1710 statutes forbade marionettes to sing; they gradually removed to the fairs, where LESAGE wrote for them.

The usual terms in England were 'mammet' and 'puppet' for the figure, and 'motion' and 'drollery' for the show. From 1562 marionettes performed all sorts of plays, from *The Prodigal Son* to *Julius Caesar*, in fairground showbooths, and managed to escape the proscription of the playhouses in 1642 and 1647; when the theatres reopened they sought (1675) the closure of the puppetshows, unsuccessfully. The leading exhibitors were Martin Powell, whose PUNCH show (1710–13) became a byword; Pinkethman, who portrayed the gods of Olympus; and Crawley, who staged the Creation of the World with a very wet Deluge.

Marionettes were somewhat displaced in popularity during the 19th century, for many of the local types could be readily performed in the streets by hand-PUPPETS. A revival occurred in artistic circles in the early 20th century. The Czech Josef Skupa (1892–1957) invented the character Spejbl, a naive, prejudiced man-in-the-street; Gustav Nosek developed his alert and active son Hurvinek: the two puppets became vehicles for anti-Nazi SATIRE, even appearing in concentration-camp pyjamas, leading the Gestapo to confiscate the original figures. Czechoslovakia has remained in the forefront of developments.

In modern stage aesthetics, marionettes have played an influential role. MAURICE MAETERLINCK's propaganda in their favour was followed by GORDON CRAIG's desideratum of an *Über-Marionette* as the ideal actor. JARRY's *Ubu* cycle was conceived as a marionette spectacle, ANTONIN ARTAUD prescribed gigantic marionettes for his Theatre of Cruelty, and MICHEL DE GHELDERODE and GARCÍA LORCA (in the tradition of GOZZI's *Love of Three Oranges*) composed plays specifically for them. On the contemporary scene, DARIO FO has suggested marionettes as agents in the proletarian revolution, Takuo Endo has applied them to performance art, and the allegorical figures of the BREAD AND PUPPET THEATRE can be seen as a logical extension.

**Marivaux, Pierre Carlet de Chamblain de** 1688–1763 French playwright, novelist and journalist. Advocating the Moderns against the Ancients, in 1720 he produced two comedies, *L'Amour et la vérité* (*Love and Truth*) and *Arlequin poli par l'amour* (*Harlequin Refined by Love*), for the COMÉDIE-ITALIENNE and a tragedy, *Annibal* (*Hannibal*), for the COMÉDIE-FRANÇAISE. Thereafter he wrote for both theatres, but most successfully for the Italian players, who responded to his nuanced dialogue in which young love and self-discovery are sensitively analysed. Marivaux is still widely performed. Amongst his most successful Italian plays were *La Surprise de l'amour* (*The Surprise of Love*, 1722), *La Double Inconstance* (*The Double Inconstancy*, 1723), *Le Prince travesti* (*The Prince in Disguise*, 1724), *Le Jeu de l'amour et du hasard* (*The Game of Love and Chance*, 1730), *Les Fausses Confidences* (*The False Confessions*, 1737) and *L'Épreuve* (*The Test*, 1740), while *La Seconde Surprise de l'amour* (*The Second Surprise of Love*, 1727) and *Le Legs* (*The Legacy*, 1736) were well received at the Comédie-Française.

**Mark Taper Forum Theatre** (Los Angeles) The giant concrete mushroom-shaped Mark Taper Forum, named after a Los Angeles financier-philanthropist, is part of the Los Angeles Music Center and home of Gordon Davidson's Center Theatre Group, which opened in 1967 and is dedicated to producing new and old musicals and dramas and new works with a West Coast flavour.

**Marlowe, Christopher** (1564–93) English playwright and poet. Educated at Cambridge University, he worked as an agent for Francis Walsingham, Elizabeth I's minister. His private life was notorious and led to accusations of atheism, blasphemy, subversion and homosexuality, but only speculation links his violent death in a Deptford (London) tavern with his activities as a spy.

Shortly after graduating as an MA, Marlowe changed the course of English drama by presenting the still-emergent professional theatre of London with the startlingly original first part of *Tamburlaine the Great* (1587), probably performed by the ADMIRAL'S MEN with EDWARD ALLEYN in the title role. This and his later plays became popular features of the company's repertoire. The second part (1587) matched the success of the first. The chronology is disputed, and Marlowe may already have collaborated with NASHE in writing *Dido, Queen of Carthage*, drawn mainly from Book Four of Virgil's *Aeneid*, for the CHILDREN OF THE CHAPEL ROYAL. He also translated Lucan's *Pharsalia* and Ovid's *Elegies*.

After *Tamburlaine*, Marlowe continued to dramatize the careers of overreaching heroes who command both admiration and condemnation. *The Jew of Malta* (c.1589), described as a tragedy on the title page of its first edition (1633), is a grotesque comedy, in which murderous excess and inflated rhetoric PARODY statesmanship and Christian authority. Interest focuses on the villain-hero

Barabas. *The Massacre at Paris* (c.1589) features the villainous Duke of Guise and treats sardonically the horrific St Bartholomew massacre of 1572. *Edward II* (c.1592) is a tragedy in which the defeat and eventual murder of a homosexual king by powerful barons are depicted with a new plainness of style. *Doctor Faustus* survives in two unsatisfactory texts (1604 and 1616), each of which shows the marks of playhouse adaptation, but the hero Faustus and his increasingly symbiotic relationship with Mephistopheles remain magnificently unaffected. *Doctor Faustus*, even more than *Tamburlaine*, *The Jew of Malta* and *Edward II*, has proved its power in many 20th-century revivals.

**Marlowe, Julia** 1866–1950 American actress. Her family migrated from England when she was five and settled in Cincinnati. Her first New York triumph came in 1899 in the title role in CLYDE FITCH's *Barbara Frietchie*. E. H. SOTHERN and Julia Marlowe first appeared together in 1904; from then until her retirement in 1924 Sothern and Marlowe were identified with SHAKESPEARE. The roles of Rosalind, Viola, Juliet, Ophelia and Portia became her property, and critics praised her verse-speaking, magnetic warmth and grace.

**Marmion, Shakerley** 1603–39 English playwright and poet. Marmion wrote three plays, the first two for Prince Charles's Men at the SALISBURY COURT THEATRE and the third for Queen Henrietta's Men at the PHOENIX. The plot of *Holland's Leaguer* (1631) features Elizabeth Holland's notorious Southwark brothel. Like this first play, *A Fine Companion* (1633) is another JONSONIAN COMEDY OF HUMOURS, less effective than *The Antiquary* (c.1635), in which the follies of old age are wittily displayed.

**Marowitz, Charles** 1934– American-born director and critic. He directed his first London production in 1958, after which he worked with PETER BROOK on a series of productions that included *King Lear* (1962), an experimental Theatre of Cruelty season based on ARTAUD and GENET (1964), and the first of his 'collage' versions of SHAKESPEARE (*Hamlet*, 1965; *Macbeth*, 1970; *Othello*, 1972; *The Taming of the Shrew*, 1973; and *Measure for Measure*, 1975). In 1968 he founded the Open Space Company, introducing avant-garde drama by contemporary North American writers (John Herbert, *Fortune and Men's Eyes*, 1968; SAM SHEPARD, *The Tooth of Crime*, 1972) as well as his own plays (*Artaud at Rodez*, 1975) and adaptations (*Woyzeck*, 1973; *Hedda*, 1980); but their London stage closed in 1979, and the company disbanded in 1981. Returning to the USA, Marowitz founded the Open Theatre of Los Angeles in 1982 and became associate director of the Los Angeles Theatre Center (1984–9). He has also gained a reputation for his theoretical writings.

**Marqués, René** 1919–79 Puerto Rican director, playwright and novelist. He studied at Columbia University and at PISCATOR's Dramatic Workshop. In 1951 he helped establish the Teatro Experimental del Ateneo in San Juan, and directed the group for three years. Devoted to maintaining the Hispanic traditions of Puerto Rico, he actively opposed the US economic and cultural invasion of the island, favouring independence instead of commonwealth status. His plays range from REALISM/NATURALISM (*La carreta*, *The Cart*, 1952) to THEATRE OF THE ABSURD (*El apartamiento*, *The Apartment/Alienation*, 1964) and to a biblical trilogy including *Sacrificio en el Monte Moriah* (*Sacrifice on Mount Moriah*, 1970). His best are *Los soles truncos* (*The Fanlights*,

1958) and *Un niño azul para esa sombra* (*A Blue Child for that Shadow*, 1970), both complex psychological works on Puerto Rican identity problems.

**Marron, Hanna** 1923– Israeli actress. Born in Germany, she started acting at the age of four and appeared in Fritz Lang's legendary film M. She emigrated to Israel at the age of ten. Trained at the HABIMAH studio, she served in the Jewish Brigade of the British army during World War II, where she performed for the soldiers; she later performed in army troupes. Marron was one of the founders of the Cameri Theatre. She lost a leg in the 1970 terrorist attack at Munich airport, but returned to the stage. She played leading roles in IBSEN's *Ghosts* (1990), *Hedda Gabler* (1966) and *A Doll's House* (1959), Leah Goldberg's *The Lady of the Manor* (1959), Moshe Shamir's *He Walked the Fields* (1948), SHAW's *Pygmalion* (1954), SENECA's *Medea* (1971), PINTER's *A Slight Ache* and *Landscape* (1975), ARTHUR MILLER's *All My Sons* (1976), BECKETT's *Happy Days* (1985) and Shulamit Lapid's *Surrogate Womb* (1992). She also played Arkadina in CHEKHOV's *The Seagull* and Queen Elizabeth in SCHILLER's *Mary Stuart* (1961).

**Mars, Mlle** [Anne Françoise Hippolyte Boutet] 1779–1847 French actress. At 16 she was part of the troupe of the COMÉDIE-FRANÇAISE. In her youth she played a series of ingénue roles, especially those of MOLIÈRE. She reintroduced MARIVAUX to the Comédie-Française repertoire, being an incomparable Sylvia in *The Game of Love and Chance*, and at her instigation all of Molière's great comedies were brought back to the stage. From 1795 to 1839 she created 109 roles at the Comédie-Française, including a number of romantic ones: the Duchesse de Guise in *Henri III et sa cour* (1829), Desdémone in *Le More de Venise* and Dona Sol in *Hernani*. She created Mademoiselle de Belle-Isle (1839) at the age of 60. Mars was the model of Parisian fashion for 30 years. When she died, she lay in state for three days and 50,000 people attended her funeral.

**Marsh, Ngaio** 1895–1982 New Zealand director, playwright and detective novelist. Educated as a Fine Arts student at Canterbury University College, she began a notable series of student SHAKESPEARE productions there with *Hamlet* in 1943, and continued to work with her students and ex-students until *Henry V* in 1972. An attempt at a more ambitious touring professional company in 1951, the British Commonwealth Theatre Company, failed. Marsh also achieved an international reputation as a writer of crime fiction, adapting some novels into plays, including *A Surfeit of Lampreys* (1950) and *False Scent* (1961).

**Marshall, Norman** 1901–80 British director, theatre manager and critic. He joined TERENCE GRAY at the Cambridge Festival Theatre in 1926. After managing the company in 1932, when he staged the first English production of O'NEILL's *Marco Millions*, he took over the GATE THEATRE in London, where he directed a series of new, partly experimental plays. After 1942 he formed his own REPERTORY company in association with CEMA, and in 1952 directed *Volpone* for the Cameri Theatre in Israel. As head of drama for Associated-Rediffusion (1955–9) he encouraged the development of theatrical programming for television (see TELEVISION DRAMA), and later played an active role in planning the NATIONAL THEATRE.

**Marston, John** 1576–1634 English playwright. Having entered the Middle Temple, he abandoned law and wrote verse SATIRES. Much of his work expresses anger at moral disorder. His first plays were written for the BOYS OF ST PAUL'S. The dark comedy of *Antonio and Mellida* (1599) was followed by its sequel, *Antonio's Revenge* (1599–1600). *Jack Drum's Entertainment* (1600) and *What You Will* (c.1601) are comparatively good-humoured satires. But Marston became embroiled, as BEN JONSON'S adversary, in the 'war of the theatres', reworking an unknown author's play, *Histriomastix*, to include a mocking portrait of Jonson, and perhaps sharing with DEKKER in the clumsy *Satiromastix* (1601). Jonson's reply in *Poetaster* (1601) was effective. Within a few years, the volatile Marston had dedicated his finest play, *The Malcontent* (published 1604), to Jonson, and collaborated with him and CHAPMAN in the lively and controversial PARODY of CITIZEN COMEDY, *Eastward Ho* (1605). The central figure of *The Malcontent*, Malevole, is a usurped and alienated duke who comments bitterly on courtly corruption. *Parasitaster; or, The Fawn* (c. 1604) is even more directly critical of James I and his court. *The Dutch Courtesan* (c.1604) is a more exuberant comedy. *Sophonisba* (1606) is a Roman tragedy. For reasons unknown, Marston was imprisoned in 1608, and on his release renounced the theatre and took holy orders.

**Marston, (John) Westland** 1819–90 British playwright and drama critic. His best-known play, *The Patrician's Daughter* (1842), was a verse tragedy, promoted and performed by W. C. MACREADY. Marston wrote intelligent theatre reviews for the *Athenaeum* in the 1860s.

**Martin, Karlheinz** 1886–1948 German director. He founded the Tribune in Berlin, where he staged TOLLER's *Transfiguration* in 1919, and the Proletarian Theatre, which influenced PISCATOR. He is best known for his film of KAISER's *From Morn to Midnight* (1920), and for a cycle of 'revolutionary classics' produced in the Grosses Schauspielhaus constructed by REINHARDT, with whom he worked after 1921.

**Martin, Mary** 1913–90 American singer and actress. Her first starring role was as a statue come to life in *One Touch of Venus* (1943). Three years later, she played the faithful wife in *Lute Song*, a musical version of a traditional Chinese play. In 1947 she headed the national company of *Annie Get Your Gun*, but had the greatest success of her career as Nellie Forbush, a native nurse from Little Rock, Arkansas, in RODGERS and HAMMERSTEIN's *South Pacific* (1949). The role was ideally suited to her sunny temperament and buoyant singing style. In 1954 she appeared in a musical version of J. M. BARRIE's *Peter Pan*. Although she was rather mature for the part of a young novice, Martin's performance in *The Sound of Music* (1959) was a favourite with audiences. She starred in the London company of *Hello, Dolly!* before appearing with Robert Preston in *I Do! I Do!* (1966). In most of her MUSICAL THEATRE roles she portrayed a warm-hearted idealist who ultimately triumphs over problems.

**Martin Beck Theatre** (New York City) Built in 1924 as a monument to its owner, the 1,300-seat playhouse was named after a leading VAUDEVILLE producer. Important productions by the THEATRE GUILD, the Irish ABBEY Players, and the D'Oyly Carte Company have been staged there, and plays by major 20th-century American dramatists.

**Martin-Harvey, John** 1863–1944 British actor-manager. He eventually established his own company and made his fortune in the provinces, after an extended apprenticeship in IRVING's LYCEUM company (1882–96). His stock pieces were a dramatization of the novel *The Only Way*, *The Breed of the Treshams* (1903), *Hamlet*, *Richard III*, *Henry V* and *The Taming of the Shrew*. His Oedipus, in REINHARDT's spectacular production of *Oedipus Rex* (1912), was the finest thing he ever did. Knighted in 1921, and one of the last of his kind, Martin-Harvey remained an actor-manager until World War II.

**Martinelli family** Italian actors. **Drusiano** (died 1606/8), a famous Arlecchino, took the first important COMMEDIA DELL'ARTE troupe to England (1577–8), and travelled to Spain in 1588. His wife **Angelica** Alberigi (or Alberghini; fl.1580–94) had her own company, the UNITI. As an actor Drusiano was overshadowed by his brother **Tristano** (c.1556–1630), the most famous Arlecchino before DOMENICO BIANCOLELLI, who boasted of numbering kings and queens among his 'gossips'. Owing to his domineering pugnacity, he shifted from company to company, appearing with the ACCESI in 1601 and in Paris with the ANDREINI (1611–13), who accused him of undermining their authority.

**Martínez, José de Jesús** 1929–91 Panamanian playwright, director and poet; born in Nicaragua. His first works included *La mentira* (The Lie), *La perrera* (The Doghouse) and *La venganza* (The Vengeance), all published in Spain in 1954. His doctoral work in metaphysics (he became professor of philosophy and mathematics at the University of Panama) clearly influenced these plays as well as *El juicio final* (Final Judgement, 1962), a monologue of contemporary human anguish. *El mendigo y el avaro* (The Beggar and the Miser, 1963) questions the false aspects of charity. *Segundo asalto* (Second Assault, 1968) and *Cero y van tres* (Zero and There Go Three, 1979) are penetrating studies of personal domination and destructiveness. In *La guerra del banano* (Banana War, 1974), he attacked capitalistic intervention in the banana industry with a play constructed on metatheatrical and collective techniques.

**Martínez Queirolo, José** 1931– Ecuadorian playwright and poet. In addition to adaptations and translations of e.g. CERVANTES, OSCAR WILDE and MROŻEK, he has written more than twenty plays. His principal works are *Réquiem por la lluvia* (Requiem for the Rain, 1960), a dramatic monologue; *Los unos vs. los otros* (Some against Others*, 1968), described as a 'sensational open-air encounter' in which socio-economic family differences are disputed within a boxing match environment; and *Q.E.P.D.* (R.I.P., 1969), with its descriptions of death and burial by two participants.

**Marx Bros** American comedy team. The first to perform were **Gummo** (Milton, 1897–1977) and **Groucho** (Julius, 1895–1977), with material written by their uncle; **Chico** (Leonard, 1891–1961) and **Harpo** (Adolph, 1893–1964) joined later. When Gummo was drafted into war service, **Zeppo** (Herbert, 1901–79) stepped in. By the time they topped the bill at New York's PALACE THEATRE in 1920, they were commanding 10,000 dollars a week for their hilarious mayhem. By then, their distinctive characteristics were in place: Zeppo the handsome, bemused straight-man; Harpo the uninhibited curly-headed mute, honking his horn, goosing show-girls and taking every metaphor literally; Chico, the saturnine Neapolitan, interrupting his con-games only to crack bad puns and play ragtime piano; and Groucho with his greasepaint moustache and eyeglasses, stooping lope and unflagging cigar, confuting reason on every plane. They moved from VAUDEVILLE to REVUE with *I'll Say She Is* (Casino, 1924), with its famous Napoleon scene in which Groucho ordered the band to strike up 'The

Mayonnaise'. Their next shows, *The Cocoanuts* (1926) and *Animal Crackers* (1928), were co-written by GEORGE S. KAUFMAN. With the filming of these productions, the brothers moved successfully to Hollywood. Not so much satirists as anarchists, they flouted normality whenever they confronted it. Their film career petered out in the 1940s; Groucho became the star of a television quiz programme and did a one-man show at Carnegie Hall in New York.

**Masefield, John** 1878-1967 British poet laureate, playwright and novelist. Masefield's verse tragedies progressed from depictions of social alienation in contemporary settings (*The Campden Wonder*, 1907; *The Tragedy of Nan*, 1908) and historical subjects (*The Tragedy of Pompey the Great*, 1910; *Philip the King*, 1914) to biblical themes (*Esther*, an adaptation of RACINE, 1921; *A King's Daughter*, based on the story of Jezebel, 1923) and religious affirmation (*The Trial of Jesus*, 1927; *Easter: A Play for Singers*, 1929). Relying on verbal imagery rather than dramatic action, they indicate some of the difficulties in finding appropriate theatrical forms for modern poetic drama, which led Masefield to experiment with Japanese models (*The Faithful*, derived from *KABUKI*) and older European traditions (*The Empress of Rome*, based on a French miracle play (see MYSTERY PLAY), 1937).

**Maskelyne family** A dynasty of British magicians. J(ohn) N(evil) Maskelyne (1839-1917) was an expert plate-spinner who staged exhibitions of illusionism at London's Crystal Palace and the ST JAMES'S THEATRE (1867, 1873) and took over Egyptian Hall, making it England's first 'home of MAGIC' (1873-1904). An ingenious mechanic, he invented the coin lock, the automatic ticket-dispensing machine, a keyboard typewriter and a cash register, as well as air-driven automata, the whist-playing 'Psycho' and the sketching 'Zoe'. His wife **Elizabeth**, sons **Archie** and **Nevil** (died 1924), and grandsons **Clive** (1895-1928), **Jasper** (1903-73), **John** and **Noel** carried on the tradition.

**Mason, Bruce** 1921-82 New Zealand playwright and actor. He wrote realistic one-act plays which caustically analysed New Zealand society. His longer plays on Maori themes include *The Pohutukawa Tree* (1957), *Awatea* (1965), *Swan Song* (1967), *The Hand on the Rail* (1967) and *Hongi* (1968). Mason also achieved celebrity with his solo works for his own performance, notably *The End of the Golden Weather* (1959), *Men of Soul* (1965), *Not Christmas but Guy Fawkes* (1976) and *Courting Blackbird* (1976). His last major work was *Blood of the Lamb* (1980); several television plays have been premiered since his death.

**Mason, Marshall W.** 1940- American director. Co-founder of the CIRCLE REPERTORY COMPANY in New York, Mason specializes in the production of new American plays, especially those of LANFORD WILSON. In 1985 his production of William M. Hoffman's *As Is*, one of the first American plays to deal with AIDS, was transferred to BROADWAY. He resigned from Circle Rep. in 1986.

**masque** English court entertainment of the late 16th and early 17th centuries. It derived from the RITUALS devised to celebrate the arrival of welcome visitors in a community, and became the pretext for display, in which music and dance were punctuated by florid speeches and accompanied by lavish COSTUME and masks. These masks gave their name to the ceremonies they adorned. BEN JONSON preferred the French spelling, 'masque', since the court entertainments which he and INIGO JONES provided for James I followed Continental precedent. Jonson's poetry and Jones's scenes and machines distinguished their work on Jacobean and Caroline masques. The collaboration lasted from 1605 to 1634, and included *The Masque of Blackness* (1605), *Oberon, the Faery Prince* (1611) and *Pleasure Reconciled to Virtue* (1618). The musician Thomas Campion, SHIRLEY and DAVENANT were other exponents. Jones, who created perspective scenery and mechanical scene changes for the Stuart court, designed the Whitehall Masquing House (1637) for Charles I and his queen. Masques were also used as devices within plays, as in KYD's *The Spanish Tragedy* (c.1589), TOURNEUR's *The Revenger's Tragedy* (c.1606) and MIDDLETON's *Women Beware Women* (c.1625). The English court masque was brought to a sudden end by the outbreak of the Civil War.

**Massey, Raymond (Hart)** 1896-1983 Canadian-born American actor and director. He began his acting career in England and made his BROADWAY debut in 1931 in BEL GEDDES's unorthodox production of *Hamlet*. His subsequent American career (he became a US citizen in 1944) ranged from SHAKESPEARE, STRINDBERG, SHAW, O'CASEY and O'NEILL in the theatre to a wide range of villains and heroes in films. His most memorable role was Lincoln in ROBERT E. SHERWOOD's *Abe Lincoln in Illinois* (1938), which suited his imposing presence, craggy handsomeness and vibrant voice. His children Daniel and Anna, born in England, have had successful careers in the theatre.

**Massinger, Philip** 1583-1640 English playwright. Massinger left Oxford University without a degree, settled in London in 1606 and may have earned his living as an actor. His earliest known plays, *The Queen of Corinth* and *The Knight of Malta* (both c.1617), were collaborations with FLETCHER and NATHAN FIELD. About 15 of the plays once ascribed to BEAUMONT and Fletcher are, in fact, the work of Fletcher and Massinger. They include *The Custom of the Country* (c.1619), *Sir John Van Olden Barnavelt* (1619), *The False One* (c.1620), *The Double Marriage* (c.1621), *The Spanish Curate* (c.1622), *The Beggar's Bush*, *The Sea Voyage* and *The Prophetess* (all 1622). These were written for performance by the King's Men (see LORD CHAMBERLAIN'S MEN), for whom Massinger wrote from 1613-40. *The Virgin Martyr* (c.1620), a collaboration with DEKKER, and *The Renegado* (1624) contain sympathetic portraits of Catholics. *The Maid of Honour* (c.1621) dared to attack the Elector Palatine and *The Bondman* (1623) satirized the powerful Duke of Buckingham, whilst the anti-Spanish *Believe As You List* (1631) was licensed only after considerable alterations. *The Roman Actor* (1626) is a tragedy about the Emperor Domitian. The central characters of *A New Way to Pay Old Debts* (c.1621) and *The City Madam* (c.1632), respectively Sir Giles Overreach and Luke Frugal, threaten by their monstrous appetites to divert comic harmony into tragic chaos.

**Master of the Revels** English title. He was the official of the English royal household responsible for the monarch's entertainment. The title was first used in 1494. The first full-time Master was Sir Thomas Cawarden (1545-59) The office became formally concerned with licensing under Edmund Tilney (1579-1610), who augmented his income by charging the companies for a licence. The revenue for reading new plays and licensing theatres made the Master the controller of London's theatrical life. When the theatres were re-opened under Charles II, most of the Master's powers were surrendered to the king's patentees, THOMAS KILLIGREW and WILLIAM DAVENANT. The

Mastership of the Revels was no longer of great significance.

**Mathews, Charles** 1776–1835 English actor. Famous as a mimic, he was a low comedian with TATE WILKINSON on the York circuit and then engaged by GEORGE COLMAN THE YOUNGER for the HAYMARKET, where his double act with JOHN LISTON was particularly popular. In the summer months he toured a one-man show, *The Mail Coach Adventure* (1808–1810), and, with a singer, *The Travellers* (1811–12). His famous series *Mr Mathews at Home* became an annual feature from 1818. A combination of mimicry, storytelling, quick-change artistry, comic songs and improvisation, his *At Homes* were equally popular in England and the USA, which Mathews toured in 1822–3 and 1834.

**Mathews, Charles James** 1803–78 English actor. Son of CHARLES MATHEWS, he wrote over 30 dramatic pieces, of which *Patter versus Clatter* (1838) was the most successful, giving him five contrasting parts. He became a popular member of the excellent OLYMPIC company, under MADAME VESTRIS, whom he married in 1838. Together they managed COVENT GARDEN (1839–42), where BOUCICAULT's *London Assurance* (1841) provided Mathews with one of his most characteristic parts as the light-tongued Dazzle. He was a new style of gentleman-comedian, relaxed and urbane, who spoke his lines without the conventional histrionic pauses. Contemporary audiences named it 'patter' after the character in which he regularly appeared. Another favourite part was Sir Charles Coldstream in Boucicault's *Used Up* (1844). The Covent Garden management ended in bankruptcy and imprisonment. A second American tour (1857–8) and a second marriage to a wealthy woman allowed Mathews to combine acting with writing and travelling for the rest of his life.

**Matkowsky, Adalbert** 1857–1909 German actor. Matkowsky began his career in 1877 at the DRESDEN COURT THEATRE; then, after a few years spent in Hamburg, he was hired in 1889 by the BERLIN ROYAL THEATRE. He stayed here until his death. He had a herculean stage presence that best suited roles such as Coriolanus, Macbeth and Karl Moor. He was widely regarded by contemporaries as the last 'romantic' actor.

**Matthews, (James) Brander** 1852–1929 American scholar, critic and playwright. As a student Matthews entered law school, but became more interested in drama and writing. From 1875 to 1895 he wrote for the *Nation*; in 1878 he penned his first original play, *Margery's Lovers*; and from 1891 until his retirement in 1924 he taught drama at Columbia University. In 1902 he was given the title of professor of dramatic literature, the first such post in American universities. He wrote 24 books, revealing his wide knowledge of French, English and American theatre. His belief that a play is intended primarily to be performed rather than read brought credibility to theatre as an academic subject.

**Matura, Mustapha** 1939– British playwright, born in Trinidad. His plays of the 1970s were much concerned with the West Indian communities in Britain. Co-founder of the Black Theatre Co-Operative, Mustapha also writes about Trinidad. In *Play Mas* (1974) a carnival brings together races and people in one grand celebration; in *Independence* (1979) he contrasts different meanings of that word. In his later plays he has described various mixed communities, telling stories which sometimes teeter on the edge of soap opera (see TELEVI-

SION DRAMA), redeemed by their sharp insights. He has written for television and created West Indian versions of European classics, such as *Trinidad Sisters* (1988) from CHEKHOV's *Three Sisters*. *Meetings* (1981, revised 1991) contrasts the values of two generations, one steeped in the old ways, the other in the new, represented by Western consumerism.

**Maugham, (William) Somerset** 1874–1965 British novelist and playwright. Maugham qualified as a surgeon. His early light comedies – from *Marriages Are Made in Heaven* (staged in Berlin, 1899) and *A Man of Honour* (produced by the STAGE SOCIETY, 1903) to *Caroline* (performed as *The Unattainable*, 1916) – reflect his view that drama is a craft rather than an art. Designed to appeal to a wide audience, the combination, in his plays, of tight construction, wit and unpretentious absence of any serious theme was so successful that in 1908 he had four running simultaneously in London: *Lady Frederick*, *Mrs Dot*, *Jack Straw* and *The Explorer*. With *Our Betters* (1917), in which adultery reveals apparent upper-class respectability as an empty façade, Maugham's comedy began to focus on social issues; and his masterpiece *The Circle* (1921) deals with repeated behaviour patterns over two generations, exposing the gap between conventional morality and personal fulfilment. However, this serious commentary on sexual relationships, continued in *The Constant Wife* (1926) and *The Breadwinner* (1930), was extended into less comfortable and unconventional areas like miscegenation (*East of Suez*, 1922) and euthanasia (*The Sacred Flame*, 1928).

His work became increasingly didactic, and after the failure of *Sheppey* (1933), which portrays the martyrdom of a common man who is condemned as insane when he attempts to live according to Christ's teaching, Maugham abandoned drama in disgust at the public response to his plays. The serious comedies of his middle period have been frequently revived since GIELGUD's production of *The Circle* in his outstanding 1944–5 season at the HAYMARKET Theatre.

**Maunder, Paul** 1945– New Zealand playwright, actor and director. Amamus Theatre, founded by Maunder and others in 1971, specialized in group-developed scripts and, touring from Wellington through the 1970s, was the major force in New Zealand group theatre. The major achievement of its last years was *Song of a Kiwi* (1977), which was developed over several years. Amamus has since evolved into Theatre of the Eighth Day, also directed by Maunder, staging *Electra* (*Thoughts during the Tour*) in 1982 and in 1984 the bilingual *Encounter at Te Puna*, dealing with Maori reactions to the first Europeans.

**Mayakovsky, Vladimir (Vladimirovich)** 1893–1930 Russian-Soviet poet and playwright. A Georgian by birth and a Bolshevik from 1908, Mayakovsky co-signed the futurist manifesto *A Slap in the Face of Public Taste* (1912) and launched his literary career. In his poetry he cultivated a dissonant style, consisting of staccato rhythms and coarsely colloquial speech, meant to embody the Russian futurist poetic. The poems dealt with love's pain and disappointment; the poet's loneliness and alienation from the bourgeois world; the concordance of art, religion and revolution. Although he never officially joined the Communist Party, he called for FUTURISM to join forces with Bolshevism in breaking with the past.

Throughout the 1920s Mayakovsky created effective propagandist art, including a series of plays and playlets mixing Russian folk idioms and Party slogans, moving-poster imagery, farcical and CIRCUS techniques – And What If?, May First Daydreams in a Bourgeois Armchair, A Small Play about Priests Who Do Not Understand What Is Meant by the Holiday, How Some People Spend Time Celebrating Holidays, The Championship of the Universal Class Struggle (all written 1920) and Moscow Is Burning (1930). Vladimir Mayakovsky, a Tragedy (1913), which he produced and acted in, is a monodrama depicting the transformation of the author as solitary artistic genius into saviour of the people. Mystery-Bouffe (1918, revised version 1921) is a neo-mystery-fantasy-satire in which the people establish paradise on earth. The premiere production was co-directed by Mayakovsky and MEYERHOLD and designed by Malevich. His two greatest plays, The Bedbug (1929) and The Bathhouse (1930), are GOGOLian social satires which sharply criticize the petty bourgeoisie and the communist bureaucracy and grotesquely parody the promised future utopia, while expressing nostalgia for the romantic revolutionary past. Both plays were coolly received. Disappointed in love and in the course that the Revolution had taken, Mayakovsky committed suicide in 1930.

**Mayfest** Scottish festival. Mayfest, which began in 1983, presents a programme of international popular music and drama in Glasgow during the first two weeks of May each year.

**Mayne, Rutherford** [Samuel Waddell] 1878–1967 Irish actor and playwright. Written for the ULSTER LITERARY THEATRE, Mayne's plays are much of their period, influenced by his experiences with the Land Commission. The Troth (1909) and Red Turf (1911) turn on landlordism and land rivalry. The Drone (1908) was probably the most popular Ulster comedy of its time. The action of Peter (1930) is largely its protagonist's dream.

**Mayo, Frank** 1839–96 American actor and manager. Mayo made his stage debut in 1856 at the American Theatre in San Francisco. He was competent in roles such as Hamlet, Iago, Othello and Jack Cade but won acclaim for his Badger in The Streets of New York. He made his New York debut in 1869, but remained an outsider, touring as a star in his own company. In 1872 he first acted the frontiersman, Davy Crockett, a part he would perform over 2,000 times. He wrote several plays in the 1880s but none were successful. In 1895 he adapted Mark Twain's Pudd'nhead Wilson for the stage and played the title role until his death the following year. In his day he was thought a 'natural' actor because he underplayed the emotional scenes. Although versatile, Mayo found success only in roles which promoted YANKEE individualism or the myth of the American frontier (see FRONTIER THEATRE).

**Mayol, Félix (Ludovic)** 1872–1941 French MUSIC-HALL performer. He attained stardom at the Paris Scala in 1902. Mayol's distinctive blond quiff, lily-of-the-valley buttonhole and eloquent hand gestures were widely imitated. He ennobled the café concert (see CAFÉ CHANTANT) style by substituting gesticulatory MIME for the usual frenetic movements, and his repertory was extensive, ranging from sentimentality to sly innuendo. He managed his own Concert Mayol from 1909 to 1914, an important venue for singers.

**Mazurier, Charles-François** 1798–1828 French acrobatic MIME artist and dancer. He made his Parisian debut at the Porte-Saint-Martin (1824; see BOULEVARD) in Polichinelle vampire, which presented the French PUNCH as a greedy, hyperactive, ebullient type. His masterpiece

was Jocko, or The Brazilian Ape (1825), a grotesque amalgam of pantomime, knockabout and MELODRAMA; audiences in Paris and London wept copiously over the death of a monkey. Mazurier's performances influenced the RAVELS, the Prices, the HANLON-LEES BROTHERS and the KIRALFYS, who preserved his repertory until 1893.

**Mda, Zakes** 1948– South African playwright, poet, critic and artist. We Shall Sing for the Fatherland (1978), Dead End (1979), The Hill (1979), Dark Voices Ring (1979) and The Road (1982) deal with labour and politics. But Mda never foregrounds political debate, rather focusing his action upon the interplay of characters. Recently he has concentrated on the uses of THEATRE FOR DEVELOPMENT.

**Meadow, Lynne** [Carolyn] 1946– American director. A graduate of the Yale School of Drama, Meadow has served as artistic director of the MANHATTAN THEATRE CLUB since 1972. Her recent directorial work includes DAVID RUDKIN's Ashes (1976), DAVID EDGAR's The Jail Diary of Albie Sachs (1979), SIMON GRAY's Close of Play (1981), AYCKBOURN's Woman in Mind (1988), Lee Blessing's Eleemosynary (1989) and Ayckbourn's A Small Family Business (1992). Her style is described as 'smooth and unobtrusive', aimed at getting 'something reduced to its essence'.

**Medebach, Girolamo** 1706–90 Italian actor-manager. In 1748 he signed up CARLO GOLDONI as house dramatist to his troupe at Venice's Sant' Angelo theatre, contracting him to write eight comedies and two operas a year. The bargain ensured Medebach an important place in Italian theatrical history, for while he was with him Goldoni drove through his reform of the Italian comic stage and wrote some of his most enduring plays, the actor-manager creating the lead male roles in many of them – e.g. Don Marzio in La bottega del caffè and the Cavaliere di Ripafratta in La locandiera. His wife, too, was, according to Goldoni's account in his Memoires, an excellent if temperamental actress. A sharp businessman, Medebach claimed the publication rights to Goldoni's work, and when the dramatist left him for the rival San Luca theatre in 1752 he replaced him with his arch-rival, CHIARI. In the late 1750s he joined the service of the Duke of Mantua as master of the court theatre.

**medicine shows** American popular entertainment. The itinerant pedlars of patent medicines, the North American descendants of the mountebanks of Renaissance Europe, enlivened their sales pitch with variety acts, ranging from simple card tricks and banjo solos to the elaborate powwows and war dances of the turn-of-the-century Kickapoo shows. To meet competition from VAUDEVILLE, the medicine show began to offer an idiosyncratic form of VARIETY only occasionally broken by a commercial message. The performances were dominated by a blackface comedian generically called Sambo or Jake. The shows themselves, a mixture of ventriloquism, chalk talks, BURLESQUE comedy, prestidigitation and banjo-picking, usually lasted two hours, the numbers interrupted by a few lectures to sell the medicine. The afterpiece, an audience favourite, was a chaotic FARCE involving a sheeted ghost. Certain medicine men like Fred Foster Bloodgood and Tommy Scott continued to play their routes well into the late 20th century.

**Medina, Louisa** c.1813–38 American playwright. She was unique in her day as a successful woman dramatist. Eleven plays have been documented, though only three have survived. All of her plays were written for Thomas S. Hamblin, manager of the BOWERY THEATRE and possibly her husband, and probably all were dramatizations of historical and adventure novels. Medina's talent for increasing the dramatic and spectacular elements of the novels made her plays successful and profitable MELODRAMAS, the staple of the Bowery. Her dramatization of ROBERT MONTGOMERY BIRD's *Nick of the Woods* had 29 performances in 1838 – the longest run on a New York stage to that date. Other successes include *The Last Days of Pompeii*, *Rienzi*, *Norman Leslie* and *Ernest Maltravers*.

**Medwall, Henry** 1461–? English playwright. His INTERLUDE, *Fulgens and Lucres* (printed c.1512) is a wholly secular play showing a lively sense of theatre in the context of its presumed presentation as a diversion at a banquet. *Nature* (printed c.1530) is a more traditional MORALITY PLAY.

**Mei Lanfang** 1894–1961 Chinese actor. Born into a traditional Beijing theatre family, he was trained in women's roles like his father and grandfather before him. His name became a household word in China. Mei created new dance plays based on historical literary themes which gave new dimensions to the repertoire. Roles in which song, dance and combat techniques were combined in solo performance were another of his innovations. He was active in breaking down the prejudices against women on the traditional stage. He took them as pupils, and a talented body of actresses became his disciples. Until 1931 he collaborated with Qi Rushan (1876–1962), a theatre scholar who became his adviser-impresario-playwright and had a deep influence on his artistic development. Mei was the first actor of artistic stature to introduce Chinese theatre to Western audiences through his tours to America in 1930 and Russia in 1935. In Moscow he gave an acting demonstration which was seen by BRECHT – with significant consequences for the German playwright's ideas on theatre.

**Meilhac, Henri** 1831–97 and **Ludovic Halévy** 1834–1908 French playwrights. Although they did some work alone or with other collaborators, their names are firmly linked as entertainers of the Second Empire and particularly as librettists for the work of Jacques Offenbach. They collaborated for the first time in 1861, on a piece for the Variétés (see BOULEVARD), *Le Menuet de Danae* (*Danae's Minuet*). Meilhac had been a caricaturist and Halévy a novelist as well as librettist, his first great success being *Orpheus in the Underworld* (1861). Together they provided librettos for Offenbach's *La Belle Hélène* (1864), *Bluebeard* (1866), *The Grand Duchess of Gerolstein* (1867) and *La Périchole* (1868). They also wrote the successful light COMEDY *Froufrou* (1869), which later provided a popular role for SARAH BERNHARDT. Meilhac excelled at the fantastic and the grotesque, whereas Halévy preferred the realism of everyday life.

**Meiningen company** German court theatre. During the last decades of the 19th century, the Meiningen Court Theatre was possibly the most widely admired and imitated company in Europe. It was developed out of the existent Meiningen Court Theatre by Georg II, Duke of Saxe-Meiningen (1826–1914), his wife Ellen Franz (1839–1923) and the director Ludwig Chronegk (1837–91). It was financed by the duke's private money. In 1874, during their first guest appearance in Berlin, the Meininger (the company members) achieved national prominence with their performances of *Julius Caesar*, *Twelfth Night* and other plays. From then until 1890, the company performed both in Meiningen and on tour in 38 German and European cities. One of the most arresting aspects of their productions was the extreme accuracy with which the historical sets and costumes were designed. The actors were also directed with a meticulous eye for the whole stage picture. The company was celebrated for the individuality of its crowd members. A rigorous standard of ensemble was constantly striven for. The Meininger were seen on tour by ANDRÉ ANTOINE and KONSTANTIN STANISLAVSKY, both of whom claimed that the company had a profound influence on their own work.

**Méliès, Georges** 1861–1938 French conjuror and filmmaker. He was the first showman to conceive of the importance of cinema as entertainment. He took over the Théâtre Robert-Houdin, Paris, in 1888, giving a series of 'fantastic evenings'. He transformed the theatre into a projection room and founded the first film studio (1896), Star-Film, using MUSIC-HALL singers and underpaid chorus girls from the Théâtre du Châtelet, since legitimate actors refused at first to appear in such a low medium. Between 1895 and 1910 he produced 4,000 reels of standard pantomime subjects and cinematic trickery, the most famous being *A Trip to the Moon* (1902). Méliès is also important for taking the first live-action films in a theatre; using 30 arc lamps, he captured PAULUS in his act.

**Mélingue, Étienne Marin** 1807–75 French actor. Mélingue was one of the most attractive, picturesque and original of the BOULEVARD performers, and his career was particularly associated with the great cloak-and-dagger parts of DUMAS *père*. In 1840 he created the title role in BOUCHARDY's *Lazare le pâtre* (*Lazarus the Shepherd*) at the Ambigu, and built his reputation with the plays of SOULIÉ. In 1847 he joined Dumas at the Théâtre Historique, where one of his great parts was Edmond Dantès in *Monte Cristo* (1848). After the collapse of Dumas's venture, Mélingue's most popular roles included Fanfan-la-Tulipe and Benvenuto Cellini. His last major role was that of Don César de Bazan in the 1872 revival of *Ruy Blas* (ODÉON). Mélingue was the idol of popular audiences, handsome and gifted with a powerful voice. He paid great attention to details of COSTUME and make-up in preparing his parts.

**melodrama** Like FARCE, melodrama is a popular form of theatre which has been denigrated by critics, so that it is associated with sensationalism and implausibility. These features make for lively theatre, however, and they sustain the mass media today.

The word 'melodrama' (*melos*, Greek, means 'a song') comes from France (see MÉLODRAME), where ROUSSEAU coined it for his *Pygmalion* (1766), in which music served as background for dialogue (in contrast to opera, where music is joined to dialogue). Since the COMÉDIE-FRANÇAISE had a monopoly on plays with spoken dialogue, the new genre was seized upon by other theatres along the Boulevard du Temple, and became the staple fare of the appropriately named Théâtre de l'Ambigu-Comique (see BOULEVARD). There, in 1800, *Coelina* by GUILBERT DE PIXÉRÉCOURT was performed, in which innocent young lovers suffer at the separation engineered by a scheming villain, but all ends happily. Within two years the play crossed the Channel as *A Tale of Mystery* by THOMAS HOLCROFT, the first English play to be labelled melodrama. In the rapidly industrializing cities of London, Paris and Berlin, melodrama played triumphantly in large theatres to illiterate audiences. Necessarily, it was a *large* genre with spectacular settings, large casts gesturing broadly, and loud music to accompany the predictable emotions.

Each of the major European capitals sported its playwright of melodrama – Pixérécourt in Paris, KOTZEBUE in Berlin and BOUCICAULT in London (and New York). By mid-century, the genre was less formulaic: crime was popular on both sides of the Channel, so that the Paris theatre row was called Boulevard du Crime; patriotism was exhibited in battles on stage; social protest took the harmless form of equating poverty with nobility and virtue; the dastardly villain persecutes the defenceless heroine, who is rescued by an intrepid hero aided by a benevolent and colloquial comic, against increasingly spectacular dangers. Boucicault, especially, had a gift for 'sensation scenes' – designing prison escapes, avalanches, explosions – but his colleagues soon introduced icebergs, air balloons and speeding trains. With technical sophistication came more sophisticated plots; innocence does not triumph in UNCLE TOM'S CABIN, and virtue is tainted in East Lynne.

By the turn of the 20th century melodrama merged into REALISM in England and France, but American melodrama was revitalized by DAVID BELASCO, who insisted on careful writing for a basic plot of poor heroine facing assorted calamities, plus weak hero, resourceful comic who was the star of the show, and a sequence of heavies who kept the plot speeding along. After World War I AGIT-PROP plays adopted the structure, but no longer the settings, of melodrama.

Historians of melodrama stress its democratic and humanitarian substratum. ERIC BENTLEY finds melodramatic elements in most great tragedies of the anglophone tradition. Others distinguish between the protagonist of tragedy, who contributes to his own undoing, and the protagonist of melodrama, who is crushed by external forces. This view necessitates reclassifying some classical tragedies as melodramas – Romeo and Juliet, for example, and The Duchess of Malfi. The righteous-victim-triumphant of socialist realism and of Chinese opera abjure the name of melodrama but adopt its all-or-nothing ethic.

*mélodrame* French term, signifying one of the many ways of manipulating speech and music in the service of drama. Spoken words are uttered either unaccompanied during intervals between instrumental movements or against a background of instrumental music. A most influential and perhaps the most famous *mélodrame* is Pygmalion (1770), with text by JEAN-JACQUES ROUSSEAU and music by Horace Coignet (1735–1821). This text was also set in 1779 by Georg Benda (1722–1821) who composed several *mélodrames*, notably Ariadne auf Naxos (1775) to words by JOHANN CHRISTIAN BRANDES and Medea (1775) to words by Friedrich Wilhelm Gotter (1736–97).

The *mélodrame* never established itself as an independent form, but passages of *mélodrame* are to be found in many operas, a notable example being in the dungeon scene of Beethoven's Fidelio. Brief snatches of spoken dialogue in otherwise completely sung operas (e.g. the few words of Ellen and Balstrode in Benjamin Britten's Peter Grimes) can only be pedantically referred to as *mélodrame*.

**Menander** c.342-c.291 BC Greek comic playwright. The most celebrated poet of the Athenian New Comedy (see GREEK THEATRE, ANCIENT), Menander wrote over 100 plays (the first probably performed in 321), but won first prize at the Great Dionysia only eight times. After his death, however, he became one of the most popular and influential of all Greek poets.

Since excavations in Egypt in the early years of this century, we now have one virtually complete play, Dyscolus (The Bad-Tempered Man, performed in 316 BC, published in 1959), more than three acts of Samia (The Girl from Samos), substantial portions of Aspis (The Shield), Epitrepontes (The Men Who Went to Arbitration), Perikeiromene (The Girl Who Had Her Hair Cut), Sicyonius (The Sicyonian) and Misoumenos (The Bête Noire), and smaller fragments of several others.

While some of Menander's characters and themes have precedents in Old Comedy, his is a very different world from that of ARISTOPHANES. His plays feature bourgeois families and their servants, striving to act decently. Unity of place and time are carefully observed. Dramatic illusion is not broken, except by the formal 'prologue speech', in which a character or god addresses the audience directly to explain the situation. This and other conventions are borrowed from the tragedy of EURIPIDES. There are five acts, usually in a single metre, with little music or singing (except between the acts, in choral performances that are not part of the text). Language, though colloquial, is never indecent.

Plots are ingeniously worked out. There is a limited range of stock character types – stern fathers, lovesick youths, innocent girls, worldly courtesans, fawning parasites, cunning slaves and clownish cooks – though there is room for variation within each type. Plot motifs, too, are drawn from a fairly restricted repertory of deceptions, misunderstandings, estrangements, recognitions and coincidences. Menander confronts his characters with socially delicate situations, and the realism, as well as the humour, lies largely in their reactions to these.

**Mendes, Sam** 1965– British director. His technical competence and virtuosity were revealed in his early twenties in FRINGE theatres. His first WEST END achievement was a production of The Cherry Orchard (Aldwych, 1989) with JUDI DENCH. An early production for the ROYAL SHAKESPEARE COMPANY was Troilus and Cressida (Swan Theatre, 1990), hailed by IRVING WARDLE as restoring 'the full glory of verse-speaking to the Stratford stage'. In 1991 he directed SEAN O'CASEY's The Plough and the Stars at the YOUNG VIC and EDWARD BOND's The Sea for the NATIONAL THEATRE. His Richard III (1992) starred Simon Russell Beale in the title role. His production of JIM CARTWRIGHT's The Rise and Fall of Little Voice (1992) transferred from London's Cottesloe to the West End. The Donmar Warehouse (London) reopened under Mendes's management in 1992, giving the British premiere of STEPHEN SONDHEIM's Assassins.

**Menén Desleal** [Menéndez Leal]**, Alvaro** 1943– El Salvadorian playwright. His surrealistic (see SURREALISM) Luz negra (Black Light, 1966) represented his country in the Olympic Theatre Festival in Mexico in 1968. In the play the two 'severed' heads that compare death with life showed clear ties with BECKETT's theatre, but with more humour.

**Menken, Adah Isaacs** [née Ada C. McCord or Adèle Theodore] ?1835-68 American actress and poet. A dancer and circus rider, she made her acting debut as Pauline in The Lady of Lyons (1857). The scandal of her bigamous marriage was compounded by her appearing in flesh-coloured tights and minimal drapery, bound to a 'wild horse of Tartary', in Milner's MELODRAMA Mazeppa (Albany, 1861). This role, which she performed throughout America, won her renown as the 'Naked Lady' and made her a star. In London, at ASTLEY's (1864), she played in *Mazeppa* and *The Child of the Sun* for the highest salary yet earned by an actress, and was lionized by DICKENS, Rossetti and Swinburne. The last phase of her career took place in Paris, in a silent equestrian role in *The Pirates of the Savannah* (Théâtre de la Gaîté); her last performance was at SADLER's WELLS, 1868.

**Mercer, David** 1928–80 British playwright. He wrote prolifically for the stage, television and films during the 1960s and early 1970s. Throughout his life, he retained an individualistic Marxist faith which he tried to reconcile with the circumstances around him as a writer from Northern working-class roots who became successful in the middle-class South. That was the theme of his first WEST END play, *Ride a Cock Horse* (1965), in which the successful writer, Peter, reverted to infantilism. Madness was the subject of his screenplay, *A Suitable Case for Treatment* (1965), and *In Two Minds* (1967). His plays also featured rebellious eccentrics, such as the agnostic vicar who runs away with a pregnant Irish girl in *Flint* (1970). Mercer's heroes are usually in retreat from societies which appal them. In *After Haggerty* (1970), a critic dislikes the new world of theatre almost as much as he rebels against the narrow-minded fundamentalism of his father's generation, while in *Cousin Vladimir* (1978) a refugee from Soviet Russia finds himself appalled by the degeneracy of modern Britain.

**Mercier, Louis-Sébastien** 1740–1814 French playwright and critic. A disciple of DIDEROT, Mercier wrote domestic dramas and comedies, with characters and incidents drawn from everyday middle-class life but often sentimental, earnest and moralizing. Notable are *Le Déserteur* (*The Deserter*, 1770), a remonstrance against war, and *La Brouette du vinaigrier* (*The Vinegar-man's Barrow*, 1775), about a misalliance between a rich girl and a working-class boy. He also wrote historical dramas and adaptations of SHAKESPEARE, giving *Romeo and Juliet* a happy ending. His critical writing anticipated the attack on classical values mounted by the romantics.

**Mercury Theatre** (London) A combination of poetic drama and dance mark the two lines that have characterized the work presented at this 150-seat theatre opened by ASHLEY DUKES in 1933. From the beginning it served as the London base of the Ballet Rambert, while its early successes included E. MARTIN BROWNE's 1935 production of ELIOT's *Murder in the Cathedral* and the 1937 premiere of *The Ascent of F6* by AUDEN and ISHERWOOD. Its reputation for verse drama was re-established by the Pilgrim Players' 1945–7 seasons under Browne's management, with productions of contemporary religious plays, followed by two popular poetic comedies, CHRISTOPHER FRY's *A Phoenix Too Frequent* and DONAGH MACDONAGH's *Happy as Larry*. Although used solely as a studio for the Ballet Rambert from 1952 to 1966, it has recently been a base for visiting companies like the International Theatre Club, the Café LA MAMA and the Other Company.

**Mercury Theatre** American repertory company. Briefly but memorably established in New York in 1937 by ORSON WELLES and JOHN HOUSEMAN, the company produced *The Shoemaker's Holiday*, *Heartbreak House* and a modern-dress *Julius Caesar* intended as an anti-Fascist tract. The final production was *Danton's Death* (1938). The ensemble included many who later appeared in Welles's film *Citizen Kane* (1940).

**Merman** [*née* Zimmerman], **Ethel** 1909–84 American singer and actress. Merman became typecast as a brassy, big-hearted nightclub singer, e.g. in *Take a Chance* (1932), *Anything Goes* (1934) and *Red, Hot and Blue* (1936), where she displayed her powerful voice and exemplary diction. She received her first solo star billing for *Panama Hattie* (1940), in which she again portrayed a nightclub singer. After playing a defence worker in *Something for the Boys* (1943), Merman appeared in IRVING BERLIN's *Annie Get Your Gun* (1946) as the Western sharpshooter Annie Oakley. Four years later she was back in another Berlin show, *Call Me Madam*, in which she portrayed a Washington hostess who is appointed ambassador to a tiny European kingdom. Her next musical, *Happy Hunting* (1956), gave her a similar role as a Philadelphia socialite. In 1959 she capped her career with her performance as Rose, the quintessential stage mother, in *Gypsy*. Both her singing and her acting received superlative reviews from the critics. A decade later Merman made her last BROADWAY appearance when she took over the title role in *Hello, Dolly!*.

**Merrick, David** 1912– American producer. Beginning with his first success in 1954, *Fanny*, Merrick produced or co-produced over 80 plays, including many imported foreign hits. They include *The Entertainer* (1958), *Gypsy* (1959), *Becket* (1960), *Stop the World – I Want to Get Off* (1962), *Luther* and *One Flew Over the Cuckoo's Nest* (1963), *Oh What a Lovely War!* and *Hello, Dolly!* (1964), *Marat/Sade* (1965), *I Do! I Do!* (1966), *Rosencrantz and Guildenstern Are Dead* (1967), *Play It Again, Sam* (1969), *Travesties* (1975) and *42nd Street* (1981). Merrick's publicity stunts for his shows are legendary on BROADWAY. To publicize *Fanny*, he commissioned a nude statue of the show's belly dancer, and had it placed in New York's Central Park, opposite a bust of SHAKESPEARE. In 1990 he produced an unsuccessful all-black revival of the musical *Oh, Kay!*.

**Merry** [*née* Brunton], **Anne** 1769–1808 British-born actress and manager. She followed her successful debut at Bath in 1785 with engagements at COVENT GARDEN until 1792. In 1796 she accepted an offer from THOMAS WIGNELL to join the CHESTNUT STREET THEATRE company in Philadelphia, which she co-managed after his death – only seven weeks after they were married. In 1806 she married WILLIAM WARREN THE ELDER. She was famous in America for her excellence in tragic roles, her gentleness, simplicity and grace on stage.

**Merson, Billy** [William Thompson] 1881–1947 British PANTOMIME and VARIETY artist. Chiefly remembered as composer and singer of 'The Spaniard that Blighted my Life', this versatile Nottingham-born performer illustrates neatly the range and skill of the MUSIC-HALL professional. He went solo in 1908. A successful career in MUSICAL COMEDY culminated in 1925 in his creation of the role of Hard Boiled Herman in *Rose Marie* at DRURY LANE. His interpretation of an ageing and unsuccessful thespian of the old school – 'They made me a present/of Mornington Crescent,/They threw it a brick at a time' – is a classic example of the music-hall comedian's ability to evoke laughter and sympathy simultaneously.

**Meskin, Aaron** 1898–1974 Russian-born Israeli actor. The son of a poor shoemaker, he joined HABIMAH in 1918 and remained with it all his life, becoming its greatest actor. Of big stature and deep voice, his most famous role was that of the man of clay in Leivik's *The Golem* (1925). He played Willy Loman in ARTHUR MILLER's *Death of a Salesman* (1951) and the father in O'NEILL's *Anna Christie* (1957), and was noted for his characterizations of Othello (1950), Macbeth (1954), King Lear (1955) and, especially, Shylock (1936, 1959).

**Messel, Oliver** 1905–78 British stage and film designer and artist. Messel started his career designing for C. B. Cochran's annual *Revues* from 1926 to 1931. Known as a colourist who frequently employed classical rules of perspective, he designed for the ballet such works as Frederick Ashton's and Ninette de Valois's *Sleeping Beauty* (1946). *A Midsummer Night's Dream* (1938), *The Lady's Not for Burning* (1949) and *Roshomon* (1959) were highlights among his stage designs. Messel's versatility is exemplified in his designs for such films as *Caesar and Cleopatra* and *Suddenly Last Summer*.

**Metastasio** [Trapassi]**, Pietro** 1698–1782 Italian poet, playwright and librettist. His first *opera seria* libretto, *Didone abbandonata* (*Dido Forsaken*), was performed in Naples in 1724. Handel later set it to music and it quickly achieved celebrity. Metastasio became the most popular and successful opera librettist of his age, enjoying a European-wide reputation as a major poet. Vivaldi, Albinoni and Mozart were among the scores of composers eager to set his work. In 1729 he was called to Vienna, where he remained official court poet for the rest of his life. Most of his subject-matter was taken from Graeco-Roman history, mythology and literature. His strengths lay in his instinct for the theatrically effective, his ability to produce fluent and mellifluous verse, and his consummate skill at wedding the needs of dramatic action and character delineation on the one hand with those of music, vocal delivery and stage spectacle on the other.

**Method** see Actors Studio; Group Theatre

**Mexican-American theatre** see Chicano theatre

**Meyerhold, Vsevolod (Emilievich)** [Karl Theodor Kasimir Meyerhold] 1874–1940 Russian-Soviet director. His career describes a trajectory from idealistic aestheticism through revolutionary experimentalism to prescriptive socialist realism. He trained in music and law before embarking on Nemirovich-Danchenko's drama course at the Moscow Philharmonia (1896–8). He joined the newly founded Moscow Art Theatre (MAT, 1898), where he first played in Chekhov's *The Seagull* and *The Three Sisters* and later toured the provinces. His growing interest in symbolist drama (see symbolism) coincided with Stanislavsky's, and the latter invited him to test new staging methods at the MAT Studio (1905).

Meyerhold believed in the primacy of movement in the theatre and in the essential difference between the rhythms of drama and of life. This resulted in what Stanislavsky considered to be puppet-like acting in Meyerhold's stagings of Maeterlinck's *Death of Tintagiles* and Hauptmann's *Schluck und Jau*, which Stanislavsky refused permission to open. The following year Meyerhold became artistic director of Vera Komissarzhevskaya's Theatre (1906–7), where his experiments with stylized methods led to his dismissal. His official work as director at St Petersburg's Imperial opera and drama theatres (1908–18) was paralleled by experimental work at various small theatres and studios under the pseudonym 'Dr Dapertutto'. He was now developing his theory of the actor-*cabotin*, a combined singer-dancer-juggler-tumbler, whose precise physicalization and mask-like presence would unite primordial and contemporary forms in a new, universal theatre.

Meyerhold embraced Bolshevism and in 1920 initiated a personal programme to make his art accessible to political themes and to the new proletarian audience.

Lunacharsky named him head of the theatre division of the People's Commissariat for Education (1920). In his productions at the Theatre of the Revolution (1922–4) and at the Meyerhold Theatre (1923–38) he discovered new forms for old and old-style plays, beginning with his production of Crommelynck's *The Magnanimous Cuckold* (1922), which utilized the first pure constructivist set (by Popova) and biomechanics, his system of kinetic, reflexive acting derived from sports, circus acrobatics, Pavlovian association and industrial time-motion studies. He also composed complex and exact 'directorial scores' for Sukhovo-Kobylin's *Tarelkin's Death* (with a famous design by Stepanova, 1922), Ostrovsky's *The Forest* (1924), Gogol's *The Inspector General* (1926) and Griboedov's *Woe from Wit* (retitled *Woe to Wit*, 1928).

Meyerhold's political productions include Mayakovsky's *Mystery-Bouffe* (1918, 1921) and Sergei Tretyakov's *Earth Rampant* (1923) and *Roar, China!* (1926). He staged impressive productions of such new Soviet plays as Mayakovsky's *The Bedbug* (1929) and *The Bathhouse* (1930), Erdman's *The Mandate* (1925) and *The Suicide* (closed at dress rehearsal, 1932), Olesha's *A List of Blessings* (1931) and Tretyakov's *I Want a Child* (refused permission to open, 1927–30). Accused of formalism, Meyerhold lost his company and the 'total theatre' that was being built for him. After some opera stagings, including a stint at the Stanislavsky Opera Theatre in Moscow (1938–9), he delivered a sadly deferential speech to the First All-Union Conference of Theatre Directors. In 1939 he was arrested and his actress-wife Zinaida Raikh was murdered in their apartment. Meyerhold was executed in a labour camp in 1940. Although he was officially rehabilitated in 1955 and has influenced Soviet directing from the 1960s to the present, a full documentary history and critical appreciation of his career is possible only now with the release of materials that were buried for decades in Soviet archives.

**Michell, Keith** 1928– Australian actor. After acting in Adelaide, he joined the Young Vic Company in 1950, and has since played many leading roles at Stratford-upon-Avon, the Old Vic, and in the West End and New York. He was artistic director of the Chichester Festival Theatre in 1974–8; appeared in Australia with the Shakespeare Memorial Theatre tour of 1952–3, in *The First Four Hundred Years* (1964), *Othello* (1978) and *La Cage aux Folles* (1985); and acted with the Queensland Theatre Company (1982). His most famous television role is Henry VIII in the BBC's *The Six Wives of Henry VIII* (1970).

**Mickery-theater** Dutch theatre company. Founded in 1965 by Ritsaert Ten Cate, the Mickery-theater in Amsterdam presented innovative productions from abroad. Performances were originally held in Ten Cate's farmhouse in Loenersloot, a village close to Amsterdam. Having been a private enterprise for five years, Mickery received subsidy for the first time in 1970 and moved to Amsterdam. Their building there (a former cinema) had no fixed area for either audience or actors.

In cooperation with foreign companies, Mickery stimulated and developed theatrical initiatives that were difficult to stage elsewhere. There were a few regulars amongst the visiting companies: Traverse Theatre (Edinburgh), La MaMa (New York), the Pip Simmons Theatre Group (London), Tenjo Tsukiji (Tokyo) and the

PEOPLE SHOW (London). Projects produced by Mickery itself showed an increasing interest in the relationship between the theatre and reality, and between theatre and audio-visual means. A spectacular system of movable cubicles, which, supported by air-cushions, allowed the audience to drift past several scenes during a performance, was employed in *Fairground* (1975), *Cloud Cuckooland* (1979, with Tenjo Sajiki), *Outside* (1979) and *Fairground '84* (produced for the HOLLAND FESTIVAL). From 1984 to 1986 research into the relationship between the theatre and video/television took a central place in the initiatives undertaken by Mickery-theater, for instance in Pip Simmons's *La Ballista*.

The company ceased to function in 1991, following a final festival called *Touchtime*, which presented a mix of well established and more recent groups from around the world.

**Mickiewicz, Adam** 1798–1855 Polish poet and playwright. From 1823 he lived in Russia, Germany, Italy and France as a political exile dedicated to the cause of Poland's freedom. His visionary work on the suffering and messianic destiny of Poland, *Forefathers' Eve* (1823, 1832; fully staged, 1901), is the national sacred drama, dreamlike in structure. His ideas for a monumental theatre based on Greek tragedy, medieval mysteries (see MYSTERY PLAY) and primeval folklore have had an enduring influence on Polish directors.

**Middle East and North Africa** It has long been assumed that theatre is a recent import to the Middle East and North Africa from the Western world. While it is certainly true that Western plays and production styles were imported to most urban parts of the region from Europe for the first time in the late 19th and early 20th centuries, earlier indigenous theatrical traditions have existed in the Middle East for many centuries. Middle Eastern traditional theatre may even have influenced the development of theatre in the West, particularly comic theatre. Most historical forms of Middle Eastern and North African theatre existed primarily as folk theatrical tradition, with little in the way of formally recorded text.

**The ancient past**

Evidence exists which suggests that dramatic performances were held in Pharaonic Egypt in temple settings, dating back as early as 2500 BC. Particularly notable are the coronation 'dramas' of ancient Egypt, which were enacted in processional style, each scene being presented at a separate station along the route. The well known Memphite 'creation drama' deals with the death and resurrection of Osiris, and was probably enacted on the first day of spring. These early works suggest that ancient Egyptian drama involved legends and religious stories which were well known to their spectators. Extant comic dialogues demonstrate the presence of humour in these early performances.

There is little mention of indigenous theatrical activity in the Middle East during the period from the 3rd century BC to the establishment of the great Mogul empires throughout the region in the 13th century. Greek and Roman civilization penetrated into most areas of Mesopotamia, Asia Minor and North Africa during the early centuries, on the heels of the conquests of Alexander the Great and through the establishment of the Eastern Roman Empire at Byzantium. The ruins of ancient theatres and colosseums are found throughout North Africa, in Syria, and as far east as central present-day Turkey, and it must be presumed that Greek and

Roman spectacles, including dramatic presentations, were performed in them (see GREEK THEATRE, ANCIENT and ROMAN THEATRE). The performance traditions of the Indian subcontinent were also known in parts of the Middle East, particularly in the Sassanian Empire of Iran (c.AD 225–652).

The Islamic conquest of the region beginning in the 7th century AD marks a period with little mention of any dramatic or theatrical activity. Orthodox Islam tended to view dramatic presentation as suspect, since it involved the depiction of personages who were imaginary or deceased. Just as images of human beings and animals were banned from plastic and pictorial arts under Islam, human images were banned from depiction in public performance. Nevertheless, the verbal arts of poetry, storytelling and recitation continued to be practised widely throughout the Islamic world. Many of these arts, such as the public recitation of epic poetry or of religious stories, took on the quality of dramatic art.

Several traditional Middle Eastern performing arts probably came into being in the centuries between the advent of Islam and the great 16th-century empires: puppet drama, particularly shadow puppet drama; narrative drama and dramatic storytelling; religious epic drama; and comic improvisatory drama.

Shadow puppet theatre similar to that found today throughout East and Southeast Asia was probably introduced to the Middle East at the time of the Mongol invasion in the 13th century. SHADOW PUPPETS are found from Japan to Greece, and vary little in their basic form of manufacture. Shadow puppet makers were able to circumvent orthodox Islamic objections by pointing out that since the figures were perforated with holes, they no longer represented animate beings. Although there is very little record of shadow puppet drama in Iran, it was known throughout the Turkish, Greek and Arabic world first as *khayāl az-zill*, then by the Turkish word *karagöz*, 'black-eye', in reference to the chief comic character, who had a black eye (see KARAGÖZ).

Narrative drama may have originated in religious preaching, but it also has pre-Islamic precedent in the Parthian storytelling practice known as *gōsān*. The epic folk tale is very ancient throughout the Middle East, and is found in all languages. The episodic organization of long epics such as the *Thousand and One Nights* suggests the storyteller's art may have served as the principle of their organization. By the 11th century storytelling had crystallized into a literary genre, the *maqāma* ('assembly'). These narratives became associated with the Islamic month of religious fasting, Ramadan.

Religious epic drama was limited to Shi'a communities, and concerned the events surrounding the death of Imam Husain, the 7th-century martyr. Known variously as *shabih* (simulation) or *ta'ziyeh* (mourning), religious epic drama may also have had its origins in pre-Islamic practices of mourning for the legendary prince Siyāvosh, a blameless hero killed unjustly by his father-in-law. These mourning practices were still observed in some parts of Iran until as recently as 1974.

Comic drama was known throughout the Middle East generically as *taqlid*, 'imitation'. However, in local areas it became better known by specific names. In the Ottoman Empire it was *orta-oyunu*, 'play in the middle' – referring to the open square, or *meidan*, where it was usually performed. Many theatrical forms of the Indian subcontinent, such as BHAVAI in Gujarat, are clearly related to these forms as well, suggesting for the traditions a long history of migration. Indeed, the traditions are almost certainly also linked to European COMMEDIA DELL'ARTE, raising the possibility that this European form may once have had Asian roots. Improvisatory comic theatre is widely distributed throughout South and Southwest Asia.

## Traditional theatre from the 16th to the 19th century

Following the Mongol invasion, two great empires arose in the Middle East – the Ottoman, centred in Istanbul (1498–1926), and the Safavid in Iran (1501–1723). The Safavids were succeeded after a short interim by the Qājar dynasty (1779–1924). Except for extreme Northwestern Africa, all of the present-day Middle East was contained under the reign of these empires until World War I.

Court life dominated the wealthy classes, and all manner of entertainments were found in the capitals of the empires. For the most part the shahs of Iran and the sultans of the Ottoman Empire were interested in patronizing the arts. They maintained performers, including actors and artists, at their courts despite general Islamic disapproval of these entertainments. At the same time, the theatrical arts flourished on a popular level outside court settings, although the historical record of the more popular forms is much less complete.

Puppet drama fared better in the Ottoman Empire than in Iran, where shadow puppet drama seems to have disappeared completely, the last vestigial performance having been recorded in 1926. *Karagöz*, by contrast, spread throughout the Ottoman Empire and adjacent lands. It was found at its peak in Egypt, Syria, Morocco, Algeria, Bosnia-Herzegovina and Greece, as well as throughout Asia Minor. By the reign of Sultan Ibrahim (1640–8) puppet drama had reached unprecedented popularity. Royal patronage continued unabated until the early 20th century. By this time, *karagöz* was being performed in coffee-houses throughout Constantinople and was a lucrative form of popular entertainment among the masses as well as at court.

Narrative drama was well established by the 13th century among the Arab populations of the Middle East. Storytellers were greatly revered at the Ottoman court, and are mentioned continually in accounts of the reigns of the sultans from the 15th century down to World War I. *Meddahs* (eulogizers) in the Ottoman Empire were ingenious parodists and satirists. They performed most often in coffee-houses in large cities. The Iranian *naqqāl* operated in a similar fashion, working from coffee-houses, or occasionally from private homes. One unusual setting for the Iranian storyteller even today is the traditional athletic club. In this setting a professional chanter, a *murshed*, accompanies the traditional athletic exercises with drum beat and recitations of deeds of bravery from the epic *Book of Kings*.

Religious epic drama in Iran probably evolved under the patronage of the Safavid shahs. They themselves had origins as a religious brotherhood, and were particularly interested in encouraging religious ritual. Mourning ceremonies for Imam Husain were patronized by them on a grand scale. During their reign enormous processions of mourners, *dasteh*, would fill the streets during the first ten days of the Islamic month of

Muharram, scourging themselves with chains, and cutting themselves with swords and knives while they chanted rhythmic dirges.

By the 19th century, *ta'ziyeh* (mourning drama) was being performed as a fully fledged genre. Huge open-air arenas called *tekiyeh* were built for royally patronized performances featuring thousands of actors and an equally large number of live animals. Members of the foreign community were regularly invited to attend. Gradually the dramas began to be performed nearly all year, not only at court but also in cities and villages throughout the country. The processional form of the mourning ceremony continues today in Shi'a communities in India and Pakistan.

Comic improvisatory theatre was also supported by the courts, with their jesters and clowns. Entertainers in *taqlid* (comic drama) would normally imitate the accents and personal characteristics of well known people of the towns and villages in which they performed. *Orta-oyunu* (one of the local names for comic drama) was active throughout the duration of the Ottoman Empire, and served as an important form of social protest. In true *taqlid* style (*taklid* in Turkish), performers in *orta-oyunu* would imitate the attitudes and accents of persons of different trades and nationalities and make fun of them. The sultan maintained a troupe at court which performed on Imperial holidays, such as the birth of a prince, his circumcision, coronations, and other state occasions. A band of actors accompanied the sultan into war, where they served to divert him from the difficulties of battle. Bands of actors also accompanied ambassadors, provincial governors and foreign legations, thus spreading theatrical practice into the provinces and other lands where Ottoman influence was felt.

During the 19th century, the Qājar and Ottoman Empires began to come under the influence of European culture. Already in the 18th century Middle Easterners had begun to tour Europe regularly, and many had been impressed with European theatre. It was at this point that European-style drama began to be performed in Lebanon, Egypt, Syria, Turkey and Iran. Traditional theatre forms have declined greatly in the 20th century, but have none the less continued to influence theatrical development in all countries in the Middle East and North Africa.

## Puppet drama

Although MARIONETTE and glove-puppet theatre has nearly disappeared in the Middle East, shadow puppet theatre, *karagöz*, is still actively performed in Turkey, Greece and several of the Arabic-speaking countries. There are dozens of stock stories presently performed by puppeteers. These have been passed down for generations, and are largely improvisatory in nature, although over time some of the scripts have been transcribed. Among some of the better known are *Kanli Kavak* (*The Bloody Poplar*), *Timarhane* (*The Madhouse*), *Yazici* (*The Public Scribe*) and *Kanli Nigâr* (*Bloody Nigâr*).

## Improvisatory comic theatre

The two principal forms of comic improvisatory theatre in the Middle East, *ru-howzi* and *orta-oyunu*, are very similar, and probably related historically. Performances are semi-improvisatory. Although in *orta-oyunu* texts have been recorded, in *ru-howzi* there is no written text. In both traditions, stock plots are most commonly transmitted through rehearsal and oral transmission and learned by troupe members. These plays are refined over years of performance, and acquire slightly different realizations for each individual troupe. One important feature of performance is that the individual play storylines are interlaced with set comic routines – *schtiks*, or, using a term from *commedia dell'arte*, LAZZI. These routines are 'set pieces' often involving pratfalls, ACROBATICS, and visual or verbal humour. Many involve satirizing other groups and dialects, and skill as a performer is often linked to the ability to mimic other languages and ethnic groups.

## Religious epic theatre

Religious epic theatre, *ta'ziyeh* or *shabih*, continues to be performed in areas of the Middle East with large Shi'a populations: Iran, Iraq, Southern Lebanon and Bahrain. In Iran performances are given both by 'professional' troupes of players and by villagers in amateur performances. Many small towns and villages have erected special buildings – *hoseinieh* – specifically for the performance of mourning ceremonies during the month of Muharram. Participants and spectators do not view *ta'ziyeh* as theatre, but rather as part of ritual mourning. Nevertheless it has many theatrical conventions. The players do not memorize their roles, but read them from strips of paper held in their hands. The parts are not welded together in a common script, but are maintained as separate scripts with cuelines for each role. The 'good' characters, on the side of Imam Husain, chant their lines in classical Persian musical modes, and wear the colour green. The 'bad' characters declaim their lines in stentorian tones and wear the colour red. Women's roles are taken by men, who wear black, and veil their faces. The performances have roles for children, played by young boys.

*Ta'ziyeh* performances have suffered a decline in the 20th century. Immensely popular, they are none the less suspect from both a religious and a political standpoint. Religious officials were always uncomfortable with the depiction of actual historical figures on stage. Political officials have never liked huge gatherings of people mourning injustice. Nevertheless, the performances continue unabated in many parts of the Shi'a world. Despite the importation of Western-style theatre to the Middle East in the 20th century, when native writers have attempted original work the most successful productions have always contained elements of these traditional performance genres.

## The 20th-century rise of national theatres

The great 19th-century empires came to an end with World War I. The Ottoman Empire was split into a dozen small states, and modern Iran emerged under the leadership of Mohammad Rezā shah Pahlavi. All of the resulting new nations looked towards Europe and the United States as models for development. The theatre was no exception. Traditional theatre forms declined rapidly in favour of Western-style theatre. Film and, later, television became important entertainment media, further speeding the decline of traditional performance forms.

For the most part the national theatres arising in 20th-century Middle Eastern nations have been pale imitations of Western theatre. It has only been in the last 20 years that new experimentation combining traditional forms of past centuries with modern directorial and acting styles has yielded a revitalized theatre. Significant theatrical development has taken place, particularly following World War I, in North Africa, Syria and Lebanon, and Iraq. More recent theatre in Turkey, Egypt and Iran has evolved as follows.

In Turkey, the principal trend in in the post-1945 period has been toward the production of more native Turkish drama. Nearly 200 new plays in Turkish have been produced in the years following the war. Traditional theatre has served as the inspiration for much of the most modern period. The trend towards theatre integrated with music and dance has been very strong in recent years, particularly in the emergence of a form known as *operet*, a kind of musical theatre.

Egypt has dominated the theatre of the Arabic-speaking world for the entire 20th century. The foundation for this domination was laid in the 19th century with the establishment of a number of successful theatrical troupes, within which actors of excellent quality developed, who then established their own troupes. The development of dramatic literature in Egypt has paralleled the development of its theatrical institutions. Tawfīq al-Hakīm (1898–1988) has been called the father of modern Egyptian drama. His works divide into three periods; in the last, after the overthrow of the Egyptian monarchy, his plays emphasized the conflict between opposing forces: compromise and heroism; tradition and modernization; idealism and realism. Whether pursuing these ideas in classical or absurdist dramatic format, his work has been continually provocative and influential. But the years following the 1967 war with Israel and the assassination of Anwar Sadāt in 1981 were not good for the development of Egyptian theatre. Difficult economic conditions during the war years were followed by an upsurge in Islamic religious fundamentalism which made stage productions difficult. During this period television and film became more prominent as vehicles for dramatic art. The growing market for Egyptian television soap operas and frothy films throughout the Arabic-speaking world eclipsed the stage. The commercial theatre, however, has continued to stage popular plays. The texts are often unpublished and the drama full of song, dance and slapstick. Muslim fundamentalists in Egypt are reported to have attacked entertainment establishments including theatres, and have even threatened the lives of actors. Some actresses have renounced their careers, donning Islamic dress. This trend constitutes yet another chapter in the struggle between conservative religious forces and dramatic artists.

In Iran, it was not until after the establishment of the National Theatre in 1911 and the constitutional revolution of 1912 that the first Western-style theatre was presented. A number of writers began to translate European stage works, and a few original plays were produced. The finest dramatic writer of the postwar years was also one of Iran's greatest novelists and short story writers, Gholām Hoseyn Sa'edi (1935–85, pen name Gohār Morād). Like many Iranian writers, he avoided CENSORSHIP by couching his work in heavy symbolism.

Several institutions formed the backdrop for dramatic work in Iran in the 1960s and 1970s. A School of Dramatic Arts was founded, and a major national theatre, the 25th of Shahrivar Hall, was opened. National Iranian Radio-Television also served as a major support for the theatre, establishing the Festival of Arts in Shiraz. Under the direction of the writer and filmmaker, Farrokh Gaffary, it became a major international showcase for avant-garde Western drama and for the traditional performance arts of Asia, Africa and Latin America. The revolution of 1978–9 stopped much of the theatrical activity that had taken place under the Pahlavi regime, making the future of theatre much less certain. Many Iranian actors and directors emigrated, and continued to produce works in Persian abroad. Interestingly, sturdy *ru-howzi* theatre (another comic form) seems to have survived the revolution, by turning its satire on the former Pahlavi regime and *ta'ziyeh* has undergone a full-blown revival.

Significant theatrical development has taken place in other Middle Eastern countries, particularly following World War 1, principally in Tunisia, Algeria, Morocco, Syria, Lebanon and Iraq. Some theatrical activity has also been seen in recent years in Kuwait.

**Middleton, Thomas** c.1580–1627 English playwright. Educated at Oxford University, he may have spent some time at Gray's Inn in London. His earliest known play, *The Phoenix* (1603–4), was written for the BOYS OF ST PAUL'S, as were the citizen comedies (see CITIZEN COMEDY), *A Trick to Catch the Old One* (c.1604), *Michaelmas Term* (c.1605) and *A Mad World, My Masters* (c.1605). *Your Five Gallants* (1607) was produced by the rival CHILDREN OF THE CHAPEL ROYAL. Two collaborations with DEKKER, both comedies, were written for the ADMIRAL'S MEN: *The Honest Whore* (1604) and *The Roaring Girl* (c.1610). Like *A Chaste Maid in Cheapside* (1611), his comic masterpiece, these collaborative works rely on the ingenious interweaving of multiple plots, but Middleton's individual voice, objective, unsentimental and quizzical, is discernible. *The Witch* (c.1612) was followed by *More Dissemblers Besides Women* (c.1615). A moral ambivalence marks some of his plays and extends to the collaborations with WILLIAM ROWLEY, *A Fair Quarrel* (c.1616), *The World Tossed at Tennis* (c.1619), the extraordinary TRAGICOMEDY *The Changeling* (1622) and *The Spanish Gipsy* (1623). As a result of the controversial anti-Spanish SATIRE, *A Game at Chess* (1624), Middleton may have been imprisoned. His appointment as City Chronologer of London (1620–7) would not have protected him, though it did reward his achievements as a writer of MASQUES and pageants. His last known play is the remarkable tragedy *Women Beware Women* (c.1625), which concludes in an almost comic scene of slaughter. Middleton is seen by many critics as a more likely author for *The Revenger's Tragedy* than TOURNEUR.

**Mielziner, Jo** 1901–76 American set and lighting designer. Mielziner created the sets for virtually every major American drama and musical from the 1930s to the 1950s, exerting a great influence not only on the field of design, but on the plays themselves. Dramas such as *A Streetcar Named Desire* and *Death of a Salesman* were in part shaped by his designs, and their success was to some degree dependent upon them. His use of scrims and a painterly style created a visual counterpart to the poetic realism of the plays of the period, notably the works of TENNESSEE WILLIAMS. The scrims together with fragmented scenic units allowed a cinematic transformation from one scene to the next through the manipulation of light, not by shifting scenery. This complemented the trend in playwriting towards a cinematic structure. He was equally capable of REALISM, as demonstrated by his set for *Street Scene* in 1929 in which he re-created the façade of a tenement and a New York City street. His designs for musicals such as *Carousel*, *Annie Get Your Gun* and *Guys and Dolls* captured the vibrancy of the American musical at its peak.

Some of his designs have outlasted the plays or are integrally entwined with them. His design for MAXWELL ANDERSON's *Winterset* – a soaring panorama of the Brooklyn Bridge receding into the fog – is better remembered than the play itself. Mielziner also lit most of his own plays in order to control light, mood and colour. He also worked as a theatre designer and consultant on many theatres, including the somewhat controversial VIVIAN BEAUMONT THEATRE in New York. (See also STAGE LIGHTING; THEATRE DESIGN.)

**Mikhoels, Solomon** 1890–1948 Yiddish actor. The leading actor and later director of the MOSCOW STATE JEWISH THEATRE, he was one of the favourite actors of the Soviet public until his death in mysterious circumstances immediately after the enforced closure of his theatre in 1948. His greatest roles were King Lear, for which he received international acclaim, Reb Alter in *An Evening of Sholom Aleichem*, Benjamin in Mendele Mocher Sforim's *The Voyage of Benjamin III* and Hostmach in GOLDFADN's *The Witch*. (See also YIDDISH THEATRE.)

**Miles, Bernard (James)** 1907–91 British actor and director. His career as an actor flourished from the 1930s onward, but it is as the founder of the Mermaid Theatre, London, that he made his greatest contribution to the British theatre. Miles had always wished to establish a resident theatre company within the City of London; the first permanent building opened on the north bank of the River Thames in 1959. The first production was his own adaptation of FIELDING's *Rape upon Rape*, called *Lock Up Your Daughters* – a rumbustious play with music. At the Mermaid he built a repertoire of classics and directed and performed in many of them. In 1987 the ROYAL SHAKESPEARE COMPANY made it the London base for productions created at the Swan Theatre in Stratford-upon-Avon. Miles also appeared in a large number of British films. He was knighted in 1969.

**Miller, Arthur** 1915– American playwright. Following the death of TENNESSEE WILLIAMS in 1983, Arthur Miller remains relatively unchallenged as America's greatest living playwright. His first produced play, *The Man Who Had All the Luck* (1944), was a consummate failure, but *All My Sons* (1947) proved that he could create powerful scenes and believable characters. His next play, *Death of a Salesman* (1949), won him lasting fame and critical acclaim. Shifting neatly between REALISM and EXPRESSIONISM, this study of an ageing drummer (commercial traveller) has subsequently been performed all over the world. His adaptation of IBSEN's *An Enemy of the People* (1950) was a thematic prelude to *The Crucible* (1953), a drama of the Salem witchcraft trials written in passionate response to Senator Joseph McCarthy's investigations of accused subversives.

*A View from the Bridge* (1955) continued his exploration of the tragedy of the common man. This time his hero is a hard-working Sicilian longshoreman who is killed because he breaks the community's law of silence about some illegal immigrants. Miller's stage voice was silent for the next eight years, during which time he divorced his wife, Marilyn Monroe (1961), and married photographer Ingeborg Morath (1962). He returned to the stage in 1964 with *After the Fall*, apparently based on his life with Monroe. *Incident at Vichy*, an examination of the Nazi–Jewish conflict during World War II, followed in the same year. *The Price* (1968), a heart-wrenching confrontation between two brothers, was the last Miller play to achieve popular success. *The Creation of the World and Other Business* (1972) and *The American Clock* (1980) failed and were hastily withdrawn.

In recent years Miller's plays have been revived or premiered in England, where he seems more popular than in the USA. In 1987 two new one-acts were presented at Lincoln Center (see VIVIAN BEAUMONT AND MITZI E. NEWHOUSE THEATRES) as *Danger: Memory!*, though they were more successful in London. *The Archbishop's Ceiling* was staged by the ROYAL SHAKESPEARE COMPANY in 1986; *The Ride Down Mount Morgan* (1991), *The Last Yankee* (1993) and *Broken Glass* (1994) opened in London (see DAVID THACKER). Throughout his career Miller has produced a rich collection of essays about the craft of playwriting, especially the nature of modern TRAGEDY, published as *The Theatre Essays of Arthur Miller* (1971).

**Miller, Gilbert Heron** 1884–1969 American producer and director. Son of the actor HENRY MILLER, he was known for his elegant staging of high comedy by such writers as PHILIP BARRY and SOMERSET MAUGHAM. He introduced to the American stage such British actors as CHARLES LAUGHTON, ALEC GUINNESS and Leslie Howard, and owned theatres in London and New York. His greatest success was *Victoria Regina* (1936) with HELEN HAYES. Other significant productions included SHERRIFF's *Journey's End* (1928), ELIOT's *The Cocktail Party* (1950) and DYLAN THOMAS's *Under Milk Wood* (1957).

**Miller, Henry** 1859–1925 American actor and manager. Born in London, he emigrated with his parents to Canada, where he made his debut in 1876. In 1893 he became leading man of CHARLES FROHMAN's new EMPIRE THEATRE Stock Company. From 1905 to 1908 he and Margaret Anglin starred under their own management, notably in *The Great Divide* by WILLIAM VAUGHN MOODY. As an actor, Miller personified the American ideal of honest, sympathetic, taciturn masculinity.

**Miller, Joaquin** [Cincinnatus Hiner Miller] 1839–1913 American poet, novelist and playwright. He spent some years among the miners and Native Americans of California and Oregon. When his early poems and stories were favourably received, he moved to San Francisco (1870), but his Byronic appearance, behaviour and writing were most popular in England. His book of poems, *Songs of the Sierras* (1871), made him famous. He also wrote four plays; *The Danites in the Sierras*, about the Mormons, was performed in a heavily revised version by Arthur McKee Rankin (1877–81).

**Miller, Jonathan (Wolfe)** 1934– British director. As an actor Miller was part of the original *Beyond the Fringe* team which added, in 1960, a new note of political SATIRE to intimate REVUE. He qualified as a doctor at Cambridge University, and his career has combined medical research with contributions to stage and television. In 1962 he directed JOHN OSBORNE's one-act play *Under Plain Cover* at the ROYAL COURT, and subsequently worked as a director in New York, at the Mermaid Theatre in London (see BERNARD MILES) and elsewhere. His 1969 production of *King Lear* with MICHAEL HORDERN introduced a scientific understanding of the ageing process and established him as a director of originality and insight. He was invited by LAURENCE OLIVIER to direct at the NATIONAL THEATRE, notably *The Merchant of Venice* with Olivier as Shylock, which led to an eventual appointment as associate director from 1973 to 1975. He left to direct a season of 'family' plays, including *Hamlet* and *Ghosts* at Greenwich Theatre in 1974, and subsequently freelanced among several regional REPERTORY theatres, including the Yvonne Arnaud Theatre in Guildford, Surrey, where he directed a memorable production of CHEKHOV's *Three Sisters*. Miller has also

directed opera with great success. In 1987 he was appointed director of the OLD VIC and launched two ambitious seasons of classics and opera in 1988 and 1989. The attempt was brave, but failed to attract sufficient box office revenue.

**Miller, Marilyn** [Marilynn; *née* Mary Ellen Reynolds] 1898–1936 American dancer and singer. Discovered as a child dancer by LEE SHUBERT, she made her BROADWAY debut in *The Passing Show of 1914*. In *Sally* (1920) she was given her first starring role as a poor dishwasher who becomes a star of the ZIEGFELD Follies. She returned to Broadway in *Sunny* (1925). Her next shows, *Rosalie* (1928) and *Smiles* (1930), were not so successful. In 1933 she made her final Broadway appearance in *As Thousands Cheer*, a REVUE with a score by IRVING BERLIN. Although her singing voice was so weak as to be inaudible at times, Miller's radiant beauty and elegant dancing made her the reigning queen of MUSICAL COMEDY in the 1920s.

**Miller, Max** [Thomas Sargent] (1895–1963) British comedian. The most celebrated of VARIETY artists, 'the Cheeky Chappie' had his London debut in 1922. By 1926 he was top of the bill at the Holborn Empire, a position he maintained for three decades. A brashly colourful figure in white trilby, two-tone shoes, kipper tie and multicoloured plus-four suit, he was accurately summed up by a reviewer as 'vulgar, loud, earthy and blue'. His act was mainly concerned with sex. The dandified appearance, preening gestures and physical display expressed total sexual confidence, the more so as his numerous asides were invariably addressed familiarly to ladies. Further, his stories were often in the first person. Miller told everybody that he was dirty, and drew them into complicity. 'I'm filthy with money,' he confided, flashing his gross dress-ring, and adding as an afterthought, 'I'm filthy without it.' His handling of an audience was masterly, his timing superb; his ability to prompt laughter and encourage it to grow by saying virtually nothing was unrivalled.

**Mills, John** [Lewis Ernest Watts] 1908– British actor and director. A popular actor in light COMEDY and musicals in the 1930s, Mills became best known as a film-star during the 1940s and 1950s, appearing in many epics and patriotic war films, representing the figure of a cheerful, stocky Englishman whose fundamental decency could always be relied on in a crisis. He took few unsympathetic or character roles. His stage career, however, indicates an emotional range beyond that of his films. He appeared in the New York production of RATTIGAN's *Ross* (1961) and in CHARLES WOOD's *Veterans* at the ROYAL COURT in 1972, a SATIRE on ageing film actors on location. He astonished audiences at the NATIONAL THEATRE in 1986 with his performance as General Sir Edmund Milne in Brian Clark's *The Petition*, an elderly right-wing hawk distressed to find that his wife after many years of marriage is a dying dove. He received the CBE in 1960 and was knighted in 1976.

**Milne, A(dam) A(lexander)** 1882–1956 British children's author and playwright. Of his many light comedies written after 1918, his satiric demolition of conservatism *Mr Pim Passes By* (1919), and *The Dover Road* and *The Truth about Blayds* – in which run-away couples are brought to realize that escape to Paris is not the path to happiness and a revered poet is discovered to be a fake (both 1921) – all became popular REPERTORY pieces. Their whimsical fantasy and sentimental humour mark Milne as the successor to BARRIE, and his best-known play *Toad of Toad Hall* (1929, based on Kenneth Grahame's *The Wind in the Willows*) is still revived almost every Christmas in London.

**mime** The terms mime and pantomime have altered in meaning and become confused over the centuries. Today they are used interchangeably to signify wordless, gestural performance; but in classical times they referred to distinct and different phenomena. Mime, from the Greek *mimos*, originally meant a form of comic folk play and then the actor who performed it. The Roman pantomime, on the other hand, whose name derives from the Greek *pantamimos* (meaning 'imitating everything'), was a male dancer who single-handedly interpreted classical literature, especially tragedies, to the accompaniment of chanted recitation and flute music, and by changing masks.

Among the Romans (see ROMAN THEATRE) the mime changed in both form and content. It gradually usurped the popularity of the Atellan farces, and could be distinguished from regular comedy by the fact that women (*mimae*) performed and masks and cothurnoi were not worn. The comic types usually included the *stupidus*, a bald-headed, soot-smeared lout, and the *sannio* or facemaker. The *mima* was often required to undress before the public. Officially, mimes were on the lowest rung of the social ladder, but their popularity was such that many of their names have been preserved, and in time they toppled tragedy and comedy from their pedestals. Their plays were slices of life, often highly satirical and earthily obscene, with an emphasis on adulteries and swindles. Political SATIRE thrived under the Republic. Comic Christians were a frequent butt. But the greater the mime's popularity, the less important the written script became; actors gesticulated and improvised their own dialogue.

Mimes and pantomimes brought the tradition of professional acting into the medieval world, although condemned by church councils and outlawed by monarchs. The mime thrived in Byzantium. Eventually, the excommunicated *mimi* were lumped with all itinerant jugglers, minstrels and showmen, and renamed *ioculatores*, goliards or VAGANTES. One curious cognate is the Elizabethan DUMB SHOW, best remembered for its appearance in *Hamlet*. This was never used as an interlude but always related to the play in which it was inserted, prefiguring action and endowing it with symbolic meaning. The COMMEDIA DELL'ARTE preserved the mimic tradition in continental Europe, with its physical but also highly verbal comedy. The association with mute expressiveness may result from the first introduction of Italian troupes into France: not knowing French, they fell back on the universal language of gesture.

Modern mime and pantomime emerged in the 18th century from French fairgrounds and minor theatres, where the dramatic monopoly constrained 'illegitimate' performers to avoid dialogue and develop a primarily physical means of expression. Such mimic shows, accompanied throughout by music, were brought to London, and soon became acclimatized as the English PANTOMIME, which developed its own idiosyncratic conventions.

Mimic gesture became an important principle of late-18th-century acting theory. After the French Revolution, for a newly proletarian audience gestural acting became a dominant partner of dialogue in MELODRAMA. Throughout the 19th century, the spectacular

pantomime was subjugated to the style of its leading actors. MAZURIER bequeathed his acrobatic style to the immensely popular RAVELS, who popularized pantomime in the United States. JEAN-GASPARD DEBURAU made PIERROT the indispensable pivot of the pantomimes at Paris's Théâtre des FUNAMBULES.

This genre declined as its favourites died out, and was replaced in popularity by the violent, so-called American pantomimes of the HANLON-LEES BROTHERS. In the 20th century, the silent film's ability to present a convincing representation of reality compelled the theatre to re-examine its own roots in search of inspiration. GORDON CRAIG with his concept of the *Über-Marionette* (1905, 1911), YEATS with his demand for an aristocratic Western NŌ theatre, and other anti-realists called for symbolic gesture. The dance reforms of Isadora Duncan and the eurhythmic exercises of Jaques-Dalcroze (see ADOLPHE APPIA) were regarded as potential sources for a new theatrical art. JACQUES COPEAU, who had always seen the *commedia dell'arte* as a fountainhead of the actor's art, founded a school in 1921 where exercises with masks worked to isolate the body as a tool of expression in preparation for the spoken drama.

ÉTIENNE DECROUX formulated 'pure mime' or *pantomime de style*, an independent art form whose (usually solo) performer creates a circumambient world and its objects wholly through movement. Hand gestures were reduced to a minimum, the face to a neutral mask, and narrative elements discarded. The mimodramas of JEAN-LOUIS BARRAULT usually depicted a struggle against time and death. Decroux's teaching was in part widely popularized by MARCEL MARCEAU. As early as 1947, Marceau's character Bip of the white face and striped jersey appeared at the Théâtre de Poche, Paris. Although fascinated by death, Marceau diluted his melancholy with wistful comedy and did not disdain to tell a story. His influence has been phenomenal, on professionals and street performers alike.

A new direction in mime was taken by the Pole Henryk Tomaszewski, who founded the Wroclaw Pantomime Theatre in 1956. Tomaszewski creates elaborate ensemble pantomimes inspired by painting, sculpture, architecture and Oriental theatre. Contemporary mime has also been invigorated with injections of choreography and CLOWNING. The dance-pantomimes of VALESKA GERT explored the type of the whore; recently, a resurgence of dance-pantomime can be discerned in the work of Pina Bausch and her Wuppertal Tanztheater.

The SAN FRANCISCO MIME TROUPE split from the Actors' Workshop in 1959 to play *commedia dell'arte* scenarios in public parks; its broadly humorous collective creativity has always served radical political ends. The same holds true of the BREAD AND PUPPET THEATRE. The most recent experiments in mime have been omniclusive, admitting words and whatever might prove expressive to expand its potential. Typical exponents of this trend are the Decroux-trained groups of Montreal, Omnibus (founded by Jean Asselin and Denise Boulanger, 1977) and Carbonne 14 (founded by Gilles Maheu) reliant on evocative imagery and text. A similar synthesis of all the actor's means to communicate is evident in such disparate artists as the Czechs Boleslav Polivka and Ctibor Turba who combine buffoonery and existential messages; the Russian group Ilkhom with its nightmarish evocation of constricted lives; and American performance artists, who range from the anarchic Ronlin Foreman to the bemused manipulator of objects, Paul Zaloom.

**Minetti, Bernhard** 1905– German actor. From 1930 to 1945 he lent villains like SCHILLER's Franz Moor (*Die Räuber*), GOETHE's Mephisto, and Angelo in *Measure for Measure* a lean, evil intelligence. After World War II he played heroic roles such as Julius Caesar (Düsseldorf) and Schiller's Wallenstein (Ruhr Festival). At the Berlin Schillertheater from 1965 until its closure in 1993 he favoured new writers. He was a fine Max in PINTER's *Homecoming*, and his glittering eye and jutting jaw in BECKETT's *Krapp's Last Tape* were unforgettable. A friend of THOMAS BERNHARD's, he created many of his manic heroes, notably himself in *Minetti*.

**minstrel show** American popular entertainment. A medley of sentimental ballads, comic dialogue and dance interludes, the minstel show was ostensibly founded on African-American life in the Southern USA. Its origin is attributed to THOMAS D. RICE, who in 1828 adopted blackface and banjo to produce the wildly popular 'Jim Crow'. At first a solo act, minstrelsy grew to four performers of violin, banjo, bones and tambourine with the Virginia Minstrels, founded by Dan Emmett (1842–3); despite the burnt cork, their repertoire drew heavily on traditional English choral singing and lugubrious parlour ballads. By the early 1850s E. P. Christy (died 1862) had evolved what was to be the standard tripartite programme: in the first part, the performers would enter in the 'walkround' until told, 'Gentlemen, be seated.' Vocal numbers, both lively and sentimental, would be sung, interspersed with comic chat from Mr Tambo and Mr Bones. Part two was a fantasia of speciality acts before the drop curtain, including the wench impersonation (see FEMALE IMPERSONATION). Part three comprised a sketch, either a plantation scene with dancing or BURLESQUES of Shakespearian plays and MELODRAMAS. Originally most of the performers and composers were white Northerners who had little first-hand acquaintance with Southern life; consequently, the blacks they portrayed were extravagant fictions, like Zip Coon the urban dandy.

After the Civil War, competition from other popular forms, especially VARIETY and MUSICAL COMEDY, compelled the minstrel show to expand and change. In 1878 J. H. Haverly combined four troupes in his United Mastodon Minstrels. Sumptuous costumes and lavish scenery became the rule. From 1880 the traditionalists complained loudly about changes, such as the omission of the blackface. A more significant change was the entry of blacks themselves into the form, first with Haverly's Coloured Minstrels. By adopting such stereotypes as the loyal uncle, warm-hearted mammy and shiftless lazybones, and by adding female performers, they perpetuated the notion that such caricatures were true to life.

The minstrel show was one of the few truly indigenous American entertainments and made a profound impression world-wide. American popular music and theatre remains influenced by it; many outstanding performers, such as EDDIE CANTOR, AL JOLSON and BERT WILLIAMS, received their training in it. Great Britain rapidly took to minstrelsy, sending its own troupes as far afield as India and Australia. St James's Hall, Piccadilly, in London, was the capital of English minstrelsy during 1859–1904. It bequeathed blackface artists like G. H. CHIRGWIN to the MUSIC-HALL and the

seaside pier, where the stereotypes were even more remote from African-American reality.

**Mira de Amescua, Antonio** 1574–1644 Spanish playwright. Of the school of LOPE DE VEGA, his plays anticipate the drama of CALDERÓN DE LA BARCA. He was also a priest, of Andalusian origin, and wrote religious and historical plays with a moral seriousness reminiscent of ALARCÓN but inferior in construction. His verse style falls between the clarity of Lope de Vega and the cultured style of Calderón de la Barca. His best play is *El esclavo del demonio* (*The Devil's Slave*, before 1612), foreshadowing Calderón de la Barca's *El mágico prodigioso*. Almost as impressive is the two-part *La próspera y la adversa fortuna de don Álvaro de Luna* (*The Rise and Fall of Álvaro de Luna*), a *COMEDIA* de privanza on the 15th-century favourite. He also wrote a number of fine comedies, such as *La fénix de Salamanca* (*The Phoenix of Salamanca*).

**miracle play** see MYSTERY PLAY

**Mirren, Helen** 1946– British actress. At the age of 19 she played a fiery Cleopatra for the NATIONAL YOUTH THEATRE. She joined the ROYAL SHAKESPEARE COMPANY, where she was chosen for such roles as Cressida in *Troilus and Cressida* and STRINDBERG's Miss Julie, which demanded her voluptuous good looks and capacity to convey a wayward temperament. In 1972 she joined PETER BROOK's International Centre of Theatre Research, touring North African desert villages in a mainly improvised story, *The Conference of Birds*. She returned to the RSC as Lady Macbeth in 1974; then played an alcoholic lead singer in DAVID HARE's *Teeth 'n' Smiles* (1975). Her maturity as an actress has been distinguished by her performances in major classic roles: in the title role in WEBSTER's *The Duchess of Malfi* (1980) for the ROYAL EXCHANGE Company in Manchester, and as Cleopatra in the RSC's studio *Antony and Cleopatra* (1983). In 1989 she appeared with Bob Peck in the YOUNG VIC premieres of two short plays by ARTHUR MILLER, *Some Kind of Love Story* and *Elegy for a Lady*. She has also appeared in many films.

*mise-en-scène* French term. Literally, that which is 'placed on the stage', it refers to the total production, including not only the physical elements of design (see THEATRE DESIGN) and the stage but the overall directorial concept and execution as well.

**Mistinguett** [Jeanne-Marie Bourgeois] 1873–1956 French music-hall star (see *CAFÉ CHANTANT*). The fabled queen of Parisian VARIETY and REVUE made her debut at the Trianon-Concert (1885), followed by a long tenure at the Eldorado (1897–1907). Her double-jointed mimicry made up for her thin voice, as she moved from singing to eccentric comedy to revue. The success of the *valse chaloupée*, danced with MAX DEARLY at the MOULIN-ROUGE (1909), made her a star, and she confirmed her status with the *valse renversante* (1912) with her partner MAURICE CHEVALIER. From 1919 to 1923 she flourished in tours of both Americas.

**Mitchell, Julian** 1854–1926 American director. After an early career as a performer, Mitchell was assistant director on several of CHARLES HOYT's FARCE comedies. He directed a number of BURLESQUES for WEBER AND FIELDS, after which he turned to the staging of elaborate comic operas such as *The Wizard of Oz* (1903) and *Babes in Toyland* (1903). From 1907 until 1914 he directed the ZIEGFELD *Follies*, and is credited with creating the chorus of beautiful, lively and individual girls that became the hallmark of those shows.

**Mitchell, (Charles) Julian (Humphrey)** 1935– British novelist and playwright. He began by writing novels in the 1960s and his first plays were adaptations of Edwardian novels by Ivy Compton-Burnett. His best-known play *Another Country* (1981) concerns the link between homosexuality and political treachery, fostered by the British public school system, and was subsequently filmed. His other plays include *Half-Life* (1977), *The Enemy Within* (1980), *Francis* (1983) and *After Aida* (1986), the latter a learned account of Verdi's relationship with Boito which was compared with PETER SHAFFER's *Amadeus*. Mitchell also writes successfully for television (see TELEVISION DRAMA).

**Mitchell, Langdon (Elwyn)** 1862–1935 American playwright. Trained as a lawyer, he is principally known for one play, *The New York Idea* (1906). This witty SATIRE on easy divorce and easy marriage prompted critics to call him 'the American SHAW'. Written for MINNIE MADDERN FISKE, it was later produced by MAX REINHARDT in Berlin (1916). Mitchell also wrote *In the Season* (1893); *Betty Sharp* (1899), an adaptation of *Vanity Fair* and a vehicle for Mrs Fiske; *The Kreutzer Sonata* (1906), an adaptation from the Yiddish of JACOB GORDIN; *The New Marriage* (1911); and *Major Pendennis* (1916), adapted from Thackeray's novel.

**Mitchell, Billy** [William] 1798–1856 English-born actor, playwright and theatre manager. A comedian in England from 1831, Mitchell appeared in New York in 1836. He managed MITCHELL's OLYMPIC from 1839 to 1850, making it a popular success when other theatres were failing. As an actor Mitchell was a favourite as Vincent Crummles in a farce created from DICKENS's *Nicholas Nickleby* entitled *The Savage and the Maiden*. When BOUCICAULT's *London Assurance* reached New York, he responded with *Olympic Insurance*; he BURLESQUED Dickens's visit in *Boz* and the EDWIN FORREST–W. C. MACREADY feud in three sketches. The greatest event at Mitchell's Olympic, however, was BENJAMIN BAKER's *A Glance at New York*, 1848, with Mose the fire b'hoy.

**Mitchell's Olympic** (New York City) Opening on BROADWAY in 1837, the Olympic was modelled on MADAME VESTRIS's famous London OLYMPIC both in physical structure and policy, presenting comedies, FARCES, VAUDEVILLES and musical pieces. In 1839, BILLY MITCHELL revived its fortunes: reduced prices and a diet of light entertainment and BURLESQUES made it the most popular theatre in town. In 1854 it burned down.

**Mitterwurzer, Friedrich** 1844–97 German actor. Mitterwurzer often played at the Vienna BURGTHEATER, renowned for his ability to play what LAUBE called 'broken characters'. His staccato acting, which revealed inconsistencies in characters, went against the general idealist interpretation of classic roles, but was eminently suited to IBSEN. Mitterwurzer was a celebrated Consul Bernick, Hjalmar Ekdal and Alfred Allmers. Some historians claim his acting foreshadowed EXPRESSIONISM.

**Mitzi E. Newhouse Theatre** see VIVIAN BEAUMONT AND MITZI E. NEWHOUSE THEATRES

**Mlama** [Muhando]**, Penina** 1948– Tanzanian playwright and director. Her published plays are in Swahili and include *Guilt* (1972), *Recognize Our Rights* (1973), *My Respect* (1974), *Decoration* (1975), *I Divorce You* (1976), *Mother the Main Pillar* (1982), *Liberation Struggles* (1982) with A. Lihamba and others, and *There is an Antidote for Rot* (1984). Mlama deals with the problems of the struggle for liberation and a just society and with more personal matters, e.g. the effects of divorce on children.

*Mother the Main Pillar* is concerned with the liberation of women. She also takes an active part in THEATRE FOR DEVELOPMENT.

**Mnouchkine, Ariane** 1939– French director. Mnouchkine is known for her successful use of *création collective* (collaboratively devised productions) and shared responsibility within her theatre group the Théâtre du SOLEIL, founded in 1964. Like ARTAUD she wanted to use the whole range of expressive means available to theatre, but her concerns are social as well as private. WESKER's *Kitchen* (1967) was an early choice, but after the upheavals of 1968 she felt the group must create its own plays. She had recourse to popular traditions in *The Clowns* (1969), but only achieved her ideal of a *collective* creation in *1789* (1970), *1793* (1972) and *L'Âge d'or* (*The Golden Age*, 1975). In her remarkable film of MOLIÈRE she confronted the problems of how a theatre company can live and work together. She returned to theatre production with her adaptation of Klaus Mann's *Mephisto* (1979), and then embarked on a cycle of SHAKESPEARE plays: *Richard II* (1981), *Twelfth Night* (1982) and *Henry IV Part 1* (1984). These were followed by epic plays about Cambodia and India by HÉLÈNE CIXOUS: *Norodom Sihanouk* (1985) and *L'Indiade* (1978), which displayed again the strong influence of Oriental theatre on her work. In 1992 her productions of plays by AESCHYLUS and EURIPIDES – *Les Atrides*, a four-part version of the *Oresteia* and *Iphigenia in Aulis* – toured to Bradford, England.

**Mochalov, Pavel (Stepanovich)** (1800–48) Russian actor. The 'Russian KEAN', he was the greatest Russian tragedian of the early 19th century. In the debate over the question of genius versus craft, his inspired but uneven performances at Moscow's Maly Theatre were favoured over those of his St Petersburg rival, the coolly technical tragedian KARATYGIN. He paid little attention to costumes and make-up, relying instead upon the power of his imagination and his physical attributes to transform him. Although MELODRAMA and neoclassical TRAGEDY by KOTZEBUE, VOLTAIRE, OZEROV, POLEVOI and KUKOLNIK were staples of his repertoire, he also played Chatsky in the original Moscow production of *Woe from Wit*. He succeeded in the roles of SCHILLER's Don Carlos (1829), Karl and Franz Moor (1828 and 1844) and Mortimer (1835), and as SHAKESPEARE's Hamlet (1837), Othello (1837), Lear (1839) and Richard III (1839). He wrote a romantic drama, *The Circassian Girl* (produced 1840), and a theoretical treatise on acting.

**Modena, Gustavo** 1803–61 Italian actor. His career is linked with the Italian struggle for independence. Political events obliged him to leave Italy in 1832, and he spent several years in exile in Switzerland, France, Belgium and England. In 1843, after his return to Italy, he formed a company of young actors that included TOMMASO SALVINI and LUIGI BELLOTTI-BON, and through them his insistence on a natural, unemphatic style and uncluttered scenic decoration profoundly affected stage presentation in Italy for several decades. He was a champion too of the stage as a means of debating social and political issues. The acting roles with which he was best associated were the stock pieces in the mid-19th-century Italian actor's repertoire: ALFIERI's Saul, DELAVIGNE's Louis XI and DUMAS's Kean.

**Modjeska** [Modrzejewska]**, Helena** 1840–1909 Polish actress. Later known for Shakespearian roles, she began her professional career in 1865 with touring companies. Recognized as a major talent in *Adrienne Lecouvreur* (SCRIBE/Legouvé), she became a star with the Warsaw

Theatre (1869–76). Exceptional beauty and ability to move audiences brought her international success. In 1876 she emigrated to the United States, and from 1877 toured in America and England with her own company, returning to Poland for guest appearances. Throughout a career lasting until 1907, she played 260 roles, including SCHILLER's Maria Stuart, DUMAS *fils*'s Marguerite Gautier, and Nora in IBSEN's *A Doll's House*, which she introduced to America in 1883.

**Moeller, Philip** 1880–1958 American director, producer and playwright. He joined the WASHINGTON SQUARE PLAYERS in 1914. His one-act plays, *Two Blind Beggars and One Less Blind* and *Helena's Husband*, were produced by the group and attracted critical attention. But Moeller made his reputation as a director, and was regarded by LAWRENCE LANGNER as one of the most brilliant American directors of COMEDY. A founder and director of the THEATRE GUILD, he staged their first production, *Bonds of Interest*, in 1919. He was especially adept with the plays of EUGENE O'NEILL. His Guild credits include *Strange Interlude* (1928), *Dynamo* (1929), *Mourning Becomes Electra* (1931) and *Ah, Wilderness!* (1933).

**Mogulesco, Sigmund** 1858–1914 Yiddish actor. Born in Bessarabia (Moldavia), he began with GOLDFADN's company before moving to America in 1886. A natural CLOWN, he specialized in comic roles besides being an accomplished musician. (See also YIDDISH THEATRE.)

**Moiseiwitsch, Tanya** 1914– British set and costume designer. She is noted for her collaborations with director TYRONE GUTHRIE and the bold thrust stage and innovative auditorium that she designed for the STRATFORD (Ontario) FESTIVAL Theatre (1957) and for the similar GUTHRIE THEATRE in Minneapolis (1963). Beginning her career in London, she then went to the ABBEY THEATRE in Dublin where she designed over 50 productions between 1935 and 1939, subsequently designing for the OLD VIC (from 1944) and at the Shakespeare Memorial Theatre in Stratford-upon-Avon (from 1949). She is most closely associated with the plays of SHAKESPEARE, but other successful productions include *Oedipus Rex* at Ontario (1954; film 1957) and *The House of Atreus* in Minneapolis (1968), both of which contained masks. Moiseiwitsch's designs have been typified by simple, direct, presentational sets that embody the visual metaphor of the play. Since she generally designed costumes as well there was a strong visual unity to her productions. With the polygonal, stepped stages at Ontario and Minneapolis that jutted into the steeply banked auditoriums, she was able to eliminate most scenery and provide a space in which her highly textured costumes could be sculpted by light.

**Moisiu, Aleksandër** [Alexander Moissi] 1879–1935 Albanian actor. Born in Kavaja (Albania), in 1904 he joined MAX REINHARDT's company in Berlin, where he quickly distinguished himself by his deep, psychological interpretations of the role he played, by his expressive, melodious voice, and by his mobile features and body. He normally performed without make-up. Fluent in English, French, German, Greek, Italian and Spanish, he attained international fame, performing in Europe, South America, Japan and the United States. He also appeared in 12 films. He was the author of a play about Napoleon, *The Prisoner*, first performed in Hamburg. His most famous stage roles were Hamlet and Othello, GOETHE's Faust, IBSEN's Oswald (in *Ghosts*), SHAW's Dubedat (in *The Doctor's Dilemma*) and LEV TOLSTOI's Fedya (in *The Living Corpse*).

**Molander, Olof** 1892–1966 Swedish director. He accomplished far-reaching reforms in Swedish direction, scenography and acting style, particularly during his leadership of DRAMATEN during the 1930s. An early admirer of GORDON CRAIG, he stressed that the director should serve the text by coordinating scenography and acting around its central idea. Molander's approach to STRINDBERG, particularly to such late plays as *A Dream Play*, *The Ghost Sonata* and *The Great Highway*, was to reject REINHARDT's forcefully expressionistic style (see EXPRESSIONISM) in favour of a blend of fantasy and selective REALISM that stressed the plays' autobiographical content. Dramaten's international reputation in the staging of O'NEILL owed much to Molander's powerful productions of *Mourning Becomes Electra*, *The Iceman Cometh* and *A Moon for the Misbegotten*.

**Molière** [Jean-Baptiste Poquelin] 1622–73 French actor-manager and playwright. The well educated son of a prosperous Paris merchant, he forsook the family's upholstery business at the age of 21 to found a short-lived company, the Illustre-Théâtre, and later toured the provinces for 13 years with MADELEINE BÉJART, a period of invaluable apprenticeship during which he also wrote his first plays, *L'Étourdi* (*The Blunderer*, 1653) and *Dépit amoureux* (*Lovers' Quarrel*, 1656), and the brief, partly improvised FARCES *La Jalousie du Barbouillé* (*The Jealousy of Barbouillé*) and *Le Médecin volant* (*The Flying Doctor*), inspired by the work of COMMEDIA troupes encountered on his travels and tailor-made for his fellow actors.

In 1658 Louis XIV was so amused by the command performance of *Le Docteur amoureux* (*The Doctor in Love*) that he granted Molière the use of the PETIT-BOURBON, where he staged his first Parisian successes, *Les Précieuses ridicules* (*The Affected Ladies*, 1659) and *Sganarelle, ou Le Cocu imaginaire* (*Sganarelle, or The Imaginary Cuckold*, 1660). In 1661 at the PALAIS-ROYAL he produced *L'École des maris* (*The School for Husbands*) and his first *comédie-ballet*, *Les Fâcheux* (*The Bores*). In 1662 he married the teenage ARMANDE BÉJART and produced *The School for Wives*, a reflection on the role of women and the incompatibility of youth and age. Its huge success provoked rivalry and accusations of immorality, but brought commissions for royal entertainments, *Le Mariage forcé* (*The Forced Marriage*) at the Louvre and *La Princesse d'Élide* at Versailles (1664), while in 1665 Molière's company was awarded a regular pension and the title of the Troupe du Roy.

Thereafter Molière and LULLY became official court entertainers: *L'Amour médecin* (*Love's the Best Doctor*, 1665), *Mélicerte* (1666), *La Pastorale comique* (1667), *Le Sicilien, ou L'Amour peintre* (*The Sicilian, or Love Makes the Painter*, 1667), *Monsieur de Pourceaugnac* (1669), *Les Amants magnifiques* (*The Magnificent Lovers*, 1670), *The Bourgeois Gentleman* (1670), *La Comtesse d'Escarbagnas* (1671), mostly couched in the form of *comédie-ballets*, and *Psyché* (1671), a *tragédie-ballet* written in collaboration with CORNEILLE and QUINAULT, were all initially performed at royal *fêtes* before being transferred to his public theatre in Paris.

Meanwhile, the comedies for the Palais-Royal met a mixed reception. Molière's study of religious hypocrisy, *Tartuffe* (Versailles, 1664), was denounced by the Church for its impiety and withheld from public performance until 1669. *Don Juan* (1665), with its cynical, free-thinking hero, was withdrawn and never re-staged in Molière's lifetime. *The Misanthrope* (1666) was received with only cool interest, while *The Miser* (1668) and *Les*

*Fourberies de Scapin* (*The Tricks of Scapin*, 1671) failed. *The Imaginary Invalid* (1673), another *comédie-ballet*, designed for the court but in fact created at the Palais-Royal, proved to be his last play: during the fourth performance Molière, ironically playing the hypochondriac Argan, was seized with a genuine coughing fit and died that night.

Molière transformed French COMEDY. His comic method is intensely physical and gives full scope to the prowess of the actor, aided only by COSTUME, personal properties and a skilful patterning of dialogue which encourages specific movement and visual display on stage. His plays gave new life to traditional French farce and Italian *commedia*, producing a satiric commentary on the society of his time and on eternal human foibles.

**Molina, Tirso de** see TIRSO DE MOLINA

**Molloy, M(ichael) J(oseph)** 1917– Irish playwright. He abandoned training for the priesthood through illness. His foremost works are his first play, *The Old Road* (1943), *The Visiting House* (1946), *The King of Friday's Men* (1948), *The Wood of the Whispering* and *The Paddy Pedlar* (1953). *The King of Friday's Men*, set in western Ireland in 1787, mourns the passage of a feudal *modus vivendi*, without ignoring its unattractive aspects. At its fluent best Molloy's dialect speech carries his often knotty plots. Though more restricted by his region than either SYNGE or FITZMAURICE, he is the last remarkable exponent of their folk drama.

**Molnár, Ferenc** 1878–1952 Hungarian playwright. He gained an international reputation for the technical mastery and sophisticated dialogue of his plays, which depict the minor pitfalls that threaten but never seriously damage the bourgeois morality of his characters. Light and clever SATIRE is tempered by sincere pathos. Many of his plays, including *The Devil* (1907), *Liliom* (1909), *The Guardsman* (1910), *The Swan* (1920) and *The Play's the Thing* (1926), were produced in Vienna, London, Paris and on BROADWAY, as well as in Hungary. *The Play's the Thing* is continually revived the world over, and the famous musical *Carousel* (1945) by RODGERS and HAMMERSTEIN is based on *Liliom*.

**Moncrieff, Gladys** 1892–1976 Australian MUSICAL COMEDY star. She appeared in musicals with the J. C. WILLIAMSON management, first starring in *Katinka* (1918), and until 1959 appeared in numerous musicals and operetta, including *The Maid of the Mountains* (1921), the London production of *The Blue Mazurka* (1926), *Rio Rita*, in which she toured Australia in 1928–30, the Australian musical *Collit's Inn* (1933), and various productions of *The Merry Widow*. To her Australian public she was affectionately known as 'our Glad'.

**Moncrieff, W(illiam) T(homas)** 1794–1857 English playwright and theatre manager. Lessee at various times of the Queen's, ASTLEY's Amphitheatre, the Coburg, Vauxhall Gardens and the City Theatre (all in London), Moncrieff was a hack writer who wrote over 100 plays to suit the time. In addition to adaptations of novels by Scott, BULWER LYTTON and DICKENS, *Tom and Jerry* (1821) was a zestful adaptation of Pierce Egan's documentary novel, *Life in London*. *The Cataract of the Ganges* (1823), using a horse troupe (see HIPPODRAMA) and real water in the cataract, was the sensation of its season at DRURY LANE.

**Monk, Meredith** 1942– American choreographer, composer and performance artist. She is the leading innovator in the so-called Next Wave (since the mid-1960s). Her dances have evolved into multimedia, nonverbal the-

atre pieces, such as *Vessel* (1971–2) and *Quarry* (1975–6) – both termed 'opera epics' – *Specimen Days* (1981), *The Games* (1983; commissioned by PETER STEIN's Schaubühne theatre in Berlin) and *Atlas* (1991).

**monopoly, theatrical** see THEATRICAL MONOPOLY

**Montansier, Mlle** [Marguerite Brunet] 1730–1820 French actress and theatre manager. Having acquired a chain of provincial theatres, she established her own theatre in the PALAIS-ROYAL in 1790. After the Revolution she built the Théâtre National, but her previous Royalist associations led to imprisonment. She narrowly missed the guillotine, but survived to open the Salle Olympique in 1801 and the celebrated Théâtre des Variétés in 1807, while running her Palais-Royal theatre as a house for acrobats and puppeteers. Several popular plays were written about her career.

**Montdory** [Guillaume des Gilberts] 1594–1653/4 French actor-manager. A powerful tragedian, D'AUBIGNAC called him 'the greatest actor of our time'. A member of VALLERAN LE CONTE's company in 1612, he toured in the plays of HARDY before bringing a new company to Paris, where he eventually settled at the MARAIS in 1634, thanks to CARDINAL RICHELIEU. Here he presented PIERRE CORNEILLE's early plays, then *Le Cid* with huge success in January 1637, playing the central role of Don Rodrigue. Shortly afterwards he retired, on a handsome pension, because of partial paralysis.

**Monteiro, (Luís de) Sttau** 1926– Portuguese playwright. Also a left-wing journalist and novelist, Monteiro came to the theatre in 1961 with *Felizmente Há Luar* (*Luckily We Still Have the Moonlight*), attacking contemporary abuses and institutions in a historical drama based on the period immediately after the Peninsular War campaigns in Portugal. *A Estátua* (*The Statue*, 1966) ridicules the hero-worship sought by and accorded to Salazar, while the *Auto da Barca do Motor fora da Borda*, of the same year, updates VICENTE's *Auto da Barca do Inferno* by providing the boat with an outboard motor and redirecting the satire against latter-day capitalists.

**Montez, Lola** [née Maria Dolores Eliza Rosanna Gilbert] 1818–61 Irish-born dancer. She performed in Europe, America and Australia. Her beauty and charm compensated for her lack of talent and musical sense. Her liaison with Ludwig I of Bavaria (1847–8) culminated in his forced abdication, and she went to the USA, making her New York debut in 1851. She toured to the Gold Rush country, performing a spider dance that shocked San Francisco audiences, and took the child actress LOTTA CRABTREE under her tutelage. After 1856 she appeared as a spiritualist and lecturer, speaking on fashion, gallantry and Roman Catholicism. She underwent a religious conversion and became a recluse after 1859.

**Montfleury** [Zacharie Jacob] c.1600–67 French actor. He remained at the HÔTEL DE BOURGOGNE throughout his career, excelling in both TRAGEDY and COMEDY. MOLIÈRE mocked his corpulence and mannered delivery in *L'Impromptu de Versailles* (1663). His death was occasioned by bursting a blood vessel while playing Oreste in RACINE's *Andromaque* (1667). He wrote one inferior tragedy, *La Mort d'Asdrubal* (*The Death of Hasdrubal*, 1647).

**Montherlant, Henry de** 1896–1972 French novelist and playwright. Montherlant was a literary stylist, as his novels show, saw drama as literary and psychological and was not interested in performance. His first big dramatic success was *La Reine morte* (*The Dead Queen*) at the COMÉDIE-FRANÇAISE in 1942, the first of several plays celebrating the Spanish GOLDEN AGE. His better plays attempt to deal with religious subjects along French neoclassical lines, e.g. *Le Maître de Santiago* (1948) and *Port-Royal* (1954). His one generally acknowledged masterpiece is *La Ville dont le prince est un enfant* (*The Town whose Prince is a Child*, written in 1951, produced in 1967), a semi-autobiographical play which depicts the passionate relationships between boys and priests in a Catholic seminary with truthfulness, restraint and force.

**Monti, Ricardo** 1944– Argentine playwright. As a participant in the vanguard theatre of the 1970s, he sought new forms for exposing old problems of the bourgeoisie through symbols and allegories. For the Laboratory Theatre he wrote *Una noche con el señor Magnus e Hijos* (*A Night with Mr Magnus and Sons*, 1970) and for the Payró Theatre in 1971, *Historia tendenciosa de la clase media argentina* (*Tendentious History of the Argentine Middle Class*). Later plays include *Visita* (*Visit*, 1977), *Marathón* (*Marathon*, 1980) and *Una pasión sudamericana* (*A South American Passion*, 1989). As a workshop director, Monti has had a major influence in forming a new generation of Argentine playwrights.

**Montigny, Adolphe Lemoine** ?1812–80 French actor, playwright and theatre manager. Beginning as an actor at the the COMÉDIE-FRANÇAISE, he moved to the BOULEVARD theatres, became a director of the Gaîté and in 1844 took over the ailing Théâtre du Gymnase, which he ran for over 30 years and restored to popularity with the talents of his wife, Rose Chéri, and the repertoire of EUGÈNE SCRIBE. A very able manager and director, he moved French theatre towards a more intimate NATURALISM. In the 1830s he collaborated on a number of *vaudevilles* and dramas. In 1847 he published his *Observations on the Théâtre-Français and the Secondary Theatres*, in which he attempted to diagnose the current ills of the Comédie-Française.

**Moody, William Vaughn** 1869–1910 American playwright and poet. He experimented with two verse plays, but turned to prose when he dramatized a story about a woman kidnapped by a band of drunken cowboys. *The Great Divide*, premiered by the actress-manager Margaret Anglin (April 1906), described the abduction of a woman from Massachusetts by a man from Arizona, successfully blending realistic motivation with poetic treatment of the national myth. Moody's final play, *The Faith Healer* (1909), was a failure in performance.

**Moore, Dora Mavor** 1888–1979 Scottish-born Canadian actress and director. One of the founders of modern Canadian theatre, she trained at RADA and had a career as an actress in the USA and England before founding the Village Players in Toronto. In 1946 the Village Players became fully professional as the New Play Society, inspired by the example of the ABBEY THEATRE. An impromptu REVUE, *Spring Thaw* (1948), became an annual Canadian institution for almost 20 years. In 1950 the NPS opened a school to provide high-level professional theatre training. The school closed in 1968, and the NPS was dissolved in 1971 after having trained and inspired a whole generation of theatre practitioners. As well as being a remarkable teacher-director, Moore was instrumental in bringing TYRONE GUTHRIE to Canada to direct the first STRATFORD FESTIVAL. The annual Toronto Theatre awards are called 'Doras' in her honour.

**Moore, Edward** 1712–57 English playwright. His first play, *The Foundling* (1748), was a humourless, sentimental comedy. He adapted LESAGE's *Gil Blas* in 1751. His major contribution was a domestic tragedy heavily influenced by LILLO, *The Gamester* (1753), where the hero, overwhelmed with gambling debts, commits suicide moments before he would have heard he had inherited a fortune. The play was adapted by DIDEROT and was a strong influence on the development of the *drame bourgeois*.

**morality play** English term. This is a recent name for a type of drama produced during the late Middle Ages in England. Morality plays present, through allegorical figures, the struggle of good and evil for the soul of man. Like the SAINTS' PLAYS, the moralities are enormously varied. Apart from fragments, the earliest English morality to have survived is the *Castle of Perseverance* (15th-century manuscript). Opening before man's birth and closing after his death, it features the seven deadly sins and the seven virtues. Its stage plan shows various scaffolds housing the World, the Flesh, the Devil; Covetousness and God on the perimeter of a circle, with the castle itself at the centre. Of the other surviving moralities, *Mankind* contains exuberant comedy while still depicting the struggle of good and evil for man's soul. *Everyman* (printed c.1510–25), the best-known of all the moralities, is a translation from the Dutch play *Elckerlijk*. It is a picture of a man's realization in the last moments of his life of what is necessary for salvation.

The usage in the rest of Western Europe, though referring to allegorical action, is not so precise and the parallel terms can cover debates or moral teaching generally. French *moralités*, traditionally viewed as comic, were also didactic in purpose. Examples are *La Condamnation des banquets*, attacking gluttony, and *Les Blasphémateurs*, attacking blasphemy. In addition there were a few political *moralités*. The genre flourished in France into the mid-16th century.

Morality plays in the Low Countries, *spelen van sinnen*, were created by the Rhetoricians.

**Moratín, Leandro Fernández de** 1760–1828 Spanish playwright, son of NICOLÁS MORATÍN. His five original comedies established the neoclassical French model in Spain for 50 years. He wrote *El viejo y la niña* (*The Old Man and the Young Girl*) in 1786, and had great success with *La comedia nueva o el café* (*The New Play, or, The Café*, 1792), satirizing establishment dramatists. This was followed by *El barón* (*The Baron*, 1803) and *La mojigata* (*The Religious Hypocrite*, 1804). His best play, *El sí de las niñas* (*The Maidens' Consent*; written 1801, produced 1806), supports free choice in marriage. In spite of its immense success it was attacked by the Inquisition, and Moratín abandoned the theatre.

**Moratín, Nicolás Fernández de** 1737–80 Spanish playwright and poet; father of LEANDRO MORATÍN. He was a critic of GOLDEN AGE theatre and a supporter of French neoclassicism. His comedy *La petimetra* (*The Fashionable Lady*, 1762) differs little from the forms of the previous century, except for its observation of the three unities (see ARISTOTLE) and the rational triumph of love over honour. Much superior are his tragedies, *Lucrecia* (1763) on the rape of Lucretia, and *Hormesinda* (1770) set in medieval Spain. They are moral in the stoic manner, with a clear condemnation of tyranny. *Guzmán el bueno* (1777) is a patriotic and more traditionally Spanish tragedy.

*moresca* Dance-drama. Belonging to the eastern Adriatic, the northern Mediterranean littoral and some of the islands, Iberia and Central America, it is sometimes associated with CARNIVAL, sometimes with a local feast, and reflects the political and commercial interplay between Christianity and Islam (in Spain it is explicitly entitled *Cristianos y moros*). Though its form varies little – a spoken prologue, sometimes with character interaction, to a spectacular sword dance – legends, inside or outside the text, frequently refer it to a particular local event. The name may have given us 'morris dance'; there is otherwise no resemblance.

**Moreto y Cabaña, Agustín** 1618–69 Spanish playwright. Of Italian parentage, he lived in Madrid and in Toledo as a monk. The best of the disciples of CALDERÓN DE LA BARCA, he had some success with serious plays, but is best known for the witty dialogue of his refined court comedies, which retained their popularity with audiences well into the 18th century. Amongst them is his masterpiece *El desdén con el desdén* (*Scorn of Scorn*, published 1654), in which a nobleman wins a cold princess by feigning complete indifference. It was the model for MOLIÈRE's *La Princesse d'Élide*. He also wrote many fine cloak-and-sword plays. *El lindo Don Diego* (*Don Diego the Dandy*, published 1662) is to some extent a *COMEDIA de figurón* whose comic character, a narcissistic fop, is diverted from the unwilling heroine by the hope of marrying a countess. *No puede ser el guardar una mujer* (*There's No Guarding a Woman*, 1659–61) wittily demonstrates that a lady will only be chaste if she wants to be, not through force. Here, as generally in Moreto, the heroine is a model of propriety who firmly but gently defends her rights.

Of his serious plays, *Antíoco y Seleuco* (published 1654) follows LOPE DE VEGA's *El castigo sin venganza* in its theme of a son who falls in love with his father's intended bride, but with a happy ending when the father allows the son to marry her.

**Morley, Robert** 1908–92 British actor and playwright. He made a reputation playing eccentric extroverts like OSCAR WILDE (GATE THEATRE, 1936), Professor Higgins in SHAW's *Pygmalion* (OLD VIC, 1937) and Sheridan Whiteside in *The Man Who Came to Dinner* by GEORGE S. KAUFMAN and MOSS HART (1941). As the author of several light comedies, including *Edward, My Son* (with Noel Langley, 1947), *Hippo Dancing* (1954), *Hook, Line and Sinker* (1958) and *A Ghost on Tiptoe* (with Rosemary Sisson, 1974), he specialized in roles written by himself as well as appearing in FARCES by Peter Ustinov, ALAN AYCKBOURN and BEN TRAVERS.

**Morosco, Oliver (Mitchell)** 1876–1945 American manager and producer. He appeared as an acrobat in the troupe of Walter Morosco in San Francisco. After adopting his mentor's name, he managed theatres in the Bay area and Los Angeles. He began producing in 1909, and later offered in New York *The Bird of Paradise* (1912), and *Peg o' My Heart* (1912), both starring LAURETTE TAYLOR; and in 1915, *The Unchastened Woman*. The SHUBERTS built and named a theatre for him in New York (1917), which he opened with his own play, *Canary Island*.

**Morris** [née Morrison], **Clara** 1846/8–1925 Canadian-born American actress. Although in the 1870s she was praised as realistic and had already developed a reputation as one of America's greatest emotional actresses, by the 1880s she was denounced by many as the queen of spasms. While a member of AUGUSTIN DALY's company she excelled, e.g. in Daly's *Article 47* in which she played Cora the Creole. She left Daly in 1873 to become a

travelling star, always more successful when playing pathetic girls in MELODRAMA that allowed her to use her 'tearful' voice.

**Mortimer, John** 1923– British playwright and journalist. A barrister by profession, during the 1950s he wrote one-act plays for radio (see RADIO DRAMA). Though emerging when a new generation was starting to transform British theatre, he was not an 'angry young man'; his tone was cool and witty – in e.g. *The Wrong Side of the Park* (1960) and *Two Stars for Comfort* (1962). He has adapted several plays from abroad for the NATIONAL THEATRE. His one full-length play to achieve critical and commercial success was *A Voyage Round My Father* (1970), a semi-autobiographical study revealing an unexpected understanding and emotional warmth. Since then he has adapted other plays and written for television (see TELEVISION DRAMA), including *Rumpole of the Bailey* from his own stories.

**Morton, Charles** 1819–1904 British MUSIC-HALL entrepreneur. His elegant Canterbury Hall in London (1852, rebuilt 1854) was the first music-hall, with its mixture of classical and popular music, to appeal to a broad middle-class public. A master of publicity, Morton initiated music-hall advertising in *The Times* and presented Sunday evening performances. He later managed the Oxford, the Philharmonic Theatre and the GAIETY, expanding into comic opera and minstrelsy; his longest tenure was at the Alhambra (1877–81, 1883–90), and on his retirement he was dubbed, somewhat inaccurately, 'the Father of the Music Hall'.

**Morton, Thomas** 1764–1838 English playwright. His first successes were at the HAYMARKET: the sentimental operetta *The Children in the Wood* (1793) and the preposterous *Zorinski* (1795). Most of his 26 plays were staged at COVENT GARDEN, beginning with a sequence of five-act comedies of which the best are *The Way to Get Married* (1796), *A Cure for the Heartache* (1797) and *Secrets Worth Knowing* (1798); and the splendid *Speed the Plough* (1800), which anticipated later domestic MELODRAMAS and is remembered for the character of Mrs Grundy, who never appears but whose possible disapproval clouds the Ashfield home. Also famous was the character of Tyke in *The School of Reform* (1805). Morton became Reader of Plays for Covent Garden and DRURY LANE. His son John Maddison Morton (1811–91) was a prolific writer of short farces, including *Box and Cox* (1847), transformed, by the addition of Sullivan's music, into *Cox and Box* (1867).

**Moscow Art Theatre (MAT)** Russian theatre company. On 21 June 1897 KONSTANTIN STANISLAVSKY, an amateur actor-director, and VLADIMIR NEMIROVICH-DANCHENKO, a playwright-teacher, joined forces with some of their acting pupils (who included OLGA KNIPPER, VSEVOLOD MEYERHOLD and IVAN MOSKVIN) to form a theatre based upon new principles. These included a realistic approach to acting to counter lazy and artificial 19th-century conventions; a harmonious ensemble dedicated to art and not to themselves or to the idea of a 'star system'; a scenic approach that utilized research into historical detail; lengthy and systematic rehearsals; education of the public to appreciate the theatre as a 'temple of art', via the elimination of the footlights, the barring of latecomers from entering the auditorium until intermission and the dispensing with curtain calls until the play's end.

MAT (originally the Moscow Art Open Theatre) opened on 14 October 1898 at the Hermitage Theatre with A. K. TOLSTOI's history play *Tsar Fyodor Ioannovich*, which proved to be an exercise in archaeological reconstruction. CHEKHOV's *The Seagull* (1898) gave the company its identity and initiated a legendary association with the playwright – *Uncle Vanya* (1899), *The Three Sisters* (1901) and *The Cherry Orchard* (1904) followed. V. A. Simov's textured, realistic settings and Stanislavsky's innovative staging helped to realize the 'theatre of mood'. In 1902 MAT began its long association with GORKY, after whom the theatre would be named in 1932. His *The Lower Depths* together with LEV TOLSTOI's *The Power of Darkness*, both produced in 1902, brought the inner lives of the lower classes to the stage and testified to the theatre's social consciousness.

MAT was aesthetically more committed to lyrical REALISM than to NATURALISM, and also made tentative forays into SYMBOLISM, as the next 30 years would prove, with productions of IBSEN, HAUPTMANN, MAETERLINCK and ANDREEV; studio work by anti-realist directors Meyerhold, VAKHTANGOV, MICHAEL CHEKHOV, K. A. MARDZHANOV, ALEXANDRE BENOIS and GORDON CRAIG; and innovative design work. This anti-realistic approach proved unpopular with the public and with Stanislavsky, who reapplied himself to developing an acting system. Overall the theatre's aesthetic and ideological profile was moderate.

MAT survived the ravages of the October Revolution and the Civil War and was named an academic theatre (1920), largely through the good offices of Lenin and LUNACHARSKY. While the theatre publicly committed itself to reinforcing Bolshevik themes in its work, its directors privately disagreed philosophically over what artistic course it should follow. Anti-realistic experimentation continued under Vakhtangov at the Third and Fourth Studios. Stanislavsky applied his acting techniques at the Bolshoi Theatre's opera studio, while Nemirovich-Danchenko opened his Musical Studio at MAT. Simultaneously, the theatre produced the new Soviet drama. BULGAKOV's *The Days of the Turbins*, despite its White sympathies, proved a favourite of Stalin's and thus was successful, as was VSEVOLOD IVANOV's *Armoured Train 14–69* (1927) and VALENTIN KATAEV's comedy, *Squaring the Circle* (1928).

The 1920s also saw influential MAT tours of Europe and the United States (1922–4). In the 1930s new productions of Russian classics were staged, some ideologically reworked, and more of the new Soviet drama was produced (AFINOGENOV, KIRSHON). Stanislavsky died in 1938. During the Thaw (1954–6) a new generation of directors emerged, including OLEG EFREMOV, who in 1972 reluctantly became MAT's new artistic director. In 1973 the company moved to its new, modern, 1,370-seat facility on Tverskoi Boulevard, while running productions concurrently in the original and the offspring theatre buildings. Efremov has guided the Chekhov MAT more successfully than actress Tatyana Doronina has led the Gorky MAT, the original theatre's rival subdivision. In the 1980–1 season, Efremov opened MAT's Little Stage for the development of a new generation of plays, playwrights and directors. The Chekhov MAT's successes include EFROS's MARX BROS-inspired staging of *Tartuffe* (1981); ROSHCHIN's patriotic war play *Troop Train* and his satirical comedy *Mother-of-Pearl Zinaida*; and Kama Ginkas's staging of Nina Pavlova's *The Club Car*, which concerns female juvenile delinquency. In 1990 the Chekhov MAT began housing Roman Kozak's Fifth Studio, formerly the Theatre-Studio Chelovek.

**Moscow State Jewish Theatre** Soviet company. Founded as the Jewish Theatrical Studio in 1919 under the leadership of Alexander Granowski, after a period of intensive training – members included Marc Chagall and Nathan Altman as designers and Alexander Krein as composer, and actors like SOLOMON MIKHOELS and Benjamin Zuskin – the company soon created a unique style and was designated a State Theatre. The problem of finding plays reflecting both the company's ethnic quality and its political fervour was solved by ruthlessly adapting the classic Jewish plays of such writers as SHOLOM ALEICHEM, Mendele Mocher Sforim and GOLDFADN. The company was particularly successful with SHAKESPEARE's plays, and *King Lear*, directed in 1935 by Sergei Radlov with Mikhoels as Lear and Zuskin as Fool, was a triumph. The theatre was closed down by an edict of Stalin in 1948 along with all Jewish theatres.

**Moshinsky, Elijah** 1946– British director. He directed THOMAS BERNHARD's *The Force of Habit* (1976) at the Lyttelton (see NATIONAL THEATRE) and *Troilus and Cressida* in the YOUNG VIC studio, before widening his range of interests to include opera and TELEVISION DRAMA. For the BBC's TV SHAKESPEARE series he provided two of the better productions, *Coriolanus* (with ALAN HOWARD) and *All's Well That Ends Well*. Moshinsky is capable of mounting spectaculars for large stages as well as interior dramas for small ones. His classical revivals for the WEST END have included *Much Ado About Nothing* (1989), *Ivanov* (1989) and *Cyrano de Bergerac* (1992) with Robert Lindsay in the title role; but his true skills were perhaps better revealed in two modern plays, both with tender, tragic plots, RONALD HARWOOD's *Another Time* (1989) and particularly William Nicholson's *Shadowlands* (1989) about C. S. Lewis's late-life marriage to the poet, Joy Davidman. Moshinsky also staged the musical *Matador* (1991) and a successful revival of JEAN ANOUILH's *Becket* (1991) with Robert Lindsay and DEREK JACOBI.

**Moskvin, Ivan (Mikhailovich)** 1874–1946 Russian-Soviet actor. One of the best character actors of his generation, he specialized in portraying native types from among the 'insulted and the injured'. Moskvin was invited to become a charter member of the MOSCOW ART THEATRE (1898). His former teacher VLADIMIR NEMIROVICH-DANCHENKO helped secure him the title role in MAT's premiere production, A. K. TOLSTOI's historical drama *Tsar Fyodor Ioannovich* (1898). From this success he went on to play a wide variety of roles at MAT, where he spent his entire professional career. These included Luka in GORKY's *The Lower Depths* (1902), Epikhodov in CHEKHOV's *The Cherry Orchard* and Snegiryov in Nemirovich-Danchenko's dramatization of Dostoevsky's *The Brothers Karamazov* (1910). He was noted for the deft comic touch and the idiosyncratic detail, betokening a richly imagined inner life, which he brought to his roles. His career extended to film acting and stage directing. In 1943 he was appointed director of MAT.

**Mostel, Zero (Samuel Joel)** 1915–77 American actor. Trained as an artist, he became an immensely talented comic actor, noted for his sagging jowls and large paunch but dancer's grace, acrobat's control and enormously expressive face. He made his BROADWAY debut in *Keep 'Em Laughing* (1942). Subsequent roles included Shu Fu in *The Good Person of Setzuan* (1956), Leopold Bloom in *Ulysses in Nighttown* (1958; 1974), Jean in *Rhinoceros* (1961), and his greatest popular triumph, Tevye in *Fiddler on the Roof* (1964; 1976).

**Moulin-Rouge, Bal du** Parisian dance hall. In 1889, a

former butcher named Charles Zidler, with Joseph Oller, opened a dance-hall-cum-*café-concert* (see CAFÉ CHANTANT) in the Place Blanche. The *quadrille naturaliste* with its *porte d'armes* (the uplifted ankle held by the dancer's hand) and *grand écart* (splits), as danced by LA GOULUE and her squalid colleagues, and the insinuating songs of YVETTE GUILBERT gave the house a reputation that enhanced the erotic prestige of Montmartre. The dance floor was reduced in 1903 to make way for a MUSIC-HALL stage; after the building burned in 1915, it reopened to offer dinner shows of cancan and ballet. Between 1925 and 1929, Jacques-Charles revived the old glories with eight spectacularly novel REVUES; it was then converted into a cinema and not reopened as a place of live entertainment until 1953.

**Mounet-Sully** [Mounet], **Jean** 1841–1916 French actor. The major late-19th century performer of TRAGEDY in France, Mounet-Sully originally trained to be a Protestant pastor. He played at the ODÉON and made his debut at the COMÉDIE-FRANÇAISE in 1872 as Oreste in RACINE's *Andromaque*, followed by Rodrigue in *Le Cid*. He became the perfect actor for the classical repertoire, audiences being overwhelmed by his passion, majestic attitudes and sheer dramatic power. His greatest roles were Hamlet, Oreste and Oedipus, but his range also included the plays of VICTOR HUGO: his Didier in *Marion de Lorme* (1873) led to his becoming a *sociétaire*, and he played a particularly fine Hernani opposite SARAH BERNHARDT. In 1889 he was decorated with the Légion d'Honneur. In 1909 he appeared as Jesus in a silent film, *The Kiss of Judas*. His brother Paul Mounet (1847–1922) excelled in older and character parts, e.g. in *Le Juif polonais* (*The Polish Jew*).

**Mowatt (Ritchie), Anna Cora (Ogden)** 1819–70 American playwright and actress. She is remembered now for *Fashion* (1845), her SATIRE on the nouveaux riches who make themselves ridiculous by aping foreign manners. After the success of *Fashion*, she toured America and England, notably as Lady Teazle, Juliet, and Pauline in BULWER LYTTON's *The Lady of Lyons*. As an actress she was admired for her naturalness, which Edgar Allan Poe found 'so pleasantly removed from the customary rant and cant'. Her second play, *Armand* (1847), was also well received. She wrote two books about the theatre and contributed regularly to magazines. She was twice married, to James Mowatt and William F. Ritchie.

**Mrożek, Sławomir** 1932– Polish playwright, essayist, comic story teller and film-maker. He has lived in Italy, France and Mexico since 1963. Using slapstick techniques of VAUDEVILLE and CABARET, he transforms concepts into model theatrical situations. *The Police* (1958) and early one-act parables – *Out at Sea* (1960), *Striptease* and *Charlie* (1961) – reveal the mechanisms of power by pushing absurd premises to logical extremes. Using SATIRE and the grotesque, he mocks national myths and parodies different theatrical styles and genres, notably the Polish romantic tradition. *Tango* (1964) traces European civilization from liberalism to totalitarianism in the form of family drama. *Vatzlav* (1970) and *Émigrés* (1974) offer ironic views of exiles from tyranny confronting freedom. Other plays include *On Foot* (1981), *Portrait* (1988), *Widows* (1990) and *Love in the Crimea* (1993).

**Müller, Heiner** 1929– German playwright and director. Müller's work falls into three categories: naturalistic plays dealing with the means of production and the cre-

ation of a socialist society like *Tractor* (1961) and *Cement* (1972, both first performed in 1975); reworkings of mythical or literary material using subjects and characters from antiquity (*Hercules 5*, 1966; *Hercules 2, or The Hydra*, 1974) together with translations and adaptations, such as *Macbeth* (1972), *Hamlet Machine* (1979) and *Desolate Shore* (*Verkommenes Ufer*, based on EURIPIDES' *Medea*, 1983); and plays focusing on German history. Marked by a fragmentary and open-ended dramaturgy presenting highly politicized collages of violence and fantasy, the most ambitious of these is *Germania – Death in Berlin* (1971, first performed 1978). *Quartet* (1982), a psychological study of social dominance in sexuality and aggression, marked a new departure. His 'historical pessimism' was heavily criticized in the GDR and his work censored during the 1960s (see CENSORSHIP), but since 1976 he has been recognized as a leading playwright. Müller's sensational 1988 DEUTSCHES THEATER production of *The Scab*, written in the 1950s, exposed the flaws that were soon to bring down the GDR. Since 1992 he has been a director of the BERLINER ENSEMBLE.

**Munday, Anthony** 1560–1633 English playwright, pamphleteer, actor and government agent, engaged in anti-Catholic espionage. Munday was a prolific journeyman-writer, translator and 'plotter', whose job it was to divide a given story into appropriate dramatic episodes. His extant plays are *Fedele and Fortunio* (c.1584), *John a Kent and John a Cumber* (1594) and the two parts of *The Downfall* and *The Death of Robert, Earl of Huntingdon* (1598), written with HENRY CHETTLE. He was involved in the revisions of *Sir Thomas More* (c.1596) and in Part 1 of *Sir John Oldcastle* (1599).

**Munford, Robert** c.1737–83 American playwright and politician. One of Virginia's more influential elected representatives, both before and after the Revolution, Munford wrote two plays which are outstanding examples of America's early comic drama and its interest in SATIRE. *The Candidates; or, The Humours of a Virginia Election* (1770) satirizes the methods by which politicians win elections. *The Patriots* (1779) attacks half-hearted and hypocritical patriots as well as Tory and Whig politics. Munford wrote mainly to air his views, creating amusing scenes with stereotypical characters. Both plays were published in 1798.

**Muni, Paul** [Muni Weisenfreund] 1896–1967 American actor. He started in the YIDDISH THEATRE at the age of 12 as Weisenfreund, playing old men parts, quickly establishing himself as a superb character actor and master of make-up. After 18 years as a leading Yiddish actor he moved to BROADWAY in English-speaking roles and then to a distinguished career in Hollywood.

**Munk, Kaj** 1892–1944 Danish playwright. A Lutheran pastor, he wrote some 35 plays vigorously exploring such moral issues as faith, the human will and the discovery of identity through courageous action; his debt to Kierkegaard and IBSEN is frequently clear. Some early plays betray a fascination with 'strong leaders', such as Herod in *An Idealist* (1924) and Henry VIII in *Cant* (1931), anticipating his brief but real attraction to Nazism. Very different views emerge in the explicitly anti-Nazi *He Sits at the Melting Pot* (1938) and in the parable of Danish resistance *Niels Ebbesen* (1940–2); its suppression led to his murder by the Gestapo in 1944. His most enduring play is *The Word* (1925), about the power of faith and the will to free humanity from prejudice.

**Murphy, Arthur** 1727–1805 Irish playwright. He began

writing plays in 1753, through friendship with SAMUEL FOOTE, and wrote an accomplished farce, *The Apprentice* (1756). Briefly an actor, playing Othello at COVENT GARDEN, he trained as a lawyer and practised as a barrister until 1788 while continuing to write plays. He translated VOLTAIRE's tragedy *The Orphan of China* (1759) but his best work, after disputes over his tragedy *The Grecian Daughter* (1772), was in comedy, including a study of married life and its attendant boredom in *The Way to Keep Him* (1760) and the more sentimental *Know Your Own Mind* (1777).

**Murphy, Tom** [Thomas] **(Bernard)** 1935– Irish playwright. Murphy's first play, *A Whistle in the Dark* (1961), concerns an Irish immigrant family in Coventry whose despairs find outlet in brutal violence. After *A Whistle* Murphy lived in London, writing television and film scripts, returning to Ireland in 1970. Outstanding among his subsequent plays are *Famine* (1968), *A Crucial Week in the Life of a Grocer's Assistant* (1969), with a tight, surrealistic structure (see SURREALISM) and Joycean wordplay; *The Morning After Optimism* (1971), in which a whore and a pimp are the shadows and finally the murderers of two idealized lovers in a debased Forest of Arden; *The Sanctuary Lamp* (1975), about three grotesque derelicts; *The Blue Macushla* (1980), a SATIRE of Irish politics set in a nightclub; *The Gigli Concert* (1983), about an Irish businessman who aspires to sing like Gigli; *Conversations on a Homecoming* (1985), which has a fugue-like structure that turns it into a lament for lost ideals; and *Bailegangaire* (1985), in which a senile crone, tended by her two granddaughters, recites an old tale of contest, death and loss. The plays explore various modifications of the straight realist stage of *A Whistle*. In *Too Late for Logic* (1989) a university philosopher interrogates those elements of his own life that led to his suicide.

The operatic range of Murphy's theatre is grounded in specifics. His is a secular world where the theological symbolism of innocence, guilt and forgiveness persists, rendered in a complex language which is also fully theatrical.

**Murray, (George) Gilbert (Aimé)** 1866–1957 British classical scholar, philosopher and playwright. He provided SHAW with the model for Cusins in *Major Barbara*. After writing two original plays, *Carlyon Sahib* (1889) and *Andromache* (1900), he turned to verse translations of Greek tragedy. His versions of EURIPIDES were staged by GRANVILLE BARKER for the STAGE SOCIETY at the ROYAL COURT THEATRE (*Hippolytus*, 1904; *The Trojan Women*, 1905; *Electra*, 1906) and at the Savoy Theatre (*Medea*, 1907), while his translation of SOPHOCLES' *Oedipus Rex* was staged by REINHARDT at COVENT GARDEN in 1912. He later turned to comedy with adaptations of ARISTOPHANES and the first reconstructions of MENANDER: *The Rape of the Locks* (*Perikeiromene*, 1914); *The Arbitration* (*Epitrepontes*, 1945).

**Murray, T(homas) C(ornelius)** 1873–1959 Irish playwright. With LENNOX ROBINSON he was one of the 'Cork realists', in the ABBEY's early years, whose work determined the theatre's characteristic style. In *Birthright* (1910), his first play, a father's jealous care for the disposition of his land becomes a mortal issue between his two sons. Murray's most successful later plays are *Aftermath* (1922), *Autumn Fire* (1924) and *Michaelmas Eve* (1932). In none of them does anyone win. In a society bound by strict Catholic teaching, which Murray approved, his characters must simply endure within the restrictions. From the tension between extreme emotional conflicts and their enforced suppression, Murray's plays derive their intense, claustrophobic atmosphere.

**Murrell, John** 1945– American-born Canadian playwright. *Waiting for the Parade* (1977), a sensitive portrayal of the lives of five women waiting for their men to come home from World War II, has been widely produced. *Memoir* (1977), depicting the last days of SARAH BERNHARDT, was first produced with the Irish actress, Siobhan McKenna, as the Divine Sarah and has since been produced in more than 20 countries. *Farther West* (1982), *New World* (1984) and *Democracy* (1991) were directed by ROBIN PHILLIPS. Murrell himself directed *October* (1988). He has also made notable translations of European classics.

**music-hall** English term. Music-hall was the Victorian term for VARIETY theatre. Under the patents system (see THEATRICAL MONOPOLY), because dialogue was forbidden them, minor theatres had perforce to offer musical entertainments. But music was available elsewhere: the public-house bar parlour or 'free-and-easy' with its weekly sing-songs, performed by amateurs, with a chairman and some professionals; the assembly-room entertainments at hotels; and the suburban London tea-garden, a middle-class version of the pleasure-gardens, where aristocratic patronage had fallen off by 1830, and which exhibited singers on a small stage. All three forms were licensed under the liberally interpreted Music and Dancing Act of George II. In London, these places of mixed entertainment, smoking and light refreshment included the Britannia in Hoxton, the Bower in the Lower Marsh (Lambeth), and the Grecian in the City Road.

The Theatres Act of 1843, which distinguished sharply between legitimate playhouses under the Lord Chamberlain's control where no smoking or drinking was allowed in the auditorium, and tavern concert-rooms under the jurisdiction of local magistrates where such practices were allowed, compelled many of the lesser resorts to make an evolutionary choice. Saloon theatres opted either to go legitimate or carry on as miscellaneous entertainments with no permission to stage plays. Typically, the Mogul tavern in Drury Lane transmuted into the Middlesex or 'Old Mo' music-hall and eventually became the grandiose Winter Garden Theatre.

The old bohemian singing-rooms in night cellars gradually disappeared, among them the Cyder Cellars in Maiden Lane and the Coal Hole in the Strand. These had been all-male resorts, featuring hearty suppers and strong drink, bawdy songs and blood-curdling performers. Respectability was the touchstone for success with many early halls: CHARLES MORTON, the intelligent manager of the Canterbury Hall in Lambeth (1852), opened it to ladies at all times and presented the first English performance of Gounod's *Faust* as an oratorio, although bookmakers still shouted odds on the premises. Morton's Oxford near St Giles's Circus, the London Pavilion in Piccadilly Circus and the Tivoli in the Strand were other important WEST END houses.

At first, music-hall programmes copied the repertory of the 'harmonic meetings', mingling madrigals and glees with lengthy BURLESQUE ballads such as SAM COWELL's 'Villikins and his Dinah' and 'The Ratcatcher's Daughter', SAM COLLINS's Irish ditties, and E. W. MACKNEY's 'Ethiopian' delineations. Women excelled at dramatic renditions. JENNY HILL, the 'Vital Spark', was typical in coming from a background of poverty, achieving fame and fortune, and retiring early because of ill health and exhaustion. Drawn from the working classes, performers shared common experience with their audiences, who were boisterous and fond of joining in the chorus and 'giving the bird'.

In 1878, the Metropolitan Board of Works required a Certificate of Suitability, which caused some 200 halls, unable to meet new standards, to close. In reaction, stock companies (see STOCK COMPANY) formed to float luxurious, well appointed houses, designed by outstanding architects like Frank Matcham. The first palatial hall was the Great Variety Theatre in Leicester Square, whose neo-Moorish building, burnt down and rebuilt as the Alhambra Palace under E. T. Smith, became famous for its ballets, managing to survive a lawsuit citing them as dramatic performances. Variety theatres continued to advance in number and importance, with improved ventilation, comfort and decoration, as well as higher prices. Soon every London neighbourhood had its local, and the journalist F. Anstey could discern four distinct levels of quality and audience in London alone: the aristocratic variety theatre in the West End, the small West End house, the large bourgeois music-hall in the outlying areas and suburbs, and that of the poor and squalid districts. In the provinces, most halls clustered in the centres, even in Manchester, Liverpool and Glasgow.

From 1879, the infusion of music-hall stars into PANTOMIME accustomed the family audience to variety material and persuaded it to attend. The middle classes took to visiting halls as the managers strove successfully to dispel the public-house image, banning sales of drinks in the auditorium, replacing tables with rows of seats, cleaning up artistes' material and taking measures to control audience behaviour. Since sanitation, elegance and safety were totems of the middle-class ethos, the music-hall sought to embody them. It was aided by new access through public transport and improved street-lighting that made it safer to venture out at night.

The average single turn seldom lasted more than 20 minutes, enabling popular performers to play several halls a night. However, to meet the increased costs, Henry de Frece in Liverpool and George Belmont in London instituted the notorious 'twice-nightly' arrangement (1885). These costs now included star salaries, for the 1890s were the heyday of the music-hall star. MARIE LLOYD with her artful innuendo, ALBERT CHEVALIER, a legitimate actor who excelled at coster impersonations, LITTLE TICH the eccentric pygmy, DAN LENO, greatest of the comedians of humble life, HARRY LAUDER with his Scottish ballads, the male impersonator VESTA TILLEY, blackface artistes G. H. CHIRGWIN and Eugene Stratton, GEORGE ROBEY of the outraged eyebrows and outrageous *double entendre*, were expensive performers to maintain.

This period of consolidation also saw some last-ditch assaults on the institution. Prostitution on the premises had always been an outrage to reformers, and Mrs Ormiston Chant attacked the London Empire for its flagrant promenade in 1895. In Manchester a combination of reform groups opposed the licence for the new Palace, and in Liverpool disputes over licensing were conducted along class lines. Another attack came from the Lord Chamberlain's office, as sketches began to play a prominent part in the music-hall bill. Parliamentary

commissions of 1866 and 1892 both recommended more liberal changes in licensing, but these were not followed up until 1912, when half-an-hour of dialogue was permitted. One result was the appearance of legitimate stars like HERBERT BEERBOHM TREE on the variety stage.

The old intimate relationship between the performer and audience began to disappear as colossal halls like Moss's London HIPPODROME with its water-tank for aquatic spectacles and the Stoll COLISEUM with its triple revolving stage were built. Programmes became filled with acrobats, trained seals and elephants, living statuary, 15-minute MELODRAMAS, mentalists and adagio dancing, edging out though not entirely displacing the solo comedian and singer who had been the music-halls' staple.

A token but important recognition of the music-hall came with the Royal Command Performance in 1912. A kind of resurgence occurred in the 1920s with the introduction of American jazz and ragtime and singers like SOPHIE TUCKER, who were already known to the public through their recordings. But it could not compete with the talking pictures, the wireless, or the wartime air raids that made going to the theatre a danger. The music-hall was still capable of fostering such talents as MAX MILLER and GRACIE FIELDS, and throve at London's Palladium till 1961. But television put paid to the process of diminution by featuring most of the surviving music-hall types on its variety programmes, and the microphone reduced the camaraderie between performer and public. Most of the extant buildings were wantonly demolished or restored for other purposes. Ironically, the tavern concerts that spawned the music-hall thrive as working men's clubs in industrial areas, whereas ersatz 'olde-tyme' music-halls forcibly demonstrate the obsolescence of the original form.

But the spirit long infused British drama, not only thematically as in JOHN OSBORNE's *The Entertainer* (1957) and TREVOR GRIFFITHS's *Comedians* (1975), but in the dialogue rhythms in BECKETT, O'CASEY, PINTER and PETER NICHOLS, as well as in performance style. A comedian like MAX WALL, excelling in *Krapp's Last Tape*, is a perfect example of this cross-fertilization.

**music-hall, French** see *CAFÉ CHANTANT*; REVUE

**musical comedy** British and American theatrical phenomenon. The term 'musical comedy', which usurped BURLESQUE, is hard to delimit, but the form probably reached its height between the 1890s and 1918.

From the providers' point of view musical comedy was a matter of showbusiness; from the consumers', a thrilling, titillating, amusing, tuneful affair making little call on credibility. What was hoped would be a box office success was cobbled together by a story deviser, a lyric writer and a composer, often with collaborators. The original material was frequently much altered during rehearsals – dialogue changed, musical numbers dropped or added, and characters eliminated or introduced. Even after the opening night, alterations were made from time to time according to audiences' reactions. *The Lucky Star* (Savoy, 1899) was advertised as 'Founded on a French original by Leterrier and Vanloo, adapted by J. Cheever Goodwin and Woolson Morse, with new dialogue by Charles H. Brookfield and new lyrics by Adrian Ross and Aubrey Hopwood, the whole revised and assembled by H. L., and with music by Ivan Caryll.' No mention was made of the fact that some of the music was borrowed from the 'French original'. A couple of months after the show opened, the *Monthly Musical Record* observed, 'The libretto has been brightened up on every page and Mr François Cellier has done wonders in touching up the music.' Such tinkering was the true but often unacknowledged fate of most musical comedies.

A simple central feature – essential if a far from intellectual audience was to remain attentive throughout – might be the love of the highly placed for the humble (who often turned out to be not so humble after all), or luck arising from a windfall, and there had to be plenty of occasions for laughter and for the admiration of elegant females, with everything set, if possible, in a modern context. The lyrics were often platitudinous and sometimes sheer nonsense. Nevertheless, some of the rhymesters displayed considerable talent, notably Adrian Ross (1859–1933), a distinguished Cambridge scholar who wrote both musical comedy lyrics and serious literature. The composers were often highly trained musicians whose facility guaranteed an instant response to a request for a new number.

The cult of 'the girl' is obvious from the very titles of the works. A short selection of British musical comedies from the years 1893 to 1913 (with the number of performances each achieved on its first appearance) could include *The Casino Girl* (196), *The Circus Girl* (497), *A Country Girl* (729), *The Earl and the Girl* (371), *A Gaiety Girl* (413), *The Girl from Kay's* (432), *The Girl from Utah* (195), *The Girl in the Taxi* (385), *The Girl in the Train* (340), *My Girl* (183), *The Pearl Girl* (254), *The Quaker Girl* (536), *The Shop Girl* (546), *The Sunshine Girl* (336) and *A Runaway Girl* (593). (A similar list could be made for the USA, e.g. *The Motor Girl, The Yankee Girl, The Wall Street Girl, The Charity Girl*, and so on.) Although 'the girl' appears so frequently, the tendency was to emphasize 'the lady'. In contrast to the tights and short skirts of Victorian burlesque, costumes were expensive and elegant. This elegance, and sometimes a studied simplicity, is well illustrated in the mass-produced photographs eagerly purchased by the public. The ladies of musical comedy are picture postcard beauties *par excellence*. Not infrequently their lives had outcomes like their roles. The Baroness Churston, the Countess of Dudley, the Countess of Drogheda, Countess Poulett, the Marchioness of Headfort and others were recruited to the peerage from the musical comedy stage.

The promoters of musical comedy aimed at long runs and big profits. *Chu-Chin-Chow* (HER [HIS] MAJESTY'S THEATRE, London;1916) achieved 2,238 performances. As well as these initial runs there were frequent revivals and touring versions played not only in Britain but in America and Australia as well. GEORGE EDWARDES (1852–1915), whose principal London theatres were the GAIETY and Daly's, is regarded as the prime architect of musical comedy. He is said to have had as many as 16 touring companies roaming Britain.

The distinctions between musical comedy and operetta on the one hand and REVUE on the other are often very blurred. A European operetta that was transmogrified into a most successful English musical comedy was *The Merry Widow* (Daly's, 1907) by Franz Lehar (1870–1948). But the years after World War I saw the gradual decline of musical comedy of the distinctive Edwardian kind. The cinema began to vie with the theatre in spectacle, the cult of the film star replaced that of the picture postcard beauty, up-to-the-minute references became the province of revue, and the somewhat effete melodiousness of the old music was challenged

by jazz. These influences were markedly American. America and England had had a musical comedy import-export relationship. Now America was growing in independence. Composers such as JEROME KERN (1885–1945) and GEORGE GERSHWIN (1898–1937) added lustre to American MUSICAL THEATRE, and native American librettists adopted an increasingly contemporary American outlook. After World War II the old kind of British musical comedy was gone, too, replaced by what was called merely 'the musical'. Musicals such as *Cabaret* (1966) and *Evita* (1978) are somewhat estranged members of the same family as *A Gaiety Girl* (1893) and *The Belle of New York* (1897).

**musical theatre, American** Despite numerous early productions of both imported and native musical entertainment, the event most often singled out as the starting point of American musical theatre is the production of *The Black Crook* in 1866. This show, created when a Faustian melodrama was augmented with dances by a French ballet company stranded in New York, is viewed as a primitive example of MUSICAL COMEDY because of its use of music and dance in the telling of its story. In the 1870s and 1880s native entertainments such as the 'Mulligan Guard' series of musical plays were created and performed by EDWARD HARRIGAN AND TONY HART. The triumphant American premiere of GILBERT and Sullivan's *HMS Pinafore* in 1879 made comic opera the most popular musical form for the rest of the century. Most distinguished of the American composers of comic opera was REGINALD DE KOVEN, whose *Robin Hood* (1891) was frequently revived. The REVUE, a form of musical theatre in which songs, dances and comedy sketches were loosely connected by a plot or recurring theme, emerged in this period, beginning with *The Passing Show* (1894).

As the 1890s progressed, signs of change began to appear on the musical stage. In 1894, the Bostonians (see BOSTON IDEAL OPERA COMPANY) presented the comic opera *Prince Ananias*, which contained the first full score by Victor Herbert, destined to be one of the most important composers of operettas for the American stage. Comic opera, operetta, and musical comedy were the dominant forms at the dawn of the new century. The most successful show of the decade was *Florodora* (1900), an English import. The native comic tradition of Harrigan and Hart was continued by GEORGE M. COHAN in a series of musical comedies. With the arrival of Franz Lehar's *The Merry Widow* in New York in 1907, a vogue for Viennese operetta was launched which lasted until World War I. In the same year, FLORENZ ZIEGFELD produced the *Follies of 1907*, the first in a series of annual revues which gradually moved that form away from topical humour towards a greater emphasis on elaborate scenery, beautifully dressed chorus girls, and star comedians and singers.

A musical idiom developed by black musicians, ragtime was first heard on the musical stage in the World War I period in the form of individual songs interpolated into shows. In 1914 IRVING BERLIN composed a ragtime score for the revue *Watch Your Step*. Meanwhile, composer JEROME KERN was revolutionizing musical comedy with his intimate Princess Theatre shows, and in the postwar years he demonstrated that contemporary American characters and situations and fresh musical styles could be effectively employed in more elaborate musical comedies.

Despite all these changes, the demand for operetta

and revues did not abate. The early 1920s also marked the reappearance of the black musical on the American stage. Although there had been a few isolated efforts since the turn of the century, African-Americans were to have their greatest impact on the BROADWAY musical in the 1920s. Beginning with SISSLE AND BLAKE's *Shuffle Along* (1921), a succession of musicals and revues popularized a form of jazz that replaced ragtime as the dominant musical comedy style, and also introduced many new dance steps. A new generation of composers began to make their mark on the Broadway stage. Writing in a jazz-influenced style GEORGE AND IRA GERSHWIN had a series of successes culminating in two political SATIRES, *Strike Up the Band* (1930) and the award-winning *Of Thee I Sing* (1931). Among the shows created by the new songwriting team of RICHARD RODGERS and LORENZ HART were *The Garrick Gaieties* (1925), *Dearest Enemy* (1925), *A Connecticut Yankee* (1927) and *Present Arms* (1928). Jerome Kern took musical theatre in another direction when he composed *Show Boat* (1927), an operetta that used American musical styles to tell a serious dramatic story about the lives of a family of showboat performers from the 1880s to the 1920s. With lyrics by OSCAR HAMMERSTEIN II, *Show Boat* pointed the way to the musical plays of the 1940s and 1950s.

The 1927–8 season, with some 250 shows, was a high point in the history of the Broadway stage. Events outside of the theatre, including the advent of sound films and the stock market crash of 1929, would prevent it from ever again reaching that level of production. At the end of the 1920s new composers and lyricists appeared: COLE PORTER wrote insinuating melodies and clever lyrics for a number of frothy musical comedies, including *Fifty Million Frenchmen* (1929), *The New Yorkers* (1930) and *Anything Goes* (1934), while the songwriting team of Arthur Schwartz and Howard Dietz brought a new, more subdued and melodic sound to their scores for the revues *The Little Show* (1929), *Three's a Crowd* (1930), and *The Band Wagon* (1931). *Porgy and Bess* (1935) by the Gershwins (with DUBOSE HEYWARD) and *On Your Toes* (1936) by Rodgers and Hart were two of the more ambitious musicals of the 1930s.

As the Depression worsened, this form of theatre began to reflect the country's growing unrest. In 1936 the GROUP THEATRE produced *Johnny Johnson*, a musical with an anti-war message, and the MERCURY THEATRE offered Mark Blitzstein's controversial capitalist versus labour parable, *The Cradle Will Rock*, in 1938. This interest in the issues of the day was short-lived, however, for with the advent of World War II the musical theatre once again turned its back on political and social commentary. The broad and lasting appeal of *Oklahoma!* (1943), the first musical by the new partnership of Richard Rodgers and Oscar Hammerstein II, was due to its affirmation of the simple values of an earlier America, combined with such departures as allowing a murder to take place on stage and using a 'dream ballet' to amplify the dramatic action. Among the subsequent 'musical plays' created by Rodgers and Hammerstein were *Carousel* (1945), *South Pacific* (1949), *The King and I* (1951), *Flower Drum Song* (1958) and *The Sound of Music* (1959).

Despite the pervasive influence of Rodgers and Hammerstein, the traditional musical comedy continued to flourish in the 1940s and early 1950s. *Annie Get Your Gun*, with a score by Irving Berlin and a bravura performance by ETHEL MERMAN as the backwoods sharp-

shooter Annie Oakley, opened to critical acclaim in 1946. FRANK LOESSER received enthusiastic notices for *Guys and Dolls* (1950), about Broadway gamblers and their perennial girlfriends. *Wonderful Town* (1953), by the team of BERNSTEIN, COMDEN AND GREEN, dealt with life in New York's Greenwich Village in the 1930s. *Pajama Game*, a musical about management labour strife in a pyjama factory, introduced the songwriting team of Richard Adler and Jerry Ross to Broadway in 1954. A year later their *Damn Yankees* combined the Faust legend with baseball, and elevated dancer GWEN VERDON to stardom.

In 1956, LERNER AND LOEWE adapted GEORGE BERNARD SHAW's comedy *Pygmalion* into the musical *My Fair Lady*, which changed the course of musical theatre: it revived the vogue for operettas set in bygone eras; it created a trend towards hiring actors rather than singers for important roles; and it led librettists to concentrate on adapting already successful plays, films, and novels rather than creating original librettos.

The two basic threads of musical theatre, operetta and musical comedy, continued to flourish from the mid-1950s and through the mid-1960s. As usual, the operettas tended to be the more ambitious works. Leonard Bernstein, ARTHUR LAURENTS, STEPHEN SONDHEIM and JEROME ROBBINS based *West Side Story* (1957) on the Romeo and Juliet legend. JERRY BOCK AND SHELDON HARNICK created one of the most popular of all American musicals, *Fiddler on the Roof* (1964). Meanwhile, the creators of musical comedy tried to vary the traditional formulas by exploring new settings and subjects. *Gypsy* (1959) was based on the life of stripper GYPSY ROSE LEE. *Cabaret* (1966) was set in the decadent Berlin of the 1930s. *Hair* (1968) brought rock music and NUDITY to the Broadway musical stage.

The only new composer-lyricist to contribute importantly to the musical theatre in the 1970s was Stephen Sondheim. His brilliant but often controversial shows of the 1970s and 1980s included *Company* (1970), *Follies* (1971), *A Little Night Music* (1973), *Pacific Overtures* (1976), *Sweeney Todd* (1979), *Merrily We Roll Along* (1981) and *Sunday in the Park with George* (1984). The work of Sondheim in collaboration with producer-director HAROLD PRINCE popularized the 'concept musical', in which the director and designers, instead of attempting to translate a pre-existing libretto and score into theatrical terms, collaborate with the composer, lyricist and librettist during the creation of the show, so that every element is conceived in terms of production. This partly accounts for the dominance of such choreographer-directors as BOB FOSSE, MICHAEL BENNETT and GOWER CHAMPION.

The period of the 1970s and 1980s was a time of reassessment of the musical theatre in the light of rising production costs and prohibitive ticket prices. Some artists and producers preferred to work in the more modest surroundings of OFF- or OFF-OFF BROADWAY, their more successful creations eventually finding their way to the Broadway theatre. Also contributing shows to Broadway were regional theatres, notably the Goodspeed Opera House in East Haddam, Connecticut, where *Annie* premiered. The current generation of musical theatre stars, such as Mandy Patinkin and Bernadette Peters, have appeared only sporadically on Broadway. The dearth of American musicals has led producers to look to Europe and Britain for new shows: *Les Misérables* and *Miss Saigon*, *Cats* and *Phantom of the Opera*.

Sometimes called the only uniquely American contribution to world theatre, the Broadway musical faces some severe economic and artistic tests in the years to come.

**Musser, Tharon** 1925– American lighting designer. Musser made her BROADWAY debut with the premiere production of *Long Day's Journey into Night*. By the late 1960s she was the dominant lighting designer on Broadway. Her versatility is apparent from her credits, which include several seasons with the AMERICAN SHAKESPEARE THEATRE Festival, all of NEIL SIMON's plays since *Prisoner of Second Avenue* (1971), and musicals such as *Mame*. Since 1975 she has teamed up with designers ROBIN WAGNER and THEONI ALDREDGE and director MICHAEL BENNETT to design *A Chorus Line*, *Dreamgirls* and several others. Her style ranges from flashy production numbers to painstakingly researched re-creations of specific light qualities and moods (such as *A Little Night Music*, 1973). (See also STAGE LIGHTING.)

**Musset, Alfred de** 1810–57 French poet and playwright. Musset's stature as a dramatist has increased during this century. His earliest plays were published rather than performed, his main creative period extending from 1833 to 1837 – with *André del Sarto* and *Les Caprices de Marianne* (1833), *Fantasio, On ne badine pas avec l'amour* (*Love Is Not to Be Trifled With*) and *Lorenzaccio* (1834), *La Quenouille de Barberine* (*Barberine's Distaff*) and *Le Chandelier* (1835), *Il ne faut jurer de rien* (*Nothing Is Certain*, 1836) and *Un Caprice* (1837). This period corresponds largely with his traumatic relationship with George Sand. Most of the plays, especially the dramatic proverbs, concern conflicts between the sexes. A number of short scenes focus on different groups of characters, rather than the traditional French construction in long unbroken acts. *Lorenzaccio*, often called the French *Hamlet*, has 34 scenes and an army of characters. Its overt attacks on the monarchy of Louis Philippe and on the bourgeoisie made it unperformable in the 1830s (see CENSORSHIP) and it only reached the stage, much adapted and reduced, with SARAH BERNHARDT in 1896, thereafter becoming an established classic. After 1847 Musset wrote directly for the stage and rewrote earlier plays. He was particularly interested in the actress RACHEL, to whom he dedicated an important essay on TRAGEDY.

**mystery** [miracle] **play** Mystery plays in England, sometimes referred to as CORPUS CHRISTI PLAYS because of their date of performance, are dramatized versions of biblical stories from the Creation to the Last Judgement. In French mysteries (*mystères*) there are fewer Old Testament episodes, and the plays usually end with the Resurrection. 'Miracle' was a contemporary medieval English term, but is better reserved for plays which deal with Christian miracles.

The mystery plays are non-liturgical and written in the vernacular. The earliest surviving English text is the fully fledged York Mystery Cycle (manuscript 1463–77). This is one of the four extant plays of this type: York (over 13,000 lines), Chester (over 11,000), Towneley (over 12,000) and N. Town (nearly 11,000). York and Chester are closely linked in many ways. Both provide the whole story of mankind from Creation to Last Judgement (as do Towneley and N. Town); both were civic plays; both were divided into a number of shorter 'pageants', performed by different craft guilds or companies; both were performed on wagons at a series of 'stations' or stopping-places around the city. The Towneley manuscript of the late 15th or early 16th century contains the plays of the so-called Wakefield Master, a playwright with a remarkable dramatic range (especially clear in the second of the Shepherds' pageants), and a strong line in ranting tyrants. The N. Town group (late-15th-century manuscript) contains a number of pageants, but also two unique plays: one on the early life of Mary (c.1,600 lines) and a two-part PASSION PLAY (c.3,000 lines). *The Mysteries* was the title chosen for TONY HARRISON's NATIONAL THEATRE adaptation of the cycles in 1985.

In France, a *miracle* might denote a secular romance, a saint's life or a Marian miracle, in which the dramatic tension is resolved by the miraculous intervention of the Virgin Mary. The *Miracles de nostres Dame par personnages*, a collection of 40 plays preserved in one manuscript, was performed annually by the Paris Guild of Goldsmiths in the 14th century. The French *mystères* were in essence historical plays. Virtually all had a religious subject. They were based on the life of a saint (see SAINTS' PLAYS) or on biblical material, in particular the life of Christ.

The term 'mystery' can loosely cover, as well as the French *mystère*, the German *Osterspiel*, the Italian SACRA RAPPRESENTAZIONE and the Spanish AUTO SACRAMENTAL – but it is not really helpful to straitjacket different national traditions.

**nadagama** Sri Lankan folk theatre. *Nadagama* was introduced to Sri Lanka by Catholic missionaries in the early 19th century. Although its original intention seems to have been to proselytize, it soon added non-religious stories to its repertory and thrived along the whole western coastal region of the island. The plays, many of which are available in script form, are long and episodic, often dealing with the exploits of heroic characters who encounter numerous dramatic challenges in love and war. Tamil and Sinhalese mix freely in the works, indicating that they were particularly popular among the Tamil-speaking minority of the region. Phillipu Sinno is regarded as the author of 13 of the plays, and the legendary father of *nadagama*. Little is known about him except that he was a popular versifier and a blacksmith born in Colombo.

The presenter (*pote gura*) describes the plot of the story and sings verses to introduce each of the stock characters, one by one and at length, accompanied by musicians. Finally, the dramatic action gets under way. A traditional *nadagama* play takes a week to enact, beginning every evening with the presentation of the stock characters, lasting from about 9 pm until midnight.

**naluyuks** Inuit mummers. Literally 'heathens', these Twelfth Night MASQUEraders of northern Labrador are groups of young masked men disguised in bear skins or sacking, who visit houses where there are children, interrogating them on their behaviour and distributing presents. In return, the children are required to sing a Christmas carol. Formal behaviour inside turns to boisterousness outside: spectators are chased and harassed, special attention being devoted to social undesirables, with the encouragement of the crowd. The tradition has both indigenous and European elements.

**Nansen, Betty** 1873–1943 Danish actress and director. In 1917 she transformed a small Copenhagen playhouse (renamed the Betty Nansen Theatre) into an art theatre specializing in IBSEN, BJØRNSON, STRINDBERG and contemporary European and American drama. She introduced PIRANDELLO's *Six Characters in Search of an Author* to Denmark, as well as plays by TOLLER, KAREL and Josef ČAPEK, O'NEILL and SHAW; she also presented new Danish plays rejected by other theatres, such as KAJ MUNK's *The Word*. As an actress she was limited by the 19th-century grand manner. Among her major roles were Hedda Gabler and Mrs Alving, which she also played in Paris.

**Napier, John** 1944– British stage designer. Primarily associated with the ROYAL SHAKESPEARE COMPANY, he studied sculpture in art school before receiving THEATRE DESIGN training under RALPH KOLTAI at London's Central School. Rejecting decorative, pictorial design conventions, his early work revealed highly selective realism and a sculptor's sense of space. More recently, he has become known for found art and pop-art assemblages with which he creates unusual stage environments frequently involving complex mechanisms and basic reconstructions of stage and auditorium. Representative productions include *Twelfth Night* (1978), *Nicholas Nickleby* (1980), *Cats* (1981), *Les Misérables* (1985), *Miss Saigon* (1989) and *Sunset Boulevard* (1993).

**Nash, 'Jolly' John** 1830 1901 British MUSIC-HALL artist. A former Gloucestershire metal-worker, he was billed as 'The Laughing Blacksmith'. An early protégé of CHARLES MORTON, he appeared at the Oxford Music Hall in London in 1861, was the first music-hall artist to perform at royal command, and one of the first British VARIETY performers to tour the USA, in 1874. He was also a musician and a specialist in silly walks; his act centred on laughing songs such as the famous 'Little Brown Jug'.

**Nashe, Thomas** 1567– c.1601 English pamphleteer and playwright. One of the UNIVERSITY WITS associated with LYLY, ROBERT GREENE and MARLOWE, he collaborated with the latter on *Dido, Queen of Carthage* (c.1587). The vigour and exuberance of Nashe's prose are displayed in the pamphlet, *Pierce Penilesse* (1592), and the picaresque tale, *The Unfortunate Traveller* (1594). His surviving play, *Summer's Last Will and Testament* (c.1593), is a courtly entertainment whose punning title alludes to Henry VIII's jester, Will Summers. Nashe's collaboration with BEN JONSON on *The Isle of Dogs* (1597) so offended the authorities that an order for the destruction of all London's theatres was issued, but luckily disobeyed.

**Nathan, George Jean** 1882–1958 American critic. Nathan became drama critic of *Smart Set* in 1909, joining H. L. Mencken who reviewed books. The two served as co-editors from 1914 to 1924, and made *Smart Set* a cult publication among young intellectuals. Their irreverence and iconoclasm seemed to epitomize a generation attempting to rid itself of the Genteel Tradition. They founded the *American Mercury* in 1923 but only Nathan continued as drama critic, until 1932. He founded and edited the *American Spectator* (1932–5). Influenced by JAMES G. HUNEKER and GEORGE BERNARD SHAW, Nathan wrote in a lively, impressionistic style and fought for a drama of ideas. He became a champion of EUGENE O'NEILL, publishing his early plays in *Smart Set*, and arranging for professional productions of his work. He reworked his criticism into books, which appeared almost every year from 1915 until 1953.

**National Theatre** (Britain) The long struggle to establish a national theatre began in the 18th century with calls from DAVID GARRICK, and continued sporadically in the following century. In 1907 a detailed scheme was prepared by WILLIAM ARCHER and HARLEY GRANVILLE BARKER. This led to the formation of a Shakespeare Memorial National Theatre committee, with broad support within the acting profession.

The funds for a building were never forthcoming, either from private or from public sources, and supporters of the OLD VIC actively opposed the SMNT campaign. In 1948 £1,000,000 from public funds were allocated to build a national theatre on the south bank of the Thames in London. These plans were delayed until LAURENCE OLIVIER lent his support to the cause. He was appointed the National Theatre's first director, and it was decided to form a National Theatre company which could operate at the Old Vic until its new theatre building was completed. The National Theatre opened at the Old Vic with a production of *Hamlet* in 1963. The first seasons were triumphantly successful, with Olivier's performance as Othello, PETER SHAFFER's *The*

*Royal Hunt of the Sun* and FARQUHAR's *The Recruiting Officer* providing highlights. Meanwhile, the architect Denys Lasdun was chosen to design a major new complex which would contain three theatres – the open-stage Olivier, the proscenium arch Lyttelton and the experimental 'black-box' Cottesloe – together with large foyers, workshops, restaurants and dressing rooms. The stage technology was considered to be in advance of its time.

The costs rose and the delays were considerable. The new National Theatre complex eventually opened piecemeal in 1976–7. Olivier had given way as director to PETER HALL in 1973, and the company found itself surrounded by controversies to do with costs, subsidy and repertoire. Hall managed to bring together a talented team of writers, directors and designers to work at the NT, including PETER GILL, DAVID HARE and BILL BRYDEN. Under RICHARD EYRE, who succeeded Hall as director in 1988, the NT went through another transformation, with a new emphasis on mainly young writers and directors in addition to the classics. This has led to some exciting experimental theatre, readings of SHAKESPEARE (such as ROBERT LEPAGE's *A Midsummer Night's Dream*, 1992), and several popular hits, although it would have astonished most NT pioneers to have found a revival of a 1940s musical playing for six months on one of the NT's main stages (*Carousel*, 1992). NICHOLAS HYTNER and STEPHEN DALDRY learned to take advantage of the technically advanced stage equipment: Daldry's productions of PRIESTLEY's *An Inspector Calls* (1992) and SOPHIE TREADWELL's *Machinal* (1993) transformed old-fashioned WELL MADE PLAYS into expressionist extravaganzas (see EXPRESSIONISM). Eyre's NT demonstrated the virtues of a postmodern national theatre, putting on glittering productions of a wide range of plays and theatrical happenings, where no distinctions were made between high and low art. It became a lively, unpompous and cheerful playground on the South Bank, where Shakespeare, ALAN BENNETT and RODGERS AND HAMMERSTEIN could meet on equal terms before (mainly) large and enthusiastic audiences.

**National Youth Theatre** (Britain) The actor, novelist and schoolmaster Michael Croft (died 1986) founded this organization in 1956, primarily to give his young school actors a chance to take part in a SHAKESPEARE play, directed to professional standards, during the summer holidays. At first the actors came from Alleyn's School in Southeast London where Croft taught and Dulwich College nearby, but after the company's successes at the EDINBURGH FESTIVAL and in London, students from all over Britain went to audition. During the 1960s the NYT summer seasons, which were held in various London theatres, began to include contemporary plays. The NYT produced DAVID HALLIWELL's *Little Malcolm* in 1965 and, with spectacular success, gave the premiere of PETER TERSON's *Zigger Zagger* in 1967, in which the songs of the football terraces mingled with a gentle warning against soccer hooliganism. The company then moved into the Shaw Theatre in Marylebone Road in central London, where they launched the Dolphin Company, a professional group. Among the many famous actors to have emerged from the ranks of the NYT are DEREK JACOBI and HELEN MIRREN.

**Nationale Scene** (Norway) The National Stage, founded in Bergen in 1876, is one of Norway's three major theatres. As the Norwegian Theatre of 1850, it had IBSEN as its resident playwright and stage director.

The theatre was from the start aggressively innovative, premiering important plays before they were seen in Oslo: *The Wild Duck* (1885), *Rosmersholm* (1887), *The Master Builder* (1894) and *Little Eyolf* (1895). Traditionally it has also been an important training ground for future stars, such as JOHANNE DYBWAD, EGIL EIDE, Ingolf Schanche and TORE SEGELCKE. Among its many inspired artistic directors have been GUNNAR HEIBERG (1884–8), HANS JACOB NILSEN (1934–9), Knut Thomassen (1967–76) and KJETIL BANG-HANSEN (1982–6). Since 1985 Tom Remlov has foregrounded new Norwegian plays there.

**Nationaltheatret** (Norway) Norway's National Theatre opened in Oslo in 1899, the result of the gradual Norwegianization of its predecessor, the originally Danish-speaking Christiania Theatre, founded in 1827. Its first director, BJØRN BJØRNSON, assembled a first-rate company; it remained an unsubsidized private company until 1927, but is now fully government-subsidized. The intimate Amphitheatre Stage opened in 1963 and in 1977 the suburban Theatre in Torshov, where innovative work was done, especially under the direction of STEIN WINGE. From 1986–8, Nationaltheatret's director was KJETIL BANG-HANSEN. Nationaltheatret began the 1990s plagued by financial and artistic crises, and was forced to close the theatre at Torshov.

**naturalism** Although naturalism and REALISM are often assumed to be synonymous, it is useful to distinguish between them. The term 'naturalism' refers to the scientifically based extension of realism propounded by ÉMILE ZOLA in the 1870s and 1880s. In naturalistic writing, medical and evolutionary theories of 19th-century science inform readings of human character and social interactions, which are seen as genetically and historically determined. The struggle of the individual to adapt to environment and the Darwinian idea of the survival of the fittest become central concerns of naturalistic fiction and drama.

Although naturalism in the arts is like realism in being a mimetic genre, it takes more explicit cognizance of environment, not merely as a setting but as an element of the action of drama. If the key play of realism is IBSEN's middle-class *Ghosts*, that of naturalism is LEV TOLSTOI's peasant *Power of Darkness*, forbidden in Russia but played in Paris in 1886. Among the plays often heralded as classics of naturalism are *The Selicke Family* of HOLZ and Schlaf, HAUPTMANN's *Weavers*, GORKY's *Lower Depths*, the minetown plays of D. H. LAWRENCE and the sea plays of EUGENE O'NEILL. These dramas depict a group protagonist in a hostile environment that is visible and sometimes palpable on stage; the group belongs to a distinctly less fortunate class than the usual bourgeois audience.

Although such plays continued to be written – e.g. ARNOLD WESKER's *Roots* – the adjective 'naturalist' has fallen into disuse, replaced in English by 'kitchen-sink drama', in French by *théâtre du* QUOTIDIEN and in German by 'new realism'.

**Naughton, Bill** 1910–92 British playwright. He started to write novels and short stories in the 1940s. His upbringing in Bolton provided the background for two gentle, ironic domestic comedies, *All in Good Time* (1963) and *Spring and Port Wine* (1964). He became the natural successor to the writers of the Manchester school, HOUGHTON, BRIGHOUSE and later Walter Greenwood. But his range was wider: *Alfie* (1963), which provided JOHN NEVILLE with one of his best roles, concerned a Cockney 'wide boy' with a gift for 'pulling the birds'.

Alfie's philandering was presented not in a spirit of moral censoriousness, but with a cool sense of tragic waste, and the play became a parable for the 'swinging sixties'. Naughton also attempted Orwellian SATIRE: *He Was Gone When We Got There* (1966).

**naumachia** (Greek, 'naval battle') Mimed sea combat. Devised by the ancient Romans as a spectacular entertainment, it was staged by constructing a basin in an amphitheatre which was then flooded. The first on record was presented by Julius Caesar on a lake in the Campus Martius (46 BC), as a fight between a Tyrian and an Egyptian fleet, involving 2,000 combatants and 4,000 rowers; the brutality was striking. The Emperors Augustus and Titus also patronized such diversions, and under Claudius (AD 52) a crew of 19,000 gladiators and condemned criminals, costumed as Rhodians and Sicilians, fought and manoeuvred to their deaths. During the Renaissance, the *naumachia* was revived for both popular festivals and noble *divertissements*, especially at weddings. One final efflorescence can be seen in the aquatic dramas produced by CHARLES DIBDIN at SADLER'S WELLS, London (1804–17).

**nautanki** Indian theatre form. Until recently this was one of the most popular kinds of theatre along the heavily populated central Indus-Ganges plain of north India, and primarily found in the villages and towns of Uttar Pradesh, Punjab, Rajasthan, Hariyana and Bihar. Its popularity is due in part to the strong singing voices of its actors, who train to reach crowds of spectators sometimes numbering thousands, and to the catchy rhythms produced on the kettle drums (*nakkaras*).

Nautanki, which may take place virtually anywhere, is organized to celebrate some special occasion, e.g. a wedding, birth of a male child, festival or fair. The plays usually stress the melodramatic and romantic and are drawn from a variety of mythological and historical sources. Their structure is either epic or narrative in form. A typical company consists of 10 to 12 actors. The stage manager (*ranga*) acts as a bridge linking diverse elements of the plot together. Following the preliminary rituals, he introduces the story, and the dramatic action follows. *Nautanki* music is a blend of classical, folk and film music. Although the actors, nowadays women as well as men, are generally Hindus of various lower castes, the musicians are Muslims. Songs dominate the plays, but dialogue is used occasionally to break up the action, and simple dances incorporating film and folk elements are performed for the sake of variety. Improvised comic skits are also used to relieve the tension of the dramas, which are usually serious and highly moralistic in tone.

Today, *nautanki* players find it difficult to survive in a society in which films dominate the public imagination and where television is on the increase.

**Nazimova, Alla** [Alla Yakovlevna Leventon] 1879–1945 Russian actress. She studied with VLADIMIR NEMIROVICH-DANCHENKO, acted with the MOSCOW ART THEATRE, and became a leading lady in St Petersburg. She toured Europe and America and in New York in 1906 she presented English performances of *Hedda Gabler*, *A Doll's House* and *The Master Builder*. She appeared different from the popular personality actresses of the day, able to transform herself externally into different characters. By 1918 her fame had faded, and she was considered another personality actress capitalizing on her sensuous exoticism. After ten years starring in Hollywood films such as *Camille* and *Salome*, she per-

formed with New York's Civic Repertory Theatre and the THEATRE GUILD. In 1935 she directed and starred in her own version of *Ghosts*, after which she returned to film-making.

**Ndao, Cheik (Sidi Ahmed)** 1933– Senegalese playwright, poet and novelist. Although French is his main literary medium, Ndao also writes in English and especially in his mother tongue, Wolof. He is best known as the author of *L'Exil d'Albouri* (*The Exile of Albouri*, 1967), which won first prize at the Pan-African Festival in Algiers in 1969 and has been performed in various parts of French-speaking Africa. He has dramatized the tragic dilemmas encountered by Senegal's 19th-century rulers when confronted by the territorial ambitions of French colonialism, as well as the theme of racialism in the United States and the failures of military dictatorship. His other plays are *La Décision* (1967), *Le Fils de l'almamy* and *La Case de l'homme* (*The Almamy's Son* and *The Hut of Manhood*, 1973), *L'Île de Bahila* (*The Island of Bahila*, 1975), *Du Sang pour un trône* (*Blood for a Throne*, 1983) and, in English, *Tears for Tears* (1977) and *Love but Educate* (1978).

**Nederlander, James** 1922– American producer. One of the major forces in the BROADWAY theatre, Nederlander owns many theatres in the USA and London, second only to the SHUBERT Organization in number. Representative Broadway productions include *Nicholas Nickleby*, *Whose Life Is It Anyway?*, *Orpheus Descending*, *Me and My Girl* and *Shadowlands*.

**Negro Ensemble Company** American company. Established in 1967, the predominantly African-American company inhabited the OFF-BROADWAY St Mark's Theatre. Under DOUGLAS TURNER WARD's inspired leadership, it began to train artists and produce plays relevant to black Americans. Although it was initially criticized for being located outside the black community and producing foreign plays, its successful nurturing of black writers, performers, directors and technicians, and the sustained excellence of its productions, brought international renown. Among its many awards are the 1982 Pulitzer Prize for *A Soldier's Play*, a Tony for *The River Niger* (1973) and 13 Obies for outstanding new plays, performances and productions such as *Dream on Monkey Mountain* (1971), *The First Breeze of Summer* (1975) and *Eden* (1976). Since 1988 the Company has been renting various Off-Broadway theatres while searching for a more permanent home. In 1993 it reopened the NEC Workshop to train students. In the same year the Company produced *Last Night at Ace High* by Kenneth Franklin Hoke-Washington. The subsequent period of financial uncertainty continues.

**Neighborhood Playhouse, The** (New York City) Like the PROVINCETOWN PLAYERS and the WASHINGTON SQUARE PLAYERS, the Neighborhood Playhouse (1915–27) was a pioneering OFF-BROADWAY theatre. Remote both geographically and temperamentally from the commercial theatre, the Playhouse, located on the Lower East Side, was an experimental outpost connected with the Henry Street Settlement House, a social agency for the area's immigrant population. The Playhouse's major interest was in exploring through folk drama the theatre's ritual, lyric, mystical roots. Among its celebrated offerings were an ancient Hindu comedy entitled *The Little Clay Cart* (1924), *The Dybbuk* (1926) and a 14th-century French MYSTERY, as well as more conventional fare such as GALSWORTHY's *The Mob* (1920), O'NEILL's *The First Man* (1922) and James Joyce's

*Exiles* (1924). Organized as an educational and philanthropic enterprise, the Playhouse achieved unexpected renown and star actors performed there, ELLEN TERRY and Ethel Barrymore (see DREW–BARRYMORE FAMILY) among others. The theatre provided an important impetus to Martha Graham and to scene designers ALINE BERNSTEIN and DONALD OENSLAGER, and it generated both the Neighborhood Playhouse School of the Theatre, begun in 1928 and still flourishing, and the Costume Institute of the Metropolitan Museum, founded in 1937.

**Neilson, Adelaide** [Elizabeth Ann Brown] 1848–80 British actress. She played Julia in *The Hunchback* for her stage debut at Margate in 1865 and Juliet for her London and New York debuts (1865 and 1872). Highly regarded as both Juliet and Viola, she was praised for her intelligent conception of the parts and the mixture of gleeful, childlike vitality and deep womanly pathos that she projected. Her other outstanding roles were SHAKESPEARE'S Rosalind, Beatrice, and Isabella; Amy Robsart in *Kenilworth* and Rebecca in *Ivanhoe*. She made several American trips and died suddenly in Paris aged 32.

**Nelson, Richard** 1950– American playwright and dramaturge. Nelson was America's most prolific dramatist during the decade of the 1980s, with such productions as *Rip Van Winkle or 'The Works'* (1981), *The Return of Pinnochio* (1983), *Between East and West* (1984) and *Principia Scriptoriae* (1986). He won awards for *Vienna Notes* (1978) and for his 'innovative programming' while Literary Manager at the Brooklyn Academy of Music. He has adapted a number of classics, such as *The Suicide* (1980), *The Marriage of Figaro* (1982) and *Three Sisters* (1984); was dramaturge for the GUTHRIE THEATRE and wrote the book for the musical *Chess* (1988). His plays have a wide following in England, where he has written radio dramas for the BBC. Both *Americans Abroad* (1989) and *Two Shakespearian Actors* (1990) were first performed at the ROYAL SHAKESPEARE COMPANY prior to Lincoln Center (see VIVIAN BEAUMONT AND MITZI E. NEWHOUSE THEATRES). In 1993 Nelson collaborated with the Russian dramatist Alexandr Gelman over *Misha's Party*. In 1994 Nelson's *New England*, which deals with a family of dispersed English expatriots in America, was staged by the RSC at the Barbican's Pit Theatre.

**Nelson** [Lewysohn], **Rudolf** 1878–1960 German VARIETY manager. By 1904 he was running the elegant CABARET Roland von Berlin. Later he founded the German Chat Noir (1907) and the Metropol-Kabarett (1910), both supplanted by the Nelson-Kunstlerspiele (1919). A gifted Offenbachian composer, he wrote the music for several operettas, and toured with his troupe during 1926–32. The rise of the Nazis exiled him to Amsterdam, where he founded La Gaieté (1934). After the war, he returned to West Berlin and undertook experimental REVUES. His style of cabaret was sophisticated rather than satiric or political.

**Nemirovich-Danchenko, Vladimir (Ivanovich)** 1858–1943 Russian-Soviet director, teacher and playwright. With STANISLAVSKY he co-founded the MOSCOW ART THEATRE (MAT, 1897). He wrote 11 plays, mostly conventional light comedies and melodramas, which achieved popular success. *The Worth of Life* (1896) won the prestigious Griboedov Prize as the season's best play, though he felt it should have gone to CHEKHOV's innovative *The Seagull*, which had been savagely received. From 1891 to 1901 he taught in the Music and

Drama School of the Moscow Philharmonia, whose prize acting students he took with him to the Moscow Art Theatre (1898). On MAT's behalf he revived *The Seagull* and enlisted GORKY to write *The Petty Bourgeoisie* and *The Lower Depths* (1902), even assisting in their creation. With Stanislavsky he co-directed *The Lower Depths* and Chekhov's plays, save for *Ivanov*, which he staged alone. As a dramatist he was especially sensitive to realizing the author's intentions and the play's essence and sought to educate Stanislavsky (who was prone to sentimentality and extraneous detail in his staging) in Chekhov's special lyricism. A number of his MAT productions reflect his penchant for poetry and mysticism, especially Dostoevsky's *The Brothers Karamazov* (1910) and *Nikolai Stavrogin* (from the novel *The Devils*, 1913).

In 1919 Nemirovich-Danchenko organized MAT's Musical Studio, bringing MAT principles of performance to his opera work, replacing the conventional singer with the 'singing actor', rethinking the role of the chorus and striving to capture the music's essence as he did a play's. He was named a People's Artist of the USSR in 1936 and became sole director of MAT following Stanislavsky's death in 1938. His book *My Life in the Russian Theatre* (1937) offers personal opinions about and memories of MAT's halcyon days.

**Nestroy, Johann (Nepomuck)** 1801–62 Austrian actor and playwright. Nestroy made his debut in Vienna at the Theater an der Wien in 1831. From then on he was the most visible and controversial figure of the Viennese theatre. His penetrating wit and fearless attitude towards the Viennese censor (see CENSORSHIP) ensured that he was continually in conflict with authority, which almost landed him in gaol.

Nestroy wrote over 80 plays: these indicate a shift of interest in the Viennese VOLKSSTÜCK from magic to consistently secular matters. The most enduring are *The Evil Spirit Lumpazivagbundus* (1833); *Zu ebener Erde und im ersten Stock* (*On the Ground Floor and the First Storey*, 1835), which employs a split stage to demonstrate class differences; *The Talisman* (1840); *The Girl from the Suburbs* (1841); *Einen Jux will er sich machen* (*He Will Go on a Spree*, 1842), best known to English audiences in THORNTON WILDER's adaptation, *The Matchmaker*; *Der Zerrissene* (*The Torn One*, 1844); and a political SATIRE, *Freedom in Krahwinkel* (1848). He was also a master of PARODY, e.g. in *Judith and Holofernes* (1849), a travesty of HEBBEL's *Judith*. Although his reputation went into steep decline after his death, the 20th century has seen a revival of interest in his work. Interest is likely to remain confined to the German-speaking world as, because of Nestroy's dependence on Viennese dialect and his extraordinarily complex verbal play, his comedies are almost impossible to translate accurately.

**Nethersole, Olga** 1870–1951 British actress-manager. She performed for 26 years, touring Britain, America, Australia and France. She first appeared in America in 1894 in Chicago in *The Transgressor*. Later successes included *Mary Magdalene* and *Camille*. In 1900 her controversial production of *Sappho* was closed by the New York police as immoral. The courts cleared Nethersole; she took the show to London – it was a huge success. She retired at the outbreak of World War I and became a nurse.

**Neuber, Caroline** 1697–1760 German actress. With her husband Johann (1697–1756), Caroline Neuber served as leader of the most successful troupe of travelling players in Germany during the 1720s and 1730s. In cooperation with GOTTSCHED, she attempted to raise the standards of contemporary theatre by abolishing improvisation and by introducing into the repertoire 'regular' tragic drama, translated from or modelled on French tragedy. She had much initial success, though her fortunes declined after breaking with Gottsched in 1741, and her final years were spent in obscurity. As an actress Neuber was most successful in comedy.

**Neville, John** 1925– British actor and director. He achieved national distinction at the OLD VIC (1953–9) as an actor in the classical mould, giving memorable performances as Romeo, Mark Antony and (alternating with RICHARD BURTON) Othello and Iago. In 1963 he became artistic director of the Nottingham Playhouse. Whilst there (for five years) he placed the theatre at the forefront of REPERTORY theatres and demonstrated the range and depth of his acting in roles as diverse as Oedipus and the homosexual barber in Charles Dyer's *Staircase*. Neville eventually moved to Canada, where he was appointed director of the Citadel Theatre, Edmonton, in 1973, and artistic director of the Neptune Theatre in Halifax in 1978. In 1986 he became artistic director of the STRATFORD FESTIVAL in Ontario. Notable television appearances include DAVID STOREY's *Home* (BBC, 1994).

**New Dramatists** American playwrights' organization. Founded in 1949 in New York by Micaela O'Harra with assistance from ROBERT W. ANDERSON, RICHARD RODGERS and HOWARD LINDSAY, New Dramatists exists to 'encourage and develop playwriting in America'. After a screening process, accepted members are provided with a cast and a director for readings of their plays. A critique session with other playwrights and professionals gives the writer a frank evaluation and suggestions for rewriting. Successful alumni include JOHN GUARE, LANFORD WILSON, WILLIAM INGE, ED BULLINS, Megan Terry, MARIA IRENE FORNÉS, PADDY CHAYEFSKY and AUGUST WILSON.

**New York City Theatres** About the mid-18th century, two theatrical companies visited New York, the second of which was composed of professional actors from London. They settled in a theatre on Nassau Street. A company assembled by DAVID DOUGLASS in Jamaica returned to New York in 1758 and built three theatres in the next nine years, including the JOHN STREET THEATRE (1767). The first substantial playhouse to be built in New York was known as the PARK (1798), a distinct improvement over the old, unattractive and uncomfortable John Street house. While the Park dominated theatrical activity through the early years of the 18th century, a more elegant theatre was built on the BOWERY, but quickly fell out of favour with the fashionable class.

By 1825, New York had emerged as the premier theatre city of America. Theatres never strayed too far from BROADWAY, the principal thoroughfare of the city. Stars from England and Europe generally made New York the first stop on their lucrative tours. When the fortunes of the Park waned, other theatres arose to take its place. The comedian BILLY MITCHELL made MITCHELL'S OLYMPIC the most popular theatre on Broadway in the late 1830s and early 1840s. Theatres tended to get bigger and more comfortable, culminating in the 4,500-seat BROADWAY THEATRE, modelled on London's HAYMARKET.

As the city pushed northward, so did the theatres. By mid-century, Broadway was no longer residential: factories, office buildings, shops and department stores mixed with theatres along its way. Playhouses became more attractive architecturally as they reflected the trends from Europe. NIBLO'S GARDEN had a grand foyer for its patrons and most theatres included refreshment stands. In the last decades of the 19th century a theatre district began to form around Union Square. In 1869, EDWIN BOOTH built his elegant theatre at the corner of Sixth Avenue and 23rd Street and provided a new look in theatres (see BOOTH'S THEATRE). CHARLES FROHMAN's EMPIRE THEATRE and Oscar Hammerstein's Olympia signalled the development of a new theatre district around Longacre (later Times) Square. From 1900 to 1928, an unprecedented boom in theatre building provided New York's population with more playhouses than it could support. The new theatres reflected the change in theatrical production. The 19th-century STOCK COMPANY resident in its own theatre was supplanted by the 'combination system', or the assembling of a cast for the presentation of a single play to be produced at a rented theatre. Some 80 theatres were built during this era, all prosceniums, filling Broadway from 39th to 54th Street. Many have been torn down or converted, falling victim to competition from movies, television and the rise of New York's alternative theatre, OFF-BROADWAY and OFF-OFF BROADWAY.

With the recognition that New York's theatres were rapidly becoming an endangered species, steps were taken to protect existing playhouses and the law was changed to permit the incorporation of theatres within tall office buildings, which resulted in the Gershwin and Minskoff Theatres in the early 1970s. Only a few have been protected by the landmark law, and the fate of the others depends heavily on the availability of plays and musicals suitable for production and the willingness of investors.

**New York Shakespeare Festival** American company. It was founded in 1954 by JOSEPH PAPP 'to encourage and cultivate interest in poetic drama with emphasis on ... SHAKESPEARE ... and to establish an annual summer Shakespeare Festival'. Papp believed that theatre should reach a broadly based public, and every summer NYSF performs two free productions in Central Park's Delacorte Theater, built for it in 1957. In 1967 NYSF established the Public Theater in New York's East Village. In 1982, he established the Festival Latino de Nueva York. From his death in 1991 until 1993 JOANNE AKALAITIS took control of the company, to be replaced by George C. Wolfe.

Apart from Shakespeare, NYSF (New York's busiest company) stages new American plays, hosts visiting companies and artists and produces American premieres of European and South American works.

**New Zealand Players** Touring professional company. Founded by Richard and Edith Campion in 1953, with the designer Raymond Boyce, the Players toured the major centres from Wellington several times a year. They offered a repertoire popular enough to compensate for their lack of subsidy (though it included few New Zealand plays) until they collapsed in 1960.

**Ngugi wa Thiong'o** 1938– Kenyan novelist and playwright. His plays in English include *The Black Hermit* (1962), *This Time Tomorrow* (1968) and *The Trial of Dedan Kimathi* (with Micere Mugo). With Ngugi wa Mirii he wrote the draft script of KAMIRIITHU Community Educational and Cultural Centre's Gikuyu play, *Ngaahika Ndeenda* (*I'll Marry When I Want*), and following that, also in Gikuyu, *Maitu Njugira* (*Mother Sing To Me*). Ngugi's work is characterized by the consistent development of early nationalist positions into an anti-imperialist commitment to the cause of peasants and workers in Kenya today; and a parallel development, from individual authorship to collective authorship in Gikuyu and other Kenyan languages. Ngugi now lives in exile. His critical essays, which address issues of language and culture in theatre and literature, are contained in *Decolonising the Mind* (1986) and *Moving the Centre* (1993).

**Niblo's Garden** (New York City) The name derives from the site in the Columbian Gardens chosen by William Niblo to build his theatre in the 1820s. Every kind of entertainment and most of the reigning stars appeared on its stage, in particular the RAVEL FAMILY of comedians and *The Black Crook*, which opened in 1866 and ran for 16 months. In 1892 the theatre was razed.

**Nichols, Anne** c.1891–1966 American playwright. She wrote numerous forgettable plays, VAUDEVILLE sketches and musicals before and after the phenomenal success of her record-breaking *Abie's Irish Rose*. The story of the mixed-up marriage between a Jewish boy and an Irish girl, it ran for 2,327 consecutive nights on BROADWAY (1922–7). Although critics attacked it as a cliché-ridden, ethnic BURLESQUE, the play made a fortune for its author-producer. Called 'the million dollar play', it was revived in 1937 and 1954, filmed in 1928 and 1946, became a radio show in the 1940s and served as the basis of a 1970s sit-com (see TELEVISION DRAMA), *Bridget Loves Bernie*.

**Nichols, Mike** [Michael Igor Peschkowsky] 1931– American actor, director and producer. Born in Berlin, Nichols fled to New York with his parents to escape the Nazis. He studied with LEE STRASBERG at the ACTORS STUDIO and began his professional career in Chicago performing with a comedy group which included Elaine May. In 1957 Nichols and May developed their own act of satirical sketches and improvisations, establishing themselves as major stars. Nichols turned to directing in 1963 with NEIL SIMON's *Barefoot in the Park*. He became renowned for his comic inventiveness in productions of the 1960s, but from the 1970s turned to more serious fare, including *Streamers* (1976), *Comedians* (1976), *The Gin Game* (1977), *The Real Thing* (1983) and *Hurlyburly* (1984). He produced the musical *Annie* (1977) and major films like *Who's Afraid of Virginia Woolf?* (1965), *The Graduate* (1968), *Catch 22* (1970), *Carnal Knowledge* (1971), *Postcards from the Edge* (1990) and *Wolf* (1994).

**Nichols, Peter (Richard)** 1927– British playwright. He started to write television plays (see TELEVISION DRAMA) in the early 1960s. His first stage success came in 1967 with *A Day in the Death of Joe Egg*, about how two parents coped, or not, with their spastic child, a 'vegetable'. This early play demonstrated Nichols's ability to take a painful theme, to handle it with humour that did not minimize despair and to write powerful acting parts. His work falls with deceptive ease into two categories. There are his broad, expansive plays, including *The National Health* (1969) set in a hospital ward for incurables, *The Freeway* (1974) about a Britain choked by a vast traffic jam, *Privates on Parade* (1977) about an army concert party in Malaya after the war which also describes the decline of British colonialism, and *Poppy* (1983) about the opium wars in China, which Nichols conceived as a tatty Victorian panto. The second, more naturalistic, category (see NATURALISM) consists of e.g. *Down Forget-Me-Not Lane* (1971), *Chez Nous* (1974), *Born in the Gardens* (1980) and *Passion Play* (1981), in which the alter egos of the partners in an adulterous marriage are

given a chance to speak. Depressed by the inappropriately lavish production of *Poppy* by the ROYAL SHAKESPEARE COMPANY, he wrote against such national theatre institutions in *A Piece of My Mind* (1986), which was not well received.

**Nicolet, Jean-Baptiste** 1728–96 Parisian showman. He inherited his father's puppet shows at the fairs of St Germain and St Laurent, and soon added live actors, playing the roles of HARLEQUINS and bankers himself. In 1759 he removed to a building in the Boulevard du Temple, amplifying his offerings of pantomimes with comic opera and pieces from the repertory of the COMÉDIE-ITALIENNE. He made an instant success, and for 30 years had to placate the jealousies of the legitimate theatres and the scrutiny of police inspectors. Outside, the theatre performed *scènes à la Momus*, farcical skits; inside, saucy plays were interspersed with acrobats, rope dancers and trained animals. In 1772 Louis XV was amused by the troupe and dubbed it the Théâtre des Grands Danseurs du Roi. Deemed by his rivals illiterate and churlish, Nicolet managed by his intuition of popular taste to amass a fortune and a large company. After the Revolution he renamed his house the Théâtre de la Gaîté and added classics, enjoying a huge success with MOLIÈRE's *Georges Dandin*.

**Nietzsche, Friedrich** 1844–1900 German philosopher. Nietzsche's most substantial contribution to the theatre, his essay *The Birth of Tragedy* (1872), argues that Greek TRAGEDY came about through the eruption of irrational, Dionysian forces into the serenity of Apollonian culture. Tragedy declined, he argued, when it was reduced in scope by EURIPIDES and clarified by Socratic rationalism. Nietzsche's version of Greek drama has often been questioned, and may more correctly be regarded as an argument in support of RICHARD WAGNER's music drama, which, to Nietzsche's mind, exercised a 'Dionysian' influence in the modern 'Socratic' world. Later, he was to repudiate both Wagner and the ideas expressed in *The Birth of Tragedy* (see also GREEK THEATRE, ANCIENT).

**Nieva, Francisco** 1927– Spanish playwright, director and designer. He began writing plays in the 1950s in Paris, but did not achieve professional stagings for more than a decade after returning to Spain. The 1976 production of *Combate de Opalos y Tasia* (*The Battle of Opalos and Tasia*) and *Carroza de plomo candente* (*The Carriage of White-Hot Lead*) won the prestigious Mayte Prize. Other prize-winning productions include his adaptation of CERVANTES's *Los baños de Argel* (*The Baths of Algiers*, 1979), written, directed and designed by Nieva; *La señora Tártara* (*Woman from the Nether Land*, 1980); and *Coronada y el toro* (*Coronada and the Bull*, 1982), staged at the Teatro Nacional María Guerrero, with direction and design by the author. In 1986 he was elected to the Royal Spanish Academy. His plays, often erotic and always wildly funny, are noted for their verbal and visual imagination and for their spirit of transgression.

**Nilsen, Hans Jacob** 1897–1957 Norwegian director and actor. He directed the NORSKE TEATRET (1933–4 and 1946–50), the NATIONALE SCENE (1934–9) and the Folketeatret (1952–5); during the war he joined the Free Norwegian Stage in Sweden. An associate of PER LINDBERG and Halfdan Christensen, Nilsen wanted a people's theatre that was socially committed. Among his major achievements were productions of important (often controversial) new plays, such as GRIEG's *Our Power and Our Glory* (1935) and the ČAPEK brothers' *The*

*Insect Comedy* (1939); and re-evaluations of classics, such as his 1948 'anti-romantic' *Peer Gynt* and his 1934 spirited, cartoon-like *Jeppe of the Hill*. As an actor he achieved particular success as Hamlet, Peer Gynt and Masterbuilder Solness.

**Ninagawa Yukio** 1935– Japanese director. Ninagawa trained as an actor in the Seihai Theatre Company, where SHINGEKI orthodoxy based on NATURALISM and REALISM was promoted. When the *angura* (underground) theatre movement evolved in Tokyo in the late 1960s, he left the STC and formed Gendaijin Gekijyō (Contemporary People's Theatre, 1967–72) and then Sakura Sha (the Sakura Troupe, 1972–4). With these companies he staged several plays by Shimitzu Kunio, including *Silliness Filled with Sincerity*, which became a milestone of contemporary Japanese theatre. In 1974 Ninagawa directed *Romeo and Juliet* for one of the largest commercial companies in Japan. In 1983 he formed the Ninagawa Studio Theatre. Productions from the European classical theatre included *Macbeth*, *Medea*, *Oedipus Rex* and *The Tempest*. From the Japanese repertoire major productions included Akimoto Matsuyo's *Tale of Chikamatsu's Love Suicide* (1989), Yukio Mishima's *Sotoba Komachi* (1990) and – for the NATIONAL THEATRE in London in 1991 – Shimitzu Kunio's *Tango at the End of Winter* (Ninagawa's first production in English). In 1994 his production of *Peer Gynt* was staged in Oslo, London and Manchester.

**nō** Japanese dance drama. *Nō* is a serious and subtle form that evolved in Japan in the 14th century out of earlier songs, dances and sketches. It was originally performed by priests attached to Buddhist temples. In performance, movement, music and words create a shifting web of tension and ambiguity. A *nō* text contains prose and poetry sections. Prose is delivered in a sonorous voice that rises gradually and evenly in pitch, then drops at the end of a phrase. This typically repeating pattern is heard in all plays and varies only slightly by character type (no attempt is made by the male actors to reproduce the female voice). Poetry sections are sung (indicated by the musical term *fushi*, melody) by the Doer (*shite*), Sideman (*waki*) or Chorus (*ji*), and make up the bulk of the text.

Acceptance of change underlies the requirement that the *nō* actor must always seek newness or freshness (*hana*, flower) in performance. The actor should never do what is expected, but rather, by analysing the performance situation – the audience, the season, the time of day, previous plays on the bill – he should choose a play and an interpretation that will elicit audience interest by being unexpected. There is no single correct way of acting, the actor-playwright-theorist ZEAMI MOTOKIYO wrote in *The Way of the Flower*; there are only more or less appropriate ways of interesting audiences under specific circumstances. It is possible to be interesting by harmonizing the performance with the situation (e.g. a celebratory play in the New Year season), but juxtaposing opposites – the Chinese theory of *yin* and *yang* – is more highly recommended: a strong demon role should be acted with a degree of gentleness; when the day is gloomy choose a lively piece. Following this theory, a male actor playing a female role in *nō* is inherently interesting because of the contrast between the actor's masculinity and the character's femininity. In all cases, says Zeami, audience approval is the aim of the actor.

The *nō* stage, which took numerous forms before 1600, became standardized around that date. It consists of a raised dancing platform about 19ft square. Above the floor of polished cyprus wood there is a temple-like roof supported by pillars at the four corners. Role types have conventional locations on the stage. Outdoor, freestanding *nō* theatres are found in the grounds of many temples and shrines and are used at festival times. The typical *nō* theatre in Japan today, however, is a conventional stage within a modern building. It is used daily for training and several days a week for public performances. There are several major *nō* theatres in Tokyo, Kyoto and Osaka.

**Noah, Mordecai M(anuel)** 1785–1851 American playwright. Noah was an active Zionist, political figure and journalist who sought diversion in the theatre. His ardent patriotism was reflected in his documentary-like plays, all based on recent events: *She Would Be a Soldier, or The Plains of Chippewa* (1819), which became a popular piece for national holidays; *The Siege of Tripoli* (1820); *Marion, or The Hero of Lake George* (1821); *The Grecian Captive* (1822) and *The Siege of Yorktown* (1824).

**Noble, Adrian (Keith)** 1950– British director. Having been an associate director of the BRISTOL OLD VIC (1976–9), he was a guest director at the ROYAL EXCHANGE THEATRE, Manchester, in 1980–1, where his productions of *The Duchess of Malfi* (1980; with HELEN MIRREN) and *A Doll's House* (1981) won critical acclaim. From 1980 to 1982, Noble was resident director with the ROYAL SHAKESPEARE COMPANY, becoming an associate director in 1982; here his productions of *King Lear* (1982) and *Henry V* (1984) were notable. To present Lear and the Fool, played by MICHAEL GAMBON and ANTHONY SHER, as a BECKETT-like couple from a Shakespearian *Waiting for Godot* was a bold gamble which nearly worked at Stratford-upon-Avon. His version of *Mephisto* (1986), without much in the way of a devil, was less happy. His compression of the three parts of *Henry IV* and *Richard III* into a trilogy, *The Plantagenets* (1988), was outstanding.

Noble took over from TERRY HANDS as RSC director in 1990, staging the two parts of *Henry IV* (1991) and three plays by SOPHOCLES, collectively known as *The Thebans* (1991). His exciting production of *Hamlet* (1992), with a virtually uncut text, featured KENNETH BRANAGH as the Prince. In the 1993/4 season he directed *King Lear* with ROBERT STEPHENS, *Macbeth* with DEREK JACOBI, *The Winter's Tale* and TOM STOPPARD's *Travesties*. Noble's ability to provide a clear, uncomplicated reading of the text, allowing an uncluttered central performance to emerge, was demonstrated with particular succcess in *King Lear*.

**Noda Hideki** 1955– Japanese playwright, director and actor. Noda's Dream Theatre Company was born in 1976 from the University of Tokyo, where he was a law student. His first play performed outside the university was *Run Merusu* (1976), since when his plays have attracted large audiences. They include *Hunting Boys* (1979), *The Capture in Zenda Castle* (1981) and *The Fallen Beasts* (1982). His rich, garrulous language blends absurd (see THEATRE OF THE ABSURD) and fantastic storylines from East and West, requiring a dynamic and athletic style of acting, and spacious and spectacular design.

**Noguchi, Isamu** 1904–88 American sculptor and designer. Although he designed almost solely for dance, his abstract design and use of objects, and his ability to focus the cubic volume of the stage space, had a significant effect on mid-20th-century design. Born in Los Angeles, Noguchi moved to Japan as a child and remained there until 1917 before returning to the USA. In 1926 he went to Paris, where he was an assistant to the sculptor Brancusi. His first theatre work was also in 1926, when he designed masks for YEATS's *At the Hawk's Well*. From 1935 to 1966 he collaborated with choreographer Martha Graham. Drawing on the tradition of NŌ and the vocabulary of his own sculptures, his designs were simple distillations of images creating psychological rather than literal space. Noguchi also designed for George Balanchine (*Orpheus*, 1948), Erick Hawkins, Merce Cunningham and the ROYAL SHAKESPEARE COMPANY (*King Lear*, 1955).

**non-profit theatre (USA)** see RESIDENT THEATRE

**Norén, Lars** 1944– Swedish playwright and poet. His widely performed plays explore relationships that have become brutal struggles for self-preservation. A recurrent motif is the child, emotionally stunted by parental neglect. Significant plays are *Demons* (1982), *Communion* (1985) and two trilogies: one of contemporary life (1981–3), consisting of *A Terrifying Joy*, *When They Burned Butterflies on the Small Stage* and *The Smile of the Underworld*; a second (1978–84) consists of the partly autobiographical plays *The Courage to Kill*, *Night Is the Mother of Day* and *Chaos Is a Neighbour of God*. Later plays include *Autumn and Winter* (1989), *Dragonflies* (1989), *And Grant Us the Shadows* (1991) and *Time is Our Home* (1992).

**Norman, (John) Frank** 1930– British playwright. Brought up in a Dr Barnardo's home, he worked as a farm labourer and with a travelling fair and served several short prison sentences for minor crimes. His two autobiographical accounts of prison life, *Bang to Rights* (1958) and *Stand on Me* (1961), earned him a reputation as an authority on low life and cockney slang. With Lionel Bart he wrote the successful musical, *Fings Ain't Wot They Used T'Be* (1959), set in London's Soho, which was produced by JOAN LITTLEWOOD at the Theatre Royal, Stratford East, and had a long WEST END run. Further musicals with Joan Littlewood's company followed, but they were less successful. In 1969, his play *Insideout* was produced at the ROYAL COURT THEATRE; but since the early 1970s he has mainly written novels, reminiscences and studies of London's underworld.

**Norman, Marsha** 1947– American playwright. Her realistic characters confront some devastation in their past to determine whether and how to survive. *Getting Out* (1978) reveals the internal conflict of a woman on parole in her choice for a new beginning, dramatized by two actresses who simultaneously portray her violent, younger self and her present, numbed self. *'night, Mother* enacts the last night in the life of a hopeless young woman as she prepares herself and her mother for her suicide and the mother's desperate attempts to prevent it. Other works include *Third and Oak: The Laundromat (and) The Pool Hall* (1978), *The Holdup* (1980), *Traveler in the Dark* (1984), *Winter Shakers* (1987), *Sarah and Abraham* (1988, a musical with Norman L. Berman), *Loving Daniel Boone* (1993), and several television plays and screenplays. An eight-year absence from BROADWAY ended with *The Secret Garden* (1991), a musical based on Frances Hodgson Burnett's classic novel, followed in 1993 with *The Red Shoes*, with lyrics and book by Norman.

**Norske Teatret** (Oslo) Norwegian company. The Norske Teatret, one of Norway's three most significant companies, is devoted to performance in Nynorsk (New Norwegian), one of two official forms of the language. Derived from provincial dialects, in contrast to the Danish-derived Norwegian of the capital, it remains part of an ongoing movement to strengthen indigenous culture. Founded in 1913, thanks to the efforts of Arne and Hulda Garborg, the theatre established other traditions in addition to those of language, including commitments to touring and new drama. It became one of the most avant-garde in Scandinavia, despite its inadequate facilities. From the start, it attracted superb actors and directors. Since 1985 it has occupied one of Europe's most modern theatres, with several stages, huge workshops and advanced equipment.

**Norton, (William) Elliot** 1903– American drama critic. Norton studied with GEORGE PIERCE BAKER at Harvard University and became drama critic on the *Boston Post* in 1934, and later on Hearst's *Record American*. He acquired the reputation of being honest and reliable about new shows that were BROADWAY-bound. He was not a great stylist nor did his reviews break new critical ground, but New York producers respected his opinion and altered their shows accordingly.

**Norton, Thomas** see SACKVILLE, THOMAS

**Novelli, Ermete** 1851–1919 Italian actor and company manager. He established his own companies from 1884, his repertoire consisting largely of stock pieces, in which he showed the wide range of his talent – from GOLDONI to DUMAS. It was for his versatility, indeed, that he was perhaps most noted. He occasionally attempted SHAKESPEARE, most successfully with *King Lear* and *The Merchant of Venice*, and toured widely in Europe and South America.

**Novo, Salvador** 1904–74 Mexican playwright. Novo was instrumental in founding the TEATRO DE ULISES with his friend XAVIER VILLAURRUTIA, thereby launching the independent theatre movement in Mexico in 1928. A serious director, actor and critic, he wrote several major plays, many of them based on classical Greek or Mexican characters. Of special note are *Yocasta, o casi* (*Jocasta, or Almost*, 1961), *Ha vuelto Ulises* (*Ulysses Has Returned*, 1961), *In Pipiltzintzin o La guerra de las gordas* (*The War of the Large Ladies*, 1963) and *In Ticitezcatl o El espejo encantado* (*The Enchanted Mirror*, 1965).

**Nowra, Louis** 1950– Australian playwright. His plays, often with exotic or historical settings, depict the private worlds of illusion, obsession and madness under pressure from external power structures, and are characterized by episodic construction, heightened language and powerful, even lurid, theatrical effects. They include two radio plays, *Albert Named Edward* (1975) and *The Song Room* (1980); *Inner Voices* (1977), *Visions* (1978), *Inside the Island* (1980), *The Precious Woman* (1980), *Sunrise* (1983); and a TELEVISION DRAMA, *Displaced Persons* (1985). He has completed two plays of a semi-autobiographical trilogy – *Summer of the Aliens* (1992), set in an outer-suburban housing estate in the 1960s, and *Cosí* (1992), about an attempt to stage Mozart's opera with a group of mental patients – as well as a SATIRE on big business, *The Temple* (1993); and *Radiance* (1993), for three Aboriginal woman performers.

**nudity** For prurient effect nudity on stage was already common in the Roman MIME, which provided undressing scenes for female performers. Christianity was scandalized by both nakedness and the theatre, and the emperor Justinian imposed trousers on all mime artists, tumblers and acrobats. The medieval Church banned public nudity, so that the Adam and Eve of the

MYSTERY PLAYS were clad in form-fitting doeskin. Princely pageants were exempt from the ecclesiastical strictures: at the entry of Charles VII into Paris in 1437 three naked girls swam in an ornamental fountain. Allegorical nudes occasionally turned up in the festivals and MASQUES of the Renaissance.

With the common acceptance of women as actors, the exposure of breasts and legs became a popular allurement, and was equated by the authorities with full nudity. 'Historical accuracy' demanded looser draperies on dancers, so tights became de rigueur c.1780, soon to be followed by trunks and the tutu. In the 19th century LIVING PICTURES and poses plastiques featured naked or semi-clothed women. FRÉDÉRIC SOULIÉ applied the principle of static nudity to drama in Christine à Fontainebleau (ODÉON, 1829) by showing a naked woman on a dissecting table. The fleshings of ADAH ISAACS MENKEN won her the billing of 'the Naked Lady' and LOLA MONTEZ created a scandal by omitting tights during her dances. But most of what passed for flesh on stage was cunningly dyed fabric: Cassive in FEYDEAU's The Lady from Maxim's (1899) appeared in bed in flesh-coloured tights under a corset and still managed to scandalize.

The strip-tease, a RITUAL wherein various garments are serially discarded leaving the performer more or less totally undressed, was, according to legend, first performed by a certain Mona at the MOULIN-ROUGE in 1893. In America legend relates that it was introduced by the trapeze artist Charmian, who inadvertently lost her tights during a performance; by 1920 it had become a BURLESQUE attraction, later perfected as a 'dance' by GYPSY ROSE LEE. Originally, at the climax a blackout or fall of the curtain supervened; certain wardrobe items, the 'pasties' that covered the nipples, would often be flung to the audience, but the cache-sexe or G-string usually stayed in place. Later, the performers at such tourist traps as Paris's Crazy-Horse Saloon (opened 1953) would leave nothing to the imagination.

Five stark-naked beauties were seen at a REVUE at the Variétés (see BOULEVARD; 1901); Colette Willy appeared stripped to the waist in the pantomime La Chair (1907); and an undressed dancer first appeared at the FOLIES-BERGÈRE in 1912. After 1918, in reaction to pre-war prudery, the Naktballett emerged in Berlin; by 1922, it had become widespread throughout Germany. Influenced by Isadora Duncan, by the physical culture movement and by sports, undraped dancing based on classical art remained popular in CABARETS until about 1927.

In the Anglo-Saxon world, however, stage nudity was permissible only if it was inert, as in the lavish tableaux staged for ZIEGFELD. In the 1960s, nudity became a tactical weapon of the alternative theatre, a direct assault on middle-class sensibilities and an alignment with 'Nature'. 1968 was its annus mirabilis, when the rock musical Hair displayed its unclad cast frontally; the LIVING THEATRE's players were arrested in San Francisco for disrobing; and Sally Kirkland became the first New York dramatic actress to appear fully nude throughout an entire play, in TERRENCE MCNALLY's Sweet Eros. The commercial theatre was quick to adopt this licence in Oh, Calcutta! (1969), whose company, male and female, shed its bathrobes in the first moments. Soon full-frontal nudity could be seen in London in DÜRRENMATT's Meteor, in Paris in Panizza's Council of Love and in Frankfurt in HANDKE's Self-Accusation. German directors have been particularly active in defoliating their lead actresses. That male nudity, at least in motion and at a state theatre, still had the power to shock was clear from the flustered overreaction to HOWARD BRENTON's The Romans in Britain (1980).

Frontal male nudity soon turned from a token of stage REALISM (as in DAVID STOREY's The Changing Room, (1971)) to a touchstone of gender identification (David Henry Hwang's M. Butterfly, (1989)). Having become a convention of homosexual drama, as in Robert Patrick's Mercy Drop (1973) and T Shirts (1978) and Terrence McNally's The Lisbon Traviata (1985), used both to shock a straight audience and appeal to a gay one, it was carried over into JOHN GUARE's mainstream comedy Six Degrees of Separation (1990).

In the US a 1991 Supreme Court decision permitted communities to ban nude dancing for reasons of 'public morality'. Such a resurgence of CENSORSHIP creates a chilling climate that compels actors to put their clothes back on. However, performance artists like Karen Finley and Annie Sprinkle exaggerate and abuse their own naked bodies to make political statements about sexual exploitation, while contemporary choreographers have attempted to abstract nudity as a formal element of composition.

**Nuevo Grupo** (New Group) Venezuelan theatre group. Created in 1967 and headed by a triumvirate, ISAAC CHOCRÓN, ROMÁN CHALBAUD and JOSÉ IGNACIO CABRUJAS, it was instrumental in establishing the standards for the contemporary theatre movement in Venezuela. The group operated two theatres, which provided the best international and national plays. Alternating as authors, directors and actors, this 'Holy Trinity', as they have been called, was at the forefront of the group until it folded in 1988.

**Núñez, José Gabriel** 1937– Venezuelan playwright and critic. He has been an active force in Venezuelan theatre and television since he began to write in 1967. Principal works are Parecido a la felicidad (Similar to Happiness, 1969), El largo camino del Edén (The Long Road to Eden, 1970), Madame Pompinette (1981) and María Cristina me quiere gobernar (María Cristina Wants to Govern Me, 1984).

**Nunn, Trevor (Robert)** 1940– British director. He started to direct plays with the Marlowe Society at Cambridge University. He joined the ROYAL SHAKESPEARE COMPANY in 1965 and succeeded PETER HALL as the RSC's artistic director in 1968. In 1978, he became chief executive and joint artistic director with TERRY HANDS. He also directed in the commercial theatre, where in 1981 he staged the hit musical, Cats, and in 1984, Starlight Express. He is perhaps the best all-round director currently working in British theatre. His range of productions at the RSC is unequalled for its richness and variety – SHAKESPEARE's 'Roman' plays in 1972, a musical version of The Comedy of Errors (1976), the studio Macbeth (1976) and his Edwardian All's Well That Ends Well (1981). In 1980 he collaborated with John Caird, DAVID EDGAR and the RSC to bring together Nicholas Nickleby in two substantial evenings, presenting a vivid picture of CHARLES DICKENS's London. Possessing a fine eye for scenic pictures on the stage, a sound instinct for style and historical appropriateness, he has rivalled American directors at staging musicals. Under his guidance the RSC became a world-renowned company. He handed over to his co-director Terry Hands in 1986, but remained prolific as a freelance, e.g. with Othello (1989), the musical Aspects of Love (1989) and

SHAW's *Heartbreak House* (1992). In 1992 he had six shows in the WEST END.

**nurseries** English training companies for young actors. Under patents granted to them, WILLIAM DAVENANT and THOMAS KILLIGREW in 1660 acquired the right to establish 'nurseries' in London. There were at least three. One was established by Killigrew in 1667 in Hatton Garden and operated until 1669. One was set up by Lady Davenant, Sir William's widow, in the Barbican in 1671. One was run by John Perin at Bun Hill in Finsbury Fields, also in 1671. At various times GEORGE JOLLY was involved in the running of the nurseries. Few of their actors appear to have graduated to the professional adult stage.

**Nušić, Branislav** 1864–1938 Serbian playwright. His comedies have been part of the national repertory for almost a century. Born and educated in law in Belgrade, Nušić was imprisoned for writing an anti-dynastic poem at the time of his first theatrical success, *A Suspicious Person* (1887). Later he was head of theatres in Belgrade and other cities. His patriotic historic tragedies and his heavily moralistic domestic dramas have remained completely overshadowed by his popular comedies, in which figures of a patriarchal Serbian mentality are shown in transition from an agrarian Oriental state towards urban and European aspirations. Nušić's incompetent bureaucrats, corrupt politicians, town gossips and con-men, his *nouveau riche* merchants and their quasi-Westernized offspring, have served as effective vehicles for generations of comic actors. Often performed in the Slavic world and in Germany, Austria and Hungary, his most significant plays are *The Cabinet Minister's Wife* (1929) and *The Bereaved Family* (1934).

**Oberammergau** Village in Upper Bavaria by whose name a PASSION PLAY is known. Following a severe outbreak of the Black Death in 1633, the inhabitants of this village vowed to perform a Passion play every ten years if they were spared from further deaths. At that time the late medieval Passion play tradition in the south of the German-speaking area was still alive. Their original play was based on the 15th-century manuscript from Augsburg known as the Augsburg Passion Play and on the Passion play by Sebastian Wild from the same city. The version of the text currently used was written originally for the 1810 performance by the Benedictine priest Othmar Weis from the nearby Ettal monastery, and the music was composed at the same time by the village schoolmaster Rochus Dedler. The text has been revised several times since; recently this has involved removal of anti-Jewish statements. The current version consists of two sessions each of some three hours' duration performed in the morning and in the late afternoon, and includes 17 *tableaux vivants* (see LIVING PICTURE) of the Glorified Christ.

**Obey, André** 1892–1975 French playwright. The COMPAGNIE DES QUINZE commissioned and staged five of his plays at the VIEUX-COLOMBIER theatre. These included his first and best play *Noah* (1931), later staged with equal success by the group's director, MICHEL SAINT-DENIS (London, 1935). Other plays included a new version of the Don Juan story, staged by COPEAU in 1937 as *Le Trompeur de Séville* and by the COMÉDIE-FRANÇAISE in 1949 as *L'Homme de cendres*. Obey was director of the Comédie-Française for one year (1946/7). His plays combine mythical archetype with modern setting in a manner reminiscent of GIRAUDOUX.

**Obraztsov, Sergei (Vladimirovich)** 1901–91 Russian actor and puppeteer. Obraztsov made his acting debut at the MOSCOW ART THEATRE Musical Studio in 1922, and the next year appeared as a solo puppeteer. In 1931 he became artistic director of the newly founded State Central Puppet Theatre, Moscow. He has staged more than 50 PUPPET plays, made documentary films and written several books, including *The Actor and the Puppet* (1938). He toured Europe (1950/1, 1966, 1970), demonstrating his virtuosity with satirical sketches and magical fantasies.

**O'Casey, Sean** 1880–1964 Irish playwright. Coming from an impoverished lower-middle-class Protestant family and having been active in the Republican and Labour movements, O'Casey became disillusioned by the shift from socialism to Catholic nationalism and withdrew from political and militant organizations, remaining a lifelong 'proletarian communist'. In 1923 the ABBEY accepted *The Shadow of a Gunman*. Its period is the Anglo-Irish war which led to the 1921 Settlement. *Juno and the Paycock* (1924), set in the Civil War after the Settlement, and *The Plough and the Stars* (1926), an antiheroic version of the 1916 Rising, completed his 'Dublin trilogy'. *The Shadow* and *Juno* were popular successes and repaired the Abbey's rocky finances. *The Plough* attracted riotous abuse.

In 1928 the Abbey directors refused *The Silver Tassie*, O'Casey's pacifist play about World War I, objecting to its expressionist second act (see EXPRESSIONISM). Now living in England, he broke with the Abbey. His later work is informed by his communist beliefs, and formally symbolic, stylized and experimental: *Within the Gates* (first production 1934), *The Star Turns Red* (1940), *Red Roses for Me* (1943), *Purple Dust* (1945), *Oak Leaves and Lavender* (1947), *Cock-a-Doodle-Dandy* (1949), *The Bishop's Bonfire* (1955) and *The Drums of Father Ned* (1958).

A common judgement has been that O'Casey's Dublin trilogy is his masterpiece, which he never again equalled: brilliant comic invention collaborates with tragic, often brutal, action. Of the later plays only *Red Roses* is set in Dublin. It movingly evokes the 1913 Lockout, effectively using song, dance and MIME. *The Star* (placed in a heavily symbolic Dublin), *Gates* and *Dust* are political allegories, restlessly seeking form appropriate to 'message'. *Bonfire*, *Cock-a-Doodle* and *Father Ned* return to Irish villages. Abbey productions of the 1970s and 1980s showed that the later plays, despite their reputation, can have a vigorous stage presence.

**October Group** French AGIT-PROP theatre company. Many of its short plays were scripted by Jacques Prévert and distinguished by playful wit and biting SATIRE. An example is *The Battle of Fontennoy* (1933), which presented World War I as a spectator sport in which lives were sacrificed in the name of hypocritical idealism while the population (the spectators) bayed for blood. The Group operated from 1933 to 1936; they represented France at the Moscow Theatre Olympiad of 1933, where they won first prize.

**Odéon, Théâtre de l'** (Paris) French theatre. The 1,900-seat theatre in the Latin quarter was built to house the COMÉDIE-FRANÇAISE in 1782. It was the first to introduce benches into the pit. BEAUMARCHAIS's *Marriage of Figaro* was first produced there in 1784. In 1789 the more revolutionary members of the troupe, including TALMA, moved to the Théâtre de la République, which became the Comédie-Française in 1799. From 1794 to 1797 the theatre was closed, then opened under the name Odéon. Twice burnt, it became the Second Théâtre-Français in 1818. Here the first plays of CASIMIR DELAVIGNE were performed. Under HAREL (1829–32) there were productions of AUGIER's *Le Ciguë* (*Hemlock*) and a move towards REALISM with George Sand's *François le Champi*. MUSSET's *Carmosine* was shown there in 1865.

In 1866 SARAH BERNHARDT became one of the leading actresses, turning it into a field hospital during the siege of Paris in 1870. In 1906 ANDRÉ ANTOINE became director for the second time, installing an up-to-date lighting system and getting rid of the old chandelier which had remained lit throughout performances. Before World War I his company set new standards of truth to life and quality of ensemble playing. The next major figure was FIRMIN GÉMIER. In 1946 the theatre became the second house of the Comédie-Française, used particularly for modern works, while the classics remained at the Salle Richelieu. In 1959 André Malraux, minister of culture under de Gaulle, installed the Renaud-BARRAULT company there instead. Here they performed some of the key plays in the recent history of French theatre, including *Rhinoceros* by IONESCO (1960) and *The Screens* by GENET (1966), provoking riots both inside and outside the theatre.

From 1967 to 1970 the performances of the THÉÂTRE DES NATIONS were given at the Odéon and for a month in 1968 the theatre was occupied by students. From 1971 onwards, the company again came under the administration of the Comédie-Française. Companies of the decentralization movement also use it as a Paris showcase for their best productions. In 1983 the theatre became, for six months of each year, the Théâtre de l'Europe under the direction of GIORGIO STREHLER; in 1990 this arrangement became full-time and Strehler was succeeded by LLUÍS PASQUAL.

**Odets, Clifford** 1906–63 American playwright. In American theatre history, Odets is the one true company playwright. He absorbed the teachings of HAROLD CLURMAN and LEE STRASBERG at the GROUP THEATRE and in 1935 they presented *Waiting for Lefty*, his incendiary play about taxi drivers driven to call a strike. In a series of short, jabbing scenes written in urban folk idiom, Odets expressed the feelings of the dispossessed working class. *Lefty* released the full potential of the new realistic acting style (see REALISM) that Group members had been investigating for four years. Later in the same year they produced two other Odets plays, *Awake and Sing!* and *Paradise Lost*, family dramas whose Jewish sufferers speak a metaphorical language of their own. Odets left for Hollywood at the end of his triumphant year, but in 1937 presented the Group with a new play, *Golden Boy*. The hero's hard choice between being a violinist and a prize fighter expresses Odets's own conflict about whether to serve art or commerce. The play proved to be the Group's biggest moneymaker. Odets's final works for the Group were *Rocket to the Moon* (1938) and *Night Music* (1940). His four remaining dramas – *Clash by Night* (1941), *The Big Knife* (1949), *The Country Girl* (1950) and *The Flowering Peach* (1954) – lack the vibrant urgency of the plays written against the background of the Depression. Odets is now regarded as the quintessential 1930s playwright, who transmuted working-class pressures into timeless drama.

**Odin Teatret** Denmark-based, international company. The Nordisk Teaterlaboratorium for Skuespillerkunst (Nordic Theatrical Arts Laboratory) is a theatrical community founded in Oslo in 1964 by the expatriate Italian EUGENIO BARBA, who had just returned from three years with GROTOWSKI in Opole. The company's first production, *Ortofilene*, toured Scandinavia with such success that the town of Holstebro, Denmark, invited them to create a permanent theatre there. Since 1966 this has been the company's base, though it also tours extensively.

The Holstebro company opened in September 1967 with *Kaspariana* (based on the strange life of Kaspar Hauser, 1812–33) and followed this in 1969 with *Ferai*, scripted by Peter Seeberg on the basis of Scandinavian mythology and EURIPIDES' *Alcestis*. Shown at the THÉÂTRE DES NATIONS in Paris, it brought them the international reputation that they have enjoyed ever since. The ideas and training methods of Grotowski remain central to the company's work: a community of actors living under a strict regime of taxing physical and vocal exercise, and at the same time involved in policy and organization; creating performances which arise from their personal confrontation with source-materials, techniques and each other; appearing before the public, often to deliberately small audiences, only when they feel that they have something to show.

In the 1970s the company began to mount CLOWN

shows, street parades and improvised musical performances, and developed its 'barter-principle', whereby, instead of paying in cash for a performance, the audience offer in return their own performance or a commitment to some local project. During the 1980s and 1990s, as well as continuing to mount anti-naturalistic productions such as *Brecht's Ashes* (1982) and *Oxyrhincus Evangelist* (1985), Odin has been a leading contributor to the work of the International School of Theatre Anthropology.

**Oehlenschläger, Adam** 1779–1850 Danish poet and playwright. His early work reflected his romantic ideals. His poem 'The Golden Horns' (1803) proclaimed a renaissance of ancient Nordic culture and mythology, which provided the subject-matter for many of the plays he wrote in imitation of GOETHE and SCHILLER, including *Hakon Jarl* and *Baldur the Good* (both 1807), *Staerkodder* (1812) and *Hagbarthe and Signe* (1815). However, in the theatre only the much more fanciful *Midsummer Night's Play* (1803) and *Aladdin* (1805) have continued to be staged into the 20th century. In the 1820s his reputation suffered from the criticisms of JOHAN LUDVIG HEIBERG.

**Oenslager, Donald** 1902–75 American set designer and teacher. His influences include GEORGE PIERCE BAKER, the work of APPIA and CRAIG which he saw in Europe in 1921, and ROBERT EDMOND JONES whom he assisted in the early 1920s. Oenslager designed some 250 productions including *Anything Goes*, *You Can't Take It with You* and *The Man Who Came to Dinner*. Although he emphasized the need to find the proper style for each play, his designs were frequently decorative and elegant. His greatest influence, however, was as a teacher – he was a professor of design at Yale University from 1925 until 1971, and many of the major figures in American design were trained by him. He is author of *Scenery Then and Now* and *Four Centuries of Theatre Design*.

**Off-Broadway** Non-Broadway New York theatre. The term was coined in the 1950s to designate the smaller theatres (100–299 seats) outside the so-called BROADWAY area surrounding Times Square. The Off-Broadway movement has roots in the early 1900s, beginning as the LITTLE THEATRE MOVEMENT among New York's intelligentsia, with groups such as the WASHINGTON SQUARE PLAYERS and the PROVINCETOWN PLAYERS staging, in an inexpensive, non-commercial atmosphere, plays that Broadway producers ignored.

In the 1950s and early 1960s Off-Broadway became an artistic magnet. Serious attention started with the 1952 revival of TENNESSEE WILLIAMS's *Summer and Smoke* by the infant CIRCLE IN THE SQUARE. Such companies as the LIVING THEATRE, Circle in the Square, Phoenix Theatre, NEW YORK SHAKESPEARE FESTIVAL, American Place Theatre, NEGRO ENSEMBLE COMPANY, Roundabout Theatre Company, Chelsea Theatre Centre, CIRCLE REPERTORY and MANHATTAN THEATRE CLUB presented premieres and revivals of neglected plays or plays that had failed on Broadway. Over the years, Off-Broadway theatres premiered such works as BECKETT's *Endgame* and *Play*, ALBEE's *The Zoo Story*, Gelber's *The Connection*, Jones and Schmidt's *The Fantasticks* (America's longest-running play, opening in 1960), GENET's *The Blacks*, ORTON's *What the Butler Saw*, Bernard Pomerance's *The Elephant Man*, CHARLES FULLER's *A Soldier's Play* and CARYL CHURCHILL's *Cloud 9* and *Fen*.

After the 1960s, Off-Broadway became a smaller version of Broadway, leaving the experimentation and discovery mostly to OFF-OFF BROADWAY. Today, Off-Broadway concentrates on commercial revivals of classics or older standards, and a few new works by established but younger playwrights. (See also NEW YORK CITY THEATRES.)

**Off-Off Broadway** Non-commercial New York theatre. The term was coined in the early 1960s to distinguish professional, commercial theatre (BROADWAY and OFF-BROADWAY) from non-commercial theatre presented in coffee houses, churches, lofts and storefronts in New York's Greenwich Village and Lower East Side. Technically, the term also refers to productions that fall under the American Actors' Equity non-profit code for performances with limited runs that feature unsalaried union actors in small theatres. Off-Off Broadway is often considered an alternative theatre movement grounded in experimentation, and questioning the limits of performance. The initial impulse was to generate new approaches and methods in a climate free from the demands of popular taste that inform commercial theatre. Frequently, though, Off-Off Broadway productions mirror commercial theatre values and standards.

CAFFE CINO became the first Off-Off Broadway theatre when Joe Cino began to present plays in his one-room coffee house in 1959. By 1965 there were several small producing organizations. The major ones include Café LA MAMA founded by Ellen Stewart in 1962 and Theatre Genesis founded in 1964 by Ralph Cook. They are devoted primarily to producing work of new American playwrights.

Theatre groups like the OPEN THEATRE, PERFORMANCE GROUP, WOOSTER GROUP, Manhattan Project, MABOU MINES, Play-House of the Ridiculous, Ridiculous Theatrical Company, Spiderwoman Theatre and BREAD AND PUPPET THEATRE are also considered Off-Off Broadway, as are individual writers, directors and actors who mount their own productions, like Jack Smith, RICHARD FOREMAN, ROBERT WILSON, Michael Kirby, SPALDING GRAY and Stuart Sherman.

**Ogilvie, George** 1931– Australian director. An actor in Melbourne, he went to London to teach and also conducted workshops for the ROYAL SHAKESPEARE COMPANY. Returning to Australia in 1966, he has directed with several major companies, including the South Australian Theatre Company, Melbourne Theatre Company, the Australian Opera and the Australian Ballet, as well as for television. His most notable recent production is John Waters's musical evocation of John Lennon, *Looking Through a Glass Onion* (1992), which toured Australia and was staged in London in 1993.

**Ogunde, Chief Hubert** 1916–90 Nigerian playwright and film-maker. The 'father of Nigerian theatre' wrote mainly in Yoruba. For nearly 40 years he travelled through Nigeria with his own company, composing over 50 operas, plays and melodramas which record all the major events in Nigeria's recent history (see YORUBA TRAVELLING THEATRES). Between 1946 and independence in 1960 he identified closely with the political struggle, and his AGIT-PROP operas were banned by the colonial authorities: *Tiger's Empire* (1946), *Strike and Hunger* (1946) and *Bread and Bullet* (1950). Later he was commissioned to write a play for the independence celebrations, *Song of Unity* (1960). His most famous political play, *Yoruba Ronu!* (*Yoruba Awake!*, 1964), resulted in his being banned from performing in the Western Region. In reply he wrote *Otito Koro* (*Truth Is Bitter*). Muritala Mohammed

(1976) refers to the assassination of that Nigerian head of state. Ogunde always sought to increase national awareness among his largely Yoruba audiences. He was a superb entertainer, transforming rather bland tales of love, heroism and evil politicians into exciting, witty theatrical performances. He also made films, e.g. *Aiye* (1980) and *Jaiyesimi* (1981).

**Ogunyemi, Chief Wale** 1939– Nigerian playwright, director and actor. Ogunyemi is one of the most prolific dramatists in Nigeria. His plays, which employ music, song, dance and dialogue, can be broadly categorized: the first group deals with traditional and mythical themes, with the intervention of gods in human affairs, including *The Scheme* (1967), *Obaluaye* (1968) and *Eshu Elegbara* (1970). *Langbodo* (1980), adapted from a novel by D. O. Fagunwa, also falls into this group and exemplifies the spectacular brilliance of Ogunyemi's stagecraft. The second category includes historical plays, and the third comprises satirical comedies, including *The Divorce* (1977), one of the most frequently performed of all English-language plays in Nigeria.

**Ōida Yoshi** 1933– Japanese actor and director. In 1968 Ōida went to Paris to work with PETER BROOK. He is trained in SHINGEKI and NŌ, which have added to the depth and distinctiveness of his performances with Brook in *The Tempest* (1968), *The Ik* (1975), *The Conference of Birds* (1979), *Mahabharata* (1985) and *The Man Who* (1994).

**O'Keeffe, John** 1747–1833 Irish playwright. He toured Ireland as actor, singer, writer of PANTOMIMES and plays. An early play, *The Shamrock*, was later successful as *The Poor Soldier* (1783). *Tony Lumpkin in Town* established his reputation and he moved to London in 1781. His next plays consisted of musical farce and comic opera – for example, *The Castle of Andalusia* (1782). His best play, *Wild Oats*, an often sentimental and genial farce with a brilliant portrait of a strolling player, Rover, was produced in 1791 and has been revived. He wrote more than 60 plays. In 1803 he sold all the copyrights in return for an annuity. His autobiography, *Recollections*, was published in 1826.

**Okhlopkov, Nikolai (Pavlovich)** 1900–67 Soviet actor and director. He is important primarily for his cinematic productions at the Realistic Theatre in the 1930s, in which he experimented with flexible stage–auditorium configurations. He studied with MEYERHOLD, at whose theatre (1923) he became the ideal biomechanical actor, in full control of his body. Meyerhold taught him about COMMEDIA DELL'ARTE, Eastern theatre techniques, ancient and folk theatres. Sergei Eisenstein, who would direct Okhlopkov in *Aleksandr Nevsky* (Okhlopkov was a film actor from 1924), helped teach him about cinematic montage. He left Meyerhold's theatre (1926) in a disagreement over the actor's role. His productions at Moscow's smallest theatre, the Realistic, of which he was artistic director (1930–7), embodied the stage dynamism, cinematic and Eastern techniques he had absorbed. For GORKY's *The Mother* (1933), he effected montage via light shifted among small square platforms surrounding the audience. His production of POGODIN's *The Aristocrats* (1935) drew upon Oriental staging techniques and pointed towards the full-scale CARNIVALization of ROSTAND's *Cyrano de Bergerac* (1943), which featured giant, silent PUPPETS as choral presences and the milling audience as a Parisian crowd. His famous *Hamlet* (1954) at the Mayakovsky Theatre was set in and around a huge pair of iron gates, symbolizing the prison that Denmark and the world had become.

**Okuni** [Izumo no Okuni] fl.1600–10 Japanese actress-dancer. The founder of *KABUKI*, she was known as Izumo no Okuni, 'Okuni from Izumo', and is reputed to have been a priestess of the Grand Shrine of Izumo. Ticket-buying audiences of commoners were captivated by her popularized version of a Buddhist prayer dance and a new dance-play, *kabuki odori*. The swaggering dandies she portrayed were known in Kyoto as *kabuki mono* (outrageous fellows) and Okuni's performance took that name. Her routines were copied by scores of female performers whose troupes toured throughout Japan, thus assuring the continuation of *kabuki* after her death. There is no evidence that Okuni was a prostitute, but her successors were. The prohibition against their performances, first promulgated in 1629, continued to bar women from Japanese stages until the 20th century.

**Old Tup** British comic ballad-drama. This traditional drama is centred on the slaughter of its eponymous animal hero, first recorded c.1845 but possibly performed as early as 1739. It is impossible to know whether the play is a dramatization of a pre-existing song or if the song derived from the play. It is performed by teenage boys and girls during the Christmas and New Year period, generally in pubs and clubs; its distribution is largely restricted to an area bounded by Chesterfield, Mansfield and Sheffield in northern England.

**Old Vic Theatre** (London) Built on the unfashionable south bank of the Thames, near Waterloo Bridge, the Coburg opened in 1818, playing MELODRAMA to packed houses. After redecoration in 1833, it was renamed the Royal Victoria and soon familiarized as the Old Vic. After a period of decline and closure, a temperance reformer, Emma Cons, opened the Royal Victoria Hall and Coffee Tavern as a concert hall in late 1880. Her niece, LILIAN BAYLIS, joined her and in 1912 took over and transformed the enterprise, initiating a scheme to present, at popular prices, all the plays in the SHAKESPEARE First Folio (1914–23). BEN GREET was the chief director and SYBIL THORNDIKE the star. From the late 1920s and throughout the 1930s the Old Vic remained a centre of excellence. GIELGUD, OLIVIER, WOLFIT, LAUGHTON, ASHCROFT, RICHARDSON, EDITH EVANS and FLORA ROBSON acted there; TYRONE GUTHRIE and MICHEL SAINT-DENIS were among the directors. Baylis died in 1937; the war closed the theatre in 1939. From 1947 to 1952 it housed the influential Old Vic School, under Saint-Denis. Michael Benthall again presented the Shakespeare First Folio plays as part of a five-year plan (1953–8).

In 1963 the Old Vic became the first home of the NATIONAL THEATRE Company under Laurence Olivier. Outstanding productions were *Othello* (1964), PETER SHAFFER's *The Royal Hunt of the Sun* (1964) and *Equus* (1973), STOPPARD's *Rosencrantz and Guildenstern Are Dead* (1967) and *Jumpers* (1972), SENECA's *Oedipus* (1968), directed by PETER BROOK, and TREVOR GRIFFITHS's *The Party* (1973). PETER HALL led the company to its new home in 1976. After a spell as the London base of the touring Prospect Theatre Company (1977–81), the Old Vic was left empty until 1983, when it was bought by a commercial speculator and embarked on a programme of REPERTORY. JONATHAN MILLER directed several notable productions there between 1987 and 1990.

**Oldfield, Anne** 1683–1730 English actress. VANBRUGH introduced her to Christopher Rich, who employed her at DRURY LANE in 1692. In 1703 COLLEY CIBBER cast her in *The Careless Husband* and her reputation was ensured.

ANNE BRACEGIRDLE retired and Mrs Oldfield triumphed over her rival Mrs Rogers. She was frequently cast in star roles by Cibber and ROWE, and proved equally good in comedy and tragedy – an example of the latter was her Andromache in PHILIPS's *The Distressed Mother*. She was buried in Westminster Abbey.

**Olesha, Yury (Karlovich)** 1899–1960 Soviet novelist, poet and playwright. The son of Polish Catholic monarchists, Olesha embraced Bolshevism and enlisted in the Red Army (1919), but grew disillusioned with the curtailments of artistic freedom under the new order. He wrote satirical verse and transformed his famous novel *Envy* (1927) into the play *The Conspiracy of Feelings* (1928) at the suggestion of the Vakhtangov Theatre, where it received a controversial expressionist staging (see EXPRESSIONISM) by Sergei Eisenstein (1929). Here Olesha externalized his conflicting feelings via two brothers – a pro-Soviet rational pragmatist and a retrograde, impractical dreamer, who fails in his attempt to destroy him. Olesha's one original play, *A List of Blessings* (1931), was staged by MEYERHOLD at his theatre as a contemporary Soviet tragedy about an egotistical Russian actress, famous for her Hamlet: ambivalent about Soviet society's treatment of the artist, she is exposed to the crass materialism of Parisian society and belatedly embraces the communist cause. Olesha adapted his fairy-tale *The Three Fat Men* (1922) for the stage, and it became a Soviet classic, spawning opera, ballet and film versions. It depicts the overthrow of the titular autocrats by a band of circus performers/revolutionaries.

**Olivier, Laurence (Kerr)** 1907–89 British actor, director and manager. A matinée idol in the 1930s, Olivier was regarded as the finest classical actor of his generation in the 1940s; he was a patron of new wave theatre in the 1950s, the first director of the NATIONAL THEATRE in the 1960s and the first actor to receive a life peerage in 1970.

Olivier joined BARRY JACKSON's BIRMINGHAM REP in 1926, then the best training ground for acting talent in the country. After playing second fiddle to NOËL COWARD in *Private Lives* (1920), he joined JOHN GIELGUD at London's New Theatre to alternate with him the parts of Romeo and Mercutio in *Romeo and Juliet* (1935). The fascinating duel, in a production directed by Gielgud which also offered PEGGY ASHCROFT's Juliet and EDITH EVANS's Nurse, immediately began to upset conventional theories about the correct playing of SHAKESPEARE. Gielgud's Romeo was a superbly controlled, musical performance, but Olivier's had more daring and virility, though his verse-speaking was considered rough. He joined the OLD VIC in 1937 where under TYRONE GUTHRIE's direction he played Hamlet, Sir Toby Belch, Macbeth and Henry V in his first season, and Iago (to RALPH RICHARDSON's Othello) and Coriolanus in his second. In 1939 he went to Hollywood where, through such films as *Wuthering Heights* and *Lady Hamilton*, he became an international film star, and married VIVIEN LEIGH, at the height of her fame from *Gone with the Wind*. His films, *The Demi-Paradise* (1943) and *Henry V* (1944), which he also directed, encouraged a national pride without lowering artistic sights.

In 1944–5 he joined Ralph Richardson to lead the Old Vic company at the New Theatre; and those seasons in which he played Richard III, Hotspur and Justice Shallow, Oedipus, and Astrov in *Uncle Vanya* have entered into the legends of British theatre – acting of the finest quality to be seen in a London ravaged by the blitz. For a few years Olivier made films with Vivien Leigh and entered into theatrical management in London. But he quickly realized that the theatre of the 1930s was no longer suitable in postwar Britain. After appearing in PETER BROOK's production of *Titus Andronicus* (1956) with Vivien Leigh at Stratford-upon-Avon, which was taken on a triumphant European tour, he returned to films, partly to escape from a theatre in which he no longer believed.

In 1957 Olivier allied himself with the new wave of British dramatists, which was then barely a ripple, by appearing in JOHN OSBORNE's *The Entertainer* as the seedy comic, Archie Rice. In the following years he played Berenger in IONESCO's *Rhinoceros*, Becket and then Henry II in ANOUILH's *Becket*, and Fred Midway in David Turner's satirical comedy, *Semi-Detached* (1962). His marriage to Vivien Leigh was dissolved in 1960 and he married JOAN PLOWRIGHT, his third wife, whom he had met at the ROYAL COURT, in 1961. He was appointed director of the first CHICHESTER FESTIVAL in 1962, which he partly used to prepare a repertoire for the newly formed National Theatre company which opened at the Old Vic in 1963. His years as the first director of the National Theatre were courageous, in that he battled against building delays, state parsimony, cancer and other major illnesses; and still managed to offer such daring acting performances as his Othello (1964), Edgar in *The Dance of Death* and James Tyrone in *Long Day's Journey into Night* (1971). In 1970 he was created a life peer, Baron Olivier of Brighton. In 1971 the governors of the National Theatre approached PETER HALL as his successor. In 1973 Olivier resigned as director, two years before the new National Theatre complex opened on the south bank of the Thames, with an auditorium that bears his name. Afterwards he appeared in films and on television, notably as King Lear in 1984.

**Ollantay** Peruvian play. An allegedly pre-Columbian play in Quechua language, it recounts love and war among the Native Americans before the arrival of the Spanish. Padre Antonio Valdés directed a performance around 1780 near Cuzco in the presence of Tupac Amaru II, the Inca chieftain who rebelled against the Spanish. The dispute centres on whether Valdés wrote the play down as the oral tradition dictated, or whether he constructed it out of the myths and legends that existed from pre-Columbian times. Its GOLDEN AGE structure favours the latter interpretation. There have been modern adaptations by César Miró and SEBASTIÁN SALAZAR BONDY. (See also *RABINAL ACHÍ*.)

**Olympic Theatre** (London) Situated off Drury Lane, the Olympic was one of London's most successful minor theatres during the 19th century. The first theatre was erected by PHILIP ASTLEY in 1805 and known as the Olympic Pavilion. Astley sold it, but after a lean period MADAME VESTRIS (1830–9) made the Olympic the genteel home of light entertainment, with PLANCHÉ as her resident dramatist and a company of comic actors, including LISTON, the KEELEYS and CHARLES JAMES MATHEWS. The theatre was destroyed by fire in 1849 and rebuilt. Under the comedian William Farren (1850–3) the extraordinary FREDERICK ROBSON made his first Olympic appearance in 1853; under the next manager, Alfred Wigan (1853–7), Robson made the Olympic famous again in a sequence of bizarre BURLESQUES. Robson was joint manager (with John Emden) from 1857 until his death in 1864, during the run of TOM TAYLOR's *The Ticket-of-Leave Man* (1863). Subsequent managers included

Horace Wigan (1864–9), Henry Neville (1873–9), GENEVIÈVE WARD (1883) and WILSON BARRETT (1890–1). The theatre closed in 1897 and was demolished in 1904.

**O'Neil, Nance** 1874–1965 American actress. She joined the Arthur McKee Rankin company in San Francisco in 1893, and he soon built her into a star. In 1900 he sponsored her world tour of *Magda*, *Fedora*, *La Tosca* and *Camille*. In 1903 she added IBSEN's *Lady Inger of Ostrat* to her repertoire. Two years later she began performing in *Hedda Gabler* and eventually took it to New York. Although billed as the great tragedienne, she was usually considered to stand in the shadow of other great emotional actresses.

**O'Neill, Eliza** 1791–1872 Irish actress. She began her remarkable five-year career at COVENT GARDEN in 1814 as Juliet. Other successes included Lady Teazle in *The School for Scandal* and the title role in Richard Lalor Shiel's tragedy, *Evadne* (1819). Shelley wrote *The Cenci* with her in mind. She retired from the stage to get married in 1819.

**O'Neill, Eugene (Gladstone)** 1888–1953 American playwright. Still regarded by many as America's finest playwright, O'Neill was the only one ever to win the Nobel Prize for Literature (1936). Like his mentor STRINDBERG, he was obsessed with his own life and family history. The son of actor JAMES O'NEILL, Eugene was immersed in a theatrical milieu from birth, although he did not begin writing until 1913. He suffered from lifelong feelings of guilt; his mother, a shy, devout Catholic, innocently became a morphine addict as a result of his birth. He was an emotional haemophiliac whose family-inflicted wounds never healed, and he became a highly subjective dramatist.

In his mid-20s he was confined to a tuberculosis sanatorium. After his recovery in 1913 he wrote plays, most of them tales of the sea and of the underside of life. In 1916 he joined a group of amateur playmakers on Cape Cod, who became known as the PROVINCETOWN PLAYERS on moving to Greenwich Village. He made his BROADWAY debut in 1920 with *Beyond the Horizon* (written in 1918), a sombre story of defeat on a farm with the sea beckoning in the background. The play won for O'Neill the first of his four Pulitzer Prizes. The others were for *Anna Christie* (written in 1920), *Strange Interlude* (1926–7) and *Long Day's Journey into Night* (1939–41).

O'Neill kept changing his style. Starting as a realist (see REALISM), with occasional returns to the genre, he also wrote expressionistic works (*The Emperor Jones*, 1920, and *The Hairy Ape*, 1921; see EXPRESSIONISM), costume drama (*The Fountain*, 1921–2, and *Marco Millions*, 1923–5), plays about STRINDBERGIAN views of marriage (*Welded*, 1922–3), biblical fables (*Lazarus Laughed*, 1925–6) and even a comedy (*Ah, Wilderness!*, 1932). He made demands on his audiences with extra-long works, namely *Strange Interlude*, nine acts; *Mourning Becomes Electra* (1929–31), a trilogy in 13 acts; and *The Iceman Cometh* (1939), twice the standard length. *The Great God Brown* (1925) is a bewildering work in which the characters constantly mask and unmask; *All God's Chillun Got Wings* (1923) is a poignant story about a white girl married to a black man; and *Desire Under the Elms* (1924) is a drama of greed, incest and infanticide. O'Neill used song, pantoMIME, dance, masks, imaginative scenic devices and novel sound effects. But his masterpieces are in the realistic mode: *The Iceman Cometh* and *Long Day's Journey into Night*.

In the 1930s he worked for years on his most ambitious project, a cycle entitled 'A Tale of Possessors Self-Possessed' that would dramatize highlights in the history of a family. In this work, envisioned as a number of plays, O'Neill aimed to show that materialism and greed had corrupted America. Ill health and despair prevented him from achieving his goal. One finished play, *A Touch of the Poet* (1935–42), survived, along with a rough draft of another, *More Stately Mansions* (1935–40), which was staged posthumously in truncated form.

**O'Neill, James** 1846–1920 Irish-American actor. Despite his great popularity in the late 19th century, he is primarily remembered today as the father of EUGENE O'NEILL. He played DUMAS *père*'s hero in CHARLES FECHTER's dramatization of *The Count of Monte Cristo* and rejoiced in his prosperity, but the role became a strait-jacket that gradually diminished his talent. Fragments of his history are woven into his son's devastating family portrait, *Long Day's Journey into Night*.

*onnagata* SEE FEMALE IMPERSONATION

**Open Theatre** (New York City) American company. This experimental OFF-OFF BROADWAY acting group lasted from 1963 to 1973. JOSEPH CHAIKIN left the LIVING THEATRE after playing Galy Gay in BRECHT's *Man Is Man* to establish a study group for exploring new styles of acting. This collection of actors, writers and dramaturges came to be known as the Open Theatre. Chaikin developed a technique that focused attention on the performer, not the character, with the actor changing from one role to another before the audience's eyes; this approach is described in his book, *The Presence of the Actor*. Gradually the group began to work on ensemble creations shaped by a single writer, resulting in *Viet Rock* by Megan Terry (1966), *The Serpent* by JEAN-CLAUDE VAN ITALLIE (1968) and *Terminal* by Susan Yankowitz (1969). They then created some chamber works, including *The Mutation Show* (1971) and *Nightwalk* (1973). But as the Open Theatre edged away from being an acting workshop towards becoming a producing company, it decided to close.

**Opitz, Martin** 1597–1639 German writer. Opitz translated Latin and Italian plays and wrote a book of poetics, published in 1624. His work helped turn the German theatre towards classicism, which was to dominate it until the middle of the 18th century.

**Oregon Shakespeare Festival** American festival. It was founded in 1935 by Angus L. Bowmer in Ashland, Oregon, to produce SHAKESPEARE's plays in an Elizabethan-style setting. The present stage, in the style of London's FORTUNE THEATRE, dates from 1959. In 1970 the Angus Bowmer Theatre was opened to house modern works, and in 1977 the 138-seat Black Swan for more experimental productions. There is an eight-month season at Ashland and a six-month season in Portland. The Festival is noted for a house style which emphasizes the clarity and beauty of the text.

**Örkény, István** 1912–79 Hungarian playwright. He has been called 'master of the grotesque'. Sent to the Russian front, he returned to Hungary in 1947 after four years as a prisoner of war. At first he depicted this dehumanizing experience in naturalistic stories. By the mid-1960s his grotesque style emerged. His plays document 20th-century Hungary, with a keen sense of the absurdities of modern life. Plays such as *Stevie in the Bloodstorm* (1969), *Blood Relations* (1974), *Keysearchers* (1977) and *Screenplay* (1979) have enjoyed great acclaim in Hungary, and the success abroad of *The Toth Family* (1967) and *Catsplay* (1971) established his international reputation.

**Orton, Joe** 1933–67 British playwright. Orton specialized in high camp comedy, whose excesses were expressed in a delicate verbal wit. His first stage play, *Entertaining Mr Sloane* (1964), caused a *succès de scandale* when it was first produced at the ARTS THEATRE Club in London. A violent young man is blackmailed into becoming the sexual pet of a respectable brother and sister whose father he has murdered. *Loot* (1966) is like an updated black farce from the 1950s, with a comic detective who will stop at nothing, the corpse of a recently deceased mother, and tons of money. His funniest play, *What the Butler Saw* (1969), succeeds on several levels – as a French FARCE, as a BURLESQUE on psychiatry and as an Edwardian comedy with the same dandified use of language. A one-act play, *Funeral Games* (1970), and two short plays, *The Ruffian on the Stair* (1967), originally written for radio, and *The Erpingham Camp* (1967), complete the short list of Orton's stage works, although his television play, *The Good and Faithful Servant* (1964), was also performed on stage. In 1967 Orton was murdered by his homosexual friend, Kenneth Halliwell, who then committed suicide.

**Osborn, Paul** 1901–88 American playwright. His best-remembered plays are *On Borrowed Time* (1938) and *Morning's at Seven* (1939). The former was a touching study of an old man's attempt to cheat death. The latter took a nostalgic look at the life of four sisters in a small American town. Most of Osborn's works to reach BROADWAY were adaptations of novels, such as *A Bell for Adano* (1944), *Point of No Return* (1951) and *The World of Suzie Wong* (1958).

**Osborne, John (James)** 1929–94 British playwright. He started as an actor in Northern repertories (see REPERTORY THEATRE), and sent his third play, *Look Back in Anger*, to the newly formed English Stage Company at the ROYAL COURT THEATRE where it received its premiere on 8 May 1956, a date often taken to signify the start of the postwar British theatre revival. The central character, Jimmy Porter, came from a working-class background but had been educated at university without afterwards finding a job to match his self-esteem. His tirades against British society led to the phrase 'angry young man', which was afterwards applied not just to Osborne but to almost all new writers who criticized the system. *Look Back in Anger* was the English Stage Company's first outright success. In 1957 Osborne wrote *The Entertainer*, which provided LAURENCE OLIVIER with the splendidly tatty part of Archie Rice, the forlorn comic of touring nude REVUES.

In the 1960s, and particularly before the death of his mentor GEORGE DEVINE, Osborne wrote plays with strong parts for major actors, notably *Luther* (1961, with ALBERT FINNEY), *Inadmissible Evidence* (1964, with Nicol Williamson) and *A Patriot for Me* (1965, with Maximilian Schell). Osborne's later plays lacked some of the original flair: *Hotel in Amsterdam* (1968), *West of Suez* (1971), *A Sense of Detachment* (1972), *The End of Me Old Cigar* (1974). *Watch It Come Down* (1976) was staged at the NATIONAL THEATRE and in 1992 he provided an angry backward look at life, *Dejavu*, which picks up the story of Jimmy Porter.

**Oskarson, Peter** 1951– Swedish director. Oskarson has sought to establish the 'art theatre' in Sweden, first at Skånska Teatern from 1973 to 1982, then at Folkteatern in Gävleborg (1982–7) and since 1993 at Orionteatern, Stockholm. As set out in the manifesto he drafted for GÖTEBORG STADSTEATER in 1981, the art theatre prioritizes art over administration, puts acting at the centre of production, and demands total commitment from all participants. It aims to restore theatre as a source of understanding and stimulus for the enrichment of spectators' lives. This potential has been demonstrated in Oskarson's own remarkable productions, especially *A Dream Play* (1984), *The Hairy Ape* (1986), *Hamlet* (1989) and *The Great Wrath* (1988), a dramatization of myths of Northern Sweden which the company spent an entire year preparing.

**Osofisan, Femi** 1946– Nigerian playwright, novelist and critic. Like other Nigerian playwrights and left-wing critics, Osofisan places contemporary political class analysis at the centre of the theatrical enterprise. His Marxist concerns, which appeal to many Nigerians since the oil boom, have involved a critique of the work of established writers like SOYINKA and J. P. CLARK-BEKEDEREMO. Soyinka, in turn, refers to this group as Nigeria's 'leftocrats'. Performances of Osofisan's plays on Nigerian university campuses have reinforced his popularity among radical students and intellectuals. First was *Red Is the Freedom Road* (1969; formerly titled *You Have Lost Your Fine Face*), followed by the publication of a satirical novel *Kolera Kolej* (1975; later dramatized) and then by a satirical version of GOGOL's *The Inspector General:Who's Afraid of Solarin?* (1978). *The Chattering and the Song* (1976), about an underground farmers' revolutionary movement, was followed by *Once upon Four Robbers* (1978) which attacks the Nigerian military. *Morountodun* (1979) combines a mythical tale with the 1969 uprising of farmers in western Nigeria. *Midnight Hotel* (1982) is a satirical adaptation of FEYDEAU's farce, *Paradise Hotel*. With publication, Osofisan's work is receiving increasing critical attention. Among the most important of his later plays are *Farewell to a Cannibal Rage* (published 1986), *Eshu and the Vagabond Minstrels* and *Aringidin and the Nightwatchmen* (both 1991). *Yungba Yungba and the Dance Contest* (1993), which has an all-female cast, is a display piece for his stagecraft. The first part of an ambitious trilogy on Nkrumah, Sékou Touré and Cabral was completed in 1993.

**Osten, Suzanne** 1944– Swedish director and playwright. Osten joined Stockholm's Stadsteater in 1970. In 1975 she founded the company Unga Klara, to write, produce and direct plays for children, and plays for adults about childhood; her work incorporates the perspective of childhood. Outstanding productions include *Medea's Children* (exemplifying 'children's tragedy', 1975), *Hitler's Childhood* (1984), *The Piggle* (1991) and *The Dolphin* (1992). She has also been acclaimed as a film director – for example, of *The Mozart Brothers* (1986) and *Speak Up! It's So Dark* (1993).

**Ostrovsky, Aleksandr (Nikolaevich)** 1823–86 Russian playwright and administrator. A native Muscovite and son of a merchant-lawyer, he became Russia's most prolific painter of mercantile society and the common people, writing well over 50 plays, mostly comedies, for the stage.

His first comedy, *The Bankrupt* (1847), later revised as *It's a Family Affair – We'll Settle It Ourselves* (1849), exposed fraudulent business practices and was banned for 11 years. In the West his best-known comedy is *Diary of a Scoundrel* (or *Enough Stupidity for Every Wise Man*, 1868), about a double-dealer. While translating classic European plays, Ostrovsky strove to further the native dramatic tradition and joined a Moscow literary circle which conducted ethnographic and historical inquiries

into Russian folk poetry and ritual. This folk quality can be found in the most famous of his three tragedies, *The Thunderstorm* (1859). Here he dramatized the struggle between oppressor and oppressed, and the corruption of innocence, with nature participating as an agent of fate. His dramatic fable, *The Snow Maiden* (1873), drew upon his knowledge of Russian folk songs, proverbs and popular poetry, blending romanticism with REALISM. These plays, *An Ardent Heart* (1869) and others, furnished Russian actresses with strong roles through which to further their craft. He often directed himself; his understanding of the actor's world is reflected in such comedies as *The Comedian of the Seventeenth Century* (1872), on the founding of the first Russian theatre in Moscow, and *The Forest* (1871), which features a pair of itinerant performers. In 1882 Ostrovsky helped to break the monopoly of the Imperial theatres, setting the tradition for the MOSCOW ART THEATRE, to follow in 1897.

Ostrovsky the dramatist tended towards the sentimental and melodramatic; his plotting was often structurally weak and his endings contrived. But he had a clear sense of environment conditioning behaviour, idiomatic expression tailored to individualized characters, and a broad view of socio-economic relationships and native traditions. His lack of sympathy towards the nobility made him popular after the 1917 Revolution, when he became the most frequently performed classical Russian dramatist.

**Ōta Shōgo** 1939– Japanese playwright and director. In 1968 Ōta was a founder member of Tenkei Theatre Company, where he worked until it was dissolved in 1988. He explores the power of language and silence in relation to the presence of actors' bodies, staging a series of plays without words, the first being *Komachi Fūden* (1977), using an original NŌ play. His trilogy of silent plays – *Mizu no Eki* (*The Water Station*, 1981; translated 1990), *Chi no Eki* (*The Earth Station*, 1985) and *Kaze no Eki* (*The Wind Station*, 1986) – has been performed in Japan and abroad.

**O'Toole, Peter** 1932– British actor. Born in Ireland, he made his reputation with the BRISTOL OLD VIC (1955–8) and at the ROYAL COURT THEATRE in *The Long and the Short and the Tall* (1959). He joined the Shakespeare Memorial Company in 1960, where he was a memorable Shylock and Petruchio, and played Hamlet in the inaugural production of the NATIONAL THEATRE company at the OLD VIC in 1963. Increasingly, however, he was drawn towards films, and starred as Lawrence in the epic, *Lawrence of Arabia* (1962). His blond hair, gaunt face and idiosyncratic vocal delivery could be compelling in the right part, but his screen career seemed to magnify his mannerisms when he returned to the stage. He appeared in a disastrous *Macbeth* for the Prospect Company at the Old Vic in 1980, but redeemed his reputation with a forceful John Tanner in a WEST END production of *Man and Superman* two years later. His most memorable comic performance was as the low-life Soho journalist in Keith Waterhouse's *Jeffrey Barnard Is Unwell* (1989), where his haggard looks gave the appearance of a dissipated corpse in hiding from God the Father.

**Otto, Teo** 1904–68 German stage designer. In 1931 he became chief designer at the Berlin State Theatre, where he worked until he emigrated to Switzerland in 1933. His association with the Schauspielhaus in Zurich led to a collaboration with BRECHT on the premiere productions of *Mother Courage* (1941), *Galileo* (1943) and *The Good Person of Setzuan* (1943). Also in Zurich he designed premiere productions of plays by DÜRRENMATT and MAX FRISCH. During the 1950s his designs could be seen in major opera houses and theatres in Austria and Germany. The most important of these productions was GRÜNDGENS's revival in Hamburg of *Faust, Part I and Part II* (1957), which moved to New York's City Center in 1961. His designs were noted for economy of architectural detail, sparse and symbolic use of properties, decorative screens and atmospheric lighting.

**Otway, Thomas** 1652–85 English playwright. His first play, *Alcibiades* (1675), gave a leading role to ELIZABETH BARRY, with whom Otway was hopelessly in love. Further heroic tragedies followed: *Don Carlos* (1676) and *Titus and Berenice* (1676), performed with his adaptation of MOLIÈRE's farce *The Cheats of Scapin. Friendship in Fashion* (1678) is a bitter comedy. His brief experience as a soldier is reflected in his comedy *The Soldier's Fortune* (1680) and its sequel *The Atheist* (1683). He also adapted SHAKESPEARE's *Romeo and Juliet* as *The History and Fall of Caius Marius* (1679). But Otway's enormous reputation in the 18th century was based on two tragedies: the tearful *The Orphan* (1680) and *Venice Preserv'd* (1682), which combines pitiable love with a remarkable analysis of a conspiracy to overthrow the corrupt Venetian state. He died in penury.

**Ouellette, Rose(-Alma)** [La Poune] 1903– French Canadian actress, comedian and theatre manager. A child singer in VARIETY shows, then a comic in early American-style BURLESQUE, in the 1920s she worked with Oliver Guimond ('Ti-Zoune'), then considered the outstanding practitioner of the art. In a genre that required great improvisational ability and little or no prepared text, La Poune rapidly became the best-known stage personality of her day. She directed Montreal's Cartier Theatre, 1928–36, and the National, 1936–53, during what is called the golden age of burlesque in Canada. She later moved to television.

**Owen, Alun (Davies)** 1926–94 British playwright. A prolific writer for television and radio (see TELEVISION DRAMA; RADIO DRAMA), Owen adapted his first play, *The Rough and Ready Lot* (1958), for the stage from the original radio script. It concerned four soldiers of fortune in South America after the end of the American Civil War, and illustrated Owen's easy command of dialogue and his gift of characterization. *Progress to the Park* (1959) was a vivid portrait of his birthplace, Liverpool, and was given a characteristically lively production by JOAN LITTLEWOOD at the Theatre Workshop, Stratford, East London. *A Little Winter Love* was produced in Dublin in 1963 and in London two years later; and he collaborated with the songwriter, Lionel Bart, in an ambitious musical about a Liverpool legend, *Maggie May* (1964).

**Owens, Rochelle** 1936– American playwright. She creates her own cultural anthropology complete with myths, ritual, chants and symbols in her experimental OFF-OFF BROADWAY plays. Her first highly controversial play was *Futz* (1967), a TRAGICOMEDY relating the sexual love of a man and his pig and the violent, demented response of his repressed neighbours to his sodomy. Owens continued to explore the conflict of individual primal impulse with a self-righteous society in such plays as *Beclch* (1967), an example of Theatre of Cruelty with its depiction of savagery and depravity. Others are *Istanboul* (1965); *Kontraption* (1970); *He Wants Shih* (1975); *Chucky's Hunch* (1981); and two surreal historical biographies (see SURREALISM), *The Karl Marx Play* (1973) and *Emma Instigated Me* (1977).

**Oyono-Mbia, Guillaume** 1939– Cameroonian playwright. Equally at home in French or English, Oyono-Mbia translates his plays himself. Three were initially written for French and British radio. They have been performed widely in Africa, and also in France and England. They combine an awareness of the comic conventions of the theatre with a sharp portrayal of social behaviour, particularly in the key realms of education, marriage, wealth and social status. His plays (dates of first publication) are: *Three Suitors: One Husband* (1964), *Until Further Notice* (1970), *Notre fille ne se mariera pas* (*Our Daughter Must Not Marry*, 1971) and *His Excellency's Special Train* (1979).

**Ozerov, Vladislav (Aleksandrovich)** 1769–1816 Russian playwright. He wrote neoclassical tragedy whose form imitated his French predecessors, but whose linguistic style and heightened subjectivism pointed towards pre-romantic schools of playwriting. The declamatory acting style and emotional demands which his plays required made them favourites of such star performers as A. S. YAKOVLEV, E. S. SEMYONOVA and V. A. KARATYGIN. The plays which followed his initial, strictly classical tragedy *Yaropolk and Oleg* (1798) enjoyed brief success for their parallels between historical and contemporary political events. *Oedipus in Athens* (1804), a reworking of *Oedipus at Colonus*, was based on a French rather than the original Greek model, which accounts for its relatively restrained happy ending. *Fingal* (1805) was inspired by the Ossianic poems. *Dmitry of the Don* (*Donskoi*, 1807) was by far his most popular work, bolstering Russians' patriotic spirit during their struggle with Napoleon by reminding them of their stirring victory over the Tartars in 1380. Ozerov's best play *Polyxena* (1809), which dramatized the eponymous heroine's tragic love for Achilles, was not a success, prompting the author to destroy the manuscript of his last complete play, *Medea*.

**Pacino, Al** 1940– American actor. A devoted student of LEE STRASBERG and a member of the ACTORS STUDIO, Pacino made a strong impression on stage in the late 1960s playing violent low-life New Yorkers, OFF-BROADWAY in *The Indian Wants the Bronx* (1968), and in his BROADWAY debut as a drug addict in *Does a Tiger Wear a Necktie?* (1969). His naturalistic style (see NATURALISM) proved ideal for film (*The Godfather, Serpico, Scarface*). In his periodic returns to the stage he has tried with limited success to overcome the typecasting of his films. His *Richard III* (1973) was brave though unavoidably contemporary. He was more comfortable as TENNESSEE WILLIAMS's Everyman in the 1970 Lincoln Center (see VIVIAN BEAUMONT AND MITZI E. NEWHOUSE THEATRES) revival of *Camino Real*; and as a shuffling crook in a revival of DAVID MAMET's *American Buffalo* (1982). In 1992 he appeared in two plays in New York, WILDE's *Salomé* and Ira Lewis's *Chinese Coffee*.

**Page, Geraldine** 1924–87 American actress. JOSÉ QUINTERO cast her as Alma in the OFF-BROADWAY production of *Summer and Smoke* at the CIRCLE IN THE SQUARE (1951–2) to rave reviews, establishing her career. Her BROADWAY debut as Lily in *Midsummer* (1953) again received critical acclaim. Her later work included Lizzie in *The Rainmaker* (1954), Alexandra del Lago in *Sweet Bird of Youth* (1959), Olga in *Three Sisters* (1964), Baroness Lemberg in *White Lies* and Clea in *Black Comedy* (1967), Marion in *Absurd Person Singular* (1974) and Mother Miriam Ruth in *Agnes of God* (1982). While Page appeared too often in neurotic roles, she was a versatile actress capable of a wide emotional range. Her numerous film appearances include *Summer and Smoke* (1961) and Woody Allen's *Interiors* (1978).

**Pak Sŭng-hi** 1901–64 Korean producer, director and playwright. He led the Towŏl-hoe Group and produced the *shinpa* plays which imitated Western sentimental MELODRAMA. Pak Sŭng-hi upgraded *shinpa* by abandoning improvisations, using fully scripted plays and demanding rigorous rehearsals. Nearly 200 new plays and adaptations have been credited to him, but most have not survived.

***Pakhomushka*** Russian folk FARCE. It is performed by young men and women at village parties, or during collective sedentary work such as sewing-bees. It concerns the humped and fanged idiot Pakhomushka and his sexually frustrated wife Pakhomikha. The hero's attempt to find a bride among the girls in the audience develops into a BURLESQUE marriage and wedding night, and finally into a farce of cuckoldry and revenge. Organization and performance are informal: roles are distributed and costumes and props improvised on the spot; by-play between actors and audience is the norm.

**Palace Theatre** (New York City) Located on BROADWAY, the 1,800-seat theatre opened on 25 March 1913 and gained popularity with the booking of SARAH BERNHARDT. It was the ambition of every American VARIETY act to play there: the record bill was for a nine-week teaming of EDDIE CANTOR and George Jessel in 1931. On 7 May 1932 the Palace became a four-a-day theatre, the live performance mingling with newsreels and cartoons, and on 16 November turned into a five-a-day cinema; this date marks the official death of VAUDEVILLE as a dominant entertainment form. The Palace was converted into a theatre for MUSICAL COMEDY in 1965.

**Palais-Royal, Théâtre du** (Paris) Originally known as the Palais-Cardinal, the first purpose-built theatre of 17th-century France was built by the architect Jacques Lemercier as a small private playhouse in RICHELIEU's palace and inaugurated in January 1641 with a performance for Louis XIII. Italian in style, it boasted a proscenium arch, machinery for scene changes and an elegant auditorium with balconies and tiered seating. After Richelieu's death, it was occasionally used for court entertainments and later by MOLIÈRE's company, who refurbished it in 1670 for the presentation of spectacular 'machine-plays'. Later it was used for operatic performance by LULLY. Destroyed by fire in 1763, it was rebuilt, then again burned down in 1781. Various theatres were built there under this name.

**Palitzsch, Peter** 1918– German director. Having trained with the BERLINER ENSEMBLE, he introduced BRECHT's theatrical methods to the West German stage when he left the GDR in 1960. He extended and modified the principles of EPIC THEATRE in productions of the classics, particularly in his adaptation of SHAKESPEARE, *The Wars of the Roses* (Stuttgart, 1967), which became an anti-illusionistic study of the dialectics of history. Palitzsch has been instrumental in promoting contemporary German drama, with influential productions of the first major plays by WALSER (*The Black Swan*, 1964), Jochen Ziem (*The Invitation*, 1967) and DORST (*Toller*, 1968). In 1992 he joined the directorate of the Berliner Ensemble.

**Palladio, Andrea** [Andrea di Pietro Monaro] 1509–80 Italian architect, one of the greatest of the Italian Renaissance. His work, most of which was done in Venice and Vicenza, was rooted in a close study of Roman remains and the writings of Vitruvius, and in the ideas of Alberti on the correspondences between architectural and musical forms. Palladio was profoundly original, and influential throughout Europe in the 17th and early 18th centuries. In 1561 and 1562 he built theatres within the hall of the basilica at Vicenza, the second being used for the production of his patron TRISSINO's *Sofonisba*. His most famous theatre is the Teatro Olimpico at Vicenza, begun in the year of his death and finished by SCAMOZZI in 1585. It represents the triumph of Renaissance academicism, a beautifully conceived and completed structure, although its Roman *scaenae frons* (see SKĒNĒ) had already been made obsolete by the development of the proscenium stage with changeable settings.

**Pallenberg, Max** 1877–1934 Austrian actor. A leading figure in REINHARDT's theatre between 1911 and 1919, he won extraordinary popularity for his comic fantasy. His range can be indicated by his two most famous roles – the title character in PISCATOR's production of *The Adventures of the Good Soldier Schweik* (1927), and Mephisto in Reinhardt's *Faust* (1933).

**Palmer, A(lbert) M(arshman)** 1838–1905 American manager. Although lacking theatrical experience, he became a leading manager, combining a keen business sense with cultivated theatrical taste. During his ten-year tenure at the Union Square Theatre (from 1872) he improved both the acting and the production standards. He also fostered and commissioned contemporary American drama. He subsequently managed the MADISON SQUARE THEATRE and WALLACK's Theatre. Among his notable productions of American plays were BRONSON HOWARD's *The Banker's Daughter* (1878), BARTLEY CAMPBELL's *My Partner* (1879), CLYDE FITCH's *Beau Brummel* (1890), JAMES A. HERNE's *Margaret Fleming* (1891) and AUGUSTUS THOMAS's *Alabama* (1891). Palmer was among the first American managers to pay foreign authors royalties for the performance of their plays.

**Palsgrave's Men** see ADMIRAL'S MEN

**p'ansori** Korean folk operetta. *P'ansori* is performed by a single singer, or KWANGDAE, with the accompaniment of a *puk*, a double-headed drum. The subjects are largely drawn from well known novels.

**pantomime** see MIME; PANTOMIME, ENGLISH

**pantomime, English** Popular entertainment. An indigenous form, it originated in the early 18th century under the influence of French fairground performers, who put on 'night scenes' with COMMEDIA DELL'ARTE characters in London. John Weaver, a dancing-master, copied these in short ballets staged at DRURY LANE in 1716, and was in turn imitated by JOHN RICH at LINCOLN's INN FIELDS. Rich's first outstanding success was *The Necromancer or Harlequin Dr Faustus* (1723), which prompted imitations at Drury Lane and the HAYMARKET. Soon pantomime settled into its customary format; the opening was drawn from classical mythology and, following a transformation of characters into such types as HARLEQUIN, Pantaloon and Columbine, the second half devolved into a knockabout harlequinade. Rich was lavish with mechanical devices, such as a coiling serpent, and his own mimic agility became proverbial. Later GEORGE COLMAN THE ELDER effectively altered the mythological opening to a fairy tale, which became standard.

By the early 19th century, these afterpieces had swollen to fill the major portion of a bill and accrued a number of traditions: the 'dame roles' (see FEMALE IMPERSONATION) were played by men, the old Harlequin costume had been transformed into a skin-tight suit of spangled lozenges, and the entertainment predominated at Christmas and Easter. CARLO DELPINI had already shifted the comic emphasis from Harlequin to PIERROT, and this moved to the CLOWN via the genius of JOSEPH GRIMALDI. Grimaldi's costume, make-up and behaviour were his legacy to future generations. This style of panto was carried to America by Charles Parsloe in 1831, but it enjoyed only a limited period of popularity, culminating in GEORGE W. L. FOX at the BOWERY THEATRE, New York (1850–67), and his *Humpty Dumpty* (1868).

In the Victorian age, pantomime, as scripted by J. R. PLANCHÉ and E. L. Blanchard, was alloyed with elements from the French FÉERIE, the BURLESQUE and operetta; the hero became the 'principal boy', played by a woman in tights (MADAME CÉLESTE may have been the first, in 1855). Certain stories proved to be worth repeating, such as *Cinderella*, *Puss in Boots*, *The Babes in the Wood*, *Dick Whittington* and *Aladdin*; standard characters like the Widow Twankey (first seen in H. J. BYRON's burlesque *Aladdin*, 1861), Baron Hardup and Buttons in *Cinderella*, the Broker's Men and Whittington's Cat were carried over from year to year. It became exclusively a Christmas-time amusement aimed primarily at a juvenile audience. Some theatres, like the Britannia,

Hoxton, and the Grecian, City Road, in London, were famous for the excellence of their pantos. Elaborate trickwork, utilizing traps, hinged properties and instantaneous transformations, were expected at the climactic moments.

The second half of the 19th century beheld the rise of the spectacular pantomime with its sumptuous processions, ballets and flying corps, the star status of the principal boy (see MALE IMPERSONATION), and the decline of the harlequinade. It became a speciality of actor clans like the CONQUESTS and the LUPINOS. Later Augustus Harris Jr (known as Druriolanus) was eager to attract middle-class audiences by familiarizing them with the stars of the less respectable MUSIC-HALL and burlesque.

After World War I pantomime was banished from Drury Lane by MUSICAL COMEDY until 1929, and from COVENT GARDEN by opera and ballet until 1938. It survived as 'rep-theatre panto', domesticated and formulaic, with such audience-participation devices as the shouts of 'Look behind you!' and the sing-along chorus. It was reinstituted at the London Palladium (1948–60); in 1961 Norman Wisdom played principal boy, an innovation repeated for a decade with male pop and rock stars until Cilla Black resumed the female prerogative in 1971. The conventional pantomime underwent some curious alterations, such as the dame taking centre stage as a glamorous drag queen (DANNY LA RUE) and the NATIONAL THEATRE adding panto to its repertory in 1983. (See also MIME.)

**Papp [Papirofsky], Joseph** 1921–91 American director and producer. Starting as a stage manager, Papp was led by his interest in bringing theatre to everyone to found the NEW YORK SHAKESPEARE FESTIVAL in 1954. Frequently taking chances, he advocated creative freedom. He directed *Cymbeline* (1954) and *The Changeling* (1956) for NYSF, thereafter directing occasionally: *Twelfth Night* (1958, 1963 and 1969), *Hamlet* (1964, 1967, 1968 and 1983), RABE's *Boom Boom Room* (1973), Thomas Babe's *Buried Inside Extra* (1983) and *Measure for Measure* (1985). For television he directed *The Merchant of Venice* (1962), *Antony and Cleopatra* (1963) and *Hamlet* (1964). From 1973 to 1977 he served as director of Lincoln Center's VIVIAN BEAUMONT AND MITZI E. NEWHOUSE THEATRES. From 1990 to 1993 JoANNE AKALAITIS was the artistic director of NYSF.

**Parigi, Giulio** 1580–1635 Italian architect and scene designer. He succeeded his mentor BUONTALENTI in 1608 as architect at the Medici court, and became responsible for the decor for court festivities. He influenced the work of German architect JOSEF FURTTENBACH and became the teacher of the English designer INIGO JONES, thus disseminating the technology of stage machinery and movable scenery to Germany and England. His most important designs included *Il Guidizio di Paride* (1608), a PASTORAL with intermezzi and NAUMACHIA in honour of Prince Cosimo's marriage to Archduchess Maria Magdalena; *Eros and Anteros* (1613); *The Liberation of Tyrrhenus* (1616), an intermezzo performed at CARNIVAL time before the Medici court; and *La Guerra d'Amore* (1616), an equestrian ballet (see HIPODRAMA) for which a wooden amphitheatre had to be constructed. In 1620 he was replaced as designer for the Medici by his son Alfonso (died 1656).

**Park Theatre** (New York City). Located on Park Row, it opened in 1798 as the New Theatre, designed European-style with three tiers of boxes and a gallery overhanging a U-shaped pit. In 1808 the Park was leased to STEPHEN PRICE, who introduced the star system by importing English actors such as GEORGE FREDERICK COOKE (1810) and EDMUND KEAN (1820). For more than a decade, the Park was considered the first theatre in the land with an outstanding resident company. In addition to English stars, it helped to create such American stars as EDWIN FORREST and CHARLOTTE CUSHMAN. In 1848 it was finally razed.

**Parker, L(ouis) N(apoleon)** 1852–1944 French-born playwright and composer. Parker's light comedies, MELODRAMAS and historical plays were staple popular fare for the English stage between 1890 and 1919. He also wrote specifically for the American stage (*The Mayflower*, 1897; *The Woman and the Sheriff*, 1911). The popularity of his plays was largely due to the strong acting parts they offered, the best of which was *Disraeli* with GEORGE ARLISS in the title role. In addition Parker devised and produced civic pageants throughout England, as well as in the Lord Mayor's procession (1907, 1908) and on patriotic themes in London during World War I, culminating in *The Pageant of Drury Lane* at the DRURY LANE Theatre in 1918.

**Parker, Stewart** 1941–88 Irish playwright. His *Spokesong* (1975) is an entertaining SATIRE, with music, on the North of Ireland's history of sectarian dispute. *Catchpenny Twist* (1977), somewhat resembling the Auden–Isherwood plays of the 1930s, views the present North of bombs and assassinations through the career of two aspiring pop musicians. From a mélange of conjuring, fairy and mystery tale, *Nightshade* (1980) presents illusion as a way of life. *Northern Star* (1984) composes a pastiche of Irish writers as part of its commentary on the 1798 rebellion. *Pentecost* (1987), literally set between warring sides, finds jazz and love to be almost sacramental ways for individuals to transcend the horrors around them. Parker's plays enunciated his 'instinct for play itself... a quintessentially ludicrous theatre', but underlying his stage and television work is a whimsically tragicomic vision of human decency persisting in the face of surrounding brutalities.

**parody** BURLESQUE, parody and SATIRE are often treated as synonyms for ridicule through distortion, but it is useful to suggest distinctions between them.

Parody is a form of mimicry. At one end of the spectrum it may approach burlesque by exaggerating mimicry into caricature. At the other end it may approach satire by enfolding a critique of social behaviour in its ridicule of an artistic form. None of the three words refers exclusively to drama; yet all have been applied to drama. The word 'parody' was the first to enter European languages, deriving through the French from the Greek, where it means a song by the side, or a mocking of another song. Setting AESCHYLUS against EURIPIDES, ARISTOPHANES parodies both of them in a famous scene in his comedy *The Frogs*. Parody caricatures a particular figure or work; occasionally it embraces a whole play. BRECHT's *Threepenny Opera* and *Arturo Ui* may be considered examples, the one parodying GAY's *The Beggars' Opera*, and the other both *Richard III* and GOETHE's *Faust*.

**Parsons, Estelle** 1927– American actress. Best known for her brash performance in the film *Bonnie and Clyde* (1967), Parsons prefers theatre. Although she was trained in LEE STRASBERG's method of psychological realism she has worked in other styles, from SHAKESPEARE to MUSICAL THEATRE. Her richest parts on

BROADWAY have been as TENNESSEE WILLIAMS's good-natured stripper in *The Seven Descents of Myrtle* (1968), as the alcoholic title character in *And Miss Reardon Drinks a Little* (1971), in New York's Public Theater's *Pirates of Penzance* (1981) and as the deranged, dictatorial schoolteacher in Roberto Athayde's *Miss Margarida's Way* (1977), a one-woman show. She has also played more experimentally OFF-BROADWAY and in the regions.

**Pasadena Playhouse** (USA) The Playhouse was founded in 1917 by Gilmour Brown, who depended upon amateur talent and volunteer help. Premieres of new works, including O'NEILL's *Lazarus Laughed* (1928), and revivals of seldom produced classics made the Playhouse famous. Beginning in 1935 it offered a series of Midsummer Drama Festivals and became a showcase for aspiring film actors (e.g. Randolph Scott, TYRONE POWER and Robert Young). Brown retired as director in 1959. In decline, the Playhouse closed in 1970; it was renovated and reopened in 1985.

**Páskándi, Géza** 1933– Hungarian playwright. A member of the Hungarian minority in Romania, he was imprisoned for political reasons (1957–63) and has lived in Budapest since 1974. His coinage, 'absurdoid', characterizes his drama, in which absurdity (see THEATRE OF THE ABSURD) is presented as an *aspect* of life. In historical dramas, e.g. *Sojourn* (1970), *The Hiding Place* (1972) and *Residents of the Windmill* (1981), Páskándi seamlessly combines psychological realism with the absurdity elicited by external and internal constraints. His *oeuvre* includes poetry, short stories and essays and has been widely translated.

***paso*** see *GÉNERO CHICO*

**Pasqual, Lluís** 1951– Spanish theatre and opera director. A major figure in Catalan theatre, he worked in Italy under GIORGIO STREHLER. In 1976, with Fabià Puigserver, he founded Teatre Lliure in Barcelona, a resident company which has featured international classic and modern theatre (BRECHT, CHEKHOV, GENET and SHAKESPEARE). In 1983 he was named director of the National Drama Centre, housed at Madrid's Teatro Nacional María Guerrero. Among his internationally acclaimed productions are *Luces de bohemia* (*Bohemian Lights*), by VALLE-INCLÁN, and *El público* (*The Audience*) and *Comedia sin título* (*Play without a Title*), avant-garde works by GARCÍA LORCA that were long considered unperformable. Since 1990 he has headed the Théâtre de l'Europe at the ODÉON in Paris. He was instrumental in introducing Spanish authors to the French stage, e.g. his own version of Valle-Inclán's novel *Tirano Banderas* and LOPE DE VEGA's *Le Chevalier d'Olmedo* (*The Knight of Olmedo*). Outstanding among his opera credits are works by Verdi performed in Spain, Italy, France and Belgium.

**Passion play** Medieval play. The 'Passion' refers specifically to the sufferings of Christ between his taking in Gethsemane and his death on the cross, though the period is sometimes extended. Popular in Europe in the 14th and 15th centuries, the Passion (play) means different things in different language areas. Like the MYSTERY PLAYS, they were not uniformly serious. Next to solemn scenes like a sermon or the Crucifixion, the audience would witness vulgar and violent action. The sources of these plays are not only the Bible and the Gospels, but also the many apocryphal gospels and other Christian legends that circulated widely during the Middle Ages in non-dramatic literature and in contemporary art. Passion plays can vary enormously in length and in style.

In Germany, what are now called Passion plays were often called Easter plays (*Österspiele*) and included scenes from Christ's life and some  from the Old Testament. The best-known is the Benediktbeuern Passion play of c.1120, which, like the *Carmina Burana* poems from the same manuscript, contains both Latin and German text. In Italy the oldest extant manuscript dates from the 12th century, from Montecassino. In the Coliseum in Rome, from 1460 to the early 16th century, there was an annual performance by the Gonfaloniere di Santa Lucia (banner-bearers of St Lucy) covering scenes from Christ's ministry, Passion and Resurrection.

**Pastor, Tony** [Antonio] 1837–1908 American VARIETY performer and manager. He made his professional debut in 1846 as an infant prodigy at BARNUM's Museum. He later travelled as a circus CLOWN, minstrel and ballad-singer, with a repertory of some 1,500 songs, arranging concerts in small towns. He first booked variety into the rowdy American Theatre at 444 Broadway (1861) and, determined to attract a respectable audience, took over the Volksgarten at 201 Bowery in 1865. Renaming it the Opera House, Pastor advertised it as 'the Great Family Resort' and invited women and children to special matinées, but even door prizes of turkeys, hams and barrels of flour were insufficient to attract a God-fearing public. The fat man with the waxed moustache and mincing step moved his clean bill of variety to 585 Broadway in 1875, and then to 14th Street in 1881. There he finally succeeded in promoting clean VAUDEVILLE to a family audience.

**pastoral** Pastorals generally depict the happy outcome of faithful love in a removed, rural setting. The form found its way into drama by way of poetry. Theocritus and Virgil provided a classical precedent. In Italy TASSO's *L'Aminta* (1573) is generally regarded as the first true pastoral play. GUARINI's *Il Pastor Fido* inspired JOHN FLETCHER. The genre is hard to define, but English dramatic examples are LYLY's *Love's Metamorphosis* (c.1589), PHILIP SIDNEY's prose romance, *Arcadia* (published 1590), PEELE's *The Old Wives Tale* (published 1595), JOHN DAY's *The Parliament of Bees* (written c.1595), SHAKESPEARE's *As You Like It* (1599) and Fletcher's *The Faithful Shepherdess* (1608). Pastoral plays survived longer in France, above all in the work of JEAN MAIRET. Milton's *Comus* (1634) also belongs to the genre.

**Paulus** [Jean Paulin Habans] 1845–1908 French music-hall (see CAFÉ CHANTANT) star. He was the first to earn a huge salary (400 francs per night in 1888). His career was a series of ups and downs in Paris and Marseilles, quarrels with managers, broken contracts and attacks by the censors (see CENSORSHIP). Then, in 1886, he won glory by adding a topical verse about General Boulanger to the song 'En revenant de la revue', which became epidemic. A strenuous performer with a stentorian voice, he founded and edited *La Revue des Concerts* (1887) as a vent for his vindictiveness; toured to London and America (1891–2); and managed the Ba-ta-clan and the Marseilles Alhambra unsuccessfully, before retiring in 1903.

***pavaikuthu [tholpavaikuthu]*** Indian puppet form. *Pavai* means 'figure of a shadow' and *kuthu* means 'play'. The *pavaikuthu* is the shadow puppet theatre of Kerala state, south India. It has unique characteristics, including the fact that the people of the region speak Malayalam whereas Tamil is the language of the drama. *Pavaikuthu* is usually performed near the *sanctum sanc-*

*torum* of Kali temples as a ritual form of entertainment for the goddess.

The puppets are short, stout silhouettes made of antelope doe-skin, thought to be holy. Because of the thick skins the puppets are not translucent, a marked deviation from the SHADOW PUPPETS found elsewhere in India. The silhouettes projected on the screen are only outlines of the figures, with minimal perforations made in the leather to delineate costume and ornament.

Performances are held in special stage houses in the temple compound. The manipulators squat below the white portion of the screen, masked by a black curtain, and operate the puppets from behind a row of lamps. After the installation ceremony two of the characters provide a summary of the previous night's story, which serves as a prologue to the events about to take place. Then the episodes of the local version of the *Ramayana* are enacted in sequence. The conclusion to the story is the grand coronation of Rama, who appears in puppet form wearing his crown.

**Pavlovsky, Eduardo** 1933– Argentine playwright, actor and director. Pavlovsky also founded a theatre group in Buenos Aires. Protesting against what he views as an absurd political 'situation, he considers himself a representative of 'exasperated REALISM' (his description). From the psychoanalytic position of early plays (he is also a psychoanalyst) such as *La espera trágica* (*Tragic Wait*, 1964) he turned to more committed sociopolitical plays with *La mueca* (*The Grimace*, 1971), *El Señor Galíndez* (*Mr Galíndez*, 1973), *Telarañas* (*Spiderwebs*, 1976) and *El Señor Laforgue* (*Mr Laforgue*, 1982). *Galíndez* and *Laforgue* are particularly outspoken about brutality, torture and repressive political actions in Argentina and Haiti, respectively. Recent plays include *Potestad* (*Power*, 1985), *Pablo* (1987), *Paso de dos* (*Pas de deux*, 1989), *El cardenal* (*The Cardinal*, 1991), *La ley de la vida* (*The Law of Life*, 1992) and *Alguna vez* (*Some Time*, 1992).

**Pavy, Salathiel (Solomon)** c.1590–c.1603 English boy-actor. He joined the CHILDREN OF THE CHAPEL ROYAL and acted in JONSON's *Cynthia's Revels* (1600) and *Poetaster* (1601). Jonson's epitaph immortalized him: though 'scarce thirteen' when he died, he was the 'stage's jewel' for 'three fill'd zodiacs', so skilled in the playing of old men that even sophisticated spectators thought him one.

**Payne, Ben Iden** 1881–1976 British director, educator and actor. His experience as an actor with F. R. BENSON's company and as stage director at the ABBEY THEATRE in Dublin directly contributed to the success of ANNIE HORNIMAN's REPERTORY company in Manchester, which he managed from its inception in 1907 until 1911. From 1913 until 1934 he was active in American theatre, directing in Chicago, New York and Philadelphia. In 1934 he became director of the SHAKESPEARE Memorial Theatre at Stratford-upon-Avon. Returning to America in 1943, he inaugurated a summer Shakespeare Festival in San Diego (1949–52) and directed at the OREGON SHAKESPEARE FESTIVAL (1956 and 1961) and in Alberta (1958–60 and 1962).

**Payne, John Howard** 1791–1852 American actor and playwright. He played Romeo and Hamlet, quickly becoming known as 'Master Payne, the American ROSCIUS', and was favourably compared with 'Master BETTY'. He is remembered now for the lyrics to 'Home, Sweet Home!' (music by H. R. Bishop) in his *Clari, or The Maid of Milan* (COVENT GARDEN, 1823). He wrote or translated and adapted from the French some 60 plays. Among the best known are *Brutus, or The Fall of Tarquin* (with EDMUND KEAN, DRURY LANE, 1818; and with EDWIN FORREST in New York, 1829); *Thérèse, or The Orphan of Geneva* (Drury Lane, 1821; and with Forrest in New York, 1829); *Clari* and two collaborations with Washington Irving, *Charles II, or The Merry Monarch* (Covent Garden, 1824) and *Richelieu* (Covent Garden, 1826).

**Peele, George** 1558–96 English playwright. He was one of the UNIVERSITY WITS, with such contemporaries as GREENE and NASHE. Peele's earliest extant play *The Arraignment of Paris* (1581–4), written for performance by the CHILDREN OF THE CHAPEL ROYAL, is a debate, distinguished only by his characteristic songs. *The Battle of Alcazar* (c.1598) provided EDWARD ALLEYN with a role reminiscent of MARLOWE's Tamburlaine. *Edward I* (c.1593) and *The Love of King David and Fair Bethsabe* (c.1594) were followed by his best-known play, *The Old Wives' Tale* (published 1595), which combines storytelling with good-humoured PARODY of contemporary dramatic styles.

**Pene du Bois, Raoul** 1914–85 American set and COSTUME designer. He began his career at the age of 14 designing costumes for the *Garrick Gaieties*. From the 1930s on he designed many shows and musicals ranging from *DuBarry Was a Lady* and *Jumbo* to *Wonderful Town* and *No, No, Nanette*. He also designed for films, ballets, ice shows and the Rockettes. His designs are typified by a strong sense of colour and a certain whimsicality of line.

**penny gaff** SEE PENNY THEATRES

**penny theatres** English playhouses. Cheap minor playhouses arose in Regency London which allowed amateurs, on payment of a fee, to play roles of their choice; DICKENS penned a classic description of them in *Sketches by Boz*. First known as 'dukeys', the earliest was an unnamed booth at the back of the Westminster Theatre in the Broadway. Hector Simpson's Vine Yard, Tooley Street, specialized in dog drama (see ANIMALS AS PERFORMERS); at Bryant's Varieties, Sloane Square, Richard III cost a fiver and the Lord Mayor six shillings to enact. Performing without a licence, these theatres were frequently closed. But the Theatres Act of 1843 spawned a spate of low-priced professional houses; their emphasis on gruesome true-crime MELODRAMAS like *Maria Marten* was another nuisance to the authorities. Legally, spoken dialogue was not permitted (see THEATRICAL MONOPOLY), but the statute was honoured more in the breach than the observance.

These theatres became known as 'penny gaffs'. The Rotunda in the Blackfriar's Road was the largest, seating 1,000 and giving two performances an evening at a top price of threepence; but the average might offer six performances of singing and dancing in a converted warehouse. The New York equivalent was the Grand Duke's Opera House, located in a Baxter Street cellar and operated by street boys, with tallow candles as footlights, wash-tubs as private boxes and a six-cent admission fee. Throughout the 1870s, it was a favourite Bohemian resort, and WEBER AND FIELDS got their start there.

**People Show** British company. The shows given by this small touring group, formed in 1966, are largely improvised around a theme or popular genre (such as TENNESSEE WILLIAMS's *Deep South* play in *People Show 95*) which is developed to its anarchic limits. One of the most influential FRINGE companies of the 1960s, it has toured Europe and contributed to the beginnings of modern performance art, to a postmodern SURREALISM and to alternative comedy.

**People's National Theatre** London company. Founded in 1930 by the actress Nancy Price, it was based on ideas similar to the New York THEATRE GUILD. Its first production was a revival of Anstey's *The Man from Blankley's* at the FORTUNE THEATRE, and in 1932 a permanent home was found at the Little Theatre. There an extensive programme of non-commercial drama was presented ranging from EURIPIDES to PIRANDELLO, though Price also staged (and acted in) Mazo de la Roche's *Whiteoaks*, which ran for two years. The venture came to an end when the Little Theatre was destroyed in 1941.

**Pepper's ghost** Theatrical effect. An actor standing in the orchestra pit below the level of the stage is lit so that his reflection is cast on a sheet of glass mounted between the audience and the stage, thus producing the impression of a phantom. The illusion was invented by a retired civil engineer named Henry Dircks, who sold it, as the Aetheroscope, in 1862 to John Henry Pepper, director of the Polytechnic Institution, London. It was first used there for a dramatic reading of DICKENS's *The Haunted Man* on Christmas Eve of that year, and the many theatres that pirated it were soon forced to pay Pepper a royalty, so that 'Pepper's ghost' became current as the term for any trick effect for raising stage spectres. It was introduced to the United States in a MELODRAMA, *True to the Last*, at WALLACK's Theatre, New York (1863), and for the next two months New York managers presented horror shows teeming with ghosts. The illusion eventually was superseded by the use of back-lit scrim.

**Pepys, Samuel** 1633–1703 English diarist. His *Diary*, which runs from 1660 to 1669, is the first English record of regular play-going and a vivid account of the plays, players, scenery and audience of the Restoration theatre. Some of his critical comments are notoriously dogmatic, but his tastes were broad and his pleasure is infectious.

**Peretz, Isaac (Loeb)** 1852–1915 Polish-born playwright. He directed the Hazomir Group in Warsaw. The most notable of his plays are *The Sisters* (1904), dealing with the extreme poverty of the Jews in Poland, and *Night in the Old Market*, an eerie, atmospheric, poetic fantasy first produced by Alexander Granowski for the MOSCOW STATE JEWISH THEATRE (1925) and offering a challenge to art theatres ever since.

**Performance Group, The** American company. One of the most controversial and visible of the environmental theatre groups of the 1960s and 1970s, it was formed in New York in 1967 by Richard Schechner (1934– ), critic, director and editor of *The Drama Review*. Influenced by GROTOWSKI, Schechner broke through traditional barriers of a text- and stage-bound theatre with productions such as *Dionysus in 69* (1968), *Makbeth* (1969), *Commune* (1970) and *The Balcony* (1979). Though only partially successful, the Group was notable for its concern with social issues and its investigation into RITUAL and the use of other cultures in the development of a new performance art. Since 1980, renamed the WOOSTER GROUP, it has continued under ELIZABETH LeCOMPTE.

*periaktoi* Ancient Greek term. Vitruvius speaks of *periaktoi* – prism-shaped scenic pieces with scenes painted on each of their three sides. By rotating the *periaktoi* a change of scene could be suggested. (See also GREEK THEATRE, ANCIENT.)

**Perkins, Osgood** 1892–1937 American stage and film actor. WINTHROP AMES cast him as Homer Cady in *Beggar on Horseback*, his BROADWAY debut. Later he appeared as Walter Burns in *The Front Page* (1928) and as Astroff in *Uncle Vanya* (1930). He was described as 'wiry, nervous, unerring in his attack'.

**Perlini, Memé** 1940– Italian actor and director. He established a major reputation as an innovative director in experimental work during the mid- and late 1970s. Although his early work included a version of SHAKESPEARE's *Othello* (1974), it was only with a production of ARISTOPHANES' *Birds* (1980) that he turned more to staging classic plays in regular theatres, including his own translation of *The Merchant of Venice* (1980) and IBSEN's *John Gabriel Borkman* (1981). He has had an enduring interest in the work of PIRANDELLO, writing and staging *Pirandello chi?* (1973) and giving imaginative reorchestrations to plays like *All'uscita* (*To the Exit*, 1989) and *Lazzaro* (*Lazarus*, 1989–90); a recent example of his interest in classical drama is *Ifigenia in Aulide* (1992).

**Peruzzi, Baldassare** 1481–1536 Italian painter and architect. He is important in theatre history as a pioneer of stage perspective and decoration, and for his use of original research on the archaeology of classical THEATRE BUILDINGS. VASARI devotes one of his *Lives* to him, indicating the range of his contribution to the early development of stage settings, theatrical machinery, festival entertainment and triumphs. His designs probably provided the models for SERLIO's influential tragic, comic and pastoral settings. (See also THEATRE DESIGN.)

**Peshkov, A.M.** see GORKY, MAKSIM

**Petit-Bourbon, Salle du** (Paris) A hall in the former palace of the Dukes of Burgundy, it was adjacent to the Louvre and used for court entertainments in 16th- and 17th-century France. A stage and balconies afforded a convenient space for court ballets and MASQUES. In 1645 the backstage area was reconstructed by TORELLI for his productions of Italian opera. In 1658 MOLIÈRE was given partial use of the theatre and staged there his earliest successes with the Parisian public. Two years later it was demolished, and Molière moved the fittings to the PALAIS-ROYAL.

**Petitclair, Pierre** 1813–60 French Canadian playwright. He wrote the first published play by a native French Canadian, *Griphon, ou La Vengeance d'un valet* (*Griphon: or A Valet's Revenge*, 1837), a three-act comedy with strong farcical elements, visibly influenced by MOLIÈRE. This work was never performed, but was followed by two others staged with repeated success: *La Donation* (*The Legal Donation*, 1842) and *Une Partie de Campagne* (*A Country Outing*, 1857), an engaging comedy of manners portraying the dangers of mimicking British speech and customs.

**Petito, Antonio** 1822–76 Italian actor and playwright. He was best-known for his performances in the mask of Pulcinella and as the not-masked character Pascariello in Neapolitan farces, many of his own devising. He first acted Pulcinella at Naples's San Carlino Theatre in 1853, and later wrote many pieces for the FARCE player SCARPETTA.

**Pétomane, Le** [Joseph Pujol] 1857–1945 French music-hall artist (see CAFÉ CHANTANT). His billing meant 'the man mad about farts'. A star at the MOULIN-ROUGE (1906–10), he earned 20,000 francs by vibrating his sphincter to imitate the characteristic eructations of a mother-in-law, various animals, and a bride on her wedding night. He also used it to smoke a cigarette, produce

music on the ocarina and blow out a candle at a distance of 20 centimetres.

**Petrolini, Ettore** 1886–1936 Italian actor, entertainer and playwright. He began his career in the *caffè-concerto* world of Rome, specializing in comic patter and songs. After World War I his art became sharper, more bitter and satirical, in a series of self-devised sketches including *Nerone, Romani de Roma, Mustafà* and *Gastone*. He formed his own company specializing in his sketches and improvisations, adaptations of comedies by dramatists like Testoni and Novelli, and embracing one-act pieces by PIRANDELLO.

**Peymann, Claus** 1938– German director. He established both HANDKE and BERNHARD on the stage with the first productions of all their earlier plays (*Offending the Audience*, 1966; *Kaspar*, 1968; *A Feast for Boris*, 1970; *The Ignoramus and the Madman*, 1972; *The Ride Across Lake Constance*, 1973), and has since gained a reputation for radically unconventional interpretations of the classics, including his 1976 production of GOETHE's *Faust* in two evenings, achieving a blend of whimsy and seriousness. He has also premiered most of HEINER MÜLLER's plays.

**Pezzana, Giacinta** 1841–1919 Italian actress. She first appeared on the stage in 1859, rising quickly to become lead actress in the company of Cesare Dondini, playing opposite ERNESTO ROSSI in a wide variety of drama, from romantic stock pieces to SHAKESPEARE. From 1870 she led her own company, touring abroad to South America, Egypt and Russia. She achieved a notable success as the mother in ZOLA's *Thérèse Raquin* (1879) at the Teatro dei Fiorentini in Naples, acting with EMANUEL and the young DUSE.

**Phelps, Samuel** 1804–78 British actor. A devoted Shakespearian, he made his first London appearance as Shylock at the HAYMARKET in 1837. He further challenged the memory of EDMUND KEAN as Hamlet, Othello, Richard III and Sir Edward Mortimer in COLMAN THE YOUNGER's *The Iron Chest*. After playing Iago to Phelps's Othello at COVENT GARDEN (1837–8), MACREADY relegated his new employee to minor parts. With the abolition of the patent monopoly (see THEATRICAL MONOPOLY) in 1843, Phelps became joint lessee of the unfashionable SADLER'S WELLS, where from 1844 to 1862 he staged all but four of SHAKESPEARE's plays and showed a rare respect for the text. His was the first London *Pericles* since the Restoration. Temperamentally austere, Phelps was the finest Lear of his generation, and although not at ease in comedy, widely admired as Bottom, Falstaff and Jaques in *As You Like It*.

**Philadelphia, Jacob** [Jacob Meyer] 1721–c.1800 American-born conjuror. He acted as a scientific jester for William Augustus, Duke of Cumberland, performing mathematical and physical experiments. After the duke's death in 1765 he went public, travelling through Europe billed as 'an Artist of Mathematics', and played before Catherine the Great, Sultan Mustafa III and Frederick the Great, who was very fond of him. A member of a secret Rosicrucian society and anti-monarchical, Philadelphia was eventually expelled from Berlin. Meanwhile, he had gained the reputation of a true sorcerer who could pass through doors, grow a second head and read minds.

**Philipe, Gérard** 1922–59 French actor. He made his name in the title role of CAMUS's *Caligula* (1945), followed by numerous film roles. In 1951 he played

Rodrigue in *Le Cid* at the AVIGNON FESTIVAL. After this he joined the THÉÂTRE NATIONAL POPULAIRE team and played leading roles, e.g. Lorenzaccio and Friedrich Prince of Hamburg. He was unique among French actors in being both praised by the critics and adored by young theatregoers.

**Philips, Ambrose** 1674–1749 English playwright. He was a Fellow of St John's College, Cambridge. In 1712 his first play, an adaptation of RACINE's *Andromaque*, retitled *The Distressed Mother*, was extraordinarily successful, an effective neoclassical tragedy. His later plays, *The Briton* (1722) and *Humphrey, Duke of Gloucester* (1723), were less noticed. He became an Irish MP in 1727.

**Phillips, Augustine** died 1605 English actor. He was one of the original sharers in the LORD CHAMBERLAIN'S MEN, with whom he remained from 1594 until his death. A musician and athlete as well as an actor, he presumably performed in his own *Jig of the Slippers* (1595).

**Phillips, Robin** 1942– British-born director. Since arriving in Canada in 1974 to assume the directorship of the STRATFORD FESTIVAL, Phillips has established a reputation as Canada's leading director of classical theatre. He resigned from Stratford in 1980, since when he has directed at several of Canada's major theatres. He is an actors' director, and his productions are renowned for their brilliant visual impact: his cinematic style of direction guides audience perception as if through the lens of a camera.

**Phillips, Stephen** 1864–1915 British playwright and poet. Of his sonorous poetic dramas, TREE staged *Herod* (1900) and *Ulysses* (1902) at HER [HIS] MAJESTY'S and GEORGE ALEXANDER produced *Paolo and Francesca* (1902) at the ST JAMES'S.

**Phoenix Theatre** (London) The first theatre of this name is better known as the COCKPIT. A second, on the corner of Charing Cross Road and Phoenix Street, was opened in 1930.

**Phrynichus** 6th-5th centuries BC Greek tragic playwright. An older contemporary of AESCHYLUS and his most prominent rival, Phrynichus is chiefly remembered for two tragedies on historical subjects: the *Capture of Miletus*, which according to Herodotus so upset the Athenians that Phrynichus was heavily fined, and the *Phoenician Women*, which influenced Aeschylus' *Persians*. Few fragments survive.

**Piaf, Édith** [Édith Giovanna Gassion] 1915–63 French singer and song-writer. The daughter of street performers, she began singing in the streets at 12, and by 17 was well ensconced in the Pigalle milieu of whores and pimps. In 1935 she was dubbed *la môme Piaf* (Kid Sparrow). By 1937 she was a star: the brassy voice blaring out of the frail, black-clad body sang of hopeless love and intense suffering. With her best numbers, 'L'Accordéoniste' and 'La Vie en rose', she became the darling of the intellectuals, their emblem of tormented devotion. Successful tours of the United States (1949, 1955) and a triumphal return to France in 1956 with 'Milord' and 'Je ne regrette rien' were vitiated by her increasing reliance on drugs. Her addiction and ill health grew until she collapsed during a concert in 1959. A biographical play by PAM GEMS, *Piaf* (1980), enjoyed a good run in London and New York.

**Picard, Louis B.** 1769–1828 French playwright, actor and theatre director. He is best known as a writer of comedies. His play *Encore des Menechmes (The Nephew as Uncle*, 1791) established him. As an actor he excelled in the roles of comic valets. His play *The Parasite (Médiocre et Rampant)*, a comedy of manners, was performed at the Théâtre Louvois in 1797 after the burning of the ODÉON. In 1799 he successfully played the lawyer, Pavaret, in his own play *Le Collatéral*. In 1801 he set up his company at the Louvois. In 1805 he staged *Bertrand et Raton* and in 1806 *Les Marionettes*, considered one of his best plays. In 1807 he was made director of the Opéra, which he left in 1815 for the Odéon, where he had a series of successes, notably *Les Deux Philibert*, *Le Capitaine Belronde*, *Une Matinée d'Henri IV*, *Vaugelas* and *La Maison en loterie*. With the Odéon fire of 1818 he moved temporarily to the Favart. In 1820 his *Les Deux Ménages (Two Households)* was successfully staged at the Odéon, and subsequently taken into the COMÉDIE-FRANÇAISE repertoire. His last play, written in conjunction with Mazères, *L'Enfant trouvé (The Foundling)*, was put on at the Odéon in 1824.

**Picasso, Pablo** 1881–1973 Spanish painter and sculptor. Perhaps the most significant figure in 20th-century art, Picasso worked primarily in France. Although much of his early work included theatrical motifs, he did not turn to THEATRE DESIGN until his cubist period, when he was asked by SERGE DIAGHILEV, probably at the suggestion of JEAN COCTEAU and Léonide Massine, to design the Ballets Russes production of *Parade* (1917). Over the following eight years he designed seven more ballets and a play, including *Le Tricorne* (1919), *Pulcinella* (1920) and *Mercure* (1924). Picasso continued to provide designs for the stage as late as 1962 (Honneger's *Icare*) but the later works were generally backdrops or simple scenery adapted from existing drawings. He also wrote two plays: *Desire Caught by the Tale* (1941) and *The Four Little Girls* (1965).

**Piccolo Teatro** see STREHLER, GIORGIO

**Picon, Molly** 1898–1992 American actress. After a stint in VAUDEVILLE she starred internationally in YIDDISH THEATRE, in cabaret and films and on BROADWAY. Known for her impish but innocent charm, she played very young women.

**Pierrot** International character. Possibly related to the *COMMEDIA DELL'ARTE* character Pedrolino, Pierrot appears first in France in the second half of the 17th century, when the characteristic loose white clothing, ruff and soft hat, with unmasked, whitened face seem to have been established. Regularly included in scripted plays and PANTOMIMES of the 18th century, and popularized in England by DELPINI, Pierrot took on in the 19th century the piquant blend of comedy and pathos now generally associated with him, in the work of the gifted French MIME artist JEAN-GASPARD DEBURAU. Imitators such as Paul Legrand at the Folies-Dramatiques further emphasized the lyrical and sentimental attributes of the role at the expense of the comic.

**Pierrot show** English seaside entertainment. Around 1890 small groups of concert singers from London would perform at houseboat parties in masks; in 1891 Clifford Essex introduced a song-and-dance group costumed as PIERROTS in loose blouses with ruffs and pompons in Southern Ireland and the Isle of Wight. These innovations were rapidly taken up at seaside resorts in the 1890s and successfully supplanted the 'nigger minstrels'. The Pierrots' freshness and exuberance were conveyed to the WEST END by H. G. Pélissier's REVUE *The Follies* (Apollo Theatre, 1908, 1910) and the 'Pierrotic entertainment', *The Co-optimists* (Royalty Theatre, 1921-7). By the time JOAN LITTLEWOOD ironically garbed the players of her anti-militaristic revue *Oh, What a Lovely War!* (1963) in Pierrot costumes, the conventions of the seaside show were regarded as fey and anti-quated.

**Pike Theatre Club** (Dublin) Established in 1953 by Alan Simpson and Carolyn Swift, its 12ft-square ingeniously lighted stage held the premiere of BRENDAN BEHAN's *The Hostage* (1954) and shared the London premiere of BECKETT's *Waiting for Godot* (1955) – adventurous presentations for the Irish theatre of the time. In 1957 Simpson gave TENNESSEE WILLIAMS's *The Rose Tattoo* for the DUBLIN INTERNATIONAL THEATRE FESTIVAL and was charged with 'presenting for gain an indecent and profane performance'. Although he was eventually acquitted, legal costs and the blow to the theatre's morale were an insuperable setback.

**Piñera, Virgilio** 1912–79 Cuban playwright, poet and fiction writer. He lived in Argentina from 1946 to 1958. His first play, *Electra Garrigó* (1948), set off a heated scandal for its bold Cuban treatment of a classical myth. His theatre is characterized by absurd (see THEATRE OF THE ABSURD), black humour and a depiction of reality in intellectual and sometimes abstract terms. On the other hand, his *Aire frío* (*Cold Air*, 1962), considered a classic Cuban play, is a totally realistic vision of a middle-class family before the Revolution. Among his most significant works are *El flaco y el gordo* (*The Thin Man and the Fat Man*, 1949), *Jesús* (1950), *El filántropo* (*The Philanthropist*, 1960) and *Dos viejos pánicos* (*Two Old Panics*, 1968).

**Pinero, Arthur Wing** 1855–1934 British playwright. He abandoned acting to commit himself wholly to authorship in 1884 and was successful in two distinct styles, FARCE and the social 'problem' play. Of the first kind are *The Magistrate* (1885), *The Schoolmistress* (1886) and *Dandy Dick* (1887). By the time he wrote *The Cabinet Minister* (1890) he had established a new reputation as a writer of comedy with the sentimental *Sweet Lavender* (1888) and *The Profligate* (1889). He proceeded to examine, if not challenge, conventional morality, highlighting the plight of women in the sensationally successful *The Second Mrs Tanqueray* (1893), in which the wayward heroine expediently commits suicide, *The Notorious Mrs Ebbsmith* (1895), *The Benefit of the Doubt* (1895), *Iris* (1901), *Letty* (1903), *His House in Order* (1906), *The Thunderbolt* (1908) and *Mid-Channel* (1909). Other effective comedies are *The Princess and the Butterfly* (1897) and *The Gay Lord Quex* (1899). His best comedy, *Trelawny of the 'Wells'* (1898), is a nostalgic celebration of the mid-Victorian theatre. Pinero was knighted in 1909.

**Pinski, David** 1872–1959 Yiddish playwright and novelist. He began writing in Warsaw and in 1899 arrived in the USA, where he wrote most of his 38 plays. In almost poetic form they search for the eternal meanings and true values of life, particularly for the poor. The most notable are *Isaac Sheftel* (1899), a naturalistic tragedy, *The Family Zevi* (1904), *The Eternal Jew* (1906) and *The Treasure*, staged first in German by REINHARDT.

**Pinter, Harold** [David Baron] 1930– British playwright, director and actor. His early plays, *The Room* (1957) and *The Birthday Party* (1958), were condemned by most critics as obscure, despite his obvious talent for creating dialogue and dramatic suspense.

Pinter was labelled a writer of the absurd (see THEATRE OF THE ABSURD), along with such dramatists as N. F. SIMPSON, EUGÈNE IONESCO and SAMUEL BECKETT. He does have affinities with Beckett: his one-act play, *A Slight Ache* (1959), has marked similarities with the second part of Beckett's novel, *Molloy*, while the tramp Davies in Pinter's *The Caretaker* (1960) is reminiscent of the tramps in *Waiting for Godot*. But whereas Beckett is trying to establish a sense of metaphysical isolation, Pinter is more influenced by the naturalistic tradition (see NATURALISM) and particularly by his Jewish childhood in Hackney at a time of Fascist demonstrations. The bullies who terrorize Stanley in *The Birthday Party* are not abstract creations but closely observed tormentors. The settings in *The Caretaker* and *The Homecoming* (1965) are precise evocations of unfashionable London. Pinter's themes accumulate layers of meanings. *The Homecoming* is ostensibly about a don who returns from a civilized university campus in the USA to his childhood home in North London, bringing his wife Ruth to meet his all-male, working-class family. Ruth's sexual fantasies are aroused by the surrounding longings. Thus she too comes 'home' to her instincts.

While the term 'Pinteresque' became common currency for anything menacing and enigmatic, Pinter started to play with ideas of time, as in *Landscape* and *Silence* (1969), a double bill first produced by the ROYAL SHAKESPEARE COMPANY, which also produced his memory play, *Old Times* (1971). His long association with PETER HALL continued at the NATIONAL THEATRE, where he became an associate director. Hall directed JOHN GIELGUD and RALPH RICHARDSON in *No Man's Land* (1975), and in 1982 a triple bill that included *A Kind of Alaska* (1982), describing sleeping sickness, an illness from which the patient can recover through the drug L-Dopa. Another short play, *One for the Road*, describes an inquisition from an agent of a totalitarian regime and illustrates the change in Pinter's style towards the less enigmatic and more direct form of storytelling, a process which began with his retrospective look at how an adultery started, *Betrayal* (1978).

Pinter's writing became more politically urgent in the 1980s, and his short plays *One for the Road* (1984), *Mountain Language* (1988) and *Party Time* (1991) all warn of the dangers of Fascist dictatorship. In 1993 his first full-length play for several years, *Moonlight*, about a dying man and his family, was performed.

As a director Pinter has been particularly associated with the plays of SIMON GRAY. In 1993 he directed the London version of DAVID MAMET's controversial two-hander, *Oleanna*.

**Pirandello, Luigi** 1867–1936 Italian playwright and novelist. A Sicilian by birth, he lived in Rome in the 1890s, publishing poetry, short stories and his first novel, *L'Esclusa* (*The Outcast*, 1893). He became a university lecturer and taught until 1922. His wife's mental health gradually deteriorated, and she was eventually confined to an asylum.

Pirandello turned to playwriting late in his career. The most important of his novels, *Il fu Mattia Pascal* (*The Late Mattia Pascal*, 1904), treated themes he was later to explore in his plays: the elusiveness of personal identity, the relativity of all values and the relationship between art and life. His one-act pieces were followed by a series of full-length plays crafted for Italian bourgeois audiences, including *Pensaci, Giacomino!* (*Think, Giacomino!*, 1916), *Liolà* (1916), *Così è (se vi pare)* (*It Is So (If You Think So)*, 1917), *Il piacere dell'onestà* (*The Pleasure of Honesty*, 1918) and *Il giuoco delle parti* (*The Rules of the Game*, 1918) – plays which made contemporary critics associate him with the TEATRO DEL GROTTESCO. *Sei personaggi in cerca d'autore* (*Six Characters in Search of an Author*, 1921), perhaps the most influential of all, provoked uproar when first performed in Rome but quickly came to be recognized as seminal, encapsulating the modernist assault on traditional theatre forms. The PITOËFF production in 1924 made an impact in Paris comparable to that of BECKETT's *Waiting for Godot* in the early 1950s. It was the first of his three so-called 'theatre in the theatre' plays; the other two, *Ciascuno a suo modo* (*Each in His Own Way*, 1924) and *Questa sera si recita a soggetto* (*Tonight We Improvise*, 1929), have never enjoyed equal success.

Throughout the 1920s and 30s Pirandello was remarkably prolific, although the quality of his work was uneven. Among the best-known plays are *Vestire gli ignudi* (*To Dress the Naked*, 1922), *Enrico IV* (1922), *La vita che ti diedi* (*The Life I Gave You*, 1923), the one-act *L'uomo dal fiore in bocca* (*The Man with the Flower in His Mouth*, 1923), *Diana e la Tuda* (*Diana and Tuda*, 1926), *Bellavita* (1927), *La nuova colonia* (*The New Colony*, 1928), *Lazzaro* (*Lazarus*, 1929), *Trovarsi* (*To Find Oneself*, 1932), *Quando si è qualcuno* (*When One Is Somebody*, 1933), *Come tu mi vuoi* (*As You Desire Me*, 1936) and *I giganti della montagna* (*The Mountain Giants*, posthumously, 1937). Some of these were written for performance by Pirandello's own company, the Teatro d'Arte, supported by the Fascist regime, with whom he was uneasily associated during his later years.

The sheer theatrical power of Pirandello's best work, in its bitter humour, emotional drive and storytelling power, is undeniable. Together with IBSEN and BRECHT he has been one of the most influential of modern dramatists, even though some works are marred by excessive discussion, explanation and an overly insistent irony. His plays dominate the repertory today in Italy and several regularly hold the stage internationally. Not all have yet been made available in English.

**Pires, José Cardoso** 1925– Portuguese playwright and novelist. His first play, *O Render dos Heróis* (*Relieving the Heroes*, 1965), deals with a reactionary peasant revolt of the 1840s. The approach and techniques are BRECHTian. *Corpo-Delito na Sala de Espelhos* (*Body of Evidence in the Hall of Mirrors*, 1979) is both Brechtian and absurd (see THEATRE OF THE ABSURD) and, with more than a touch of the GENET of *Le Balcon*, evokes the nightmare of the PIDE (the dictator Salazar's secret police).

**Piron, Alexis** 1689–1773 French playwright and poet. He wrote a series of plays for the COMÉDIE-FRANÇAISE, including *La Métromanie* (*Metromania*, 1738), a lively, original comedy featuring a young provincial poet much like Piron himself.

**Pisarev, Aleksandr (Ivanovich)** 1803–28 Russian playwright. In his short career he became known as the best Russian *vaudeville* dramatist, combining farcical situations with effective characterization and even some early social criticism. During the reactionary reign of Nikolai I when freedom of speech and of the press was largely curtailed, the disarming medium of the *vaudeville* became one of the few avenues for superficial criticism. Most of Pisarev's 23 plays were translations or adaptations of French neoclassical models. Basically a conservative in literary matters, Pisarev aligned himself with the classically minded SHAKHOVSKOI circle. MIKHAIL SHCHEPKIN, the father of Russian realistic acting (see REALISM), took a serious approach to the playing of roles in Pisarev's *vaudevilles The Tutor and the Pupil* (1824) and *The Busybody* (1825). Two of his works, *The Caliph's Amusements* (1825) and *The Magic Nose, or The Talisman and the Dates* (1825), were dubbed 'vaudeville-operas', indicating a greater emphasis on spectacle-

scenic transformations, COSTUMES and dances which was well suited to their Oriental stories.

**Piscator, Erwin (Friedrich Max)** 1893–1966 German director. Piscator's concept of political theatre formed one of the most significant creative forces in German drama during the 1920s as well as in the 1960s. He succeeded KARLHEINZ MARTIN as director of the Proletarian Theatre and developed a form of AGIT-PROP suited to the German context which culminated in a historical REVUE, *Despite All!* (1925), a polemic panorama of events of World War I in a simultaneous montage of authentic speeches, news extracts, photographs and film sequences. He aimed to influence voters and clarify communist policy, and the standards of authenticity and contemporaneity carried over into his productions for the VOLKSBÜHNE.

Dismissed in 1927, he founded the Piscator-Bühne in opposition to the Volksbühne. There he mounted a series of striking multimedia productions designed to present complex economic and social forces in concrete terms. TOLLER's *Hurrah, We Live!* (1927) was performed on a four-storey structure on to which filmed scenes were projected; *Rasputin*, later the same year, used a revolving hemisphere with scenes played within its opening segments, film and photographs integrated with the action, and texts or dates projected on screens flanking the stage. The technology provided a model of EPIC THEATRE that influenced BRECHT – who collaborated on the *Rasputin* production and that of *The Adventures of the Good Soldier Schweik* (1928) – as well as containing all the techniques of the modern documentary drama. It also influenced the Theatre Workshop of JOAN LITTLEWOOD in England and the LIVING NEWSPAPER productions of the FEDERAL THEATRE PROJECT in the USA (through Piscator's book on *The Political Theatre*,1929).

After teaching in New York during World War II, where he first staged his adaptation of *War and Peace* (1942), Piscator returned to Germany and became director of the new Freie Volksbühne in 1962. There he was instrumental in developing the documentary plays of HOCHHUTH, KIPPHARDT and WEISS.

**Pisemsky, Aleksei (Feofilaktovich)** 1821–81 Russian playwright and novelist. With his friend OSTROVSKY, he brought the common people on to the Russian stage. His play *A Bitter Fate* (1859) is sometimes called the first Russian realistic tragedy (see REALISM). Antecedent in plot, character and theme to LEV TOLSTOI's *The Power of Darkness*, Pisemsky's dramatization of a provincial *ménage à trois* with fatal consequences is largely devoid of Tolstoi's moral didacticism. His later plays were mostly historical MELODRAMAS and SATIRES on incipient capitalism in the 1860s and 1870s (e.g. *Baal*, 1873). His narrative works include the novels *The Muff* (1850), *A Thousand Souls* (1858) and *Troubled Seas* (1863). He continued the GOGOLian tradition of exposing the baser side of humanity and shared with this author a malady that was the subject of his first stage comedy, *The Hypochondriac* (1852).

**Pitoëff family** Russian-French theatrical producers and actors. **Georges** (1884–1939) and **Ludmilla** (1895–1951) Pitoëff left Russia, where they had known STANISLAVSKY and MEYERHOLD, for Switzerland (1915–21) and then Paris, where Georges's productions were some of the most significant of the interwar period. A member of the CARTEL, Georges was an outstandingly inventive director, particularly of PIRANDELLO (*Six Characters in Search of an Author*, 1923) and Chekhov, but his repertoire was wide-ranging and international. He brought both Lenormand and Anouilh to public notice. Ludmilla, his wife, was an outstanding actress and something of a mystic. She starred in Chekhov, in Shaw's *St Joan* (1925) and in Claudel's *L'Échange* (1937 and 1946). Their son, **Sacha** (1920– ), is a powerful stage and film actor who has also produced Pirandello and Chekhov.

**Pix, Mary** 1666–1709 English playwright. Her first plays appeared in 1696, the tragedy *Ibrahim* and the lively farce *The Spanish Wives*. By 1697 she and other women playwrights were mocked in *The Female Wits*. Her fast-paced comedy *The Deceiver Deceived* (1698) was plagiarized by George Powell for *The Imposture Defeated*. In all she wrote 12 plays, tragedies of heroic sentiment and comedies of witty intrigue, all displaying a concern to defend the independence of her heroines.

**Pixérécourt, (René Charles) Guilbert de** 1773–1844 French playwright. Destitute at the Revolution, he turned to the theatre to make a living, and within a few years had become the acknowledged father of the new genre, the melodrama. Among his 120 works there were also *vaudevilles* and comic operas, but the most successful were melodramas, many of which he directed. From 1825–35 he managed the Gaîté (see boulevard). *Victor; ou L'Enfant de la forêt* (*Victor, or The Child of the Forest*, 1797), in which a virtuous youth discovers his father to be a brigand, shows Pixérécourt's sententious moralizing. *Coelina; ou L'Enfant du mystère* (1800), adapted into English by Holcroft as *A Tale of Mystery*, set the pattern for melodrama. It exploits the idea of a mutilated 'hero', has an innocent persecuted heroine, a good comic role, an exciting chase and conflict above a ravine, and the final triumph of virtue. The mood of the action is reflected in the scenery and the behaviour of nature. *L'Homme à trois visages* (*The Man with Three Faces*, 1801), with its Venetian setting, conspiracies, and hero who is obliged to play three different roles, established another pattern in the early melodrama. His last major play, and one of his most important, *Latude; ou trente-cinq ans de captivité* (*Latude, or Thirty-five Years of Captivity*, 1834), was an episodic account of a true story about an unjust imprisonment.

Pixérécourt had an excellent sense of theatre, but his dialogue barely supported the action, and most of his plays died with him. He also strove to ensure the payment of proper royalties to authors.

**Pla, Josefina** 1909– Paraguayan playwright, poet, journalist and critic. Born in the Canary Islands, she has lived in Paraguay since 1927. She has written more than 40 plays, some in collaboration with Roque Centurión Miranda, with whom in 1948 she created the Municipal School of Dramatic Art in Asunción. Her best-known play is *Historia de un número* (*Story of a Number*, 1949), an expressionistic (see expressionism), sentimental farce; other plays range from local themes, written in Guaraní (the non-official language), to classical tragedies such as *Alcestes*.

**Placide family** American actors. **Alexander** Placide (?–1812), a French rope dancer and pantomimist, emigrated to the United States during the Revolution and appeared at the John Street Theatre, New York, in 1792. He managed theatres in Charleston and Richmond. Of his many children **Henry** Placide (1799–1870) was considered one of the finest American character actors, remaining at the Park Theatre for most of his career. American audiences considered him

best in traditional English comedy, e.g. as Sir Peter Teazle.

Henry Placide's older sister Caroline (1789–1881) married William Rufus Blake, and his siblings **Eliza** (?–1874) and **Thomas** (1808–77) both had theatrical careers, Thomas managing the Park Theatre for some years. **Jane** (1804–35), another sister, played in New Orleans for a decade as a singer and comic actress, where she was referred to as 'Queen of the Drama', her Lady Macbeth and Cordelia being especially admired.

**Planché, J(ames) R(obinson)** 1795–1880 British playwright and musician. Planché's adaptation from the French of *The Vampire* (1820) at the London Lyceum brought him into prominence. He designed accurate historical costumes for a revival of *King John* (1823), his research in the field culminating in *The History of British Costume* (1834). His antiquarian activities showed in his theatrical practice and his 150 plays and librettos. Planché's most original dramatic work was written for Madame Vestris at the Olympic from 1830 to 1839. *Olympic Revels* (1830) initiated a sequence of charming extravaganzas, wittily rhymed and prettily costumed, based on classical mythology, and influential in the development of English pantomime (see pantomime, English). In 1845 he embellished Vestris's Haymarket season with *The Golden Fleece*.

**Planchon, Roger** 1931– French director, actor and playwright. Planchon is of working-class origins and largely self-educated in the theatre. At 21 he founded his first company in a disused printing works in Lyon. One of the first directors to produce Brecht in France (*The Good Person of Setzuan*, 1954), with Adamov he evolved a Marxist theatre style. He coined the term *écriture scénique* (scenic writing) to describe the director's work, which should complement the author's dramatic writing. His first production to be shown in Paris was Adamov's *Paolo-Paoli* (1957), which demystified the *belle époque* and divided the critics. In 1957 he moved to the large municipal theatre in Lyon's workers' suburb of Villeurbanne, where he remained. Here he made Marxist reinterpretations of plays by Shakespeare (*Henry IV*, 1957, *Troilus and Cressida*, 1964, *Richard III*, 1966), Molière (*George Dandin*, 1958, *Le Tartuffe*, 1962 and 1973, *Dom Juan*, 1980), Marivaux (*La Seconde Surprise de l'amour*, 1959) and Racine (*Bérénice*, 1966, *Athalie*, 1980). Since 1962 he has written over a dozen plays, in many of which he has directed and performed, notably *La Remise* (1962), *Bleus blancs rouges, ou Les Libertins* (1967), *L'Infâme* (1969), *Le Cochon noir* (1973), *Gilles de Rais* (1976), *Fragile forêt* and *Le Vieil Hiver* (1991). In 1972 Planchon's theatre was entitled Théâtre National Populaire and so the mantle of Vilar passed to him. In the 1980s and early 1990s his energies became increasingly taken up with his work as a film director. In 1995 he was dismissed from his post at the TNP.

***platea*** see mansion and *platea*

**Plater, Alan (Frederick)** 1935– British playwright. In 1970 he co-founded the Hull Arts Centre. He began writing television plays (see television drama), several of which he adapted for the stage. *A Smashing Day* (1965) received a brief London run; *See the Pretty Lights* (1970) is a tender story of love between a middle-aged man and a teenage girl. But Plater's true vitality as a writer only emerged when he started to work with song-writers such as Alex Glasgow and in a style of regional 'epics' which owed much to Joan Littlewood, combining songs, music-hall sketches and comedy gags into what were often serious social themes. The most successful of these local documentaries was *Close the Coalhouse Door* (1968), based on stories by Sid Chaplin, which described the history of coal mining as seen through the eyes of the Milburn family. Recently Plater has written mainly for television, but two plays were provided for the Theatre Royal, Stratford, London: *Rent Party* (1989), a jazz musical set in 1930s Harlem, and I *Thought I Heard a Rustling* (1991), about *agents provocateurs* in a threatened local library.

**platt** Elizabethan theatrical term. It refers to the outline or 'plot' of a play. The platt was a physical object: the BOOK-KEEPER wrote out the detail of the plot, to be hung up and consulted by actors and stage-hands. A few have survived, sometimes matching names of actors with their characters and providing notes about properties and sound effects.

**Plautus** [Titus Maccius Plautus] died c.184 BC Roman playwright. Plautus was the first Roman dramatist to specialize solely in COMEDY, and the first whose work survives (see ROMAN THEATRE). His name is uncertain; it is usually given as Titus Maccius Plautus, but all three may be nicknames. After his death there were said to be 130 plays circulating in his name, but the 21 preserved, completely or partly, in medieval manuscripts are regarded as authentic.

Of the 21, one (*Vidularia, The Wallet Play*) is a mere fragment. Only two are firmly dated, *Stichus* to 200 and *Pseudolus* to 192 BC. The others are *Amphitruo, Asinaria* (*The Ass Play*), *Aulularia* (*The Jar Play*), *Bacchides* (*The Bacchises*), *Captivi* (*The Prisoners*), *Casina, Cistellaria* (*The Casket Play*), *Curculio, Epidicus, Menaechmi* (*The Menaechmuses*), *Mercator* (*The Merchant*), *Miles Gloriosus* (*The Braggart Soldier*), *Mostellaria* (*The Spook Play*), *Persa* (*The Persian*), *Poenulus* (*The Wretch from Carthage*), *Pseudolus, Rudens* (*The Rope*), *Trinummus* (*Threepence*) and *Truculentus*. All are adapted from Greek originals (three by MENANDER).

Plautus' style is far more jokey than that of his models, being full of puns, alliteration, coinages, bizarre imagery and other tricks of language. Even the more serious figures are allowed to come out of character for the sake of a joke. The role of the Cunning Slave – a likeable rogue who solves all his master's problems with his trickery – is built up enormously, and this character may give his name to a play (e.g. *Epidicus, Pseudolus, Stichus*) as he never does in Greek drama. Address to the audience is frequent, especially from the Cunning Slave; sometimes this is thinly disguised as soliloquy, but Plautus is quite prepared to break the 'dramatic illusion' altogether by acknowledging the audience's presence. The pathos and moral delicacy of Menander are abandoned or undercut, as the cynicism and deceitfulness of the Cunning Slave prevail over all. Meters are far more varied than in Menander, large sections of most of the plays being written for musical accompaniment.

Names of persons and places are Greek (or sometimes a comic PARODY of Greek), but Greek institutions and customs are generally Romanized. *Amphitruo* is the only ancient comedy to survive on a mythical theme, but even here the focus is on intrigue and deception and the characters are familiar Plautine types.

In some plays, such as *Aulularia* and *Menaechmi* (the source of SHAKESPEARE's *Comedy of Errors*), the plot is well sustained and more or less consistent; in others, such as *Stichus*, it is ragged and unimportant besides the

elements of FARCE and slapstick. No doubt the former plays are closer to their Greek models than the latter. Plautus was writing scripts for theatrical performance, and it is obvious that he knew his theatre and his audience intimately, and provided exactly what was wanted.

**Plavilshchikov, Pyotr (Alekseevich)** 1760–1812 Russian playwright, actor and teacher. His looks and bearing made him ideally suited for the impersonation of positive heroes, kings and moralizers in tragedy, but his real talent was expressed in roles drawn from bourgeois drama and *bytovoi* (daily life) comedies, where he showed simplicity, naturalness and sincerity of feeling. These works were closer in style and tone to his own bourgeois dramas and doleful comedies on Russian themes. His comic opera, *The Miller and the Mead-Seller as Rivals* (1782), a sequel to KNYAZHNIN's *The Mead-Seller* and Ablesimov's comic opera *The Miller*, favours the miller for his more total Russianness. His comedy, *Kuteikin's Agreement* (1789), is a sequel to FONVIZIN's classic Russian national comedy, *The Minor. The Landless Peasant* (1790) sentimentally depicts the relationship between master and serfs. *The Shopman* (1804) offers a satirical treatment of the Russian merchant class in a state of moral decline, foreshadowing OSTROVSKY.

Plavilshchikov was also an impressive administrator. In 1781 he succeeded Dmitrevsky as supervisor of the Russian theatre in St Petersburg. Later he trained companies of serf actors (see SERF THEATRES). Everywhere he worked he tried to enhance the standard repertory with new dramatic offerings.

**play** Play is central to the health and the growth of individual and community. Through play human beings both celebrate and shape their world. It is a dynamic which permeates culture; more a process, a relationship and an attitude than a thing in itself. Play is a free activity, intrinsically self-motivated and non-utilitarian, where attention is voluntarily limited. For the player, absorption may lead to an altered sense of time and/or space, a fusion of action and awareness, and an enhanced feeling of competence, energy and discovery. The activity is often felt to be different, set apart, from everyday life, and in Protestant cultures this division has been rigidified in the opposition of work and play. The uselessness of play is an irritant to a moralistic work ethic, and this rigidity has nurtured a considerable anti-theatrical prejudice.

In many languages the word or words used to express play are at root associated with swift movement, with leaping, dancing, joking. Motion through space and time, fun and make-believe, the flow of appearance and experience, are constituent elements of theatre, and from an early period in England the Anglo-Saxon words *pleg* and *gamen* were used to describe theatrical events of all kinds. Throughout medieval and Tudor times the live performance, that unique meeting between actor and spectators, was known in the vernacular as a play or a game. For this sport, a 'play-ground' or 'play-house' was required and usually, along with other 'play-stuff', a 'play-book' (sometimes with separate 'rolls' for individual players). Many of the artifacts needed for the practice of theatre took on terms related to the central activity. A play in the sense of a literary text is a late and special use of the word.

A play as a script can take many forms. It may be a record written down after the event, like numerous British folk plays transcribed in the 19th and 20th centuries by enthusiastic collectors. It may be an elaborate narrative written down, after a period of oral transmission, in order to stabilize the story but with little concern for the way it is staged, like the manuscripts of Tibetan harvest festival dramas. It may be a schematic aid to performance – outlining plot, characters, entrances and exits, and the disposition of 'props' – like the scenarios of the COMMEDIA DELL'ARTE. Or it may be a literary composition in dialogue form with either implicit and explicit instructions for the players or, as with SHAW and O'NEILL, lengthy novelistic stage directions intended primarily for the reader. This preparation of a text for a reading public alongside the principal aim of notation for performance creates a double focus. Rules and conventions alien to the play as event shape the play as script. For example, the notion of the division of playing time into five acts comes from the world of reading. The performances of PLAUTUS and TERENCE were continuous. In England, the Renaissance interest in this pattern at first affected the printing, far more than the playing, of plays. However, the development of scenic illusion, and the gradual division of actors and audience into separate acoustic spaces, meant that act structure became a substantive part of the play as experienced.

This double focus can lead in literate societies to an undue emphasis on 'interpretation', to a conviction that the play is in essence literature, and, more seriously, to a division of labour which excludes the living writer from direct involvement in theatre-making. Early records in Britain refer to 'devisers', 'doers' and 'makers' of plays and games. These unnamed creators share with most great dramatists, many of whom were actors, a common interest and involvement in the actual activity of play. A playwright is one who works play. That is both the craft and the essence of theatre.

**Playfair, Nigel** see LYRIC THEATRE, HAMMERSMITH

**Playwrights Horizons** 1971– American writers' theatre. Founded in New York in 1971 by Robert Moss, it exists to develop and produce new scripts. Working in two small theatres on THEATRE ROW (West 42nd Street), the organization has presented more than 250 new plays including *Kennedy's Children, Gemini, Sister Mary Ignatius Explains It All for You, The Dining Room, Sunday in the Park with George, Driving Miss Daisy* and *The Heidi Chronicles*. The stable group of nine resident playwrights has included CHRISTOPHER DURANG, A. R. GURNEY JR, Albert Innaurato and WENDY WASSERSTEIN.

**Pleasants, Jack** 1874–1923 British comedian. 'The Bashful Limit' was the epitome of the shy comedian, the beauty of whose act lies in the spectacle of one so ostensibly ill-at-ease and tongue-tied exhibiting himself solo before a packed house (at the other end of the spectrum lies the brash persona of a MAX MILLER). He opened his professional career at the Varieties, Leeds, in 1884. Following a big success in PANTOMIME at the Theatre Royal in his native Bradford in 1906, he expanded his career outside his northern stamping ground to become a nationally known dialect comedian. He 'wore a costume suggestive of the charity boy who had outgrown his clothes', and carried or sported in his buttonhole his whimsical trademark, a large white daisy. Remembered chiefly for the naive gaiety of 'Twenty-one Today' and the sexual gaucheness of his keynote song 'I'm Shy, Mary Ellen, I'm Shy', he contributed to the longstanding and questionable tradition of regional gormlessness on the English stage.

**Pleasence, Donald** 1919–95 British actor. He joined the BIRMINGHAM REPERTORY THEATRE (1948–50) and the BRISTOL OLD VIC in 1951, and in 1953 wrote and appeared in his play, *Ebb Tide*, which transferred from the EDINBURGH FESTIVAL to the ROYAL COURT. His voice, soft and expressive, and his slightly plump appearance brought him into demand as a character actor throughout the 1950s, in plays by ANOUILH and PIRANDELLO; but it was not until he played the tramp in HAROLD PINTER's *The Caretaker* (1960, triumphantly revived in 1991), alternately cringing and sinister, that he became a star in London and New York. Two other major roles followed, in Anouilh's *Poor Bitos* and as Eichmann in Robert Shaw's play, *The Man in the Glass Booth* (1967). His film and television appearances were numerous, often as sinister German officers in war dramas or master criminals; and this stereotyping tended to conceal the range of his acting abilities.

**Plowright, Joan (Anne)** [Lady Olivier] 1929– British actress. She trained at the OLD VIC Theatre School in the late 1940s and joined GEORGE DEVINE's original English Stage Company in 1956. She emerged as a leading actress when creating the part of Beatie in WESKER's *Roots* in 1959. She met LAURENCE OLIVIER at the ROYAL COURT and played Daisy in IONESCO's *Rhinoceros* (1960), opposite Olivier's Berenger. They married in 1961. She joined the NATIONAL THEATRE company when it was formed in 1963, playing major roles including Joan in SHAW's *St Joan*, Hilde in IBSEN's *The Master Builder* and Portia in *The Merchant of Venice* (1970). Her particular quality lies in down-to-earth directness showing few mannerisms and little fuss, but good technical control and much emotional warmth – assets which were particularly helpful in two plays by EDUARDO DE FILIPPO, *Saturday, Sunday, Monday*, produced at the National Theatre in 1973, and *Filumena* (WEST END, 1977). In addition to her television and film roles she appeared in BEN TRAVERS's last comedy, *The Bed before Yesterday* (1975), in ALAN BENNETT's *Enjoy* (1980) and as Poncia in GARCÍA LORCA's *The House of Bernarda Alba* (1987).

**Plummer, (Arthur) Christopher (Orme)** 1929– Canadian-born actor. After a spell with the Canadian Repertory Theatre, he made his New York debut in 1954. In the 1950s and 1960s his speciality was SHAKESPEARE; he appeared at the AMERICAN SHAKESPEARE THEATRE, the STRATFORD (Ontario) FESTIVAL and with the ROYAL SHAKESPEARE COMPANY (1961). He was Pizarro in *The Royal Hunt of the Sun* (1965) and Chekhov in NEIL SIMON's *The Good Doctor* (1973), among other roles. In London he played King Henry in *Becket* (1961). He joined the NATIONAL THEATRE in New York in 1971.

**Plyuchek, V(alentin) N(ikolaevich)** 1909– Soviet director. One of MEYERHOLD's pupils, in 1939 he co-founded with ALEKSEI ARBUZOV an experimental Moscow studio which in 1941 became a front-line theatre, and in 1942 he was made director of the Theatre of the Northern Fleet. He directed the Moscow Touring Theatre (1945–50) and staged plays at the Moscow Theatre of Satire (1950–7), where he has been artistic director since 1957. Founded in 1925 on the site of BALIEV's former Bat CABARET, the Theatre of Satire at first duplicated that organization's VARIETY-sketch format. Plyuchek's arrival at the theatre coincided with the Thaw, the new order being announced by his productions of MAYAKOVSKY's now classic SATIRES, *The Bathhouse* (1954), *The Bedbug* (1955) and *Mystery-Bouffe* (1957). His controversial constructivist stagings (see THEATRE DESIGN) remained in the repertory. He became a specialist in producing plays by Russian satirists Ilf and Petrov, poet-editor Aleksandr Tvarkovsky, GEORGE BERNARD SHAW, BEAUMARCHAIS, BRECHT (who received the Stalin Prize in 1954 and thereafter became 'performable' in the Soviet Union), OSTROVSKY, Aleksandr Shtein, ERDMAN and ROZOV. In 1964 Plyuchek was named a People's Artist of the Russian Soviet Federated Socialist Republic.

**Poel [Pole], William** 1852–1934 British actor and director. Poel pioneered the return from the restrictions of the picture-frame stage to the bare Elizabethan stage. For a while he managed the future OLD VIC and stage-managed for F. R. BENSON (1884). But his staging of the bad quarto of *Hamlet* on a bare platform in London's St George's Hall (1881) began his true career. Poel's work for the Elizabethan Stage Society (1895–1905) was original and immediately influential on HARLEY GRANVILLE BARKER and on 20th-century theatrical ideas. Beginning with *Twelfth Night* (1895), and including a notable production of *Everyman* (1901) as well as neglected work by FORD, MARLOWE, FLETCHER, JONSON, MIDDLETON, and even CALDERÓN DE LA BARCA, Coleridge and Swinburne, this unique venture ended with *Romeo and Juliet* (1905). The Elizabethan Stage Society performed in halls, lecture-rooms and courtyards rather than theatres. Poel's fanatical views on voice production were less sympathetically received, and delayed his critical recognition. His selected writings are published in *Shakespeare in the Theatre* (1913).

**Poesía en Voz Alta** (Poetry Out Loud) Mexican theatre group. Dating from 1956 to 1963, founded by Juan José Arreola, Octavio Paz, Juan Soriano and Leonora Carrington, all writers and painters, this experimental and controversial theatre project was dedicated to the importance of language and poetry in the theatre. Its eight programmes in eight years, with total or partial support from the National University, conceptualized theatre as a game. Despite its stormy trajectory, the movement inspired experimentation in other formats and produced a new generation of talented directors, including Héctor Mendoza.

**Pogodin [Stukalov], Nikolai (Fyodorovich)** 1900–62 Soviet journalist and playwright. He was a prolific (almost 30 plays), prize-winning conformist who embraced socialist realism and monumentalism. His schematic, 'conflictless' plays demonstrate the conversion of recalcitrant types to the noble cause of 'socialist construction'. *Tempo* (1929), his first play, depicts the inspiring construction work of the first Five-Year Plan (1928–33). *Aristocrats* (1934), produced by OKHLOPKOV at the Realistic Theatre, depicts the reclamation for Soviet society of prison camp inmates, who became inspired by their work on the Baltic–White Sea Canal project. Part of Pogodin's creative programme to glorify and humanize the Soviet leadership is his Lenin cycle – *The Man with a Gun* (1937), *The Kremlin Chimes* (1942), *The Third* and *Pathétique* (both 1959). His most atypical play, *A Petrarchan Sonnet* (1957), concerns the corruption of a platonic affair by hypocritical busybodies and broaches the subject, so relevant under Stalin, of the individual's right to the privacy of his emotional life. Its theme and open-ended conclusion identify this as a drama of the 'year of protest' (1956).

**Polaire [Émilie-Marie Bouchard]** 1877–1939 Algerian-born French singer and actress. Her singing career began in Paris at the age of 14, and her minuscule waist, doe's eyes and bobbed hair (20 years ahead of its time)

caught the public's attention. She introduced 'Ta-ra-ra-boom-de-ay' to France, and was taken up by Colette whose *Claudine à Paris* she played (1906). She was also seen in London and New York (1910). After World War I she devoted herself exclusively to acting.

**Polevoi, Nikolai (Alekseevich)** 1796–1846 Russian critic and playwright. Editor of the progressive journal the *Moscow Telegraph* (which folded in 1834), he also wrote plays which contributed to the 'officially nationalistic' drama of the time. His translation of *Hamlet* was staged in 1837 in Moscow and St Petersburg. The charge of sentimentalism was levelled against virtually all of the 38 plays that he hastily composed over the last eight years of his life. Of these negligible works, which enjoyed audience and official popularity to match their critical disfavour, the most characteristic was *The Grandfather of the Russian Fleet* (1838), a specimen of reactionary romanticism.

**Poliakoff, Stephen** 1952– British playwright. Three plays produced by the BUSH THEATRE, *The Carnation Gang* (1973), *Hitting Town* (1975) and *City Sugar* (1975), together with *Heroes* (1975), established him as a prolific, original playwright with an instinct for powerful contemporary metaphors. He was appointed writer-in-residence to the NATIONAL THEATRE in 1976–7, during which time he wrote *Strawberry Fields* (1977), but *Shout Across the River* (1978, produced by the ROYAL SHAKESPEARE COMPANY), in which an agoraphobic mother fails to protect her delinquent daughter from the horrors of big city life, revealed a new dimension to his work. *Favourite Nights* (1981), about a girl addicted to gambling, was more loosely constructed. In *Breaking the Silence* (1984), produced by the RSC, he wrote a compelling story about the early days of the Russian Revolution, prompted by the experiences of his grandfather. More recent plays include *Coming in to Land* (1987), *Playing with Trains* (1989) and *Sienna Red* (1992).

**Polichinelle** see PUNCH

**Polin [Pierre-Paul Marsalès]** 1863–1927 French music-hall (see CAFÉ CHANTANT) performer. For 20 years a favourite comic singer at the Paris Scala, he popularized the type of the ingenuous private, his cap at a rakish angle. His songs 'Ah, Mademoiselle Rose' and 'La Petite Tonkinoise' became classics. After World War I, he appeared on the legitimate stage.

**Pollock, Sharon** 1936– Canadian playwright, actress and director. *Walsh* (1973) is an epic retelling of the treatment accorded Chief Sitting Bull in Canada after his defeat of General Custer. Despite the historical settings, Pollock's commitment to important social issues here was clear, and it was again demonstrated in *The Komagata Maru Incident* (1976), condemning Canada's racist immigration policy, and in *One Tiger to Kill* (1980), based on a contemporary prison hostage-taking incident. *Blood Relations* (1980), her version of the famous Lizzie Borden story, marked a shift to further exploration of personal issues in *Doc* (1984) and *Fair Liberty's Call* (1993).

**Ponsard, François** 1814–67 French playwright. At a time when romantic drama was going out of fashion, Ponsard revived neoclassical tragedy with *Lucrèce* (ODÉON, 1843). In 1846 *Agnès de Méranie* returned to more fashionable medieval themes and in 1850, with *Charlotte Corday*, often regarded as his best work, he was accepted by the COMÉDIE-FRANÇAISE. The play explores different approaches to the Revolution. In 1853 and in 1856 he produced two important satirical comedies on contemporary life, *L'Honneur et l'argent* (*Honour and Money*) and *La Bourse* (*The Stock-Exchange*). *Le Lion amoureux* (*The Lion in Love*, 1866) was an attempt to write a new 'scientific' tragedy.

**Popov, Oleg (Konstantinovich)** 1930– Russian CLOWN. Having mastered ACROBATICS and juggling (see JUGGLER), he excelled at parodies of CIRCUS acts and naive spectators. His type embodies the simple-minded booby Ivanushka of Russian folklore, with his blond Dutch-boy haircut and checked cap. Although adept at satiric sketches, he prefers to fill the pauses between acts, rather than create elaborate numbers.

**Popova, Lyubov (Sergeevna)** 1889–1924 Russian-Soviet scene and COSTUME designer. She progressed through several creative phases prior to constructivism (see THEATRE DESIGN). In a series of 'plastic paintings' (1915), reliefs, graphics and linocuts (1920–1) she anticipated her design for MEYERHOLD's production of Crommelynck's *The Magnanimous Cuckold* (1922), considered to be the first pure constructivist stage set. It was a configuration of moving wheels, ramps, slides, ladders, stairways and platforms, which interpreted the actions in the script kinetically, in keeping with Meyerhold's 'biomechanical' approach to the acting. This design greatly influenced others, e.g. VARVARA STEPANOVA's for the Meyerhold production of *Tarelkin's Death* (1922). Popova's less successful design for SERGEI TRETYAKOV's *Earth Rampant* (1923), also directed by Meyerhold, was a montage of real objects – modes of transport, weapons, telephones, a screen – on which were projected slides and films. Popova's other theatrical designs include fantastic pictorial sets and costumes for TAIROV's *Romeo and Juliet* (Kamerny Theatre, 1921) and an unrealized collaborative design with Meyerhold and Vesnin for the mass spectacle *Struggle and Victory* (1921).

**pornographic theatre** Participants in pornographic theatre graphically depict sexual acts, allying exhibitionism with voyeurism. It is only when eroticism has been divorced from any religious, poetic or symbolic significance (or American law's 'redeeming social value') that a performance can be deemed truly pornographic, though moralists have tried to apply that label to erotic manifestations in the theatre throughout history. The Romans of the Empire solicited such exhibitions from their MIME artists, and the Byzantine empress Theodora gave public displays of genital acrobatics during her early days as a circus girl (5th century AD).

Although the Restoration stage has enjoyed a reputation for licentiousness, its one wholly pornographic play, *Sodom, or The Quintessence of Debauchery* (c.1684), a medley of fornication, buggery and incest couched in heroic couplets and attributed erroneously to John Wilmot, Earl of Rochester, was probably never staged. Throughout the 18th century brothels were the usual arenas for sexual exhibition in London, Berlin and Amsterdam. The first exclusively pornographic theatre may have been that run by the Parisian brothel-keeper Lacroix in 1741, but private erotic theatres soon became a fad of the French nobility. In Russia, a rougher equivalent was the erotic shows put on by dissolute landowners in their SERF THEATRES.

Times of social upheaval are particularly ripe for this sort of exhibition, and in 1791, after the outbreak of Revolution, a pair of so-called savages did the deed in the PALAIS-ROYAL as a public show. But the 19th century returned such displays to the brothel. The Theatron

Erotikon, or Théâtre Érotique, of the rue de la Santé, founded in 1862, was a PUPPET-show playing smutty one-acts for a select gathering. In England, such plays were circulated *sub rosa* but not put on, in an age when IBSEN's *Ghosts* was attacked by conservatives as pornographic.

Secret erotic theatres sprang up in Germany after World War I as part of the black market, but it was not until the so-called 'sexual revolution' of the 1960s that ordinary titillation was augmented by programmatic exploitation of 'deviant' practices. FERNANDO ARRABAL used taboo-breaking simulation of sadism and *bestialité érotique* to rouse audiences from their torpor, and the works of Sade himself were dramatized. Lennox Raphael's *Che!* (1969) featured a nude Uncle Sam whose involvement in oral sex and sodomy caused the whole cast to be arrested by the New York police. Much of this blatant sexuality was performed in the name of theatrical experimentation and dadaism, and much in protest, as with Tuli Kupferberg's anti-war spectacle *Fuck Nam*. But a good deal was purely commercial, like the clubs that sprang up in West Germany to show simulated sexual acts, while the real thing was offered in United States nightspots. KENNETH TYNAN's REVUE *Oh, Calcutta!* (1968) garnered contributions from BECKETT, Gore Vidal, JULES FEIFFER and others in its celebration of copulation. The boundaries between Establishment and Underground were effaced, but the buggering of a naked druid in HOWARD BRENTON's *The Romans in Britain* (NATIONAL THEATRE, 1980), though meant as a metaphor for imperialist rape, proved too literal for many. The prevalence of pornography in film and videotape has somewhat reduced its allure in the live theatre, freeing playwrights to use the sexual act or leave it alone as dramatic need arises.

Throughout the 1980s, actual rather than simulated copulation took place in porno palaces such as Show World in Times Square, New York; mildly comic REVUE sketches were pretexts for graphic enactment. The two styles of porno presentation popular in Tokyo during the 1970s and early 1980s, *nudo gekijo*, a strip-tease theatre in which the voyeurs were invited to become participants during the 'open stage' segment, and *honban manaita* (chopping board), shows of genital acrobatics, are now officially illegal. When the AIDS epidemic jeopardized promiscuity, sexual congress was replaced by sado-masochistic demonstrations encouraging audience participation, such as those offered by the Project and Belle de Jour at private New York clubs.

Feminists are divided between condemning pornography as a degradation of women and promoting it as a life-enhancing liberation. The latter attitude prevails in the performance art of Karen Finley, Annie Sprinkle, and others who PARODY standard responses by grotesque caricature. This approach has been widely misconstrued by conservatives, who take the parody to be the real thing, and in the USA neo-Puritanism has even demanded the CENSORSHIP of simulated masturbation on the radio.

**Porter, Cole** 1891–1964 American composer and lyricist. He contributed songs to the Broadway musical *See America First* in 1916. Living in Europe for most of the 1920s, he wrote songs for two BROADWAY shows with French settings: *Paris* (1928) and *Fifty Million Frenchmen* (1929). In the 1930s Porter wrote the scores for a series of frothy musical comedies (see MUSICAL COMEDY), including *Gay Divorce* (1932), *Anything Goes* (1934), *Red, Hot and*

*Blue!* (1936), *Leave It to Me!* (1938) and *Du Barry Was a Lady* (1939), his songs generally characterized by ingenious lyrics and unusual rhythms. In 1948 he created what many consider to be his most theatrically effective and versatile score, *Kiss Me, Kate*, a musical version of SHAKESPEARE's *The Taming of the Shrew*. During the 1950s he wrote his last two hit shows: *Can-Can* (1953) and *Silk Stockings* (1955).

**pose plastique** see LIVING PICTURE; NUDITY

**Potier, Charles** 1774–1838 French actor. A great comic performer, he drew maximum advantage from a weak voice and emaciated figure. He showed his versatility at the Variétés (see BOULEVARD) in such plays as *Les Anglaises pour rire* (*English Ladies for a Joke*, 1814). In 1818 he moved to the Porte-Saint-Martin, where he created the role of Père Sournois in *Les Petites Danaïdes* (*The Little Danaides*). One of his most popular roles was in *Le Ci-devant Jeune Homme* (*The Young Man from the Old Regime*, 1812).

**Potter, Dennis (Christopher George)** 1935–94 British television playwright. Although he wrote for the stage (and adapted some of his television plays), it was as a television playwright that Potter was distinguished. From *Vote, Vote, Vote for Nigel Barton* (1965) to *The Singing Detective* (1986) he created a body of work that used the medium with ingenuity and imagination. *Son of Man* (1969) was a bold portrayal of a 'human' Christ anguished by self-doubt; *Pennies from Heaven* (1978) anticipated *The Singing Detective* by an extraordinary use of popular songs to form, divert and generate the action. *Blue Remembered Hills* (1979) cast adults as children, giving their games played in the context of World War II a rare fantasy.

*The Singing Detective* featured MICHAEL GAMBON as a hospital patient suffering from a skin disease who sees himself as Raymond Chandler's Philip Marlowe in a dream-like evocation of a musical film *noir*. Nostalgia, loneliness and sexual longing were themes in *Blackeyes* (1989), less well received. *Lipstick on your Collar* (1993) showed Potter returning to form. By the time of his death he had completed two four-part serials, *Karaoke* (for the BBC) and *Cold Lazarus* (for Channel 4), due to be screened in 1996. The first is a classic thriller about a writer who finds that his literary inventions start to happen in his own life; in the second, the writer dies of cancer (as Potter did), is scientifically frozen for 400 years and then brought back to life. (See also TELEVISION DRAMA.)

**Poulsen, Emil** 1842–1911 Danish actor. He played some 250 roles at the KONGELIGE TEATER, including SHAKESPEARE, MOLIÈRE, HOLBERG and IBSEN. His astonishingly wide range accommodated such lyrical roles as Romeo as well as the inner torment of Shylock, Macbeth and Ibsen's Bishop Nicholas. He had some success in comedy (especially as Tartuffe) and from the late 1870s regularly appeared in Danish premieres of Ibsen: Consul Bernick, Torvald Helmer (in the world premiere of *A Doll's House*, 1879), Dr Stockmann, Hjalmar Ekdal, Ejlert Lovborg, Alfred Allmers, Dr Wangel, Masterbuilder Solness and John Gabriel Borkman. His brother Olaf was a Holberg specialist in the same company and his sons Adam and JOHANNES were actors and directors.

**Poulsen, Johannes** 1881–1938 Danish actor and director. Son of EMIL POULSEN, he was with the KONGELIGE TEATER from 1909. He was a forceful actor rather than subtle, able to establish a character in a few vigorous strokes. His successes included comic roles by SHAKESPEARE and HOLBERG, OEHLENSCHLÄGER's Aladdin, IBSEN's Peer Gynt and Bishop Nicholas, and KAJ MUNK's Henry VIII. As a director he countered NATURALISM with a form of spectacular theatricalism partly imitative of REINHARDT, as in his 1914 *Everyman* (revived in Hollywood in 1936) and a revival of Oehlenschläger's *Aladdin* that swamped the text with Oriental extravagance. His most unusual initiative was to engage GORDON CRAIG to design his 1926 revival of Ibsen's *The Pretenders*.

**Power family** Irish-American actors. Tyrone Power (1795–1841) successfully played stage Irishmen in London and wrote comedies until 1833, when he went to the United States and was a great success. Tyrone's grandson (**Frederick**) **Tyrone** (**Edmond**) (1869–1931) was a leading man in DALY's company. For a time he appeared with MINNIE MADDERN FISKE, his Lord Steyne in *Becky Sharp* being especially well received. His son Tyrone (1914–58) won his most substantial reputation as a film actor. He made his debut as Benvolio in KATHARINE CORNELL's production of *Romeo and Juliet*. After his film career began he appeared in *John Brown's Body* and *The Dark Is Light Enough*. His son, **Tyrone Jr**, is also an actor.

**Praga, Marco** 1862–1929 Italian playwright and critic. After a modest success with *La moglie ideale* (*The Ideal Wife*, 1891), in which DUSE appeared, he was prolific in the 1890s, writing either alone or in collaboration, treating middle-class psychology and manners and the woman with a past. His work is marked by considerable technical skill and some mordant social comment, but his morality was too conventional seriously to question the values of the society he depicted in plays like *L'innamorata* (1894), *La crisi* (*The Crisis*, 1905), *La porta chiusa* (*The Closed Door*, 1914) in which Duse scored a great success, and *Divorzio* (1915). His theatre criticism in *L'Illustrazione Italiana* was highly influential.

**Prampolini, Enrico** 1894–1956 Italian painter, sculptor, stage designer and director. An early member of the futurist movement, with MARINETTI he wrote many of its major manifestos, and advanced the movement through the exhibitions he organized and the journals he edited, like *Noi* and *Stile Futurista*. From 1921 he was particularly active in theatre, designing scenes and COSTUMES for the Teatro Sintetico Futurista, then collaborating with BRAGAGLIA's Teatro degli Indipendenti. The grand and visionary range of his ideas for art work outside the theatre is well seen in his *Manifesto dell'Aeropittura* (1929). Avoiding many of the political associations that FUTURISM had in the 1920s and 1930s, he remained committed to its artistic principles throughout his life.

**Prehauser, Gottfried** 1699–1769 Austrian actor. He inherited and cultivated the role of HANSWURST, beginning in 1720 in Salzburg. He succeeded STRANITZKY and became the Hanswurst of the Vienna Kärntnertortheater from 1725, refining the type into a polished Viennese gallant. According to EDUARD DEVRIENT: 'His caricatures always remain recognizable human beings and never sink to BURLESQUE.'

**Preston, Thomas** ?16th century English playwright. His TRAGICOMEDY *Cambyses King of Persia* illustrates the bridge in English drama from the medieval to the Elizabethan periods, offering a historical tale rather than a MORALITY PLAY. That play was written around 1569 and Preston wrote others, but details are unreliable.

**Prevelákis, Pantelís** 1909–86 Greek playwright. Like his mentor KAZANTZÁKIS, Prevelákis was a versatile author who wrote plays and translated Spanish, Italian and French dramas into Greek. His main characters are people posing existential questions, in search of their better identity. The early and the late plays are set in contemporary Greece, while the trilogy *The Sickness of the Century* (referring to the moral crisis of Western civilization) combines biblical, Renaissance and modern settings. In the first part of the trilogy, *The Holy Sacrifice* (1952), the protagonist Juliano dei Medici sacrifices his life to purge himself and those around him. *The Hands of the Living God* (1952) treats a theme drawn from Dostoevsky. *Lazarus* (1954), which concludes the trilogy, penetrates the spiritual aspect of a physical miracle. *The Volcano* (1962) develops a heroic theme from Crete's struggle of liberation from the Turkish yoke.

**Price, Stephen** 1783–1840 American manager. He was the first successful American theatre manager who was neither a playwright nor an actor. Price began gaining control of the PARK THEATRE in New York in 1808 and in 1810 began importing English stars. This practice gradually destroyed the resident repertory tradition in America. From 1826 to 1830 he managed DRURY LANE in London, gaining a monopoly over English stars. He drained the London stage of its talent to supply visiting stars for the Park. Shrewd, even unscrupulous in his dealings, 'King Stephen' nevertheless gave audiences on both sides of the Atlantic their money's worth.

**Priestley, J(ohn) B(oynton)** 1894–1984 British playwright, novelist and critic. After the success of the dramatization of his best-selling novel *The Good Companions* (1931, adapted with Edward Knoblok), a sentimental comedy about an acting troupe, Priestley began to develop his characteristic themes in *Dangerous Corner* (1932). The idea of relativity, two alternative sequences of events following from the same incident, was transferred to time in two 1937 plays, *Time and the Conways* and *I Have Been Here Before*. Though viewed as strikingly original at the time, the concepts are used as dramatic devices rather than posing serious intellectual questions. In 1938 he took over the Westminster Theatre with his own company, the London Mask Theatre, which performed his more experimental works like *Music at Night* and the modern MORALITY PLAY *Johnson over Jordan* (both 1939) – four-dimensional dramas using expressionistic techniques (see EXPRESSIONISM). His comedies include *Laburnum Grove* (1933), satirizing middle-class suburbia, and *When We Are Married* (1938) which borders on farce. In 1943 came a socialist allegory – *They Came to a City*. After the war, during which he became a popular radio broadcaster, he continued the same mixture of dramas based on relativity and the spirit world (*An Inspector Calls*, 1946) or exploring political attitudes (*The Linden Tree*, 1947), experimental works (*Dragon's Mouth*, 1952, a play for voices written with Jacquetta Hawkes) and comedy. One of the last of his 49 plays, a dramatization of Iris Murdoch's novel *A Severed Head* (written in collaboration with her, 1963), ran for two years in the WEST END, and his work has continued to be a staple of English REPERTORY THEATRE.

**Prince, Harold** 1928– American producer and director. Launching his career as a producer in partnership with Robert E. Griffith and Frederic Brisson, Prince had immediate success with *The Pajama Game* (1954) and *Damn Yankees* (1955). With Griffith he produced *West Side Story* (1957) and *Fiorello* (1961), and on his own produced *Fiddler on the Roof* (1964). Beginning with *She Loves Me* (1963), he served as both producer and director of a number of successful musicals. His most notable contribution to the musical stage was the series of 'concept musicals' which he produced and directed in conjunction with composer-lyricist STEPHEN SONDHEIM: *Company* (1970), *Follies* (1971), *A Little Night Music* (1973), *Pacific Overtures* (1976), *Sweeney Todd* (1979) and *Merrily We Roll Along* (1981). He directed LLOYD WEBBER's *Phantom of the Opera* ( London, 1986; New York, 1988). *Kiss of the Spider Woman* was first performed at the State University of New York at Purchase (1990) and revised for its 1992 productions in Toronto and London. In 1992 Prince also adapted and staged an OFF-BROADWAY play, *Grandchild of Kings*, the first of three projected plays based on SEAN O'CASEY's autobiography. *Kiss of the Spider Woman* (London, 1992; BROADWAY, 1993) was followed in 1993 by a new production of *Show Boat* (Toronto, 1993; Broadway, 1994).

**Prince Henry's Men** see ADMIRAL'S MEN

**Princess's Theatre** (London) Opening in Oxford Street in 1828, it was named the Princess's in 1840. Its most distinguished period was that of CHARLES KEAN's management (1851–9), when it became London's most fashionable theatre. Kean mixed gentlemanly MELODRAMA with grandly pictorial productions of SHAKESPEARE and Lord BYRON. In the enlarged house (1880) WILSON BARRETT had his most successful years in London management (1881–6). The Princess's was demolished in 1931.

**principal boy** see PANTOMIME, ENGLISH; MALE IMPERSONATION

**Pritchard, Hannah** 1711–68 English actress. She was a leading member of GARRICK's company at DRURY LANE from 1748 almost to her death. Her most acclaimed performance was as Lady Macbeth opposite Garrick. Before then she had mainly been associated with comedy roles, and contemporary reports indicate an actress of charm and gentleness, wit and intelligence. They also unkindly draw attention to her stoutness, against which she fought a losing battle in her later years.

**private theatres** English playhouses. These indoor playhouses of Elizabethan, Jacobean and Caroline London are to be distinguished from the open-air PUBLIC THEATRES. The term, used to ensure against civic interference, is misleading. They were, in fact, open to the fee-paying public. The main private theatres were the unknown home of the BOYS OF ST PAUL'S (c.1575), the first BLACKFRIARS (1576), the second Blackfriars (1600), the WHITEFRIARS (1605–8), the COCKPIT or Phoenix (1616) and the SALISBURY COURT (1629).

**producer** In the professional theatre (as in television and film) the producer brings together the financial and artistic resources that are necessary to create a production. The producer may have the original idea for a production, or commission others to develop an idea. In amateur theatre the term is often used to describe the function of the person more correctly known as the director.

**Prokopovich, Feofan** 1681–1736 Ukrainian clergyman, humanist and playwright. Via his sermons, orations, literary-theoretical treatises (*De arte libri tres*, written 1705, published 1786) and political school dramas, he championed Peter the Great's programme of reform. A man of great learning, he assumed monastic orders, became rector of Kiev Academy (1710), bishop of

Pskov (1718), archbishop of Novgorod (1720) and vice-president of the Synod, co-organizer of St Petersburg's Academy of Sciences and from 1715 ecclesiastical adviser to Peter's reform programme. His TRAGICOMEDY *Vladimir, Duke and Ruler of Slavic Russian Lands Led by the Holy Ghost from the Darkness of Unbelief to Evangelical Light, in the Year 988 after the Birth of Christ* (1705), a verse drama on the introduction of Christianity into Old Russia, is actually allegorical propaganda in praise of Tsar Peter against unenlightened opposition. In an effort to secularize the school drama, Prokopovich introduced into his play comic characters, musical interludes, more natural dialogue and satirical commentary on daily life.

**proscenium** Theatrical term. It comes from the Greek *proskēnē* meaning the place in front of the scene building (see GREEK THEATRE, ANCIENT); in ROMAN THEATRE *proscenium* referred to the raised stage in front of the *scaenae frons* (see SKĒNĒ). As the scenic stage developed in the Renaissance it became necessary to mask the stage devices and the wings, and this led to the development of a frame known as the proscenium arch. By the 19th century the entire stage was contained behind the proscenium arch and was known simply as a proscenium stage or, occasionally, as a picture-frame stage. Today proscenium staging refers to a type of illusionistic theatre in which the stage space is separated from the auditorium by a proscenium arch. (See also THEATRE DESIGN.)

**Provincetown Players** American company. Led by George Cram Cook, an enthusiastic visionary from Iowa, in 1915 a band of amateurs staged several of their own plays in Provincetown, Massachusetts. The following year, after EUGENE O'NEILL joined the group and contributed the outstanding work *Bound East for Cardiff*, they decided to move their playmaking to Greenwich Village, New York City. Launched in an apartment in Macdougal Street in November 1916, the Provincetown Players initially featured short works, with O'Neill and SUSAN GLASPELL as their leading writers. Cook himself had literary ambitions and envied O'Neill's growing fame. In 1922 he and Glaspell, his wife, sailed for Greece, where he died two years later. After a hiatus (1922–3), the Players were headed by a triumvirate of O'Neill, Kenneth Macgowan and ROBERT EDMOND JONES, who in turn were succeeded by James Light as director. A casualty of the stock market crash and the Depression, the Players folded in 1929.

**Prowse, Philip** 1937– British designer-director, for long associated with the Glasgow CITIZENS' THEATRE. He trained in THEATRE DESIGN at the Slade School of Art, and worked at COVENT GARDEN and Watford (1967–9) before moving to Glasgow (1969). Although primarily a designer of plays, he has also worked in opera and ballet with other companies and abroad. Prowse's stage settings are marked by their highly expressive, architectonic character. Rather than merely indicating the place where action occurs, his sets tend to function dramatically during the course of the action. Since the mid-1970s he has combined designing with the direction of his own productions, notable examples being *Phèdre* (1984) and *The Duchess of Malfi* (1985), both of which were produced in London, and the following in Glasgow: *Anna Karenina* (1987), *Mother Courage* (1990) and *Edward II* (1992).

**Pryce, Jonathan** 1947– British actor. At Nottingham Playhouse he played Gethin Price in TREVOR GRIFFITHS's *Comedians* (1975), a production that went on to tour internationally. His Hamlet at the ROYAL COURT was made remarkable by the manner in which Pryce also played the Ghost as a regurgitated voice from within Hamlet, and his Macbeth for the ROYAL SHAKESPEARE COMPANY (1987) was played as a hearty soldier. In *Miss Saigon* (1989) he scored a personal triumph as the Engineer, a Vietnamese pimp whose dreams hold the large-scale musical together. He has worked in film and television, and as a director. He played Fagin in the revival of Lionel Bart's *Oliver!* (London, 1994–5).

**Prynne, William** 1600–69 English Puritan and pamphleteer. His *Histriomastix* (1632) is a famous anti-theatrical tract. It was thought by Archbishop Laud to contain attacks on the king and queen, for which Prynne was fined, pilloried, had his ears cut off and was sentenced to life imprisonment. Freed in 1640, he became a Member of Parliament.

**public theatres** English playhouses. These open-air theatres of Elizabethan, Jacobean and Caroline London are to be distinguished from the equally public but more exclusive indoor PRIVATE THEATRES. The public theatres were the THEATRE (1576), the CURTAIN (1577), a theatre of unknown name in Newington Butts (c.1580), the ROSE (c.1587), the SWAN (1595), the GLOBE (1599), the BOAR'S HEAD (c.1599), the FORTUNE (1600), the RED BULL (1605), the second Globe (1614), the HOPE (1614) and the second Fortune (1623).

**Pulcinella** see PUNCH

**Punch** English puppet. The name is short for Punchinello, itself from the Italian Policinella. The Neapolitan COMMEDIA DELL'ARTE figure, Pulcinella, was a shrill, cowardly, oafish peasant, given to mischief and sententiousness. The French Polichinelle first appears as a marionette in the 17th-century show of the toothdrawer Jean Brioché; cleverer than his Italian counterpart, this little wooden character was soon adapted to political SATIRE. Versions also crop up in Nuremberg and Spain. After a lapse in popularity, the early 19th century saw a Polichinelle revival: the dancer MAZURIER imitated the puppet and the MIME artist Vautier made him a major character at the THÉÂTRE DES FUNAMBULES.

The English Punch is the most celebrated of English PUPPETS. He probably came over during the Restoration, for the word was in common use by 1669 to describe something short and thick. PEPYS and Evelyn both witnessed a MARIONETTE Punch. The English Punch inherited many of the traits of the medieval Vice and was linked with all sorts of traditional themes: he took part in the creation of the world (Bartholomew Fair, 1703), the Deluge (1709) and, as the hero of Martin Powell's puppet-show at COVENT GARDEN (1710), he associated with paladins and danced a minuet with a pig.

By 1780, the glove-puppet Punch had become a familiar street show, played in a curtained booth. A conventional scenario had taken shape: Punch, a kind of anarchic Falstaff, lying, bragging and bullying, in a series of confrontations with representatives of the social order – wife, beadle, doctor, executioner – wins out by sheer egoistic brazenness. His dog Toby, first wooden, then real, is a silent observer of the mayhem. The first Punchman to be taken up by the literati was Giovanni Piccini (died 1835), whose script was published by John Payne Collier with engravings by George Cruikshank in 1828. In 1962, the 300th anniversary of Punch's advent in England (dated from Pepys's diary entry) was celebrated at St Paul's Cathedral, London; but of late he has been under attack by feminists and educationists for his wife-beating and child abuse.

**puppets** A puppet performance involves a doll or figure which imitates human behaviour, often in a parodic or alienated manner. Live manipulators animate the figures dexterously to produce an impression of life upon the spectators; the paradox is that the puppeteer remains hidden or obscured, while his creation takes centre stage as a vivid individual. The art may have arisen out of masked religious ceremonials, and the use of miniature human figurines for magical purposes. The earliest to develop were the stringed puppets or MARIONETTES, which appear to have been known to the early Egyptians, Hindus and Greeks. Other common types are hand or glove puppets, SHADOW PUPPETS (e.g. KARAGÖZ in the Middle East) and rod puppets.

Hand puppetry, in which the puppeteer cannot see the public's reaction, is portrayed as early as 1340 in the Oxford MS *Li romans du bon roi Alexandre* by the Fleming Jehan de Grise, but is probably much older. Three, rarely five, fingers are used, and the stage concealing the manipulator is a booth with three walls, known in the Romance languages as *castelet*, *castillo* and *castello*. The 'motions' of Elizabethan and Jacobean England, reproduced in BEN JONSON's *Bartholomew Fair* (1614), presented anachronistic legends chock-full of slapstick, violence and bawdry. Hand puppets were a favourite instrument of the Russian *SKOMOROKHI*, being easily portable and wielded by one man, and devolved into the popular figure Petrushka. Indeed, the most enduring national types of puppet – PUNCH in England, GUIGNOL in France, KASPER in Germany and Austria – were portrayed most commonly by hand puppets. The leading 20th-century performer was SERGEI OBRAZTSOV.

Rod puppets, more characteristic of the Orient, may have been created in Bengal and, with the spread of Hinduism, became the popular *wayang golek* of Sunda, Java and Thailand. In China, the *tiexian kuilei* are first mentioned during the Tang Era (618–906). The three leading types are the big heads from Sichuan, the medium-sized from Hunan, Shanxi and Beijing, and the miniature variety from Shandong. Except for the clowns, most have no feet and the faces are painted in the style of Beijing opera (see *JINGXI*), the colour combination indicating the complexity of the character.

In Japan, the BUNRAKU is a separate genre of the drama, with its own repertory. The large but lightweight figures are moved by a principal operator, assisted by two hooded auxiliaries, by means of a control stick and various levers manipulating arms, fingers, eyes, eyebrows, mouth and so on. The voices are provided by a *joruri* reciter, who spins the narrative to samisen accompaniment. This style flourished during the Tokugawa period (1600–1868).

In the 19th century, puppets engaged the imagination of literary Europe. George Sand created a Théâtre des Amis for hand puppets at her estate at Nohant; Henry Monnier opened a pornographic puppet theatre in 1862; and Count Franz Pocci, intendant of the Munich court theatre, composed plays for Kasper. The notion of the actor as puppet gained ground among the European avant-garde. In 1888, Henri Signoret opened a Petit Théâtre des Marionettes, which presented ARISTOPHANES, CERVANTES and SHAKESPEARE. MAURICE MAETERLINCK wrote three plays for puppets in 1894 (*Alladine et Palomides*, *Intérieur* and *La Mort de Tintagiles*), claiming that actors were too obtuse to convey his metaphysical concerns. JARRY's *Ubu Roi* was performed at the Théâtre des Pantins in 1898 with puppets by the painter Bonnard, and GORDON CRAIG hoped in 1905 and 1911 that the actor would acquire the technique and egoless grace of an *Über-Marionette*. Erwin Piscator staged *The Adventures of the Good Soldier Schweik* with figures devised by George Grosz (1928). Such oversized manikins became a popular AGIT-PROP device, taken to heights of ingenious creativity in the United States during the anti-Vietnam War protests by the BREAD AND PUPPET THEATRE.

**Purim play** Jewish folk drama. Purim, a Jewish festival held in late March and early April, celebrates the thwarting by Esther and Mordecai of Haman's planned massacre of the Jews in Persia under Artaxerxes (Ahasuerus). From earliest times, it constituted a Jewish equivalent to CARNIVAL, with masquerades and cross-dressing. By the late 15th century jesters and mummers were performing public enactments and selecting a 'King of Purim'. This gave rise to the only true Jewish folk drama. Significantly, the first Judaeo-Spanish play is *Esther* by Solomon Usque and Lazara Gratiano (1567). *Purimspiele* were of long standing among the German Jews; the first to be published was *Ahasweroshspiel* (Frankfurt, 1708). The Rabbinical authorities frequently forbade performances and burnt the texts, because they parodied serious portions of the ritual.

Ephraim Lauter's 1925 Purim play initiated the first YIDDISH THEATRE in the Ukraine. By this time, it had become a vehicle for the *badchen*, the improvising master of ceremonies of Jewish weddings and celebrations; the term 'Purim play' had become synonymous with crude Yiddish productions and 'Purim author' with a hack playwright.

**Purvis, Billy** c.1781–1853 Scottish-born English showman. A CLOWN, conjuror, dancer and virtuoso of the Northumbrian pipes, in 1818 he established a company (subsequently and grandly known as the 'Victorian Theatre') which toured the fairs and races of the north of England and lowland Scotland presenting PANTOMIME plays, MELODRAMAS and cut versions of SHAKESPEARE – interspersed with local songs, dances and music, and introduced by Billy himself, grotesque in clown's pantaloons, skull cap and round glasses. At his death his former employee NED CORVAN penned an affectionate elegy which refers to a number of Billy's skills and GAGS, notably his routine of 'stealing the bundle', a simple *LAZZO* with improvised asides to the audience in which the clown robbed an unsuspecting bumpkin of his possessions.

**Pushkin, Aleksandr (Sergeevich)** 1799–1837 Russian poet, playwright and dramatic theorist. The greatest national poet also pioneered historical, romantic drama in opposition to the prevailing French neo-classical model. His dramatic output, while not large, is ambitious, progressive and even revolutionary. He forged a hybrid Russian literary language suitable for comic and tragic scenes and character-specific for individuals of every class and profession.

Pushkin's dramatic *magnum opus*, *Boris Godunov* (written 1825, produced 1870), is an episodic blank verse TRAGEDY, patterned after SHAKESPEARE'S HISTORY PLAYS. It illustrates Pushkin's thesis that the object of tragedy is 'man's fate and the people's destinies'. He dwells on the tragic relationship between ruler and ruled, the struggle against tyranny and the yielding to power. A ban on both publication and performance, together with a long-standing myth concerning its unstageability, has kept the play less popular than Mussorgsky's operatic treatment of it (1873). In his *Little Tragedies* (written 1823–30, published 1832–9) Pushkin presents a series of short, self-contained character sketches of familiar European literary types – the miser; the artistic genius and his rival; the legendary Don Juan. These pieces are seldom performed. His *Rusalka* (1831), a REVENGE TRAGEDY on a fairy-tale theme which provided tragedienne MARIYA ERMOLOVA with an artistic success, and the unfinished *Scenes from the Age of Chivalry* (1835), on peasant rebellion and the impoverished nobility, round off his playwriting career. Several theatres in Moscow and Leningrad today bear his name.

**Pyat, Félix** 1810–89 French journalist and playwright. A prominent utopian socialist, he made three brief incursions into government and hoped to create a popular theatre. He subscribed to the moral virtues of MELODRAMA, the form of most of his ten major plays. *Ango* (1835) was a virulent attack on the monarchy in the person of François I and was soon banned (see CENSORSHIP). With *Les Deux Serruriers* (*The Two Locksmiths*, 1841) and *Le Chiffonnier de Paris* (*The Rag-Picker of Paris*, 1847), starring FRÉDÉRICK LEMAÎTRE, he turned to a drama of modern society. The latter was his most popular work and contains the common opposition between poverty and virtue in a garret and wealth and corruption in an affluent drawing-room.

**Q Theatre** (London) Opened by Jack de Leon in 1924, it gained a reputation for trying out of new plays, e.g. TERENCE RATTIGAN's earliest work *First Episode* (1934) and PRIESTLEY's *Bright Shadow* (1950), as well as for giving a chance to new actors, including Max Adrian, ANTHONY QUAYLE and Dirk Bogarde. The death of de Leon in 1956 ended a campaign for funds to modernize the building, which had been refused a performance licence a year earlier, and it was demolished in 1958.

**Quayle, (John) Anthony** 1913–89 British actor and director. A stalwart member, but not a star of the OLD VIC company in the 1930s, he took a leading part in the reconstruction of British theatre in the postwar years. He succeeded BARRY JACKSON as the director of the Shakespeare Memorial Theatre at Stratford-upon-Avon. During his eight years there he earned the company an international reputation with such productions as *Titus Andronicus* (1956), directed by PETER BROOK and starring LAURENCE OLIVIER, in which he played Aaron. His Stratford policy was criticized for being too star-orientated; he acted in many productions himself, notably as Falstaff in *Henry IV Parts 1 and 2* (1951), in *Coriolanus* (1952) and in *Othello* (1954). On leaving Stratford in 1957, he acted in contemporary plays, e.g. as Galileo in BRECHT's play in New York in 1967. He also directed Dostoevsky's *The Idiot* (1970) for the NATIONAL THEATRE. He appeared in numerous films, usually in major supporting roles: his normally restrained acting style was not one which commanded centre-stage attention. With PEGGY ASHCROFT as his partner, he provided a memorable account of ALEKSEI ARBUZOV's *Old World* in 1978. That year he joined the Prospect Theatre Company to direct *The Rivals* and play King Lear; and when Prospect eventually collapsed as Britain's major touring classical company, he formed an unsubsidized alternative, Orbit, in 1981.

**Queen Elizabeth's Men** English company. Elizabeth I gave her name to this new theatre company, formed primarily for the purpose of performing at court, in 1583.

RICHARD TARLTON and ROBERT WILSON were prominent performers. It was disbanded in 1594.

**Questors Theatre** (Ealing, West London) British amateur theatre group. Founded in 1929, its tireless leader for the first 40 years of its existence was Alfred Emmet, who distrusted commercial theatre and wanted to present intellectually stimulating plays in competent productions. From 1933 until the late 1950s the company used a disused chapel, then acquired the site and built a new 400-seat theatre. Questors Theatre has facilities beyond the range of most amateur companies; it also has a proud reputation for discovering new plays and dramatists, JAMES SAUNDERS being perhaps the best-known. Emmet died in 1990, but members of his family are still involved with the group, which has proved to be a sympathetic training ground for all kinds of theatre artists, for over half a century.

**Quin, James** 1693–1766 English actor. Contemporary records show that in matters of costume and vocal projection 'Bellower Quin' favoured the grand style. At LINCOLN'S INN FIELDS from 1718 to 1732 he played the major Shakespearian tragic heroes. He remained working in London, at COVENT GARDEN and finally DRURY LANE, until 1751, his manner of playing becoming less and less fashionable but a powerful reminder of the heroic tastes of the Restoration theatre.

**Quinault, Philippe** 1635–88 French playwright and librettist. TRISTAN L'HERMITE encouraged his natural ability. Quinault produced a series of plays for the HÔTEL DE BOURGOGNE and the MARAIS, the most successful of which were the TRAGEDY *Astrate, roi de Tyr* (*Astrates, King of Tyre*, 1664) and the COMEDY *La Mère coquette* (*The Flirtatious Mother*, 1665). With the foundation of the Paris Opéra in 1672 he became LULLY's collaborator, producing librettos for a dozen large-scale works which dominated operatic tradition for many years. He also collaborated with MOLIÈRE and PIERRE CORNEILLE on the lyrics for the *tragédie-ballet Psyché* in 1671.

**Quiñones de Benavente, Luis** ?1593–1651 Spanish

playwright. He was the greatest exponent of the *entremés* (see *GÉNERO CHICO*): his name became so linked with the genre that many are falsely attributed to him, though he composed hundreds. He began writing about 1609 and had stopped by 1645 when his friend Manuel Vargas published a collection of his playlets. These have been divided into the realistic, taking the form of a miniature *COMEDIA*, and the fantastic, usually sung. A frequent character is Juan Rana, a comic doctor, lawyer or mayor, played with enormous success at the time by the actor Cosme Pérez.

**Quintero, José** 1924– Panamanian-born American director. Quintero and Theodore Mann launched CIRCLE IN THE SQUARE in Greenwich Village, New York, in 1951. First drawn to theatre for its passion, Quintero demands 'depth of feeling and commitment' from his collaborators, and a belief that the collective product is more important than any individual contribution. He specializes in the plays of O'NEILL, and his productions include the definitive *The Iceman Cometh* with JASON ROBARDS JR (1956), *Long Day's Journey into Night* (premiere, BROADWAY, 1956), *A Moon for the Misbegotten* (Spoleto, Italy, 1958; Broadway, 1973), *Strange Interlude* (for the ACTORS STUDIO, 1963) and *A Touch of the Poet* (Broadway, 1977). Other Quintero productions include the famous Circle revival of TENNESSEE WILLIAMS's *Summer and Smoke* (1952), BEHAN's *The Hostage* (1954) and *The Quare Fellow* (1958), Leoncavallo's *I pagliacci* and Mascagni's *Cavalleria rusticana* (Metropolitan Opera, 1966), JULES FEIFFER's *Knock Knock* (1976) and COCTEAU's *The Human Voice* (1978, Melbourne, Australia; 1979, Broadway). After the Broadway failure of Tennessee Williams's last play, *Clothes for a Summer Hotel* (1980), Quintero left New York.

**quotidien, théâtre du** French genre. The name was given to a style of French theatre influenced partly by German-language playwrights, e.g. FASSBINDER, KROETZ, SPERR and HANDKE, and pioneered in the 1970s by the Comédie de Caen and the Théâtre National de Strasbourg. The plays characteristically show inarticulate people in everyday situations presented with a heightened REALISM so that powerful theatrical images express, often brutally, the desires and needs which they are unable to express in spoken language. Plots are fragmentary and characters are often controlled by language that is imposed upon them from outside – e.g. the language of the sports business in René Kalisky's *Skandalon* (1970), about a champion racing cyclist controlled entirely by the interests of others. Georges Michel is often seen as the first of these playwrights, though his success *La Promenade du dimanche* (*The Sunday Walk*, 1966) also owes much to the THEATRE OF THE ABSURD. He has written several plays on the theme of alienation in the consumer society, of which the best is *Un Petit Nid d'amour* (*A Little Love Nest*, 1970). The major *quotidien* playwrights of the 1970s were Michel Deutsch and Jean-Paul Wenzel.

**quyi** Chinese storytelling. *Quyi* is a generic description for the different styles of Chinese storytelling and balladry. There are said to be some 350 forms extant today. Performers sing or recite to the accompaniment of drums, wooden clappers or stringed instruments. Chinese storytellers are superb mimics. Repertoires are based on the classical epics and romantic novels of China's past, but there is also an extensive range of contemporary material. It ranges from comic skits to social commentary enlivened with sly digs and allusions. In the past the storytellers worked the street pitches, market-places and tea-house theatres. In contemporary China they hold a prestigious position in the hierarchy of performing arts. They were forced into silence during the Cultural Revolution but are back in full force today.

**Rabe, David** 1940– American playwright and screen-writer. Rabe attended Villanova University, Philadelphia, where a number of his early plays were performed. Drafted in 1965, he was sent to Vietnam and became known and respected for his writing about the war there. JOSEPH PAPP discovered him and had five of his early plays staged by the NEW YORK SHAKESPEARE FESTIVAL. His trilogy about Vietnam includes *The Basic Training of Pavlo Hummel* and *Sticks and Bones*, which ran simultaneously in 1971, and *Streamers* (1976). Far less successful were *In the Boom Boom Room* (1973–4), about the victimization of a Philadelphia go-go dancer, and *The Orphan* (1974), Rabe's adaptation of the *Oresteia*. He is, however, more than a Vietnam War playwright: *Goose and Tomtom* (1982) is an existential comedy about a bizarre robbery; *Hurlyburly* (1984) is about Hollywood image-making and failed dreams. *Those the River Keeps* was premiered in 1991. His plays, filled with violence, racism and foolish heroism, combine grotesque comedy, surreal fantasy (see SURREALISM) and bitter SATIRE.

**Rabémanajara, Jacques (Félicien)** 1914–89 Malagasy playwright and poet. Twice exiled to France for political reasons, Rabémanajara associated with the black writers of his generation, particularly the Senegalese poet Léopold Senghor. Though more famous as a poet, he also wrote three substantial, rather literary plays based on the legend and history of Madagascar, in the French tradition of heroic classical drama: *Les Dieux malgaches* (The Malagasy Gods, 1964), *Les Boutriers de l'aurore* (The Boatmen of the Dawn, 1957), *Agapes des dieux, Tritriva* (Reunion of the Gods, Tritriva, 1962). In spite of their undoubted power, they are seldom performed.

**Rabinal Achí** Guatemalan play. The *Rabinal Achí* is the only indisputably authentic dramatic work of the pre-Colombian New World. (The OLLANTAY of Peru and the *Güegüence* of Nicaragua show later influences.) Created as the *Dance of Tun* by the Maya-Quiché Indians, it shows no European influence. Music and spectacle are integral to the repetitious, stylized dialogue involving two primary characters, the Quiché Warrior and the Rabinal Warrior, engaged in ceremonial battle over death with honour. Preserved through oral tradition, the play was first recorded in 1850, and subsequently translated into French, Spanish and English. A part of the rich folkloric tradition of Guatemala, it is still performed annually at the end of January in the city of Rabinal.

**Rachel** [Élisa Félix] 1820–58 French tragic actress. This star of the 19th century was the daughter of a pedlar. The actor SAMSON taught her at the Conservatoire, and she made her debut at the COMÉDIE-FRANÇAISE in 1838 as Camille in CORNEILLE's *Horace*. ALFRED DE MUSSET became one of her many lovers. Rachel's demands and caprices, plus her increasingly frequent absences on lucrative tours to England, led to difficulties and eventual resignation from the Comédie-Française. Her greatest roles were classical, but she was able to endow them with a strong human quality. In 1838 she played Hermione in *Andromaque*, Émilie in *Cinna* and Roxanne in *Bajazet*. She had very clear diction, a sense of musical rhythms and an economy of gesture, particularly compared when with the larger gestures of contemporary MELODRAMA. She played Bérénice (1844) and Athalie (1847), and Agrippine in *Britannicus* (1848), but among RACINE's plays her greatest triumph was as Phèdre, first performed in 1843. She also succeeded in the modern repertoire, in SCRIBE's *Adrienne Lecouvreur*. In her later years she was often compared unfavourably to the Italian actress RISTORI by those who preferred a more romantic style.

**Racine, Jean** 1639–99 French poet and playwright. Orphaned as a child, he received a classical education at the Jansenist schools at Port-Royal. Having failed to secure an ecclesiastical living he moved to Paris, where MOLIÈRE agreed to present his first play, *La Thébaïde, ou Les Frères ennemis* (The Thebaïd, or The Enemy Brothers, 1664). When a second tragedy, *Alexandre le Grand* (Alexander the Great, 1665), premiered by Molière at the PALAIS-ROYAL, proved successful, the ambitious Racine transferred it to Molière's rivals at the HÔTEL DE BOURGOGNE, the recognized performers of TRAGEDY. His mistress, the tragic actress Mlle du Parc, played the lead in his next tragedy *Andromaque* at the Hôtel de Bourgogne in 1667. In addition to the COMEDY *Les Plaideurs* (The Litigants, 1668), he produced six tragedies in only ten years, all of them masterpieces: *Britannicus* (1668), *Bérénice* (1670), *Bajazet* (1672), *Mithridate* (1673), *Iphigénie en Aulide* (1674) and *Phèdre* (1677).

Racine was soon acknowledged to have outstripped the ageing PIERRE CORNEILLE. He was elected to the Académie-Française in 1673. But he had made enemies and in 1677 a tragedy entitled *Phèdre et Hippolyte* by Pradon opened in direct opposition to his own play and was more favourably received. Racine retired from the theatrical scene and subsequently wrote only a court *divertissement* to music by LULLY, *Idylle sur la paix* (Idyll on Peace, 1685), and two tragedies on biblical subjects, *Esther* (1689) and *Athalie* (1691).

Racine was the most gifted tragedian of his century. His *oeuvre* observes and transcends neoclassical dramaturgy. Powerful tragic feeling is contained within a defined emotional spectrum, a precise convention of language and a rigid structural form. The centre of interest is the characters and their weak or vacillating psychologies, particularly the female roles, which have attracted leading actresses of every generation.

**radio drama** Immediately after the end of World War I, radio began to establish itself internationally as a medium of mass communication, and its potential for drama was quickly appreciated by the pioneers of broadcasting. Indeed, some theorists of the media believe that it is in the nature of both radio and television to aspire to the condition of drama. Comedy series and sit-coms, including such major BBC ones as Tommy Handley's *ITMA* in the 1940s, *Hancock's Half Hour* and *The Goon Show* in the 1950s, and the more recent *Dad's Army* and *Yes, Minister*, are undoubtedly dramatic in their employment of narrative and character creation. Several students of radio have argued that *The Goon Show* has claims to be one of the most dramatically innovative programmes in the history of sound broadcasting, since it exploits the representational possibilities and limitations of radio to the full.

Academic attempts to reserve the term 'radio drama'

for the more serious and highbrow end of the radio-drama spectrum soon founder on the impossibility of clear-cut demarcations when analysing a popular mass medium reaching millions. Is the BBC's long-running daily serial in fifteen-minute instalments, *The Archers*, radio drama or not? If not, what is it? But the problem of definition is not restricted to manifestly fictional output. Documentary slides very easily into what has become known as 'docudrama'; quiz programmes, confrontational discussions and interviews, actuality reportage, and even illustrated accounts of yesterday's proceedings in parliament (a non-stop theatre with a cast of hundreds) do develop dramatic momentum and tension, helping to sustain listeners' interest.

## 'Drama' and 'features'

From the 1930s, the Features Department of the BBC existed alongside the Drama Department before they were eventually merged in the mid-1960s, and credit for exploring the unique dramatic potential of radio during the 1930s, 1940s and early 1950s is rightly accorded to Features rather than to Drama, which in its earlier days concentrated on conventional, theatre-like plays. The word 'feature' suggests a factual basis as opposed to an entirely fictional construct, but in practice the BBC Features Department blurred any clear-cut distinction between fact and fiction. Long before the word 'faction' was coined to describe a mode of writing in which the techniques of fiction were applied to real-life stories, this is precisely what Features specialized in. Among the principal writer-producers of radio features were a number of poets, notably Louis MacNeice. Some of the most famous and seminal productions by Features, including D. G. Bridson's *The March of the '45* (1936) and MacNeice's *Christopher Columbus* (1942), resemble Elizabethan chronicle history plays in existing as both dramatized history and poetic drama, documentary and fiction. Yet Features also produced entirely fictional work, including two of the most renowned radio plays in the history of broadcasting, MacNeice's *The Dark Tower* (1946) and DYLAN THOMAS's even more revered *Under Milk Wood* (1954). Such works were the province of BBC Features rather than Radio Drama because they totally violate conventional ideas of well made realistic drama and accord with the free, radiogenic form of the feature. MacNeice shapes his work as a poetic, saga-like quest with rapid shifts from episode to episode, while Thomas uses a narrative structure with dramatized inserts involving numerous characters.

The fluidity of 'radio drama' and the concomitant problem of fixing frontiers have been an almost universal phenomenon. In some countries, such as Australia, this indeterminacy is virtually institutionalized in the official nomenclature: the ABC has a Radio Drama and Features Department, a name simultaneously acknowledging a distinction and closely linking the two modes under one umbrella, with the same production staff. The most famous American radio broadcast ever – and probably in the world – illustrates radio's uncertainty principle in a startling way. At Hallowe'en in 1938, one of the Columbia Broadcasting System's radio-drama series, 'Mercury Theatre on the Air', put out an adaptation by ORSON WELLES of H. G. Wells's novel, *The War of the Worlds*. Not only did this occupy a regular drama slot that should have established it as fiction; it was also science fiction, a fantasy about a Martian invasion of the Earth. Yet millions of Americans reacted to it as though it were actually happening; there was widespread mass

hysteria, and people fled from their homes and cities in panic and terror. The truth proved to be much stranger than the totally fabricated and far-fetched fiction that caused it, a fiction interpreted by many listeners as fact.

Although a newcomer to radio, Welles grasped the actuality techniques characteristic of American radio drama in the 1930s, which were designed to promote realism and conviction, and were identical to those employed in radio journalism and other factual investigations; in *The War of the Worlds* he employed them to give as much authenticity as possible to a highly improbable story. Welles and his colleagues did not for a moment imagine that the broadcast would have the extraordinary effect it did, but the 'Mercury Theatre' production demonstrates how powerful an illusion of reality radio can create, and how different radio drama is from drama with a visual dimension, whether stage, television or big screen. None of these media could have produced an equivalent response; in Welles's hands, the 'blindness' of radio turned out to be its greatest asset.

## Radio versus stage, television and cinema

This much discussed 'blindness' is the most significant factor in distinguishing radio drama from any other dramatic form. Historically, most drama from the Ancient World onwards has been intended for performance in visual as well as aural terms. SENECA has been claimed as a forerunner of radio drama because his plays were performed by readers as sound plays, not by actors as stage plays. In the recent past a number of influential theorists have stressed the visual side of theatre at the expense of other elements, which has in turn provoked other theorists to reassert the primacy of language. On radio, 'showing', or ostension (to use the technical term), is achieved largely through language, which is why radio drama is thought of as more of a writer's medium than theatre itself: somewhere between an entirely verbal form, such as the novel, and stage drama. It is possible for radio drama to dispense with speech altogether and rely solely on sound effects, as in Andrew Sachs's pursuit play *The Revenge*, which caused a considerable stir when broadcast by BBC Radio 3 in 1978; but its self-imposed limitations as a narrative make it a curiosity, not a feasible model for further development.

The sightlessness of radio makes impossible a number of elements we take for granted in drama on stage: in addition to scenery, costumes, lighting and visual symbols, there are proxemics and kinesics – the positioning and movement of actors as well as their physical gestures and facial expressions. In the very early days of radio, attempts were made to broadcast live stage performances, from both 'straight' theatre and MUSIC-HALL, but these were disastrous because in unadapted form they proved to be very difficult to follow without visual definition. On radio, settings, including the time of day, have to be conveyed principally through language; without a verbal context, the usefulness of sound effects is severely restricted owing to their inherent imprecision and ambiguity. The notorious BBC seagull implies water but does not, in itself, tell us whether the setting is on land or at sea, a beach or a small sailing boat, a dockside or a luxury liner. This is why Elizabethan and Jacobean drama, with its verbal scene painting and other descriptive devices necessitated by the theatrical conventions of the time, transfers to radio much more easily than some stage plays in the naturalistic and expressionistic traditions (see NATU-RALISM; EXPRESSIONISM), which rely heavily on visual presentation.

An actor on radio is a voice, and identification by an audience is entirely aural. This makes it difficult to mount plays with large casts on radio, especially if there are a number of equally important characters using roughly the same linguistic register, because the unaided ear cannot keep track of more than a few voices. Whereas a silent character on stage can have a powerful visual presence, a silent character on radio is an absence and simply does not exist. Pauses and hesitations can be extremely expressive in stage plays (CHEKHOV, BECKETT), but only because we can see the characters. On radio, an unfilled break in the dialogue is more likely to be interpreted as a fault in transmission than a meaningful silence.

There are a number of ways in which radio obviously cannot compete with the stage, television or cinema as a medium for drama, but the comparison is by no means to its disadvantage. It has been claimed that radio is a visual medium because it stimulates the inward eye by denying the eye itself anything to hold its attention. Listeners are actively involved in creating a fictional reality from the acoustic information provided by a broadcast play. In this respect, the process more closely resembles the reading of fiction than the viewing of drama, although listeners have to respond to a variety of other acoustic signals, sometimes including music as well as effects. Radio's stage is in the mind, and each listener, like each reader of a novel, constructs his or her own imaginary world without having it fixed, as in any visual form, by the physical appearance of the actors, the decor, and the sequence of images decided by the director.

There is an important difference between drama *on* radio and drama *for* radio, a distinction disguised by the term 'radio drama'. The German word *Hörspiel*, stressing the mode of sensory apprehension (hearing) rather than the mode of transmission (radio), is more exact in designating a work written for the medium, but unfortunately there is no English equivalent: the word 'earplay', coined by the Canadian producer Fletcher Markle as a radio-drama series title for American National (Public) Radio in 1978 as part of the attempt to revive the form in the USA during the 1970s, comes very close, but like TYRONE GUTHRIE's much earlier term 'microphone play' it has not entered the critical vocabulary. A good example of *Hörspiel* is the first play written for the new medium to be broadcast by the BBC, Richard Hughes's *Danger* (1924), which is set in total darkness, a coalmine following an accident that has literally put out the light. Because there is nothing to see, *Danger* is unstageable: it is 'a play for voices', to use the phrase Dylan Thomas attached to *Under Milk Wood*, which can be staged, though never without a considerable degree of awkwardness (even more than Chekhov on radio).

Unlike *Danger* and *Under Milk Wood*, many broadcast plays fall into the category of 'drama on radio' (stage plays and plays written in the hope of stage and television production but not achieving it), but there is also a considerable body of 'drama for radio', exploiting its ability to go places and do things either impossible or unsatisfactory in live theatre or even in the more visually flexible media of film and television. Sound effects can suggest large-scale catastrophes (the destruction of Pompeii, the fire-bombing of Dresden) and, at the other end of the scale, inner states of mind such as mental anguish (noises in the head). In comedy, too, invisibility can be a great help rather than a hindrance, especially when it comes to sound effects. The surreal humour (see SURREALISM) of *The Goon Show*, which perfected this technique, depends on hilarious patterns of sound that have no exact visual analogues and could function in no other medium.

In discovering what was radiogenic and what was not, early producers were influenced, strangely enough, by the methods of the silent cinema. For a short time in the 1920s, drama in a new medium that could be seen but not heard coincided with drama in an even newer medium that could be heard but not seen. Radio writers borrowed from cinema many of the techniques that distinguished it from theatre, including montage and superimposition, and adapted them to suit a presentation in sound alone. The visual flexibility of cinema, moving from scene to scene with a single cut, sliding between past and present with a dissolve, and placing characters in situations impossible in theatre (Charlie Chaplin in the precariously balanced hut in *The Gold Rush*), has its counterpart in the aural flexibility of radio. Even moving from long shot to close-up can be paralleled in sound since radio can create a sense of distance and also enter the minds of characters, the latter much more readily than any visual medium. Such devices as the soliloquy and aside are, of course, entirely satisfactory in small doses on an Elizabethan thrust stage, however clumsy they may appear in a proscenium-arch picture frame, but radio focuses very naturally on the interior workings of consciousness and can relay mental processes at length without any sense of strain. Since we do not see the actor speaking, the words seem to come straight from the mind, not the mouth. This accounts for the great intimacy of radio drama.

Arguably the best of the three 'microphone plays' Tyrone Guthrie wrote within a couple of years while working for the BBC, *The Flowers Are Not for You to Pick* (1930), exemplifies how gifted writers in the early days of radio seized on a cinematic method that could readily be adapted for radio, while also indulging to the full the new medium's novelistic ability to render the inner lives of people. Guthrie's play is all in the mind of its central character, who as a drowning man in the middle of an ocean is located realistically in a position unrealizable in the theatre, except in a highly stylized way. To capture the man's dying review of his entire life, Guthrie employs a sequence of flashbacks, a collage of memories involving fast transitions in time and place. Even more unstageable are the contemporary 'radiophonic' experiments by Lance Sieveking, notably *Kaleidoscope I* (1928), a decidedly original montage of speech and sound owing little to theatrical tradition but indebted to the principles of cinematic editing. What makes the achievement of these avant-garde figures so remarkable is that their complex works were broadcast live without benefit of magnetic tape, in conditions and using equipment that now seem primitive.

An important and uncinematic feature of radio drama is narration, relatively rare in Western theatre, in spite of the importance of the Chorus in Greek tragedy and BRECHT's influence on recent drama. What makes narration so natural on radio is, as with some other aspects of the genre, the invisibility of the speaker. Excessive reliance on narration in radio drama did lead to a reaction against it by the new writers of the 1950s and 1960s, such as GILES COOPER and Samuel Beckett, but it has been making a strong comeback since the heyday of the absurdists. Narration can certainly be an over-easy way of solving problems, but handled with skill, as in *Under Milk Wood*, it functions as a verbal camera, suggesting another, though oblique and unexpected, cinematic analogue. On radio, a narrator can establish with a few words a fictional reality that might cost a fortune to provide visually: mention Ancient Rome or an elaborate sci-fi supercity in space, add appropriate effects, and they exist in sound. In his enormously popular radio-drama serial, *The Hitch-Hiker's Guide to the Galaxy* (1978), which acquired cult status, Douglas Adams made brilliant use of narration. This self-reflexive cosmic fantasy, accommodating a major character with two heads, numerous time warps, visits to a number of bizarre planets, a variety of weird life forms, not to mention chatty computers, presented radio with marvellous opportunities rather than problems. Its triumphant success led to a television adaptation, which was vastly inferior because what was imaginatively stimulating on radio inevitably became gauche when translated into visual images.

Radio excels in creating fantasy and symbolic worlds, indeterminate characters who may or may not be real, and interior monologue. Although Mervyn Peake was a gifted painter and his prose is strongly visual, a dramatic adaptation of his grotesque *Gormenghast* novels into theatrical or filmic terms would be fraught with near-insoluble difficulties, whereas the BBC radio version is among the Drama Department's triumphs of the 1980s. John Huston's famous film of *Moby Dick* is far from contemptible, but it reduces the allegorical dimensions of Melville's novel to a thin realism, the white whale being no more than a white whale, an artificial one to boot. Henry Reed's 1947 radio adaptation, on the other hand, is among the masterpieces of radio. Among the imaginary worlds that radio has no problem in establishing are the ones giving speech to voiceless things, whether animate or inanimate: in Don Haworth's *On a Day in a Garden in Summer* (1975), for example, the speakers or 'characters' are plants. The nearest visual equivalent would almost certainly be whimsically twee and his serious purpose completely subverted. The ghosts of Elizabethan and Jacobean tragedy, such as Hamlet's father and Banquo, present a radio producer with none of the hard decisions a stage director has to make about whether they should be represented physically, even if through a glass darkly or as electronic flickerings. Because it presents six disembodied consciousnesses rather than six characters, Virginia Woolf's most abstract work of fiction, *The Waves*, probably defies transformation into a visual medium more than any major novel apart from *Finnegans Wake*, but her six voices might almost have been designed for radio, as MacNeice's celebrated adaptation reveals. *Finnegans Wake* itself was given the full radio treatment by that least inhibited of experimenters, John Cage, in his extraordinary *Roaratorio*, subtitled 'an Irish Circus' and based on James Joyce's novel.

## Germany

In various parts of Europe, radio got off to an enterprising start during the 1920s, but with the spread of totalitarian regimes, both right and left, it increasingly became a propaganda tool and an instrument of state control. As a mass-medium art form, radio drama inevitably suffered badly. Germany was in the forefront of radio-drama development during the post-World War I Weimar period, but Hitler's rise to power in 1933 put an end to this momentum and stifled experiment. It was some time after World War II before German radio recaptured something of its early imaginative energy, by which time it was under pressure from television. Today, Germany is one of the main producers of radio drama, and the *Hörspiel* probably has a higher artistic status there than radio drama does in any other country, including Britain, but Germany is one of a number of countries conspicuously lacking in the so-called Golden Age of radio (including drama) in the anglophone world.

## The Golden Age of radio

The period from the early 1930s to the early or mid-1950s in such nations as Australia, Britain, Canada and the USA depended on the stability and continuity of democratic institutions, something denied to continental Europe except for non-combatant Sweden and Switzerland. Ironically, World War II was a crucial factor in the making of the Golden Age since it effectively postponed the domination of television for more than a decade. Television transmissions began in the 1930s, well before radio had even come of age, but the war curtailed these experimental broadcasts, and in Britain, for example, the television audience did not overtake the radio audience until the televising of Elizabeth II's coronation in 1953, an event that encouraged millions of people to buy television sets. In some countries, radio drama did not have to compete with television for considerably longer because the introduction of the latter was delayed for political reasons. This explains why radio drama remains a viable form in South Africa, whereas in the USA it is again on the extreme edge of extinction.

## The USA

The ability of radio drama to withstand the assault of television varied according to the broadcasting system involved. From the beginning, the American system was based on commercial sponsorship, and the bulk of radio drama was unashamedly popular: soap operas, variety series, mystery and detective series. What happened with the advent of television was that all such forms deserted radio for the newer medium, leaving a vacuum to be filled by pop music. Although the output of serious radio drama in the USA was relatively small, the work of the three directorial giants of the 1930s and 1940s, Norman Corwin, Arch Oboler and Orson Welles, was of a consistently high quality and was widely appreciated. Nevertheless, even in the Golden Age, serious drama led a fairly embattled existence, with worthwhile series being set up and dropped almost at whim, and there was no structure to save it from the tidal wave of television. American radio drama did limp on throughout the 1950s, but was apparently laid to rest about 1960, only to be tentatively resurrected by Elliot Lewis and a few others in the mid-1970s. This was not a new dawn, but the example of Earplay in the 1970s, broadcasting ambitious work nationwide on public radio stations, encouraged others to keep the genre alive and even to explore its potential in the style of the German *Hörspiel*. Chief among these have been Everett Frost with Voices International in New York and Eric Bauersfeld with BARD (Bay Area Radio Drama) in Berkeley, California. Radio drama in the USA has survived in a handful of urban centres, including Boston, Chicago and Los Angeles.

## Australia and Canada

The American experience of a rapid rise and an equally rapid decline in the fortunes of radio drama has been partly paralleled in countries such as Australia and Canada where commercial sponsorship has had an important, sometimes dominant, role in broadcasting alongside a public-service sector akin to the BBC (in Australia, the ABC; in Canada, the CBC). It has been estimated that fewer than one in ten of the Australian population ever tune in to an ABC radio broadcast; the CBC, however, commands considerably greater loyalty from Canadians. In both Australia and Canada, television arrived later than in the USA, its spread was slower, and consequently its impact was not so immediately overwhelming. It has been argued that the Golden Age of radio drama in Canada did not begin until the mid-1940s, when television arrived in the USA, and lasted until the mid-1960s, by which time American radio drama was little more than a memory.

Yet despite the commitment of both ABC and CBC to maintain drama as a presence on radio, output has declined steadily although not dried up altogether. Audiences have shrunk, and in enormous countries with small populations this absence of listeners is more conspicuous than in much smaller European countries with much larger populations, such as Britain and Germany. The conditions that encouraged the poet Douglas Stewart, a New Zealander by birth but Australian by adoption, to write in verse one of the finest radio plays ever broadcast, *The Fire on the Snow*, first produced by the ABC in 1941, no longer appertain. Yet some young writers in Australia and Canada have been attracted to radio during the 1970s and 1980s, partly as a reaction against television. The celebrated intimacy of radio and its existence as spoken language still have appeal for literary artists, and the ABC and CBC continue to provide a limited outlet for them. In addition to mainstream radio drama, both organizations continue to encourage a small amount of radical innovation in the vein of the *Hörspiel*.

## Britain

The reasons for Britain's pre-eminence in radio drama should now be clear: on the one hand, political stability, continuity and openness; on the other, the BBC's monopoly in nationwide broadcasting as a public-service institution. Whereas commercial television began transmissions in 1955 on a national basis, commercial radio stations were not allowed to operate until 1973, and then only to serve strictly circumscribed localities. Proposals for national commercial radio were not seriously put forward until the mid-1980s and as yet have come to nothing. During the 1960s and 1970s, it was fashionable to sneer at the Reithian doctrines enshrined in the theory and practice of the BBC from the 1920s to the 1950s as elitist and patronizing, but it is now obvious that without such commitment to excellence in all areas of broadcasting and to disseminating high culture as well as popular entertainment the BBC would not enjoy its international reputation as, arguably, the most reliable and most imaginative broadcasting institution in the world.

The idea of radio being a national theatre of the air, in the absence of a bricks-and-mortar national theatre, developed early in BBC history: radio could bring the theatre to the people in their homes, making available the masterpieces of world drama from AESCHYLUS to IBSEN to millions who either had no access to live the-atre or lacked the theatregoing habit, especially when it came to the classics. The BBC has undergone several major reorganizations since World War II, but its policy for serious radio drama, as opposed to light-entertainment drama, has survived more or less intact; although audiences have declined considerably, output has remained remarkably buoyant. Despite cutbacks during the 1980s, plenty of stage classics and adaptations of classic novels are still broadcast, as are plenty of new plays. Radio-drama production is absurdly cheap by the standards of television, and radio can therefore take risks and attempt experiments that would be out of the question in television. Indeed, as TV drama becomes more anodyne, with a plethora of stereotypical soap operas and mini-series, as older viewers yearn nostalgically for the good old days of TV drama in the 1960s and 1970s, the virtues of radio drama are increasingly obvious in the 1990s.

The BBC's strong tradition of radio drama and feature production has been a vital factor in enabling these forms to survive so well in the television era, despite all the talk about a dying art during the past 30 years. One crucial change, following the recommendations of audience research, has been to move drama away from prime-viewing times (previously peak listening times) to afternoon and early evening slots, and even morning and late-at-night ones. Yet developments in drama itself helped to give radio a new lease of life as a dramatic medium when television was taking over as *the* mass medium in the 1950s. Several critics have argued that radio is the natural home for the THEATRE OF THE ABSURD, and there was something approaching a revolution in radio drama between the mid-1950s and the mid-1960s, with Giles Cooper, Samuel Beckett, Rhys Adrian, Frederick Bradnum, HAROLD PINTER, JAMES SAUNDERS, Barry Bermange, JOE ORTON and TOM STOPPARD. Until this time, there was a tendency for some of the best radio writers to compensate for its blindness by providing rich verbal textures, colours for the ear, as in *The Dark Tower* and *Under Milk Wood*. The new writers demonstrated that radio drama could function just as well without such compensation, that minimalism could be as radiogenic as the work of poets such as MacNeice and Thomas.

Indeed, radio proved to be the training ground for a new generation of British playwrights, who subsequently made their names in the theatre, television and film. Radio continues to do this, but the momentum of the 1960s is now something to be recollected in tranquillity. Yet plays of the stature of DAVID RUDKIN's *Cries from Casement As His Bones Are Brought to Dublin* (1973) and JOHN ARDEN's *Pearl* (1978), Robert Ferguson's *Transfigured Night* (1984) and HOWARD BARKER's *Scenes from an Execution* (1984) are reminders that, if radio is a dying or dead art in some countries, it is still thriving in others, notably in Britain and Germany. There, at least, it is dying by millimetres if it is dying at all.

**Radlov, Sergei (Ernestovich)** 1892–1958 Russian-Soviet director. He was a leader in the movement to unite folk theatrical forms with modern 'urban eccentrism' in order to create a new popular theatre. His techniques derived primarily from COMMEDIA DELL'ARTE, CIRCUS and silent screen comedy. He received his early training from MEYERHOLD during the latter's *commedia* period. In 1920 he co-directed the mass spectacle *Towards a World Commune* and founded with Vladimir Solovyov the Theatre of Popular Comedy, which operated until 1922. The latter utilized circus performers in a series of 'circus comedies' and 'circus pantomimes' on anti-capitalist themes: *The Corpse's Bride* and *The Monkey Who Was an Informer* (1919), *The Sultan and the Devil* and *The Adopted Son* (1920), and *Love and Gold* (1921). Drawing upon American detective and adventure serials, Radlov experimented with multiple and simultaneous staging in order to create a sense of continuous flow. He employed similar means in his productions of classic comedies by MOLIÈRE, Hans Sachs, CALDERÓN DE LA BARCA, LABICHE and especially SHAKESPEARE. He staged a number of notable productions of Shakespeare in the 1930s, including *King Lear* (1935) at the MOSCOW STATE JEWISH THEATRE, starring SOLOMON MIKHOELS.

**Radok, Alfred** 1914–1976 Czech director. His successes were frequently interrupted by political pressures. An assistant to E. F. BURIAN in the late 1930s, he was a founder of the postwar Theatre of the Fifth of May, which produced provocative new versions of established drama and musical theatre. Essentially an apolitical artist with an innate genius for theatrical metaphor and multimedia, he struggled to survive in the ideological minefields of a dogmatic regime, often being shunted from one position to another at the National, the Municipal and provincial theatres, while directing landmark productions for the stage (*The Entertainer*, 1957; *Marriage*, 1963; *Game of Love and Death*, 1964), in film (*Distant Journey*, 1949) and for the mixed media, above all, the hybrid form of LATERNA MAGIKA (1958), a technically sophisticated offspring of Radok's talent for juxtaposing realistic elements in striking, often poetic configurations. The Soviet bloc invasion of Czechoslovakia in 1968 triggered his self-exile, and he worked in more limited fashion abroad, chiefly in Sweden, until his death.

**Radrigán, Juan** 1937– Chilean playwright. Radrigán is affiliated with theatre of the marginal classes. His plays are brutal and violent portrayals of contemporary society, written in the vernacular but with poetic imagery. Since he burst on the theatre scene with *Testimonios sobre la muerte de Sabina* (*Testimonies on the Death of Sabina*) in 1979, he has become one of Chile's most prolific writers. Other major plays are *Viva Somoza* (*Long Live Somoza*) written in collaboration with Gustavo Meza in 1980, *El loco y la triste* (*The Crazy One and the Sad One*, 1980), *Hechos consumados* (*Accomplished Deeds*, 1981), *El toro por las astas* (*The Bull by the Horns*, 1982) and *Las voces de la ira* (*Voices of Anger*, 1984).

**Radzinsky, Edvard (Stanislavovich)** 1938– Soviet-Russian playwright. His plays present the philosophical dilemmas of the intelligentsia and of youth in conflict with the values of their elders. His first popular success was the bittersweet romance *104 Pages about Love* (1964), staged by ANATOLY EFROS. It has been widely performed, and made into a ballet and a film. *Making a Movie* (1965) deals with a film director's difficulties in maintaining his integrity in art, love and life. Radzinsky's historical plays of conscience include *Conversations with Socrates* (1975), *Lunin* (1977, about a Decembrist conspirator) and *Theatre in the Time of Nero and Seneca* (1980). In *The Seducer Kolobashkin* (1968) and *Don Juan Continued ...* (1979), the idea of time travel suggests the flight of the creative persona from false and banal reality. With the highly popular *She, in the Absence of Love and Death* (1980), Radzinsky returned to the difficulties of the young in reconciling their ideals with contemporary, unromantic reality. Following the 1986 premiere of *Jogging* (*Sporting Scenes*,

1981), a battle-of-the-sexes exposé of the children of the ruling elite, he became one of the most frequently produced native playwrights in modern Russia. *An Old Actress in the Role of Dostoevsky's Wife*, a Pirandellian battle of wits and realities between a role-playing man and woman in an institution for the aged, had its US premiere in 1992.

**Raikin, Arkadi (Isaakovich)** 1911–88 Soviet-Russian CLOWN. He began his career as an actor and MIME artist and in 1938 shifted to CABARET, becoming the director of the Leningrad Theatre of Miniatures. There he combined drama, operetta, VARIETY and pantomime into an idiosyncratic style. Despite the bluntness of his SATIRE and his Jewish ancestry, Raikin managed to avoid persecution because of his immense popularity. His range extended from full-length shows such as *Around the World in 80 Days* (1951) to one-man quick-change concerts. He was seen in London in 1964.

**Raimund, Ferdinand** 1790–1836 Austrian actor and playwright. After an unsuccessful start as a tragic actor, Raimund won acclaim in the comic roles that he played in Vienna. He wrote plays that represented a sustained attempt to employ the Viennese VOLKSSTÜCK, especially in the *Zauberstück*, to express serious romantic themes. They represent the high point of that Austrian dramatic tradition, originating in the JESUITENDRAMA, that explored the interrelationship of spiritual and secular spheres of being. Of the nine plays Raimund wrote, *The Peasant as Millionaire* (1826), *The King of the Alps and the Misanthrope* (1828) and the ambitious, serious comedy *The Spendthrift* (1834) have proved to be remarkably durable.

**Rajatabla** Venezuelan theatre group. A subsidiary of the Ateneo de Caracas (Caracas Atheneum), it was created in 1971 and headed for years by Carlos Giménez (1945–93), an Argentine director long established in Venezuela. Rajatabla has been a major experimental force in Caracas.

**Rame, Franca** 1929– Italian actress and playwright. Rame was born into the profession; her early experience was on the VARIETY stage. From 1953 her career has been inseparably entwined with that of her husband DARIO FO, with whom she worked on television in the 1960s and in nearly all of whose plays she has appeared; she has also collaborated with him as playwright. That fruitful collaboration, however, has not obscured her own distinctive acting and writing talents, evident in her performances in the plays of other dramatists, e.g. SHAW's *Mrs Warren's Profession* (1981), and in her own work – expressive of vigorously held feminist views – notably *Parti femminili* (*Female Parts*, 1988) and *Coppia aperta, quasi spalancata* (1991).

***ramlila*** Indian theatre form. Literally translated, *ramlila* means the 'play of Rama', the hero of the SANSKRIT epic the *Ramayana*. The celebration of Rama through the depiction of dramatic episodes from his life is an all-India phenomenon, particularly in the months of September, October and November. *Ramlila* is popular in villages and cities in the north, though the manner of performance differs considerably from place to place. The form may have originated in ancient India. Clear historical evidence for its beginning is not found until the early 17th century. Centres for large-scale *ramlilas* include the cities of Ramnagar, Allahabad, Mathura and Delhi, where many performances are organized, each attracting thousands of spectators. In Ramnagar alone, the public spectacles and processions attract over a million pilgrims.

*Ramlila* falls within the province of amateur performers drawn from the community. In some areas, actors have come from the same Brahmin families for centuries. It is customary for the roles of the five chief characters to be played by Brahmin boys who have not yet reached the age of puberty. The person who trains the boys and who heads the entire *ramlila* performance is called the *liladhari*. The approach to the stage space varies depending on the city and the community. In Ramnagar, which literally means 'Rama's city', 30 days are assigned to the *ramlila*, each with its own particular events. The maharaja often travels from one event to another in his own horse-drawn carriage or on his elephant. Hundreds of youths take part in the great battle scenes between the monkey soldiers of Rama and the demon soldiers of Ravana, the symbolic representative of evil. The spectacle ends in the burning of effigies, four to five storeys tall, of Ravana and his demon brothers. At the end of the evening they are shot with burning arrows, then burst into flames and explode with fireworks, falling in a heap at the feet of the actor playing Rama, as the crowd fervently chants 'Victory to Rama!'

People from many walks of life participate in the *ramlila* – Hindus, Muslims, Christians, Sikhs and Parsees, rich and poor alike, maharajas and beggars – whoever comes to witness the events may participate.

**Ramos-Perea, Roberto** 1956– Puerto Rican playwright, essayist and short story writer. In addition to *Los 200 no* (*The 200 Noes*, 1983), a violent encounter between a university student and a professor, and *Ese punto de vista* (*That Point of View*, 1984), his work includes a major historical trilogy: *Revolución en el infierno* (*Revolution in Hell*), based on the Ponce massacre of 1937; *Módulo 104, Revolución en el purgatorio* (*Module 104, Revolution in Purgatory*), based on the Puerto Rican penal system during the years 1980–2; and *Cueva de ladrones, Revolución en el paraíso* (*Thieves' Cave, Revolution in Paradise*), based on the radical student movement. Later plays include *Obsesión* (*Obsession*, 1988) and *Llanto de luna* (*Moon Lament*, 1989).

**Rana, Juan** see QUIÑONES DE BENAVENTE, LUIS

**Randolph, Thomas** 1605–35 English playwright and poet. He was educated at Cambridge University. His PASTORAL play, *Amyntas* (1630), is enlivened by its comic scenes. His other full-length piece is *The Jealous Lovers* (1632). Randolph also wrote witty dramatic sketches (e.g. *Aristippus, or The Jovial Philospher*, c.1629, which proposes that the philosophy of drinking be added to the university syllabus) and a monologue, *The Conceited Pedlar* (1627). *The Muses' Looking-Glass* (1630), in which an actor out-argues Puritan opposition to the theatre, reflects the influence of BEN JONSON.

**Rascón Banda, Víctor Hugo** 1950– Mexican playwright. His portrayal of middle- and lower-class situations and problems has brought him popularity, even when the plays are MELODRAMAtic or unrealistic. Major successes include *Las armas blancas* (*White Arms*, 1982) and *Máscara vs. Cabellera* (*Mask vs. Head of Hair*, 1985), a portrait of a wrestling idol.

**rasdhari** Indian theatre form. The people who originally organized the RASLILA performances in Rajasthan were known as *rasdharis*, and eventually the word came to indicate their theatre form, with its own unique features and characteristics. Today village productions by itinerant troupes of actors and musicians take place in any open meeting area in the village. Spectators generally close in on the performers, lean out of the doors and windows of surrounding houses or perch anywhere that affords them a better view of the show. Musicians sit among the spectators, and entrances and exits are negotiated by the actors through the crowd.

The songs and musical accompaniment are borrowed from other styles of music and theatre popular in the region. Improvisation is freely used in dialogue, dance and song as the actors test the interest of the audience in particular themes or dramatic action. The simplicity of the form allows considerable latitude in interpreting and altering the classical stories and in reinforcing moral behaviour.

**raslila** Indian theatre form. This generic term is used widely throughout India to describe various dances and dance dramas that have a particular theme. It takes on special significance in several regions as a form of theatre. The term *ras* refers to Lord Krishna's joyous, melodious, circular dance with the wives of Brahmin cowherds of Vrindavan, a holy city south of Delhi in north India, described in mythological sources. *Lila* means 'play' and implies more than just dramatic literature, referring to the god's playful tryst with man and earthly beings.

The *raslila* of Vrindavan is the best-known form of *raslila* in all of India. There are also other forms, such as those of Manipur, the KRISHNATTAM of Kerala and the ANKIYA NAT of Assam. *Raslila* of Vrindavan is a devotional dance drama. Krishna is thought to have been born in the city of Mathura, a few miles distant from Vrindavan, the place where he spent his childhood and youth. Thus, the whole area is considered holy ground and the enactment of the dance drama is an extension of the religious fervour of the inhabitants and the thousands of pilgrims who flock to the area every year. The performances centre on Krishna, his chief consort, Radha, and aspects of his earthly life, lovers and devotees. When particular sections are well executed the spectators shower verbal praise on the gods, not on the artists. Nearly 150 *lilas* are said to have been composed, from which the company may choose only one a night to perform, because of time constraints. Often the choice is dictated by the particular audience and the season. Plays concern episodes connected with Krishna's birth, his mischievous childhood, his sport with the young milkmaids of Vrindavan and his adult life.

Performances usually last only two and a half hours. Unlike many forms of rural theatre, *raslila* must be completed before midnight. Since it is regarded as a religious RITUAL and not just an entertainment, etiquette, such as the removing of shoes, must be adhered to by the spectators; smoking and talking are strictly forbidden. The proper place for *raslila* performances is a temple, a private garden, a bungalow or holy resting place for travellers. It is not considered appropriate to perform such a sacred event in the street. The actors are all men or boys, who study with a teacher (*swami*) who serves as the leader of the troupe. The text of the songs and the *lilas* are taught orally to those who are not literate. In a full-scale performance, actors often seem to drop out of character, staring at the audience indiscriminately. No standard of excellence exists, even though the companies are professional. The religious fervour of the experience seems to outweigh any aesthetic consideration.

**Rastell, John** c.1475–1536 English playwright. Brother-in-law of Sir Thomas More and father-in-law of JOHN

HEYWOOD, Rastell is regarded not as a particularly good writer, but as an important one in terms of the movement of English drama away from MORALITY PLAYS to more secular themes. Plays believed to be by him include *The Nature of the Four Elements* (c.1517) in which the leading character is offered the benefits of the new Renaissance education, despite alternative temptations; *The Dialogue of Gentleness and Nobility* (c.1527); and *Calisto and Melibea* (c.1527), taken from Fernando de Rojas's *La Celestina*. Rastell and his son William were printers, and published the INTERLUDES of other writers, including Heywood.

**Rastelli, Enrico** 1896–1931 Italian JUGGLER. Born into a CIRCUS family, he made his juggling debut at the Circo Gatti in 1922, breaking a world record by juggling ten rubber balls in one hand and ten table mats in the other. Unequalled for accuracy and number in balancing spheres, he usually performed in football shorts and ended his act with a one-man soccer game that sent the balls into the audience.

**Rattigan, Terence** 1911–77 British playwright. He established a reputation for light COMEDY with *French without Tears* (1936), *While the Sun Shines* (1943) and *Love in Idleness* (played by the LUNTS in 1944, and in New York as *O Mistress Mine*, 1946). The autobiographical play about his wartime experiences, *Flare Path* (1942), began to introduce serious themes, which became the keynote of social dramas that made him the leading playwright of the immediate postwar period. These ranged from dramatizations of notorious miscarriages of justice, in *The Winslow Boy* (1946) dealing with a schoolboy accused of theft and in *Cause Célèbre* (1977) based on a murder case, and provocative moral issues – *Ross* (1960) dramatizing homosexuality through the life of T. E. Lawrence, and *A Bequest to the Nation* (1970) on the relationship between Nelson and Lady Hamilton – to sensitive studies of psychological domination in *The Browning Version* (performed together with *Harlequinade* under the title of *Playbill*, 1948) and *Separate Tables* (1954). He also continued to write comedy, with *The Sleeping Prince* (1956), and contributed a number of successful film scripts.

By the time Rattigan was knighted in 1971, his works were already being criticized as conventional 'problem play' treatments catering to unsophisticated popular taste, but his skilful craftsmanship and subtle characterization have been recognized in numerous revivals.

**Raucourt, Françoise** [Marie Antoinette Josephe Saucerotte] 1756–1815 French actress. Endowed with a fine voice, bearing and beauty, she made her debut at the Théâtre-Français (see COMÉDIE-FRANÇAISE) in 1772 in the role of Dido. Her popularity with the public was mitigated by her strong masculine tendencies and scandals associated with her private life. She played roles of mothers and queens and was magnificent as Athalie and Cléopâtre (*Rodogune*), but less good in roles requiring the depiction of motherly love. An ardent royalist, she was imprisoned in 1793 and later tried to rally the conservative elements for a second Théâtre-Français. From 1807 to 1814 she organized a French company to tour Italy. Fifteen thousand people attended her funeral, but the curé agreed to a Christian burial only under orders from the king.

**Raupach, Ernst** 1784–1852 German playwright. Referred to by LAUBE as 'the SHAKESPEARE of triviality', Raupach was by far the most popular and fertile dramatist of his day. He wrote several MELODRAMAS, but was most celebrated for his skilfully constructed history plays, of which the 16-play cycle, *The Hohenstaufens* (1837), was the best-known.

***ravana chhaya*** Indian puppet form. One of three kinds of SHADOW PUPPET theatre in India, *ravana chhaya* struggles to survive in Orissa State in eastern India. The term *ravana* refers to the demon-king of Lanka who is a principal character in the epic *Ramayana*. *Chhaya* means 'shadow'. The puppets are simple figures, without moveable parts, between six and eight inches tall. Unusually, the puppet of Ravana is much more interesting and larger than that created for Rama. The form has only one story in its repertory, the life of Rama and his struggles with Ravana. Besides the characters of the epic, there are the stock characters of the village barber and his grandson, and numerous properties and scenic items. The dialogue and songs of the puppeteers are accompanied by music, the performance blending Oriyan folk and classical melodies set to lively rhythmic patterns.

**Ravel family** French MIME artists and dancers. They were among the most popular and influential performers in early-19th-century America. **Gabriel** (1810–82), an excellent pantomimist and rope dancer, was the chief businessman of the troupe; **Jérome** (1814–90) wrote such durable scenarios as *The Green Monster, Mazulme, or The Night Owl, Pongo the Intelligent Ape* and *Raoul, or The Magic Star*. The other siblings were **Angélique** (1813–95), **Antoine** (1812–82) and **François** (1823–81). After training in Italy, they had earned fame in Paris by 1828 and created a furore at DRURY LANE in 1830 with pantos, inspired by MAZURIER, that combined skilled ACROBATICS, graceful dance and advanced trick-work. They appeared at the PARK THEATRE, New York, in 1836–7, and then became a fixture at NIBLO'S GARDEN in 1842–6, 1849–50 and 1857–60. In 1850 the troupe divided, with Jérome and Antoine touring the United States and François and Gabriel playing in Europe.

**Ravenscroft, Edward** 1643–1707 English playwright. He gave up the law after the success of his first play, an adaptation of MOLIÈRE's *Le Bourgeois Gentilhomme* as *The Citizen Turned Gentleman* (1672). Ravenscroft tried most genres, including COMMEDIA DELL'ARTE characters in *Scaramouche a Philosopher* (1677), and a good FARCE, *The Anatomist* (1697). By far his most successful play, *The London Cuckolds* (1681), a bawdy mockery of sexual ambition, was so popular that it was performed annually on the Lord Mayor's Day until Garrick stopped the practice at DRURY LANE in 1751.

**Raznovich, Diana** 1945– Argentine poet, novelist, essayist and playwright. Her dozen or so plays include *Buscapiés* (*Fireworks*, 1968) and *Plaza hay una sola* (*There's Only one Plaza*, 1969), a collection of eight short plays under one title, and *Jardín de otoño* (*Autumn Garden*, 1983), her best-known play, with its two women madly enamoured of a television personality. Her *Casa matriz* (*Mother Centre*, 1991) shows the depths of consumerism through a 'rent-a-mother' agency that assuages basic emotional needs.

**Reade, Charles** 1814–84 British playwright and novelist. Usually remembered for his historical novel, *The Cloister and the Hearth* (1861), Reade was also a social campaigner and playwright whose early performed work included a highly successful collaboration with TOM TAYLOR on *Masks and Faces* (1852) at the HAYMARKET. *It Is Never Too Late to Mend*, a typically pugnacious criticism of the brutal British penal system, was dramatized in 1868. *Foul Play* (1868), a collaboration with BOUCICAULT, and *Griffith Gaunt* (1867) also appeared as both novels and plays. Reade adapted ZOLA's novel, *L'Assommoir*, as *Drink* (1879). *The Lyons Mail* (1854), an effective adaptation from the French, passed from the repertoire of FECHTER to that of IRVING and on to MARTIN-HARVEY.

**realism** Although realism and NATURALISM are often assumed to be synonymous, it is useful to distinguish between them. The term realism was first used in France in the 1850s to characterize works concerned with representing the world as it is rather than as it ought to be. What realism and naturalism share is an allegiance to an art of representation or imitation of unheroic everyday contemporary life. It is now clear that realism is a style no closer to reality than the several movements that rose in reaction against it, each claiming to approach reality more closely.

The 19th-century European novel is a bastion of realism, but its techniques entered the theatre gradually. Towards the middle of the 19th century came real objects on a stage that resembled a room with the fourth wall removed – the so-called picture-frame stage. T. W. ROBERTSON introduced real bread and real tea to the London stage of the 1860s. ANDRÉ ANTOINE founded the Théâtre Libre in Paris in 1887, where he provided authentic settings with real objects – most famously, a side of beef – for slice-of-life dramas that eschewed the tight suspenseful structure of the WELL MADE PLAY. Inspired by him, OTTO BRAHM founded the FREIE BÜHNE in Berlin in 1889, and J. T. Grein his Independent Theatre Society in London in 1891. For these three avant-garde theatres, Ibsen's *Ghosts* was the key realistic play. Realism as a dramatic movement spanned the 30 years between IBSEN's first socially-realistic play, *The Pillars of Society* (1877), and SHAW's *The Doctor's Dilemma* (1906).

Variously ill received in their day, realistic plays are now acknowledged as the beginning of the modern repertory. After NEMIROVICH-DANCHENKO and STANISLAVSKY founded the MOSCOW ART THEATRE in 1898, an understated, psychologically-based style of acting accommodated realistic plays; through STRASBERG's 'Method' adaptation of Stanislavsky, such acting now dominates film. The impact of the realistic movement was powerful and is still evident: realism is the dominant style of modern drama, recognizable in verisimilitude of setting, coherence of character, modernity of problems and prosaic quality of dialogue.

**Reaney, James** 1926– Canadian poet and playwright. His first play, *The Killdeer* (1960), established most of the themes and methods that permeate his more than 30 theatre works: a focus on local settings and local myths, childish play, the movement from innocence to experience, an almost surrealistic approach (see SURREALISM) to realistic stories, and a rich poetic imagery often expressed in incantatory chanting. These features are found in *Listen to the Wind* (1966) and in *Colours in the Dark* (1967), produced at the STRATFORD FESTIVAL by JOHN HIRSCH. With *Sticks and Stones* (1973) Reaney's plays moved from the poetic to the historic. It is the first play in a trilogy entitled *The Donnellys* about a bitter blood-feud. *Sticks and Stones, The St Nicholas Hotel* (1974) and *Handcuffs* (1975) were developed in workshops and first produced at Toronto's TARRAGON THEATRE. More recently, Reaney has written for opera and begun work in video and film.

**Red Bull Theatre** (London) Elizabethan theatre. An inn in Clerkenwell used for occasional theatrical produc-tions, the Red Bull was converted into a distinctive theatre – a square yard surrounded by galleries – in 1605. During its occupation by Queen Anne's Men (1605–19) it was notorious for the boisterousness of its audiences. THOMAS HEYWOOD provided much successful material. After the queen's death and the defection of CHRISTOPHER BEESTON it housed various companies; even during the Interregnum there were illegal productions and PUPPET-plays. It was demolished c.1665.

**Red Lion Theatre** (London) Elizabethan playhouse. The discovery, in 1983, of legal documents relating to the building of a 'scaffold or stage for INTERLUDES or plays' in the Red Lion in Stepney has revised our knowledge of this enterprise. In 1567, nine years before his brother-in-law JAMES BURBAGE, JOHN BRAYNE envisaged a specialized structure dedicated to the performance of plays. We know that it was a farmhouse, not an inn, and that Brayne financed the conversion work in the yard, with instructions to build a stage 5ft high, 30ft deep and at least 40ft wide. There was to be a trap-door and a 'turret' or tower 30ft high, presumably to serve as a TIR-ING HOUSE. There is, however, no solid evidence that the structure was ever used, or even completed.

**Redgrave, Michael (Scudamore)** 1908–85 British actor. Born into a theatrical family, he joined the LIVERPOOL PLAYHOUSE company in 1934, where he met and married the actress, Rachel Kempson. In 1936 they went to the OLD VIC, then under the direction of TYRONE GUTHRIE, where Redgrave played such roles as Orlando in *As You Like It*, Horner in WYCHERLEY's *The Country Wife* and Laertes in *Hamlet*. He was a member of JOHN GIELGUD's repertory company at the Queen's Theatre in 1937 and played Harry in T. S. ELIOT's *The Family Reunion* in 1939, his first major part in a contemporary play.

His handsome presence, polite but somewhat studious manner and gentle speaking voice were equally well suited to stage and screen, and he appeared in several patriotic wartime films. He created the part of Crocker-Harris in TERENCE RATTIGAN's *The Browning Version* (1948) and joined the Shakespeare Memorial Company in 1951, playing Richard II, followed by notable performances as Prospero, Hotspur, Antony and King Lear. In 1959 he appeared in his own adaptation of HENRY JAMES's *The Aspern Papers*. In 1962 he joined LAURENCE OLIVIER's company in the first CHICHESTER FESTIVAL season, playing the title role in *Uncle Vanya*. Subsequently he played Hobson in *Hobson's Choice* and Solness in *The Master Builder* at the NATIONAL THEATRE, before ill-health forced him to leave the company. He returned in 1972 to play the silent, ageing academic in SIMON GRAY's *Close of Play*. His books on acting reveal his intelligent approach to his craft. He was knighted in 1959.

Redgrave's three children, VANESSA, Corin (1939– ) and Lynn (1943– ), all became successful actors, as are two of his grandchildren by Vanessa Redgrave (Richardson).

**Redgrave, Vanessa** 1937– British actress, daughter of MICHAEL REDGRAVE and Rachel Kempson. Her Rosalind in MICHAEL ELLIOT's production of *As You Like It* (1961) at Stratford-upon-Avon was acclaimed, and she appeared in other Elliot productions including as Ellida in *The Lady from the Sea* (1982). She played Nina in *The Seagull* (1964), directed by Tony Richardson who was then her husband, and in 1966 achieved a triumphant success as Miss Brodie the Scottish schoolmistress in the stage version of Muriel Spark's novel, *The Prime of Miss Jean Brodie*.

Her membership of the Workers' Revolutionary Party and her passionate advocacy of political causes have attracted much publicity; but her dedication and sincerity, two outstanding qualities also of her acting, have rarely been questioned. Her tall, willowy appearance, expressive voice and, not least, her marvellous comic sense have made her one of the leading international actresses of her time, both on stage and on screen. In recent years she has specialized in roles from modern American drama, including works by O'NEILL and TENNESSEE WILLIAMS and two plays by Martin Sherman, *A Madhouse in Goa* (1989) and *When She Danced* (1991). In 1989 her company Vanessa Redgrave Enterprises brought over from Moscow to London the powerful Vakhtangov Theatre version of Mikhail Shatrov's *Peace of Brest*, banned in the former Soviet Union for its unattractive portrayal of Lenin.

**Régio, José** 1901–69 Portuguese playwright. With only four dramas and three further one-act plays to his credit, Régio was nevertheless his country's greatest dramatist of the mid-century. The theme of duality – either of identity, or that of living in a dualistic world between spirit and matter, between God and the devil – recurs poetically and dramatically over the 20 years between the MYSTERY PLAY *Jacob e o Anjo* (*Jacob and the Angel*, 1941, performed in 1952 in Paris) and the one-act *Mário ou Eu-Próprio-o-Outro* (*Mário/or/Myself-the-Other-Person*, 1957). Although 'literary', Régio's works have performed well. In 1974 a successful film was made of *A Virgem Benilde* (*The Virgin Benilde*, 1947).

**Regnard, Jean-François** 1655–1709 French playwright. His first efforts were FARCES and light comedies for the COMÉDIE-ITALIENNE. His later, more substantial comedies for the COMÉDIE-FRANÇAISE retain the same Italianate spirit with echoes of MOLIÈRE. *Le Joueur* (1696), concerning an incurable gambler, and *Le Légataire universel* (*The Residuary Legatee*, 1708), which subordinates love to the profit motive, are interestingly amoral but alive with comic energy.

**Rehan** [Crehan], **Ada** 1860–1916 Irish-born American actress. Her family migrated to Brooklyn from Ireland when she was five. She made her debut at 13. From 1878 to 1899 she was AUGUSTIN DALY's leading lady. During her 31 years on stage in the USA and in England she played over 200 roles, ranging from the title role in Daly's *Odette* (1882) and Lady Teazle in *The School for Scandal* (1894) to a host of Shakespearian parts: Katherina, Rosalind, Viola, Beatrice, Miranda and Portia. After Daly's death she toured again with OTIS SKINNER in *The Taming of the Shrew* (1904–5). ELLEN TERRY described her as 'the most lovely, humorous darling I have ever seen on the stage'.

**Reicher, Emanuel** 1849–1924 German actor. In 1887 Reicher was hired by the Berlin Residenztheater. Here his performance as Pastor Manders in *Ghosts* established him as a leading naturalistic actor (see NATURALISM). From 1895, he acted under BRAHM at the DEUTSCHES THEATER. Here he was celebrated for the minute psychological accuracy of his roles, especially in IBSEN's plays. From 1917 he directed at the Garden Theatre in New York.

**Reid, (J.) Graham** 1945– Irish playwright. Reid's plays centre on the violence in the North of Ireland. His first two, *The Death of Humpty-Dumpty* (1979) and *The Closed Door* (1980), tell equally harrowing stories of victims on the periphery of terrorist violence, and the widening circle of loss. The terrorism, rape and torture in *Dorothy* (1980) proved too strong for the ABBEY, Reid's main venue. He has since written a successful trilogy for television, *Billy* (1982, adapted for the stage in 1990), and the stage plays, *The Hidden Curriculum* (1982) and *Remembrance* (LYRIC THEATRE, Belfast, 1984), a somewhat gentler piece, exploring sectarian family pressures on middle-aged lovers from opposite sides of the political divide.

**Reid, Kate** 1930–93 Canadian actress. She appeared at the STRATFORD FESTIVAL from 1959 to 1962. Noted for her work in roles demanding intense emotional energy, in 1962 she played Martha in New York in EDWARD ALBEE's *Who's Afraid of Virginia Woolf?*, and in 1964 appeared opposite ALEC GUINNESS in *Dylan*. She co-starred in TENNESSEE WILLIAMS's *Slapstick Tragedy* (1966) and spent almost two years in ARTHUR MILLER's *The Price* in New York and London. For the AMERICAN SHAKESPEARE [THEATRE] Festival she has played several Shakespearian roles. In 1985 she appeared opposite DUSTIN HOFFMAN in a major revival of *Death of a Salesman*. She also had a successful film and television career, primarily in the USA.

In Canada she played Madame Ranevskaya in *The Cherry Orchard* at Stratford in 1965 and returned to the Festival in 1970 and 1980, primarily in modern plays. Other important Canadian appearances were in *Mrs Warren's Profession* at the SHAW FESTIVAL in 1976 and as Clytemnestra in the National Arts Centre's 1983 production of the *Oresteia*. She also had a successful film and television career, primarily in the USA.

**Reinhardt, Max** 1873–1943 Austrian director. In his youth Reinhardt was an actor, mainly of old men's roles, first at the Salzburg Town Theatre, then at the DEUTSCHES THEATER in Berlin under the direction of OTTO BRAHM. In 1903 he gave up acting to concentrate on directing, and over the next decade became the most celebrated stage director in Europe. Although he absorbed the latest developments in scenic design, employing designers such as GORDON CRAIG and Ernst Stern (1876–1954), and exploited advances in actorial training and technique, he always maintained an illusionistic stage (see THEATRE DESIGN). This illusionism is the unifying element in his otherwise eclectic work, ranging from intimate chamber drama through vivid productions of SHAKESPEARE and the classics, to vast spectacles staged in arenas throughout Germany and Europe.

During these years Reinhardt was director of the Deutsches Theater, a post he kept until 1933. From 1917 on, he was closely involved with running the newly established Salzburg Festival; here he employed both theatres and extra-theatrical settings such as churches and the cathedral square for his productions. During the 1920s, his career increasingly became centred on Salzburg and Vienna, where he was director of the Theater in der Josefstadt. In 1933, with the coming to power of the Nazis, he spent more and more of his time in the USA, where he worked both in Hollywood and on BROADWAY. His most significant work in these later years was his film of *A Midsummer Night's Dream* (1935).

**Reinshagen, Gerlind** 1926– German playwright. She came to the theatre after writing RADIO DRAMA. Her scrupulously observed plays invest the mechanisms of everyday life with an unobtrusive significance. *Doppelkopf* (*Rummy*, 1968) shows the fall of a careerist during an office party, and *Eisenherz* (*Ironheart*, 1982) exposes emotional tensions behind the professional rivalries of office life. *Leben und Tod der Marilyn Monroe* (*Life and Death of Marilyn Monroe*, 1971) dramatizes the legend of Reinshagen's film heroine from slums to suicide. In *Himmel und Erde* (*Heaven and Earth*, 1974) a waitress's reflections on the men she has served are terminated by a heart attack. Reinshagen's best play is *Sonntagskinder* (*Sunday's Children*, 1976), an evocation of childhood during the war years in Germany, showing the domestic impact of distant carnage. Like *Das Frühlingsfest* (*Spring Festival*, 1980), which looks at the shady side of the German 'economic miracle' in the 1950s, it places a young woman of integrity in an atmosphere of casual corruption. Both plays are in part autobiographical.

**Réjane** [Gabrielle Réju] 1856–1920 French actress. Réjane became the star of the BOULEVARD. She excelled in light and polished COMEDY but her range included broader popular roles, such as SARDOU's Madame Sans-Gêne (1893) and carefully observed naturalistic parts (see NATURALISM). Her most important years were spent at the Vaudeville, whose director, Porel, she married in 1893. *Madame Sans-Gêne* was followed by BECQUE's *La Parisienne*. In the following year she was the first French Nora in IBSEN's *A Doll's House*. One of her greatest parts was in Paul Hervieu's *Course au flambeau* (1901). In 1908 she took over the Théâtre Nouveau as the Théâtre Réjane, where she staged *John Gabriel Borkman*. She was also involved in film-making, notably *Madame Sans-Gêne*.

**Remizov, Aleksei (Mikhailovich)** 1877–1957 Russian novelist, critic and playwright. He was a superb literary craftsman; his novels, stories and plays reflect his interest in ancient rituals and folklore, children's games and fairy tales, dreams, etymology and Old Russia. He served as literary manager of MEYERHOLD's Fellowship of the New Drama in Kherson, South Russia (1903–4), and wrote several plays, contemporary stylizations of ancient legends. *The Devil Play* (1907) is a modernization of a medieval Kievan legend. Although it captured the spirit and style of the original, Remizov was booed off the stage. *The Tragedy of Judas, Prince of Iscariot* (1909) combines an apocryphal Judas legend, the Oedipus myth and Russian folkloric imagery and stylization. *Tsar Maximilian* (1919) is Remizov's version of a well known and much rewritten Russian folk drama. His prose works formed the bulk of his writing and include a major critical work on Russian literature, *The Fire of Things* (1954). He emigrated to Berlin in 1921 and to Paris in 1923.

**Rene, Roy** [Harry van der Sluys; 'Mo'] 1892–1954 Australian comedian. As 'Master Roy' he sang and appeared in PANTOMIME, and later in suburban MINSTREL SHOWS, from which he adapted Mo's characteristic black-and-white make-up. Partnered from 1916 to 1928 by Nat Phillips ('Stiffy'), he dominated Australian VAUDEVILLE in the 1920s–30s with a distinctive earthy humour and outrageous innuendo; his catch-phrase 'Strike me lucky!' became a household term. In the 1940s he appeared in the radio comedy (see RADIO DRAMA) series 'McCackie Mansions'; his last stage appearance was in *Hellzapoppin'* in 1949–50.

**Rengifo, César** 1915–80 Venezuelan playwright, director, politician and journalist. Author of more than 60 plays (from 1942), Rengifo wrote trilogies on Venezuelan history and the petroleum industry. The periods that he dealt with are the Conquest, pre-independence, the wars of Federation and the petroleum period. A revisionist historian, he made strong critical statements about injustices in contemporary society. His leftist political orientation led him to experiment with BRECHTian techniques, balancing aesthetics

against ideology to avoid outright propaganda. His *Manuelote* (1952) is widely known; other major plays include *El vendaval amarillo* (*Yellow Wind*, 1959), *Lo que dejó la tempestad* (*What the Storm Left*, 1961) and *Las torres y el viento* (*Towers and Wind*, 1970).

**repertory theatre (Britain)** The repertory movement in Britain is now the major provider of theatre in the regions. The campaigns and experiments at the turn of the century which led to its establishment were essentially reactions against the commercial touring system and all that went with it: the actor-managers, the 'stars', the long runs, the domination of London, the priority of profit over experiment and new work – all these features were seen as stultifying and a hindrance to the healthy development of theatre as a social force. Looking back to the days of the resident stock companies (see STOCK COMPANY) and abroad to the accomplishments of the well endowed national and state theatres (the COMÉDIE-FRANÇAISE, in particular), men such as HARLEY GRANVILLE BARKER and WILLIAM ARCHER, during the early years of this century, argued forcefully for the establishment of a National Repertory Theatre in London, to be followed later by regional theatres on similar lines if smaller in scale.

In its ideal form, a repertory theatre would offer to the public a wide variety of the very best of drama, old and new, British and foreign, popular and minority-interest. Commercial considerations ought not to govern the repertoire and for this reason, it was claimed, the theatre would need to be well funded, either by private benefactors or, preferably, by national or local government (just as were museums and libraries). A large stock of productions would be maintained and presented on a regular, rotating basis (the 'true repertory' model) by a permanent, resident company of actors able to play as an ensemble and to keep plays fresh in performance, freed from the deadening constraints of the long run. Barker's famous seasons at the ROYAL COURT THEATRE, 1904–7, were an early attempt to put some of the ideas to the test. But with London entrenched in the very system that repertory was endeavouring to oppose, it was in cities outside the capital that full scale repertory companies were to be established. The repertory movement was henceforward essentially *regional* in character and in philosophy.

Within a space of just seven years, five repertory ventures had been initiated: at Manchester in 1907 (ANNIE HORNIMAN's company, which based itself in the refurbished GAIETY THEATRE from 1908); at Glasgow in 1909; at Liverpool in 1911; at Birmingham in 1913 (under BARRY JACKSON); and briefly, at Bristol in 1914. These early companies set the pattern for future growth, successfully building reputations for their high-quality ensemble playing, for their provision of a varied repertoire and for their encouragement of new writers.

After World War I, the movement diversified and lost some momentum. But there was the adventurousness of TERENCE GRAY's Cambridge Festival Theatre (1926–33) and his experiments in 'presentational' stage design. Birmingham and Liverpool provided the inspiration for the founding of a dozen more genuine repertory theatres across the country. The handful of outstanding companies – in Bristol, Oxford, Cambridge, Sheffield and Northampton especially, in addition to Birmingham and Liverpool – ensured a firm basis for the stronger national network of repertory theatres after World War II.

Schemes emerged for new repertory theatre buildings at Coventry, Nottingham, Birmingham and elsewhere, financed by the local authorities, often with additional money from the ARTS COUNCIL and public subscription. Coventry's Belgrade Theatre (1958) was the first purpose-built repertory theatre for 20 years. By 1980 some 40 new theatres (or major conversions of pre-existing buildings) had been completed, most of which were designed for regional repertory. The buildings were often prestigious in character, sometimes too large but sometimes imaginative and exciting in design: Sheffield Crucible Theatre's thrust stage, the Manchester ROYAL EXCHANGE's in-the-round auditorium and the spacious foyers and auditoria of the West Yorkshire Playhouse (Leeds) are good examples. Arts Council money freed companies from the tyranny of 'weekly rep' (the dominant practice of weekly changes in the bill to maximize box-office income). More and more theatres changed to two- and then three-week runs, increased rehearsal time and so improved their standards. At the same time ticket prices could be kept at reasonable levels and new or experimental work risked more frequently.

Of special note have been the seasons directed by JOHN NEVILLE, Stuart Burge and RICHARD EYRE at the Nottingham Playhouse (between 1963 and 1978); Peter Cheeseman's series of local documentaries at the VICTORIA THEATRE, Stoke-on-Trent; and the unique, assertively theatrical style pursued at the CITIZENS' THEATRE, Glasgow, since 1970.

The repertory concept had, by the mid-1960s, begun to widen out to take on a more strategic, 'audience-centred' significance – less associated now with providing a varied selection of plays for regular, traditional theatregoers, more with the function of *regional* theatres serving a multiplicity of interests and tastes, communities and age groups – and as such claiming and earning public subsidy for a public service. Community touring and THEATRE-IN-EDUCATION units made significant strides in bringing theatre to new audiences.

Not all the aims of the original proponents of repertory have been achieved. The permanent acting company can rarely be afforded by theatres other than the NATIONAL and the Royal Shakespeare (see ROYAL SHAKESPEARE COMPANY) Theatres and rarely are plays presented in 'true repertory' (i.e. on a rotational basis): actors are now usually cast play-by-play and 'short runs' are the norm. None the less, since the war artistic standards have undoubtedly been raised, the repertoire broadened, much new work generated, the principle of subsidy (if not its correct level) agreed and a decentralized network of some 60 regional theatres firmly established.

In the recession of the late 1980s and early 1990s, subsidy standstills and the increasingly market-driven economy had a narrowing effect upon the repertoire and audience attendance began to decline.

**resident theatre (USA)** This movement, which gained its greatest momentum in the 1960s, has variously been called the regional, repertory and resident theatre movement. The initial impetus was to create an alternative, decentralized theatre network in the United States outside of New York. Its non-profit-making status is significant in that box office profit is not of prime concern; rather, the focus is on the art of the theatre, the development of theatre artists, craftsmen and administrators dedicated to establishing a new American theatre, and the production of classical and innovative contemporary drama. Most resident theatres have a set season with subscribers and are established in their own building.

Claiming as antecedents the amateur LITTLE THEATRE MOVEMENT of the 1920s, the GROUP THEATRE of the 1930s and the FEDERAL THEATRE PROJECT of the Depression, the resident theatre movement began with the founding of the Cleveland Play House in 1915, still in existence, although its impetus and inspiration are credited to MARGO JONES who in the 1940s devised the prototype for the regional theatre with her Theatre '47 in Dallas, Texas. From a handful of theatres two decades ago, today there are more than 200 playing to over 15 million people annually. These theatres are the chief originators of significant theatre in America, and many of the notable plays of the 1970s and 1980s began life in them before transferring to New York. A number of playwrights owe allegiance to the resident theatre: e.g. Chicago's GOODMAN THEATRE has energetically fostered the talents of DAVID MAMET and JOHN GUARE. Writers as diverse as SAM SHEPARD, LANFORD WILSON and CHARLES FULLER have been nurtured by the non-profit theatre. However, the resident theatres, surviving through private and public subsidy, have been in jeopardy since the mid-1980s because of the erratic pattern of support that has failed to close the growing gap between income and expenses, intensified by the recession of recent years.

**Reumert, Poul** 1883–1968 Danish actor. He had a long and glorious career at the KONGELIGE TEATER, most of it in a legendary partnership with Bodil Ipsen. He specialized in complex tragicomic roles, contrasting well with her exuberant, provocative style; they were especially successful as Edgar and Alice in *The Dance of Death*, and as Ill and Madame Zachanassian in *The Visit*. Perfectly fluent in French, Reumert had a special affinity with the plays of MOLIÈRE, whose *Précieuses Ridicules* he translated. An outstanding Scapin, a very sensual Tartuffe and a controversially grave Alceste, he acted Molière throughout Scandinavia and in Paris.

**Reutter** [Pfützenreuter], **Otto** 1870–1931 German MUSIC-HALL singer and song-writer. His career began at Berlin's Apollo Theatre in 1895. Basically a minstrel of the proletariat, conservative and patriotic, occasionally topically satirical, he displayed wit and feeling in his reflections on the workaday world, unlike more sophisticated song-writers. He played all the major music-halls in Germany, and wrote the words and music to thousands of numbers, the most famous being 'Ick wundre mir über gar nischt mehr' ('Nothing Surprises Me No More') and 'In fünfzig Jahren ist alles vorbei' ('It'll All Be Over in Fifty Years').

**revenge tragedy** Elizabethan and Jacobean theatrical genre. A revenge tragedy, modelled on the success of KYD's *The Spanish Tragedy* (c.1589), begins with the appearance of the ghost of a wronged and/or murdered man to a living descendant or associate who hears the ghost's story and assumes the role of avenger. Elizabethan playwrights incorporated some features of the prototype and abandoned others. SHAKESPEARE's *Titus Andronicus* (c.1592) and *Hamlet* (c.1601) exhibit and surpass the full range. Other notable examples are TOURNEUR's *The Revenger's Tragedy* (c.1606) and *The Atheist's Tragedy* (published 1611); WEBSTER's *The White Devil* (c.1612) and *The Duchess of Malfi* (c.1613); MIDDLETON's *The Changeling* (1622) and *Women Beware Women* (c.1625); MARSTON's *Antonio's Revenge* (1600) and

SHIRLEY's *The Traitor* (1631). But the theme of revenge so dominated the tragedies of the period that the list could be substantially extended.

**revista** Portuguese genre. The *revista* ranges from intimate sketch to mini-musical. Characteristically, it has played in the larger theatres, more particularly in Lisbon. The first *revista*, an imitation of the early-19th-century REVUE, *Fossilismo e Progresso* (*Fossil-Worship and Progress*, 1859), started a tradition of an annual *Revista do Ano* (*Review of the Year*). Initially just a series of brief sketches, they were the theatrical equivalents of lampoon and caricature: the queen might be depicted squawking out a *fado* (popular ballad), the government furtively picking the lock of the Treasury. By the end of the century, the *revista* had acquired the framework of a story (usually mythological in theme) for its political SATIRE, a chorus line and orchestra, and could expect long runs: *Sal e Pimenta* (*Salt and Pepper*) ran for more than 200 performances.

The satire, often vitriolic, was fired against the dictator Franco in the first decade of the new century, and against over-heavy policing under the republic. The *revista* gained popularity and importance under the dictator Salazar's corporatist regime, c.1928–74, being the only political theatre with any continuity in the nation's life. In the five decades following 1920, there was a high of 122 new shows in the 1930s and a relative low of 68 in the 1960s. In 1991 Felipe La Féria's anthology *Passa por Mim no Rossio* (*It's All Here, in the Rossio* – Lisbon's historic central square, where the theatre is) celebrated 150 years of *revista* .

**revue** Episodic programme of songs and COMEDY sketches. Revue features also MIME, dance and instrumental music, ostensibly organized around topical and satirical subject-matter, occasionally connected by a single theme or by a master of ceremonies. The term first appears at a French fairground theatre with *La Revue des théâtres* (1728). The end-of-year survey became an annual Parisian feature at the Théâtre de la Porte-Saint-Martin (1828–48; see BOULEVARD) and Berlin continued the tradition at the Metropol-Theater (1903–14).

At the turn of the century the spectacular revue arrived, a dance-dominated form that substitutes nostalgia, sentimentality and visual effects for SATIRE. In the *revue à grand spectacle* each tableau contributes to an overwhelming sense of glamour. The first was *Place aux jeunes* (1886) at the FOLIES-BERGÈRE, Paris, which became a leading purveyor of this form: by 1928 the show boasted 80 tableaux, 500 performers and 1,200 costumes.

In Germany and Austria the revue became the second half of VARIETY programmes and occasionally transmuted into operetta; jazz bands, nude women and light shows were regular features after World War I. The form's loose-knit structure attracted the theatrical avant-garde. MAX REINHARDT's pantomimic spectacles *Sumurun* (1910) and *The Miracle* (1911) owed much to it, and ERWIN PISCATOR's *Revue Rote Rummel* (1924) adapted it to leftist political ends, inspiring ERNST TOLLER's *Trotz Alledem* (1925) and the AGIT-PROP Red Revues of the German Communist Party. BRECHT in Berlin, MAYAKOVSKY and MEYERHOLD in Moscow and VOSKOVEC AND WERICH in Prague also took it as a model.

The revue did not catch on in England until shortly before World War I; the wartime thirst for light entertainment confirmed its success, when OSWALD STOLL imported French revues to London's HIPPODROME. The impresarios André Charlot and C. B. COCHRAN specialized in more intimate showcases for such talents as NOËL COWARD, BEATRICE LILLIE and GERTRUDE LAWRENCE (*Cheep*, 1917; *London Calling*, 1923; *Charlot's Revue*, 1924; *On with the Dance*, 1925; *Words and Music*, 1932). The basic unit became the 'black-out' sketch, a short comic scene ending with a punchline and a rapid lights-out. The smart WEST END revue (or 'review') flourished well into the 1960s and proved to be a nursery for comedians, singers and dancers whose personalities suited the cosy, saucy style of the genre: e.g. Cicely Courtneidge, Cyril Ritchard, Hermione Gingold and JOYCE GRENFELL. Eventually it succumbed to television and a blacker brand of satire, more akin to CABARET.

In New York some 200 revues opened between 1900 and 1930, often originating in the after-hours roof gardens of legitimate theatres. These included both the spectacular – e.g. the ZIEGFELD Follies, the SHUBERT BROTHERS' *Passing Show*, GEORGE WHITE's *Scandals*; and the intimate – e.g. *Greenwich Village Follies*, *Music Box Revue*, *Garrick Gaieties*. As *Thousands Cheer* (1933) was one of the first revues to feature a female black star, ETHEL WATERS, in a white cast. The decline of the intimate revue is due in part to the disappearance of a homogeneous audience that shares similar tastes and a certain level of urbanity.

After 1945, the spectacular revue diversified into nightclub and floor shows, strip-tease (see NUDITY); ice and fashion shows. Much of its function had already been usurped by the revue film, exemplified by the work of Busby Berkeley. The topical revue became a feature of television, while the intimate revue was narrowed to a survey of a single composer's work (*Oh, Coward!*, 1972; *Side by Side by Sondheim*, 1976). In the 1960s, revue techniques once more inspired experimental theatre: Poland's LATERNA MAGIKA, JOAN LITTLEWOOD's *Oh, What a Lovely War!* (1963), PETER BROOK's *US* (1966), JEAN-LOUIS BARRAULT's *Rabelais* (1968), LUCA RONCONI's *Orlando Furioso* (1969) and ARIANE MNOUCHKINE's *1789* (1970) have drawn on the revue format. Much contemporary street and alternative performance is organized as a deliberate perversion of outmoded revue traditions.

**Reyes, Carlos José** 1941– Colombian playwright and director. He collaborated with SANTIAGO GARCÍA to establish the Casa de Cultura de Bogotá, later the Teatro La Candelaria. He has operated his own theatre, El Alacrán, which merged in 1984 with the Popular Theatre of Bogotá. He also writes plays for children and historical drama for television. Among his major plays are *Soldados* (*Soldiers*, 1967), a gripping account of Colombian violence based on a chapter of Alvaro Cepeda Zamudio's novel, and *La casa grande* (*The Big House*). *Los viejos baúles empolvados que nuestros padres nos prohibieron abrir* (*The Dusty Old Trunks our Parents Forbade Us to Open*, 1968) and *Variaciones sobre la Metamorfosis* (*Variations on Metamorphosis*), a play structured around Kafka's work *Metamorphosis*, are later examples. Recent works include *La voz* (*The Voice*, 1990) and *Función nocturna* (*Night Function*, 1991).

**Ribeyro, Julio Ramón** 1929– Peruvian novelist and playwright. He is principally known for his play *Santiago, el pajarero* (*Santiago, the Bird Dealer*, 1970), inspired by a *tradición* of Ricardo Palma, which criticizes governmental systems in an 18th-century setting. His other plays include *El sótano* (*The Basement*, 1959), *Fin de semana* (*Weekend*, 1961), *Los caracoles* (*The Snails*, 1964) and

*Atusparia* (1979), a work based on an indigenous revolt in 1885.

**Ribman, Ronald** 1932– American playwright. Ribman attracted critical attention in 1965 with his *Harry, Noon and Night* at the American Place Theatre in New York, followed by *The Journey of the Fifth Horse* (1966). Other plays include *The Ceremony of Innocence* (1965), *Passing Through from Exotic Places* (1969), *Fingernails Blue as Flowers* (1971), *A Break in the Skin* (1972), *The Poison Tree* (1973) and *Cold Storage* (1977, an award-winning comedy about the function of death), *Buck* (1983) and *Sweet Table at Richelieu* (1987). More respected than loved, Ribman's plays deal with man's entrapment by a universe he cannot change.

**Riccoboni family** Italian actors. The founder of the dynasty, **Antonio** (fl.1655–95), was seen in London as Pantalone in 1679. His son **Luigi Andreas** (1676–1753), known as **Lélio**, in 1716 reopened the COMÉDIE-ITALIENNE in Paris, where he won acclaim for his expressive acting, especially in MARIVAUX's plays. He also toured to London in 1727–8. His works include a history of the Italian theatre, a study of European acting and calls for theatre reform in support of sentimental comedy.

His son **Antoine-François-Valentin** (1707–72), known as Lélio *fils*, worked with the Comédie-Italienne during 1726–50 as first lover, dancer and choreographer; he wrote several comedies, a discourse on PARODY (1746) promoting opera over tragedy, and *L'Art du théâtre* (1750), which raised questions of the actor's emotional involvement in his role. His wife Marie-Jeanne de La Boras, known as **Madame Riccoboni** (1713–92), was a friend of DIDEROT and wrote comedies in the style of Marivaux.

**Rice** [McLaren], **Dan** 1823–1900 American CLOWN. He began as a showman in 1841 with 'Lord Byron', 'the most sapient of pigs'. His debut as clown was made in Galena, Illinois, in 1844, and he was soon a favourite for his native American humour and SATIRE of local politicians. His red-and-white striped costume, top-hat and chin-whiskers later became attributes of Uncle Sam. Rice popularized the term 'one-horse show', originally an insult flung at him by a journalist, and as the 'Great Shakespearian clown' bandied mangled quotations with his audience. He was half-seriously nominated for president in 1868; alcoholism undermined his abilities, and his last public appearances were as a temperance lecturer in the 1870s.

**Rice** [Reizenstein], **Elmer** 1892–1967 American playwright. Rice trained as a lawyer and used his legal knowledge in several plays and in theatre disputes. He served various causes, from Marxism in the 1930s to the American Civil Liberties Union. His career started in 1914 with *On Trial*, an experimental play using a courtroom scene for flashbacks into the crime being tried. His work with the FEDERAL THEATRE PROJECT was threatened with government CENSORSHIP, leading to his resignation. In 1938 he and four other playwrights – ROBERT E. SHERWOOD, S. N. BEHRMAN, SIDNEY HOWARD and MAXWELL ANDERSON – founded the Playwrights' Company.

Rice's best work is *The Adding Machine* (1923), an expressionistic play (see EXPRESSIONISM) about the dehumanization of mankind. In *Street Scene* (1929) a character exclaims: 'Everywhere you look, oppression and cruelty!' *We, the People* (1933), a bitter attack on Depression times, ended in an AGIT-PROP call for democratic ideals. In *Judgment Day* (1934) Rice scourged Nazi Fascism, and in *Between Two Worlds* (1934) contrasted the political systems of Russia and America. Finally, in *American Landscape* (1938), disillusioned with both Marxism and American commercial theatre, he continued to support American idealism. He went on writing after World War II (*The Grand Tour*, 1951, *Winners*, 1954, and *Cue for Passion*, 1958), but less successfully. Always a liberal idealist, Rice preached individual freedom from all tyranny.

**Rice, Thomas D(artmouth)** ['Daddy'] 1806–60 American blackface performer. Between 1828 and 1831 Rice, according to tradition, observed a crippled Negro stableman sing a refrain and dance with a jerky jump – thus 'Jump Jim Crow', after the slave's name. From this single song and dance he developed full-length entertainments called 'Ethiopian operas'; he is considered the 'father of American minstrelsy' (see MINSTREL SHOW). He also toured Great Britain. In 1858, he played the title role at the BOWERY THEATRE in *UNCLE TOM'S CABIN* (1850).

**Rice, Tim(othy Miles Bindon)** 1944– British lyricist. He teamed up with ANDREW LLOYD WEBBER while still at school to write *Joseph and the Amazing Technicolour Dreamcoat*, which was eventually seen in London in a professional production in 1968. Rice is a skilful if unconventional lyricist, whose off-rhymes and unusual rhythms contributed to the success of two further Lloyd Webber musicals, *Jesus Christ Superstar* (1970) and *Evita* (1976); but *Blondel* (1983), written with Stephen Oliver, received only a short run at London's Aldwych Theatre. *Chess* (1986) told a love story against a background of Cold War politics in sport. He has written lyrics for such composers as Paul McCartney and Marvin Hamlisch, and written and edited books on cricket. He is also well known in Britain as a television presenter.

**Rich, Frank** 1949– American drama critic. Rich was co-founder, reporter and editor of the *Richmond Mercury* (Virginia, 1972–3); the senior editor and film critic of *New Times Magazine* (New York, 1973–5); film critic of the *New York Post* (1975–7); film and television critic of *Time* magazine (1977–80); and chief drama critic of the *New York Times* (1980– ). As daily critic of the *New York Times*, Rich is arguably the most influential drama critic in the USA. Intelligent, demanding and generally knowledgeable about theatre and popular culture, Rich writes for the literate reader with style, authority and a hard intellectual edge and – in the estimation of the New York theatre community – little sympathy or affection for the theatre.

**Rich, John** [John Lun] ?1682–1761 English actor and manager. He inherited from his father, the unscrupulous Christopher Rich, the patent for LINCOLN'S INN FIELDS THEATRE and opened in 1714. In 1716 he began the tradition of an annual PANTOMIME with extraordinary success, starring himself as HARLEQUIN. In 1728 he accepted GAY's *The Beggar's Opera* which made 'Gay rich and Rich gay'. In 1730 he raised money to open a new theatre in COVENT GARDEN. Though he was illiterate, Rich's business acumen ensured the commercial profitability and popularity of his theatres.

**Richards, Lloyd** 1923– African-American actor, director and educator. Richards began his professional career as an actor OFF-BROADWAY and as resident director at regional theatres. His breakthrough as a director came with the legendary success of *A Raisin in the Sun* (1959). In 1968 he was named artistic director of the National Playwrights' Conference at the Eugene O'Neill Theatre Center in Waterford, Connecticut, for the development of new plays. Appointed dean of the Yale Drama School and artistic director of the YALE REPERTORY THEATRE (1979–91), he used his positions of leadership to promote the work of contemporary playwrights, the most prominent being Lee Blessing, AUGUST WILSON and the South African ATHOL FUGARD.

**Richardson, Ian** 1934– British actor. He was born and trained in Scotland. His substantial reputation rests on his Shakespearian work (see SHAKESPEARE): he played Hamlet at BIRMINGHAM REPERTORY THEATRE in the 1958–9 season, and in 1960 went to the Shakespeare Memorial Theatre in Stratford-upon-Avon. For the next 15 years he performed across the range of the repertoire, including Sir Andrew Aguecheek (1960), Oberon (1962), Edmund (in PETER BROOK's *King Lear*, 1964), Chorus in *Henry V* (1966), Richard II (1973) and Richard III (1973). He had notable successes in *The Duchess of Malfi* (Count Malatesti, 1960) and in WEISS's *Marat/Sade* (1965). He has also worked extensively in film and television, most recently as the Machiavellian politician whom everyone trusted in *House of Cards*. It was screened in 1990 (and had a sequel in 1993) at a time when, to many people's surprise, Margaret Thatcher was ousted as the British prime minister; but this was a strange coincidence.

**Richardson, John** see RICHARDSON'S SHOW

**Richardson, Ralph (David)** 1902–83 British actor. He joined the BIRMINGHAM REPERTORY THEATRE company in 1926 and in 1930 the OLD VIC company, where he showed his versatility as an actor in roles which ranged from Caliban to Henry V. He was not, however, ideally suited to the major classical parts, having neither the exceptional musicality of JOHN GIELGUD nor the dynamic sex appeal of LAURENCE OLIVIER, his two great contemporaries. Richardson's qualities emerged through his performances in contemporary plays, by MAUGHAM (*For Services Rendered*, 1932, and *Sheppey*, 1933) and J. B. PRIESTLEY (*Eden End*, 1934, and *Cornelius*, 1935). As Johnson in Priestley's *Johnson over Jordan* (1939) he gave a memorable performance as a modern Everyman, recollecting at the moment of death the vagaries of his life.

Richardson excelled as the ordinary man with a natural decency and even innocence; his Othello (1938), partnered by Olivier's homosexual Iago, was a notable example of miscasting. In 1944 he was invited to lead a revitalized Old Vic company at the New Theatre. With Olivier he provided four outstanding Old Vic seasons, in which his personal successes came as Peer Gynt, Falstaff and Inspector Goole in J. B. Priestley's *An Inspector Calls*. He was knighted in 1947. In the 1950s he continued to play major roles in both the classical repertory, such as Prospero (1952) and Timon (1956), and contemporary WEST END successes, such as Cherry in ROBERT BOLT's *Flowering Cherry* (1957). He enjoyed a bumbling eccentricity in WILLIAM DOUGLAS HOME's *Lloyd George Knew My Father* (1972). With John Gielgud he starred in DAVID STOREY's *Home* (1970) and in HAROLD PINTER's *No Man's Land* (1975), in which he played the elderly wealthy writer, Hirst. As a member of the NATIONAL THEATRE company he played in *The Wild Duck* and the title role in *John Gabriel Borkman* (1975), but his last major role came as the elder statesman contemplating his political career without much affection in David Storey's *Early Days* (1980).

**Richardson's Show** English fairground theatre. As a touring theatre it was responsible for spreading popular drama beyond London in the early 19th century. John Richardson (1766–1836) opened his first showbooth at Bartholomew Fair in 1798, with scenery from DRURY LANE and three blind Scotsmen as musicians. The narrow theatre (100ft long by 30ft wide) was said to contain 1,500 lamps and a thousand spectators. The average offering presented an overture, a MELODRAMA (with three murders and a ghost, according to DICKENS), a PANTOMIME, a comic song and incidental music in the space of 25 minutes. The young EDMUND KEAN worked there.

**Richelieu, Armand-Jean du Plessis, Cardinal (de)** 1585–1642 Chief minister of Louis XIII. A generous patron of the arts, Richelieu strongly influenced 17th-century French literature and theatre, which he adored. In 1634 he formed the Académie-Française to guard French language and culture. That same year he helped to establish MONTDORY's company at the MARAIS, and in 1641 inspired a royal decree authorizing the 'rehabilitation' of actors. He also commissioned five dramatists (Boisrobert, Colletet, PIERRE CORNEILLE, Claude de l'Estoile and ROTROU) to write plays, perhaps intending them for performance in the private theatre he built within his palace, later known as the PALAIS-ROYAL.

**Ridley, George** 1835–64 British performer and songwriter. Famous for composing 'Blaydon Races' in particular, in his naturalistically costumed and highly characterized performances he belonged to the new and growing tradition of the MUSIC-HALL; his penny songbooks, effectively chapbooks (complete with crude woodcuts), look back to an older tradition of ballad publication.

**Rigg, Diana** 1938– British actress. She joined the Shakespeare Memorial Company in 1959 and remained until 1964. She became a popular television star through *The Avengers* series in which she played Emma Peel, returning to the stage in 1966 to appear as a memorable Viola in the ROYAL SHAKESPEARE COMPANY's *Twelfth Night*. She joined the NATIONAL THEATRE in 1972 to appear in TOM STOPPARD's *Jumpers* (1972), as Lady Macbeth to Denis Quilley's Macbeth and, with particular success, in MOLIÈRE's *The Misanthrope* (1973) where she played Célimène to ALEC MCCOWEN's Alceste, directed by JOHN DEXTER. The same Rigg-McCowen-Dexter team appeared in a WEST END production of *Pygmalion* (1974), while in 1975 she returned to the National Theatre in a modernization by TONY HARRISON of RACINE's *Phèdre – Phaedra Britannica*. A more recent challenge was her role as EURIPIDES' Medea (1993) in the West End.

A strikingly attractive actress, Rigg excels in roles which bring out her gift for ironic comedy, usually understressed, revealing a natural gift for timing. In 1978 she starred in Tom Stoppard's play, *Night and Day*. In recent years she has appeared rarely in national companies. She played Cleopatra in a revival of DRYDEN's *All for Love* at London's Almeida Theatre (1991), and the Almeida production of *Medea*, with Rigg in the title role, moved to the West End in 1993. She was made DBE in 1994.

**Ringelnatz, Joachim** [Hanns Bötticher] 1883–1934 German poet and CABARET artist. He entered the Munich cabaret Simplicissimus as 'house poet' in 1909. He was renowned as a reciter at Berlin's Schall und Rauch during the 1920s, performing his poetry, particularly the scurrilous exploits of the mythical seaman

Kuttel Daddeldu. His style lies somewhere between nonsense verse and topical SATIRE, and influenced BRECHT. In 1933 his performances were declared 'undesirable' by the Nazis, and he died the following year of tuberculosis.

**Ringwood, Gwen Pharis** 1910–84 American-born Canadian playwright and teacher. Her first play, *The Dragon of Kent*, was produced at the Banff School of Fine Arts in 1935. In 1937 she went to the USA. Four of her plays were produced by the Carolina Playmakers including her classic, *Still Stands the House* (1938). From 1939 she taught playwriting at the University of Alberta and continued to write. Her prairie tragedy, *Dark Harvest* (1945), was produced at the University of Winnipeg. Many of her plays were based on local history. Her move to a remote town in British Columbia in 1953 removed her from the mainstream of Canadian drama.

**Ristori, Adelaide** 1822–1906 Italian actress. Born into the profession, she entered the major Compagnia Reale Sarda at the age of 15 and soon became its leading actress. In the 1840s she was *prima attrice* to many of the prominent actor-managers of the day, before retiring for several years following her marriage to an Italian nobleman.

To this point her reputation had been won largely in native Italian drama – from GOLDONI, through ALFIERI, to contemporary writers and adapters of French plays. In 1853 she returned to the stage, again with the Reale Sarda, and the mid-1850s saw her established as an actress of international standing; in 1855 she triumphed in Paris, benefiting from French critical hostility to the waning star, RACHEL. This success she repeated in 1856, adding Lady Macbeth to her repertoire. In 1857 she appeared for the first time in London, winning acclaim for her powerfully 'realistic' interpretation of Legouvé's Medea and SHAKESPEARE's Lady Macbeth. She toured to North and South America, North Africa and most of Europe. The plays in her repertoire were likewise international, including Alfieri's *Mirra*, SCHILLER's *Maria Stuart*, RACINE's *Phèdre* and GIACOMETTI's *Elisabetta regina d'Inghilterra*. In 1882 she undertook the part of Lady Macbeth again, this time in English.

Her great strength lay in her combination of classical appearance, pose and deportment, and acute psychological REALISM. In common with her younger contemporary, TOMMASO SALVINI, she studied her parts in depth, developing a subtle, emotionally powerful characterization through the accumulation of small but significant detail. Her prompt books, memoirs and occasional writings on theatre reveal the seriousness of her approach to her art.

**rite of passage** Anthropological term. It celebrates and effects the transition of an individual from one social position to the next. Naming ceremonies, puberty rites, weddings and funerals are typical and virtually universal examples, but occupational RITUALS such as degree ceremonies and the transformation of an apprentice into a craftsman are also included. Their structure is invariably tripartite: the separation of the individual from his/her existing network of relationships, a liminal period during which he/she stands outside normality, and his/her incorporation into a new network of rights and obligations.

**Rittner, Rudolf** 1869–1943 German actor. He was the naturalistic actor (see NATURALISM) who most completely fulfilled OTTO BRAHM's conception of acting. He created many of HAUPTMANN's leading roles under Brahm's direction at the FREIE BÜHNE, the DEUTSCHES THEATER and the Lessingtheater in Berlin.

**ritual** The relationship between ritual and theatre is a keystone of theatre history and dramatic analysis. Both drama and ritual deal with social relationships, and both do so in the most direct way possible, through the enactment of those relationships by living people. God may be held by believers to be present in the wafer and wine; everyone can agree immediately that a priest holding a chalice is present as a focus of attention. Similarly, it may be a matter of endless debate whether or not the spectator in a theatre suspends his/her disbelief, willingly or otherwise, and what exactly that might mean; it is not a matter of debate that an actor representing a murderer mimics the assassination of an actor representing a victim. Further, in both modes, social relationships are given very high definition.

Social relationships are not something that can be observed. What we observe are forms of greeting, expressions of deference, gestures of affection. Most of these, if not all of them, are 'ritualistic' in the sense that their form and meaning are culturally determined and inherited, not spontaneously generated. But even the simplest of routine actions will shift its meaning according to context. In Western cultures, to hold a door open and let somebody pass through is, at its simplest, merely a routine courtesy; if one is a man and one a woman, whether they are acquainted or not, a different significance is present which derives from a whole bundle of notions about the roles of men and women. Status is involved as well as sex. Both ritual and drama take these routine acts and their contextually determined meanings – the small change of social currency – exaggerate them, stylize them, refine them, and set them into a pattern of expressive sequences of visual and auditory symbols.

There, however, the identity between them stops: ritual and theatre lie at the opposite poles of a functional continuum. While theatre confines itself to saying things about social relationships, ritual also does things with them; and what it does is to reinforce or change them.

This function, and the distinction between theatre and ritual, are clearly seen in the RITE OF PASSAGE, such as the wedding ceremony. The young woman who dresses in ceremonial clothes to play Hippolyta in the final act of *A Midsummer Night's Dream* is clearly an actress representing a bride, and she will do so repeatedly during the run. The young woman who dresses in ceremonial clothes on the morning of her wedding day *is* a 'bride', from that moment, and will remain so until she and her 'groom' are pronounced 'man and wife'. Nor, in principle, is her action replicable. No woman who has participated in a valid ritual can revert to the status of 'maiden' or 'spinster'. Further, not only the bride and groom are involved in an event which changes their relationship to each other; so too, if less radically, are their kinsfolk, and even their friends. Not just two individuals but two extended families are conjoined in a relationship not previously existing, and certain obligations will follow.

The interest of such a ceremony is that it creates new social arrangements in an actual sense and that it does this by theatrical means. For it is crucial to the event that there be not merely protagonists and a master of ceremonies, but an audience, whose presence as witnesses ratifies the validity of the ceremony. Further, just as in the theatre the audience contracts to accept a fiction, so in the wedding ceremony the congregation condones *en masse*, both by its silence and by its vocal participation when called upon, not merely the particular act but a whole framework of values within which it exists. As a congregation, whether they suspend their disbelief or not, they silence it, and their silence gives consent. This it is that makes ritual such a powerful conservative force, even while it effects pragmatic change.

Ritual is never an unambiguously progressive force. Its effectiveness depends on the public acceptance of a status quo, whatever the participant's private reservations may be; its symbols, though often complex and diffuse, are never avant-garde (a dual consideration which might give pause to exponents of 'ritual' theatre). It is a commonplace that rituals are often tied to seasons and cycles. Annual festivities mark out time as signposts and fences mark out space, lending a comforting air of continuity to human life. Laid over this inexorable terrestrial rhythm is the changing of the human seasons, the movement from the cradle to the grave celebrated in the life-cycle rituals. It is important to note here a further distinction between ritual and theatre: whereas the latter almost always sets its action in fictional time, the action of the former always exists in real time, and it is arguable that it would otherwise lose its point.

Certain 'ritualistic' elements in court proceedings have often been noticed: the elaborate formal courtesies, the use of a specialized language, the stylization of the presentation of evidence into a FLYTING between 'prosecution' and 'defence', the vital role of the citizenry – as represented by 12 good men and true – in redefining the status of the 'accused', who occupies a liminal position for as long as he or she bears that name. Less frequently noted is the element of time. In English courts this is manifest in the partly archaic dress worn by the legal specialists. Just as a priest's vestments give him an identity beyond the personal one, going back in mythological terms to Melchizedek, so the robes and wigs of judge and counsel declare them to be representatives of the Law, an abstract value and an institution whose existence stretches back beyond their birth (and by implication forward beyond their death) and which pre-empts any personal views they may have on the matter in hand.

The judicial sentence of death is an extreme example of ritual's ability to manage social time and space; and it is no surprise that the public execution was a popular and complex event all over Europe. Vast crowds flocked to witness the 'MORALITY PLAY' of public justice, in which the crimes of the condemned were re-enacted on his own body, in which public confessions (sometimes in verse) were given from the scaffold and the condemned might be harried beyond death in the ghastly practices of quartering and decapitation. The gibbeted body or the head displayed on a spike would remain as an eerie puppet-like image of the consequences of wickedness. At the same time, the event had a strangely festive air, a cross between a grand parade and a chartered fair. In 18th-century London, a condemned man would often dress as a bridegroom for his final ride to Tyburn; he was a hero in the theatrical sense, and the events of the day the last act of his tragedy. His white-trimmed garments declared him to be about to be wedded to death, and ironically evoked the idea of human seasonality explicit in the rite of passage.

The widespread juridical ritual of the CHARIVARI was organized not by the state but by the community, and applied not to criminal offences but to antisocial acts such as sharp practice in trade, marital disharmony, or unsuitable marriages such as that between an old widower and a young virgin. Characteristically the community or its representatives would express their disapproval by a procession with rough music to the dwelling of the wrong-doer, usually early in the morning or late at night so as to cause maximum embarrassment to the offender. In more elaborate forms, the procession would include an effigy of the offender, riding backwards on a donkey or mounted on a pole, which would subsequently be hanged or burned. The offender had two choices: either to correct his or her behaviour, or, if this was impossible (e.g. the old widower), to buy the rough musicians off – effectively a fine or even, in this case, financial compensation for their loss of a potential bride. Either way, re-incorporation into decent society would follow.

To ritual, convention is all. There are rituals which invert status or turn normal values inside out in a more comprehensive sense – the 12-day Christmas period of Misrule in medieval and early modern Europe springs to mind. But normality reasserts itself as soon as the defined period of licence comes to an end. CARNIVAL, because more open-ended in its time-span and its expressive activities, has sometimes got out of hand; so that over the six centuries which separate *böse Fastnacht* in Basle from London's Notting Hill Carnival in the 1970s, participants have tried to make a reality out of the idea of the world turned upside-down. But without exception Lent returns and triumphs; the authorities, temporarily shaken, reassert their control, break a few heads, gaol a few ringleaders and clear the streets of broken glass. And what happens is not revolution, but a reversion to status quo for another year.

**Rivel, Charlie** [Josep Andreu i Lasserre] 1896–1983 Spanish (Catalan) CLOWN. In 1929 he won world fame at the London Olympia and the Cirque d'Hiver, Paris, in a parody of Charlie Chaplin on the flying trapeze. At the age of 16, as the traditional august, the red-nosed fall-guy clown, he joined two of his brothers to form the Three Rivels. His standard outfit was an ankle-length, sleeveless red jersey, a bald pate and a square red nose. Like GROCK, a musical-acrobatic clown of few words, he emitted at regular intervals the cry: 'Akrobat–schööööön!'

**Riverside Studios** (London) Arts centre in Hammersmith. It was founded as an independent trust in 1975 with PETER GILL as its first artistic director and for ten years was the most adventurous centre of its kind in Britain, bringing over avant-garde companies from abroad and providing a London venue for British touring companies. When Gill moved to the NATIONAL THEATRE in 1980, the Riverside Studios came under threat from the local authorities. David Lefeaux joined David Gothard in 1982 and directed several ambitious plays there, but in 1984 their long campaign to protect the Studios came to an end with their departures. It is now a receiving house for a variety of artists.

**Rix, Brian** 1924– British actor-manager. Under Rix London's Whitehall Theatre established a reputation for FARCE between 1950 and 1967 that rivalled the Aldwych farces of the 1930s. The first of the Whitehall farces, Colin Morris's *Reluctant Heroes*, ran for four years, as did *Dry Rot* (1954), which was followed by *Simple*

*Spymen* (1958, both by John Chapman) and by Ray Cooney's *One for the Pot* (1961) and *Chase Me, Comrade* (1964). After a further series of successful farces at the Garrick and Cambridge Theatres in London, Rix left the stage for charity work with the mentally handicapped in 1980, for which he was honoured with a life peerage in 1992.

**Robards, Jason, Jr** 1922– American actor. Praised for his rich voice and intense characterizations, he played Hickey in a now legendary production of O'NEILL's *The Iceman Cometh* (1956) at the CIRCLE IN THE SQUARE. He became a star as James Tyrone in *Long Day's Journey into Night* (1956). Another triumph was as Quentin in ARTHUR MILLER's *After the Fall*. In 1991–2 he appeared in New York in HOROVITZ's *Park Your Car in Harvard Yard*.

**Robbins, Carrie** 1943– American COSTUME designer. Robbins began her professional career in the late 1960s. Her best work comprises detailed yet theatrical period costumes such as those for the 1971 *Beggar's Opera*, or lavish operatic ones such as those for *Samson et Dalila* for the San Francisco Opera, which combined a 19th-century sensibility with a biblical epic style. Her work is typified by rich textures and bold lines and her sketches are detailed and almost frenetic, creating a sense of energy and movement. She has frequently collaborated with set designer Douglas Schmidt, notably on *Grease* and *Frankenstein*.

**Robbins, Jerome** 1918– American choreographer and director. Trained in the techniques of classical ballet, Robbins joined the American Ballet Theatre in 1940. In 1944 he choreographed *Fancy Free*, a ballet with music by LEONARD BERNSTEIN, later transformed into the BROADWAY musical *On the Town*. In 1947 he created a hilarious Keystone Kops ballet for *High Button Shoes* that remains one of the few masterpieces of comic choreography in the American MUSICAL THEATRE. Among his other memorable dances of the period was the 'Small House of Uncle Thomas' ballet for *The King and I* (1951). For the teenage gang members of *West Side Story* (1957) he created a restless, explosive yet balletic style of movement. He directed and choreographed two other acclaimed musicals: *Gypsy* (1959) and *Fiddler on the Roof* (1964). In 1989 he re-created his most successful numbers in the retrospective *Jerome Robbins' Broadway*.

**Robert-Houdin** [Jean-Eugène Robert] 1805–71 French conjuror. He transformed the performance of MAGIC. Married to the daughter of a watchmaker named Houdin, in 1845 he gave up watchmaking and opened the Théâtre des Soirées Fantastiques de Robert-Houdin, in the Palais-Royal, Paris, where for seven years he played to full houses. There he turned what had been a fairground amusement into a salon entertainment by doing away with obvious fakery and verbose commentary. He is also said to have invented the matinée performance. During the conquest of Algeria, the French government employed him to overawe the rebels with his Invincible Man act, in which he seemed impervious to bullets.

**Robertson, Agnes** see BOUCICAULT, DION

**Robertson** [Étienne-Gaspard Robert] 1763–1837 Belgian-born illusionist. He was the first to present animated projections using the *fantascope*, a magic lantern on wheels (1798). At a deconsecrated Capuchin monastery in Paris he terrified audiences with 'supernatural' evocations of François Villon, William Tell, VOLTAIRE, ROUSSEAU and Marat, who seemed to approach and withdraw. SHADOW PUPPET techniques

allowed Robertson to give the illusion of legs moving and other rudimentary actions.

**Robertson, T(homas) W(illiam)** 1829–71 British playwright and journalist. Robertson travelled the Lincoln circuit with his parents and siblings, acting and writing. After prolonged struggles as a playwright, bit-player, prompter and stage manager, he retired from the theatre c.1859. In 1865 his friend H. J. BYRON persuaded MARIE WILTON to stage Robertson's play *Society* at the Prince of Wales's. The production gave birth to 'cup-and-saucer drama', the reproduction on stage of the indoor customs of Victorian England. Robertson had perceived the potential purchase on the public imagination of a style of writing and acting that would replace the blatantly theatrical with the persuasively accurate. The making of a roly-poly pudding in *Ours* (1866), immediate successor to *Society*, is a brilliant domestic adaptation of the melodramatic sensation scene such as BOUCICAULT might have written. The tea-and-sandwiches of Act I of *Caste* (1867) are a comic *tour de force*. Robertson never matched *Caste* again, though *Play* (1868), particularly *School* (1869) and *M.P.* (1870) all had successful runs at the Prince of Wales's, and his modest innovations admitted a new REALISM to the writing and acting of plays in the last decades of the 19th century.

**Robeson, Paul** 1898–1976 African-American actor. A Columbia Law School graduate, Robeson gained prominence in 1924 when he appeared in the PROVINCETOWN PLAYERS' revival of *The Emperor Jones* and as Jim Harris, the black lawyer who marries white in O'NEILL's controversial play, *All God's Chillun Got Wings*. He took the lead in *Black Boy* (1926), played Crown in *Porgy and Bess* (1927), and was Joe in the London performance of *Show Boat* (1928) in which he sang 'Ol' Man River', the song he refashioned into a lifelong protest against oppression. With a commanding physique, deep, resonant voice and humane spirit, Robeson was a magnificent Othello, a role he played in London (1930), in New York (1943) and at Stratford-upon-Avon (1959). He was also renowned as a concert artist and film actor. His outspoken opposition to racial discrimination and his communist sympathies led to professional ostracism at home and the withdrawal of his passport. In failing health, he retired from public life in the 1960s.

**Robey [Wade], George** 1869–1954 British comedian. His WEST END debut came in 1891; by the end of 1892 'the Prime Minister of Mirth' was top of the bill, and there he stayed through a long and varied career in MUSIC-HALL, VARIETY, PANTOMIME, REVUE, operetta and MUSICAL COMEDY. At the age of 66 he tried his hand at SHAKESPEARE, appearing to critical acclaim as Falstaff in *Henry IV, Part 1* at His Majesty's (see HER/HIS MAJESTY'S THEATRE). In addition to live theatre, he worked extensively in radio and television, played Sancho Panza opposite Chaliapin in Pabst's 1932 film *Don Quichotte*, and made a brief retrospective appearance as the dying Falstaff in OLIVIER's film of *Henry V*. He was still touring in variety and comedy at the age of 82. He was knighted in the year of his death.

Fundamentally a high-status comedian, he employed an orotund but crystal-clear middle-class diction, eschewed the egalitarian matiness of a CHIRGWIN and the low-status bashfulness of JACK PLEASANTS, and constantly ordered his audience to 'desist' from laughing – an injunction utterly undermined by his exaggerated air of dignity, his mobile face and his famous raised eyebrows.

**Robin, Henri** [Henrik Joseph Donckel] 1811–74 Dutch illusionist. As early as 1847 he displayed a 'Living Phantasmagoria' in Paris, using the plate-glass principle to conjure up phantoms which he then fought; this well established trick later prevented PEPPER'S GHOST from getting a French patent. Robin performed in England during 1850–3 (with a command performance at Windsor Castle), and in 1861 gave the first full evening's show of MAGIC at the Egyptian Hall, London. He successfully managed his own theatre in the Boulevard du Temple in Paris (1862–9). His famous illusion here was 'The Medium of Inkerman', a drum on a tripod which, allegedly beaten by the spirit of a slain drummer, tapped out answers to questions from the audience.

**Robin Hood plays** English plays. These popular dramatizations of episodes from the life of the great English outlaw related to and possibly derived from ballads about him, and were associated with May games. Allusions to the playing of Robin Hood exist in the 15th and 16th centuries, and two (possibly three) texts are extant: 'Robin Hood and the Friar' (c.1560), which may be an amalgamation of two plays, and the fragmentary 'Robin Hood and the Sheriff' (c.1475). References cease early in the 17th century; later 'Robin Hood plays' are ecotypes of the HERO-COMBAT.

**Robins, Elizabeth** 1862–1952 American-born English actress and author. She made her acting debut with the BOSTON MUSEUM Stock Company in 1885 and subsequently toured with EDWIN BOOTH, LAWRENCE BARRETT and JAMES O'NEILL. She visited London in 1889 and remained there. Soon she became known for the introduction of IBSEN to the English stage, playing Martha Bernick in *Pillars of Society* (1889), Mrs Linde in a revival of *A Doll's House* (1891), Hedda (1891), Hilda in *The Master Builder* (1893), Rebecca West in *Rosmersholm* (1893), Agnes in *Brand* (1893), Astra in *Little Eyolf* (1896) and Ella in *John Gabriel Borkman* (1897); she held the stage rights to many of these plays. She retired from the stage in 1902. Using the *nom de plume* C. E. Raemond she published several novels as well as the suffragist play *Votes for Women* (1907). In later years she wrote *Ibsen and the Actress* (1928), *Theatre and Friendship* (1932) and *Both Sides of the Curtain* (1940).

**Robinson, (Esmé Stuart) Lennox** 1886–1958 Irish playwright. The year after his first play – *The Clancy Name* (1908), a gloomy exercise in the 'Cork realist' manner – Robinson became the ABBEY's play director until 1914. Reappointed in 1919, he founded the DUBLIN DRAMA LEAGUE and was the Abbey's main play director until 1934, when HUGH HUNT succeeded him. His early plays are unremittingly cheerless, as he acknowledged: *Harvest* (1910) manages to turn a situation promising comic development into bitter despair. His talent was in fact for satiric comedy, as he demonstrated in *The Whiteheaded Boy* (1916) and *Drama at Inish* (1934). Yet he ranged widely: *The Big House* (1926) movingly chronicles the fortunes of an Ascendancy family; *Church Street* (1934) draws effectively on PIRANDELLO, as a young Irish dramatist invents plots for his family's lives.

**Robson, Flora** 1902–84 British actress. Although she never dominated the great female roles, she always offered sensitive, witty and intelligent portrayals in a wide range of styles. For the OLD VIC in 1933 she played Gwendoline in WILDE's *The Importance of Being Earnest*, and over 30 years later, in 1968, played Miss Prism in the same play in London's WEST END. She worked extensively in America (including Hollywood), playing Lady Macbeth in New York in 1948, a part she had previously played in 1933. Her Shakespearian roles were few, but for JOHN GIELGUD's production of *The Winter's Tale* (1951) she created what many critics describe as her best performance, typically in a supporting role, Paulina. She was made DBE in 1960.

**Robson, Frederick** [Thomas Brownbill] 1821–64 British actor. His years at the OLYMPIC (1853–63) were among the most astonishing success stories of the 19th-century theatre. His singing of 'Vilikens and his Dinah' in the character of Jem Bags in Henry Mayhew's revived *The Wandering Minstrel* turned him into a star. Robson was only five feet tall and J. R. PLANCHÉ, for example, wrote for him the title role of Gam-Bogie in *The Yellow Dwarf* (1854), exploiting both his diminutiveness and his ability to combine COMEDY and terror. Another famous role was the suicidal Job Wort in TOM TAYLOR's *A Blighted Being* (1854), in which he grounded extravagant comedy on a base of pathos.

**Robson, Stuart** [Henry Robson Stuart] 1836–1903 American actor. He made his stage debut as Horace Courtney in *Uncle Tom's Cabin as It Is*, a dramatic retort to UNCLE TOM'S CABIN, in 1852. Subsequently he appeared with numerous stock companies (see STOCK COMPANY). From 1877 until 1889 he teamed with W. H. Crane, starring in such FARCES as *Our Bachelors* and *Our Boarding House*, but also in *A Comedy of Errors* as the two Dromios, and *The Merry Wives of Windsor* as Falstaff (Crane) and Slender (Robson). BRONSON HOWARD's *The Henrietta* was especially written for them. After 1890 Robson starred on his own, most notably as Tony Lumpkin in *She Stoops to Conquer*.

**Roche, Billy** 1949– Irish playwright. Roche's televised Wexford trilogy originated as stage plays: *A Handful of Stars* (1988), *Poor Beast in the Rain* (1989) and *Belfry* (1991). In strong local dialect he proclaims the tension between rebellious individual desire and the comfortable miseries of small-town life. *Amphibians* (1992) uses similar characters to describe the masculine search for mythic rites. *The Cavalcaders* (1993) is an accomplished exploration, through the fragmentation of a working men's singing group, of the complex betrayals of friendship and heterosexual desire.

**Rodgers, Richard** 1902–79 American composer. Rodgers teamed up with lyricist LORENZ HART in 1919. After their first successful score for *The Garrick Gaieties* (1925), they created an almost unbroken stream of hit musicals, including *Dearest Enemy* (1925), *The Girl Friend* (1926), *Peggy-Ann* (1926) and *A Connecticut Yankee* (1927). Rodgers composed bouncy, jazz-influenced music that complemented the clever lyrics of Hart. In the early 1930s Rodgers and Hart wrote the songs for several Hollywood musical films, then returned to BROADWAY to create some of the most popular scores of the late 1930s and early 1940s, including *Jumbo* (1935), *On Your Toes* (1936), *Babes in Arms* (1937), *I'd Rather Be Right* (1937), *I Married an Angel* (1938), *The Boys from Syracuse* (1938), *Too Many Girls* (1939) and *By Jupiter* (1942). *Pal Joey* (1940), a musical chronicling the adventures of an amoral nightclub owner, was initially unpopular with critics and audiences, but more successful in its 1952 revival.

From 1943 Rodgers partnered lyricist-librettist OSCAR HAMMERSTEIN II and wrote dramatic, emotionally expansive scores for his 'musical plays' of the 1940s and 1950s. Their first show was *Oklahoma!*, one of the most popular and influential of all American musicals, which was followed by e.g. *Flower Drum Song* (1958) and

*The Sound of Music* (1959). Their shows were noted for the care with which music and dance were integrated with the libretto.

**Rodrigues, Nelson** 1912–81 Brazilian playwright. He was known for sensational and provocative topics. His first major success, *O Vestido de Noiva* (*Wedding Gown*; 1942), was the play that marked the renovation of the contemporary Brazilian theatre through an ingenious staging by Zbigniew Ziembinski, a Polish émigré director. Rodrigues's plays often give a melodramatic treatment to taboo topics such as incest, homosexuality and adultery, as in *Album de Família* (*Family Album*), *Anjo Negro* (*Black Angel*), *Toda Desnudez Será Castigada* (*Nudity will be Punished*) and *O Beijo no Asfalto* (*Kiss on the Pavement*). He is now Brazil's most widely staged playwright; the 1981 production of *O Eterno Retorno* (*The Eternal Return*) by Antunes Filho triggered a resurgence of interest in professional productions of his works.

**Rogers, Will(iam Penn Adair)** 1879–1935 American folk hero. He began in WILD WEST EXHIBITIONS billed as 'the Cherokee Kid, the wonderful Lasso-Artist', dazzling audiences by circling a horse and rider with a lasso in each hand. He made his first appearance in New York in 1905 with a trick roping and riding company (Madison Square Garden), and gradually evolved his technique of commenting drolly on current events in his slow Oklahoma drawl while he played with his lariat. His stage personality, free from make-up or comic properties, was an extension of his own warm, gum-chewing self. Rogers appeared in musicals, VAUDEVILLE and films. In 1991, *The Will Rogers Follies* (lyrics by BETTY COMDEN AND ADOLF GREEN) opened in New York for a successful run.

**Rojas Zorrilla, Francisco de** 1607–48 Spanish playwright. From the School of CALDERÓN DE LA BARCA, he lived in Madrid and was admitted to the Order of Santiago in 1645. Of more than 80 plays ascribed to him only about 30 are certainly his, including comedies, serious plays and SENECAN revenge tragedies (see REVENGE TRAGEDY). His best-known play is *Del rey abajo ninguno* (*None but the King*, published 1650), on the dilemma of a peasant who believes that the king, on whom he cannot avenge himself, is attempting to seduce his wife. In *Cada cual lo que le toca* (*To Each His Just Deserts*), a woman raped before marriage restores her husband's honour by killing the attacker herself – a solution which aroused the hostility of the contemporary audience. The Senecan tragedies include *Morir pensando matar* (*Killers Turned Victims*, published 1642) and *Lucrecia y Tarquino* on the rape of Lucretia. His comedies include *Entre bobos anda el juego* (*A Fool's Game*, 1638), a *comedia de figurón*, and *capa y espada* plays (see COMEDIA).

**Rolland, Romain** 1866–1944 French novelist and playwright. He was one of the first to advocate the *théâtre populaire*, in an essay on *Le Théâtre du peuple* (1903) – a major reference point for subsequent practitioners. He also wrote less influential plays about the French Revolution, notably *Danton* (1900) and *Le 14 juillet* (1902).

**Romains, Jules** 1885–1972 French novelist and playwright. His most important plays were social SATIRES on the theme of imposture, propaganda and trickery. Influenced by unanimism, *Crommedeyre le vieil* (*Old Crommedeyre*) was produced by COPEAU in 1920, but JOUVET acted in and produced his most successful play *Dr Knock, ou Le Triomphe de la médicine* (*Dr Knock, or The Triumph of Medicine*) in 1923, a comedy satirizing the mystifying tendencies of medicine.

## Roman theatre
### Origins of drama
Patriotic Romans such as Livy and HORACE liked to claim that Rome possessed an indigenous dramatic tradition, which had developed from religious ceremonies and from the ritual abuse ('Fescennine verses') which accompanied them. Certainly the festivals of the Roman calendar, at which aristocratic magistrates vied with each other to finance shows that would win the favour of the electorate, provided good opportunities for drama to develop and flourish. From an early date, however, Rome was in contact with the Greek colonies of southern Italy, and these colonies (notably Tarentum) had a thriving tradition of drama, both literary and subliterary (see GREEK THEATRE, ANCIENT). And even the most popular and informal types of drama at Rome seem to have had non-Roman origins.

These types were the MIME and the Atellan FARCE, both of which were established at Rome by the late 3rd century BC. The mime was a Romanized version of a widespread Greek form, a vulgar, often improvised low-life episode performed by a small group of unmasked actors. The Atellan farce (*fabula Atellana*) was believed to be an import from the Oscan town of Atellae in Campania, which would itself have had close connections with the Greek colonies. It was a boisterous entertainment performed by a stock troupe of masked clowns, reminiscent of the COMMEDIA DELL'ARTE.

Literary drama at Rome probably dates from 240 BC, when the Romanized Greek LIVIUS ANDRONICUS first produced a Latin adaptation of a Greek play at the Ludi Romani (one of the annual festivals). Such adaptations became popular, and the conventions of Roman drama were quickly established. Andronicus and his immediate successors, Naevius and QUINTUS ENNIUS, differed from the Greek dramatists in writing both TRAGEDY and COMEDY, as well as non-dramatic works.

### Tragedy, historical drama and pantomime
We possess only fragments and play titles from the work of the great tragedians of the Roman Republic – the 3rd-century pioneers Andronicus and Gnaeus Naevius, and the 2nd-century classics Quintus Ennius, Marcus Pacuvius and Lucius Accius. Tragedies were almost always based on Greek originals. The plays of EURIPIDES were especially favoured as models, and there was a general preference for warlike and melodramatic themes. The interest in the supernatural (ghosts, dreams and portents) and in madness, which is prominent in SENECA, can be traced back to this period. Though the Greek mythical settings were retained, the values expressed and celebrated – courage, endurance and piety, especially in the service of the state – were distinctively Roman; and Stoic philosophy became influential at an early date. Above all, Roman tragedy was strongly rhetorical, and seems to have aimed more at solemn grandeur than at the intellectual stimulation and provocation found in the best work of Euripides.

The metre of spoken dialogue, the iambic *senarius*, was adapted from the main dialogue metre of Greek tragedy, but was less strict. Large sections of the actors' parts, however, were sung, chanted or declaimed to the accompaniment of the pipe or *tibia* (the Greek *aulos*). The Chorus was retained, but no attempt was made to imitate the complex metres of Greek choral songs.

From the time of Naevius onward, the tragedians occasionally wrote plays on subjects from Roman history, whether legendary or recent. These *fabulae praetextae* (plays performed in the *toga praetexta*, the bordered toga of Roman magistrates) had a precedent in Greek historical tragedies such as AESCHYLUS' *Persians*, but the plots naturally had to be freely invented by the Roman dramatists. In the 1st century BC, revivals of existing Latin tragedies continued to be popular, but we hear less of the composition of new works for the stage. At the same time poets started to write tragedies merely as literary exercises, intended for declamation (like other Roman poetry), not for staged performance. The *Thyestes* of Varius Rufus, performed in 29 BC, is the last tragedy known to have been produced on stage; the *Medea* of Ovid (43 BC to AD 17) was evidently not produced. By the time of Seneca the stage was regarded with contempt by respectable Romans, but the word 'tragedy' had a lofty sound and the form was one in which the contemporary taste for blood, rhetoric and melodrama could be indulged to the full.

One reason for the decline of staged tragedy was doubtless the rise of the pantomime, which was introduced in the reign of Augustus. This was a performance in dumb-show by a masked dancer (the *pantomimus* himself) to the accompaniment of a kind of cantata sung by a chorus. The subject was normally taken from Greek myth, but the libretto was unimportant; what mattered was the grace of the dancer and his skill in mimicking the actions described. This curious form of entertainment was despised by the best-educated Romans, but remained extremely popular as long as the Western Empire lasted, and survived in the East well into the Byzantine period.

### Comedy, farce and mime

The most admired writers of Roman comedy were PLAUTUS, Caecilius Statius and TERENCE. Like Livius Andronicus, Naevius and Ennius, they adapted their plays from the New Comedy of 4th- and 3rd-century Greece. These plays became known as *fabulae palliatae*, plays performed in the Greek cloak. The action usually takes place in a city street, and always in front of one, two or three houses, each with a visible door. The Greek plots were handled with considerable freedom. The Chorus, already vestigial in MENANDER, was dropped altogether (though a trace remains in Plautus' *Rudens*). Those Greek institutions and customs which would have puzzled the Roman audience are either Romanized (especially in Plautus) or played down (especially in Terence). Plautus constantly enlivens his plays with jokes, puns, topical allusions, audience address and vulgarities of various kinds (but not political satire, which was restricted by libel laws (see CENSORSHIP) and for which Naevius had been prosecuted). The verse forms are much more varied than those of Greek New Comedy, and similar to those of Roman tragedy, showing that large sections of each play were accompanied on the *tibia*. The writing of *palliatae* came to an end with the work of Sextus Turpilius, who died in 103 BC. Revivals of the old plays remained popular in Cicero's day (mid-1st century BC), but are not heard of thereafter.

A more popular form of comedy was the *fabula togata*, or drama in Roman dress, of Titinius, Afranius and Atta. This was set among the lower classes in Italian towns, and the fragments suggest that the plays resembled Plautus', with much vulgar abuse between the characters and with plot motifs of love, intrigue and misunderstanding borrowed from the *palliata*. The writing of *togatae* seems to have come to an end with Atta, who is said to have died in 77 BC, though we hear of later revivals.

In the late Republican period attempts were made to give literary form to the Atellan farce and the mime. Both forms seem to have been used as tailpieces after more serious plays. Atellan titles such as *Maccus as Soldier*, *Bucco as Gladiator*, *The Pig*, *The Farmer*, show how the stock troupe of clowns could be put to various uses, and evoke the plays' homely and rustic settings. Adultery was a frequent theme of the mime, which by now employed actresses as well as male actors; and mime-actors might also indulge in ribald political SATIRE, which could not be risked in respectable types of drama.

### Shows and spectacles

From the earliest times the Romans used shows of various kinds to mark the annual religious festivals, as well as special events such as triumphs and important funerals. Dancing, acrobatics and gymnastic contests must always have existed, but in 264 BC such harmless entertainments were supplemented by the introduction of gladiatorial fights from Etruria. Gladiators were prisoners, condemned criminals or otherwise desperate men, who, having nothing to lose, were prepared to fight to the death in the hope of winning fame and popularity if they survived. By the end of the Republic the main types of spectacle were well established: the gladiatorial fight, the wild-beast show (all manner of exotic animals being pitted against men or against each other; see BAITING), the mock sea-battle (see *NAUMACHIA*) and the chariot race. As the population of Rome grew, as wealth flowed in from wars of conquest and an expanding empire, and as struggles for power among the nobility grew more and more desperate, greater and greater sums were spent on buying the favour of the Roman mob. Under the emperors this expenditure continued, since the largely unemployed populace of Rome and other cities had to be kept quiet by being given the entertainments which it had come to expect.

### Roman theatres and amphitheatres

The earliest Roman theatres were temporary wooden constructions, erected when needed at the different sites of the various festivals. The scenic resources required by the plays of Plautus and Terence are very simple: the stage has merely to be backed by a building with up to three doors, representing entrances to different houses. Plautus' *Amphitruo* shows that it was possible to climb to the roof of the building. Similar resources were presumably used in tragedy and farce. The first stone theatre at Rome was the Theatre of Pompey, opened in 55 BC. Others followed in the time of Augustus, and under the emperors theatres became widespread throughout most of the Empire. There are particularly well preserved examples at Aspendus in Turkey, Orange in France, and Sabratha and Leptis Magna in North Africa. It comes as a disappointment to realize that all these were built at a time when comedy and tragedy had been largely replaced by mime and pantomime; indeed, there is no proof that any surviving Roman play was ever performed in any surviving theatre. Often the theatres must have been used merely for public assemblies or (in place of amphitheatres) for gladiatorial contests and wild-beast shows; one writer complains that even the Theatre of Dionysus at Athens has been subjected to this indignity.

In a Roman theatre the *scaena* (scene-building) rises

to the full height of the *cavea* (seating) or higher, and is integrally connected to it. While Greek theatres had to be built against hillsides, the engineering skills of the Romans enabled them to build free-standing theatres on level ground. The stone-floored *orchēstra* no longer used for dancing, was reduced to a small semicircle, and might be occupied by additional seating. The wood-floored stage was broader, deeper and lower than that of Hellenistic Greece. Behind it rose the imposing façade, the *scaenae frons* (see SKĒNĒ) richly ornamented with pillars, niches and statues.

There might be a roof over the stage, and an awning might be spread over the entire theatre. Small theatres, called *odea*, were completely roofed, and were housed in rectangular buildings. Vitruvius, an architectural writer of the Augustan period, gives instructions for the design of a Roman theatre, distinguishing it from the Greek type. These instructions were closely studied by PALLADIO and other theatre-builders of the Renaissance. He also describes painted scenery, with perspective effects, for tragedy, comedy and satyr play.

Amphitheatres were used for gladiatorial contests and wild-beast fights, and some could be flooded to accommodate mock sea-battles. They consisted of an oval arena (beneath which there might be concealed pits to house equipment and animals) completely surrounded by seating. Thus, as the name implies, the shape was roughly that of two theatres facing each other. Greatest of all was the Flavian Amphitheatre or Colosseum at Rome, which was built in the first century AD and could seat about 45,000 spectators.

## Actors and musicians

The usual word for 'actor', *histrio*, apparently derives from an Etruscan word for a masked dancer. The earliest Roman dramatists are said to have acted in their own plays, like the earliest Greek ones. By the time of Plautus and Terence, however, there were permanent troupes of professional actors, each led by an actor-manager, and a dramatist had to win the patronage of one of these if his plays were to be staged. At the end of the Republic acting was still a respectable enough profession for QUINTUS ROSCIUS GALLUS, a famous actor who performed in both tragedy and comedy, to be the friend and protégé of Cicero.

## Masks and costumes

Surviving representations and descriptions of actors and masks show that the Romans followed, or exaggerated, the practice of the Hellenistic Greek theatre. Thus tragic actors had their height increased by means of raised soles to their boots (*cothurni*) and a raised forehead (*onkos*) on the mask, and wore padding under their robes so that their build was proportional to their height. The mask of the *pantomimus* had a closed mouth. Comic actors wore the costume of everyday life, whether Greek or Roman. Masks of slaves, old men and other figures of fun had gaping mouths and comically exaggerated features, while those of young men and maidens were more realistic.

**Romeril, John** 1945– Australian playwright. He was initially a writer for La Mama and the Pram Factory, Melbourne. His plays, often with strong political or social content, range from the surreal absurdity (see SURREALISM; THEATRE OF THE ABSURD) of *I Don't Know Who to Feel Sorry For* (1969) and the REALISM of *Bastardy* (1972) to cartoon-like EXPRESSIONISM in *Chicago Chicago* (1971) and *The Floating World* (1974), and the musical adaptation of a novel, *Jonah Jones* (1985). He now works chiefly

with the Melbourne Workers Theatre, creating performances related to workplace issues.

**Romero, Mariela** 1949– Venezuelan playwright and essayist. Her major plays include *El juego* (*The Game*, 1977), the bifurcated experiences of two characters named Ana. *Rosa de la noche* (*Rose of the Night*, 1980) takes place in the seedy Caracas underworld of pimps and prostitutes. In *El vendedor* (*The Salesman*, 1981), the world of a lonely woman without love is invaded by an aggressive type pretending to be a salesman.

**Ronconi, Luca** 1933– Italian actor and director. After a career as an actor he turned to direction with a version of GOLDONI's *La buona moglie* (*The Good Wife*) in 1963. In the course of the 1960s he evolved a distinctive and highly theatrical production style particularly of Renaissance drama, including SHAKESPEARE's *Measure for Measure* and *Richard III*, Bruno's *Il candelaio* (*The Candle Maker*) and TOURNEUR's *The Revenger's Tragedy*. Perhaps his most ambitious work of the 1960s was a spectacular stage treatment in 1968 of ARIOSTO's epic poem *Orlando Furioso*, which he co-scripted with the poet Eduardo Sanguinetti. The range of his work in the 1970s and 1980s has been considerable, including productions of AESCHYLUS' *Oresteia*, MIDDLETON's *A Game at Chess* and IBSEN's *Ghosts*. Ronconi has also had a distinguished career in opera, including productions of Gounod's *Faust*, WAGNER's *Siegfried*, Gluck's *Orpheus and Eurydice* and Mozart's *Idomeneo*, the last at La Scala in 1990. Outstanding recent stage productions have included a version of Georges Bernanos's *Dialogues des Carmélites* (1988), CHEKHOV's *The Three Sisters* (1989), EUGENE O'NEILL's *Strange Interlude* (1990) a further production of *Measure for Measure* (1992) and a staging of TASSO's *Aminta* (1994). In 1992 he established a School of Theatre, attached to the Teatro Stabile of Turin.

**Roscius Gallus, Quintus** c.120–62 BC Roman actor. His reputation in plays by PLAUTUS and TERENCE was of the highest, and it is suggested that he took great care in the preparation of his roles. His name has been conferred as an accolade of virtuosity on a number of more recent actors, not always with good cause. For instance SAM COWELL was dubbed the Young American Roscius, and IRA ALDRIDGE, the black American actor, the African Roscius.

**Rose Theatre** (London) The foundations of this playhouse, built in 1587 close to the south bank of the Thames, were uncovered and excavated in 1989. We now know that the inner yard had a diameter of about 49ft, that the stage (built at the northern end of the yard) was about 38ft wide along the TIRING HOUSE façade (tapering to perhaps 25ft at the front) and 18ft deep and that the front half of the yard sloped down to the stage, presumably to improve sightlines for the standing audience. This precious and unique evidence of the physical dimensions of one Elizabethan playhouse has, after a vigorous public campaign, been preserved. The Rose was built and owned by PHILIP Henslowe, whose 1592 alterations to the interior can be traced in the foundations. From 1592 to 1594 STRANGE's MEN were the main users, but after 1594 the Rose was the London base of the ADMIRAL's MEN under the leadership of EDWARD ALLEYN. MARLOWE's plays were regularly revived there. In 1600 the company moved to the FORTUNE, leaving the Rose to Worcester's Men. The playhouse was demolished in 1605–6.

**Rosencof, Mauricio** 1933– Uruguayan playwright, journalist and short story writer. In 1961 *Las ranas* (*The*

*Frogs*) brought him public attention for its realistic presentation of human misery in a lower-class neighbourhood. In a brief incursion into children's theatre he also dealt with social themes, and *La valija* (*The Suitcase*, 1964) has been frequently anthologized and translated. His major work is *Los caballos* (*The Horses*, 1967), in which he follows the REALISM of his earlier plays but experiments with elements of fantasy with considerable success. During the period of military repression in Uruguay in the 1970s–80s, Rosencof was imprisoned for his writings and activities.

**Rosenthal, Jean** 1912–69 American lighting designer. When she began working with ORSON WELLES and JOHN HOUSEMAN in the FEDERAL THEATRE PROJECT there were no lighting designers; the job was done by the set designer or electrician. In 1938 she began working for Martha Graham as lighting and production supervisor (and continued until her death). Aware of the dependence of dance on light, Rosenthal was able to develop the new art of lighting design (see STAGE LIGHTING). A common element in all her designs is an evocative sense of mood. Her hundreds of theatre designs include *West Side Story* and *The Sound of Music*. She also designed the architectural lighting for theatres and projects ranging from airline terminals to hotels.

**Roshchin, Mikhail** 1933– Soviet playwright. Roshchin published his first book at 23 and his first play, *The Seven Feats of Heracles*, on the cleaning of the Augean Stables, seven years later. In 1968 he wrote both the very popular *A Rainbow in Winter* (1968) and the more problematic *The Old New Year*. The latter, the first Soviet SATIRE for some time, was produced at the MOSCOW ART THEATRE in 1973, largely owing to the success there of Roshchin's 1971 youth play, *Valentin and Valentina*. A contemporary Soviet Romeo and Juliet, the young lovers are impeded by a society which has overlooked personal problems in favour of social ideology and productivity. *Troop Train* (1975), Roshchin's emotional commemoration of the 30th anniversary of World War II and of his mother's personal experience aboard a crowded troop train, has an almost entirely female cast, and was successfully staged by ANATOLY EFROS at the Moscow Art Theatre. Other plays include *Husband and Wife*, a *Valentin and Valentina* update on the problems of young marrieds; *The Galoshes of Happiness*, a censored adaptation of Hans Christian Andersen's tale; *Mother-of-Pearl Zinaida*, a satirical comedy about a writer named Aladdin; *Hurry to Do Good*; and an adaptation of TOLSTOI's *Anna Karenina*, all of which were staged in the early 1980s.

**Rossi, Ernesto** 1827–96 Italian actor-manager. From the 1860s to the end of his career he acted mainly with his own companies in a large repertoire that included the major Italian stock pieces of the century. SHAKESPEARE figured prominently in his list of lead roles, which included Othello and Hamlet (1856), Macbeth, King Lear, Richard III, Shylock, Romeo and Coriolanus. He translated and adapted *Julius Caesar* for his own stage interpretation. He toured to North and South America and throughout Europe. In 1876 he took several of his Shakespeare productions to London, but he never enjoyed the same success there as his contemporary SALVINI, and a return visit in 1882, when he performed the part of Lear in Italian with English players acting the rest of the play in English, was a disaster. But his contribution in the area of stage-management, and in acclimatizing Shakespeare to the Italian stage, is underrated. Of solid, rather stocky appearance and of

limited vocal range, he had a lively, demonstrative mode of playing that well suited him to romantic roles, and a fondness for interpolating engaging, if often extraneous, stage-business.

**Rostand, Edmond** 1868–1918 French playwright. Compared with the dominant NATURALISM of the time, Rostand's plays were romantic and patriotic in spirit, especially *Cyrano de Bergerac* (1897) and *L'Aiglon* (1900). His comedy *Les Romanesques* (*The Fantasticks*, COMÉDIE-FRANÇAISE, 1894) had light and witty dialogue reminiscent of ALFRED DE MUSSET. *La Princesse lointaine* (*The Distant Princess*, 1895) provided a role for SARAH BERNHARDT, as Mélissinde, the princess of its poet hero's idealized dream. Sarah again played the lead role in *La Samaritaine* (*The Woman of Samaria*, 1897), a biblical piece. *Cyrano de Bergerac*, created by COQUELIN at the Porte-Saint-Martin (see BOULEVARD), was his most popular play, combining nostalgia for the 17th century with swashbuckling heroism, a romantic love theme and lyrical verse. *L'Aiglon* offered another major role to Bernhardt as the sickly prince, Napoleon's son. Rostand's last major play, *Chantecler* (1910), was based on the *Roman de Renart*, with actors dressed as farmyard animals. Like VICTOR HUGO, he was often more poet than dramatist, but his romanticism was tinged with REALISM and SATIRE.

**Rostovsky, St Dmitry** [Danylo (Savych) Tuptalo; Dmitry of Rostov] 1651–1709 Ukrainian poet, playwright and ecclesiastic. His popular school dramas, based on medieval MYSTERY and MORALITY PLAYS, mixed biblical and allegorical characters with low comic types. These include *Nativity Play* (produced 1702, Rostov), *The Dormition Play*, *Esther and Ahasuerus*, *The Resurrection of Christ* and *A Sinner's Repentance*. The last was performed at court in 1752 and established FYODOR VOLKOV's Yaroslavl troupe in St Petersburg, an important step in the development of the formal Russian theatre. Rostovsky was canonized in 1757.

**Rote Sprachrohr, Das** German company. 'The Red Megaphone', the first and most important AGIT-PROP troupe in Weimar Germany, was founded in 1927 by M. Valletin, using members of communist youth groups. It performed choral works, didactic plays and REVUES at workers' gatherings. *Hallo, Kollege Jungarbeiter* (*Hello, Young Colleagues*, 1928) depicted workers struggling against exploitation in episodic scenes, and a choral piece *Dritte Internationale* (*Third International*, 1929), with songs by Hanns Eisler, toured the USSR. After 1930, the group moved towards EPIC THEATRE techniques with *Song of the Red United Front* and *General Strike* (both 1931). After the Nazi seizure of power, members were arrested or emigrated.

**Rotimi, Ola** 1936– Nigerian playwright and director. His plays fall between academic drama and popular Yoruba-language folk operas. The first, *Our Husband Has Gone Mad Again*, a comedy set in Nigeria during the throes of a general election, was premiered at Yale in 1966, where Rotimi had studied. He founded the Ori Olokun Acting Company at Ife University, working in conjunction with the composer Akin Euba. The first production there was *The Gods Are Not to Blame* (1968), Rotimi's version of SOPHOCLES' *Oedipus the King* and an allegory of the Nigerian Civil War. *Kurunmi* (1969), about the 19th-century Yoruba wars, was followed in 1971 by *Ovonramwen Nogbaisi*, a tragic reappraisal of the sack of Benin by the British in 1897. *Holding Talks: An Absurdist Drama* (published in 1979) was popularly received. If

(1979), concerned with a group of working-class Nigerians, typifies Rotimi's craft: strong theatricality combined with music and MELODRAMA building to a tragic climax. *Hopes of the Living Dead* (1985) is about a leper, whose disease becomes a metaphor for social and psychological disease. From 1992–3 he ran a company, African Theatre Cradle, based in Ife.

**Rotrou, Jean de** 1609–50 French playwright. PIERRE CORNEILLE's only serious contemporary rival was resident playwright at the HÔTEL DE BOURGOGNE in succession to HARDY. Thirty-five plays survive, mostly freewheeling tragicomedies of multiple incident and blithe disregard for the three unities (see ARISTOTLE). He also wrote comedies, the best of which is a version of the Amphitryon story entitled *Les Sosies* (*The Doubles*, 1636), and several tragedies, amongst them *Hercule mourant* (*Hercules Dying*, 1634), which helped to introduce a more regular neoclassical form of tragedy. He was one of RICHELIEU's group of five commissioned dramatists, though his most mature work was produced after his return to his native Dreux: the TRAGICOMEDY *Venceslas* (1647), the regular tragedy *Cosroès* (1648), and his most imaginative tragedy *Le Véritable Saint Genest* (1645), derived from LOPE DE VEGA, which depicts the conversion of the Roman actor Genesius.

**Rousseau, Jean-Jacques** 1712–78 Swiss-born French philosopher and man of letters. Although the author of several operatic works, notably *Le Devin du village* (*The Village Soothsayer*, 1753) and *Pygmalion* (1770), and a comedy *Narcisse* (1752), presented at the COMÉDIE-FRANÇAISE, Rousseau condemned the theatre – whose aim is to please, not to instruct – in his philosophical writings. In his *Lettre à d'Alembert* (1758) he denounces both TRAGEDY and COMEDY for inviting interest in characters whose excessive behaviour is beyond our own experience, for laying too much stress on love and for presenting vice in a sympathetic light. His ideological position is directly opposed to that of DIDEROT.

**Roux, Jean-Louis** 1923– French Canadian director, playwright and actor. He helped found Montreal's enduring THÉÂTRE DU NOUVEAU MONDE (1951), becoming its artistic director (1966–82) and guiding it towards a modern, diversified repertoire. He was director of the École Nationale du Théâtre (1981–7). His brilliant career as an actor has included major stage, radio and television plays. He has adapted many works for Quebec audiences, notably SHAKESPEARE's *Julius Caesar* (*Jules César*, 1971), and is the author of *Rose Latulippe* (1951), dealing with a popular Canadian legend, and *Les Bois-brûlés* (*Halfbreeds*, 1967), a historical drama.

**Rovina, Hanna** 1889–1980 Russian-born Jewish actress. The First Lady of the Hebrew stage, with NAHUM ZEMACH and Menahem Gnessin she founded the original HABIMAH Studio, emigrated with it to Palestine in 1931 and remained an active member of the Habimah theatre all her life. She gained international fame as Leah, the possessed bride in ANSKI's *The Dybbuk*. She played memorable mother roles in *The Eternal Jew* by DAVID PINSKI (1923), *The Mother* by KAREL ČAPEK (1939), *Mirele Efros* by JACOB GORDIN (1939), *In the Wastes of the Negev* by Yigal Mossinson (1949) and *Hanna Szenes* by Aaron Megged (1958). Among her great roles were also EURIPIDES' *Medea* (1955) and the Old Lady in DÜRRENMATT's *The Visit* (1959).

**Rovinski, Samuel** 1932– Costa Rican playwright. His motivation derives from a sense of justice and the need to raise the consciousness of those responsible for intol-

erable situations. His plays include *Gobierno de alcoba* (*Bedroom Government*, 1971); *Las fisgonas de Paso Ancho* (*The Busybodies of Paso Ancho*, 1971), a caricature of a wide variety of social ills; *Un modelo para Rosaura* (*A Model for Rosaura*, 1974); and *El martirio del pastor* (*Pastoral Martyrdom*, 1984), which dealt with the assassination in El Salvador of Monsignor Romero.

**Rovner, Eduardo** 1942– Argentine playwright and director. Based in Buenos Aires, Rovner is author of a dozen or so plays, beginning with a realistic style in *Una pareja* (*A Couple*, 1976) and *Ultimo premio* (*Last Prize*, 1981). Within the so-called 'satiric absurd' (see THEATRE OF THE ABSURD) are *¿Una foto... ?* (*A Photo... ?*, 1977) and *Cuarteto* (*Quartet*, 1991). Plays that function as FARCES include *Compañía* (*Company*, 1989) and *Volvió una noche* (*She Returned One Night*, 1990).

**Rowe, Nicholas** 1674–1718 English playwright and editor. *The Ambitious Stepmother* (1700) established his serious neoclassical style; *Tamerlane* (1701) celebrates William III. He adapted MASSINGER's *The Fatal Dowry* as *The Fair Penitent* (1703). His later work is influenced by the 'she-tragedies' of BANKS, centring on the plight of a virtuous woman and aiming at pathos. His best play in this form, *The Tragedy of Jane Shore* (1714), combines *Richard III* with political and pathetic tragedy. But his drama was markedly unsentimental. In 1709 Rowe published his edition of SHAKESPEARE in six volumes. In the first serious attempt to edit Shakespeare since 1623, he aimed to remove textual corruption and added stage directions, as well as regularizing act and scene divisions according to neoclassical five-act form.

**Rowley, Samuel** c.1575–1624 English actor and playwright. He was a leading member of the ADMIRAL'S MEN from c.1597 to 1613. His only known surviving play is a chronicle about Henry VIII, *When You See Me, You Know Me* (1603). Rowley is associated with the lost *The Taming of a Shrew* (c.1589) and probably supplied 'additions' to MARLOWE's *Doctor Faustus*.

**Rowley, William** c.1585–1626 English actor and playwright. A leading member of Prince Charles's Men and, on occasions, the King's Men (see LORD CHAMBERLAIN'S MEN) – where he was also a company manager – he is known to have played comic parts relying on his large frame, e.g. the Fat Bishop in MIDDLETON's *A Game at Chess* (1624). He collaborated with Middleton, notably on *The Changeling* (1622), with DEKKER and FORD on *The Witch of Edmonton* (1621) and with FLETCHER on *The Maid in the Mill* (1623). His own citizen comedies (see CITIZEN COMEDY) are *A New Wonder: A Woman Never Vexed* (published 1632) and *A Match at Midnight* (published 1633).

**Royal Court Theatre** (London) The present theatre opened in 1888. After PINERO's *Trelawny of the Wells* (1898), its most distinctive early contributions to English theatre were the seasons under the joint management of J. E. VEDRENNE and HARLEY GRANVILLE BARKER (1904–7), which established SHAW and introduced the Continental avant-garde. Away from London's WEST END theatres and smaller than them, it was forced by financial hazards to convert into a cinema (1932–52). In 1956 the English Stage Company appointed as artistic director GEORGE DEVINE, who was committed to staging new, controversial plays and was triumphantly vindicated by the success of JOHN OSBORNE's *Look Back in Anger* (1956). But the Royal Court was not just a home for 'angry young men': it staged plays by BRECHT, IONESCO, WESKER, N. F. SIMPSON and JOHN ARDEN. It maintained its leadership of the New

Drama under Devine's successor, WILLIAM GASKILL (1965–72), who with LINDSAY ANDERSON gave prominence to plays by DAVID STOREY and EDWARD BOND as well as reviving the neglected work of D. H. LAWRENCE. The challenging lead has been maintained by recent artistic directors, especially with the provision of the Small Theatre Upstairs in 1969. In 1977 Stuart Burge took over from Oscar Lewenstein as artistic director, and was in turn replaced by Max Stafford-Clark in 1979. Since 1993 STEPHEN DALDRY has been in charge.

**Royal Exchange Theatre** (Manchester) One of the premier regional theatres in Britain (see REPERTORY THEATRE), the building itself is a remarkable piece of theatre design: a theatre-in-the-round built of steel tubing and glass suspended within the vast hall of Manchester's old Royal Exchange – a unique combination of new and old. The company began life as the 69 Theatre Company, based in the Manchester University Theatre (1968–73), and transferred to the new theatre in 1976. High-quality productions, especially of the classics and modern classics, often with star names in the cast, have been the hallmark of its policy; notable productions have included *The Rivals* (1976), *The Duchess of Malfi* (1980), *The Dresser* (1980) and *The Three Sisters* (1985). There has never, apart from one season, been a resident acting company, but continuity is provided by the multiple artistic directorship which has included MICHAEL ELLIOT.

**Royal Shakespeare Company (RSC)** British company. The first Shakespeare Memorial Theatre at Stratford-upon-Avon was opened in 1879 and destroyed by fire in 1926. The present building, designed by Elizabeth Scott, opened in 1932. It was renamed the Royal Shakespeare Theatre in 1961. It has a 29ft proscenium stage and can accommodate 1,500 spectators. The transformation of what had been a seasonal festival theatre at Stratford-upon-Avon, the Shakespeare Memorial Theatre, into the home for Britain's first *de facto* national theatre company can be largely credited to the determination of two men, Fordham Flower and PETER HALL.

Fordham Flower led the theatre through the difficult postwar years to its comparative prosperity and expansion during the 1950s. In 1946, he appointed BARRY JACKSON as director; Jackson responded by introducing such young directors and actors as PETER BROOK and PAUL SCOFIELD. When Jackson retired in 1948 he turned to ANTHONY QUAYLE, the actor-director, who brought in stars from London such as the Oliviers. Quayle exploited the relative decline in the fortunes of the OLD VIC; and such spectacular successes as Peter Brook's *Titus Andronicus*, with LAURENCE OLIVIER as Titus, in 1955 established the Stratford theatre as a Mecca for Shakespearian production. When Quayle resigned in 1957 he was succeeded briefly by Glen Byam Shaw, who had joined him in the leadership of the company in 1953.

Peter Hall was appointed to succeed Shaw as director in 1960, proposing to establish a large semi-permanent company, with actors on two- or three-year contracts, who would be encouraged to stay by the prospect of also playing in a second theatre, in London, the Aldwych. Stratford programmes would concentrate on the work of SHAKESPEARE and his contemporaries, while those at the Aldwych would include modern plays from Britain and abroad, together with transfers from Stratford. The new company would actively pursue state support at a level appropriate to its planned national status. To that end, the old pious but somewhat funereal title was dropped and replaced in 1961 by the Royal Shakespeare Company, and the royal charter of 1925 was amended to this effect.

The first annual subsidy from the ARTS COUNCIL came in 1963; the deficits and the grants continued to grow in future years. By the time of Peter Hall's departure in 1968 the audiences had trebled and, in addition to running its two theatres, the RSC ran experimental seasons at smaller theatres, such as the influential Arts Theatre season in 1962 and the Theatre of Cruelty collage at LAMDA (the London Academy of Music and Dramatic Art) in 1964. The company's reputation had soared, led by such Peter Brook productions as PETER WEISS's *The Marat/Sade* (1964) and *US* (1966) and by the Hall–JOHN BARTON adaptation of Shakespeare's early HISTORY PLAYS, *The Wars of the Roses* (1963). A rivalry developed between the RSC, regarded as a 'directors' theatre', and the newly formed NATIONAL THEATRE under Laurence Olivier, an 'actors' theatre' with higher subsidies.

Like the National Theatre, the RSC sought a new London theatre as its metropolitan home, which eventually opened in 1982 as part of the Barbican Arts Centre. Hall handed over the RSC's directorship in 1968 to TREVOR NUNN. In 1978 TERRY HANDS became with Nunn joint artistic director, a post made necessary by the continuing expansion of the company. Notable among Nunn's achievements was the establishment of two studio theatres in London and Stratford, where vigorous programmes of new and experimental productions could be pursued. In London the studios were at The Place, then at the Donmar Warehouse and then, after the move into the Barbican, the Pit; while at Stratford a converted store and rehearsal room became known as The Other Place (1974).

Despite the record of new plays by EDWARD BOND, HOWARD BARKER and DUSTY HUGHES, among other contemporary writers, the studio productions of *Hamlet* (1975) and *Macbeth* (1976) were particularly memorable and reflected a growing dissatisfaction with over-decorated versions of Shakespeare. The RSC's regional responsibilities included small-scale touring productions and seasons at Newcastle upon Tyne. It also became internationally known for the bold scale of its ventures, such as the cycle of Roman plays directed by Trevor Nunn in 1972, the *Henry VI* trilogy directed by Terry Hands in 1977 and the collective efforts at historical reconstruction reflected in *Nicholas Nickleby* (1982) and *Les Misérables* (1985).

In 1986 an anonymous benefaction made possible the opening of a third theatre in Stratford, the Swan – an open-stage playhouse in the shell of the auditorium of the old Memorial Theatre. The Swan is dedicated to exploring the work of Shakespeare's contemporaries.

In 1986 Trevor Nunn stepped back from the leadership and his co-director Terry Hands took over. The RSC's empire, with five theatres under its control and some major musicals in the WEST END, greatly outstripped its resources from grant-funding. The financial plight led to the closure of the Barbican Theatre for four months in 1990. Hands resigned and ADRIAN NOBLE became director. His initial impact was to pull the RSC back from its more speculative schemes and to return to a star-studded classic repertoire, such as *Henry IV, Parts 1 and 2* (1991, with ROBERT STEPHENS as Falstaff), *Hamlet* (1992, with KENNETH BRANAGH) and *King Lear* (1993, also with Robert Stephens).

**Rozenberg, Lev S.** see BAKST, LÉON

**Rozenmacher, Germán** 1936–71 Argentine playwright. He dealt with Jewish values and traditions in such plays as *Réquiem para un viernes a la noche* (*Requiem for a Friday Night*, 1964). He collaborated with COSSA, SOMIGLIANA and TALESNIK in the creation of *El avión negro* (*The Black Aeroplane*, 1970), a play that in various scenes anticipated Perón's return to Argentina.

**Różewicz, Tadeusz** 1921–90 Polish playwright, poet and prose writer. He fought in a guerrilla unit during the Nazi occupation. Judging both traditional and avant-garde drama as obsolete, Różewicz created plays out of fragments of daily life, newspapers and conversational clichés, as collages from the refuse heap of modern civilization. Practising open dramaturgy in which director and actors were invited to collaborate, he mixed genres and created extensive stage directions that are arguments with the theatre. Major plays are *The Card File* (1960), *The Old Woman Broods* (1968), *White Marriage* (1974), *Dead and Buried* (1979) and *The Trap* (1982).

**Rozov, Viktor (Sergeevich)** 1913– Soviet playwright. Extremely popular and prolific, he is important in the movement to rehumanize the Soviet theatre by focusing on real, often anti-heroic, personalities and their problems. His first play, *Her Friends* (1949), initiated an association with the director ANATOLY EFROS. The majority of his plays deal with the painful necessity of compromise and realism, while maintaining personal integrity and a belief in the power of love. His characters' successes are measured in terms of personal fulfilment rather than professional advancement or ideological correctness. Examples are *Good Luck!* (1954), *On the Wedding Day* (1964), *The Reunion* (1967) and *From Night to Noon* (1969). *Alive Forever* (1956), a revised version of his 1943 play *The Serebrisky Family*, treats the small-scale human dramas which occur around the edges of war. It remains the signature piece of Moscow's Sovremennik Theatre (1957) and was made into the film *The Cranes Are Flying*. His 1979 family drama, *The Nest of the Woodgrouse* (*Meet My Model Family*), is about the conflict between generations and confronts the problems of moral decay among top-level bureaucrats. It was eventually staged in 1981 in Moscow and later at the NEW YORK SHAKESPEARE FESTIVAL's Public Theater. *The Back of Beyond* (1983) is based on an actual incident, in which the corrupt officials of a small town covered up a father's murder of his son.

**Rudkin, (James) David** 1936– British playwright. His first play, *Afore Night Come* (1960), revealed an instinct for high tragedy and myth. The story concerned an itinerant Irish tramp who is murdered by a gang of fruit-pickers on a Midlands farm, but the heightened language evoked themes of ritual slaughter, infertility and the suppression of the imagination (and Ireland) by British imperialism. The relationship between Ireland and England is the subject of *Cries from Casement as His Bones Are Brought to Dublin* (1973) and *Ashes* (1974), his best-known play, about a Belfast couple whose infertility is mysteriously linked to the struggle in Ulster. In *Sons of Light* (1976) Rudkin's allegorical assessment of contemporary man is part-fable, part-science fiction. More recent plays include *The Triumph of Death* (1981), about organized Christianity and its association with temporal powers, *Space Invaders* (1983), *Will's Way* (1984) and *The Saxon Shore* (1986). Rudkin has written extensively for radio and television (see RADIO DRAMA; TELEVISION DRAMA), is an accomplished linguist and musician and has translated and adapted European classics for the ROYAL SHAKESPEARE COMPANY.

**Rudman, Michael (Edward)** 1939– American-born director. He moved to Britain to study at Oxford University. After gaining experience as an associate director at the Nottingham and Newcastle Playhouses (1964–8) and at the ROYAL SHAKESPEARE COMPANY (1968), he became artistic director of the influential TRAVERSE THEATRE Club in Edinburgh from 1970 to 1973, where his international outlook and championship of such Scottish dramatists as C. P. TAYLOR and EVELING became a major feature of the annual EDINBURGH FESTIVAL. He moved to a London theatre club of similar size, HAMPSTEAD, in 1973, where for five years he produced and directed such plays as HANDKE's *Ride across Lake Constance*, Taylor's *The Black and White Minstrels* and Eveling's *Union Jack (and Bonzo)*, FRAYN's *Clouds*, *Alphabetical Order* and *Donkey's Years*, and PAM GEMS's first play, *Dusa, Fish, Stas and Vi*. He joined the NATIONAL THEATRE in 1979, as director in charge of the Lyttelton Theatre. He left the NT in 1988. Briefly director of the CHICHESTER FESTIVAL THEATRE (1990), he was appointed director of the Crucible Theatre, Sheffield, in 1992.

**Rueda, Lope de** ?1509–65 Spanish playwright. One of the first actor-managers of the GOLDEN AGE, he toured with his company throughout Spain, acting in innyards, squares and palace halls. CERVANTES praised his comic acting and his poetry, though his description of Rueda's company exaggerates the simplicity of the performances. Four of his *COMEDIAS*, showing strong Italian influences, and two PASTORALS were published in 1567, as well as seven prose *pasos* or *entremeses* (see GÉNERO CHICO) under the title of *El deleitoso* (*The Delightful One*). Rueda's short works are very witty and far superior to his longer plays.

**Rueda, Manuel** 1921– Dominican Republic poet, musician, playwright and fiction writer. He is one of his country's most important writers. His play *La trinitaria blanca* (*The White Flower*, 1957) was anthologized in 1968 along with *Vacaciones en el cielo* (*Vacations in Heaven*), *La tía Beatriz hace un milagro* (*Aunt Beatriz Works a Miracle*), and *Entre alambradas* (*Inside Fences*), the latter dealing with the US occupation of the Dominican Republic in 1965. Rueda's theatre is characterized by his balance of form, poetic language, humour and dramatic action. *El rey Clinejas* (*King Clinejas*, 1979) is an example of popular theatre, successfully combining poetry and fantasy.

**Ruggeri, Ruggero** 1871–1953 Italian actor. From 1888 he had a long professional career, working with many of the major players of his day including NOVELLI, Talli and Grammatica. A forceful actor with a striking presence, he is best-remembered for his acting in the plays of PIRANDELLO, playing lead roles in, among others, *Il giuoco delle parti* (*The Rules of the Game*, 1918), *Sei personaggi in cerca d'autore* (*Six Characters in Search of an Author*, 1921) and *Enrico IV* (1922). A member of the company that Pirandello took to Paris in 1925, he played the lead role in *Enrico IV* with spectacular success.

**Ruiz de Alarcón (y Mendoza), Juan** c.1580–1639 Mexican-born Spanish playwright. He settled in Madrid in 1615. In 1628 and 1634 he published two collections of plays which stand out for their castigation of the vices of Spanish society and for the nonconformity of their protagonists. They did not appeal to Spanish audiences. His best-known play, *La verdad sospechosa* (*Suspect Truth*), condemns the vice of lying, and is the source of

CORNEILLE's *Le Menteur* and several English plays. *Las paredes oyen* (*Walls Have Ears*) castigates slander, and *No hay mal que por bien no venga* (*It's an Ill Wind ...*) portrays an outsider who refuses to conform to standards of behaviour which he sees as pointless. *Los pechos privilegiados* (*Privileged Hearts*) gives the ideal of what a king's favourite should be, while *Ganar amigos* (*Winning Friends*) promotes the virtue of returning good for evil.

**Russell, Annie** 1864–1936 British-born American actress. She established her career with a brilliant portrayal of the title character in *Esmeralda* (1881). Compared with ELEONORA DUSE for her simplicity and naturalism, she was effective especially in emotional and comic roles, and the ideal ingénue. In 1905 she created SHAW's heroine in *Major Barbara* and gave memorable performances of Puck in *A Midsummer Night's Dream* (1906), Viola in *Twelfth Night* (1909), Beatrice in *Much Ado* (1912) and Lady Teazle in *The School for Scandal* (1914).

**Russell, Henry** 1812–1900 British entertainer and songwriter. After studying music with Rossini and Bellini, he made a debut as a ballad singer (1837) and soon became hugely popular, offering the first solo vocal programmes in America aimed at the common man. He not only sang in a pleasant baritone and accompanied himself on the piano, but composed his entire repertory. This included *Cheer, Boys, Cheer!*, *Woodman! Spare That Tree*, *A Life on the Ocean Wave* and *The Old Armchair*, as well as temperance, anti-slavery and humanitarian ballads. He performed in England and America until the early 1860s.

**Russell, Lillian** [*née* Helen Louise Leonard] 1861–1922 American singer and actress. Her name is synonymous with one of her show titles, *An American Beauty*. Rising from obscurity in Iowa, she became a much sought-after star in comic opera, BURLESQUE and VAUDEVILLE across America and in England. She performed in *The Pie Rats of Penn Yan*, PASTOR's burlesque of *The Pirates of Penzance*; *The Snake Charmer*, *The Sorcerer*, *The Princess of Trebizonde*, *Iolanthe* and *The Princess Nicotine*. With WEBER AND FIELDS's celebrated troupe she enjoyed five seasons, 1899–1904. Roles in *Lady Teazle* (musical version of *The School for Scandal*), *The Butterfly* and *Wildfire* furthered her already flourishing reputation.

**Russell, Willy** [William] **(Martin)** 1947– British playwright. Born and educated in Liverpool, he took many jobs, including that of hairdresser, before becoming a full-time writer in 1971. His first three short plays, *Blind Scouse*, appeared in 1971–2; but his first success came with a musical biography of the Beatles, *John, Paul, George, Ringo and ... Bert* (1974), which transferred to London. The cheerful humour of his comedies, *Breezeblock Park* (1975), *One for the Road* (1976) and *Stags and Hens* (1978), brought him popularity as an observer of Liverpudlian life; but *Educating Rita* (1979) proved to be much less parochial in its appeal, a study of a pupil–teacher relationship where the attractive and intelligent student eventually takes control. *Shirley Valentine* (1986) concerns a woman approaching middle age who succeeds in breaking away from her humdrum life. Both were successful as stage plays and as films. Russell has also written casual, informal musicals, such as *Blood Brothers* (1983) and *Our Day Out* (1984).

**Rustaveli Theatre** see STURUA, ROBERT (ROBERTOVICH)

**Ruzzante** [Ruzante; Angelo Beolco] ?1502–43 Italian amateur actor and playwright. (Il) Ruzzante (the Chatterbox) was head of a travelling company which performed in Padua, Venice and Ferrara at CARNIVAL time from 1520. He incarnated the type of garrulous, critical, grumbling peasant. His comedies united the experiments of court theatre such as the PASTORAL eclogue and the Terentian comedy (see TERENCE) with the indigenous *momarie* of urban Venice and the *mariazi* of the Paduan countryside. In his own time, his reputation as an actor overwhelmed his fame as a playwright, but his plays paved the way for the COMMEDIA DELL'ARTE. JACQUES COPEAU revived his *Ancontana* (1522?) in 1927; the Teatro Stabile of Turin staged his *Moschetta* (1528) in 1960; and in England *Il Reduce*, his caustic anti-war monologue, has occasionally been revived.

**Ryga, George** 1932–87 Canadian playwright, poet and novelist. He applies surrealistic techniques (see SURREALISM) to powerful and realistic stories of injustice and oppression. *The Ecstasy of Rita Joe* (1967), his most successful work, is a grim indictment of Canada's treatment of its native people. It has been widely produced across Canada, in Britain and the USA, and was even turned into a ballet. *Grass and Wild Strawberries* (1969) explores the generational conflicts of the 1960s. *Captives of the Faceless Drummer* (1971) depicts the kidnapping of a diplomat by revolutionaries, provoking a storm of controversy. Much of Ryga's later work was in television and the novel.

**Sabbattini, Nicola** 1574–1654 Italian architect and engineer. Sabbattini was born and died in Pesaro and for many years was architect for the Duke of Urbino. Although most of his work was on civil and military projects, he also designed and built theatres – which at the time meant transforming great halls – and scenery. The one theatre specifically attributed to him is the Teatro del Sol at Pesaro, built in 1637 for the production of *L'Asmondo*. His importance lies in his book, *Pratica di fabricar scene e machine ne'teatri* (1638), which documents the theatre machinery and technology of the day. It was widely read and influenced theatre practice throughout Europe.

**Sacco [Sacchi], (Giovanni) Antonio** 1708–88 Italian actor. A famous Truffaldino, he travelled with his COMMEDIA DELL'ARTE troupe throughout half of Europe (1738–62). In Venice he played at the Teatro Sant' Angelo, where, at his urging, GOLDONI wrote for him *The Servant of Two Masters* (1745), *Truffaldino's 32 Mishaps* (1738–40) and *Truffaldino's Son Lost and Found* (1746). GOZZI followed suit with *The Love of Three Oranges* (1761), an enormous success. GARRICK and Casanova spoke highly of Sacco's talents, especially in improvised COMEDY.

**Sackville, Thomas** 1536–1608 English playwright. With Thomas Norton he wrote *The Tragedy of Gorboduc* (1561). This is usually considered the first English TRAGEDY, drawing upon classical precedent in some respects (chorus, reported action) but otherwise showing an inclination to freer form and to political comment that was to be a feature of classic Elizabethan tragedy.

*sacra rappresentazione* Fifteenth-century Florentine play. It was a development of the Italian *LAUDA* but written by an individual and performed outside the liturgical calendar. These didactic dramas sometimes had a contemporary framework and were largely written for boy performers, e.g. the stories of Isaac, Joseph and the Prodigal Son.

**Sadler's Wells Theatre** (London) A surveyor of highways and theatrical impresario named Sadler (whether his name was Dick or Thomas is disputed) opened a Musick-House in 1683 on a site in Finsbury, aiming to provide cheap entertainment in north London. In 1764–5 Thomas Rosoman replaced the old wooden hall with a brick theatre (capacity 2,600) and Sadler's Wells was acknowledged as one of the 'minor theatres', a home for PANTOMIME, illegitimate drama, music and acrobatic displays. Under Tom King's control (1772–85), the theatre earned a fashionable reputation for patriotic spectacle, musical innovations (CHARLES DIBDIN) and good wine. The infant JOSEPH GRIMALDI began his long association with Sadler's Wells in 1781. From 1799 to 1819 the driving force was Charles Dibdin the younger, who exploited the theatre's aquatic potential in 1803 by installing a large water tank on the stage, but the opening success of *The Siege of Gibraltar* (1804) proved hard to follow. By the time of Grimaldi's retirement (1828), MELODRAMA was the rage. From 1844 to 1862 SAMUEL PHELPS staged a classical repertoire, including 31 of SHAKESPEARE's plays, and attracted discerning audiences, but after he retired the theatre declined.

Eventually, in 1931, in a new building on the site designed to seat 1,550, LILIAN BAYLIS opened her north London operations, in association with the OLD VIC in south London. By 1934 Sadler's Wells was devoted almost exclusively to opera and ballet. The policy continued after wartime closure until the ballet company moved to COVENT GARDEN in 1956 to provide the nucleus of the Royal Ballet. In 1968, the opera company moved to the Coliseum as part of the English National Opera. After a period of uncertainty, the theatre became the home of the Sadler's Wells Royal Ballet in 1977.

**Sadovsky [Ermilov], Prov (Mikhailovich)** 1818–72 Russian actor. Scion of a century-old family of actors at the Maly Theatre, he was the primary interpreter of OSTROVSKY and succeeded SHCHEPKIN in developing naturalness and psychological veracity as the cornerstones of Russian realistic acting. Shchepkin discovered him, arranging for his Moscow debut in 1839. He was most believable playing Russians or characters like the gravedigger in *Hamlet* whom he could transform into earthy Russian types. He performed 29 roles in 28 plays by Ostrovsky, and in works by e.g. GOGOL, PISEMSKY, TURGENEV and SUKHOVO-KOBYLIN. His commonness made Sadovsky's Osip in *The Inspector General* (1845) so believable that observers thought he had become the role. He belonged to the literary circle which championed native culture over Western influences.

*sainete* see *GÉNERO CHICO*

**St Charles Theatre** (New Orleans) Built in 1835, the St Charles was the largest, handsomest American theatre to that date. The original STOCK COMPANY included CHARLOTTE CUSHMAN. During its highwater years, most American and English stars played at the theatre and JUNIUS BRUTUS BOOTH's last performance occurred on its stage. Latterly it became a VAUDEVILLE and then a movie house.

**Saint-Denis, Michel** 1897–1971 French director. The nephew of COPEAU, Saint-Denis first directed with the COMPAGNIE DES QUINZE. In 1935 he went to London to direct *Noah* by OBEY and stayed on to found the London Theatre Studio, a theatre school modelled on Copeau's ideas, hoping to develop an art theatre. The venture failed, but his production of CHEKHOV's *Three Sisters* in 1939 is still remembered. During the war he worked for the BBC and then helped, with HUGH HUNT and GEORGE DEVINE, to revive the OLD VIC and establish its theatre school. He left England in 1951 and in 1952 became director of one of the new decentralized theatres, the Comédie de l'Est. He founded the first theatre school outside Paris and moved both theatre and school to Strasbourg in 1953, where both have since acquired an international reputation. Later he became co-director of the Juilliard School at the Lincoln Center, New York. In 1960 he published *Theatre: A Rediscovery of Style*, in which methods and approaches derived from Copeau are set out.

**St James Theatre** (New York City) Known as the Erlanger, after its builder, it opened in 1927 and was later bought by the SHUBERTS, who ran it until 1957. Built as a musical house with about 1,600 seats, the RODGERS and HAMMERSTEIN musicals *Oklahoma!* (1943)

and *The King and I* (1951) held the stage for five and three years respectively. Their *Flower Drum Song* followed in 1958. Other notable musicals have included *Hello Dolly!* (1964), *Barnum* (1980) and *My One and Only* (1983).

**St James's Theatre** (London) Close to Piccadilly, the theatre opened in 1835. In 1879 it was taken over by JOHN HARE and the KENDALS, who produced comedies about fashionable society, including PINERO's early plays. Its most brilliant years ran from 1891 to 1917 with the management of GEORGE ALEXANDER and the productions of Pinero's *The Second Mrs Tanqueray* (1893), WILDE's *The Importance of Being Earnest* (1895), HENRY JAMES's *Guy Domville* (1895), STEPHEN PHILLIPS's *Paolo and Francesca* (1902) and Pinero's *His House in Order* (1906). Such plays appealed to the intelligent middle-class audience by their judicious mixture of audaciousness and reassurance. LAURENCE OLIVIER and VIVIEN LEIGH hired St James's in 1950–1, opening with CHRISTOPHER FRY's *Venus Observed*. RATTIGAN's *Separate Tables* (1954) broke the theatre's long-run record. But St James's closed in 1957.

**Saint-Subber, Arnold** 1918–93 American producer. He served as assistant to John Murray Anderson for numerous productions including the ZIEGFELD *Follies* of 1943. His close association with playwright NEIL SIMON established him on BROADWAY in the 1960s. Of the shows he produced or co-produced, the more notable are *Kiss Me Kate* (1948), *The Grass Harp* (1952), *My Three Angels* (1953), *Dark at the Top of the Stairs* (1957), *The Tenth Man* (1959), *Barefoot in the Park* (1963), *The Odd Couple* (1965), *Plaza Suite* (1968), *Last of the Red Hot Lovers* (1969), *The Prisoner of Second Avenue* (1971), *Gigi* (1973) and *1600 Pennsylvania Avenue* (1978).

**saints' plays** [saint's plays; saint plays] Medieval plays based on the lives of saints occurred all over Europe from the 12th to the 15th century. Nearly 40 French examples have survived. The saints chosen were often those whose cult was limited to a particular area or town. Two extant English texts are *Mary Magdalen* and *The Conversion of St Paul* from late-15th- or early-16th-century East Anglia.

**Saks, Gene** 1921– American director and actor. He made his New York debut in 1947 as Joxer in O'CASEY's *Juno and the Paycock*, turning to directing in 1963 and becoming famous for comedy. His major directing credits include *Nobody Loves an Albatross* (1963), *Generation* (1965), *Mame* (1966), *Sheep on the Runway* (1970), *How the Other Half Loves* (1971), *Sometime, Next Year* (1975), *I Love My Wife* (1977), *Supporting Cast* (1981), *Special Occasions* (1982), *Brighton Beach Memoirs* (1983), *Biloxi Blues* (1984) and *Lost in Yonkers* (1991).

**Salacrou, Armand** 1899–1989 French playwright. He sold a profitable advertising business to devote himself to writing. DULLIN directed many of his plays, notably *Patchouli* (1930), *Atlas-Hotel* (1931) and *La Terre est ronde* (*The World Is Round*, 1938). BARRAULT staged *Les Nuits de la colère* (*Nights of Anger*, 1946), about resistance and collaboration. *L'Archipel Lenoir* (*The Lenoir Archipelago*, 1947) satirized the bourgeoisie and *Boulevard Durand* (1961) was a documentary drama about Jules Durand, a trade union activist sentenced to death in 1910 for a murder he did not commit. Salacrou was a fine craftsman of plot and character. He anticipated the social drama that flourished in the decentralization movement after World War II.

**Salazar Bondy, Sebastián** 1924–65 Peruvian playwright and poet. He founded the Club de Teatro

(Theatre Club) in Lima in 1953 with Reynaldo D'Amore. His first play, *Amor, gran laberinto* (*Love, the Great Labyrinth*, 1947), revealed his affinity for satirical FARCE. *Rodil* (1952) and *Flora Tristán* (1958) dealt with aspects of Peruvian social history. *El fabricante de deudas* (*The Debt Arranger*, 1962), inspired by Balzac, used humour and BRECHTian techniques to uncover bourgeois economics. His masterpiece was *El Rabdomante* (*The Diviner*, 1965), a play that incorporated his earlier techniques of SATIRE, social commentary and humour into an absurdist mould (see THEATRE OF THE ABSURD). His several one-act plays, which he called 'games' and 'toys', are also important.

**Salisbury Court Theatre** (London) This indoor theatre, built of brick and stone, was the last to be erected before the Civil War. It was opened in 1630 as a home for the Children of the King's Revels. A surviving drawing may be INIGO JONES's design; it shows a semicircular stage in a rectangular frame 53ft by 37ft. Prince Charles's Men and Queen Henrietta's Men played there before 1642. During and after the Interregnum WILLIAM BEESTON staged performances there, before it was destroyed in the Great Fire of 1666.

**Salle des Machines** (Paris) A large theatre in the Tuileries palace, it was lavishly equipped by GASPARE VIGARANI for celebrations surrounding the marriage of Louis XIV in 1660. It was then used for court opera and spectacles, directed successively by the younger Vigarani, BERAIN and SERVANDONI. It housed the Opéra between 1763 and 1770 and, briefly, the COMÉDIE-FRANÇAISE after 1770.

**Saltykov-Shchedrin, Mikhail (Evgrafovich)** [N. Shchedrin] 1826–89 Russian satirist, novelist, playwright and journalist. He exposed hypocrisy, petty tyranny, and spiritual and moral bankruptcy at all levels of tsarist society. Once a provincial governor, he became a journalist in the liberal press. His major narrative works include *Provincial Sketches* (1856), an anti-bureaucratic SATIRE; *History of a Town* (1869), a PARODY of Russian history and an attack on tsarist tyranny via the study of a mythical town named 'Stupidville'; *The Golovlyovs* (1880), a gloomy chronicle of a family's gradual self-destruction; and *Fables* (1869–86), which employs the traditional Russian device of Aesopian language to criticize the status quo. His writings were staged during his lifetime. His two plays met with more resistance. *Pazukhin's Death* (1857), which depicts another monstrous family, received its provincial and Moscow premieres in 1889 and 1893, respectively. *Shadows* (1862–5), another satire on the world of clerks and bureaucrats, was first staged in 1914. Saltykov's satire was tentatively embraced by the Soviet regime.

**Salvini, Tommaso** 1829–1915 Italian actor-manager. Born into the profession, he joined the young company of GUSTAVO MODENA, whose stage reforms in favour of simplicity, naturalness and psychological truth greatly influenced his development. By his late teens he was playing lead roles opposite the principal actresses of the age, including RISTORI. In 1856 he gave one of the first significant performances of a SHAKESPEARE play in Italy when he played Othello at Vicenza; shortly afterwards he appeared as Hamlet. His repertoire was never large and these roles (to which he later added Macbeth, King Lear and Coriolanus), along with a handful of Italian parts – like Corrado in GIACOMETTI's *La morte civile* (*Civil Death*) and the title role in ALFIERI's *Saul* – formed the cornerstone of his later foreign touring repertoire. He became the most internationally celebrated actor of his age, enjoying a triumphant histrionic progress from 1869 onwards to his retirement, through North and South America, Western Europe and Russia. The opening performance of his Othello at the Boston Conservatoire in 1873 was an unqualified triumph, repeated two years later in London, where the gradually unleashed savage animality of his Moor astonished critics and public alike.

Endowed with rich physical attributes – a powerful, sonorous voice, a striking and muscular figure, and perfect command of gesture and movement – he brought intelligence and imaginative perception to his preparation and execution of roles, on occasions retiring from the stage for months at a time in order to study a new piece. Critics and practitioners, from Henry James and THÉOPHILE GAUTIER to BERNARD SHAW, from Ristori to BERNHARDT to STANISLAVSKY, were unanimous in his praise. The success of his British tour in 1876 through a dozen provincial cities is witness to the spell he could exercise on spectators wholly ignorant of the language in which he performed.

**Samson, Joseph Isidore** 1793–1871 French actor. His career was particularly associated with the COMÉDIE-FRANÇAISE. He had his first successes in the repertoire of SCRIBE, with Bertrand de Rantzau in *Bertrand et Raton* (1833) and the doctor in *L'Ambitieux* (*The Ambitious Man*, 1834). He also wrote a number of plays and helped to found the Society for Dramatic Artistes. Later roles included André in *Le Chandelier* (*The Candleholder*, 1852) and the marquis in *Mlle de Seiglière* (1851). He had a fine reputation as a teacher at the Conservatoire, where RACHEL was one of his protégés.

**San Francisco Mime Troupe** American collective. The group had existed in embryonic form since 1955, but was founded in 1962 by R. G. Davis, who moved to San Francisco after studying MIME in Paris. Over the years it moved from silent mime to avant-garde happenings to outdoor COMMEDIA DELL'ARTE performance and on to radical politics. The collective, a medium for expression of the members' social and political concerns, is based on the highly physical techniques of *commedia dell'arte* and Davis's dance and mime training. The amplified aesthetic suits the outdoor venues in which the troupe regularly performs. Davis left the troupe in 1970; Joan Holden has been the chief resident playwright since 1967. In recent years the troupe has undertaken extensive touring in the USA as well as in Europe and in Central America, including the successful *I Ain't Yo' Uncle*, an African-American deconstruction of *UNCLE TOM'S CABIN*.

**Sánchez, Florencio** 1875–1910 Uruguayan playwright. He later settled in Argentina. The self-taught Sánchez was a faithful observer of daily life, of the customs and people of his time. During the so-called Golden Decade (1900–10) he wrote plays that reflected traditional values in an age when the predominance of urban life and immigrant population signalled rapid change in lifestyles. *La gringa* (*The Foreign Girl*, 1904) and *Barranca abajo* (*Down the Gully*, 1905) are his two masterpieces, depicting characters who struggle against insurmountable obstacles. Don Zoilo in the latter play is a memorable figure whose despair leads him to suicide.

**Sánchez, Luis Rafael** 1936– Puerto Rican playwright and novelist. Influenced by IONESCO and by his compatriot, RENÉ MARQUÉS, his *Sol 13, Interior* (*Sol 13, Inside*, 1961) consisted of *La hiel nuestra de cada día* (*Our Daily*

*Gall*) and *Los ángeles se han fatigado* (*The Angels Are Tired*), plays in contemporary working-class Puerto Rican settings, thematically linked to classical motifs. *O casi el alma* (*Or Almost the Soul*, 1964) posits Christ in a theological discussion on Puerto Rico. *La pasión según Antígona Pérez* (*The Passion according to Antígona Pérez*, 1968) is an 'American chronicle' of Latin American revolution using BRECHTian techniques and the Antigone dilemma. *Quíntuples* (*Quintuplets*, 1984) consists of interlocking monologues that characterize the foibles of the Morrison quintuplets.

***sandae-gǔk*** ('mountain or hillside ritual') Korean masked dance-drama. A generic term, *sandae-gǔk* is performed on a high stage, or uses a mound of earth for a stage. It is preserved by local performers through oral tradition. Performances are RITUAL occasions specific to the village or area.

**Sandow, Eugen** [Ernst Friedrich Möller] 1867–1925 German strong-man. Sandow was the first stage Hercules to turn his physique into a commercial property. He developed a system of body-building through attention to individual muscle groups. At his London debut at the Royal Aquarium (1889), he wrestled the champion Samson. Later his weight-lifting included a 312lb dumb-bell and a 600lb cart-horse. At the Chicago Columbian Exposition of 1893, FLORENZ ZIEGFELD glorified him with spectacular publicity, abbreviated costumes and such stunts as having him lift his pianist with the grand piano. Sandow advertised products like corsets and health oils and promoted several physical culture magazines. He retired in 1907.

**Sangallo, Bastiano da** [Aristotile] 1481–1551 Italian architect and stage designer. He was a crucially influential figure in the evolution of perspective staging and scenic effects; few examples of his scenic work have survived. Both BUONTALENTI and VASARI were his pupils and learned much from him.

**Sanger, 'Lord' George** 1827–1911 English showman. His first CIRCUS opened in Kings Lynn, and in 1860 he originated the first three-ring circus at Plymouth Hoe. In 1871 he bought ASTLEY's Amphitheatre, enlarged it and opened it as Sanger's Grand National Amphitheatre with the PANTOMIME *Lady Godiva*. He staged mammoth spectaculars that earned him a fortune. In 1893 he let the Ecclesiastical Commissioners pull down Astley's, but carried on his gigantic TENT SHOW until 1905.

**Sanquirico, Alessandro** 1777–1849 Italian scene designer. From 1817 to 1832 Sanquirico was the sole designer and chief scene painter for La Scala in Milan. He designed operas by Bellini, Donizetti, Mozart, Meyerbeer and Rossini, thus exerting great influence on the development of grand opera. The most important included the premieres of Rossini's *La Gazza Ladra* (1827), Bellini's *Norma* (1831) and Donizetti's *Lucretia Borgia* (1834). His settings were on a vast scale, using a richly decorated architectural foreground and opening out to a broad landscape view painted with a single-point perspective. Gas lighting evoked the correct atmosphere against his painted scenery. His work created a standard for opera design in Italy and elsewhere in the mid-19th century.

**Sanskrit theatre** Ancient Indian theatre. It is difficult to date the origin of Sanskrit theatre. Fragments of the earliest known plays have been traced to the 1st century AD, but their sophistication suggests that a living theatre tradition must have existed earlier in India.

The period between 1000 and 100 BC saw the rise of the great Hindu epic literature, particularly the *Mahabharata*, the longest and most comprehensive document of ancient Indian life; the *Ramayana*, a somewhat shorter but no less important epic work; and the *Puranas*, a major collection of stories dealing with the life and exploits of Krishna, incarnation of the god Vishnu.

Sanskrit theatre has left no tangible evidence of its early history. It is possible to glean the outlines of the Sanskrit theatre only in the surviving plays and descriptions from other sources. The most important single source is the *Natyasastra* of Bharata Muni, a work which has been variously dated to between 200 BC and AD 200. *Natya* means 'drama' or 'theatre'. *Sastra* is a generic term referring to any authoritative text. The author of the *Natyasastra* bears the name of the first tribe of India and his name has come to mean 'actor' as one of an occupational group. Theatre is said to have been the inspiration of Brahma, the god of creation. In chapter one, Bharata describes – as follows – how theatre came into being.

When the world was given over to sensual pleasure, Indra, king of the gods (one of India's earliest major deities), approached Brahma and asked that he create a form of diversion that could be seen as well as heard and that would be accessible to the four occupational (colour) groups (*varnas*) – priests, warriors, tradesmen and peasants. Out of his state of meditation, Brahma created drama (*natya*), which he referred to as a fifth *Veda*, or sacred text. Brahma requested that Indra compose plays and have the gods enact them. Not considering it appropriate for gods to act, Indra asked that the priests (*brahmanas*) be recruited to take on this task. Bharata and his sons were summoned by Brahma and persuaded to serve as the first actors, which they willingly agreed to do. And Brahma, knowing what he had in mind when he created theatre, taught them the art himself.

To fulfil additional personnel needs, Brahma created heavenly nymphs to act and dance, and musicians were recruited to play and sing to accompany the show. The occasion of the first performance was established to depict and coincide with the defeat of the demons by the gods, celebrating Indra's victorious leadership. Brahma explains the purpose of drama – that it is meant to educate and entertain – and thus no subject may be excluded from consideration; those who correctly observe the ritual sacrifices connected with performance will be protected from evil and will enjoy success.

Bharata's simple story reveals many important facts about Sanskrit theatre: (1) it is composed of sacred material; (2) a specialist should witness it; (3) it should be performed by members of the priestly caste, the top rank in the hierarchy of the caste system; (4) it requires special knowledge and skill to execute it; (5) training is a hereditary process passing from father to son and descending directly from God; (6) special skills are necessary to execute theatre, such as dance, music, recitation and ritual knowledge; (7) it should be performed on consecrated ground; (8) its purpose is to entertain as well as to educate.

The *Natyasastra* is broad in scope – broader than ARISTOTLE's *Poetics*, the other major document of theatre practice surviving from the ancient world. It covers acting, theatre architecture, costuming, make-up, properties, dance, music and play construction, as well as the organization of theatre companies, audiences, dramatic competitions, the community of actors and RITUAL practices, to name only a few of the more important subjects of the book.

Within the theatre companies, the actors studied under the guidance of a drama teacher (*natyacharya*), probably the stage manager; under his guidance, it was their job to keep physically and vocally fit for performance by undergoing rigorous training. Men and women both seem to have been permitted to act together or in separate troupes of their own sex. The Sanskrit plays that survive confirm the use of stock character types such as the hero (*nayaka*), heroine (*nayika*) and clown (*vidushaka*). Two styles of acting appear to have been common – the realistic (*lokadharmi*) and the conventional (*natyadharmi*), the latter receiving almost exclusive attention in the text.

The well rounded actor of Sanskrit plays was expected to go beyond external representation of character through correct execution of movement, speech and ornamentation. Although acting is obviously a very important part of theatre, the social status of the actors does not seem to have been particularly high in ancient India. Bharata may have been a Brahmin priest, but Sanskrit actors were classed with bandits and prostitutes, according to most ancient authorities. Among the musicians were male and female vocalists, flautists who performed on bamboo instruments, and players of stringed instruments.

Sanskrit theatre was performed to celebrate important religious occasions, in connection with temple festivals. The *Natyasastra* calls the performance of plays a visual sacrifice (*yajna*) to the gods and thus clearly identifies it as a sacred event. And yet we also know that performances were organized to celebrate coronations, marriages, the birth of children, the return of a traveller and the defeat of an enemy. Literally hundreds of plays were written from the 1st to the 10th century AD, the high point of Sanskrit dramatic output. The author for whom we have the greatest abundance of works is BHASA, whose 13 surviving plays cover a wide range of subject-matter and at least one of which, *The Vision of Vasavadatta* (*Svapnavasavatta*), is among the most important works of Sanskrit dramatic literature.

One of the most popular works of ancient India is *The Little Clay Cart* (*Mrcchakatika*), attributed to Sudraka. No other works have been traced to Sudraka and yet it is hard to believe that a writer could have produced only one brilliant work and remained silent the rest of his life. The preface to the play describes the author in considerable detail, indicating that he was a king, a mathematician, knowledgeable in love and skilled in the training of elephants.

Arguably, India's greatest playwright is KALIDASA, whose life and dates remain a mystery. He could have been court poet of King Chandragupta II of Ujjain in the mid-5th century AD. His undisputed literary masterpiece is *Abhijnanasakuntala* (*Sakuntala and the Ring of Recognition*), which, like *The Little Clay Cart*, has been produced frequently in modern times. Kalidasa's craftsmanship is regarded as the best example of the adherence of a Sanskrit poet to the classical rules without sacrificing his own artistic integrity. The play is a delicate exploration of human love. The source of the story may be found in the *Mahabharata*. Among the major playwrights of a later period of Sanskrit drama,

Bhavabhuti stands out above the others. He appears to have lived around AD 700 and was a member of the court of a north Indian king. His *The Latter History of Rama* is among the best Sanskrit plays: it adapts incidents from the epic *Ramayana* and develops unique and creative twists to the plot. Like other later writers, Bhavabhuti succumbs to the temptation to embellish his writing with lengthy poetic expressions.

Rather than serving as a reflection of life in ancient India, Sanskrit drama served as a model of ideal human behaviour. The idealization of the characters, their values and actions, all point to this lofty ultimate aim. It was not a drama of protest or of reaction; guided by the *Natyasastra*'s rules, the writers cooperated and lived within their society rather than breaking down barriers or exhibiting individualistic points of view.

The 10th century marks the end of Sanskrit theatre as an active force in Indian art.

**Santana, Rodolfo** 1944– Venezuelan playwright. Santana has written more than 50 plays, most of them performed and/or published. An early period was dominated by metaphysical, absurdist (see THEATRE OF THE ABSURD) and science-fiction plays. Later he used Kafkaesque techniques to examine cruelty, violence, sex and revolution in contemporary society: *La muerte de Alfredo Gris* (*The Death of Alfredo Gris*, 1968) and *El sitio* (*The Siege*, 1969) are examples. A third, more eclectic, period included experimentation with historical materials (*Barbarroja*, 1970) as well as sociopolitical issues. Other works include the monologue *La empresa perdona un momento de locura* (*The Company Allows a Moment of Madness*, 1979), *El animador* (*The MC*, 1980) and a play about boxing, *Fin del Round* (*End of the Round*, 1981).

**Santareno, Bernardo** [Antonio Martinho do Rosario] 1920–80 Portuguese playwright. Driven by indignation against all forms of exploitation and injustice, Santareno was the dramatist who reflected most closely the aspirations of the people in the Salazar era. In the theatre he developed a highly naturalistic and compelling dramatic construction and dialogue, from *A Promessa* (*The Promise*, 1957), through most of the 18 plays he wrote, up to the unpublished *O Punho* (*The Fist*). Many plays were banned or withdrawn (see CENSORSHIP). His *Crime de Aldeia Velha* (1959) shows superstition, rural backwardness and mass hysteria leading to a witch trial and burning, every bit as powerfully as MILLER's *The Crucible*. *O Judeu* (*The Jew*, 1966) is a harrowing reconstruction of the infamous Inquisition trial of the 18th-century dramatist DA SILVA, and of the society which could countenance such an institutional crime.

**Saqui, Madame** [Marguerite-Antoinette-Sévère Lalane; La Belle Nini] 1777–1866 French rope-dancer. At 15 she made a thunderous debut at the CIRQUE OLYMPIQUE. In 1809 she married the acrobat and impresario Saqui. Her exploits included vaulting over 24 armed soldiers and dancing on a cord stretched between the towers of Notre Dame. When she performed before Napoleon, she was set ablaze by the fireworks. From 1816 she performed quick-change roles in her own booth on the Boulevard du Temple. Penniless, she returned to touring, amassing 32,000 francs, which were stolen by highway robbers when she was 75. She returned to Paris and could be seen in the Champ de Mars pushing a child in a wheelbarrow across the tightrope.

**Sarcey, Francisque** 1827–99 French critic. From 1860 he was drama critic for *L'Opinion Nationale* and in 1867 he

took on Sainte-Beuve's Monday column in *Le Temps*, which he continued until his death. His criticisms were published as *Quarante Ans de théâtre* (1900–2). Sarcey was much respected by actors, who knew him as 'uncle' Sarcey, and noted for his impartiality. His tastes were conservative and he placed great emphasis on common sense and professionalism. He believed that the critic should go with the current of popular opinion and try to shape it, rather than offer absolute principles, and that a play should be judged according to its own conventions.

**Sardou, Victorien** 1831–1908 French playwright. Like SCRIBE, Sardou was a master-craftsman of the theatre. He developed the WELL MADE PLAY by exploiting successful formulae (G. B. SHAW coined the term 'Sardoodledom'). For instance, every exit and entrance has a distinct purpose for the development of the plot. He wrote large-scale historical plays and comedies reflecting French society towards the end of the Second Empire. After a couple of early attempts, *A Scrap of Paper* (*Pattes de Mouches*, 1860), at the Théâtre du Gymnase, established his reputation as a master of stagecraft and skilfully manipulated intrigue. Other comedies are *La Famille Benoîton* (1865), *Nos Bons Villageois* (*Our Good Villagers*, 1866), *Rabagas* (1872), a hard-hitting political SATIRE; and the *vaudeville Let's Get a Divorce* (1880). *Patrie* (*Fatherland*, 1869) and *La Haine* (*Hatred*, 1874) are historical dramas. He wrote a series of plays for SARAH BERNHARDT: *La Tosca* (1887), *Cléopâtre* (1890) and *Gismonda* (1894); his historical comedy *Madame Sans-Gêne* was played first by RÉJANE in 1893, showing him to be more at home in historical comedy than in more serious works, where his psychology lacks depth. Two of his late plays, *Robespierre* (1899) and *Dante* (1903), were written to be staged by IRVING. *L'Affaire des poisons* (1907) exploited a particularly seamy side of the court of Louis XIV.

**Saroyan, William** 1908–81 American playwright. This Californian Armenian made his debut as a playwright with *My Heart's in the Highlands* (1939). Both the GROUP THEATRE and the THEATRE GUILD had a hand in its production, and although most playgoers were baffled by its loose allegorical form, the play established Saroyan as the leading avant-garde playwright of the day. His next play, *The Time of Your Life* (1939), became a modern American classic, with its wit, humanity and local San Francisco colour. He continued to write for the stage through the late 1950s, his later works including *Love's Old Sweet Song* (1940), *The Beautiful People* (1941), *Hello Out There* (1942, a one-act play), *Get Away Old Man* (1943) and *The Cave Dwellers* (1957), but none of them matching the success of his first two.

**Sartre, Jean-Paul** 1905–80 French philosopher, novelist and playwright. Sartre proposed a 'theatre of situations' in which characters are defined not by their psychological states, but by their choices and actions. In his world of interpersonal relations each person struggles to control the other, and this makes for exciting dramatic situations – well exemplified in *Huis clos* (*In Camera*, 1944), which has become a masterpiece of the modern theatre. Sartre's career as a playwright began with *Les Mouches* (*The Flies*, directed by DULLIN, 1943), a modern version of the Electra story which was seen in occupied Paris as a call to resistance. In the late 1940s he wrote many plays, including *Les Mains sales* (*Dirty Hands*, 1948) about political expediency and *Le Diable et le bon Dieu* (*The Devil and the Good Lord*, 1951). In *Les Séquestrés* d'Altona (*The Condemned of Altona*, 1959) he came nearest to writing a tragedy of modern times with the story of a young German whose attempts at free choice during the Hitler period were falsified by the subsequent turn of historical events. Despite his lifelong interest in Greek tragedy (e.g. his adaptation of EURIPIDES' *Trojan Women*), Sartre's imagination was essentially melodramatic, in the manner of ALEXANDRE DUMAS *père*, whose work he brilliantly adapted.

**Sastre, Alfonso** 1926– Spanish playwright and theorist. Influenced by such authors as CAMUS and PIRANDELLO, he is known for his plays of social awareness. He founded Teatro de Agitación Social in 1950, publishing his ideas on socially committed theatre as an instrument of reform in *Drama y sociedad* (1956). In 1956 he founded the Grupo de Teatro Realista, performing his own and others' works.

Sastre's plays are not outspoken or overtly political – rather, suggestive and symbolic, a necessary concession during the Franco regime (1939–75). Several were banned (see CENSORSHIP), including *Escuadra hacia la muerte* (*Death Squad*, 1953), a play set in a bunker 'during the next war', and *En la red* (*In the Web*, 1961), inspired by the Algerian war. A long period of conflict with the Franco regime culminated in his imprisonment two decades later. Other plays from this period are *Prólogo patético* (*Pathetic Prologue*, 1949), about the morality of terrorist action; *El cuervo* (*The Raven*, 1957), a 'time-slip' play of suspense; and *La cornada* (*Death Thrust*, 1960), describing the last hours of a bullfighter and his exploitative manager. Among his most widely performed plays are *Guillermo Tell tiene los ojos tristes* (*Sad Are the Eyes of William Tell*, 1962), an ironic inversion of the historical tale, and *Historia de una muñeca abandonada* (*Story of an Abandoned Doll*, 1964).

Dating from the mid-1960s are his 'complex tragedies', which combine elements of classic TRAGEDY with BRECHTian techniques and a use of the grotesque reminiscent of VALLE-INCLÁN. Two historical plays from this group, *La sangre y la ceniza* (*Blood and Ashes*, 1967) and *Crónicas romanas* (*Roman Chronicles*, 1970), have been performed successfully abroad. Sastre's long-awaited integration into mainstream Spanish theatre came in 1985 when he was awarded the National Theatre Prize for *La taberna fantástica* (*The Fantastic Tavern*, 1966).

**satire** BURLESQUE, PARODY and satire are often treated as synonyms for ridicule through distortion, but it is useful to suggest distinctions between them. None of the three words refers exclusively to drama; yet all have been applied to drama. Although sometimes confused with the Greek satyr play (see GREEK THEATRE, ANCIENT), the word 'satire' is of Roman origin, meaning a dish of mixed fruit, and the long poems first called satires mixed several literary techniques. The satirical technique, however, is already evident in the Greek comedies of ARISTOPHANES.

Satirists tend to assume some moral or social norms by which degrees of wickedness or folly can be measured, offering ridicule with a moral, meliorative intention. Sometimes claimed as a genre distinct from comedy, satire can vary from the gentle mockery of SHAKESPEARE or MOLIÈRE to the bitter thrust of MARSTON or LESAGE. Perhaps the most celebrated modern satirist is SHAW, but BRECHT also draws upon its long tradition in such plays as *Man Is Man*.

**satyr play** see GREEK THEATRE, ANCIENT

**Satz, Ludwig** 1895–1944 American Yiddish comedian.

He was a much loved leading star of the American YIDDISH THEATRE from 1918 until his death. Billed as 'the man who makes you laugh with tears and cry with a smile', he was a master of characterization, improvisation and make-up.

**Saunders, James** 1925– British playwright. His early plays were influenced both by English poetic drama and by the French absurdists (see THEATRE OF THE ABSURD). His first stage success came with *Next Time I'll Sing to You* (1963), suggested by the life of an Essex hermit, Jimmy Mason. The actors, who discuss the recluse, act episodes from his life and wonder what they are supposed to be doing, are themselves presented as lonely individuals. Loneliness is also a theme in *A Scent of Flowers* (1964), about a young girl who died from lack of love. Literary experiment is a feature of Saunders's prolific output, with echoes of IONESCO, PIRANDELLO, BECKETT and even BEAUMONT and FLETCHER (in *The Borage Pigeon Affair*, 1969). He collaborated with Iris Murdoch in adapting her novel, *The Italian Girl* (1968), for the stage. He has worked primarily among the smaller theatres around London and has been a strong supporter of the amateur QUESTORS THEATRE. His major WEST END success was *Bodies* (1978), about two middle-aged couples facing crises in their lives. *Making It Better* (1992) was a comedy about a World Service radio producer at the time of the Velvet Revolution in Czechoslovakia.

**Savary, Jérôme** 1942– French actor, director, playwright and film-maker. Savary founded (with ARRABAL) the Grand Théâtre Panique. This became the Grand Magic Circus in 1968 and produced a series of highly successful shows, part CABARET, part social SATIRE, usually performed in unconventional theatre spaces. In 1981 he applied his irreverent performance techniques to MOLIÈRE's *Le Bourgeois Gentilhomme*. In 1982 he became director of a new Maison de la Culture at Béziers, and in 1988 artistic director of the Théâtre National de CHAILLOT.

**Savits, Jocza** 1847–1915 German director. Savits pioneered the 'SHAKESPEARE-stage' in the Munich Court Theatre between 1888 and 1906. With it he attempted, without much success, to re-create the non-illusionistic playing conditions of the Elizabethan theatre. Despite the incompleteness of his achievement, his experiments pre-dated those of the Englishman WILLIAM POEL and also influenced GEORG FUCHS in his founding of the Munich Artists' Theatre.

**Saxe-Meiningen, Duke of** see MEININGEN COMPANY

**scaenae frons** see SKĒNĒ

**Scamozzi, Vincenzo** 1552–1616 Italian architect and stage designer. From the school of PALLADIO, on the latter's death he completed the Teatro Olimpico at Vicenza (1585), and was responsible for the Teatro Olimpico at Sabbioneta, completed in 1590. His work on both theatres shows his original and imaginative borrowing from classical models; both are supreme examples of late Renaissance theatrical architecture.

**Scaparro, Maurizio** 1932– Italian director. He began his career as a theatre critic for the socialist newspaper *Avanti!*, moving on to practical stage work in Bologna. A highly informed director – with a literary as well as a theatrical instinct, and a talent for drawing out in production the social implications of the plays he directs – he has always displayed a keen interest in recovering neglected work from the Italian repertory, including lesser-known GOLDONI pieces and rarely performed

Renaissance plays, like ARIOSTO's *La Lena* (1964) and the anonymous *La Venexiana* (1984), as well as pieces from the modern repertory, like PIRANDELLO's *Liolà* (1992). His major SHAKESPEARE productions have included *Hamlet* and *Richard II*. Since 1982 he has been co-director, with GIORGIO STREHLER, of the Paris-based Théâtre de L'Europe, and in 1983 succeeded LUIGI SQUARZINA as the director of the Teatro Stabile in Rome, where his productions include an adaptation of Marguerite Yourcenar's *The Memoirs of Hadrian* (1989).

**Scarpetta, Eduardo** 1853–1925 Italian actor and playwright. At an early age he rose to fame in the Neapolitan theatre with a FARCE character type, Don Felice Sciosciammocca. For several years he worked closely with the actor-writer ANTONIO PETITO, writing and staging pieces in Neapolitan dialect. After Petito's death he formed his own company, performing in several Neapolitan theatres and producing work like *Lo Scarflietto* (*The Bed Warmer*, 1881), *Il romanzo di un farmacista povero* (*The Story of a Poor Chemist*, 1882) and, particularly, *Miseria e nobilità* (*Poverty and Nobility*, 1888). Although much of his work was a Neapolitanization of French farce, he reformed the theatre by eliminating the gratuitous LAZZI of the old tradition and rooting comedy in recognizable local life. He retired in 1914, having dominated the Neapolitan stage for some 40 years. His successor as a master of Neapolitan comedy, EDUARDO DE FILIPPO, was a member of his company in its last years.

**Scarron, Paul** 1610–60 French playwright and man of letters. Rheumatic disability gave him a capacity for self-mockery. He published collections of BURLESQUE verse and his first play was in that vein: *Jodelet, ou Le Maître-Valet* (*Jodelet, or The Master-Servant*), a vehicle for the comedian JODELET at the MARAIS in 1645. More comedies followed, some adapted from Spanish originals, including *Don Japhet d'Arménie* (1647), his best play, and *L'Écolier de Salamanque* (*The Student of Salamanca*, 1654). Their verbal wit and stylistic incongruity make them less accessible now, except for *Le Roman comique* (*The Comical Romance*), a long picaresque romance in two parts (1651 and 1657) about a troupe of strolling players.

***scena per angolo*** Italian scenic device. FERDINANDO BIBIENA is credited with this Renaissance innovation in stage design, the *scena per angolo* or multipoint (angled) perspective, in 1703. Until this time, all perspective scenery had a single vanishing point – for a spectator seated in an ideal position, the scenery seemed to disappear at a single point in the distance. Because of this, the scenery also appeared to be an extension of the auditorium; it was in the same scale as the spectators. Multipoint perspective, as the name implies, could have several vanishing points. This freed the stage from the auditorium. The scene behind the proscenium no longer had to conform to the scale of the spectators: it could be larger than life. There was no need for symmetry; a scene could be shown from any point of view. The designs of the Bibienas in the 18th century were marked by soaring splendour, as seemingly vast rooms and colonnades disappeared in the heights above the proscenium and divergent corridors seemed to dissolve into the far depths of the stage.

**scenic design** see THEATRE DESIGN

**Schechner, Richard** see PERFORMANCE GROUP; THEATRE DESIGN

***Schembartläufer*** Austrian masked figures. They are associated with Bavarian and Austrian CARNIVAL, partic-

ularly Nuremberg. Their name, as well as denoting obvious attributes of their appearance and behaviour (they are bearded (in German, *Bart*), and 'run' (*Läufer*, runner) through the streets), also suggests that they are phantoms. Their masks, though always bearded, are female as well as male; they carry staves or lances, and their behaviour is wild and threatening. They are recorded as throwing ashes, and sometimes burning embers, into the crowd.

***Schicksaltragödie*** ('fate tragedy') German theatrical genre. This form of play, popular in Germany during the romantic period, represents *in extremis* the Sophoclean concept of fate (see SOPHOCLES) as an inescapable force. The most celebrated *Schicksaltragödie* was ZACHARIAS WERNER's *The 24th of February* (1810), which owed much to GEORGE LILLO's *Fatal Curiosity* and itself influenced ALBERT CAMUS's *Le Malentendu*. GRILLPARZER's first play *The Ancestress*, though of a far higher standard than most *Schicksaltragödien*, has affinity with some popular plays of this genre.

**Schikaneder, Emanuel** 1751–1812 Austrian actor and singer. Schikaneder, a highly successful impresario in the Viennese popular theatre, is best known today as the librettist for Mozart's *The Magic Flute* (1791). Partly as a result of the immense popularity of this opera, he was able to build the Theater an der Wien.

**Schiller, Friedrich** 1759–1805 German playwright, historian and aesthetician. Schiller's contribution to the development of German drama is equal in quality and importance to that of GOETHE, with whom he was closely associated during the last nine years of his life. Schiller's first play, *The Robbers* (1781), written while he was a disaffected recruit in the military academy in Württemberg, is among the greatest of all first plays. Though dependent on SHAKESPEARE and imitative of the STURM UND DRANG movement of the previous decade, it is in its depiction of the Moor brothers, one of whom is a monster of malice, the other of titanic disaffection, *The Robbers* has a unique power. Of his next two plays, written while he was house dramatist at Mannheim, *Fiesko* (1781–2) and *Love and Intrigue* (1782–3), the latter is still stageworthy despite its strident tone, because of Schiller's intense sense of outrage at the injustice of the class system. *Don Carlos* (1787) has an unwieldy plot, and changes in tone half-way through: the first part, involving Don Carlos's fear and hatred of his father Philip II, belongs to *Sturm und Drang*; the second part elevates the tragedy to a more complex plane.

The next ten years Schiller devoted to the study of history, philosophy and aesthetics, in 1789 becoming professor of history at Jena University, close to Weimar. His trilogy on the Thirty Years War general, Wallenstein – *Wallenstein's Camp*, *The Piccolomini* and *Wallenstein's Death* (all 1799) – is a tragedy that belongs to the rank of world drama. He labelled his next play, *Maria Stuart* (1800), a 'romantic tragedy' possibly because of the disquieting appeal of his beautiful heroine and his dispassionate portrayal of the political forces to which she falls victim. *The Bride of Messina* (1803) was a deliberate revival of Greek tragedy (see GREEK THEATRE, ANCIENT). His final completed work was the ever-popular *Wilhelm Tell* (1804), which throws doubt upon the viability of the romantic personality embodied in the enigmatic figure of Tell. Schiller possessed a surer understanding of the practical stage than Goethe, and his tragedies have proved more durable than much of Goethe's dramatic work. As a result, Schiller is widely regarded as the national dramatist of Germany.

**Schiller, Leon** 1887-1954 Polish director, manager and composer. Influenced by GORDON CRAIG, he assimilated his views into the Polish tradition of MICKIEWICZ and WYSPIAŃSKI. He began directing in his mid-30s, staging old Polish nativities and mysteries (see MYSTERY PLAY). He founded the Bogusławski Theatre (1924-6), where he developed a monumental style based on the Polish romantic repertory and combining elements of EXPRESSIONISM, constructivism and cubism with the use of large crowds, PISCATOR's technique of montage, and revolutionary themes. In the 1930s he moved to radical political theatre and neo-REALISM. After the war, he created the State Theatre Institute. Major productions are Miciński's *Revolt of the Potemkin* (1925), Wyspiański's *Achilleis* (1925), Krasiński's *Undivine Comedy* (1926), BRECHT's *Threepenny Opera* (1929), SŁOWACKI's *Kordian* (1930), Mickiewicz's *Forefathers' Eve* (1932) and TRETYAKOV's *Roar, China* (1932).

**Schlegel, A(ugust) W(ilhelm)** 1767-1845 German literary historian and translator. Schlegel's work did much to familiarize the public with the ideas of the romantics. In particular, his *Lectures on Dramatic Art and Literature*, first delivered in Vienna in 1808, covered the whole field of Western drama, creating an awareness of how genuinely popular the theatre had been in past ages. The ideal of such a theatre was shared by many romantics. Schlegel was also a translator of genius, and his versions of 17 of SHAKESPEARE's plays, published between 1797 and 1810 (the series was completed by Dorothea Tieck and Wolf von Baudissin in 1833), are regarded by some as being as close in quality as can possibly be to the original. Schlegel also adapted EURIPIDES' *Ion*, which was produced by GOETHE at Weimar in 1802.

**Schlegel, J(ohann) E(lias)** 1719-49 German playwright and aesthetician. Although he was associated with GOTTSCHED, Schlegel had a strong appreciation of SHAKESPEARE and of his works as an alternative to the neoclassical tradition. However, as a playwright he is known as 'the German RACINE'. Of his several neoclassical tragedies, *Canute* (1746) is possibly the most original.

**Schlemmer, Oskar** 1888-1943 German sculptor, painter and designer. Basing his work upon mathematical analysis of the geometric shapes that the body (or parts of the body) makes as it moves through space, Schlemmer created masks and costumes that suggested, in Walter Gropius's words, 'moving architecture'. The most complete integration of his ideas was achieved in the *Triadic Ballet* (1912-22), a highly structured and schematized series of dance scenes. His work with the Bauhaus, where he was head of the stage workshop from 1923 to 1929, influenced postwar design and modern dance. Schlemmer also designed for the commercial theatre and dance - notably the KOKOSCHKA-Hindemith opera, *Mörder, Hoffnung der Frauen* (Murder, Hope of Women), creating settings in the style of the expressionist painters (see EXPRESSIONISM).

**Schmidhuber de la Mora, Guillermo** 1943- Mexican playwright. He was for many years director of the Alfa Technological Museum in Monterrey. His major works include *Nuestro señor Quetzalcóatl* (Our Lord Quetzalcóatl, 1974), *Todos somos el rey Lear* (We Are All King Lear, 1979), *Los herederos de Segismundo* (Segismundo's Heirs, 1980) with its attribution to CALDERÓN DE LA BARCA's *Life Is a Dream*, *El día que Mona Lisa dejó de sonreír* (The Day Mona Lisa Stopped Smiling, 1987) about the death of Leonardo da Vinci, and *El quinto viaje de Colón* (Columbus's Fifth Voyage, 1992).

**Schneider, Alan** [Abram (Leopoldovich) Schneider] 1917-84 Russian-born American director and critic. Known as BECKETT's American interpreter, Schneider made his debut as a director with SAROYAN's *Jim Dandy* (1941) and worked at Washington's ARENA STAGE and New York's NEIGHBORHOOD PLAYHOUSE. He was also drama critic for the *New Leader* until 1965. Director of the Juilliard Theater Center (1976-9) and at his death a co-artistic director of the ACTING COMPANY, he believed his main function was to serve as intermediary between the playwright and production.

Schneider directed premieres of, among others, Beckett's *Waiting for Godot* (Miami, Florida, 1956), *Endgame* (1958), *Happy Days* (1961), *Play* (1964) and the movie *Film* starring Buster Keaton (1964). He also received acclaim for The PINTER Plays (*The Collection* and *The Dumb Waiter*, 1962), ALBEE's *Who's Afraid of Virginia Woolf?* (1963), *Tiny Alice* (1965) and *A Delicate Balance* (1967) and ROBERT W. ANDERSON's *You Know I Can't Hear You When the Water's Running* (1968).

**Schnitzler, Arthur** 1862-1931 Austrian playwright and short story writer. Schnitzler's training as a doctor is often considered to have influenced fundamentally his attitude as a dramatist. His plays are mainly ironic analyses of life in contemporary Vienna. *Anatol* (1893) and *La Ronde* (1900), both cycles of one-act plays that disclose the anxieties lying behind the gracious appearance and easy sexual mores of the city's life, are best-known internationally. But his greatest achievement probably lies in his full-length plays - in the moving and tragic VOLKSSTÜCK, *Liebelei* (The Game of Love, 1895); the melancholy drama, *The Lonely Way* (1904); the bitterly satirical survey of Viennese society, *The Vast Country* (1911); and the powerful play on antisemitism in Vienna, *Professor Bernhardi* (1912). Though he was only slightly acquainted with Freud, there is a remarkable concordance between Freud's and Schnitzler's perceptions of the human condition, one Freud himself acknowledged.

**Schönemann, Johann (Friedrich)** 1704-82 German actor. Schönemann took over the leadership of the Neuber troupe after CAROLINE NEUBER had broken with GOTTSCHED. He continued for several years to perpetuate the LEIPZIG STYLE of acting, though his pre-eminence in the profession declined as a result of the rise of REALISM in acting, associated with EKHOF.

**Schönherr, Karl** 1867-1943 Austrian playwright. Schönherr was best-known for his grim and powerful realistic dramas about peasant life in the Tyrol. Among the most successful of his plays are *The Picture Carvers* (1900), *Midsummer Day* (1902), *Carnival People* (1905) and *Faith and the Homeland* (1910).

**Schreyvogel, Josef** 1788-1832 Austrian director. From 1815 Schreyvogel was artistic director of the BURGTHEATER. During this time he established the famous ensemble style of the company, translated and produced important Spanish plays, and introduced the plays of GRILLPARZER.

**Schröder, Friedrich (Ludwig)** 1744-1816 German actor and playwright. The stepson of KONRAD ACKERMANN, Schröder spent most of his youth as a comic actor in Ackermann's troupe, which he took over on his stepfather's death in 1771. In 1776, he established it on a permanent basis at the Hamburg Town Theatre. From 1780 to 1784 he was with the Vienna

BURGTHEATER, returning finally to Hamburg. As an actor, Schröder was famous for his unvarnished realism, powerful climaxes and distinct characterization. Such acting was referred to as the HAMBURG STYLE, and was later regarded as antithetical to the WEIMAR STYLE. In Hamburg he introduced to the stage several STURM UND DRANG plays and, most importantly, many of SHAKESPEARE's works, which he adapted. His production of Hamlet in 1776, with BROCKMANN as Hamlet and himself as the Ghost, was a landmark in the introduction of Shakespeare to the German stage. Schröder was a skilled playwright and adapted the work of several other English dramatists, including SHERIDAN, for German audiences. He was the original for the figure of the actor-manager Serlo in Goethe's novel Wilhelm Meister's Apprenticeship.

**Schröder, Sophie** 1781–1868 German actress. The most important years of Sophie Schröder's career were between 1815 and 1829 when she was a leading actress at the BURGTHEATER under SCHREYVOGEL. Here she gave the first performance, in 1818, of GRILLPARZER's Sappho and, in 1821, of his Medea. In these and in classic roles, her acting was regarded as the epitome of romanticism.

**Schwartz, Maurice** ?1890–1960 American Yiddish actor, director and playwright. Starting in 1906, he soon achieved success and founded the YIDDISH ART THEATRE in 1918 at the Irving Place Theatre in New York, where his carefully selected company included Celia Adler, JACOB BEN-AMI, BERTHA GERSTEIN, Anna Apfel and LUDWIG SATZ, and where he set the highest standards in play selection, production values and acting. From a long sequence of great roles, his Yoshe Kalb, Shylock and Tevye stand out. His company appeared several times on BROADWAY in both Yiddish and English, and toured the world. (See also YIDDISH THEATRE.)

**Scofield, (David) Paul** 1922– British actor. His first substantial work dates from 1942 when he joined the BIRMINGHAM REPERTORY THEATRE under the direction of BARRY JACKSON, whom he followed to the Shakespeare Memorial Theatre in Stratford-upon-Avon in 1946. A series of Shakespearian roles have included one of his most renowned performances, Lear in PETER BROOK's production of 1962 (subsequently filmed, 1969) for the ROYAL SHAKESPEARE COMPANY, and portrayals of Macbeth (RSC, 1967), Prospero in The Tempest (Leeds Playhouse, 1974), Othello (NATIONAL THEATRE, 1980) and Oberon (National Theatre, 1982). But he has not been limited to Shakespearian roles. His Sir Thomas More in BOLT's A Man for All Seasons (Globe Theatre, London, 1960; filmed, 1966) remains one of the great performances in postwar British theatre, and work in plays by contemporary playwrights (OSBORNE's Hotel in Amsterdam (1968), HAMPTON's Savages (1973), SHAFFER's Amadeus (1979), for instance) has given evidence of Scofield's power, range and versatility. He starred in Jeffrey Archer's Fleet Street drama Exclusive (1989) and played Shotover in TREVOR NUNN's production of SHAW's Heartbreak House (1992). In 1994 he was memorable as both Chuzzlewit brothers in the BBC adaptation of DICKENS's novel.

**Scott, George C.** 1927– American actor and director. Noted for his artistic integrity and intense acting style, Scott has combined stage work with an outstanding film career. He made his New York debut as Richard III in the New York Shakespeare Festival (1957), followed by Children of Darkness (1958). He appeared as Ephraim Cabot in Desire under the Elms (1963). Sly Fox (1976), based

on Volpone, was a BROADWAY success. He directed and starred in NOËL COWARD's Present Laughter in 1982, directed Design for Living in 1984 and directed and starred in PAUL OSBORN's On Borrowed Time in 1991. He has also played Antony and Shylock with the NEW YORK SHAKESPEARE FESTIVAL.

**Scribe, (Augustin) Eugène** 1791–1861 French playwright and librettist. One of the most prolific writers of the 19th-century theatre, Scribe is considered the creator of the WELL MADE PLAY, much imitated by LABICHE and SARDOU. He tried every genre, often in collaboration, but his favourite was the vaudeville (nearly 250 pieces, over half of his total output), in which he observed the bourgeoisie of his day with great accuracy. His characters are not highly developed, but are sustained by the sheer force of the dramatic action: he prepares a situation, prolongs it, and finally sorts it out.

In 1821 he was contracted as a house dramatist to the Théâtre du Gymnase, recently opened as a fashionable BOULEVARD theatre, and over the next ten years turned out some 150 plays for it. L'Héritière (The Heiress, 1823), written with G. Delavigne, became a classic of the Gymnase repertoire. Bertrand et Suzette; ou Le Mariage de raison (1826), in which a girl leaves the man she loves in favour of a mercenary marriage, created a scandal, but is one of his best plays. He explored this theme further in a play for the COMÉDIE-FRANÇAISE, Le Mariage d'argent (The Mercenary Marriage, 1827). Also for the Comédie-Française, Scribe developed a new type of political-historical comedy in which the characterization is more sustained than in the vaudevilles, including The School for Politicians (Bertrand et Raton; ou L'Art de conspirer, 1833), La Camaraderie (1837), La Calomnie (1840), The Glass of Water (1840), Une Chaîne (1841), Adrienne Lecouvreur (1849), specially written for RACHEL, and The Ladies' Battle (1850). He was also librettist for some 28 operas as well as nearly 100 opéras-comiques.

**Scudéry, Georges de** 1601–67 French playwright and poet. Formerly a soldier, he wrote tragedies, tragicomedies and comedies – irregularly constructed, rhetorical and full of extravagant or violent incidents – for the companies at the HÔTEL DE BOURGOGNE and the MARAIS. La Comédie des Comédiens (The Actors' Comedy, 1635) presents on stage the company of actors under MONTDORY who performed it. In 1637 he published his adverse comments on PIERRE CORNEILLE's Le Cid, thus initiating the influential literary controversy. He was elected to the Académie-Française in 1649.

**seaside entertainment** see PIERROT SHOWS

**Sedaine, Michel-Jean** 1719–97 French playwright and poet. A former stonemason by trade and largely self-educated, he shared the views of his friend DIDEROT on widening the subject-matter and social range of contemporary drama. Le Philosophe sans le savoir (A Philosopher without Knowing It, COMÉDIE-FRANÇAISE, 1765), his most progressive play, is a serious bourgeois COMEDY, mixing domestic realism with sentiment. This and his one-act comedy La Gageure imprévue (The Unforeseen Gamble, 1768) were well received. The bulk of his output consisted of opéras-comiques, or comedies with music, on which he collaborated with various composers for performance at the COMÉDIE-ITALIENNE and the theatres of the Paris fairs.

**Segelcke, Tore** 1901–79 Norwegian actress. With her colleagues Gerd Egede Nissen and Aase Bye, she dominated the female repertoire at the NATIONALTHEATRET from the 1930s to the 1950s. Specializing in roles demanding both inner strength and emotional spontaneity, she was particularly successful in O'NEILL (Nina Leeds, Lavinia Mannon and Josie Hogan) and IBSEN. Her Nora was admired for its clear through-line and she was an especially strong Agnes in *Brand*. Among her later successes were Mrs Alving and the role of Pelagea Vlassova in BRECHT's *The Mother*. She was much acclaimed during her 1956 tour of the USA.

**Segura, Manuel Ascencio** 1805–71 Peruvian playwright. His lively and spontaneous efforts to capture local colour and life in a popular vein resulted in the best-known, most played, Peruvian work of all time – *Ña Catita* (1856), a portrait of a Lima matchmaker.

**Seibel, Beatriz** 1934– Argentine critic, director and playwright. She has had success with children's theatre – *De gatos y lunas* (*Of Cats and Moons*, 1965) – and with adult theatre such as *Siete veces Eva* (*Seven Times Eve*, 1982) and *Canto latinoamericano* (*Latin American Song*, 1985). She often incorporates historical and literary items into her theatre.

**Sellars, Peter** 1958– American director. Sellars, who had directed over 100 productions by the age of 27, first came to prominence as a Harvard undergraduate when he directed *The Inspector General* for the AMERICAN REPERTORY THEATRE (1980–1). Briefly artistic director of the Boston Shakespeare Company (1983–4), he then became head of the American National Theatre Company at the JOHN F. KENNEDY CENTER in Washington, DC, a post which he left in 1986, becoming head of the Los Angeles Festival in 1990. Among Sellars's ambitious and controversial productions have been Handel's *Orlando* (1982), BRECHT's *The Visions of Simone Machard* (1983), a GORKY–GERSHWIN mélange at the GUTHRIE called *Hang On to Me* (1984), *The Count of Monte Cristo* (1985) and Sophocles's *Ajax* (1986), featuring a Rambo-type Vietnam general. Since the late 1980s he has concentrated on directing opera, on both sides of the Atlantic. A memorable and controversial production of *The Merchant of Venice* (1994) came briefly to London's Barbican Theatre.

**Semyonova, Ekaterina (Semyonovna)** 1786–1849 Russian actress. A favourite of PUSHKIN, she was often compared to MLLE GEORGE, whose singsong, declamatory delivery she emulated in a rich contralto voice. A female serf, Semyonova was trained by DMITREVSKY and, beginning in 1803, excelled in the roles of tragic heroines to which she brought ardent emotionalism. Her career is closely linked with those of ALEKSANDR SHAKHOVSKOI and of OZEROV, whose plays she performed in the 1810s. Although she played Sofia in the original St Petersburg cast of *Woe from Wit* by GRIBOEDOV, her career suffered when classical tragedy gave way to romantic drama on the Russian stage. She and her famous fellow company member A. S. YAKOVLEV straddled the line between two acting traditions, one artificial, the other more realistic. During 1820–2 she temporarily retired from the stage. In 1826 she married Prince S. Gagarin, thereafter using her power to terrorize her enemies and rivals, especially young actresses. Her notable roles include RACINE's Clytemnestra and Phaedra, VOLTAIRE's Mérope and SCHILLER's Mary Stuart.

**Seneca** [Lucius Annaeus Seneca; Seneca the younger] c.4 BC–AD 65 Roman playwright. Seneca won fame as an orator and Stoic philosopher, and, after a period of exile, was made tutor to the young Nero, over whom he exercised a benign influence for some years, while amassing immense wealth for himself. He retired from public life in AD 62, and in 65 was accused of complicity in the Conspiracy of Piso and forced to commit suicide.

Ten plays are ascribed to Seneca in medieval manuscripts. The probably authentic ones are *Hercules Furens*, *Troades* (*Trojan Women*), *Phoenissae* (*Phoenician Women*), *Medea*, *Phaedra*, *Oedipus*, *Agamemnon* and *Thyestes*. *Oedipus* is based on SOPHOCLES (*Oedipus Tyrannus*), *Agamemnon* on AESCHYLUS, *Thyestes* on an unknown (perhaps Latin) source, the rest on EURIPIDES. The adaptation, however, is always free, as Seneca selects only those scenes of the original plays which suit his purpose, and makes many additions and rearrangements. Of the plays considered spurious, *Octavia* is of interest as the only surviving *fabula praetexta*, or play on a historical subject (see ROMAN THEATRE). It concerns events in AD 62, when Nero divorced his wife Octavia and then ordered her execution, and was evidently written after Nero's death, which it prophesies.

It is disputed whether the plays were written for stage performance or merely (like most non-dramatic Latin poetry) for recitation to a small private audience. They contain nothing that can not be staged, but dramatic realities are persistently neglected; often, for instance, it is impossible to determine when a character enters, as he turns out to be present only when he starts to speak. It is anyway probable that Seneca would have thought it beneath his dignity to write for the theatre. Certainly his main concern is with the rhetoric of speeches. He portrays the heightened passion throughout, while striving at the same time for neatness and cleverness in his epigrams and rhetorical conceits. These purposes work against each other, giving, to modern tastes, an extremely artificial effect and eliminating all possibility of subtle characterization. The plays in general are Stoic in their portrayal of the evils stemming from passion and ambition, but evil always prevails. Every tragedy builds up to a violent climax, related in extravagant terms by a messenger towards the end.

Senecan tragedy came into its own in the Renaissance, when the plays were sometimes performed at universities. Among the tragedies of Elizabethan and Jacobean England Senecan influence is most obvious in inferior plays; but without that influence, the tragedy of the period might not have existed at all.

**Serban, Andrei** 1943– Romanian-born American director. He made his debut in the USA with *Arden of Feversham* at LA MAMA in 1970 and, after a year with PETER BROOK, staged *Medea*, *The Trojan Women* and *Electra* (1974), becoming one of the prominent figures in contemporary American theatre. His productions are noted for their minimalism and simplicity of detail. Among notable examples are a controversial comic interpretation of *The Cherry Orchard* in an all-white setting (NEW YORK SHAKESPEARE FESTIVAL, 1976); *Agamemnon* (Lincoln Center, 1977); *The Ghost Sonata* at the YALE REPERTORY THEATRE, where he worked in 1977–8; *The Marriage of Figaro* (GUTHRIE THEATRE, 1982); and *Uncle Vanya*, with JOSEPH CHAIKIN (La MaMa, 1983). He has worked frequently at the AMERICAN REPERTORY THEATRE, e.g. GOZZI's *The King Stag* and *The Love for Three Oranges* (1984) and BULGAKOV's *The Master and Margarita* (1986) and *The Serpent Woman* (1989). He has also directed operas. While continuing to direct in the West, in 1990 he was appointed head of the National Theatre of

Bucharest. Romanian productions include *An Ancient Trilogy, Twelfth Night* and *The Cherry Orchard*. Since 1992 he has taught at Columbia University, New York.

**serf theatres** (Russia) Serfs – Russian servants, or slaves – were attached to the land and belonged to their owners. Catherine the Great's 1762 charter freed the landowning gentry from state obligations; left with time on their hands, some of their energies were given over to the creation of spectacular entertainments, which fed their egos and promoted their image among their social peers and the visiting dignitaries who were sometimes in attendance. This led to the beginning of the serf theatre, in which indentured performers were treated as gifted children and had bestowed upon them monetary and amorous favours alternating with torture and public humiliation. Eventually numbering 173 venues, the serf theatres of Prince Yusupov, NIKOLAI SHEREMETIEV and others were the best-equipped and most lavishly appointed facilities in the land. In the 1840s the rising fortunes of the Imperial municipal theatres and falling rural landowners' profits caused these theatres to close or be absorbed into touring companies, the latter precipitating the birth of the provincial repertory system. The spectre of serfdom, abolished in 1861, haunts CHEKHOV's plays, and the lot of the provincial actor is well described by OSTROVSKY.

**Serlio, Sebastiano** 1475–1554 Italian architect. In 1525 he went to Rome to work with BALDASSARE PERUZZI. Before going to Paris in 1541 he designed a temporary wooden theatre in Vicenza, said at the time to be the world's largest, the only specific theatre architecture Serlio is known to have been responsible for. *Architettura* (1537–51), his seven-volume commentary on Vitruvius' *De Architectura*, was probably the most influential and significant Renaissance work on architecture. Book 2, published in 1545, contained a short section on theatre architecture and design which formed the basis for theatre practice throughout Europe for the next two centuries.

Serlio combined his study of antiquity with Renaissance aesthetics and technology, thereby creating the foundation for the development of the proscenium stage and illusionistic scenery. His theatre plan included a long, narrow stage and semicircular arrangement of seats taken from the classical Roman theatre. But he also assumed that the theatre would be contained in a rectangular space, so that the seating plan was truncated. More importantly, the main stage was backed by a deep, raked, scenic stage that contained stock perspective scenery on flat frames enhanced by 'wooden relief'. The three scenes were the tragic, comic and satyric. The first contained a street with stately houses, statuary and the like. The comic was a street containing houses of ordinary citizens and was to include a tavern, a courtesan's house and a church. And the satyric depicted a PASTORAL setting. By 1620 his writings on theatre were translated into five languages. (See also THEATRE BUILDINGS; THEATRE DESIGN)

**Serreau, Jean-Marie** 1915–73 French director. Having trained with DULLIN, Serreau contributed to the success of the THEATRE OF THE ABSURD, directing plays by ADAMOV, GENET, IONESCO and BECKETT. But he also directed one of the first plays by BRECHT to be performed in France (*The Exception and the Rule*, 1947) and in the 1960s became identified with the post-Brechtian political theatre of writers such as CÉSAIRE and YACINE. In the 1960s his innovative approach led to a series of experiments in multi-media performance, attempting to find a synthesis between science and poetry.

**Serulle, Haffe** 1947– Dominican Republic fiction writer and playwright. *Duarte* (1975) and *El hatero del Seybo* (*Pedro Santana*, 1976) are historical plays. His others denounce a variety of secular evils: *La danza de Mingó* (*Mingó's Dance*, 1977), *Prostitución en la casa de Dios* (*Prostitution in God's House*, 1978), *Testimonio de un pueblo oprimido* (*Testimony of an Oppressed People*, 1980), *Miriam la buena* (*The Good Miriam*, 1982) and *Bianto y su señor* (*Bianto and his Master*, 1984).

**Serumaga, Robert** 1940–81 Ugandan playwright. Educated at Trinity College, Dublin, he returned to Uganda in 1966 and founded the semi-professional Theatre Ltd, later known as the Abafumi Players. Subsequently he created notable dance dramas with a group of school-leavers whom he trained as professional performers and with whom he travelled widely. His published plays are *A Play* (1967), *The Elephants* (1970) and *Majangwa* (1971).

**Servandoni, Giovanni (Niccolò)** [Jean Nicolas Servan] 1695–1766 Italian architect, painter and stage designer. He moved to Paris in 1724, and from 1728 was principal designer at the Paris Opéra. Between 1738 and 1742 and again in the 1750s he mounted in the SALLE DES MACHINES displays of spectacular changeable scenery, machines and lighting effects with his own scenarios. He also painted scenery at COVENT GARDEN (1749) and at Württemberg (1763). Servandoni's designs, with their impressive perspectives and diagonal vistas, mark the high point of illusionistic scenery.

**Settle, Elkanah** 1647–1724 English playwright. His tragedy *The Empress of Morocco* (1669) was the first play published in England with illustrations of the performance. He wrote numerous heroic tragedies, including *The Female Prelate* (1680), a play on Pope Joan, before turning to operatic spectacle. His adaptation of *A Midsummer Night's Dream* as *The Fairy Queen* with music by Purcell (1692) contains spectacular scenes of music and dancing. In 1679 his comedy *The World on the Moon* was performed with extravagant machine effects. From 1683 Settle also wrote drolls, shortened comic versions of plays for fairground performance. In 1691 he became city poet and produced city pageants for London until 1708.

**Séveste, Pierre-Jacques** 1773–1825 French theatre manager. In 1817, after the restoration of the monarchy (1814), he was granted a licence to erect theatres in the Parisian suburbs. His first was the Théâtre Montparnasse (1819), followed by the larger Théâtre de Montmartre (1822). His actors were usually badly paid, and often of semi-amateur status. After his death his family continued to exploit their monopoly of suburban theatres until 1851, by which time they were becoming the real 'popular' theatres of Paris.

**Sewell, Stephen** 1953– Australian playwright. His plays, written from a Marxist perspective, share an episodic structure, powerful theatrical effects and a preoccupation with the tension between political commitment and private emotion. They include *The Father We Loved on a Beach by the Sea* (1976), *Traitors* (1979), *Welcome the Bright World* (1982), *The Blind Giant Is Dancing* (1983), *Dreams in an Empty City* (1986), *Sisters* (1991), *King Golgruther* (1991), a grotesque allegory-fantasy of corporate greed; and a TELEVISION DRAMA, *The Long Way Home* (1985). His less overtly political work focuses on family relationships in *Sisters* (1991) and *The Garden of Granddaughters* (1993).

**Seydelmann, Karl** 1793–1843 German actor. He was one of the greatest virtuosi of the 19th century. His interpretation of classic roles, especially Carlos in *Clavigo*, Mephistopheles, King Philip in *Don Carlos*, and Shylock, were distinguished for the dryness and individuality of his approach. For some of his critics, Seydelmann acted with little attention to the role's context within the play; for others, he was the epitome of the 'thinking' intellectual actor.

**Seymour, William** 1855–1933 American actor, director and stage manager. Among Seymour's many management positions figured the Union Square Theatre, the MADISON SQUARE THEATRE, the Metropolitan Opera House, CHARLES FROHMAN'S EMPIRE THEATRE in New York; and the BOSTON MUSEUM, where he spent a decade (1879–88).

**shadow puppets, shadow theatre** Form of entertainment in which flat figures of a non- or semi-transparent material reflect stylized shadows against a screen, and are moved to music or chant. All Oriental shadow theatres began as illustrations to narration. In Indonesia (Java and Bali) the figures of the *wayang* (i.e. silhouette) theatre are usually of water-buffalo hide: the *wayang klitik* figures are flat with one movable arm; those of the *wayang golek* are three-dimensional with movable heads and arms. The forms of the characters are traditional, the differences in size and colour indicating their type and temper. The *dalangs*, or showman-reciters, perform only by invitation and are used to spread religious and dynastic propaganda; they now present drawing-room versions of traditional plays. The tales are drawn from South Indian myth and RITUAL. The play is performed on a screen 13ft long and 5ft high set up in an inner verandah; it begins at sundown after a long musical introduction, and goes on into the night.

The *piyingxi* of China is a form of miniature opera. The translucent figures of coloured parchment cast coloured shadows in this synthesis of painting, song, music and manual choreography. The technique originated in the song era (960–1279) as depictions of the folkloric tales *shuo-shu*, but soon evolved a distinct repertory of historic and Buddhist themes. During the Japanese occupation, it was used for Resistance propaganda, and during the Korean War the communist government exploited it in training soldiers. For a short period in the 1950s it was influenced by the American comic strip, but has reverted to the traditional love stories, criminal cases and battles.

**Shadwell, Thomas** c.1642–92 English playwright. Most famous as the target of DRYDEN'S SATIRE *MacFlecknoe* (1678), Shadwell in fact succeeded Dryden as Poet Laureate after 1688. His adaptation of MOLIÈRE'S *Les Fâcheux* as *The Sullen Lovers* (1668) was followed by *The Humorists* (1670) and *Epsom Wells* (1672) in the style of JONSON. The best of his satiric comedies are *The Virtuoso* (1676), which includes mockery of the pseudo-science of the Royal Society; *The Squire of Alsatia* (1688), with its virtuoso display of the language of the criminal underworld; and *Bury Fair* (1689), which explores provincial aping of London manners. His dark comic version of the Don Juan story, *The Libertine*, was performed in 1675, and his contemporary political version of SHAKESPEARE'S *Timon of Athens* in 1678.

**Shaffer, Peter (Levin)** 1926– British playwright. His early play, *Five Finger Exercise*, was successfully produced in 1958. This demonstrated a command of drawing-room comedies and drama, suggesting that Shaffer was a natural successor to TERENCE RATTIGAN. The first stage play to fully combine his flair for craftsmanship with his wider preoccupations – which include an interest in music and in religious and philosophical subjects – was *The Royal Hunt of the Sun* (NATIONAL THEATRE, 1964), about the destruction of the Inca civilization in Peru by the Spanish Conquistadores led by Pizarro; and the contrast between the Inca god-king, Atahuallpa, and Pizarro anticipated future moral conflicts in later plays. An amusing FARCE, *Black Comedy* (1965), was another NT hit, and later matched with *White Lies* (1968) to form a double bill in the WEST END. Although *The Battle of Shrivings* (1970) was less successful, Shaffer's two subsequent plays, *Equus* (1973) and *Amadeus* (1979), both produced at the NT, were acclaimed as masterpieces. In *Equus*, a weary psychoanalyst attempts to grapple with the mysteriously Dionysian faiths of a delinquent youth, while in *Amadeus* the composer Salieri bitterly watches the progress of his divinely inspired rival, Mozart. Both plays contrast reason with faith, materialism with inspiration. *Yonadab* (1985) echoes some of these themes without providing so powerful a myth. In his comedy *Lettice and Lovage* (1987) a romantic historical tour guide converts a pedantic, fact-bound historian. *The Gift of the Gorgon* (1992), about a Dionysian dead playwright and his Apollonian widow, attracted polarized reviews – familiar in criticism of Shaffer.

His twin brother, Anthony, is also a dramatist and a novelist, and they have collaborated on three detective novels, published in the early 1950s.

**Shakespeare, William** 1564–1616 English playwright. Though Shakespeare's plays are better known than those of any other playwright in the world, knowledge of his life relies on a few surviving scraps of evidence. Born in Stratford-upon-Avon, Warwickshire, son of a prosperous glover who became Chief Alderman in 1571, he is assumed to have attended the local grammar school. Within six months of his marriage to Anne Hathaway (1582) their daughter Susanna was born. The family was completed with the birth of twins, Judith and Hamnet, in 1585. Hamnet died in 1596.

Shakespeare's supposed life as an actor in London is unrecorded before ROBERT GREENE'S jibe at the 'upstart crow' in 1592. Greene, a university man, may have resented Shakespeare's part in the writing of the three *Henry VI* plays. In 1594 Shakespeare purchased a share in the newly formed LORD CHAMBERLAIN'S MEN, possibly helped by his patron Henry Wriothesley, Earl of Southampton, to whom the narrative poem *Venus and Adonis* (1593) had been dedicated. By 1594 he had also written at least three comedies, *The Comedy of Errors*, *The Two Gentlemen of Verona* and *The Taming of the Shrew*, and two tragedies, *Titus Andronicus* and *Richard III*, as well as a second narrative poem, *The Rape of Lucrece*. His hand has also been detected in the collaborative play *Sir Thomas More* (c.1595).

About this time Shakespeare was writing approximately two plays per year for the Lord Chamberlain's Men at the THEATRE. The period 1594–8 may have seen the first productions of *King John* (sometimes dated as early as 1589); the middle comedies, *Love's Labour's Lost*, *A Midsummer Night's Dream* and *The Merchant of Venice*; the popular tragedy *Romeo and Juliet*; and the cycle of English HISTORY PLAYS comprising *Richard II*, the two parts of *Henry IV* and *Henry V*. In 1597 he bought New Place, one of the finest houses in Stratford. At the end of

1598 his company were forced to leave the Theatre and erected the GLOBE.

Shakespeare wrote most of his greatest plays during the first decade (1599–1608) at the Globe. They include the mature comedies, *Much Ado About Nothing* (which may shortly pre-date the move), *As You Like It* and *Twelfth Night*; the darker comedies, *All's Well that Ends Well*, *Measure for Measure* and *Troilus and Cressida*; a pot-boiler, *The Merry Wives of Windsor*, written in response to demands for more of Falstaff; and the major tragedies, *Julius Caesar, Hamlet, Othello, King Lear, Macbeth, Antony and Cleopatra, Coriolanus* and *Timon of Athens*. In this period the Lord Chamberlain's Men were honoured with the title of King's Men and confirmed in their ascendancy at court.

The Jacobean taste for sensation and spectacle was more easily satisfied in the indoor BLACKFRIARS, which the King's Men added to the outdoor Globe in 1608. Shakespeare's last plays, *Pericles, Prince of Tyre* (on which he collaborated, probably with George Wilkins), *Cymbeline, The Winter's Tale* and *The Tempest*, take account of the revived interest in romance and magic whilst giving scope for scenic spectacle. At the end of his career he returned to collaborative work, joining forces with FLETCHER on *Henry VIII, The Two Noble Kinsmen* and the lost *Cardenio*. By 1613, when the Globe was destroyed by fire, his hold on the London theatre was slipping. He spent his last years in Stratford.

**Texts**
Only 16, less than half of Shakespeare's plays, were published during his own life. Plays were held in low esteem as literature and acting companies guarded their possessions from other companies. There were unauthorized, 'pirated' publications of unreliable texts, like the famous 'bad' Quarto of *Hamlet* (1603). So it was an act of singular homage when two of the King's Men, JOHN HEMINGES and HENRY CONDELL, oversaw the publication, in lavish Folio form, of 36 plays by their late colleague. The First Folio (1623, reprinted 1632, 1664 and 1685) includes 20 plays which might otherwise never have been published. The first critical edition was that of NICHOLAS ROWE (1709), who, using the Fourth Folio as his authority, respected Shakespeare's text but regularized the plays' division into scenes and acts. Later 18th-century editors, including Alexander Pope (1725), LEWIS THEOBALD (1734), SAMUEL JOHNSON (1765) and Edmond Malone (1790), followed Rowe's pattern. Modern editors are served by the Variorum editions pioneered by H. H. Furness in 1871. There are reliable single-volume collections and an expurgated 'Family Shakespeare' produced by Thomas Bowdler in 1818.

In the late 20th century there has been a movement away from the notion of a single perfect text for a Shakespeare play, claiming that different versions may be the result of revisions made by the playwright or his company during the process of rehearsal and performance. Outstanding among 20th-century series are the variously edited Arden, New Cambridge, Penguin and Oxford Shakespeares.

**Shakespeare performance in England**
From the early days of the Restoration theatre until well into the 19th century it was normal practice to hack, reshape and plunder Shakespeare's texts to suit prevailing tastes: e.g. NAHUM TATE's *King Lear* (1681) and COLLEY CIBBER's *Richard III* (1700). THOMAS BETTERTON doctored the texts himself, setting a precedent which would be followed by later actor-managers from DAVID GARRICK

through JOHN PHILIP KEMBLE, W. C. MACREADY, CHARLES KEAN and HENRY IRVING, to BEERBOHM TREE and the 20th century. Betterton's versions used changeable scenery. The actors' formal delivery at the front of the stage, in the full light of the candelabra, enacted through gesture the passions expressed in their lines. Garrick's memorable debut as Richard III (1741) was an energetic, and eventually decisive, challenge to the old-school conventions.

As the London theatres got bigger only a presence as imposing as that of SARAH SIDDONS or as charismatic as that of EDMUND KEAN could command an audience of over 3,000. With the advent of gas lighting during the 1830s came greater visibility, allowing actors to play inside, rather than in front of, the scenery. 'Pictorial Shakespeare' under the various regimes of Macready, MADAME VESTRIS, Charles Kean, Irving and Tree made the visual elements of Shakespearian production as important as the aural. The splendour of the crowded 19th-century stage of SAMUEL PHELPS was finally challenged by WILLIAM POEL's sequence of bare-stage productions for the Elizabethan Stage Society in 1894.

The replacement of the actor-manager by the director distinguishes 20th-century Shakespearian production. GRANVILLE BARKER's work at the Savoy (1912–14) demonstrated how the text could be released by the clearing of the cluttered stage. TYRONE GUTHRIE dared radically to reinterpret Shakespeare's plays. At the rebuilt Shakespeare Memorial Theatre KOMISSARZHEVSKY's unconventionally designed productions (1933–9) brought Stratford-upon-Avon into new prominence, and in 1960 PETER HALL became the managing director of the newly named ROYAL SHAKESPEARE COMPANY. Most of the major English actors and directors have worked at Stratford, or at the company's London bases, the Aldwych (1960–82) and the Barbican (since 1982). The conventions of modern Shakespearian production – that the director should discover the leading idea or ideas of a play and reinforce them through design (see THEATRE DESIGN) and COSTUME on a stage that permits the free flow of scenes – have been authorized by the Royal Shakespeare Company.

**Shakhovskoi, Prince Aleksandr (Aleksandrovich)**
1777–1846 Russian director and playwright. An indefatigable force in the 19th-century theatre, he was director of the repertory section of the Imperial Theatre (1802–26); author of over 100 plays; an acting teacher, whose famous pupils included E. S. SEMYONOVA, V. A. KARATYGIN and I. I. SOSNITSKY; a translator-adapter from French, German and English; and one of Russia's first serious *régisseurs*.

Shakhovskoi forged an acting style based on French models. His dramatic output includes tragedies, MELODRAMAS, *vaudevilles*, opera librettos, patriotic historical dramas; and, most notably, satirical comedies of manners, the first of which was *A Woman's Jest* (1796). *The New Sterne* (1805) made him famous. His most controversial comedy, *Lesson for Coquettes, or The Lipetsk Spa* (1815) was also the first five-act Russian play to set its entire action out of doors.

Initially concerned to preserve old literary forms, Shakhovskoi eventually embraced romanticism, co-authoring a comedy *All in the Family, or The Married Fiancée* (1817) with GRIBOEDOV, whose early work he had influenced, and KHMELNITSKY. In *Seigneurial Pursuits, or Home Theatre* (1808) he characterized the SERF THEATRE and introduced the stage type of the upstart landowner, reprised in his *Tranchirin's Boast* (1822) which marked the acting debut of MIKHAIL SHCHEPKIN. Shakhovskoi's *The Cossack Poet* (1812) is generally considered to be the first Russian *vaudeville*. His longest-running play, *The Bigamous Wife* (1830), was an early attempt to portray the merchant class on stage.

**shaman** Witch-doctor, medicine man, cunning person or professional sorcerer. His (less frequently her) skills are various: human and veterinary medicine, the location of lost goods and people, the identification of witches and counter-measures against them, the ability to harm an enemy magically. The method of work is usually a RITUAL performance employing literary, musical, dramatic or choreographic techniques. Typically, the shaman is one whose own affliction has been cured by a shamanic ritual.

**Shange, Ntozake** [*née* Paulette Williams] 1948– African-American playwright and novelist. Shange's first play *For Colored Girls Who Have Considered Suicide When the Rainbow Is Enuf* (1976) brought immediate acclaim. The play called for seven women to recount their life experiences. More conventional was *A Photograph: A Study in Cruelty* (1977), followed by *Spell #7* (1978), an extended choreopoem of character revelations using poetry, song, dance and masks; *Boogie Woogie Landscapes* (1980); a revisionist adaptation of BRECHT's *Mother Courage* (1980); and a rhythm-and-blues musical collaboration *Betsey Brown* (1991), based on her 1985 novel. *The Love Space Demands* was performed in 1992. Her novel, *Liliane*, was published in 1994.

**Shank, John** died 1636 English actor. He joined the King's Men (see LORD CHAMBERLAIN'S MEN) at some point between 1613 and 1619 and, in the old comic tradition of gagging CLOWNS, performed JIGS and wrote at least one, *Shank's Ordinary* (1624). The most provocatively interesting of the parts allotted to him is that of the waiting-woman Petella in a revival of FLETCHER's *The Wild Goose Chase*, exploiting the broad comic potential of the clown in a female role.

**Sharaff, Irene** 1910–93 American COSTUME designer. By the early 1930s she was designing major BROADWAY plays and, primarily, musicals such as *As Thousands Cheer* and *On Your Toes*. Through the 1960s she designed many significant musicals including *The King and I* and *West Side Story*. Her Hollywood career began in 1944 with *Meet Me in St Louis* and later included *An American in Paris*, *Cleopatra* and *Who's Afraid of Virginia Woolf?*. Although the latter demonstrated her ability to create pedestrian costumes, she is best known for stylish design and her use of colour. She also had the unusual ability to translate stage productions into film.

**Sharman, Jim** 1945– Australian director. Based in London in the early 1970s, he worked at the ROYAL COURT THEATRE and directed large-scale productions, including *Hair*, *Jesus Christ Superstar* and *The Rocky Horror Show* in London, America and Japan. Returning to Australia in 1975, he specialized in staging PATRICK WHITE's work and has directed with several major companies. In 1992 the Royal Queensland Theatre Company staged his epic drama *Shadow and Splendour*.

**Shaw, Fiona** 1959– British actress. One of a group of striking and individualistic performers (among them JULIET STEVENSON), Shaw grew in stature during the 1980s, through roles to which she could bring her passion and nervous intelligence. She was a free-thinking Mary Shelley in HOWARD BRENTON's *Bloody Poetry* (1984) for the touring company Foco Nova, and a less than sub-

missive Celia in *As You Like It* (ROYAL SHAKESPEARE COMPANY, 1985). She played in CHRISTOPHER HAMPTON's version of *Les Liaisons Dangereuses* (1986). In 1988 she was Electra in DEBORAH WARNER's version of SOPHOCLES' play, prowling the stage with a haggard ferocity. She successfully tackled the role of Hedda Gabler in Warner's production of IBSEN's play for the ABBEY THEATRE (1991). She came to represent women angry at their inferior status in a man's world. Her greatest triumph in the battlefield of the genders came in 1993 with STEPHEN DALDRY's revival of a little-known play by the American Sophie Treadwell, *Machinal*, at the NATIONAL THEATRE, in which she played a woman sent to the electric chair for murdering her husband. In 1995 she played Richard II at the NT.

**Shaw, George Bernard** 1856–1950 Irish-born playwright and critic. He left Dublin for London in 1876, declaring himself a socialist in 1882 and joining the Fabian Society in 1884. Already a prolific writer, he began to develop his witty iconoclasm while music critic for the *Star* (1888–90) and the *World* (1890–4).

The play that he undertook to provide J. T. Grein's INDEPENDENT THEATRE with began as a collaboration with WILLIAM ARCHER, whose interest in IBSEN Shaw shared and had expressed in *The Quintessence of Ibsenism* (1891). But his analysis was too individualistic for Archer. *Widowers' Houses* (1892), with its diagnosis of slum-landlordism, announced Shaw's combative dramatic intentions. Too heretical for the contemporary theatre to accommodate, he had to rely on readings, private production and publication to mount his attack on the entrenched actor-managers and the traditional deceits of the received drama. *Plays Unpleasant* (1898) contained *Widowers' Houses*, the controversial *Mrs Warren's Profession* (first performed 1902) and *The Philanderer* (first performed 1905). More palatable challenges to conventional drama were the *Plays Pleasant* (1898), *Arms and the Man* (1894), *Candida* (1897), *The Man of Destiny* (1897) and *You Never Can Tell* (1899). The *Three Plays for Puritans* (1901), *The Devil's Disciple* (1897), *Captain Brassbound's Conversion* (1900) and *Caesar and Cleopatra* (1907) illustrate the Shavian dictum that 'decency is indecency's conspiracy of silence' and are imbued with his perception of the intellectual flabbiness of the English 19th-century theatre. They complement the dramatic criticisms he contributed to the *Saturday Review* (1895–8), collected in *Our Theatre in the Nineties* (3 vols., 1932), and the published *Prefaces* to his plays (1934).

The regular performance of his plays had to await the seasons at the ROYAL COURT THEATRE (1904–7) under HARLEY GRANVILLE BARKER and J. E. VEDRENNE, who revived earlier plays and mounted new ones which dramatized debates on social and political issues of national importance. *John Bull's Other Island* (1904) drew attention to the persistent Irish question. In *Man and Superman* (1905), a socialist hero outmanoeuvres all his political adversaries but surrenders to the rival life-force of a woman. *Major Barbara* (1905) sets social conscience against conscienceless social reform in a dazzling debate. Beside it, *The Doctor's Dilemma* (1906) seems merely clever.

Further discussion plays like *Getting Married* (1908) and *Misalliance* (1910) maintained Shaw's hold on London theatre. Religious conversion is a major theme in his plays from *Candida* to *Androcles and the Lion* (1913) and beyond, but the satirical account of a thoroughly secular conversion brought him his first popular triumph, *Pygmalion* (1914). Staged by HERBERT BEERBOHM TREE and starring MRS PATRICK CAMPBELL as the flower seller who conquers society through elocution, *Pygmalion* established Shaw as England's leading playwright. Between the outbreak of World War I and his death he wrote more than 30 new plays, but only a few have lasted. They include his most complex discussion play, *Heartbreak House* (1920), the extraordinary philosophical *Back to Methuselah* (1922), the startlingly original historical tragedy, *Saint Joan* (1923), three plays which he termed 'political extravaganzas' – *The Apple Cart* (1929), *Too True to Be Good* (1932) and *Geneva* (1938) – and an underrated comedy, *The Millionairess* (1936). There has also been a revival of interest in *Good King Charles's Golden Days* (1939). Shaw's command of the English-speaking theatre has weakened in recent years, not least because of the birth of a modern political drama to reinforce what used to be his lonely voice.

**Shaw Festival** (Canada) An annual summer festival in Niagara-on-the-Lake, Ontario, devoted to presenting the works of GEORGE BERNARD SHAW and his contemporaries, and home to one of the finest acting ensembles in North America. Inspired by Brian Docherty, the Festival began over four weekends in 1962, and became an annual event. In 1973 an elegant red-brick Shaw Festival Theatre supplemented the company's original home in the historic Court House. By the 1980s the season had stretched to five months. A typical Shaw festival season, under the directorship of Christopher Newton, contains only a handful of plays by Shaw, the remainder being selected from works written during Shaw's considerable lifespan. Newton has assembled a strong core of actors, who are encouraged to return to the Festival for successive seasons.

**Shchepkin, Mikhail (Semyonovich)** 1788–1863 Ukrainian actor. A former serf actor (see SERF THEATRES), he became the acknowledged father of Russian realistic acting and a major influence upon STANISLAVSKY via the latter's teacher GLIKERIYA FEDOTOVA. Shchepkin's professional career began in the provinces in 1805; he later moved to Moscow (1822) and the Maly Theatre (1824). He counted a wide assortment of artist-intellectuals among his personal friends, collaborating with them in the creation of native characters; they included GRIBOEDOV, PUSHKIN, TURGENEV, SUKHOVO-KOBYLIN and, especially, fellow Ukrainian GOGOL. Shchepkin's squat, rotund physiognomy and natural exuberance targeted him from youth for the 'comic old man', to which he added natural warmth and humour, emotional expressiveness, personal dignity and moral strength. By the 1840s he had won acclaim as Famusov in *Woe from Wit* (1830) and as the Mayor in *The Inspector General* (1836). By the 1860s, however, the 'House of Shchepkin', as the Maly was called, became the 'House of OSTROVSKY', in honour of the dramatist whose brand of photographic REALISM achieved success via the performances of a new generation of actors headed by PROV SADOVSKY. In 1897 the Shchepkin legacy passed to the MOSCOW ART THEATRE, to be systematized by Stanislavsky.

**Sheldon, Edward (Brewster)** 1886–1946 American playwright. A graduate of GEORGE PIERCE BAKER's Workshop 47 at Harvard College, Sheldon was an early proponent of social REALISM in America with *Salvation Nell* (1908), a love story involving characters from the Salvation Army at work among New York's squalid immigrant underclass; *The Nigger* (1909), concerned

with the struggle of a southern governor who discovers that his grandmother was an octoroon slave; and *The Boss* (1911), a drama of labour-management conflicts. More obviously romantic plays are *The High Road* (1912), a search for beauty, and *Romance* (1913), where an American clergyman explains his love for an Italian diva. Sheldon also collaborated with such dramatists as SIDNEY HOWARD (*Bewitched*, 1924) and Charles MacArthur (*Lulu Belle*, 1926).

**Shepard, Sam** [Samuel Shepard Rogers] 1943– American playwright, film actor and screenwriter. Although he has not scored a major commercial BROADWAY success, Shepard is arguably the most critically acclaimed, if the most obscure and undisciplined, American dramatist of the past 20 years. He is inventive in language and revolutionary in craft, and his subject-matter is contemporary and American, ranging from myths of the American West, American stereotypes and the death or betrayal of the American dream to the search for roots, influenced by rock and roll, the pop and counter-cultures, Hollywood and hallucinatory experiences. Among his 40-odd plays are *La Turista* (1966); *The Tooth of Crime* (1972), a rock drama written during a four-year period in London; *Curse of the Starving Class* (1978); *Buried Child* (1978); *True West* (1980) and *Fool for Love* (1979), both originally staged at the Magic Theatre in San Francisco where he was playwright-in-residence for several years; *A Lie of the Mind* (1985) and *The States of Shock* (1991), an ambiguous look at post-Vietnam America. In 1994 he directed his play *Simpatico* at New York's Public Theater. Shepard has appeared in several successful films, including his own *Fool for Love*, and wrote the screenplay for *Paris, Texas*.

**Sher, Antony** 1951– South-African born British actor. He trained in London and Manchester and established his reputation with a series of roles between 1975 and 1981, especially as Klestakov in GOGOL's *The Inspector General* (Edinburgh, 1975) and Muhammad, the confused Arab businessman, in MIKE LEIGH's *Goose-Pimples* (1981). He joined the ROYAL SHAKESPEARE COMPANY in 1982 and his Fool in *King Lear* was the first of his brilliantly theatrical creations of Shakespearian characters. Richard III in 1984 was another. Sher has starred (for the RSC) in PETER BARNES's *Red Noses* (1985), and in *The Merchant of Venice* (1988) and *Tamburlaine the Great* (1992), and (for the NATIONAL THEATRE) in STEVE BERKOFF's *The Trial* (1991) and BRECHT's *The Resistible Rise of Arturo Ui* (1991). He is a truly exciting actor, taking risks that are usually triumphantly vindicated.

**Sheremetiev, Count Nikolai (Petrovich)** 1751–1809 Russian manager. He owned the largest and most sumptuous SERF THEATRES in Russia. Familiar with European theatres, he turned his father's serf company on his estate at Kuskuvo, a Moscow suburb, into a fully fledged theatrical enterprise rivalling St Petersburg's court theatres and far surpassing Moscow's public theatres. Sheremetiev imported leading Moscow actors to instruct his company of 95 serf actors, and leading musicians from abroad to train his serf orchestra. A scenic designer (see THEATRE DESIGN) and translator were on staff. Ballets, comedies and *vaudevilles* were staged, but operas were the most popular. In 1801 the count married his leading lady, the serf actress Praskovya Ivanovna (died 1803), to whom he gave the stage name Zhemchugova ('the Pearl'). In order to remove his new wife from her serf environment, he moved his company to the Moscow suburb of Ostankino. There two serf architects erected a theatre with a seating capacity of 300 and a stage equipped with trapdoors, *periaktoi*, flying machines and all manner of special effects. The count treated his serf actors better than those belonging to other landowners and far better than his other serfs.

**Sheridan, Richard Brinsley** 1751–1816 Irish playwright and theatre manager. Born in Dublin, educated at Harrow, he lived in Bath and moved to London, where in 1775 his first three plays were produced. *The Rivals* uses Bath as a setting for a tangled plot in which Lydia Languish's mockery of sentimentalism is pitted against the serious lovers, Faulkland and Julia; the play includes the famous figure of Mrs Malaprop. The other two plays of 1775 were a FARCE, *St Patrick's Day*, and a successful comic opera, *The Duenna*. In 1776 he became manager of DRURY LANE, though he was never a success there. In 1777 he adapted VANBRUGH's *The Relapse* as *A Trip to Scarborough*; and his best play, *The School for Scandal*, was performed. In it he returns to the satiric methods of Restoration comedy, but optimistically reconciles the Teazles after Lady Teazle's flirtation with adultery. His mockery of contemporary drama, *The Critic* (1779), continues the tradition of BUCKINGHAM's *The Rehearsal*. In 1780 he became an MP and took an active part in the proceedings surrounding the impeachment of Warren Hastings. He finally gave up management of Drury Lane after the fire of 1809.

**Sherriff, R(obert) C(edric)** 1896–1975 British playwright and novelist. Sherriff's bitterly realistic depiction of the pressures on front-line soldiers in a dug-out preparing for an attack, *Journey's End*, was performed by the STAGE SOCIETY in 1928 and had a wide international impact. The immediacy and public commitment were missing in his treatment of historical subjects like the last years of Roman Britain and Napoleon (*The Long Sunset*, 1955; *St Helena*, 1935), his study of amnesia (*Home at Seven*, 1953) and his rustic comedy about village cricket (*Badger's Green*, 1930) – although these plays provided impressive roles for an actor like RALPH RICHARDSON.

**Sherwood, Robert E(mmet)** 1896–1955 American playwright and screenwriter. His career started with *The Road to Rome* (1927) and continued with such plays as *Reunion in Vienna* (1931), both sentimental comedies. With *The Petrified Forest* (1935), a story of frustrated idealism, *Idiot's Delight* (1936), an anti-war play, and *Abe Lincoln in Illinois* (1938) Sherwood won three Pulitzer Prizes. In 1938 he helped found the Playwrights' Company. He changed his pacifist stance with the advent of war in Europe. *There Shall Be No Night* (1940) is a militant condemnation of American isolationism, trumpeted across America by actors LUNT AND FONTANNE. Sherwood became a speech-writer for President Roosevelt. After the war he wrote *The Rugged Path* (1945) and *Small War on Murray Hill* (1957).

**Shields, Ella** 1879–1952 American singer, comedienne and male impersonator (see MALE IMPERSONATION). Initially a 'coon singer', she began a 25-year career on the British VARIETY stage in 1904. She rapidly moved into PANTOMIME, and in 1910 at the London Palladium made her first appearance in top-hat and tails, *à la* VESTA TILLEY. Many of her songs became popular classics, notably 'If You Knew Susie' and the celebrated 'Burlington Bertie from Bow', written by her husband William Hargreaves.

**Shiels [Morshiel], George** 1886–1949 Irish playwright. Permanently crippled in 1913, Shiels took to writing. His earliest plays (one-acters) were produced by the ULSTER LITERARY THEATRE. The ABBEY presented his first full-length play, *Paul Twyning* (1922). Thereafter Shiels supplied the Abbey with a string of box-office successes whose popularity owed much to the theatre's broadly farcical interpretation of them. They include *Professor Tim* (1925), *Cartney and Kevney* (1927), *The New Gossoon* (1930), *The Passing Day* (1936), *The Old Broom* (Group Theatre, Belfast, 1944), *Tenants at Will* (1945) and *The Caretakers* (1948). *Tenants at Will*, called 'a comedy in three acts', is a tragedy of 19th-century peasant miseries. In *The Passing Day*, memorably directed by TYRONE GUTHRIE at the 1951 Festival of Britain, a dying man manipulates and is manipulated by his family and business circles. From the dramatist there is no moral judgement – 'not the playwright's business'.

Shiels's plays have their funny, even farcical, scenes, but the laughter does not conceal the ironic reserve noted and disliked by YEATS. Although his range is narrow, with recurring situations, characters and contemporary Northern Irish settings, Shiels's dispassionate observation of human meanness and folly conveys unsettling but not depressing truths.

***shingeki*** Japanese term. Literally 'new drama', *shingeki* is the generic word for modern theatre and drama in Japan, to be distinguished from traditional forms like NŌ and KABUKI. At the same time, and more narrowly, *shingeki* refers to one kind of modern theatre: the realistic, Western-based drama performed by companies like the People's Art Theatre, the Literary Theatre and the Actors' Theatre.

**Shirley, James** 1596–1666 English playwright. He took holy orders and was briefly headmaster of a grammar school, a post which he forfeited in 1625 by his conversion to Roman Catholicism. Turning to playwriting, he completed at least 36 plays before 1642. He sided with the Royalists during the Civil War and died of exposure in the Great Fire of London.

Shirley's comedies involve multiple plots, e.g. *The Witty Fair One* (1628), *Hyde Park* (1632), *The Gamester* (1633), *The Lady of Pleasure* (1635), *The Imposture* (1640) and *The Sisters* (1642). The social values and witty dialogue anticipate Restoration comedy. His tragedies include *The Traitor* (1631), *The Politician* (c.1639) and *The Cardinal* (1641). A few of his MASQUES survive, among them *The Triumph of Peace* (1634), one of the showiest of its kind, as well as a modest volume of *Poems* (1646).

**Sholom Aleichem [Solomon Rappaport]** 1859–1916 Yiddish playwright. His homely plays, filled with lovable philosophical comic characters, provided artistic and financial successes for theatre companies all over the world. *Tevye the Milkman* (made into the American musical *Fiddler on the Roof*) is probably the best-known. *200,000*, sometimes called *The Big Win*, is a comedy filled with social significance, whilst in *Hard to Be a Jew* two students, one Jewish and one not, change places for a year to find out whether it is indeed hard to be a Jew. Other plays include *Scattered and Dispersed*, about the dissemination of the Jewish people at the turn of the century, and many dramatizations of his novels. (See also YIDDISH THEATRE.)

**showboats** American floating entertainment. From the early 19th century, flatboats, then steamers and paddlewheelers, plied the Mississippi and Ohio rivers, offering entertainment to the residents along the banks. The first intentionally designed showboat was that of William Chapman Sr, launched at Pittsburgh in 1831. The Chapman family in their Floating Theatre, a rude shed set on a barge and poled downriver, soon became a familiar sight, making annual tours of the major waterways with a repertory of KOTZEBUE, SHAKESPEARE and musical FARCES. They set the style of similar enterprises, although imitators sometimes offered lighter entertainment. The crafts ranged from ramshackle scows to grandiose arks. CIRCUS boats, led by Spalding and Rogers's Floating Circus Palace (1851), were capable of seating up to 3,400 spectators and offered MINSTREL SHOWS and a museum of curiosities in addition to sawdust acts.

After the disastrous hiatus of the Civil War, a new period of prosperity came to the showboat. The leading entrepreneur was Augustus Byron French, whose five 'floating palaces' from 1878 to 1901 offered lavish VARIETY bills; the only full-length drama ever offered was UNCLE TOM'S CABIN. The reliance on variety was challenged by the Eisenbarth-Henderson Temple of Amusement, which purveyed drama exclusively, including Faust, lit by electricity.

There were 26 showboats (as they had come to be known) active in 1910, 14 in 1928, and 5 in 1938. The last recorded by Philip Graham was The Goldenrod, tied up in St Louis in 1943. The decline can be attributed to the closure of the frontier; unable to compete with the urban entertainments that sprang up in the wake of civilization, the owners suffered greatly from the Depression of 1929. Behind the fashion even in their heyday, the boats became nostalgic artifacts. It was JEROME KERN's and OSCAR HAMMERSTEIN's musical adaptation of Show Boat (1927), a novel by Edna Ferber, that simultaneously immortalized the phenomenon and encased it in an aura of quaintness.

**Shubert brothers** American theatre owners and producers. The family business, the Shubert Organization, was founded by three brothers – Sam S. (1879–1905), Lee (1875–1953) and Jacob J. (1880–1963) Shubert – in the late 19th century. The brothers moved to New York City in 1900 and began acquiring theatres, including the Herald Square and the CASINO. After Sam's death his brothers continued the business, coming into conflict with the THEATRICAL SYNDICATE, a rival group. They built the Sam S. Shubert Theatre, which became the flagship of the Shubert enterprises and home for their own brand of musical drama and comedies.

By 1916 the Shuberts had become the nation's most important and powerful theatre owners and managers. They built many of BROADWAY's theatres, including the WINTER GARDEN and the Imperial, and owned or managed more than 100 others across the country. They were especially well known for their productions of operettas and annual REVUES such as The Passing Show (1912–1924) and Artists and Models (1923–43). Badly hurt by the Depression, they nevertheless continued to produce musicals, revues and popular straight plays throughout the 1930s and 1940s. In 1956 they were forced by the government to give up a number of theatres. The Shubert Organization currently owns and manages 16 of the operating Broadway theatres, and owns or controls others in Chicago, Philadelphia, Boston, Los Angeles and Washington, DC. In recent years it has once again become involved in Broadway productions, such as Amadeus (1980), Children of a Lesser God (1980), Dream Girls (1981), Nicholas Nickleby (1981), Cats (1982), Glengarry Glen Ross (1984) and Sunday in the Park with George (1984), The Heidi Chronicles (1989) and Someone Who'll Watch Over Me (1992).

**shund theatre** ('rubbish theatre') Yiddish term. It describes the popular sentimental and melodramatic YIDDISH THEATRE in America, designed to please the mass audience of unsophisticated immigrants from 1890 onwards.

**Shvarts, Evgeny (Lvovich)** 1896–1958 Soviet playwright and writer. He wrote witty adult fairy tales, political SATIRES that were unique during the period of socialist realism (1934–53). The son of liberal Jewish intellectuals in Kazan, he eventually settled in Leningrad. His first play, Underwood (1929), is about a witch who steals a typewriter and the orphan who retrieves it.

Shvarts's plays were not condemned outright because their exact satirical meanings could be flexible. Also, he balanced his fantasy output with realistic, patriotic plays extolling the courage and resourcefulness of the Russian people. Such plays include The Treasure (1933); Brother and Sister (1936); Our Hospitality (1939, unproduced); One Night (1941), about the bombing of Leningrad; and Far Land (1943), dedicated to the Leningrad children separated from their parents during the evacuation from the Nazi blockade.

The first of his major fairy-tale satires, The Naked King (1934), drawn from several Andersen stories, exposes the pettiness and fakery of all dictators and was banned from the stage until 1960 when the Sovremennik Theatre produced it. His best and most philosophical play, The Shadow (1940), based on Andersen's 'Peter Schlemeil', contemplates man's capacity for good and evil, and the relativity of truth and reality which makes simple solutions unwise. The play was beautifully realized by designer-director NIKOLAI AKIMOV in 1940 at the Leningrad Theatre of Comedy. The Dragon (1944), his most political play, attacks the conspiracy to tyranny between ruler and ruled. Staged by Akimov in 1944, it was banned until 1960. An Ordinary Miracle (1956), Shvarts's Tempest, about a senior magician who learns that love is the real magic, was also staged by Akimov in 1956. His remaining work includes the fairy-tale plays Adventures of Hohenstaufen (1932), Little Red Riding Hood (1937), The Snow Queen (1938) and Two Maples (1954), which preach the value of the collective and the dangers of capitalism; and several screenplays and PUPPET plays.

**Shverubovich, V. I.** see KACHALOV, VASILY

**Siddons, Sarah** 1755–1831 English actress. Probably the greatest English tragic actress, she was an infant star and learned her art in Manchester, touring on TATE WILKINSON's circuit in Yorkshire and in Bath; she appeared in London in a triumphant debut as Isabella in GARRICK's version of SOUTHERNE's The Fatal Marriage in 1782. In 1784 she was painted by Sir Joshua Reynolds as 'The Tragic Muse'. Her declamatory delivery and dignified presence were offset by the eloquence of her face and the concentration of her performances. She toured to Dublin and Edinburgh with equal success, then returned to London where her brother JOHN PHILIP KEMBLE was now acting. In 1785 she played Lady Macbeth for the first time, perhaps her greatest role. By 1790 she had left DRURY LANE (where she had first appeared in 1775), moving to COVENT GARDEN in 1801. She retired in 1812, playing Lady Macbeth in her last performance. Apart from this role, she was famous as Jane Shore in ROWE's play, as Belvidera in OTWAY's Venice Preserv'd and in other classical English parts.

**Sidney, Philip** 1554–86 Elizabethan poet, critic and courtier. Sidney's doubts about the status of plays as literature are evident in *The Apology for Poetry* (c.1580), which demonstrates the cultured scepticism soon to be challenged by MARLOWE and the UNIVERSITY WITS. Sidney died before the golden age of English drama.

**Sieveking, Alejandro** 1934– Chilean playwright and director. Sieveking presented his first play, *Encuentro con las sombras* (*Meeting with Shadows*), at an amateur festival in 1955. He is an accomplished writer and director; his work tends towards realistic psychological drama, as in *Mi hermano Cristián* (*My Brother Christian*, 1957), presenting the case of a man victimized by his invalid sibling. *Parecido a la felicidad* (*Akin to Happiness*, 1959) was about intimate personal relations, before the violence of *La madre de los conejos* (*Mother Rabbit*, 1961), a family study in sibling rape with two suicides. During the 1960s Sieveking continued to explore folkloric and poetic tendencies in *Animas de día claro* (*Fair Weather Souls*, 1962), a successful musical *La remolienda* (*The Carousing*, 1965) and *La mantis religiosa* (*The Praying Mantis*, 1971). Like his contemporaries, he has also dealt with sociopolitical issues, as in *Tres tristes tigres* (*Three Sad Tigers*, 1967). A versatile and prolific writer and director, Sieveking normally works within a realistic framework. From 1974 to 1984 he and his wife, Bélgica Castro, the lead actress for whom he often writes, maintained the Teatro del Angel in San José, Costa Rica, during the post-Allende period of Chile.

**Sigurjónsson, Jóhann** 1880–1919 Icelandic playwright. Sigurjónsson is today considered the classic Icelandic playwright; his first success came with the 1908 production in Reykjavík of *The Hraun Farm*, which marks the beginning of an era of Icelandic playwriting. Subsequent plays, originally staged by the Royal Theatre, Copenhagen, were written simultaneously in Icelandic and Danish, in order to reach a bigger audience. His masterpiece, the neo-romantic tragedy *Eyvind of the Mountains* (1911), was produced in 12 countries on both sides of the Atlantic and was filmed as *The Outlaw and His Wife* (1917). *The Wish* (1914) was based on an Icelandic Faustian legend, but World War I prevented its going beyond Scandinavia. Sigurjónsson's last play was *The Liar* (1917).

**Silva, António José da** see DA SILVA, ANTÓNIO JOSÉ

**Simeon Polotsky** [Samuil (Emelyanovich) Petrovskii-Sitniyanovich] 1629–80 Russian poet and playwright. The first court poet and founder of didactic school drama, he entered a monastery and became tutor to Tsar Aleksei Mikhailovich's children. He revised JOHANN GREGORY's dramatic repertoire and in the 1670s wrote two plays of his own, ostensibly on biblical themes after the *JESUITENDRAMA* – *The Comedy-Parable of the Prodigal Son* (published 1685) and *Of Nebuchadnezzar, the Golden Calf, and the Three Youths Who Were Not Burned in the Furnace*. The first play criticized the rowdy behaviour of young nobles travelling abroad to secure an education; the second shows a wise and just king, meant to resemble Aleksei Mikhailovich, opposing a tyrant, who is the cause of national suffering. Simeon Polotsky enlivened his plays with music, dancing and scenic effects.

**Simon, (Marvin) Neil** 1927– American playwright. Critical acclaim has come slowly for Simon, who has had more smash hits than any other American playwright. Even with almost a hit a year since 1961, he fights a reputation of being a GAG writer who caters to the moral hang-ups and material greed of middle-class America.

Simon learned his craft by writing comic material for radio and television personalities. His first full-length COMEDY, *Come Blow Your Horn* (1961), was followed by the musical FARCE *Little Me* (1962). After *Barefoot in the Park* (1963) he wrote *The Odd Couple* (1965), and a year later added the musical *Sweet Charity* and *The Star-Spangled Girl*. With four shows running simultaneously on BROADWAY, he was the most successful playwright of the 1960s. He added *Plaza Suite* to his list of successes in 1968 together with the musical *Promises, Promises*. After *Last of the Red Hot Lovers* (1969) he wrote *The Gingerbread Lady* (1970), which attempted to deal honestly with alcoholism, but was unpopular with audiences. Two bittersweet comedies followed: *The Prisoner of Second Avenue* and *The Sunshine Boys* (both 1972). In 1973, he reached a low point in his career with two failures: *The Good Doctor* (1973), adapted from short stories by ANTON CHEKHOV, and *God's Favorite*, adapted from the Bible (1976). But a move to California resulted in another hit, *California Suite* (1976), a Beverly Hills version of *Plaza Suite*. *Chapter Two* (1977) was critically acclaimed. His fourth musical, *They're Playing Our Song*, proved popular in 1979 but his next three were unsuccessful. Simon then returned to his own past for a charming *Brighton Beach Memoirs* (1983) and the award-winning *Biloxi Blues* (1984). *Broadway Bound* (1986) was another popular success, followed by two failures, *Rumours* (1988) and *Jake's Women* (1990). *Lost in Yonkers* (1991) is his most critically admired play to date. *Laughter on the 23rd Floor* (1993) harks back to his days as a young television comic writer. *London Suite* premiered in Seattle in 1994.

**Simonov, Konstantin (Kirill Mikhailovich)** 1915–79 Soviet journalist, novelist, poet and playwright. He survived Stalinism and achieved international repute by his literary editing of Soviet journals and his patriotic war stories and anti-capitalist partisan tales, strong on romance, heroism and strict adherence to the Party line. His poetry and novels – *Comrade in Arms* (1952) and the trilogy consisting of *Days and Nights* (1943–4), *The Living and the Dead* (1959–71) and *Soldiers Are Not Born* (1963–4) – relate to the war and were of great importance to the Russian people during the 1940s and 1950s. The same can be said of his 10 plays. His best-known war play, *The Russian People* (1942), about the heroic potential of ordinary people, appealed to CLIFFORD ODETS, who prepared an American acting edition for New York's THEATRE GUILD. *Under the Chestnut Trees of Prague* (1945) is a postwar play demonstrating the necessity of Soviet guidance in the democratization of its satellite countries; *The Russian Question* (1947) is an anti-capitalist piece set in New York City.

**Simonson, Lee** 1888–1967 American set designer. Simonson studied in Paris and, like ROBERT EDMOND JONES, returned to the USA with great excitement about the New Stagecraft. He advocated simplified REALISM – while creating sets that were based in realism, he stripped away all scenic elements that were unnecessary for mood or information. As founding member, director and resident designer for the THEATRE GUILD he designed over half their productions, including *Heartbreak House*, *Liliom* and *Green Grow the Lilacs*. His designs for *The Adding Machine* were among the most successful examples of EXPRESSIONISM on the American stage.

**Simpson, N(orman) F(rederick)** 1919– British playwright. His most successful plays were written in the late 1950s (*The Resounding Tinkle*, 1957; *The Hole*, 1958; and *One Way Pendulum*, 1959) and were staged at the ROYAL COURT THEATRE. These plays, distinguished by anarchic comedy, were seen as peculiarly British versions of the THEATRE OF THE ABSURD. Later work (*The Cresta Run*, 1965; *Playback 625* – in collaboration with Leopoldo Maler – 1970; and *Was He Anyone?*, 1972) failed to make the impact of the earlier plays, but Simpson continued a writing career in television and film. He translated EDUARDO DE FILIPPO's *Napoli milionaria* from which Peter Tinniswood adapted the acting version for RICHARD EYRE's NATIONAL THEATRE production (1991).

**Sinden, Donald (Alfred)** 1923– British actor. His distinctive vocal qualities and broad style have emphasized Sinden's reputation as a fine comedy actor. But as a classical actor he has produced exciting and often adventurous performances, as, for instance, in his role as Richard Plantagenet in JOHN BARTON's *The Wars of the Roses* (ROYAL SHAKESPEARE COMPANY, 1963). He has played Lear and Othello for the RSC (1977 and 1979 respectively) as well as creating witty character studies in such roles as Lord Foppington (VANBRUGH's *The Relapse*, RSC, 1967) and Sir Peter Teazle (SHERIDAN's *The School for Scandal*, 1983). His skills in demanding, naturalistic roles have been shown in appearances as Vanya in CHEKHOV's *Uncle Vanya* (1982) and Doctor Stockmann in IBSEN's *An Enemy of the People* (1975). His most challenging part in recent years was as the Duke of Altair in the CHICHESTER FESTIVAL THEATRE's revival of CHRISTOPHER FRY's *Venus Observed* (1992), tackling LAURENCE OLIVIER's well remembered part.

**Singspiel** German musical drama. A popular form, it arose in Germany during the mid-18th century as a result of the popularity of GAY's *Beggar's Opera* (1728). Most *Singspiele* have a popular setting and comprise light, tuneful songs connected by dialogue that is spoken, not sung. Several dramatists wrote *Singspiele*, notably GOETHE, but the most consummate achievements in the genre are Mozart's *The Abduction from the Seraglio* (1782) and *The Magic Flute* (1791). The operetta of the 19th century evolved in part from the *Singspiel*.

**Sissle, Noble** 1889–1975 and **Eubie Blake** 1883–1983 American singer-lyricist and pianist-composer. Blake met Sissle in 1915. For several years they performed in VAUDEVILLE in an act featuring their own songs. In 1921 they joined with the vaudeville comedy team of Flournoy Miller and Aubrey Lyles to create the first black musical to play a major BROADWAY theatre during the regular theatrical season, *Shuffle Along*. Nothing they did later matched that early success, but with the rediscovery of ragtime in the 1960s and 1970s Sissle and Blake songs were again heard on Broadway in *Doctor Jazz* (1975), *Bubbling Brown Sugar* (1976) and *Eubie* (1978).

**sit-com** SEE TELEVISION DRAMA

**Sjöberg, Alf** 1903–80 Swedish director. His 50-year career at DRAMATEN was a decisive force in modern theatre. He combined a belief in the moral and intellectual function of theatre with a mastery of modern stage technology. He is best known for his productions of SHAKESPEARE, STRINDBERG and modern European dramatists such as CLAUDEL, IONESCO, BRECHT, GOMBROWICZ and WITKIEWICZ. Typically, he balanced analysis of a play's historical context with its contemporary relevance. An accomplished designer, he made light and space particularly vital elements in his fluid staging. Some of his most inventive work, such as his

adaptations of C. J. L. Almqvist's novels *Amorina* and *The Queen's Jewel*, was done within the limited resources of Dramaten's Little Stage.

**Skármeta, Antonio** 1940– Chilean novelist, short story writer and playwright. His single but stunning play, *Ardiente paciencia* (*Burning Patience*, 1982), demythifies the life of Pablo Neruda, Nobel laureate, through the eyes of his young postman.

**Skelton, John** c.1460–1529 English poet and playwright. Among his plays only *Magnyfycence* (printed by JOHN RASTELL in 1530) has survived. Though classed as a MORALITY PLAY, it is not concerned with the struggle of good and evil for the soul of a generalized mankind but with good and evil counsel struggling for power over the ruler, the Magnyfycence of the title.

***skēnē/scaenae frons*** Greek/Roman term. Sometime in the mid-5th century BC a *skēnē*, or scene building, was introduced into open-air Greek theatre (see GREEK THEATRE, ANCIENT). It was probably a temporary wooden structure which later became more elaborate and permanent. But whatever its form, the *skēnē* provided playwrights and performers with greatly expanded possibilities. About two-thirds of the extant tragedies occur before a temple or palace, which could be represented by the *skēnē*. The door (perhaps three doors by the end of the 5th century) allowed for exits and entrances, and the possibility of concealment and surprise. The roof of the *skēnē* provided a raised stage, e.g. for the appearance of gods.

When Roman theatres were constructed the Greek *skéné* became the *scaenae frons*, a three-tiered façade of pillars, niches and statuary with three doors, and one door at either side of the stage (see ROMAN THEATRE).

**Skinner, Cornelia Otis** 1901–79 American actress and author. Daughter of actor OTIS SKINNER, she established her reputation in the 1920s, touring the USA and Britain in monodramas that she wrote and staged herself. These included *The Wives of Henry VIII* (1931), *The Empress Eugenie* (1932), *The Loves of Charles II* (1933) and *Paris '90* (1952). She also appeared in more traditional theatre, and wrote memoirs, light verse, essays and theatrical biography, including *Madame Sarah*, a life of SARAH BERNHARDT (1967).

**Skinner, Otis** 1858–1942 American actor. One of America's most versatile performers, Skinner played over 140 roles between 1877 and 1879 with the resident companies of the Philadelphia Museum and the WALNUT STREET THEATRE. Between 1879 and 1892 he played in the companies of EDWIN BOOTH, LAWRENCE BARRETT, AUGUSTIN DALY, HELENA MODJESKA and JOSEPH JEFFERSON III. From 1892 he was a confirmed and popular star. He is best-remembered for the role of Hajj, the beggar, in *Kismet*, which he created in 1911. Skinner and his actress daughter, CORNELIA OTIS SKINNER, were both prolific authors.

***skomorokhi*** Itinerant players of Old Russia. Musicians, boxers and dancers with long hair and tunics had been portrayed in the frescos of the Sophia Cathedral in Kiev in 1037; however, the Church opposed them as pagan and immoral. Their antics at Easter with made-up faces and old clothes, and their disguises as women or animals on New Year's Eve, proclaimed the *skomorokhi*'s heathen origins. By the late 16th and early 17th centuries they had become hugely popular, some troupes consisting of over 100 men. They excelled as puppeteers, bear-leaders, dog and rat trainers and storytellers. The most famous, Foma and Erema, entered folklore.

Following an uprising in Moscow, Tsar Aleksei Mikhailovich, first of the Romanovs, banned them 'and all manner of devilish sports' (1648); this ban was strictly enforced and they were exiled to the northern hinterlands, where the traditions were long upheld. Some became private jesters, some entertainers at weddings and parties. They exercised an immeasurable influence on the Russian PUPPET theatre and the fairground booth and, through them, on Russian CIRCUS and VARIETY.

**Słowacki, Juliusz** 1809–49 Polish poet and playwright. From 1831 he lived in political exile in Switzerland, Italy and France. He wrote over 20 verse dramas dealing with European and Polish history and legend, folklore and fairy tale, which blend the mystical and cruel, the cosmic and grotesque, in loose, fragmentary scenes. Major works are *Maria Stuart* (1832), *Kordian* (1834), *Beatrix Cenci* (1839), *Balladyna* (1839), *Mazeppa* (1840) and *Fantazy* (1841).

**Sly, William** died 1608 English actor. In 1590 he was with STRANGE'S MEN in TARLTON'S *The Seven Deadly Sins*. After a spell with the ADMIRAL'S MEN, he joined the LORD CHAMBERLAIN'S MEN, perhaps from the company's foundation in 1594, becoming a sharer after the death of AUGUSTINE PHILLIPS. There is a portrait of Sly in the Dulwich Picture Gallery, London. It is not known what parts he played.

**Smit, Bartho** 1924–86 South African playwright and critic. Arguably the most prominent Afrikaans dramatist, Smit was a controversial figure, his plays frequently censored in South Africa (see CENSORSHIP). His work spans three decades, from *Moeder Hanna* (*Mother Hanna*, 1959), a drama about the futility of war, to *Die Verminktes* (*The Maimed*, 1960), to *Die Kaiser* (*The Emperor*, 1977), which adapts the fable of *The Emperor's New Clothes* to satirize the absurdities of social mores. His best-known play is *Christine* (first produced 1973), which focuses on Nazi Germany and develops themes of Calvinist guilt and racial prejudice.

**Smith, Albert Richard** 1816–60 British writer and entertainer. A popular humorist and journalist, in 1850 he presented his panorama-lecture *The Overland Mail*, studded with songs, anecdotes and impersonations, at Willis's Rooms, London. Aided by his brother Arthur (1825–61), he presented *The Ascent of Mont Blanc* (1852) at London's Egyptian Hall, complete even to the sound effects of popping champagne corks. It was one of the greatest hits of the Victorian amusement scene and ran for 2,000 performances. It was followed by *Mont Blanc to China* (1858–9).

**Smith, Anna Deavere** 1951– American actress and playwright. Since 1983 Smith has developed a series of unique one-person performance pieces collectively called *On the Road: A Search for American Character*, based on interviews about controversial events or subjects. But her work was not widely known until May 1992 when *Fires in the Mirror: Crown Heights, Brooklyn, and Other Identities*, the 13th in this series, was presented at the JOSEPH PAPP Public Theater in New York. This was based on the 1991 stabbing of a Hasidic scholar by a group of young black men in Brooklyn. Smith's human collage of over 20 individuals, acclaimed as a remarkable theatrical event, won her multiple awards. *Twilight: Los Angeles, 1992*, focusing on racial tension in LA, was produced in Los Angeles (1993) and New York (1994).

**Smith, Maggie** [Mrs Margaret Natalie Cross] 1934– British actress. She starred with Kenneth Williams in the Bamber Gascoigne REVUE, *Share My Lettuce* (1956). Her attractive wit and lively personality gave her a considerable WEST END success. She joined the OLD VIC company for the 1959–60 season, playing in *As You Like It* and *Richard II*; and then appeared in ANOUILH's *The Rehearsal* (1961) and PETER SHAFFER's *The Private Ear* and *The Public Eye* (1962), two award-winning parts in a double bill. She was invited to join OLIVIER's NATIONAL THEATRE company for the opening seasons, playing memorably as Desdemona to Olivier's Othello.

She began her film career in 1963, and with *The Prime of Miss Jean Brodie* (1968), which won her an Oscar, became a major film star. Her sensitive face, husky voice and ironic delivery helped her to excel in comedies of manners from all periods: in NOËL COWARD's plays (*Design for Living*, 1971; *Private Lives*, 1972) and in CONGREVE's *The Way of the World*, as Millamant (1984). Although less highly regarded as a tragic actress, her Hedda Gabler (1970) was much admired. In 1976 she joined the STRATFORD (Ontario) FESTIVAL company in Canada, where she played in *Virginia* (1981), a study of the life of Virginia Woolf. Another wildly eccentric character was her flamboyantly romantic historical guide in Shaffer's *Lettice and Lovage* (1987). In 1970 she was awarded the CBE.

**Smith, Oliver** 1918–94 American set-designer and producer. He began his career designing for dance. Starting with the 1944 production of *On the Town* (which he also co-produced), Smith designed a steady stream of long-running musicals including *My Fair Lady*, *West Side Story* and *Hello Dolly!*. From 1941 onwards, he designed some 400 theatre, dance, opera and film productions. He served as co-director of the American Ballet Theatre from 1945 to 1981. For him, scenery was an integral part of choreography. In terms of style he frequently mixed painterly backgrounds with sculptural scenic elements, with an almost formulaic approach to the arrangement of scenic elements and space.

**Smith, Sol(omon Franklin)** 1801–69 American manager and actor. From 1823 he managed his own company for four years, then toured the Mississippi valley with JAMES H. CALDWELL, and in 1835 entered into a partnership with NOAH LUDLOW. They dominated the FRONTIER THEATRE of their time, but ended the partnership in 1853. As an actor, Smith, affectionately known as 'Old Sol', was particularly effective as a low comedian in such roles as Mawworm in *The Hypocrite*. He eventually went into law and became a Missouri state senator. His three autobiographical volumes give valuable insights into theatrical conditions of the time.

**Smithson, Harriet (Constance)** 1800–54 Irish-born British actress. She made her debut at DRURY LANE in 1818. Her impact on London audiences was slight, but in Paris, where she played Juliet, Ophelia and NICHOLAS ROWE's Jane Shore in the company of CHARLES KEMBLE in 1827, she was a sensation. The adulation of Frenchmen such as GAUTIER, DUMAS *père* and HUGO contributed to the rise of the French romantic theatre. Smithson married Berlioz in 1833 and soon retired from the stage.

**soap opera** SEE TELEVISION DRAMA

**Sofola, Zulu** 1935– Nigerian playwright and director. Her plays employ elements of MAGIC, RITUAL and myth to examine conflicts between traditionalism and modernism in which male supremacy persists. Her most frequently performed plays are *Wedlock of the Gods* (1972) and *The Sweet Trap* (1977). In the former, the heroine feels liberated after the death of a husband she has never loved; but she and her new lover are hunted down after breaking their society's marital taboos. Critics are divided about Sofola's treatment of women's rights and of class difference: does her work offer a blueprint for liberation or is it inherently conservative? Recent plays include *Memories in the Moonlight* (1986) and *Song of a Maiden* (1991).

**sokari** Sri Lankan theatre form. One of the oldest kinds of theatre in Sri Lanka, it is performed after the Sinhalese New Year in offering to the goddess Pattini. Performances are confined to the remote hilly regions and the performers are all male peasants. Any open spot in the village, usually the threshing ground, is used for the all-night show. Dancing and music punctuate the lively events, and full face masks are used by some performers.

The story differs in details from place to place, but in essence it tells of Guru Hami, a north Indian, and Sokari his wife, along with Paraya their comic servant, who are disenfranchised, build a boat and sail to Sri Lanka; here they experience various comic adventures. Sokari, who is young and seductive, elopes with a local doctor who has been summoned to treat Guru Hami's dog bite; she eventually returns and delivers a child. The ending, along with the recurrent sexual symbolism and the obscenities that feature throughout the performance, suggest that *sokari* may be a dramatic elaboration of an archaic fertility RITUAL.

**Solari Swayne, Enrique** 1915– Peruvian playwright. For years a university professor of psychology in Lima, he is known primarily for *Collacocha* (1955), about the tragic struggle of an engineer, Echecopar, to conquer the forces of nature. *La mazorca* (*The Corn*, 1964), set in a Peruvian jungle plantation, echoed similar telluric concerns. *Ayax Telemonio* (1969) used a classical motif to criticize current social and political issues.

**Soleil, Théâtre du** French company. It was founded in 1964 by ARIANE MNOUCHKINE and a group of friends, who adopted a cooperative structure of *création collective*, or collaborative devising of productions, at a disused warehouse at Vincennes. Their most famous production *1789* (1970) combined historical research and improvisation. It told the story of the French Revolution from the point of view of the people and was highly successful with audiences in the wake of the political upheavals of 1968. It was performed on stages placed around the audience, who were free to move about. *1789* was followed by two further collective creations – *1793* (1972) and *L'Âge d'or* (*The Golden Age*, 1975). *L'Âge d'or* owed much to MEYERHOLD and the *COMMEDIA DELL'ARTE*. *Mephisto* (1979) was a dramatization of Klaus Mann's novel. This was followed in the early 1980s by a cycle of SHAKESPEARE plays, *Richard II*, *Henry IV Part 1* and *Twelfth Night*, physically expressive productions that also suggested the remote, hieratic quality of Shakespeare's nobles by borrowings from Oriental theatre styles, costumes and so on. A contemporary play about Southeast Asia, *Norodom Sihanouk* (1985), was followed by a play about India, *L'Indiade* (1988); the text for both plays was by HÉLÈNE CIXOUS. In 1990–92 the company returned to Eastern performance style for productions of plays by AESCHYLUS and EURIPIDES.

**Sologub, Fyodor** [Fyodor Kuzmich Teternikov] 1863–1927 Russian poet, novelist, short story writer and playwright. A pessimist bordering on nihilism, Sologub envisioned an inverted cosmos in which God rules an evil world of matter and desire, while Satan governs a calm realm of beauty and death. His art, in the manner of the symbolists (see SYMBOLISM), remythologizes ancient legends, making them revolve around sex, sadism and the humiliation of beauty. His idea of theatre is expressed in the essay 'The Theatre of One Will' (1908). Although he advocated a bare stage, Sologub's 18 plays offer theatrical levels and devices, and interesting shifts in perspective, focus and pacing – which attracted MEYERHOLD, who achieved a rare success for symbolist drama with his staging of *The Triumph of Death* (1907) at VERA KOMISSARZHEVSKAYA's Theatre. Meyerhold's staging of *The Hostages of Life* (1912) marked the first production of a symbolist play at a traditional theatre, the Aleksandrinsky. EVREINOV presented *Nocturnal Dances* (1908), with choreography by Mikhail Fokine, at his Merry Theatre for Grown-up Children (1909). Sologub's most popular play was a dramatization of his novel *The Petty Demon* (1907) for Nezlobin's Theatre (1910).

**Solórzano, Carlos** 1922– Guatemalan-born Mexican playwright and critic. He spent 1948–50 in Europe, where he met ALBERT CAMUS, MICHEL DE GHELDERODE and existentialism. In Mexico he became artistic director of the Professional University Theatre and later professor at the National University. His major plays are *Doña Beatriz* (1952), *El hechicero* (*The Sorcerer*, 1954) and his masterpiece, *Las manos de Dios* (*The Hands of God*, 1956), plus several one-act plays. He has written books on Latin American theatre and a weekly column in a major Mexican journal.

**Somigliana, Carlos** 1932–87 Argentine playwright and journalist. He was a prominent figure in the realist generation (see REALISM) of Argentine theatre of the 1960s; his major plays include *Amarillo* (*Yellow*, 1965), *El avión negro* (*The Black Aeroplane*, 1970), written in collaboration with COSSA, ROZENMACHER and TALESNIK; and short plays for TEATRO ABIERTO from 1981.

**Sondheim, Stephen** 1930– American lyricist and composer. After an apprenticeship with OSCAR HAMMERSTEIN II, Sondheim created the lyrics for *West Side Story* (1957) and *Gypsy* (1959). In 1962 he wrote both music and lyrics for *A Funny Thing Happened on the Way to the Forum*. In the 1970s he startled the MUSICAL THEATRE world with the scores for a series of highly experimental shows. *Company* (1970) was a collage of musical vignettes about married life in contemporary New York. *Follies* (1971) used a reunion of MUSICAL COMEDY performers to examine the effects of middle age on love and marriage. *A Little Night Music* (1973) had a score written entirely in three-four time. *Pacific Overtures* (1976) employed the conventions of Japanese KABUKI theatre and an all-Oriental cast to tell of the opening of Japan to the West. *Sweeney Todd* (1979) adapted Victorian MELODRAMA to modern sensibilities by suggesting the tormented soul behind the 'demon barber of Fleet Street'. *Merrily We Roll Along* (1981) examined the myth of the American success story by tracing the lives of its central characters backwards from middle age to youth. *Sunday in the Park with George* (1984) explored the process of artistic creation by bringing to life the work of French painter Georges Seurat.

Sondheim's scores for each of these shows were characterized by brilliant, often cerebral lyrics and driving, unsentimental music. He is generally considered the most distinguished composer-lyricist in the musical theatre of the 1970s and 1980s. Recent works include

*Into the Woods* (1987), exploring the darker aspects of classic fairy tales, *Assassins* (1991) and *Passion* (1994).

**Sonnenfels, Josef von** 1733–1817 Austrian critic. Strongly influenced by GOTTSCHED, Sonnenfels's *Letters on the Viennese Stage* (1768) attacked the local, improvised comedy and advocated a more decorous, scripted theatre. Although he did not succeed in dislodging the popular theatre, he had considerable influence on the founding of the BURGTHEATER and on the development of its ideals of ensemble.

**Sophocles** c.496–406/5 BC Greek tragic playwright. Sophocles came from Colonus, near Athens. He produced his first set of plays in 468, and won first prize in the Great Dionysia (see GREEK THEATRE, ANCIENT) although he was competing against AESCHYLUS. He produced 132 plays (we know the titles of over 110) and probably won 18 victories at the Great Dionysia and others at the Lenaea. He is said to have been responsible for introducing the third actor (though this is also attributed to Aeschylus) and for increasing the size of the tragic Chorus from 12 to 15. He took an active part in public life, and his offices included a generalship (an elective one-year post) in 440/1 as a colleague of the statesman Pericles. In later times he had a reputation for piety, illustrated by various anecdotes.

The chronology of the seven surviving plays is uncertain. There is evidence dating *Antigone* to c.442; *Ajax* and *Trachiniae* (*Women of Trachis*, concerning the death of Heracles) are probably earlier than this. *Oedipus Tyrannus* (*King Oedipus*) perhaps dates from the 420s. *Philoctetes* is securely dated to 409, and *Electra* may not be much earlier. *Oedipus at Colonus* was not produced until 401, after Sophocles' death. Thus even the earliest surviving plays may not have been written until Sophocles was in his 50s, and he seems to have written the latest well into his 80s. We also possess about half of a satyr play, *Ichneutae* (*Trackers*, concerning the childhood of Hermes), and various shorter fragments.

Sophocles was concerned with plots as complete and coherent sequences of events, linked together by principles of cause and effect and of plausible human motivation. With this goes the importance of prophecy: by the end of a play it generally turns out that the prophecy of an oracle or seer has been fulfilled, in a way that at least some of the characters did not expect or intend.

Each of the plays is concerned with death (at least the possibility of it, though in *Philoctetes* no one actually dies), with human suffering, and with abrupt changes of fortune, whether for good or ill (the mutability of fortune being a staple theme of Sophoclean moralizing). There is fruitful tension between this grim material and the harmonious form of the plays. The gods do not act justly in any human sense; their perfect knowledge is set against the inevitably limited knowledge of mortals.

Each play contains a major character who, while he may be less attractive morally than those around him, wins our respect by his uncompromising adherence to some purpose, whatever the opposition and whatever the cost. Thus Ajax insists on suicide, Antigone on burying her brother, Oedipus (*Tyrannus*) on learning the truth about the killing of Laius and his own identity, and so on. When this intransigence is set against the forces of change and illusion, the result is often the death of the 'hero'; but, as he remains morally undefeated, his courage attains a paradoxical value which transcends death itself. There is further paradox in the fact that two of these characters are women (the defiance of Antigone and Electra must have startled the Greek audience) while two others are destitute outcasts (Philoctetes and Oedipus (*at Colonus*)).

Characterization is always strong enough to provide a criterion by which actions may be judged plausible, but does not extend to psychologically detailed portraiture. In the choral odes Sophocles' style can be almost as ornate as that of Aeschylus; in dialogue it is simpler, combining dignity with great suppleness and vigour.

**Sorge, Reinhard (Johannes)** 1892–1916 German playwright and poet. His visionary play *The Beggar* (1912, staged by REINHARDT in 1917) was the first fully developed work in the 'ecstatic' line of EXPRESSIONISM. Its subjective intensity, episodic structure and portrayal of the spiritual regeneration of mankind through the poet-hero's murder of his technologically obsessed father typified the movement.

**Sorma, Agnes** 1865–1927 German actress. She was a woman of extraordinary grace and beauty. Her poetic style on stage complemented exactly the acting of JOSEF KAINZ, with whom she was a colleague at the DEUTSCHES THEATER from 1883 to 1899. Later she worked with MAX REINHARDT, specializing in both classical and contemporary leads.

**Sosnitsky, Ivan (Ivanovich)** 1794–1872 Russian actor. Along with KARATYGIN, he was one of the two leading St Petersburg actors of his day. An attractive, charming and popular performer, who often paid more attention to polish than to feeling, he excelled as lovers, officers, rakes and dandies in light comedies and *vaudevilles*. He inherited some of SHCHEPKIN's 'old man' roles. Sosnitsky and Shchepkin each played the role of the Mayor in *The Inspector General* in the St Petersburg and Moscow premieres, respectively. The latter's portrayal was realistic, whereas the former's was in the spirit of *vaudeville*. The rivalry undermined their friendship. Other rogues in Sosnitsky's gallery included Figaro, Tartuffe and Repetilov (*Woe from Wit*).

**Sothern, E(dward) A(skew)** 1826–81 and **E(dward) H(ugh) Sothern** (1859–1933) American actors. Beginning his career as an eccentric comedian on English stages, the elder Sothern made his American debut as Dr Pangloss in *The Heir at Law* in 1852. He achieved American star status as Lord Dundreary in TOM TAYLOR's *Our American Cousin* in 1858. In 1861, after 400 consecutive performances, Londoners indulged in frequent 'Dundrearyisms' and his distinctive sidewhiskers, known as 'Dundrearies', became popular. Other Sothern parts included Dundreary's Brother Sam in the play of that name (1862) and the title roles in T. W. ROBERTSON's *David Garrick* (1864) and H. J. BYRON's *The Crushed Tragedian* (1878). Excelling in original comic business, E. A. Sothern remained popular on both sides of the Atlantic.

In 1879 his American-born son, E. H. Sothern, made his debut in New York in a small role in *Brother Sam*. In 1887 DANIEL FROHMAN engaged him for the newly formed company at the LYCEUM THEATRE. He quickly established himself as a dashing romantic hero in such roles as Prince Rudolph in *The Prisoner of Zenda* (1895), and broadened his range to poetic drama in 1900 as the hero in HAUPTMANN's *The Sunken Bell* and as Hamlet. Under the management of CHARLES FROHMAN, Sothern first appeared with JULIA MARLOWE, whom he later married, in *Romeo and Juliet* (1904). Together they reigned for a decade as America's foremost Shakespearian players.

**sottie** Short, medieval French comic play. The characters were unnamed *sots*, or fools, with identifying costumes. Many *sotties* had no real plot, but consisted of lively banter, ACROBATICS and slapstick. The titles reveal the nature of the *sottie*, e.g. *La Sottie des sots ecclésiastiques qui jouent leur bénéfice au content*. The aim was to produce riotous laughter, often using satirical allegory directed at social, political or religious abuses.

**Soulié, Frédéric** 1800–47 French playwright and novelist. He wrote a successful trilogy on French history from the Revolution to the reign of Louis Philippe: *Diane de Chivri* (Renaissance Theatre, 1839), *Le Fils de la folle* (*The Son of the Madwoman*) and *Le Proscrit* (*The Workman*, 1840). The last began a series of highly profitable MELODRAMAS for the Ambigu-Comique in which villains, robbers and virtuous workers feature. With *Gaetan, Il Mammone* (1842) he provided an excellent role for the popular BOULEVARD actor, MÉLINGUE. *Eulalie Pontois* (1843) was pure melodrama; *Les Amants de Murcie* (1844) was a romantic Spanish version of *Romeo and Juliet*; *Les Talismans* (1845) included good and bad angels in a variety of guises. *Les Étudiants* (1845) was a lighter piece. Soulié's last, and major, work was *La Closerie des genêts* (1846), adapted by BOUCICAULT as *The Willow Copse*, which ran for hundreds of performances and took five hours to play: the complicated plot looks seriously at social attitudes to illegitimacy and also introduces a particularly unpleasant villainess, Leona.

**sound effects** Sound effects are used in the theatre for a variety of reasons:
1 to establish (a) locale (b) time of year (c) day or night (d) weather conditions;
2 to evoke atmosphere;
3 to link scenes;
4 to provide an emotional stimulus;
5 to reproduce physical happenings: cars arriving, babies crying, clocks striking and so on.

In the days before microphones, gramophone records and tape recorders, sound in the theatre depended upon mechanical and live effects. The creation of these was a great art and was usually the domain of the property department. Even in the mid-1950s, although gramophone records had very much taken over, live effects were still employed. Rather than hire expensive sound equipment and records, producers would insist, say, that mechanical wind or wave machines, clock chimes or metal thunder sheets be used.

Certain sounds are more convincingly produced 'live' or manually. For example, a pistol shot with a real gun and a blank cartridge has a sharpness and immediacy difficult to achieve with an electronic sound system. The sounds of door bells, phone bells, door chimes and door knockers are usually more easily achieved live. Glass and crockery crashes are also better with the real thing.

One of the most famous of all sound effects sequences was for *The Ghost Train* by Arnold Ridley. First produced at the St Martin's Theatre in London in 1925, it is still a firm favourite with repertory and amateur companies. The stage directions in the original script call for an assortment of tubular bells, garden rollers, galvanized iron tanks, thunder sheets, drums, air cylinders, whistles, milk churns, mallets and wire brushes, and require six carefully rehearsed stage-hands to create the various train sounds.

During the late 1940s and into the 1950s the use of 78rpm sound effects discs was prevalent. The sounds were selected from specialist libraries and transferred to lacquer disc. Usually only two or three items were recorded on each single-side to allow for maximum flexibility during replay. Music was still obtainable only on 78rpm commercial discs since the new long-playing record was only introduced in the mid-1950s. The turntable units for the 78rpm effects discs were rugged affairs, in Britain known as 'panatropes': instead of 'sound cues' stage managers used to write 'pan cues' in their prompt scripts. A selection of sound effects discs was very convenient during rehearsals because the director could call for any combination, sequence and balance of effects *in situ*. The BBC radio drama department still uses sound effects discs if rehearsing and broadcasting a play on the same day.

American theatre was a few years ahead of Britain with the transition from disc to tape. The first major production in London to use tape machinery was *My Fair Lady*, which transferred from BROADWAY to the Theatre Royal, DRURY LANE, in 1957. From around this period UK theatres began to employ recording tape.

Standard tape cassette recorders have not proved very successful because of the difficulty of 'cueing-in' accurately and the impossibility of editing. Tape cartridge recorders, on the other hand, have become popular since the early 1980s because they are compact, mechanically silent and extremely accurate in operation. These machines were developed particularly for use in radio stations for the convenient handling of jingles and commercials. But they are slow to rewind or fast-forward, and difficult to edit. DAT (digital audio tape) cassette recorders are suitable for theatre but not widely employed. Larger subsidized theatre companies have been moving towards solid state digital tapeless sound, producing high-quality sound, instantaneous access, and flexibility. The effect in question, cleaned up and edited, can be assigned to a key on the keyboard.

Most of the everyday sounds of weather, traffic, birds, animals, aircraft, bells, people, and so on can be obtained on commercial recordings. However, these recordings are limited both in the range of available sounds and in the duration of the tracks. With portable recording equipment many natural sounds can be captured. But it can be very time-consuming and sometimes impossible to record the wanted sound devoid of other background noises; and in the theatre it is essential to have clean sound effects. It is often necessary to simulate effects in front of a microphone, where extraneous noises can be eliminated altogether.

Because one is usually putting a single sound on to a single loudspeaker, theatre recordings are more often than not monaural. But there are exceptions. For example, in most cases music is enhanced by stereo. Stereo can also be useful for providing breadth and perspective to e.g. crowd, battle, traffic and sea effects. Travelling sounds like cars, aeroplanes and trains can, of course, be recorded in stereo, but will be fixed in their timing. It is much more flexible to have the same mono sound on twin tracks fed separately by two loudspeakers. Then, by adjusting the relative gains, the effect can be moved from one loudspeaker to the other at will. Twin tracks may also be used for two different continuous effects of indeterminate length: e.g. rain on one track and wind on the other. This leaves a second tape machine free for superimposing other effects.

**Southerne, Thomas** 1660–1746 Irish playwright.

Beginning with *The Loyal Brother* in 1682, he went on writing until 1726. *Sir Anthony Love* (1690) gave Susanna Mountfort a virtuoso role in a BREECHES PART as the disguised woman playing at being a rake. *The Wives' Excuse* (1691), Southerne's best play, depicts the unfortunate wife who refuses adultery as revenge for her husband's treatment of her. *The Maid's Last Prayer* (1693) is an even more vicious SATIRE. Southerne's two tragedies from this period were both long-lasting successes and both based on novellas by APHRA BEHN: *The Fatal Marriage* (1695) from *The Nun* anticipates a more sentimental form of tragedy; *Oroonoko* (1695) is a fine example of the sentimental noble savage play. Southerne was admired by contemporary writers and frequently helped younger dramatists.

**Southwark Theatre** (Philadelphia) In 1766 DAVID DOUGLASS erected America's first substantial theatre and presented the first play by a native American, Thomas Godfrey's *The Prince of Parthia* (1767). The playhouse was two and a half storeys high, painted red, brick in its lower storey and surmounted by a cupola. In 1774 it was closed by the Continental Congress, used briefly as a hospital, then by British occupation troops for entertainments to benefit widows and orphans. In 1784, LEWIS HALLAM JR reoccupied it, avoiding the laws against play-acting by presenting 'moral lectures'. The ban was lifted in 1789, but the theatre was outmoded and abandoned by 1817.

**Sowande, Bode** 1948– Nigerian playwright, director and novelist. He was a founding member of the Ori Olokun Acting Company. His first successful work was the trilogy comprising *The Night Before*, *Farewell to Babylon* and *Flamingoes* (1972–82). These deal with the totalitarian state and with problems of loyalty and leadership among a radical group. In the 1980s Sowande's plays embraced BRECHTian techniques of dislocation, e.g. in *Afamako – the Workhorse* (1978) and *Monkey's Gold* (1993). *Tornadoes Full of Dreams* (1990) is a large-scale treatment of the Haitian revolution. *Mammy-Water's Wedding* and *Ajantala-Pinocchio* were performed in 1992.

**Soya, Carl-Erik** 1896–1983 Danish playwright and novelist. He wrote some 35 plays, including several suites of shorter plays. Popular in the 1930s, Soya uses the theatre to juggle fancifully with major ideas, whose magnitude he often contrasts with human pettiness. Several plays, including *Pieces of a Pattern* (1940) and *Two Threads* (1943), explore the possibly deterministic nature of existence. Others, like *Who Am I?* (1932) and *Purpose, Faith and Point of View* (1938), deal with individual identity and guilt. The popular *Lion With a Corset* (1950) looks sceptically at the roots of aggression and war. While Soya's tone is persistently playful, it also frequently intimates an underlying despair.

**Soyinka, Wole** 1934– Nigerian playwright, poet and novelist. Soyinka is generally considered Africa's greatest living playwright. After a university education in Ibadan and Leeds, he became a play-reader at the ROYAL COURT THEATRE, London (1957–9), and had three pieces performed there. On returning to Nigeria he founded the 1960 Masks, which presented his play *A Dance of the Forests* for the independence celebrations. Many of Soyinka's themes are foreshadowed in this complex work: the notion of three parallel and interlocking worlds of the past, the present and the future; the need for sacrifice; the role of the artist in society; the presence of the god, Ogun.

A political, though not a didactic playwright, he demonstrates in his work the dialectic within the term 'political art'. In the early 1960s he published *The Trials of Brother Jero*, a satirical comedy recounting the adventures of a mendicant Christian preacher; *The Strong Breed*, an ironical exposition of the context for human sacrifice today; and *The Road*, which gives a contemporary context for the ancient Egungun masquerade. *Kongi's Harvest* (1966) discovers the tyrant's ability to corrupt a whole people. Detained without trial from 1967–9, Soyinka wrote and later published *The Man Died* (1972):'The man dies,' he wrote, 'in all who keep silent in the face of tyranny.' *Madmen and Specialists* (1970) is set in the Biafran war. While in exile, he wrote a version of *The Bacchae of Euripides* for the NATIONAL THEATRE in London (1973). At Cambridge he wrote *Death and the King's Horseman* (1975), involving a ritual Yoruba suicide halted by a British district officer.

Soyinka returned to Ife in 1976 and set up the Guerilla Theatre Unit in order to confront post-independence tyranny and corruption. In 1977 he produced *Opera Wonyosi*, a direct satirical attack on the self-crowned emperor of the short-lived Central African Empire. *A Play of Giants* (1985) parodies some of Africa's worst modern tyrants. *Requiem for a Futurologist* (1985) is a SATIRE on the cult of bogus fortune-tellers and false prophets. Soyinka was awarded the Nobel Prize for Literature in 1986. Since the mid-1980s his major publications have been poetry collections, and essays on drama and literature. *From Zia with Love* (first performed in Italy, 1992) focuses again on civil rights abuses under Nigeria's military regime, the action taking place in a prison cell.

**Spencer, Gabriel** died 1598 English actor. He joined the ADMIRAL'S MEN after the dissolution of Pembroke's Men in 1597. Spencer is remembered only for his death – 'slain in Hogsdon fields by the hands of Benjamin Jonson bricklayer', as HENSLOWE wrote. The cause of his quarrel with JONSON is unknown.

**Sperr, Martin** 1944– German playwright. His first play, *Hunting Scenes from Lower Bavaria* (1966), provides the earliest example of the VOLKSSTÜCK revival. Using village life as a microcosm of social attitudes, it focuses on the persecution of a homosexual. Influenced by EDWARD BOND, his extreme REALISM is designed as 'shock theatre'. As with WOLFGANG BAUER, his use of sex games and sadism results in sensationalism and made his plays notorious. But the ironically idyllic endings of *Tales from Landshut* (1967) and *Munich Freedom* (1971), showing capitalism as literally murderous or suicidal, owe more to HORVÁTH.

**Spurling, John** 1936– British playwright. *MacRune's Guevara* (1969, produced by the NATIONAL THEATRE) gives an account of the life of the Bolivian revolutionary hero, Che Guevara, as interpreted by a dead Scottish Marxist artist, MacRune, and the narrator. Spurling discusses the nature of political myths again in *In the Heart of the British Museum* (1971), which considers three kinds of cultural revolution – in China during the 1960s, in Ovid's Rome and in the Aztec Empire. *The British Empire, Part One* (1980) vividly contrasted different episodes of British colonial history by placing them on side platforms, with a promenade audience. A witty and sophisticated writer, Spurling has likened his ideal theatre to an art gallery. His plays, which include *Shades of Heathcliff* (1971), *Death of Captain Doughty* (1973), *Coming Ashore in Guadaloupe* (1976) and *Antigone through a Looking Glass* (1979), have been staged mainly in studio and FRINGE theatres.

**Squarzina, Luigi** 1922– Italian director and playwright. Since the late 1940s he has been one of the most active and versatile directors in the Italian theatre, for both classic and modern drama. Between 1962 and 1976 he was artistic director of the Teatro Stabile in Genoa, and from 1976 to 1983 of the Teatro Stabile in Rome. His work on classic texts, in particular those of GOLDONI, PIRANDELLO and SHAKESPEARE, has been marked by an intelligent and sensitive orchestration that both serves and illuminates the plays. He was one of the first to re-explore the stage possibilities of D'ANNUNZIO's plays after their modern neglect. Among his notable productions of Shakespeare are *Timon of Athens* (1983) and *The Merchant of Venice* (1992), from his own translation. His many productions of Pirandello include *Ciascuno a suo modo* (*Each in His Own Way*, 1984) and *Come prima meglio di prima* (*As Before Better than Before*, 1990). He has written a number of plays on social and political themes and is a perceptive commentator on the modern Italian stage. His sophisticated comedy *Siamo momentaneamente assenti* (*We Are Temporarily Absent*, 1991) was highly praised.

**stage lighting** Stage lighting, particularly in the 100 years since the first use of electricity in the theatre, has had a profound effect upon staging, scenery, styles of production and acting, and even upon the shape of the theatre building itself. But its impact must be seen against a continuum that takes us back centuries.

Sophisticated electric lighting now employs computers and precisely focused lighting instruments subtly to control the composition, intensity and colour of light. Such control allows atmospheric light to fill the theatrical space, to reveal the living actor and unify him with his stage environment. Its development has encouraged the new, specialist profession of the lighting designer.

Theatre has always used the technology of its period. Stage lighting did not begin with electricity. During the days of candle, oil lamp and gas, great ingenuity was employed to illuminate the stage and provide atmosphere and effects. Primitive theatre used natural light. In ancient Greek outdoor theatre, lighting, of course, came from the sun, and the playwrights learned to utilize natural phenomena. Performances commenced at dawn, and several plays incorporate the sunrise into the script. AESCHYLUS' *Agamemnon*, for example, begins with the Watchman waiting for a beacon that will announce the capture of Troy: in his opening speech he refers to the waning stars, the morning dew and the sunrise. The earliest custom-built English theatres were also open to the elements and natural light. For indoor performances light was admitted or shuttered and artificial light kindled or put out, according to the show, the time of day and the ingenuity of the organizers.

Religious ceremony has always employed the symbolism of light, but the 15th century marks a significant beginning in the employment of artificial light. A Russian bishop describes a display by the architect Brunelleschi (1377–1446) in the church of San Felice, Florence, of *The Annunciation*. From a revolving globe, surrounded by circles of light illuminating translucent clouds, which supported eight cherubim, was lowered another, internally lit globe, containing the Angel Gabriel. This could be darkened by remote control as he stepped out to speak to Mary. As the angel returned and rose into the air, the light blazed forth again.

**The influence of Italy**

The Italian Renaissance theatre became the cradle of stage lighting. The courts of 16th-century Italy provided the opportunity. GUARINI extols the virtue and economy of good lighting for his plays: 'Without artificial lighting, the scene will be deprived of its beauty ... besides, expenses will be reduced ... for the beauty that can be created by light can be made up only by great expense in adorning devices.' In 1545 SERLIO published his *Architettura*, which discusses contemporary theatrical methods. He describes 'general stage light', which lights the whole stage; 'decorative light', ornamenting the perspective picture; and 'mobile light', that often simulates the sun or moon moving across the sky. General light is achieved by torches and chandeliers hung above and to the front of the stage; the chandeliers have reflective glass vessels filled with liquid to aim the light towards the stage. 'A large number of lights are placed leaning at the front of the scene' – the first mention of footlights?

The first recorded stage lighting instrument was the *bozze*. This was a glass vessel of various convex and concave shapes, filled either with oil and wick when used as a lamp, or with coloured liquids as a colour medium, lens or reflector. A number of these, fixed to boards behind holes in the scene, would light up the windows of the street or the many coloured silk transparencies of the pastoral scene. When a strong light was needed 'you put a torch behind a glass and, behind, a barber's basin well burnished'. Thus the spotlight had also arrived. The stage, glowing with multicoloured, flickering light, shimmering with encrusted and translucent scenery and jewel-bedecked costumes, must have been an astonishing and lovely spectacle.

In about 1565 LEONE DE' SOMMI, a dramatist and stage designer of Mantua, anticipated GORDON CRAIG by 350 years when he wrote *Four Dialogues on Scenic Representation* in which his protagonists discourse upon mood and atmosphere. From a stage expressing joy, brightness and life with brilliant and glowing colours, they discuss the onset of tragedy with much of the lighting dimmed or put out. 'This created a profound impression of horror ... and won universal praise.' De' Sommi pointed out that the coloured lens-like *bozze* not only coloured the light effectively but also reduced glare. He recommended the use of mirrors to amplify the lights, but also to allow them to be placed further from the stage, hidden from view behind the wings, to reduce obnoxious smoke. Smoke and heat were severe problems for hundreds of years. De' Sommi also championed the darkened auditorium: 'A man in the shade sees more distinctly an object illuminated from afar.' Further: 'You obviate smoke fumes and render the seeing clearer...you save the Duke fifty ducats in respect of the torches usually set.' Stage lighting had begun!

Angelo Ingeneri (1550–1613) was the scene designer for the famed Teatro Olimpico in Vicenza in 1585. He described lighting in 1598 as 'one matter of supreme theatrical importance'. He also said, 'The darker the auditorium, the more luminous seems the stage.' He wanted light sources concealed and was concerned that the actors' faces be well lit. To this end he proposed the first flown lighting position over the front of the stage: 'a valance ... on the inner side fitted with lamps having tinsel reflectors'. Ingeneri described the use of gauze to give an effect of mystery and stressed the creative use of light and darkness to enhance the drama.

Stage lighting was becoming systematized, and SABBATTINI in his *Manual for Theatrical Scenes and*

*Machines* (1638) describes that system in words and drawings. He started a discussion of the problems of footlights that was to last for over 300 years. JOSEF FURTTENBACH, a German who studied in Italy, and published *Architectura Recreationis* in 1640, gives a detailed description of lighting which includes *bozzi* with reflectors in a seven-foot-deep upstage pit, as well as, for the first time, rows of lamps overhead 'between the clouds'. This completed the repertoire of Renaissance lighting that created precedents for patterns of thought and practice that still pertain today.

Italian influence spread across Europe, with each country emphasizing one aspect or another according to their own theatrical tradition. In England, INIGO JONES bought and used some *bozzi* in 1609. He opened English theatre to Italian-style spectacle and employed multicoloured lights in profusion, but his more old-fashioned flambeaux torches, used in the Whitehall Banqueting Room, so damaged the ceiling paintings that theatrical performances there were stopped.

The Puritan revolution brought English theatre to a halt, but the future King Charles II, living in France, saw much of theatrical development in the French court. With the English Restoration, London theatres were built and restored, but were now indoors. The COCKPIT (1660) had two chandeliers and five pairs of sconces. In the Hall Theatre (1665) tin lanterns and reflectors are described, but a few years later these were supplanted by 130 candlesticks with reflectors. Footlights, too, are described in February 1670. The frontispiece to *The Wits*, 1672, shows an indoor stage but with an almost Elizabethan thrust, lit with chandeliers and footlights.

In France, the court led the way to innovation. Detailed descriptions of the *Ballet Comique de La Reine* (1581) tell of scenery glittering with gold and jewels, illuminated by many lamps. In 1641 in Paris, CARDINAL RICHELIEU began the horseshoe-shaped PALAIS-ROYAL theatre, where MOLIÈRE was later to perform. Footlights with 50 lamps, each with five flames, supplemented candles on vertical lighting poles at either side of the stage and chandeliers in the auditorium. The French theatre blazed with light throughout, unlike the Italian, where more frequently the auditorium was darkened to increase the impact of the stage.

In Italy FERDINANDO BIBIENA and his family led the movement that produced astonishing vistas on the stage. GIOVANNI SERVANDONI, who worked extensively in Paris, developed further the use of distorted perspective and transparencies to create the impression of vast distances and spectacle. In 1738 he opened his Spectacle d'Optique in the SALLE DES MACHINES, Paris, with a stage 40 metres deep. From a darkened auditorium, spectators watched performances depicting mythological events, which used live and painted figures in gigantic settings. 'A large number of lamps were so well arranged that it all resembled a tableau of a perfectly arranged chiaroscuro.' Outside the conventional theatre, such spectacles, under the direction of leading stage designers such as DE LOUTHERBOURG (in 1781) and Daguerre (in 1822), proved their popularity time and again. Their value as an occasion for experiment, which returns benefit to the theatre, has parallels for today, where high-budget, industrial theatre and rock-and-roll spectacle provide a similar opportunity for development.

England's great actor and director, DAVID GARRICK, travelled to the Continent in 1765 and returned determined to modernize the lighting at his Theatre Royal, DRURY LANE. He introduced wing- and footlights with reflectors and removed the overhanging chandeliers. His great scene designer, De Loutherbourg, used colour-changing silks on his side lighting.

Stage lighting was growing ever brighter. Tallow candles in the footlights were replaced by more expensive but efficient wax candles. In 1784 the Argand oil lamp was developed, with a chimney. It was as bright as a dozen wax candles. Used with reflectors, it created new conditions on the stage, which contributed towards the reduction of make-up and the introduction of new styles of COSTUME, and encouraged another step towards more naturalistic acting.

## Gaslight

In 1803 the LYCEUM THEATRE, London, was the scene of a historic demonstration: lighting by gas. It was not until 1817 that the stage of this theatre was to be the first in England lit by the new substance. A month later, the Drury Lane stage blazed with the new light; and across the Atlantic, the CHESTNUT STREET THEATRE, Philadelphia, had installed gas the year before. The owners, it was reported, 'flatter themselves that its superior safety, brilliance and neatness will be satisfactory'.

The gas burned with a bare flame, for the mantle would not be invented until the end of the 19th century. Albeit dependent on the quality of the gas, the light it produced was brighter and whiter than even the Argand lamp. It burned without changing intensity and required no trimming of wicks – and, most vitally, it was easier to control. The brightness could be varied by regulating the gas supply, and a 'gas table' that allowed control of separate parts of the stage became the first 'stage switchboard'. At the Paris Opéra in 1822 the former ballet-master wrote, 'This light is perfect for the stage. One can obtain gradation of brightness that is really magical.' But there were problems. The smell of gas could be offensive and the danger from heat was more serious than ever. Bare gas jets next to wood and canvas presented a major hazard. The Chestnut Street Theatre was one of the first of hundreds to burn down.

Gaslight could not provide a beam or shaft of light any better than its predecessors could. But in 1826 a new light source, limelight, was invented. W. C. MACREADY tested it in his PANTOMIME *Peeping Tom of Coventry* at COVENT GARDEN in 1837. Limelight used a block of limestone heated by an oxygen/hydrogen flame to provide an intense point source that could be installed in a hand-operated spotlight. This, for the first time, was used to provide strong accents of light across the stage.

The practice of darkening the auditorium during the performance was introduced in England by HENRY IRVING, who was a great innovator in stage lighting and sought to enhance his productions with the imaginative use of light and shade. Bram Stoker, his lighting assistant, said, 'It became an easy matter to throw any special part of the stage into greater prominence.' Irving had extensive lighting rehearsals, without actors but attended by the staff, which included his 30 gasmen and eight limelight operators. In 1857, Charles Garnier's new Paris Opéra had opened. It contained a lighting system with 28 miles of piping, feeding 960 gas jets from a gas table of 88 stopcocks. A Parisian lighting catalogue of 1877 contains details of many types of instrument, including carbon-arc spotlights which ranged from versions that could flood the whole stage to small hand-held follow spotlights.

## Electric light

In 1881 the Savoy Theatre in London opened with an electric lighting installation. It used 1,158 incandescent lamps, of which 824 were on the stage, controlled by six dimmers. Richard D'Oyly Carte appeared before the curtain and demonstrated the new safety of electricity by smashing a lit lamp wrapped in muslin. This was greeted with tumultuous cheers.

The electrical revolution quickly spread across the world. David Belasco tells us that the first theatre in the USA to be equipped with electricity was the California in San Francisco. However, for many years electric light was used only to replace the gas jets. When the footlights, battens and vertical strips at the side of the stage were converted to the new electricity, the light was brighter, had no smell and was much safer. Despite frequent criticism of excessive, harsh brightness, theatres rapidly increased the number of lamps used. But it was many years before the spotlight, coupled to the dimmer, began to offer new opportunities.

Meanwhile, in reaction against the flat glare of early electric light, GORDON CRAIG and ADOLPHE APPIA were dreaming of a new stage lighting. Both rejected the increasingly realistic scenery of their time, and both, inspired by the beauty and evocative power of natural light, imagined a stage with the actor within an environment unified by being filled with three-dimensional light. Craig and Appia were more influential with their writings than their all too few productions. Others, perhaps without realizing it, took up the challenge that their inspiration posed.

In the USA DAVID BELASCO was the first director of the 20th century to pay great attention to lighting. Lighting rehearsals for his productions could take weeks, and he established a lighting laboratory to plan the lighting in advance. His lighting engineer Louis Hartmann was responsible for the development of the first incandescent spotlights. This team also introduced indirect overhead lighting by shining spotlights into reflective silver-coated bowls, which produced a soft, naturalistic impression of light from the sky. Today, a multiplicity of carefully focused spotlights creates an equally soft and potentially naturalistic impression, but with the advantage of precise control.

In 1917 Hartmann's baby spotlights were first introduced in England by the director BASIL DEAN. He, like Belasco, was intensely concerned with stage lighting, and also introduced German equipment such as the acting-area flood. In 1923 he installed a Schwabe cyclorama system at the St Martin's Theatre, London, and in *R.U.R.* used scene projection in England for the first time. In 1939 he directed J. B. PRIESTLEY's *Johnson over Jordan*, devising with his electrician, Bill Lorraine, an English version of Hartmann's reflected light.

A giant of the German theatre who shared Dean's conviction of the importance of lighting was the director MAX REINHARDT. His versatility made him a master of the stage, in the Gordon Craig tradition, with productions that ranged from the vast and spectacular like *The Miracle* to the most intimate, such as his work at the Redoutensaal recital room in Vienna. 'Lighting must replace the decorations,' he wrote in 1901. In Germany the practice of repertoire, with a different performance every night, led to large stages equipped with bridges hung over the stage to carry the lighting, which could thus be readily reached and reset by electricians. Equipment was large but finely engineered. High-quality optics and spacious stages encouraged developments in large-scale scene projection. Linnebach, Haseit and other German engineers developed a pattern of stage lighting which, from the 1920s, was to remain largely unchanged for many years. Meanwhile in the USA and later in England, lighting in the form of electric lamps in rows of battens (or X-rays) and footlights imitating the soft overall lighting of the age of gas began to change. (The oldest specialist stage lighting manufacturer is Kliegl Bros of New York, founded in 1896. In England, Strand Electric was founded in 1914 and remained the leading British company in the field for over 80 years.)

Intensity control of electric light was achieved with dimmers, variable resistances or auto-transformers, the operation of which was synchronized by increasingly sophisticated mechanical linkage systems. A grand master control allowed dimmers to be connected via shafts and clutches to a central lever or wheel. Frederick Bentham, inspired by a lifelong enthusiasm for 'colour music', mixing light to music, conceived that lighting should be controlled in a way that was analogous to music. He developed the light console – one man instead of many could control several hundred dimmers. Remote control systems were installed by WEST END commercial managements a decade before such systems were adopted by BROADWAY. The emerging, and wealthy, television industry in Britain adopted the principle of dimmer control for each light, and installed similar control systems. The advent of the computer led to the first memory control.

In the USA, Ed Kook founded Century Lighting. He developed the compact ellipsoidal spotlight, often colloquially named the Leko, after himself and his partner Levy. More significantly, Kook supported the emergence of the new professional in the theatre, the lighting designer. While in England between the wars lighting was the province of the director, with men such as TERENCE GRAY and NORMAN MARSHALL working with their electrician Harold Ridge, in the USA lighting remained the designer's responsibility. LEE SIMONSON, NORMAN BEL GEDDES, ROBERT EDMOND JONES, DONALD OENSLAGER and JO MIELZINER all extended the use of lighting as an integral part of their scene designs.

## Lighting design

In 1925, Stanley McCandless was appointed to teach stage lighting at Yale University. Specialists in lighting design including JEAN ROSENTHAL began to establish a profession around the lighting process. In the UK Richard Pilbrow founded Theatre Projects in 1957. He introduced methods of pre-planning lighting as well as equipment from America and Germany. He also developed a team of lighting designers, and in so doing established the lighting design profession in Britain. Through the 1980s, with the impact of CAMERON MACKINTOSH's worldwide work as producer of the English 'mega-hit' musicals (*Cats, Les Misérables, Miss Saigon, Phantom of the Opera* and *Sunset Boulevard*), this lighting influence went international. The spectacular productions demonstrated dramatic stage lighting, employing all the resources of modern technology to enhance and underpin the drama of story and song.

Government financial support of regional and national theatres in the 1970s and 1980s in the UK led to considerable improvement in stage design and lighting. And there were other factors that led to an explosion of lighting opportunity, such as commercial presentations and the emergence of the popular music industry, introducing techniques that later influenced theatrical practice. In the USA, unlike Britain, major universities offer training in stage lighting design. Just as 18th-century designers took their work outside the theatre, so today the lighting designer's skills find a wider audience. Designed lighting in architecture shows the significant impact of theatre practice, as does lighting for television. Rock-and-roll concert lighting and industrial theatre and exhibitions have been fruitful areas of operation for the designer, and have also offered opportunity for experiment.

British and American techniques increasingly merged in the 1980s. Lighting is now achieved with a multiplicity of spotlights which may be coloured with a choice of hundreds of different shades of plastic colour media. Accent light is provided by low-voltage beam projectors or PAR (parabolic reflector sealed beam) reflector lamps. Instruments are still usually positioned overhead on pipes in rows across the stage and vertically at the side. In the 1950s probably 200 instruments were commonplace, but in 1995 between 600 and 1200 units, of an average power of 1000 watts, are the norm.

The advent of the computer has brought the ability to memorize at the touch of a button a complete lighting picture. As theatre consultant to the NATIONAL THEATRE Richard Pilbrow designed Lightboard, establishing a standard for most of the subsequent control systems. Lightboard developed Bentham's 'playability', but with a new freedom to mix pre-recorded lighting images or 'groups'; it offered for the first time a control that combined intensity recording with remote-control focusing. Only in the mid-1990s, as a consequence of the greater memory, speed and cheapness of micro-processors, does the prospect of another leap forward in lighting control appear possible, as computer power promises to use graphics and computer modelling techniques to close the loop between the visual image on the stage and the mind processes of the designer.

The centuries-old argument over footlights and the need for light from the front and above the actor is long over. Front-of-house spotlighting was first mounted on the front of the balconies, then invaded the audience boxes, and now hundreds of instruments may be used. New theatres make elaborate provision, with bridges in the ceiling and slots in the walls, to allow light to reach the stage with the greatest possible freedom of angle.

In Europe (even in Germany), lighting design has generally not made such creative advances as in Britain and the USA, except in the work of some exceptional artists. WIELAND WAGNER, in directing his grandfather's operas at BAYREUTH, created memorable images with light. JOSEF SVOBODA, the Czech scenographer, has opened new vistas. The emergence of the professional lighting designer has been slow to gain acceptance in central Europe, in part because of union traditions, but this is now finally changing in the 1990s thanks to the pioneer work of such as Munich's Max Keller, as well as to the influence of visiting British designers.

Each step of progress in lighting – candle to oil lamp, oil lamp to gas, gas to electricity – has brought change. Each step has been followed by changes in acting technique and ever more subtle and often more realistic scenery, costumes and make-up. The actor's scenic environment has become more three-dimensional. Physical thickness, depth and texture, used with light, have replaced much of the painted detail of previous ages. But the most significant change has been in the theatres themselves, and in the relationship between the actor and the audience. Only in the late 19th century did it become normal to darken the auditorium: the desire for increased NATURALISM and audience concentration on the stage made dimming the houselights symbol of the play's commencement. The actor had to perform upstage of the proscenium lighting in order to be seen, and a gulf grew between him and the darkened audience. Almost immediately visionary directors realized that this broke the fragile bond of communication that lay at the heart of live theatre, which is the interplay between performer and spectator.

The coming of the spotlight, which illuminated space from a distance, not only allowed the actors' faces to be lit from the auditorium, but allowed the actor to work in lit space that could be placed within the audience. So a re-examination of antique and new forms of theatre began. Theatre-in-the-round, and thrust, transverse, environmental and open stages all became legitimate means of theatrical expression. All were enabled by lighting to place actor and audience in the same space, while allowing the proper focus of attention to remain with the performer. Once more the actor is able to be at the heart of his audience. At a point in theatre history where new, electronic means of storytelling challenge the live theatre as never before, this rediscovered intimacy, this living contact, continues to give theatre its uniqueness in a world of ever more dazzling media.

**Stage Society, Incorporated** (London) The successor to Grein's INDEPENDENT THEATRE SOCIETY was founded in 1899 to produce modern plays that had been refused a licence for public performance, in professional stage conditions on Sunday nights when the theatres were otherwise closed. It was the first to produce SHAW's early plays, opening with *You Never Can Tell* and successfully asserting its freedom from stage CENSORSHIP with *Mrs Warren's Profession* (1902). As well as opening the theatre to other new English works like GRANVILLE BARKER's *Waste* (1907), the Society introduced a whole range of major European dramatists – from the NATURALISM of HAUPTMANN, GORKY and TOLSTOI to forerunners of EXPRESSIONISM like KAISER and WEDEKIND. It provided the impetus for the influential 1904–7 ROYAL COURT seasons of VEDRENNE and Granville Barker, who gained his experience as an actor and director in early Stage Society productions. It also initiated the Phoenix Society. This was formed to continue the revivals of Restoration comedy that had been started in 1915, and was instrumental in bringing early English drama back to the public stage between 1919 and 1925 with a series of productions ranging from MARLOWE and JONSON to DRYDEN and WYCHERLEY.

In the interwar period the Stage Society continued its function of championing new and unlicensed works – including the plays of James Joyce, D. H. LAWRENCE, John Van Druten and R. C. SHERRIFF as well as PIRANDELLO, COCTEAU, ODETS and GARCÍA LORCA (*Blood Wedding* being its final production in 1939) – although by that time it was no longer unique and its role had been largely taken over by the GROUP THEATRE and by Peter Godfrey and NORMAN MARSHALL at the GATE THEATRE.

**Stainless Stephen** [Arthur Baynes] 1892–1971 British comedian. Sheffield-born and an ex-schoolteacher, he built into his act both his regional identity – stainless steel shirt front and bowler hat band – and his former professional pedantry – through the technique of speaking the punctuation of his script (not to mention his own stage directions) as if giving dictation.

**Stanfield, Clarkson** 1793–1867 English scene-painter. Stanfield was at sea from 1808 to 1815, and seascapes remained a feature of his later painting. ELLISTON employed him at DRURY LANE in 1823 in order to challenge the supremacy of JOHN HENDERSON GRIEVE's family at COVENT GARDEN. Admired as a marine and landscape artist, he was elected to the Royal Academy in 1835. MACREADY persuaded Stanfield to paint scenes for him at Covent Garden, the 1839 diorama for *Henry V* being particularly famous. Among the finest of his many dioramas were his Plymouth Breakwater (1823) and his Venice (1831), admired for the depiction of the subtle textures and colourings of water. In all he made over 550 recorded scenes.

**Stanislavsky** [Alekseev], **Konstantin (Sergeevich)** 1863–1938 Russian actor, director and teacher. He created the most influential 'system' of acting in the Western world. In 1888 Stanislavsky (he adopted this stage name in 1885) co-founded the amateur Moscow Society of Art and Literature (1888), where he acted a variety of roles.

His first directorial effort for the Society, LEV TOLSTOI's *The Fruits of Enlightenment* (1891), was admired by VLADIMIR NEMIROVICH-DANCHENKO. In 1897 they founded the MOSCOW ART THEATRE, dedicated to the highest ideals of ensemble art, naturalness, simplicity, the alternation of large and small roles for each performer and the detailed realization of the essence of the play. The company opened with an antiquarian-set, naturalistically staged (see NATURALISM) production of A. K. TOLSTOI's historical drama, *Tsar Fyodor Ioannovich* (1898). MAT's second production, CHEKHOV's *The Seagull*, featured sensitive acting and a rich overlay of sound, lighting and scenic effects deemed necessary by Stanislavsky, if not by Chekhov. In this production Stanislavsky scored a personal triumph as Trigorin.

As an actor, he excelled in all of Chekhov's plays for MAT – as Astrov in *Uncle Vanya* (1899), Vershinin in *The Three Sisters* (1901), Gaev in *The Cherry Orchard* (1904) – as well as in plays by IBSEN, GORKY, GRIBOEDOV and MOLIÈRE, roles which required in-depth preparation and total transformation of his physical appearance. He also became interested in new symbolist staging (see SYMBOLISM) and invited GORDON CRAIG, ALEXANDRE BENOIS and VSEVOLOD MEYERHOLD to direct with MAT.

Stanislavsky's own 'system' was tested and developed at MAT's First Studio (1912), and the theatre enjoyed its first post-revolutionary success – *Twelfth Night* – in 1917. Stanislavsky side-stepped the effects of the Revolution by working at the Bolshoi Theatre's opera studio, continuing to supervise experimental studio work and administering MAT's European and American tours (1922–4). His productions of OSTROVSKY's *The Ardent Heart* (1926) and BEAUMARCHAIS's *The Marriage of Figaro* (1927) embraced the grotesque even as he began to record the tenets of his realistic acting system (see REALISM).

To publicize the American tour he hastily and somewhat carelessly assembled the autobiographical *My Life in Art*, which he revised in 1926 and 1936. The first part of his text *The Actor's Work on Himself* was completed in 1937, at which point he began the second part. Stanislavsky advocated a balance between the actor's inner experiencing of the role (*perezhivaniye*) and its precisely attuned physical and vocal expression. He was named a People's Artist of the USSR in 1936 and, save for occasional lapses in popularity, his system has remained the basis of Russian acting. The confused publication history of his acting text in the United States and Americans' penchant for self-analysis and self-expression led to the psychologically and emotionally based 'Method' approach of New York's ACTORS STUDIO, which has been mistaken for the original system. The misleading Russian editions of Stanislavsky's text and the similarly inaccurate American texts (*An Actor Prepares*, *Building a Character* and *Creating a Role*), translated and edited by Elizabeth Reynolds Hapgood, are being replaced by complete editions of the original work in Russian and English.

**Stapleton, Maureen** 1925– American actress. Among her outstanding roles has been Serafina in *The Rose Tattoo* (1951), Flora in *27 Wagons Full of Cotton* (1955), Lady Torrance in *Orpheus Descending* (1957) and Carrie in *Toys in the Attic* (1960). Her performance as Eva, the alcoholic performer in NEIL SIMON's *The Gingerbread Lady* (1970), was described as 'remorselessly honest'.

**Steele, Sir Richard** 1672–1729 Irish playwright and essayist. He responded to the criticisms of JEREMY COLLIER by producing a drama that was both entertaining and moral. *The Funeral* (1701) was a FARCE about undertaking, but *The Lying Lover* (1703) and *The Tender Husband* (1703) were serious studies of virtue in a comic world – to be strong influences on the development of sentimental comedy. But the plays were not successful and Steele began editing a series of periodicals, including *The Tatler* (1709–11), *The Spectator* (1711–12), *The Guardian* (1713), *The Englishman* (1713–15), *Town Talk* (1715) and *The Theatre* (1720), all of which frequently discussed theatre and drama, advocating new plays and satirizing the stage. In 1715 he became manager of DRURY LANE. His fourth and last play, *The Conscious Lovers* (1722), was a serious, influential sentimental comedy founded on middle-class morality.

**Stein, Gertrude** (1874–1946) American literary figure. A novelist, playwright, poet and American icon, Stein produced over 500 titles, 75 of them plays published in three collections: *Geography and Plays* (1922), *Operas and Plays* (1932) and *Last Operas and Plays* (1949). Most were never produced because of the obscurity of the writing, which represented in words the surrealistic techniques (see SURREALISM) of modern art. *Yes Is for a Very Young Man* (1944), *The Mother of Us All* (1945), and *Four Saints in Three Acts* (1934), the last two with music by Virgil Thomson, are sometimes produced.

**Stein, Peter** 1937– German director. Stein's collective productions at the Berlin Schaubühne, which he established in 1970, have provided some of the most interesting work in contemporary German theatre. Highly political, his approach has been based on meticulous research into the social and political context of a text. This creative rehearsal method has culminated in independent performances exploring the ethos of an era, such as KLEIST's *Prince of Homburg* (1972) and the double-evening Total Theatre spectacle *Shakespeare's Memory* (1976), which presented the background material for the ensemble's staging of *As You Like It* (1977). His strikingly objective interpretations of the classics (IBSEN's *Peer Gynt*, 1971; GORKY's *Summer Folk*, 1974; AESCHYLUS'

*Oresteia*, 1980; CHEKHOV's *Three Sisters*, 1984, and *The Cherry Orchard*, 1989) expose the contemporary relevance of historical attitudes. The Schaubühne's preeminence faded in the 1980s. Since Stein resigned in 1985 he has directed for the Welsh National Opera and in 1992 produced *Julius Caesar* at the Salzburg Festival.

**Steiner, Rolando** 1935– Nicaraguan playwright, journalist and critic. He returned to Managua from study in Spain to work for *La Prensa*, the major newspaper. His three one-act plays, *Judith, Un drama corriente* (*An Ordinary Drama*) and *La puerta* (*The Door*), were collected under the title *La trilogía del matrimonio* (*The Matrimonial Trilogy*) and published in 1970.

**Steinsson, Gudmundur** 1925– Icelandic playwright. His tragicomic *A Brief Respite* (1979) broke box-office records in Iceland and has since been produced in eight countries. Essentially a critique of the consumer society mentality, the play depicts an average urban family caught in the rat race, where there is no time for anything – not even for death. Another popular play is the farcical *Viva España* (1976), which describes holidaymakers in Spain, their boredom, alienation and sexual frustration under a veneer of marital bliss. A satirist, some of his works are large-scale allegories. Important plays include *Matthew* (1975), *The Garden Party* (1982) and *The Wedding Portrait* (1986).

**Stepanova, Varvara (Fyodorovna)** 1894–1958 Soviet designer. One of the original group of constructivist designers (see LYUBOV POPOVA), she is remembered for her distinctive work on MEYERHOLD's production of SUKHOVO-KOBYLIN's *Tarelkin's Death* (24 November 1922). Indebted to Popova's design for *The Magnanimous Cuckold* (1922), the *Tarelkin* set consisted of pieces of booby-trapped, white-painted wooden furniture. Whereas Popova had designed the entire space, Stepanova simply inhabited hers with designed objects. The CARNIVAL-esque tone of the production is representative of the 'eccentrist' trend of the day.

**Stephens, Robert** 1931–95 British actor. At the ROYAL COURT THEATRE he played in *The Crucible* (1956) with the English Stage Company, in OSBORNE's *The Entertainer* (1957) and *Epitaph for George Dillon* (1958). He was often cast as a smooth young man, perhaps untrustworthy. The range of his talents was not recognized until after LAURENCE OLIVIER invited him to join the NATIONAL THEATRE company in 1963. He appeared in the NT's *Hamlet, St Joan* and *The Recruiting Officer*, but his first great success came as Atahuallpa in PETER SHAFFER's *The Royal Hunt of the Sun* (1964). Through arduous physical training and brilliant vocal and MIME control, Stephens transformed himself into an image of the Sun God of the Incas. Other major roles followed in such NT productions as *Armstrong's Last Goodnight, Trelawny of the 'Wells', A Bond Honoured* and *The Dance of Death*. He continued his NT career under PETER HALL, appearing in *The Cherry Orchard* (1978) and *Brand* (1978), but by the mid-1970s he was equally well known as a television and film star. He was a memorable Falstaff in ADRIAN NOBLE's *Henry IV, Parts 1 and 2* (ROYAL SHAKESPEARE COMPANY, 1991). His performance as Lear in Noble's RSC production (1993) demonstrated his commanding stage presence, rarely used by the British national companies since the 1960s.

**Sternheim, Carl** 1878–1942 German playwright. His eight comedies under the title *Scenes from the Heroic Life of the Middle Classes* have become modern classics. Sometimes listed as a forerunner of EXPRESSIONISM, his

work is more in the tradition of MOLIÈRE, although the closest German counterpart is the satiric sketches of Georg Grosz. Chronicling the rise of the Maske family over three generations from *The Knickers* (1911) to *1913* and *Tabula Rasa* (1919), this cycle portrays the moral anarchy of a soulless society in figures who have no core of personality behind their materialistic obsessions and whose language is fragmented cliché, transforming the commonplace into the grotesque. In some ways anticipating the THEATRE OF THE ABSURD beneath their naturalistic surface, the plays were repeatedly banned, but *The Snob*, originally produced by REINHARDT in 1914, was the first play to be staged in Berlin when the theatres reopened after 1945.

**Stevens, Roger (Lacey)** 1910– American producer. Since producing *Twelfth Night* on BROADWAY in 1949, Stevens has been associated with many of the leading theatrical groups of the USA, including the ACTORS STUDIO Theatre and the AMERICAN SHAKESPEARE (Festival) THEATRE. His productions have won numerous awards. He chaired the National Council on the Arts during 1964–9. Until 1988 he headed the JOHN F. KENNEDY CENTER FOR THE PERFORMING ARTS in Washington, DC.

**Stevenson, Juliet** 1956– British actress. She emerged to stardom through the ranks of the ROYAL SHAKESPEARE COMPANY. In 1981/2 she played leading roles in three RSC productions: *A Midsummer Night's Dream, The Witch of Edmonton* and EDWARD BULWER LYTTON's *Money*, before moving to the ROYAL COURT to appear in ROBERT HOLMAN's *Other Worlds* (1983). She returned to the RSC to play Isabella in *Measure for Measure* (1983) and appeared in STEPHEN POLIAKOFF's *Breaking the Silence* (1984). In 1986, she played La Présidente de Tourvel in CHRISTOPHER HAMPTON's adaptation of Laclos's *Les Liaisons Dangereuses* in the RSC's studio, the Pit. She played Cressida in the RSC's *Troilus and Cressida* (1986) as a feminist role-model, a cool, wary girl taking her chances among male war games; while at the other extreme, she was an anguished Yerma in a revival of GARCÍA LORCA's play at the NATIONAL THEATRE's Cottesloe. She is a precise actress with an element of surprise in her playing. She holds back her expressions of feeling until the point when they are so long-awaited as to seem inevitable; and then she erupts in fury or passion, e.g. her performance as Hedda Gabler in the NT's production of IBSEN's play in 1989. Her Paulina in Ariel Dorfman's *Death and the Maiden* (1991), a part that could have veered towards MELODRAMA, she kept under strict control. She has also performed in film and on television.

**Stewart, Nellie** [Eleanor] 1858–1931 Australian actress. Daughter of the actress Theodosia Yates (Mrs Guerin), she appeared aged five with CHARLES KEAN in Melbourne, and in childhood toured internationally in *Rainbow Revels*, written for the Stewart family. She first starred in the PANTOMIME *Sinbad* in 1880, and was identified with many musical roles, including Griolet in *La Fille du Tambour Major*, Sweet Nell of Old Drury and Cinderella. Her lifelong companion George Musgrove managed her career in Australia, England and America. An enchanting performer even in old age, she played Romeo in the balcony scene shortly before her death.

**stock company** Nineteenth-century play production in England and the USA was typified by the independent stock company of a permanent troupe of actors headed by an actor-manager and performing a number of different works in REPERTORY rotation, either in a permanent house or on tour. Actors were cast according to type or 'line', which usually resulted in 'stock' characterizations, and productions were mounted from the company's meagre collection or 'stock' of scenery and props (actors furnished COSTUMES).

Economically undermined by the advent of expensive, visiting international stars (mainly from Britain), American stock companies were further diminished by the 1880s when rail travel facilitated the growth of combination companies, which travelled complete with star, full cast, scenery and costumes. By the end of the century most professional theatre production was centralized in New York City and most American theatres were controlled by the THEATRICAL SYNDICATE, an infamous booking outfit.

**Stoll, Oswald (Gray)** 1866–1942 British manager. Born in Australia, he had various provincial successes in management before he took over the London COLISEUM (1904), which in his hands became a home for giant CIRCUSES, gargantuan musicals and MAX REINHARDT's epics. In 1911 he left Moss Empires and joined Walter Gibbons's Variety Theatres Consolidated, thereby gaining 29 halls. He was knighted in 1919.

**Stone, John Augustus** 1800–34 American playwright and actor. Stone's *Metamora, or The Last of Wampanoags* (1829) won EDWIN FORREST's first playwriting contest and became Forrest's property and his 'war-horse' piece, with over 200 performances. The Stone–Forrest Indian chief epitomized the natural goodness of the 'noble savage': brave, chivalrous, gentle towards his squaw. As an actor Stone mostly played eccentric comics or bluff old men. He wrote nine other unsuccessful plays.

**Stoppard [Straussler], Tom** 1937– British playwright. Born in Czechoslovakia, he emigrated to Britain with his family in 1946. After working as a journalist Stoppard began to write plays for television and radio (see TELEVISION DRAMA; RADIO DRAMA), and his first television play, *A Walk on the Water* (1963), was later adapted for the stage as *Enter a Free Man* (1968). In much of his work the influence of Polish and Czech absurdist writers (see THEATRE OF THE ABSURD) can be felt.

His first major success came with *Rozencrantz and Guildenstern Are Dead* (1966), which was originally produced on the EDINBURGH FESTIVAL FRINGE but later staged by the NATIONAL THEATRE. The story of *Hamlet* is seen through the eyes of two attendant courtiers who do not know, to the point of their deaths, what is going on; through Stoppard's wit and technical virtuosity, this sad farce about the human condition became a powerful myth for British audiences. The professor of moral philosophy, George, in *Jumpers* (1972) is similarly out of touch with the politics of a brave new world; while Henry Carr in *Travesties* (1974) is a minor British consular official in Zurich in 1917, a city visited by Lenin, James Joyce and Tristan Tzara, of whose significance Carr is sublimely unaware. Stoppard's political agnosticism and his sympathy with the underdog led to a concern for those imprisoned by totalitarian regimes, as manifested in his play (with music by André Previn), *Every Good Boy Deserves Favour* (1977); his liberal scepticism permeates *Night and Day* (1978), about politics and Western journalism in an African state.

But his zest for language and skilful plotting also generate an atmosphere of sheer fun, as in his Whitehall FARCE *Dirty Linen* (1976), *Dogg's Hamlet* and

*Cahoot's Macbeth* (1979), and his adaptation of a play by the Austrian playwright JOHANN NESTROY, *On the Razzle* (1981). His serious comedy about adultery, *The Real Thing* (1982), was equally successful in the WEST END and on BROADWAY. *Hapgood* (1988) was a mixture of spy novel and farce, while *Artist Descending a Staircase* (1988) was a comic homage to the surrealists. *Arcadia* (1993) was a high comedy of ideas, with insight and laughter inseparable. *Indian Ink* (1995) assesses Anglo-Indian relations over 50 years.

**Storey, David (Malcolm)** 1933– British playwright and novelist. His early novels (including *This Sporting Life*, 1960) describe the Yorkshire working-class background which permeates his later plays. *The Restoration of Arnold Middleton*, first shown at the ROYAL COURT THEATRE in 1967, shows a provincial schoolmaster, driven to madness through an unhappy marriage and homesickness for his lost Northern childhood. When Storey teamed up with his sympathetic director, LINDSAY ANDERSON, his plays gained in sharpness and dramatic effect. *In Celebration* (1969) ironically contrasts the lifestyles of two generations of the Shaw family. Storey's observation of working environments provided the framework for *The Contractor* (1969), in which a large wedding marquee is raised and lowered on stage; *The Changing Room* (1971), about a rugby team; *The Farm* (1973); and *Life Class* (1974). *Home* (1970), in which JOHN GIELGUD and RALPH RICHARDSON appeared, describes a rest home for the near-senile, a model for Britain itself. This satirical, allegorical vein appears in *Cromwell* (1973), the curious black sex farce *Mother's Day* (1976) and *Sisters* (1978). *Early Days* (1980) provided Ralph Richardson with a fine role as an elder statesman contemplating his past life. *The March on Russia* (1989) and *Stages* (1992) continue to show Storey's understanding of class alienation.

**Strange's Men** English company. A prominent Elizabethan household theatre, it first appeared at Elizabeth I's court in 1582. Its patron was the son of the Earl of Derby. Strange's Men often amalgamated with other companies, e.g. with the ADMIRAL'S MEN at the THEATRE in 1590–1 and at the ROSE in 1592–3. Among prominent players were RICHARD BURBAGE, WILLIAM SLY and AUGUSTINE PHILLIPS. SHAKESPEARE associated with these three to form the nucleus of the LORD CHAMBERLAIN'S MEN in 1594. His early plays were possibly in the repertoire of Strange's Men.

**Stranitzky, Josef Anton** 1676–1726 Austrian actor. An itinerant comedian, he moved in 1705 to Vienna, where he acted with Johann Baptist Hilverding's troupe at a fair booth and created the part of a Salzburg peasant, the comic character HANSWURST. This became a leading role when he took over the company in 1706 and moved it to the new Kärntnertor Theatre in 1711. Stranitzky's Hanswurst was earthy and foul-mouthed, improvising irreverently even in the lofty HAUPT- UND STAATSAKTIONEN. He made a fortune and, as actor-author, founded a tradition that would descend to NESTROY.

**Strasberg, Lee** 1901–82 American director and acting teacher. Strasberg studied at the AMERICAN LABORATORY THEATRE, acted with the THEATRE GUILD and in 1931 helped found and directed for the GROUP THEATRE, espousing the work of the Russian director, KONSTANTIN STANISLAVSKY. Among his directorial successes were *The House of Connelly*, *Night over Taos*, *Men in White* and *Clash by Night*. In 1950 he became a director for the ACTORS

STUDIO and emerged as the leading exponent of the Method, based on the Stanislavsky system. In 1965 he directed a highly controversial *Three Sisters* at the Aldwych Theatre in London. Many of America's leading film and stage actors studied with Strasberg, among them MARLON BRANDO, whose 'internal' style as Stanley in *A Streetcar Named Desire* became popularly associated with Method acting. Others were Montgomery Clift, ANNE BANCROFT, Shelley Winters, Paul Newman and Joanne Woodward. Although his methods and results excited great controversy, Strasberg had a major effect on modern acting.

**Stratford Festival** (Canada) An annual summer festival in Stratford, Ontario, and the leading classical repertory theatre in North America. In 1952 a group of Stratford citizens invited TYRONE GUTHRIE to help them establish a summer SHAKESPEARE Festival. He and designer TANYA MOISEIWITSCH created an architecturally complete apron stage and then built a theatre round it, initially under a canvas roof. From the opening night of *Richard III* on 13 July 1953, the daring concept and high standards of production made the Festival an immense critical and popular success.

Guthrie's flair and originality maintained the excitement over three seasons before he handed control to MICHAEL LANGHAM who, over the next ten years, consolidated Guthrie's achievements and built the company into a superb acting ensemble. In 1957 a permanent building replaced the earlier tent, and the Festival soon took over a second theatre with a conventional proscenium. JEAN GASCON succeeded Langham in 1968. The Gascon era was a time of ambitious expansion. The repertoire grew to include not only MOLIÈRE and other European classics but also JONSON, WEBSTER, and the less familiar Shakespeare such as *Cymbeline* and *Pericles*. In 1970 Gascon established the smaller Third Stage for new and experimental works. The Festival company toured extensively in Canada, the USA, Europe, the USSR and Australia.

When Gascon resigned in 1974, the young English director ROBIN PHILLIPS was appointed to succeed him, releasing a storm of nationalist outrage. Phillips relied heavily on imported stars and centralized control. His resignation in 1980 provoked a dangerous crisis. After many months of turmoil, bitterness and accusations of betrayal on all sides, JOHN HIRSCH (1981–5)was finally appointed as artistic director. During his tenure, the Festival never fully recovered from the unseemly débâcle. Many leading actors boycotted Stratford in protest, the company was demoralized, much of the public was alienated, and artistic crises were replaced by financial ones. In 1986 JOHN NEVILLE succeeded Hirsch. Then came David William (1990–3) and Richard Monette (1994–).

The Stratford Festival's importance to world theatre lies in the influence of its stage and staging techniques. In London, CHICHESTER and Sheffield, in New York and Minneapolis, new theatres have been consciously modelled after it though none has been as successful. As the biggest and most important of the open stages, it has contributed a great deal to the loosening of the grip of the proscenium arch in modern theatre architecture everywhere. The Stratford Festival's importance to Canadian theatre is twofold. Initially it provided training and inspiration for a generation of theatre artists and established the highest production standards for the emerging professional theatre. In more recent years

it has provided an irresistible target for the attacks of the 'alternative theatre movement' which, in some measure, grew out of a reaction against Stratford and all that it represented.

**Strauss, Botho** 1944– German playwright and critic. Co-editor of *Theater Heute* from 1967 to 1970, he was then dramaturge for the Berlin Schaubühne under PETER STEIN, for whom he adapted IBSEN's *Peer Gynt*, KLEIST's *Prince of Homburg* and GORKY's *Summer Folk*. After quasi-absurd exercises (see THEATRE OF THE ABSURD) like *The Hypochondriacs* (1971), in 1976 he gained international acclaim with *Three Acts of Recognition*, which questions the relationship between art and experience. *Great and Small* (1978) added a political dimension, which is extended in *Kalldewey Farce* (1982). *Der Park* (1984) transposed *A Midsummer Night's Dream* to a sordid urban park in present-day Germany. *Visitors, Time and the Room* and *Seven Doors* (published 1988) abandon plot but retain a surreal coherence (see SURREALISM). The three-part *Final Chorus* (1991) was his comment on German reunification. Strauss's esoteric comedies are played all over continental Europe, but not in Britain.

**Streep, Meryl** 1949– American film and stage actress. She made her New York debut as Imogen in *Trelawny of the 'Wells'* (1975). For the Phoenix she played Flora in *27 Wagons Full of Cotton* and Patricia in *A Memory of Two Mondays* in 1976, also appearing in *Secret Service*. Over the next two years she played Katharine in *Henry V*, Isabella in *Measure for Measure*, Dunyasha in *The Cherry Orchard*, Lillian in *Happy End* and Katharina in *The Taming of the Shrew*. Soon after, she began a brilliant film career. Equally at ease in drama or farce, she is noted for meticulous preparation and a wide-ranging intellect.

**Strehler, Giorgio** 1921– Italian director. One of the major figures in post-World War II theatre in Italy, Strehler, jointly with Paolo Grassi, established in Milan in 1947 the first fully fledged Italian *teatro stabile*, the Piccolo Teatro. A subsidized theatre, it tried to reach a socially more heterogeneous audience than had traditional urban theatre. Strehler has mainly been based there, although in the 1980s he was equally involved in the work of the Théâtre de l'Europe, for which he has directed plays like BRECHT's *The Threepenny Opera*.

Strehler's productions in the musical and regular theatre number more than 200. A seminal influence was the work of Brecht's BERLINER ENSEMBLE and its European tour of 1956. Strehler later mounted important Italian productions of such plays as *The Good Person of Setzuan*, *The Good Soldier Schweik* and *Galileo*. SHAKESPEARE has been an ongoing interest, from 1948 (*The Tempest*) through the 1950s when he staged a number of the HISTORY PLAYS like *Richard III* (1950), *Henry IV* (1951), *Julius Caesar* (1953) and *Coriolanus* (1957), to the metaphysical and poetically evocative productions of *King Lear* (1972) and *The Tempest* (1978).

His work on the Italian repertoire has included notable reorchestrations and rediscoveries, among them FERRARI's 19th-century piece *Goldoni e le sue sedici commedie nuove* (*Goldoni and His Sixteen New Comedies*, 1958), turn-of-the-century plays by PRAGA and Bertolazzi, an influential revival of PIRANDELLO's *I giganti della montagna* (*The Mountain Giants*, 1951), and a string of plays by GOLDONI: *Gli innamorati* (*The Lovers*, 1950), *L'amante militare* (*The Military Lover*, 1951), *La trilogia della Villeggiatura* (*The Villeggiatura Trilogy*, 1954), *Le baruffe chiozzotte* (*The Chioggian Squabbles*, 1964) and several reworkings of *Arlecchino, servitore di due padroni*

(*Arlecchino, Servant of Two Masters*, from 1947) in which he has revived the masked tradition of the settecento for modern audiences. He has also worked on the modern repertory, with EDUARDO DE FILIPPO's *La grande magia* (*The Great Sorcery*, 1990). He devised the two parts of the *Progetto Faust* for the Piccolo's Studio Theatre (1989–90) and staged Beethoven's *Fidelio* at La Scala (1990).

Strehler's fascination with the mid-18th century is evident too in his many productions of Mozart's operas. His current work straddles activity in Paris and Milan. Under the joint aegis of the Piccolo Teatro and the Théâtre de l'Europe he created a further production of *Le baruffe chiozzotte* (1992), a highly balletic staging which toured to the British NATIONAL THEATRE. In 1992 Strehler resigned from the directorship of the Piccolo Teatro, but continued to direct, making notable contributions to the Goldoni bicentenary in 1993.

**Strindberg, August** 1849–1912 Swedish playwright, novelist and essayist. He began as an actor. Two of his first plays, *In Rome* (1870) and *The Outlaw* (1871), were staged by DRAMATEN; both were indebted to OEHLENSCHLÄGER's history plays. Paradoxically, the same theatre rejected his first major play, the remarkable *Master Olof*, which had to wait until AUGUST LINDBERG's six-hour production in 1881 – Strindberg's real breakthrough in the Swedish theatre. Meanwhile, in the 1870s he had abandoned a university education, married his first wife Siri von Essen and written his first novel *The Red Room* (1879). In the 1880s Dramaten produced *The Secret of the Guild* and Ludvig Josephson's New Theatre staged *Master Olof*, *Sir Bengt's Wife* and *Lucky Per's Journey*.

Strindberg responded to ZOLA's call for NATURALISM in the theatre in a typically personal way. *The Father* (1887) employed a naturalism which Strindberg claimed was larger than real life – focusing on 'the struggles between natural forces'. While he gives his naturalistic plays a psychological basis, explained in the two essays 'On Psychic Murder' (1887) and 'On Modern Drama and the Modern Theatre' (1889), he takes psychology to a level of symbolic, elemental action. The schematic patterns and mythic references of the apparently naturalistic *Miss Julie* (1888) lift it beyond the literal to the symbolic (see SYMBOLISM). Strindberg's dream of having his own theatre was briefly realized in Copenhagen in 1889, with the Scandinavian Experimental Theatre, modelled on ANTOINE's Théâtre Libre. After the banning of *Miss Julie* by the Danish censor (see CENSORSHIP), the theatre's single programme consisted of *Creditors* and two of his better one-act plays, *The Stronger* and *Pariah*.

He spent much of the 1890s in Berlin (where he met his second wife Frida Uhl), Austria and Paris, devoting himself obsessively to scientific experiments and occult studies. Between 1894 and 1896 occurred his 'Inferno crisis', a sequence of psychotic episodes culminating in his hospitalization and eventual return to Sweden. His recovery was partly aided by his discovery of the 18th-century Swedish mystic, Emmanuel Swedenborg. Determined to be 'the Zola of the Occult', Strindberg assembled masses of esoteric phenomena in his *Occult Diary*, which provided much of the detail in his post-Inferno plays.

In 1898 he wrote Part 1 of *To Damascus*, the first of a new type of drama, exploring mankind's spiritual progress in a divine context. The 34 plays that followed in the next 14 years are remarkable for their diversity

and innovation. Some, like the *Damascus* trilogy and *The Great Highway* (1909), are large psycho-spiritual pilgrimage dramas with dream-like settings and action. Others, such as *A Dream Play* (1902), use dream structure to reformulate experience. Strindberg also resumed writing history plays, producing 11 on Swedish topics, and made plans for *The Saga of Mankind*, an ambitious world-history cycle of which four plays were completed.

From 1907 he was actively involved in running the tiny Intimate Theatre, which he had opened with the actor August Falck in imitation of REINHARDT's Kammerspielhaus. He wrote special 'chamber plays', attempting to create the dramatic equivalent of chamber music. Four of these – *Storm Weather*, *The Burned House*, *The Ghost Sonata* and *The Pelican* – explore the encounter with death as a kind of painful awakening from a life of sleep-walking illusion. As a practising painter, he experimented with ways to 'dematerialize' settings, using drapery, tapestry and coloured lighting.

Strindberg's entire career was marked by the urge to experiment and redefine. He exploded the narrow limits of Zola's naturalism; his history plays established a new kind of relationship between background events and the personal drama in the foreground; and his dream and fantasy plays anticipated and paved the way for surrealistic, expressionistic and absurdist theatre (see SURREALISM; EXPRESSIONISM; THEATRE OF THE ABSURD).

**strip-tease** see BURLESQUE; NUDITY

**Stubbes, Philip** c.1555–91 English printer and minor poet. He is best known for his attack on London's immorality in *The Anatomy of Abuses* (1583), which incidentally gives information about contemporary popular entertainments. Part of the book was directed against the public theatres. NASHE responded with *The Anatomy of Absurdity* (1589).

**Stukalov, N. F.** see POGODIN, NIKOLAI

**Sturm und Drang** ('storm and stress') German theatrical term. It denotes the work of certain German dramatists and writers of the 1770s. *Sturm und Drang* drama represents a reaction to the rational drama of the Enlightenment. It was written under the influence of ROUSSEAU's natural philosophy and of the plays of SHAKESPEARE, which at that time were being translated into German and introduced to the stage. In *Sturm und Drang* the rights of the individual are expressed and heroes attract a following by the sheer force of their personalities. Themes are often sensational, dealing with incest, infanticide, extreme suffering and radical disaffection with the world. Dramaturgically the plays are indebted to the 'epic' form of Shakespeare rather than to the carefully composed work of playwrights such as LESSING.

GOETHE was a leader among these writers in the first half of the 1770s, his *Götz von Berlichingen* being one of the most accomplished and characteristic specimens. The plays of LENZ are also durable examples. Other prominent writers in the movement were Heinrich Leopold Wagner (1747–79), who wrote two plays of considerable power, *Repentance after the Deed* (1775) and *The Child Killer* (1776); and Friedrich Klinger (1752–1831), who was known for *The Twins* (1776) and the play that has been used to give the movement its name, *Storm and Stress* (1776). The works of the young SCHILLER, *The Robbers, Fiesko* and *Love and Intrigue*, although written in the 1780s, show many of the characteristic features of *Sturm und Drang*. Several of the plays were given their first performances either by DÖBBELIN in Berlin or FRIEDRICH SCHRÖDER in Hamburg. The acting of Schröder was especially suited to the jagged, harsh characterizations in these plays.

**Sturua, Robert (Robertovich)** 1938– Georgian director. Since 1963 he has run Tblisi's Rustaveli Theatre. Sturua became a Deputy of the Supreme Soviet of the Georgian Soviet Socialist Republic. He mounted spectacular, offbeat productions of *The Caucasian Chalk Circle* (1975), *Richard III* (London and Edinburgh, 1979–80) and *King Lear* (New York, 1990). His Richard, a casually murderous, clownish embodiment of totalitarian evil, defeated a slobbering, Brezhnev-like King Edward and duelled with his omnipresent understudy Richmond through a giant map of Great Britain. Sturua staged Shatrov's historically revisionist plays *The Peace of Brest-Litovsk* (as a near-vaudevillian spectacle in Moscow, 1987, and Chicago, 1990) and *Blue Horses on Red Grass*, which ran briefly in Moscow. In 1992 he produced CHEKHOV's *Three Sisters* in London, starring VANESSA, Lynn and Jemma REDGRAVE.

**Suassuna, Ariano** 1927– Brazilian playwright. His *Auto da compadecida* (*The Rogue's Trial*) in 1957 vaulted him into national prominence in Rio and São Paulo for its ingenious mixture of popular, religious and folkloric elements. Other plays in similar vein, although less successful, are *O Arco Desolado* (*The Desolate Arch*), *O Casamento Suspeitoso* (*The Suspicious Marriage*) and *O Santo e a Porca* (*The Saint and the Pig*), the latter a treatment of the classical miser, borrowing freely from PLAUTUS and MOLIÈRE but with a uniquely Brazilian flavour.

**Sudermann, Hermann** 1857–1928 German playwright. At the height of his fame over the turn of the century, Sudermann was regarded by many as a playwright equivalent in stature to IBSEN. His naturalistic dramas (see NATURALISM) *Honour* (1889), *Sodom's End* (1890) and *Heimat* (*Homeland*, 1893 – known in English as *Magda*) were celebrated, the last providing a powerful central role which appealed to the prominent actresses of the time. As the naturalist movement ebbed, Sudermann moved unsuccessfully into poetic drama.

**Sukhovo-Kobylin, Aleksandr (Vasilievich)** 1817–1903 Russian playwright, trained in philosophy. Sukhovo-Kobylin was falsely indicted for the murder of his estranged French mistress and dragged through the courts for seven years before being acquitted. His experiences resulted in the dramatic trilogy for which he is famous. Published in 1869 under the collective title *Tableaux of the Past*, each of the three plays is written in a distinct style and revolves around an interlocking set of characters. *Krechinsky's Wedding* (written in prison, 1854) is a WELL MADE PLAY about a gambler-poseur who deceives a young girl and her family and is unmasked. *The Case* (1861) grimly chronicles the spiralling events that trap and ruin the girl and her father when they are embroiled in the tsarist legal system. Here the tone is harshly satirical, the structure, language and environment more realistic. *Tarelkin's Death* (1869) is a phantasmagoria featuring two petty-bureaucratic vultures who, having disposed of the hapless family in the previous play, now attempt to cheat one another. While *Krechinsky* premiered in 1855, *Case* was not staged until 1882 as *Bygone Times* (stressing its 'pastness') and *Tarelkin* until 1900 as *Rasplyuev's Merry Days*. The most famous single production was MEYERHOLD's *Tarelkin* in 1922, which featured the director's experiments in biomechanics and circus play.

**Sumarokov, Aleksei (Petrovich)** 1717–77 Russian playwright, poet and critic. 'The Russian BOILEAU', his 'Epistle on Poetry' (1748) was the rough equivalent of *L' Art poétique*. He was (for his time) an enlightened noble and humanist, convinced of the theatre's importance as an agent for social and moral education. He was one of the first graduates of St Petersburg's Noble College of Land Cadets (1740), where his best TRAGEDY, *Khorev* (1747), was played under his direction. This was the first Russian neoclassical play to be performed by Russians and, like his eight other tragedies, it adhered to the three unities (see ARISTOTLE), the five-act play structure, the rhetorical language and the heroic tone of the French models. Of some interest are his *Hamlet* (1748), based on French translations, and *Dmitry the Pretender* (1771), which previews the historical events treated by PUSHKIN in *Boris Godunov*. His 12 comedies of character and situation, inspired by MOLIÈRE, attack the commonly depicted vices of his day, including Gallomania, judicial corruption, the idleness and cruelty of landowners and the abuses of serfdom. Of these, *The Odd Fellows*, *Nartsiss* and *Tresotinius*, all from 1750, are characteristic. From 1756 to 1761 he was director of St Petersburg's Russian Patent Theatre, the first permanent Russian professional public theatre.

**surrealism** After rejecting the word 'surnaturalism', the poet Guillaume Apollinaire in 1917 invented the word 'surrealism' in the preface to his play *The Breasts of Tiresias*: 'When man wanted to imitate walking, he created the wheel, which does not resemble a leg. He thus made surrealism without being aware of it.' Apollinaire thus founded an art movement, without being aware of it.

The seed, as opposed to the name, of surrealism had been planted in neutral Zurich in 1916. Young artists, refugees from World War I, viewed all art with a jaundiced eye and voiced their disapproval. Romanian Tristan Tzara established correspondence channels with a rebellious avant-garde among the futurists in Italy and the cubists in Paris. Apparently choosing their name 'dada' by opening a dictionary at random, these temperamentally theatrical artists opposed dada to art, process to product. Nevertheless, Tzara penned a play, *The First Celestial Adventure of M. Antipyrine*, which was first performed in Zurich, and four years later in Paris, when Tzara moved to that bastion of the avant-garde.

Paris had seen not only Apollinaire's *Breasts* in 1917, but the PICASSO–COCTEAU–DIAGHILEV *Parade* and the publication by André Breton and Philippe Soupault of their *Magnetic Fields*, a dialogue obtained by 'automatic writing'. Chance, spontaneity and deliberate shock were the tactics of the year 1920, with more or less collective participation. By 1924 Tzara and Breton were rivals and the latter, seizing upon the neologism of Apollinaire, 'the patron saint of surrealism', published the movement's first manifesto. An heir of SYMBOLISM in its opposition to reason and REALISM, a sibling of dada in its espousal of the unconscious, the erotic, the shocking, surrealism was more ambitiously a lifestyle that sought through images to pierce to man's deepest centre. Programmatically hostile to theatre, in 1926 Breton expelled ARTAUD and VITRAC from the movement. Excluding dada performances and the unreconstructed dadaist Georges Ribemont-Dessaignes, there were scarcely a dozen surrealist performances, but the emphasis upon spontaneity and imagery was nevertheless a lasting legacy of surrealism to the theatre. Above all, surrealism's impact on the theatre came through the mediacy of its first director of research, Antonin Artaud.

**Sutherland, Efua Theodora** 1924– Ghanaian playwright and director. Since independence she has dominated Ghanaian theatre, writing a wide range of plays in Akan and English, directing traditional and modern experimental drama and inspiring various projects: e.g. the innovative *kodzidan* (the 'story house'), built by community effort in rural Atwia; the Ghana Drama Studio in Accra; and research into traditional performance at the Institute of African Studies in the University of Ghana. She later developed *Anansegoro* (dramatic versions of Ananse, the traditional spider folk-hero). *The Marriage of Anansewa* was published in 1975. Her earlier stage plays, *Foriwa* (1962) and *Edufa* (1962), show an eclectic interest in Western dramatic modes.

**Sütő, András** 1927– Hungarian playwright. Sütő is the leading writer of the Hungarian minority in Romania. His dramas probe the duty of the individual, confronted by arbitrary authority, to preserve his dignity and identity even at the cost of his life. *The Palm Sunday of a Horse Dealer* (1974), *Star at the Stake* (1975) and *The Wedding Feast at Susa* (1981) are historical dramas; these and *Cain and Abel* (1977) have had numerous productions in Hungary and Transylvania. Their success is due as much to the lyrical beauty of Sütő's language as to their subject-matter. He is also well known for his prose works.

**Sutro, Alfred** 1863–1933 British playwright. One of the most popular exponents of the WELL MADE PLAY after PINERO, he wrote more than 50 works. He was also responsible for translating MAETERLINCK's plays.

**Suzman, Janet** 1939– South-African born British actress. The niece of a leading political opponent of apartheid, Helen Suzman, she moved to London to study drama and joined the ROYAL SHAKESPEARE COMPANY in 1963, playing Joan la Pucelle in *The Wars of the Roses* (1963–4). For the next 15 years she played major classical roles with the company, including Rosalind and Portia (1965), Ophelia (1965–6), Cleopatra (1972), and Clytemnestra and Helen in JOHN BARTON's cycle, *The Greeks* (1980). Her most notable achievements, however, have come in more recently written plays – as an outstanding Hedda in *Hedda Gabler* (1972), Masha in JONATHAN MILLER's production of *Three Sisters* (1976) and Hesta in ATHOL FUGARD's *Hello and Goodbye* (1973). She has been equally successful in films and television, notably in *The Draughtsman's Contract* (1981) and the TV serial *Clayhanger* (1975–6). She appeared in the title role of RACINE's *Andromache*, directed by Jonathan Miller in 1988, and in EURIPIDES' *Hippolytus* (1991). She has also directed. Strikingly tall and attractive, Suzman nevertheless commands attention as an actress more through the subtlety of her voice inflexions and the intelligent ironies of her interpretations.

**Suzuki, Tadashi** 1939– Japanese director and theorist. Suzuki originally established his reputation directing experimental works by post-*SHINGEKI* playwrights like BETSUYAKU MINORU at Tokyo's Waseda Little Theatre, which he founded with Betsuyaku and actor Ono Seki. In 1969 his fertile collaboration with actress Shiraishi Kayoko began, and he moved away from a text-centred to an actor-centred theatre. He assembled dramatic collages to showcase Shiraishi's talents, and out of these grew the actor-training method for which he subsequently became famous. In 1976 he moved his troupe out of Tokyo to the village of Toga, and later changed its

name to SCOT (Suzuki Company of Toga). Since 1982, he has organized an annual international theatre festival at Toga. Suzuki's reputation as a director rests on his renditions of Western classics. *The Trojan Women* (1974), *The Bacchae* (1978) and *Clytemnestra* (1983) are representative. He has also staged bilingual productions, using Japanese and American actors, including *The Tale of Lear* (1988).

***svanga*** [swang; sang; sangeet] Indian theatre form. This kind of rural theatre is found in Harayana, Uttar Pradesh and Punjab, all states of north India. Hindu festivals and family celebrations, especially marriages and the birth of a son, provide the occasion for a *svanga*. Stories of love, honour and duty abound. Performances take place in an open space of the village or on the veranda of a patron's house. The actors, who are all male, wear exaggerated headdresses and brightly coloured cloth pieces, false hair and beards. The characters express their feelings in the dialogue of the region and punctuate their emotions with songs that have a strong poetic line.

**Svoboda, Josef** 1920– Czech stage designer (though he prefers the term 'scenographer' to describe his profession). Trained as an architect, he was for nearly thirty years chief designer and head of technical operations in the National Theatre; since the early 1980s he has been head of the LATERNA MAGIKA operation, now with its own independent state theatre. Svoboda's work is based on a metaphoric rather than realistic approach to design, and on the use of a wide range of contemporary equipment, materials and techniques. Outstanding among his more than 500 international productions have been *Hamlet* (Brussels, 1958), *Carmen* (New York, 1972), WAGNER's *Ring* (London, 1974–6; Geneva, 1975–7; Orange, 1988), *Idomeneo* (Ottawa, 1983), CLAUDEL's *Partage de midi* (Louvain, 1984), GOETHE's *Faust* (Milan, 1989), and *La Traviata* (Macerata, 1992).

**Swan Theatre** (London) The significance of this theatre, built in c.1595 on the south bank of the Thames, lies in the surviving sketch of its interior, made in 1596 by a visiting Dutchman, Johannes de Witt. This sketch, the only substantial visual evidence of the inside of an Elizabethan playhouse, shows a round, or polygonal, building with three galleries surrounding an open yard. An almost square stage, supported by stout timbers, occupies half of the yard. Access for actors is provided by two double doors, and the unadorned platform is backed by a gallery and partly roofed. Pillars support the roof. A ban on plays in London followed a performance of JONSON's *Isle of Dogs* at the Swan in 1597, after which the theatre sank into obscurity. MIDDLETON's *A Chaste Maid in Cheapside* was performed there (c.1611).

In 1986 the ROYAL SHAKESPEARE COMPANY opened a new Swan Theatre, designed with an open stage, at Stratford-upon-Avon. This new Swan stages plays by SHAKESPEARE, his contemporaries and the playwrights of the Restoration.

**Swanston, Elliard** [Eyllaerdt] died 1651 English actor. A leading member of the King's Men (see LORD CHAMBERLAIN's MEN) from 1624 until 1642, he created many of MASSINGER's main roles and played Othello, Richard III and CHAPMAN's Bussy d'Ambois in revivals. Unlike most actors he was on the Parliamentary side in the Civil War, appearing later on the Restoration stage, e.g. in SHADWELL's *The Virtuoso* (1676).

**symbolism** Symbolism in theatre is probably as old as

theatre itself, but the widely symbolic must not be confused with the self-styled French symbolists of the last decade of the 19th century and the Russian playwrights of the first two decades of the 20th.

The French symbolist poet-playwrights admired a man of the theatre, RICHARD WAGNER, and a philosopher (of theatre, among other matters), FRIEDRICH NIETZSCHE. The major symbolist poet and thinker was Stéphane Mallarmé, who viewed *Hamlet* as a drama of the mind, and who urged the creation of a new drama that would reflect the mental or spiritual life rather than the crude world of the senses. Through Mallarmé the symbolists viewed art not only as expression, but primarily as a mode of cognition.

Disdaining everyday reality and the REALISM that reflected it, symbolism came to the theatre in reaction against ANTOINE's Théâtre Libre (whose repertory was not, though, exclusively realist). The 18-year-old poet Paul Fort founded his Art Theatre in 1890 and committed it to symbolism the following year, notably with the production of MAETERLINCK's *Intruder* (death) and *The Blind* (who are blind to death) – short, static plays in which the interior life is conveyed mainly through atmospheric effect. Fort was fortunate in securing the services of actor AURÉLIEN LUGNÉ-POE (the Poe affixed in admiration for the American poet), but the young theatre manager was unable to sustain his symbolist theatre, which he dissolved before producing *Axel* by the recently deceased Villiers de l'Isle Adam. This operatic work presented sensitive aristocrats in a Gothic landscape of forest, moonlight and castle, which would also be found in the work of such symbolist playwrights as HOFMANNSTHAL, early YEATS and, with modifications, PAUL CLAUDEL. When Fort retired at age 20, Lugné-Poe raised the symbolist banner over his Théâtre de l'Oeuvre, which lasted till 1929.

The Russian symbolists' erudite, static and visionary dramas, beginning with Nikolai Minsky's *Alma* (1900), included VYACHESLAV IVANOV's 'theatre of congregate action'; VALERY BRIUSOV's *uslovny* (self-conscious, conventional) theatre; ANDREI BELY's neo-mystery plays; INNOKENTY ANNENSKY's and ALEKSEI REMIZOV's mythic and Russian folkloric themes; FYODOR SOLOGUB's fatalism and author-centred 'theatre of one will'; and MIKHAIL KUZMIN's darkly dandyish *commedia*. The greatest Russian symbolist dramatist, ALEKSANDR BLOK, posited theatricalism as an alternative faith to symbolist mysticism in his harlequinade *The Little Showbooth* (1906); so too did such marginally symbolist writers as NIKOLAI EVREINOV, in his monodramas and in his major play *The Chief Thing* (1921), and LEONID ANDREEV, in his Poe-like meditations on death's proximity and life's vacuity (e.g. *He Who Gets Slapped*, 1915).

The symbolist theatre is noteworthy as the first modern Western theatre to look beyond the stage to occult powers – what Baudelaire in a famous sonnet called *correspondances* between the natural and the supernatural, the visible and the invisible, the material and the mystical.

**Syndicate, Theatrical** see THEATRICAL SYNDICATE (USA)

**Synge, J(ohn) M(illington)** 1871–1909 Irish playwright. From 1895 to 1903 he lived mainly in Paris, while making forays into the west of Ireland and to the Aran islands. The last seven years of Synge's life were intensely productive. In 1902 he wrote *In the Shadow of the Glen* (staged by Frank and Willie Fay, 1903) and *Riders to the Sea* (Irish National Theatre Society, 1904), and drafted *The Tinker's Wedding*, whose anticlericalism frightened the ABBEY (it went unproduced until 1971). *The Well of the Saints* was produced in 1905; *The Playboy of the Western World*, which occasioned riots, in 1907; and his last play, *Deirdre*, posthumously in 1910.

Synge was a force in the Abbey directorate from 1905, but he was racked and eventually killed by Hodgkins disease. His travels prompted his creative urge. He scorned the experimental drama of IBSEN and MAETERLINCK, but responded to a tragic joy in the endurance of the Aran islanders. His characters assert their destinies. Deirdre exalts her death into 'a story will be told forever'. In *The Well of the Saints* the blind and outcast Douls see in their 'own minds...lakes, and broadening rivers, and hills are waiting for the spade'.

Berated for defaming the purity of Irish morals, Synge was also attacked on the grounds that his language travestied and coarsened Irish speech. He defended its authenticity, but his aim was not faithful transcription. His achievement was the greater one of forging a dramatic rhetoric from imaginative fidelity to its source. It is a splendid convention, as artificial as SHAKESPEARE's blank verse. The speech of Synge's plays invests their realist stage with a poetry both lyrical and mocking.

**Szajna, Józef** 1922– Polish director and artist. From 1955 Szajna designed plays at the People's Theatre, Nowa Huta – e.g. *Princess Turandot* (1956) and *Of Mice and Men* (1956). He was its director from 1963 to 1966. After moving to Warsaw he worked on GROTOWSKI's revival of WYSPIAŃSKI's *Acropolis* (1966), and in 1971 became director-designer for the Studio Theatre. A total theatre artist in the spirit of GORDON CRAIG, Szajna has been a playwright and dramaturge, developing scripts from sections of literary texts, such as his productions of *Faust* (1971), *Dante* (1974) and *Cervantes* (1976), as well as *Macbeth* (1963, England). His production of *Death on a Pear Tree* (1978) was toured throughout Europe and North America. Until 1982 he taught scenography at the Academy of Fine Arts in Cracow.

**Tabarin** [Antoine Girard] c.1584–1626 French CLOWN. In Paris, about 1618, he set up a booth stage in the Place Dauphine with a few other performers, regaling passers-by with comic monologues and knockabout farces designed to alternate with and promote the sale of medicaments. Tabarin's stage name derived from the short cloak (or *tabar*) which he wore over a belted smock and baggy trousers, together with a wooden sword and his most famous prop, a floppy felt hat capable of multiple metamorphoses. By 1622 rival publishers brought out two collections of his material, mostly improvised in performance and owing much to COMMEDIA routines. Unlike other booth performers such as BRUSCAMBILLE, Tabarin did not belong to a theatre company, but his name has become synonymous with street performance.

***tableau vivant*** see LIVING PICTURE; NUDITY

**Tagore, Rabindranath** 1861–1940 Indian poet, painter and playwright. Winner of the 1913 Nobel Prize for Literature (and author of India's national anthem), Tagore is perhaps India's best-known modern playwright. He founded a unique school, Santiniketan, in 1901 in rural Bengal aiming to mix the best of Indian and Western culture, and in 1935 founded Visva-Bharati University, dedicated to the arts. He travelled and lectured widely in Europe, America and the East. Although his many plays are not frequently produced outside Bengal today, they constitute an important contribution to dramatic literature. They include *Chitra* (*Chitrangada*, 1892), *The King of the Dark Chamber* (*Raja*, 1910), *The Post Office* (*Dakghar*, 1913) and *Red Oleanders* (*Raktakarabi*, 1924).

**Tairov** [Kornblit]**, Aleksandr (Yakovlevich)** 1885–1950 Russian-Soviet director. Having begun his acting career in Kiev, Tairov joined VERA KOMISSARZHEVSKAYA's Theatre in St Petersburg for the 1906–7 season. Disillusioned with the artistic director MEYERHOLD's idea of the actor, he left. With his actress-wife ALISA KOONEN he founded the Moscow Kamerny (Chamber) Theatre (1914), a venue for highly sophisticated productions featuring innovative cubist and constructivist designs (see THEATRE DESIGN).

If Meyerhold's theatre often resembled a circus – purposely crude and gymnastic – Tairov's consistently suggested a controlled, exquisite ballet. All movement was choreographed, dialogue intoned. While the Kamerny's opening production, the Pavel Kuznetsov-designed *Sakuntala* (1914), failed to realize Tairov's vision, ALEKSANDRA EKSTER's cubist-designed *Thamira, the Cither Player* (1916) by ANNENSKY and Aleksandr Vesnin's severely constructivist *Phaedra* (1922) came closer. The Kamerny production of E. T. A. HOFFMANN's *Princess Brambilla* (1920), designed in a HARLEQUIN's motley of swirling colours, approached Tairov's intended synthesis of theatrical elements and forms.

The Kamerny also helped introduce Western classics to the Soviet stage, including WILDE's *Salomé* (1917), G. K. Chesterton's *The Man Who Was Thursday* (1923) and plays by SHAW and O'NEILL. Tairov's productions of Soviet plays ranged from BULGAKOV's *The Crimson Island* (1928) and Semyonov's *Natalya Tarpova* (1929), anti-establishment works which were quickly removed from the repertoire, to VISHNEVSKY's orthodox *An Optimistic Tragedy* (1934), which helped win the director the honour of People's Artist of the USSR (1935). The Kamerny, despite periods of government intervention and supervision, remained open until shortly before the director's death.

**Talesnik, Ricardo** 1935– Argentine playwright, actor and director. After an auspicious beginning in television, he wrote *La fiaca* (*The Doldrums*, 1967), a dramatization on the theme of lack of individual freedom experienced by a man suffering from Monday morning 'blahs'. The play was an instant success: it was staged throughout Europe and Latin America and filmed in 1968. Major later plays include *Cien veces no debo* (*A Hundred Times I Ought Not*, 1970) and *Los japoneses no esperan* (*The Japanese Don't Wait*, 1973), both taking anti-bourgeois postures. Talesnik has experimented with MUSICAL COMEDY, PANTOMIME and one-person shows, and was a collaborator with ROZENMACHER, SOMIGLIANA and COSSA in *El avión negro* (*The Black Aeroplane*, 1970), a play based on myths regarding Perón's proposed return to Argentina.

**Talli, Virgilio** 1858–1928 Italian actor and company manager. His importance as an actor-manager lies particularly in his contribution to stage-management, in which his activities prefigured those of the director in the Italian theatre in concern for the unity of a production and insistence on subordinating the personality playing of lead actors to the requirements of the play. From 1885 he managed a number of fine companies and was responsible for the first stagings of plays like GIACOSA's *Come le foglie* (*Like the Leaves*, 1900) and D'ANNUNZIO's *La figlia d'Iorio* (*Iorio's Daughter*, 1904).

**Talma, François Joseph** 1763–1826 French actor. He was Napoleon's favourite actor and contributed to a revival of interest in neoclassical tragedy which accorded with Napoleon's own attempt to create an empire inspired by ancient Rome. Talma, whose early years were spent in England (where he trained to be a dentist), made his debut at the COMÉDIE-FRANÇAISE in VOLTAIRE's *Mahomet* in 1787. In 1789 he played the title role in *Charles IX*, Marie-Joseph Chénier's violently anti-monarchical and anticlerical play. He took the part because no one else wanted it; it allowed him to portray the darker passions of fury and despair, which he would use to advantage in the DUCIS adaptations of *Othello*, *Hamlet* and *Macbeth*, as well as in the roles of Néron in RACINE's *Britannicus* and Oreste in *Andromaque*.

*Charles IX* was the occasion of a split in the Comédie-Française. Talma espoused the revolutionary cause and left the fundamentally royalist institution with a group of other dissidents to take up residence at the former Variétés Amusantes, the Théâtre de la République (the present Comédie-Française), in 1791. He came to know and admire Napoleon, who had a considerable interest in the theatre and a taste for neoclassical plays. Talma once more became part of the Comédie-Française when the various factions were brought together in 1799. From 1802 onwards he was frequently on tour. In 1816 the king renewed the pension that Napoleon had granted him.

In England he had seen reforms in stage COSTUME

which he then introduced to France, appearing in authentic Roman dress in Voltaire's *Brutus* (1789), which lead to a rapid costume revolution at the Comédie-Française. His experience of the English theatre led him towards a more natural style of delivery than the traditional declamation normally reserved for tragedy. His most popular roles were PIERRE CORNEILLE's Cinna, Manlius in Lafosse's *Manlius Capitolinus* (1806) and Oreste in Racine's *Andromaque*. Talma was almost a symbol of the Empire. He was also the actor who made the bridge between neoclassical tragedy and the romantic drama.

**tamasha** Indian theatre form. The term is a Persian word meaning 'fun', 'play' and 'entertainment', and was probably introduced, by the Urdu-speaking soldiers of the Mogul armies. Of India's many kinds of rural theatre, few stress humour as a dominant feature of their content as extensively as does *tamasha*. *Tamasha* satirizes and pokes fun at contemporary society, often at the expense of politicians and businessmen, priests and prophets, under the guise of historical or mythological stories. It is a major rural theatre genre in the state of Maharashtra in west central India. Estimates suggest that approximately 10,000 artists from around 450 *tamasha* troupes service a population of about 62 million people. In sheer numbers alone, this makes *tamasha*, which developed in the 16th century as a bawdy entertainment, one of the more popular theatrical forms in India.

After a devotional song in praise of the deities comes the *gaulan*, a dramatic episode in which Krishna and his clown attendant waylay milkmaids on their journey to market. Their conversation with the milkmaids and their old aunt provides considerable cause for mirth. Following this is the *vag*, a short dialogue play drawn from historical and mythological sources, laced with satirical incidents and broad slapstick humour. There are also hugely popular love songs (*lavani*) which are interpreted through dancing as well as singing, nowadays by girls whose physical charms, as much as their vocal abilities, help to sell a song.

During the 18th century the poet-singers (*shahirs*) raised the artistic level of the narratives and love songs, and helped to improve the reputation of the *tamasha* artists above that of prostitutes and outcasts – which, for historical reasons, was the image that the public had had of them. The *shahir* tradition continued throughout the independence movement, and brought the idea of freedom from British rule, achieved in 1947, to the heartland of India. As political differences had begun to emerge in the 1930s and 1940s, some popular *shahirs* had become associated with communist causes.

Like other forms of rural theatre, *tamasha* has served as a source of inspiration to modern urban directors and actors, some of whose productions have imitated the *tamasha* technique. Among the most prominent in recent years have been Vijaya Mehta's Marathi versions of *The Caucasian Chalk Circle*, *The Little Clay Cart* and Girish Karnad's *Hayavadana*; Vijay Tendulkar's *Ghashiram Kotwal*, directed by Jabbar Patel; and *Teen Paishacha Tamasha*, also directed by Patel and adapted from BRECHT's *Threepenny Opera*.

**Tamayo y Baus, Manuel** 1829–98 Spanish playwright. His attempts to halt the decline of the theatre, assailed on one side by romanticism and on the other by REALISM, led to the establishment of the *alta COMEDIA*. After adapting French and German plays he had his first orig-inal success with *Virginia* (1853), a tragedy in the manner of ALFIERI. He tried historical dramas in verse and prose, then changed to thesis plays of social morality with *La bola de nieve* (*The Snowball*, 1853), attacking the vice of jealousy. Similarly, *Lances de honor* (*Affairs of Honour*, 1863) attacks duelling. His best play is generally considered to be *Un drama nuevo* (*A New Play*, 1867), depicting the hidden passions among actors of SHAKESPEARE's company rehearsing a new play by the master.

**Tandy, Jessica** 1909–94 Anglo-American actress. Tandy trained and made her debut in England, joining the BIRMINGHAM REPERTORY Company in 1928. She made her debut on BROADWAY as Toni Rakonitz in 1930 in *The Matriarch*. Among her outstanding roles were Ophelia to JOHN GIELGUD's Hamlet (1934) and Blanche Dubois in TENNESSEE WILLIAMS's *A Streetcar Named Desire* (1947). As Blanche she won rave reviews and achieved Broadway stardom. In 1942 she married HUME CRONYN, with whom she co-starred on Broadway. At the GUTHRIE THEATRE Tandy played such roles as Linda in *Death of a Salesman*, Gertrude in *Hamlet*, and Madam Ranevskaya in *The Cherry Orchard*. Latterly she devoted more time to films, e.g. *Driving Miss Daisy*, which gave her her first major film role at the age of 80.

**Tang Xianzu** 1550–1616 Chinese playwright. A native of Jiangxi, he abandoned government service in 1598 to devote himself to his writing. Tang was a romantic and an individualist who sidestepped the rigid rules of orthodox metrical usage in favour of a freer, more sensual use of poetic diction. His contemporary and rival Shen Jing (1553–1610), in contrast, adhered strictly to the traditional forms of metrical composition. The two represented two main schools of thought which contributed to the development of KUNQU as a dramatic form. Tang's major contribution to drama was a quartet of plays with a dream motif. One of these, *The Peony Pavilion* (*Mudan ting*) in 55 scenes, is one of the longest of its kind. The theme of romantic love expounded in a supernatural context had a great emotional impact on the audiences of the day, and excerpts have been constantly performed on the traditional stage.

**Tapia y Rivera, Alejandro** 1826–82 Puerto Rican playwright. The acknowledged founder of Puerto Rican theatre, he wrote several plays, some historical, including *Roberto D'Evreux* (1854), for which he was censured for trying to humanize the English royal family; and *La cuarterona* (*The Quadroon*, 1867), which dealt with racial issues on the island.

**Tara Arts** British company. The first professional theatre company to be established and run by Asian immigrants in Britain, it was founded in South London in 1976 by a small group of artists led by Sunil Saggar, Ovais Kadri and Jatinder Verma. The first production (1977) was of the classic Bengali play by RABINDRANATH TAGORE, *Sacrifice*. But the company also wanted to establish a new tradition, reflecting a community that was losing touch with its Asian roots while at the same time needing to assert its identity in Britain. It now fuses classical traditions from East and West, is developing its own form of AGIT-PROP community drama and has toured widely in Britain and around the world. The little-known 8th-century classic, Shudraka's *The Little Clay Cart* (1991), was performed at the NATIONAL THEATRE. *The Jackal's Cackle* (1991), derived from the *Panchatantra*, told its story through classical Indian dance, MIME and masks. *Heer and Romeo* (1991–2) brought together *Romeo* *and Juliet* and Varis Shah's *Heer and Ranjha* into one play; while *Monsters and Minotaurs* (1992–3) used puppetry and dance to combine the Greek story of the Minotaur with tales from India.

**Tarkington, Booth** 1869–1946 American novelist and playwright. Although better known as a novelist, Tarkington was the author of 21 produced plays. He liked to write for actors: *Monsieur Beaucaire* (1900) for RICHARD MANSFIELD, *Master Antonio* (1916) for OTIS SKINNER, *Poldekin* (1920) for GEORGE ARLISS. His most successful play, *Clarence* (1919), showing the disruption of a normal household by a handsome, bumbling hero, was written for ALFRED LUNT and HELEN HAYES. After their success with *The Man from Home* (1907), Tarkington and Harry Leon Wilson collaborated on nine more plays.

**Tarlton [Tarleton], Richard** died 1588 English CLOWN and playwright. The finest popular entertainer of his generation and a favourite at court, Tarlton became a legend in his own lifetime. The posthumously published *Tarlton's Jests* (1611) provides biographical information. Among his lost works are *Tarlton's Toys* and *Tarlton's Tragical Treatises* (both 1576). Of his popular play, *The Seven Deadly Sins* (1585), an outline plot (or PLATT) survives. It was performed by QUEEN ELIZABETH'S MEN, which Tarlton joined in 1583 after a spell with LEICESTER'S MEN. He was more suited to solo or extempore performance than to scripted drama. He specialized in the JIG, was a Master of Fence and a skilled musician. The drawing by John Scottowe shows him playing a pipe while beating a tabor, the image of a rustic clown.

**Tarragon Theatre** (Toronto) The most solidly established of Toronto's so-called alternative theatres, Tarragon, under the direction of its founder Bill Glassco, was a major source of new work in the 1970s, particularly the plays of DAVID FRENCH, MICHEL TREMBLAY and JAMES REANEY. Since 1982 it has been directed by Urjo Kareda, a former drama critic, dramaturge and briefly co-artistic director of the STRATFORD FESTIVAL. While still maintaining a commitment to new Canadian works, he has considerably broadened its repertoire.

**Tasso, Torquato** 1544–95 Italian poet and playwright. Most of his dramatic writing was done for court entertainment, celebrations and festivals. Two plays are particularly important: *Re Torrismondo* (*King Torrismondo*, 1578, but written earlier), a quasi-baroque verse TRAGEDY in emulation of SOPHOCLES that treats of the disastrous consequences ensuing from an illicit passion; and *Aminta*, the most celebrated and influential dramatic PASTORAL of the Renaissance, first performed at Ferrara in 1573 by the GELOSI company. Tasso was one of the most admired of Italian poets abroad; his influence was strongly felt in the work of many 16th- and 17th-century English writers.

**Tate, Harry [Ronald Macdonald Hutchinson]** 1872–1940 Scottish comedian. As the man who was 'always in control of the situation', he reduced his environment to utter chaos. At golf, billiards, motoring, fishing, flying or broadcasting he was invariably defeated by the malice of objects, including his recalcitrant moustache, and by obstructive fellow creatures like his obnoxious son and mute, staring little boys. His sketches became classics and influenced W. C. FIELDS.

**Tate, Nahum** 1652–1715 Irish playwright and poet. In 1680 his adaptation of SHAKESPEARE's *Richard III* was banned (see CENSORSHIP) for its study of usurpation and

abdication: Tate disguised it as *The Sicilian Usurper*. In 1681 his version of *King Lear* was performed and effectively kept Shakespeare's play off the stage until 1838. Tate's work eliminates the Fool, introduces a love plot between Edgar and Cordelia, and finally restores Lear to to the throne in an honest attempt to graft new conventions of decorum on to a work that he admired. In the same year he turned *Coriolanus* into *The Ingratitude of a Commonwealth*. His farce, *A Duke and No Duke*, was performed in 1684; the second edition (1693) contains an important defence of FARCE by Tate. He also wrote the libretto for Purcell's *Dido and Aeneas* (1689). In 1692 he was appointed Poet Laureate.

**Taylor, C(ecil) P(hilip)** 1928–81 British playwright. Throughout his life he kept faith with the socialism of his Glasgow Jewish childhood, but the revolutionary flavour of his early plays, such as his first *Aa Went to Blaydon Races* (1962), gave way to the warm humour of such plays as *Allergy*, a one-act comedy about the downfall of a Trotskyist paper with a very small circulation, or *The Black and White Minstrels* (1972). Taylor was a prolific dramatist, adapting plays by STERNHEIM and IBSEN as well as writing for the stage and television. For many years he stayed with regional companies in Newcastle, Liverpool and in Scotland. His *Schippel* (adapted from a Sternheim comedy) was seen as *The Plumber's Progress* (1975) in London, while *Bread and Butter* (1966), *Bandits* (1977), *And a Nightingale Sang ...* (1979) and his last play, *Bring Me Sunshine, Bring Me Smiles* (1982), had brief London runs. His most successful play, *Good*, about a liberal German professor in the 1930s whose moral cowardice leads to a military career and a job in Auschwitz, was first staged by the ROYAL SHAKESPEARE COMPANY in 1981.

**Taylor, Joseph** 1586–1652 English actor. He joined the King's Men (see LORD CHAMBERLAIN'S MEN) in 1619, possibly to replace RICHARD BURBAGE, and after 1630 shared the business management with LOWIN. He created many of MASSINGER's leading roles and played Hamlet, Iago, and Ferdinand in WEBSTER's *The Duchess of Malfi*. He was versatile enough to be an outstanding Mosca in a revival of JONSON's *Volpone*.

**Taylor, Laurette (Cooney)** 1884–1946 American actress. She first appeared in New York in 1903, achieving stardom in 1912 in the title role of *Peg O'My Heart*, a script by J. Hartley Manners, who married Taylor in 1911. Later roles included Nell Gwynne in *Sweet Nell of Old Drury* and Rose Trelawny in *Trelawny of the Wells*. She co-starred in 1945 in *The Glass Menagerie*, becoming once more the toast of BROADWAY.

**Taylor, Tom** 1817–80 British playwright, journalist and art critic. Taylor's phenomenal energy accounts for his various careers. He was professor of English at the University of London from 1845 to 1847, during which time he was called to the Bar and had eight plays staged at the LYCEUM; he was on the newly created Board of Health until 1871, by which time he had written a further 60 plays and established himself as art critic of *The Times* and a popular contributor to *Punch*, of which he later became editor. In addition he wrote plays for the OLYMPIC from 1853 to 1865 and for the HAYMARKET from 1859 to 1861. He gratified popular taste with BURLESQUES and PANTOMIMES and, like many contemporaries, with adaptations from French, such as his most famous MELODRAMA, *The Ticket-of-Leave Man* (1863), and his moral comedy *Still Waters Run Deep* (1855). Taylor's most ambitious work for the theatre was the succession of HISTORY PLAYS, some in blank verse, which began with 'Twixt Axe and Crown (1870) and ended with Anne Boleyn (1876). Our American Cousin (1858) was the outstanding popular success of his lifetime.

**Tchelitchew, Pavel** 1898–1957 Russian-American theatrical designer and artist. Tchelitchew studied abstract art and stage design under ALEKSANDRA EKSTER, but eventually renounced his cubist style and moved to Berlin in 1921, where he designed the opera Le coq d'or and met SERGE DIAGHILEV. In Paris in 1923 he embraced a neo-romantic style and developed his controversial technique of multiple perspectives, which gave his representational painting a surreal quality (see SURREALISM). In 1934 he designed LOUIS JOUVET's production of Ondine in Paris, and subsequently moved to the United States where he eventually acquired citizenship. His designs for ballet included Nobilissima visione (1938) and Balustrade (1940) for George Balanchine.

**Teatro Abierto** (Open Theatre) Argentine theatre phenomenon. It was organized by OSVALDO DRAGÚN and others in 1981 in response to an oppressive political regime. Designed to revitalize a stagnant stage, the first promotion in 1981 resulted in 21 new one-act plays by as many authors, staged by 21 directors, in a seven-day cycle. The Teatro Picadero mysteriously caught fire at the end of a week, but the fierce determination of the group, coupled with great public enthusiasm for the event, enabled them to continue in the Teatro Tabarís almost immediately. The 1982 cycle was overshadowed by the Falklands (Malvinas) War. Events scheduled for subsequent years became less compelling because of the Alfonsín election in 1983 and the return to democratic procedures in Argentina.

**Teatro Campesino, El** (The Farmworkers' Theatre) Chicano company. It was founded by LUIS VALDÉZ in 1965 to support Filipino and Mexican-American strikers against the grape farmers of the San Joaquin valley, California. Initially an AGIT-PROP group tailoring its actos (short plays) to the issues and needs of the moment in a style at once cartoon-like, comic and realistic, the company took on a wider political involvement during the Vietnam War. In the 1970s El Centro Campesino Cultural was created on 40 acres of farmland at San Juan Bautista, south of San Francisco, for Valdéz and his people to research American Indian myth and RITUAL as a basis for life and theatre. In performance, the early actos were replaced by mitos ('myths') such as El baile de los gigantes (The Dance of the Giants, 1974), though the basic principle of a bilingual theatre using a vivid physical style remained the same. Valdéz's drama of racial violence, Zoot Suit (1978), was acclaimed in Los Angeles. During the 1990s several productions have been mounted and toured annually. (See also CHICANO THEATRE.)

**Teatro de Orientación** Mexican theatre group. With objectives similar to those of the TEATRO DE ULISES, this group was established (1932–4 and 1938–9) with a governmental subvention under the direction of CELESTINO GOROSTIZA.

**Teatro de Ulises** Mexican theatre group. Co-founded in 1928 by XAVIER VILLAURRUTIA and SALVADOR NOVO, the group broke with the old traditions of Castilian accent, prompter's box and star system in order to stress the overall coordination role of the director and a poetic, conceptual theatre. New lighting and staging techniques were adopted from the European masters – CRAIG, REINHARDT, STANISLAVSKY, PISCATOR and others.

Defunct by 1929, the group presented six plays, mostly French translations, and managed to give new impetus to the renovation of Mexican drama and new spirit to Mexican playwrights and directors.

*teatro del grottesco* Italian genre. This name was given to a body of plays by Italian dramatists of the second and third decades of the 20th century. Never a movement, 'theatre of the grotesque' sought an anti-naturalistic (see NATURALISM) renewal of the bourgeois theatre via the development of ironic, parodistic and grotesque situations; by the use of an author's spokesman or raisonneur; and by emphasis upon the public and private faces of dramatic characters. The best-known plays of this theatre include the widely translated and performed La maschera e il volto (The Mask and the Face, 1916) by LUIGI CHIARELLI, and Rosso di San Secondo's Marionette che passione! (Puppets, What Passion!, 1918). PIRANDELLO is considered by many to have written some of his early plays in this vein, and his essay on humour, L'umorismo (1908), was a seminal influence.

**Teatro Español** (Madrid) The municipal theatre, built on the site of a CORRAL DE COMEDIA, celebrated its 400th anniversary in 1983. The present building was modernized in the mid-1800s. Its venerable history embraces Spain's greatest authors, actors and directors. In the early 20th century, Benito Pérez Galdós and BENAVENTE premiered major works there, and the theatre witnessed the brilliant career of the María Guerrero–Fernando Díaz de Mendoza company. In the 1930s, MARGARITA XIRGU and artistic director Cipriano de Rivas Cherif administered it for five years, creating a model national theatre. They premiered GARCÍA LORCA's La zapatera prodigiosa (The Shoemaker's Prodigious Wife) and Yerma, and VALLE-INCLÁN's Divinas palabras (Divine Words). In 1949 BUERO-VALLEJO's Historia de una escalera (Story of a Stairway) announced the revival of the postwar stage. Among important directors of recent decades are José Tamayo (1950s), Miguel Narros (1960s and 1980s), Alberto González Vergel (1970s), José Luis Gómez (1980s) and Gustavo Pérez Puig (1990s).

**Teatro Nacional D. Maria II** (Lisbon) Portuguese National Theatre. It is the most visible result of a decision taken in 1836 by the newly formed and fragile liberal regime to further the theatrical arts. The theatre was sited at the head of the Rossio, the central and historically most important square in Lisbon. The first director, ALMEIDA GARRETT, concurrently inspector-general of theatres, supervised its building, provided its first successful plays, transformed the professional training of actors and launched it as the home for the national drama. Even during the Salazar regime it strove to maintain high standards, with Portuguese and foreign classics and moderns. The prestige and imaginative direction of the company in the latter years enabled it to soar above the crasser CENSORSHIP and conformist social pressures, even if it tended to play safe.

Garrett's beautiful theatre was gutted by fire in 1964, but was reopened in 1978. To the more traditional main auditorium it has now added a sala experimental (workshop theatre). Recently the theatre has been in celebratory mode, hosting a REVISTA retrospective. Recently the theatre has been in celebratory mode, hosting a REVISTA retrospective. 1994 was Lisbon's turn to be Cultural Capital of Europe. This national theatre put on a half-dozen special productions, of which the most theatrically brilliant was F. la Féria's adaptation of a novel by Agustina Bessa Luís, As Fúrias (The Furies).

**Teje, Tora** 1893–1970 Swedish actress. The national tragedienne of her times, she was noted for her musicality (occasionally over-exploited) and her physical authority and expressiveness. From the 1920s to the early 50s she was DRAMATEN's natural choice for such roles as Medea, Phèdre and Queen Margaret in *Richard III*. Among her important STRINDBERG roles were Indra's daughter in OLOF MOLANDER's revolutionary 1935 production of *A Dream Play* and Alice in *The Dance of Death*. She was admired for her early work in O'NEILL (Nina Leeds in *Strange Interlude* and Abbie Putnam in *Desire Under the Elms*).

**television drama** Over most of the world today, more people are being exposed to more drama than ever before. This drama is not that of the theatre or even that of the cinema: it comes to them on the domestic screen in their own homes or – as is sometimes the case in Third World countries – in communal venues. This drama-in-the-home may reach them from terrestrial, cable or satellite sources; often it will be recorded on videocassette and played back at the viewer's leisure. This is an unprecedented invasion of the private sphere by a previously public activity.

Television may of course be merely a means of transmitting pre-existing material. The simplest form of electronic drama is obtained by putting one or more cameras in front of a stage and recording a theatrical event. At a more ambitious level, stage drama may be adapted for the specific interpretative possibilities of the medium. SHAKESPEARE has proved to be effective on the small screen in many countries. The BBC presented the entire 37-play canon in a six-year plan begun in 1978 jointly with Time-Life Films, a prestige project massively backed by major US corporations. In France, the COMÉDIE-FRANÇAISE has presented MOLIÈRE, MARIVAUX, BEAUMARCHAIS and other classics on TV; in Greece, Channel ERT 1 has recorded some of the dramas of antiquity, including all the plays of ARISTOPHANES and EURIPIDES, in the theatres of Epidaurus and Herodes Atticus. The German ZDF network has shown not only German playwrights like LESSING, KLEIST, HAUPTMANN and BRECHT but also GOLDONI, STRINDBERG and SYNGE, among many others. Japan's public-service network NHK televises *KABUKI* plays as well as items from the more esoteric *BUGAKU* and *NŌ* repertoire.

Television has its own potential, which is somewhat distinct from that of the other dramatic media. But drama written for TV did not properly emerge until the late 1940s and early 1950s. At that time such plays were exclusively produced in the studio. The difference between film and television studio production was that, whereas for film a single camera would take each shot discontinuously, to be edited afterwards, for television two, three or more cameras would shoot the action in an unbroken run. TV plays, normally set indoors, would go out 'live', i.e. they were seen at the actual moment of performance. Exterior scenes, if needed at all, were filmed beforehand and then inserted into the transmission. In other words, television drama shared with theatre the element of 'real time' untouched by any editing process (other than the vision-mixer's switch from one camera image to another).

The coming of videotape in 1958 was to change all that. Plays could now be recorded and edited, first physically (by actually cutting the tape) and then electronically: this made a more cinematic construction possible. Indeed, in the 1960s many television writers

and directors turned directly to film in order to break out of the studio. The fact that by the 1980s lightweight video cameras had to an extent replaced film cameras has not affected this basic approach to production: single-camera operation of whatever kind retains the visual mobility and structural flexibility of the cinema film. From the viewers' standpoint, an even more visible change in the 1960s and 1970s was the introduction of colour. These innovations have meant that television drama, even in the strict sense of a medium-specific form, can now draw on a wide range of techniques: studio and/or location, monochrome and/or colour, film (of different gauges) and/or videotape (of different formats), as well as a wide range of electronic special effects.

It follows that the defining characteristic of television drama is not so much the mode of production as the mode of reception. The viewer does not make any special effort: drama is offered to him in the home, surrounded by everyday distractions. The play may at times even be resented as an intruder, breaching family taboos. Small screen size and imperfect image resolution make the television experience less overwhelming than that of the cinema: the viewer has the choice at any time to switch over or off. A television play, then, has to grab him quickly to retain his attention; the response is rarely going to be as compelling as that experienced by a crowd in the theatre or the cinema. TV drama speaks to its audience as individuals or at best as members of small groups.

But perhaps the significant point is not so much the impact of any one play but that of television drama as a whole. Embedded in a continuous stream of electronic information (news, weather reports and so on), it forms part of the viewer's alternative world, an extension or even a partial replacement of first-hand experience. Is this enriching or enfeebling? That will of course depend on the overall context of programming, the sense of social reality it conveys, the imaginative enrichment it brings. Even the advertising messages on commercial channels that punctuate plays will subliminally colour their reception. The sheer quantity of television drama available for consumption in itself becomes problematic. In the United States, somewhere between 30 and 70 channels may be available: the viewer is literally spoilt for choice.

**The social framework**

TV drama in different countries varies according to differing socio-economic, technological and cultural/political conditions. Some Third World countries cannot as yet afford television at all. Others are so poor, with thin network coverage and few sets in private ownership, as to make television – drama or whatever – a negligible influence. For instance, in India where regular broadcasts started only in 1965 and colour was not introduced until 1982, the impact of TV drama cannot begin to compare with that of its flourishing film industry, the world's largest.

The cultural/political climate cannot fail to be a major factor in the tone and quality of television drama. South African television, long hampered by divisive internal policies, has tended to rely on imports for the bulk of its programmes. In the former East European bloc the government line would carry more weight in broadcasting policy than would 'merely' pleasing the viewers. Much of Soviet television drama used to derive from stage plays. Official guidelines frowned on scenes of sex, violence and racism. Since the dissolution of the USSR in 1991, Western soap operas, including Latin American ones, have flooded Russian TV screens. The early period of Chinese TV drama – over 80 mono-chrome plays broadcast live between 1958 and 1966 – was terminated by the Cultural Revolution. For ten years only the eight revolutionary operas approved by Mme Mao were featured on Chinese television. The top-pling of the 'Gang of Four' ushered in a new era, techno-logically as well as ideologically. Modern production methods came in: plays were at last recorded on tape in specialized drama studios, and production expanded at a dizzy rate. Since 1986, China's more than 500 stations have produced an average of 2,000 plays per annum; in 1991 this figure rose to 5,000. Here, too, Western dra-mas began to invade the screen, including the BBC's Shakespeare series. Cultural factors which may not be directly political will also colour a country's TV drama output. Hong Kong is as addicted to martial arts pro-grammes as Japan is to samurai epics. Britain's meticu-lously researched and expertly produced period dramas (which have a rich overseas sales potential) owe not a lit-tle to post-imperial nostalgia.

The actual organization of broadcasting institutions is bound to be crucial. Out-and-out commercialism as in the USA; a state-run service as in Cuba or the former communist countries of Eastern Europe; a duopoly, partly a public service and partly independent, as in Great Britain, Sweden and Japan; stations run by spe-cial-interest groups (Catholic and socialist) as in the Netherlands; or any of the possible range of variants of these, with regulations tough or permissive as the case may be – all make for very different kinds of drama out-put.

In the former West Germany, television presents a unique picture. Authority in the first channel (ARD) is vested in the regional (*Länder*) governments. The second channel (ZDF) is jointly controlled by federal govern-ment, *Länder* and various interest groups. This arrrange-ment leaves an occasional space for delving into controversial areas. In the 1960s there were plays dedi-cated to coming to terms with the Nazi past. In the early 1970s the regional station WDR screened several tele-films dealing sympathetically with working-class top-ics, such as Klaus Wiese and Christina Ziewer's *Dear Mother, I'm OK* and *Snowdrops Bloom in September*. R. W. FASSBINDER's five-part series *Eight Hours Don't Make a Day*, which examined the link in working-class life between work, home and leisure, antagonized critics both left and right. A regular platform for experimental telefilms has been provided by ZDF's weekly slot, 'Das kleine Fernsehspiel' ('The Little Television Play'), which puts out work of minority interest.

The world's largest producer of TV drama, chiefly of the entertainment variety, is the United States. The domestic strength of the industry makes it the leading exporter, able to offer its programmes abroad at irre-sistible prices. An oligopoly of three networks – ABC, CBS and NBC – has dominated the numerous local sta-tions, which get 70 per cent of their material from the Big Three. There is a solid home market: in 1979, 98 per cent of the population owned a set; in 30 million homes there were two, and in 10 million homes three or more sets. By 1992, average daily viewing had risen to the daunting figure of over seven hours. Since the purpose of commercial television is to sell air time to advertis-ers, the criteria of success are 'ratings' (i.e. viewer num-

bers) or, at a more sophisticated level, 'demographic profiles' (i.e. the socio-economic slice of the market reached). The networks produce only a fraction of their own material and buy in telefilms from six major Hollywood studios (Columbia, Paramount, MGM, 20th Century Fox, Universal and Warner Brothers) or inde-pendent TV film production companies. The bulk of these productions comes from the West Coast; their style and ethos is that of Hollywood. Production values count for a great deal, cultural prestige for rather less. In the ceaseless competition for a slice of the market, the principle of Least Objectionable Programming is held in high regard. There have, of course, been notable exceptions to this generalization. For example, the *Hallmark Hall of Fame*, begun in 1952 and continued into the 1990s, mixed prestigious theatrical offerings with plays specially written for TV; associated for 27 years with NBC, this show switched in the 1979–80 season to CBS. The (privately supported) Public Broadcasting Service (PBS), which is dedicated to transmitting 'qual-ity' work, only reaches some 2–3 per cent of American viewers; much of its material is of British origin.

At times ideological considerations do, of course, supplement purely commercial ones. When ABC's *Roots*, the dramatization of the Alex Haley novel which traced the progress of an African-American family over several generations from slavery to post-bellum Reconstruction, was shown for eight successive nights in January 1977, its impact was immense. This 12-hour indictment of white America's treatment of its black population struck a chord: the mayors of over 30 cities proclaimed a 'Roots Week', and some 250 colleges were to offer courses based on the book and the mini-series. A comparable blockbuster with educational intent was NBC's *Holocaust* (1978), which won 107 million viewers in the USA and an estimated 220 million in 50 other countries. This story of the Nazi persecution of a family of Berlin Jews, shot wholly on location in Germany and Austria, was criticized by some on grounds of taste but undoubtedly brought home to many viewers, in Germany and elsewhere, genocidal horrors the mem-ory of which had been repressed until then.

## Away from theatre

In Britain, where the BBC, guided by the Reithian pub-lic-service ethos, used to enjoy a monopoly of the air, television drama tended at first to be little more than televised theatre. But in the early 1950s attempts were made to ginger things up; Nigel Kneale's science-fiction serial, *The Quatermass Experiment*, caused much excite-ment in 1953. This alarming preview of the dire conse-quences of space flight was followed by sequels, culminating as late as 1979 in *Quatermass 4*.

The coming, after a vigorous debate, of commercial television in 1955 opened up British broadcasting to more popular tastes. The United States had shown the way. The American networks, originally broadcasting from New York, had encouraged a spate of fresh TV play-writing, probably to persuade people in the higher income brackets to buy receivers. The competition between 'The Philco Playhouse' (NBC) and 'Studio One' (CBS) in the late 1940s and early 1950s brought on what in retrospect glowed like a golden age of television drama. Writers like Gore Vidal and N. Richard Nash made their mark. Reginald Rose's courtroom drama, *Twelve Angry Men* (CBS, 1954), came out with a powerful liberal plea for even-handed justice. PADDY CHAYEFSKY's *Marty* (NBC, 1953) depicted an unglamorous butcher's longing for love; other plays of his such as *The Catered Affair*, *The Bachelor Party* and *Middle of the Night* revelled in what he called 'the marvellous world of the ordinary'. A similar outburst of creativity took place in Canadian television.

In seeking out more popular material, Britain – both the BBC and the drama-orientated independent company ABC – bought in a large number of North American scripts. ABC's 'Armchair Theatre' changed the tone of drama on the small screen; writers like ALUN OWEN, Clive Exton and BILL NAUGHTON gave it a contemporary and British accent. Associated Television, ATV and Granada also promoted original TV playwriting. In 1964 the BBC started 'The Wednesday Play', a title changed in 1970 to 'Play for Today'. This became a platform for innovative (and, to some timid souls, alarming) drama, presenting the work of MICHAEL FRAYN, SIMON GRAY, PETER TERSON and many other writers. DAVID MERCER's *In Two Minds* (1967) questioned the conventional wisdom about schizophrenia. PETER NICHOLS's *The Common* (1973) mixed domestic with political intrigues. One of the instant hits was Jeremy Sandford's *Cathy Come Home* (1966), brilliantly directed by Ken Loach. This story of young Cathy and Reg, filmed on location in cinéma-vérité style, brought the plight of the homeless close to millions of viewers and implied, in the author's words, that 'our State is needlessly cruel'. The verisimilitude of *Cathy* and other documentary dramas (an ill-defined category that runs all the way from the biopic to personalized reportage) gave rise to some anxiety: would viewers be fooled into thinking the play was *real*? Curiously, such fears were aroused only by plays with a radical thrust.

It is not to underrate the contribution made by producers, directors, actors and designers to say that it was above all the writers who raised the prestige of British television drama from the 1960s onwards. Established literary figures like TERENCE RATTIGAN and J. B. PRIESTLEY were attracted to the new medium; authors like JOHN OSBORNE, JOHN MORTIMER and TOM STOPPARD were all to write for it. The success on the domestic screen of *A Night Out* (ABC, 1960) gave HAROLD PINTER a wider hearing than his first stage plays had commanded. John Hopkins's quartet, *Talking to a Stranger* (BBC, 1966), was described as 'the first authentic masterpiece written directly for television'. The politically committed playwright and screenwriter TREVOR GRIFFITHS favoured the small screen – when granted access to it – as giving him the widest audience. His 11-episode *Bill Brand* looked at left-wing politics from the inside. Jim Allen's *Days of Hope* (BBC, 1976), a four-part chronicle of British working-class history up to the General Strike of 1926, unleashed a storm of protest in the press: the issues raised were far from merely historical. Author-director MIKE LEIGH successfully transferred his improvisational playmaking technique to television with naturalistic and satirical pictures of English life. The Irish novelist William Trevor played variations on the theme of loneliness in his TV plays; Elaine Morgan showed great skill in dramatized biographies. The highly productive ALAN PLATER, initially inspired by Paddy Chayefsky, at first used his north-country background to create regional speech and characters of great authority, but then diversified; he has expertly dramatized many novels. His fellow Northerner ALAN BENNETT – actor, REVUE artist, writer for stage and screen – has created affectionate and shrewdly observed cameos of 'ordinary' people without disguising the melancholy beneath his laughter.

DENNIS POTTER, originally a television critic, began a spectacular and highly productive TV playwriting career with *The Confidence Course* (BBC) in 1965. His work increasingly veered away from mainstream NATURALISM, most notably perhaps in the trilogy which employed popular music in a startlingly novel way: *Pennies from Heaven* (BBC, 1978), *The Singing Detective* (BBC, 1986) and *Lipstick on Your Collar* (Whistling Gypsy for Channel 4, 1993). The first of these serials harked back to the songs of the 1930s, the second to those of the 1940s, the third to the 1950s. The irruption of songs into the action had the reverse effect of that of MUSICAL COMEDY: it was an alienating device which questioned, while at the same time sympathizing with, the very emotions being expressed.

This literary flavour of much British television contrasts with American television, where a script like ARTHUR MILLER's play set in Auschwitz, *Playing for Time* (CBS, 1980), tends to be the exception. In Britain the single play was long held to be the key to dramatic innovation; all the alarm bells would ring whenever that was in danger of being crowded out by the series or the serial. In fact, it was not until the 1980s that the single play finally took a very modest back seat in programming, with ratings looming ever larger in the more competitive climate of Thatcherism. Up to the 1970s, the BBC's freedom from commercial pressures allowed it to take risks (principally in the area of the single play) and to set standards that the independent companies had to acknowledge and follow. Even so, there were unstated limits as to how far drama might go. Peter Watkins's *The War Game* (1965), a by no means sensationalized vision of how Britain might fare in a nuclear war, was banned on the grounds that 'it had the power to produce unpredictable emotions'.

If over the years the BBC was to become somewhat less enterprising, the creation in 1982 of Channel 4, with a brief to innovate, to cater for minority tastes and to commission rather than produce programmes itself, gave British television drama a new fillip. A number of production companies sprang up to fill the programming gap. The funding provided by Film on Four increasingly blurred the distinction between the telefilm and the cinema film: many of the films it commissioned were shown on the large as well as the small screen. By the end of the 1980s, Film on Four had been involved in over 150 full-length features, a godsend to the ailing British film industry.

## Television genres

Once American television play production had moved to the West Coast, the series replaced the single play. Commercially the change-over made sense: cast, location and sets can be used repeatedly, and captive audiences 'delivered' to advertisers with a high degree of certainty. A crude ratings approach gave way in the early 1970s to demographic considerations: in order to retain upmarket viewers, networks had to provide something better than what one critic called 'mind candy'. Standards improved without actually departing from a broad consensus of taste.

Like Hollywood movies, series quickly took on genre patterns. The Western proved to be as popular on TV as it had in the cinema. *Wagon Trail* (NBC) began its long, largely studio-bound career in 1957, some of its episodes improbably inspired by *Pride and Prejudice* and *Great*

*Expectations*. Owen Wister's 1902 novel, *The Virginian*, had spawned some films for the cinema; now NBC was to run a series under that title (1962–9), with guest performers like GEORGE C. SCOTT, Bette Davis and Robert Redford. *Bonanza* (NBC, 1959–71) was a sort of Western soap opera.

In the movies, crime had been depicted largely from the gangster's perspective. On television it is policemen or detectives who carry the action: long-term identification has to be with the side of law and order. ABC's *Dragnet* (begun in 1952) was based on actual case histories; Sergeant Joe Friday's 'Just the facts, ma'am' entered the language. *Kojak* (CBS, 1973–7) fought crime while licking a lollipop. *Hill Street Blues* (NBC, 1980–7) took a disenchanted look at a police station in a deprived East Coast city. The same company's *Miami Vice* (1984–9) stressed formal values, some sequences resembling pop promos.

Indeed, villainy has a worldwide appeal. A series on Radio-Television Hong Kong dramatizing real crimes enjoyed the collaboration of the police. The Australian Broadcasting Corporation's *Phoenix* (1991) aimed to give a gritty look to its portrayal of the inner working of the Major Crime Squad. The British version of the genre was at first rather benign. *Dixon of Dock Green* (BBC), a cosy cop show devised by Ted (later Lord) Willis, ran from 1955 until 1976, by which time its avuncular lead Jack Warner was well beyond retirement age. But *Z Cars* (BBC, 1960–78), as well as its spin-off *Softly, Softly* (BBC, 1966–76), gave a more down-to-earth picture of police work. Thames TV's *The Sweeny* (1974–8) portrayed Scotland Yard's Flying Squad in action-packed mid-Atlantic terms. The BBC's *Juliet Bravo* (from 1980) featured a woman police officer – a breakthrough in a traditionally macho genre. *The Bill* (Thames TV, from 1985) has also included women police constables in its cast, and this has now become standard practice.

The detective is a television hero in many countries. In the French series *The Last Five Minutes* (ORTF, 1958) Inspector Bourrel always solved his case just in the nick of time. In the late 1950s the BBC's *Maigret* series, based on Simenon's famous sleuth, conjured up a satisfyingly French atmosphere; many of the scripts were by GILES COOPER. The lead created by Rupert Davies was reincarnated on the small screen some 30 years later by the versatile MICHAEL GAMBON. The image of the British detective was to become increasingly differentiated – Taggart and Bergerac representing opposite ends of the UK, Glasgow and the Channel Islands respectively; there was even a Chinese detective. A number of British TV sleuths derive from crime fiction: Miss Marples out of Agatha Christie, Chief Inspector Wexford out of Ruth Rendell, Commander Adam Dalgliesh out of P. D. James, Chief Inspector Morse out of Colin Dexter. The last, played by John Thaw, was to become a cult figure. Made by Zenith for Central Television, *Morse* (1987–93) regularly played to 15 million UK viewers and a worldwide audience of 75 million in over 50 countries. Far from being the usual police detective, Morse – Oxford-based, literate and opera-loving – often barked up the wrong tree. The solution of the crime would leave him melancholy rather than elated. His trademark, a 1960 Mark Two Jaguar, has become famous.

The medical show, too, had a well established Hollywood history. MGM, which had made as many as nine films between 1938 and 1947 on Dr Kildare, a young intern under the mentorship of a crusty old doctor, went on to make a television *Dr Kildare* series for NBC (1961–6). In Britain, *Emergency –Ward 10* kept ATV viewers tranquillized from 1957 onwards; *Casualty* (BBC, from 1986) has scored high marks for REALISM in situation as well as make-up: the gashes and contusions look clinically accurate.

Science fiction, a well established literary genre since the days of Jules Verne, had been popular in the cinema before it blasted off on the TV screen. *Star Trek*, NBC's sci-fi serial which started in 1966, has taken a positive view of space exploration, borne aloft by confidence in America's cosmic mission. Moral dilemmas have tended to be confronted from a liberal perspective. The extraterrestrial Mr Spock's pointed ears and the simple but recurrent dematerialization effects endeared the programme to viewers in many countries. This long-running serial had been anticipated in Britain by the evergreen *Doctor Who*, launched by the BBC in 1963; originally aimed at children, this soon conquered audiences within a broad spectrum of age and status. The ongoing tale of an eccentric doctor who travels through time and space in the TARDIS, his supertechnological spacecraft disguised as a police box, proved to be highly marketable around the world and built up a devoted following. Until its demise in 1986, the serial adapted to evolving audience requirements by periodic changes of writers and lead actors.

The most important of the lighter sorts of television drama is situation comedy – sit-com for short. Its format is based on the need to spin (often initially an unpredictable number of) episodes out of a more or less constant situation. Its ancestor is radio comedy with its weekly instalments. In a sit-com a group of people assembled within a fixed framework (family, workplace, pub, corner grocery shop or boarding-house) are made to strike sparks from each other: the performers' personalities are the key to success. Though normally close to reality, with some inevitable stereotyping, it may well verge on farce; John Cleese's misadventures as the manic hotel owner of *Fawlty Towers* (BBC, 1975–9) were pure latter-day FEYDEAU.

American sit-coms, usually backed by the deplorable device of the 'laugh track', have often been built around a female character. CBS starred the effervescent and indestructible Lucille Ball in *I Love Lucy* (1951–5), *The Lucy Show* (1962–8) and *Here's Lucy* (1968–73). *The Golden Girls* (NBC, from 1985) are a group of irrepressible middle-class old-age pensioners in Miami; *Roseanne* (ABC, from 1988) features Roseanne Barr as an equally irrepressible working-class wife.

In Britain sit-com had its first flowering with the prickly Tony Hancock. *Hancock's Half Hour*, scripted by Alan Simpson and Ray Galton, produced notable delights on radio as well as BBC television between 1954 and 1961; in the same co-authors' *Steptoe and Son* (BBC, 1964–73), a rag-and-bone man bickered incessantly with his son and partner. In Johnny Speight's *Till Death Us Do Part* (BBC, 1966–74) the preposterous views of Alf Garnett, a working-class reactionary played by Warren Mitchell, were held up to ridicule. Archie Bunker, his counterpart in the American adaptation, *All in the Family* (CBS, 1971–9), though equally foul-mouthed was more of a wisecracker. At the other end of the social spectrum, Antony Jay and Jonathan Lynn's *Yes, Minister* (BBC, 1980–5) and its sequel *Yes, Prime Minister* (1986–9) gave a keyhole view of the Whitehall corridors of power, allegedly very close to the real thing.

A subdivision of sit-com found on both sides of the Atlantic is the military comedy. Jimmy Perry and David Croft's *Dad's Army* (BBC, 1967-77) poked fun at an ineffectual but lovable Home Guard platoon which went through the motions of guarding England against the Nazi invader. *M\*A\*S\*H* (CBS, 1972-83), a medical-cum-army sit-com, was set in a medical army surgical hospital during the Korean War. The war lasted three years; *M\*A\*S\*H* ran for eleven. When the last of its 251 episodes went out in the United States it was watched by 125 million viewers. A similar glorious finale in terms of viewing figures was scored by *Cheers* (Paramount Television for NBC, 1982-93). With a run as long as that of its military predecessor, this sharply written sit-com based on a group of regulars in a Boston bar collected as many as 26 Emmy awards.

## The soap opera

A genre of American derivation but of truly universal appeal is the soap opera, so called because its radio predecessor in the 1930s was mainly sponsored by soap powder firms. Its hold on the American public is such that addicts can read a *Soap Opera Digest* or dial a 24-hour 'Soap by Phone' service to bring themselves up to date on any episodes they might have missed. In 1979 there were as many as 12 soaps a day on tap. This family- or community-based type of narrative has a beginning but no end, and hence no middle: ARISTOTLE would not have approved. A soap opera dies of inanition rather than for any dramaturgical reasons. Its tone is a mixture of the melodramatic and the mundane. Viewer identification is essential, hence narrative time and viewing time generally coincide: when it is Christmas in the story it is actually Christmastime. A common feature is the interweaving of several narrative strands in any one instalment so as to keep track of the group as a whole. Cliffhanger endings characterize not only the end of episodes but even the moment before the commercial breaks: the viewer must not be let off the hook.

With their Hollywood gloss, American soaps have lathered their way into the hearts of much of mankind. Perhaps none has had a greater impact than *Dallas*, made by Lorimar for CBS (1978-82), with an international audience of some 300 million viewers. The feuding among the Ewing family, Texan oil multimillionaires, kept the telemasses spellbound. The shooting of the baddie, J. R. Ewing, hyped by a lavish publicity campaign, echoed around the world. Other soaps in tycoon country satisfied a similar appetite. *Dynasty* (ABC, 1981-9) was also set in an oil-rich family, British-born Joan Collins playing Alexis, the woman you love to hate. The show's weekly wardrobe budget alone came to $10,000.

In Britain, too, soap opera had its roots in radio (see RADIO DRAMA) - serials like *Mrs Dale's Diary* (1948-69) and *The Archers*, broadcast daily since 1 January 1951. British soap opera keeps some grip on social and regional realities. While the suburban lower-middle-class *Grove Family* (BBC, 1953-6) led the way, quite the greatest success among British soap operas (though its makers reject the label) has been *Coronation Street*, the Granada serial with a Lancashire working-class setting. Launched on 9 December 1960, it was originally scheduled to run for a mere 13 weeks - but it never stopped. The Rovers Return must be the best-known pub in the country; the fame of Bet Lynch, Elsie Tanner and Hilda Ogden rivals that of royalty. The biographies of the saga's characters are chronicled by an archivist for the benefit of succeeding generations of scriptwriters. Studiously contemporary in external detail, *Coronation Street* plays on nostalgia for older, more settled values. Throughout the 1980s, viewing figures oscillated around the 16 million mark; a matrimonial cliffhanger in February 1983 clocked up an audience of 29 million.

*Crossroads* (ATV/Central, 1964-87) also counted its followers in millions, but it never enjoyed the critical esteem of *Coronation Street*. *Emmerdale Farm* (Yorkshire TV, since 1972) combines studio work with location shooting in the country. The village where its exteriors are filmed has become a tourist mecca. Scottish Television joined the chorus in 1980 with *Take the High Road*. Merseyside Television's *Brookside*, broadcast on Channel 4 since 1982, has a decidedly topical look. Shot on location in an actual housing estate near Liverpool, it has confronted problems such as unemployment and rape. *EastEnders* (BBC, from 1985, created by Julia Smith and Tony Holland) has made Albert Square the Cockney equivalent of Coronation Street. The viewing figures of this serial rival those of its northern elder brother. Australia, too, has its soap operas. The middle-class appeal of *Neighbours* works its charm not only at home but overseas as well, e.g. on as many as 14 million viewers in Britain.

Soap opera is, of course, not confined to the English-speaking world. On Egyptian television the more popular programmes are known as 'street cleaners' because crowds tend to disappear off the streets during transmission times. Though the Egyptian state broadcasting company ERT takes a good deal of foreign, chiefly American, material it also commissions TV drama from local independent producers. The first country in Africa to have colour TV, which was introduced in 1971, Egypt has had a fully established film industry since well before World War II, and television can draw on a pool of creative and technical talent. Being far and away the strongest producer of TV drama in the Arab world, it exports a great many programmes to other Arabic-speaking countries. Egyptian soap operas pose no political or moral challenges. In addition to tales of everyday life, ERT also presents serials with a patriotic or religious thrust: for several years it filled the screens during the month of Ramadan with 30-part serials on the lives of the prophets, ending the cycle with a lavishly mounted biography of Mohammed himself.

In some countries soap opera may be more than mere entertainment. Thus, *Cockcrow at Dawn*, broadcast by the Nigerian Television Authority since 1980, is the story of the Bello family, country folk who fail to adapt to city life and return to the land where they settle down as small farmers. Without being overtly didactic, the serial has slipped in practical hints about modern farming methods. In Japan, there is a vast and eager public for soap operas. NHK puts out a 15-minute 'novel serial' at 8.15 a.m. from Monday to Saturday - a form of breakfast television watched by nearly 50 per cent of the viewing audience. The kind of Japanese serial termed 'home drama' frequently features plucky women who keep the family together. *O Shin* (1983) was set in the Meiji era rather than in the present; but this MELODRAMA of a woman from a poor farming background who achieves success after countless tribulations became a national obsession quite in the manner of soap opera.

Initially, Mexico was the chief producer of long-running *telenovelas*, exporting them to other Latin American countries; in the 1970s Brazil was to sprint into the lead. Brazil's high illiteracy rate has given a peculiar importance to television drama. TV Tupi, a São Paolo station which has since gone out of business, launched *Beto Rockefeller* in 1968, the tale of a poor man who makes his way to the top. Fantasies of social climbing were to be a major ingredient of the genre. The length of *telenovelas* is prodigious: DIAS GOMES's *The Well Beloved* the saga of politics in a town in Bahia, ran for 177 episodes.

These Brazilian *telenovelas* are close to the traditional soap opera in that they are constantly evolving, new episodes being written in response to viewer reactions. The chief purveyor is the Globo TV Network – the world's fourth-largest. A family enterprise, it is part of an immensely powerful communications empire. With a TV drama output of feature-film proportions, Globo is far from indifferent to quality: it employs leading writers, directors, designers and musicians. It has as many as 500 actors on staff or under contract. In 1993 it opened Latin America's largest production centre in Rio de Janeiro. Its serials achieve viewing figures of up to 50 million – more Brazilians having access to a TV screen than to clean drinking water. Some of the subjects of these serials plunge boldly into controversy. *Gabriela*, a feminist story based on a Jorge Amado novel, proved enormously popular not only at home but also in Portugal – where a bishop denounced it for subverting the family. The fact that Globo exports its telefilms to more than 80 countries suggests that US (and even UK) preponderance in the world market for TV drama is not written on tablets of stone.

Indeed, the American industry has been transformed rapidly in the last two decades of the 20th century. All the Big Three networks changed hands in the 1980s, their new ownership more attuned to a tough-minded corporate culture than ever; and a great many old-established media corporations went out of business. But this was merely part of a worldwide media revolution. The boundaries in which regulations used to flourish can easily be leapt over by satellite broadcasting; the use of videocassettes has meant that wider consumer choice has partially replaced the drama seen only at the actual time of transmission. Interactive television-on-demand is a technical possibility. The interconnectedness of the various TV systems has more and more taken the shape of co-productions, at any rate in the case of high-budget prestige serials. This has obvious advantages, but it may well threaten the national flavour of drama.

## 'Quality' television

Although British television was to find itself under increasing pressure during the 1980s, partly from a worsening economic climate and partly from the attitude of a government unsympathetic to the public-service ethos, many outstanding programmes were achieved nevertheless. Financially strong enough to go in for large-scale prestige telefilms, Granada in 1981 presented a 13-episode adaptation (by JOHN MORTIMER) of Evelyn Waugh's *Brideshead Revisited*, with glittering production values and stars of the calibre of CLAIRE BLOOM, JOHN GIELGUD and LAURENCE OLIVIER; it followed this up in 1984 with the equally dazzling 14-episode *The Jewel in the Crown*, based on Paul Scott's 'Raj Quartet'. The latter serial tackled a delicate subject, the last days of British rule in India, with considerable complexity and a wealth of narrative detail. The BBC's blockbuster reply to all this came in 1987 with *The*

*Fortunes of War*, the adaptation (by Alan Plater) of Olivia Manning's 'Balkan Trilogy' and 'Levant Trilogy'. This serial, which brought the actors KENNETH BRANAGH and Emma Thompson to prominence, was, however, a co-production with two American companies.

Equally notable, though in a wholly different key, was ALAN BLEASDALE's 5-episode *Boys from the Blackstuff* (BBC, 1982). In this angry, compassionate study of a group of unemployed Liverpool workers and their families, each man in turn came to the fore in successive episodes. The style moved from NATURALISM to something almost surreal (see SURREALISM) in a desolate picture of 1980s society. The death of a militant old worker while being pushed in a wheelchair through the ruins of Liverpool's dockland sounded a requiem for a whole era. The series was universally praised. Not so Bleasdale's next BBC serial, *The Monocled Mutineer* (1986), a World War I story denounced by the right-wing press as less than respectful of the British army. Other dissident productions that stood out in an increasingly conformist decade were Troy Kennedy Martin's *Edge of Darkness* (BBC, 1985), a police thriller which developed into a story of nuclear skulduggery, and Alan Plater's adaptation of a novel by Chris Mullin MP, *A Very British Coup* (Skreba for Channel 4, 1988), in which Establishment machinations against a possible Labour victory at the polls were unmasked.

Undeniably, television drama is a significant social phenomenon; but is it aesthetically significant? The bulk of it may be trivial; but then so is the bulk of stage plays and films. A critical problem is that popular and minority tastes, regrettably perhaps, tend to diverge. Both levels have their separate justification; both should ideally be catered for in a mass medium such as TV drama. An outstanding German example of a serial which did manage to do this – and at the same time to straddle the divide between cinema and TV – was Edgar Reitz's *Heimat* (*Homeland*; WDR, 1984). This 11-part, 16-hour epic, which follows the history from 1919 to 1982 of the Simon family and their neighbours in a fictitious village in the Hunsrück district, has the sweep and amplitude of a 19th-century novel. The result of some two years' location shooting in the area, *Heimat* places personal destinies in the wider context of the nation's history. Technological, political and social transformations shape the lives of the villagers, who are moved from a patriarchal lifestyle into the modern age. The sequel is set in the 1960s: an even longer epic, which shows the adventures of the younger generation whose homeland is no longer the village but the wider world of art.

Television drama may at times threaten to become socially enervating by its very quantity. Its essentially domestic appeal may be stripping dramatic performances of their former sense of festive occasion. But against that, plays that enter virtually every home can, in ideal circumstances, have the power to move a whole nation, or indeed many nations together. Constantly evolving, television drama is an ineluctable fact of contemporary life: a possible danger, perhaps, but a great opportunity for imaginative enrichment and deeper self-understanding if, collectively, that is what we choose to have.

**Téllez, Gabriel** see TIRSO DE MOLINA

**Tennyson, Alfred,** Lord 1809–92 British poet. When he was 65 his first play, *Queen Mary*, was staged at the LYCEUM (1876), with IRVING as Philip of Spain. A second historical verse drama, *Harold*, remained unperformed until 1928, when LAURENCE OLIVIER took the title role at the ROYAL COURT. A third, *Becket*, also opened after Tennyson's death, and the part of Becket remained in Irving's repertoire until his death. There were four others: *The Falcon* (1879), *The Cup* (1881), *The Promise of May* (1882) and *The Foresters* (1892).

**tent show** American touring entertainment. These plays or VARIETY shows, dating from the 1850s, were staged under canvas. By the late 19th century, travelling troupes with repertories extensive enough to provide a week's worth of entertainment had become popular in the summer, when local opera houses were too poorly ventilated to attract the public. The Chautauqua circuit, offering lecture meetings of an educational or religious nature, performed in brown tents to distinguish them from the white canvas of the show tents, which were 50 or 60 feet wide, with bare benches or bleachers and a platform stage designed for portability.

The earliest repertoires were imitations, often pirated, of the standard domestic fare, primarily MELO-DRAMA. Later tent showmen composed their own plays, carpentered to a limited company and the familiar themes of rural life. The standbys of this repertory include Charles Harrison's *Saintly Hypocrites and Honest Sinners* (1915) and W. C. Herman's *Call of the Woods*, which pitted homespun virtue against urban corruption. The comic character TOBY, developed c.1911, became the popular hero of these works.

After World War I, motor vehicles replaced rail transport, and tent shows proliferated. Some 400 shows were travelling through the United States by 1927. But the catastrophic effects of the Depression, dust storms, unionization and competition from local cinemas led to the closure of hundreds of companies in the 1930s. The FEDERAL THEATRE PROJECT absorbed many of these entertainers, and in the 1950s only some dozen troupes survived.

**Ter-Arutunian, Rouben** 1920–92 Armenian-American set and COSTUME designer. Born in Tbilisi, Georgia, of Armenian parents, he was educated in Paris and Berlin and emigrated to the USA in 1951. In addition to theatre and opera, Ter-Arutunian designed for television in the 1950s. His work falls primarily into two categories: 'decorative' (or painterly), such as his famous *Nutcracker* for the New York City Ballet; or sculptural, such as *Ricercare* for American Ballet Theatre. The latter style allows him to create space around a minimal amount of scenery. He claims to design the visual counterpart to drama, poetry, music and movement 'with simplicity, clarity, and a certain element of mystery'.

**Terence** [Publius Terentius Afer] c.184–159 BC Roman playwright. He is said to have been a freed slave from Carthage, but biographical evidence is scanty. The six comedies which survive appear to be all he ever wrote. They are *Andria* (*The Girl from Andros*, 166 BC); *Hecyra* (*The Mother-in-Law*, 165); *Heauton Timoroumenos* (*The Self-Tormentor*, 163); *Eunuchus* (*The Eunuch*, 161); *Phormio* (161) and *Adelphoe* (*The Brothers*, 160). *Hecyra* and *Phormio* were adapted from plays by Apollodorus of Carystus, a follower of MENANDER, the others from plays by Menander himself.

The broad and farcical humour which PLAUTUS had introduced into his plays was largely eliminated by Terence, who sought to bring Menandrean restraint and refinement to Roman comedy. While *Eunuchus* and *Adelphoe* contain farcical scenes, and *Phormio* has a clever trickster as its central character, the humour of Terence's work is generally a subtle consequence of the interplay of character and situation. *Hecyra* is a largely serious and realistic exploration of domestic difficulties, with little, apart from the happy ending, to qualify it as a comedy at all.

Terence tried in various ways to improve on his Greek models. His prologues, for example, stand entirely outside the drama and serve the special purpose of explaining his aims, complaining of the audience's past failure to appreciate his work, and replying to the attacks of a jealous rival. They reveal a new artistic self-consciousness and afford a glimpse of the theatrical conditions of the period.

While self-conscious moralizing is avoided, the plays have a distinctly high-minded tone. Most characters try to act for the best; their problems are held up for sympathy rather than ridicule, and their foibles are exposed with genial tolerance. Terence shows insight and understanding in his portrayal of women, and has a particular interest in relations between fathers and sons. The 'humanity' for which he is famous can now be seen to be largely an inheritance from Menander, but it is at least an inheritance that he preserved intact, to be passed on to such admirers as MOLIÈRE. (See also ROMAN THEATRE.)

**Terriss, William** [William Charles James Lewin] 1847–97 British actor. Terriss had been a merchant seaman, a tea-planter in Assam and a sheep-farmer in the Falkland Islands – where his daughter, the actress Ellaline Terriss (1871–1971), was born – before his first significant stage success as Squire Thornhill in a dramatization of GOLDSMITH's *The Vicar of Wakefield*. After his engagement with IRVING at the LYCEUM (1880–5), where he played several Shakespearian roles, he found his natural home at the ADELPHI, where he featured in a succession of muscular MELODRAMAS, beginning with *The Harbour Lights* (1885). Terriss's swashbuckling athleticism earned him the nickname of 'Breezy Bill' – there was no subtlety about his acting. He was stabbed to death by a deranged actor at the stage door of the Adelphi.

**Terry, Ellen (Alice)** 1847–1928 British actress. Born into a theatrical family, she played Mamillius for CHARLES KEAN at the PRINCESS's in 1856 and the 'shrew' to IRVING's Petruchio at the Queen's (1867). In 1875 she made her first major Shakespearian appearance, as Portia in the BANCROFTS' production of *The Merchant of Venice*. Her beauty and the apparent spontaneity of her verse-speaking continued to charm audiences for 50 years.

In 1878, having just seen Terry playing the sentimental title role in W. G. WILLS's *Olivia* (this version of GOLDSMITH's *The Vicar of Wakefield* was still in her repertoire 30 years later), Irving invited her to join him at the LYCEUM, where she remained for 25 years as England's leading actress. She was Irving's Ophelia (1878), Portia (1879), Desdemona (1881), Juliet (1882), Beatrice (1882), Viola (1884), Lady Macbeth (1888), Queen Katharine (1892), Cordelia (1892), Imogen (1896) and Volumnia (1901); but never his Rosalind, since *As You Like It* had no satisfactory part for him. This imbalance, her agreement to play second fiddle, antagonized GEORGE BERNARD SHAW, whose long and loving correspondence with Terry was published in 1931. Eventually she played the part Shaw wrote for her as Lady Cicely Waynflete in *Captain Brassbound's Conversion* (1906). By then Irving was dead, and Terry had staged IBSEN's *The Vikings* (1903) – as a production, a costly failure – in sets designed by her son, GORDON CRAIG. Her Hermione for BEERBOHM TREE at HER [HIS] MAJESTY's (1906) was her last Shakespearian role. She wrote an autobiography, *The Story of My Life* (1908), and a series of lectures on SHAKESPEARE's heroines that became a regular part of her programme from 1910 to 1921. In 1925 she was appointed DBE. Few stage personalities have ever been so loved.

Three of Ellen's sisters, Kate (1844–1924), Marion (1852–1930) and Florence (1855–96), had distinguished stage careers, as did her brother Fred (1864–1932). From her liaison with the married architect E. W. Godwin she had two extraordinary children, Gordon and EDITH CRAIG. Of her other descendants, JOHN GIELGUD is the best-known.

**Terson [Patterson], Peter** 1932– British playwright. He was a teacher for ten years before his first play, *A Night to Make the Angels Weep* (1964), was produced at the VICTORIA THEATRE, Stoke-on-Trent. This play, together with *The Mighty Reservoy* (1964), revealed him to be an amusing observer of life in the Midlands and the North of England, with the instinctive ability to seize on a symbolic idea, which raised his NATURALISM towards myth. He became resident dramatist at Stoke-on-Trent in 1966. Several of his plays transferred to little theatres around London, including *Mooney and his Caravans* (1968) and *Zigger Zagger* (1967), about football fans and hooligans, written for the NATIONAL YOUTH THEATRE. Terson wrote other NYT successes such as *The Apprentices* (1968), *Spring Heeled Jack* (1970) and *Good Lads at Heart* (1971). His work has always retained its background in regional, local and community situations. *Strippers* (1984), describing the life of women in high areas of unemployment, received a successful WEST END run.

**Tesfaye Gessesse** 1937– Ethiopian playwright, actor and director. He studied drama in the United States and then worked at the Haile Selassie I Theatre in Addis Ababa University. After the 1974 revolution he took charge of the AGER FIKIR theatre and in 1976 assumed control of the Ethiopian National Theatre until 1983. In addition to short stories he has written a number of plays in Amharic, including *Yeshi* (1962), about urban prostitution, *Iqaw* (1975), *Renaissance* (1979) and *The Verdict Is Yours* (1984).

**Teternikov, F. K.** see SOLOGUB, FYODOR

**Thacker, David** 1950– British director. Having studied and directed at the University of York, he joined the Theatre Royal, York, established the Rolling Stock Theatre, a touring Young People's Theatre company (1978; see THEATRE-IN-EDUCATION), and became director of the Duke's Playhouse in Lancaster. In 1984 he was appointed director of the YOUNG VIC in London, which, under Thacker's leadership, became the best place in London to take students of all ages to see intelligent SHAKESPEARE productions. His own productions included *Othello* and *Macbeth* (1984), *Hamlet* and *Measure for Measure* (1985), *Julius Caesar* (1986) and *Romeo and Juliet* (1987).

Thacker is also adept at directing modern plays with challenging themes, particularly from America. His production of IBSEN's *Ghosts* (1986) with VANESSA REDGRAVE transferred to the WEST END. His revival of ARTHUR MILLER's *The Crucible* (1985) led to a special relationship with the author. At the Young Vic he directed the world premieres of *Two-Way Mirror* (1989) and *The Last Yankee* (1993), which transferred to the West End. In 1989 he directed *Pericles* for the ROYAL SHAKESPEARE COMPANY. This led to mainstage RSC productions of *As You Like It*, *The Merry Wives of Windsor* and *Two Gentlemen of Verona* in 1992. He was appointed director in residence at the RSC, where three of his productions were seen in the 1993/4 season – *The Merchant of Venice*, *Julius Caesar* and *Two Gentlemen of Verona*. In 1994 Thacker directed the premiere of Arthur Miller's *Broken Glass* at the NATIONAL THEATRE.

**Theatre, The** (London) This, the first dedicated public playhouse in England, was situated in Shoreditch, outside the city walls. Opened in 1576 by JAMES BURBAGE, it became the favourite home of the LORD CHAMBERLAIN's MEN and many of SHAKESPEARE's plays were first staged there. When Burbage's lease ran out in 1597, the Theatre was dismantled and its timbers carried over the Thames to provide building material for the GLOBE. It was probably a polygonal building, with three galleries surrounding an open yard.

**theatre buildings** (Europe and anglophone nations) Theatre buildings are not essential for theatre performances. The roots of drama lie in the interaction between actor and audience, and there are regular pleas to return to these roots. But a common slogan of the fundamentalists – Two Planks and a Passion – includes recognition of some of the basic reasons for organizing theatre space. Planks assist the actor to project passion by enhancing visibility and audibility. And they also help to delineate the acting area.

To improve visibility and audibility as the size of the audience increases, the options are to raise the actors or the audience, or both. Early drama discovered the usefulness of performing on a hillside, and this became the normal positioning for the Greeks (see GREEK THEATRE, ANCIENT). By the time that the Greek theatre was evolving into the Roman model (see ROMAN THEATRE), all the basic features of every subsequent theatre, including those of today, had been incorporated. Something like ten centuries spanned the period from the emergence of the Greek theatre until the collapse of Rome. It would be another ten centuries before dramatic performances would again require permanent purpose-built theatres – at least, in the West. In India and the Orient, performances had a very formal structure but, being more intimate, could be housed in less ambitious buildings. Nevertheless, the proportions of the respective areas for actor and audience were meticulously specified, and development in the East continued throughout the thousand years when Western drama was moving haphazardly towards its renaissance.

**The Middle Ages**

The form of today's theatre buildings was established during the 16th century, when the general cultural renaissance included a surge of interest in drama which stimulated a simultaneous revival of theatre building in Europe. Although formal theatre buildings had disappeared during the Middle Ages, the art and craft of the actor had survived with the mimes, minstrels, acrobats, conjurors and ballad singers performing wherever the need arose. LITURGICAL DRAMA had found an obvious home in the churches, often developing quite complex productions, with the actors moving through the audience and involving them in the action. But the most organized medieval dramas were the MYSTERY PLAYS, for which a sequence of MANSIONS appropriate to each episode were built on temporary platforms arranged formally or scattered around a market square.

Alternatively, as in most of the English mysteries, the episodes could be built on wagons and moved from station to station around the town.

## The Renaissance

The 16th-century Italian humanists, wishing to restore to the stage the classical dramas of the ancients, looked back to the architectural forms of the theatres of antiquity. Combining a study of the architectural books of Vitruvius with their observations of the remains of the Roman theatres, they created temporary open-air theatres in courtyards on the Roman model. Temporary Renaissance outdoor theatres were followed by permanent indoor theatres, and in Vicenza we still have PALLADIO's Teatro Olimpico with its monumental *scaenae frons* (see SKĒNĒ) backing an acting stage facing an orchestra, and an audience *cavea* whose semicircle has been flattened to fit the site. Beyond the five openings in the *scaenae frons* still stand the perspective street scenes designed by SCAMOZZI for the opening performance in 1585 of SOPHOCLES' *Oedipus Tyrannus*. These represent the other line of Italian Renaissance development – the concept of perspective scenery developed by SERLIO, whose illustrated writings on theatre architecture were probably the most influential source for Renaissance theatre builders.

Outside Italy new theatres were designed to accommodate the growth of indigenous drama. The surge of theatre growth that began in Elizabethan England and continued until the closure of the theatres under the Commonwealth in 1642 bred two forms of theatre building. Outdoor theatres such as the CURTAIN, SWAN, GLOBE and FORTUNE developed out of the methods used for temporary staging in inn yards and bear-baiting pits. A thrust stage in an encircling courtyard was surrounded by an audience in galleries and on the ground. This was the theatre that SHAKESPEARE wrote for, with virtually no representational scenery. The indoor theatres such as the COCKPIT had a Palladian-inspired *scaenae frons* resulting from INIGO JONES's 1613 visit to Vicenza's Teatro Olimpico. As designer of temporary stagings for the court MASQUES in Whitehall, Jones was also heavily influenced by Serlio and developed a scenic style of wings and back shutters opening to reveal 'relieves', vistas in three-dimensional relief.

Meanwhile, the shape of theatres outdoors in Madrid and indoors in Paris had been developing in a form much closer to that which would be standard for a long period as the English playhouse and even longer as the Italian opera house. The first permanent Spanish theatre since the Romans (whose theatre in Merida still stands) was the 1582 Corral Príncipe in Madrid, with a stage set squarely across the end of a rectangular auditorium galleried all around and with rows of seats at ground level. Whereas the Spaniards had adapted the configuration of an inn yard, the French fitted their early theatres into the space of a tennis court. In 1548 a roofed rectangular theatre had been built on the site of the HÔTEL DE BOURGOGNE to house mystery plays, and the development of indoor courtyard theatres can be traced through the successive alterations to its stage – from simple end platform supporting the *mansions* of the medieval mysteries, to the angled perspective wings of Serlio, to the early-18th-century sliding wings of painted changeable scenery.

The growth of Italian opera in the 17th century moulded theatre building in the same basic form that was emerging everywhere – the proscenium-framed scenic stage facing a galleried auditorium. Indeed, auditorium shape across Europe, and in those countries colonized by Europeans, became relatively stabilized throughout the 18th and much of the 19th centuries. English actors continued throughout the Georgian period to play in something of a residual tradition of the ancient theatre and its early Renaissance revival, by acting on an apron stage, thrust forward through a proscenium arch flanked by 'doors of entrance' and framing a background of changeable scenery. Although this forestage was gradually cut back, it lasted well into the 19th century, when public taste for a more spectacular entertainment forced the actors somewhat reluctantly back into a scenic environment.

Throughout the 18th and early 19th centuries the British playhouse remained relatively simple in structure and unadorned in decoration, with its architectural roots in the concept of a simple shell building furnished by a carpenter. Elsewhere in Europe, however, particularly in Italy and Germany, theatre auditoria became places for artists like the BIBIENAS to lavish the grandeurs of the baroque and the elegances of the rococo. The simplicity of British theatres resulted partly from their being predominantly dramatic rather than lyric, entrepreneurial rather than court or civic, and in a country generally less committed to art than was Central Europe.

Financial considerations led in the latter part of the 19th century to a further drifting apart between Britain and much of the rest of Europe. British theatre was to remain unsubsidized until the mid-20th century, whereas in Central Europe a grid of court theatres developed into municipal theatres, supported financially as civic amenities. Proscenium theatres are most successful when the balconies remain shallow with preferably only two or three, but certainly not more than four or five, rows of seats. In Britain financial pressures forced the balconies to deepen until their overhangs produced a tunnel effect that broke contact between actor and audience. When cantilever engineering made supporting pillars redundant, deep balconies became ever more popular.

## The return to sightlines

In the mid-19th century RICHARD WAGNER reacted strongly against the virtually universal Western concept of a theatre audience hung on every available wall space, irrespective of its view of the stage. Wagner called for universally perfect sightlines from every seat to a scenic stage, and in 1876 built his BAYREUTH Festspielhaus with a single wedge of raked seating. The result was excellent when applied to the new, epic music drama but less satisfactory for more intimate performance. The preoccupation with sightlines became an increasing feature of the debate: the suggestion that boxes enabled the audience to be seen rather than to see was an obvious battle cry for those who sought a new serious role for the drama and pursued a democratic theatre based on purity of sightline from all seats.

## Technological influences

Meanwhile, theatre technology was advancing. In nearly two centuries there had been only one really major development in the backstage area: the full-height flying towers that became standard in the second half of the 19th century. Most scenery had continued to move in one plane, parallel to the front of the stage – whether it came down from the flies, up through sloats (slotes) or traps in the floor, or slid on from the sides. Here again there were differences between British practice and the rest of Europe, mostly attributable to their respective traditions of subsidized opera or commercial drama. In Central Europe the scenic wing flats were simultaneously changed by elaborate carriage systems running on rails in the basement under slots in the stage, whereas British wings moved in simple wooden grooves fixed to the stage and suspended from the flies. Towards the end of the 19th century various factors produced a shift away from perspective painting towards solid three-dimensional scenery. One was the introduction of electricity, which was less sympathetic to painted scenery than the soft gaslight that preceded it, but perhaps more important was that three-dimensional scenery was more appropriate to a new drama that pursued REALISM rather than rhetoric.

The growth in the use of three-dimensional scenery required new methods when it came to changing it. Complex technologies were developed in Germany, particularly – e.g. the turntable stage, which enabled a sequence of scenes to be revolved towards the proscenium opening. Britain's Victorian theatre was based on 'runs' or performances of the same play. This was unlike most of Europe, where the repertoire system remained, requiring sophisticated changing, storage, rehearsal and production manufacturing facilities of all kinds. The Italians stood aside from all this, continuing with simple stages and a system of scenery based on painted canvas stored in rolls and temporarily battened out on simple timber framing when required for a performance. However, because opera was (and still is) a matter of popular importance in Italy, the public areas were as extensive as in Germany and in other countries where a theatre was an important civic building.

European concepts of theatre architecture were carried forth into the New World by colonists who sought, at least initially, only to create a theatre in the image that they knew. The earliest American theatres were firmly based on the British Georgian playhouse, but by quite early in the 18th century the basic form was already showing signs of the widening of stage and auditorium that would in the early 19th and 20th centuries give a characteristic shape to BROADWAY and the road houses across America, which were fed with tours from the New York base. This configuration brought a higher proportion of the audience closer to the stage by adopting a short, wide format rather than the long, narrow shape more common in Europe.

## The 19th century

Today, most of Britain's remaining stock of 'old' theatres dates from this period, which came to an end in the years leading up to World War I. Outside London's WEST END, with its open-ended runs of the same play, these theatres were intended for a touring system of plays and musicals based on a weekly run (or multiples of one week) in each town. Their stage arrangements lacked storage and workshops, while their seating capacities were geared to a commercial system whereby a couple of reasonable houses on Friday and Saturday could comfortably clear the costs, leaving the rest of the week as profits. This required the sort of capacities (1,000 was small) which could only be achieved by making the balconies deep and steep. Sightlines to the stage were often clear (after cantilevers had removed the need for pillars), but the view could be from far away

and often funnelled by the overhang of the balcony above. The commercial basis of such theatres also required that they be built on a minimum site area, and the most prolific architect of the period, Frank Matcham, was renowned for his skill in extracting maximum usage from small, irregularly shaped sites. He was also adept at contriving the rich decorative treatment which a popular theatre needed to offer as an escape from the social conditions of a rapidly developed industrialization.

## The 20th century

Art centuries rarely tally with neat spans of a hundred years: the 20th century for theatre architecture got under way in the 1920s and was, inevitably, heavily influenced by the cinema. Boxes on the side walls disappeared altogether, or became so vestigial that they were intended as decoration rather than for audience. Out went the plasterer's excesses of Victorian and Edwardian quasi-baroque and in came the new clean lines of modernity. A single rake of auditorium seating with the possible addition of not more than one deep balcony became the norm. Everyone could see, from seats which became cheaper as the stage became ever more distant. Outside the majority of theatres built on this norm, there were many exceptions. Everywhere that MAX REINHARDT went, an interesting theatre seemed to emerge: in Berlin the Grosses Schauspielhaus wrapped its 3,000 audience around a huge arena stage thrusting forward from a restrained proscenium; in London, Olympia became a cathedral, while in Salzburg the cathedral square became a theatre, as did the 17th-century rock-hewn riding school. On a smaller scale, COPEAU in Paris and TERENCE GRAY in Cambridge were amongst those who thrust through the proscenium arch and discarded it totally. Visionaries such as GROPIUS and NORMAN BEL GEDDES produced exciting schemes which were rather too advanced to build – and by the time that their philosophies were adopted some 50 years later, a reaction had already set in. However, developments in STAGE LIGHTING, particularly the limitless spatial backgrounds of Fortuny's cyclorama, helped to realize a stage design revolution sought by APPIA and CRAIG, whose visual concepts had initially been frustrated by the available technology.

By the time that World War II loomed, no magazine was complete without an article on adaptable theatres or the actor–audience relationship, and the correspondence even bred new professionals – theatre consultants, sharing at least equal responsibility with the architect for the theatrical form of the building.

In 1945 Europe was devastated, with many theatres destroyed or disabled. In Germany, particularly, the rebuilding began almost immediately with performances restarting in improvised theatres. In Britain, old theatres temporarily saved by the wartime surge in demand for entertainment now entered a downward spiral of decreasing quality, increasing costs and lack of maintenance. But the REPERTORY THEATRE movement, slowly established between the wars, now blossomed with ARTS COUNCIL funding, and there was a growing demand for new theatres with their own resident acting companies in every town of consequence. In the USA the universities were developing drama faculties which needed housing, and each campus became the focus for a regional theatre movement that first complemented and then began to replace the old touring houses in all but the biggest centres of population. In Australasia the old theatres were coming down, to be replaced within new commercial developments, and there was a growing demand for major opera-house-sized theatres in the major centres. Third World countries gaining independence often regarded a National Theatre as a desirable acquisition. Even Great Britain once again revived its long-smouldering NATIONAL THEATRE ambitions.

But what was to be the shape and substance of the new theatres? The modern medium, concrete, has finality, and this has helped to fuel demand for an adaptable theatre that can cope with every style of production – from intimate drama to grand opera – and with audiences of widely varying sizes.

The new German opera houses generally opted to hang the audience on the walls, but adopted a fan-shaped auditorium so that the ascending tiers of boxes faced the stage. Most *Grosse Häuser* had a *Kleines Haus* attached and this tended to be a more flexible space, increasingly moving towards the neutral black box concept that represented an ideal for many people in the 1960s and 1970s. In the USA mainstream theatres got bigger and bigger: the perfect sightline was supreme. Australia built, in Sydney's Opera House, the only new theatre to be instantly recognizable by everyone across the world, whether or not they ever went to a theatre. The other main Australian cities then built simple, large theatre complexes which are probably the best of the world's pure sightline theatres. In Britain the new theatre building comprised almost entirely regional playhouses with seating in the 350–650 bracket, usually with a studio attached for about 100 people – the wedge-shaped single tier being the most popular, and at its most effective, capable of up to about 500 seats. The proscenium was unstressed, being formed by the natural termination of the walls and ceiling. It became standard to have a flexible area in front of the stage, which could be optional forestage, flat floor or sunken orchestra pit. The National Theatre was finally built. Of its three auditoria, the third and smallest (the Cottesloe) has most caught the imagination and stimulated an almost inevitable rediscovery of what has been labelled 'the courtyard form'.

The courtyard revival is a response to the isolation that can be experienced by an individual member of the audience in a theatre designed to give everyone a direct, clean and uninterrupted view of the stage. Indeed, it almost follows from defining a pure sightline that an individual will not be aware of fellow members of the audience. Hang some on the walls, and those in the central seats will be aware, out of the corners of their eyes, of the response of those hanging over their balcony rails to see the stage. This may not be an ideal in a theatre with democratic aims, but many would hold that, for the cheaper seats, close contact is more important than a view that is clear but remote. Consequently an increasing number of theatres are being built to concepts against which Wagner started the reaction.

## The future

So where does theatre architecture go next? As we approach the end of the 20th century, a particularly hectic 50 years of intensive theatre building has slowed down. The postwar renewal-and-development phase is complete and economic stagnation has concentrated diminishing resources on maintaining performances on existing stages rather than creating new ones. In today's theatres there are so many overlapping cycles of

rediscovery and reaction that all forms, from the simplest to the most sophisticated, coexist. There is no reason to suppose that this will change. A whole series of stylistic options for realizing a text in performance will require a similarly wide series of architectural options. Meanwhile, simple or complex, we would do well to bear in mind the definition that has been offered by John Orrell: 'The essence of theatre design is to bring players and audience together in a fruitful collaboration, never allowing the two elements to become remote from each other, nor yet so mingling them together that the audience loses its capacity for wonder.'

**Théâtre de Complicité** British touring company. Founded in 1983, they are devoted to 'physical theatre'. Influenced by the French MIME director JACQUES LECOQ, they have concentrated on athletic acting and the grotesque. *Help! I'm Alive* (1990) was an agile version of a 16th-century Italian farce by RUZZANTE. Their brilliantly expressionistic version (see EXPRESSIONISM) of DÜRRENMATT's *The Visit* (NATIONAL THEATRE, 1991) established the company's reputation as an innovative force in British theatre. Since then they have produced an acrobatic *Winter's Tale* (1992) and an adaptation of short stories by the Polish writer Bruno Schultz, *The Street of Crocodiles* (1992), which was a triumph at the NT.

**Théâtre des Nations** French theatre festival. This international event was held for two months of each year in Paris between 1957 and 1968 and had a strong influence on the development of French theatre styles. It began as the Festival de Paris in 1954, when the BERLINER ENSEMBLE gave its first performance in the West. The festival has since become peripatetic.

**theatre design** This essay does not attempt a history of theatre design (see *The Cambridge Guide to Theatre*, 2nd edition, edited by Martin Banham), but simply accounts for some common features and principles.

While the necessary ingredients for a theatrical event vary depending upon the needs and expectations of particular societies in particular eras, there are only two elements essential for theatre to occur: a performer and a spectator. But a performance must occur *somewhere*, and if there is space there is, inherently, design.

The design may range from a circular piece of ground surrounded by standing spectators – as in much street theatre, RITUAL performance and, probably, pre-Aeschylean Greek dance and dithyrambs – to the lavish settings and computerized mechanisms of grand opera performed for spectators in surroundings of baroque splendour. In both cases someone has made decisions about the space, about its delineation, about the relationship of the performer to the space and the space to the spectator, and about the role the space plays in the spectators' responses. All of this is design, and no theatre exists without it.

While there are periods in theatre history in which it is possible to talk about scenic design separately from stage architecture – the painterly style of, say, the romantic scenic artists, or the distorted and exaggerated sets of the German expressionists – in most cases there is an indivisible connection between the stage, the overall space of the theatre (see THEATRE BUILDINGS), and the elements that comprise the scenic design. In most of the classic periods of theatre history – ancient Greece and Rome, the 15th-century NŌ era of Japan, Elizabethan England, 17th-century France and Spain – there is little scenery *per se*, but formal, architectural stages instead: platforms on which to act. Scenery, by which we normally mean some sort of stage decoration, tends to be either illusionistic – pretending to be something it is not, such as a room or a forest – emblematic, or evocative. Formal stages emphasize their own theatricality, constantly reminding the audience that what they are seeing is taking place in a theatre. Such stages also throw focus on to the performers and the language.

Theatre architecture or space is generally classified according to the relationship of the stage to the audience. Scenic design is usually categorized by its style. There are two broad categories of staging: frontal and environmental. In the former, the audience sees a performance directly in front of it; in the latter, the audience is surrounded to some degree by the performance space. Most theatre, of course, is frontal and this category can be subdivided into end stage – usually a raised stage at one end of a rectangular theatre, directly facing an audience; thrust – a stage surrounded on three sides by audience; and arena – a stage completely surrounded by the audience. Needless to say, there are many variants on this arrangement, most notably the booth or trestle stage generally associated with popular entertainment and certain forms of medieval staging. It consists of a raised stage, usually with a curtain or scenic backdrop at the rear creating a 'backstage' area for costume changes, storage and entrances. It differs from an endstage only in that it is most frequently used outdoors or as a temporary structure in spaces not normally used for theatre.

It might be noted that outdoor theatre (which includes most theatre throughout approximately the first 2,000 years of both occidental and oriental theatre history) tends to blur the distinction between frontal and environmental staging. Many plays and theatre structures in such surroundings incorporate natural events and topography into the design and production in a way that indoor theatres rarely do, leading the spectator to perceive him or herself as surrounded by the 'design'.

Design is broadly categorized as presentational or representational. Representational theatre tries to create an illusion of reality. Presentational theatre emphasizes theatricality and acknowledges the theatre as theatre – there is no illusion. This is perhaps best expressed in the *Natyasastra* of Bharata Muni, the ancient Sanskrit treatise on theatre: 'Some accessories ... will be Realistic, while others will be Conventional. Anything following its natural form is called Realistic, while any deviation from the same will be known as Conventional.' Just as in the history of art, there are many individual styles. Three general classifications are worth noting: architectural, sculptural and painterly. Architectural stages – such as those of ancient Greece and Rome, Elizabethan England, and most of the permanent stages of classic Indian, Chinese and Japanese theatres – are the result of a marriage between design and architecture. The features of the stage – arches, platforms, doors, steps, and so on – are permanently built into the stage space. While specific scenery and set pieces may be used within a production to transform the stage into a specific place, the designer and performers are limited by the basic architecture.

Sculptural settings see the stage space as a cubic volume and, like sculptures, emphasize the fact by organizing the space around themselves. They emphasize three-dimensionality of the stage space (rather than

creating an *illusion* of depth) by the use of three-dimensional forms and the sculpting of space with light. This is largely a 20th-century phenomenon and is typified by the use of geometric forms, abstract structures, platforms and steps. It is sometimes referred to as a structural stage.

Painterly, as the name suggests, relies on painted images, usually to create an illusion of place or to evoke a particular mood or sensibility. Painterly designs of one style or another dominated much Western theatre design from the Renaissance until fairly recently.

## Proscenium, open and thrust stages

The encapsulation of the actor and setting within the proscenium arch can forfeit a sense of intimacy and communion between stage and audience. In the 1840s there was a definite movement away from the pictorial realism of the proscenium stage and towards other forms. In Germany, Ludwig Tieck and Karl Immermann both advocated an open stage based upon their understandings of Shakespearian staging. In the second half of the 19th century, a greater interest and knowledge of oriental theatre developed that reinforced this trend. One of the first elements borrowed from the East was the revolving stage of the *kabuki* theatre, which was first used by Karl Lautenschläger in Munich in 1896. The *no* and *kabuki* of Japan also used thrust stages; runways into the audience; simple, stylized and emblematic scenery; a starkly presentational style; and a formal, minutely prescribed theatre architecture. This influenced the major theoreticians and practitioners of 20th-century design and staging.

The reaction against the proscenium went in several directions. The most successful involved thrust stages and architectural stages, but there were also fanciful projects involving revolving auditoriums, stages or spectators suspended in the centre of spherical theatres and so on. Most of the latter, of course, were never built, but detailed plans and even models exist for such projects as Walter Gropius's *Totaltheater*, the Spherical Theatre of his Bauhaus colleague Andreas Weininger, Frederick Kiesler's Endless Theatre, and the several projects of Norman Bel Geddes. Of the theatres that were constructed, the most notable and influential were Max Reinhardt's Grosses Schauspielhaus and the Redoutensaal, and Jacques Copeau's Vieux-Colombier Theatre.

By the 1950s the architectural thrust stage and the pictorial thrust stage (a combination of a scenic end stage with a thrust) seemed to be the standard for all new theatre spaces.

## Constructivism

In terms of theatre design, some of the most notable anti-illusionistic movements came from Russia and were associated with the dynamic avant-garde art movements of the first three decades of the century. The most significant figure was director, actor and theoretician Vsevolod Meyerhold. Strongly influenced by Appia in his early years, Meyerhold was a central figure of Futurism and constructivism in the theatre but worked in many styles. Constructivism emerged about 1920, and was clearly influenced by futurism and cubism. The movement sought an art based on 'space and time' and using 'kinetic and dynamic elements'. This was manifested in skeletal sets of wood and metal with platforms, ramps, steps and various kinetic elements, often on stages otherwise stripped bare. Meyerhold called these sets 'machines for acting'.

Constructivist design was also the predominant form at the Kamerny Theatre of ALEKSANDR TAIROV, although the sets by ALEKSANDRA EKSTER, his primary collaborator, were seldom as stark or 'home-made'-looking as most constructivist design. Pure constructivism in stage design lasted only briefly (although variations on the idea can be seen to this day), but it was a major contributor towards the predominance of theatricality over illusion and was especially notable for settings that sat like islands in the midst of the stage with no connection, literally or metaphorically, with the wings or flyspace.

## Expressionist design

The most dominant theatrical force during the early decades of the century was EXPRESSIONISM. Clearly influenced by Appia, expressionist design frequently reduced the stage to its bare essentials, often little more than a few scenic elements and black drapes on an otherwise bare stage. Light became the most important aspect of design. The movement of light reinforced the stream-of-consciousness imagery of many expressionist plays, and allowed the smooth transition through episodic scenes. The light frequently cut a swath through the dark void of black-curtained stages (see also STAGE LIGHTING). The contrast of light and shadow, unusual angles and unrealistic colours of light contributed to the nightmare quality of the productions. Images were distorted and exaggerated; walls tilted at precarious angles; oversized set and prop pieces and bold blocks of colour wrenched the image out of objective reality into a subjective view of the world.

Expressionist design is frequently associated with the work of director LEOPOLD JESSNER who, working primarily with designer Emil Pirchan, created architectural/structural settings of steps and platforms that changed through the use of lights and curtains. Jessner's reliance on this formula led to cliché and quickly became known as *Jessnertreppen* (Jessner steps).

## Sculptural design

From the Renaissance until the end of the 19th century design was essentially pictorial – a two-dimensional image creating the illusion of depth or volume. Building upon the foundations of Appia and constructivism, however, many designers rejected any form of REALISM for sculptural design. Their images varied greatly. Geometric masses, architectonic structures, fanciful versions of classical columns, ramps, platforms and steps intersecting on a multitude of planes, scaffold-like structures – all found their way on to the stage. The work of TANYA MOISEIWITSCH, Nadine Baylis, MING CHO LEE, SANTO LOQUASTO and others typify much of this aesthetic.

## Environmental theatre

The concept of the spectator and performer sharing the space of the theatre, or the inclusion of the spectator within the performance space, has been current since at least the Middle Ages, but the term was coined by American director and theoretician Richard Schechner. The roots of modern environmental theatre can be traced to the productions in the 1930s of Szygmunt Tonecki in Poland and NIKOLAI OKHLOPKOV in the USSR. The most significant examples in the postwar era are the works of JERZY GROTOWSKI (and his sometime collaborator, JOSEF SZAJNA) in Poland, ARIANE MNOUCHKINE at the Théâtre du SOLEIL in Paris, LUCA RONCONI in Italy and Schechner's PERFORMANCE GROUP in the USA.

## Conceptual design, or theatricalism

Related to environmental theatre, this movement of the 1970s and 1980s was primarily a European development. Its designs tend to be for classical plays and operas created either by a director working closely with a designer, or a single individual assuming both roles, such as FRANCO ZEFFIRELLI or JEAN-PIERRE PONNELLE. In either case, one individual is generally responsible for all aspects of design, not just sets, and from this comes the term 'scenographer' which implies a more unified and far-reaching involvement than the term 'designer' does. Typically, the setting is a single image – or a single basic setting that can transform into variations of the single image – that embodies the central concept of the production, in which the directorial concept is usually more significant or more pronounced than the playwright's script – if, indeed, one exists. The impulse for this approach is traceable to REINHARDT and MEYERHOLD and the practices of BRECHT. The productions of the BERLINER ENSEMBLE have been an acknowledged influence on many contemporary designers.

Theatricalist sets are frequently distinguished by high walls that soar into the flyspace and seemingly overwhelm the performers; and by overwhelming images or emblems whose visual power suffuses the sets and costumes. Examples can be found in the work of Karl von Appen, Achim Freyer, ANDRÉ ACQUART, JOHN NAPIER, JOHN BURY, RALPH KOLTAI, EUGENE LEE and WIELAND WAGNER, and in the productions of BENNO BESSON, GIORGIO STREHLER, PATRICE CHÉREAU, LIVIU CIULEI, ANDREI SERBAN, PETER STEIN, ROBERT WILSON and RICHARD FOREMAN.

## Postmodern design

Whereas modern design sought an aesthetic and organic unity in which the stage picture functioned as a metaphor for the world of the play, postmodern design cries out that unity is impossible in the contemporary world. It is a pan-historical, omnistylistic aesthetic in which the world is seen as a multiplicity of competing, often incongruous and conflicting elements and images. Using discordance, juxtaposition and even ugliness, postmodern design often makes reference to other productions, to other works of art and to the world beyond the play, with only the stage frame as a unifying element.

Patrice Chéreau's production of WAGNER's 'Ring Cycle' at BAYREUTH in 1976 is often cited as a landmark. Visually the production referred to a range of industrial, technological and sociopolitical images from the 19th and 20th centuries, thus grounding the production in Wagner's time and its historical aftermath. The approach has been further exemplified in the designs of John Conklin, Robert Israel, Adrianne Lobel and George Tsypin in the USA; Richard Hudson in the UK; Yannis Kokkos and Richard Peduzzi in France; and Bert Neumann, Karl Kneidl and Jochen Finke in Germany.

**Théâtre du Nouveau Monde** French Canadian company. The most respected and influential in French Canada, it was founded in Montreal in 1951. Under JEAN GASCON it began staging French classics, especially works of MOLIÈRE; by the end of the decade it was offering at least one Canadian play each season, notably the works of MARCEL DUBÉ. In 1966 Gascon was replaced by JEAN-LOUIS ROUX, under whose direction the company moved towards a more varied repertoire, including experimental plays and musical REVUES. The economic difficulties of the later 1970s and the 1980s had serious effects upon the TNM, but the threat against its survival has now receded.

**theatre-for-development** Theatre used by oppressed Third World people to achieve justice and development for themselves. There are now thousands of organized groups of landless peasants, urban workers and threatened minorities, in Africa, the Americas and Asia, who use theatre to confront the problems in their lives.

These initiatives occurred quite separately in the late 1970s all over the Third World, as economic and social conditions worsened for the very poor and activists came to despair of conventional solutions. Drama, as a process of collective improvisation, can be the means by which very poor people analyse their difficulties: those involved in the drama form their own analysis, which grows out of collective thought, rather than being handed down from the top. This theatre is also concerned with cultural identity among threatened minorities: Native populations in the Americas (for example, the Inuit in Canada; the Caribs in Dominica), and Aboriginal peoples in Australasia. Despite common perspectives and intentions there are also considerable differences between these groups, resulting from the cultural and political forces of the particular regions.

Examples of the movement are Teatro Nixtayolero in Nicaragua, which developed among rural peasant farmers; the theatre workshops of TAREA, a popular education support group in the *barrios* of Lima, Peru; Sistren, in Kingston, Jamaica, who have enabled severely oppressed working-class women to articulate before a wide audience their growing consciousness and confidence; the drama project of the people of KAMIRIITHU in Kenya; and the work by and among Harijans (so-called 'Untouchables') in Tamil Nadu, India, which uses drama to analyse issues and devise and rehearse strategies, which are then carried out.

**Theatre Guild** American organization. In 1919 a lawyer and playwright named LAWRENCE LANGNER restructured the WASHINGTON SQUARE PLAYERS as the Theatre Guild. Langner and his board, which included PHILIP MOELLER (who was to become the Guild's leading director), THERESA HELBURN (a playreader soon to be made executive director), an actress, a banker and the scene designer LEE SIMONSON, were determined to shed their amateur downtown status and to present challenging full-length plays on BROADWAY.

In its first few years the Guild's notable achievements were with European EXPRESSIONISM (KAISER's *Man and the Masses*, 1924) and with the world premieres of several plays by SHAW (*Heartbreak House*, 1920; *Back to Methuselah*, 1922; *Saint Joan*, 1923; and *Caesar and Cleopatra*, 1925). Although it was criticized for neglecting American writers, two experimental American plays were presented early in its history – ELMER RICE's *The Adding Machine* (1923) and JOHN HOWARD LAWSON's *Processional* (1925). Later in the 1920s, and for the following three decades, the Guild produced the work of major American dramatists including SIDNEY HOWARD (*They Knew What They Wanted*, 1924, and *The Silver Cord*, 1926); S. N. BEHRMAN (*The Second Man*, 1927, and *Biography*, 1932); ROBERT E. SHERWOOD (*Reunion in Vienna*, 1931, and *Idiot's Delight*, 1936); and MAXWELL ANDERSON (*Elizabeth the Queen*, 1930 and *Mary of Scotland*, 1933). In 1928, with *Strange Interlude* and *Marco Millions*, the organization began regularly to produce EUGENE O'NEILL's plays.

In 1931 some of the its younger members defected to form the GROUP THEATRE, with a plan to train actors into a true ensemble and encourage the development of socially relevant plays – highlighting two areas where the Guild had failed. Throughout the 1930s and 1940s it had to rely on musicals and popular shows, depending on its in-house stars, the LUNTS, to rescue it from a financial abyss. But through its subscription policy and its extensive national tours the Guild brought more worthwhile, well produced plays to a greater number of people, and over a longer period of time, than any other theatrical organization.

**theatre-in-education (TIE)** (Britain) Young People's Theatre (YPT) is an umbrella term to cover all forms of theatre work for and with young people. There are two major kinds: children's theatre, which is professional theatre mainly for the younger age range (up to 14), consisting of self-contained performances given by touring or building-based companies before large numbers of children; and theatre-in-education (TIE).

TIE is professional theatre work with specific educational aims, offering a unique educational resource to schools and colleges. Although it has roots in the work of such pioneers as JOAN LITTLEWOOD, it began with a pilot educational project at the Belgrade Theatre, Coventry, in 1965. The aim was to forge new links between the theatre and local schools, and to this end a small unit of 'actor-teachers' was formed to take programmes of work into classrooms and school halls. The objectives were educational and the means theatrical. The success of the scheme together with the availability of new money from the ARTS COUNCIL for YPT led over the next five years to the formation of similar teams at REPERTORY theatres in Bolton, Leeds, Nottingham, Edinburgh and Glasgow. The scale and adventurousness of the work grew, and soon a number of education authorities set up TIE units of their own, the Cockpit team within the Inner London Educational Authority being the most notable example. In due course some repertory-based teams found their relationship with their parent theatre inhibiting and became independent YPT or community/YPT companies. In 1992 there were about 30 TIE companies, or YPT companies with a strong commitment to TIE. In 1994 the number is closer to 20. Many other community and touring companies include TIE within their schedules on a more occasional basis.

Kinds of TIE work range from straight performance of a play – devised specially for children of a particular age and followed by a workshop on its themes or a follow-up programme of work organized by the teacher in consultation with the company – to full participation programmes. It is the latter for which TIE won its reputation as a pioneering force in education. Such programmes may last anything from one hour to a full day or even to a series of visits made to each class over a four-week period. The pupils are involved in an experience *with* the characters – e.g. as witnesses or in role – and confronted with a series of problems to be solved, dilemmas faced, decisions reached. Learning through experience is a crucial tenet of the work. Subject-matter ranges from conventional curriculum areas, such as local history or study of themes from an examination set text, to more general, sometimes sensitive, matters of social concern such as racial prejudice, drugs or the environment.

In its early years TIE was a uniquely British phenomenon; there are now, however, companies established in Eire, Scandinavia, Kenya, Nigeria, Australia and the USA, and interest in TIE continues to grow.

**Théâtre Libre** see ANTOINE, ANDRÉ

**Théâtre National Populaire** French National People's Theatre, founded by FIRMIN GÉMIER in 1920 after campaigning by ROLLAND and other advocates of *le théâtre populaire*. The state subsidy included a theatre (see CHAILLOT) but not the means to run a producing company. After Gémier's death in 1933 the TNP remained moribund until the appointment of VILAR in 1951. He believed in an uncluttered theatre, making use of bold movement, lavish COSTUME and complex lighting (see STAGE LIGHTING). Furthermore, Parisian theatre-going was simplified: evening dress and tipping were abolished, performances began on time with latecomers excluded, and the text of the play was sold in place of glossy programmes. The repertoire combined vigorous productions of French and other world classics unfamiliar in the France of the 1950s. First-class actors were attracted to the TNP – e.g. GÉRARD PHILIPE and MARIA CASARÈS. Georges Wilson succeeded Vilar in 1963 but was overtaken by politics: young and committed audiences were looking for new formulae, and Wilson's audience figures dropped disastrously. In 1972 the crisis was solved by transferring the title of TNP to PLANCHON's company in Lyon. With his new co-director CHÉREAU, their company continued its policy of adventurous revivals and new plays, often of a demanding nature. In 1986 Georges Lavaudant succeeded Chéreau as co-director.

**theatre of the absurd** Theatrical genre. Literally meaning 'out of harmony', 'absurd' was ALBERT CAMUS's designation for the situation of modern humanity – strangers in an inhuman universe. Recognizing such strangers in stage characters of the 1950s, the critic Martin Esslin in 1961 published his influential *Theatre of the Absurd*. He defined plays of the absurd as those that present man's metaphysical absurdity in aberrant dramatic style that mirrors the human situation. It was never a formal movement. The playwrights of the absurd were centred in postwar Paris, but they soared to international fame with the unexpected success of BECKETT's *Waiting for Godot*. Journalists soon seized upon the label, confusing it with the everyday meaning of 'absurd' as outrageously comic. Esslin's main absurdists are Beckett, ADAMOV, IONESCO and GENET, with less attention paid to ALBEE and PINTER.

Since then almost every non-realistic modern dramatist has had this label affixed. Certain absurdist techniques have, nevertheless, established themselves in the contemporary theatre, and it is in this formal sense, rather than in a philosophical one, that the idea of 'theatre of the absurd' has been maintained in critical currency. Among these techniques are the rejection of narrative continuity, of character coherence and of the rigidity of logic, leading to ridiculous conclusions; scepticism about the meaning of language; bizarre relationship of stage properties to dramatic situation. Such techniques have occasionally resulted in memorable stage images. Residual absurdism may be seen in such images as the Vampire in CARYL CHURCHILL's *Mad Forest* or the Angel in TONY KUSHNER's *Angels in America*. (See also REALISM; NATURALISM; SYMBOLISM; EXPRESSIONISM; SURREALISM.)

**theatre of the ridiculous** American movement. In 1967 the Play-House of the Ridiculous opened on OFF-OFF BROADWAY with *The Life of Lady Godiva*, written by Ronald Tavel, directed by John Vaccaro, and featuring CHARLES LUDLAM as actor. Though these three men did not stay together long, they independently continued their 'ridiculous' work, a self-consciously wild dramaturgy full of witty word-play, sexual ambiguity, flamboyance and bad taste. Tavel left the Play-House within a year to pursue a writing career, and in 1967 Vaccaro directed two Ludlam works, *Big Hotel* and *Conquest of the Universe*, before Ludlam left to become actor-manager of his own company. Vaccaro toured Europe with the Play-House and then operated it out of LA MAMA until 1972, when he closed his theatre. At the Ridiculous Theatrical Company Ludlam went on to write, direct and perform in plays such as *Turds in Hell* (1968), *Camille* (1973) and *Der Ring Gott Farblonjet* (1977).

**Théâtre Ouvert** French organization. It was set up by Lucien Attoun in 1971 at the AVIGNON FESTIVAL to promote new work by playwrights. Gradually activities were extended and in 1981 the organization moved into a permanent studio theatre at the Winter Garden in Montmartre. Here authors are given a chance to try out plays with actors, possibly leading to public performance. Théâtre Ouvert has been a significant force in encouraging new French playwriting.

**TPR (Théâtre Populaire Romand)** see JORIS, CHARLES

**Theatre Row** (New York City) An alternative theatre district west of BROADWAY on West 42nd Street, it was officially launched in 1978. A block owned by a quasi-governmental agency was rented out to ten OFF-OFF-BROADWAY theatre companies representing diverse artistic goals and ethnic backgrounds (later, other members were added). The theatres and companies utilize a collective box office, Ticket Central, and Theatre Row provides a testing ground for actors, directors, playwrights and designers, many of whom move their activities to Broadway, OFF-BROADWAY and regional theatre. The theatres and companies comprising Theatre Row are the Samuel Beckett, the Harold Clurman, the Judith Anderson, PLAYWRIGHTS HORIZONS, Theatre Row Theatre, Intar Hispanic American Arts Centre, the ACTING COMPANY, Alice's Fourth Floor, Theatre Arielle, the Douglas Fairbanks, Nat Horne Musical Theatre, the George S. Kaufman and the John Houseman Theatre Centre.

**theatrical monopoly** Under patents granted by Charles II to WILLIAM DAVENANT and THOMAS KILLIGREW in 1662, which were interpreted as giving them and their successors the exclusive right to perform drama in London, this so-called monopoly beleaguered the theatre for well over 150 years. The proprietors of DRURY LANE and COVENT GARDEN theatres, on whom the patents devolved, had their claims reinforced by the terms of the 1737 Licensing Act, which, in addition to the imposition of formal CENSORSHIP by the Lord Chamberlain, restricted plays to the City of Westminster and 'places of His Majesties residence'.

The appearance of a theatre at SADLER'S WELLS in the 1780s was the first real challenge to the monopoly; later a number of 'minor theatres' emerged to cater for the huge population increase in London in the early 19th century. To avoid direct conflict with the 'majors' (which had begun by this time to include the HAYMARKET as a summer patent theatre), these theatres restricted their performances to burlettas, loosely defined as plays with musical accompaniment – from this arose the distinction between 'legitimate' and 'illegitimate' drama. But by the 1820s some theatres, like the ADELPHI and OLYMPIC, which were tolerated by the Lord Chamberlain's Office, were in virtually open conflict with the patent theatres' exclusivity, and damaging their box-office receipts.

The patent theatres' claim to be the upholders of Britain's dramatic heritage was by the 1830s a somewhat empty one, but the law was intermittently invoked by the patentees. In 1832 a parliamentary inquiry under EDWARD BULWER LYTTON concluded that the monopoly, having 'neither preserved the dignity of the Drama, nor ... been of much advantage to the Proprietors of the Theatres themselves', should be abolished forthwith. In practical terms it was already dying; but legislation guaranteeing free competition on the London stage was delayed another 11 years until the Theatre Regulation Act of 1843.

**Theatrical Syndicate** American theatrical trust. The origins of the Syndicate lay in the combination system of producing. The expansion of railways after the Civil War made it possible to tour a production anywhere in America. This proved more profitable than the previous system of resident companies hosting visiting stars. Consequently, by 1885 nearly all the first-class stock companies (see STOCK COMPANY) had been replaced by combinations from New York City, and both producers and regional theatre owners had opened booking offices there to arrange these tours. In 1896 the producer CHARLES FROHMAN joined the booking agency of Marc Klaw and Abraham Erlanger in a partnership with Alfred Hayman, who leased the most important theatres in the West, and with Fred Nixon and Fred Zimmerman, who controlled Philadelphia and the mid-Atlantic region. This arrangement was called the Theatrical Syndicate. By 1903 it governed first-class theatrical production in America.

The Syndicate was a means of maximizing profit, not a vehicle for artistic innovation or social welfare. Consequently, it ran on 'big business' principles, and was ruthless and rapacious. Its monopoly was broken by even more ruthless monopolists, the SHUBERT BROTHERS, who by 1913 controlled twice as many theatres as the Syndicate. The Syndicate agreement expired soon after the death of Frohman in 1915; the Shubert organization has remained a vital force.

**theatrum mundi** Mechanical theatre. Figurines are moved horizontally by means of strings along a track in a flat wing-and-border set by a single performer (in German, *Mechanikus*). This forerunner of the newsreel re-created current events, such as natural disasters, battles or scenes from everyday life. Brown's Theatre of Arts toured British fairs (1830–40) with miniatures of Napoleon's campaigns. GOETHE owned such a theatre.

**Theobald, Lewis** 1688–1744 English playwright and critic. In 1726 he attacked Pope's edition of SHAKESPEARE in *Shakespeare Restored*, the first book ever published on Shakespeare alone. Though mocked, Theobald's attempts to restore Shakespeare's texts were intelligent and effective, and he published an edition in 1734. In 1727 his play *The Double Falsehood* was performed. His claim that it was an adaptation of Shakespeare's lost play *Cardenio* (written with JOHN FLETCHER and performed in 1613) is disputed. He adapted WEBSTER's *The Duchess of Malfi* as *The Fatal Secret* (1733). He was appointed Poet Laureate in 1730.

**Thérésa** [Eugénie Emma Valadon] (1837–1913) French music-hall star (see CAFÉ CHANTANT). She made her stage debut in Paris in 1856 at the Théâtre de la Porte-Saint-Martin. Fame arrived in 1863 at the Alcazar; already known for sentimental ballads, she decided to PARODY

one with a comic yodel and was cheered to the echo. For almost 30 years she kept audiences in stitches with such favourites as 'Nothing Is Sacred to a Sapper' and 'The Bearded Lady'. She also appeared in FÉERIEs and comic operas (*La Reine des Halles*, 1881) before her retirement in 1893.

**therukoothu** Indian theatre form. *Theru* means 'street' and *koothu* is a play. *Therukoothu* has a rustic origin and is popular among the lower-class urban and rural people of Tamil Nadu, south India. Very few companies remain today. The players, too, come from the lower strata of society and perform in any open space, often in a village. The make-up of central characters is bright blue and red, accentuated with white and black lines. As part of the village RITUAL, the actors parade through the streets along with the temple deities. Following an all-night show, they participate in the symbolic destruction of evil under the watchful eye of the temple effigies and thousands of enthusiastic villagers who participate in the ceremony, which concludes when they walk across beds of hot coals to prove their faith in God.

Among the popular fun-loving figures in *therukoothu* is the *kattiakaran*, a clown figure who combines the function of the fool with that of the stage manager. About half of the performance is made up of high-pitched songs. The other half is improvised prose dialogue spoken in Tamil. The dance steps are simple, violent movements. The plays centre primarily on stories drawn from the epic literature.

**Thespis** 6th century BC Greek tragic playwright. The earliest tragedian whose name was known to ancient scholars (see GREEK THEATRE, ANCIENT), Thespis is said to have won a victory with a play produced c.534 and to have been the first to introduce an actor (the dramatist himself) conversing with the Chorus. He is also credited with inventing the mask. Since none of his plays were preserved for posterity, no authentic fragments survive, and it is impossible to assess the value of the traditions concerning him.

**Thimig family** Viennese actors. **Hugo** (1854–1944) was a leading comic actor at the BURGTHEATER. His daughter **Helene** (1889–1974), a versatile actress, was married to MAX REINHARDT; she did much to perpetuate her husband's method of training actors. Hugo's two sons, **Hermann** (b.1890) and **Hans** (b.1900), also acted with the Burgtheater.

**Thoma, Ludwig** 1867–1928 German playwright and novelist. Thoma wrote several comedies about life in rural Bavaria. The most popular is *The Local Train* (1902), which is still revived.

**Thomas, Augustus** 1857–1934 American playwright. Thomas tackled well documented American scenes in such plays as *Alabama* (1891), *In Mizzoura* (1893) and *Arizona* (1899). *The Copperhead* (1918), which made Lionel Barrymore (see DREW–BARRYMORE FAMILY) a star, details the story of an Illinois farmer who, at the request of President Lincoln, pretends to be a sympathizer with the Confederacy. Many plays explored contemporary issues: capital and labour in *New Blood* (1894), politics in *The Capitol* (1895), hypnotism in *The Witching Hour* (1907) and mental healing in *As a Man Thinks* (1911).

**Thomas, (Walter) Brandon** 1856–1914 British actor and playwright. A prominent member of the HARE/KENDAL company at the ST JAMES's, he wrote a dozen or so plays but is remembered only for *Charley's Aunt* (1892), an immensely popular FARCE which describes the escapades of three Oxford undergraduates, one of whom is cajoled into playing the part of a rich woman in order to advance the marital ambitions of the other two.

**Thomas, Dylan (Marlais)** 1914–53 Welsh poet and playwright. He was at one time an actor in REPERTORY theatre. His expressionistic (see EXPRESSIONISM) radio 'play for voices' *Under Milk Wood* (first staged in 1953) has gained a wide reputation. (See also RADIO DRAMA.)

**Thomashefsky** [Tomashevsky], **Boris** 1868–1939 Russian-born American Yiddish actor-manager. He was a flamboyant personality and matinée idol of the New York SHUND THEATRE. Though large and fat, he played romantic hero parts in MUSICAL COMEDY and MELO-DRAMA. His mellifluous tenor voice and florid good looks were especially suited to the costume operettas popular through the first half of his career.

**Thompson, Judith** 1954– Canadian playwright. Her plays blend NATURALISM and SURREALISM in showing the struggle between the conscious and the unconscious mind. *The Crackwalker* (1980) presents the violation of an ordinary regional setting by repressed images of sordidness and madness. *White Biting Dog* (1984) is a complex metaphor for the relationships surrounding a mother and son. *I Am Yours* (1987) envelops characters and audience in a dream-like experience of demonic possession and maternal repression.

**Thompson, Lydia** 1836–1908 British actress. She had already made a name for herself as a dancer and comedienne when she took her troupe of British Blondes to New York (1868). Her production of *Ixion, or The Man at the Wheel*, the first modern BURLESQUE in more than one act, created the 'leg show'. A strict taskmistress to her underlings and a shrewd businesswoman, she toured the USA several times, retaining her popularity on both sides of the Atlantic. Her last appearance was with MRS PATRICK CAMPBELL in *A Queen's Romance* (Imperial Theatre, London, 1904).

**Thompson, Mervyn** 1936–92 New Zealand playwright and director. Co-founder of the Court Theatre, Christchurch, artistic director of DOWNSTAGE THEATRE, Wellington (1975–6) and lecturer in drama at the University of Auckland (1977–89), he is best-known for solo plays for his own performance – *Coaltown Blues* (1984) and *Passing Through* (1991) – and for his unique form of 'songplay', *O! Temperance!* (1972), *Songs to Uncle Scrim* (1976) and *Songs to the Judges* (1980). His last work was *Jean and Richard* (1992), a whimsical fantasy about the pioneer aviators Batten and Pearse.

**Thompson, Sam** 1916–65 Irish playwright. A shipyard painter, Thompson began writing for BBC radio. The soberly observed realities of *Over the Bridge* (1960), denouncing mob bigotry and murder, outraged the Unionist establishment in the (Belfast) GROUP THEATRE's directorate. It was independently produced. *The Evangelist* (1963), whose butt is commercialized religion, was effective theatre. In a posthumously discovered manuscript, *The Masquerade*, three characters act out Nazi fantasies in a London basement.

**Thorndike, (Agnes) Sybil** 1882–1976 British actress. She made her name in a number of modern plays by MAUGHAM, GRANVILLE BARKER, HOUGHTON and ST JOHN ERVINE before joining the OLD VIC, where she not only played Shakespearian and Restoration heroines but also Prince Hal in *Henry IV, Part 1*, Ferdinand in *The Tempest*, the Fool in *King Lear* and Launcelot Gobbo in *The Merchant of Venice*. She extended her range still further with a repertoire of CLAUDEL and GILBERT MURRAY's translations of EURIPIDES (1919–20), then a season of GRAND-GUIGNOL (1920–2), but her major successes in the interwar period were in the title roles of SHAW's *Candida* (1920), *St Joan* (a part written specifically for her, 1924) and a revival of *Major Barbara* (1929). She also gave striking performances in plays by John Van Druten, EMLYN WILLIAMS and PRIESTLEY.

During and after World War II she toured widely with the Old Vic company for ENSA, and latterly she frequently appeared with her husband, LEWIS CASSON. She was appointed DBE in 1931 and Companion of Honour in 1970; her final performance in 1966 inaugurated a new theatre in Surrey named after her.

**Throckmorton, Cleon** 1897–1965 American set designer. Throckmorton began his career with the PROVINCETOWN PLAYERS and designed many of EUGENE O'NEILL's early plays including *Emperor Jones* and *The Hairy Ape*. In the same way that O'Neill was experimenting with EXPRESSIONISM, Throckmorton employed stylized settings in the manner of various European movements. He designed several plays for the THEATRE GUILD, including *Porgy*.

**Thurston, Howard (Franklin)** 1869–1936 American MAGICIAN. He began as a card manipulator in New York, but developed into a specialist in spectacular illusions, making horses and people vanish; in 'The Triple Mystery' he made a girl materialize in a nested box, suspended her in a mummy case above the stage, and then caused her to appear in a roped trunk above the spectators' heads. He came to London in 1900, purchased HARRY KELLAR's show in 1907, and introduced his version of the Indian rope trick in 1926.

**Tidblad, Inga** 1901–75 Swedish actress. Particularly admired for roles in Shakespearian comedy (Rosalind, Viola, Beatrice and Portia), she never played major classical tragedy but specialized increasingly in STRINDBERG, IBSEN and EUGENE O'NEILL. Her Miss Julie (which she played in New York at 61) and Queen Christina were greatly admired for their poise and complexity, as were her roles in world premieres of O'Neill: Mary Tyrone in *Long Day's Journey into Night* (1956) and Deborah in both *A Touch of the Poet* (1957) and *More Stately Mansions* (1962).

**Tieck, Ludwig** 1773–1853 German playwright, novelist and essayist. His plays exhibit the same failings as those of other early romantic writers. While they are wonderfully inventive, they defy effective staging, though his comedies *Puss in Boots* (1797) and *The World Upside Down* (1798) have done well in modern revivals. His vast dramatic fantasy, *Emperor Octavian* (1804), cannot be properly represented on stage.

Throughout his life, Tieck was profoundly interested in SHAKESPEARE and the Elizabethan playwrights. He translated some of the plays, notably *The Tempest* (1795), and was involved in the completion of A. W. SCHLEGEL's translations of Shakespeare. As a result of a visit to England in 1817, he became interested in the physical arrangement of the Elizabethan theatre. In 1836, with the help of the architect Gottfried Semper, he reconstructed on paper London's FORTUNE THEATRE. In 1843 he produced *A Midsummer Night's Dream* in Berlin, utilizing many features of the Elizabethan stage. As dramaturge of the DRESDEN COURT THEATRE from 1824, he tried to create a simpler approach to staging than was currently fashionable. His writings on the theatre are collected in the four volumes of *Critical Writings* published in 1848.

**Tilley, Vesta** [Matilda Alice Victoria Powles] 1864–1952 British male impersonator. The most popular of her kind (see MALE IMPERSONATION), she first appeared in trousers as the Pocket Sims Reeves. Her first London appearance was in 1878. Although she was a celebrated principal boy in PANTOMIME, her chief contribution was as an elegant young man-about-town, singing such numbers as 'Following in Father's Footsteps' and 'The Midnight Son'. Her natty masculine attire, specially tailored for her, set the fashion; her transvestism was made palatable for a newly genteel audience by her soprano voice.

**Tingeltangel** German MUSIC-HALL. A generic term for a lower-class Berlin entertainment, it derives from a song the comedian Tange sang at the Triangel Theater. Female singers and comedians would sit on a small stage and come forward to deliver their numbers, accompanied solely by a piano. The verses were usually ribald and called for the almost exclusively male audience of artisans, small tradesmen and students to join in the chorus and goose-step round the platform. At the end of the 19th century the most famous were Moors Academy of Music, the Silberhalle and Elysium, the Kuhstall, the Klosterstiebel and the Singspielhalle.

**Tipton, Jennifer** 1937– American lighting designer (see STAGE LIGHTING). Tipton's early interest in dance led to an appreciation of the potential of light, and its uses and impact on performance. Since 1965 she has designed every production by choreographer Twyla Tharp. In theatre she has designed frequently for the NEW YORK SHAKESPEARE FESTIVAL and the GOODMAN THEATRE. Her preference for more 'abstract' theatre has led to collaboration with MABOU MINES, ROBERT WILSON and ANDREI SERBAN. In 1991 she directed *The Tempest* at the GUTHRIE THEATRE. Tipton's work is typified by a sense of sculptured and textured space.

**tireman** English term. He was the wardrobe master of Elizabethan theatre companies. Whilst leading actors possessed their own COSTUMES, the tireman would supply and maintain clothes for the hired men and for the boys playing women's parts.

**tiring house** English term. The tiring house was the section of an Elizabethan theatre building directly behind and giving access to the stage, where the actors 'attired' themselves for performance. It may also have contained a wardrobe, property store, play collection and meeting-rooms. Its façade served as the upstage wall of the platform, so that actors entered directly from the tiring house on to the stage.

**Tirso de Molina** [Gabriel Téllez] c.1579–1648 Spanish playwright. He joined the Mercedarian order in 1600, spent some time in Toledo and two years in the West Indies, and lived in Madrid from 1621 to 1625. His best plays were probably written from about 1612 to 1625. From 1625 to 1634 he was exiled by his order to their remote house at Trujillo, and forbidden to write plays. He returned to Toledo in 1634 and to Madrid, but in 1640 he was again banished, this time to Soria, where he was made prior.

Ranking with CALDERÓN DE LA BARCA and LOPE DE VEGA as a GOLDEN AGE dramatist, Tirso claimed to have written 300 plays by 1621, but about 80 remain today. In particular he is noted for his portrayal of strong-minded heroines, frank and outspoken in their attitudes to love. Amongst many high-spirited comedies, two set in the court are *Don Gil de las calzas verdes* (*Don Gil of the Green Breeches*) and *El vergonzoso en palacio* (*The Shy Man at Court*).

He also wrote numerous *capa y espada* (see COMEDIA) plays, including *Marta la piadosa* (*Pious Martha*) whose heroine feigns an attack of piety in order to avoid an unwelcome match, and *Por el sótano y el torno* (*Through Basement and Hatch*) in which a woman tries to preserve the honour of her brazen sister.

Among a few plays dealing with the theme of adultery and honour is *El celoso prudente* (*Jealous but Prudent*) in which the protagonist learns just in time that his wife is innocent. Among his freely treated historical plays is a trilogy on the fortunes of the Pizarro family in which he is critical of authority, apparently making veiled attacks on Philip IV's favourite Olivares in *Tanto es lo de más como lo de menos* (*Too Much Is as Bad as Too Little*), which may have led to his exile in 1625. Another fine historical play, *La prudencia en la mujer* (*Prudence in Women*), portrays the efforts of a young widowed queen to keep the throne for her young son.

Tirso wrote several serious plays based on Old Testament stories, including *La venganza de Tamar* (*Tamar's Vengeance*) and *La mujer que manda en casa* (*The Woman who Rules the Roost*) on the story of Jezebel. Perhaps his most important play is *El burlador de Sevilla y convidado de piedra* (*The Trickster of Seville and the Stone Guest*), the first great treatment of the Don Juan Tenorio legend, without the comic or sympathetic approach of later versions. *El condenado por desconfiado* (*Damned for Lack of Faith*) contrasts a great sinner saved by last-minute repentance and a saintly hermit who despairs and becomes a brigand, and is damned when he refuses to repent.

**Toby** American character. The principal figure in the North American TENT SHOW, Toby was a redhaired, freckle-faced farm boy. His dramatic function was to provide laughs while contributing to the happy ending. The character grew gradually more grotesque. Harley Sadler turned him into a Texas cowpoke and Neil Schaffner into an awkward dude whose large freckles and blacked-out front teeth constituted a kind of COMMEDIA mask. The female equivalent was Sis Hopkins, created by Rose Melville c.1898, an 'Indiana jay' in pigtails and a pinafore; the type became known as Susie. The growing predominance of Toby and his antics to the detriment of the dramas in which he appeared has been cited as a factor in the declining popularity of the tent show.

**Toller, Ernst** 1893–1939 German playwright and poet. His life was characterized by radical political commitment. A pacifist in World War I, he became president of the first short-lived Bavarian Soviet Republic, then commander of its Red Army. Imprisoned after the Republic's fall in 1919, he subsequently campaigned for judicial reform and for refugee relief. His plays, which are among the most significant works of EXPRESSIONISM, reflect this experience yet transpose it to a universal level. *Transfiguration* (staged by KARLHEINZ MARTIN, 1919) presents graphic images of war in following the protagonist's conversion from patriotism to militant pacifism, alternating REALISM with dream sequences. *Masses and Man* (1920) and *The Machine Wreckers* (1922) deal with revolution through strike action. In *Hinkemann* (1923), a revolutionary is released from prison to find an intolerable discrepancy between grotesque reality and his ideals.

*Hoppla We're Alive* (1927) presented a contemporary cross-section of Berlin. The forces of Fascism drove Toller into exile in 1933, where he produced *Draw the Fires* (1935), a protest against the coming war based on a

1917 naval mutiny. His last play was *Pastor Hall* (1939). Toller committed suicide on the outbreak of war. His artistic predicament, the gap between idealistic drama and political actuality, is characteristic of the expressionists, and forms the subject of TANKRED DORST's play *Toller* (1968).

**tollu bommalu** [*tholu bommalatta*] Indian puppet theatre. One of the oldest and best-known forms of puppetry in India, it is found in several regions of Andhra Pradesh in south India. *Tollu* means 'doll' and *bommalu* means 'leather'. The SHADOW PUPPETS are cut from the hide of goats, deer and buffalo. Typically, humans and saints are made of goat skin, demons are made of buffalo hide and gods and heroes are cut from deer skin. Puppets are generally large, translucent and multicoloured. Many have movable parts.

Only the songs have a written text. Dialogue sections are improvised and continue as long as the puppeteers think the audience is interested. The musical accompaniment includes drums, cymbals and harmonium. During performance the puppeteers chant and speak their dialogue to each other rather than through the puppets. The puppets seem to act only as symbols of the characters portrayed. Special effects may include the decapitation of a puppet by a string, to the sound of loud thuds on the drums. Among the more popular characters are the clowns, Katikayata, the drunken lecher and womanizer, and Bangavaka, his fat, scandal-mongering wife. The pair provide comic interludes, breaking the monotony of the familiar epic stories which are drawn from the *Ramayana*, the *Mahabharata* and the *Puranas*.

**Tolstoi, Aleksei (Konstantinovich)** [Kozma Prutkov] 1817–75 Russian playwright, poet and novelist. He began his literary career in 1841 with one of three vampire tales which may have provided source material for SUKHOVO-KOBYLIN's *Tarelkin's Death*. From 1853 to 1863 he published nonsense verse, satirical prose and verse and theatrical parodies. His popular romantic historical novel, *Prince Serebryany* (1862), is set during the reign of Ivan the Terrible. His reputation as a dramatist rests on his popular blank-verse historical trilogy on three of Russia's feudal monarchs (1533–1605): *The Death of Ivan the Terrible* (1864), *Tsar Fyodor Ioannovich* (1868) and *Tsar Boris* (1870). In each of these self-contained dramas, Tolstoi humanizes history by focusing upon the personal psychology and morality of the ruler's political crisis.

**Tolstoi, Aleksei (Nikolaevich)** 1883–1945 Soviet novelist, short story writer and playwright. A nobleman by birth and an anti-Bolshevik at the time of the Revolution, Tolstoi, later known as the 'Red Count', accommodated himself totally to the new regime and became an apologist for Stalin following an interlude in Parisian exile (1918–23). Before 1917 he produced symbolist poetry (see SYMBOLISM), novels and short story collections. He wrote 28 plays, beginning in 1908. His pre-revolutionary plays are farces and comedies satirizing the landed gentry and the merchant class. Seven received Moscow stagings, and his dramatic fairy tale *The Sorcerer's Daughter and the Enchanted Prince* was produced at MEYERHOLD's theatre of small forms, the Strand (1908). In the 1920s Tolstoi wrote historical dramas, the science fiction play *The Revolt of the Machines* (1924) and the first part of his Peter the Great trilogy – *On the Rack* (1929), rewritten as *Peter the First* (first version, 1935; second version, 1939) – which parallels his

unfinished three-part historical novel *Peter the First* (1930, 1934, 1945). His evolving presentation of Peter as tyrant, modernizer and finally national hero reflects the shift in official perspective which likened Peter to Stalin. His two-part historical play *Ivan the Terrible* (*The Eagle and Its Mate*, 1944; *The Difficult Years*, 1946) is a somewhat idealized view. Tolstoi received three Stalin Prizes.

**Tolstoi, Lev (Nikolaevich)** 1828–1910 Russian novelist and playwright. A titled noble, Tolstoi rejected his class and became one of Russia's greatest novelists and a social dramatist. In 1878, following the completion of his novels *War and Peace* (1869) and *Anna Karenina* (1877), he underwent a celebrated spiritual crisis, resulting in his rejection of Orthodox Christianity. His new ethical philosophy manifests itself in all of his remaining work – religious treatises, social polemics, aesthetic essays and dramas.

Tolstoi rejected theatre's sham and self-indulgence but embraced its potential for educating and uplifting a popular audience. His earliest plays – *A Contaminated Family* (1864), *The Nihilist* (1866) and *The First Distiller* (1886) – two SATIRES and a moral fable, treated such contemporary evils as women's rights, nihilism and alcoholism. In *What Is Art?* (1897–8), 'On Shakespeare and the Drama' (1903–4) and other aesthetic and critical works he distinguished between true and counterfeit art. True art is universal, moral, but not excessive in emotional and scenographic detail. False art, which includes the works of SHAKESPEARE, GOETHE, HUGO and others, violates these criteria.

Tolstoi condemned his own naturalistic peasant tragedy (see NATURALISM), *The Power of Darkness* (1886), for wallowing in extraneous detail, but it remains a powerful indictment of the inhumanity and moral degeneracy brought on by the ignorance and squalor of Russian peasant life. Based upon a contemporary criminal case, it relates a tale of adultery and infanticide and features a typically meek Tolstoyan *raisonneur* and climactic confession-conversion. It was banned from the Russian stage until 1895, premiering instead at ANTOINE's Théâtre Libre in 1888. *The Fruits of Enlightenment* (1889) satirized the unenlightened attitude of the Russian landed nobility towards the peasantry, despite the abolition of serfdom in 1861. *The Living Corpse* (1900) exposed the inadequacy of laws governing marriage and divorce. *The Light Shines in the Darkness* (1900) is an unfinished autobiographical tale of an aristocrat whose adherence to a transparently Tolstoyan ethic puts him at odds with his family and society. *The Cause of It All* (1910) is another anti-alcohol tract. Much of Tolstoi's narrative writing has also been adapted for the stage.

**Tomaszewski, Henryk** see MIME

**Toole, J(ohn) L(aurence)** 1830–1906 British actor. He was the leading low comedian of the late 19th century. Toole's long friendship with HENRY IRVING began in 1857 and they performed together as the squat extrovert comedian and the gaunt introverted tragedian. Toole was the star of ADELPHI FARCES and BURLESQUES from 1859–67, at his best in roles combining eccentric comedy and pathos: Caleb Plummer in BOUCICAULT's *Dot* (1862) and Michael Garner in H. J. BYRON's *Dearer than Life* (1868). In 1882 Toole rechristened the Charing Cross Theatre Toole's Theatre, where he proved a shrewd manager. He was the first to present J. M. BARRIE's plays.

**Topol, Haim** 1935– Israeli actor. He now lives in England. In Israel his greatest roles were Azdak in

BRECHT's *The Caucasian Chalk Circle* (1962 and again in 1992) and Sallah Shabbati in the film of that name (1964) by EPHRAIM KISHON. In London and on BROADWAY he rose to fame with his portrayal of Tevye the Milkman in the musical *Fiddler on the Roof* (1967), based on SHOLOM ALEICHEM's Yiddish novel. He starred in the 1972 film adaptation of the play and has also tried directing. He played Othello at the 1975 CHICHESTER FESTIVAL. In 1994 he recreated the role of Tevye in a memorable London revival.

**Torelli, Giacomo** 1608–78 Italian architect, engineer and stage designer. Torelli revolutionized French *mise-en-scène*. He was responsible for the chariot-and-pole system of changeable scenery: wing flats were attached through slits in the stage floor to rolling wagons in the cellar beneath; by an arrangement of pulleys and ropes wound on a common drum all the flats could move smoothly and simultaneously under the control of a single stage-hand, while overhead borders were similarly operated by counterweights. The result was a swift, magical transformation of one scene to the next, which had a profound effect on design and on the evolution of opera and intermezzi. Torelli had already designed the Teatro Novissimo in Venice when he was summoned to Paris by Mazarin in 1645. There he re-equipped the PETIT-BOURBON and designed Italian opera, 'machine-plays' and court ballets. Rivalry with GASPARE VIGARANI forced him to return to his native Fano. His drawings established an Italianate tradition of spectacular staging for opera and ballet which was to be maintained by Vigarani, BERAIN and SERVANDONI.

**Torres Naharro, Bartolomé de** c.1485-c.1520 Spanish playwright and theorist. He wrote most of his plays in Italy. A collection of plays and verse, the *Propalladia (First Fruits of Pallas)*, was published in Rome in 1517. He returned to Spain, and added further plays to later editions. The work was banned by the Roman Catholic Index of 1559 (see CENSORSHIP), but an expurgated edition was published in Madrid in 1573. With one exception, his nine plays are in five acts with an introduction, using one verse form throughout. In *Prohemio* he gives his views on the theatre, discussing classical theory and types of plot. His plays – especially *Himenea (Hymen)*, with its plot foreshadowing that of the typical cloak-and-sword play – influenced later writers.

**Totò** [Antonio de Curtis] 1898–1967 Italian comedian and actor-manager. As an actor-manager he specialized in COMEDY and REVUE, which exploited his mimic genius, perfect timing of lines, and skill with frenetic stage 'business'. Often compared to screen comedians like Chaplin and Keaton, he was a brilliant improviser whose impact was more visual than verbal, thanks to his expressive face and hand gestures. In the 1950s he rapidly became established as one of the most popular Italian film comedians in films like *Napoli milionaria (Affluent Naples*, 1950), *Guardie e ladri* (1951) and *L'oro di Napoli (The Gold of Naples*, 1954), a reputation he enjoyed until his death.

**Tourneur, Cyril** c.1575–1626 English playwright. He is celebrated for *The Revenger's Tragedy* (c.1606), though many believe this sombrely ironic play to be by MIDDLETON. The details of Tourneur's life are obscure, but he is known to have written a lost play, *The Nobleman* (c.1607), and *The Atheist's Tragedy* (published 1611), a mechanical REVENGE TRAGEDY.

**Tovstonogov, Georgy (Aleksandrovich)** 1915–89 Soviet director. In 1938 he became artistic director of the Tbilisi Russian Theatre. From 1946 to 1949 he directed the Moscow Children's Theatre, and between 1950 and 1956 he was chief director of Leningrad's Lenin Komsomol Theatre, where he developed the successful policy of mixing Soviet dramas, Russian classics and Western literature, which he took with him to the Bolshoi Dramatic Theatre (BTD, or the Gorky) in 1956, transforming it into the best theatre in Leningrad.

A craftsman with a lush, romantic pictorial style, Tovstonogov staged orthodox Soviet productions in the later 1950s and 1960s and several examples of post-Thaw 'new lyricism' and intimate, human drama: VOLODIN's *Five Evenings* (1959) and *My Elder Sister* (1961); ARBUZOV's *Irkutsk Story* (1960) and *Happy Days of an Unhappy Man* (1968); and ROZOV's *The Reunion* (1964). Best were his readings of classical texts, justly celebrated for their brilliant ensemble play: Dostoevsky's *The Idiot* (1957; London, 1966); GRIBOEDOV's *Woe from Wit* (1962); CHEKHOV's *The Three Sisters* (1965); GORKY's *The Petty Bourgeoisie* (1967), the Gorky's longest-running production; SHAKESPEARE's *Henry IV, Parts 1 and 2* (1969), condensed into a single evening, and GOGOL's *The Inspector General* (1972); and *The Story of a Horse* (adapted from LEV TOLSTOI's narrative 'Kholstomer' by co-director Mark Rozovsky, 1975), a treatment of the man's-inhumanity-to-man theme from the perspective of a horse. The play's immense popularity extended to America, where it has been widely produced. In 1984 Tovstonogov premiered a musical version of SUKHOVO-KOBYLIN's *Tarelkin's Death*. He also produced many modern Western classics by e.g. BRECHT, O'NEILL and ARTHUR MILLER.

**toy theatre** [juvenile drama] Theatre for children involving models of playhouses. Toy theatre originated in early-19th-century London with the full-length coloured theatrical portraits of Robert Dighton. Sheets of characters from current London productions, 'a penny plain and tuppence coloured', began to appear. Sets of sheets providing all the major poses, scenery and properties, along with a book of words, enabled children to re-create the stage of their time. The images were cut out, pasted on cardboard and mounted on wire slides, and manipulated in miniature wooden playhouses, lit by candles or small oil-wicks. Often the characters' costumes would be ornamented with gilt and tinsel. The early sheets are of great historical importance, preserving the look of Regency MELODRAMA, operetta and PANTOMIME; the most popular and frequently reprinted plays were M. G. Lewis's *Timour the Tartar* (1811), an equestrian spectacle (see HIPPODRAMA), and Isaac Pocock's *The Miller and His Men* (1813), with its climactic explosion of gunpowder stores.

Germany was a late starter in the 1830s, but by mid-century dominated the English market with elegant sets, based on fairy tales and operas. France, Spain and Denmark also produced toy theatres, but their repertory was not drawn from actual stage productions; the USA, with Seltz's American Boy's Theatre, was content to copy English models.

**tragedy** Almost every culture offers an audience pleasure – paradoxically – through an art based on human suffering. In Western culture a significant form of such art is tragedy, a word whose meaning changes with time and place of text or performance. Through the centuries, too, the very word 'tragedy' has acquired a valorizing resonance, which is unique for an art form. Ancient and modern critics have contrasted tragedy with COMEDY; and more recently with MELODRAMA. Early critics – pre-eminently ARISTOTLE – focused on tragic action, whereas recent critics dwell on tragic vision. After centuries of commentary on Greek elements of tragedy, more recent approaches have shifted to abstruse semiotics and ideological codes of tragedy.

Tragedy (tragōidia) means goat-song, but there is no caproic trace in what we know of Greek tragedy. Performed annually to celebrate the god Dionysus, Attic tragedy of the 5th century BC was based on Greek myth. Formally, each tragedy was a verse exchange between a Chorus and a small number of actors (usually three). The episodes of the plot were punctuated by choral songs, and the ending was not necessarily unhappy. Of the three Greek tragic playwrights whose works are extant, only AESCHYLUS wrote tetralogies, i.e. three sequential tragedies followed by a satyr play. Between Aeschylus and EURIPIDES the scope of tragedy narrowed from cosmic moral questions to more personal passions (see GREEK THEATRE, ANCIENT).

It was Aristotle in the 4th century BC who first praised tragedy as the highest form of poetry. Preferring SOPHOCLES to other dramatists, and Oedipus to other tragedies, Aristotle began the comparative evaluation of works, which has since become a major tool of criticism. Although Aristotle was descriptive rather than prescriptive, he bequeathed to posterity terms that today elude exact definition – hamartia (error), catharsis (purgation), mimesis (imitation) – as well as the more familiar pity and fear. Aside from criticism, later homage to Greek tragedy was seen in imitation. The Roman SENECA accomplished this so sensationally that his nine plays became the strongest influence upon subsequent European tragedy. Later tragedy is indebted to Seneca for the five-act structure, the violent catastrophic ending, and the clash of characters speaking stichomythia (under emotional stress, each character utters a line that is rhythmically matched to the one preceding it).

In medieval theatre, tragedy came to mean the downfall of a person of high degree. With the Renaissance, the genre gained importance both in theory and practice. Italy and especially France looked back and up to the pagan classics. Senecan imitation (in Latin) began in the 14th century, but after the defeat of Constantinople in 1453 Greek tragedy gradually became the model, and a misunderstood Aristotle became the rule. GIRALDI and Scaliger set forth the unities of time, place and action. The architect SERLIO in 1545 distinguished between tragic, comic and satyric settings. Italian Renaissance tragedy, as opposed to comedy, is of only scholarly interest, and not until ALFIERI in the 18th century did Italy produce a playable tragedy.

France took a similar path a century later, with MAIRET in 1630 prescribing the three unities. Other dramatists voluntarily donned this straitjacket. Since PIERRE CORNEILLE's Cid violated the unities, it gave rise to the 'Querelle du Cid', which was terminated when the Academie-Française laid down the rules of tragedy. Self-consciously noble, neoclassical verse tragedy with its strict decorum dominated not only French but most other Continental drama for the next 150 years. In England and Spain, however, popular traditions outweighed the learned, encouraging 'impure' tragedy. Although the first English tragedy Gorboduc is sternly regular, MARLOWE and SHAKESPEARE soon rattled the stage with their action-packed tragedies, towering pro-

tagonists, ironies, images and final catastrophes. KYD's Spanish Tragedy is usually cited as the first REVENGE TRAGEDY, a subgenre of which Hamlet is the crowning achievement.

When James I succeeded Elizabeth, the tragic genre grew darker and more sceptical. Good and Bad Angels underline the moral conflict of Marlowe's Dr Faustus, but WEBSTER, TOURNEUR and CHAPMAN question the very basis of moral judgement in tragedy. Moreover, alongside these dramas of the unfortunate mighty a few so-called domestic tragedies dramatized the suffering of common people, and this departure from the tragic tradition was to culminate in the 18th-century London Merchant (LILLO), a source of middle-class drama throughout Europe, so that noble tragedy suffered an eclipse. Before then, however, during the court-centred theatre of the Restoration, English tragedy briefly adapted the French form into heroic tragedy, a violence-filled struggle between love and honour neatly encapsulated in couplets.

With romantic bardolatry, tragedy returned loquaciously but untheatrically to literature, since almost every romantic poet of every European country tried his (left) hand at verse tragedy. Along with these efforts came a resurgence of theory, in the works of the SCHLEGEL brothers, LESSING, and HUGO's preface to his Cromwell, with its blatant rejection of decorum. During the same period the philosopher Hegel enunciated his view of tragedy as 'the collision of equally justified ethical claims'. Towards the end of the 19th century NIETZSCHE rejected a moral approach to tragedy, and instead he praised the Dionysian irrational element that paralleled the spirit of music. Realists refused to limit tragedy to privileged protagonists, and the director ANTOINE found nothing incompatible between REALISM and tragedy, while STRINDBERG called his Miss Julie 'a naturalistic tragedy'. Whether or not they were preoccupied with genre, several modern playwrights have been labelled tragic – IBSEN, CHEKHOV, O'NEILL, GARCÍA LORCA and BECKETT.

In the voluminous 20th-century literature on tragedy, two major questions recur. First, is tragedy possible in an anarchic age like ours which lacks a community of belief? Second, is the ordinary individual a fitting subject for tragedy in our democratic age? Perhaps the most resounding negative reply to the first question is George Steiner's Death of Tragedy, whereas ARTHUR MILLER has uttered as resounding an affirmative answer to the second question. Although contemporary dramatists may care little about genre designations for their plays, tragedy is still of deep concern to many contemporary critics – not only those of drama.

**tragicomedy** The word conjures up a mixture of sadness and merriment, but the genre has meant different mixtures at different periods in the Western theatre. The word was coined by PLAUTUS in the Prologue to his Amphitryon; spoken by the god Mercury, who high-handedly designates a new genre in which kings (who frequent TRAGEDY) mix with slaves (who frequent COMEDY). Another fissure of classical decorum had earlier been noted by ARISTOTLE, in the happy endings of several tragedies by EURIPIDES (seven extant to our time), but these plays were not called tragicomedies until the Renaissance.

From late classical to late medieval times, genre terminology was loose, and we cannot recapture today the meaning of such sporadic labels as *tragicomoedia, comoedotragoedia* and *comoedia tragica*. Often unlabelled, popular drama mixed the funny and the sad, the common and the divine. The seriocomic *Second Shepherd's Play* was contemporary with Latin school plays of serious main plot and comic subplot. These different mixtures – neoclassical and popular – flourished indiscriminately in the playing spaces of England, France and the Low Countries, but Italian playwright-critics tried to systematize the amorphous practice. GIRALDI spurned the word 'tragicomedy' for his tragedies with happy endings, preferring 'mixed tragedy'. It was, however, GUARINI whose PASTORAL tragicomedy *Il Pastor Fido* (1590) and critical defence *Compendio della poesia tragicomica* (1601) raised a lively little storm. As playwrights, both evolved labyrinthine plots that twisted their way to a happy and romantic ending, but those of Giraldi were solemn, whereas Guarini sounded an occasional comic note in such figures as a satyr. Both playwrights cited a host of classical authorities to justify the breach of classical decorum. The genre proved eminently exportable, and in the early 17th century tragicomedy (for the most part removed to court from pasture) bloomed happily in England, France and Spain, counting among its practitioners FLETCHER, SHAKESPEARE, HEYWOOD, MARSTON, MASSINGER, SHIRLEY; GARNIER, HARDY, MAIRET, CORNEILLE, ROTROU; LOPE DE VEGA, TIRSO DE MOLINA and ZORRILLA.

Renaissance verse tragicomedy was set exotically, plotted suspensefully and resolved satisfactorily; as the 17th century rolled on, the violent action of tragicomedy departed more and more from the inner thrust of tragedy, while more or less comic elements provided entertaining distraction. Although lacklustre dramatists tried to prolong its life into the 18th century, popular prose theatre soon displaced it. The ghost of tragicomedy nevertheless infiltrated into Gothic MELODRAMA of the 19th century.

Modern tragicomedy derives from a minor attribute of the Renaissance variety – comic elements in the basically serious action. There is, however, no clean lineage; there rarely is in theatre. If one seeks a history of a merry-melancholy genre, much depends on the mixture. Almost all English Renaissance tragedies have a comic component, but the mixture became programmatic in the romantic movements of France and Germany. Melodrama, the mass medium of the time, thrived on a comic character who helped the hero defeat the villain. Throughout the 19th century English verse drama tended towards solemnity, and perhaps for that reason rarely reached a theatre; but in prose and verse, comic notes sound increasingly loud in plays by Germans LENZ, GRABBE, BÜCHNER and even KLEIST.

With the advent of REALISM in the late 19th century, classical genre designations were all but forgotten, and most serious plays supported a comic component without reducing it formulaically, as in melodrama. SHAW recognized: 'IBSEN was the dramatic poet who firmly established tragicomedy as a much deeper and grimmer entertainment than tragedy.' Although neither Shaw nor Ibsen (who designated *The Wild Duck* as tragicomedy) defines the modern genre, it overlaps with such terms as irony, humorism, the grotesque and the absurd (see THEATRE OF THE ABSURD).

The critic ERIC BENTLEY in *Life of the Drama* instructively classifies modern tragicomedy into (1) tragedy transcended (as opposed to Renaissance 'tragedy averted'), for example STRINDBERG's *Dream Play*; and (2) comedy with an unhappy or indeterminate ending, for example BECKETT's *Waiting for Godot*. Contemporary dramatists tend to express their tragic vision with comic devices, creating tragicomedy that is funny without being foolish, serious without being solemn.

**Travers, Ben** 1886–1980 British playwright and novelist. He made his reputation with the ten 'Aldwych FARCES', a label given to his plays because they occupied the stage of London's Aldwych Theatre continuously – from *A Cuckoo in the Nest* (1925), *Rookery Nook* (1926) and *Thark* (1927), to *Dirty Work* (1932) and *A Bit of a Test* (1933). Combining absurdly improbable situations, eccentric characters and broad humour with social SATIRE, his work has survived well and has been adapted for film and television. In 1976 there were three of his plays on the London stage. His last, *The Bed before Yesterday*, opened in 1975 with JOAN PLOWRIGHT as an outspoken middle-aged woman who belatedly discovers the joy of sex.

**Traverse Theatre** (Edinburgh) Britain's first studio theatre, the Traverse (so called because its audiences were seated either side of the stage) was started in 1963 with the aim of providing an experimental theatre club offering creative opportunities for theatre artists the whole year round and not merely during the EDINBURGH FESTIVAL. Its founder was the American director Jim Haynes. He introduced to the British stage many of the plays of such international writers as ARRABAL, WEISS, KROETZ and SHEPARD, and commissioned new work from British playwrights. This policy remains central to the club's work. In 1969 and then again in 1992 the Traverse moved to new premises and now operates two auditoria. New work premiered at the Traverse includes Jimmy Boyle's and Tom McGrath's *The Hardman*, Clare Luckham's *Trafford Tanzi*, C. P. TAYLOR's *Bread and Butter* and STEVE BERKOFF's *East*.

**Treadwell, Sophie** 1885–1970 American playwright and journalist (and war correspondent during 1916–18). Although other plays of hers were produced – *Gringo* (1922), *Plumes in the Dust* (1936) and *Hope for a Harvest* (1941) – Treadwell's reputation rests predominantly on her innovative *Machinal* (1928; Moscow, 1933), revived successfully in New York (1990) and London (1993). In nine expressionistic scenes (see EXPRESSIONISM), the play perfectly combines form and content, telling the story of a woman who is robotized by life.

**Tree, Herbert (Draper) Beerbohm** 1853–1917 British actor and theatre manager. The half-brother of Max Beerbohm, he had his first success in farce and entered into management in 1887, briefly at London's Comedy Theatre and then at the HAYMARKET (1887–96). Tree was no literary purist, but liked plays with plenty of action and a dash of scandal, such as those by HENRY ARTHUR JONES, WILDE and IBSEN. His *Hamlet* (1892) was deemed by W. S. GILBERT to be 'funny without being vulgar'. The outstanding Haymarket productions were the last two, Paul Potter's dramatization of *Trilby* (1895), with Tree as Svengali, and *Henry IV, Part 1* (1896), with Tree as Falstaff. He was one of the great make-up artists and a shameless dominator of the stage. He planned and managed HER [HIS] MAJESTY'S THEATRE from 1897 to 1915 and it became the home of 14 lavish Shakespearian productions, the last surviving monument of pictorial SHAKESPEARE. At His Majesty's Tree also created the great costume role of Fagin (1905). SHAW's *Pygmalion* opened there in 1914, with Tree as Henry Higgins partly obliterated by Mrs Patrick Campbell's Eliza Doolittle. Tree was a witty and humane man. Despite his major role in the foundation of the Royal Academy of Dramatic Art (1904), he was less a student of acting than a brilliant opportunist. He was knighted in 1907.

**Tremblay, Michel** 1942– Quebec playwright and novelist. He first achieved national prominence with *Les Belles-soeurs (The Sisters-in-Law)* in 1968, transposing to the stage the profound frustrations of Montreal's urban proletariat. Set in one tawdry flat, his characters, all female, express their despair in pure *joual*, the impoverished popular idiom of Quebec. Stylized monologues and choreographed choruses transform a seemingly banal plot into poignant tragedy. The influence of this play has been remarkable, a whole generation of young dramatists following Tremblay's lead in the use of *joual* without, however, attaining his dramatic and poetic intensity.

In nine plays composed over the next decade he continued to portray Montreal peopled by transvestites, homosexuals and misfits. Some characters reappear, in works such as *En pièces pétachées (Broken Pieces*, 1969), *À toi pour toujours, ta Marie-Lou (Forever Yours, Marie-Lou*, 1971), *Hosanna* (1973), *Sainte Carmen de la Main (Saint Carmen of Main Street*, 1976) and *Damnée Manon, Sacrée Sandra (Damned Manon, Holy Sandra*, 1977).

His own move to an affluent section of the city, along with the election of an independent Parti Québécois government in 1976, have affected his evolution. A fervent separatist, he appears to avoid embarrassing the government. Plays such as *L'Impromptu d'Outremont (The Impromptu of Outremont*, 1980) deal with middle-class concerns, while *Albertine en cinq temps (Albertine in Five Times*, 1984) is timeless, portraying brilliantly the universal problem of ageing. A new departure was his opera *Nelligan* (1990), dealing with the Quebec poet of that name. Tremblay's plays have been widely translated and performed. He is French Canada's outstanding dramatist to date.

**Trenyov, Konstantin (Andreevich)** 1876–1945 Soviet short story writer and playwright. He achieved fame with the Moscow Art Theatre production of *Pugachyov Times* (1924). This monumentalist play was made controversial by the author's unexpectedly harsh depiction of the popular hero of the 18th-century peasant revolt. His classic Civil War drama, *Lyubov Yarovaya* (1926), presents as heroine a strong-minded schoolteacher who sacrifices her beloved White Russian husband for her Bolshevik beliefs. The role became a prototype for revolutionary women in Soviet dramas. First produced at Moscow's Maly Theatre (1926), it was revised under Stalin in 1936. Trenyov's remaining plays were primarily anti-bourgeois satires and Soviet problem plays. *On the Banks of the Neva* (1937), set during the Revolution, marked an early appearance by Lenin on the Soviet stage. Trenyov's final play, *The Commander* (1945), about General Kutuzov, hero of the War of 1812, represented his return to the epic historical drama.

**Tretyakov, Sergei (Mikhailovich)** 1892–1939 Soviet poet, journalist, translator and playwright. Tretyakov became an aggressive spokesman for utilitarian art and constructivist design (see THEATRE DESIGN), best known for his post-revolutionary theatrical collaborations with Meyerhold and Sergei Eisenstein. His first theatrical work with Eisenstein (at the Proletkult Theatre) was their version of Ostrovsky's *Enough Stupidity for Every Wise Man* (1923), staged as a satirical REVUE featuring CLOWNing, ACROBATICS, caricature and film clips. Eisenstein's version of Tretyakov's *Gas Masks* (1923) was actually staged in a Moscow gas-works. Tretyakov's *Earth Rampant* (1923) was staged by Meyerhold with a constructivist design by Lyubov Popova, incorporating elements of the mass spectacle. *Roar, China!* (1926), a great success at Meyerhold's theatre, was based on a real incident concerning colonialist brutalization of the Chinese. Its effectiveness as a propaganda vehicle led to productions throughout Europe and in New York by the Theatre Guild in 1930.

Tretyakov's *I Want a Child* recommended socially based eugenics to achieve perfect proletarian children in Soviet society. Meyerhold's production (1927–30) was denied permission by Glavrepertkom (the Main Repertory Committee), which considered the play to be ahead of its time. Brecht, who met Tretyakov on the 1930 *Roar, China!* tour in Berlin, called him 'my teacher' and adapted *I Want a Child* for the German stage, where it never played. Tretyakov translated Brecht's *St Joan of the Stockyards*, *The Measures Taken* and *The Mother* into Russian (1936). Arrested and executed in 1939, Tretyakov was rehabilitated in the 1960s, when the influence of his collaboration with Meyerhold could be seen in Yury Lyubimov's staging of *Ten Days that Shook the World* and in other productions at Moscow's Taganka Theatre.

**Triana, José** 1931– Cuban playwright. His first plays, *Medea en el espejo (Medea in the Mirror*, 1960) and *La muerte del ñeque (Death of the Strong Man*, 1963), both employ classical Greek tragic figures in a lower-class Cuban environment. Violence and criminality prefigure the game symbolism in his later theatre. His masterpiece and Cuba's best-known play internationally is *La noche de los asesinos (The Night of the Assassins*, 1965), a brutal work involving three adolescents in the myth, ritual and exorcism of killing their parents. No other plays appeared until Triana, originally a revolutionary, defected on a trip to Paris in 1980. *Ceremonial de guerra (War Ceremony*, written 1968–73) and *Diálogo de mujeres (Women's Dialogue*, 1979–80) are both set in Cuba at the turn of the century. The Royal Shakespeare Company staged his *Worlds Apart*, a study of Cuba in the period 1894–1914, in 1986 at Stratford-upon-Avon. His one-act monologue, *Cruzando el puente (Crossing the Bridge*, 1992) was followed by *La fiesta, o Comedia para un delirio (The Party, or Comedy for a Delirium)* in 1993.

**Trinidad carnival** (See also CARNIVAL.) In its 200-year history the pre-Lenten Trinidad carnival has encompassed many theatrical forms. Essentially an annual parade of original costumes worn by bands of masked revellers, the carnival over the years acquired ancillary exhibitions of music, song, dance, MIME and the spoken word that have made it a grand theatrical spectacle and a repository of the nation's performing arts.

Carnival was transported to Spanish-held Trinidad by French colonial planters in the 1780s. Under British rule it continued to be observed by the white elite as a European-type festival, the free coloureds and black slaves having no part in it. When slavery ended in 1834, the black and coloured masses took over the festival and transformed it into an expression of their newfound freedom. Among the principal 19th-century masquerades were canboulay (*cannes-brûlées*, burnt canes) revellers re-enacting scenes from slavery, dread stick-fighters whose music, dance and pungent argot survive on the contemporary stage, military bands that satirized the armed forces, indigenous creatures of myth and folk-tale, and the ubiquitous calypsonian who emerged as carnival songster and public commentator. During this period repeated attempts by government to suppress the masquerade as a rowdy and indecent exhibition were strenuously resisted, sometimes with rioting and loss of life.

In the 20th century conditions slowly improved as English replaced French patois in song lyrics and the street parade gained respectability. Calypsonians, now universally recognized professional singers, gave nightly concerts which often ended with a comic sketch that recounted in song a topical event of recent date. On carnival streets traditional maskers like the Midnight Robber harangued spectators with hair-raising encounters and threats until paid off. The Dragon Band performed an elaborate street ballet, the Pierrot Grenade gave its version of a spelling bee contest, military bands exhibited precise drills or made furious assaults on an imaginary enemy.

Carnival music kept pace with developments. Skin drums and wooden clappers used to accompany *canboulay* trampers and stick-fighters gave way to shack-shack (gourd rattle) and bottle-and-spoon ensembles when drum beating was restricted. Then came the bamboo bands and finally the steel orchestras, made from discarded petrol drums, which have extended their musical repertoire from calypsoes to classics and have spread to countries abroad.

In recent years traditional performing masquerades have dwindled as newly conceived bands enrol thousands of members. Detailed ornamentation in costuming and theatrical presentation has been replaced by massed colour effects, with the exception of the extravagant costumes of the competing carnival kings and queens. Some traditional masquerade bands have been presented as dramatic spectacles to pantomime contemporary concerns such as environmental pollution and nuclear war.

**Trissino, Gian Giorgio** 1478–1550 Italian playwright and literary theorist. His two plays, the tragedy *Sofonisba* (1514–15) and the comedy *I simillimi* (1548), written under strong classical influence, were highly regarded in their day, especially the former which was widely imitated. LUIGI RICCOBONI tried unsuccessfully to revive Italian interest in tragedy by staging the play in Venice in 1713. Trissino was an active patron of the architect PALLADIO.

**Tristan** [François] **l'Hermite** c.1601–55 French poet and playwright. His first, and perhaps best, tragedy *La Mariane*, on the subject of Herod's jealous love for his doomed wife, was performed with great success at the MARAIS only months before PIERRE CORNEILLE's *Le Cid*. *La Mort de Sénèque* (*The Death of Seneca*, 1644) and an entertaining comedy, *Le Parasite* (1654), were among his later works, which were well received. He was elected to the Académie-Française in 1649. There have been several revivals of late.

**Trotter, Catharine** 1679–1749 English playwright. She was highly educated and precocious; her first poems and novels were published in 1693, when she was 14. Her first play, *Agnes de Castro*, a romantic tragedy in classical style and centred on a pathetic heroine, was performed in 1695. She was mocked with MARY PIX and Mrs Manley in *The Female Wits* in 1696. Her plays, mostly 'she-tragedies', were often revised with help from CONGREVE. In 1703 she published a pamphlet defending John

Locke's *Essay on Human Understanding*. Her marriage to a clergyman in 1708 ended her career as a playwright.

**Tsegaye Gebre-Medhin** 1936– Ethiopian playwright. In 1960 he was appointed director of the Haile Selassie I Theatre in Addis Ababa, where many of his plays were staged. Their criticism of the feudal regime led to imprisonment and dismissal. After the revolution his translations and original plays in Amharic, characterized by strong nationalism, established him as Ethiopia's foremost playwright: *A Man of the Future*, first performed before the revolution in 1964; *ABC in Six Months*, an inspiring revolutionary drama (1974); *Otello* (1982); and *Tewodros*, an epic about an emperor defeated by the British (1983). *Oda Oak Oracle* (1965) and *Collision of Altars* (1975) have been published in English. By the 1980s his work was increasingly critical of the Marxist government and he was forced into silence by the censors (see CENSORSHIP). In 1992 he produced a new play *ABC or XYZ?*, celebrating the overthrow of the previous government but also making some criticism of the new transitional government of Ethiopia.

**Tsodzo, Thompson** 1947– Zimbabwean playwright and novelist. Many of his plays in Shona have been televised. Published plays include *The Talking Calabash* (1976), *Tsano* (*The Brother-in-law*, 1982) and *Shanduko* (*Changes*, 1983). His focus is generally moralistic though *The Storm* (1982), which commemorates the struggle for Zimbabwean independence, and *Shanduko* show an interest in modern political developments.

**Tsuka Kōhei** 1948– Japanese playwright and director. Tsuka best represents the climate of the 1970s in Japan, following the underground theatre movement of the 1960s. In 1974 he formed Tsuka Kōhei's Office, for which he composed not written scripts but *kuchidate* (word-of-mouth) performances, the method often used in traditional Japanese theatre. He uses a simple bare stage and his plays include ironic comment on political or social matters, e.g. *For the Father Who Could Not Kill Himself in the War* (1972), *The Departure* (1974), *Murder in Atami* (1973), *Stripper Story* (1975) and *The Kamata March* (1980).

**Tucker, Sophie** [*née* Sophia Kalish] 1884–1966 Russian-born American VAUDEVILLE singer. Known as 'the Last of the Red-Hot Mammas', she made her professional debut in 1906 in blackface and won a reputation as a 'Coon Shouter', singing ragtime melodies. In 1911 she introduced 'Some of These Days', which became her theme song. She moved easily from ragtime to jazz, made a huge success in England beginning in 1922, and appeared in the musicals *Leave It to Me* (1938) and *High Kickers* (1941).

**Tukak Teatret** Danish-based company. Founded in 1975 under the guidance of Norwegian actor-director Reidar Nilsson, this experimental theatre company is based in the remote village of Fjaltring on the northwest coast of Jutland, Denmark. Its early identity grew primarily from its training of Greenlandic actors and its attempt to rediscover and adapt to the modern theatre (without falling into a nostalgic folklorism) the lost paratheatrical forms (including drum dances, masks and storytelling) of Inuit Greenland before its colonization by Denmark. By the early 1980s, partly as a result of its successful international tours, it had broadened into an international theatre of and for native peoples in general, including North American Indians and Inuit. By the mid-1980s, ex-company-members were involved in establishing the first permanent theatre company in the Greenlandic capital Nuuk. Among Tukak's major productions have been *Inuit, Tupilak, Man and the Mask* and *Sinnattoq*. In 1980 the company participated in the founding of the Indigenous People's Theatre Association.

**Turgenev, Ivan (Sergeevich)** 1818–83 Russian novelist and playwright. A liberal and a Westernizer, Turgenev absorbed the romantic idealism of the 1840s without embracing its radicalism. With the publication of his great novel *Fathers and Sons* (1862), which alienated Slavophiles and Westernizers alike, he went into more or less permanent exile in France. He became the first Russian writer to find a large Western following for his work. Although he considered himself to be primarily a novelist, he came to drama first, writing a total of ten plays. His early efforts are GOGOLian SATIRES, genre parodies and *vaudevilles* of no real distinction. A number of them, including *The Charity Case* (1845), *Where It's Thin, There It Breaks* (1847), *The Bachelor* (1849) and *The Provincial Lady* (1850), were written with his friend the comic actor SHCHEPKIN in mind. They feature the 'insulted and injured' little man in whom are mingled the humour and pathos that were the actor's strong suit. His best play, the classic *A Month in the Country* (1850), clearly foreshadows CHEKHOV in its conversational misdirection, leisurely pacing and sense of uneventfulness in an oppressive rural environment. Turgenev's subtle, lyrical character studies shifted the narrative focus to internal action and helped pave the way for Chekhov's psychological REALISM.

*turlupinades* French FARCES, played at the HÔTEL DE BOURGOGNE, Paris, from 1618 to about 1630 by a famous trio of comedians. GROS-GUILLAUME was round and fat and played a foul-mouthed, good-natured drunkard; GAULTIER-GARGUILLE was a modified Pantalone; Turlupin (Henri Le Grand, c.1587–1637) was a witty and malicious improviser who wore a brick-red beard and a striped costume like Brighella's (see *COMMEDIA DELL'ARTE*).

**Turrini, Peter** 1944– Austrian playwright. *Rozzenjogd* (*Rathunt*, 1971) and *Sauschlachten* (*Pigslaughter*, 1972) belong to the *VOLKSSTÜCK* revival, cynically showing an underclass degraded by the consumer society – in *Sauschlachten* a mute peasant lad is treated, then slaughtered as a pig by other villagers. These plays explore simple situations in crude but vigorous dialect. *Der tollste Tag* (*The Maddest Day*, 1972) is a coarsened, sharpened adaptation of BEAUMARCHAIS's *Marriage of Figaro*. To reach the '90 per cent of Austrians that theatre never touches' Turrini with W. Pevny turned to television with *Alpensaga*, the six-part story of the intrusion of politics and industry into an Alpine village between 1900 and 1950. He came back to theatre with *Der Minderleister* (*The Underperformer*, 1988), which explores the torment of a redundant steel-worker with surreal stage metaphors (see SURREALISM), dream scenes and explicit sex. With *Tod und Teufel* (*Death and the Devil*, 1990) and *Alpenglühen* (*Alpine Glow*, 1993) he achieved BURGTHEATER status, though these plays, like *Grillparzer im Pornoladen* (*Grillparzer in the Porn Shop*, 1993) continue to scourge the Establishment in flamboyant, anarchic vein.

**Tussaud, Madame** see WAXWORKS

**Tutin, Dorothy** 1931– British actress. She joined the Shakespeare Memorial Theatre at Stratford-upon-Avon in 1958 and played Ophelia, Viola and Juliet. In 1961 she played the tormented Sister Jeanne in JOHN WHITING's *The Devils* at the Aldwych Theatre. She stayed with the ROYAL SHAKESPEARE COMPANY to play Desdemona, Varya in *The Cherry Orchard*, Polly Peachum in *The Beggar's Opera* and to appear in JOHN BARTON's Shakespearian anthology on kingship, *The Hollow Crown*. This grounding in classical theatre helped her in her first major WEST END success, as Queen Victoria in *Portrait of a Queen* (1965), which went to New York in 1968; and her cool, controlled timing was a memorable feature of HAROLD PINTER's *Old Times* at the Aldwych in 1971. Lady Plyant in *The Double Dealer* (1978) was one of several roles played at the NATIONAL THEATRE in the late 1970s, including Madam Ranevsky in *The Cherry Orchard*. She played Hester in a revival of TERENCE RATTIGAN's *The Deep Blue Sea* (1981) and appeared in the West End production of Pinter's *A Kind of Alaska* (1985). Among her film parts were Sophie Breska in *Savage Messiah*. She has appeared in two recent Pinter plays, *Mountain Language* and *Party Time* (1991). In 1967 she was awarded the CBE.

**Tyler, George (Crouse)** 1867–1946 American manager and producer. In 1897 he joined forces with Theodore A. Liebler to found Liebler and Company in New York, which for the next 17 years produced some 300 plays; brought to America MRS PATRICK CAMPBELL, ELEONORA DUSE, RÉJANE and the ABBEY THEATRE; and managed stars such as ARNOLD DALY, JAMES O'NEILL and Gertrude Elliott. Tyler became an independent producer in 1918 and his productions included BOOTH TARKINGTON's *Clarence* (1919), EUGENE O'NEILL's *Anna Christie* (1921), KAUFMAN and CONNELLY's *Dulcy* (1921) and O'CASEY's *The Plough and the Stars* (1927). His revival of *Macbeth* in 1928 was designed by GORDON CRAIG. Tyler is noted for attracting European talent to the United States, and for preferring new works to revivals.

**Tyler, Royall** 1758–1826 American playwright. Educated at Harvard, Tyler wrote *The Contrast* (1787) in three weeks after seeing his first stage production, a New York performance of *The School for Scandal*. *The Contrast* was the first script by an American to receive a successful professional production. Despite an uninspiring plot, by dint of lively and humorous dialogue it contrasts the effete world of fashion with more macho types. Jonathan, a low comedy role played by WIGNELL, introduced the YANKEE character to the American stage.

**Tynan, Kenneth (Peacock)** 1927–80 British theatre critic. Briefly the director of the Lichfield Repertory Company and an actor, he then turned to journalism where his wit and unorthodox left-wing views made a powerful impression in the *Evening Standard* and, from 1954 to 1958, the *Observer*, where his theatre columns were outstanding. His liveliest journalism dates from this period, although he also wrote eloquently for the *New Yorker* (1958–60), the *Observer* again (1960–3) and as a freelance commentator (until his death). LAURENCE OLIVIER invited him to become literary adviser to the NATIONAL THEATRE (1963–9), and Tynan's influence was felt in the radical tone of the early seasons. He was an advocate of BRECHT and BECKETT, although he underrated HAROLD PINTER. He brought together an evening of 'elegant erotica', *Oh, Calcutta!*, the first and most successful sex REVUE which came in the wake of the abolition of CENSORSHIP in 1968. He published several essay and review collections, including *He That Plays the King* (1950), *Curtains* (1961) and *The Sound of Two Hands Clapping* (1975).

**Udall, Nicholas** 1505–56 English playwright. The most famous of his plays is *Ralph Roister Doister*, a comedy about the amorous manoeuvrings of its broadly drawn characters, possessing the robustness of the comedies of TERENCE and PLAUTUS which it imitated and adapted to a truly English context. Udall wrote other plays, but only *Ralph Roister Doister* can be attributed to him with any certainty, and its date of performance is not fully established. He taught at both Eton and Westminster schools, and the play seems to have been written for and performed by the boys at one of these.

**Ullmann, Liv** 1938– Norwegian actress. Ullmann's stage work is often mentioned as a footnote to her films (particularly those with INGMAR BERGMAN). However, she acted at Rogaland Teater, the NORSKE TEATRET and NATIONALTHEATRET, playing Anne Frank, Juliet and Saint Joan, before her international breakthrough in Bergman's film *Persona*. Some of her most important work has been in BRECHT at the Norske Teatret, including Grusha in *The Caucasian Chalk Circle* and Mother Courage. While she has typically been cast in roles that emphasize suffering, she individualizes it with great intensity, often incorporating a volatile anger.

**Ulster Literary Theatre** Irish company (from 1915 the Ulster Theatre). Founded in 1902, it proposed to enunciate a regional identity, a variant of the ABBEY's work, often in good-humoured SATIRE. The company toured England and Ireland and gave the premieres of some 50 Northern Irish plays. Apart from RUTHERFORD MAYNE, it cultivated no important dramatist and remained amateur to the end, though working to professional standards. Its demise in 1934 was due to the lack of either private or government financing.

***Uncle Tom's Cabin*** American novel and play. Harriet Beecher Stowe's novel, serialized from 1851, was first dramatized in Baltimore in January 1852. No American play has had such a remarkable stage history. The third version, by GEORGE L. AIKEN (now the accepted version), was performed by the HOWARD FAMILY in Troy, New York, in September 1852. In 1852–3 there were also productions in London, Berlin and Paris. The Howards made a life's work of 'Tomming', as did a host of American actors. 'Tom shows' under canvas were on the road in 1854; in the 1890s some 400 troupes were barnstorming across the country. Bloodhounds, dancers, singers and dioramas were among the theatrical novelties featured in Tom shows, of which there were still a dozen companies on the road in 1927.

**Uniti, Compagnia degli** COMMEDIA DELL'ARTE troupe. Said to have been founded in the late 16th century, it circulated throughout northern Italy under the protection of Vincenzo Gonzaga, Duke of Ferrara, and never toured abroad; it combined with the CONFIDENTI in 1583. Its leading players included, in 1584, ISABELLA ANDREINI; in 1593, DRUSIANO MARTINELLI as Arlecchino; and, in 1614, SILVIO FIORILLO as Captain Matamoros. The last notice of it occurs in 1640.

**Unity Theatre** London company and theatre. Developed from the Workers' Theatre Movement, it opened its first stage in a converted church hall in 1936 with the English premiere of ODETS's *Waiting for Lefty*, which became a model for left-wing theatre of the time with its AGIT-PROP form, audience participation and theme of strikers' solidarity. When it moved to a small 200-seat auditorium in 1937, Unity's political line was firmly established with the first of BRECHT's plays to be performed in London (*Señora Carrer's Rifles*); a satiric 'political pantomime' (*Babes in the Woods*); and the first English example of a LIVING NEWSPAPER, as well as the London GROUP THEATRE's production of Spender's *Trial of a Judge* in 1938. Unity continued to introduce new radical works, including O'CASEY's *The Star Turns Red* (1940), SARTRE's *Nekrassov* (1956), ADAMOV's *Spring '71* (1962) and Shatrov's *The Bolsheviks* (1970), until it was burnt down in 1975.

**University Wits** Name popularly given to a group of Elizabethan playwrights, among whom MARLOWE, GREENE, NASHE and PEELE are the most prominent, who were educated at Oxford or Cambridge University, lived in London and contributed significantly to the development of English drama. Most of them were hostile to the rising generation of playwrights, which included JONSON and SHAKESPEARE, who had lacked their educational advantages.

**Urban, Joseph** 1871–1933 Austrian-American set designer. Many of the approaches and techniques adopted by ROBERT EDMOND JONES, LEE SIMONSON and others were first introduced in America by Urban. In 1904 he began to work with the Vienna BURGTHEATER and then designed operas throughout Europe. He moved to the USA in 1912 to design for the Boston Opera. He was discovered by showman FLORENZ ZIEGFELD, who persuaded him to design for the *Follies*. Urban's designs were simple in terms of line, but vibrant colour created a sense of lushness and complexity. He applied pointillist techniques to scene painting, which added new dimensions and allowed parts of the image to appear or disappear under different coloured lights. He was also one of the first to use platforms and portals – arched scenic units at the side of the stage, connected at the top. This framed and focused the stage while providing continuous elements for unit sets.

**Usigli, Rodolfo** 1905–79 Mexican playwright and poet. During the 1930s and 1940s he launched Mexican dramaturgy with plays of lasting significance. Unaffiliated with the independence theatre movement in Mexico, Usigli emulated the best of world theatre and earned accolades from GEORGE BERNARD SHAW. His first major success was *El gesticulador* (*The Impostor*; written 1937, performed 1947), a study of hypocrisy. *Corona de sombre* (*Crown of Shadow*; written 1943, performed 1947) is a revisionist historical play on the period of Maximilian and Carlota in Mexico. It forms a trilogy with *Corona de luz* (*Crown of Light*, 1960) and *Corona de fuego* (*Crown of Fire*, 1961), which deal with the Virgin of Guadalupe and Cuauhtémoc, respectively. Other major works include *El niño y la niebla* (*The Boy and the Mist*, 1936–51), *Jano es una muchacha* (*Jano Is a Girl*, 1952) and *Buenos días, señor presidente* (*Good Morning, Mr President*, 1972), the latter rooted in CALDERÓN DE LA BARCA's *La vida es sueño* (*Life Is a Dream*) and growing out of the 1968 Tlatelolco massacre in Mexico. Known also for his explanatory prologues and epilogues, Usigli wrote more than 40 plays in addition to several substantial books on the theatre.

**vagantes** Travelling clerics. In medieval documents the term applies to disaffected and homeless clerics, students and Latin teachers, to distinguish them from ordinary rovers. They travelled throughout England, France and Germany in the 12th and 13th centuries, reciting disputatious poems and rollicking songs composed in vulgar Latin. In France these clerics were known as *goliards*, and the goliardic ballads are often forceful and obscene, sometimes anticlerical in tone, praising wine and women in song. One set, the *Carmina burana*, was put to music by Carl Orff (1936). The *vagantes* were important in disseminating a classical influence throughout the folk culture of their time.

**Vakhtangov, Evgeny (Bagrationovich)** 1883–1923 Armenian-born Russian director, actor and teacher. In 1911 Vakhtangov was accepted as an actor into the MOSCOW ART THEATRE (MAT), where he eventually became one of the leading teachers of the STANISLAVSKY system. His acting often featured an expressive, grotesque outer form developed from a psychological basis in such roles as Feste in *Twelfth Night* (1919). He believed in the actor's primacy in the theatre, his personality and imagination being his most significant tools in creating a performance somewhere between the poles of mere impersonation (Stanislavsky) and stylization (MEYERHOLD). His performance must include the skills of singing, dancing, vaudeville and MUSICAL COMEDY. A man of prodigious talent, energy and enthusiasm, at the height of his brief career and in the face of serious personal illness and national famine, Vakhtangov taught and directed at 14 theatres and studios, in addition to his work at MAT and its First and Second Studios. His best work was done at MAT's Third Studio (after 1926, the Vakhtangov Theatre) – CHEKHOV's *The Wedding* (1920), MAETERLINCK's *The Miracle of St Anthony* (1921), GOZZI's *Princess Turandot* (1922) – and with the Jewish HABIMAH Theatre on SOLOMON ANSKI's *The Dybbuk* (1922). GOZZI's *Princess Turandot* (1922), Vakhtangov's final and most famous production, spoofed the play's romanticism via frank theatricality, oriental conventions and a cubist set by Ignaty Nivinsky.

**Valdéz, Luis** 1940– Chicano director and playwright. Valdéz is responsible for the CHICANO THEATRE revolution. He visited Cuba before joining the SAN FRANCISCO MIME TROUPE in 1964. Knowledgeable about *COMMEDIA DELL'ARTE*, BRECHT and pantoMIME, he used bilingual theatre to help organize the migrant workers around Delano, California, in 1965. His efforts led to the *actos*, one-act revolutionary pieces, and the creation of EL TEATRO CAMPESINO (Farmworkers' Theatre), which in turn inspired the formation of other Chicano theatre groups. His early titles include *Las dos caras del patroncito* (*The Boss's Two Faces*), *Quinta temporada* (*Fifth Season*), *No saco nada de la escuela* (*I Don't Get Anything out of School*), *Vietnam campesino* (*Vietnam Farmer*), *Soldado razo* (*Buck Private*) and *Huelguistas* (*Strikers*). *Zoot Suit* (1978), based on the Sleepy Lagoon murder trial during World War II, dramatized the stereotypical *pachuco*. Valdéz's folk musical *Corridos*, based on popular Mexican folk ballad traditions, opened in 1983. Each season El Teatro Campesino stages *La Pastorela*, his adaptation from

Mexican folklore of the journey of the shepherds to the manger. In 1994 his musical about the bandit-hero, Tiburcio Vasquez, was staged in Los Angeles.

**Valentin, Karl** [Valentin Ludwig Fey] 1882–1948 German comedian. By 1907 he was the leading Munich comedian in his own monologues and sketches. In 1911 he met Liesl Karlstadt (Elisabeth Welleno, 1892–1961) who was his partner for 35 years, playing both male and female roles. They worked together until 1941, in Munich and on tour in Zurich, Vienna and Berlin. Lanky, cranky Valentin created more than 500 skits and FARCES that raised Bavarian folk comedy to a sphere of universal significance. His comic world comprised the recalcitrance of inanimate objects, cross-purposes of language and the malignity of human nature. Often, by a scene's end, the stage – a record shop, a radio studio or a variety stage – would be totally demolished, in the wake of monstrous physical and logical complications. His admirers included BRECHT, who compared him to Chaplin.

**Valle-Inclán, Ramón del** 1866–1936 Spanish novelist and playwright. From Galicia, he moved to Madrid. His first play, *Cenizas* (*Ashes*, 1899), was a poetic melodrama revised as *El yermo de las almas* (*The Desert of Souls*) in 1908. This was followed by a rural Galician trilogy, *Comedias bárbaras* (*Barbaric Comedies*), depicting the fossilized nobility of the region: *Aguila de blasón* (*The Emblazoned Eagle*, 1907), *Romance de lobos* (*Ballad of Wolves*, 1908) and *Cara de plata* (*Silver Face*, 1922). His growing interest in FARCES and the grotesque was evident from *La marquesa Rosalinda* (1912). Later farces included *La enamorada del rey* (*The Girl Who Loved the King*, 1920) and *Farsa y licencia de la reina castiza* (*Farce of the True Spanish Queen*, 1922), which satirizes the decadent and licentious court of Isabel II.

In 1920 *Luces de Bohemia* (*Lights of Bohemia*) was the first play to which Valle-Inclán gave the title *esperpento*, which he described as the systematic distortion of the norms of theatre and novel through the mathematics of the concave mirror. This he felt was necessary to portray corrupt society with enhanced truth, and foreshadows many elements of the THEATRE OF THE ABSURD. The play is a sombre evocation of the last days of the Bohemian poet Alejandro Sawa. Other *esperpento* plays are *Divinas palabras* (*Divine Words*, 1920) and *Los cuernos de don Friolero* (*Don Friolero the Cuckold*, 1921), a sour farce on the decadence of the military, using PUPPETS and actors. These plays have since been seen as his most original and important contribution to the theatre. They were published together as *Martes de carnaval* (*Shrove Tuesday*,1930).

**Valleran le Conte** fl.1590–1614 French actor-manager. One of the earliest of his kind to be documented, he began as a strolling provincial player. In 1599 he brought a company to Paris and signed a three-month lease at the HÔTEL DE BOURGOGNE, but prosperity eluded him. The bulk of his repertoire probably consisted of tragedies and tragicomedies by ALEXANDRE HARDY, whom he made company dramatist.

**Vampilov, Aleksandr (Valentinovich)** 1937–72 Soviet playwright. On the basis of a few plays, Vampilov, a native Siberian, has been called the greatest playwright of his generation. His one-act comedy *The House Overlooking a Field* (1964) was published in the influential Moscow journal *Theatre*, and was soon followed by *Farewell in June*. Whereas the young protagonists of *Farewell in June* and *The Elder Son* (1967) are still capable of making a moral choice, the confirmed middle-aged egoists of Vampilov's two best plays, *Duck Hunting* (1967) and *Last Summer in Chulimsk* (1971), either no longer care or are no longer able to do so. In *Duck Hunting*, the last of his plays to be staged in the USSR (at the Theatre of Russian Drama in Riga, 1976) and the most bitter, he created a model of the 'urban grotesque' which has been adapted by other Soviet dramatists such as Lyudmila Petrushevskaya, Semyon Zlotnikov, Mark Rozovsky, Viktor Slavkin, ARBUZOV and VOLODIN. The anti-hero of *Duck Hunting* is a crippled personality, regarded as an aberration like the old duck who can no longer migrate. This theme is echoed in *Last Summer in Chulimsk*, about people living at the edge of the Siberian wilderness. Vampilov's indebtedness to the traditional FARCE-*vaudeville* is demonstrated in his unfinished *vaudeville The Incomparable Nakonechnikov* (1971) and in the two plays published under the title *Provincial Anecdotes* (1971) – *Twenty Minutes with an Angel* (1962) and *An Incident with a Typesetter* (1970).

**Van Itallie, Jean-Claude** 1936– Belgian-born American playwright and director. Van Itallie took American citizenship in 1952. In 1963 he wrote *War*. His *Motel* and *Pavanne* were produced at the Café LA MAMA in 1965. *American Hurrah* appeared at the Pocket Theatre, New York, in 1966. *The Serpent* premiered in Rome in 1968 and was produced by the OPEN THEATRE, New York, in 1969. Other scripts include *King of the US* (1972), *Mystery Play* (1973), and adaptations of Chekhov scripts. His 1991 play about the effects of AIDS, *Ancient Boys* (La MaMa), was not well received. Van Itallie's affiliation with JOSEPH CHAIKIN and the Open Theatre placed him at the forefront of experimental dramaturgy in the 1960s and 1970s, when he was seen to merge European traditions with a poetic vision of American experience.

**Vanbrugh, Sir John** 1664–1726 English playwright and architect. While still an army captain he wrote *The Relapse* (1696), a comic sequel to COLLEY CIBBER's *Love's Last Shift*. In 1697 his SATIRE on contemporary society, *Aesop*, was performed, as well as *The Provoked Wife*, in which Vanbrugh analyses loveless marriage and divorce. Attacked by JEREMY COLLIER for immorality, he defended himself wittily in *A Short Vindication of The Relapse and The Provoked Wife* (1698). He adapted a play by DANCOURT as a FARCE, *The Country House* (1698), FLETCHER's *The Pilgrim* (1700), another Dancourt play as *The Confederacy* (1705) and a MOLIÈRE comedy as *Squire Trelooby* (1704). His last unfinished comedy was completed by Cibber as *The Provoked Husband* in 1728.

His career as an architect began in 1699 with Castle Howard. He designed and managed the Queen's Theatre in the Haymarket, which opened in 1705, and Blenheim Palace, for which he was Surveyor from 1705 to 1716. He was knighted in 1714.

**Vargas Llosa, Mario** 1936– Peruvian novelist and playwright. Primarily known for his outstanding novels, he also wrote *La señorita de Tacna* (*The Girl from Tacna*, 1981), dramatizing the process of storytelling, followed by *Kathie y el hipopótamo* (*Kathie and the Hippopotamus*, 1983) and *La Chunga* (1986).

**variety** Popular entertainment. Variety was the most widespread and widely attended form of urban enter-

tainment in the 19th and early 20th centuries. The element of variety is common to popular theatre, which seeks to engage limited attention spans with a diversity of skills. Egypt in the 5th century BC had its sequences of musicians, dancers, acrobats and female JUGGLERS performing for rich men's guests; and the wandering minstrel of the Middle Ages was capable of a broad range of diversions. As a distinct genre, variety was organized in the 19th century in the music-halls and public houses of Europe and America, took on elements of CIRCUS, and ramified into CABARET and REVUE. A major contributory factor to its prominence was a new proletarian public, who had lost their communal village traditions and were receptive to less demanding, cheaper and more colourful amusement than the 'legitimate' theatre offered. Innovative forms of publicity and presentation developed, to exploit the form's commercial potential.

Variety can be identified by its series of attractions, 'turns' or 'numbers', unconnected by any theme. In contrast to the modern dramatic theatre, the audience is encouraged to eat, drink and smoke during the performance. In Great Britain, the common form was the MUSIC-HALL, which took to calling itself 'variety' as it gained respectability; in America, in contrast, 'variety' preferred to be known as VAUDEVILLE. Nomenclature is confused: the chief European terms are, in France, the *café concert* and *CAFÉ CHANTANT* and, later, the revue-like music-hall; in Germany, the low *SINGSPIEL*halle and *TINGELTANGEL* and the more circus-like and spectacular *variété*; in Russia, the disreputable *myuzik-kholl* and the all-encompassing *estrada*. In Spain variety remained closely linked to folkloric dance and song, in Italy to circus. Variety's apogee came before World War I; afterwards, it had to compete with and was absorbed by cinema, radio and television. Its influence on the literary drama has been enormous (e.g. BRECHT), but more especially it has been a constant inspiration for experimental theatrical innovators, from the Italian futurists of the 1910s to radical feminist groups of the 1980s.

**Vasari, Giorgio** 1511–74 Italian architect, painter, stage designer and biographer. One of the key figures in the development of perspective stage setting, he worked in Venice on a production of ARETINO's *La Talanta* (1541) and later, in Florence, built the wooden theatre of the Palazzo Vecchio and devised the spectacular entertainments to celebrate the marriage of Francesco de'Medici and Giovanna d'Austria in 1566. In 1569 he introduced an important innovation in stage decoration with a system of rotating PERIAKTOI. His *Vite de'piu eccellenti pittori, scultori ed architetti* (*Lives of the Most Excellent Painters, Sculptors and Architects*, 1530–68) is an invaluable source of information.

**vaudeville** American popular entertainment. This form of variety has nothing to do with the French *vaudeville*, a farce studded with songs set to popular tunes; rather, the term attempted to lend a veneer of elegance to what was originally rough and ready entertainment. The usual venue for VARIETY performances in the late 1860s was the concert saloon, where broad comedy and exuberant dance predominated. This 'honky tonk' style permutated into the BURLESQUE SHOW, while respectable variety gained greater professionalism and urbanity between 1876 and 1893 to become vaudeville.

The birth of vaudeville was 24 October 1881, when TONY PASTOR, hoping to lure a family audience with promises of clean amusement, opened his 14th Street

Theatre, New York. The innovation was enlarged and expanded by B. F. Keith (1846–1914) and his associate Edward F. Albee (1857–1930). Keith and Albee owned several theatres and in 1894 opened the first exclusively vaudeville house, the Boston Colonial, typical of the opulent palaces designed to lure the middle-class spectator into a fairy-tale world of luxury. Keith and Albee eliminated offensive material, fining offenders, and introduced the continuous show, so that one could enter the theatre at any time between 9.30 a.m. and 10.30 p.m. and see a performance.

The Keith–Albee circuit dominated the eastern United States through its many theatres (over 400 by 1920) and booking offices; Martin Beck's Orpheum circuit played the West, though he also built the New York PALACE, which soon was regarded as vaudeville's Valhalla. In addition, there were thousands of small houses scattered throughout the nation, enabling performers to play one-night stands all through the season. Vaudevillians became a nomadic race, living much of the year in railway carriages and on platforms and in dreary boarding-houses.

By 1900 the typical 'polite vaudeville' bill had grown formulaic, and was divided into two parts by an intermission. Turns or 'numbers' seldom lasted more than 10 to 20 minutes, although some popular egoists like HARRY LAUDER and AL JOLSON might usurp a whole hour. According to George Burns, a performer needed only 17 good minutes, which he could play year in, year out across the country. In addition to the song-and-dance and comedy acts, there were MIME artists, ventriloquists, eccentrics, musical virtuosi, acrobats and JUGGLERS, male and female impersonators (see MALE and FEMALE IMPERSONATION), miniature musicals, monologuists, trained animals (see ANIMALS AS PERFORMERS), conjurors, demonstrations of new inventions, and even famous criminals discoursing on their lurid past.

Much of the comedy in vaudeville dealt in racial stereotypes, with the Dutch, Irish, Jewish, blackface, Swedish and Italian comics the most familiar, reflecting the melting-pot nature of urban American society. Low comedy was categorized as 'jazz', a fast routine to speed up an act; 'hokum', crude fun verging on vulgarity. Dance tended to be acrobatic until World War I, when adagio and exhibition ballroom dancing and even imitations of the Ballets Russes arrived. Among the leading performers spawned by vaudeville or trained in its excellent school were W. C. FIELDS, who moved from juggling to comic skits; EDDIE CANTOR and Al Jolson, who retained the corked face of minstrelsy (see MINSTREL SHOW), as did the black comedian BERT WILLIAMS; GEORGE M. COHAN, whose family had been variety pioneers; WILL ROGERS with his low-key commentary; and GEORGE BURNS AND GRACIE ALLEN. As vaudeville increased in respectability and popularity, stars of the 'legit', like LILLIE LANGTRY, Ethel Barrymore (see DREW–BARRYMORE FAMILY) and ALLA NAZIMOVA, played 'tab' versions of their dramatic hits on the circuits.

Vaudeville was the dominant form of American entertainment by 1890, and grew exponentially: in 1896 New York had seven vaudeville theatres; by 1910, 22. It came to be clearly differentiated into the Big Time, with its two-a-day offerings of an eight- or nine-act bill, and the Small Time with fewer acts and a film played continuously.

The decline of vaudeville is attributable to a number of factors. Between 1905 and 1912 the Big Time had grown in sophistication, putting its emphasis on glamour, novelty and lavish wardrobes; the influence of MUSICAL COMEDY and REVUE could be felt. Before 1925, vaudeville reached its period of greatest growth, but the cinema proved a powerful rival for the working-class audiences. By the mid-1920s many vaudeville houses were converted to cinemas, and the succumbing of the Palace in 1932, its *coup de grâce* delivered by the Depression, is considered the symbolic terminus of the form.

**Vauthier, Jean** 1910– Belgian playwright. He is remembered for the creation of Capitaine Bada, a cross between the common man and the writer who struggles for control of his life and his language but becomes lost in a welter of baroque poetic prose. BARRAULT scored a personal triumph in *Le Personnage combattant* (*The Fighting Character*, 1956) and in 1966 *Capitaine Bada* was revived by Marcel Maréchal, who also commissioned *Le Sang* (*Blood*, 1970).

**Vedrenne, J(ohn) E(ugene)** 1867–1930 British theatre manager. He became manager of the ROYAL COURT THEATRE, where he brought in GRANVILLE BARKER for the 1904 season. There and, in 1907, at the Savoy they mounted a series of productions that influenced the whole development of British theatre – not only establishing SHAW on the public stage, but introducing GALSWORTHY and HAUPTMANN. Their example encouraged the formation of the new REPERTORY THEATRE movement in Britain, while Vedrenne's insistence on a fixed, modest expense allowance per production enforced simplified settings that focused attention on ensemble acting. After the partnership was dissolved in 1911 he became manager of the Royalty Theatre, and in 1920 of the Little Theatre (London).

***veedhi natakam*** Indian theatre form. The term *veedhi* means 'street'. *Natakam* means 'drama'. Once a popular genre of traditional theatre in Andhra Pradesh, a state in south India, it is now on the decline. The stories performed in *veedhi natakam* are drawn from the epics and the *Puranas*. Troupes of players perform from November to May, playing in the open air, usually in squares or before village temples. Today exponents adapt popular film music in place of traditional folk melodies to the dramatic action. The actors sing all the songs and a chorus of musicians repeats various lines and phrases for emphasis. A harmonium provides the basic melodic line and the *tabla* drums keep the tempo.

**Vega (Carpio), Lope (Félix) de** 1562–1635 Spanish playwright, poet and novelist. He rivals CALDERÓN DE LA BARCA as the greatest dramatist of the GOLDEN AGE. A child prodigy, he was famous as a poet in his twenties, his great plays being written from his late thirties. He had many scandalous affairs with actresses, even after becoming a priest in 1614 on the death of his second wife. He wrote little after 1625.

Five hundred plays ascribed to him have survived; at least 314 are accepted as his by modern critics. Lope developed and established the three-act verse COMEDIA as the standard Spanish play of the period. The range of subjects treated was enormous, including COMEDY, TRAGEDY, FARCE, lives of saints, PASTORAL and historical, though he tended to blur the distinctions. He varied the metre according to the type of scene, favouring the eight-syllable ballad metre. Some of his views on drama are given in the laconic and ironical *Arte nuevo de hacer comedias en este tiempo* (*New Art of Playwriting for Today*) published in 1609. In this poem he defends his art against the attacks of the classicists, including his mixing of comic and tragic scenes, following GUARINI; he recommends the unity of action, though not those of place and time; he comments on types of theme, on plot construction and on metre. Throughout he defends what practice has shown to be successful rather than the demands of theorists.

The largest group of Lope's plays are *capa y espada* comedies (a kind of *comedia*) such as *El acero de Madrid* (*Madrid Spa*, 1602–12), in which a gallant disguises himself as a doctor and prescribes daily visits to the spa for his lady so that they can meet. Lope also wrote court comedies, including the brilliant *El perro del hortelano* (*The Dog in the Manger*, 1613–15) in which a countess falls in love with her secretary, a commoner.

Some of the most famous of Lope's plays are those in which a peasant is forced to defend his honour and his wife against a tyrannical overlord. In *Fuenteovejuna* (1612–14) the people of the town of that name rise in revolt against their lord and murder him and his servants. Under torture they will only say, 'Fuenteovejuna did it', and are eventually pardoned by the king since no culprit can be identified. *Peribáñez* (1605–8) and *El mejor alcalde el rey* (*The King Is the Best Justice*, 1620–3) emphasize the need for a strong bond between monarch and peasant. Other plays, on the theme of adultery and honour, range from the witty *El castigo del discreto* (*The Wise Man's Punishment*, 1598–1601) to the bloody, ballad-inspired *Los comendadores de Córdoba* (*The Knights-Commander of Córdoba*, 1596). In *El castigo sin venganza* (*Punishment without Revenge*, 1631) an elderly libidinous duke is obliged to procure the deaths of his young wife and his illegitimate son when he discovers their affair, which is a direct result of his neglect. In doing so he also loses any chance of an heir. Other fine tragedies include *El duque de Viseo* (*The Duke of Viseo*, 1608–9?) and the lyrical *El caballero de Olmedo* (*The Knight of Olmedo*, 1620–5?).

Lope's vivid characterization and apparent REALISM have made him frequently more popular than the supposedly more cerebral Calderón de la Barca.

**Velten, Johannes** 1640–?93 German actor. From 1685 Velten led a troupe of players under the patronage of the Elector of Saxony. He did much to raise standards of acting and of repertoire. He introduced, in German adaptation, plays of CORNEILLE, RACINE and MOLIÈRE. His troupe combined both improvisational and scripted acting. Some years after his death, it was taken over by CAROLINE NEUBER.

**Verdon, Gwen** 1926– American dancer, singer and actress. Considered to be the finest MUSICAL COMEDY dancer of the 1950s, Verdon made her BROADWAY debut as a dancer in *Alive and Kicking* (1950). Following her success as the seductive Lola in *Damn Yankees* (1955), she showed her acting skill in *New Girl in Town* (1957), a musical version of EUGENE O'NEILL's *Anna Christie*. She next appeared in *Redhead*, a vehicle written especially for her. In 1966 she created the role of Charity Hope Valentine in *Sweet Charity*, directed by her husband, BOB FOSSE. Her only musical of the 1970s was *Chicago* (1975). Verdon's sinuous, energetic style of dance ideally suited the jazz choreography created for her by Fosse and JACK COLE.

**Verga, Giovanni** 1840–1922 Italian novelist and playwright. He was the foremost representative of late-19th-century Italian literary naturalism (*VERISMO*). Much of his work depicted the lives of the peasants and fisher folk of his native Sicily, in a poetic and highly original

prose. In addition to his better-known non-dramatic work, he achieved success on the stage with *Cavalleria rusticana* (*Rustic Chivalry*, 1884), in which DUSE enjoyed one of her greatest triumphs. Derived from one of his own short stories, this one-act play was justly praised for the originality of its setting (a Sicilian village square) and formal qualities. *La lupa* (1896), likewise taken from a short story, was a vehicle for strong female leads. A more ambitious three-act play, *Dal tuo al mio* (*From Yours to Mine* 1903), attempted to treat of class conflict on a broader social canvas and provoked some controversy, but won only limited success.

***verismo*** Italian artistic and literary movement. It flourished in the late 19th and early 20th centuries, indebted to French NATURALISM. The most significant figures in the Italian theatre were the dramatists GIACOSA and VERGA. Important too were the ideas of the Sicilian writer CAPUANA. In drama *verismo* had two broad manifestations. One was a region-based drama rooted in the observation of local life, sometimes in dialect, occasionally marred by folkloristic simplification, but at its best a powerful representation of elemental passions and social conflict. Examples are Verga's *Cavalleria rusticana* (*Rustic Chivalry*) and *La lupa*, BRACCO's *Don Pietro Caruso* and Bertolazzi's *El nost Milan*, Capuana's *Malia* and De Roberto's *Il rosario*. The other manifestation was a bourgeois naturalistic drama, e.g. PRAGA's *La moglie ideale* (*The Ideal Wife*), Rovetta's *I disonesti*, Giacosa's *Tristi amori* (*Sad Loves*) and *Come le foglie* (*Like the Leaves*). Verismo produced the first distinctively national drama in Italy after decades of rather passive imitation of French drame. It helped to breed a new school of actors who drew upon romantic REALISM but accommodated that to more familiar locales and subject-matter.

**Vestris,** Madame [Lucy Elizabeth Bartolozzi] 1797–1856 English actress, singer and theatre manager. Briefly married to the French ballet dancer, Armand Vestris (1787–1825), she became a star in the 1820 revival of W. T. MONCRIEFF's *Giovanni in London* (1817) at DRURY LANE. Showing her legs as well as her voice to best advantage, she starred in BREECHES PARTS such as Macheath in *The Beggar's Opera*. In 1830 she boldly leased the OLYMPIC. From 1831to 1839 her innovations in COSTUME and stage decoration gave new impetus to pictorial staging. There is some dispute about whether she was the first manager to employ a BOX SET. J. R. PLANCHÉ's exquisite BURLESQUE extravaganzas were the outstanding features of the Olympic repertoire and her company included LISTON, the KEELEYS and CHARLES JAMES MATHEWS, whom Vestris married. They toured America together (1838), jointly managed COVENT GARDEN (1839–42), and later, after debt and imprisonment, the London LYCEUM (1847–55).

**Vianna Filho, Oduvaldo** 1936–74 Brazilian playwright and actor. Son of playwright Oduvaldo Vianna, in 1956 he joined São Paulo's Arena Theatre which produced his early plays. In 1964 he co-founded Rio's Opinion Theatre which, with Arena and Workshop, led the *engagé* theatre movement of the 1960s. *Se Correr o Bicho Pega, se Ficar o Bicho Come* (*If You Run the Beast Will Catch You, If You Stay the Beast Will Eat You*, 1965) was a veiled reference to the military dictatorship (1964). Before his death, CENSORSHIP prevented productions of his later plays, but *Rasga Coração* (*Heart Stopping*, 1974), staged in 1979 by Arena founder José Renato, was a posthumous success. Along with BOAL and GUARNIERI he established a legacy of well crafted plays that communicated social consciousness through a Brazilian fusion of BRECHTian technique and intense emotion.

**Viau, Théophile de** 1590–1626 French poet and playwright. One play has survived, the tragedy *Pyrame et Thisbe*. Published in 1623 but probably first performed earlier at the HÔTEL DE BOURGOGNE, it is a fine example of baroque verse tragedy, with medieval-style multiple-stage setting and decor provided by MAHELOT.

**Vicente, Gil** c.1460–c.1539 Portuguese playwright and actor. He also wrote a number of plays wholly or partly in Spanish. Vicente was the founder of the Portuguese theatre, and its major dramatist. He was connected with the court, probably before the death of King John II in 1495, contributing to musical and poetic spectacles. His first play, the *Monólogo do Vaquiero* (*Monologue of the Cowherd*), was recited or acted, possibly by Vicente himself, on the occasion of the birth of the future king John III in 1502. As in a similar play by ENCINA, a cowherd stumbles into the royal bedchamber and with rustic humour and simplicity makes an offer of produce to the baby prince on behalf of the nation. Vicente's other PASTORAL plays are less memorable, with the exception of the *Auto da Sibila Cassandra* (*Sibyl Cassandra's Play*, 1513). The *Monólogo* is the first of over 40 works of varying lengths that he wrote and produced for the court.

Vicente's religious theatre synthesizes the themes and staging of the Middle Ages. It includes the *Auto da Alma* (*Play of the Soul*, 1518), a MORALITY PLAY, with Soul making her way to the safety of Mother Church; the trilogy known as the *Barcas* (*The Ship of Hell*, 1516; *The Ship of Purgatory*, 1518; *The Ship of Heaven*, 1519), which puts the whole of humanity into the dock of individual judgement at the point of death; and the *Breve Sumário da História de Deus* (*A Brief Summary of the Story of God*), in which Time and World preside over the passage of humanity from Adam to Christ, in a play calling for split-level simultaneous staging.

His many *farsas* (FARCES) deal with human, social and institutional foibles and abuses. The eponymous heroine of *Inês Pereira* (1523) buries her first husband, then marries a dolt of a yeoman and literally rides off at the end of the play to his cuckolding. The protagonist of the *Juiz da Beira* (*The J. P. from Beira*, 1526) is a figure very much in the mould of BRECHT's Azdak in his ambivalent sentencings.

In these religious plays and comedies, as well as in chivalresque tragicomedies and court MASQUES, Vicente deployed theatrical skills that were not equalled anywhere in Europe for another 60 or 70 years.

**Victoria Theatre** (Stoke-on-Trent) Britain's first permanent theatre-in-the-round began life as STEPHEN JOSEPH's touring Studio Theatre Company. In 1962 it became based in a converted cinema on the border between Stoke and Newcastle-under-Lyme. Peter Cheeseman has been its director since 1966. The company is best known for its documentary plays – entertaining blends of music, song and dramatized research into actual events in the area, including the building of the local railways (*The Knotty*) and the threatened closure of the nearby steelworks (*Fight for Shelton Bar*). These have created strong bonds with the surrounding communities. The repertoire also includes the classics and new plays (sometimes by resident dramatists, such as PETER TERSON) and each season is organized on a true REPERTORY basis. 1986 saw the opening of the New Victoria Theatre, a purpose-built theatre-in-the-round.

**Viertel, Berthold** 1885–1955 Austrian director.

Instrumental in promoting the plays of HASENCLEVER, BRONNEN and KAISER, he produced BRECHT's *Fear and Suffering in the Third Reich* under the title of *The Private Life of the Master Race* in New York in 1945, and worked at the BERLINER ENSEMBLE before becoming director of the Vienna BURGTHEATER in 1951.

**Vieux-Colombier Theatre** (Paris) This 19th-century theatre building in the street of that name on the left bank of the Seine was renovated by COPEAU in 1913 as the launching pad for his renewal of French theatre. It was again remodelled by JOUVET after World War I so as to approximate an Elizabethan stage, and Copeau's company performed there between 1920 and 1924. It was occupied by the COMPAGNIE DES QUINZE in 1931 and then continued under commercial management until it closed in 1972. It saw the first Paris performances of such influential plays as SARTRE's *Huis Clos* (*In Camera*, 1944), T. S. ELIOT's *Murder in the Cathedral* (1945) and ADAMOV's *Paolo Paoli* (1957). In 1993 the theatre was rescued, restored and reopened as the second house of the COMÉDIE-FRANÇAISE.

**Viganò, Salvatore** 1769–1821 Italian choreographer and dancer. He made his debut as a choreographer at the age of 17 with an intermezzo. Later at the San Samuele Theatre in Venice he scored signal success as dancer and choreographer. In Vienna he created some of his most significant works, including *Die Gasehöpfe der Prometheus* (1801) to Beethoven's music, brilliantly fantastic and allegorical ballets. His Shakespearian subjects included an *Othello* in 1818.

**Vigarani, Gaspare** 1586–1663 Italian theatre architect and stage designer. Although he had a well established reputation in Italy, particularly for his theatre at Modena (1654), his most famous work was done in Paris, where he designed a new theatre to replace the PETIT-BOURBON. The result was the SALLE DES MACHINES, based on the Modena theatre and constructed in the Tuileries Palace. When it opened in 1662 with *Ercole Amante* (*Hercules in Love*) it was the largest theatre in Europe. It accommodated 7,000 spectators and had a stage 140 feet deep. The elaborate settings and machinery included a device that raised the entire royal family above the stage. Vigarani was very jealous of his rival GIACOMO TORELLI and had the latter's machinery removed from the Petit-Bourbon before it was demolished, ostensibly to use it in the new theatre. Instead, he had it burned. After his death Vigarani was succeeded at court by his son Carlo (1623–1713), who held the post until 1680 and designed primarily at the Palace of Versailles. Carlo Vigarani's best-known work was MOLIÈRE and LULLY's *Les Plaisirs de l'Île Enchantée* (*Pleasures of the Enchanted Isle*, 1664), a spectacular three-day celebration.

**Vigny, Alfred de** 1797–1863 French poet, playwright and novelist. He was a leading figure in the French romantic movement. Vigny's reputation as a dramatist rests on two plays: *Le More de Venise, Othello* (1829) and *Chatterton* (1835), both performed at the Théâtre-Français (see COMÉDIE-FRANÇAISE). At this time, SHAKESPEARE was being re-evaluated in France: Vigny, in his *Othello*, did not attempt to turn Shakespeare's play into a neoclassical tragedy, as DUCIS had done; he made a free, but generally faithful, translation. He also wrote a three-act version of *The Merchant of Venice*. In 1831 his historical drama, *La Maréchale d'Ancre*, with MLLE GEORGE in the title role, was performed at the ODÉON. *Chatterton*, with its theme of a poet driven to suicide by a philistine society, was one of the great successes of the romantic theatre and offered a superb role to MARIE DORVAL (Vigny's mistress) as a sensitive soul who dies of a love she cannot express.

**Vilar, Jean** 1912–71 French actor and director. Vilar trained with DULLIN and began to direct avant-garde productions in Paris during the Occupation. In 1947 he founded the AVIGNON FESTIVAL, where he developed the virtues of COPEAU's bare stage, performing in the courtyard of the papal palace. His uncluttered production style suited heroic tragedy, but also enabled him to present MOLIÈRE, MARIVAUX and MUSSET in a new light. As an actor of mature roles he complemented the young GÉRARD PHILIPE. In 1951 he was put in control of the THÉÂTRE NATIONAL POPULAIRE at CHAILLOT. He insisted that theatre should be 'a public service' available to all. His repertoire consisted of classics and modern classics but his few attempts at new plays were box-office failures. In 1963 he left the TNP to devote himself to the Avignon festival, but in 1968 he was fiercely attacked by young revolutionaries who mistook his lifelong left-wing commitment for compromise. His attempt to reconcile social and political commitment with high-class theatre art influenced many practitioners, notably MNOUCHKINE, PLANCHON and VITEZ.

**Villaurrutia, Xavier** 1903–50 Mexican playwright and poet. With SALVADOR NOVO he co-founded the TEATRO DE ULISES in 1928. Villaurrutia experimented with the most recent European techniques and, after the early demise of the Ulysses theatre, continued with TEATRO DE ORIENTACIÓN in the same mould. His plays often show the influence of GIRAUDOUX and LENORMAND. The *Autos profanos* (1933–7) are five short humorous pieces with strong philosophical foundations. Major plays are *La hiedra* (*The Ivy*, 1942) based on RACINE's *Phèdre* and *Invitación a la muerte* (*Invitation to Death*, 1940), with overtones of *Hamlet*.

**Villegas, Oscar** 1943– Mexican playwright. His plays are highly experimental in form and language, greatly influenced by rock music in theme and structure. They include *El renacimiento* (*The Renaissance*, 1967), *Santa Catarina* (*St Catherine*, 1969) and *Mucho gusto en conocerlo* (*Pleased to Meet You*, 1985). His major work is *Atlántida* (*Atlantis*, 1976), a full-length play which examines values among youth outside mainstream society. The techniques used are daring and innovative; major themes are aspects of individual freedom and expression. *La eternidad acaba mañana* (*Eternity Ends Tomorrow*) was shown in 1994.

**Vilna Troupe** Yiddish company. This celebrated cooperative company opened in Russia in 1916 with two immediately successful productions of SHOLOM ASCH's *The Landsman* and PERETZ HIRSHBEIN's *The Forsaken Nook*. With DAVID HERMAN as director and JACOB BEN-AMI as leading actor, the company's achievements soon brought a much needed dignity to European YIDDISH THEATRE, and various 'wings', or detachments, set out on world tours. Its most famous production, SOLOMON ANSKI's *The Dybbuk*, toured continuously for many years. The Warsaw wing achieved its greatest success with Sholom Asch's *Kiddush Hashem*, whilst the Berlin wing toured a particularly striking production of Peretz Hirshbein's *The Haunted Inn*. There were also Romanian and American wings.

**Vinaver, Michel** 1927– French novelist and playwright. An early play, *Les Coréens* (*The Koreans*, 1956), had some success. Between *Iphigénie Hôtel* (written in 1959) and *Par-dessus bord* (*Overboard*, written in 1969; directed

by PLANCHON, 1973) he wrote no plays, devoting himself to business, the world which provides the material for most of his later plays – e.g. *La Demande d'emploi* (*Situation Vacant*, 1973); *Les Travaux et les jours* (*Works and Days*, 1979); *À la renverse* (*Bending over Backwards*, 1980). These consist of minimal plot and ambiguous, fragmentary dialogues interweaving different streams of consciousness. Vinaver has been associated with the *théâtre du* QUOTIDIEN because of the everyday concerns and realistic nature of his characters, but in his more ambitious plays such as *Par-dessus bord* mythical archetypes underlie modern stories and NATURALISM alternates with sequences which question the possibility of representation. JACQUES LASSALLE directed a COMÉDIE-FRANÇAISE company in his major play *L'Émission de télévision* at the ODÉON in 1990, produced in 1992 at London's GATE THEATRE as *The Television Programme*.

**Vincent, Jean-Pierre** 1942– French director. He founded the Théâtre de l'Espérance at the Montmartre Palace Theatre in 1972 in collaboration with Jean Jourdheuil. Here he produced BRECHT, BÜCHNER and VISHNEVSKY, as well as modern French works. In 1975 he became director of the Théâtre National de Strasbourg, staging translations of new German writing and French plays of the QUOTIDIEN. In 1983 he was appointed director of the COMÉDIE-FRANÇAISE, but resigned three years later to return to freelance directing. In 1990 he was appointed to succeed PATRICE CHÉREAU at the Théâtre des Amandiers at Nanterre.

**Visconti, Luchino** 1906–76 Italian film and theatre director. Best known for his films, including *Morte a Venezia* (*Death in Venice*, 1971), he was also a distinguished director in the 'straight' and musical theatre. He came to prominence after World War II directing plays by e.g. ARTHUR MILLER, TENNESSEE WILLIAMS, SARTRE and ANOUILH, and discovering in classic plays dimensions of social REALISM hitherto ignored, as in his stage re-evaluation of GOLDONI's *La locandiera* (1952). His early productions of SHAKESPEARE included *Troilus and Cressida* (1949) and *Macbeth* (1958). At once lyrical and realistic, flamboyant and analytical, his work often aroused vigorous enthusiasm or hostility. He also staged operas, particularly those of Verdi. Among his notable stage productions of the 1960s and 1970s were CHEKHOV's *The Cherry Orchard* (1965) and PINTER's *Old Times* (1973), in which he explored the passage of time and its effects with an underlying melancholy that became increasingly prominent, too, in his film work.

**Visé, Jean Donneau de** 1638–1710 French man of letters, critic and journalist. He fomented the hostile reaction to MOLIÈRE's *L'École des femmes* (*The School for Wives*) in 1663. Nevertheless, several of his later plays were performed by Molière's company, and he collaborated with THOMAS CORNEILLE, e.g. on *La Devineresse* (*The Fortune-Teller*, 1679). In 1672 he founded *Le Mercure Galant*, the gazette of French social and literary life.

**Vishnevsky, Vsevolod (Vitalievich)** 1900–51 Soviet playwright. He drew upon his experiences as a member of the Red Army in composing dramas of epic sweep and heroism. *The First Horse Army* (1929) commemorates and mythologizes Red Cavalry leader Marshal Semyon Budyony. His most famous play, *An Optimistic Tragedy* (1934), about a heroic female commissar's sacrifice of her own life to instil discipline in a motley group of seamen during the Civil War, gave its name to a new type of play. Vishnevsky points towards the 'conflictless dramas' of socialist realism. TAIROV's famous 1934 production at the Kamerny Theatre, with his wife ALISA KOONEN as the commissar, established the model for succeeding productions. Vishnevsky blatantly falsified history in his last play *Unforgotten 1919* (1949), which fabricates a heroic role for Stalin in the Revolution.

**Vitez, Antoine** 1930–90 French actor and director. Russian in origin, with strong communist sympathies, he first acted and directed in the decentralized theatres. Vitez achieved his effects by unusual direction of actors, encouraging them to go for unexpected body movements, to play against the text, to break accepted conventions. From 1968 he was an influential teacher at the Conservatoire. His choice of repertoire was broad – classical and modern. In 1981 he became director of the CHAILLOT THEATRE, where he continued to direct experimental productions with his famous slogan: 'elite theatre for all'. In 1988 he was appointed administrator-director of the COMÉDIE-FRANÇAISE and embarked on an ambitious programme of reforms, cut short by his death.

**Vitrac, Roger** 1899–1952 French poet and playwright. Active in the dada movement, he founded the Théâtre Alfred Jarry with ARTAUD in 1926. Here two of his plays were performed, *Les Mystères de l'amour* (*The Mysteries of Love*, 1927) and *Victor, ou Les enfants au pouvoir* (*Victor, or Power to Children*, 1928). The latter is a masterpiece of surrealist theatre (see SURREALISM), evidenced in the 1962 revival by ANOUILH. Set in 1909, *Victor* satirizes middle-class manners, patriotism and the conventions of BOULEVARD comedy by means of a grotesque child, Victor, who is nine years old but already six feet tall and can see through all the social pretence that surrounds him.

**Vivian Beaumont** and **Mitzi E. Newhouse Theatres** (New York City) Part of the Lincoln Center for the Performing Arts, the repertory theatre with its experimental appendage began under the aegis of ELIA KAZAN and Robert Whitehead. Named after its benefactress, the Vivian Beaumont opened in 1965. With 11,000 square feet of stage space, it was intended to convert from PROSCENIUM to thrust stage. The smaller stage (originally the Forum) was intended for experimental productions. JOSEPH PAPP (1973–7) obtained funds from Mitzi E. Newhouse, and renamed the Forum accordingly. After Papp's departure, the theatres were reopened only intermittently, until 1985 when Gregory Mosher and Bernard Gersten took over. In 1992 André Bishop, formerly of PLAYWRIGHTS HORIZONS, began his leadership.

**Viviani, Raffaele** 1888–1950 Italian actor, director and playwright. Naples is the setting for many realistic plays of powerful social criticism, written in the Neapolitan dialect, among the most outstanding of which are *'O vico* (*The Alley*, 1917), *Tuledu'e notte* (*Tuledu by Night*, 1918) and *Festa di 'Piedigrotta* (*The Festival of Piedigrotta*, 1919). They present sharp and realistic portraits of working-class life. One of the major figures of the Italian stage between the two world wars, Viviani was extremely versatile, combining the talents of playwright, director, composer and actor-manager.

**Voaden, Herman** 1903–84 Canadian playwright. He combined a teaching career with important work in the community and the Little Theatre movement. In the late 1920s he conducted a crusade for a true Canadian drama and a new Canadian theatrical art. During the 1930s he began writing and producing his own innovative and experimental multimedia works in a style he called 'symphonic EXPRESSIONISM', which tried to develop the ideas of APPIA and CRAIG with a distinctively Canadian production of ELIOT's *Murder in the Cathedral*. After the war he was a founder and first president of the Canadian Arts Council, which led to the expansion of government support of the arts.

**Vodanović, Sergio** 1926– Chilean playwright. Born to Yugoslavian immigrant parents, he trained as a lawyer. His first major works are *El senador no es honorable* (*The Senator Is Not Honourable*, 1952) and *Deja que los perros ladren* (*Let the Dogs Bark*, 1959), criticizing political intrigue and corruption through well drawn characters. *Los fugitivos* (*The Fugitives*, 1965), with the young lover/older woman syndrome, resonates of *Tea and Sympathy*. In his later plays, Vodanović becomes more virulent in his sociopolitical commentaries: *Perdón ... ¡Estamos en guerra!* (*Sorry ... We're at War!*, 1966) and *Nos tomamos la universidad* (*We Took the University*, 1970). *¿Cuántos años tiene un día?* (*How Many Years in a Day?*, 1978), written in conjunction with the company ICTUS, contrasts the liberty of expression of former years with the oppression of television news reporters under Pinochet.

**Volkov, Fyodor (Grigorievich)** 1729–63 Russian actor. Named 'the father of the Russian theatre', he established a public theatre in his native Yaroslavl (1750). In 1752 his troupe, which included his brother Grigory and IVAN DMITREVSKY, was brought to St Petersburg to perform the MORALITY PLAY *A Sinner's Repentance* by DMITRY ROSTOVSKY and some tragedies by ALEKSEI SUMAROKOV. What was to have been a court theatre instead became in 1756 the Russian Patent Theatre, Russia's first permanent professional public theatre, under the direction of Sumarokov. Volkov became the company's leading tragic actor, impersonating the heroes in Sumarokov's plays, most notably Khorev and Hamlet. Recognizing Volkov's singular talent, his passionate temperament and naturalness of expression, Sumarokov adjusted his neoclassical verse form to accommodate him. Volkov took over the direction of the theatre in 1761. He and his brother took part in the plot to overthrow Peter III, for which they were rewarded with court offices. While organizing the festivities for the coronation of Catherine the Great (1763), which included the masquerade *Minerva Triumphant*, Volkov caught cold and died.

**Volksbühne** [Freie Volksbühne] (People's Theatre) German cultural movement. The generic label for a wide movement, it is also the name of those theatres affiliated with it. It was founded in 1890 in Berlin as a subscription organization, its first title, the Freie (Free) Volksbühne, reveals its origins as well as its unique contribution in bringing theatre to a mass audience. Growing out of OTTO BRAHM's FREIE BÜHNE, it was dedicated to providing art for the working classes and brought out the social content in the new NATURALISM. The tension between ideological and artistic aims split the organization in 1892, and it took over two decades to create a working compromise. Disagreement reached a head with the productions of ERWIN PISCATOR, and produced two parallel organizations in 1927.

The organization built two major Berlin theatres specifically for its needs. The first opened as the Volksbühne on Bülowplatz in 1914, with 2,000 seats and a 130ft-wide stage with a huge revolve, in which a permanent company could produce socially committed work. By 1930 there were over 300 local organizations,

with a nationwide membership of half a million. As one of the dominant forces in the Weimar Republic, it helped to shape the direction of modern drama by employing such directors as REINHARDT, Jürgen Fehling and Piscator at the beginning of their careers, and by supporting new plays from a wide range of dramatists, including BARLACH and TOLLER, and more recently HOCHHUTH and KIPPHARDT. The educational lectures that accompanied its first productions developed into influential periodicals, *Die Volksbühne* and *Die Schaubühne*.

The Nazis dissolved the Volksbühne in 1937. Re-established in 1947, it ceased to exist as a subscription organization in East Germany in 1957. The contemporary Freie Volksbühne was founded in 1949 in West Berlin, and moved into a newly designed theatre under Piscator in 1963.

**Volksstück** Viennese theatrical genre. A *Volksstück* is a play written for a popular audience in local dialect. Although several German cities have a *Volksstück* tradition, the genre is associated most consistently with Vienna, where, throughout the 18th and much of the 19th century, it flourished in the city's commercial theatres. Originating in the improvisational work of JOSEF STRANITZKY and GOTTFRIED PREHAUSER, the *Volksstück* gradually came to be scripted. The end of the 18th century saw the production of the single most famous example of the genre, Mozart and SCHIKANEDER's opera *The Magic Flute* (1791). Over the turn of the century, the theatres most associated with the performance of the *Volksstück* were established. Of these the Theater in der Josefstadt, founded in 1788, and the Theater an der Wien, founded by Schikaneder in 1801, are still in use.

In the 19th century, two distinct subgenres of the *Volksstück* can be distinguished. First there is the *Zauberstück*, a 'magic play' with music and spectacle, generally chronicling the adventures of the ordinary Viennese citizen in a fairy-world, of which the plays of FERDINAND RAIMUND are the best example. Then there is the *Lokalstück*, a more realistic play that treats, sometimes moralistically, sometimes farcically, the local customs and habits of the Viennese. The vigorous, witty and caustic comedies of JOHANN NESTROY are the finest examples of such comedy. Towards the end of the 19th century, the *Volksstück* tradition began to lose its identity, being transformed on the one hand into operetta, on the other into commercial comedy.

In the 1920s FLEISSER, HORVÁTH and ZUCKMAYER adapted the *Volksstück* as a vehicle for social comment, as did Brecht with *Mr Puntila and His Man Matti*. Horváth defined it as a play about common people, for common people, in the language of common people. In the late 1960s BAUER, FASSBINDER, KROETZ, SPERR and TURRINI returned to the genre to bring the lives of the underprivileged to the stage.

**Volodin** [Lifshits]**, Aleksandr (Moiseevich)** 1919– Soviet playwright. His lyrical dramas on the personal lives of ordinary people, related with a combination of gently ironic humour and pathos, are characteristic of the post-Thaw period. Trained as a scenarist, Volodin writes highly cinematic plays, with montage-like editing and dissolving of episodes, split-staging and parallel plotting, voice-over narration and musical accompaniment. His restless characters must discover personal happiness and spiritual values for themselves – a task made difficult by an ideologically based society, the pressure of work, the fallibility of the human heart and the failure of such institutions as marriage. This basic situation is manifested in *The Factory Girl* (1956), *Five Evenings* (1957), *The Elder Sister* (1961), *The Idealist* (1962), *The Appointment* (1963) and *Never Part from Your Loved Ones* (1972). Volodin has written three highly successful parable plays, *Two Arrows*, *Little Lizard* and *Dulcinea of El Toboso* (1973), the last concerning Aldonsa and Sancho Panza's lives following Don Quixote's death, and the basis for a highly popular stage musical at Leningrad's Lensoviet Theatre. Two of his most recent plays, *Dialogs* and *The Mother of Jesus*, premiered at small amateur and studio theatres and included spontaneous verbal exchanges between the author, the performers and the audience. Volodin has also written several film scenarios, including *Autumn Marathon* and *The Blonde*.

**Voltaire** [François-Marie Arouet] 1694–1778 French poet, playwright, historian and philosopher. Voltaire's manifold interests and irritable outspokenness led to periods of imprisonment and self-imposed exile, interrupting his career as a playwright, which began with a tragedy, *Oedipe* (1718), and, after three further plays in the next decade, resumed with vigour in the early 1730s and again in the 1740s, continuing intermittently until his last performed tragedy, *Irène*, in 1778. He wrote librettos, comedies and domestic dramas, but was most respected for his tragedies, though none are performed today. In his tenacious neoclassicism he emulated PIERRE CORNEILLE and RACINE, but without their creative originality. Even his innovative choice of subject-matter from native French history (e.g. *Adélaïde du Guesclin*, 1734) or from exotic climes (e.g. *Alzire, ou Les Américains*, 1736, set in Peru; *L'Orphelin de la Chine* (*The Chinese Orphan*, 1755)) introduced only a superficial local colour. *Zaïre* (1732), a Turkish tragedy of love, is considered his masterpiece. Voltaire helped to popularize SHAKESPEARE in France, before disavowing him. He used his own plays as propaganda against religious bigotry and tyranny and also wrote dramatic criticism, notably the prefaces to his plays and the *Commentaires sur Corneille* (1764). His genuine love of the stage led to the building of several private theatres and his patronage of individual players, such as ADRIENNE LECOUVREUR and LEKAIN.

**Von Sydow, Max** [Carl Adolf] 1929– Swedish actor. While best known internationally for his many films, Von Sydow has had an outstanding stage career. In 1955 he joined INGMAR BERGMAN's MALMÖ STADSTEATER company, giving powerful performances as Erik XIV, Peer Gynt, Alceste and Faust. After several years in film, his stage career resumed in the 1970s at DRAMATEN, where Bergman directed him in unnerving performances of the Lawyer in STRINDBERG's *A Dream Play* and Gregers in IBSEN's *The Wild Duck*. His volatile physical presence on stage is matched by a remarkably clear focus; both were in evidence in his 1991–2 performances as Eugene O'Neill in NORÉN's *And Give us the Shadows*.

**Vondel, Joost van den** 1587–1679 Dutch playwright and poet. Influenced by SENECA, SOPHOCLES and EURIPIDES, in his turn he gave international status to the Dutch Golden Age and had some influence on German baroque. In 1637, van den Vondel wrote *Gijsbrecht van Aemstel* to mark the opening of Amsterdam's new municipal theatre in 1638. It was performed there annually on New Year's Day, from 1638 until 1968. In 1641 he was converted to the Roman Catholic Church. Many of the plays that followed display deep religious feeling and draw on the Bible. Some, such as *Lucifer* (1654) and *Adam in Exile* (1664), are still performed today.

**Vormingstoneel** Dutch movement. Meaning 'educational drama', this movement among Dutch theatre companies aims to produce work with a strong political tendency. Since 1970 (see AKTIE TOMAAT) companies like Proloog (1964–83), De Nieuwe Komedie (1969–85) and Sater (1971–85) and, in Belgium, INTERNATIONALE NIEUWE SCENE, Mannen van de Dam (Men of the Dam) and Trojaanse Paard (the Trojan Horse), inspired by BRECHT and Marx, have aimed to stimulate an audience's social awareness and emancipation through the theatre.

The plays are often collaborative and deal with the problems of a specific social group. After the performance, the company invites discussion. To reach a potential audience, acting space is created in all kinds of locations: at schools, factories and local meeting centres, and at demonstrations. In the 1980s, the Dutch companies involved lost their subsidies, a decision which has caused the disappearance of an outspoken segment of Dutch theatre.

**Voskovec, Jiří (Wachsmann)** 1905–81 and **Jan Werich** 1905–80 Czech actors, playwrights and CABARET performers. With the composer Jaroslav Ježek, they founded the Liberated Theatre, where they staged SATIRES and political REVUES until 1938, mixing parodies of film and theatrical clichés with social commentary. Werich usually played the robust, instinctual clown to Voskovec's more rational straight-man, and their verbal comedy attacked middle-class values and Fascist ideology. In 1938 they emigrated to the USA, but returned to Prague in 1946 to perform in their own theatre. After 1948 Voskovec settled in the USA; Werich retired from the Prague Theatre of Satire in 1968.

**Voss, Gert** 1942– German actor. Voss worked in CLAUS PEYMANN's companies in Stuttgart, Bochum and Vienna. After his acclaimed Hermann in KLEIST's *Hermannsschlacht* (1987), he achieved star status at the BURGTHEATER, playing Richard III, Prospero and Macbeth under Peymann, Shylock as a hard-boiled 1980s businessman in braces, and CHEKHOV's Ivanov, both under ZADEK. He created Mr Jay with shambling self-irony in George Tabori's *Goldberg Variations*. THOMAS BERNHARD wrote *Ritter, Dene, Voss* for him. In 1994 Voss joined Zadek at the BERLINER ENSEMBLE, making his debut as Antony in *Antony and Cleopatra*.

**Vychodil, Ladislav** 1920– Slovak designer. From 1945 he was primary designer and technical chief of the Slovak National Theatre in Bratislava. Vychodil describes his work as 'poetism' – a lyrical yet restrained form with an emphasis on props and details over traditional decor. Except for a period of imposed socialist realism in the early 1950s, his work is typified by a complex treatment of the floor and cyclorama with an emphasis on light and colour, and the use of flown scenic pieces creating a layered look. When, in the late 1970s, he began working with director ALFRED RADOK, the result was a more spare look and an almost total deemphasis of obvious design.

**Vysotsky, Vladimir (Semyonovich)** 1938–80 Russian actor and singer. He became a national idol shortly after joining the Taganka Theatre in Moscow. Closely associated with its director YURY LYUBIMOV, he played the aviator in *The Good Person of Setzuan* (1964), Kerensky in *Ten Days That Shook the World* (1965), Pugachev in a curtailed and cancelled play of that name by Esenin (1967), Hamlet (1971), and Svidrigailov in *Crime and Punishment* (his last role, 1979) as well as Lopakhin in ANATOLY EFROS's staging of *The Cherry Orchard* at the Taganka (1975). His more than 900 songs and poems were a chronicle of 20 years of daily life in the Soviet Union.

**Wagner, (Wilhelm) Richard** (1813–83) German composer and librettist. His contribution to drama was such that NIETZSCHE referred to him as 'the most outstanding theatrical genius that the Germans have ever had'. His major theatrical works, operas of which he wrote both librettos and scores, include *Rienzi* (written in 1838–40; performed 1842), *The Flying Dutchman* (1841; 1843), *Tannhäuser* (1843–5; 1845), *Lohengrin* (1846–8; 1850), *Tristan and Isolde* (1857–9; 1865), *The Mastersingers of Nuremberg* (1862–7; 1868), *Parsifal* (1877–82; 1882),*The Rhinegold* (1853–4; 1869), *The Valkyrie* (1854–6; 1870), *Siegfried* (1856–71; 1876) and *The Twilight of the Gods* (1869–74; 1876). Four of these operas (*Rhinegold, Valkyrie, Siegfried* and *Twilight of the Gods*) were components of the great cycle *The Ring of the Nibelungs*, which did not receive its first integral performance until 1876, under Wagner's own direction at the theatre in BAYREUTH.

Wagner aimed to write music dramas, the very term emphasizing his view that the effect of opera should be above all dramatic. He abhorred the gratuitous in opera, and in this he included display singing and arias that were almost free-standing items, stage effects striking by their spectacle alone – in fact, everything theatrical that was not justified by its contribution to the drama or that interrupted its organic unity. He strove for a continuous flow of music in which voices express greater or less feeling, the mundane or the transcendent, as the progress of the drama demands. His orchestra was not a mere accompanist, but the definer of the ambience of the characters, the prop and stay of their world. In spite of his aspirations towards the total work of art (*Gesamtkunstwerk*) in which all the arts were to find expression, his own works are authentic operas in which the essential elements are the music and the characters.

Wagner's prose works run to some ten volumes. They include *Art and Revolution* (1849), *The Artwork of the Future* (1849) and *Opera and Drama* (1851). His writings as a whole do not express a single, unchanging and uncontradictory view and they are often tortuous in expression, but they display practical interests and skills. His essays *On the Performing of Tannhäuser* and *Remarks on Performing the Opera, The Flying Dutchman* (both 1852–3) are careful guides to rehearsals, playing, singing, acting and staging.

**Wagner, Robin** 1933– American set designer. Wagner has been associated with some of the most successful musicals of the post-1960 period including *Hair, A Chorus Line* and *Dreamgirls*. His work at the ARENA STAGE in the mid-1960s led to explorations of stage space and moving scenery. He is generally associated with spectacular sets and stylish decor, but by and large his sets are minimal. It is the way in which the sets move and are integrated into the production that gives the illusion of a great deal of scenery. His best-known set was for *A Chorus Line*. For most of the show it consisted of only a white line on the floor; in the final scene the upstage wall revealed Mylar mirrors. This seemingly simple set was the result of over a year of stripping away excess and unnecessary scenic elements to arrive at a design that simply and boldly expressed the essence of the play. Wagner also designed the BROADWAY productions of TONY KUSHNER's two-part *Angels in America* (1992–3).

**Wagner, Wieland** 1917–66 German director and designer; grandson of RICHARD WAGNER. He staged all the major productions of his grandfather's operas at BAYREUTH after its reopening in 1951, and established the contemporary style of Wagnerian interpretation with his *Ring* cycle in the same year. Freeing the operas from NATURALISM, he introduced symbolic lighting, sets and rhythms corresponding to the theories of ADOLPHE APPIA.

**Walcott, Derek (Alton)** 1930– West Indian playwright, poet and director. Born in St Lucia, he founded the St Lucia Arts Guild which performed his first published play, *Henri Christophe* (1950), about the Haitian revolutionary leader. While working as a journalist and theatre critic, in 1957 he was commissioned to write an epic drama – *Drums and Colours* (1958) – for the arts festival that heralded the birth of the West Indies Federation. He wrote *The Sea at Dauphin* (1954) and *Ti Jean and His Brothers* (1958) before he founded and became director of the Trinidad Theatre Workshop (1959), where for 17 years he wrote and directed plays including the highly acclaimed *Dream on Monkey Mountain* (1967), *The Joker of Seville* (1974), *O, Babylon!* (1976) and *Remembrance* (1977). *Three Plays* (published 1982) includes *The Last Pantomime, Beef, No Chicken* and *A Branch of the Blue Nile*. In 1984 he directed an open-air production of his play, *Haitian Earth*, in St Lucia. His plays have also been produced by theatre organizations in the United States and England. *The Odyssey* was staged by the ROYAL SHAKESPEARE COMPANY in 1992.

A world-ranking playwright and poet (author of some dozen volumes of poetry), Walcott dramatizes a tension between instinct and intellect – the racial instinct stemming from an African heritage in conflict with an undiminished admiration for European intellectual and artistic achievement. He was awarded the Nobel Prize for Literature in 1992.

**Waldoff, Claire** [Clara Wortmann] 1884–1957 German MUSIC-HALL performer. She had a phenomenally successful CABARET debut in Berlin in 1907. In 1910 she became the star of the Linden-Cabaret, personifying the lower-class types drawn by Heinrich Zille. Her throaty voice, red pageboy haircut and mannish suits contributed to the effect of such hits as 'Hermann heest er' ('Is Name's 'Erman'). A symbol of Berlin wit and *joie de vivre*, she appeared in London in 1913 and 1933. After the latter tour, the Nazis banned her from the theatre, and she retired to lower Bavaria to live out her life in obscurity.

**Walker, George** see WILLIAMS, BERT

**Walker, George F.** 1947– Canadian playwright. His early plays, including *Beyond Mozambique* (1974), were produced by the Factory Theatre Lab in Toronto. *Gossip* (1977) and his gothic comedy, *Zastrozzi* (1977) were first seen at the Toronto Free Theatre, and have enjoyed several other productions in the USA, Britain and Australia. His first directorial attempt was with his own *Ramona and the White Slaves* (1976). His plays are profoundly influenced by electronic media and popular culture and, in his own words, 'try to walk that fine line between the serious and the comic'. *Gossip* was the first in a trilogy of 'Power Plays', which was completed by

*Filthy Rich* (1979) and *The Art of War* (1983). His other major trilogy, the 'East End Plays' – *Criminals in Love* (1985), *Better Living* (1986) and *Beautiful City* (1987) – explore urban life in Toronto. In 1992 Walker expanded the trilogy with *Escape from Happiness. Nothing Sacred* (1988) was a reworking of Turgenev's *Fathers and Sons*.

**Wall, Max** [Maxwell George Lorimer] 1908–90 British actor and comedian. With a voice as mobile and disjointed as his limbs, with trousers too high and jackets too tight, and a face that expressed a fathomless range of experience, Wall turned the simplest act and the most innocent comment into anarchic and often disturbing comedy. His early reputation was established in the MUSIC-HALL and on radio from the 1920s to the 1950s. Thereafter he turned increasingly to 'straight' plays, appearing in such roles as Père Ubu (ROYAL COURT THEATRE, 1966), Archie Rice (Greenwich Theatre, London, 1974) and as Bludgeon in JOHN ARDEN's *Sergeant Musgrave's Dance* (OLD VIC, 1984). He had a special affinity for BECKETT, memorably instanced by his portrayal of Vladimir in the Manchester ROYAL EXCHANGE THEATRE production of *Waiting for Godot* (1981). Wall often appeared as a solo artist, inventing Professor Wallofski and presenting his one-man show *Aspects of Max Wall* (1974 and after).

**Wallace, Edgar (Horatio)** 1875–1932 British novelist and playwright. His experience as a crime reporter gave a realistic basis to the ingenious plots of his popular detective thrillers, the most successful of which were *The Ringer* (1926), *On the Spot* (1930) and *The Case of the Frightened Lady* (1931).

**Wallace, Nellie** [Eleanor] **(Jane)** 1870–1948 Scottish comedienne. She began her MUSIC-HALL career clog-dancing at the age of 12 and, billed as 'the Essence of Eccentricity', was a star shortly after her first London appearance in 1903. Portraying a moth-eaten spinster with buck teeth and a ratty fur-piece ('my little bit of vermin'), she was one of the few actresses grotesque enough to play a PANTOMIME dame successfully. Her best songs included 'The Blasted Oak', 'Tally Ho', 'A Boy's Best Friend Is His Mother' and 'Let's Have a Tiddley at the Milk Bar'. She last performed publicly at the Royal Command Performance of 1948.

**Wallach, Eli** 1915– American actor. He won stardom as Alvaro Mangiacavallo, a sexually driven truck driver in TENNESSEE WILLIAMS's *The Rose Tattoo* (1951). Wallach and Anne Jackson (b.1926), studied at the ACTORS STUDIO and had successful careers before they married in 1948. They were later acclaimed as an acting duo in *The Typists* and *The Tiger* (1963), *Luv* (1964), a revival of *The Waltz of the Toreadors* (1973), *Twice around the Park* (1982), and in a revival of ODET's *The Flowering Peach* (1994).

**Wallack family** American actor-managers. Of English origin, the Wallack family was linked with the history of the New York stage for over 50 years. Versatile and accomplished, Henry John Wallack (1790–1870) moved to the USA in 1819 and in 1824 became leading man at the Chatham Theatre, though he continued to go back and forth to England. Two of his sisters were also actresses. His brother J(ames) W(illiam) Wallack (?1795–1864), known as the elder to distinguish him from his nephew, appeared first in the USA at the PARK THEATRE as Macbeth in 1818. For the next 35 years he shuttled between the USA and England, though he was best-known on the American stage. Exceedingly handsome, he was admired for roles in TRAGEDY and COMEDY, especially the latter. Although most historians catego-

rize him as a member of the KEMBLE school, he has been dubbed 'the first romantic actor of America'. His Shylock and Jaques in *As You Like It* were considered innovative.

In 1852 he assumed control of the theatre he called Wallack's. For nine years this theatre prospered. For almost 35 years his company was the leading American ensemble, first under his leadership and later under his son Lester. In 1861 he built the second Wallack's on BROADWAY. His nephew, J(ames) W(illiam) Wallack Jr (1818–73), son of Henry, acted in tragedy, mostly outside New York, spreading the Wallack name to all the major American theatrical centres. Next to James the elder, **Lester** Wallack (John Johnstone; 1820–88), his nephew, made the greatest contribution to the American stage. During his career with the Wallack company he played nearly 300 roles, excelling as Benedick, Charles Surface, Sir Andrew Aguecheek, and Sir Elliott Grey in his own adaptation of *Rosedale* (1863). Lester became the manager of the second Wallack's Theatre until 1882 when he opened a new Wallack's, remaining there until 1887.

**Waller, Lewis** 1860–1915 British actor-manager. He became the supreme matinée idol at the turn of the century, his repertoire constrained by the need to gratify the KOW (Keen on Waller) Brigade. He produced *An Ideal Husband* at the HAYMARKET in 1895. D'Artagnan (1898) and the eponymous hero of BOOTH TARKINGTON's *Monsieur Beaucaire* (1902) became the basis of his repertoire, but Waller would have preferred more Shakespearian roles: he was excellent as Brutus, Faulconbridge, Henry V and Hotspur. During his management of the Imperial (1903–6) and London's LYRIC (1907–11) he also played Othello.

**Walnut Street Theatre** (Philadelphia) The oldest functioning playhouse in America, opened in 1809, was transformed from a CIRCUS arena into a workable theatre (the Olympic) and in 1820 renamed the Walnut Street. It briefly housed a company that rivalled the CHESTNUT STREET. It passed to the ownership of EDWIN BOOTH's brother-in-law, the actor-manager John Sleeper Clarke (1833–99). In 1968 its 1828 Greek-revival façade was restored, but the interior was modernized.

**Walser, Martin** 1927– German playwright and novelist. Influenced by Kafka as well as BRECHT, his characteristic work presents an absurdist perspective (see THEATRE OF THE ABSURD) on contemporary society with its roots in the Nazi era. After his first play *The Detour* (1961), in which marital infidelity represents the absence of values, a theme he returned to in *Home Front* (*Die Zimmerschlacht*, 1967), he turned to parable drama with *Rabbit Race* (*Eiche und Angora*, 1962) and *The Black Swan* (1964). These form the initial parts of an abandoned 'German Chronicle', the first a PARODY of the final days of the war, the second a symbolic fable of the younger generation's traumatic guilt for the actions of their parents. Rejecting documentary drama as well as the overt theatricality of HANDKE, Walser's plays alternate between grotesque NATURALISM and psychological parable, as in *Child's Play* (1970) and *In Goethe's Hand* (1982).

**Walter, Eugene** 1874–1941 American playwright and screenwriter. A business manager involved with MINSTREL SHOWS, CIRCUSES and symphony orchestras, Walter wrote a score of successful realistic MELODRAMAS. He portrayed the victims of overwhelming social and personal forces: the political machine in New York City (*The Undertow*, 1906); the power of business (*Paid in Full*, 1908); money as corruption (*Fine Feathers*, 1913). His best play, *The Easiest Way* (1908), remembered for a realistic production by DAVID BELASCO, features a weak woman who understands her frailty. Walter's dramatic techniques were easily adapted to the writing of numerous film scenarios.

**Wälterlin, Oskar** 1895–1961 Swiss director and actor. In 1919 he directed his first opera, Pergolesi's *La serva padrona*. His association with the Basel Stadttheater continued until his death: 1919–25, as an actor; 1925–32 and 1942–4 as artistic director (a post which he was to take up for a third time in 1961). In Basle he is particularly remembered for WAGNER's *Ring* which he had prepared with ADOLPHE APPIA for 1924–5, but only *Rhinegold* and *The Valkyrie* were presented, following a hostile conservative outcry. In 1938 he became artistic and administrative director of the Schauspielhaus, Zurich, where he remained until 1961, creating an impressive ensemble and establishing the Schauspielhaus as the main centre of German theatre from the late 1930s to the early 1960s. Under Wälterlin, Zurich saw the world premieres of BRECHT's *Mother Courage* (1942), *The Good Person of Setzuan* (1947), *Galileo* (1947) and *Puntila* (1949); ZUCKMAYER's *Barbara Blomberg* (1948); the first German performance of THORNTON WILDER's *Our Town* and the first plays of two emerging Swiss playwrights – FRISCH's *Don Juan or The Love of Geometry* (1952) and *The Fire-Raisers* (1957), and DÜRRENMATT's *The Visit* (1955).

**Walters, Sam** 1939– British director. He went to Jamaica to found the state's first theatre and acting school and then launched the small Orange Tree Theatre in Richmond, Surrey, which, although on the FRINGE, won a reputation for its ambitious programmes, high production standards and encouragement of new writers such as MARTIN CRIMP, David Cregan, JAMES SAUNDERS, Fay Weldon and Olwen Wymark. Walters opened the new Orange Tree in 1991. The combination of unusual revivals (JOHN MARSTON's *The Dutch Courtesan*, 1993), drama from Eastern Europe, new British plays and major classics reflects the range of his enthusiasms.

**Walton, Tony** 1934– British-born American set and COSTUME designer. He has designed for theatre, film, television, opera and ballet. Walton began work at the Wimbledon Theatre; his first New York production was in 1957. He soon became associated in the USA with a range of witty and elegant musicals, including *A Funny Thing Happened on the Way to the Forum, Pippin, Grand Hotel: The Musical, The Will Rogers Follies,* a revival of *Guys and Dolls* (1992) and *She's Loves Me* (1993). Walton's style – like that of his idol BORIS ARONSON – is mutable, often whimsical and always inventive. With over 45 New York productions to his credit, including *The Real Thing, Hurlyburly, Six Degrees of Separation, Conversations With My Father, Death and the Maiden* and the 1994 *Christmas Carol,* Walton is one of the most active designers in New York theatre today. *Fool's Paradise, The Ginger Man, Most Happy Fella, Caligula* and *Triple Bill* number among his London designs, while his film credits include *Mary Poppins* and DUSTIN HOFFMAN's *Death of a Salesman.*

**Wanamaker, Sam** 1919–93 American actor and director. After 1952 most of Wanamaker's work was in and for the English theatre. Born in Chicago, he made his BROADWAY debut in 1942. He went to London during the run of CLIFFORD ODETS's *The Country Girl,* and a period of acting and directing there culminated in a ROYAL COURT production of BRECHT's *The Threepenny Opera.* In 1957 he

was appointed artistic director of the New Shakespeare Theatre in Liverpool. In 1959 he played Iago to PAUL ROBESON's Othello at Stratford. His enthusiasm for SHAKESPEARE became a magnificent obsession, leading him to found the Globe Playhouse Trust and World Centre for Shakespeare Studies (1970). Wanamaker died shortly before the opening of his dreamed-of 'replica' of Shakespeare's second GLOBE THEATRE, not far from its original site.

His daughter, Zoë Wanamaker, is a well known stage and screen actress.

**Ward, Douglas Turner** 1930– African-American actor, director and playwright. He acted in OFF-BROADWAY plays before accepting a minor role on BROADWAY in *A Raisin in the Sun* (1959). In 1965 he produced his two one-act satiric comedies, *Happy Ending* and *Day of Absence,* for a 14-month Off-Broadway run. In 1968 Ward, Robert Hooks and Gerald Krone founded the NEGRO ENSEMBLE COMPANY where Ward continues as artistic director. He has directed and played leading roles in many of the company's productions, notably *Ceremonies in Dark Old Men* (1969) and *The River Niger* (1972), and has also written *The Reckoning* (1969) and *Brotherhood* (1970).

**Ward, Geneviève (Teresa)** [Ginevra Guerrabella] 1838–1922 American-born British actress. Her career belongs to the British theatre, where she made her reputation in a forgotten play by Herman Merivale and F. C. Grove, *Forget-Me-Not* (1879), playing a high-society Frenchwoman. She toured the English-speaking world, returning to the London stage to play Eleanor of Aquitaine in IRVING's production of *Becket* (1893) and Morgan le Fay to Irving's King in the LYCEUM's lavish *King Arthur* (1895). She played Queen Margaret for JOHN MARTIN-HARVEY in his 1916 *Richard III,* the part in which she made her farewell appearance with the F. R. BENSON company in 1920, at the age of 82. She was created DBE in 1921, the first actress to be so honoured.

**Ward, Nick** 1962– British playwright and director. He won the George Devine Award in 1987 for his plays *Apart from George* (1987) and *The Strangeness of Others* (1988). On leaving Cambridge University he ran two small theatre companies, winning a 'Fringe First' at the EDINBURGH FESTIVAL for his adaptation of a D. H. LAWRENCE short story, *Eastwood* (1985). He was taken into the NATIONAL THEATRE Studio by its director, PETER GILL, where he directed his own translation of STRINDBERG's *The Ghost Sonata.* With his bleak vision of Britain today, Ward has an exceptional ability to evoke desolate land- or cityscape; but his terse dialogue, written for semi-articulate characters, has provided so far only rather arid experiences in the theatre.

**Wardle, (John) Irving** 1929– British theatre critic. He entered journalism as a sub-editor on the *Times Educational Supplement* in 1956, and became the deputy drama critic on the *Observer* in 1960. In 1963 he joined *The Times,* where his thoughtful, persuasive columns set the standards for daily reviewing until 1989 when he joined the *Independent on Sunday.* As a critic he weighs each side to an argument; his knowledge and integrity are rarely questioned, and best revealed in his biography of GEORGE DEVINE, *The Theatres of George Devine* (1978). Wardle's early play, *The Houseboy* (1974), received a successful production at London's Open Space and was later seen on television. From 1973 to 1975, he was the editor of the theatre magazine, *Gambit.* In 1992 he published a book on *Theatre Criticism.*

**Warfield, David** 1866–1951 American actor. BELASCO's

one great male star was a native of San Francisco. In New York he became a specialist in musical PARODY at the CASINO THEATRE, which led to an engagement as an eccentric ethnic comic. Belasco coached him in a series of pathetic older parts in which he was always the gentle, slightly humorous, forgiving victim. His first vehicle was *The Auctioneer* (1901), followed by *The Music Master* (1904) and *The Return of Peter Grimm* (1911); his career culminated in an unsuccessful production of *The Merchant of Venice* (1924).

**Warner, Deborah** 1959– British director. She formed the Kick Theatre Company in 1980, which, in common with CHEEK BY JOWL but unlike the small groups of the 1970s, concentrated on staging classic plays with style and economy – e.g. *King Lear* (1985) and *Coriolanus* (1986). In 1987 she was invited to direct *Titus Andronicus* for the ROYAL SHAKESPEARE COMPANY, a production widely hailed as the best interpretation of the play since PETER BROOK's in 1955. In 1988 she directed *Electra* for the RSC. Warner excels in providing the settings for outstanding performances and for coaxing actors to reach beyond their normal limits, particularly Brian Cox (Titus, Lear, 1990) and Fiona Shaw (Electra, Shen Te in *The Good Person of Setzuan* (1989), Hedda (1991), the title role in *Richard II* (1995)). In 1993 she was invited to direct *Coriolanus* at the Salzburg Festival.

**Warren, Mercy Otis** 1728–1814 American patriot and political satirist. She represents 'the War of Belles Lettres' during the Revolutionary War. Her propaganda plays, really dialogues without plot, character development or women, satirized British officials and American Loyalists and were published anonymously in Massachusetts periodicals and as political pamphlets. Several plays have been falsely attributed to Warren; she acknowledged authorship of only *The Group* (1775). Other plays which are identified as her work include *The Adulateur: A Tragedy: As It Is Now Acted in Upper Servia* (1772), which refers to the Boston Massacre and attacks Governor Thomas Hutchison; *The Defeat* (1773); and two blank-verse historical tragedies, *The Ladies of Castille* and *The Sack of Rome*, both published in *Poems, Dramatic and Miscellaneous* (1790).

**Warren, William,** the elder 1767–1832 British-born American actor and manager. When engaged by TATE WILKINSON for his provincial company in 1788, Warren acted with SARAH SIDDONS. In 1796 he joined THOMAS WIGNELL's company. At the CHESTNUT STREET THEATRE he first appeared as Friar Lawrence in *Romeo and Juliet* and as Bundle in *The Waterman*. His remaining career was associated with the theatres in Baltimore and Philadelphia. Warren was especially adept at old men in COMEDY, but he was also capable in TRAGEDY. He was noted especially for his performances as Old Dornton, Sir Robert Bramble, Falstaff and Sir Toby Belch.

**Warren, William,** the younger 1812–88 American actor; son of WILLIAM WARREN THE ELDER. His career is thoroughly identified with the BOSTON MUSEUM, the STOCK COMPANY he joined in 1847. He won respect and affection from the public, showing a special talent for eccentric comic roles including Dogberry, Polonius, Bob Acres, Sir Peter Teazle, Micawber, Touchstone and Launcelot Gobbo.

**Washington Square Players** American producing agency. The Players were founded in 1915 by a group of actors and playwrights, including LAWRENCE LANGNER, to improve the level of drama in New York City. For three seasons they produced distinctly modern one-act plays

at low cost for small audiences. They then moved to the Comedy Theatre, seating 600, where they presented the first BROADWAY production of EUGENE O'NEILL's *In the Zone*. Important American actors worked with the Washington Square Players, e.g. KATHARINE CORNELL. In 1918 the group disbanded, but reorganized in 1919 as the THEATRE GUILD.

**Wasserstein, Wendy** 1950– American playwright. She portrays with wit and understanding the plight of the modern woman caught between feminism and traditionalism. *Uncommon Women and Others* (1977) depicts the reunion of five women graduates of Mount Holyoke, Massachusetts, and their reflections on their college days. *Isn't It Romantic* (1983) follows two such women as they confront their parents, their lovers and their own futures. *The Heidi Chronicles* (1989) traces the history of the women's movement through the life of one woman and her friends. *The Sisters Rosensweig* (New York, 1992; London, 1994) explores the relationship between three Jewish sisters.

**Waterhouse, Keith** see HALL, WILLIS

**Waters, Ethel** 1896–1977 African-American singer and actress. In 1933 she featured in IRVING BERLIN's REVUE, *As Thousands Cheer*. Moving from honky-tonks to cellar cafés to New York socialite clubs, Waters attained a glowing reputation as comedienne and singer of such songs as 'St Louis Blues', 'Dinah' and 'Stormy Weather'. She emerged as a dramatic actress of warmth and sensitivity in stage or film productions of *Mamba's Daughters* (1939), *Cabin in the Sky* (1940), *Pinky* (1949) and *The Member of the Wedding* (1950).

**Waterston, Sam(uel Atkinson)** 1940– American actor. In 1963 Waterston began a long association with the NEW YORK SHAKESPEARE FESTIVAL as Silvius in *As You Like It*, returning in 1968 as Prince Hal in *Henry IV, Parts 1 and 2*, and in 1971 as Cloten in *Cymbeline*. In 1972 his Benedick in *Much Ado* drew critical acclaim as a superb comic performance. He added Prospero in 1974 and Hamlet the following year, described in the *New York Times* as 'easy to like' but intellectually unsatisfying. Waterston has also appeared on BROADWAY and OFF- it, and in numerous films.

**waxworks** Public exhibition of waxen effigies. First found in 16th-century Amsterdam, this form of popular entertainment has two sources: anatomical cabinets for the display of medical anomalies, and state portraits that permit subjects a symbolic audience with their monarch. It was the portrait from life of Louis XIV by the Parisian Antoine Benoist (1632–1717) that popularized wax as a medium for such shows. The Cabinet Palais-Royal (1783) of Johann Christian Curtius (Creutz) exhibited figures of the nobility, while his Caverne des grands voleurs in the Boulevard du Temple in Paris was a resort of the people.

During the French Revolution, Curtius had licence to take death masks of heads fresh from the guillotine, a task carried out by his niece Marie Grosholtz (1760–1850). With this legacy of gruesome mementos, and as Madame Tussaud, she opened a gallery in London in 1833 which soon became world-famous. Its Chamber of Horrors, displaying the latest in murderers, is a forerunner of the news photo. Her success was soon emulated by the Musée Grévin, Paris (where the Raft of the Medusa boasted a wave effect produced by clever lighting); the Hamburg Panoptikum (still extant); Emil E. Harmer's Munich Panoptikum; Präuscher's Enkel Museum, Vienna; and the Eden Musée, New York. These housed historical tableaux along with the grotesque and unnerving models of foetuses and venereal afflictions usually found in so-called 'medical museums'. Tigerpark, founded in Singapore in 1946, enhanced the traditional terrors of Hell and scenes from Chinese myth with up-to-date technology. Disneyland and Disneyworld have added synthetic flesh and computer-controlled movement and speech without appreciably surpassing the artistic results of their precursors.

**wayang** see SHADOW PUPPETS

**Wayburn, Ned** [Edward Claudius Weyburn] 1874–1942 American director and choreographer. Among the shows he staged in New York were two editions of *The Passing Show* (1912, 1913) and six of *The Ziegfeld Follies* (1916–19, 1922, 1923). In addition to producing and staging hundreds of musicals, Wayburn operated dance studios which trained many of the MUSICAL THEATRE's finest dancers.

**Webb, John** 1611–72 English architect and scene-designer. As INIGO JONES's pupil he helped to prepare MASQUES for the court of Charles I. He designed the scenery for DAVENANT's *The Siege of Rhodes* (1656) – probably the first use of perspective scenery on a public stage. Surviving drawings by Webb suggest that he was beginning a movement towards scenic REALISM.

**Weber, Joseph** 1867–1942 and **Lew Fields** [Lewis Maurice Shanfield] 1867–1941 American comedians. After learning their craft as child performers, Weber and Fields evolved a knockabout act in which the short, rotund, innocent Weber was the foil for the tall, skinny, bullying Fields. In 1896 they opened the Weber and Fields Music Hall, where they offered hilarious BURLESQUES of current BROADWAY successes, choosing talented writers, designers and directors to assist them. The rough, acrobatic comic style of Weber and Fields, coupled with the fractured English they spoke in their 'Dutch' personas, made them favourites in both legitimate theatres and VAUDEVILLE houses across the USA.

**Webster, Benjamin (Nottingham)** 1798–1882 English actor and theatre manager. Beginning as a dancer, he got his first chance to display his skill in comedy with MADAME VESTRIS at the OLYMPIC in 1832. As manager of the HAYMARKET (1837–53) he demonstrated his exemplary concern to find good plays, such as those by SHERIDAN KNOWLES, JERROLD, BOUCICAULT, BULWER LYTTON, TOM TAYLOR and CHARLES READE, and to stage them conscientiously. No other theatre could match the repertoire of the Haymarket during Webster's management. His production of *The Taming of the Shrew* (1844) defied the taste for pictorial SHAKESPEARE by setting the play on an Elizabethan-style stage – 40 years before WILLIAM POEL's first experiments in this field. From 1844 to 1874 he was also manager of the lower-brow ADELPHI, initially with MADAME CÉLESTE.

**Webster, John** c.1580–1634 English playwright. Son of a prosperous coachmaker, Webster was trained at the Middle Temple. He wrote the Induction to MARSTON's *The Malcontent* when the play was revived by the King's Men (see LORD CHAMBERLAIN's MEN) in 1604 and collaborated with DEKKER on *Westward Ho* (1604) for the BOYS OF ST PAUL's. The two were less successful with *Northward Ho* (1605). A previous collaboration with Dekker, on *The Famous History of Sir Thomas Wyatt* (not published until 1607), produced an untidy history play.

Webster's poetic gift and dramatic ingenuity were supremely exhibited in the two tragedies which he wrote alone, *The White Devil*, performed at the RED BULL

in 1612, and *The Duchess of Malfi*, offered to the more sophisticated audience of the King's Men at the GLOBE and BLACKFRIARS (c.1614). Violent and sensational according to the prevailing taste, both plays are also eloquent and compassionate. Webster chose his plots from the catchpenny translations of Italian novellas, but he perceived an almost Aeschylean pattern (see AESCHYLUS) in these squalid stories of bloodthirsty family vengeance. It seems that he kept a careful commonplace book of striking lines from the work of other writers, improving almost everything that he stole.

Webster's remaining extant work is less impressive: *The Devil's Law Case* (published 1623) is a TRAGICOMEDY; *Monuments of Honour* (1624) is a Lord Mayor's pageant. He collaborated with THOMAS HEYWOOD on *Appius and Virginia* (c.1608), with MIDDLETON on *Any Thing for a Quiet Life* (c.1621) and with WILLIAM ROWLEY on *A Cure for a Cuckold* (c.1624).

**Webster, Margaret** 1905–72 British actress and director. She was the last member of a 150-year-old theatrical dynasty. She joined the OLD VIC in 1929, returning to play Lady Macbeth in 1932–3. In 1934 she began to direct, mostly in America. Notable productions included *Richard II* with MAURICE EVANS (1937), *Hamlet* (1938), *Twelfth Night* (1940), *Othello* with PAUL ROBESON (1943), *The Cherry Orchard* (1944) and *The Tempest* with CANADA LEE as Caliban (1945). She founded with EVA LE GALLIENNE and CHERYL CRAWFORD the AMERICAN REPERTORY THEATRE (1946–8). In 1950 she began directing operas, becoming the first woman to direct at the New York Metropolitan Opera.

**Wedekind, Frank** 1864–1918 German playwright. Wedekind was influenced initially by the naturalists and their views on biological imperatives. But his plays were not rigorously realistic. Instead, adopting an episodic approach to plot and presenting character frequently through the means of grotesque caricature, he foreshadowed the expressionists (see NATURALISM; EXPRESSIONISM). His first major play, *Spring Awakening* (1891), was not produced until 1906 because of the bold and shocking manner in which he unfolded his theme, which was the need for a repressive society to recognize the stirrings of puberty in its children. The 'Lulu' plays, *Earth Spirit* (1895) and *Pandora's Box* (1904), striking in their depiction of a society riven by the demands of lust and greed, are more ambiguous over the issue of sexuality. Of his several other plays, the one-act *The Court Singer* (1899) and *The Marquis of Keith* (1901) have been widely performed. In the past 20 years there has been a significant revival of Wedekind in the German and English theatres.

**Wei Liangfu** fl.1522–73 Chinese musician. His dates are controversial and biographical data scanty. It is known that he worked in Jiangsu province, carrying out innovative research on the several musical modes which flourished in the south at that time. He created the mellifluous, somewhat plaintive, singing to flute accompaniment which characterizes the musical content of *KUNQU* drama. Wei was assisted in his researches by Zhang Yetang, who was an authority on the northern modal repertoire. An accomplished singer, Wei created a new musical vogue which influenced style and practice in the theatre.

**Weigel, Helene** 1900–71 Austrian-born actress and theatre manager. She worked under JESSNER and was BRECHT's leading actress, becoming his second wife in 1928. Her performances in *The Mother* (1932) and *Mother*

*Courage and Her Children* (1949) gave the definitive interpretation of his female proletarian characters. The nominal director of the BERLINER ENSEMBLE, she took control of the company after Brecht's death and the tours she mounted established his international reputation.

**Weill, Kurt** 1900–50 German composer. He directed a small opera company before collaborating with BERTOLT BRECHT on such works as *The Threepenny Opera* and *The Rise and Fall of the City of Mahagonny*. With his wife, the actress Lotte Lenya, he went to America in 1935. He composed scores for *Johnny Johnson* (1936), *Knickerbocker Holiday* (1938), *Lady in the Dark* (1941), *One Touch of Venus* (1943), the opera *Street Scene* (1947) and *Lost in the Stars* (1949). His IRVING BERLIN shows have also been frequently revived in America. Although Weill's compositions for the American stage were more lyrical and optimistic than his Berlin scores, he worked with such noted writers as PAUL GREEN, MAXWELL ANDERSON and LANGSTON HUGHES in creating shows that tackled serious issues in an uncompromising way.

**Weimar style** German acting tradition. The term refers to the style of tragic acting cultivated by GOETHE while he was director of the Weimar Court Theatre between 1791 and 1817, and which was described in the 'Rules for Actors' which he wrote down as guidelines. Goethe expected his actors to be models of decorum on stage, scrupulously attentive to articulation, especially in the delivery of verse, and with constant grace and formality in stature and gesture. His rules were read by actors throughout the 19th century, and the style of acting they suggested was widely copied.

**Weise, Christian** 1642–1708 German schoolmaster and playwright. His plays, which were written for his students at the Zittau gymnasium, demonstrate a striking REALISM in contrast to the formal, often turgid drama of the baroque era. Among his best-known works are the tragedy *Masaniello* (1683) and the comedy *Peasant Machiavel* (1679).

**Weisenborn, Günter** 1902–63 German playwright and novelist. He made his name with *Submarine S4* (1928), the earliest example of a LIVING NEWSPAPER, dealing with the sinking of an American naval vessel. He continued this trend with works such as *Outside the Law* (1945), the first play about the Nazi period to be performed in Berlin after the war.

**Weiss, Peter** 1916–82 German playwright, novelist and graphic artist. Weiss's play the *Marat/Sade* (1964) brought him wide international recognition. The complexity of its structure is represented in the full title, *The Persecution and Assassination of Marat as Performed by the Inmates of the Asylum of Charenton under the Direction of the Marquis de Sade*. The multi-layered action combines the two contrasting poles of 20th-century theatre, ARTAUD and BRECHT, to present conflicting themes of revolution and repression, psychological freedom and social equality, in the framework of a madhouse world. PETER BROOK produced the London version in 1965.

Weiss's commitment to Marxism underlies *The Investigation* (produced by PISCATOR in 1965). Using transcripts from the 1964 Frankfurt War Crimes trials, it shows that genocide was the logical extension of capitalism. Subsequent plays extended the genre of documentary theatre to its limits and created a new form of psychological documentary. *The Song of the Lusitanian Bogey* (1967) and *Vietnam Discourse* (1968) deal with the history of colonialism using masks, songs and REVUE

elements. Weiss turned to analysing the role of the revolutionary writer in *Trotsky in Exile* (1970), a piece reflecting his own exile in Sweden, where he lived after 1939. *Hölderlin* (1971) presents the artist as the conscience of the revolution and reuses the image of madness to expose the moral grotesqueness of 19th-century society. Weiss returned again to earlier themes in his final play *The New Investigation* (1981).

**Weisse, Christian Felix** 1726–1804 German playwright. His highly successful *Richard III* (1759) was written, he claimed, without any knowledge of SHAKESPEARE's play. He also adapted, very severely, *Romeo and Juliet* (1767), which was the version most frequently performed in the 18th century. Weisse's SINGSPIELe, especially *Hell Is Let Loose* (1752) and *The Hunt* (1770), were also very popular.

**Wekwerth, Manfred** 1929– German director. From the former East Germany, he was manager of the BERLINER ENSEMBLE (1977–89) and director for that company from 1951. His *Coriolanus* for the NATIONAL THEATRE in London in 1971 complemented his production of BRECHT's version, which he had directed in Berlin and brought to London in 1965.

**Welfare State International** British company. Formed in Leeds in 1968 and now based in Ulverston, Cumbria, this loosely knit group of actors, sculptors, musicians, painters and pyrotechnologists, under the direction of John Fox and Boris Howarth, has fulfilled the 1960s dream of taking theatre to a mass audience. Their performances are constructed around some local concern or festivity, and members of the local community are involved in their planning and realization. Aesthetically, a Welfare State performance is not a 'play' but an event incorporating processions, dramatic pieces, firework displays, social dancing and communal eating and drinking, with a strong emphasis on visual images.

**well made play** A translation of the French *pièce bien faite*, the well made play was first codified by EUGÈNE SCRIBE (1791–1861). Since he (with assorted collaborators) wrote some 400 plays, he had little time for such frivolities as theory. By the mid-19th century, when the term came into common use, it was already derogatory, and yet its formulae have moulded some 150 years of Western drama.

The well made play is skilfully crafted to arouse suspense. It is an outgrowth of the comedy of intrigue: its action is propelled through a concatenation of causally related events. Beginning with a detailed, faintly disguised exposition, it gathers momentum through complications and crises, with each act closing on a climactic curtain. A series of perils for the protagonist leads to the revelation of a secret in an obligatory scene – named and analysed by the French critic FRANCISQUE SARCEY some half-century after Scribe codified the practice. The well made play then closes swiftly in a logical and plausible resolution. Technically, it thrives on fortuitous entrances and exits, mistaken identity and quid pro quos.

Scribe's structural influence is everywhere evident in 19th-century France – in SARDOU, AUGIER, DUMAS *fils*, LABICHE, FEYDEAU – and the formula swiftly crossed the English Channel and is seen in plays by BULWER LYTTON, TOM TAYLOR and T. W. ROBERTSON, not to mention HENRY JAMES and HENRIK IBSEN. Even SHAW, who fulminated against 'Sardoodledom', manipulated the formula in both his Pleasant and his Unpleasant Plays, and its carpentry has been learned by craftsmen as various as LILLIAN HELLMAN, TERENCE RATTIGAN, JEAN ANOUILH and HARVEY FIERSTEIN. Shaw's dismissal of the obligatory scene has been widely quoted: 'Once this scene was invented, nothing remained for the author to do except to prepare for it in a first act, and to use up its backwash in a third.' Yet that 'nothing' took considerable doing on the part of playwrights.

**Weller, Michael** 1942– American playwright. After productions at the EDINBURGH FESTIVAL FRINGE and at CHARLES MAROWITZ's Open Space (London) in 1969, he premiered *Cancer* at the ROYAL COURT in 1970. Renamed *Moonchildren*, it opened at the ARENA STAGE (Washington) in 1971 and depicts the hang-ups and idealism of the 'children of the sixties', a subject Weller returned to with *Loose Ends* (1979), which expresses the disillusionment of the 1970s as young people attempt to reconcile their ideals with the demands of careers, marriages and families. His other plays include *23 Years Later*, *Fishing*, *At Home*, *Spoils of War* and *Lake No Bottom* (1990), about the relationship of artist and critic. He wrote the screenplays for *Hair* (1979) and *Ragtime* (1980). His play *Help* was staged in 1994 at the Ensemble Theatre of Cincinnati.

**Welles, (George) Orson** 1915–85 American actor and director. Welles's acting career began in Dublin in 1931 and he made his New York debut in 1934. In 1936, as director of the Negro People's Theatre, New York, he staged a controversial 'voodoo' version of *Macbeth* with an all-black cast. In 1937, when appointed a director of the FEDERAL THEATRE PROJECT, he directed notable productions of *Dr Faustus* (and acted the title role) and *The Cradle Will Rock*. With JOHN HOUSEMAN he co-founded the same year New York's MERCURY THEATRE, remembered primarily for its modern-dress production of *Julius Caesar*. His radio version of H. G. Wells's *The War of the Worlds* (1938) inadvertently created a national panic (see RADIO DRAMA). He directed, co-authored and starred in *Citizen Kane* (1940), one of the most influential films in cinema history.

Welles's theatre impact lessened after World War II, although he is remembered for his 1946 version of *Around the World in Eighty Days*, his first appearance in London as Othello (1951), his adaptation and direction of *Moby Dick* in London (1955) and New York (1962), his direction and acting in *King Lear* (1956) at New York's City Center and his direction at London's ROYAL COURT THEATRE of *Rhinoceros* (1960).

**Wemyss, Francis Courtney** 1797–1859 English-born American actor and manager. A year after his first London appearance in 1821, Wemyss made his American debut at the CHESTNUT STREET THEATRE. His forte was COMEDY and FARCE, in roles such as Vapid in *The Dramatists*, Marplot in *The Busy Body* and Rover in *Wild Oats*. He later acted in New York with CHARLOTTE CUSHMAN, W. C. MACREADY, JOSEPH JEFFERSON III and LAURA KEENE. In 1827 he turned to management. He founded the Theatrical Fund to aid needy actors, edited 16 volumes of plays and wrote an informative autobiography, *Twenty-six Years of the Life of an Actor and Manager* (1847).

**Werfel, Franz** 1890–1945 Austrian playwright, novelist and poet. His early works are among the most interesting examples of EXPRESSIONISM, with their contemporary perspective on classical themes. His strongly pacifist adaptation of EURIPIDES' *Trojan Women* (1915) was followed by a 'magic trilogy' updating GOETHE's

*Faust* – *The Mirror Man* (1921), *The Goat Song* (1922), *The Silent One* (1923) – in which the revolt against authority typified by the plays of BRONNEN and HASENCLEVER is given a highly critical perspective. The tragic history of the Habsburg emperor in Mexico, *Juarez and Maximilian* (1925), won him an international reputation. *The Goat Song* was produced by the New York THEATRE GUILD in 1926, as was his wartime comedy on the rescue of an antisemitic Polish officer by a Jewish refugee, *Jacobowsky and the Colonel* (BROADWAY, 1944). His verse tragedy on the history of Jewish suffering, *The Eternal Road*, was staged by REINHARDT at the Manhattan Opera House in 1937. But Werfel is primarily remembered for his 1941 novel *The Song of Bernadette*.

**Werich, Jan** see VOSKOVEC, JIŘÍ

**Werkteater** (Work Theatre) Dutch cooperative society. Founded in Amsterdam in 1970, the Werkteater receives subsidy to investigate new possibilities in the theatre (see AKTIE TOMAAT; VORMINGSTONEEL). The aims are to find alternatives for acting methods taught at drama schools or used in repertory theatre and to investigate the relationship between actors and audience. The working method is democratic and collective; many of the performances develop from improvisations.

The Werkteater bears comparison with the LIVING THEATRE (the actor as a person merges with his part into a unity) and with JERZY GROTOWSKI (the actor is trained to develop his physical abilities, because the language of the body is considered to be *the* language of the theatre). The society's strong social involvement – apparent through plays like *Toestanden* (*Situations*, 1972), about situations in mental hospitals, *Bosch en Lucht* (*Forest and Air*, 1979), a play about 'ordinary' and mentally deficient people, and *Avondrood* (*Sunset Sky*, 1973), dealing with the issue of senior citizenship – is unlike the sharp line of approach seen in Vormingstoneel. In the early 1980s, some members left and set up solo projects, of which Joop Admiraal's *U bent mijn moeder* (*You Are My Mother*) was acclaimed in the Netherlands and abroad. In the mid-1980s Shireen Strooker and a new generation of actors performed existing plays, but after a few seasons they turned again to their own material and to improvisation.

**Werner, Zacharias** 1763–1823 German playwright. Werner was the only romantic dramatist to achieve popular recognition. His most widely performed play, *The Consecration of Power* (1807), is a five-act verse tragedy on the life of Martin Luther. His most famous, or notorious, play was the one-act SCHICKSALTRAGÖDIE, *The 24th of February* (1810), which dramatizes with mordant and unrelieved grimness the working-out of a family curse.

**Wertenbaker, Timberlake** Anglo-American playwright, resident in Britain. Her first plays provided feminist parables: *New Anatomies* (1981) was about two Victorian women who dressed as men; *Abel's Sister* (1984) concerns the effects on the mind of physical (and political) disabilities; *The Grace of Mary Traverse* (1985), set in the 18th century, is an exuberant study of women defying conventional roles. In *The Love of a Nightingale* (1988), a version of the myth of Philomel and Procne, Wertenbaker's interest in Greek theatre became apparent; she later adapted the two *Oedipus* plays and *Antigone* by SOPHOCLES to provide a trilogy for the ROYAL SHAKESPEARE COMPANY, *The Theban Plays* (1991). Her two most successful works, *Our Country's Good* (1988, based on Thomas Keneally's novel *The Playmaker*) and *Three*

*Birds Alighting in a Field* (1991) were directed by Max Stafford-Clark at the ROYAL COURT. The former, one of the outstanding plays of the decade, was a tribute to the redemptive power of theatre.

**Wesker, Arnold** 1932– British playwright. Wesker was, with OSBORNE, PINTER, LITTLEWOOD and DEVINE, one of the pioneers of modern British theatre. His first three plays, *Chicken Soup with Barley* (1958), *Roots* (1959) and *I'm Talking about Jerusalem* (1960), were a partly autobiographical trilogy. All three expressed the unforced socialism of his childhood, where the enemy was Fascism and the key to social progress lay in mass education. The trilogy was performed at the ROYAL COURT THEATRE in London, where JOAN PLOWRIGHT scored a personal triumph in *Roots* as Beatie, the Norfolk girl inspired by learning. In *The Kitchen* (1959, notably revived at the Court in 1994 by STEPHEN DALDRY) and *Chips with Everything* (1962), Wesker drew on his own experiences to provide vivid dramatic pictures of working lives. He became the founder-director of Centre 42, an arts centre established at the Round House at Chalk Farm, North London, deriving its name from Clause 42 in the Trade Union Charter. *Their Very Own and Golden City* (1965) and *The Friends* (1970) mourn the decline of utopian socialism in Britain.

Wesker's writing was moving towards a more lyrical, disillusioned and sometimes introverted, theatre. *The Four Seasons* (1965) is concerned with the waxing and waning of love, while *Love Letters on Blue Paper* (1976), *Caritas* (1981) and the one-woman trilogy of short plays, *Annie Wobbler* (1984), all concentrate on a particular person or state of mind. *The Journalists* (1975) and *The Merchant* (1976) tackle major themes but, with their large casts, have yet to be seen in London. He also directs and has written extensively about the craft of writing.

**West End** London theatre district. The centre of English commercial theatre gains its name from its geographical relationship to the City of London. It contains over 25 theatres within a relatively small area, ranging in size from the COLISEUM or the London Palladium with over 2,300 seats to the Windmill with 326 (though at one period the smallest was the Little Theatre, originally with only 250 seats), and in age from DRURY LANE where the first theatre was erected in 1663 to the Westminster, converted from a cinema in 1931. The older buildings have all been demolished, reconstructed and restored several times; but over half the theatres in the district were built between 1889 and 1909. Two, the Coliseum and COVENT GARDEN, are now opera houses, while others have seldom held anything but musicals and REVUES, like the Shaftesbury or the Windmill (which became a theatre-restaurant in 1981).

The reputations and the types of drama performed on West End stages have changed with successive managements, and some have never had an identifiable policy. But commercial pressures have taken their toll, and an increasing number of theatres have been taken over for musical spectaculars, such as the productions by ANDREW LLOYD WEBBER. As a result, in general it has been theatres outside the West End, with non-commercial policies, or subsidized companies, that have established standards, recovered the heritage of traditional drama or constituted the leading edge of modern English developments – the OLD VIC up to 1981, the LYRIC in Hammersmith during the 1920s, the Greenwich Theatre since 1969 and, in particular, the ROYAL COURT.

**West, Mae** 1893–1980 American actress and playwright. Her pose of unabashed but self-mocking sensuality made her a cult figure. She achieved notoriety in her first play *Sex* (1926), in which she took the lead. Attacked by the censors (see CENSORSHIP), she continued to defy them with *The Drag* (1927), the first American drama to depict a homosexual party; *Diamond Lil* (1928), a MELODRAMATIC comedy about white slavery; and *The Constant Sinner* (1931). Her Hollywood career in the 1930s increased her fame, but the limitations forced on her by production codes brought her back to BROADWAY in *Catherine Was Great* (1944). West always located her insatiable, man-eating temptresses safely in past eras, and her own attitude was one of worldly bemusement.

**Western, (Pauline) Lucille** 1843–77 American actress. Born of theatrical parents, she performed as a child with her sister in a piece designed to show off their dancing and farcical impersonations. As an adult, she excelled in emotional roles such as Lady Isabel in *East Lynne*, Marguerite Gautier in *Camille*, the title roles in *Lucretia Borgia* and *Leah the Forsaken*, and her most popular role, Nancy, in *Oliver Twist*. A dark-eyed beauty, she relied on inspiration more than art and gave the impression of being impulsive and untamed.

**Wheatley, William** 1816–76 American theatre manager and actor. Wheatley made his stage debut at the age of ten in 1826 at the PARK THEATRE, New York, as young Albert in W. C. MACREADY's production of *William Tell*. He later played the title role in *Tom Thumb*, establishing himself as a leading juvenile actor. He excelled as Nicholas Nickleby and Charles in *London Assurance*. In 1853 he became co-manager of the ARCH STREET THEATRE with John Drew (see DREW–BARRYMORE FAMILY) and later with John Sleeper Clarke until the outbreak of the Civil War. In 1862 he returned to New York and leased NIBLO'S GARDEN, where he produced elaborate romantic dramas including *The Duke's Motto* and *Arrah-na-pogue*. His biggest hit came in 1866 when *The Black Crook* began its 475-performance run, creating a vogue for elaborate musical spectacle and making Wheatley a rich man.

**Wheeler, Andrew C(arpenter)** [Trinculo; Nym Crinkle; J. P. Mowbray] 1832–1903 American drama critic. From 1869 he reviewed plays for various papers including the *Sunday World*, the *Leader*, the *Sun*, the *Dramatic Mirror*, the *Theatre* and the *World*. He was known also as a playwright, novelist, and essayist on nature (under the Mowbray pen-name). Wheeler popularized an aggressive style marked by devastating sarcasm. He opposed the Genteel Tradition, the aesthete views of WILLIAM WINTER, and the cultural shift of the country away from rugged individualism.

**White, George** 1890–1968 American dancer and producer. As a producer of successful musical REVUES in the 1920s, White provided stiff competition for FLORENZ ZIEGFELD. He started out as a dancer, and in 1919 produced the *Scandals of 1919*, the first revue in a series of 13. He introduced black dance steps such as the Charleston and the Black Bottom to white audiences. His fast-paced revues were also noted for the jazz music of GEORGE GERSHWIN and DeSylva, Brown and Henderson.

**White, Jane** 1922– African-American actress. White came early to BROADWAY as the female lead in *Strange Fruit* (1945). Thereafter she played mostly in OFF-BROADWAY and regional theatres, taking lead roles in *Blithe Spirit*, *The Taming of the Shrew*, and *Dark of the Moon* in 1948–9. In 1964 she appeared in three productions for the NEW YORK SHAKESPEARE FESTIVAL: *Love's Labour's Lost*, *Troilus and Cressida* and *Coriolanus* (as Volumnia). She played Clytemnestra in the Off-Broadway *Iphigenia in Aulis* (1967). As Goneril to MORRIS CARNOVSKY's King Lear (1975) she was hailed for her commanding intelligence, style and rich contralto voice. In 1991 she again played the role of Volumnia in *Coriolanus* (Folger Theatre, Washington), for which she had won an award 25 years earlier.

**White, Patrick (Victor Martindale)** 1912–90 Australian novelist and playwright. He was already an internationally known novelist when his four plays *The Ham Funeral* (1961), written in 1947, *The Season at Sarsaparilla* (1962), *A Cheery Soul* (1963) and *Night on Bald Mountain* (1964) were staged by university theatres in Adelaide and Melbourne. All make use of heightened language, expressionistic devices (see EXPRESSIONISM) and larger-than-life characterization. Later plays were *Big Toys* (1977), a comedy of Sydney high society; *Signal Driver* (1982) and *Netherwood* (1983). White was awarded the Nobel Prize for Literature in 1973.

**Whitefriars Theatre** (London) Part of the old Whitefriars monastery, it was used as a theatre by the CHILDREN OF THE CHAPEL ROYAL in 1608 when they had lost control of their BLACKFRIARS venue. The Children of the King's Revels and later the Children of the Queen's Revels played there. Two of JONSON's finest plays, *Epicoene* and *Bartholomew Fair*, were probably first performed at this obscure theatre, which fell into disuse after 1614.

**Whitehead, Ted** [Edward] **(Anthony)** 1933– British playwright. His plays for television and the theatre have concentrated on changing sexual manners, within and outside marriage, in contemporary Britain – e.g. *The Foursome* (1971) and *Alpha Beta* (1972), which describes the slow disintegration of a marriage over nine years. The horror of sexual frustration and despair extends on occasions to black FARCE, as in *Old Flames* (1975), where girlfriends congregate to eat their common boyfriend in a celebratory feast; but Whitehead is seen at his best in his bleakly naturalistic studies (see NATURALISM) which sometimes acquire, as in *The Sea-Anchor* (1974), a haunting atmosphere of loves lost and won.

**Whitelaw, Billie** 1932– British actress. She has worked extensively with both the NATIONAL THEATRE and the ROYAL SHAKESPEARE COMPANY, but it is her various appearances in the plays of SAMUEL BECKETT that have been of special importance. These have included *Play* (NT at the OLD VIC, 1964), *Not I* (ROYAL COURT, 1973 and 1975), *Footfalls* (Royal Court, 1976), *Happy Days* (Royal Court, 1979), *Rockaby* and *Enough* (NT, 1982). No other English actor has established such an authoritative command of the special qualities of Beckett's work. This emphasis should not, however, detract from the range of character and classical work which she has also undertaken, on stage and television, from Desdemona to Maggie Hobson (*Hobson's Choice*), and to Martha in ALBEE's *Who's Afraid of Virginia Woolf?* (1987).

**Whiting, John (Robert)** 1917–63 British playwright. Although his output as a stage dramatist was small, consisting of four major plays, he also wrote screenplays for films and television and adapted some French plays (by OBEY and ANOUILH) for the British stage. At a time when proletarian roughness was in vogue, he aspired towards elegant language, subtlety of thought and intricacy of dramatic techniques. His early plays were reminiscent of CHRISTOPHER FRY, erring towards flippancy in *A Penny for a Song* (1952) and religiosity in *Saint's Day* (1951). *Marching Song* (1954) handled the subject of postwar military guilt with originality and insight; while his best-known play, *The Devils*, based on Aldous Huxley's book *The Devils of Loudun*, was an early success at London's Aldwych Theatre (Shakespeare Memorial Company, 1961). *The Devils* proved that Whiting was ahead of his time in handling a complex historical narrative on an open stage, and that he was broadly liberal in his views, against all kinds of bigotry and intolerance.

**Wiehe, Michael** 1820–64 Danish actor. A leading actor at the KONGELIGE TEATER, he was much admired by IBSEN. Amongst his varied repertoire (including SHAKESPEARE, SCHILLER and HOLBERG), he excelled as melancholy romantic lovers, especially opposite JOHANNE LUISE HEIBERG whose ironic style contrasted well with his apparent vulnerability. He temporarily rebelled against what he felt was the Kongelige's frivolous repertoire by joining Frederik Høedt in his rival season at Christiansborg Court Theatre in 1855–6. His brother Wilhelm was also a successful actor.

**Wieth, Mogens** 1919–62 Danish actor. With his unusually expressive voice, Wieth established himself early at the KONGELIGE TEATER as a specialist in such lyrical roles as Peer Gynt and Orpheus in ANOUILH's *Eurydice*. In the late 1940s he shared brilliant seasons with Bodil Kjer at the Kongelige's New Stage, highlighted by *The Waltz of the Toreadors* and *The Misanthrope*. He was active in radio, TV and film, both in Scandinavia and in England, where his stage roles included a much admired Torvald in *A Doll's House*.

**Wignell, Thomas** 1753–1803 English-born American actor and manager. He joined his cousin LEWIS HALLAM's American Company in 1774 and soon became its leading man. Known primarily as a comedian, he played the role of Jonathan in the original production of ROYALL TYLER's *The Contrast* and created the prototype of the YANKEE character. In 1791 he joined the musician Alexander Reinagle to form the CHESTNUT STREET THEATRE. Wignell recruited English players including JAMES FENNELL, WILLIAM WARREN THE ELDER and THOMAS A. COOPER, making Philadelphia the theatrical capital of America and developing a touring circuit. When Wignell died, management of the company was assumed by actors Warren and WILLIAM B. WOOD. Warren married Mrs Wignell in 1806, and Wood joined him as owner of the company upon Reinagle's death in 1809. They finally disbanded in 1828.

**Wild West exhibition** A recreation of American FRONTIER life and skills popular in the late 19th century. P. T. BARNUM billed his Wild West extravaganza *Indian Life, or A Chance for a Wife* in 1874 as a 'thrilling arenic contest'. The genre took its definitive shape under the guidance of Col. (William Frederick) Buffalo Bill Cody (1846–1917), a former Indian fighter and buffalo hunter. He and Dr W. F. Carver organized a travelling show, *The Wild West*, which featured a programme of shooting, roping and riding, and an attack on the Deadwood stagecoach. In 1884 it went on the road. From the first, it presented the white frontiersman as a civilizing factor in overcoming the savage elements of Nature and American Indians. A European tour in 1887 (and again in 1903–6) made a deep impact, influencing the young BERTOLT BRECHT.

The cinema eventually took over and expanded the

depiction of cowboys and Indians, while authentic skills were relegated to the rodeo and CIRCUS 'after-shows'. One of Cody's stars, the sharp-shooter Annie Oakley (Phoebe Ann Moses, 1866–1926), was to inspire the IRVING BERLIN MUSICAL COMEDY *Annie Get Your Gun* (1946). ARTHUR KOPIT's play *Indians* (1969) paints a sardonic picture of the relationship between Cody's exhibitions and the plight of the Native American.

**Wildbrandt, Adolf** 1837–1911 German playwright and director. During the 1870s and 1880s Wildbrandt was closely associated with the BURGTHEATER, first as a writer of historical plays and of comedies, then, between 1881 and 1887, as director. His finest play, *The Master of Palmyra* (1889), was written after he had retired from the Burgtheater.

**Wilde, Oscar** [Fingal O'Flahertie Wills] 1854–1900 Anglo-Irish playwright, poet, novelist, essayist and wit. Wilde's first play, *Vera: or, The Nihilists* (1883), is a MELODRAMA about a group of Russian revolutionary terrorists. His second, *The Duchess of Padua* (1891), is a costume TRAGEDY in blank verse, first staged, like *Vera*, in New York. He began to find his own voice in drama after the publication of his controversial novel, *The Picture of Dorian Gray* (1891). *Lady Windermere's Fan* (1892), produced by GEORGE ALEXANDER at the ST JAMES'S, is a formal example of the WELL MADE PLAY, in which the heroine's reputation rests on the discreet recovery of a fan. *A Woman of No Importance* (1893) and *An Ideal Husband* (1895) are fairly conventional in terms of plot and subject-matter; but the lively work of Wilde's plays is done in the dialogue. His upper-class dandies and dowagers have made so merry with the values that the plays purport to uphold that the saving of a marriage has, by the time it is achieved, little more significance than the saving of a cigarette card.

In his brilliant masterpiece, *The Importance of Being Earnest* (1895), the conventions of dramatic fiction become the subject rather than the disguise of the plot, turning the title on its head. Shortly after *Earnest's* opening at the St James's, the first of two sensational trials began. As the evidence of Wilde's homosexual practices was revealed in court, George Alexander removed Wilde's name from posters and programmes and then withdrew the play altogether. It was during Wilde's spell of imprisonment in Reading Gaol that he begged SARAH BERNHARDT to produce *Salomé* in Paris (1896). LUGNÉ-POE staged it instead. Written some years earlier, it is a symbolist extravaganza (see SYMBOLISM) about the killing of John the Baptist. The Chamberlain's office banned the play in England until 1931 (see CENSORSHIP), when the English version translated by Wilde's lover, Lord Alfred Douglas, was first publicly shown.

Wilde was known to have planned several plays in prison; in the sad aftermath he wrote only part of a one-act piece, *A Florentine Tragedy*, subsequently completed by T. Sturge Moore and produced in London in 1906.

**Wildenbruch, Ernst von** 1845–1909 German playwright. In the course of an active military and diplomatic career, Wildenbruch wrote several popular, nationalistic plays with historical settings, which were performed by the MEININGEN COMPANY. *The Quitzows* (1888), about the Hohenzollerns, was the most acclaimed, though his trilogy about the Emperor Henry IV (1896) was also a success.

**Wilder, Clinton** 1920–86 American producer. Wilder began his professional career as a stage manager for *A*

*Streetcar Named Desire* in 1947. He turned to producing and later joined with Richard Barr to form a production company, Theatre 1960 (later 1961, 1962, and so on), to present non-commercial avant-garde plays. Their achievements include *The American Dream*, *The Death of Bessie Smith* and *Happy Days* (1961); *Who's Afraid of Virginia Woolf?*, *Endgame*, *The Sandbox*, *Death-watch* and *Zoo Story* (1962). Joined by EDWARD ALBEE in 1963, they offered *The Dutchman* and *Tiny Alice* (1964), *Malcolm* and *The Long Christmas Dinner* (1966), *A Delicate Balance*, *Rimers of Eldritch* and *Everything in the Garden* (1967), and *Seascape* (1975).

**Wilder, Thornton (Niven)** 1897–1975 American playwright and novelist. While Wilder may be considered one of America's top ten playwrights, his reputation rests upon three full-length plays and a half-dozen one-acts, beginning in 1931 with the publication of *The Long Christmas Dinner & Other Plays in One Act* – three realistic and three radically experimental sketches. In 1938 his Pulitzer Prize-winning *Our Town* opened on BROADWAY, employing many of the experimental techniques Wilder had used in his one-acts: minimal scenery, narrative descriptions. *Our Town*, which has been endlessly revived, opens by examining small-town life in Grover's Corners, New Hampshire, in 1901; succeeding acts fulfil the cycle of marriage, birth and death, ending with Emily Gibbs's conversation with the dead whom she has just joined. Wilder's next play, *The Merchant of Yonkers* (revised as *The Matchmaker*, 1954), was unsuccessful until converted into the musical *Hello, Dolly!* (1964). *The Skin of Our Teeth* (1942), a parable of the world's history centred on the Antrobus family, was highly acclaimed.

**Wilkie, Allan** ?1889–1970 Scottish-born actor and manager. His first Australian SHAKESPEARE season was in 1916, and from 1920 to 1930 he toured Australia and New Zealand, mainly in Shakespeare. Wilkie's company, with his wife Frediswyde Hunter-Watts as leading lady, was known for its fine acting, with economical settings and elegant COSTUMES. Unable to survive the Depression after 1930, the Wilkies moved to Canada and travelled through North America in Shakespeare recitals, eventually returning to Scotland.

**Wilkinson, Tate** 1739–1803 English actor and manager. He was famed for his mimicry of other actors, such as PEG WOFFINGTON; his imitation of GARRICK at COVENT GARDEN cost Wilkinson his friendship. In 1770 he took on sole management of the York circuit of six theatres in the North of England. He reformed abuses in the theatres and employed most rising stars, including JOHN PHILIP KEMBLE and his sister SARAH SIDDONS. His engaging *Memoirs* were published in 1790 and his account of the Yorkshire circuit, *The Wandering Patentee*, in 1795.

**Williams, Bert** [Egbert Austin Williams] 1874–1922 African-American comedian. Born in Nassau, British West Indies, he began in MINSTREL SHOWS, where he had to affect blackface to conceal his light complexion, and to learn the standard 'stage-darky' dialect. From 1893 to 1908 he teamed with George Walker (1873–1911), who played the flashy free-spending urban sport to Williams's melancholy, shuffling fall-guy, both in VAUDEVILLE and in a series of successful all-black musicals, including *Sons of Ham* (1900), *In Dahomey* (1902) and *Bandana Land* (1908). Williams was known nationwide for such lugubrious songs as 'I'm a Jonah Man' and 'Nobody'. He became the first black performer in the ZIEGFELD *Follies*, in which he played from 1910 to 1919.

'The funniest man I ever saw and the saddest man I ever knew', as W. C. FIELDS called him, played in tandem with Leon Errol and EDDIE CANTOR, and never failed with his one-man poker game.

**Williams, Emlyn** 1905–87 Welsh playwright and actor. He established the psychological thriller with *A Murder Has Been Arranged* (1930) and *Night Must Fall* (1935), a line he continued with plays like *Someone Waiting* (1953). His best work is the semi-autobiographical study of the relationship between a young Welsh miner and his schoolteacher, *The Corn Is Green*, which ran for two years with himself in the lead role when first performed in 1935. His numerous other plays range from behind-the-scenes drama in SHAKESPEARE's theatre (*Spring 1600*, 1934) to the supernatural and religious (*The Wind of Heaven*, 1945; *Trespass*, 1947). He also made adaptations, including his first farcical success *The Late Christopher Bean* (1933) and *The Master Builder* (for OLIVIER at the NATIONAL THEATRE, 1964). Williams also won international success as a performer, e.g. in his one-man shows as DICKENS (from 1951) and in *Growing Up*, based on readings from DYLAN THOMAS (from 1955).

**Williams, Tennessee** [Thomas Lanier] 1911–83 American playwright. From 1945, with his first success *The Glass Menagerie*, Tennessee Williams has had a deep impact on the American theatre, bringing to it an original lyric voice and a new level of sexual frankness. Among American playwrights his achievement is equalled only by that of EUGENE O'NEILL.

The pleasure and the pain of sex constituted the subject of both his work and his life, and he returned repeatedly to the same neurotic conflicts embedded within the same character types: the spirits of Blanche Du Bois and Stanley Kowalski, the fierce antagonists of *A Streetcar Named Desire* (1947), haunt practically all of his fables and have provided vehicles for bravura acting. As in *Streetcar*, the battle between repression and release, between the puritan and the cavalier, is at the heart of Williams's work (*Summer and Smoke*, 1948; *The Rose Tattoo*, 1951; and *Battle of Angels*, 1940, rewritten as *Orpheus Descending*, 1957). In some plays (*Battle of Angels* and *You Touched Me*, 1945; *Sweet Bird of Youth*, 1959) lusty men reanimate languishing women; in others (*Cat on a Hot Tin Roof*, 1955; *The Milk Train Doesn't Stop Here Anymore*, 1963) the refusal of desirable males to satisfy deprived women provides the central conflict. Sometimes, as in *Suddenly Last Summer* (1958), men withhold sex from women because they are homosexual: in the American theatre of the 1950s and 1960s Williams was unable to write openly about his own homosexual passion.

After *The Night of the Iguana* (1961), an uncharacteristic play of resolution and completion, Williams's work was less successful as he became increasingly dependent on drugs and alcohol. Some of his plays, notably *The Gnädiges Fräulein* (1966), *In the Bar of a Tokyo Hotel* (1969) and *Outcry* (1973), chronicle the despair of creators who have lost control of their art. Others such as *Small-Craft Warnings* (1972) and especially *Vieux Carré* (1978) are attempts at self-restoration in which he returns to the delicacy of *The Glass Menagerie*, displaying compassion not only for others but also for himself as a young man.

**Williamson, David (Keith)** 1942– Australian playwright. His early plays *The Coming of Stork* (1970) and *The Removalists* (1971) were written while he was a thermodynamics lecturer. His astute observation of contemporary Australian society and his ear for the vernacular's ironies and self-betrayals make him Australia's most successful playwright. His plays include *Don's Party* (1971), *What if You Died Tomorrow* (1973), *The Club* (1977), *Travelling North* (1979) and *The Perfectionist* (1982); *Sons of Cain* (1985), dealing with political corruption; *Emerald City* (1987), exploring a screenwriter's conflict between artistic integrity and commercialism; *Money and Friends* (1991) and *Brilliant Lies* (1993), dealing with sexual harassment. He also wrote the TELEVISION DRAMA miniseries *The Last Bastion* (1984).

**Williamson, J(ames) C(assius)** 1845–1913 Australian entrepreneur. Born in Pennsylvania, he was an actor-dancer in New York and San Francisco before touring Australia in 1874 in *Struck Oil*. Returning to settle in 1879, he soon became Australia's leading manager, largely through importing overseas successes; his enforcing of his rights to *HMS Pinafore* and other pieces confirmed British COPYRIGHT laws in Australia. Through various partnerships he established a firm which dominated Australian theatre until 1976. When he died, all Australian theatres remained dark for a night in his memory.

**Williamson, Nicol** 1938– British actor. His first major success came in 1964 as Maitland the tormented solicitor in JOHN OSBORNE's *Inadmissible Evidence*, which revealed his talents to express a powerful if introverted personality – the inwardness which later, in 1969, allowed Williamson to become one of the most celebrated Hamlets of his generation. He is also an excellent comic actor, as in the New York production of *Plaza Suite* (1969), and appeared in a wide variety of films. He took the title roles in *Coriolanus* and *Macbeth* ( Royal Shakespeare Company, 1973) and in a studio performance of *Uncle Vanya* (RSC, 1974). He also developed a solo performance, involving poetry readings, extracts from plays and singing in a quiet, intense style, which made him a highly effective CABARET performer.

**Willis, Nathaniel Parker** 1806–67 American essayist and playwright. Willis began an intense but brief association with the theatre with *Bianca Visconti* (1837), the winner of actress Josephine Clifton's $1,000 competition. *The Kentucky Heiress* (1837), also written for Clifton, failed. In 1839 Willis wrote *Tortesa the Usurer* for J. W. WALLACK, the story of a rich man who bargains for an aristocratic wife but accepts a glover's daughter. Audiences, however, did not appreciate his literary comedy, and star actors did not want plays with several starring roles. Enjoying a reputation as the foremost essayist in America, Willis stopped writing plays.

**Wills, W(illiam) G(orman)** 1828–91 Anglo-Irish playwright and painter. Wills provided HENRY IRVING with many of his LYCEUM successes. These included *Charles I* (1872), *Eugene Aram* (1873), *Vanderdecken* (1878) and *Faust* (1885). From his attempts to combine poetry with drama the only enduring success was *Olivia* (1878), an adaptation of GOLDSMITH's novel, *The Vicar of Wakefield*, in which ELLEN TERRY performed.

**Wilson, August** 1945– African-American playwright. He has written a series of plays, each set in a different decade, which he terms his 'view of the black experience of the 20th century', drawing on his own experience of growing up in a black slum district of Pittsburgh, Pennsylvania. His work has been fostered in the regions, with premieres at the YALE REPERTORY THEATRE, beginning with *Ma Rainey's Black Bottom* (1984) and including *Joe Turner's Come and Gone* (1986), *Fences* (1987), *The Piano Lesson* (1988) and *Two Trains Running*

(1990). The latter, set in 1968 at a restaurant in Pittsburgh opposite a funeral home and a meat market, focuses on disenfranchised characters looking back nostalgically and with some confusion at their limited 'progress'. Wilson's 1940s play, *Seven Guitars*, which centres on the lives of a blues musician, premiered in 1995 at Chicago's GOODMAN THEATRE. He has transcended the categorization of 'black' playwright to reach a broad-based audience.

**Wilson, Francis** 1854–1935 American comedian and singer. From 1885 to 1889 he appeared in comic operas with the McCaull Opera Company, then established his own company. His greatest role was that of Cadeaux in *Erminie* (1886), a part he played nearly 1,300 times over 35 years. His other successes included *The Merry Monarch* (1890), *The Lion Tamer* (1891), *Half a King* (1896) and *The Toreador* (1902). Because of his early training in a STOCK COMPANY, Wilson brought to his musical roles the skills of a character actor, carefully preparing each move and gesture rather than trusting to improvisation.

**Wilson, Lanford** 1937– American playwright. Wilson began writing plays at university and then became part of a group of playwrights at the Caffé Cino in New York, where his first script was produced, *So Long at the Fair* (1963). Since then his plays have been produced at the CIRCLE REPERTORY COMPANY, which he helped to found, at Café LA MAMA in New York, in London and on BROADWAY. Among the more successful are *The Madness of Lady Bright* (1964), *Balm in Gilead* and *This Is the Rill Speaking* (1965), *Rimers of Eldritch* (1966), *Lemon Sky* (1970), *The Great Nebula in Orion* (1971), *The Hot l Baltimore* (1973), *5th of July* (1978), and *Talley's Folly* (1979). His 1983 *Angel's Fall* was a critical, but not popular, success. In 1988 his *Burn This* appeared on Broadway, then four years later in London. *Redwood Curtain* dates from 1992.

**Wilson, Robert** died 1600 English actor and playwright. Famous as an extemporizer, Wilson was with LEICESTER'S MEN after 1572 and with QUEEN ELIZABETH'S MEN after 1583. His three surviving plays, *The Three Ladies of London* (c.1581), *The Three Lords and Three Ladies of London* (c.1589) and *The Cobbler's Prophecy* (c.1594), show a professional ability to adapt mid-century drama to the changing taste of the early PUBLIC THEATRES.

**Wilson, Robert** 1941– American director and designer. Wilson's training as a painter and architect is evident in his painterly theatre compositions. His work with brain-damaged children, using physical activity to stimulate mental activity, also influenced his dreamy pieces with their slow pace and repetition of simple movements, e.g. *A Letter to Queen Victoria* (1974) and *Einstein on the Beach* (1976), composed with the help of an autistic adolescent. Operatic in scale, Wilson's streams of visual and aural images lack plots and characters in any conventional sense and often employ massive scenery, animals and complex lighting effects. *Deafman Glance* (1970) lasted eight hours and *Overture to Ka Mountain*, created for the 1972 Shiraz Festival in Iran, lasted a week. In the 1980s he began to work in Europe, where it was easier to find funding. There he created *The Man in the Raincoat* (1981, Cologne), *Great Day in the Morning* (1982, Paris), *The Golden Windows* (1982, Munich), *the CIVIL warS* (1983, five countries) and *The Black Rider: The Casting of Magic Bullets* (1990, Hamburg; 1993, New York). In recent years Wilson has directed classic plays and operas. In conjunction with his direction of IBSEN's *When We Dead Awaken* at the AMERICAN REPERTORY THEATRE in 1991, a retrospective of his work was mounted at Boston's Museum of Fine Arts.

**Wilton, Marie (Effie)** 1839–1921 British actress and manager. Known as the 'Queen of BURLESQUE' at London's Strand Theatre (1858–64), she determined on a career in legitimate drama and entered into theatre management at the age of 25, borrowing money to buy the lease of the disreputable Queen's Theatre and sharing the management with H. J. BYRON. In the renamed Prince of Wales's she re-created the atmosphere of decorous Victorian domesticity, with ornamental flowers, anti-macassars, carpeted aisles and chintz. Audiences responded with enthusiasm. The crowning achievement was her annual staging from 1865 to 1870 of six comedies by T. W. ROBERTSON, including *Caste* (1867), in which she created one of her finest roles, that of Polly Eccles. Her Captain Hawtree was SQUIRE BANCROFT, whom she married and to whom she relinquished the management. She contributed to the growth of ensemble acting, the raising of the status of actors and the increasing appropriateness of stage decor. From 1880 to 1885 the Bancrofts managed the HAYMARKET.

**Winge, Stein** 1940– Norwegian director. Winge became prominent in the 1970s with highly physical productions of SHAKESPEARE, IBSEN and GOETHE. More recent examples include a provocative, unnerving *Hamlet* in the NORSKE TEATRET's Rehearsal Hall (1987) and a boldly expressionistic (see EXPRESSIONISM) *Inspector General* at GÖTEBORGS STADSTEATER (1993). His six-hour production of DORST's *Merlin* in 1989 was overwhelming. He works entirely within institutional theatres, but in innovative ways: at NATIONALTHEATRET he founded the experimental Teatret på Torshov in 1977, and as director there (1990–2) promoted new approaches to IBSEN.

**Winter, William** [Mercutio] 1836–1917 American drama critic. Winter took charge of the *Albion*'s dramatic department (1861–5), writing under the name of Mercutio. From 1865 to 1909 he was chief critic for the *New York Tribune*, establishing himself as the leader of his generation. His critical beliefs were essentially Aristotelian, tempered with 19th-century romantic idealism (later called 'the Genteel Tradition'); he considered acting the primary art of theatre, and the standard drama preferable to modern plays. Beauty and morality were inseparable in art; he rejected the notion that art should depict real life and saw IBSENism as a 'rank, deadly pessimism'. Winter prepared acting versions of SHAKESPEARE's plays for EDWIN BOOTH and AUGUSTIN DALY, and among other critical works wrote lengthy biographies of Booth (1893), ADA REHAN (1898), RICHARD MANSFIELD (1910), JOSEPH JEFFERSON III (1913) and TYRONE POWER (the father of the film actor, 1913).

**Winter Garden Theatre** (New York City) An important BROADWAY musical house, designed for the SHUBERT BROTHERS, it opened in 1911 and was decorated with a garden motif. In 1912 the Winter Garden became the home of *The Passing Show* (an annual Shubert REVUE designed to compete with FLORENZ ZIEGFELD's *Follies*), which was presented regularly until 1924. During the 1910s and early 1920s the theatre featured light musicals, vehicles for AL JOLSON. It has since been the home of such major musicals as *West Side Story* (1957), *Gypsy* (1959) and *Cats* (1982, and still playing in 1995). The Winter Garden, which seats some 1,500 spectators, is owned by the Shubert Organization.

**Witkiewicz** [Witkacy], **Stanisław Ignacy** 1885–1939 Polish playwright, painter, novelist and philosopher.

Unrecognized by his contemporaries, he has emerged since 1956 as a seminal figure. Having served in the Russian army, witnessing the Revolution of 1917, he wrote over 30 plays between 1918 and 1926, many unpublished and unperformed. His theory of *Pure Form in the Theatre* (1920) seeks to liberate drama from storytelling and traditional psychology, and give it the formal possibilities of modern art and music. His works present an apocalyptic vision of the loss of metaphysical feelings in the coming anthill civilization, viewed with mocking irreverence and self-irony. Major plays are *They* (1920), *Gyubal Wahazar*, *The Water Hen* (1921), *The Madman and the Nun*, *The Crazy Locomotive* (1923), *The Mother* (1924), *The Beelzebub Sonata* (1925) and *The Shoemakers* (1934).

**Wodehouse, P(elham) G(renville)** 1881–1975 English novelist and playwright. Famous for his novels, he worked with Guy Bolton on many of the most successful English musical comedies between 1917 and 1935 (see MUSICAL COMEDY), such as *Have a Heart* (1917) and *Leave It to Jane* (1917), as well as collaborating with GEORGE GROSSMITH and Ian Hay on a series of FARCES.

**Woffington, Peg** [Margaret] ?1714–60 Irish actress. In 1737 she was starring at Dublin's Smock Alley Theatre. In 1740 she was triumphant in the BREECHES PART of Sir Harry Wildair in FARQUHAR's *The Constant Couple*. In 1742 she was Lady Anne to GARRICK's Richard III. She became his mistress and lived with him but they never married. She left DRURY LANE in 1748 and started to play tragic roles. Rivalry with GEORGE ANNE BELLAMY reached a climax with a fight when they were playing *The Rival Queens* in 1756. She collapsed on stage as Rosalind when delivering the epilogue to *As You Like It* in 1757.

**Wolf, Friedrich** 1888–1953 German playwright. His topical plays – *Cyanide* (1929), dealing with abortion from his experience as a medical practitioner, and *Tai Yang Awakes*, on the Shanghai workers' uprising of 1927, staged by PISCATOR in 1931 – made him the rival of BRECHT as the most significant political dramatist in the Weimar Republic. He later published the journal *Volk und Kunst* and was GDR ambassador to Poland.

**Wolfe, George C.** 1955– African-American playwright and director. Wolfe's first New York show, the musical *Paradise!* (1985), presented at PLAYWRIGHTS HORIZONS, was unsuccessful, but he followed it with *The Colored Museum* (1986), a hilarious lampoon of black experience topics. In 1990 he directed his play *Spunk* at the Public Theater, based on three Zora Neale Hurston short stories, followed the same year by his Public Theater production of BRECHT's *The Caucasian Chalk Circle* (set in Haiti). He became one of three resident directors at the NEW YORK SHAKESPEARE FESTIVAL. His musical about Jelly Roll Morton, *Jelly's Last Jam*, premiered in Los Angeles (1991) before opening on BROADWAY (1992). Shortly before his direction of the acclaimed *Angels in America* (for which he won the 1993 Tony for direction), Wolfe was appointed producer of the NYSF.

**Wolff, Egon** 1926– Chilean playwright. Born of German parents, he is a chemical engineer who owns a small factory in Santiago. His early plays focus on psychological problems, generational conflicts and social issues. Among many titles, two stand out. *Los invasores* (*The Invaders*, 1962), with a surrealistic technique (see SURREALISM) and a touch of J. B. PRIESTLEY's *An Inspector Calls*, portrays violently the threat of class revolution if the bourgeoisie continues to ignore social concerns. *Flores de papel* (*Paper Flowers*, 1970) deals with gratuitous violence in an obtuse class struggle. Later titles include *Kindergarten* (1977), *Espejismos* (*Mirages*, 1978), *José* (1980) and *La balsa de la Medusa* (*Medusa's Raft*, 1984, the third part of his famous trilogy). *Háblame de Laura* (*Tell Me about Laura*, 1986) was followed by *Invitacíon a comer* (*Invitation to Lunch*) and *Cicatrices* (*Stars*, 1993).

**Wolff, Pius Alexander** 1782–1828 German actor. According to GOETHE, Wolff was the only actor who fully mastered the WEIMAR STYLE. He left the Weimar Court Theatre in 1816 for the BERLIN ROYAL THEATRE. Here his interpretations of Hamlet became legendary. Wolff was the author of the highly popular comedy, *Preziosa* (1821).

**Wolfit, Donald** 1902–68 British actor-manager. He established a reputation as a Shakespearian actor with the OLD VIC in 1929–30, at Stratford-upon-Avon in 1936, and with his own company from 1937. He toured widely, giving memorable performances not only as Shylock in *The Merchant of Venice*, Macbeth and Lear, but also in the title role of JONSON's *Volpone* and in MASSINGER's *A New Way to Pay Old Debts*. He also offered striking interpretations of modern plays, including HOCHWÄLDER's *The Strong Are Lonely* (1955), IBSEN's *Ghosts* (1959) and *John Gabriel Borkman* (1963), as well as classical drama such as *Oedipus Rex* and *Oedipus at Colonus* (1953). He was knighted in 1957.

**Wood, Charles (Gerald)** 1933– British playwright. Wood, who served as a soldier, has written attacks on militarism, British imperialism and the class system embodied in the army ranks. *Dingo* (1967), set in North Africa during World War II, and *H: Being Monologues at Front of Burning Cities* (1969), about the 'Christian' General Havelock who commanded the British forces in India at the time of the Indian mutiny, are epic tirades on the folly and hypocrisies of war. In a lighter vein he has written amusing comedies about a run-down REPERTORY THEATRE, *Fill the Stage with Happy Hours* (1966), the welfare state (*Meals on Wheels*) and Hollywood, including *Veterans* (1972), *Has 'Washington' Legs?* (1978) and *Across from the Garden of Allah* (1986). He has written widely for television; *Tumbledown* (1988), about the treatment of a wounded officer during the Falklands War, aroused much controversy when it was produced by the BBC (see TELEVISION DRAMA).

**Wood, John** British actor. Tall and lean and with a characteristic acerbic delivery, Wood joined the joined the OLD VIC Company in 1954. After joining the ROYAL SHAKESPEARE COMPANY in 1971 he was offered parts in both Shakespearian and modern plays which revealed his exceptional intelligence and expressivity. In 1974, as Carr in TOM STOPPARD's *Travesties*, he provided a brilliantly comic study of a bemused minor Foreign Office official. Other roles include Richard III (NATIONAL THEATRE, 1979), Prospero in *The Tempest* (1989), Solness in *The Master Builder* (1989), Sheridan Whiteside in the GEORGE S. KAUFMAN and MOSS HART comedy *The Man Who Came to Dinner* (1989) and the title role in NICHOLAS HYTNER's production of *King Lear* (1990). He has also made film appearances, e.g. as a 1930s actor in Woody Allen's *The Purple Rose of Cairo*.

**Wood, Mrs John** [née Matilda Charlotte Vining] 1831–1915 British-born actress and manager. After a career in provincial English theatre she married the actor John Wood and went to Boston (1854), where they became regulars with the Boston Company. She played at WALLACK's Theatre in 1856, creating the role of Minnehaha in Charles Walcot's *Hiawatha*. Afterwards, having separated from her husband, she played starring engagements. In 1863 she began a three-year stint as manager of the Olympic Theatre. She returned to England in 1866 and acted only once more (1872–3) in America. Saucy, impudent and fun-loving, Mrs Wood was described as one of the best ever BURLESQUE actresses on the American stage.

**Wood, William B(urke)** 1779–1861 American actor and manager. Born of English parents in Montreal, Canada, he joined THOMAS WIGNELL's Philadelphia company, ultimately finding his niche in management, becoming assistant to WILLIAM WARREN THE ELDER at the CHESTNUT STREET THEATRE. Warren and Wood brought their Philadelphia, Baltimore and Washington theatres to international eminence during the 1820s-40s.

**Woollcott, Alexander** 1887–1943 American drama critic. Woollcott made his debut as a critic for the *New York Times* in 1914. His battles with the SHUBERT BROTHERS in 1915 made him a celebrity. He helped establish that witty 'vicious circle' that met for lunch at the 'Algonquin Round Table'. In 1929 he established his 'Shouts and Murmurs' column in the *New Yorker*, began his radio show, and collaborated on a play with GEORGE S. KAUFMAN. He appeared frequently as an actor, playing, according to BROOKS ATKINSON, 'a sort of virtuoso fat man'. Woollcott remains best known as the model for Sheridan Whiteside in Kaufman and MOSS HART's *The Man Who Came to Dinner*. Vitality and urbanity were his trademarks.

**Wooster Group** New York company. Formed in 1975 by successors to Richard Schechner's PERFORMANCE GROUP, the Wooster Group is politically radical and composes multimedia theatre pieces, often exploring suppressed and disturbing elements of society and culture, restructuring the spectator–performer relationship unconventionally. The Group's other members include SPALDING GRAY. Notable pieces include the tetralogy *Three Places in Rhode Island* (1975–9), the trilogy *The Road to Immortality* (1981–7) and its epilogue *Brace Up!* (1990).

**Worth, Irene** 1916– American-born actress. Known equally on both sides of the Atlantic, she has been especially praised for the musicality of her voice and her commanding stage presence. She made her professional debut in the USA, but went to London in 1944 for a classical training. She appeared as Celia in the premiere of *The Cocktail Party* at the EDINBURGH FESTIVAL (1949). After working with the OLD VIC Company (1951–3), with TYRONE GUTHRIE and ALEC GUINNESS she helped found the STRATFORD FESTIVAL (Ontario) in 1953. She joined the ROYAL SHAKESPEARE COMPANY, appearing as Goneril in PETER BROOK's production of *King Lear* (1962). Other notable appearances have included *Tiny Alice* (New York, 1964; Royal Shakespeare Company, 1970), as a 'majestically unruffled' Volumnia in *Coriolanus* at London's NATIONAL THEATRE (1984), and as Grandma Kurnitz in NEIL SIMON's *Lost in Yonkers* (1991).

**Wycherley, William** 1641–1715 English playwright. He trained for the law. His first play, *Love in a Wood* (1671), gained him a high literary reputation. After *The Gentleman Dancing-Master* for the Duke's Company (1672), Wycherley wrote the two masterpieces that confirmed his reputation as the most brilliant satiric dramatist of his day – *The Country Wife* (1675) and *The Plain Dealer* (1676). The genial SATIRE of his first plays reached a climax in *The Country Wife* where the hero, Horner, pretends castration as a cover for his affairs, exposing the follies of society. *The Plain Dealer* is a darker version of MOLIÈRE's *The Misanthrope*, a powerful play tracing the deceptions of love and friendship through a central figure, Manley, an obsessive and savage satirist. From this point Wycherley's career went downhill; he lost favour at court for many years, was imprisoned for debt and did not write another play. He wrote mediocre poems, published a massive volume of them in 1704, and was later helped by Pope in his revisions of later poems. On his release from prison, James II gave him a pension.

**Wyndham, Charles** [Charles Culverwell] 1837–1919 British actor and manager. From 1870 to 1872 he toured his own Comedy Company around the Midwest theatres of the USA, presenting plays by T. W. ROBERTSON and JAMES ALBERY and establishing his reputation as an actor in BRONSON HOWARD's *Saratoga*. Returning to England, in 1875 he became manager of London's Criterion, in which he retained an interest for the rest of his life. Wyndham exploited the intimacy of the small basement theatre in a series of society FARCES. His favourite part was the title-role of T. W. Robertson's *David Garrick*, but the Criterion was associated rather with the society comedies of HENRY ARTHUR JONES, particularly *The Case of Rebellious Susan* (1894) and *The Liars* (1897), in both of which Wyndham excelled. In 1899 he assumed the management of the new Wyndham's Theatre, which later housed Jones's *Mrs Dane's Defence* (1900) and the first English performance of ROSTAND's *Cyrano de Bergerac* (1903). He was knighted in 1902, and in 1903 the New Theatre opened under his management.

**Wynn, Ed** [Isaiah Edwin Leopold] 1886–1966 American comedian. Wynn began in VAUDEVILLE and found a comfortable solo niche in MUSICAL COMEDY, including *The Perfect Fool* (1921), which became his nickname, *Simple Simon* (1930), *The Laugh Parade* (1931) and *Hurray for What?* (1937). His stage persona wore horn-rimmed glasses and a tiny pork-pie hat, spoke with a lisp, giggled and walked with a mincing gait. Many of his GAGS were predicated on an inability to complete an anecdote or a piece of music; his insane inventions included a typewriter carriage for eating corn-on-the-cob and a cigarette lighter that pointed out the nearest matches. He later appeared on radio, film and television.

**Wyspiański, Stanisław** 1869–1907 Polish painter, poet and playwright. Drawing upon Polish romantic drama, particularly MICKIEWICZ's ideas, he revolutionized stage design and production in his work for the Cracow theatre. His *Study of Hamlet* (1905) calls for a synthesis of the arts, with stress on setting and COSTUME. His plays, symbolist in orientation (see SYMBOLISM), interweave the real and fantastic, and join Polish history to Greek and biblical myth. Plays on national issues include *Song of Warsaw* (1898), *The Wedding*, *Deliverance* (1901), *November Night* (1903), *Acropolis* (1904) and *Legend* (1905); those on mythological themes are *Protesilas and Laodamia*, *Achilleis* (1903) and *The Return of Odysseus* (1907).

## X

**Xirgu, Margarita** 1888–1969 Spanish actress, director and teacher. A legendary figure in Hispanic stage history, she began acting at the age of 12 in Catalan theatre. As head of her own company, she premiered plays by García Lorca, Valle-Inclán, Casona and Rafael Alberti. In 1933 her version of *Medea* inaugurated modern use of the Roman theatre in Mérida, the site of annual festivals of classical theatre. Exiled in Latin America after the Civil War (1936–9), she promoted Spanish authors while also strengthening ties with the French stage. She made a major contribution in Argentina, established Chile's first theatre arts school, and served as director of the School of Dramatic Art in Montevideo, Uruguay.

## Y

**Yacine, Kateb** 1929–89 Algerian francophone playwright. His work is densely poetic and firmly political. Criticism of French colonial policies led to the banning of his early plays in the 1950s (see CENSORSHIP), but SERREAU succeeded in producing *Le Cadavre encerclé* (*The Surrounded Corpse*) in 1958 and *Les Ancêtres redoublent de férocité* (*Ancestors Become More Ferocious*) in 1967 at the THÉÂTRE NATIONAL POPULAIRE. His play celebrating Ho Chi Minh, *L'Homme aux sandales de caoutchouc* (*The Man with Rubber Sandals*), was deemed subversive enough for the mayor of Lyon to cut Marcel Maréchal's subsidy when he produced it in 1971.

**Yakovlev, Aleksei (Semyonovich)** 1773–1817 Russian actor. With E. S. SEMYONOVA he was one of the great St Petersburg actors of the day and a forerunner of the later romantic performance style. A pupil of DMITREVSKY, Yakovlev was not one for careful preparation of a role or the continued development of his craft over the course of his career. Instead he brought inspired emotionalism, manly good looks, a sonorous voice and wildly uneven play to his impersonation of KOTZEBUE's sentimental characters and OZEROV's noble heroes (Oedipus, Fingal and Dmitry Donskoi). He was the first Russian actor to appear in a series of roles adapted from SHAKESPEARE and SCHILLER, including Othello in a translated French version (1806), Edgar in Gnedich's *King Lear* (1807), and Karl Moor (1814).

**yakshagana** Indian theatre genre. *Yakshagana* refers to a variety of different theatre forms of south India, the best-known of which is found in Mysore state. The term means 'songs of the demi-gods'. *Yakshagana* is popular with rural audiences. All the companies are itinerant organizations under the management of temple authorities, and the festival season lasts from November to May.

*Yakshagana* is a lively, fast-paced genre in which songs, dances and improvised dialogue mix according to a prescribed structure. At the heart of the *yakshagana* are the poetic songs (*prasanga*) sung by the chief musician (*bhagavata*), who controls the pace of the show. Popular *prasangas* have been transcribed and published, even those from hundreds of years ago; and, with their particular melody (*raga*) and metre intact, they constitute a major part of the historical record of the dramatic literature. The improvised dialogue changes from night to night, but most of the *prasangas* are based on stories from the great Hindu epics the *Mahabharata* and the *Ramayana* and from the *Puranas*, and concern serious events from the lives of well known epic figures. Humour is injected into the performance by the clowns (*hasyagar*).

Costumes and make-up for the *yakshagana* of this region are unique. Large heart-shaped headdresses are worn by the warriors, crowns of wood covered with tinsel are worn by kings, and the demons, whose spiky make-up distorts the actors' facial features beyond recognition, also wear large, impressive headdresses.

**Yale Repertory Theatre** American theatre. An adjunct to the Yale School of Drama in New Haven, Connecticut, this important non-profit professional RESIDENT THEATRE was founded in 1966 by ROBERT BRUSTEIN. In 1968 it moved into a church converted into a theatre with a thrust stage. Among important new works premiered at Yale have been ROBERT LOWELL's version of *Prometheus Bound* (1967), KOPIT's *Wings* (1978), three plays by EDWARD BOND, several by ATHOL FUGARD in the 1980s (*A Lesson from Aloes, Master Harold, The Road to Mecca*) and all of AUGUST WILSON's plays.

**Yankee theatre** (USA) Yankee actors achieved their greatest popularity between 1825 and 1855, though Yankee characters appeared both earlier and later. The first notable – 'Jonathan' was the most common nickname – was in ROYALL TYLER's *The Contrast* (1787); the last, Joshua Whitcomb in DENMAN THOMPSON's *The Old Homestead* (1886). The stage Yankee possessed characteristics ascribed to rustic New Englanders: he was simple, blundering, sentimental, parsimonious, patriotic, shrewd, critical of city folks and devoted to picturesque speech. The English comedian CHARLES MATHEWS was the first to exploit the Yankee in his *Trip to America* (1824) and *Jonathan in England* (1824), and four American actors quickly followed his lead: J. H. HACKETT, GEORGE HANDEL HILL, DANFORTH MARBLE and Joshua Silsbee. The Yankee actors were extremely popular in London in the 1930s and 1940s; the critics found them not unlike 'our own canny Yorkshire lads'.

**Yeats, W(illiam) B(utler)** 1865–1939 Irish poet, playwright and critic. His work is now considered to be the most important in the revival of Irish literature. Yeats's ambition for Irish theatre was that it should stimulate, through his own plays, a poetic celebration of Irish legend and history, heroic and mythic in scale yet with the ironic tone he admired in SYNGE. So in Yeats's *On Baile's Strand* (1904) the Blind Man and the Fool parody Conchubar and Cuchulain.

Formally, Yeats rejected the dominant theatrical REALISM, contemporary subjects and painstakingly authentic sets. A bare stage with merely suggestive properties – a blue cloth for a well – would enable verse to make drama a sacred rite, expressed also through dance, music and masks. For this drama 'close to pure music' Yeats found precedents in the French symbolists and in Japanese NŌ plays. But his drama was not insulated from life. The early plays are in part political parables. *The Countess Cathleen* (1899) belongs to his myth of the Anglo-Irish aristocracy; *Cathleen ni Houlihan* (1903) is a patriotic allegory; and *The King's Threshold* (1903) asserts the poet Seanchan's place among the lawmakers.

The burden of ABBEY THEATRE management impeded Yeats's own work. Between 1904 and 1910 his only major plays were *Deirdre* (1906), *The Golden Helmet* (1908) and its verse adaptation *The Green Helmet* (1910). Apart from *The Words upon the Window Pane* (1930), conjuring Swift's ghost to a seance, in prose and with a realistic setting, his later work experiments with verse and symbolist theatre (see SYMBOLISM). There are effective dramatic moments. In *At the Hawk's Well* (1916) words unite with songs, Edmund Dulac's masks and the hawk-dance performed by Michio Ito, to enact Cuchulain's heroic resolution. In *The Dreaming of the Bones* (1931) the dance and parting of Diarmuid and Grania, traitors 700 years dead, are memorably succinct. *Purgatory* (1938 – Yeats's last appearance at the Abbey) embodies in its fable of murderous family decadence his bitter judgement on modern Ireland. The problem remains, however, of a verse that is lyrical, expository, meditative – not dramatic.

Yeats's plays, infrequently performed, never won the popular audience for which he hoped. Nor did they revive verse drama in the 20th century. They are astonishing sketches, by an indisputably great poet, for a verse drama never fully realized. He was awarded the Nobel Prize in 1923.

**Yiddish Art Theatre** American company. Founded by MAURICE SCHWARTZ, it opened at the Irving Place Theatre in New York in 1918, subsequently moving to the Garden Theatre. Members rejected the improvisations of *SHUND* THEATRE in favour of carefully rehearsed plays of quality, ensemble acting and a high standard of presentation. The first successes came with PERETZ HIRSHBEIN's earthy PASTORAL play *The Forgotten Nook*, followed by the same writer's *The Blacksmith's Daughter*, another delicate, idyllic play of village life. During the second year 15 plays were added to the repertoire, including SHOLOM ALEICHEM's *Tevye the Milkman* and four of JACOB GORDIN's plays including *God, Man and Devil*, based on the Faust legend. Inevitably stars were

created, like BERTHA GERSTEIN, LUDWIG SATZ, Muni Weisenfreund (PAUL MUNI) and Anna Apfel. Several productions in English translation transferred to BROADWAY including Schwartz's greatest personal triumph, Israel Joshua Singer's *Yoshe Kalb*. The company continued until the late 1930s.

**Yiddish theatre** Indigenous Jewish theatre. It was not until the last quarter of the 19th century that a general movement away from religious restriction had spread sufficiently to allow the belated beginnings of an endemic Jewish theatre.

There had been plays written and published sporadically, the two of greatest historical importance being *Reb Henoch* by Isaac Eichel which appeared in Germany in 1793 and Solomon Ettinger's *Serkele*, written in Russia in 1825 (published 36 years later). AVROM GOLDFADN, later to earn the title of 'father of the Yiddish theatre' bravely presented – in Romania – the first public performance of a Yiddish play in October 1876, *The Recruits*, a Schweik type of broad comedy, although the subject was anything but funny at the time. Goldfadn had included many of his own songs, thus setting a pattern of musical theatre that was to last. The venture was a great success and the theatrical floodgates burst open. New companies sprang up everywhere, split up and multiplied, all following Goldfadn's pattern of musical plays written at a simple, folksy, emotional level, each company employing a resident 'writer' to supply story-lines and songs. The rest was improvised.

Stylistic traditions were adopted by all the companies. Thus a doctor always wore rimless spectacles, a simpleton had his shirt-tail hanging out, marriage-brokers carried an umbrella, students held a book and rich men a cane. Colour had special significance: villains wore red wigs and heroes black ones. The atmosphere at performances was close to that of a family gathering or a communal celebration, with a quite unique emotional rapport between actors and audience.

With the banning of all Yiddish theatre in Russia following the assassination of Tsar Alexander II in 1883, and the escalation of Jewish persecution in Europe, a general exodus began. The theatre companies went with the people, establishing themselves in countries such as England, France and the Argentine, but particularly in America, where performances quickly became a vital social, educational and cultural influence amongst rapidly growing Yiddish-speaking communities. Theatres appeared in most of the large cities, particularly Chicago, Boston, Philadelphia and San Francisco. Soon no fewer than 11 Yiddish theatres were functioning in New York alone. Prolific writers like MOISHE HURWITZ and Jacob Lateiner began churning out potboilers. Extrovert actor-managers like BORIS THOMASHEFSKY and MAURICE SCHWARTZ became matinée idols.

The more cultured members of the community looked down upon this popular theatre as unworthy, and movements towards a Jewish art theatre materialized in Europe and later in America. It first manifested itself in Odessa in 1908, on the lifting of the 25-year ban on performances, when PERETZ HIRSHBEIN formed the Hirshbein Troupe, with JACOB BEN-AMI as leading actor. Rejecting improvisation, he directed plays by JACOB GORDIN, SHOLOM ASCH, ISAAC PERETZ, DAVID PINSKI and SHOLOM ALEICHEM, in addition to his own. Hirshbein disbanded the company after two seminal years, but the main fruits of his labours were to come later in Vilna, Moscow and New York.

In 1916 the celebrated VILNA TROUPE appeared, quickly achieving a style and character of its own, under the direction of DAVID HERMAN. At about the same time ESTHER KAMIŃSKA and her Warsaw company were producing some remarkable work, which was continued by her daughter IDA KAMIŃSKA until the 1939 Nazi invasion. The company was re-formed after the war as the Polish State Yiddish Theatre and is one of the two remaining state-funded full-time Yiddish theatres, the other being the Romanian State Yiddish Theatre. The MOSCOW STATE JEWISH THEATRE resulted from the wave of creative enthusiasm which followed the Russian Revolution in 1917, and achieved world fame with productions of plays by Sholom Aleichem, Mendele Mocher Sforim, Goldfadn and, particularly, SHAKESPEARE.

In America a high-quality Yiddish theatre flourished for two decades following World War I, led by Maurice Schwartz and his YIDDISH ART THEATRE. Jacob Ben-Ami's short-lived JEWISH ART THEATRE reached probably the highest point of theatrical achievement. Yiddish theatre went into a worldwide decline in the 1930s, by which time the Yiddish language had virtually fallen into disuse. A large body of plays remains, many of which will hold their own in any company.

**Yoruba travelling theatres** Nigerian companies. These professional, wholly commercial groups traditionally travel around Nigeria performing to Yoruba-speaking audiences. The Yoruba have a long theatre history. The Yoruba travelling theatres reflect and cater for the need for a Yoruba urban identity within the Nigerian polity: a sense of a Yoruba past with a contemporary urban style and morality. They started with the establishment of the OGUNDE Theatre in 1945 and by 1988 there were 150 separate companies. From the early 1980s they turned increasingly away from live theatre towards film, television and video production. Companies include MOSES OLAIYA ADEJUMO's Alawada Theatre.

**Young, Stark** 1881–1963 American drama critic, translator, playwright and director. Associate editor of *Theatre Arts* magazine from 1921 to 1940 and chief drama critic of the *New Republic* from 1922 to 1947, Young was an advocate of the New Stagecraft movement, and worked closely with EUGENE O'NEILL, Kenneth Macgowan and ROBERT EDMOND JONES at the Provincetown Playhouse. He staged the premiere of O'Neill's *Welded* in 1924 and wrote several plays, none successful. He is better remembered for his translations of CHEKHOV's plays, especially of *The Seagull* for the LUNTS in 1938, and for his books about theatre.

**Young Vic** (Britain) There have been two Young Vic schemes. The first was initiated by GEORGE DEVINE as a touring children's theatre attached to the OLD VIC company. Its first production was in December 1946 and it ran until 1951, with audiences mainly from 9 to 15 years of age.

The second scheme began, as part of the NATIONAL THEATRE's programme for young people, with the opening in London of the Young Vic Theatre – the first purpose-built young people's theatre in Britain – in 1970. The auditorium seats 450–500 people around a central (or sometimes a thrust) stage, and there is now additionally (since 1984) a small studio theatre seating 110. The purpose has been to make theatre of the highest

standard – classics, specially written plays and experimental work – available to students and young people in an unpatronizing, exciting manner and at affordable prices. FRANK DUNLOP, the theatre's first director, established it as a completely independent organization in 1974.

**Yu Ch'i-jin** 1905–74 Korean playwright, director and producer. Educated in Japan, in 1931 he became one of the founding members of the Kŭgyesul Yŏnguhoe Group. His first successful play was *T'omak* (*The Earthen Hut*, 1932). He wrote more than 30 plays ranging from tragedy to comedy, becoming the most influential playwright until the 1950s. The most important subjects of his plays are the struggle against Japanese colonial policy and against occupying foreign military forces, SATIRE against political feuds, and the national insistence upon ethnic identity. In 1950 he was appointed the first director of the newly established National Theatre. In 1962 he opened the Drama Centre, which failed within a year. Some of his representative plays are *Maŭi t'aeja* (*Prince Maŭi*), *So* (*The Cow*), *Choguk* (*The Fatherland*), *Wŏnsulrang* and *Pyŏl* (*The Star*).

**Yu Zhenfei** 1902–92 Chinese actor. Trained under both KUNQU and JINGXI master actors, he turned professional on the *jingxi* stage where he was quickly acclaimed for his interpretations of the young scholar-hero roles of the classical Beijing repertoire, regularly partnering MEI LANFANG in this capacity. Yu worked indefatigably for the preservation and performance of *kunqu*. During the 1950s he trained a new generation of performers at the Shanghai Municipal Academy of Dramatic Art. He has also written a treatise on *kunqu* techniques.

***yueju*** (Guangdong opera) Chinese opera form. This regional form of music drama of Guangdong Province is also popular in southern Guangxi, Hong Kong and Macao and among those Overseas Chinese communities of North America, Australia and elsewhere whose ancestors came from Guangdong. This *yueju* should not be confused with the *YUEJU* of Shaoxing opera, a completely different style of Chinese music drama. (Although the two names sound identical, the first of the two characters is different in Chinese.)

*Yueju* has its origins in the 18th century with the actor Zhang Wu, who established a troupe. Because of Guangdong's proximity to the British colony of Hong Kong, Guangdong opera has been more subject to foreign influences, especially film, than any other form of Chinese music drama. Early in this century urban actors began to experiment with more naturalistic movements and gestures, and to discard the traditional embroidery in favour of the more realistic costumes being used in the spoken drama and film. For the first time they used scenery on the stage. Some new items were directly political in their content, such as one in praise of the female anti-Manchu revolutionary Qiu Jin, who was beheaded in 1907.

Except for the Cultural Revolution decade (1966–76), Guangdong opera has done well under the People's Republic. The state-run Guangdong Provincial Opera Company was established in 1958. There has been a tendency to return to traditional usage in some aspects of stagecraft such as costuming, movements and gestures.

***yueju*** (Shaoxing opera) Chinese opera form. This Chinese regional music drama is not to be confused with the identically sounding *YUEJU*, Cantonese or Guangdong opera (the first character of which is quite different in Chinese). Shaoxing opera arose quite recently and does not belong to any of the major systems of local Chinese drama. It developed from peasant balladeers singing local folk-songs early in the 20th century. Some formed themselves into drama troupes but the scale was small. The musical accompaniment was percussion or chorus.

In 1916 the actor Wang Jinshui brought Shaoxing opera to Shanghai. He and others greatly expanded the scope of this form of music drama by adding stringed and other instruments to the accompanying orchestra and expanding the available rhythmic structures. In 1923 a training school for girls was set up in Sheng County, and from 1928 all-female companies began their period of prosperity in Shanghai. They competed with the male companies. By the mid-1930s the best-known feature of Shaoxing opera was that virtually all performers were female.

As a result, romantic love stories are the strong point of Shaoxing opera. Military scenes and acrobatics are totally absent. During the Cultural Revolution the Shaoxing opera companies were closed down. But with the fall of the 'gang of four' in 1976 the genre has revived like all other Chinese regional styles. Actors now perform some male roles, especially evil ones, but actresses dominate strongly in most items, and in particular the scholar/lover (*xiaosheng*) roles are usually played by women.

**Yurka, Blanche** 1893–1974 Czech-born American actress. She went to the USA as an infant. She shifted from tragic (Gina in *The Wild Duck*, 1925) to strong-willed roles, winning praise for her emotional depth and vocal timbre, e.g. as Gertrude to John Barrymore's (see DREW–BARRYMORE FAMILY) Hamlet. She was also an active member and organizer of Actors' Equity.

**Zacconi, Ermete** 1857–1948 Italian actor and company manager. Influenced by the naturalistic style (see NATURALISM) of GIOVANNI EMANUEL, in 1897 he formed his own company, and his repertoire included much modern drama in the naturalistic vein (including IBSEN, TOLSTOI and GIACOSA) as well as Shakespearian tragedy, in which he was notable as Macbeth, Othello, Lear and Hamlet. For a time he worked with DUSE in her attempts to launch the new poetic drama of D'ANNUNZIO, and later appeared with her in Ibsen's *The Lady from the Sea* (1921). He continued to be a lead actor in film and in the Italian theatre until World War II.

**Zadek, Peter** 1926– German theatre and film director. Zadek's fast-paced, highly theatrical and politically unconventional stagings of SHAKESPEARE, BRENDAN BEHAN and O'CASEY gave him a reputation as a radical iconoclast during his time as artistic director in Bremen (1964–7) and Bochum (1972–5). His most successful productions have been his own adaptations of novels by Hans Fallada into satiric REVUES of the Nazi period, *Little Man – What Now?* (1972, together with TANKRED DORST) and *Each Dies for Himself Alone* (1981). Zadek was director of the Hamburg Schauspielhaus (1985–9) and since 1992 has been a director of the BERLINER ENSEMBLE.

***zaju*** Chinese variety play. This is a generic term for a style of entertainment in which dance, song, monologue, balladry and farcical skits were given an integrated presentation. *Zaju* reached its creative peak during the Yuan dynasty (1234–1368), resulting in the emergence of a structured four-act style of play, the first definitive synthesis of song, music, versification and acting. A vigorous school of playwrights arose during the 13th century. Only the leading performer, whether male or female, sang. The ancillary performers carried on the dialogue and action between the singing as well as enforcing the comic pace. Surviving playscripts indicate that Yuan drama was a thriving popular entertainment catering for all levels of society. The Beijing theatre (*JINGXI*) of modern times is a legitimate descendant.

**Zaks, Jerry** 1946– German-born American director. His American directing credits include the highly acclaimed *Lend Me a Tenor* (1989). Zaks became known as an outstanding director of comedy, with productions noted for pace, style, wit and exceptional ensemble acting. In 1990 he left Lincoln Center, where he had been director-in-residence, to work for the Jujamcyn Theaters; his first production was STEPHEN SONDHEIM's musical *Assassins* at PLAYWRIGHTS HORIZONS, followed in 1992 by a critically acclaimed Tony-winning revival of *Guys and Dolls* on BROADWAY.

**Zamyatin, Evgeny (Ivanovich)** 1884–1937 Russian-Soviet novelist, critic and playwright. He is best known in the West for his anti-utopian novel *We* (1920), which inspired Orwell's *1984*. He wrote satirically and passionately on artistic freedom, social ills and literary craft. He was an early Bolshevik, but his anti-philistine polemical writing of the 1920s led to mounting official criticism of his work, culminating in the banning of his books (see CENSORSHIP) and his emigration to Paris in 1931.

Zamyatin wrote eight plays of which three were original works and five adaptations. His earliest play *The Society of Honorary Bell Ringers* (1925), derived from his novel *Islanders*, was produced at Leningrad's Mikhailovsky Theatre in 1925. That same year the MOSCOW ART THEATRE's Second Studio invited him to dramatize Nikolai Leskov's short story, which he turned into *The Flea*, a COMMEDIA-style depiction of Tsarist Russia and Victorian England. The tragedy *Attila* (1928), his last play, presents the Hun leader in a positive light and in poetic style. It was banned while in rehearsal at the Leningrad Bolshoi Dramatic Theatre (1928), at which point Zamyatin returned to narrative writing. His essay 'The Modern Russian Theatre' (1932) includes a comparison of the methods and influence of STANISLAVSKY and MEYERHOLD.

**zanni** (both singular and plural) Italian term. The *zanni* were the two servants in the *COMMEDIA DELL'ARTE*; originally from Bergamo and speaking the local patois, they soon differentiated into two distinct types. The first became the clever, domineering intriguer, who motivated the plot through schemings and brainstorms; often characterized as an urban lackey, he wore first a bright jerkin, later a stylized livery. His names were Brighella, Buffetto, Flautino and Coviello. The second was a knave from the village or the garden, a dolt not devoid of mother-wit, whose function was to be the fall-guy and provide the prat-falls. His clothes were patched or mended, and turned in time into a costume of polychrome rhomboids. His names were Arlecchino (see HARLEQUIN), Truffaldino, Pasquino, Tabarino, Tortellino, Mezzetino, Trappolino, Trivellino, Bagolino and Fritellino, and gradually he became the more important of the two.

**Zapolska, Gabriela** 1860–1921 Polish actress, director, manager, playwright and novelist. She is credited with introducing IBSEN into Russia, playing Nora in *A Doll's House* during a guest appearance of the Warsaw Theatre in 1883. She studied acting in Paris and appeared in minor roles at the Théâtre Libre (1892–4), returning to Poland as a proponent of NATURALISM. Her most popular play is *The Morality of Mrs Dulska* (1906), a mordant SATIRE on bourgeois hypocrisy. *Maĺka Szwarcenkopf* (1897) portrays lower-class Jewish life; *Miss Maliczewska* (1910) deals with a young actress victimized by predatory males.

**zarzuela** Spanish MUSICAL COMEDY. The genre was probably invented by CALDERÓN DE LA BARCA; *El mayor encanto amor* (*Love the Great Enchanter*, 1635) was one of the earliest examples. Usually performed in the open air, in one to three acts, it took its name from the Palacio de la Zarzuela outside Madrid. Developing from the *sainete* (see GÉNERO CHICO), the musical element became the most important with aria and recitative alternating, in a stylized and often allegorical form. It enjoyed enormous popularity, culminating in the first decades of the 20th century. Director José Tamayo's spectacular *Anthology of the Zarzuela* has been touring the world since 1966.

**Zavadsky, Yury (Aleksandrovich)** 1894–1977 Russian-Soviet director. His training as a designer later manifested itself in his attention to the outer form of his stage productions, many of which employed music generously. While acting at the MOSCOW ART THEATRE (1924–31), Zavadsky formed his own studio (1924), using an approach to acting based on STANISLAVSKY and VAKHTANGOV. The studio moved to Rostov in 1936, where it formed the core of the Gorky Theatre, and Zavadsky became its head (1936–40). From 1940 until the late 1970s he was artistic director of Moscow's Mossoviet Theatre.

Zavadsky attempted to recreate Vakhtangov's lyrical merger of psychological REALISM and vibrant theatricalism. His many productions at the Mossoviet include SHAKESPEARE's *The Merry Wives of Windsor* (1957, 1967) and LERMONTOV's *Masquerade* (1952, 1963, 1967); *Petersburg Dreams*, adapted from Dostoevsky's *Crime and Punishment* (1969), a popular success with its romanti-

cized Raskolnikov; classics by CHEKHOV, GOLDONI, OSTROVSKY, Jack London and SHAW; and Soviet dramas by AFINOGENOV, SIMONOV, KORNEICHUK, LEONOV, Shtein, ZORIN and Virta. Among his students was Polish director JERZY GROTOWSKI.

**Zeami** [Seami] **Motokiyo** 1363–1443 Japanese actor, playwright, composer, choreographer and theorist. Zeami is the foremost figure in the history of NŌ, the form he refined during 34 years in the Kyoto court under Shogun Yoshimitsu's patronage. He moved beyond playing a role to striving for a mysterious beauty tinged with sadness. Representative works attributed to him are *The Damask Drum*, *The Old Pine*, *Kiyotsune*, *Visiting Lady Komachi* and *Lady Yuya*.

Zeami was a practical theatre person, concerned with finding means to attract a varied audience through novelty, by doing the unexpected (following the yin–yang theory of opposites) and by cultivating a 'beginner's heart'. Over the last 30 years of his life he wrote 21 'secret' treatises on training, play structure, acting and how to run a professional troupe. Much of his advice applies to any theatre. He claimed there was no single correct way of acting; audience approval is the proper criterion of success.

**Zeffirelli, Franco** 1923– Italian stage and film designer and director. Zeffirelli began his career in 1945 as an actor, but after two years he became a designer. He worked primarily on plays and films for LUCHINO VISCONTI. In 1951 he became a stage director and subsequently worked on such operas as *La Cenerentola* (La Scala, 1953) and *Don Giovanni* (COVENT GARDEN, 1962), and such SHAKESPEARE plays as *Romeo and Juliet* (1960) and *Much Ado About Nothing* (1965). In his work as film director, Zeffirelli's abundantly romantic, yet realistically detailed, style is evident in his widely acclaimed *Romeo and Juliet* (1968) as well as *The Taming of the Shrew* (1967), *La Traviata* (1982), *Otello* (1986) and *Hamlet* (1989).

**Zemach, Nahum** 1887–1939 Russian-born Israeli director. Founder of the HABIMAH Theatre, he was an ardent Zionist and lover of the Hebrew language. He conceived the idea of a professional Hebrew theatre which would disseminate the Zionist idea and ultimately settle in Palestine. Under his guidance, the collective of actors achieved world fame. But in 1927, during its tour of the USA, the troupe split in two, the majority of senior members going to Palestine and the minority, headed by Zemach, remaining in New York. Zemach, whose dream of establishing a Hebrew theatre in the land of Israel had come true, ended his life staging performances in Yiddish and English in New York.

**Ziegfeld, Florenz** 1869–1932 American producer. Ziegfeld's first venture into show business was as manager of SANDOW, a VAUDEVILLE strongman. After meeting singer Anna Held in Europe, Ziegfeld brought her to New York and presented her in several musicals. At her suggestion, he created a Parisian-style REVUE called *Follies of 1907*, the first in a series that he continued to produce for the next quarter of a century. Initially presented on a modest scale, the *Follies* grew increasingly elaborate, eventually moving to the New Amsterdam Theatre, where designers such as JOSEPH URBAN created ornate scenery and lavish costumes. In 1913 the show's title was changed to *The Ziegfeld Follies*. The motto 'Glorifying the American Girl' underlines the *Follies*' emphasis on choruses of beautiful women in glittering production numbers. Many of the shows also featured first-rate comedians, popular singers and dancers.

Ziegfeld also presented some of the most successful musical comedies (see MUSICAL COMEDY) and operettas of the 1920s, including *Sally* (1920), *Kid Boots* (1923), *Sunny* (1925), *Rio Rita* (1927), *Show Boat* (1927), *Rosalie* (1928), *The Three Musketeers* (1928) and *Whoopee* (1928). Rarely innovative in his choice of material or his production methods, Ziegfeld built his reputation as a producer on his ability to discover and nurture talented performers, and the care and expense with which he mounted his shows.

**Zindel, Paul** 1936– American playwright. He is known for two plays that provide actresses with challenging roles. The first, *The Effect of Gamma Rays on Man-in-the-Moon Marigolds* (1970), was first produced in Houston, Texas. The less successful second, *And Miss Reardon Drinks a Little* (1971), continued his examination of fragile people who become a part of the madness surrounding them. Recently Zindel has turned to writing television plays and screenplays as well as novels.

**Zipprodt, Patricia** 1925– American COSTUME designer. Zipprodt became well known in the 1960s with such productions as *Fiddler on the Roof*, *Cabaret* and *Pippin*, and the film *The Graduate*. She developed a technique of creating layers of paint and dye that gave a vibrant or shimmering sense of colour to costumes that would otherwise be drab. This approach continued through *Sunday in the Park with George* (1984), in which costumes were heavily textured with dye, paint, brocade and lace.

**Zola, Émile** 1840–1902 French novelist and critic. Zola is famous for his series of novels which chronicle life under the Second Empire, one of which, *L'Assommoir* (1877), established him at the head of the naturalist movement (see NATURALISM). Also interested in the theatre, he was the major influence on ANTOINE's Théâtre Libre. Melodramatic adaptations of some of his novels drew large audiences to the Ambigu (see BOULEVARD); and *Thérèse Raquin* (1873), an adaptation of his novel, though not very successful on the stage, became a model for the naturalist play both in France and abroad. Between 1873 and 1880 he was drama critic for various journals and used his columns to promote the new drama and to develop a critical methodology. He believed in the social and educational value of theatre. For the WELL MADE PLAY he wished to substitute a drama of observation and scientific fact, using an analytic approach like novelists such as Balzac, Flaubert and himself and offering 'an anatomical study of each human being'. Scenery should take on the role of description in the novel, with a real function in the analysis of facts and characters. He objected to the conventional paraphernalia of wings and backdrops and even foresaw the abandonment of footlights. In his last years Zola devoted his attention to socialist and humanitarian propaganda.

**Zorin, Leonid (Genrikhovich)** 1924– Soviet-Russian playwright. One of the post-Thaw generation, he brought a new lyricism and focus on personal relationships and ethical concerns to the theatre. Zorin's first play *Falcons* was produced in 1941 at the Baku Russian theatre (he was a native of Baku). In 1949 *Youth* was staged at the Maly Theatre in Moscow. *The Guests* (1954) identifies a class of ruthless, privileged bureaucrats to which the son of a revolutionary father belongs, thus reversing the idea of earlier Soviet plays that the younger generation is more enlightened than the elder. The play was attacked by the Ministry of Culture and by literary conservatives. *A Roman Comedy* (*Dion*, 1964) is a SATIRE about a plainspoken ancient Roman poet-pundit and his relationship with the emperor. *A Warsaw Melody* (1967) is a story of unfulfilled love between two young students, a Russian boy and a Polish girl. A typical 1960s drama, it played over 4,000 times during the 1968–9 season. *The Decembrists* is part of a trilogy commemorating the 50th anniversary of the October Revolution (1967) – the other parts being A. Svobodin's *The Populists* and Mikhail Shatrov's *The Bolsheviks* – which considers the use of terror in revolution and was premiered at Moscow's Sovremennik Theatre.

**Zorrilla, José** 1817–93 Spanish poet and playwright. Apart from two unsuccessful classical tragedies, his 33 plays are on Spanish history and legend. His most famous is the mediocre *Don Juan Tenorio* (1844), a sentimental treatment of the legend ending in repentance and salvation, and still performed every year in Spain around All Souls' Day. Much better is the two-part *El zapatero y el rey* (*The Shoemaker and the King*, 1840–2) on Pedro the Cruel and the shoemaker Diego Pérez, while the one-act MELODRAMA *El puñal del godo* (*The Dagger of the Goth*, 1843) is also interesting.

**Zuckmayer, Carl** 1896–1977 German playwright and novelist, who became a Swiss citizen in 1966. His reputation is based on *The Captain from Köpenick* (1931), which has become a modern classic. Based on a true incident, its SATIRE of Prussian militarism is a classic formulation of the common man's struggle against state bureaucracy. Recognized by HAUPTMANN as his successor, Zuckmayer completed Hauptmann's unfinished play, *Herbert Engelmann*. But his naturalistic treatments (see NATURALISM) of the conflict between patriotic duty and resistance to the Nazi regime (*The Devil's General*, 1946) or between nuclear physics and moral responsibility (*The Cold Light*, 1956) seem dated now by comparison with less conventional treatments of the same subjects by WEISS or KIPPHARDT; while his experiment with a poetic 'requiem', *The Song in the Fiery Furnace* (1950), was only partially successful in coming to terms with the modern dramaturgy developed by THORNTON WILDER and FRISCH.

3